The Billboard Book of
NUMBER ONE
ADULT CONTEMPORARY HITS

WESLEY HYATT

BILLBOARD BOOKS
an imprint of Watson-Guptill Publications/
New York

To all my aunts and uncles both past and present—Joe and Christine Eshelmen, Carma and Tom Charping, Laura and Jack Clinard, Mary and Don Harrison, Norma and Henry Moorefield, Betty and Bill Swaim, Rex and Polly Willard, Richard and Patsy Willard, Clyde and Shirley Willard, and Harold and Linda Willard—who taught me to appreciate music, even if I don't sing or play instruments very well.

Senior editor: Bob Nirkind
Production manager: Hector Campbell
Book and cover design: Bob Fillie

Copyright ©1999 by Wesley Hyatt

Published in 1999 by Watson-Guptill Publications
1515 Broadway
New York, NY 10036

Library of Congress Cataloging-in-Publication Data
Hyatt, Wesley.
    The Billboard book of number one adult contemporary hits/ Wesley Hyatt
        p.   cm.
    Includes bibliographical references (p.) and indexes.
    ISBN 0-8230-7693-8
    1. Popular music—United States—Discography.
    I. Billboard (Cincinnati, Ohio:1963) II. Title.
    ML156.4.P6H93   1999
    016.78164'0266—dc21   99-11660
                                                                        CIP

Manufactured in the United States

First printing, 1999

1 2 3 4 5 6 7 8 9 / 07 06 05 04 03 02 01 00 99

Photo Credits

FROM *BILLBOARD* PHOTO ARCHIVES:

Ray Charles, p . 9; Bobby Vinton, p. 10; Barbra Streisand, p. 25; Elvis Presley, p. 34; Tom Jones, p. 81; Anne Murray, p. 87, p. 119; Elton John, p. 122; Olivia Newton-John, p. 146, p. 174; Barry Manilow, p. 153, p. 187; Elton John, p. 201; Bette Midler, p. 240; Dionne Warwick, p. 244; Dan Fogelberg, p. 259; Kenny Rogers, p. 261; Stevie Wonder, p. 287; Bruce Springsteen, p. 302; Huey Lewis and the News, pp. 310–311; George Michael, p. 334; Bee Gees, p. 350; Cher, p. 351; Mariah Carey, p. 360; Richard Marx, p. 373; Celine Dion, p. 381, p. 413; the Rembrandts, p. 400

FROM *PHOTOFEST:*

Al Martino, p. 17; Chad and Jeremy, p. 30; Dean Martin, p. 31; Herb Alpert and the Tijuana Brass, p. 38; Ray Conniff and the Singers, p. 46; Jack Jones and Nancy Sinatra, p. 51; Ed Ames, p. 54; Petula Clark, p. 56; Vikki Carr, p. 59; John Gary, p. 61; Bobby Goldsboro, p. 65; Glen Campbell, p. 69; Andy Williams, p. 73; Perry Como, p. 89; Englebert Humperdinck, p. 93; The Carpenters, p. 95; Roberta Flack, p. 106; The 5th Dimension, p. 112; Lobo, p. 117; Tony Orlando and Dawn, p. 120; Paul and Linda McCartney, p. 123; Helen Reddy, p. 126; Art Garfunkel, p. 129; Marie Osmond, p. 130; Jim Croce, p. 132; John Denver, p. 136; Charlie Rich, p. 137; Joni Mitchell, p. 140; Gardon Lightfoot, p. 148; Neil Sedaka, p. 150; Helen Reddy, p. 160; The Captain and Tennille, pp. 166–167, p. 189; The Carpenters, pp. 184–185; David Soul, p. 205; James Taylor, p. 210; Neil Diamond, pp. 215, 257; Al Stewart, p. 224; Billy Joel, p. 243; ABBA, p. 248; John Denver, p. 263; Juice Newton, p. 267; Stephen Bishop, p. 273; Toto, p. 274; Phil Collins, p. 293, p. 358; Miami Sound Machine, p. 309; Madonna, p. 320, 393; Whitney Houston, p. 325; Patrick Swayze, p. 330; Sheryl Crow, p. 395; Michael Bolton, p. 409; Shawn Colvin, p. 410

OTHER CREDITS:

Dan Klores Associates Inc.: Peter, Paul and Mary, p. 19
B. J. Thomas: B. J. Thomas, p. 79
Henry Jerome: Bobbi Martin, p. 83
Julia Hepfer: Joan Baez, p. 98; .38 Special, p. 347
Selwyn Miller: Bread, p. 101
Columbia Tristar Television: Marie Osmond, p. 130
Gino Empry: Roger Whittaker, p. 162
Gloria Jenett: Paul Anka, p. 179
Jeanne Bot: George Baker Selection, p. 181
    Randy Vanwarmer, p. 229
Harry Wayne Casey: Terry DeSario with KC, p. 236
    Michael Johnson, p. 219
Rogers & Cowan: Lionel Richie, p. 317
Archive Photos: Roberta Flack, p. 220
Wesley Hyatt: Frank Sinatra, p. 45; Lou Rawls, p. 193;
    Tina Turner, p. 389

ACKNOWLEDGMENTS

Though I proposed the idea and wrote this book, it would be far less entertaining and enlightening without the help of several individuals. I am greatly indebted foremost to the work of two music personalities in Miami who lent special help. First is my boss Harry Wayne Casey, KC of KC and the Sunshine Band, who not only told me more than I knew before about his #1 AC hit "Yes I'm Ready" but also told me about people and sources of information in the industry he knew which might be of help to me. His efforts helped me get in contact with Yvonne Elliman, the Commodores, and Jack Wagner, to name just three sources. The other is Tom Dowd, one of the great pop and R&B music producers of the 20th century. Though Tom's work is sadly unrepresented at the top of the AC chart, he nevertheless took time to tell me how to get in contact with several other producers.

I contacted public relations firms, business managers, personal managers, and related types to locate many musicians with whom I spoke for this book. Sad to say, not all cooperated in letting their artist(s) talk briefly about their hit(s) or failed or refused (I haven't figured exactly which!) to set up an interview, even after repeated requests via phone or fax. Yet most did so, and I thank them profusely for their help, which in some cases included providing photos and press kits in addition to helping me get in touch with their artists.

In the order in which one of their clients appears chronologically in the book, they and the artist(s) they represent are: Mike Church of Mike Church Entertainment (Connie Francis); Kent Arwood of Kathy Gangwisch & Associates Inc. (Ray Stevens); Dorran Kelly (The Lettermen); Frank Cassidy of Mr. Acker Bilk and His Paramount Jazz Band Fan Club (Mr. Acker Bilk); Jackie Monaghan of Morningstar P.R. (Brenda Lee); Tennyson Flowers (Andy Williams); Andy Morris of Dan Klores Associates (Peter, Paul and Mary); Larry Spellman of Larry Spellman Entertainment (Al Martino); Peggy Stegman (Al Hirt); Anna of the Mars Talent Agency (Gary Lewis, John Ford Coley); Gerard W. Purcell of Gerard W. Purcell Associates Ltd. (Eddy Arnold); Rob Wilcox (Roger Williams, Tony Orlando); Paradise Artists (Ed Ames); Melinda Garza of ViCar Entertainment (Vikki Carr); Jim Stephany of Jim Stephany Management (Bobby Goldsboro); Beth Brightbill of Ken Hill Productions, Inc. (The Vogues); Sanford Brokaw of the Brokaw Company (Glen Campbell, Marilyn McCoo, and Billy Davis Jr.); Larry Dorr of Music Avenue Inc. (Blood, Sweat and Tears); Mercy Keefe of Gloria Thomas Inc. (B.J. Thomas); Laura Williams of Double Exposure (Dionne Warwick); Marlene Palmer of Palmer Publicity Ink, Ltd. (Anne Murray); Early Morning Productions (Gordon Lightfoot); Selwyn Miller (Bread); HK Management (Chicago); William R. McKenzie of the McKenzie Accounting Corporation (Three Dog Night); Susan Greene of Helen Reddy Productions (Helen Reddy); Jill Willis (Donny Osmond); Chevy Nash, Gallin-Morey Associates (America); Karen Simpson (Neil Sedaka); Dave Kirby of the Agency Group (Phoebe Snow); Gino Empry (Roger Whittaker); Sherry Ingram and Associates (The Captain and Tennille); Gloria Jewett of Paul Anka Productions (Paul Anka); Brian Gannon (The Brotherhood of Man); Paulette Desouza (WAR); Great West Entertainment Management (Firefall); Tim Wilson of Show Corporation (Rita Coolidge); Jo Shank of Gates Music (Chuck Mangione); Fred Kewley of Fred Kewley Management (Michael Johnson); Steve Chapman and Co. Management (Al Stewart); Larry Larson of Larry Larson and Associates (Poco); Sheryl Kagan of Rogers & Cowan (Kenny Rogers); Celia Bellmund of Crosseyed Bear Productions Inc. (Spyro Gyra); Jeffrey Lane (Maureen McGovern); Alison Auerbach of Rogers & Cowan (Pure Prairie League); Tammy Wise of Ronnie Milsap Enterprises (Ronnie Milsap); Barry Ormes (Patti Austin); Fitzgerald Hartley (Toto); Chris Schuckei of *The Late Show Starring David Letterman* (Paul Shaffer of the Honeydrippers); Ken Adamany (Frankie Sullivan of Survivor); Stephan Galfas (Kool and the Gang); the Direct Management Company (Boy Meets Girl); Garry George of Garry George Management (Gloria Loring); Bob Brown Management (Huey Lewis); Lianne Malterre, A&M Records (Amy Grant); Kell Houston of the Good Music Company (The Jets); David Cohen (Bill Medley); John "J.T." Thomas (Gioia Bruno of Exposé); Tim Ansell of Gold Mountain Records (Susanna Hoffs of the Bangles); Julia Hepfer of the Mark Spector Company (.38 Special); Dennis Arfa, QBQ Entertainment (Richard Marx); Joe Lennane (Taylor Dayne); and George Dassinger (John Dittrich of Restless Heart).

Also thanks to Mark Ford, communications director for Nashville Songwriters Association International, who put me in contact with Randy Vanwarmer, Fred Knobloch, and several other writers as well; Arthur Thomas of SCE Group for getting me in contact with members of the Jordanaires for the Elvis Presley entries; Doreen V. Dorion and Jasmine Arakel of Realsongs, who got me faxed answers from songwriter Diane Warren during a busy time for all parties involved; Kelly Newby of Jeff Wald Entertainment for getting me a few minutes of Paul Williams' time; and Carl Schunk for helping me get Jack Morgan of the Russ Morgan Orchestra. And last but certainly not least, thanks to my father Dr. Ronald Hyatt, who had the connections to help me locate Oliver (I owe you one, Dad!). I contacted the other people quoted in the book personally through my own connections or those provided by others interviewed.

To all the artists, writers, and producers who took the time to give me the stories behind their songs, some of which they have told literally hundreds of times to interviewers, I offer my highest and most sincere gratitude for their time and comments. I only wish I had more room to include your insightful and entertaining anecdotes.

I owe special thanks to two individuals who I have yet to meet but who provided the foundation and framework of this book. The first is Fred Bronson, whose *Billboard Book of Number One Hits*, the first *Billboard* chart book to include essays about each of the hits, proved there was a market for this kind of information. The other is Joel Whitburn, whose compilations of *Billboard* chart data—standard references in the industry—were invaluable, providing information on how many versions of a #1 song hit the other charts, on songs artists had on the adult contemporary, pop, country, and rhythm and blues charts, and various details about the artists and records themselves. For his titles and other works I consulted while I was working on this book, see the Bibliography.

Individual photo credits are listed on the facing page, but special thanks are due to two sources who delivered a good chunk of them—Dylan Siegler of the Billboard Photo Archives, and once again Ronald Mandelbaum and his crack staff at Photofest in New York.

And last but never ever least, I once again salute my editor Bob Nirkind, who got behind the concept of the book wholeheartedly and thought I could do it justice. I'd sing him a song about how much I appreciate his help, but since I want to keep working for him, I think I'll just stop with my praise in written form here.

WESLEY HYATT
January 1999

CONTENTS

1964

36	There! I've Said It Again	*Bobby Vinton*
37	For You	*Rick Nelson*
38	Java	*Al Hirt*
39	Navy Blue	*Diane Renay*
40	Hello, Dolly!	*Louis Armstrong*
41	Love Me With All Your Heart (Cuando Calienta El Sol)	*The Ray Charles Singers*
42	People	*Barbra Streisand*
43	The Girl From Ipanema	*Stan Getz/Astrud Gilberto*
44	Everybody Loves Somebody	*Dean Martin*
45	We'll Sing in the Sunshine	*Gale Garnett*
46	The Door Is Still Open to My Heart	*Dean Martin*
47	Ringo	*Lorne Green*

1965

48	The Wedding	*Julie Rogers*
49	Willow Weep for Me	*Chad and Jeremy*
50	You're Nobody Till Somebody Loves You	*Dean Martin*
51	Have You Looked Into Your Heart	*Jerry Vale*
52	King of the Road	*Roger Miller*
53	The Race Is On	*Jack Jones*
54	Cast Your Fate to the Wind	*Sounds Orchestral*
55	Crying in the Chapel	*Elvis Presley*
56	A Walk in the Black Forest	*Horst Jankowski*
57	(Such An) Easy Question	*Elvis Presley*
58	Save Your Heart for Me	*Gary Lewis and the Playboys*
59	Hold Me, Thrill Me, Kiss Me	*Mel Carter*
60	You Were On My Mind	*We Five*
61	I'm Yours	*Elvis Presley*
62	Taste of Honey	*Herb Alpert and the Tijuana Brass*
63	Make the World Go Away	*Eddy Arnold*

1966

64	England Swings	*Roger Miller*
65	Spanish Eyes	*Al Martino*
66	It Was a Very Good Year	*Frank Sinatra*
67	Crying Time	*Ray Charles*
68	The Ballad of the Green Berets	*Staff/Sgt. Barry Sadler*
69	I Want to Go With You	*Eddy Arnold*
70	Together Again	*Ray Charles*
71	Band of Gold	*Mel Carter*
72	Strangers in the Night	*Frank Sinatra*
73	The Impossible Dream (The Quest)	*Jack Jones*
74	Somewhere, My Love	*Ray Conniff and the Singers*
75	I Couldn't Live Without Your Love	*Petula Clark*
76	Born Free	*Roger Williams*
77	In the Arms of Love	*Andy Williams*
78	Summer Wind	*Frank Sinatra*

121	I'll Never Fall in Love Again	*Tom Jones*
122	Jean	*Oliver*
123	Is That All There Is	*Peggy Lee*
124	Wedding Bell Blues	*The 5th Dimension*
125	Try a Little Kindness	*Glen Campbell*
126	Leaving on a Jet Plane	*Peter, Paul and Mary*
127	Raindrops Keep Fallin' on My Head	*B. J. Thomas*

1970

128	Without Love (There Is Nothing)	*Tom Jones*
129	I'll Never Fall in Love Again	*Dionne Warwick*
130	Bridge Over Troubled Water	*Simon and Garfunkel*
131	Let It Be	*The Beatles*
132	For the Love of Him	*Bobbi Martin*
133	Everything Is Beautiful	*Ray Stevens*
134	Daughter of Darkness	*Tom Jones*
135	The Wonder of You	*Elvis Presley*
136	A Song of Joy	*Miguel Rios*
137	(They Long to Be) Close to You	*The Carpenters*
138	I Just Can't Help Believing	*B. J. Thomas*
139	Snowbird	*Anne Murray*
140	We've Only Just Begun	*The Carpenters*
141	You Don't Have to Say You Love Me	*Elvis Presley*
142	It's Impossible	*Perry Como*

1971

143	One Less Bell to Answer	*The 5th Dimension*
144	Watching Scotty Grow	*Bobby Goldsboro*
145	If You Could Read My Mind	*Gordon Lightfoot*
146	For All We Know	*The Carpenters*
147	(Where Do I Begin) Love Story	*Andy Williams*
148	When There's No You	*Englebert Humperdinck*
149	If	*Bread*
150	Me and You and a Dog Named Boo	*Lobo*
151	Rainy Days and Mondays	*The Carpenters*
152	It's Too Late	*Carole King*
153	You've Got a Friend	*James Taylor*
154	If Not for You	*Olivia Newton-John*
155	Beginnings	*Chicago*
156	The Night They Drove Old Dixie Down	*Joan Baez*
157	Superstar	*The Carpenters*
158	Never My Love	*The 5th Dimension*
159	Peace Train	*Cat Stevens*
160	Baby I'm-A Want You	*Bread*
161	All I Ever Need Is You	*Sonny and Cher*

1972

162	An Old Fashioned Love Song	*Three Dog Night*
163	Cherish	*David Cassidy*
164	American Pie—Parts I and II	*Don McLean*
165	Hurting Each Other	*The Carpenters*
166	Without You	*Nilsson*
167	Rock and Roll Lullaby	*B. J. Thomas*
168	The First Time Ever I Saw Your Face	*Roberta Flack*
169	Morning Has Broken	*Cat Stevens*
170	The Candy Man	*Sammy Davis Jr.*
171	Song Sung Blue	*Neil Diamond*
172	Where Is the Love	*Roberta Flack and Donny Hathaway*
173	Alone Again (Naturally)	*Gilbert O'Sullivan*
174	The Guitar Man	*Bread*
175	Baby Don't Get Hooked on Me	*Mac Davis*
176	Black and White	*Three Dog Night*
177	Garden Party	*Rick Nelson and the Stone Canyon Band*
178	If I Could Reach You	*The 5th Dimension*
179	I Can See Clearly Now	*Johnny Nash*
180	I'd Love You to Want Me	*Lobo*
181	Clair	*Gilbert O'Sullivan*
182	Sweet Surrender	*Bread*

1973

183	Been to Canaan	*Carole King*
184	You're So Vain	*Carly Simon*
185	Don't Expect Me to Be Your Friend	*Lobo*
186	Dueling Banjos	*Eric Weissberg and Steve Mandell*
187	Last Song	*Edward Bear*
188	Danny's Song	*Anne Murray*
189	Sing	*The Carpenters*
190	Tie a Yellow Ribbon Round the Ole Oak Tree	*Tony Orlando and Dawn*
191	You Are the Sunshine of My Life	*Stevie Wonder*
192	Daniel	*Elton John*
193	And I Love You So	*Perry Como*
194	My Love	*Paul McCartney and Wings*
195	Boogie Woogie Bugle Boy	*Bette Midler*
196	Yesterday Once More	*The Carpenters*
197	Touch Me in the Morning	*Diana Ross*
198	Delta Dawn	*Helen Reddy*
199	Say, Has Anybody Seen My Sweet Gypsy Rose	*Tony Orlando and Dawn*
200	Loves Me Like a Rock	*Paul Simon*
201	My Maria	*B. W. Stevenson*
202	I'm Coming Home	*Johnny Mathis*
203	All I Know	*Art Garfunkel*
204	Paper Roses	*Marie Osmond*
205	The Most Beautiful Girl	*Charlie Rich*
206	Leave Me Alone (Ruby Red Dress)	*Helen Reddy*
207	Time in a Bottle	*Jim Croce*

1974

208	The Way We Were	*Barbra Streisand*
209	Love's Theme	*The Love Unlimited Orchestra*
210	Love Song	*Anne Murray*
211	Last Time I Saw Him	*Diana Ross*
212	Seasons in the Sun	*Terry Jacks*
213	Sunshine on My Shoulders	*John Denver*
214	A Very Special Love Song	*Charlie Rich*
215	Keep On Singing	*Helen Reddy*
216	I'll Have to Say I Love You in a Song	*Jim Croce*
217	TSOP (The Sound of Philadelphia)	*MFSB featuring the Three Degrees*
218	The Entertainer	*Marvin Hamlisch*
219	Help Me	*Joni Mitchell*
220	I Won't Last a Day Without You	*The Carpenters*
221	Sundown	*Gordon Lightfoot*
222	You Won't See Me	*Anne Murray*
223	Annie's Song	*John Denver*
224	You and Me Against the World	*Helen Reddy*
225	Please Come to Boston	*Dave Loggins*
226	Feel Like Makin' Love	*Roberta Flack*
227	Call on Me	*Chicago*
228	I'm Leaving It (All) Up to You	*Donny and Marie Osmond*
229	I Love My Friend	*Charlie Rich*
230	I Honestly Love You	*Olivia Newton-John*
231	Tin Man	*America*
232	Stop and Smell the Roses	*Mac Davis*
233	Carefree Highway	*Gordon Lightfoot*
234	Back Home Again	*John Denver*
235	My Melody of Love	*Bobby Vinton*
236	Longfellow Serenade	*Neil Diamond*
237	Laughter in the Rain	*Neil Sedaka*
238	Angie Baby	*Helen Reddy*
239	When Will I See You Again	*The Three Degrees*
240	Wishing You Were Here	*Chicago*
241	Mandy	*Barry Manilow*

1975

242	Only You	*Ringo Starr*
243	Please Mr. Postman	*The Carpenters*
244	Morning Side of the Mountain	*Donny and Marie Osmond*
245	Best of My Love	*The Eagles*
246	Sweet Surrender	*John Denver*
247	Lonely People	*America*
248	Nightingale	*Carole King*
249	Poetry Man	*Phoebe Snow*
250	Have You Never Been Mellow	*Olivia Newton-John*
251	I've Been This Way Before	*Neil Diamond*
252	(Hey Won't You Play) Another Somebody Done Somebody Wrong Song	*B. J. Thomas*

1976

1983

1984

1985

476	Axel F	Harold Faltermeyer
477	The Search Is Over	Survivor
478	Who's Holding Donna Now	DeBarge
479	Everytime You Go Away	Paul Young
480	Cherish	Kool and the Gang
481	Saving All My Love for You	Whitney Houston
482	Part-Time Lover	Stevie Wonder
483	Separate Lives	Phil Collins and Marilyn Martin
484	Say You, Say Me	Lionel Richie

1986

485	That's What Friends Are For	Dionne and Friends
486	Go Home	Stevie Wonder
487	My Hometown	Bruce Springsteen
488	The Sweetest Taboo	Sade
489	How Will I Know	Whitney Houston
490	Sara	Starship
491	These Dreams	Heart
492	Secret Lovers	Atlantic Starr
493	Overjoyed	Stevie Wonder
494	Greatest Love of All	Whitney Houston
495	Live to Tell	Madonna
496	There'll Be Sad Songs (to Make You Cry)	Billy Ocean
497	No One Is to Blame	Howard Jones
498	Your Wildest Dreams	The Moody Blues
499	Glory of Love	Peter Cetera
500	Words Get in the Way	Miami Sound Machine
501	Friends and Lovers	Gloria Loring and Carl Anderson
502	Stuck With You	Huey Lewis and the News
503	Throwing It All Away	Genesis
504	I'll Be Over You	Toto
505	The Next Time I Fall	Peter Cetera with Amy Grant
506	Love Will Conquer All	Lionel Richie
507	The Way It Is	Bruce Hornsby and the Range
508	Love Is Forever	Billy Ocean

1987

509	This Is the Time	Billy Joel
510	At This Moment	Billy Vera and the Beaters
511	Ballerina Girl	Lionel Richie
512	You Got It All	The Jets
513	Mandolin Rain	Bruce Hornsby and the Range
514	Nothing's Gonna Stop Us Now	Starship
515	The Finer Things	Steve Winwood
516	Just to See Her	Smokey Robinson
517	La Isla Bonita	Madonna
518	Always	Atlantic Starr
519	In Too Deep	Genesis
520	I Wanna Dance With Somebody (Who Loves Me)	Whitney Houston

566	Everlasting Love	*Howard Jones*
567	If You Don't Know Me by Now	*Simply Red*
568	Right Here Waiting	*Richard Marx*
569	One	*The Bee Gees*
570	If I Could Turn Back Time	*Cher*
571	Cherish	*Madonna*
572	Healing Hands	*Elton John*
573	Don't Know Much	*Linda Ronstadt featuring Aaron Neville*
574	Another Day in Paradise	*Phil Collins*

1990

575	How Am I Supposed to Live Without You	*Michael Bolton*
576	Downtown Train	*Rod Stewart*
577	Here We Are	*Gloria Estefan*
578	All My Life	*Linda Ronstadt featuring Aaron Neville*
579	Love Will Lead You Back	*Taylor Dayne*
580	This Old Heart of Mine	*Rod Stewart (with Ronald Isley)*
581	Hold On	*Wilson Phillips*
582	Do You Remember?	*Phil Collins*
583	When I'm Back on My Feet Again	*Michael Bolton*
584	Cuts Both Ways	*Gloria Estefan*
585	Vision of Love	*Mariah Carey*
586	Come Back to Me	*Janet Jackson*
587	Release Me	*Wilson Phillips*
588	Oh Girl	*Paul Young*
589	Unchained Melody	*The Righteous Brothers*
590	Love Takes Time	*Mariah Carey*
591	From a Distance	*Bette Midler*
592	You Gotta Love Someone	*Elton John*

1991

593	Because I Love You (The Postman Song)	*Stevie B*
594	The First Time	*Surface*
595	All the Man That I Need	*Whitney Houston*
596	Coming Out of the Dark	*Gloria Estefan*
597	You're in Love	*Wilson Phillips*
598	Cry for Help	*Rick Astley*
599	Baby Baby	*Amy Grant*
600	Love Is a Wonderful Thing	*Michael Bolton*
601	I Don't Wanna Cry	*Mariah Carey*
602	Rush, Rush	*Paula Abdul*
603	(Everything I Do) I Do It for You	*Bryan Adams*
604	Time, Love and Tenderness	*Michael Bolton*
605	Everybody Plays the Fool	*Aaron Neville*
606	Too Many Walls	*Cathy Dennis*
607	When a Man Loves a Woman	*Michael Bolton*
608	That's What Love Is For	*Amy Grant*
609	Keep Coming Back	*Richard Marx*

1992

610	Can't Let Go	*Mariah Carey*
611	Don't Let the Sun Go Down on Me	*George Michael with Elton John*
612	What Becomes of the Brokenhearted	*Paul Young*
613	Missing You Now	*Michael Bolton featuring Kenny G*
614	Save the Best for Last	*Vanessa Williams*
615	Tears in Heaven	*Eric Clapton*
616	Hazard	*Richard Marx*
617	Hold On My Heart	*Genesis*
618	If You Asked Me To	*Celine Dion*
619	I'll Be There	*Mariah Carey*
620	The One	*Elton John*
621	Restless Heart	*Peter Cetera*
622	Sometimes Love Just Ain't Enough	*Patty Smyth with Don Henley*
623	Nothing Broken but My Heart	*Celine Dion*
624	Am I The Same Girl	*Swing Out Sister*
625	I Will Be Here for You	*Michael W. Smith*
626	To Love Somebody	*Michael Bolton*
627	I Will Always Love You	*Whitney Houston*

1993

628	A Whole New World (Aladdin's Theme)	*Peabo Bryson and Regina Belle*
629	Forever in Love	*Kenny G*
630	Simple Life	*Elton John*
631	Love Is	*Vanessa Williams and Brian McKnight*
632	I Have Nothing	*Whitney Houston*
633	Tell Me What You Dream	*Restless Heart featuring Warren Hill*
634	Have I Told You Lately	*Rod Stewart*
635	By the Time This Night Is Over	*Kenny G and Peabo Bryson*
636	I'll Never Get Over You (Getting Over Me)	*Exposé*
637	I Don't Wanna Fight	*Tina Turner*
638	The River of Dreams	*Billy Joel*
639	Said I Loved You . . . But I Lied	*Michael Bolton*

1994

640	The Power of Love	*Celine Dion*
641	Now and Forever	*Richard Marx*
642	I'll Remember	*Madonna*
643	Can You Feel the Love Tonight	*Elton John*
644	Wild Night	*John Mellencamp/Me'shell Ndegeocello*
645	All I Wanna Do	*Sheryl Crow*
646	I'll Make Love to You	*Boys II Men*

1995

647	I'm the Only One	*Melissa Etheridge*
648	Love Will Keep Us Alive	*The Eagles*
649	Take a Bow	*Madonna*

INTRODUCTION

When it became apparent by the late 1950s that rock and roll definitely was here to stay, some radio stations were in a quandary. They wanted to keep playing current hits, a format which had appealed to their listeners for decades, yet they did not want to play that frenetic beat. A programming approach emerged whereby airplay was given to songs without the heavy sounds. Those songs became known in the music industry as "easy listening" or "middle of the road" tunes.

Having written several articles about the phenomenon, *Billboard*, the leading periodical covering the industry, decided to list the top records in this genre just as it had done previously for years with the pop, R&B (rhythm and blues, also known earlier as "race" and later as "soul" or "black" music), and country charts. In the issue dated July 17, 1961, the magazine unveiled its first Easy Listening chart of the top 20 most-played tunes on easy listening radio stations. It remained a top 20 chart through the issue dated October 17, 1964, with the only changes being the name of the chart, which became Middle-Road Singles on November 3, 1962 and Pop-Standard Singles on May 2, 1964.

From October 24, 1964 through May 29, 1965, the chart fluctuated between 15 to 25 singles listed per week under the title Middle-Road Singles until the month of May 1965, when the title was again Pop-Standard Singles. Then in the June 5, 1965 issue, *Billboard* revamped the chart again, listing 40 positions under the title of Easy Listening. At the same time, the chart went from being largely a compilation of the top pop singles of each week minus those with rock overtones to a list that better reflected what easy listening stations were actually programming. Whereas previously the Easy Listening chart had listed as #1 records only those which had been at least top 10 pop hits the same week they peaked on the chart, now there were more discrepancies between the chart and the pop roster. Some #1 Easy Listening singles, such as "It's Such a Pretty World Today" by Andy Russell and "Cold" by John Gary, both in 1967, even failed to make the pop chart at all. The "generation gap" between the music loved by the older easy listening bunch and the younger pop crowd was particularly wide during the years between 1965 and 1967. Names like Jack Jones, Dean Martin, and Andy Williams had far more success on the Easy Listening chart than on the pop chart, and very few #1 songs from the former also made #1 on the latter. (For example, in 1965 there were no crossover #1 hits, and in 1967 there was just one.)

In the late 1960s and early 1970s, however, there was often a strong correlation between top performances by singles on the pop and Easy Listening charts. This was partially due to the mellow quality of some of the popular hits of the time done by artists like the Carpenters, Glen Campbell, and Bread, but also because fewer people who considered themselves easy listening fans were requesting previous favorites like Frank Sinatra and Ed Ames. The easy listening format grew in popularity during in this period, and to reflect that fact *Billboard* expanded the chart to 50 singles per week starting on the July 7, 1973 issue. It was not until the April 7, 1979 issue that the chart became known as Adult Contemporary, the name it would carry for the next two decades.

After 1979, the only significant changes on the Adult Contemporary chart (hereafter abbreviated as "AC chart"), involved its size. In the October 20, 1984 issue it shrunk to 40 positions, then went back to 50 again the week of September 19, 1987. It was back to 40 positions for the July 17, 1993 issue. Then in the March 16, 1996 edition, *Billboard* restructured the listing so that there were now 25 records listed for Adult Contemporary. At the same time *Billboard* created a new category, Adult Top 40, reporting that the Adult Top 40 chart would reflect a broader spectrum of artists than the AC chart. In this book, only records topping the AC chart have been listed.

The Billboard Book of Number One Adult Contemporary Hits lists chronologically each record to top the AC chart since the first listing in 1961 through January 1999—a total of 38 years. For each chart-topper are given the title, artist, label and catalog number when it was #1 AC, the week it first made #1 AC and how many weeks it stayed there, plus the writers and producers of each record. Whenever possible I have identified which writers did the melody and which did the lyrics.

For each of the 677 records which went to #1 AC, I have given a little background on the artist(s) involved and told highlights of the story behind the song's creation. I have also provided information on its performance if any on *Billboard*'s pop, R&B, and/or country charts, other versions of the songs, and any major Grammy or Oscar nominations and awards collected by the record.

A few brief notes on terminology are in order. As noted before, *easy listening, middle of the road, adult contemporary*, and *AC* are all synonymous. *Single* and *45* are both used to describe records released with just one primary tune on it. In the old pre-CD days, singles came out on vinyl and had one song on each side; the *A-side* was designated by the record company as the intended hit, and the other side, the *flip*, was known as the *B-side*. As you will see, some B-sides ended up being AC hits. I use the old-fashioned terms *album* and *LP* to describe collections of songs. Certain tracks from these collections are released as singles in order to get radio airplay and encourage listeners to buy the albums.

Regarding charts, I use *pop* and *Hot 100* interchangeably to describe the tunes played on top 40 radio stations, and often I make mention of the song's pop performance in comparison with its AC peak to compare and contrast how it did on the other main chart in *Billboard*. For 45s which hit #2 or #3 pop, I list the songs ahead of them which kept them from the top pop post, and for all top 10 pop singles I list the week(s) in which they peaked. On the other end of the scale, *bubbling under* refers to the list *Billboard* kept of songs that seemed to have potential to break into the Hot 100. If a single has a *bubbling under* designation, it peaked below the Hot 100.

I hope anyone reading this book will be encouraged to seek out the singles or their albums, as they will provide a fascinating overview of how the AC market has changed and developed within the course of a few decades. The AC station of today might balk at playing some of the earlier hits as being too sweet for the current audience, and likewise I cannot imagine such surprisingly tough tunes as Melissa Etheridge's "I'm the Only One" or the Rembrandts' jangly "I'll Be There for You" being accepted on any AC station during the 1960s or maybe even the 1970s. But they all made it to the top at one time or another, and these are their stories. Enjoy.

1 The Boll Weevil Song

BROOK BENTON

Mercury 71820

July 17, 1961 (3 weeks)

Writer: Brook Benton, Clyde Otis

Producer: Not Listed

The honor of the first #1 AC hit goes to Brook Benton, a mellow singer/songwriter born Benjamin Franklin Peay in Camden, South Carolina, on September 19, 1931. He spent the early part of his professional singing career with gospel groups, first the Camden Jubilee Singers in the 1940s, then Bill Langford's Langfordaires in New York in the late 1940s, followed by the Jerusalem Stars in 1951. In 1953 he cut his first solo recordings but did not crack the pop chart until 1958 with "A Million Miles From Nowhere," which reached #82. He stayed afloat through that time writing hit songs for other artists, such as "A Lover's Question," a #6 pop and #1 R&B hit for Clyde McPhatter in 1958.

His first hit came in 1959 with "It's Just a Matter of Time," a #3 pop smash that year which spent nine weeks at #1 R&B (surprisingly, it was his first R&B chart entry). He wrote that hit along with Clyde Otis, a manager of artists at Mercury Records. Over the next few years, Benton and Otis created, and Benton recorded, several other top pop and R&B triumphs, including "Endlessly" (#12 pop, #3 R&B) and "Thank You Pretty Baby" (#16 pop, #1 R&B for four weeks) in 1959, "Kiddio" (#7 pop, #1 R&B for nine weeks) in 1960, and "The Boll Weevil Song" in 1961.

"The Boll Weevil Song" was an adaptation of a traditional American tune, but with a novelty slant. It peaked at #2 on both the R&B and pop charts, stopping at the latter for three weeks starting July 10, 1961, behind "Tossin' and Turnin'" by Bobby Lewis, in addition to its three-week stint atop the AC chart.

Benton had 16 other entries on the AC chart through 1968, with the highest charting of them on the listing after "The Boll Weevil Song" being its follow-up, "Frankie and Johnny," at #6 in 1961. Its flip side, "It's Just a House Without You," also made the AC chart that year at #8. In 1970 Benton came the closest he ever did to getting back to #1 when "Rainy Night in Georgia" made #2 AC for three weeks as well as #4 pop and #1 R&B. He had his 21st and last AC entry with "Shoes" at #18 in 1971.

He continued to record throughout the 1970s but only made the R&B chart once more—in 1978 at #49 with "Makin' Love Is Good for You" on Olde World Records. He last recorded in 1979 for Polydor Records. In the 1980s he spent time touring the oldies circuit.

On April 9, 1988, Benton died of complications from spinal meningitis. He was 56 years old.

2 Together

CONNIE FRANCIS

MGM 13019

August 7, 1961 (1 week)

Writer: B.G. DeSylva and Lew Brown (words and music),
*   Ray Henderson (music)*

Producer: Not Listed

The top female vocalist on the AC chart in the 1960s was Connie Francis, born Concetta Rosa Maria Franconero in Newark, New Jersey, on December 12, 1938. She began her recording career at MGM Records in 1955 but had no success there and nearly left the music business until her father encouraged her to take a gamble on his approach.

"After my father had chosen 'Who's Sorry Now' for me, that was when my career took off," Francis said. "He told me it was a song the adults already know, and if we added a triplet beat, the kids would dance to it." She had her doubts, but having nothing to lose, she recorded it his way. "Who's Sorry Now" went to #4 in early 1958 and became the first of 16 top 10 hits for the artist.

Francis had already notched two #1 pop hits in 1960 ("Everybody's Somebody's Fool" and "My Heart Has a Mind of Its Own") when "Together" became her first entry and first #1 on the AC chart. Like "Who's Sorry Now," the tune was an old favorite that had been a #1 record for Paul Whiteman and His Orchestra in 1928, though other versions recorded that year by Cliff Edwards and Nick Lucas fared well too. There had been a surge of interest in the song previously (in 1944) for some reason too, with Guy Lombardo, Dinah Shore, and the duo of Helen Forrest and Dick Haymes all doing hit renditions of it.

Recalling how she found "Together," Francis said, "I was stuck for a song and I didn't have anything for the session. If I didn't have a song, I would take a book called *Musicians Handbook* and look up old songs to consider to record." There she found "Together," heard a copy of the record and thought it was beautiful, and then went to record it.

The musical arranger for "Together" was Cliff Parman, who Francis described as "wonderful." She also remembered that "We did that one in Nashville. . . .All the musicians in Nashville are so for you. They all come up with suggestions to make it better."

"Together" peaked at #6 pop the week of August 7, 1961. Its flip side was "Too Many Rules," which crept to #72 pop while the A-side peaked at #1 AC. In 1964 P. J. Proby tried to revive "Together" again, but all his version could do was go to #117 bubbling under. Francis said she still performs the song today as part of a hit medley in her concert act.

Following "Together," Francis had a double-sided pop and AC hit, "When the Boy in Your Arms (Is the Boy in Your Heart)," which went to #2 AC and #10 pop, backed with "Baby's First Christmas," which made #7 AC and #26 pop. The next single gave her a #1 hit on both the AC and pop charts [see 12—"Don't Break the Heart That Loves You"].

3 Wooden Heart

JOE DOWELL

Smash 1708

August 14, 1961 (3 weeks)

Writers: Bert Kaempfert, Kay Twomey, Fred Wise,
*   Ben Weisman*

Producer: Shelby Singleton Jr.

A song first sung by Elvis Presley hit #1 AC five months before the King of Rock was able to reach the same peak on that chart. It was Joe Dowell who took "Wooden Heart," which Presley introduced in his 1960 movie *G.I. Blues*, to the top of the AC and pop chart, the latter for the week of August 28, 1961 only.

Joe Dowell was born in Bloomington, Indiana, on January 23, 1940. His path to recording fame came when producer Shelby Singleton Jr. signed him to his Smash label and looked for material for the young artist to record. When Singleton heard "Wooden Heart" in *G.I. Blues* and realized it had not been released, he quickly planned to cover it with Dowell. The tune was based on a German folk song titled "Muss I Denn." One of its adaptors, Bert Kaempfert, later co-wrote another #1 AC and pop record [see 72—"Strangers in the Night"].

Playing organ on the Dowell record was Ray Stevens, who remembered the session came at the end of a productive stretch. "It was an amazing day, because at 10 a.m. I played on 'Ahab the Arab,' and then at 2 p.m. I played on Leroy Van Dyke's 'Walk on By,' and then at 6 p.m. I played on 'Wooden Heart,'" he said. All three records hit the pop top five.

Like Dowell, Stevens found help from Singleton in his musical career, although he was allowed to do more work for the record company, including playing on songs like "Wooden Heart." Stevens said he has good memories of Dowell. "He seemed like a real nice guy, personable and friendly," he said.

But Stevens admitted he did not see much of Dowell outside of the "Wooden Heart" session because in the wake of his "Ahab the Arab" success, "I kind of drifted away" from working with Singleton. Dowell ended up having two follow-ups make the Hot 100—"The Bridge of Love" in 1960 (#50 pop, #10 AC) and "Little Red Rented Rowboat" in 1962 (#23 pop)—while Stevens went on to greater success, including a #1 AC record of his own [see 133—"Everything Is Beautiful"].

The Presley version of "Wooden Heart" was not released when Dowell's cover became a success, but it did appear twice as the B-side of later singles, first on his version of "Blue Christmas," where it bubbled under at #107 in 1964, and then on "Puppet on a String," where it bubbled under again to #110 in 1965. The only artist who came close to challenging Dowell with a cover version in America in 1961 was Gus Backus, whose "Wooden Heart" bubbled under to #102. In the United Kingdom, however, Presley's rendition became the hit single and stayed at #1 there for six weeks in 1961.

In 1975 Bobby Vinton brought "Wooden Heart" back into the Hot 100. It peaked at #58 pop and went to #23 AC.

4 Michael
THE HIGHWAYMEN

United Artists 258

September 4, 1961 (5 weeks)

Writer: Dave Fisher, from a traditional tune

Producer: Dave Fisher

The Highwaymen were Robert Burnett from Mystic, Connecticut, Steve Butts from New York City, Chan Daniels from Buenos Aires, Argentina, Dave Fisher from New Haven, Connecticut, and Steve Trott from Mexico City. "We were all classmates and fraternity brothers at Wesleyan [in Middletown, Connecticut] in 1958," recalled Burnett of their first meeting. A year later, the group was performing professionally.

All sang tenor except Butts, a bass, and Daniels, a baritone. Burnett played bongos and maracas, Daniels the charango (an instrument made from an armadillo shell), Fisher the banjo, and Trott the guitar. "Dave did all our arranging back then," Burnett said. "Michael," an 1800s folk song, became part of their repertoire when it was added at the last minute at one concert.

In their sophomore year, the Highwaymen went to New York City to see a booking agent contacted by Trott's father. "A guy named Ken Greengrass saw us," Burnett said. "He arranged for the recording date that year [1960]."

When the group recorded its first LP, they thought the hit single from it would be "Santiano," which Burnett termed an "upbeat folk song." On its B-side was "Michael." "We recorded it in early 1960," Burnett recalled. Released in January 1961, the record did nothing for half a year, until WORC in Worcester, Massachusetts, gave it airtime. By September 4 "Michael" was #1 pop and AC, staying atop the former chart one more week and atop the latter chart four more weeks.

All members of the Highwaymen were 21 when "Michael" became a hit. After the song's success, the Highwaymen stayed in college but did shows weekends before returning to Wesleyan Sundays. They had three more AC and pop entries through 1962—"The Gypsy Rover" (#12 AC, #42 pop) backed with "Cotton Fields" (#3 AC, #13 pop), and "The Bird Man" (#19 AC, #64 pop)—before vanishing from those charts entirely. The group graduated in 1962 but didn't disband until 1964, when Trott went to law school.

Trott served in the U.S. Justice Department during the Reagan administration in the 1980s and is now an appellate judge for the 9th Circuit. Burnett became first vice president at Bank Boston in Rhode Island. Butts became an academic planner at Lawrence College in Appleton, Wisconsin. Fisher wrote music for movies and TV shows in Los Angeles. Daniels died on August 2, 1975.

In 1990, the members sued Johnny Cash, Waylon Jennings, Kris Kristofferson, and Willie Nelson for copyright infringement for recording and touring under the group name the Highwaymen. When it appeared no one would be a winner as the case dragged on, Jennings proposed a truce, to be sealed by having both groups do a concert in Los Angeles in October 1990. "Ever since then, we've been singing together four or five times a year, usually at charities or conventions," Burnett said.

5 Mexico
BOB MOORE AND HIS ORCHESTRA

Monument 446

October 9, 1961 (1 week)

Writers: Felice and Boudleaux Bryant

Producer: Not Known

The first of many instrumental #1 hits on the AC charts was "Mexico," popularized by Bob Moore. Born in Nashville, Tennessee, on November 30, 1932, Moore was best known before the tune hit as a leading bass player in the home of country music both at clubs and recording sessions. He could play several styles of music, and the artists he accompanied ranged from country great Red Foley to Connie Francis.

Moore had talents evident beyond just playing bass, which Monument Records President Fred Foster realized when he employed Moore as music director for the label in 1959. One of his most productive tasks was leading the orchestra backing Roy Orbison at recording sessions. Orbison, previously signed to Sun Records, flourished as Moore's orchestrations helped him score such top 10 pop hits as "Only the Lonely" and "Blue Angel" in 1960 and "Running Scared" and "Crying" in 1961. By the time of the 1961 hits, Moore had his own deal to record instrumentals for Monument based largely on how well Orbison was doing on the Hot 100.

The first single under Moore's name was "Theme From My Three Sons," which went nowhere despite *My Three Sons* being one of the most popular new TV series at the time (Lawrence Welk did have a rendition make #55 pop that year). But his next release was "Mexico," which broke him out of the pack. It was written by the top songwriting team of Felice and Boudleaux Bryant, perhaps best known for their late 1950s pop hit compositions for the Everly Brothers such as "Wake Up Little Susie" and "All I Have to Do Is Dream."

"Mexico" made #7 pop the week of October 2, 1961, in addition to #1 AC and even went to #22 R&B. But Moore's other instrumentals never made any of those charts again. The best he could manage to do with a single was in 1963, when "Kentucky" bubbled under to #101.

Sensing the inevitable, Moore quit attempting to establish his own solo career and went back to being a bassist or music director for others. He left Monument for the Hickory label later in the 1960s and went on to work with artists ranging from Bob Dylan to Don McLean in the 1970s before retiring from the music business.

Bob Moore should not be confused with two other similarly named pop acts. Saxophonist Bobby Moore and the Rhythm Aces were an R&B septet who went to #27 pop in 1966 with "Searching for My Love," while another Bobby Moore was a session bassist and singer in the 1960s and 1970s who went to #99 pop in 1975 with "(Call Me Your) Anything Man."

6 Sad Movies (Make Me Cry)
SUE THOMPSON

Hickory 1153

October 16, 1961 (1 week)

Writer: John D. Loudermilk

Producer: Not Listed

John D. Loudermilk, a writer who first made the pop chart at #38 as "Johnny Dee" singing "Sittin' in the Balcony" in 1957, remembered meeting the woman who gave him his first #1 on any *Billboard* chart. "I had a new artist. We were working with Hickory Records then. She was Sue Thompson, and she had a little girl's voice," he said. Thompson, born Eva Sue McKee on a farm near Nevada, Missouri, on July 19, 1926, was raised in Sheridan and San Jose, California. She recorded for Mercury, Columbia, and Decca before Hickory, but no releases on those labels made any chart.

Loudermilk presented Thompson with his tune "Sad Movies (Make Me Cry)," which he had not written for anyone specifically. "I had the song first, and then I gave it to her," he said. "It just kind of fit her."

The song was inspired by something his girlfriend at the time said. "I was in a movie theater. *Spartacus* was the movie. After the movie went off, they turned the bright lights on, and it was just an ambience killer. The person I was with had tears in her eyes and said, 'Sad movies make me cry.'"

"Sad Movies (Make Me Cry)" reached #1 AC plus #5 pop the week of October 23, 1961. A cover by the Lennon Sisters peaked at #13 AC and #56 pop that same year. And most astonishingly, Loudermilk noted, "Brigitte Bardot had a record of it."

Thompson's follow-up, "Norman," also written by Loudermilk, was a bigger pop hit than "Sad Movies," stalling at #3 on the Hot 100 in early 1962. It missed the AC chart, but the next Thompson 45, "Two of a Kind," hit #8 AC and #42 pop in 1962, and the single after that, "Have a Good Time," went to #9 AC and #31 pop.

Over the next three years Thompson had four songs hit the Hot 100, the last being another Loudermilk composition, "Paper Tiger," at #23 pop in 1965. Refashioning herself as a country artist, she made her debut in the world of country music in 1971 with "The Two of Us Together," a duet with Don Gibson which went to #72. With and without Gibson she made the country chart 12 times through 1976, the highest entry being 1974's "Good Old Fashioned Country Love" at #31. She also made the AC chart one last time, with "Big Mabel Murphy," a #40 AC and #50 country entry in 1975.

By the late 1990s, Thompson had retired from show business and was living in Las Vegas. Loudermilk has remained active in Nashville as a songwriter, with many hits to his credit including "Then You Can Tell Me Goodbye" [see 297].

7 Big Bad John
JIMMY DEAN

Columbia 42175

October 23, 1961 (10 weeks)

Writer: Jimmy Dean

Producer: Don Law

Jimmy Dean, born in Plainview, Texas, on August 10, 1928, was no stranger to the *Billboard* charts when "Big Bad John" hit, although that was his first AC entry. He hit the country chart in 1953, a year after he began recording, with "Bumming Around," which went to #5. His first pop hit, 1957's "Deep Blue Sea," went to #67. But apart from "Little Sandy Sleighfoot," which went to #32 pop after its release during the Yuletide season in 1957, no Dean single cracked any chart thereafter until "Big Bad John."

Dean discussed the song with Dorothy Horstman in *Sing Your Heart Out, Country Boy*. "While appearing in summer stock in *Destry Rides Again*, I became acquainted with an actor by the name of John. He was six-feet-five and built like a football player. He was the only guy in the group I had to look up to, so I started calling him 'Big John.' Then while flying to a recording session in Nashville, and needing a fourth side to record, I started writing this song that had been going round in my mind. I always thought that 'Big John' had a powerful ring to it, so, in an hour and a half, I had put 'Big John' in a mine and killed him. And there you have 'Big Bad John.'"

"Big Bad John" was #1 on the AC, pop, and country charts simultaneously for a time. It arrived atop the Hot 100 November 6, 1961 and stayed there for five weeks, while on the country chart it reached the limit the weeks of November 20 and 27, 1961. *Billboard* reported the single sold 400,000 copies the first two and a half weeks of release and then averaged sales of around 40,000 a day. Its 10-week run at #1 AC was not matched until Roger Miller's "King of the Road" came out in 1965 [see 52], and neither were surpassed until Paul Mauriat's "Love Is Blue" [1968; see 103].

At the Grammys, "Big Bad John" won Best Country and Western Recording plus nominations for Record and Song of the Year and Best Male Solo Vocal Performance. Dean resurrected John as a character in his 1962 single "The Cajun Queen," which went to #4 AC, #16 country, and #22 pop. "Big Bad John" also reappeared as the title song for a 1990 movie starring Dean. It was not a hit.

Dean remained a fairly constant presence on the country chart for the next decade, but rarely charted on the AC or pop charts after 1962. The exceptions were "The First Thing Ev'ry Morning (and the Last Thing Ev'ry Night)" in 1965 (#1 country, #19 AC, and #91 pop), "Sweet Misery" in 1967 (#16 country, #13 AC), and "I.O.U." in 1976 (#9 country, #35 pop, and #47 AC). Dean last charted in 1983 when a rerelease of "I.O.U." went to #77 country. He remained a popular occasional guest on several shows on The Nashville Network (TNN) cable channel in the 1990s.

8 When I Fall in Love

THE LETTERMEN

Capitol 4658

January 6, 1962 (1 week)

Writers: Edward Heyman (words), Victor Young (music)

Producer: Nick Venet

1962

The first Lettermen did get sweaters with letters for their ath-
letic abilities in high school, but that was not how the group
got its name, according to founder Tony Butala. "I looked around
to see what was around, and all the others had school-type names—
the Four Preps, Danny and the Juniors. . . .The name 'Lettermen'
came to me from a friend whose group had used the name for two
nights," he said.

Butala's idea for the group was to "get three guys and do some
sound between the raucous rock and roll and the smooth big band
sound." Original partners Mike Barnett and Talmadge Russell lettered in football and baseball respectively, while Butala lettered in
baseball. The three appeared in a Las Vegas revue in 1958 titled
Newcomers of 1958. "It was the first time that the Lettermen name
was on the marquee," Butala said. Barnett and Russell left that
same year.

By 1960 the Lettermen were Butala, Jim Pike, and Bob Engemann. Butala met Pike in a lounge act in Las Vegas, and actress
Connie Stevens introduced Butala to her then-boyfriend Engemann, who she thought sounded like her high school pal Butala. In
1961 the trio's "The Way You Look Tonight" gave them their AC
and pop debuts, peaking at #3 AC and #13 pop.

"When I Fall in Love" came next. It was an instrumental in the
1952 movie *One Minute to Zero*, and had gone to #20 pop that same
year in Doris Day's vocal version. The idea for the Lettermen to
do it came from producer Nick Venet, who had Butala sing lead
because he liked what Butala called his "breathy, Bobby Vinton
voice." Butala loved the song, noting that "Those lyrics can't be
dated. We did vocal arrangements similar to 'The Way You Look
Tonight.'"

"When I Fall in Love" also went to #7 pop, which tied their
highest peak there along with 1967's "Goin' Out of My Head/Can't
Take My Eyes Off You." "When I Fall in Love" returned often to
the pop and AC charts, hitting the latter in covers by Donny
Osmond in 1973 (#31), Linda Ronstadt in 1985 (#24), Natalie Cole
in 1988 (#14), and Celine Dion and Clive Griffin in 1993 (#6).

The Lettermen's last pop entry, 1971's "Love," went to #42
pop and #8 AC, while their 29th and last AC entry was 1975's "You
Are My Sunshine Girl" at #28. Engemann left the group in 1966
and was replaced by Gary Pike, one of Jim's two younger brothers.
In early 1969 Jim developed a vocal problem, and his other
younger brother, Donnie, replaced him. The younger Pikes stayed
with Butala until 1980.

The latest Lettermen are Donovan Scott Tea, who joined in
1984, and Darren Dowler, who joined in 1995. "We've gone 38
years without a break," Butala said of his group. "We do about 150
shows a year. We just finished our 69th album." When not working Butala lives in his hometown of Sharon, Pennsylvania, where he
is working on a Vocal Group Hall of Fame to spotlight the music
and careers of easy listening groups in the 20th century.

9 Can't Help Falling in Love

ELVIS PRESLEY

RCA 47-7968

January 13, 1962 (6 weeks)

Writers: George Weiss, Hugo Peretti, Luigi Creatore

Producer: Steve Sholes

For anyone who attended an Elvis Presley concert in the 1970s, the song ending the show was invariably "Can't Help Falling in Love." It was not his biggest hit; despite its AC peak it could not dislodge Joey Dee and the Starliters' "Peppermint Twist" from #1 on the Hot 100 and so stopped at #2 pop the week of February 3, 1962 (it did hit #1 in the U.K.). And though it appeared in his film *Blue Hawaii*, it was not his only ballad that came from a movie; the title song from 1956's *Love Me Tender* holds that honor. So why did Presley like this tune so much?

A possible answer was provided by Gordon Stoker, a member of the Jordanaires vocal quartet which backed Presley on "Can't Help Falling in Love." "He told us about meeting Priscilla [Beaulieu] when doing that session," Stoker recalled. Presley later married Priscilla Beaulieu, in 1967 (although they divorced in 1973, Elvis never remarried). The happiness Elvis felt during that period, combined with the fact that he just enjoyed singing "Can't Help Falling in Love," made the session a memorable one, according to Stoker.

Another Jordanaire, Neal Matthews, recalled that "The four of us [the Jordanaires] and a Hawaiian group sung on that. There were eight voices on it." The result gave the song a deep layer of harmony that can be heard particularly well near the end.

"Can't Help Falling in Love" was based on "Plaisir d'Amour," a French tune written by Giovanni Martini sometime during the 18th century. The updating by George Weiss, Hugo Peretti, and Luigi Creatore was eligible for both Oscar and Grammy nominations yet somehow snagged neither despite the song's massive popularity.

Billboard reviewed "Can't Help Falling in Love" as the B-side to "Rock-A-Hula Baby," a song recorded during the same session as the former on March 23, 1961, in Hollywood and not surprisingly also used in *Blue Hawaii*. "Rock-A-Hula Baby" did not make the AC chart but did go to #23 pop.

Though "Can't Help Falling in Love" remains strongly identified with Presley, many other artists have covered the tune. The ones making the charts with their versions include Al Martino in 1970 (#5 AC, #51 pop), Andy Williams in 1970 (#28 AC, #88 pop), the Soft Tones in 1973 (#56 R&B), the Stylistics in 1976 (#52 R&B), Englebert Humperdinck in 1979 (#44 AC), Jimmy Castor in 1980 (#93 R&B), Slim Whitman in 1981 (#54 country), and Corey Hart in 1987 (#24 both AC and pop). In 1993 UB40's rendition, heard in the film *Sliver*, actually surpassed Presley's showing on the Hot 100 and peaked at #1 pop for seven weeks starting June 24, 1993 (on the AC chart it made only #11).

Presley would make #1 AC five more times. The next of these was "Crying in the Chapel" [see 55].

10 A Little Bitty Tear

BURL IVES

Decca 31330

February 24, 1962 (1 week)

Writer: Hank Cochran

Producer: Not Listed

Rotund, goateed Burl Ives was a multitalented individual who made his mark in several fields. He made 30 movies between 1946 (*Smoky*) and 1988 (*Two Moon Junction*). He won an Oscar for Best Supporting Actor for his role in 1958's *The Big Country*. He also made numerous TV appearances from the 1950s through the 1980s, and starred in his own situation comedy, *O.K. Crackerby*, from 1965–66 and in the drama *The Lawyers* from 1969–72. These thespian efforts have overshadowed in some people's minds his music, the field which originally brought Ives to national attention.

Born Burle Icle Ivanhoes in Hunt Township, Illinois, on June 14, 1909, Ives was a folksinger going by the title "The Wayfaring Stranger" when he had his first hit record, 1948's "Blue Tail Fly" with the Andrews Sisters, which went to #24. His record entries were rather sparse over the next 13 years, and only six singles made the pop chart. After "Mari-anne" went to #84 in 1957, it was over four years before Ives returned on the Hot 100 with "A Little Bitty Tear."

The writer of "A Little Bitty Tear" was Hank Cochran, who told *Billboard* in 1965 that he composed most of his songs driving home from work, where it was quiet and nothing could bother him. He said he composed "A Little Bitty Tear" in the car within about 15 minutes. "Nothing prompted the idea for it," he said. "It just came into my mind."

"A Little Bitty Tear" went up the charts almost as effortlessly as it had been composed. Besides its #1 AC peak, it climbed to #9 pop the week of February 10, 1962, plus stayed at #2 on the country chart for two weeks in early 1962. Ives won Grammy nominations for Best Male Solo Vocal Performance and Best Country and Western Recording for the record. Around the same time Wanda Jackson covered "A Little Bitty Tear," but all she could do was reach #84 pop. When Hank Cochran revived his own tune in 1980 it went to #57 country.

Cochran also composed the follow-up to "A Little Bitty Tear," "Funny Way of Laughin.' " "Funny. . ." went to #3 AC, #9 country, and #10 pop and won Ives his only Grammy for Best Country and Western Recording. A few other entries in 1962 did well, but after that Ives fared rather poorly on the charts, peaking in the lower regions and having several miss the Hot 100. His last chart entry anywhere was "I'll Be Your Baby Tonight," which made #35 AC and bubbled under to #133 in the summer of 1968.

From the 1970s on the bulk of Ives' airplay was around the Yuletide season, when stations played his "A Holly Jolly Christmas." He also did the song on the annual TV special *Rudolph the Red-Nosed Reindeer*, which first aired on December 6, 1964 and was still being broadcast even after Ives' death, on April 14, 1995.

11 Midnight in Moscow

KENNY BALL AND HIS JAZZMEN

Kapp 442

March 3, 1962 (3 weeks)

*Writers: Kenny Ball, Jan Burgers; based on a tune
    by Vassili Soloviev-Sedoi*

Producer: Not Listed

The early 1960s British fad for "trad" jazz—traditional New Orleans–style jazz played by English artists—never took off in America, with the exception of "Midnight in Moscow." Originally titled "Padmeskoveeye Vietchera," translated as "Moscow Nights," the song was a standard in Russia, typically played as a ballad in that country.

Kenny Ball heard the tune while on a trip to Brussels in the summer of 1961. "A Hungarian goulash band was playin' it. I was gassed!" he told *Newsweek* enthusiastically in trad-ese. But as he did not speak Russian, he could not understand the title of the song from the announcer. Luckily, he took down the notes of the main theme on his airline ticket and eventually matched the tune with the title.

"I knew from the first it was a solid trad jazz number," Ball recalled. Apparently so did other imitators, for by the time it was out in America after peaking at #2 in the United Kingdom in December 1961, Ball's record had spawned at least three other instrumental covers of the tune. There was also a vocal version by Julius LaRosa called "You Can't Keep Me From Loving You," with words by Oscar Brand and Paul Nassau (the Russian standard had words by N. Matusovsky). But none of them managed even a sliver of the success of Ball's version, which peaked on the Hot 100 at #2 behind Bruce Channel's "Hey! Baby" the week of March 17, 1962.

Kenneth Daniel Ball was born in Ilford, England, on May 20, 1930. He formed his first trad band in 1958 after four years of being a professional musician, but did not get a recording contract until their group auditioned successfully for Pye Records three years later. Their first entry on the British chart was "Samantha," which peaked at #13 in 1961. "Midnight in Moscow" later that year was the group's highest-charting record in the United Kingdom. On that record Ball played trumpet and harmonica, joined by his Jazzmen Colin Bates on piano, Johnny Bennett on trombone, Ron Bowden on drums, Diz Disley on banjo, Dave Jones on clarinet, and Vic Pitts on bass.

Though the group never made the AC chart again, two of their follow-ups in 1962, "March of the Siamese Children" and "The Green Leaves of Summer," hit #88 and #87 respectively on the Hot 100. Ball last charted in America in 1963 when he bubbled under to #119 with "Heartaches." (His version of "Sukiyaki" that year was a hit in England but was eclipsed in America by the original from Kyu Sakamoto—see 29.) Also in 1963, he became the first Englishman to become an honorary citizen of New Orleans.

Ball continued to chart in the United Kingdom through 1964 with "When I'm 64." Though his career remained low-key after that, he continued to tour into the 1990s.

12 Don't Break the Heart That Loves You

CONNIE FRANCIS

MGM 13059

March 24, 1962 (4 weeks)

Writers: Benny Davis, Ted Murray

Producers: Arnold Maxin, Danny Davis

As with "Who's Sorry Now" and some of Connie Francis' other hits, Connie's dad was a key factor in getting her to record "Don't Break the Heart That Loves You." As she recalled, "One day he came into the office and said, 'Connie, you've got to hear this song. There are two songwriters out here who want to meet you.' I said, 'Who are they?'" When he told her they were in their late seventies, Francis was anything but excited. Who needed to hear anything new from two old timers? But when her dad explained that they were Benny Davis and Ted Murray, the duo which created such standards as "Baby Face" and "There Goes My Heart," she reconsidered.

"So I said, 'Send them in.' I heard 'Don't Break the Heart That Loves You' played once and said, 'That's a hit song.'" Indeed it was, though Francis gives credit to work done by Don Costa, "My favorite arranger. He could do anything." In fact, she added, in terms of what they contributed to her records, "All of the arrangers who did my songs should have been listed as producers."

"Don't Break the Heart That Loves You" went to top the Hot 100 the week of March 31, 1962 while still atop the AC chart. Later, Margo Smith recorded a version which topped the country chart in 1978. As for Francis, she kept making AC hits throughout the rest of the 1960s, although after 1965 they began to be in the lower regions, as did her entries on the Hot 100. Among her follow-ups were two other new Davis-Murray compositions, 1963's "Follow the Boys" (#7 AC, #17 pop) and 1965's "Whose Heart Are You Breaking Tonight" (#7 AC, #43 pop).

It was during the 1970s that Francis endured the toughest phase of her career. She had no records entering the chart (1969's "The Wedding Cake" was her last Hot 100 entry, peaking there at #91, and her last AC entry for 12 years, stopping there at #19). Even worse, she endured a rape on November 8, 1974, following a concert in Westbury, New York, and found herself unable to sing following the trauma. She did not return to touring and recording until 1981, when she released a new LP. Unfortunately, its title song, "I'm Me Again," went only to #40 AC as a single and failed to chart anywhere else, and Francis was relegated to doing mostly her 1950s and 1960s hits in concerts.

In early 1998 Francis found time to relocate near Boca Raton, Florida, in the middle of a busy touring schedule. "I've been doing shows all over the place," she said. She was happy touring and doing her old songs for her fans and noted, "I love to work. I want to die when I'm 99 on that stage, because there's nothing like it."

13 Stranger on the Shore
MR. ACKER BILK

Atco 6217

April 21, 1962 (7 weeks)

Writer: Acker Bilk

Producer: Dennis Preston

"I think 'Stranger on the Shore' was good for jazz. People come to jazz concerts because of 'Stranger,' which lasts three minutes, and end up listening to two hours of jazz." So wrote Mr. Acker Bilk in a fax sent to me in 1998 by Frank Cassidy, secretary of the Mr. Acker Bilk and His Paramount Jazz Band Fan Club. "Stranger on the Shore" was Bilk's main claim to fame in America, but he had other hits in his native England. He deserves credit for getting "Stranger on the Shore" atop the AC and pop charts during the pre-Beatles music era when few British acts had a transatlantic hit.

Born in the country village of Pensford, Avon, England, on January 28, 1929, Bernard Stanley Bilk earned the nickname of "Acker," meaning "mate." He lost his two front teeth in a school fight, but that did not dissuade him from starting to play the clarinet in 1948. He didn't front his first band until 1958 in Bristol, England. That group, which became known as the Paramount Jazz Band, was still with Bilk 40 years later. His United Kingdom chart debut was 1960's "Summer Set," which hit #5 as well as #104, bubbling under in America. Five more singles charted in his homeland before "Stranger on the Shore" peaked at #2 in Great Britain.

The inspiration for "Stranger on the Shore" was, oddly enough, the crying of Bilk's 6-month-old daughter Jenny. In fact, the tune's original title was "Jenny," but when the British Broadcasting Corporation used it as the theme for a TV series called *Stranger on the Shore*, the instrumental was renamed in honor of the show.

The sixth week "Stranger on the Shore" led the AC listings, on May 26, 1962, it was also #1 pop in America. Incredibly, it even made #7 R&B. Regarding this stateside success, Bilk wrote, "I was very pleased." But only one more single entered both charts, 1962's "Above the Stars" at #19 AC and #59 pop. Two more instrumentals made the bottom third of the Hot 100 through 1963, followed by one last single to bubble under in 1964, "The Harem" (#125). Asked why he could not create another "Stranger on the Shore" in America, Bilk wrote, "I was too busy, so I didn't try."

Also in 1962, two vocal versions of "Strangers on the Shore" made the charts, one by Andy Williams (#9 AC, #38 pop) and one by the Drifters (#19 AC, #73 pop). Bilk's "Stranger on the Shore" earned him a Grammy nomination for Best Performance by an Orchestra or Instrumentalist with Orchestra, Not Jazz or Dancing.

Off the charts over a decade, in 1976 Bilk had a mini-comeback with "Aria," which made #5 in England and #41 AC in America. He was still recording in 1994, when he released an LP called *Chalumenu—That's My Home* on Apricot Music. When not touring, Bilk resides in Somerset, England.

14 I Can't Stop Loving You
RAY CHARLES

ABC–Paramount 10330

June 9, 1962 (5 weeks nonconsecutive)

Writer: Don Gibson

Producer: Sid Feller

The idea of movie teen idol Tab Hunter beating Ray Charles in a cover battle sounds ridiculous today, but that's what ABC–Paramount Records was worrying about in 1962 when Charles' "I Can't Stop Loving You" competed against a note-by-note cover from Hunter. When Charles agreed to have his version released as an edited single from his LP *Modern Sounds in Country and Western Music*, it went to #1 AC, pop, and R&B in 1962 (without charting country, by the way) and stopped Hunter's version from charting anywhere.

The release of the country album was controversial in and of itself at ABC–Paramount. As Charles explained in his autobiography *Brother Ray* with David Ritz, he had been planning that kind of LP for several years when he realized that his contract with the label was nearing its end and he would be able to test the faith of the company's executives in him with his proposal.

"They told me how this might injure my career," he wrote. "They told me how all my fans had been loyal to me. They explained how I might irritate some people, how I might lose my following. And even though I listened and understood what they were saying, I ignored them and made the record anyway. We had no contract problems."

Charles' producer Sid Feller brought copies of the greatest country hits he knew for Charles to record. "I Can't Stop Loving You" was included as the fifth tune on the LP's B-side. "This song was written in Knoxville [Tennessee] in a house trailer on the Clinton highway," Don Gibson told Dorothy Horstman in *Sing Your Heart Out, Country Boy*. "I sat down to write a lost love ballad. After writing several lines to the song, I looked back and saw the line 'I can't stop loving you.' I said, 'That would be a good title,' so I went ahead and rewrote it in its present form."

Gibson took his version of the tune to #7 country and #81 pop in 1958. Kitty Wells also did a rendition that year which went to #3 country. Later revivals of "I Can't Stop Loving You" on the country chart were by Conway Twitty in 1972 (#1), Sammi Smith in 1977 (#27), and Mary K. Miller in 1978 (#28). On the pop chart, Count Basie did a rendition that hit #77 in 1963. But none of them gained the widespread appeal of Charles' record, which was #1 R&B for 10 weeks starting the week of May 26, 1962, and #1 pop for five weeks starting June 2, 1962, in addition to its AC triumph.

"I Can't Stop Loving You" also won a Grammy for Best Rhythm and Blues Recording and a nomination for Record of the Year. The LP from which it came, *Modern Sounds in Country and Western Music*, also had a nomination for Album of the Year. Another cut from it provided Charles with his second #1 AC hit [see 17—"You Don't Know Me"].

15 The Stripper

DAVID ROSE

MGM 13064

July 7, 1962 (2 weeks)

Writer: David Rose

Producer: Jesse Kaye

This big instrumental hit of 1962 was a seven-year-old song recorded in 1958 and never intended for release. "The Stripper" has quite an interesting background, and the same can be said about its composer, David Rose.

Born in London on June 15, 1910, Rose came to America when he was 7. In the 1930s Hollywood Rose did find some work, but was known by the public chiefly through his brief marriages to the often-wed Martha Raye and Judy Garland. His musical talent finally achieved wide acceptance in 1943 when his instrumental "Holiday for Strings" hit #2 and sold a million copies. That song later became the main theme on radio and television for *The Red Skelton Show*, and Rose stayed as musical director for Skelton for more than 20 years until the series ended in 1971.

Rose also contributed scores to more than 1,000 TV episodes, one of which was the 1955 drama "Burlesque" on the CBS nighttime anthology series *Shower of Stars*. He wrote eight measures as background music for the show. Three years later, doing an album featuring a brass section, Rose had time left in the recording session and had his musicians play that same bit of bump-and-grind music, which featured both blaring brass and a thumping percussion section. But MGM, Rose's record company, felt it was inappropriate to release the song, so it stayed hidden away.

Then in 1962, Rose recorded "Ebb Tide" to promote a version of that song in MGM's new film *Sweet Bird of Youth*. When a song was needed for the single's B-side, an unknown office worker picked "The Stripper." Though not intended to be a hit, the tune intrigued comedian Robert Q. Lewis, who served as a disc jockey in Los Angeles. Lewis played the song repeatedly for 45 minutes in one stretch, and Rose credited that incident for popularizing the record.

As "The Stripper" headed up the AC and pop charts to peak at #1 (it did so only for the week of July 7, 1962, on the Hot 100), *Newsweek* asked MGM Records Vice President and producer of "The Stripper" Jesse Kaye to explain the song's appeal. "It's because it's well done with a big orchestra, but still has the feel of walking down the runway in a strip joint," he said. "You listen to those little three- and four-piece combos in a strip joint and the music is dirty. This isn't. It's naughty—naughty and nice. It's the kind of music which would be played in a million-dollar strip joint, if there was one."

"The Stripper" compiled Grammy nominations for Best Performance by an Orchestra for Dancing, Best Instrumental Theme, and Best Instrumental Arrangement. It went to #12 R&B, but marked the last appearance for Rose on that or any other chart. He concentrated instead on his TV work well into the 1980s, doing the theme for the Michael Landon series *Highway to Heaven*. He died on August 23, 1990 at the age of 80.

16 Roses Are Red (My Love)

BOBBY VINTON

Epic 9505

July 28, 1962 (4 weeks)

Writers: Paul Evans, Al Byron

Producer: Bob Morgan

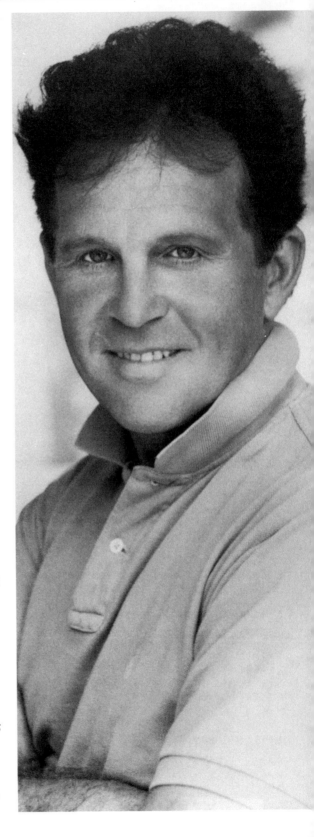

After letting him record two flop LPs of instrumental band music, Epic Records officials planned to wind up their contract with bandleader Bobby Vinton. But Vinton knew his contract called for him to record two more singles before the term of the agreement was over. Waiting in an office while officials mulled their options, Vinton noticed a pile of rejected records.

"As I looked through the stack, I spotted an interesting title, 'Roses Are Red.' Out of all the songs there I decided to play this one. As soon as I heard it, I said to myself, 'I'm not really a singer, but this sounds to me like a song that could go over.' I thought I could sell enough records with that song to get us out of a deficit and have the chance to make another band album," Vinton wrote in his autobiography, *The Polish Prince*.

Vinton convinced Epic executives that the tune, along with a song he wrote while in the Army called "Mr. Lonely," were worthy of being done by him for release. They assigned him a new producer, Bob Morgan, and the two of them tried some "rock and roll tricks," as Vinton put it, on "Roses Are Red" before deciding their efforts were terrible and that the song needed a straight-ahead interpretation.

It took one take to do "Mr. Lonely" and two or three to finish "Roses Are Red." But Epic considered a tune called "You and I" to be hit material, so "Roses Are Red" became the B-side of it, as the latter song's references to yearbooks fit perfectly with the graduation time release of the single. However, when Vinton's old pal Joe Gorlack told him how "Roses Are Red" got to him emotionally, Vinton resolved to push that side instead.

After buying about 1,000 copies of the single, Vinton sold them personally to people in western Pennsylvania, Ohio, and West Virginia. (The tri-state area was familiar to him, as he was born in Canonsburg, Pennsylvania, as Stanley Robert Vinton on April 16, 1935.) Then he hired a woman to deliver a dozen red roses to radio station deejays in Pittsburgh. The gimmick worked, and "Roses Are Red" went on to peak at #1 pop for four weeks starting July 14, 1962, before doing the same on the AC chart. It even crossed over to the R&B chart and hit #5 there. And when it hit #1 in West Germany, Vinton recorded the song in German.

"Roses Are Red" prompted an answer record by Florraine Darlin called "Long As the Rose Is Red," which peaked at #15 AC and #62 pop in 1962. As for "Mr. Lonely," Epic had Buddy Greco cover it. It went to #64 pop in 1962. Epic released Vinton's version in late 1964, and it went to #1 pop and #3 AC. Vinton's official follow-up to "Roses Are Red" was "Rain Rain Go Away," which hit #4 AC and #12 pop. He returned to #1 AC with "Blue Velvet" [see 32].

17 You Don't Know Me

RAY CHARLES

ABC-Paramount 10345

August 25, 1962 (3 weeks)

Writers: Cindy Walker, Eddy Arnold

Producer: Sid Feller

"You Don't Know Me" came close to repeating the same triumphs of the single which paved the way for its release, "I Can't Stop Loving You" [see 14]. As with the latter record, "You Don't Know Me" was a remake of a country tune which hit #1 AC and came from Ray Charles' 1962 LP *Modern Sounds in Country and Western Music*, which spent 14 weeks at #1 on the mono album chart. Both songs also had a B-side which did fairly well on its own. "Born to Lose," the flip of "I Can't Stop Loving You," made #13 AC and #41 pop, and "Careless Love," on the opposite side of "You Don't Know Me," went to #19 AC and #60 pop.

However, "You Don't Know Me" fell short of "I Can't Stop Loving You" in terms of performance on other charts. It missed the high mark on the Hot 100 when it peaked at #2 the week of September 8, 1962, behind Tommy Roe's "Sheila," and also only reached #5 on the R&B chart.

The tune originally was a hit for its co-writer Eddy Arnold, who took it to #10 country in 1956. Jerry Vale covered the record that year and went to #14 pop. Charles had the highest-charting pop version. Other renditions to make the music charts were by Lenny Welch in 1960 (#28 R&B, #45 pop), Elvis Presley in 1967 (#34 AC, #44 pop), Ray Pennington in 1970 (#61 country), and Mickey Gilley in 1981 (#1 country, #12 AC, #55 pop). Charles also sang the song again in his 1965 album *Live in Concert*, but it was not released as a single.

Those used to hearing Ray Charles do such shouters as "Hit the Road Jack" (#1 pop for two weeks in 1961) were puzzled by the switch to "I Can't Stop Loving You" and "You Don't Know Me," with their airy choirs and strings. He noted his fans' concerns in his autobiography with David Ritz, *Brother Ray*: "Many people are confused about my decision to do country music. They think ABC dictated to me. They think ABC produced these albums for me. Not true. For better or worse, the records were my ideas. Anyone who knows me understands that I really like this music. Not for show, not for shock, but for my own pleasure."

Charles continued in the country vein over the next three years, and most of his biggest AC hits during that time were country covers. They included "Your Cheating Heart" (#7 AC in 1962) and "Take These Chains From My Heart" (#3 AC in 1963), both #1 country hits for Hank Williams in 1953, and "No One to Cry To" (#8 AC in 1964), a #6 country hit for the Sons of the Pioneers in 1946. It would be another song written by a country artist which gave him his third #1 AC hit [see 67—"Crying Time"].

18 Ramblin' Rose

NAT "KING" COLE

Capitol 4804

September 15, 1962 (5 weeks)

Writers: Noel Sherman, Joe Sherman

Producer: Lee Gillette

Suave, smooth-voiced Nathaniel Adams "King" Cole, born in Montgomery, Alabama, on March 17, 1917, never was wild about rock and roll, yet he achieved some of his biggest musical successes when that genre was flourishing in the 1950s and 1960s. As a jazz pianist, he first recorded in 1936 in a band led by his brother Benny, then formed the Nat King Cole Trio in 1939 with Oscar Moore on guitar and Wesley Prince on bass. They recorded on the independent label Armour until signing with Capitol in 1942. They began to make the pop chart in 1943 with Nat singing lead and hit #1 with "(I Love You) for Sentimental Reasons" in 1946 and "Nature Boy" in 1948. Nat went solo in 1950 and hit #1 again that year with "Mona Lisa." He returned to the spot a year later with "Too Young."

Cole continued to have pop top 10 hits regularly through 1958, but then found himself hitting the Hot 100 at the lower rungs for the next four years until "Ramblin' Rose." The brother team of Joe and Noel Sherman wrote the tune within a half hour, and while they liked their composition, it took longer to convince Cole it could be a hit.

As Cole told Ren Grevatt in *Billboard*, "Sometimes the more you want a hit, the harder it is to get one. I look for a good song. Jackie Gale, who runs my publishing firm, brought 'Ramblin' Rose' to the [West] Coast. I'll admit I wasn't too excited by it. I could have blown it. But we cut it and you know the rest. Joe and Noel Sherman wrote a good song and a good song always has a chance."

While ruling the AC chart roost, "Ramblin' Rose" peaked at #2 pop the weeks of September 22 and 29, 1962, behind "Sherry" by the Four Seasons. Its success led to an album named after the song which stayed on the LP chart for 162 weeks and peaked at #3. The song also earned a Grammy nomination as Record of the Year. While it made #7 on the R&B chart, "Ramblin' Rose" failed to cross over to the country chart. However, the tune landed there later in versions by Johnny Lee in 1977, which peaked at #37, and Hank Snow in 1978, which peaked at #93.

Cole had first made the AC chart with "Take a Fool's Advice" in 1961, which peaked at #14 (#71 pop). He remained a regular presence on the chart until his death from lung cancer on February 15, 1965. A few posthumous singles made both the AC and pop charts, ending with 1966's "Let Me Tell You, Babe" (#20 AC, #90 pop). Then in 1991, with his vocals dubbed from his 1952 original recording, Nat appeared one last time on the charts, singing with his daughter Natalie on "Unforgettable" (#3 AC, #14 pop). (For more on her career, see 565—"Miss You Like Crazy.")

19 | I Remember You

FRANK IFIELD

Vee-Jay 457

October 20, 1962 (1 week)

Writers: Johnny Mercer (words), Victor Schertzinger (music)

Producer: Norrie Paramor

Frank Ifield was born in Coventry, England, on November 30, 1936, then emigrated to Australia shortly after World War II broke out. He had developed his vocal style by the time he was in his early teens. In 1951 he released his first record, "Did You See My Daddy Over There?" and followed it with more than 40 singles over the next eight years. Ifield also appeared on several radio and TV series in Australia during the decade.

He returned to England in 1959 and got a small hit with "Lucky Devil" at #22 the following year. "Gotta Get a Date" made #49 in September 1960, then nearly two years passed before Ifield had his biggest triumph with "I Remember You."

"I Remember You" was one of several tunes Johnny Mercer and Victor Schertzinger composed for the 1942 film *The Fleet's In*. Doing the song in the movie was Jimmy Dorsey and His Orchestra, whose version went to #9 pop in 1942. That same year Harry James and His Orchestra took their interpretation, with a vocal by Helen Forrest, to #24 pop.

Ifield's version sold over a million copies in the United Kingdom alone as well as hitting #1 there for seven weeks starting July 26, 1962. Reportedly his producer, Norrie Paramor, thought Ifield had changed the song beyond recognition (Ifield yodeled the title, for example) and initially did not want his name on it.

In America, the record went to #5 pop the weeks of October 13 and 20, 1962, a great achievement for a British record at the time. In 1966 "I Remember You" went to #49 on the country chart in a version by Slim Whitman, which also hit #44 country when rereleased in 1981. Glen Campbell's remake made #32 country in 1988.

Three of Ifield's follow-ups to "I Remember You" made #1 in Great Britain: "Lovesick Blues" (1962); "The Wayward Wind" (1963); and "Confessin'" (1963). He last charted in England in 1967 with "Call Her Your Sweetheart," which went to #24. In the United States "Confessin'" came out as "I'm Confessin' (That I Love You)" and made #16 AC and #58 pop. It was his last AC entry, and after "Please" reached #71 pop in early 1964, he had no other singles on the Hot 100 either. Three years later he had a single bubble under to #132, the appropriately titled "Out of Nowhere," before vanishing from the American music charts. However, he continued to sing often in England.

He had a brief comeback in the United Kingdom in 1991 when a remix of the British B-side of "I Remember You," "The Yodeling Song," hit #40. It was billed as being by Frank Ifield featuring the Backroom Boys. Ifield continued to perform actively in England, and in 1998 his LP *The Fire Still Burns* was released there; it was not released in America.

20 | Only Love Can Break a Heart

GENE PITNEY

Musicor 1022

October 27, 1962 (2 weeks)

Writers: Hal David (words), Burt Bacharach (music)

Producers: Wally Gold, Aaron Schroeder

Only when Gene Francis Allan Pitney used his own first and last names did he finally have success in the music industry. Pitney, born in Hartford, Connecticut, on February 17, 1941, formed a band in high school while growing up in Rockville, Maryland, called Gene Pitney and the Genials. A manager spotted him at a Genials concert and had Pitney record his first sessions in 1959 with Ginny Arnell (real name Ginny Mazarro) under the pseudonym "Jamie and Jane," but their "Strolling" followed by "Classical Rock and Roll" were not chartbusters. In late 1959 he tried again, pressured by his manager to bill himself as "Billy Bryan," but "Cradle of My Arms" bombed too.

In 1960, tired of pseudonyms but wanting a recording career, he went to New York City and hooked up with music publisher Aaron Schroeder. Schroeder placed some of Pitney's tunes with other artists rather quickly, with the biggest early hit being "Rubber Ball," a #6 pop hit for Bobby Vee in 1960. The next year he made his Hot 100 debut as an artist with "(I Wanna) Love My Life Away" at #39. Three more songs made the pop chart over the next year, including "Town Without Pity" at #13 and "(The Man Who Shot) Liberty Valance" at #4, before the release of "Only Love Can Break a Heart."

"Only Love Can Break a Heart" was meant to be the B-side of "If I Didn't Have a Dime (to Play the Juke Box)," which ended up making #58 pop. "The guy who wrote that song, Bert Berns, came into my office and sang that song to me," Pitney recalled to Dawn Eden in *Goldmine* in 1993. "He had an acoustic guitar, and when he strummed that guitar, he also hit the box of the guitar—with his ring, I think it was—and it was the greatest sound."

As for "Only Love Can Break a Heart," co-writer Burt Bacharach arranged and conducted the session, but the whistling on the record was Pitney. It peaked at #2 pop the week of November 3, 1962, behind "He's a Rebel" by the Crystals—a tune written by Pitney himself! The song also hit #16 R&B. In the 1970s Sonny James took it to #2 country, while Dionne Warwick got it to #109 bubbling under in 1977 and Kenny Dale made it to #7 country in 1979.

Pitney had only four more entries on the AC chart, ending with "Twenty Four Hours from Tulsa" in 1963, but all made the top 10 on the listing. He had no pop hit as big as "Only Love Can Break a Heart," but remained constantly on the chart through 1969's "She Lets Her Hair Down (Early in the Morning)" at #89. He continued to record through 1972, but there was more interest in him overseas than in the United States, and it was not until 1993 that he started doing shows in America again. Toward the end of the 1990s he was touring roughly half of each year.

21 All Alone Am I

BRENDA LEE

Decca 31424

November 10, 1962 (5 weeks)

Writers: Arthur Altman (words–English),
*   Manos Hajidakis (music)*

Producer: Owen Bradley

Brenda Mae Tarpley, born in Lithonia, Georgia, on December 11, 1944, was christened Brenda Lee by "a little gentleman in Augusta, Georgia, affiliated with a TV station down there" who thought Brenda Lee would be a more recognizable name. European music fans nicknamed her "Little Miss Dynamite" after her success with her second charted pop single, 1957's "Dynamite" (her first entry, "One Step at a Time," hit #43 in early 1957). No matter what anybody called her, chart statistics bear out that in the 1960s she was the #1 pop female vocalist and the #2 AC female vocalist, behind Connie Francis on the AC charts.

Lee's string of 1960s hits began when "Sweet Nothin's" went to #4 pop. She had two more #1 pop hits later that year, "I'm Sorry" and "I Want to Be Wanted." Her AC debut, "Everybody Loves Me but You," hit #2 for a week in 1962. Two singles later, she topped the chart with "All Alone Am I."

"It came from *Never on Sunday*," Lee recalled, referring to the movie starring Merlina Mercouri as a prostitute. A music publisher, whose name Lee said she has forgotten, sent one of the melodies in the picture to her organization for consideration as a tune. "We loved the song and had it translated and recorded it," Lee said. As for the movie, Lee said, "I didn't see it till later on in life," as its adult subject matter was judged unsuitable for a teenager to see at the time.

Billboard reviewed "All Alone Am I" as the B-side to "Save All Your Lovin' for Me," but Lee said "All Alone Am I" was the song intended as the hit side. "Save All Your Lovin' for Me" did not make the AC chart but did hit #53 pop. "All Alone Am I" peaked on the pop chart at #3 the week of November 24, 1962, behind the Four Seasons' "Big Girls Don't Cry" at #1 and Elvis Presley's "Return to Sender" at #2.

Lee racked up 14 more AC hits through 1965's "Johnny One Time," which hit #3 AC and #41 pop. Thereafter the hits became sparse for her on the AC and pop charts. Her last AC entry, "I Think I Love You Again," hit #37 AC and #97 pop in 1970. The following year, Lee turned her attention to the country chart and compiled 32 entries there through 1986. Her biggest country hit was 1974's "Big Four Poster Bed," which went to #4.

Lee spent most of 1997 singing with Mel Tillis at his theater in Branson, Missouri. She got a long-overdue honor that year, when she was inducted into the Country Music Hall of Fame. She also found time to rerecord 24 of her biggest hits with her original producer Owen Bradley, including "All Alone Am I," for release in 1998. Sadly, Bradley died before Lee was able to get an album deal to release the material.

22 Go Away Little Girl

STEVE LAWRENCE

Columbia 42601

December 15, 1962 (6 weeks)

Writers: Gerry Goffin, Carole King

Producer: Al Kasha

"Go Away Little Girl" was the first song to be #1 on the Hot 100 by two different artists. Donny Osmond took it to the pop top again in 1971, when it hit #14 AC, but Steve Lawrence arrived there first with it eight years earlier, where oddly it made #14 too, but on the R&B chart. Lawrence's version topped the AC chart for six weeks, holding the same position concurrently on the pop chart for the last two of those weeks. Despite this success, one of its co-writers was not thrilled with the record.

"Steve Lawrence was one of Don Kirshner's pets," Gerry Goffin told Joe Smith in *Off the Record*. "The song 'Go Away Little Girl' was originally written for Bobby Vee. Some great American work of literature. It should have died in the closet, but it didn't. I was never happy with the song, but I am happy for the money I received on it. It's sort of a shame, though. 'Go Away Little Girl' was our biggest song. . . .Took a half hour to write."

Other versions of "Go Away Little Girl" also charted. The biggest runner-up was by the Happenings, who went to #12 with their effort in 1966. And two revivals used the song as part of medleys. The Tokens combined it with "Young Girl" to bubble under at #118 in 1969. Then in 1977, Marlena Shaw altered the tune's gender and segued "Yu-Ma" into "Go Away Little Boy" for a #21 R&B hit.

But Steve Lawrence's version remains the biggest hit and most frequently played rendition of the song. Born in Brooklyn, New York, on July 8, 1935, as Sidney Leibowitz, Lawrence first charted in 1952 with "Poinciana," which hit #21. A year later, he became a regular singer on *The Tonight Show With Steve Allen*. Another singer on the show was Eydie Gorme, and her first chart hit, "Fini," went to #19 in 1954. Three years later, Lawrence and Gorme married.

Lawrence and Gorme had their own pop hits through the AC chart's debut in 1961, but Lawrence charted there first, with "My Claire de Lune" (#13 AC, #68 pop) backed with "In Time" (#19 AC, #94 pop) making the AC chart during its first month of existence. Gorme's AC debut, "Don't Try to Fight It, Baby" (#18 AC, #53 pop), was in 1963, just two months before the first charting duet by the couple. Billing themselves thereafter as "Steve and Eydie," they took "I Want to Stay Here" to #8 AC and #28 pop.

The two eschewed rock for middle-of-the-road tunes, a decision which virtually banished them from the Hot 100 after 1964, but they continued to make the AC chart fairly consistently through the mid-1970s as soloists and as a duo. They last charted in 1979 as "Parker & Penny" singing "Hallelujah," which peaked at #46. Two decades later, Steve and Eydie remain a popular nightclub act despite their lack of hit singles.

23 Walk Right In
THE ROOFTOP SINGERS

Vanguard 35017

January 26, 1963 (5 weeks)

Writers: Gus Cannon, Hosie Woods

Producers: Erik Darling, Bill Svanoe

The Rooftop Singers' mastermind was Erik Darling, born in Baltimore, Maryland, on September 25, 1933. He sang with the folk trio the Tarriers from 1956–58 (they had a #4 pop hit in 1957 with "The Banana Boat Song") and then with the legendary folk group the Weavers, replacing Pete Seeger in 1958. But his greatest commercial success came after he went solo in 1962.

"After I left the Weavers, I went on to pursue a solo career singing in coffeehouses and clubs across the country and in Canada," Darling told Kristin Baggelaar and Donald Milton in *Folk Music: More Than a Song*. "Meanwhile, I had found this song, 'Walk Right In,' on an old recording of a jug band, Gus Cannon and His Jug Stompers, and I thought that it had to be a hit if done in a certain way with a new group." Darling brought together two friends, Bill Svanoe and Lynne Taylor, to record "Walk Right In," a tune first recorded in 1929.

Svanoe was a folksinger studying economics at Oberlin College. Taylor had been a professional vocalist since the age of 14, and had sung in the bands of Benny Goodman and Buddy Rich. Besides the trio's harmony on the tune, the record featured two 12-string guitars, a sound that Darling had deliberately gone after.

"Before 'Walk Right In' was a hit, you couldn't buy a 12-string guitar," he said. "The only ones that you could find then were in pawnshops and quite old. Eventually, I ordered one from the Gibson Company, but in order to record 'Walk Right In' with two 12-strings, we had to wait for the company to build a second one for Bill!"

"Walk Right In" topped the AC and pop charts for two weeks simultaneously starting January 26, 1963. It also peaked at #4 R&B and #23 country. The Moments (not the soul group with the 1970 hit "Love on a Two-Way Street") covered the song in early 1963 and went to #82 pop. Additionally, the Rooftop Singers' LP titled after the song got a Grammy nomination for Best Folk Recording.

But, as Darling later noted, the trio coalesced specifically to record "Walk Right In" and could never find another tune to equal it. Two follow-ups made the Hot 100 in 1963—"Tom Cat" (#20) and "Mama Don't Allow" (#55 pop, #20 AC)—and the group recorded three LPs, but basically the Rooftop Singers coasted on the success of "Walk Right In" until they disbanded in 1967. Toward the end, Taylor's part went to Mindy Stuart and then Patricia Street. Darling and Street recorded an LP for Vanguard titled *The Possible Dream* in 1975. Prior to that album, Darling did a few solo albums, but they all failed.

"Walk Right In" made a minor comeback in 1977 when Dr. Hook took it to #39 AC, #46 pop, and #92 country.

24 Rhythm of the Rain
THE CASCADES

Valiant 6026

March 2, 1963 (2 weeks)

Writer: John Gummoe

Producer: Not Listed

The Cascades were a vocal/instrumental quintet from San Diego which consisted of guitarist John Gummoe, pianist Eddie Snyder, bassist David Stevens, saxophonist David Wilson, and drummer David Zabo. Gummoe was the group's lead singer and songwriter. After a successful audition with Valiant Records, the five gentlemen prepared to record three songs for the label in 1962. One was Gummoe's composition "Rhythm of the Rain."

Perry Botkin Jr., arranger of the first session for the Cascades, talked to Bob Gilbert and Gary Theroux in *The Top Ten* about recording "Rhythm of the Rain" with the group. "I think my biggest contribution was a little sort of musical figure behind the tune," he said. "All the way through you hear a celeste piano thing that goes 'Deet doo deet doo—deet doo, deet doo deet-doo.' I remember sitting at the piano and finding that figure and everybody saying, 'Oh yeah, that's great!'" Botkin also speculated that the thunderclap sound effect heard at the start of the song was used by Phil Spector when the latter produced the Ronettes' #24 pop hit of 1964 "Walking in the Rain," since Spector recorded that song at the same studio.

"Rhythm of the Rain" went to #3 pop behind "Walk Like a Man" by the Four Seasons at #1 and "Ruby Baby" by Dion at #2 the week of March 9, 1963, while riding high on the AC chart. It also hit #7 on the R&B chart.

The tune was revived several times over the years. It was the last Hot 100 entry for Gary Lewis and the Playboys [see 58—"Save Your Heart for Me"] in 1969, peaking at #63. On the country chart, Pat Roberts took it to #34 in 1972, Floyd Cramer to #67 in 1977, and Jacky Ward to #11 in 1978. It reappeared on the AC chart at #37 in 1984 when done by Neil Sedaka and at #3 in 1990 when Dan Fogelberg recorded it in a medley with the Beatles' "Rain." And in the United Kingdom, where the Cascades' version peaked at #5 in 1963, Jason Donovan took the tune to #9 in 1990.

The Cascades never made the U.K. chart after "Rhythm of the Rain," or the AC or R&B charts. Their follow-ups made only the lower rings of the Hot 100 or bubbled under. In chronological order, they were "The Last Leaf" in 1963 (#60) and its flip side "Shy Girl" (#91), then "A Little Like Lovin'" (#116) in late 1963, "For Your Sweet Love" (#86) in early 1964, "Cheryl's Goin' Home" (#131) in 1966, and "Maybe the Rain Will Fall" (#61) in 1969.

As for their engineer, Botkin hit #8 on both the AC and pop charts in 1976 with his partner Barry DeVorzon with their instrumental "Nadia's Theme (The Young and the Restless)." The song served as background music for Olympic gold medalist Nadia Comaneci and as the theme to the CBS-TV daily soap opera *The Young and the Restless*.

25 The End of the World
SKEETER DAVIS

RCA 8098

March 16, 1963 (4 weeks)

Writers: Sylvia Dee (lyrics), Arthur Kent (music)

Producer: Chet Atkins

Though "The End of the World" was not written specifically for Skeeter Davis, she has said that the song has special meaning to her in reflecting the feelings she had over the death of her pal and fellow (unrelated) performer Betty Jack Davis in a car crash on August 2, 1953. The two recorded as the Davis Sisters and were about to have their biggest hit, "I Forgot More Than You'll Ever Know," which hit #1 country for eight weeks in late 1953, when the accident occurred. Skeeter survived the crash and went on to work with Betty's sister Georgia as the Davis Sisters, but the two disbanded in 1956. Skeeter then pursued a successful solo career in country music which peaked with "The End of the World."

"The End of the World" was written by Sylvia Dee in honor of her late father. It was an across-the-board smash for Skeeter, hitting #1 AC, #2 both country and pop (held out of #1 on the Hot 100 on March 23, 1963, by Ruby and the Romantics' "Our Day Will Come"), and even #4 R&B. Skeeter wrote in her autobiography, *Bus Fare to Kentucky*, that "Scott Muni, the pop disc jockey on WABC in New York, had played the record and, I believe, was the one who should receive credit for the record's dramatic breakout."

One deejay who did not play the tune, to Skeeter's distress, was her then-husband Ralph Emery, who instead aired the nonhit B-side "Somebody Loves You" on his show on WSM Nashville. It was one of several points of contention between Davis and Emery, who later gained fame as host of *Nashville Now*, the nightly country music show on cable's The Nashville Network (TNN) from 1983–93. Davis claimed that during their marriage (1960–64), Emery used speed and fathered a daughter by another woman, among other indiscretions. She later wed Joey Stampinato, bassist with the band NRBQ.

Good chart performance was not the only positive thing about "The End of the World," according to Davis. When during a performance in Atlanta she discovered that her backing band didn't know the song, she decided to create her own band to play behind her on tours. This proved to be a wise move, as Davis continued to chart on the country scene through 1976's "I Love Us." (On the AC chart, "The End of the World" was the first of five entries there, ending when "Gonna Get Along Without You Now" hit #15 in 1964.)

Born Mary Francis Penick on Glencoe, Kentucky, on December 30, 1931, Skeeter earned her nickname and later professional name for being as hyperactive as a mosquito as a child. She used the name throughout her career, which included stints on the Grand Ole Opry beginning in 1959. She could still be seen at that venue and did some recording in the 1990s. RCA rereleased Davis' "The End of the World" in 1973, but it sold poorly. In 1982 Jody Taylor revived the tune and it peaked at #70 country.

26 Can't Get Used to Losing You

ANDY WILLIAMS

Columbia 42674

April 13, 1963 (4 weeks)

Writers: Doc Pomus, Mort Shuman

Producer: Robert Mersey

The Academy Awards named it Best Song. So did the Grammys, as well as judging it Record of the Year. But despite the critical acclaim, Andy Williams' rendition of "The Days of Wine and Roses" fared only modestly on the charts in 1963, reaching #9 AC and #26 pop. It was the other side of the single, "Can't Get Used to Losing You," which got the most airplay then as now on radio stations.

The singer was not certain in recalling whether "Can't Get Used to Losing You" was really supposed to be the flip side or if it was released with the hope of becoming a double-sided hit. "I never thought of it as being a B-side," Williams said. "I guess maybe it was considered the B-side."

He *was* sure that "The Days of Wine and Roses" was intended to be a hit. Columbia, remembering the success that Williams' album *Moon River and Other Movie Themes* had enjoyed after Williams sang the Oscar-winning Best Song of 1961, "Moon River," at the Academy Awards, took a gamble. They knew Williams would be singing "The Days of Wine and Roses" at the Oscars in 1963. Hoping that the tune would win Best Song too, they released it as a single. It did win an Oscar, but "Can't Get Used to Losing You" became the hit.

Williams said he got the latter song "through Robert Mersey, the producer. He knew Doc Pomus, and he brought the song to me." Williams recalled that the song ("just a couple of little verses and a chorus") did not have much on paper that impressed him. But he gave it a go. Then Mersey put together an arrangement emphasizing strings at the beginning and interlude of the song, and Williams was impressed.

"In this case, I think the arrangement had to do with it being a hit, the plucking sounds. . . .Once I had heard what he had done with it, I saw what it was," he said.

"Can't Get Used to Losing You" held at #2 pop for four weeks while heading the AC chart. It did not reach the summit of the Hot 100 thanks to the Chiffons' "He's So Fine" the weeks of April 13 and 20, 1963, and Little Peggy March's "I Will Follow Him" the weeks of April 27 and May 3, 1963. Incredibly, the song also became a #7 R&B hit, the highest Williams ever charted in that genre. And the album on which it appeared, *Days of Wine and Roses*, became Williams' biggest LP, staying at #1 for 16 weeks.

With "Can't Get Used to Losing You," Williams had the first of four #1 AC hits he would compile over an eight-year period. His next #1 AC entry did not come until 1966 [see 77—"In the Arms of Love"].

27 Puff the Magic Dragon

PETER, PAUL AND MARY

Warner 5348

May 11, 1963 (2 weeks)

Writers: Peter Yarrow, Leonard Lipton

Producer: Albert Grossman

"There's a misconception that Peter, Paul and Mary are 'protest singers,' " insisted Peter Yarrow. As evidence, he cited several of their songs not in that vein, including "Puff the Magic Dragon." And, added Yarrow, despite what many critics claimed over the years, "Puff. . ." was not a song with drug allusions. (Among other questionable claims was the rumor that the title words were really "Puff the Magic Drag On.") "It's not at all about anything other than that sad loss of sweetness and innocence that we all experience," Yarrow said.

The impetus for the composition came when Yarrow was a senior at Cornell University in 1959 and invited his freshman pal Lenny Lipton to visit his apartment in Ithaca, New York. "He sat down at the typewriter and typed something off the top of his head and began a part of what the song became," Yarrow recalled.

A few years later, Yarrow came across what Lipton had typed once again. "I looked at it and said, 'Oh, this could be a terrific song' and wrote more lyrics to it," Yarrow noted. But it needed the approval of his fellow singers Paul Stookey and Mary Travers in order to get them to record it. Luckily for Yarrow, that was no problem.

"'Puff the Magic Dragon' was very easily embraced by the group," he said. "It was embraced because they liked it. It moved them." They were not the only ones, as "Puff the Magic Dragon" went all the way to #2 pop the week of May 11, 1963, behind "I Will Follow Him" by Little Peggy March and even #10 R&B in addition to #1 AC. It became a standard part of the repertoire for Peter, Paul and Mary, and they mocked the drug-lyric believers in concert in later years by explaining how it was possible to interpret "The Star Spangled Banner" as promoting the use of illegal substances.

Peter Yarrow, born in New York City on May 31, 1936, had been a solo singer in Greenwich Village in 1961 before joining forces with Paul Stookey, born in Baltimore, Maryland, on December 30, 1937, and Mary Travers, born in Louisville, Kentucky, on November 7, 1937. They had seven months of rehearsal before Warner Brothers Records signed them as an act in early 1962.

Prior to "Puff the Magic Dragon," which was billed as just "Puff" on some singles, the trio had two songs which made both the AC and pop charts, "Lemon Tree" in 1962 (#12 AC, #35 pop) and "Settle Down (Goin' Down That Highway)" in 1963 (#14 AC, #56 pop). The single after "Puff" became their second consecutive #1 AC hit [see 31—"Blowin' in the Wind"].

I Love You Because

AL MARTINO

Capitol 4930

May 25, 1963 (2 weeks)

Writer: Leon Payne

Producer: Voyle Gilmore

Blind country music singer and writer Leon Payne had his only solo hit with "I Love You Because," which made #1 on the country jockey chart for two weeks starting January 14, 1950. In *Sing Your Heart Out, Country Boy*, his widow Myrtie Payne told Dorothy Horstman that "Leon said he wrote this song for me." However, the sentiments he sang were so universal that "I Love You Because" became one of the most frequently recorded tunes to make the country chart. Covers of the song appeared in 1950 by Ernest Tubb, who took it to #2, and Clyde Moody, who went to #8. Ten years later, Johnny Cash had a version which hit #20.

But "I Love You Because" did not make the pop chart until 1963, when Al Martino tried a less countrified take on the tune. "It was my idea to do it that way," he said. "At the time, I was listening to Eddy Arnold, and I found it on his album."

Martino asked his pal and fellow Capitol artist Nat "King" Cole who he would recommend to do the arrangement, and Cole suggested Belford Hendricks. Martino came to New York to record the tune with Hendricks, who told Martino he needed to make an adjustment to do the tune properly for a final cut. "He thought it would be a good idea if I lowered my key," Martino said. After a few days of work, Martino's "I Love You Because" was ready for public consumption.

The record was not expected to take off like a rocket, given that Martino's last entry was a reprise of his #1 hit "Here in My Heart," which made #86 pop and #17 AC (his first AC entry) in the summer of 1961. But something about "I Love You Because" appealed to love-starved radio listeners and record buyers, and by June 1, 1963, it hit #3 pop behind Lesley Gore's "It's My Party" at #1 and Jimmy Soul's "If You Wanna Be Happy" at #2 while finishing its second week at #1 AC.

While no other tries with "I Love You Because" have entered the AC or pop charts, the song did return several more times to the country chart over the next two decades, including renditions from Carl Smith (#14 in 1969), Jim Reeves (a posthumous #54 in 1976 for the singer who died in 1964; the record was a huge hit in Great Britain in 1964 as well, spending weeks on the chart), Don Gibson (#61 in 1978), and Roger Whittaker (#91 in 1983). In addition, "I Love You Because" was one of the first songs Elvis Presley recorded during his sessions at Sun Studios in Memphis, Tennessee, in 1954.

As for Martino, 39 more of his singles made the AC chart after "I Love You Because"; three of those were #1 AC hits too, with the first being "Spanish Eyes" [see 65].

29 Sukiyaki
KYU SAKAMOTO

Capitol 4945

June 8, 1963 (5 weeks)

Writers: Rokusuke Ei, Hachidai Nakamura

Producer: Koji Kusano

He acted in at least 10 movies and had more than 15 hit songs in his native country. But most Americans who remember Kyu Sakamoto identify him with the bouncy "Sukiyaki," which hit #1 on the Hot 100 and ran atop the AC chart concurrently for three weeks starting June 15, 1963. Born in Kawasaki in 1941 the ninth child of a Toyko restaurateur, Kyu had been recording in Japan four years before "Sukiyaki" became an Eastern-to-Western favorite.

The song's original title, "Ue O Muite Aruko," actually translated as "I Look Up When I Walk," but to keep the Japanese flavor Western countries heard the tune under the title "Sukiyaki." Sakamoto took it in stride, telling *Newsweek*, "At least 'Sukiyaki' is a Japanese word." As "Sukiyaki," the tune was covered by Kenny Ball and His Jazzmen [see 11] when the head of Pye Records in England heard the original version, and Ball took it to #10 in early 1963. Later that year came Sakamoto's single, and it hit #6 in Great Britain.

Its success in America has been attributed to disk jockey Rich Osborne of KORD in Pasco, Washington, playing Sakamoto's single to acclaim from his audience. But in his memoirs titled *Playback*, Capitol A&R (artists and repertoire) producer Dave Dexter, Jr., claimed that a deejay in Fresno, California, played "Sukiyaki" first as part of his programming for his sizable Japanese-American audience, and that was where its popularity started. A curious Dexter found out who sang the song by asking Capitol's contacts in Japan, then agreed to release the tune. Dexter said it took the company two hours to ready the master for release to American stations plus a little promotion before "Sukiyaki" took off.

Dexter also noted, "I still don't know what 'Sukiyaki' had that others lacked. A mood, I suppose. But none of Kyu's follow-up records had it. We tried two or three. Few were sold. I haven't heard his name mentioned in years." Sakamoto did register again in America with "China Nights (Shina No Yoru)," which hit #19 AC and #58 pop in 1963 before disappearing from the charts. In 1975 he recorded 12 songs in English at North Hollywood's Amigo Studios, but the tunes went nowhere. He was one of 520 people who died on a Japan Airlines plane crash near Tokyo on August 12, 1985.

Sakamoto's "Sukiyaki" also hit #18 R&B in 1963. The song would make all three charts again in two different renditions in later decades, both by American artists. The first was by A Taste of Honey in 1981, where it became the first AC song to hit #1 by two different artists [see 403 for more details]. Then in 1995 the Baltimore, Maryland, male quartet 4 P.M. took it to #8 pop, #17 AC, and #75 soul. "Sukiyaki" even made the country charts, first at #21 in 1963 by Clyde Beavers and at #96 in 1986 by Boots Clements. All later versions were in English.

30 Tie Me Kangaroo Down, Sport
ROLF HARRIS

Epic 9596

July 13, 1963 (3 weeks)

Writer: Rolf Harris

Producer: Not Listed

Take a flippant attitude by a musician from Down Under. Add liberally the sound of a "wobble board." Then put a touch of inspiration from a song popularized by Harry Belafonte. Presto! You have "Tie Me Kangaroo Down, Sport," the biggest novelty hit by an Australian act.

While listening to "Hold 'Em Joe," a #30 pop hit in America in 1954 by Harry Belafonte, Rolf Harris wrote a song about the passing of a stockman in the Outback. But Harris, born in Perth, Australia, on March 30, 1930, backed it with the odd, wobbly sound he discovered in 1958 when he let a Masonite board dry on an oil heater and shook it to cool it down. The resultant twang gave "Tie Me Kangaroo Down, Sport" a melody as offbeat as its storyline.

Despite some terms that not all U.S. listeners understood, such as "abos" (aborigines) and "didgeridoo" (an aboriginal wind instrument), the record topped the AC chart and peaked at #3 on the Hot 100 the week of July 13, 1963, behind the Essex's "Easier Said Than Done" at #1 and Jan and Dean's "Surf City" at #2. The song also hit #19 on the R&B chart. Its popularity stateside came three years after the record hit #9 in the United Kingdom. Fox Records released the single in America in 1960, but it bombed at the time.

When the song hit in 1963, Harris told *Newsweek*, "I'm aggressively Australian. I'm also a bit weird. But maybe that's because I embody the Australian attitude toward humor—and that's new and strange to outsiders. In 'Kangaroo' I'm singing about an old guy dying and making fun of it. Out in the bush, Australians tend to develop a callous disregard for life. . . . There gets to be a funny side to suffering."

Harris was not quite as Australian as portrayed in the interview, however. His parents emigrated from Wales, and he left Australia at age 22 to pursue his musical and artistic career in Great Britain. In America, Harris first cracked the Hot 100 with "Sun Arise," which went to #61, before "Tie Me. . ." hit. In England, "Sun Arise" reached #3 as the follow-up to "Tie Me. . .".

One other Harris single, "Nick Teen and Al K. Hall," made the Hot 100, hitting #95 in late 1963. Harris concentrated on TV shows in England and on one of them introduced "Two Little Boys." That tune was the last #1 record of 1969 in the United Kingdom, holding the spot for six weeks. In America, it bubbled under at #119 and made #19 AC in 1970, becoming the second and last AC entry for Harris.

Nearly a quarter century after that success, Harris surprised everyone by going to #7 in the United Kingdom in 1993 with a remake of Led Zeppelin's "Stairway to Heaven." The wobble-board sound was still there, more than 30 years after he first popularized it with "Tie Me Kangaroo Down, Sport."

31 Blowin' in the Wind

PETER, PAUL AND MARY

Warner 5368

August 3, 1963 (5 weeks)

Writer: Bob Dylan

Producer: Albert Grossman

It's amazing but true: Bob Dylan's single of "Blowin' in the Wind" backed with "Don't Think Twice, It's All Right" failed even to bubble under in 1963. Yet the folk singer's 45 did make its way to the attention of fellow Greenwich Village performers Peter, Paul and Mary, and they made them into two of their biggest hits ever.

Recalling the group's reaction to the songs, Peter Yarrow said, "Noel [Paul Stookey] was most attracted by 'Don't Think Twice.' 'Blowin' in the Wind' was my immediate favorite." Yarrow won out in having the group do the latter song first, and as he recalled, "It was the first, and I think the only song, that we just put out as a single without an album at the same time."

Yarrow said he particularly likes one touch on the trio's recording of the song. "Right in the middle of the verse, Mary went from singing two lead lines in a melody and went to high harmony on the third line while I sang melody, bringing the melody to another pitch."

With its popularity and theme about social change, Peter, Paul and Mary soon found themselves singing "Blowin' in the Wind" at nearly every major civil rights event of the 1960s and later years. They heard requests for it seemingly from everyone except the man who wrote it. "I don't remember Bobby ever coming up and saying, 'Wow, I love your version,'" admitted Yarrow. But his group did sing it with Dylan and Stevie Wonder at a celebration for establishing Martin Luther King Jr. Day as a national holiday, and they definitely respected Dylan, with Yarrow calling him "the premier folk poet of his generation."

"Blowin' in the Wind" peaked at #2 pop the week of August 17, 1963, behind "Fingertips—Pt. 2" by Little Stevie Wonder. Ironically, Wonder's cover of "Blowin' in the Wind" four years later went to #9 pop and #1 R&B. Later charted versions were by Stan Getz in 1964 (#110 bubbling under) and the Edwin Hawkins Singers in 1969 (#100 bubbling under).

In addition, Peter, Paul and Mary's album *In the Wind*, which featured "Blowin' in the Wind," went to #1 on the LP chart for five weeks starting November 2, 1963. And the trio won Grammys for the song for Best Performance by a Vocal Group and Best Folk Recording.

Peter, Paul and Mary followed "Blowin' in the Wind" with their "Don't Think Twice, It's All Right," which made #2 AC and #9 pop. But after 1963, Peter, Paul and Mary dropped considerably in popularity on the Hot 100 for most of the rest of the 1960s, scoring only one top 20 hit, 1967's "I Dig Rock and Roll Music." They did have three top 10 entries on the AC chart between 1964–66, including "Tell It On the Mountain," "For Lovin' Me," and "The Cruel War." Finally, in late 1969, they managed to lead both charts with "Leaving on a Jet Plane" [see 126].

32 Blue Velvet
BOBBY VINTON

Epic 9509

September 7, 1963 (8 weeks)

Writer: Lee Morris, Bernie Wayne

Producer: Bob Morgan

Bobby Vinton was feeling blue in 1963. No, not the down-and-out kind of blue, but rather the urge to do songs with the word "blue" in the title for a themed album. When "Blue on Blue" became a hit in 1963, reaching #3 pop and #2 AC, he decided to look for similar tunes.

"Burt Bacharach wrote 'Blue on Blue' for me, so I was not that excited to record 'Blue Velvet' when I heard the song," Vinton told Joe Smith in *Off the Record*. "But Al Gallico [a music publisher] was there in Nashville, where we were recording at the time, and he said, 'Why don't you do "Blue Velvet"? I'll send a girl out for the lead sheet.' I did the song in 10 minutes. I had no idea it would be one of the biggest records of 1964 [actually 1963]."

"Blue Velvet" was Vinton's second double #1 AC and pop hit, topping the latter chart for three weeks starting September 21, 1963. It was written in 1951 and originally went to #16 pop that year when done by Tony Bennett. Four years later, the Clovers took it to #14 R&B. Five years after that in 1960, the Statues reached #84 pop and the Paragons bubbled under to #103 with their versions. The song charted one more time prior to Vinton when Lawrence Welk's instrumental cut bubbled under to #103.

On the heels of the popularity of his version, Vinton ran into Dean Martin at the health club in the Sands Hotel in Las Vegas. As he recounted in his autobiography *The Polish Prince*, Vinton introduced himself as the singer of "Blue Velvet."

"I've never heard of it," Martin said. "But it's all over the radio—it's number one in *Billboard*," Vinton told him. "I never read *Billboard* if I don't have a record out," Martin responded.

"Well, *Billboard* has just awarded me the 'most programmed' male vocalist award. And [Frank] Sinatra is second," said Vinton. "Sinatra is second and you're first!" Martin exclaimed. Vinton added, "I'm only trying to tell you what the deejays said." Unfortunately and unbeknownst to Vinton, Sinatra just happened to be next to Martin under a sheet— not the best way for Vinton to make a first impression.

"Blue Velvet" later became the title for a controversial 1986 film directed by David Lynch. The song was included in the film but did not chart again. However, when it was used in a skin cream commercial on British television in 1990, Vinton's "Blue Velvet" went to #2 in the United Kingdom that year after failing to chart during its original release there. Only two other Vinton records made the U.K. chart—his first U.S. #1 hit "Roses Are Red (My Love)," which went to #15 in 1962 and reentered at #71 in 1990 [see 16], and his next double #1 AC and pop hit, "There! I've Said It Again" [see 36], which hit #34 in 1964.

33 Washington Square
THE VILLAGE STOMPERS

Epic 9617

November 2, 1963 (3 weeks)

Writers: Bob Goldstein, David Shire

Producer: Joe Sherman

The Village Stompers was an octet of veteran session and performing jazz musicians who played at the Basin Street East club in the Greenwich Village area of New York City in the early 1960s. It featured Dick Brady on trombone, Ralph Casale on banjo and guitar, Don Coates on piano, Frank Hubbell on trumpet, Mitchell May on bass, Joe Muranyi on clarinet, Al McManus on drums, and Lenny Pogan on guitar.

Hubbell was the ostensible leader of the group ("He had the personality to be a leader," May noted). Hubbell had headed a jazz band called the Sun City Six before using his friends and their friends in the jazz world to form the Village Stompers. "I had not known Hubbell, but I knew Joe Muranyi and Brady and Pogan," May recalled. May himself had been playing bass since he finished serving in the Army in 1959.

The tune which introduced them to the world was "Washington Square," which May believed existed as a composition under that title by Bob Goldstein and David Shire before it was found an appropriate match for the Village Stompers, as Washington Square was located in Greenwich Village. "Duke Niles, I remember, was this hot-shot agent for the group. I think he paid the guys $50 for the tune," May said.

Under Joe Sherman's production and arrangement, "Washington Square" introduced the world to the Village Stompers. It went all the way to #2 pop the week of November 23, 1963, held out of the top by "I'm Leaving It Up to You" [see 34]. The song got a Grammy nomination for Best Instrumental Theme. Also, the Ames Brothers tried to make a comeback with a vocal version of "Washington Square," but they only made #129 bubbling under, while the Kirby Stone Four's cover did not chart at all. In 1971 James Last took "Washington Square" to #22 AC.

"I personally wasn't surprised," May said of the success of "Washington Square." "The strangest things became hits."

But due to the Village Stompers' lack of successful follow-ups to "Washington Square," the "folk-Dixie band," as May called it, decided to disband around 1965. They had only two other AC entries, the title tune to the Broadway musical *Fiddler on the Roof* (#19 AC, #97 pop) in 1964 and the title tune to the movie *Those Magnificent Men in Their Flying Machines* (#35 AC, #130 bubbling under) in 1965.

May continued as a bassist and often worked with Brady, Coates, Muranyi, and Hubbell at various sessions the rest of the 1960s. Then, he said, "In the early 1970s the music became so rock-oriented, there was no more 12 months of work for me." He sought help to deal with his anger about his loss of work and ended up becoming a psychoanalyst himself. In the late 1990s he was still living in New York City. He said he saw Dick Brady most often among those connected to their one-time hit "Washington Square."

34 I'm Leaving It Up to You
DALE & GRACE

Montel 921

November 23, 1963 (2 weeks)

Writers: Don Harris, Dewey Terry, Jr.

Producer: Sam Montel

The duo of Don and Dewey sparked little notice in 1956 when they recorded their composition "I'm Leaving It Up to You," but Louisiana music producer Sam Montel remembered it when he met singing hopeful Dale Houston from Baton Rouge, Louisiana. But Houston's solo vocal left something to be desired, so he brought in another 19-year-old singer he knew, Grace Broussard, a native of Prairieville, Louisiana, who had also sung in Baton Rouge for a few years, albeit with her brother Dan.

Montel recorded them and sent out promo copies to radio stations. A deejay at one of them, Paul Berlin of KNUZ in Houston, Texas, said the seven deejays there made it their pick of the week. "I said, 'Wait a minute, Paul, I'm going to change the violins because they're recorded in B-natural and they're supposed to be B-flat. I made a mistake,'" Montel related in *The Billboard Book of Number One Hits* by Fred Bronson. "He said, 'If you tell me you're gonna change anything on this record after seven experts say this is gonna be a number one song, you are crazy—or using reverse psychology.' I took his advice and never changed it."

"I'm Leaving It Up to You" came out on Montel's local label Michele first. When the Jaimie/Guyden label gave it national distribution, it came out on the Montel label. It peaked at #1 AC and pop simultaneously the weeks of November 23 and 30, 1963. The same year the record hit #6 R&B, and might have gone even higher there had not *Billboard* stopped publishing an R&B chart the week of November 30, 1963 (that hiatus lasted until January 30, 1965).

The follow-up to "I'm Leaving It Up to You" was the similar-sounding "Stop and Think It Over," which made #3 AC and #8 pop in 1964. It was their last entry on the AC chart. The next 45 out was "The Loneliest Night," which reached #65 pop in the summer of 1964, followed by "Darling It's Wonderful," which petered out at #114 bubbling under in the fall of 1964. Around that time Dale and Grace were fighting on tour often and eventually decided not to work together anymore. Both tried solo careers on Montel's label but ended up with nothing resembling a hit. After years apart, in the mid-1990s Dale and Grace reunited briefly to perform a few dates in America.

"I'm Leaving It Up to You" was the first #1 AC song to return to that position in a different version, the one by Donny and Marie Osmond in 1974 [see 228].

35 Dominique
THE SINGING NUN

Philips 40152

December 7, 1963 (4 weeks)

Writer: Soeur Sourire

Producer: Not Listed

Who would have guessed that the hottest name in American music in late 1963 would be a shy 30-year-old woman from a convent in Fichermont, Belgium? The Singing Nun, Sister Luc-Gabrielle, was a freak hit in the industry, popular with both teenagers and adults.

Born Jeanine Deckers, the Singing Nun had joined the convent in 1959 and brought to it her love of music. She could not write songs but was able to compose them on guitar. Her tunes caught the fancy of her fellow sisters and they decided to record them at Philips Records' studio in Brussels, with Sister Luc-Gabrielle joined by three other nuns at the session.

Philips executives thought what they heard was so good that they distributed her album across Europe and dubbed her Sister Smile, or Soeur Sourire. Seeing its success, American officials with Philips decided to release the album as well, plus the song "Dominique" as a single. Americans who did not speak French probably did not realize it was written for her Mother Superior's Saint Day to eulogize Saint Dominic (1170–1221), founder of the Order of Preaching Friars. All they knew was it was catchy and upbeat and repeated "Dominique" a lot.

The run at #1 for "Dominique" was the same on the pop and AC charts—four weeks starting December 7, 1963. Even more impressive, the Singing Nun was the first artist to have simultaneously a #1 pop single and a #1 album.

The LP, *The Singing Nun*, stayed atop the album chart for 10 weeks starting December 7, 1963. She won a Grammy for Gospel or Other Religious Recording (Musical), plus a nomination for Best Female Vocal Performance.

As her popularity peaked, Philips Records sales manager Lou Simon told *Billboard* that Philips "has enough recorded material to do at least one other [Singing Nun] LP." But attention to the Singing Nun plummeted dramatically in the pop world in 1964 when the Beatles arrived. As a result, all her follow-up song, "Tous Les Chemins (All the Roads)," could do was reach #115 the week of February 8, 1964, before dropping out of the Bubbling Under chart. When the second Singing Nun LP, titled *Her Joy, Her Songs*, was released, it managed to hit only #90 in 1964 during 14 weeks on the chart.

The Singing Nun eventually dropped out of the convent and returned to civilian life. A movie made about her story titled *The Singing Nun* came out in 1966 with Debbie Reynolds in the title role. Reynolds sang "Dominique" on the soundtrack, which went to #23 on the LP chart in 1966.

Deckers recorded a new version of "Dominique" in 1983 which went nowhere. She committed suicide with a female friend on March 31, 1985, claiming in a note that tax problems had been bothering them.

BOBBY VINTON

Epic 9638

January 4, 1964 (5 weeks)

Writers: Redd Evans, Dave Mann

Producer: Bob Morgan

"When I did 'There! I've Said It Again,' I walked into the studio, the session started at 7 p.m. I sang the song at 7:15, one take, and I said, 'Good night, everybody. This is a Number 1 record. We could stay here all night, but all we'd do is mess it up."

Vinton's instinct, as quoted when he talked to Joe Smith in *Off the Record*, proved to be correct in chart terms. "There! I've Said It Again" became his third double #1 AC and Hot 100 hit, arriving atop both charts the week of January 4, 1964 but staying on top of the pop chart only four weeks. No one else scored a trio of simultaneous #1 AC and pop hits until John Denver did it in 1974–75 with "Sunshine on My Shoulders," "Annie's Song," and "I'm Sorry."

"There! I've Said It Again" came to the attention of Vinton when a deejay at a Cincinnati rock concert yelled to him that he should cover the song if he wanted a hit. The tune was introduced in 1941 by the Benny Carter Orchestra, but it was not a hit for the group. In 1945 it went to #1 pop when cut by Vaughn Monroe, #8 pop by Jimmy Dorsey, and #11 pop by the Modernaires with Paula Kelly. Sam Cooke took it to #81 pop and #25 R&B in 1959. Mickey Gilley revived the property in 1989 and got to #53 country.

The way Vinton recorded "There! I've Said It Again" probably was quite different from how Gilley did his rendition. As Vinton told Smith, "That record was done live, all at the same time. Today it's tough for me to get a hit because of all the overdubbing. I'm a master at performing live. When they took away that style of recording, I lost the magic."

Luckily for him, that change did not occur overnight. Vinton found himself able to withstand the British invasion that knocked out many American artists from the competitive race for the top of the charts. (In fact he had the last #1 pop record before the Beatles got their first with "I Want to Hold Your Hand.") He had six consecutive top 10 AC records through 1965's "L-O-N-E-L-Y," and continued to make the AC chart at least once every year for the next decade.

By the late 1960s and early 1970s, most of Vinton's hits were remakes of earlier songs. His biggest success was "I Love How You Love Me," a remake of the #5 pop hit by the Paris Sisters in 1961, which hit #2 AC for six weeks and #9 pop in late 1968. But as the mid-1970s approached, Vinton's heyday appeared past as the hits decreased. His only entry in 1973 was "Hurt," another top five hit in 1961 but for Timi Yuro, which went to #40 AC and bubbled under to #106. Then came a song that took him back to the top once again [see 235—"My Melody of Love"].

1964

37 For You

RICK NELSON

Decca 31574

February 8, 1964 (2 weeks)

Writers: Al Dubin (words), Joe Burke (music)

Producer: Not Listed

Most Americans became acquainted with Rick Nelson first as an actor playing himself on *The Adventures of Ozzie and Harriet*, a comedy on which he, his older brother David, his father Ozzie, and mother Harriet starred on ABC-TV from 1952–66. Born Eric Hilliard Nelson in Teaneck, New Jersey, on May 8, 1940, he actually started acting with his family when they did their show on radio in 1949. But it's singing and not acting for which he is remembered best, and he started that career in 1957 with a double-sided pop hit, "A Teenager's Romance" (#2) backed with "I'm Walking" (#4).

Nelson scored two #1 pop hits, "Poor Little Fool" in 1958 and "Travelin' Man" in 1961, before changing his billing from Ricky to the more mature-sounding Rick. He got onto the AC chart twice in 1962 with "Teen Age Idol" (#2 AC, #5 pop) and "It's Up to You" (#4 AC, #6 pop), then vanished from it until he moved from the Imperial label after six years to Decca and redid the chestnut "For You," a #9 pop hit for John Boles in 1930 and a #13 pop hit for Joe Green in 1931.

James Burton, who played guitar for Nelson all the way back to "Stood Up," a #2 pop hit in 1958, believed that Ozzie Nelson played a key role in selecting "For You" for his son to record. "His dad, who was a big bandleader at one time, was into that production era of music, and he had the idea of remaking those old tunes," Burton said.

Besides Burton, other longtime band members playing with Nelson on "For You" were bassist Joe Osborne and drummer Richie Frost. They "modernized" old tunes like "For You" for pop audiences of the 1960s, according to Burton. They all also could be seen at the end of many episodes of *The Adventures of Ozzie and Harriet* playing a tune, and Burton said sometimes they filmed the songs live on the set shortly after recording them in a studio.

"For You" reached #6 pop the week of February 15, 1964 at the same time it was #1 AC. It would be Nelson's last top 20 pop hit until 1972, when he came back with "Garden Party" [see 177]. Between "For You" and "Garden Party" there were only two other AC entries, both in 1964, "The Very Thought of You" (#11) and "There's Nothing I Can Say" (#18).

While Nelson's career languished in the late 1960s, Burton was doing well, having left Nelson in the mid-1960s to work on the ABC-TV series *Shindig*; later, in the 1970s, he joined Elvis Presley. He had high regard for his former boss and considered many of the records they did together ahead of their time in terms of production. "The guy made history," Burton said. "If you think about it, Elvis was #1 and Ricky was #2. That's pretty good, being a close second."

38 Java

AL HIRT

RCA 8280

February 22, 1964 (2 weeks)

Writers: Freddy Friday (real name: Murray Sporn), Allen Toussaint, Alvin Tyler

Producer: Chet Atkins

"Java" had the right brew to make New Orleans trumpeter Al Hirt a household name in 1964. Its composer was fellow New Orleans native Allen Toussaint, but Hirt did not know that at first. "As I remember, I went to work in Nashville a great deal with Chet Atkins," Hirt said. "He used to get a stack of tunes submitted and he and I went through tunes we liked. We heard 'Java' and he said, 'Hey, this is a catchy little tune.'. . .I didn't know Toussaint until I saw his name on it. He was still in Fort Hood, Texas, in the service then."

Originally "Java" was a piano instrumental Toussaint debuted on his 1958 album *The Wild Side of New Orleans*, where it was credited to "Al Tousan." Another piano instrumental version by Floyd Cramer went to #12 AC and #49 pop in 1963.

But only Hirt and his horn made "Java" a hit. "The tune caught everybody's fancy, maybe because it was a cute song," he said. "Deejays loved it because it was less than two minutes long and they could play it wherever they needed to."

Hirt's "Java" peaked at #1 AC plus #4 pop the week of February 29, 1964. It won him a Grammy for Best Performance by an Orchestra or Instrumentalist with Orchestra—Not Jazz or Dancing. A vocal version by Donna Lynn, "Java Jones," only bubbled under to #129 later in 1964.

Hirt maintained a sense of humor about his success with "Java." He said he never learned what inspired Toussaint to write it because "I was afraid to ask him." He did recall meeting Toussaint in the mid-1980s. "I said, 'Allen, when are you going to write me another song like "Java," because you promised me one 20 years ago!?' "

"Java" was the first AC and pop entry for Alois Maxwell Hirt, born in New Orleans on November 7, 1922. He started playing the trumpet at age 6, and at age 16 he made his professional debut locally. He studied the horn under Dr. Frank Simon, a teacher at the Cincinnati Conservatory who had been a cornet soloist with John Philip Souza before emerging as a trumpeter with various bands in the 1950s.

His first solo album was for RCA in 1961. With the success of "Java" he became a prominent fixture on the AC and pop charts through 1969, though none of his later singles had the impact of "Java." He also did the title theme for the ABC-TV series *The Green Hornet* (1966–67), but it just bubbled under to #126 in 1966. The only thing that rankled him during this period was RCA billing him as "Al (He's the King) Hirt." "I don't consider myself the greatest in the world," he said.

Since the 1970s Hirt has on occasion played on records and toured some while remaining a large presence in New Orleans (literally large too—the 6-foot-2 Hirt has weighed over 300 pounds at times). As for the future, he said, "I'll never stop playing the horn."

39 Navy Blue
DIANE RENAY

20th Century 456

March 21, 1964 (1 week)

Writers: Bob Crewe, Eddie Rambeau (born Edward Flurie),
*   Bud Rehak (born Andrew Racheck)*

Producer: Bob Crewe

Lesley Gore soundalike Diane Renay rode her quick crest of success with "Navy Blue," a song about how upset she was about her boyfriend going to serve at sea. Born and raised in Philadelphia as Renee Diane Kushner, she began doing dance and voice lessons in 1954. At age 15 she won a talent competition by a local beauty pageant that led to a deal with Atlantic Records and the release of her first single, "Little White Lies." After that 45 and her follow-up "Tender" bombed, she snagged a contract with 20th Century Fox Records via manager/producer Bob Crewe.

"Navy Blue" was cut when Diane was only 18 years old. "I heard it on the radio wherever I'd go. I was amazed," she told *People* magazine. It peaked at #6 on the Hot 100 the weeks of March 14 and 21, 1964, during the time when "Beatlemania" was reaching its peak (the Beatles held the top three spots at the time with "I Want to Hold Your Hand," "She Loves You," and "Please Please Me"). But also keeping her from the top five was "Dawn (Go Away)" by the Four Seasons—produced by Renay's producer Bob Crewe!

On the heels of the triumph of "Navy Blue" came follow-up "Kiss Me Sailor," which reached #29 pop. It did not enter the AC chart, and after "Kiss Me Sailor," no other singles would make the Hot 100 either. However, both songs did appear on her *Navy Blue* album, which peaked at #54 in 1964. The nautical theme running through her singles was kept intact by the cover photo showing Renay poking her head through a life preserver, and the military angle was maintained by tunes like "Bell Bottom Trousers" and "Soldier Boy."

Crewe remained with Renay as they tried hard to capitalize on "Navy Blue," but they had little success. She had three singles bubble under later in 1964—"Growin' Up Too Fast" (#124) and "It's in Your Hands" (#131) on the 20th Century label and "Watch Out Sally" (#101) on MGM Records. The duo would get a few more record deals with other companies over the next few years, but by 1968 Renay had had enough of the music world and left show business.

In 1969 the 23-year-old Renay married and went to live in New Jersey. Years later she divorced and moved to Las Vegas. In 1992 she remarried. She went to work as a business manager for her husband Chris Eagen's company, and kept a low profile about her past career. In 1996 Renay told *People* magazine that she enjoyed her current life and did not want to live in the past, so those hoping to hear her do "Navy Blue" again in public will have to be content with hearing it on the radio or stereo for the time being.

40 Hello, Dolly!
LOUIS ARMSTRONG

Kapp 573

March 28, 1964 (9 weeks)

Writer: Jerry Herman

Producer: Mickey Kapp

Following his success with the Broadway musical *Milk and Honey* in 1961, Jerry Herman began composing the score for a musical version of the play *The Matchmaker*. Even after the book was finished, Herman found it difficult to come up with appropriate songs to drop into the slots reserved for them, but he persevered. In one of them, "Hello, Dolly!" protagonist Dolly Levi is saluted in a big production number by waiters at the Harmonia Gardens restaurant in New York City when she arrives from Yonkers to complete her matchmaking tasks. It became such a showstopper that the musical's original title, *Call on Dolly*, became *Hello, Dolly!* when it debuted on Broadway on January 16, 1964.

Famed bandleader Louis Armstrong, born in New Orleans on August 4, 1901, received the song to record by default. The music publisher for "Hello, Dolly!" had to pay for Armstrong's recording session to get "Satchmo" (Armstrong's nickname) to do it. The session did not even have an arrangement, and virtually every major label turned down the record except Kapp. To everyone's astonishment, the record was a huge hit, even knocking the Beatles out of #1 on the Hot 100 on the week of May 9, 1964. It was Armstrong's first chart entry since "Blueberry Hill" peaked at #29 in 1956, and the biggest hit ever for the jazz musical giant, who first started recording with his own band in 1926.

The follow-up was another show tune, "I Still Get Jealous," from 1947's *High Button Shoes*, in which Armstrong dropped Dolly's name into the mix. It peaked at #45 pop and #7 AC. He sang another show title tune written by Herman, "Mame," which reached #81 pop and #7 AC in 1966. In 1968 he sang part of "Hello, Dolly!" to Barbra Streisand in the movie adaptation of the musical.

Armstrong died on July 6, 1971, but, incredibly, made the charts posthumously 17 years later when his 1967 recording "What a Wonderful World" (which had hit #1 in Great Britain but only #12 AC in America) was revived in the Robin Williams movie *Good Morning, Vietnam* and peaked at #32 pop and #7 AC. In 1990 Armstrong was named to the Rock and Roll Hall of Fame as a forefather of rock music.

As for "Hello, Dolly!" it never went away for long. In 1964 ardent Democrat Carol Channing, who starred in the musical, sang it as "Hello, Lyndon!" to promote Johnson's presidential campaign. In 1965 Bobby Darin covered the tune and it went to #79 pop and #18 AC. Its luster dimmed somewhat when Herman was found guilty of plagiarizing the 1949 pop hit "Sunflower" for the tune, but that did not affect the popularity of the musical, which ran for 2,844 performances originally. And more than 30 years after Armstrong made it a hit, "Hello Dolly!" sung once again by Carol Channing, could be heard on Broadway and touring revivals of the show.

41 Love Me With All Your Heart (Cuando Calienta El Sol)

THE RAY CHARLES SINGERS

Command 4046

May 30, 1964 (4 weeks)

Writers: Michael Vaughn (words–English), Carlos Rigual (music)

Producer: Enoch Light

Astute viewers of some TV variety shows from the 1950s to the 1970s noticed in their credits a musical director billed as "the other Ray Charles," to distinguish him from the great soul singer. That person was born Charles Raymond Offenberg in Chicago, Illinois, on September 13, 1918. He sang on radio in the 1940s before going into conducting and arranging. In the 1950s he was a top behind-the-scenes music man on such TV shows as *Your Hit Parade* from 1950–57, where he was choral director, and *The Perry Como Show*, where from 1950–63 he led the orchestra plus created a vocal group known as the Ray Charles Singers.

The Ray Charles Singers first recorded on Essex in the early 1950s, followed by MGM and Decca, but their only release to make the pop chart until 1964 was 1955's "Autumn Leaves" at #55. Charles' concept for the group was to make a collection of singers sound like just one vocalist.

"My whole theory of singing is that you were singing to someone no more than two feet away, like a lover. Don't scream at me!" Charles told Joseph Lanza in *Elevator Music*. "Any choir is a multivoiced extension of myself. I had a big argument with the engineer on our first recording date because I wanted soft, almost whispering sounds. They kept arguing that you could not hear it through the surface noise on the record. I told them it was their problem."

"Love Me With All Your Heart" was a typical example of Charles' approach. Steve Allen first charted at #85 pop in 1963 with the original foreign lyrics of the song ("Cuanda Calienta El Sol" is translated as "When the Sun Is Hot"). Using new English lyrics, the Ray Charles Singers got "Love Me With All Your Heart" to #1 AC and #3 pop, peaking on the latter the week of June 13, 1964, behind the Dixie Cups' "Chapel of Love" at #1 and Peter and Gordon's "A World Without Love" at #2. It also won a Grammy nomination for Best Performance by a Chorus. In 1966 a cover by Irish vocal trio the Bachelors got to #3 AC and #38 pop.

After "Love Me With All Your Heart," the Ray Charles Singers had frequent AC 45s, even though the group had nearly vanished from the Hot 100 by early 1965. In 1970 their 12th charted AC single, "Move Me, O Wondrous Music" at #26, was their AC swan song as well as final pop entry (#99 for one week). Charles' "many people—one vocal sound" approach resulted in innumerable personnel changes during the group's chart runs.

As for Charles, he kept doing TV variety shows into the 1980s. One of his last onscreen appearances was playing on *The Steve Allen Show* in 1980—the same Steve Allen who first did "Cuando Caliente El Sol."

42 People

BARBRA STREISAND

Columbia 42965

June 27, 1964 (3 weeks)

Writers: Bob Merrill (words), Jule Styne (music)

Producer: Robert Mersey

Nervous tension abounded at a recording session on December 20, 1963. Barbra Streisand was to sing four tunes from *Funny Girl*, the Broadway-bound musical about the life of Fanny Brice in which she starred. The show's

composer Jule Styne wanted to release a single to promote *Funny Girl*, but the song he liked the most was one Streisand did not care much about and the show's directors had asked to be dropped several times—"People."

Styne came up with the melody. Then librettist Bob Merrill took the phrase "a very special person," which appeared in the script to describe Brice, as the basis for lyrics for the song. "Everyone said it didn't progress the story, which a show song should," Merrill told Shaun Considine in *Barbra Streisand: The Woman, The Myth, The Music*. "I felt it was a good ballad and had a special kind of magic, but none of the directors had any faith in it."

Nonetheless, "People" was done in at least two takes at the session with 30 musicians led by arranger-conductor Peter Matz. "There was a wrong note on the ninth bar in the French horn. We didn't fix it till the second time though," Matz told Considine. However, Columbia released the first take because Streisand's vocal was better on it. Some also wanted to delete the interlude where Streisand sang out of tempo accompanied only by piano, as it made the record nearly four minutes long. It stayed.

On January 21, 1964, while *Funny Girl* was tried out in Boston, Columbia released "People" as the B-side to another song in the show, "I Am Woman." Upset, Styne pitched "People" to others, and Nat "King" Cole agreed to cut it. By the time *Funny Girl* opened on Broadway March 26, 1964 to ecstatic reviews for Streisand, Columbia Records President Goddard Lieberson read a review in *Billboard* of Cole's single. Worried his artist would lose a hit she sang in her show, he had his publicity personnel promote Streisand's version of "People" immediately.

"I Am Woman" (not the Helen Reddy tune) went only to #114, while Streisand's "People" reached the AC summit on June 27, 1964, the first of two consecutive weeks where it peaked at #5 pop. It was her first entry on both charts. Cole's rendition made only #100 pop the week of April 11, 1964. In 1968 the Tymes took it to #39 pop and #33 R&B, and in 1969 Tony Bennett went to #27 AC with it.

But "People" remains indelibly linked to Streisand. It won her a Grammy for Best Female Vocal Performance ("People" also got nominations for Record of the Year and Song of the Year), and it served as the title tune to a 1964 LP, her first to reach #1. In fact, by 1973 "People" had appeared in some form on seven Streisand albums, including her first "greatest hits" LP and the 1968 film soundtrack for *Funny Girl*. She did not have her next #1 AC until 1974 [see 208—"The Way We Were"].

43 The Girl From Ipanema
STAN GETZ/ASTRUD GILBERTO

Verve 10323

July 18, 1964 (2 weeks)

Writers: Antonio Carlos Jobim (music), Norman Gimbel (lyrics–English)

Producer: Creed Taylor

The bossa nova craze of the early 1960s affected nearly everyone in the musical industry. Even Elvis Presley sang "Bossa Nova Baby," a top 10 pop hit in 1963. The man credited with popularizing the music form in America was Stan Getz. Born Stan Gayetzsky in Philadelphia on February 2, 1927, the tenor saxophonist won much acclaim in the 1940s for his work with, in chronological order, the bands of Stan Kenton, Jimmy Dorsey, Benny Goodman, and Woody Herman. After 13 years as a solo act, his 1962 collaboration with guitarist Charlie Byrd resulted in a #1 album, *Jazz Samba*, which included their hit single "Desafinado" (#15 pop, #4 AC).

Wanting to follow the success of his bossa nova sound, Getz asked Brazilian Antonio Carlos Jobim, the writer of "Desafinado," for more music. One tune Jobim created was "The Girl From Ipanema," with English lyrics supplied by Norman Gimbel. Jobim's inspiration was a beautiful 19-year-old girl, Helo Pinheiro, although she was not named in the song.

Jobim brought the song to a March 1963 recording session along with guitarist João Gilberto, who did fine playing the tune but could not speak anything but Portuguese. As Getz wanted a vocal for the record, the situation looked hopeless until he requested that Joao's wife Astrud, a 24-year-old native of Bahia, try her luck at it. The request was bizarre, as Astrud had never sung professionally before and came to the studio only as a favor to her husband. But she gave it a shot, as she did have some reason to lay claim to the tune.

"I lived in Panama for 20 years," she was quoted in Dylan Jones' *Ultra Lounge: The Lexicon of Easy Listening* as saying: "So I guess I was a girl from Ipanema, but not the girl—that girl could have been anyone, and it probably was. I love the song and I really don't mind if people associate it with me because it has become a standard. The bossa nova has come to signify all the happy things in life: at the movies, whenever you hear a bossa nova song start to play, you know that the boy and girl are going to kiss. It's so sexy."

"The Girl From Ipanema" single from the LP *Getz/Gilberto* peaked at #5 pop for two weeks in late July 1964. Astrud was credited as the vocalist on the single, but not on the album. The following year the record won a Grammy for Record of the Year and got Astrud a nomination for Best Female Vocal Performance. *Getz/Gilberto* was named Album of the Year and also won Getz a Grammy for Best Instrumental Jazz Performance.

Getz had no other AC or pop entries after this collaboration, while Gilberto managed only one other entry, "I Had the Craziest Dream," which made #31 AC in 1967 without cracking the Hot 100. Getz died on June 6, 1991 from liver cancer, while Gilberto continued to tour and record into the late 1990s.

By the way, the *Miami Herald* reported in 1997 that the song's real inspiration, Helo Pinheiro, was doing well financially as a businesswoman in Rio de Janiero. One of the more than 120 products she was promoting was Girl from Ipanema Iced Tea.

44 Everybody Loves Somebody

DEAN MARTIN

Reprise 0281

August 1, 1964 (8 weeks)

Writers: Ken Lane, Irving Taylor

Producer: Jimmy Bowen

Everybody Loves Somebody" by Frank Sinatra made its debut on a *Billboard* chart the week of July 3, 1948, when it peaked at #25 and then promptly fell off the chart the following week, as did the song on the other side of the record, "Just for Now," which peaked at #21.

Sixteen years later, producer Jimmy Bowen looked for a hit he could cut with Dean Martin, who despite considerable success in films and TV specials in the early 1960s had been dead recording-wise, having only a few lower-rung entries on both the album and pop charts and nothing at all on the AC chart. Martin agreed to do whatever Bowen wanted on the condition that he could do an LP of smooth standards which would be called *Dream With Dean* first. Bowen accepted the deal.

Eleven cuts made the grade, but Dean disliked the 12th and final track and refused to do it at the session. Martin's longtime pianist Ken Lane then plunked out a song he had co-written in 20 minutes years before with Irving Taylor— "Everybody Loves Somebody." Something about the tune sparked Bowen into doing it both as a slow, moody version for that session, then trying it later with a big orchestra behind Martin as a single release.

So 10 days after *Dream With Dean* was complete, Bowen redid "Everybody Loves Somebody." Bowen recalled in his autobiography *Rough Mix* that at that session some of the microphones used for the strings and horn also picked up some of the drumbeat, "but even that worked in our favor." Martin needed only two takes to do the song, and after some intensive promotion by Warner Brothers Records, which owned Reprise, "Everybody Loves Somebody" reached the pole position of the Hot 100 the week of August 15, 1964, while riding high on the AC chart at the same time. It was Martin's first #1 pop hit since "Memories Are Made of This" in 1956. The irony of it all was that the Dean Martin recording was on Reprise, a label set up by the original singer of "Everybody Loves Somebody"—Frank Sinatra.

"Everybody Loves Somebody" appeared in the slow version on *Dream With Dean* and the hit version on an LP titled after it; the former peaked at #15 while the latter reached #2 for four weeks behind Barbra Streisand's *People* LP [see 42]. In addition, Martin would get his only Grammy nomination from the song for Best Male Vocal Performance. And "Everybody Loves Somebody" lingered on, serving as the theme song for Martin's TV variety show on NBC from 1965–74.

The tune was the first of five #1 AC hits Martin had, followed by "The Door Is Still Open to My Heart" [see 46]. Maybe not everyone loved Martin, but easy listening programmers of the mid-1960s sure did.

45 We'll Sing in the Sunshine

GALE GARNETT

RCA 8388

September 26, 1964 (7 weeks)

Writer: Gale Garnett

Producer: Andy Wiswell

Gale Garnett has the distinction of being the first #1 AC artist from New Zealand, where she was born in Auckland on July 17, 1942. She came to America with her family when she was nine, eventually settling in New York City. Her father died in 1956, and although she was only 14, she got her own apartment so she could pursue an acting career. After a few months being a waitress and a charwoman, she got her first professional job at age 15 and eventually made it to Hollywood, where she appeared on *Hawaiian Eye*, 77 *Sunset Strip*, and *Adventures in Paradise* among her more than 60 TV show guest credits.

In the early 1960s Garnett made her professional singing debut at the Garrett Club in Los Angeles. Three months later, she went to audition for RCA armed with more than 20 folk songs which she had composed. The label signed her, and Garnett's first release was "We'll Sing in the Sunshine," which made #1 AC and #4 pop, the latter for the weeks of October 17, 24, and 31, 1964, and also #43 country. "We'll Sing in the Sunshine" earned a Grammy for Best Folk Recording as well as nominations for Best Female Vocal Performance and Best Accompaniment Arrangement for Vocalist(s) or Instrumentalist(s).

Billboard carried an ad for her new single "Lovin' Place" in the November 28, 1964 issue, but that effort flopped. The best she could do was bubble under to #108 in the spring of 1965 with the perhaps appropriately titled "I'll Cry Alone." She kept recording singles for RCA through 1967, but none charted.

Garnett tried a different tack in 1968 and 1969, doing two LPs of hippie music on Columbia backed by a group called the Gentle Reign. That failed to chart, but Garnett continued to do the club circuit in America through the mid-1970s at least before fading into the mists of obscurity.

The one person who really got a push from "We'll Sing in the Sunshine" was its producer Andy Wiswell. Two records he produced thereafter in the 1960s found their way to the top of the AC chart, Staff Sgt. Barry Sadler's "The Ballad of the Green Berets" [see 68] and Perry Como's "Stop! And Think It Over" [see 88]. As far as the tune itself was concerned, "We'll Sing in the Sunshine" got fair airplay on oldies radio stations into the 1990s and even generated a few other renditions by artists. In 1970 LaWanda Lindsey took her remake to #63 country, followed two years later by a cover from Alice Creech which hit #34.

46 The Door Is Still Open to My Heart

DEAN MARTIN

Reprise 0307

November 14, 1964 (1 week)

Writer: Chuck Willis

Producer: Jimmy Bowen

In 1955 Dean Martin had been recording eight years and working nine years as a straight man with comedian Jerry Lewis when "The Door Is Still Open to My Heart" became a hit. Originally titled "The Door Is Still Open," the song went to #4 R&B when done by a Baltimore act called the Cardinals, who had formed in 1946 as the Mellotones. The Cardinals had no further success after "The Door. . .," and in fact had only two previous chart entries, both R&B— "Shouldn't I Know?" (#7, 1951) and "The Wheel of Fortune" (#6, 1952). The song's writer, Chuck Willis, managed to score on both the pop and R&B charts in the 1950s before his death from a perforated ulcer on April 10, 1958 at age 30. His best-remembered hits as a singer were "C.C. Rider" (#1 R&B, #12 pop in 1957) and "What Am I Living For" (#1 R&B, #9 pop in 1958).

But back to "The Door Is Still Open to My Heart." The probable reason why the Cardinals did not make the pop chart with it was that Don Cornell released his own version, and in 1955 covers of black artists' records by white artists generally favored more airplay if not sales for the latter. The tune actually was the official B-side to Cornell's cover of another R&B hit, the Moonglows' "Most of All," which peaked at #5 for that group that year. Cornell took both tunes to #14 on *Billboard*'s Most Played by Jockeys pop listings. But Cornell could not handle the onslaught of rock and roll, and his last charted record came two years later with "Mama Guitar."

Nine years later, fresh off Martin's unexpected success with "Everybody Loves Somebody" [see 44], Dean's producer Jimmy Bowen held a brainstorming session to come up with a follow-up record. Helping him was his old chum Don "Dirt" Lanier, who also served as Bowen's contractor to book musicians for sessions. In his autobiography *Rough Mix*, Bowen recalled that Lanier pulled out "The Door Is Still Open to My Heart" at around 3 a.m. during their meeting and played it on a guitar. They were enthusiastic about the song's prospects, and so was Martin when Lanier performed the tune in front of him the next day.

Fans were also enthusiastic, and "The Door Is Still Open to My Heart" climbed the summit of the AC chart *and* peaked at #6 pop the week of November 14, 1964. Its success proved Martin's comeback was not a fluke, as he now had two back-to-back singles make the pop top 10 for the first time in his career. Even the B-side, "Every Minute Every Hour," managed to bubble under at #123. Martin made it three in a row #1 AC hits with his next release, "You're Nobody Till Somebody Loves You" [see 50].

47 Ringo

LORNE GREENE

RCA 8444

November 21, 1964 (6 weeks)

Writers: Don Robertson, Hal Blair

Producer: Joe Reisman

His movie and TV acting career stretched from the 1950s to the 1980s, but Lorne Greene, born in Ottawa, Canada, on February 12, 1914, is best remembered as the star of the NBC-TV series *Bonanza* from 1959–73. The success of *Bonanza* led RCA Records to sign Greene to do an album of western songs consistent with his image on the show. His producer Joe Reisman contacted Don Robertson to write songs for the LP.

In a 1998 letter to this author, Robertson continued the story: "Joe added that singing was not Lorne's strong suit, so songs with a lot of talking and a minimum of singing would be desirable. I had a strong feeling that Hal Blair, with his long and successful background in writing songs for cowboy movies, would be an ideal collaborator for his project. I called Hal and asked him if he would be interested in working on it with me. He was. This would have been sometime early in 1963.

"Not long after, Hal called me and told me he had a couple of ideas for Lorne. I went over to Hal's house in North Hollywood. Hal already had the title, 'Ringo,' and those great opening lines. We began working out the story and putting lines together. We really didn't worry about the music at that point, except that the structure and meter and the rhythmic flow of the lyric was fundamental. . . .When we had the story and the lyric lines worked out to our satisfaction, I worked on the music and the arrangement till we were both satisfied."

Robertson did a piano and vocal demo of "Ringo" and took it to Reisman in March 1963. In the fall Reisman recorded "Ringo," and Blair and Robertson loved Greene's delivery and Reisman's arrangements. Greene's *Welcome to the Ponderosa* LP came out in September 1964.

"As I mentioned, RCA had no plans for releasing singles from this album, but apparently one of their branch distributors in Texas ordered custom singles," wrote Robertson. "A local Texas DJ had been playing the 'Ringo' track and had received enthusiastic listener response, and the local distributor thought he could sell some singles. It then spread like wildfire from area to area around the country."

"Ringo" went to #1 AC and pop, topping the latter the week of December 5, 1964 only. It also hit #24 country. Greene did a version of it in French too. But Greene found "Ringo" hard to top. He had only three other AC entries after it—"The Man" in 1965 (#16 AC, #72 pop), and "Five Card Stud" (#36 AC, #112 bubbling under) and "Waco" (#35 AC) in 1966. He did his last album in 1967. He died on September 11, 1987.

"In the past couple of years 'Ringo' (with parody lyrics) was running in two different Southwest Airlines TV and radio commercials with Jack Palance," wrote Robertson. "Here it is thirty-four years later and 'Ringo' is still very much alive! Hal and I are indeed a couple of very grateful songwriters."

48 The Wedding

JULIE ROGERS

Mercury 72332

January 2, 1965 (3 weeks)

Writers: Fred Jay (words–English), Joaquin Prieto (music)

Producer: Not Known

"The Wedding" originated from a tune written by Joaquin Prieto in Argentina in 1960 as "La Novia." Fred Jay wrote English lyrics in 1961, and though the song was recorded by several artists including Anita Bryant, who released it as a single on Columbia in 1961, it never became a hit at the time. However, one British woman did hear the tune then and wound up cutting a hit version of the song three years later. Her name was Julie Rogers.

Rogers, born Julie Rolls in Bermondsey, London, England, on April 6, 1943, worked at a variety of jobs from age 16 until she recorded "The Wedding." She had been a dancer in Spain, a secretary, and even a flight attendant before she decided to pursue a singing career. British bandleader Teddy Foster signed her to sing with his group in the early 1960s before teaming with her as a duo.

While Rogers and Foster played dates in London, the director of A&R (artists and repertoire) for Mercury Records in the United Kingdom, Johnny Franz, noticed Rogers and signed her to the label. Her debut release "It's Magic" did not live up to its title and came and went without notice, but "The Wedding" had its own magic and became a big British hit at #3 on the United Kingdom in 1964. Backing her on the record were the Johnny Arthey Orchestra and Chorus.

As all things British seemed to be the rage in the United States following the popularity of the Beatles, "The Wedding" received a decent shot on Mercury's American label and made #10 pop the weeks of January 2 and 9, 1965. Its softer (detractors may say gushier) sound than most of the English product circulating at the time made it a natural to top the AC chart at the same time.

Rogers followed up "The Wedding" with two singles which made the British chart in 1965, "Like a Child" at #21 and "Hawaiian Wedding Song" at #31. In the United States "Like a Child" made it to #12 AC and #67 pop, but that was it in terms of chart action for Rogers. After 1965, she disappeared from both the English and American charts and went into general obscurity.

Yet "The Wedding" remained a strong seller. A decade after it had become a hit for Rogers, consumers worldwide had reportedly purchased more than 7 million copies of the record. Airplay for the song was not as strong, but for many years it continued to be a favorite choice for couples to have played at their weddings.

1965

49 Willow Weep for Me

CHAD AND JEREMY

World Artists 1027

January 23, 1965 (1 week)

Writer: Ann Ronnell

Producer: Not Listed

The male duo of Chad Stuart, born December 10, 1943, and Jeremy Clyde, born March 22, 1944, have the distinction of being the only "British invasion" group of the mid-1960s to head the AC chart, probably because they had the softest pop sounds of all the bands coming from Great Britain. Both were Englishmen, with Jeremy's grandfather being the Duke of Wellington. Their American debut, on which they were billed by their full names, was "Yesterday's Gone," a #21 pop hit in the summer of 1964. "A Summer Song" came next and nearly brought them to the AC peak; they did hold at #2 AC for six weeks while hitting #7 pop.

After "A Summer Song" came "Willow Weep for Me," a remake of a tune which charted first in 1932 at #17 pop when done by Ted Fio Rito and His Orchestra and then a year later at #2 pop by Paul Whiteman and His Orchestra with a vocal by Irene Taylor. Chad and Jeremy's version became a moderate hit when it made #15 on the Hot 100 at the same time it hit #1 AC.

Chad and Jeremy were a fixture on the AC and pop listings throughout 1965. The songs that came closest to recapturing the success of "Willow Weep for Me" were "If I Loved You" from the Broadway musical *Carousel* (#6 AC, #23 pop) and "Before and After" (#4 AC, #17 pop). The two stopped making the AC chart at year's end but remained on the Hot 100 in 1966 with two other singles, "Distant Shores" (#30) and "You Are She" (#87). They also made several appearances on American television, not just on music shows but also basically playing themselves on such comedies as *Batman* and *The Dick Van Dyke Show*.

After 1966, Chad and Jeremy's appeal faded quickly. Two early art-rock albums, *Cabbages and Kings* followed by *The Ark*, generated little sales or airplay, and by 1969 the two had gone their separate ways. Recalling their rocky music career, Chad told Ethlie Ann Vare in *Goldmine* in 1984 that "You had no instruction books, you had no way of knowing what was coming or how to meet the next challenge. Everything was tough. . . .You got too sidetracked by the fans and the fan mags and the applause. I remember as if I was frantically faking my way through life."

Jeremy returned to his acting roots in England in the 1970s and early 1980s, appearing in such films as *The Silver Bears* and *ffolkes*. During the same period Chad stayed in the U.S. music industry, and at one time was a staff producer at A&M Records.

In 1984 the duo reunited to release an album called *Chad Stuart and Jeremy Clyde* for a small label, Rochsire Records. It failed. Then, as in the past, the two men refused to tour in 1960s revival shows, so it is unlikely that fans will ever hear them perform "Willow Weep for Me" again.

You're Nobody Till Somebody Loves You

DEAN MARTIN

Reprise 0333

January 30, 1965 (1 week)

Writers: Russ Morgan, Larry Stock, James Cavanaugh

Producer: Jimmy Bowen

"That song, my mother in Las Vegas has 600 renditions of that," said Jack Morgan of "You're Nobody Till Somebody Loves You," co-written by his late father Russ Morgan. The elder Morgan was the first to popularize the tune, taking it to #14 pop in early 1946 as leader of the Russ Morgan Orchestra, but his son acknowledged the tune has been covered so often by so many different artists, including Dean Martin, that "Everybody knows the song, but not many people realize he wrote it."

What little Jack Morgan remembers about the creation of the tune was that "When dad wrote it in New York City, he had just had breakfast or lunch at Lindy's Deli in New York City." He does recall that his father allowed such major singers as the Mills Brothers in 1949 and Roberta Sherwood in 1951 to do their own interpretation of the song. Others who have cut the tune include Sam Cooke and Little Richard.

The Morgans had a certain familiarity with Dean Martin. "We were living in Beverly Hills, and they were living there too," recalled Jack. "Their kids went to the same schools I did." And, although the Morgans did not hear personally from Martin regarding his take on the song, they did appreciate the money they got from its success.

Martin's version of "You're Nobody Till Somebody Loves You" was the highest charting of three covers of the tune to make the Hot 100 during the 1960s. It reached #25 as well as #1 AC. The other two pop entries were by Dinah Washington in 1962 (#87) and the Wonder Who?, a pseudonym for the Four Seasons, in 1966 (#96). In 1986 Ray Price's version went to #60 country.

Morgan, who began working in his father's orchestra in 1958 and took over leading it following his father's death in 1969, said "You're Nobody Till Somebody Loves You" remained an integral part of the group's act before and after Martin's record came out. "We do it every night," he said. He also noted that it is in a medley of songs the

orchestra performs while telling the audience that although they may not associate those tunes with the Russ Morgan orchestra, they were in fact hits for them. "You're Nobody Till Somebody Loves You" ends the medley. Jack Morgan does this revue quite often, for when he is not at his home in Illinois, "I'm on the road ten and a half to eleven months a year."

"You're Nobody Till Somebody Loves You" marked Martin's third consecutive #1 AC hit. Its B-side, "You'll Always Be the One I Love," made #13 AC and #64 pop. The follow-up, "Send Me the Pillow You Dream On," ended Martin's streak by stopping at #5 AC, but Martin returned to the top two years later [see 92—"In the Chapel in the Moonlight"].

51 Have You Looked Into Your Heart

JERRY VALE

Columbia 43181

February 6, 1965 (1 week)

Writers: Teddy Randazzo, Bobby Weinstein, Billy Barberis

Producer: Ernie Altschuler

Singer/songwriter/producer Teddy Randazzo saw his singing career take a dip while his writing profile increased thanks to the odd situation he faced with "Have You Looked Into Your Heart." He had minor pop successes in the late 1950s and early 1960s prior to that song, with the biggest being "The Way of a Clown" (#44, 1960) and "Big Wide World" (#51, 1963). Recalling the creation of "Have You Looked Into Your Heart," he said, "I was going across the country to Seattle, Washington. I wrote both melodies, that and 'Big Wide World.'"

Randazzo also came up with the chorus for the song but found he needed help from his backup musicians Bobby Weinstein and Billy Barberis to complete the tune when he performed it in public at the Thunderbird in Las Vegas. Then he recorded the song in California as part of an LP he was doing for Colpix Records. "I had signed with Colpix and put out 'Big Wide World.' And that was sort of a hit, so I got an album deal," he said.

But Randazzo said when Don Kirschner took over operations at Colpix, he canceled the singer's album. Undaunted, he said, "I brought it to Columbia to Jerry Vale. . . . They took basically my record and did the arrangement the same."

Vale, born in the Bronx, New York, on July 8, 1932, as Genaro Louis Vitaliano, hardly seemed the candidate to make the song a success. While he had been making the pop charts as early as 1953 with "You Can Never Give Me Back My Heart," which stopped at #29, he had been off the listings since 1958. Yet his version of "Have You Looked Into Your Heart" had enough appeal to top the AC chart and reach #24 pop. "He did a fine job," Randazzo said.

The popularity of "Have You Looked Into Your Heart" led to four more pop singles for Vale through 1966, though none came close to capturing a sliver of its appeal. The song did make Vale a mainstay on the AC chart, however, on which he compiled a total of 27 entries ending with "My Little Girl (Angel All A-Glow)," which peaked at #36 in 1971. He remained a steady nightclub performer after that time, although the most often his name appeared in papers was in 1998, when reporters noted his attendance at the deaths of two fellow Italian-American singers, Sonny Bono and Frank Sinatra.

Randazzo decided to shift his interest to behind-the-scenes work in the music industry following Vale's hit with "Have You Looked Into Your Heart." Speaking from his home in Orlando, Florida, in 1998, he said, "I still write, I still arrange and when I get a chance to produce I do that too. . . . I got plenty to say."

52 King of the Road

ROGER MILLER

Smash 1965

February 13, 1965 (10 weeks)

Writer: Roger Miller

Producer: Jerry Kennedy

"If you have the song idea clearly in your mind, the actual writing can be done rapidly," Roger Miller told Paul Ackerman in *Billboard* in 1965 while discussing his method of composing. One example of his approach was "King of the Road." Miller saw the phrase "Trailer for sale or rent" on the side of a barn. "Sometimes a single phrase is the catalyst, and the words flow, and I began to wonder how a cheap hotel room might be," he told Ackerman. But it was not until he saw a hobo in a Boise, Idaho, airport gift shop that he completed "King of the Road," the story of a "man of means by no means" which became one of the biggest smash country crossovers ever.

"King of the Road," complete with finger snaps provided by Buddy Killen and guitarist Thumbs Carlisle, topped the country chart for five weeks beginning the week of March 27, 1965. A week before that, Miller's record peaked at #4 pop. But its biggest success was on the AC chart. Its 10-week run at #1 tied with "Big Bad John" and later "This Guy's in Love With You" and "Time Passages" as the second longest-running #1 AC hit through 1992, surpassed only by "Love Is Blue" with 11 weeks in 1968.

Another precedent set by "King of the Road" was at the 1965 Grammys. The song helped Miller nab nine nominations and win six awards, the biggest number in both categories by one artist in a year until Michael Jackson surpassed them with his *Thriller* LP in 1983. Miller won for Best Contemporary Single, Best Contemporary Male Vocal Performance, Best Country & Western Album, Best Country & Western Single, Best Country & Western Song, and Best Country & Western Male Vocal Performance.

Such acclaim was an honor for Miller, who was born in Fort Worth, Texas, on January 2, 1936. He began writing songs at age 5 while growing up in Erick, Oklahoma. His idols were Hank Williams and Will Rogers. He came to Nashville to sing in the mid-1950s but found the going tough for a few years, having to get by at one point as a bellhop at the Andrew Jackson Hotel.

He cracked the country chart as a solo performer in 1960 with "You Don't Want My Love," which went to #14. But his career did not really take hold until 1964's "Dang Me" hit #1 country for six weeks and made #7 pop as well, the first of many hits on both charts for him. "Chug-a-Lug" (#3 country, #9 pop) and "Do-Wacka-Do" (#15 country, #31 pop) followed before he made "King of the Road," which was his first AC entry.

In the fall of 1966 Mickie Finn reached #35 AC with her banjo instrumental version of "King of the Road." But before that charted, Miller had one more song which returned him to #1 AC [see 64—"England Swings"].

53 The Race Is On

JACK JONES

Kapp 651

April 24, 1965 (1 week)

Writer: Don Rollins

Producer: Michael Kapp

Singer Allan Jones had two nice bits of fortune strike him in 1938. He had his biggest record ever with "The Donkey Serenade," which made #8 pop, and his wife, actress Irene Hervey, gave birth to their son Jack in Los Angeles, California, on January 14 that year. Nobody knew it at the time, but Jack would end up having a more successful and longer-lasting musical career than his father.

For a year after graduating from high school, Jack's professional music career consisted of singing with his father in nightclubs, but Jack became a solo act after his parents divorced in 1957. He insisted he got no special treatment because of who he was, even though Capitol signed him to record in 1959.

"One of the things people don't realize is that it can also be an obstacle to be a well-known singer's son," Jones told Edith Efron in *TV Guide*. "The agent says, 'Allan Jones' kid? Oh, yeah,' and yawns, bored. He figures you've got no talent, that you're trying to trade on your father's name."

The indifferent reaction described by the younger Jones at first extended to his recording efforts. Although Capitol tried to make him into a rock star, Jack went into the Air Force and did not make the AC or pop chart until 1962 with "Lollipops and Roses" on the Kapp label (#12 AC, #66 pop), which despite its mediocre performance won him the Grammy for Best Male Vocal Performance. He followed it the next year with his version of "Call Me Irresponsible," the Oscar-winning Best Song of 1963 from the movie *Papa's Delicate Condition* which made #75 pop. Then came "Wives and Lovers," which became his highest-charting pop hit at #14 in 1964 while going to #9 AC. Over the next two years he did several singles, most being title songs from movies, but the only one to crack the AC top 10 or pop top 50 was "Dear Heart" at #6 AC and #30 pop in early 1965. His next release was "The Race Is On."

First done by George Jones in 1964, "The Race Is On" went to #3 on the country chart that year, plus got to #96 on the Hot 100 the week of January 23, 1965. Regarding the tune, Jack Jones told Will Friedwald in the former's 1995 *Greatest Hits* LP liner notes that "Mickey Kapp brought me the George Jones (no relation) record of this and said, 'What do you think?' and I said, 'I love it!' However, we couldn't understand the lyrics so we had to slow down the turntable to take the words off. Actually, this song was a hit three times, because it hit again later for Sawyer Brown." Indeed, in 1989 the group Sawyer Brown took their cover to #5 country.

The pop version by Jones got to #1 AC and #15 on the Hot 100. He would return to #1 AC the next year [see 73— "The Impossible Dream"].

54 Cast Your Fate to the Wind

SOUNDS ORCHESTRAL

Parkway 942

May 1, 1965 (3 weeks)

Writers: Vince Guaraldi

Producer: Not Known

Jazz pianist Vince Guaraldi is probably best known among the general public as the composer to the music of several *Peanuts* TV cartoon specials first aired in the 1960s and 1970s but still rerun today. However, he did have his own hit in 1963, the instrumental "Cast Your Fate to the Wind," which made #9 AC and #22 pop. An instrumental cover by Martin Denny came out at the same time but only bubbled under to #124 in late 1962.

"Cast Your Fate to the Wind" went on to become one of the most frequently charting tunes on the AC chart. In 1965 pop singer Steve Alaimo reached #22 AC and #89 pop with his vocal version, with words written by Frank Werber. "I just happened to ask if there any words to it, and there were," Alaimo told this author about his record in 1997. "I almost died. I thought the lyrics were fantastic."

The next year Shelby Flint also sang "Cast Your Fate to the Wind," making #11 AC and #61 pop. A decade later, Roger Williams did an instrumental rendition that hit #39 AC in 1976. But the highest charting of all these efforts came from Sounds Orchestral, a group created by British producer John Schroeder to make contemporary music both teens and adults could enjoy.

Schroeder featured Johnny Pearson as pianist on his cut, with the other musicians including drummer Kenny Clare and bass players Frank Clark, Pete McGurk, and Tony Reeves. It became a #5 hit in the United Kingdom in 1964 before being released in America, where it made #1 AC plus #10 pop the week of May 8, 1965.

Pearson, born in Plaistow, London, England, on June 18, 1925, made his name in his native country as the founder and member of the Malcolm Mitchell Trio from 1948–54. He then freelanced as a pianist for several acts including Lena Horne in concerts and recording sessions before moving into arranging, conducting, and composing music. Pearson provided songs for several radio and TV series in Great Britain in addition to his recording activities. He also made the AC chart at #23 under his own name in 1972 with an instrumental titled "Sleepy Shores."

Several singles came out under the Sounds Orchestral name after "Cast Your Fate to the Wind," but they fared so poorly that they are unlikely to be remembered by anyone but record enthusiasts. The first follow-up was "Canadian Sunset," which stopped at #14 AC and #76 pop, then came "A Boy and a Girl" at #30 AC and #104 bubbling under near the end of 1965. Five years passed before Sounds Orchestral had its final AC entry. Ironically, a project formed to promote "good music" ended up covering the Kingsmen's rock classic "Louie Louie" and got to #39 in 1970 on the Janus label in America.

55 Crying in the Chapel

ELVIS PRESLEY

RCA 447-0643

May 22, 1965 (7 weeks)

Writer: Artie Glenn

Producer: Steve Sholes

Artie Glenn composed "Crying in the Chapel" in 1953 for his 16-year-old son Darrell to record. The younger Glenn took it to #6 pop that year but was outcharted by a version from June Valli which made #4 pop. "Crying in the Chapel" made the hit parade often that year, with covers by Rex Allen (#8), the Orioles (#11), Ella Fitzgerald (#15), and Art Lund (#23). But it took Elvis Presley to make the most successful rendition of "Crying in the Chapel."

On November 30, 1960, Elvis Presley cut his version with plans to put it on the *His Hands to Mine* gospel album. But that LP came out by the start of 1961 without the tune. RCA held "Crying in the Chapel" back because it could not make a deal with the publishing company who owned the tune until its release as a single in 1965. It did not appear on a Presley album until his second LP of religious music, 1967's *How Great Thou Art*.

Neal Matthews, first tenor with the Jordanaires, recalled singing background vocals for the record with Presley. "'Crying in the Chapel' was done in Nashville," he said. "I think the session was called at 6 o'clock in the evening, but we didn't record it until 3 in the morning."

Matthews explained the delay was that Presley liked to take it easy in the recording studio at the time and "played around a lot on the session." The Jordanaires were worn out by the time they cut the tune but regrouped and got themselves together in time for a relatively easy job. "I think we cut it in three takes, and I think they used the third take," Matthews said.

When it comes to the subject of Presley and his gospel music, Matthews firmly believed that the King of Rock and Roll was a devoutly religious man. "He tried out for two quartets but didn't get into gospel groups. I think he sings religious songs great. In fact, I think he sings everything fine." (It should be noted that the three Grammys Presley received in his lifetime were all for his gospel albums.)

Presley's "Crying in the Chapel" peaked at #3 pop the week of June 12, 1965, behind the Supremes' "Back in My Arms Again" at #1 and "Wooly Bully" by Sam the Sham and the Pharoahs at #2. It did hit #1 in the United Kingdom. And "Crying in the Chapel" was his first top 10 pop hit since 1963's "Bossa Nova Baby" peaked at #8 and his last top 10 pop hit until "In the Ghetto" hit #3 in 1969.

Also, earlier in 1965 Adam Wade took his "Crying in the Chapel" to #20 AC and #88 pop. Two years before that, Little Richard did a rendition which bubbled under to #119. And in 1967 Presley released "Indescribably Blue," a tune written by Darrell Glenn, the original singer of "Crying in the Chapel."

56 A Walk in the Black Forest
HORST JANKOWSKI

Mercury 72425

July 10, 1965 (2 weeks)

Writer: Horst Jankowski

Producer: Not Listed

He may be considered a one-hit wonder in America (the one hit being his composition "A Walk in the Black Forest"), but in his native Germany Horst Jankowski had a reputation as one of the best jazz pianists in the country during the 1950s and 1960s. He played with such notables as Ella Fitzgerald, Benny Goodman, and Miles Davis and is credited with popularizing jazz in his homeland, among his more notable achievements.

Born in Berlin, Germany, on January 30, 1936, Jankowski moved with his family out of the city when it was bombed during World War II. After the war they returned home and his mother got him into the Berlin Conservatory of Music, where he earned a concert pianist degree as well as studying tenor saxophone, contrabass, and trumpet.

When he was 16 Jankowski started touring Europe, backing singer Caterina Valente. He toured with her for two years, then arranged and wrote for the German orchestra of Erwin Leha as well as formed his own jazz combo. In 1957 his reputation in Germany was so well established he was voted the top jazz pianist in the country, an honor he held for at least nine consecutive years.

In 1960 Jankowski branched out as an orchestral director for such visiting musicians as Gerry Mulligan, plus formed his own 18-member choir of amateur singers (65 people auditioned to be part of the group). But he remained unknown in most other countries until the 1965 release of his 1962 composition "Eine Schwarzwaldfarht," which was released in English as "A Walk in the Black Forest." It sold a quarter of a million copies in the United Kingdom and made #12 pop as well as #1 AC in America.

"A Walk in the Black Forest" also earned Grammy nominations for Best Instrumental Arrangement and Best Instrumental Performance, Non-Jazz. Its presence on the album *The Genius of Jankowski* aided the LP in become a million seller worldwide. Critics were not too impressed by the mellow mood music it contained, including instrumental versions of "My Yiddishe Momme" and "The Donkey Serenade." The British music paper *Melody Maker* termed the LP "inoffensive background music for tea and scones."

Another cut from *The Genius of Jankowski* written by the pianist, "Simple Gimpel," made #15 AC and #91 pop in the fall of 1965. It was his last Hot 100 entry. He had seven more albums released in America on Mercury through the 1960s, with five singles from them making only the AC chart, including "Black Forest Holiday" at #21 in 1966. His last AC entry was "Zabadak" at #27 in the summer of 1968, after which Jankowski concentrated his activities mainly in Europe.

Jankowski died June 29, 1998 of cancer in Germany. He was 62 years old.

57 (Such An) Easy Question
ELVIS PRESLEY

RCA 47-8585

July 24, 1965 (2 weeks)

Writer: Otis Blackwell, Winfield Scott

Producer: Not Listed

"That was a piece of crap," Jordanaire member Gordon Stoker stated bluntly in recalling "(Such An) Easy Question." He added that Elvis, who sang the tune while Stoker and the other Jordanaires provided backing vocals, agreed with him. "He called them all a piece of junk, because most of them were."

The "them" which Stoker mentioned were songs Presley began doing around 1962 when movies took priority over music in his career. Though "(Such An) Easy Question" actually was recorded in Nashville on March 18, 1962, for Presley's *Pot Luck* LP that year, Stoker contends it was among the sort of tunes Presley was forced into recording at the time for movies. The Jordanaires and others urged Elvis not to accept what he was given, but he did not feel like arguing with anyone. So he and the others persevered and tried to make what tunes he received sound as good as they could. "We would take each one of those songs and do something catchy," Stoker said.

"(Such An) Easy Question," which peaked at #11 pop, did appear in Presley's 1965 film *Tickle Me*, but though that probably led to the idea of releasing the song as a single three years after it was recorded, for some reason the only soundtrack to *Tickle Me* was an EP (a record which resembled a 45 but had more than one tune on a side) that did not include "(Such An) Easy Question." The flip side of "(Such An) Easy Question," "It Feels So Right," did not make the AC chart but did hit #55 pop. But "(Such An) Easy Question" did set an unlikely precedent in giving Elvis Presley the most #1 AC hits up to mid-1965, a shocking development given his status as the King of Rock and Roll.

All the information on the early part of Presley's career is readily available elsewhere. For brevity's sake we'll just repeat that he was born in Tupelo, Mississippi, on January 8, 1935, raised on country and R&B music in Memphis, and first recorded for Sun Records in 1954. A year later he cracked the country chart with the two-sided hit "Baby Let's Play House" backed with "I'm Left, You're Right, She's Gone," and by the end of 1955 RCA had bought out his contract from Sun. The next year "Heartbreak Hotel" became the first of 18 #1 pop hits for Presley, none of which reached the same peak on the AC chart.

Presley's AC debut was "(Marie's the Name) His Latest Flame," which made #2 for two weeks in 1961. Then came "Can't Help Falling in Love" [see 9], and between that and his next #1 AC, "Crying in the Chapel" [see 55], which preceded "(Such An) Easy Question," Elvis had four AC entries, all in 1962, ending with "She's Not You" at #2 for two weeks and its flip "Just Tell Her Jim Said Hello" at #14. His single after "(Such An) Easy Question" went to #1 AC [see 61—"I'm Yours"].

58 Save Your Heart for Me
GARY LEWIS AND THE PLAYBOYS

Liberty 55809

August 7, 1965 (2 weeks)

Writers: Gary Geld, Peter Udell

Producer: Snuff Garrett

Born the first son of comedian Jerry Lewis in New York City on July 31, 1945, Gary Lewis formed his band in 1964 with keyboardist David Walker, bassist David Costell, and guitarists Al Ramsey and John West. Snuff Garrett, the Lewises' next-door neighbor, signed the group and produced the first release, "This Diamond Ring," which hit #1 pop on February 20, 1965. "Count Me In" followed and went to #2 pop for two weeks in 1965 behind "Mrs. Brown You've Got a Lovely Daughter" by Herman's Hermits.

Feeling the group's third single should be a ballad, Garrett picked "Save Your Heart for Me" by Gary Geld and Peter Udell. "They wrote 'Save Your Heart for Me' for Brian Hyland," said Lewis. "Brian Hyland ended up putting it on an album and not a single, and it was kind of buried."

Lewis credited the marketing savvy of Garrett for making the song a hit, as well as its short running time of 1 minute and 52 seconds. "It was played everywhere. Deejays loved it," he said. Indeed, "Save Your Heart for Me" almost topped the pop chart as well as AC, peaking at #2 behind Sonny and Cher's "I Got You Babe" the week of August 21, 1965. Despite rumors to the contrary, Gary Lewis and the Playboys played on this and other records. "The Playboys always put down the basic tracks," Lewis said. "Whatever overdubbing Snuff wanted, he put down."

But the group's recording activity stalled when Lewis was inducted into the Army to serve in the Vietnam War on January 1, 1967. During leave time Garrett got him into the studio to record songs, including "Sealed With a Kiss," his only other AC entry, which went to #32 there in 1968. Though not wild about recording the song ("I went, 'Oh, man, Brian Hyland again!'" said Lewis, recalling that Hyland had a #3 pop hit with the tune in 1962), it did give him his last pop chart success when it peaked at #19 in 1968.

By then Lewis was out of the Army, and he reactivated the Playboys with two new LPs for Liberty Records. "We had a couple of $8,000 failures," he noted. A lawsuit with the company ensued, and Lewis eventually settled, but no new recording contract surfaced for the group. Nonetheless, Lewis and crew toured for a few more years.

As the mid-1970s rolled around, "I just said, 'Hey, to hell with this' and started a music store in the San Fernando Valley [in California]," Lewis recalled. "That happened until about '82, when agents said I was very bookable again." With a new lineup of Playboys, Lewis went back on tour.

"We've been playing about 100 dates a year, which is wonderful. We're playing more now than in the '60s," noted Lewis in 1997. And yes, "Save Your Heart for Me" was part of the repertoire.

59 Hold Me, Thrill Me, Kiss Me
MEL CARTER

Imperial 66113

August 28, 1965 (1 week)

Writer: Harry Noble

Producer: Nick DeCaro

Like Sam Cooke, the man who served as his pop music mentor, Mel Carter's first professional music experience was in gospel groups. Born in Cincinnati, Ohio, on April 22, 1939, Carter sang on local radio shows starting at age 4. By the early 1950s he had joined the all-male Raymond Rasberry Singers gospel band.

In the mid-1950s Carter won a scholarship to the Conservatory of Music in Cincinnati, and soon after formed his own gospel unit called the Carvetts. He went on to become assistant director of the Greater Cincinnati Youth and Young Adult Choral Union, but by the end of the 1950s he found himself pulled toward the world of pop. With a young Quincy Jones helping on production, Carter cut "I Need You So" for Mercury in 1959. The next year he did "I'm Coming Home" for the Arwin label, but neither song really did much for his career.

Luckily for Carter, Sam Cooke saw him perform in a club and signed him to Derby, a label which Cooke owned. The first single Carter did was "When a Boy Falls in Love," a song co-written by Cooke which became Carter's initial pop entry when it hit #44 and his only R&B entry when it made #30 in 1963. But two Derby follow-ups did not do well, and a switch to Imperial Records in 1964 did not pull him out of his recording slump either.

Then came "Hold Me, Thrill Me, Kiss Me," first recorded by its composer Harry Noble before it became a hit in 1953 for Karen Chandler, who took it to #5 pop. Carter took it back to prominence 12 years later, but his head did not swell with pride from the remake's success at all. "When my record was top 10, my mother had me carrying the garbage out," he told Eric Eberwein in *Goldmine* in 1985.

"Hold Me, Thrill Me, Kiss Me" by Carter hit #8 pop the week of August 28, 1965, in addition to #1 AC, his first entry on the latter chart. The song later had revivals on the country chart by Johnny and Jonie Mosby in 1969 (#38) and by Micki Fuhrman in 1980 (#60), and on the AC chart by Bobby Vinton in 1977 (#43).

The popularity of "Hold Me, Thrill Me, Kiss Me" allowed Carter to make several follow-ups that reached both the AC and pop charts. The first was "(All of a Sudden) My Heart Sings," another remake of an oldie, in this case a #7 pop hit for Johnnie Johnston in 1945. Carter's rendition made #3 AC and #38 pop. After that came "Love Is All We Need," which went to #21 AC and #50 pop. The next single returned Carter back to the top of the AC lineup [see 71—"Band of Gold"].

60 You Were On My Mind
WE FIVE

A&M 770

September 4, 1965 (5 weeks)

Writer: Sylvia Fricker

Producer: Frank Werber

"We started as the Ridge Runners in the Claremont [California] area," Pete Fullerton recalled of his group We Five. After relocating to San Francisco, the group got a contract with A&M Records. But their manager, Frank Werber, felt the name "Ridge Runners" was wrong. He considered the Clive Five ("My real name is Clive," said Fullerton, who objected to the moniker for the group), then settled on We Five to describe the quintet. Besides bassist Fullerton, the other members were Beverly Bivens, lead singer, who played tambourine and hit the high registers along with Fullerton; Michael Stewart, brother of Kingston Trio member and later solo singer John Stewart, who played rhythm guitar and drums and sang the low registers; Bob Jones, who played lead guitar; and Jerry Burgan, who played rhythm guitar. "The very first song we recorded was 'You Were on My Mind,'" said Fullerton. "It took 13 takes, and we used the 13th." The 13th one was lucky for them, as "You Were On My Mind" hit #1 AC and #3 pop, behind Barry McGuire's "Eve of Destruction" at #1 and the McCoys' "Hang On Sloopy" at #2 at its peak week there on September 25, 1965. It also merited them a Grammy nomination for Best Performance by a Vocal Group.

Sylvia Fricker of the husband and wife duo Ian and Sylvia, who wrote "You Were on My Mind," had performed it with her husband prior to We Five's effort. "Michael Stewart came up with the idea of doing that song," Fullerton said. "We said, 'Yeah, let's do it.' We added a little salsa to it and added a little drums."

"You Were On My Mind" was We Five's only AC entry. They had one more pop entry with "Let's Get Together," which hit #31 in late 1965. (The Youngbloods' remake, titled "Get Together," made #37 AC and #5 pop in 1969.) Fullerton said the group worked together until the end of 1968, when "We all went our separate ways." For a time he, Bivens, and Burgan toured some as the We Five.

Burgan retained rights for the group's name and occasionally recorded but mostly did club dates as We Five over the following years while living in Glendale, California. The other members lived in the San Francisco area except for Jones, who moved to Hawaii. Fullerton became an urban minister of an enterprise called the Truck of Love in San Jose. "I work with emergency situations, situations that fall into the cracks for social needs," he said. Of his time with We Five, he said, "It was a great, wonderful experience. I wouldn't have changed it for anything."

"You Were On My Mind" returned to the charts in 1967, when Crispian St. Peters took it to #36 pop, and in 1971, when Bobby Penn's version made #51 country.

61 I'm Yours
ELVIS PRESLEY

RCA 47-8657

October 9, 1965 (3 weeks)

Writers: Don Robertson, Hal Blair

Producer: Not Listed

Like "(Such An) Easy Question" [see 57], "I'm Yours" appeared for the 1962 LP *Pot Luck* (the "I'm Yours" session took place in Nashville on June 26, 1961) and turned up in 1965 in the movie *Tickle Me*. Both songs went to #1 AC and #11 pop. However, the *Pot Luck* album version included narration not on the single, and the B-side to "I'm Yours," "(It's a) Long Lonely Highway," only bubbled under to #112.

Interestingly, "I'm Yours" was meant to appear in Presley's 1961 film *Blue Hawaii*. Writer Don Robertson recalled in a letter to this author that he received the film's script from Presley's New York production office, which needed a song to be sung by the groom, played by Presley, at a wedding. "I discussed the project with super-songwriter and close friend Hal Blair, and we decided to try to come up with something together that would be appropriate for that scene," Robertson wrote. "I don't recall which one of us suggested the title 'I'm Yours,' but it seemed like a nice idea for a wedding song.

"We got together in my office on Hollywood Boulevard in Los Angeles, and we worked as we had so many times before. I sat at the piano and Hal pulled up a chair beside me. I started improvising, exploring musical elements, and we both liked one of the patterns I played. We bounced lyric lines back and forth and the song gradually evolved. . . .After several hours, we had a rough draft.

"During the next few days I sang and played it at the piano over and over, honing the details and the phrasing and working out an arrangement for a demo. I performed it for Hal and he was happy with it." Hal and Robertson's wife Irene helped Robertson pick the best take. But after he submitted the demo, the final decision was to use "Hawaiian Wedding Song" in *Blue Hawaii* and use "I'm Yours" elsewhere.

Over a period of seven years, Presley recorded 14 of Robertson's songs. "We had a warm rapport, personally and musically," Robertson wrote.

"I'm Yours" was the last #1 AC hit Presley had for five years. In fact, he went nearly two years without strong AC entries (1967–69) until he returned with "Memories," which made #7 AC. Soon after that, Presley found himself without the Jordanaires, the quartet who did backing vocals for him for 15 years, because they didn't want to do the rigorous live Las Vegas concert schedule. The decision did not mean they lacked work, however. "Only about 10 percent of our workload was with Elvis," recalled Jordanaire first tenor Neal Matthews. "Some people think we were part of Elvis's group, but we were not on salary with him at all."

After the Jordanaires went their own way (they continued to tour through the 1990s), Presley did find success in Las Vegas. His next #1 AC tune was recorded there live [see 135—"The Wonder of You"].

62 Taste of Honey
HERB ALPERT AND THE TIJUANA BRASS

A&M 775

October 30, 1965 (5 weeks)

Writer: Bobby Scott

Producers: Herb Alpert, Jerry Moss

The record company executive most familiar to the public in the 1960s was A&M founder Herb Alpert, whose peppy trumpet playing on instrumentals led to five #1 albums and four #1 AC hits during the decade. His group first hit the Hot 100 in 1962 as the Tijuana Brass featuring Herb Alpert with "The Lonely Bull," which went to #6. The next year they became Herb Alpert's Tijuana Brass and made #96 with "Marching Through Madrid."

The Brass did not make the AC chart until "Mexican Drumming Man" entered at #19 in 1964. A year later, the newly titled Herb Alpert and the Tijuana Brass returned to the pop top 10 with a theme first introduced by its writer Bobby Scott as the title tune in a 1960 Broadway show which became a movie the next year.

"Taste of Honey" had been recorded several times prior to Alpert's take in both instrumental and vocal versions (Ric Marlow wrote the lyrics). In 1962 two tries without words made the charts, with Martin Denny and His Orchestra going to #50 pop and #13 AC while the Victor Feldman Quartet went to #88 on the Hot 100 the week of September 1, 1962. Two years later Tony Bennett lent his voice to a single which went to #19 AC and #94 pop, and even the Beatles sang the tune then as a track on their #2 album *Introducing. . .The Beatles.*

"I thought it was a wonderful melody," Alpert told Thomas O'Neil in *The Grammys: For the Record* about "Taste of Honey." "It was written as a waltz and I did it as a shuffle, which I thought was unique and would have an interesting, original flair to it."

The Brass's rendition of "The Third Man Theme" (a #1 pop hit both for Anton Karas and Guy Lombardo when the movie from which it came was released in 1950) made the charts first, and went to #7 AC and #47 pop in 1965. But it was the single's B-side, "Taste of Honey," which garnered the greatest critical and commercial approval. Besides being #1 AC, its #7 showing on the Hot 100 for two weeks beginning November 27, 1965 was the highest position Alpert reached on that chart until 1968 [see 106—"This Guy's in Love With You"].

"Taste of Honey" won Grammys for Record of the Year, Best Instrumental Arrangement, Best Instrumental Performance, Non-Jazz, and Best Engineered Recording. The LP on which it appeared, *Whipped Cream and Other Delights*, got a Grammy nomination for Album of the Year and stayed at #1 for eight weeks starting November 27, 1965. The only other single from the LP was "Whipped Cream," which came out before "Taste of Honey" in the spring of 1965 and went to #13 AC and #68 pop. The group returned to #1 AC two years later [see 86—"Casino Royale"].

63 Make the World Go Away
EDDY ARNOLD

RCA Victor 8679

December 4, 1965 (4 weeks)

Writer: Hank Cochran

Producer: Chet Atkins

His nickname was "The Tennessee Plowboy," but farming is not what made Eddy Arnold (born Richard Edward Arnold near Henderson, Tennessee, on May 15, 1918) famous. He is one of the most successful country artists of all time, and his debut began just a year after *Billboard* started its first chart for country music singles in 1944. "Each Minute Seems a Million Years" went to #5 in 1945 and was the first of 145 singles by him on the country chart, including 92 top 10 hits and 28 #1 hits. One of the latter was "Make the World Go Away," his biggest pop and first #1 AC hit.

"Make the World Go Away" was Arnold's third entry on the AC chart. His first was "What's He Doing in My World," which went to #18 in 1965 and also made #1 country, his first there since 1955's "That Do Make It Nice," and #60 pop, his highest crossover on the Hot 100 since "Tennessee Stud" hit #48 in 1959. Next came "I'm Letting You Go," which went to #33 AC and #15 country and bubbled under at #135 pop. Then Arnold decided to do "Make the World Go Away," which had made the charts just two years before in versions by Ray Price (#2 country and #100 pop) and Timi Yuro (#8 AC and #24 pop).

"I really wasn't aware of Ray's, but I did hear Timi Yuro's," Arnold said of the recordings. "I found out she had sold 50,000 records, which didn't sound to me like a hit. And I thought, 'I've got a chance then.'" Once Arnold decided to do the song, he hit on a novel approach. "I said, 'Hey, what I need to do is do a song that's more or less like the songs I've done before with violins added.'" The use of strings and the large chorale backing of the Anita Kerr Singers made "Make the World Go Away" one of the first so-called "countrypolitan" hits, a country song which sounded almost as uptown as downhome due to its pop influences.

Arnold admitted some other country artists were aghast at what he had done. "They said, 'Aw, you shouldn't do that.' But then they did it. Gladly did it. And it brought me back to prominence." He took the criticism lightly and added with a laugh, "I cried all the way to the bank."

A #1 country hit for three weeks starting the week of December 4, 1965, "Make the World Go Away" peaked at #6 pop the week of December 25, 1965. The record also earned Grammy nominations for Best Country & Western Single and for Arnold for Best Male Country & Western Vocal Performance.

Other versions of "Make the World Go Away" charted later, including Donny and Marie Osmond's in 1974 (#31 AC, #44 pop, #71 country) and Charly McClain's in 1977 (#73 country). As for Arnold, he returned to #1 AC with "I Want to Go With You" [see 69].

64 England Swings

ROGER MILLER

Smash 2010

January 1, 1966 (1 week)

Writer: Roger Miller

Producer: Jerry Kennedy

The novelty number "England Swings," which composer Roger Miller sang as "Eng-guh-lund Swings," went to #1 AC, #3 country, and #8 pop, peaking on the latter the weeks of December 18 and 25, 1965. It was his fifth AC entry after he debuted on the chart with "King of the Road" [see 52]. The songs between the two hits on the AC chart were "Engine Engine #9" (#2 AC for three weeks, #7 pop), the double-sided "One Dyin' and A Buryin'" (#8 AC, #34 pop) backed with "It Just Happened That Way" (#26 AC, #105 bubbling under), and "Kansas City Star" (#3 AC, #31 pop).

After "England Swings," Miller had two more AC singles in 1966, "Husbands and Wives" (#2 AC, #26 pop) and "You Can't Roller Skate in a Buffalo Herd" (#17 AC, #40 pop). After the chart run of the latter ended, NBC-TV aired *The Roger Miller Show*, a musical variety program, from September 12, 1966 through December 26, 1966, with "King of the Road" as its theme. Miller's successes following that hit, including "England Swings," had led to the idea for the show, but it didn't win a large enough audience to convince NBC to let it go a full season. On the official Web site on the Internet for Miller operated by his estate, he was quoted as saying about the show's cancellation that "It set my career back two years. It must have sent the network back ten years."

Miller was joking, of course, but his popularity as a musician on the AC and pop charts was winding down. After 1967's "Walkin' in the Sunshine" (#6 AC, #37 pop) and 1968's "Little Green Apples" (#5 AC, #39 pop) and "Vance" (#15 AC, #80 pop), Miller was off the Hot 100 and had only one more AC single, the 1973 release "Open Up Your Heart," which made #20.

He continued to be a regular on the country chart through 1975, although his last top 10 on that listing was back in 1968 with "Little Green Apples" at #6. He then had six singles make the chart through 1986's "Some Hearts Get All the Breaks" at #81. By that time Miller was garnering much acclaim and a Tony Award for his work doing the music for the 1985 Broadway musical *Big River*, based on Mark Twain's novel *Huckleberry Finn*. Later, in 1988, Ricky Van Shelton had a #1 country hit covering Miller's 1970 tune "Didn't We All Have the Right."

Roger Miller died on October 25, 1992 from cancer. He was 56 years old. A quotation from Miller's Web site was typical of his whimsical manner: "If I had to live my life over. . .I wouldn't have time."

1966

65 Spanish Eyes

AL MARTINO

Capital 5542

January 8, 1966 (4 weeks)

Writers: Eddie Snyder and Charlie Singleton (words),
  Bert Kaempfert (music)

Producer: Tom Morgan

In 1965 Bert Kaempfert had his fifth instrumental single make the AC chart. "Moon Over Naples" went to #6 on the listings as well as #59 on the Hot 100. Later that year, the same composition would become a bigger success when Al Martino sang it as "Spanish Eyes."

"Bert Kaempfert sent me a copy of his instrumental. I listened to it and thought it was a hit melody, but it had no lyrics," Martino recalled. He later heard a record containing lyrics for the song, but Martino told Kaempfert's music publisher he did not like the words.

Faced with this opposition and wanting Martino to give the song a shot, Eddie Snyder and Charles Singleton became the new designated writers for the instrumental. "I liked it very much," Martino said of the revised composition. He made plans to record what was now "Spanish Eyes," but there was one more person he felt he needed for the session. "I called up Bert Kaempfert and asked him to come up to New York to help us," Martino said. "We liked him. He had a certain sound. We wanted to keep it."

With the composer playing on the record, "Spanish Eyes" saw its way to #15 pop in addition to its four-week run on the AC chart. It also proved to be a hot seller in Germany, where Kaempfert was based, with at least 800,000 copies sold there.

Interestingly, "Spanish Eyes" had a strange afterlife in the United Kingdom. In 1970 the song entered the British chart for one week at #49, then came back even stronger three years later when it peaked at #5 in the summer of 1973. Martino said he believes a deejay in the country took a chance on playing the tune one time, and the response he got from doing it led to the record's rerelease. It became the last entry for Martino on that chart, coming 21 years after his "Here in My Heart" was the first British #1 single when it debuted there in 1952.

Martino said he did another tune by Kaempfert, Snyder, and Singleton, "Strangers in the Night" [see 72], before Frank Sinatra recorded it in 1966. However, when Sinatra cut the tune and was promoting it to radio stations, Martino was out of the country and so lost the chance to make a hit of his version.

Luckily, Martino did have a few other successes waiting in the wings during and after that period. One of them, "Mary in the Morning," became his third #1 AC hit [see 89].

66 It Was a Very Good Year

FRANK SINATRA

Reprise 0429

February 5, 1966 (1 week)

Writer: Ervin Drake

Producer: Sonny Burke

"The Voice," "The Chairman of the Board," "Ol' Blue Eyes"—the nicknames proliferated, but for his fans and many music lovers Francis Albert Sinatra, born in Hoboken, New Jersey, on December 12, 1915, was simply the finest pop singer of his generation, perhaps of the 20th century. Establishing himself as a singer with the orchestras of Harry James in 1939–40 and then Tommy Dorsey from 1940–42, Sinatra then broke out as a solo performer whose unique phrasings made him a chart favorite for the next 25 years. One of his best-remembered later efforts was his initial #1 AC single—"It Was a Very Good Year"—a song which became an immediate Sinatra standard after its release.

When "It Was a Very Good Year" first appeared on record in 1961 as a track on the Kingston Trio's LP Goin' Places (which peaked at #3 on the album chart), it generated little recognition. But reportedly when Sinatra heard the tune played one day on the radio, he thought it had potential and chose to record the song for September of My Years, a 1965 album whose concept about middle age and growing older coincided with Sinatra's 50th birthday.

In "It Was a Very Good Year," Sinatra sang about the times he had had at various ages in his life, starting at 17, devoting a chorus to each age. Arranger Gordon Jenkins provided a smooth background of strings and oboes to complement Sinatra's voice and make the transitions between keys seem effortless. "Gordon had his identity and his sound," pianist Lou Levy told Will Friedwald in Sinatra! The Song Is You. "Everything was sort of a wail and a moan. He had a way of getting that kind of sound. I could take only so much of it, but with Sinatra, it worked. And I know Frank liked it. How can you knock an arrangement like '[It Was a] Very Good Year'? That's really sort of a masterpiece."

While it peaked at #1 AC, "It Was a Very Good Year" made only #28 pop in early 1966, which nonetheless was Sinatra's best chart performance since "Softly, As I Leave You" went to #4 AC and #27 pop in 1964. Its flip side, "Moment to Moment," went to #18 AC and bubbled under at #115. Sinatra also won a Grammy for Best Male Vocal Performance for the song, but "It Was a Very Good Year" did not earn a nomination for Song of the Year, while the title tune from September of My Years, which was never released as a single, did. Understandably, writer Ervin Drake complained to National Recording Arts and Sciences President Francis Scott. (While the song did not get a Grammy, the LP September of My Years won for Album of the Year.)

In September 1966 Della Reese took "It Was a Very Good Year" to #99 pop, her last Hot 100 entry. Sinatra had better luck, continuing to be a favorite on the AC and pop charts. In fact, his next release topped both charts [see 72—"Strangers in the Night"].

67 Crying Time

RAY CHARLES

ABC-Paramount 10739

February 12, 1966 (3 weeks)

Writer: Buck Owens

Producer: Sid Feller

Country singer Buck Owens composed "Crying Time," but it was not even an entry for him on the country chart. It was Ray Charles who had the most success on record with the tune, reaching #1 AC for the third time. All Charles' #1 AC songs were written by country artists, and he had no compunctions about doing the tunes even if they were identified strongly with other artists.

"As a genuine fan of country music, there were other songs I knew and associated with certain singers I loved," Charles told David Ritz in the liner notes to the 1997 anthology *Ray Charles Genius & Soul: The 50th Anniversary Collection*. "Take 'Your Cheating Heart.' That's Hank Williams. Now Hank was great, Hank was an original, but I was stupid enough to figure I could do Hank in my own way. Same goes for Buck Owens' 'Crying Time' and 'Together Again.' Didn't sing the songs out of disrespect for Buck. I'm crazy about Buck. But I heard something that fit my style. The key was keeping my style while watching my style work in different ways."

With backing vocals from the Jack Halloran Singers, "Crying Time" went top 10 AC, pop, and R&B, stopping on the latter at #5. Incredibly, "Crying Time" was Charles' last single to make the pop top 10 when it rested at #6 the week of February 19, 1966. "Crying Time" also won Charles Grammys for Best Rhythm and Blues Recording and Best Rhythm and Blues Solo Vocal Performance, Male or Female.

The success of "Crying Time" returned Charles to prominence after two years of rather unexceptional singles. Only devout Charles fans can recall the following tunes which hit the AC chart during 1964–65: "No One to Cry To" (#8 AC, #55 pop); "A Tear Fell" (#6 AC, #50 pop); "Smack Dab in the Middle" (#13 AC, #52 pop); "Makin' Whoopee" (#11 AC, #46 pop); "Cry" (#11 AC, #58 pop); "I'm a Fool to Care" (#22 AC, #84 pop); and the theme to the movie "The Cincinnati Kid" (#19 AC, #115 bubbling under).

Luckily, "Crying Time" was a hit and encouraged Charles to record the Buck Owens song he mentioned earlier, "Together Again" [see 70]. It became the fourth #1 AC single for the man born Ray Charles Robinson in Albany, Georgia, on September 23, 1930. Completely blind since age 7 as a result of glaucoma, he studied at the State School for Blind and Deaf Children in St. Augustine, Florida, from 1937–45.

Charles first made the R&B chart in 1949 at #2 with "Confession Blues" as part of the Maxin Trio, then went solo and hit #5 R&B in 1951 with "Baby Let Me Hold Your Hand." He made his pop chart debut at #34 in 1957 with "Swanee River Rock." Two years later "What'd I Say" hit #6 pop and #1 R&B, and the legendary talent of Ray Charles solidified from that point onward.

68 The Ballad of the Green Berets

STAFF SGT. BARRY SADLER

RCA 8739

March 5, 1966 (5 weeks)

Writer: Robin Moore, Barry Sadler

Producer: Andy Wiswell

"The Ballad of the Green Berets," an ode to the famous Army Special Forces (Airborne) unit that became best known for its role in the Vietnam War, was released at the right time: In 1966 the major protests against America's involvement in the war were yet to come. The singer had himself fought in Vietnam, though he was stationed stateside when he created, recorded, and promoted the song.

Staff Sergeant Barry Sadler was born in Carlsbad, New Mexico, on November 1, 1940. He joined the Air Force at age 18, and four years later he reenlisted in the Army, where he spent a year in training to become a Green Beret. He spent 37 weeks of his training studying medicine, his specialty. But the interest in music which he had shown as a teenager remained, and when he recuperated from wounds suffered in Vietnam, he decided to pursue that interest.

His cohort Robin Moore, who wrote a book called *The Green Berets*, told Dorothy Horstman in *Sing Your Heart Out, Country Boy* his side of how their tune developed. "Barry Sadler and I were both members of the Special Forces—the Green Berets—stationed at Fort Bragg [near Fayetteville, North Carolina]. He was always singing and playing his guitar. Barry got the idea for the song in 1963, and we wrote it together. It was published in 1965 and released January 1, 1966, long before the Vietnam War had run its course."

"The Ballad of the Green Berets" was a rare simultaneous #1 on the AC and pop charts for five weeks starting March 5, 1966. The song also went to #2 on the country chart. An album titled after the tune went to #1 on the LP chart for five weeks starting March 12, 1966. The song led to a very brief fad for items connected to it and Sadler in the spring of 1966. In its May 2, 1966 issue, *Newsweek* reported a comic strip called "The Green Berets" could be seen in the newspapers of some 25 major cities, plus there was a Barry Sadler fan club which numbered more than 200,000 members. One officially sanctioned endeavor was the Barry Sadler Foundation, which provided scholarships to children of American soldiers killed while serving their tour of duty in Vietnam.

The mania for Sadler died out rather quickly, however. The follow-up single "The 'A' Team" went to #8 AC, #28 pop, and #46 country, but it was his last 45 to make each of those charts. And *The "A" Team* LP only went to #130 in mid-1966 before it—and Sadler's musical career—faded quickly. Sadler died on November 5, 1989, from heart failure. He had been hospitalized for more than a year after being shot in his head during a robbery attempt in Guatamala on September 7, 1988.

69 I Want to Go With You

EDDY ARNOLD

RCA Victor 8749

April 9, 1966 (3 weeks)

Writer: Hank Cochran

Producer: Chet Atkins

As with Eddy Arnold's first #1 AC hit "Make the World Go Away" [see 63], "I Want to Go With You" was written by Hank Cochran. Typical of many follow-up records during the 1960s, "I Want to Go With You" had a similar sound to the previous hit, yet had its own distinctive touches, in this case, a heavier drum line and fancy piano playing.

Asked if Cochran had said anything about how he felt about Arnold's interpretation of his songs, Arnold said, "He was delighted, although he hadn't pitched me 'Make the World Go Away.' But he did pitch me 'I Want to Go With You.'" Ever the jokester, Arnold said that Cochran is so appreciative of his work on the tunes that "When I see him, he bows to me."

Surprisingly, Cochran has never had much luck as a recording artist even though he composed some of the biggest country hits of all time, including "A Little Bitty Tear" [see 10]. He has had only a few entries on the country chart as a vocalist, with the biggest being "Sally Was a Good Old Girl," which went to #20 there in 1962.

Arnold's rendition of "I Want to Go With You" reached #1 on the country chart for six weeks starting April 9, 1966. On the pop chart it went to #36. That same year, Arnold was elected to the Country Music Hall of Fame. The country crooner continued to make the AC and pop charts through 1969. His last #1 country hit was "Then You Can Tell Me Goodbye" in 1968, which went to #6 AC and #84 pop. His last pop entry was "They Don't Make Love Like They Used To" in 1969 (#10 country, #19 AC, and #99 pop), and his final single on the AC chart was "Soul Deep" in 1970 (#28 AC, #22 country).

"The Blues Don't Care Who's Got 'Em" was as of press time Arnold's last entry on the country chart, where it went to #76 in 1983. That gave him the distinction of being one of only a few country artists to chart in the 1940s, 1950s, 1960s, 1970s, and 1980s, along with Roy Acuff, Hank Snow, and Hank Thompson. "I hope I have one more hit in this decade," Arnold noted. "If I do, that will make me have a hit in six decades. That's what I hope to do. And then I'm going off in the cornfield."

There's that sense of humor again. Actually, Arnold remained quite active in the 1990s as a host, guest, or presenter on various series and specials on cable television's The Nashville Network (TNN), and many of the newer talents appearing on these shows with him cite him as a major influence on their lives. He has truly earned the overused but in his case appropriate title of "living legend."

70 Together Again

RAY CHARLES

ABC-Paramount 10785

April 30, 1966 (3 weeks)

Writer: Buck Owens

Producer: Sid Feller

Buck Owens wrote "Together Again" in the wee hours one morning in 1963 at his piano. He told *Billboard* in 1966 he considered the song his best composition at the time because ". . .[it] keeps getting recorded over and over. It's now being recorded at the rate of one and a half times a month." One of the people heard singing it at the time was Ray Charles, who took the song to #1 AC after Owens' original version went to #1 country for two weeks starting June 6, 1964.

The Charles version of "Together Again" also went to #10 R&B and #19 pop. The record's B-side, "You're Just About to Lose Your Clown," went to #91 pop for two weeks in the spring of 1966. Ten years later, Emmylou Harris took "Together Again" to #1 again on the country chart the week of April 24, 1976. Yet another take on "Together Again" came in 1984 when Kenny Rogers and Dottie West went to #19 country.

Charles remained a consistent presence on the AC, pop, and R&B charts through 1973, although he placed more singles on the latter two listings. He did not break into the upper echelon of the AC chart during this period; his highest-charting outings were two singles which stopped at #20, 1972's "What Am I Living For" (#54 pop) and 1973's "Come Live With Me" (#82 pop). Charles became hard to find even on the R&B chart through the end of the 1970s, and in 1980 he turned his full attention to country music. He did eventually make the country chart, even getting to #1 there on March 23, 1985, with "Seven Spanish Angels," a duet with Willie Nelson.

Around the same time, Charles' impassioned delivery near the end of the all-star benefit record "We Are the World" [see 472] reminded fellow singers how much they appreciated and had been influenced by him. One of them, Billy Joel, teamed with Charles to do "Baby Grand" in 1987. It became Charles' first single on the AC and pop charts since the 1970s, peaking at #3 AC and #75 pop. Three years later, a remake of the Brothers Johnson's "I'll Be Good to You," produced by Quincy Jones and also sung by Chaka Khan, made #1 R&B for two weeks starting January 20, 1990, plus #18 pop and #30 AC.

Three years after "I'll Be Good to You," Charles made the AC chart one more time with another song from the 1970s, "A Song for You," which peaked at #9 AC despite a poor sales showing of #104 bubbling under. No other tunes hit the AC chart after that, but Charles was still touring and working on records toward the end of the 1990s, not content to rest on his laurels or his reputation as a musical genius. As he told David Ritz in the liner notes to *Ray Charles Genius & Soul: The 50th Anniversary Collection*, "I've still got a lifetime of music ahead of me."

71 Band of Gold

MEL CARTER

Imperial 66165

May 21, 1966 (2 weeks)

Writers: Bob Musel (words), Jack Taylor (music)

Producer: Nick DeCaro

Like his previous #1 AC hit "Hold Me, Thrill Me, Kiss Me" [see 59], Mel Carter's "Band of Gold" was a cover of a 1950s hit. Don Cherry had the biggest success with the song originally, reaching #4 pop in 1956, but the same year it also charted as a single done by Kit Carson (#11) and the Hi-Fi Four (#93). Also, a group called the Roomates (sic) bubbled under to #119 with their version in 1961. A different tune with the same title hit #3 pop in 1970 when done by Freda Payne.

Carter's version made #32 on the Hot 100 and was his last top 40 pop hit. He had two more entries on the Hot 100 in 1966 before disappearing from the chart, "You You You" (#49 pop plus #11 AC) and "Take Good Care of Her" (#78 pop only). He made the AC chart the next year with "Be My Love," a remake of the Mario Lanza #1 hit of 1951, which went to #23 and became one of Carter's favorites. In 1968 he made the AC chart again with "I Pretend," which peaked at #38. But after three failed singles on the Amos label in 1969, Carter's recording output became irregular.

Carter had several acting stints on nighttime TV series such as Marcus Welby M.D. and Sanford and Son during the 1970s. During the same period he attempted comebacks on several labels, but the best he could muster was #39 AC in 1974 with "I Only Have Eyes for You" on Romar Records and #47 AC with "My Coloring Book" on Private Stock in 1976. The latter single was his last to make the AC chart, and as before both tunes were remakes of previous hits.

In 1980 Carter made two singles for the Cream label, "You Changed My Life" and "Who's Right Who's Wrong," both of which sank quickly. He tried yet again in 1984 with a dance record called "Love Test" on Airwave Records, but it attracted little attention. He generated better press that same year with his album Willing, his first LP of new material since 1969. While the record did not bring him back on the charts, Carter did receive his first Grammy nomination for the LP for Best Male Soul Gospel Performance.

While his singing career never returned to the heights of his mid-1960s hits, Carter maintained enough clout to tour into the 1990s. He told Eric Eberwein in Goldmine in 1985 that he had no regrets about what happened in his professional life, saying that "I'm still alive, I'm kicking, and I thank God for having given me the talent to have experienced some of the things in my life that I've seen and been a part of. . . .I'm thankful for that."

72 Strangers in the Night

FRANK SINATRA

Reprise 0470

June 4, 1966 (7 weeks)

Writers: Bert Kaempfert, Charlie Singleton, Eddie Snyder

Producer: Jimmy Bowen

Frank Sinatra's biggest solo hit of the 1960s was "Strangers in the Night," which apart from being #1 AC also topped the Hot 100 the week of July 2, 1966, plus hit #1 in seven other countries, including the United Kingdom and Argentina. Though the song came across as tailor-made for Sinatra, he was not the first to record it, and his version very nearly failed to come out in time to be a hit.

When music publisher Hal Fine sent record producer Jimmy Bowen a copy of the soundtrack for the film A Man Could Get Killed, an instrumental passage on one cut struck Bowen as perfect for Sinatra. Bowen asked Fine to put a lyric on the piece, and after two rejected tries "Strangers in the Night" was born. Bowen planned a recording session for the night of April 11, 1966. Earlier the same day, he ran into singer Jack Jones, who mentioned casually that he was going to record "Strangers in the Night" the next day. Quietly startled, Bowen went into overdrive to get the song done before Jones could get his version out. Bowen's first difficulty in the studio was Sinatra's inability to get a half-tone change of key two-thirds the way through the song. In Bowen's autobiography, Rough Mix, he recounts how he came up with the solution. He told Sinatra, "Frank, sing it right up to the key change and cut. Then we'll give you a bell tone and we'll go from there in the new key to the end." As planned, Bowen stopped the master tape, rang the bell and then started the tape again as Sinatra sang in the new key, resulting in a finished take.

After Sinatra and the musicians left, Bowen spent the night with his engineer splicing in the key change, mixing the tracks, and mastering the songs onto acetate dubs. The latter produced high-quality sound yet lasted only about 10 plays. Bowen had the acetates given to runners in packages to be hand-delivered to the top deejays in all 50 major markets the next day. The result was that Jones' version never charted, nor did one by Bobby Darin which already had been cut but not released.

While Sinatra's vocal rendition had the charts to itself, Bert Kaempfert recorded an instrumental of the composition he did for the movie and it reached #8 AC and bubbled under to #124. Ten years later, Bette Midler revived the standard to take it to #45 AC.

"Strangers in the Night" by Sinatra won Grammys for Record of the Year, Best Male Vocal Performance, and Best Arrangement Accompanying Vocalist or Instrumentalist, the latter going to Ernie Freeman. Its success prompted the release of an LP bearing the song's name which went to #1 on the album chart the week of July 23, 1966. On that LP was Sinatra's follow-up and next #1 AC hit, "Summer Wind" [see 78].

The Impossible Dream (The Quest)

JACK JONES

Kapp 755

July 23, 1966 (1 week)

Writers: Joe Darion (words and music), Mitch Leigh (music)

Producer: David Kapp

The man who lost out with "Strangers in the Night" ended up following Frank Sinatra's version of that tune at the #1 AC spot with "The Impossible Dream (The Quest)." Because of Sinatra's preemptive strike with his "Strangers. . ." 45, Jack Jones' version became the B-side for his rendition of "The Impossible Dream," but the latter did very well for itself, getting to #1 AC and #35 pop plus earning a Grammy nomination for Best Male Vocal Performance.

"The Impossible Dream" came from the Broadway musical *Man of La Mancha*. It was a highlight in the show summing up the ambitions of its lead character Don Quixote, played originally by Richard Kiley. In his *Greatest Hits* album, Jones told Will Friedwald that he had his doubts about covering the song. "I didn't even want to sing this song," he said. "I love Richard Kiley, but when I saw the show, I didn't think I could make the song work for me. Obviously today, I can see where I didn't take advantage of some of the lyrics. It should be sung by somebody who's really been through it all. I think that this interpretation clicked for me because it was, again, so pure, that it worked for a young man singing this song. I wouldn't say that I intentionally thought of doing it like that, it just came out that way. There are only very few times when one makes deliberate choices. You just do the songs the way you feel them; you lay them out and you arrange them, and then your interpretation comes from honesty."

Under the musical direction of Pete King, Jones cut "The Impossible Dream" on April 4, 1966. Two years later a pair of remakes of the tune hit the charts. The Hesitations took it to #14 R&B and #42 pop in 1968, while the same year an instrumental version by Roger Williams went to #5 AC and #55 pop.

By now it was obvious to chart watchers that while Jones struggled to crack the pop top 40 with his singles, he had no problem whatsoever on the AC chart. For example, of the four 45s of his released between "The Race Is On" [his first #1 AC hit—see 53] and "The Impossible Dream," three of them made the AC top 10—"Seein' the Right Love Go Wrong" (#9) and "Just Yesterday" (#5) in 1965 and "Love Bug" in 1966 (#5). Only "The Weekend," which followed "Love Bug," underperformed in this period, making just #20 on the roster.

After "The Impossible Dream" came "A Day in the Life of a Fool," which hit #4 AC and #62 pop. But Jones' biggest AC hit was his next release, "Lady" [see 84].

74 Somewhere, My Love
RAY CONNIFF AND THE SINGERS

Columbia 43626

July 30, 1966 (4 weeks)

Writers: Paul Francis Webster (words), Maurice Jarre (music)

Producer: Ernie Altschuler

Born in Attleboro, Massachusetts, on November 6, 1916, Ray Conniff followed in his father's footsteps and became a trombonist. His first paying job was in 1938 for 15 months as trombonist and arranger for Bunny Berigan's band. He worked for the bands of Bob Crosby, Artie Shaw, and Harry James in the 1940s as well as the Armed Forces Radio Services.

In 1951 Mitch Miller hired him as an arranger for Columbia Records, which he did for such artists as Guy Mitchell, Marty Robbins, and Johnny Mathis. His first " and the Singers" album came out in 1957, but his first two charted pop singles, "'S Wonderful" at #73 in 1957 and "Midnight Lace—Part I" at #92 in 1960, were instrumentals.

"I wasn't the first to use voices as instruments. . . .But I believe I was the first to put voices right alongside instruments until you couldn't tell them apart," he told Joseph Lanza about his group in *Elevator Music*. "Trumpets and girls go together, because they operate on almost identical frequency ranges. Male voices blend better with tenor and baritone saxophones." His "Singers" were usually 13 male and 12 female vocalists backed by eight musicians.

After "Midnight Lace," Conniff had no chart entries until "Invisible Tears," his first charted 45 with the Singers, went to #10 AC and #57 pop in 1964. The next year "Happiness Is" got to #26 AC only. Then came "Somewhere, My Love," also known as "Lara's Theme" from the movie *Doctor Zhivago*. It went to #1 AC and then #9 pop the week of August 13, 1966. It won Ray Conniff and the Singers a Grammy for Best Performance by a Chorus plus a Grammy nomination for Song of the Year. Other covers which charted were all 1966 instrumentals: Roger Williams (#5 AC, #65 pop), the MGM Singing Strings (#28 AC), and the Brass Ring (#36 AC, #126 bubbling under).

"Somewhere, My Love" pushed Conniff's LP named after it to #3 on the album chart, the highest peak for any Conniff LP. (The soundtrack to *Doctor Zhivago* with the original instrumental version did even better, hitting #1 on the album chart the week of November 5, 1966.) Conniff had virtually no pop 45s after "Somewhere, My Love," but did get 12 more AC entries through 1969 plus three more through 1977's "Rain On" at #48, a remarkably long run for an act in the rock era.

"Instead of playing trombone solos that other musicians liked, I made an about-face and wrote my arrangements with a view to making the masses understand and buy records," he told Lanza. "From that point, I became very successful. I use the word success both financially and as a person. . . .I could have gone on as I did with the big bands and be a little over the head of the general buying public, but this is a better way to go."

Conniff has released more than 100 albums and still averages at least one LP a year. He is currently signed with PolyGram.

75 I Couldn't Live Without Your Love
PETULA CLARK

Warner 5835

August 27, 1966 (1 week)

Writers: Jackie Trent (words), Tony Hatch (music)

Producer: Tony Hatch

No female vocalist in the British invasion in the mid-1960s was as popular as Petula Sally Clark, known familiarly by her fans worldwide as "Pet." Clark, born in Epsom, England, on November 15, 1932, sang professionally before she was 10 years old and was quite popular in her native country for nearly 20 years before "Downtown" went to #1 pop in 1965 and launched her career in America.

Clark came to prominence singing in the early 1940s, doing radio shows and entertaining British soldiers, who nicknamed her "The Forces Girl," during World War II. In 1944 she made her film debut in *Medal for the General* and did more than a dozen others for a decade until she wearied of the ingenue roles she played in them. She did not do records until 1949. "Put Your Shoes On, Lucy" was her first single released in Great Britain.

Coral Records tried her "Song of the Mermaid" in America in 1951, but nobody cared. The King, MGM, Imperial, Warwick, Laurie, and London labels took shots with her 45s in the United States through 1964 but nothing charted, even though in England Clark had hit #1 with "Sailor" in 1961 and had six other top 10 songs from 1954–62. Then her #2 English hit "Downtown" broke out when Warner tried it in 1964, although not on the AC chart, as it was considered rock and roll (!). The follow-up, "I Know a Place," gave Clark her AC debut at #16 as well as #3 pop. She then had three top five AC 45s through 1966—"You'd Better Come Home," "My Love," and "A Sign of the Times."

In the summer of 1966, Clark got a variety series on the British Broadcasting Corporation called *This Is Petula Clark*. Her husband Claude Wolff told her producer Tony Hatch the show was an excellent opportunity for her to sing her latest single. To that end, Hatch used a ballad he created with his writing partner Jackie Trent, a onetime client of his who became his wife.

"Jackie wrote the words of 'I Couldn't Live Without Your Love' as a private tribute to me," Hatch told Don Charles in *Goldmine* in 1990. "She was appearing in Birmingham [England] at the time, and wrote the music one day for no particular reason. She loved it and asked me to put it on a cassette for her. [Driving] up to Birmingham, she played the music to herself in the car and wrote the lyrics [as] a way of expressing the personal relationship we shared."

But Trent and Clark did not get along well, and Trent insisted that she get writer's credit if Hatch gave the song to Clark. Clark loved the tune so much she consented, and "I Couldn't Live Without Your Love" became a #1 AC hit and a top 10 entry in Britain and America, where it made #9 pop the weeks of August 20 and 27, 1966. She returned to #1 AC the next summer [see 90—"Don't Sleep in the Subway"].

76 Born Free
ROGER WILLIAMS

Kapp 767

September 3, 1966 (6 weeks nonconsecutive)

Writers: Don Black (words), John Barry (music)

Producer: Hy Grill

In 1955, Roger Williams' "Autumn Leaves" topped the Best Seller chart for four weeks. Eleven years later on a different chart, the pianist had another #1 hit with "Born Free," the title song from the movie about a lion raised by humans in Africa.

Williams, born in Omaha, Nebraska, on October 1, 1924 as Louis Weertz ("Everybody called me Lou," he said), was a musical prodigy who played the piano at age 3. Following extensive music education, he signed with Kapp Records as a solo artist in 1952. "Autumn Leaves" was his chart debut, and he charted fairly often until 1962, when "Maria" from the musical *West Side Story* became his first AC entry at #11 (it made #48 pop), followed by "Amor" (#16 AC, #88 pop). His next chart entry wasn't until an update of his first hit, "Autumn Leaves—1965," hit #10 AC and #92 pop.

In 1966, Kapp asked Williams to record "Born Free." "Kapp called me on it and he said, 'It's a song about a lion.' I said, 'OK,'" Williams laughed. To establish a "lionlike" quality at the start of the song, Williams said, "I used a double glissando from the bottom of the piano, and it kind of roars." Williams said he played the tune once at a symphony in Toledo, Ohio, near a zoo and the lions started to roar when the tune began, prompting laughter from the audience.

Toward the end of the record, studio musicians sang some of Don Black's lyrics, making "Born Free" not purely an instrumental. The result impressed Williams, who noted that while one never can predict whether a record will be a hit, "To tell you the truth, I thought it would do something." "Born Free" certainly did do something. It peaked at #7 pop the week of December 17, 1966, after having topped the AC chart three months earlier. Williams played the song at the Academy Awards ceremony on April 10, 1967, where it was nominated for and won the Oscar for Best Song. He also earned a Grammy nomination for Best Instrumental Performance (Other Than Jazz) for the tune.

Though Matt Munro, who sang the song in the film, took "Born Free" to #35 AC in 1966 and the Hesitations vocal group's version went to #38 pop and #4 R&B in 1968, Williams is the artist most strongly associated with the tune. Williams charted entries in both AC and pop through 1969, but his last AC appearance was another movie song, 1977's "Main Theme From 'King Kong,'" which reached #32. He continued to record after that, and his 110th LP, *Roger Williams Plays Popular Melodies That Will Live Forever*, was released by Reader's Digest in 1997.

Based in Encino, California, Williams still tours constantly. "I'm playing with a lot of symphonies, doing a lot of jazz now," he noted. With plenty of concerts and records planned for the future, Williams is nowhere near retiring as he enters his mid-seventies.

77 In the Arms of Love

ANDY WILLIAMS

Columbia 43737

October 1, 1966 (2 weeks)

Writers: Ray Evans and Jay Livingston (words),
*   Henry Mancini (music)*

Producer: Robert Mersey

The 1965 movie *What Did You Do in the War, Daddy?* was not a hit, and Andy Williams never saw the movie. But there was one motivating factor for him to sing the song "In the Arms of Love" from the film, and that was that its composer was Henry Mancini. "I just had such a track record with Henry that there was no reason not do it," Williams said, citing his success in recording Mancini's themes from other movies such as "Moon River" from *Breakfast at Tiffany's* and the title songs for *Charade* and *The Days of Wine and Roses* [see 26—"Can't Get Used to Losing You"].

"In the Arms of Love" was not a pop hit in spite of its AC triumph, reaching only #49 on the Hot 100. However, he and his producer felt enough confidence in the song to make it the title tune of Williams' latest LP released in the fall of 1966. "It was mostly Mersey and me who determined that [what song would be an album's title tune]," Williams said. "Columbia gave a free rein."

Williams added that Mersey and most of his other producers picked what songs he could consider cutting. "They got most of the material to me, and if I liked them, I'd do them," he said. He relied on his producer's judgment because by 1966 he was starting his fifth season as host of his own weekly variety series on NBC-TV, and the activities associated with the show cut into the amount of time he had to find music for his LPs. "During those times, I recorded about three albums a year," he said. "We'd just do them in the evenings."

Williams had not always been that busy. He was born Howard Andrew Williams in Wall Lake, Iowa, on December 3, with his birth year given by sources anywhere from 1927 to 1932. (When asked by this author if he wanted to confirm any of those years, he said, "I'll pass.") He and his brothers formed a quartet that was singing professionally by the time the Williamses moved to Los Angeles in the early 1940s.

The quartet's big break was being the chorus for Bing Crosby on "Swinging on a Star," a #1 pop hit for nine weeks in 1944. That same year, a rumor spread that Williams provided the singing voice for Lauren Bacall in the movie *To Have and Have Not*. "I sang for her in the movie, but according to her book, they took off my voice and used hers instead in the final version," he said.

By 1952, the Williams Brothers Quartet had disbanded. Andy pursued a solo career which got him a job as a regular singer on NBC-TV's *The Tonight Show Starring Steve Allen* from 1954–57. The exposure led to his first pop entry, 1956's "Walk Hand in Hand," which hit #54.

Williams' next #1 AC hit after "In the Arms of Love" was "Happy Heart" [see 116].

78 Summer Wind

FRANK SINATRA

Reprise 0509

October 15, 1966 (1 week)

Writers: Johnny Mercer (lyrics–English), Henry Mayer (music)

Producer: Sonny Burke

Originally written in West Germany with words by Hans Bradtke, "Summer Wind" had acquired English lyrics by Johnny Mercer before it was adapted for use by several American artists in 1965. Wayne Newton took it to #9 AC and #78 pop that year, while Roger Williams joined with the Harry Simeone Chorale to reach #20 AC and #109 bubbled under. But it was not until bobbysoxers' favorite Frank Sinatra sang the tune that it reached the top.

Sinatra recorded "Summer Wind" on May 16, 1966, without doing the second chorus. What it did have were prominent jazz organ and other instrumental passages handled skillfully by Nelson Riddle, Sinatra's favorite arranger of the 1950s to whom the singer returned in 1963 for some recording work. In *Sinatra! The Song Is You*, Will Friedwald opined that "Summer Wind" was the best Sinatra-Riddle collaboration of the 1960s and described how the band backing Sinatra took the role of the wind in the record. "This figure is first stated on the organ and then repeated by various voices in the band—the high reeds, the low reeds, the baritone sax in solo—and then becomes a countermelody and background riff to Sinatra's exposition," Friedwald wrote. "The summer wind, as depicted in this figure, is a symbol of loss. "At first the breeze blows in gently, illustrating to the protagonist what has been and what is. As Sinatra's emotions mount, the wind and the music waft upward into a crescendo of hurricanelike intensity with the help of two modulations. Like a tornado, it reduces the hero's happiness to rubble and then softly drifts away, as tenderly and as cruelly as it entered."

Released as the follow-up to "Strangers in the Night" [see 72] from the album of the same name, "Summer Wind" wafted to #25 pop at its peak while becoming Sinatra's third consecutive #1 AC record. It became a fan favorite at Sinatra concerts after its inclusion in the 1984 movie *The Pope of Greenwich Village*. Sinatra remade the tune on his 1993 *Duets LP* singing with Julio Iglesias.

"Summer Wind" was the 18th Sinatra song to make the AC chart. He debuted there on the chart's debut, July 17, 1961, at #15 with "Granada," which went to #64 pop. Twenty-one years earlier he had been #1 on *Billboard*'s first Best-Selling Retail Records chart with "I'll Never Smile Again," on which he sang lead for Jimmy Dorsey and His Orchestra. When Sinatra became a solo artist in 1942, he remained a constant pop favorite into the 1960s, though only four of his songs hit #1 on any *Billboard* music chart before 1966—"Oh! What It Seemed to Be" (1946), "Five Minutes More" (1946), "Mam'selle" (1947), and "Learnin' the Blues" (1955).

Sinatra would end up having six #1 hits on the AC chart alone between 1966–67, with "Summer Wind" being followed by "That's Life" [see 81].

79 The Wheel of Hurt
MARGARET WHITING

London 101

November 5, 1966 (4 weeks)

Writers: Charles Singleton, Eddie Snyder

Producer: Arnold Goland

One of the most popular female vocalists of the prerock era (before 1955, in other words) was Margaret Whiting. Her 1966 comeback single "The Wheel of Hurt" was the result of a determined plan to return to the musical forefront, and though its success was relatively short-lived, it did propel her back into the spotlight as a favorite cabaret attraction well into the 1990s.

Born in Detroit, Michigan, on July 22, 1924, Margaret Whiting grew up in Los Angeles. She was the daughter of popular 1930s composer Richard Whiting ("Hooray for Hollywood," "On the Good Ship Lollipop"). By age 18 she was singing lead for Freddie Slack and His Orchestra in a 1943 top 10 pop hit "That Old Black Magic." In 1946 she started her solo career and was quite successful over the next eight years, notching 41 singles, including two #1 pop hits, 1948's "A Tree in the Meadow" and 1949's "Slippin' Around" with Jimmy Wakely. But after 1956's "The Money Tree" went to #20, she had only one more entry through the next decade, 1958's "I Can't Help It," which crept to #74.

Whiting got some attention in 1955 when she starred in a comedy TV series for CBS called *Those Whiting Girls*, which CBS repeated in 1957. After that, even though she recorded for Verve and then Dot Records, Whiting was virtually out of sight until 1966, when she felt the time was right for her return. As she told Claude Hall in *Billboard* in 1966, "I wanted to have a hit record again. Bobby Darin and Frank Sinatra proved it could be done." She and producers Jack Gold and Arnold Goland cut "Somewhere There's Love." Top 40 radio programmers liked the tune at first, "but," said Whiting, "when they found out it was Margaret Whiting, they turned the record down." She faced no such harsh judgment by AC operators and debuted on that chart in early 1966, when "Somewhere. . ." got to #29.

Reassessing what they needed to do and how to promote their music to pop stations, Whiting and crew's next single, "The Wheel of Hurt," got her back on the chart and up to #25 pop while topping the AC chart. It might have gone even higher had not a competing version by Al Martino made #12 AC and #59 pop at the same time. Whiting credited her producers for making the song a hit and told Hall that they were very important to her professionally because "I work a month on a record now, and I never did that in my life."

Whiting had 10 more AC entries after "The Wheel of Hurt," though only 1967's "Only Love Can Break a Heart" [see 20] made the Hot 100 too. Her last AC single was, appropriately, 1970's "Until It's Time for You to Go." She has since toured the United States often, making personal appearances, and remained a favorite guest on nostalgia TV shows heading into the 21st century.

80 Winchester Cathedral
THE NEW VAUDEVILLE BAND

Fontana 1562

December 3, 1966 (4 weeks)

Writer: Geoff Stephens

Producer: Geoff Stephens

With lines like "vo-de-oh-doe" sung into a megaphone, "Winchester Cathedral" sounded like something one would have heard Rudy Vallee do on his radio show in the 1930s rather than a typical 1960s record. In reality the tune was a contemporary creation from British songwriter Geoff Stephens. He did get the inspiration from old tunes for the music for "Winchester Cathedral," but the lyrics hit him when he spotted a picture of a cathedral on a calendar hanging at the music publishing company where he worked.

Stephens, born in London, England, on October 1, 1934, told *Time* he created a group named the New Vaudeville Band to do the song and decided to sing lead "just for a giggle." But it turned out to be no laughing matter when it peaked at #4 in the United Kingdom in the fall of 1966. In America it fared even better, hitting #1 on the AC and pop charts and staying atop the Hot 100 for three weeks starting December 3, 1966.

The record garnered a Grammy nomination for Record of the Year. It also *won* the award for Best Contemporary (Rock and Roll) Recording, beating out the likes of "Eleanor Rigby" by the Beatles, "Good Vibrations" by the Beach Boys, and "Monday, Monday" by the Mamas and the Papas.

Originally, session musicians backed Stephens on the song, but its success led to requests for appearances on shows as diverse as *The Tonight Show Starring Johnny Carson* and *The CBS Evening News*. To accommodate them, Stephens hired seven men between the ages of 19 and 26 to serve as the touring New Vaudeville Band. Alan Klein, sometimes billed as "Tristam VII" or "Tristam, seventh Earl of Cricklewood," replaced Stephens as lead singer, while the rest of the group had musicians who played guitar, bass, drums, saxophone, trombone and piano.

The success of "Winchester Cathedral" led to a spate of more than 400 covers from the famous (Frank Sinatra, who sang it on his *That's Life* LP) to the forgotten (anyone recall of the Palm Beach Band Boys?). The only ones to chart came in 1966 by singer Dana Rollin at #71 pop and by a group called the New Happiness which bubbled under with its version to #112. But the New Vaudeville Band found following up on the hit was tough. In 1967, the group charted with "Peek-A-Boo" (#16 AC, #72 pop) and "Finchley Central" (#24 AC, #102 bubbling under). Their last chart entry was "The Bonnie and Clyde," which bubbled under to #122 in 1968.

Despite the paucity of hits, various groups calling themselves the New Vaudeville Band went on to tour America, Canada, and England into the 1990s. Geoff Stephens concentrated his efforts on other songwriting ventures, including co-writing Tom Jones' #1 AC hit of 1970, "Daughter of Darkness" [see 134].

FRANK SINATRA

Reprise 0531

December 31, 1966 (3 weeks)

Writers: Dean Kay, Kelly Gordon

Producer: Jimmy Bowen

1967

When Warner Brothers executive Russ Regan heard "That's Life," he knew exactly who should cut the song. "A guy named Kelly Gordon. . .brought the song to me," he told Joe Smith in *Off the Record*. "He was a co-writer and he wanted a record deal. I listened to it and I said, 'My God, this is a hit for Frank Sinatra.' I looked at Kelly and I said, 'How badly do you want to sing this song?' He wanted to know what I meant. I said, 'What if Frank Sinatra records it?' "He said, 'Here it is. Take it and run.' Then he said, 'But I do want you to know it's already been recorded by O.C. Smith on CBS.' I told him it didn't matter, and I took the record into Mo Ostin. Mo listened to it, called his secretary in, and said, 'Thelma, get ABC Messenger and send this over to Frank.'"

Sinatra loved the demo. The record was to be the follow-up to "Strangers in the Night" [see 72], but his marriage to Mia Farrow and a trip to London to film the movie *The Naked Runners* forced Reprise to release "Summer Wind" instead [see 78]. Finally, on October 18, 1966, his producer Jimmy Bowen cut it as his first eight-track record. A problem developed when the studio was miked for the session: somehow only the rhythm section made the tape, although the rest of the instruments could be heard clearly in the studio and in the headphones. Sinatra's arrival at the studio a half-hour earlier than expected and insistence that the record be done as soon as possible didn't help matters.

After two takes with Sinatra, Bowen was not pleased. "They didn't work," he said in his autobiography *Rough Mix*. "They sounded too hip and pretty. I was after an arrangement with balls and bite." Bowen thought Sinatra's mellow vocal was encouraging the rhythm section to slow down as well. To press him, Bowen told Sinatra he had to do it one more time if he wanted a hit, and a somewhat peeved Sinatra punched up the song, as did the rhythm section, resulting in the final take.

When the finished product came out, Sinatra called Bowen to thank him for doing a great job on the record. Obviously, many agreed with that assessment. In addition to its AC success the song went to #4 pop and #25 R&B, while O.C. Smith's version only managed to bubble under at #127. Twenty years later, David Lee Roth took his rendition to #85 pop.

While it peaked on the pop chart on December 31, 1966, the song behind it at #5 was the one which would succeed him on the AC chart—"Sugar Town" by his daughter Nancy Sinatra. It was the first time a father and daughter had their own hits in the top five of the pop chart. The two set another record by being the first father-daughter duo to top that chart a few months later, with "Something Stupid" [see 85].

Sugar Town
NANCY SINATRA

Reprise 0527

January 21, 1967 (2 weeks)

Writer: Lee Hazlewood

Producer: Lee Hazlewood

Frank Sinatra Jr.'s attempt to follow in the musical footsteps of his famous father met with middling success at best, but his sister Nancy emerged as one of the top female vocalists of the 1960s. Born in Jersey City, New Jersey, on June 8, 1940, Nancy was the first child of Frank and his first wife Nancy. When they moved to Los Angeles in the mid-1940s, Nancy Jr. decided to learn music just like her father and studied dance, piano, and vocals. She continued studying music and voice during the 1950s, and in 1961 signed with her father's record company Reprise, hoping to launch a full-fledged singing career. Although her chances for professional success appeared bleak when her output during 1961–64 produced no entries on the Hot 100, "So Long Babe" made #86 pop in 1965, which was enough to convince Reprise executives to keep her on the label.

Then came "These Boots Are Made for Walkin'" at #1 pop in 1966, and Nancy was off and running. She compiled three more pop chart singles through 1966, then Nancy and he decided to aim for a softer sound. "We had been doing only Lee's songs as singles at the time, and many of them were written to sound somewhat like 'Boots,'" she told Todd Everett in the liner notes to the 1986 Rhino album *Nancy Sinatra: The Hit Years*. "'Sugar Town,' which I liked a lot, was an exception." It was also an exception by becoming her first AC entry. "Sugar Town" went to #5 pop for three weeks beginning December 31, 1966 before topping the AC chart. Its B-side, "Summer Wine" with Lee Hazlewood, also charted at #49 pop in 1967.

Nancy compiled 10 more AC entries on the AC chart from 1967–71, including two with her father [see 85—"Somethin' Stupid"]. In 1972 she

switched from Reprise to RCA but got only to #120 bubbling under with her single "Down From Dover." She had no chart entries after that. Though she stopped touring in 1974, she did release a few singles on the Private Stock label in 1975 and 1976, but they all sank without a trace.

In the late 1980s through the 1990s Sinatra tried a variety of ways to reinvigorate her career (she had told Everett that "I miss recording so much that I ache. I love music."). These efforts ranged from playing herself on the Vietnam War TV series *China Beach* to posing nude in *Playboy* in 1995. Following her father's death in 1998, she announced plans for a national music museum in his honor, plus the release of a CD and tape of her old material.

Jack Jones and
Nancy Sinatra

83 My Cup Runneth Over

ED AMES

RCA 9002

February 4, 1967 (4 weeks)

Writers: Tom Jones (words), Harvey Schmidt (music)

Producers: Jim Foglesong, Joe Reisman

Ed Ames (born Edmund Dantes Urick in Malden, Massachusetts, on July 9, 1927) first attracted the attention of American record buyers as one of the Ames Brothers, a vocal quartet that really was related. Ed was the youngest, Gene the oldest, and Joe and Vic the middle brothers, and all were separated by a year. They formed as a singing unit in 1947, although they did not become the Urick Brothers.

So how did the Uricks become the Ames Brothers? As Ed explained, "When we got to New York, Abe Burrows, the writer of *Guys and Dolls*, he just gave us that name. He said the 'A' would give us top billing." The Ameses did not have to worry about where they would appear in alphabetical order, though, for they began a string of successful records with 1948's "A Tree in the Meadow," which they sang with Monica Lewis and took to #21. They notched #1 hits in 1950 with the double-sided entry "Rag Mop" and "Sentimental Me," and in 1953 with "You You You." They had their own TV variety series, which was sold to individual stations in 1955, among many other television appearances, and continued charting annually until they broke up by the start of 1960. "China Doll" in the spring of that year became their last pop entry, peaking at #38.

Ed decided to pursue an acting career and nabbed a role in the long-running off-Broadway musical *The Fantasticks*. He gained more national attention in 1964 when he began to play the role of Mingo on *Daniel Boone*, a western on NBC-TV Thursday nights. But his singing abilities emerged soon thereafter when "Try to Remember," a tune from *The Fantasticks*, returned him to the pop chart when it peaked at #73 in early 1965. It also went to #17 AC, becoming the first of 17 entries for him on that chart.

Almost two years after "Try to Remember," Ed did another show tune. "The same writers who wrote 'Try to Remember' from *The Fantasticks* wrote 'My Cup Runneth Over,' which came from another musical," he said. That musical was *I Do, I Do*, about a married couple played originally on Broadway by Mary Martin and Robert Preston.

Ames was still acting on *Daniel Boone* when "My Cup Runneth Over" came out, so promoting the tune took some effort. "It wasn't easy," he recalled. "On my periods off, I'd go out on planes and promote it. . . .Somehow or other it fell through and one disk jockey started playing it, and it caught on."

"My Cup Runneth Over" peaked at #8 on the Hot 100 the week of March 25, 1967, becoming the only pop top 10 solo hit for Ed. He earned Grammy nominations for Record and Best Pop Vocal of the Year with the tune, and the LP on which it was the title tune was nominated for Album of the Year as well. Ed followed it with another #1 song, "Time, Time" [see 87].

84 Lady

JACK JONES

Kapp 800

March 4, 1967 (4 weeks)

Words: Larry Kusik and Charles Singleton (words),
Bert Kaempfert and Herbert Rehbein (music)

Producer: Not Listed

With an orchestra led by Ralph Carmichael, who also arranged the session, "Lady" went to #1 AC and #39 pop. It was the last of Jack Jones' three #1 AC hits and also the last of his songs to make the pop top 70. Recalling the session for the tune to Will Friedwald in the liner notes to his *Greatest Hits* CD in 1995, Jones said, "In this particular song, the range seemed to be uncomfortable for me. I said, 'I don't want to do it, it's too low.' And they said, 'Go into the studio and try it out. If you don't like it, we won't put it out.' And we liked it!"

No doubt Jones did not like the fact that after "Lady" he faced a severe dropoff in attention on the Hot 100. During the year after "Lady" peaked he had five minor singles, then was off the listing forever. Ironically, the first of these five was titled "I'm Indestructible," which went to #81 pop while its flip side, "Afterthoughts," got to #19 AC, and the last in 1968 was titled "If You Ever Leave Me" at #92 pop plus #5 AC. Among his post-"Lady" singles, Jones fared best on both charts with 1967's "Now I Know" at #3 AC and #73 pop.

Now signed to RCA rather than Kapp, he continued to make the AC chart pretty regularly through 1970, although after 1968 none of his singles made the top 10 on the roster. After 1970, Jones' AC entries were spotty. There was "Let Me Be the One" (#18) in 1971, "She Doesn't Live Here Anymore" (#45) and "What I Did for Love" from the Broadway musical *A Chorus Line* (#25) in 1975, and "With One More Look at You" from the film *A Star Is Born* (#21) in 1977. That same last year, Jones sang what probably is his most familiar tune to latter-day listeners—the theme for the TV series *The Love Boat*, which ran on ABC from 1977–86. Jones' vocal was used on the show until the last season, when a version by Dionne Warwick replaced it. Released as a single on MGM in 1980, "Love Boat Theme" went to #37 AC and became his swan song on the chart.

Jones continued singing in the 1980s and 1990s, with his activities slanted more to live performances than recording. (He did, however, make a cameo in the 1982 movie comedy *Airplane II*, singing the "Love Boat Theme.") Though his commercial heyday appears over, Jones can take pride in the fact that he was one of the most successful AC artists during the 1960s and still commands a sizable audience at club dates across America.

85 Somethin' Stupid

NANCY SINATRA AND FRANK SINATRA

Reprise 0561

April 1, 1967 (9 weeks)

Writer: C. Carson Parks

Producers: Jimmy Bowen, Jim Hazlewood

"The Incest Song" was the nickname record label wags gave to this pairing of Frank Sinatra with his daughter Nancy, which topped the Hot 100 four weeks concurrently with the AC chart starting the week of April 15, 1967 and also hit #1 in England for two weeks at the same time. The reason for that tag was the lyrics: the "something stupid" being said between the two was "I love you." Consumers and deejays proved to be less perverse than record executives and read no sexual connotations into a song they thought reflected familial bonds instead, as did Frank and Nancy.

Though many people think "Somethin' Stupid" was written especially for the Sinatras, it first appeared on an album by writer C. Carson Parks and his wife Gaile Foote in 1966 on Kapp Records. An associate of Frank's, Sarge Weiss, heard the tune and offered it to Frank to do as a duet with his daughter. Another false impression given from some sources is that the two recorded their parts at different sessions, a claim that co-producer Jimmy Bowen refuted in *Sinatra! The Song Is You* by Will Friedwald. Bowen told Friedwald that "we had two microphones set up in the studio, and they were singing side by side. It should have been filmed. It would have been a great TV spot."

Most sources claim the session took only about a half hour to complete. It was decided to use both Nancy and Frank's producers jointly for the song, and Bowen and Lee Hazlewood worked together on the venture with no major problems reported. In her book *Frank Sinatra: An American Legend,* Nancy recalled the recording session, which took place February 1, 1967. "On the first take, Dad got so silly, sounding his S's like Daffy Duck for fun, so we had to do a second take," she wrote. "Mo Ostin, the president of Reprise, bet him $200 it would bomb. He lost his money: It went to number one, selling several million copies." It also merited a Grammy nomination for Record of the Year.

"Somethin' Stupid" was the last of two AC number ones for Nancy [see 82—"Sugar Town"], and the fifth of six for Frank. The two sang again on a pair of singles released in 1971, but neither came close to matching the success of "Somethin' Stupid." "Feelin' Kinda Sunday" hit #30 AC and would be Nancy's last entry on that chart, while "Life's a Trippy Thing" failed to chart anywhere. Frank later revived the concept of "Somethin' Stupid" by recording with other vocalists on his appropriately titled LPs *Duets* (1993) and *Duets II* (1994).

86 Casino Royale

HERB ALPERT AND THE TIJUANA BRASS

A&M 850

June 3, 1967 (2 weeks)

Writer: Burt Bacharach

Producers: Herb Alpert, Jerry Moss

In his *The Complete James Bond Movie Encyclopedia,* author Steven Jay Rubin called Herb Alpert's work for *Casino Royale* one of the few high points for the muddled film spoof of Agent 007. In fact, the title theme became the first from a "James Bond" movie to top the AC chart, although many Bond purists would scoff at counting the motion picture as part of the series, as it was done by a different production company. In any event, one fact that cannot be disputed is that "Casino Royale" was the second #1 AC hit for Alpert and his Tijuana Brass.

The tune was actually written by the team of Hal David (who wrote lyrics not used in Alpert's record) and Burt Bacharach, and, technically, it involved only Alpert and no members of the Brass. "Bacharach recorded it in London and apparently he didn't like the end result," Alpert told Craig Rosen in *The Billboard Book of Number One Albums.* "He sent me a tape of the song and the arrangements and I liked it a lot. So he sent me the multitracks and I added in my trumpet. That song has a real special quality."

"Casino Royale" fared modestly on the pop chart in comparison to its AC peak, landing at #27 in 1967. But it and its predecessor, "Wade in the Water," which climbed to #5 AC and #37 pop in the spring of 1967, did well enough to entice album consumers to buy the LP on which they appeared, *Sounds Like...,* which hit #1 the week of June 17, 1967.

Because it was an instrumental without lyrics, "Casino Royale" was ineligible to be nominated for an Oscar for Best Song. But at the Grammys the record won nominations for Best Instrumental Theme, Best Instrumental Arrangement, and Best Instrumental Performance, while the soundtrack to *Casino Royale* was nominated for Best Original Score Written for a Motion Picture or TV Show. Another single from the soundtrack, "The Look of Love" sung by Dusty Springfield, did get an Oscar nomination for Best Song while hitting #22 pop and #31 AC.

Though "Casino Royale" marked the first time Herb Alpert and the Tijuana Brass recorded a tune for a motion picture, it was not the debut in the medium for Alpert himself. He played trumpet on the soundtrack and even did a small bit as a drummer going down a mountain with Moses in the 1956 epic *The Ten Commandments.* And in the 1959 film *Say One for Me,* he could be glimpsed playing trumpet in a band at a club.

Alpert and crew used another movie tune to follow up "Casino Royale." "The Happening," an instrumental version of the #1 pop hit by the Supremes from the movie of the same name, went to #4 AC and #32 pop. After that came another #1 AC hit, "A Banda" [see 94]. In 1968 Alpert performed another Bacharach and David tune, and its popularity dwarfed that of "Casino Royale" [see 106—"This Guy's in Love With You"].

87 Time, Time

ED AMES

RCA 9178

June 17, 1967 (1 week)

*Writers: Earl Shuman (words–English), Michel Jordan
(words–French), Armand Canfora, Jose Baselli (music)*

Producer: Jim Foglesong

E d Ames' follow-up to his first #1 AC hit, "My Cup Runneth Over" [see 83], was "Time, Time," an adaptation of a French tune written in 1963 with words in
that language by Michel Jourdan (Earl Shuman provided the English translation). Ames did not recall
the original title in French for the tune but did
remember how it got to him. "My producer just
brought it to me," he said. "Jim Foglesong presented it to me, I liked it, and we recorded it."

Ames trusted and had a good relationship
with Foglesong, his producer. "He was great.
He was the best. He had no hidden agendas. He
would play songs for me to consider. If I didn't
like the song, we wouldn't do it. If I did like the
song, we would do it. We weren't always right
about them commercially, but we were right some
of the time." He later elaborated how Foglesong
drew tunes from people pushing songs. "They'd
come to the record company," he said. "He was the
A&R [artists and repertoire] man [for RCA]. Most of
the time, the publishers or the songwriters thought
their work would be good for me, and that's how they
came to us."

"Time, Time" did moderately well on the pop
chart, peaking at #61 in the spring of 1967. As
with "My Cup Runneth Over," it served as
the title tune for an album by Ames.
Ed recalled that Foglesong
and/or RCA representatives
usually took whatever
song appealed most
strongly to him as the
title tune for his LPs. In
addition, he said his
albums were done at a
rate that would
astound many artists
today, as it typically
took less than two
days for him to do the
vocals and have the
instruments recorded
for an album rather
than the weeks,
months, sometimes
even years that some
singers or groups take
at present.

The successor to "Time, Time" on the AC chart was
"Timeless Love," a concoction written by folk singer Buffy
Sainte-Marie, who had her biggest pop hit and only AC entry
as a solo singer in 1972 with "Mister Can't You See" (it went
to #29 AC and #38 pop). "Timeless Love" nearly became
Ames' third #1 AC entry in a row, but it fell one shy of the
top and peaked at #2 for a week in the fall of 1967. However,
the song failed to enter the Hot 100.

The record after "Timeless Love" both returned Ames to
the pop chart and gave him his third #1 AC hit; see 97—
"When the Snow Is on the Roses."

88 Stop! And Think It Over

PERRY COMO

RCA 9165

June 24, 1967 (1 week)

Writers: Sid Topper, Roy C. Bennett

Producer: Andy Wiswell

Often regarded (or lampooned) as the most "casual" vocalist in the music industry, Perry Como, born Pierino Como in Canonsburg, Pennsylvania, on May 18, 1912, built an impressive show business career not only singing on record but also in movies and on radio and television. He was a barber in his hometown when he decided to join Freddie Carlone's band in 1933. In 1936 he joined Ted Weems and His Orchestra as a featured singer until it broke up in 1942, then went out on his own and made the *Billboard* pop chart the first time as a soloist with "Goodbye, Sue" backed with "There'll Soon Be a Rainbow," which hit #18 in 1943.

By the late 1940s Como was one of the leading singers in America and had transferred his successful radio show to television, where it lasted until 1963. He also appeared in several films, such as 1948's *Words and Music*. During that same period he compiled numerous million-selling singles from "Till the End of Time" (1945) to "Catch a Falling Star" (1958), but his rate of success had started to drop by the early 1960s.

Como's AC debut was in 1962 with "Caterina," which reached #6 while halting at #23 pop. He had four more entries after that before "Stop! And Think It Over" gave him his first #1 AC single, the biggest being 1965's "Dream On Little Dreamer," which got to #3 AC and #25 pop.

"Andy showed Perry a bunch of songs, and that was one of the songs he selected," recalled Mickey Glass, Como's manager from 1950 to the present, about "Stop! And Think It Over." "That wasn't a big hit." Indeed, it was not on the pop chart at least, reaching only #92, the lowest peak on the Hot 100 for any #1 AC song to that point. Producing it was Andy Wiswell, director of A&R (artists and repertoire) for RCA Records.

Como continued to struggle pop-wise through the rest of the 1960s, although several of his singles which failed to make the Hot 100 did reach the AC chart. One of those non-Hot 100 entries, "You Made It That Way (Watermelon Summer)," went to #2 AC for two weeks in late 1967. He had his first top 40 pop hit in four years in 1969 when "Seattle," the theme of the ABC-TV series *Here Come the Brides*, went to #38 on the Hot 100 as well as #2 AC for one week. That single's B-side, "Sunshine Wine," also received some AC airplay and arrived at #18 on the listing.

Less than two years later, Como finally did another song that was nearly as big on the pop chart as it was on the AC roster. [See 142—"It's Impossible."]

89 Mary in the Morning

AL MARTINO

Capitol 5904

July 1, 1967 (2 weeks)

Writers: Johnny Cymbal, Mike Lendell

Producers: Tom Morgan, Arvin Holtzman

Unlike his first two #1 AC hits, "I Love You Because" [see 28] and "Spanish Eyes" [see 65], Al Martino did not actively seek out the tune "Mary in the Morning." The demo came to him from representatives of his label, Capitol, and Martino enjoyed what he heard.

However, the first effort at doing the song did not please him due to what he heard coming from the instruments. As Martino was a firm believer that the writers who cut the demo made the song sound the way they wanted to hear it, he had guitarist Johnny Cymbal, the tune's co-writer, who had played on the demo, play on the record's second and final take, which Martino liked much better. "It's the sound I wanted when I first recorded it," he said. Incidentally Cymbal, who also recorded under the name of Derek, made the Hot 100 as a recording artist several times, with one of his tunes making the AC chart too, 1963's "Teenage Heaven" (#19 AC, #58 pop).

Martino remembered that the first radio station to get behind "Mary in the Morning" was Jim Hillard at WFIL in his hometown of Philadelphia. "He just loved it and said, 'Al, I'll make this a hit.' And he did." The record made #27 pop nationally as well as #1 AC.

"Mary in the Morning" was Martino's first #1 on the AC chart, but nearly all the songs he had there before its release in 1967 had peaked at least at #12. The exception was 1965's "My Cherie," which made only #26. Those which came close to topping the AC chart were "Painted, Tainted Rose" (#3 in 1963), "I Love You More and More Every Day" (#3 in 1964), "Think I'll Go Somewhere and Cry Myself to Sleep" (#2 for one week in 1966), and "Daddy's Little Girl" (#2 for two weeks in 1967). Of these, "I Love You More and More Every Day" made the pop top 10 as well, going to #9 on the Hot 100 the week of March 21, 1964.

All this success was a long way from Martino's modest start. Born Alfred Cini in Philadelphia on October 7, 1927, he was encouraged to go into singing after seeing the success of his childhood chum, opera singer Mario Lanza. After winning on the CBS-TV variety series *Arthur Godfrey's Talent Scouts*, Martino had a #1 hit in America and England with "Here in My Heart" in 1952.

After "Here in My Heart," his music career was shaky for almost a decade. Following three more entries, including 1953's "When You're Mine" (#27), Martino did not return to the pop chart until 1959's "I Can't Get You Out of My Heart," which made #44. It was only after "I Love You Because" in 1963 that he became a fairly regular visitor on the AC and pop charts through the 1970s. His follow-up to "Mary in the Morning" also hit #1 AC [see 96—"More Than the Eye Can See"].

90 Don't Sleep in the Subway

PETULA CLARK

Warner 7049

July 15, 1967 (3 weeks)

Writers: Jackie Trent (words), Tony Hatch (music)

Producer: Tony Hatch

With the success of "I Couldn't Live Without Your Love" [see 75], producer Tony Hatch began writing more songs with his wife Jackie Trent listed as lyricist, and the result was continued hits for Petula Clark in 1966 and 1967 with "Who Am I" (#31 AC, #21 pop) and "Color My World" (#10 AC, #16 pop). However, Clark's husband Claude Wolff had a particular distaste for Trent and did not like the idea of her writing words for his wife to sing, and the fact that Trent was now attending Clark's sessions in the studios riled him even more. Therefore, when film legend Charlie Chaplin offered Clark the chance to record the theme song he had written for his new movie *A Countess From Hong Kong*, "This Is My Song," in 1967, Wolff endorsed the idea strongly, but when it came time for Clark to record the song, Wolff picked American arranger Ernie Freeman to produce it. Clark sang the tune in several languages and generated an international smash, with the single going to #2 AC for four weeks and #3 pop. Plans were made for Chaplin to write another ballad for her, but it never materialized.

Needing a follow-up fast, Wolff swallowed his pride and went back to Hatch and Trent, but stipulated that the song should not be too up-tempo. The result was "Don't Sleep in the Subway," which for some reason had an off-color working title of "Don't S__t in the Custard" before Trent came up with more radio- and listener-friendly lyrics.

"Don't Sleep in the Subway" peaked at #5 pop the weeks of July 8 and 15, 1967 while going to #1 AC. It earned Grammy nominations for Best Contemporary Single, Best Female Vocal Performance, and Best Contemporary Female Solo Vocal Performance. It was Clark's second and final #1 AC hit and also her last top 10 pop hit.

Clark did better on the AC chart during the rest of the 1960s, scoring four consecutive top 10 AC entries after "Don't Sleep in the Subway" through 1968, including "Kiss Me Goodbye." But shortly after 1969's "Look at Mine" went to #14 AC and #89 pop, Wolff severed ties with Hatch. The result was that Clark went through several producers over the next few years, and the hits virtually dried up.

In 1972 Clark left Warner Records and got a deal with MGM in America, where she scored three AC entries, the biggest being "Wedding Song (There Is Love)" at #9 AC and #61 pop in 1972. But after "Loving Arms" went to #12 AC in 1975, Clark found herself without an American distributor until 1981, when Scotti Brothers released her "Natural Love," which got to #24 AC and #66 pop in 1982. Clark recorded infrequently after that, but remained much in demand internationally for personal appearances through the late 1990s. She had residences in Switzerland and the United States.

91 It's Such a Pretty World Today

ANDY RUSSELL

Capitol 5917

August 5, 1967 (1 week)

Writer: Dale Noe

Producer: Al de Lory

Though largely forgotten today, Andy Russell was one of the most promising male vocalists of the 1940s. Born Andres Rabago in East Los Angeles, California, on September 16, 1919, Russell worked as a drummer and vocalist with Gus Arnheim's orchestra before he graduated high school. With the group, Russell inaugurated a tradition of singing parts of songs in Spanish.

In the 1940s Russell distinguished himself as a solo singer on several fronts. He was a regular on radio's *Your Hit Parade* from 1946–48, among many appearances on the medium. During the same period he popped up in three movies, *The Stork Club* (1945), *Breakfast in Hollywood* (1946), and *Copacabana* (1947). He also notched 12 entries on the pop music chart, from 1944's "Besame Mucho" at #10 to 1948's "Underneath the Arches" at #13.

A few years later, Russell and his then-wife Anna starred in a five-minute daily musical show on ABC-TV from 1950–51. But the marriage had gone sour by 1955, and when Andy and Anna split, members of the Roman Catholic clergy objected to the divorce. The public outcry led Andy to relocate to Mexico and later Buenos Aires for more than a decade.

On March 30, 1967, Russell made his first appearance in America in 12 years at the Chateau Madrid in New York City. Reviewing the concert for *Billboard*, Claude Hall wrote, "The second time around may turn out to be the best time around for Russell." Shortly thereafter Capitol released "It's Such a Pretty World Today," Russell's cover of a #1 country hit for Wynn Stewart the weeks of June 3 and 10, 1967. Despite reaching #1 AC, Russell's version only bubbled under to #119, becoming the first AC chart topper not to make the Hot 100.

Three other records by Russell made the AC chart over the next year, although none even bubbled under. They were "I'm Still Not Through Missin' You" at #10 and "Your Love Is Everywhere" at #32, both in 1967, and 1968's "If My Heart Had Windows," which stopped at #29. Unable to really crack the American market this time around, Russell concentrated once more on the Latin market and worked south of the United States border.

In the mid-1970s, resisting pressure to become a citizen of Mexico, Russell returned to America, where he was nowhere near the star he had been. Living in Encino, California, in the early 1980s, he bemoaned to Richard Lamparski in *Whatever Became Of. . .? Ninth Series* that "But now I'm hard to sell in my own country—except to those who already know me."

Russell died on April 16, 1992. He was 72 years old.

92 In the Chapel in the Moonlight

DEAN MARTIN

Reprise 0601

August 12, 1967 (3 weeks)

Writer: Billy Hill

Producer: Jimmy Bowen

"In the Chapel in the Moonlight" was first done in 1936 by Shep Fields and His Orchestra, who took their version to #1 pop. Three covers that appeared around the same time were by Richard Himber (#7 pop), Mal Hallet (#11 pop), and Ruth Etting (#20 pop). In 1954 two competing versions emerged, one by Kitty Kallen (#4 pop) and the other by the Four Knights (#30 pop). Thirteen years later Dean Martin's version became his fourth #1 AC hit as well as #25 pop, although an ad for the song in the June 24, 1967, issue of *Billboard* indicated that Reprise did not initially intend to release it as a single until a radio station programmer started playing it. The promotion read, "Thanks to Bob Van Camp, WSB, Atlanta, Georgia, for 'discovering' the track!"

By the time Martin cut "In the Chapel in the Moonlight" with his producer Jimmy Bowen, the two men had worked out a routine for picking songs, which they described to *Billboard*. Both listened to the radio for potential songs to cover, and also reviewed the hundreds of songs submitted to Martin, but Bowen made the final decisions on which 10 to 12 songs to do for an album. Bowen said the majority of songs they did were in a "pop-country" vein.

For recording each song, Martin had a practice of cutting the tunes with only a rhythm section present, meaning a piano, bass, drums, and guitar. Later Bowen would tape a full orchestra and overdub their tracks onto the final record. Martin told *Billboard* he liked recording by this method because it was "Much easier that way. I don't bother anybody, and nobody bothers me. Anyhow, it sounds better."

Bowen did not object to this unconventional approach, nor did he mind that Martin never spent more than two sessions singing on an album, typically doing a record in no more than two or three takes. He felt the quickness of the recording dates encouraged Martin to be spontaneously creative in the studio. "Dean changes the lyrics as he goes along, just the way he does on the television show," Bowen said. "He can get away with scrambling the words or rearranging the melody right in the middle of a take and nobody minds. In fact, they love it."

AC radio stations apparently loved it too, for "In the Chapel in the Moonlight" was the 14th top 10 AC song Martin had in just over a three-year period. "In the Chapel in the Moonlight" would be Martin's next-to-last top 40 pop hit, with its follow-up "Little Ole Wine Drinker, Me" bowing out at #38 pop and #5 AC. The record after that would be his last #1 AC entry [see 100—"In the Misty Moonlight"].

93 The World We Knew (Over and Over)

FRANK SINATRA

Reprise 0610

September 2, 1967 (5 weeks)

*Writers: Carl Sigman (words–English), Bert Kaempfert,
   Herbert Rehbein (music)*

Producer: Jimmy Bowen

Recorded on June 29, 1967, "The World We Knew (Over and Over)" was the sixth consecutive #1 AC single for Frank Sinatra. The first four words of the title became the name of a Sinatra LP featuring that tune and Sinatra's previous hit with his daughter Nancy, "Somethin' Stupid" [see 85]. (The LP was also known simply as *Frank Sinatra*.) But not surprisingly the song itself was in the style of "Strangers in the Night" [see 72], as, like that record, it was based on a composition from German musician Bert Kaempfert.

"Sinatra used to laugh at me. I think he was just challenging me to see if we could do it or not," producer Jimmy Bowen told Will Friedwald about the tune in *Sinatra! The Song Is You*. "And he used to laugh because Kaempfert's melodies were always testy. 'Strangers in the Night' is not easy to sing. And 'The World We Knew'—oh, God, what a hard song to sing!"

As usual, Sinatra polished off "The World We Knew" with ease, and it revolved its way to #30 on the Hot 100 during its five-week stint at #1 AC. Another song from the album followed, but "This Town" from the film *The Cool Ones* reached only #17 AC and #53 pop in late 1967, Sinatra's worst chart performance since 1965's "I'll Only Miss Her When I Think of Her," which made #18 AC and #131 bubbling under.

Jimmy Bowen's departure from Reprise Records in 1968 ended his working relationship with Sinatra, and unknowingly to the artist at the time, brought about a downward slide in Sinatra's chart performance which the singer never did reverse. True, he did have two songs make #2 AC for three weeks each—1968's "Cycles" and 1969's "My Way," later to become Sinatra's signature song—but they were the only 45s to surpass the top 30 pop peak of "The World We Knew (Over and Over)," with "Cycles" hitting #23 and "My Way" going to #27.

Going into the 1970s, Sinatra's showings on the AC and pop chart became sporadic. He retired from show business in 1971 only to return in 1973, but concert performances took up more of his time and consideration than did recording work. His highest-charting effort of the decade came in 1975 with "I Believe I'm Gonna Love You," which went to #2 AC and #47 pop. After 1977's "Everybody Ought to Be in Love," which made only #29 AC, Sinatra was off the AC chart until 1980's "Theme from New York, New York," which went to #10 AC and #32 pop, the last time Sinatra appeared on the Hot 100. Its follow-up, "You and Me (We Wanted It All)," reached #42 AC. Sinatra's final AC entry was 1984's "L.A. Is My Lady," at #34.

By 1995 ill health kept Sinatra from performing or recording, and rumors abounded for three years about how serious his condition was. He died on May 14, 1998, at the age of 82.

94 A Banda (Ah Bahn-da)

HERB ALPERT AND THE TIJUANA BRASS

A&M 870

October 7, 1967 (2 weeks)

Writer: Chico Buarque de Hollandu

Producers: Herb Alpert, Jerry Moss

If you heard the Herb Alpert version of a tune written originally with Portuguese lyrics by Chico Buarque de Hollandu on an AC radio station in 1967, then you heard "A Banda (Ah Bahn-da)." But if you heard the vocal version with English lyrics by Bob Russell sung by Sue Raney around the same time, then you heard "Parade." "A Banda (Ah Bahn-da)" was the first of two same-song-in-English-with-two-different-titles situations on the AC chart; the second came 25 years later, with "Am I the Same Girl?"[see 624].

Though not one of the Tijuana Brass's better-remembered tunes, "A Banda" did respectably in its time, peaking at #35 pop as well as topping the AC chart in the fall of 1967. "Parade" was nowhere near as popular as "A Banda," making only #22 AC near the end of 1967. It was the middle of three AC-only entries for Sue Raney. To further complicate matters, "A Banda" and the previous Herb Alpert and the Tijuana Brass #1 AC entry "Casino Royale" [see 86] competed for Best Instrumental Theme at the 1967 Grammy Awards. It was a composer's award, however, so it technically was not the Brass versus the Brass but rather de Hollandu versus Burt Bacharach and Hal David. (Lalo Schifrin claimed the statuette for his theme to TV's *Mission: Impossible*.)

"A Banda" was the third #1 AC hit for Alpert and the Brass, but that figure could easily have been seven, as four other singles halted their rise only at #2. "Zorba the Greek" stayed at #2 for three weeks in 1966, as did "The Work Song" that same year. 1966's "What Now My Love" and 1967's "Mame" both had one-week stays at the runner-up post. In fact, "A Banda" was the 13th consecutive song by Herb Alpert and the Tijuana Brass to make the top 10 on the AC chart, an impressive feat.

This success did not go unnoticed by adults who enjoyed the group's music and felt like they were "with it" musically while not having to endure rock and roll. In the fall of 1966 Herb Alpert and the Tijuana Brass even rated a mention in Congress, when Senator Thomas H. Kuchel (R—California) extolled them by saying, "In a day when discordant sounds and irregular beats seemingly have provocation attraction for unknown numbers, it is rewarding that a musical organization specializes in what may be called joyous music."

Alpert and the Brass's "joyous music" kept coming. Early in 1968 "Carmen" peaked at #3 AC, and by mid-1968, Alpert and crew had scored their fourth #1 AC entry [see 106—"This Guy's in Love With You"].

95 It Must Be Him

VIKKI CARR

Liberty 55986

October 21, 1967 (3 weeks)

*Writers: Mack David (words–English), Maurice Vidalin
(words–French), Gilbert Becaud (music)*

Producer: Dave Pell

Phil Spector's version of "He's a Rebel" kept Vikki Carr's first single from becoming a hit. As Carr explained, "That was a song that was a hit for the Crystals [whose producer was Spector] in the States, but I had a hit with it in Australia." The Crystals covered Carr's rendition and went to #1 pop in America while Carr only bubbled under to #115 in the fall of 1962. It took five more years before Carr finally broke onto the Hot 100 with "It Must Be Him."

After her Australian success, Carr worked overseas more than in America. "When 'It Must Be Him' was happening, I was very well liked in England," she said. Therefore, in 1966 when she recorded "It Must Be Him," she promoted it there first even though some executives had told her the single would not be a hit. Her manager at the time, Arnie Mills, got the tune from his composer pal Mack David, who had translated the lyrics into English after hearing original composer Gilbert Becaud sing the tune in French. "He [Mills] felt for my kind of singing, it would be a great song for me," she said.

Following five weeks of promotion in England, she returned to the United States. Back in the U.K., "It Must Be Him" made the charts in June 1967 and crested at #2 on Liberty Records. Al Bennett, the president of Liberty in America, was in England as "It Must Be Him" hit. Carr's only U.S. chart action up to that point had been four songs that made the AC chart only in minor slots from late 1966 to early 1967, but Bennett felt this one had the possibility of being a smash. "He said, 'We are going to rerelease this record or heads are going to roll. This kid did it all by herself,'" she said.

The majestic "It Must Be Him" peaked at #1 AC and #3 pop, holding at the latter the weeks of November 4 and 11, 1967, behind Lulu's "To Sir With Love" at #1 and Sam and Dave's "Soul Man" at #2. To Carr's dismay and later amusement, American TV censors in 1967 would not let her sing the line "God, let it please be him," as some considered it an inappropriate use of the Lord's name.

Carr said the song still gets a standing ovation at many of her concerts, and much to her surprise, her younger fans are often leading the cheers. Also a surprise—this one unpleasant—was not winning any Grammy nominations she had for 1967: Album of the Year, Best Female Vocal Performance, and Best Contemporary Female Solo Vocal Performance. "I lost out that year and I couldn't believe it," Carr admitted. She racked up five Grammy defeats before winning in 1985 for Best Mexican/American Performance, but the pain of the earlier losses still lingered and she noted it at the time: "When I accepted it in New York, I said, 'It was a long time since 'It Must Be Him'!"

96 More Than the Eye Can See

AL MARTINO

Capitol 5989

November 11, 1967 (2 weeks)

Writers: Bob Crewe, Larry Weiss

Producers: Tom Morgan, Marv Holtzman

"More Than the Eye Can See" was the fourth and final #1 AC single for Al Martino. The tune was the result of a collaboration between Bob Crewe, who also wrote "Navy Blue" [see 39] and Larry Weiss, later to write "Rhinestone Cowboy" [see 268]. "It was Peter DeAngelis, I think, who submitted the song to me," Martino said. DeAngelis also served as the arranger when Martino cut "More Than the Eye Can See."

Peaking at #54 on the Hot 100, "More Than the Eye Can See" was one of the lesser pop singles for Martino, but the vocalist would fare better there in the future. He remained fairly consistent in making both charts through 1970, with his highest-charting effort after "More Than the Eye Can See" being "Love Is Blue" [see 103], which as sung by Martino went to #3 AC and #57 pop. Most of his tunes in the 1970s made only the AC chart, but there were a few exceptions.

In 1972 Martino portrayed the Frank Sinatraesque character Johnny Fontane in the film *The Godfather*, but despite the movie's wide appeal Martino's rendition of its theme, "Speak Softly Love," went only to #24 AC and #80 pop. He had more success in 1975 when "To the Door of the Sun (Alle Porte Del Sol)" went to #7 AC and #17 pop and "Volare" reached #9 AC and #33 pop. He still made both charts through 1978, although on the Hot 100 "The Next Hundred Years" was his farewell, hitting #49 pop as well as #6 AC, while his follow-up to that single, "One Last Time," lived up to its name by becoming his final entry on the AC chart at #44.

Overall, Martino had stayed on the charts for over 25 years, an impressive achievement especially given that he had started to chart before the rock era. He believed his versatility played a part in his longevity. "What I tried to do was adapt my style to certain things at the time," he said. "I can do folk, I can do pop, I can do classical, I can even do opera."

Another reason, he believed, was that he usually performed the recording "according to the writer's rendition. . . .Nobody knows better than the writer how to do the rendition."

Martino remained active as a performing artist in the 1990s, doing several dates in Las Vegas in 1998 alone. He presently resides in southern California, and has one main hope heading into the next century. "My goal is another recording contract," he said. "Somewhere there's got to be a recording company that wants me." He may also do an autobiography which, he assured me, will be quite interesting should it ever reach print.

97 When The Snow Is on the Roses

ED AMES

RCA 9319

November 25, 1967 (4 weeks)

Writers: Larry Kusik and Eddie Snyder (words–English),
Ernst Bader (words–West Germany), James Last (music)

Producer: Jim Foglesong

Like Ed Ames' previous #1 AC hit, "Time, Time" [see 87], "When the Snow Is on the Roses" came from a foreign country. This time it was West Germany, where Ernst Bader did the lyrics. Larry Kusik and Eddie Snyder provided an English rendition. And, again like "Time, Time," Ames did not remember the title of the foreign version but knew his producer Jim Foglesong discovered it for him. Five years later, Sonny James covered "When the Snow Is on the Roses," taking it to #1 country the week of September 16, 1972. "I wasn't aware of that," Ed said.

Ames' "When the Snow Is on the Roses" did much better on the AC chart than the pop one. On the latter, the tune peaked at only #98 with two weeks on the chart beginning the week of September 30, 1967, the same time it started its climb up to the top of the AC listings two months later. Ames hit a higher pop peak when his next single, "Who Will Answer?" went to #19 on the Hot 100 in early 1968 (it made #6 AC).

Ames' continuing musical success and large amount of fan mail for his work as Mingo on *Daniel Boone* encouraged him to leave the series in the summer of 1968 to pursue other career options. (*Daniel Boone* ended in 1970.) But his hit-making days were over. He had only two more entries make the Hot 100, 1968's "Apologize," which went to #79 pop and #10 AC, and 1969's "Son of a Travelin' Man," which reached #92 pop and #21 AC. Between those two songs he hit the AC chart only with "All My Love's Laughter" (#12), "Kiss Her Now" (#22), and "Changing, Changing" (#11). Six releases after "Son of a Travelin' Man," "Chippewa Town" was the last Ames entry on the AC chart, peaking at #36 in the summer of 1970.

During the 1970s, Ames said, "I was in a lot of concerts and theatrical stuff. I kind of stopped recording when my contract ran out with RCA." He did a few one-night performances but was not out on the road touring much. "And I didn't want to be," he said. "I have a horse ranch and a place in Beverly Hills, and I didn't need to tour." But in early 1998 he mentioned that he was talking with several labels about returning to the studio, although nothing was definite. "I may do some single records, some new material," he said.

Oh, nearly forgot. Ed does not get residuals from his often-seen 1964 guest shot on *The Tonight Show Starring Johnny Carson*, where he convulsed the host and the audience when he threw a tomahawk squarely into the crotch of a drawing of a man. He said he did more than 30 shows with Carson but none had the same impact. "He repeated it every chance he could," Ed said. "He loved that thing. It's a very funny thing."

98 Cold

JOHN GARY

RCA 9361

December 23, 1967 (2 weeks)

Writers: Charles Jones, Norma Helms

Producer: Joe Reisman

"Catch Cold," trumpeted the full-page ad in the October 28, 1967 issue of *Billboard* for John Gary's latest single. Few did, for despite being a *Billboard*-recommended pick to hit the Hot 100, the tune failed even to bubble under while it made the top of the AC chart. It was the worst pop showing of any single to reach #1 and signaled the end of what looked at one point to be a promising singing career for John Gary.

Born John Gary Strader in Watertown, New York, on November 29, 1932, the vocalist entered amateur talent contests as a child and became part of a USO tour when he was 14. When the tour arrived in Hollywood, gossip columnist Hedda Hopper became a fan and introduced him to Ken Murray, who put him in his "Blackouts" revue in Los Angeles for a year and a half until his voice changed. After finishing high school he joined the Marine Corps and sang at various engagements during the 1950s, including one season on the popular national radio show *Don McNeill's Breakfast Club*.

Tired of his inability to get a recording contract, Gary came to New York in 1962 and gave himself six months to get a company to sign him. On his fifth month in town, while struggling just to eat, RCA signed him. Some major nightclub bookings and TV guest shots followed, and in 1964 he had his first AC entry and only Hot 100 single, "Soon I'll Wed My Love" (#19 AC, #89 pop). After two more AC songs ("Don't Throw the Roses Away" at #27 in 1965 and "Don't Let the Music Play" in 1966), he got his own musical variety series on CBS-TV in 1966 as the summer replacement for *The Danny Kaye Show*. But he still did only moderately well on the AC chart thereafter, with "Everybody Say Peace" going to #10 AC in the summer of 1967 before "Cold" arrived.

Gary, who was once considered to have so much potential that he earned an entry in 1967's *Current Biography* book series, suffered a distinct dropoff in popularity when it became obvious he was not fulfilling the hopes of those who had thought he would become a top-drawing crooner. Gary had no more AC entries after "Cold," his 1968 TV series flopped, and his TV appearances continued to dwindle through the 1970s.

In the 1980s, Gary, based in Dallas, Texas, handled real estate holdings with his wife. He bemoaned to Richard Lamparski in *Whatever Became Of. . .?* that "These are not the best of times for balladeers, especially when you're trying to reactivate your career from Texas." Gary never did manage a comeback. He died in Dallas on January 4, 1998, at age 65.

99 Chattanooga Choo Choo

HARPERS BIZARRE

Warner 7090

January 6, 1968 (2 weeks)

Writers: Mack Gordon (words), Harry Warren (music)

Producer: Lenny Waronker

Harpers Bizarre began in 1965 as the Tikis, four men in their teens or thereabouts based in Santa Cruz, California. They were singer Dick Scoppettone, drummer and singer Ted Templeman, lead guitarist Eddie James, and bassist Dick Yount. They auditioned for San Francisco–based Autumn Records "at least 20 times," according to Scoppettone. Finally, when the label had some hits with the Beau Brummels ("Laugh Laugh," "Just a Little"), they signed the Tikis. "Right after that, they went bankrupt," Scoppettone said.

In 1966 the Tikis moved to Warner Records while ex-Beau Brummels drummer John Peterson joined the group so that Templeman could concentrate more on singing. Warner gave the Tikis to producer Lenny Waronker. He had them do "The 59th Street Bridge Song (Feelin' Groovy)" before its writer Paul Simon got it out on a single with his partner Art Garfunkel, and the record became the group's first hit, going to #4 AC and #13 pop in 1967. (Simon and Garfunkel's version was on the B-side of "At the Zoo," a #16 pop hit in 1967.) For that record, the group's name became Harpers Bizarre on the recommendation of a secretary at Warner.

After "Feelin' Groovy," James left the band and studio musicians performed on tracks while the group sang in the studio. "We never again played musical instruments on our records," Scoppettone said. Then Waronker decided the theme for the band's second album, in late 1967, would be primarily 1930s and 1940s music, including "Chattanooga Choo Choo," a #1 pop hit in 1941 for the Glenn Miller Orchestra, who first performed it in the film *Sun Valley Serenade.* Waronker also used Joe Smith, a vice president at Warner, to add to the atmosphere. "Joe Smith used to be an old radio deejay, and Lenny asked Joe to write an opening pitch to read like an old-time announcer," Scoppettone said. Smith did so gladly.

"Chattanooga Choo Choo" went only to #45 pop while topping the AC chart. Later singles did worse. The group's last 45 on the AC and pop listings was "Battle of New Orleans" in 1968 (#21 AC, #95 pop). Seeing their records' continuing poor showings, the group broke up in 1970.

In the 1970s Templeman became the producer for the Doobie Brothers. But Scoppettone revived the group in 1976 for an LP called *As Time Goes By* on his label the Forest Bay Company. "I started my own record company at that point and wanted to see how much money I could lose," he joked. He, James, Peterson, and Yount posed for the cover photo, but "They didn't participate in the album as such. I did all the vocals." The revival faded quickly.

In the 1990s Scoppettone worked in the Santa Cruz area as a travel agent. In 1998 he told me that Dick Yount wanted to re-form the group to go on the road, but that, after the 1976 reunion debacle, he would leave it up to Yount to work out the details. "I'm not really getting involved," said Scoppettone.

1968

100 In the Misty Moonlight

DEAN MARTIN

Reprise 0640

January 20, 1968 (2 weeks)

Writer: Cindy Walker

Producer: Jimmy Bowen

Jerry Wallace nearly topped the AC chart when his rendition of "In the Misty Moonlight" hit #2 on the chart in 1964 (on the pop chart, it went to #19). But it took chart favorite Dean Martin to take it to the top three years later. It became Martin's fifth and last #1 AC hit. George Morgan revived the tune in 1975 and made #65 country.

Martin, born Dino Crocetti in Steubenville, Ohio, on June 7, 1917, was a solo vocalist performing under his stage name by 1940 yet generated little attention until he played the straight man to Jerry Lewis in a comedy act which began in 1946. He first made the pop chart in 1948 with a humorous record with Lewis called "That Certain Party." It reached #22 pop. The following year, Martin landed on the chart with his first straight singing record, "Powder Your Face With Sunshine (Smile, Smile, Smile)," which went to #10. For the next decade he was a fairly regular visitor on the chart, with his biggest hits being "That's Amore" (#2 for five weeks starting in 1953), "Memories Are Made of This" (#1 pop for five weeks in early 1956), and "Return to Me" (#4 in 1958).

His career took a dip for a few years once he and Lewis broke up in 1956, but by the early 1960s he had established a strong career of acting in movies and making personal appearances, and by 1964 he had come out with another hit [see 44—"Everybody Loves Somebody"]. The next year he began the first of nine years hosting his own variety series on NBC-TV, which cemented Martin's image in the public eye as a devil-may-care, somewhat lazy hedonist who rarely got through a sketch or song without fooling around on some level.

The act had begun to wear thin by the early 1970s, on television as well as records. He last made the pop chart in 1969 with "I Take a Lot of Pride in What I Am" (#75 pop, #15 AC). Four more records made the AC charts through his swan song in 1973, "Get On With Your Livin'." A decade later, he was still recording, but his last *Billboard* chart appearance was his only country entry, 1983's "My First Country Song," which stalled at #35.

Martin remained a popular TV guest and live performer, particularly in Las Vegas, through the mid-1980s. After that he became increasingly reclusive, particularly after the death of his son Dean Paul Martin in 1987. Out of the public eye for many years, Martin died on Christmas Day 1995 at age 78.

101 Am I That Easy to Forget

ENGELBERT HUMPERDINCK

Parrot 40023

February 3, 1968 (1 week)

Writers: Carl Belew, W.S. Stevenson, Shelby Singleton

Producer: Peter Sullivan

Prior to 1967, if you had asked anyone other than a student of classical music who Engelbert Humperdinck was, you most likely would have gotten a blank stare. (An opera lover might have told you that was the name of the German composer who wrote the opera *Hansel and Gretel* in 1893.) After 1967, however, when another musician with the same name hit it big on the charts, a large segment of the general public in the United States could probably have given you an answer.

Arnold George Dorsey, born in Madras, India, on May 2, 1936, had been in Great Britain since 1947 and recording unsuccessfully since 1958. But in 1965 manager Gordon Mills, then hot with Tom Jones [see 121—"I'll Never Fall in Love Again"], got hold of him and promised him great rewards. For Dorsey, who was just about to turn 30, the possibility of getting out of the minor nightclubs where he was performing—and going nowhere—was a big incentive. Yet he was not prepared for the stage name Mills picked for him.

"When Gordon said the new name was Engelbert Humperdinck, I said, 'You must be joking,'" he told Robert Musel in *TV Guide*. "He had to spell it to me, and I took it down on a piece of paper and went and showed it to the boys in the bands at the club. They fell about laughing. I didn't like it at all to start with." Neither did Decca, who did not realize when they signed Humperdinck they were getting the same artist they had dropped earlier when he was Dorsey.

Despite the moniker, or possibly because of it, Humperdinck drew worldwide attention in 1967 with two huge hits in many countries—"Release Me (And Let Me Love Again)," his American chart debut, which made #28 AC and #4 pop, and "The Last Waltz," which went to #6 AC and #25 pop. However, it was his follow-up to "The Last Waltz" which became his first #1 AC hit.

Co-writer Carl Belew first recorded "Am I That Easy to Forget" and got to #9 country in 1959. Debbie Reynolds covered the song in 1960 and amazingly had a #13 R&B entry with it as well as #25 pop. That same year Skeeter Davis did a version which made #11 country. Other country covers were a posthumous Jim Reeves release in 1973 (#12) and Orion in 1980 (#65).

Humperdinck's version employed an arrangement done for Esther Phillips' noncharting rendition. His record made #18 pop as well as #1 AC. After "Am I That Easy to Forget," he had nine consecutive top 10 AC entries. One of them, "When There's No You," became Humperdinck's second #1 AC hit [see 148].

102 The Lesson
VIKKI CARR

Liberty 56012
February 10, 1968 (1 week)
Writer: Mack David
Producer: Tommy Oliver

"It's amazing how many people remember that song," Vikki Carr said, referring to "The Lesson," her first single released in the wake of her huge hit "It Must Be Him" [see 95]. Though not quite as popular, "The Lesson" did hit #1 AC and got to #34 pop, a perfectly respectable peak for a follow-up record. Like "It Must Be Him," "The Lesson" was the creation of writer Mack David, who submitted the tune after the former became a hit. But while there was no change in writer, "The Lesson" employed Tommy Oliver as producer rather than Dave Pell, who did "It Must Be Him." Carr insisted it was not a slight against Pell or a working problem with the producer. "I think it was just a case of trying someone new at the company," she said.

Carr was less nervous about what to do immediately after "It Must Be Him" than she was about its overall effect on her career. "The thing is, you get typecast," she said. "The difficulty was trying to get out of that mold." She felt that her versatility as an artist was suffering and that she was beginning to be seen mainly as a ballad singer, a problem which was exacerbated when she left Liberty for Columbia in 1970. Particularly irksome was Columbia's attitude about her practice of always doing a few songs in Spanish, something she had done since her first album with Liberty. Columbia felt she should do English-only lyrics. "They just couldn't understand the importance that Latin music had," she said.

Though Carr's pop success quickly faded after "The Lesson," she remained constantly on the AC chart through 1972, but her efforts there in the 1970s did not crack the top 25 save for 1971's "I'll Be Home," which went to #7 AC and became her last pop entry at #96. In 1974 she did her last English-language LP for Columbia, which included her single "Wind Me Up," which climbed to #45 AC in early 1975. It was her 18th and final AC single, her first having been 1966's "My Heart Reminds Me," which made #31.

In 1980 Carr signed with Columbia's operations in Mexico to sing for the Latin market. "When they learned I sing in Spanish, it was like all the doors opened for me," she said. She became a top seller in the field through the late 1990s, but was eventually frustrated again because she was still a one-language recording artist, this time in Spanish. Carr mentioned trying a jazz album in English-only and noted, "I'm going to do it. I don't know what company it will be, but I'm going to do it. Maybe that time will come about soon." She also clarified that "I've been very happy that I've been able to maintain myself in Spanish and English."

Vikki Carr was born Florencia Martinez Cardona in El Paso, Texas, on July 19, 1941. She currently is based in her hometown when not performing across North and South America.

103 Love Is Blue
PAUL MAURIAT

Philips 40495
February 17, 1968 (11 weeks)
Writer: Andre Popp, Pierre Cour
Producer: Not Listed

"Love Is Blue" is the instrumental with the most weeks at #1 on the AC chart and held the longest-running record at #1 AC until 1993, when the first of several releases, "The River of Dreams," passed that mark. ["River of Dreams" —see 638—held at #1 for 12 weeks; "Because You Loved Me" —see 657—has the record, 19 weeks.] Its success is all the more remarkable given that Paul Mauriat had been releasing material in America with little popularity prior to the record and that other artists had done the tune before he did it.

Born in 1925, Mauriat began working in European recording studios in 1958, providing orchestrations for French artists like Charles Aznavour as well as his own records. Beginning in 1966 he had his LPs released in America as well. As Lou Simon, product manager at the time for Philips Records, told Craig Rosen in *The Billboard Book of Number One Albums*, "Part of our plan was to have a working relationship with all of our licensees in Europe. The idea was to cross-fertilize as much product from the U.S. [to Europe] as from there to here. When the Paul Mauriat material came from our French organization, we thought the orchestrations were interesting."

Nothing in the way of major sales or airplay occurred in America until Mauriat covered "Love Is Blue," a song which placed fourth in 1967 in the Eurovision contest, an annual event wherein European nations submitted one song from their country so that judges could pick the best for that year. Vicki Leandros sang the song, which represented Luxembourg and appeared originally with French lyrics as "L'Amour Est Bleu." Then she tried to sell it in 19 different languages including English with little luck. But with a celeste piano and lush strings, Mauriat transformed the tune into an international hit. In America, the record made #1 pop a week before it did so on the AC chart and stayed atop the Hot 100 for five weeks. Its drawing power led Mauriat's album *Blooming Hits* to #1 on the LP chart for five weeks starting March 2, 1968. The song also inspired a wave of covers, many of them with vocals. On the AC chart in 1968, Al Martino took it to #3 and Claudine Longet hit #28. Three years later, Steve Lawrence and Eydie Gorme got to #37 AC as part of a medley with "Autumn Leaves."

In late 1968 Mauriat's streak on the Hot 100 ended with the only two successful pop follow-ups to "Love Is Blue," "Love in Every Room" (#60 pop, #7 AC) and "Chitty Chitty Bang Bang" (#76 pop, #24 AC). On the AC chart he continued to have entries through 1972's "Après Toi (Come What May)," which peaked at #21. Coincidentally, the song was the Eurovision winner for 1972 for Luxembourg as sung by Vicki Leandros.

The best Mauriat could do after "Après Toi. . ." was in 1977, when he bubbled under at #109 with "Love Is Still Blue," a jazz version of his old hit.

104 Honey

BOBBY GOLDSBORO

United Artists 50283

May 4, 1968 (2 weeks)

Writer: Bobby Russell

Producers: Bob Montgomery, Bobby Goldsboro

Bobby Goldsboro can recall how he first heard the initial version of his biggest hit, "Honey." "A friend of mine, Larry Henley, lead singer of the Newbeats ['Bread and Butter'], told me he liked a record he had just heard by Bob Shane of the Kingston Trio written by Bobby Russell," Goldsboro said. Henley's endorsement of the tune was enough for Goldsboro to take a listen, but he was not too impressed. "I felt the song was overproduced with drums and so on," he said. Shortly thereafter Russell visited Goldsboro and played him some potential tunes for the artist to sing, which he rejected as being "teenybopper." But when Russell played "Honey" on guitar and Goldsboro could hear the lyrics more clearly than on the Shane version, he was hooked. Goldsboro wanted to do the song as a single immediately, but Russell told him he had to wait four weeks to give Shane's take a shot on the marketplace.

The recording of "Honey" produced something Goldsboro had never seen: At the end of the first take, all the musicians listened to the playback because they felt it sounded so good. A second take was done for insurance, but Goldsboro said, "We actually took the first take."

Shane's "Honey" only bubbled under to #104, while Goldsboro's single really took off, selling over a million copies within four weeks. Goldsboro's label, United Artists, reported it was their fastest-selling record ever; it was so popular that the company took requests for orders only until noon each day. The single went to #1 AC, pop, and country, spending five weeks atop the Hot 100 starting April 13, 1968, and then going to the peak of the country chart for three weeks on May 25, 1968. It was Goldsboro's first of several country entries.

Goldsboro did not believe his singing was responsible for the success of "Honey." "I really feel it was the arrangement Don Tweedy wrote for me," he said. He felt that Tweedy's arrangement was so solid that if Shane had used it he too could have had a hit.

A few other artists did versions of "Honey." An instrumental group called the Distant Galaxy performed "Honey" in a medley with the "Elvira Madigan Theme" that reached #39 AC later in 1968. O.C. Smith took it to #44 pop in 1969. Orion included it as part of a double-sided entry with "Ebony Eyes" which made #89 country in 1979. And even an answer record, "Honey (I Miss You Too)" by Margaret Lewis, made #74 country in 1968.

But Goldsboro's "Honey" remained the best-remembered and most-honored version, earning Grammy nominations for Record of the Year, Song of the Year, and Best Male Contemporary Pop Vocal Performance. Summing up its impact on him, Goldsboro said, "I was just completely blown away. I had no idea what it was going to do. I knew it was going to be a hit, but not that big!"

105 The Good, the Bad and the Ugly

HUGO MONTENEGRO

RCA 9423

May 18, 1968 (3 weeks)

Writer: Ennio Morricone

Producer: Neely Plumb

When Italian director Sergio Leone's three spaghetti westerns starring Clint Eastwood ambushed movie screens in the 1960s, what often stuck in people's minds was Ennio Morricone's haunting scores. One of the title themes, that for *The Good, the Bad and the Ugly*, became a hit on its own through a cover done by Hugo Montenegro.

Born on September 2, 1925, Montenegro had begun arranging music by 1945, but his records did not generate much radio or sales activity. He gained more popularity during the 1960s doing the scores for movies like *Hurry Sundown* and TV shows like *The Big Valley*. Joining up with him to do the latter was session musician Tommy Morgen, whose career stretched back to dates with the Andrews Sisters in the early 1940s. Morgen was a key member when Montenegro nailed his biggest hit ever, "The Good, the Bad and the Ugly."

"That album was done in one day," Morgen recalled in 1998. "I think it was all day one Saturday at RCA." Its majestic volume belied the fact that Montenegro did it only with a few studio musicians.

The main sound in the chorus, which resembled an owl's hoot, was played on the ocarina by Art Smith. Morgen responded to each "hoot" with his electric harmonica. "I knew it was live, so I had to do this hand thing, the 'wah-wah-wah' sound," he said. Between the choruses Montenegro grunted something which came out like "rep, rup, rep, rup, rep." Also heard were Elliot Fisher's electric violin, Manny Klein's piccolo trumpet, and Muzzy Marcellino's whistles (Marcellino was the man behind the whistles on the soundtrack to the 1954 John Wayne film *The High and the Mighty*).

Morgen said he had no idea how the cover would do after he recorded it. "You really don't know what's going to be a hit," he said. "And as a studio player, you walk in, you give total concentration, do the best you can....You're not sure what's going to become a monster." But "The Good, the Bad and the Ugly" was monstrous indeed. Beside reaching #1 AC, it nearly led the Hot 100, held at #2 pop only behind "Mrs. Robinson" by Paul Simon and Art Garfunkel the week of June 1, 1968. With its success, Montenegro had Morgen and crew do two weekends of concerts with him, one in Orange County, California, and the other in San Francisco.

Only two Montenegro follow-ups charted—"Hang 'Em High," the title tune from another Eastwood western, at #6 AC and #82 pop later in 1968, and a remake of the Turtles' #1 pop hit from 1967, "Happy Together," at #29 AC and #112 bubbling under in 1969. Montenegro died of emphysema on February 6, 1981.

"Hugo was a very interesting man," Morgen said. "He liked to be surrounded by friends. He and I got along very well....He was a very accomplished arranger/recorder."

106 This Guy's in Love With You

HERB ALPERT

A&M 929

June 8, 1968 (10 weeks)

Writers: Burt Bacharach, Hal David

Producers: Herb Alpert, Jerry Moss

Though known best as a trumpeter, Herb Alpert did record as a vocalist for Dot Records in 1962 with "Tell It to the Birds" under the name Dore Alpert. But when he started putting out records with the Tijuana Brass, Alpert released only instrumentals, although "Mame," a #2 AC and #19 pop single in 1966, did have voices on it chanting a few lyrics. The group's instrumental-only status changed almost overnight after Alpert starred in his own TV special on CBS. On the show, which aired on April 22, 1968, he did more than just play his established hits. "I wanted to use my wife somehow, Alpert told *Newsweek*. The idea came up, why not sing her a song?" He went through 50 submitted tunes before selecting "This Guy's in Love With You." Viewers loved it and requested the song immediately.

Released as a single two days later, "This Guy's in Love With You" spent four of the same weeks it helmed the AC chart atop the pop standings beginning the week of June 22, 1968. The album from which it came, *Beat of the Brass*, also hit #1 for two weeks beginning July 26, 1968. (Another single on the album, an instrumental version of the title tune of the Broadway musical *Cabaret* that had been released earlier, went only to #13 AC and #72 pop, while its B-side "Slick" made #36 AC and #119 bubbling under.) Alpert recorded versions of the tune in Spanish and Italian that summer as well.

"This Guy's in Love With You" also went to #22 AC in 1968 in, ironically, an instrumental version by Tony Mottola. Switching genders to "This Girl's...," Eydie Gorme also went to #22 AC, while Dionne Warwick went to #2 AC for four weeks and #7 both pop and R&B in 1969 with her cover. And a noncharting rendition earned the Johnny Mann Singers a Grammy nomination for Best Contemporary, Pop Performance by a Chorus.

Alpert followed "This Guy's..." with two other vocal efforts, "To Wait for Love" (#2 AC for three weeks, #51 pop) in 1968 and "Without Her" (#5 AC, #63 pop) in 1969. Both 45s were about the highest-charting efforts Alpert had in the wake of "This Guy's..." for nearly 10 years. Most singles from 1969 through the early 1970s missed the AC top 10 and the Hot 100 altogether, with the only exception being "Jerusalem" at #6 AC and #74 pop in 1970.

The group's name became just Herb Alpert and the T.J.B. by 1973's "Last Tango in Paris" (#22 AC, #77 pop), but over the next two years the new moniker produced only four other AC entries, with just one making the Hot 100, 1974's "Fox Hunt" (#14 AC, #84 pop). After 1975's "El Bimbo" made #28 AC, four years went by without another Alpert single on any chart. But Alpert did come back in 1979, and he did it with his fifth #1 AC hit [see 372—"Rise"]

107 Classical Gas
MASON WILLIAMS

Warner 7190

August 17, 1968 (3 weeks)

Writer: Mason Williams

Producer: Mike Post

No one accused Mason Williams of being a limited talent in 1968. His main job then was chief writer and occasional regular on camera for *The Smothers Brothers Show*, having known Tommy and Dick Smothers since their sister Sherry brought him to their attention. In addition, he had written eight books, created a poster on display at the Museum of Modern Art in New York City, and co-wrote with Nancy Ames "Cinderella Rockefella," a song which reportedly sold 6 million copies worldwide even though it reached only #68 on the Hot 100 when done by Esther and Abi Ofarim in 1968. So it should have surprised none of his associates when he ended up with his own hit instrumental recording.

"Classical Gas" emerged out of Williams' attempt to imitate the riffs of a Brazilian guitarist he met. "I never did figure them out," he told *Newsweek*. "But after a couple of months of trying, I wrote 'Classical Gas.'" The title of the composition is appropriate, given its baroque stylings and emphasis on strings and brass, featuring instruments common to most classical and rock tunes.

According to producer Jimmy Bowen in his autobiography *Rough Mix*, credit for the instrumentation, as well as most of the record's appeal, should go to Mike Post, whom Bowen leased out to serve as producer and arranger of "Classical Gas." Bowen remembered that he was not thrilled with the initial cut for the tune but liked Post's changes, which included dropping some drum, piano, and guitar pieces from the background plus adding a "weird bridge of Wagnerian horns to break up a tedious stretch of music." Williams did not appreciate what Post did, however, and did not work with him again.

In any event, "Classical Gas" led the AC chart two weeks after it peaked at #2 on the Hot 100 on August 3 and 10, 1968, behind the Doors' "Hello, I Love You." Williams cleaned up at the Grammy Awards that year, winning three statuettes for the 45 for Best Contemporary Pop Instrumental Performance, Best Instrumental Theme, and Best Instrumental Arrangement. The tune reappeared on the AC chart at #20 in 1969 when the Alan Copeland Singers combined it as a medley with "Scarborough Fair." Williams also found ways to use the song as background music for a few bits on *The Smothers Brothers Show*.

Williams was born in Abilene, Texas, on August 24, 1938. After his two-year stint with *The Smothers Brothers Show* ended with CBS canceling the program in 1969, Williams found his musical success waning. "Greensleeves" that year was his last of four Hot 100 entries, peaking at #90 there and #13 AC. Only two other Williams records then made the AC chart, "A Gift of Song" at #33 in 1969 and "Jose's Piece" at #31 in 1970.

In 1987 Williams teamed with the Mannheim Steamroller instrumental group to do a new version of "Classical Gas." Their joint LP named after the song peaked at #118.

108 The Fool on the Hill
SERGIO MENDES AND BRASIL '66

A&M 961

September 7, 1968 (6 weeks)

Writers: John Lennon, Paul McCartney

Producer: Sergio Mendes, Herb Alpert

It started as Sergio Mendes and Brasil '65 on Capitol, then became Brasil '66 the following year when Mendes made his AC and pop debut on A&M Records with "Mas Que Nada" at #4 pop and #47 AC. Thereafter the last two digits of Mendes' group changed every few years, roughly, but not always, to correspond with the time when the song was released. For example, there was a Brasil '77 as early as 1973, but then Brasil '86 actually showed up in 1986. Whatever the reasoning behind this idiosyncracy, Mendes managed to record his easy-listening brand of music on A&M well into the 1990s.

Born in Niterol, Brazil, on February 11, 1941, Mendes studied music in his native country, emigrating to America in 1965. For three years his releases fared better on the AC chart than the Hot 100, but he finally got his first top 40 pop entry, "The Look of Love," in 1968, a tune which made #4 pop and #2 AC for five weeks. His next release gave him back-to-back top 10 hits on both charts.

"The Fool on the Hill," a track from the Beatles' 1967 album *Magical Mystery Tour*, was not released by that quartet as a single. In fact, no tunes from the LP became a 45 despite heavily sales and airplay. Some covers soon appeared, such as one by Eddie Fisher early in 1968 which generated little response. But Mendes released a version of another Beatles tune, "With a Little Help From My Friends," around the same time, managing to get to #31 AC, which may have helped pave the way for his cover of "The Fool on the Hill."

To do "The Fool on the Hill," Mendes employed 4 trumpets, 4 flutes, and 20 stringed instruments to augment his own electric piano and the vocals of Lani Hill. An offbeat touch had the tune done in a normal 2/4 samba rhythm but played in 3/4 time. Describing his alterations, he told *Billboard* that "I'm open to sounds. Jazz is a natural element for me. I always have a little jazz tag or blues intro."

"The Fool on the Hill" went to #1 AC and #6 pop the week of September 28, 1968. It gave him the top spot on the AC chart before the Beatles themselves finally made it two years later [see 131—"Let It Be"]. In 1970 Mendes covered another Beatles tune, "Norwegian Wood," and made #32 AC and #107 bubbling under.

Mendes continued to make the AC chart sporadically in the 1970s, but none of his singles made the Hot 100 until his next #1 AC hit, "Never Gonna Let Go" [see 440].

109 My Special Angel
THE VOGUES

Reprise 0766

October 19, 1968 (2 weeks)

Writer: Jimmy Duncan

Producer: Dick Glasser

A smooth, mellow vocal quartet, the Vogues prospered in the mid- to late-1960s. The group coalesced in 1960 in high school at Turtle Creek, Pennsylvania, located near Pittsburgh, when Bill Burkette, Chuck Blasko, Hugh Geyer and Don Miller first sung together as the Val-Aires. Bill was lead baritone, Geyer first tenor, Blasko second tenor, and Miller baritone.

Their first single on the Hot 100 came in 1965. "You're the One" hit #4, as did the follow-up, "Five O'Clock World." But four singles released in 1966 did progressively worse on the chart, ending with "That's the Tune," which went only to #99 the week of December 24, 1966. The Vogues came back strong in 1968, offering a new, more melodic tone with "Turn Around, Look at Me." It hit #7 pop and became the first of the Vogues' 18 AC entries, peaking at #3. Next came "My Special Angel," which also went to #7 pop while hitting #1 AC. After "My Special Angel," the Vogues started to slide again on the pop chart; they got six more decreasingly popular entries through 1969's "Green Fields," which peaked at #92. But the group consistently made the AC chart, their last entry being 1974's "Prisoner of Love," which hit #37.

In 1972 Geyer and Miller left the Vogues. They were replaced by one singer as the Vogues became a trio. Current lead singer Terry Brightbill, who joined the Vogues in 1985, said the band changed members several times before the last original member, Chuck Blasko, dropped out in 1986.

By 1997 the Vogues consisted of Brightbill, Stan Elich, and Jim Campagna as singers, with Brightbill's wife Beth serving as drummer. Elich joined in 1988, and Campagna in 1996. All were based in Franklin, Pennsylvania. "We do about 120 dates a year," Brightbill said of the Vogues' touring schedule. Brightbill and crew tour everywhere but Pittsburgh, where Blasko still performs occasionally with other musicians as the Vogues. And now and then founding Vogue Bill Burkette does a date with Brightbill's Vogues.

Asked if "My Special Angel" remained part of the act, Brightbill said, "Very much so. It's a big crowd pleaser. In fact, probably more people relate us to that tune than to Bobby Helms." Helms first popularized the song in 1957; like the Vogues' version, it hit #7 pop but also went to #8 R&B and #1 country for four weeks starting December 9, 1957.

"My Special Angel" was inspired by writer Jimmy Duncan's love for his 4-year-old daughter Sherry. He wrote it in less than 10 minutes and came up with the melody and arrangement a half hour later. Besides the Vogues and Helms renditions, the song also made the country chart at #53 in 1976 by Bobby G. Rice and at #82 in 1985 by James and Michael Younger.

110 Those Were the Days
MARY HOPKIN

Apple 1801

November 2, 1968 (6 weeks)

Writer: Gene Ruskin (adaptation of folk song)

Producer: Paul McCartney

For Mary Hopkin, the key phrase to success was *Opportunity Knocks.* That was the title of the British TV series on which she appeared in 1968 to sing "Turn, Turn, Turn." The famous model Twiggy saw the show and told Paul McCartney to audition the lass. So again opportunity knocked—or rather rang—when McCartney called Hopkin at her home in Pontardwe, Wales, where she was born on May 3, 1950, and asked her to record for the Beatles' new record label Apple.

For her U.K. debut (Hopkin had previously recorded for a small independent Welsh label) McCartney produced a song he had heard in 1966 in a London cabaret sung by Gene Ruskin, a former Columbia University architecture teacher. "Those Were the Days" was a Russian folk tune titled "Darogoi Dimmoyo" (in English, "Dear for Me") to which Ruskin had given English lyrics. His version had been put on record earlier in 1962 on an LP by the American folk group the Limeliters, while the original Russian tune had been recorded first in the 1920s by Alexander Wertinsky.

"Those Were the Days" was one of the first four releases on Apple Records along with the Beatles' "Hey Jude," "Sour Milk Sea" by Jackie Lomax, and "Thingummybob" by the Black Dyke Mills brass band. Apple officials had the records hand-delivered in gift boxes to the British Royal Family to celebrate the label's kickoff.

The single was a powerhouse on both sides of the Atlantic. In England "Those Were the Days" knocked "Hey Jude" out of #1 on September 25, 1968, and stayed at the top for six weeks. In America it nearly peaked on the Hot 100 just as it did on the AC chart, holding at #2 for three weeks starting November 2, 1968, just behind "Hey Jude." The single also nabbed Hopkin a Grammy nomination for Best Contemporary Pop Vocal Performance by a Female.

Hopkin had further success with other records produced by McCartney, including "Goodbye" in 1969 (#2 in the U.K., #6 AC, and #13 pop) and "Temma Harbour" in 1970 (#6 U.K., #4 AC, and #39 pop). But without McCartney's help she floundered. She last hit the AC and pop charts in America in 1972 with "Knock Knock Who's There" (#11 AC, #92 pop), which also was her last top 10 song in Britain, where it peaked at #2 in 1970. Her last entry in England was "If You Love Me" at #32 in 1976, ending a five-year drought of hits there.

In 1983, she tried to revive her career by joining a group called Oasis, but the effort flopped badly everywhere. Hopkin has been heard little since then. For a woman whom British critic Tony Palmer of the *London Observer* newspaper called in 1968 "potentially the greatest lady vocalist since Edith Piaf," "Those Were the Days" stands as an ironic comment on the state of her music career.

111 Wichita Lineman

GLEN CAMPBELL

Capitol 2302

December 14, 1968 (6 weeks)

Writer: Jimmy Webb

Producer: Al de Lory

Glen Campbell and
Sarah Campbell

After spending much of the 1960s behind the scenes as a session musician, Glen Campbell burst from the pack in 1968 with his first #1 AC and first top 10 pop hit "Wichita Lineman." The song was a shining example of what Campbell called his "country-based pop" musical style, and it set a pattern seen in many of the seven other singles which were to top the AC chart over the next decade. Jimmy Webb wrote "Wichita Lineman" following a 50-mile drive he took along the drab panhandle part of the Oklahoma-Kansas border as a tribute to a lineman he saw working on one of the endless telephone poles along the side of the road.

Despite what one source claimed, Campbell said he was the first to receive and record "Wichita Lineman" from Webb. "Jimmy Webb wrote that one for me," he said. "I was the only person he did that for." Campbell previously had a hit with Webb's "By the Time I Get to Phoenix," which went to #12 AC and #26 pop in late 1967.

Campbell remembered there was a problem in doing "Wichita Lineman" in the studio when they tried to reproduce what he had heard when Webb played him the song on his Hammond organ. "We just couldn't get it down in the studio," he said. So to achieve the desired sound, the production company carted Webb's organ from his house to the studio.

Released in the fall of 1968, "Wichita Lineman" made #1 on both the AC and country charts, topping the latter the weeks of December 21 and 28, 1968. On the pop chart "Wichita Lineman" stopped at #3 the week of January 11, 1969, behind Marvin Gaye's "I Heard It Through the Grapevine" at #1 and the Supremes and the Temptations' "I'm Gonna Make You Love Me" at #2. The song also became the title tune of an album for Campbell which went to #1 for five weeks beginning December 21, 1968. In addition, Campbell got a Grammy nomination for Best Male Contemporary Pop Vocal Performance, and "Wichita Lineman" merited nominations for Record of the Year and Best Arrangement Accompanying Vocalists and a win for Best Engineered Recording (Other Than Classical).

"Wichita Lineman" was revived in 1969 by Sergio Mendes and Brasil '66, who took it to #34 AC and #95 pop, and an instrumental version by the Larry Page Orchestra which made #33 AC. By the time the former peaked, Campbell already had his second #1 AC hit [see 114—"Galveston"].

112 I've Gotta Be Me

SAMMY DAVIS JR.

Reprise 0779

January 25, 1969 (7 weeks)

Writer: Walter Marks

Producer: Jimmy Bowen

Sammy Davis Jr. was one of the preeminent entertainers of the 20th century. Born in New York City on December 8, 1925, the dynamic performer first made the pop chart in 1954 with "Hey There" from the Broadway musical *The Pajama Game*. He had several other 45s make it through 1956, then found himself without an entry until 1962's "What Kind of Fool Am I." That was another show tune, this time from the Broadway musical *Stop the World—I Want to Get Off*, and it peaked at #17 pop and #6 AC, making it the first of his 15 entries on the latter chart.

But apart from "The Shelter of Your Arms," which peaked at #7 AC and #17 pop in 1964, Davis had little action on either chart until 1968, when yet another stage song took him back to hit status. Like his other hits, "I've Gotta Be Me," which came from the musical *Golden Rainbow*, was not done on stage by Davis, nor was he the only artist to sing it. It was Steve Lawrence, the star of the Broadway show, who took his version of the song to #6 AC in early 1968.

Around the same time, producer Jimmy Bowen began to work with Davis to find him the hit that had so far eluded the artist while his pals in the Rat Pack on the Reprise roster like Dean Martin and Frank Sinatra were prospering. Their collaboration on "Lonely Is the Name" brought Davis back to the charts in 1968, but the peaks of #93 pop and #12 AC were not outstanding, and Bowen, after cutting a few more tunes with Davis, began to get antsy for a hit.

Then toward the end of 1968, Bowen heard "I've Gotta Be Me" and planned to talk with Davis about it when the latter came to see him in Hollywood. As Bowen recalled in his autobiography *Rough Mix*, before he could speak to Davis, the artist said, "Listen, man, this isn't like a hit song, but I got a thing I just gotta do—from a Broadway show. It's called 'I've Gotta Be Me.'"

Both men were behind the record, but not other Reprise officials, who preferred the B-side. Bowen went around them by getting Davis's latest LP to be titled after the song and hiring independent promotion men to publicize the song to deejays. Once influential Los Angeles radio station KRLA started playing it, "I've Gotta Be Me" not only topped the AC chart but also went to #11 pop.

Despite its Broadway origins and a cover by Tony Bennett that went to #29 AC in late 1969, "I've Gotta Be Me" is identified indelibly with Davis. Its opening line of "Whether I'm right/Or whether I'm wrong" and general theme of individualism suited his gung-ho approach to show business perfectly. In fact, it was the song played during his funeral. But Davis was to manage to score one more #1 AC hit before that happened [see 170—"The Candy Man"].

1969

113 You Gave Me a Mountain

FRANKIE LAINE

ABC 11174

March 15, 1969 (2 weeks)

Writer: Marty Robbins

Producer: Jimmy Bowen

Frankie Laine, born Francesco Paolo LoVecchio in Chicago, Illinois, on March 30, 1913, decided to be a singer at age 17, but it took him another 17 years before he had a hit. From 1930–46, his biggest accomplishments were winning a dance marathon in 1932 that got him into *The Guinness Book of World Records* for its length (145 days) and getting his professional name while singing on WINS radio in New York City in 1938. The station's program director dubbed him "Frankie Lane," but the artist added an "i" to the surname to "individualize it," as he put it.

In 1947 "That's My Desire" took Laine to #4 pop. He remained a constant hit maker for the next decade, scoring #1 hits with "That Lucky Old Sun" and "Mule Train" in 1949 and "The Cry of the Wild Goose" in 1950. The arrival of rock and roll and departure of his longtime producer Mitch Miller in the late 1950s sent his musical career downward for a time. His least successful efforts came in the mid-1960s at Capitol Records where Laine and his producer differed in their musical tastes. Laine claims he could have recorded "The Impossible Dream" [see 73], but his producer rejected the song.

His fortunes changed in 1967 at ABC Records. "I'll Take Care of Your Cares" was his first Hot 100 entry in four years, peaking at #39, and it also went to #2 AC. It was the first of a string of 11 songs by Laine to hit the latter chart, culminating with "You Gave Me a Mountain."

"Marty Robbins once told me that he'd been trying to bring 'You Gave Me a Mountain' to my attention for several years before he finally succeeded in November 1968," Laine recalled in his autobiography *That Lucky Old Son.* "I wish he'd been quicker about it. There were many times in the mid-60s when I longed for a song of its quality."

However, Laine objected to the line "Despised and ignored by my father," as his own beloved dad had died two months prior to the recording session. "Deprived of the love of my father" was used instead. "Still, every time I reached that line it brought back mental images of Pa in his casket and they broke me up inside. 'Mountain' remains a difficult number for me to get through today," Laine wrote.

Despite what Laine claims was a lack of promotion by ABC Records, "You Gave Me a Mountain" scaled to the top of the AC chart and peaked at #24 pop. A version by Johnny Bush went to #7 country in 1969. And Elvis Presley included his version in his 1972 LP *Aloha From Hawaii Via Satellite.*

"You Gave Me a Mountain" turned out to be Laine's last AC entry and next-to-last Hot 100 record. Laine continued to record into the 1990s plus tour 15 weeks each year while living in San Diego, California, with "You Gave Me a Mountain" always included in his repertoire.

114 Galveston

GLEN CAMPBELL

Capitol 2428

March 29, 1969 (6 weeks)

Writer: Jimmy Webb

Producer: Al de Lory

Though he had scored with such tunes by Jimmy Webb as "By the Time I Get to Phoenix" and "Wichita Lineman" [see 111], Glen Campbell was not the first to record Webb's tune "Galveston." That distinction belonged to Don Ho, the Hawaiian balladeer best known for his single "Tiny Bubbles (In the Wine)," which made #14 AC and #57 pop in 1967.

"He did it as a ballad," Campbell recalled. "I heard it more up-tempo."

When Ho's version of "Galveston" flopped, Ho let Campbell cut a new rendition of the song. As to why Ho did the song in the first place even though he was such an unlikely artist to be singing about being a Texas native and having opinions about the Vietnam War, Campbell said that Johnny Rivers, Webb's publisher at the time, also had Don Ho as a client, so he gave "Galveston" to Ho.

The Gulf Coast town of Galveston, Texas, was one which Campbell had visited as a youth with several musicians prior to singing about it as an adult. "We played down there when I was a kid," he said. "I was 15 years old." The "down there" reference came from the fact that Campbell was born north of Galveston, but not too far. He was born on April 22, 1936, in an Arkansas community called Billstown, which consisted of a church and two stores. To help people who wanted to locate his birthplace on a map, he often claimed that he was born in Delight, Arkansas, which was 4 miles away from Billstown.

As for "Galveston" the song, it became Campbell's second #1 AC hit, third #1 country hit (three weeks there starting April 19, 1969), and second top 10 pop hit (it peaked at #4 the week of April 12, 1969). An instrumental version of "Galveston" by Roger Williams made #21 AC and #99 pop in the summer of 1969.

Campbell related an interesting story regarding this hit and "Wichita Lineman." It seems that when the two U.S. ships with the same names as the Campbell hits, the USS *Galveston* and the USS *Wichita,* met or passed each other, each blared out the appropriate theme. Given that kind of free publicity, one wonders why he and Webb did not try to do more songs named after places. As it stood, he released two more singles written by Webb after "Galveston," 1969's "Where's the Playground Susie" (#10 AC, #26 pop) and 1970's "Honey Come Back" (#4 AC, #19 pop).

That activity was not the sum total of Campbell's involvement with Webb, however. "I'm getting ready to do a DVD Surround Sound album with old songs, and I'll be doing five songs of Jimmy's plus 'Wichita Lineman' and 'Galveston,'" Campbell said in 1998.

Aquarius/Let the Sunshine In
THE 5TH DIMENSION

Happy Heart
ANDY WILLIAMS

Soul City 772

May 10, 1969 (2 weeks)

Writers: James Rado, Gerome Ragni, Galt MacDermot

Producer: Bones Howe

Columbia 44818

May 24, 1969 (2 weeks)

Writer: Jackie Rae (words), James Last (music)

Producer: Jerry Fuller

The biggest hit medley ever on the AC and pop charts was "Aquarius/Let the Sunshine In," a combination of two melodies from the Broadway musical *Hair*. The story of how the Fifth Dimension came to do the tune is a classic tale of coincidence. Group member Billy Davis Jr. accidentally left his wallet in a taxi while the Fifth Dimension performed in New York City in 1968. The taxi's next passenger was Ed Gifford, a producer of *Hair*, who found the wallet and called Davis.

"It sounds like a fantasy, doesn't it?" Davis recalled. "But it's the truth. . . .I think he must have looked in my wallet and saw an AFTRA card. He said, 'You must be Billy Davis Jr., the entertainer.'" Davis confirmed he was part of the Fifth Dimension and invited Gifford and his wife to see them to thank him for getting his wallet.

After the show, Gifford revealed to Davis and the other four members of the Fifth Dimension (Florence La Rue, Marilyn McCoo, Lamonte McLemore, and Ron Townson) that he was a producer of *Hair* and offered them tickets to the show. One moment in the musical stood out for all of them: "We heard Ronnie Dyson singing 'Aquarius,'" Davis said. "During intermission we all ran out and said, 'We've got to do this song. It's a beautiful song.'"

They called their producer Bones Howe, who was less enthusiastic than the quintet, saying it already had been done by others (e.g., the Staples Singers for one). A week later, he told the group they would cut "Aquarius." McCoo noted that Howe also told them, "But we're going to add 'Let the Sunshine In.'"

The latter tune, also from *Hair*, had not impressed Davis or McCoo as much as "Aquarius" had. As McCoo said, "When they did it as part of 'The Flesh Failures' [the real title of the song], it was not as joyous a sound." But they went along with Howe and recorded the medley; it was originally over five minutes long, but was later edited for single release. Kept intact on all versions was Davis shouting out such ad-libbed phrases as "Sing along with the Fifth Dimension," all of which he said were his creations.

The final production went to #1 both on the AC and pop charts, peaking on the latter for six weeks starting April 12, 1969, and #6 on the R&B chart. It won them Grammys for Record of the Year and Best Group Contemporary Vocal Performance. They also got thank-you notes from the producers of *Hair*.

McCoo and Davis were not caught totally off guard by the success of the medley. "In our hearts we felt it would be a major hit," McCoo said. But Davis said, "I didn't think it would be as big as it was." "We didn't know it would define a generation," McCoo added.

Though he had a fine rapport with producer Robert Mersey, Andy Williams decided not to work with him after 1966's "In the Arms of Love" [see 77]. He decided to use other producers "just to make a change," as he put it. He and new producer Jerry Fuller decided that "Happy Heart" had potential as a hit single and title tune for an album, so it became both in 1969. As an entry on the pop chart it fared pretty well, hitting #22 on the Hot 100, the highest position on that chart for Williams since "Dear Heart" hit #24 in 1965.

Like his other #1 AC tunes, "Happy Heart" was recorded rather quickly so that Williams would have time for his TV work (his variety series on NBC ended in 1967 after five years but resumed again in the fall of 1969 after he did several specials for the network). "We'd go in and get three a day," he said of the number of songs cut. "We'd get three in within four hours."

Williams also promoted his songs heavily on his TV series and specials. Regarding the former, he said, "We did a section called 'The Wonderful World of Albums,' and I'd sing a song, usually from one of my albums, and walk through a cutout of the album onstage," he said. Virtually no other AC artist had the same kind of forum that Williams had for promoting his or her latest releases on television.

The first Williams record to make the AC chart was the double-sided entry "Danny Boy" (#15) and "Fly by Night" (#20) in 1961. This followed five years of pop entries where his biggest success was a song called "Butterfly" which hit #1 on the Most Played by Jockeys listing in 1957. On the AC chart Williams would compile 44 entries over 15 years, and while four fell one shy of that mark to peak at #2. Those were the aforementioned "Dear Heart" (one week in 1965), "Music to Watch Girls By" (one week in 1967), "More and More" (four weeks in 1967), and "One Day of Your Life" (two weeks in 1970).

In 1971 Williams notched his last #1 AC entry, "Where Do I Begin (Love Story)" [see 147]. Like his 1966 chart topper "In the Arms of Love," the tune was a movie theme and, also like that song, Williams did not see the film in which the song originated before he cut the record. With "Where Do I Begin" that put him in a distinct minority, as it was from the tremendously popular hit film *Love Story*.

Lauri Wright and
Andy Williams

117 Love Theme From *Romeo and Juliet*

HENRY MANCINI

RCA 0131

June 7, 1969 (8 weeks)

Writer: Nina Rota

Producer: Joe Reisman

The designated hit side of Henry Mancini's first single release of 1969 was "The Windmills of Your Mind," the tune from the film *The Thomas Crown Affair* which won the 1968 Oscar for Best Song. That song became a vocal hit for Dusty Springfield instead, peaking at #3 AC and #31 pop in 1969, while deejays and record buyers preferred the B-side of the Mancini record. The tune there was "Love Theme From *Romeo and Juliet*," taken from the 1968 film of the same name. Ironically, Mancini did not write the theme even though he had in the past composed and released as singles such memorable movie music as "Moon River" from *Breakfast at Tiffany's* and "The Pink Panther Theme."

Mancini got the idea to do the song after seeing *Romeo and Juliet* in late 1968. "I liked the picture very much, and in the background there was this lovely piece of music," he was quoted as saying in *The Billboard Book of Number One Hits* by Fred Bronson. "I left the movie very impressed by the score, and I started asking . . .why this hasn't been recorded." He learned that there had been a recording of the main theme which flopped. Undeterred, he made his own version, and even played the piano for the first time on record.

What saved Mancini's effort from dying was massive airplay of the song on an Orlando, Florida, radio station one night, bringing many requests from listeners and leading to other heavy airplay later on. "Love Theme From *Romeo and Juliet*" went on to #1 on both the AC and Hot 100 charts, arriving on the latter four weeks after it hit #1 AC on June 28, 1969. It stayed at #1 pop for two weeks.

"Love Theme From *Romeo and Juliet*" won Grammy nominations for Record of the Year and Song of the Year. Mancini got his 18th Grammy, a record at the time, for Best Instrumental Arrangement for the tune. A cover by the Percy Faith Orchestra and Chorus won a Grammy for Best Contemporary Performance by a Group.

Johnny Mathis also covered the tune in a vocal version subtitled "A Time for Us," which hit #8 AC and #96 pop in 1969. The lyrics, written by Larry Kusik and Eddie Snyder, were heard in the movie too.

Henry Mancini was born in Cleveland, Ohio, on April 16, 1924, and raised in Aliquippa, Pennsylvania. In 1952 he became a staff composer at Universal Pictures, but became a freelancer in 1958, after the success of his thumping theme for the *Peter Gunn* TV series. He had singles on the AC chart each year from 1961's "Moon River" (#3) through 1977's "Theme From *Charlie's Angels*" (#22).

Mancini was diagnosed with cancer while adapting for a Broadway musical his score for the 1982 film *Victor/Victoria*, which had won him an Oscar for Best Score. He told those at his 70th birthday celebration he hoped to live long enough to see the 21st century. Sadly, he did not attain that goal, as he died on June 14, 1994.

118 Spinning Wheel
BLOOD, SWEAT AND TEARS

Columbia 44871

August 2, 1969 (2 weeks)

Writer: David Clayton-Thomas

Producer: James William Guercio

After Blood, Sweat and Tears released their 1967 debut LP *Child Is Father to the Man*, lead singer Al Kooper, who had formed the group with Bobby Colomby and others, left. Colomby found a vocalist recommended by Judy Collins, David Clayton-Thomas. Born David Henry Thomsett in Surrey, England, on September 13, 1941, Clayton-Thomas went to Toronto, Canada, at age 4 and began his musical career in 1962. His singing and songwriting talents made "Spinning Wheel" a big early hit for the band.

"It was written in an age when psychedelic imagery was all over lyrics," Clayton-Thomas recalled. The Beatles' *Sgt. Pepper's Lonely Hearts Club Band* was one inspiration. The line about "ride a painted pony" came from "Both Sides Now," a #3 AC and #8 pop hit for Judy Collins in 1968. The lyrics also warned against being obsessed with the idea of social revolution. "It was my way of kind of saying, 'Don't get too caught up, because everything comes full circle,' " he noted.

Apart from lyrics, "Spinning Wheel" stood out with its heavy use of horns. Clayton-Thomas credited that to arranger Fred Lipsius. Edited from the single but heard on the album and often played on radio was the ending where the band spontaneously went into a riff with woodwinds and horns, followed by organist Dick Halligan saying, "That wasn't very good, was it?" amid laughter. "He had a very dry sense of humor," Clayton-Thomas said.

One of three songs to peak at #2 pop from the LP *Blood, Sweat and Tears*, which itself hit #1 on the album chart for seven weeks starting March 29, 1969, "Spinning Wheel" was kept from #1 for three weeks from July 5–19, 1969, the first week by "Love Theme From *Romeo and Juliet*" [see 117] and the last two by "In the Year 2525" [see 119]. It also went to #45 R&B. At the Grammys the group had 10 nominations, with "Spinning Wheel" nominated for Record of the Year and Song of the Year and winning for Best Arrangement Accompanying Vocalists for Lipsius's work.

Most of the 8 to 10 musicians in Blood, Sweat and Tears preferred touring over recording. Although they made more money over the short term, by the early 1970s it had led to a drop in popularity. By 1976 all the original band members had left at least once, including Clayton-Thomas, who tried—unsuccessfully—for a solo career in 1972 (his only AC entry, "Magnificent Sanctuary Band," went to #36 that year). He returned to the band in 1974.

Sales continued to decline in the 1970s. But Clayton-Thomas stayed with the band during the 1980s and 1990s even though it rarely recorded new material. In 1997 he released his first solo LP in a decade, *Blue Plate Special*, and recorded another in 1998 while still fronting Blood, Sweat and Tears. The band is currently based in New York City.

119 In the Year 2525 (Exordium and Terminus)
ZAGER AND EVANS

RCA 0174

August 16, 1969 (2 weeks)

Writer: Rick Evans

Producers: Rick Evans, Denny Zager

"In the Year 2525" begins with comments about life on Earth some 500 years in the future, "if man is still alive," and successive verses describe the dehumanization taking place at roughly 1,000-year intervals. It culminates in the year 10,000 A.D., with mankind's reign over the world finished. Probably no other hit ever painted such a nihilistic view of the future, but in the year 1969 many regarded the tune as hip and happening, and it topped not only the AC chart but also the Hot 100 for six weeks beginning July 12, 1969.

The saga of Zager and Evans started in 1961 when Denny Zager organized a quartet called the Eccentrics in his hometown of Lincoln, Nebraska. Both Zager and Rick Evans, one of the other members, sang and played guitar. In 1964 Evans wrote "In the Year 2525," but no one else in the group wanted to sing it. (Zager had already left the group to form another band, the Devilles.) Four years later, both men had grown disgusted with their groups and decided to become a duo. One of the songs they tried out was Evans' old composition "In the Year 2525." The song became popular in local clubs, and Zager and Evans went to Odessa, Texas, in November 1968 to record the tune. They pressed 1,000 copies on their own label, Truth Records, then printed up 10,000 more as they began to get local airplay with the tune. They sent copies to major record companies to see if any were interested in putting out the increasingly successful song and hit paydirt with RCA's Ernie Altschuler, who became executive producer for the record.

With RCA's promotional push, "In the Year 2525" became a hit and Zager and Evans looked to be a major rising act. A *Time* reporter, who described "In the Year 2525" as having "a simple and schmaltzy tune and a chugging, nostalgic background right out of the 1950s," wrote about the group. Evans boasted about their upcoming LP that "Nearly every song is profound." That profundity apparently escaped everyone else, as Zager and Evans' popularity soon declined dramatically.

Because "In the Year 2525" also topped the British charts in August 1969, Zager and Evans geared up for the release of their follow-up, which everyone expected to capture at least a glimmer of the first record's popularity. But "Mr. Turnkey" was a depressing song about a jailed prisoner which crept only to #106 in October 1969 before disappearing.

Zager and Evans broke up shortly thereafter. Their only legacy, "In the Year 2525," has the dubious distinction of having generated what *Miami Herald* columnist Dave Barry described as "violent hatred" in readers responding to Barry's early 1990s survey asking them to name what they considered the worst songs of all time.

120 A Boy Named Sue

JOHNNY CASH

Columbia 44944

August 30, 1969 (2 weeks)

Writer: Shel Silverstein

Producer: Bob Johnston

A joke circulating around the late 1960s had it that a prison riot once started when the inmates learned they had to hear Johnny Cash sing again. The "Man in Black" has indeed been a regular performer at jails since 1957, and it was at a prison concert that he first sang his highest-charting single on the AC and pop charts.

A week before a date at the San Quentin prison, where Cash had played as early as 1958, he and his wife June Carter Cash had a party at their house where he heard Shel Silverstein's novelty tune "A Boy Named Sue," about the insults a man endured because of his feminine name. He enjoyed the tune but thought nothing more about it at the time.

"When I went to San Quentin, June asked if I had it," Cash told Bill Flanagan in *Musician*. "I said, 'Yeah, but I haven't had a chance to rehearse it, I can't do it.' She said, 'Take the lyrics, put it on a music stand, and read it off as you sing it. They'll love it.'" The convicts certainly did, especially when Cash used the phrase "son of a bitch," which was bleeped out of the final record and became a source of embarrassment to him in retrospect.

"A Boy Named Sue" hit #1 both AC and country, topping the latter for five weeks beginning August 23, 1969, and it stopped at #2 pop for three weeks starting August 23, 1969 behind the Rolling Stones' "Honky Tonk Women."

Born in Kingsland, Arkansas, on February 26, 1932, Cash grew up in Dyess, Arkansas, and served in the Air Force in the early 1950s before signing with Sun Records in Memphis in 1955. "I Walk the Line" became his pop debut when it made #17 on the Best Sellers chart in 1956. In 1958 Cash signed with Columbia and did well both on the country and pop charts through the mid-1960s. One of those records, "The Matador," was his first AC entry, going to #13 in 1963.

Cash had a resurgence of popularity in 1968 sparked by his live recordings in concert at prisons, and the success of "A Boy Named Sue" led to his own variety series on ABC-TV from 1969–71. Although his pop and AC appeal faded, with Cash's last entry on both charts being "One Piece at a Time" in 1976 (#6 AC, #29 pop), he remained a giant on the country chart.

He made news in the 1980s and 1990s more for winning a slew of lifetime achievement awards and discussing his substance abuse problems than for his recordings. In 1997 he released his second autobiography and announced he was suffering from a debilitating disease. But he still had enough fire in him in 1998 to take out a *Billboard* ad thanking country deejays who played his latest Grammy-winning tune. It actually had received little airplay, so Cash used an early picture of him extending his middle finger to the camera. Cash had people laughing again, but at a far more serious message than that of "A Boy Named Sue."

121 I'll Never Fall in Love Again

TOM JONES

Parrot 40018

September 13, 1969 (1 week)

Writers: Lonnie Donegan, Jimmy Currie

Producer: Peter Sullivan

T homas Woodward was born in Pontypridd, South Wales, on June 7, 1940. His coal miner father has this advice for his son growing up: Stay out of the mines if you can. His son did avoid the coal mines, instead working at a paper mill and building site, but his real passion was singing. Billing himself as Tommy Scott, he tried to support a wife, whom he wed at age 16, by performing.

The aspiring vocalist looked to be going nowhere when Gordon Mills, his future manager, spotted him at a club in 1964 leading a group called the Senators. Mills noted the audience's enthusiastic reaction to the band's version of "Spanish Harlem" and attributed much of its appeal to the gyrations of the lead singer. The only thing which left Mills cold was the name Tommy Scott. Using his real first name plus his mother's maiden name as his surname, Tommy Scott became Tommy Jones.

Signed to Decca in England, the first single issued with Jones was "Chills and Fever," a flop. But then came the driving "It's Not Unusual," which hit not only in the United Kingdom but also in America, where it reached #3 AC and #10 pop in 1965. It was the first in a long line of records for Jones on both charts, and it helped him win the Grammy for Best New Artist.

But material for Jones varied widely over the next two years, and he had only one other genuine hit during that period, 1965's #3 pop hit "What's New Pussycat?" "Tom is the most versatile singer in the world," Mills boasted to *Life*. "Sometimes the trouble with Tom is he's too versatile. He can sing anything—ballad, R&B, country-western, anything." With that in mind, the decision was made to cast Jones in a more adult mold, but with his sensuality intact. The first single to use this approach, "Green, Green Grass of Home" in early 1967, was a success, going to #12 AC and #11 pop.

Following that was "I'll Never Fall in Love Again," which was not the Dionne Warwick song [for information on that record, see 129]. Though credited to Lonnie Donegan and Jimmy Currie, the tune sounded like the same melody as the #11 pop entry "Wanderin'" by Sammy Kaye in 1950. "I'll Never Fall in Love Again" went to #28 AC and #49 pop in its initial release in 1967, but a rerelease of the same single two years later made #1 AC and #6 pop, peaking on the latter chart the weeks of September 13 and 20, 1969. By the time the new version made #1 AC, Jones had spent four weeks at #2 AC with the previous single "Love Me Tonight" in the summer of 1969. The second shot of "I'll Never Fall in Love Again" was followed by another #1 AC entry [see 128—"Without Love (There Is Nothing)"].

122 Jean
OLIVER

Crewe 334

September 20, 1969 (4 weeks)

Writer: Rod McKuen

Producer: Bob Crewe

When it came time for him to become a solo vocalist, William Swofford, born in North Wilkesboro, North Carolina, on February 22, 1945, became known professionally by only his middle name of Oliver. He had not envisioned singing by himself on stage when he pursued a musical career while a student at the University of North Carolina in the mid-1960s, however. "I was a member of a harmony trio that began at Chapel Hill," he recalled. The group, called the Good Earth, headed to New York City after they graduated in 1967 and gained the attention of producer Bob Crewe, who put out a Good Earth album on Dot Records which did little business.

"Eventually the group underwent some personnel changes," Swofford said. "I was the only constant member. Then we broke up." But Crewe, who liked him, encouraged Swofford to become a soloist and had him record "Good Morning Starshine" from the Broadway musical *Hair*. It hit #3 both AC and pop in 1969 and led to the production of an album named after the song.

"'Jean' was chosen as an album song. We had no idea it would be a single," said Swofford. "It was a 3/4 ballad in the psychedelic era." But when Crewe asked deejays what song from the album should follow "Good Morning Starshine," "Jean" was their overwhelming favorite. It ended up nearly topping the pop chart as well as AC, ending at #2 on October 4 and 11, 1969, behind the Archies' "Sugar, Sugar."

"Jean," from the movie *The Prime of Miss Jean Brodie*, was an Oscar nominee for Best Song. Swofford attributed some of the song's success to the movie's popularity, but noted that Rod McKuen, who sang "Jean" in the film, released his version as a 45 before Swofford's and it bombed. "I think it was just so different at the time. There weren't a lot of records of that type competing then. . . .It was a beautiful arrangement," noted Swofford in explaining what he thought was his record's appeal.

Swofford never had another hit. The best he could do was reach #14 AC and #35 pop with "Sunday Mornin'" in 1970, his next-to-last pop entry. A year later, "Early Mornin' Rain" was his final AC single, stopping at #38.

"I performed for a living until 1984," Swofford said. He toured with the hope of getting another record contract until, as he put it, "I came to the realization of that happening again being very unlikely." Aware that he had other skills, he started work in sales and as of 1998 was a business manager at the Merck Pharmaceutical Company in Louisiana, handling the company's business for half of the state. Swofford occasionally gets contacted by promoters to perform again but turns them down. "I have all I can do in my present life," he said. "I have a very good life."

123 Is That All There Is
PEGGY LEE

Capitol 2602

October 18, 1969 (2 weeks)

Writers: Jerry Leiber, Mike Stoller

Producers: Jerry Leiber, Mike Stoller

In 1969, after being two of the hottest tunesmiths in rock and roll in the 1950s with such hits as "Jailhouse Rock" and "Hound Dog" for Elvis Presley, songwriters Jerry Leiber and Mike Stoller were still recovering from the 1966 dissolution of their record company Red Bird after only two years in operation. By penning the anthem to middle-age disillusionment "Is That All There Is," they were reflecting on recent events in their life—sort of.

Talking to John Tobler and Stuart Grundy in *The Record Producers*, Leiber said, "Despite what has been said elsewhere, I didn't write that song as a reaction to our feelings at the end of the Red Bird period—I think that's a little narrow. It was more of a reaction to the problems I was experiencing in living in general." Both men were in fact looking for an older audience, but were not sure how big a one existed for their music.

Peggy Lee had some of the same fears. Lee, born Norma Jean Egstrom in Jamestown, North Dakota, on May 26, 1920, admired the duo, having recorded two of their songs, "Fever" (#8 pop, 1958) and "I'm a Woman" (#54 pop, 1963). The latter was one of only three hot Hot 100 entries from 1959–68 (the other two were even lower on the ladder), but she did hit the AC chart eight times from 1965–67, including "Big Spender" from the musical *Sweet Charity* (#9, 1966) and "I Feel It" (#8, 1967). Still, at the end of the 1960s it looked bleak hitwise for Lee, who had enjoyed strong sales during her years with Benny Goodman in the 1940s and had put out solo hits like "Manana" in the 1950s.

In her autobiography *Miss Peggy Lee* she noted, "When I came to record 'Is That All There Is,' there was resistance everywhere. They said it was too far out, they said it was too long, they said. . . .So I went to Glenn Wallichs [co-founder of Capitol Records] with a demo (something I hadn't done before), and Glenn seemed embarrassed. 'Peggy, you don't have to play a demo, you helped build this Capitol Tower. You just record anything you want.'"

Georgia Brown first performed the tune on a 1966 TV show for the British Broadcasting Corporation but never recorded it. Lee's single, arranged by Randy Newman, was the first version released even though it took 36 takes and the engineer accidentally erased the best take. It peaked at #11 pop as well as #1 AC. Lee won the Grammy for Best Female Contemporary Vocal Performance, and the tune also got a nomination for Record of the Year.

Unfortunately, that was all there was for Lee in terms of hitting the Hot 100, but she did make the AC chart six more times, with the last entry being "Let's Love," a #22 song in 1974 written for her by Paul McCartney. Leiber and Stoller also produced and wrote her 1975 LP *Mirrors*. She continued to tour and record into the 1990s.

124 Wedding Bell Blues
THE 5TH DIMENSION

Soul City 779

November 1, 1969 (2 weeks)

Writer: Laura Nyro

Producer: Bones Howe

One lucky songwriter for the Fifth Dimension to cover was Laura Nyro. Her "Sweet Blindness" and "Stoned Soul Picnic" were top 15 pop hits for the quintet, although neither made the AC chart. That changed when Nyro's "Wedding Bell Blues" helmed both the AC and pop charts, staying three weeks atop the latter starting November 8, 1969.

The Fifth Dimension had met Nyro first in the mid-1960s when both acts were struggling. "We were working at this little club and Laura was staying in the same building the guys were staying," Marilyn McCoo recalled.

When "Wedding Bell Blues" came along with the opening line of "Bill, I love you so," it seemed perfect for the group to do as an in joke, as McCoo was planning to marry Davis. "Bones [Howe, the group's producer], when we were having one of our listening sessions, said, 'Marilyn, why don't you sing the song?' I think it was a lark," she said. But Davis recalled that Howe told him, "I'm going to have Marilyn sing this song for you."

Whatever the case, "Wedding Bell Blues" did present a conundrum for the Fifth Dimension because of its arrangement. "There was some discussion about us recording a song being by a soloist," McCoo said. "Up to that point, all of the singles had been group vocals." But the record company assured them the tune would only be an album track and not set a precedent for the group, so McCoo sang lead.

But demand for the song to be released as a single grew, which confused the group, as they had thought Nyro's version was a national hit. (In reality, it was a hit for her only in California; nationally, it bubbled under to #103 in 1966.) "Wedding Bell Blues" ended up being their second double #1 AC and pop hit after "Aquarius/Let the Sunshine In" [see 115], and hit #23 R&B as well. "We were all pleasantly surprised when it happened," McCoo said.

As it happened, the Davis-McCoo wedding occurred not long before the song hit. "The timing was so close, because we got married in July and it peaked in October," McCoo said. And any potential problem with using McCoo as the lead singer in future records, never materialized, because McCoo underwent surgery that same year, the four others toured as the Fifth Dimension, and the group's other female, Florence LaRue, singing "Wedding Bell Blues." None of the audiences seemed to notice the difference. "I thought, 'Well!' It did hurt my ego a little bit," laughed McCoo.

After "Wedding Bell Blues," the group did no other singles written by Nyro, who died at 49 in 1997 without ever gaining much success as an artist. Instead, they went to Burt Bacharach and Hal David for their next #1 AC hit, "One Less Bell to Answer" [see 143].

125 Try a Little Kindness
GLEN CAMPBELL

Capitol 2659

November 15, 1969 (1 week)

Writers: Bobby Allen Austin, Thomas Curt Spaugh

Producer: Al de Lory

"Try a Little Kindness" was credited to Bobby Allen Austin and Thomas Curt Spaugh, but Glen Campbell said he helped rewrite some of the lyrics. Rather than take writer's credit, however, he took half of the publishing rights instead.

Campbell also claimed that "'Try a Little Kindness' was the most played song on radio in 1969." He said its positive message of love made it gain airplay on religious stations as well as Campbell's main station base at the time of AC, pop, and country. While the "most played" label is questionable, "Try a Little Kindness" did do very well on the AC and country charts, reaching #2 on the latter (it did fall somewhat short on the pop chart, reaching only #23).

Of aid to Campbell in turning songs like "Try a Little Kindness" into hits was having his own TV variety series, *The Glen Campbell Goodtime Hour*, which aired on CBS from January 29, 1969 through June 13, 1972, and allowed him to promote his songs. "It was amazing," he said, recalling its impact in 1969. "I had five albums on the pop chart and eight albums on the country chart because of the TV show."

Handling his work on the TV show and in the recording studio was not too difficult, according to Campbell. "I would learn the songs at the [TV] studio and just go in and do them at the sessions," he said. Campbell claimed this method allowed him to do an album's worth of material within a matter of days. His producer Al de Lory also contributed to the swiftness of getting Campbell's records together. "We worked together great, because I could go in and could do my part in a couple of takes and he would just put strings and horns on them," Campbell said.

Besides being producer, de Lory also served as Campbell's conductor and arranger on his records. He held those positions with Campbell from 1967–71. Prior to that time, Campbell had only spotty success as a solo singer. His AC and pop debut was "Turn Around, Look at Me," which stalled at #15 AC and #62 pop in early 1962. While Campbell did not make the AC chart again until 1967 ("By the Time I Get to Phoenix"), he did have two other pop entries before 1967, "Too Late to Worry—Too Blue to Cry" in 1962 (#76) and "The Universal Soldier" in 1965 (#45). He also had two country entries before 1967, the earliest being "Kentucky Mean Paradise" with the Green River Boys, which reached #20 in 1963. During those struggling years in the 1960s, Campbell worked as a session musician with everyone from the Beach Boys to Frank Sinatra.

After de Lory's departure, followed quickly by the cancellation of *The Glen Campbell Goodtime Hour* in 1972, Campbell's recording career took a general downswing on the AC, pop, and country charts. Yet in 1975 he released a record that wound up topping all three [see 268—"Rhinestone Cowboy"].

126 Leaving on a Jet Plane

PETER, PAUL AND MARY

Warner Brothers 7340

November 22, 1969 (3 weeks)

Writer: John Denver

Producers: Albert Grossman, Milt Okun

The first track of "Leaving on a Jet Plane" was on the Chad Mitchell Trio's LP *Mitchell Trio Alive*, released before its writer, John Denver, decided to leave the group, not necessarily on a jet plane, in 1969. Denver had written and recorded the tune for private use two years earlier, as he recalled in his autobiography *Take Me Home*.

"I was playing around with an idea," Denver wrote. "I had a six-pack of beer and a couple of sandwiches. And then I picked up my guitar and wrote a song with my soul wide open and my mind picturing the scene as if it stood before me, real enough to touch. I called it 'Oh, Babe, I Hate to Go.' I wrote the song not so much out of the experience of feeling that way for someone as out of the longing to have someone to love. When I got through, I knew I'd written my best song yet."

Milt Okun, later Denver's producer when the singer's solo career took off in the 1970s, liked the song but hated the title, so it became "Leaving on a Jet Plane." He played it to Peter, Paul and Mary, and, Yarrow recalled, "Mary immediately fell in love with that one."

Initially a track on the trio's 1967 LP *Album 1700*, "Leaving on a Jet Plane," which consisted of only one guitar, one bass, and three voices, did not make an impact as a single until two years later. "As with 'Puff the Magic Dragon,' all of a sudden radio stations started playing it," Yarrow said. He believed the first station to air it was in Denver. Eventually it spread nationwide, and after finishing its run atop the AC chart it hit #1 on the Hot 100 the week of December 20, 1969. "Leaving on a Jet Plane" also went to #52 on the country chart in 1970 when done by the Kendalls, a father and daughter duo.

Yarrow said the song was popular with servicemen and their families during the Vietnam War. Peter, Paul and Mary opposed America's involvement in the conflict, but they understood its appeal with military members ("They said it was a very important link to home") and reconciled their opinions in light of the situation. "Everybody in this country was injured in some way by the war," he noted. Of the song's writer John Denver, Yarrow said, "We loved him very much. He was a great friend."

"Leaving on a Jet Plane" was the last AC and pop entry for Peter, Paul and Mary. The group disbanded in 1971 and didn't make another record until their 1978 LP *Reunion*. Their next albums were three on the Gold Castle label from 1986–90, followed by three albums for Warner Brothers through 1996. Nowadays they perform both individually and as a group, doing about 45 dates a year as Peter, Paul and Mary. They look forward to continuing their singing and work on social justice into the 21st century.

127 Raindrops Keep Fallin' on My Head

B.J. THOMAS

Scepter 12265

December 13, 1969 (7 weeks)

Writers: Burt Bacharach, Hal David

Producers: Burt Bacharach, Hal David

"Raindrops...," written for the 1969 movie hit *Butch Cassidy and the Sundance Kid*, went through three drafts before Hal David was satisfied with the lyrics. He and Burt Bacharach had Ray Stevens in mind to do the song originally, but circumstances prevented that from happening.

"I should have cut 'Raindrops [Keep Falling on My Head],'" said Stevens. "I should have known with the talent involved and that it was for a major movie that it was going to be a winner. I just had my feet in the wrong place. I had just spent endless hours in the studio doing 'Sunday Morning Coming Down,'" Stevens recalled. He was so sure that song would be a hit that he turned down "Raindrops Keep Falling on My Head" for fear of competition in airplay for the songs. Much to Stevens' chagrin, "Sunday Morning Coming Down" only went to #55 country and #81 pop in late 1969 while "Raindrops..." soared to #1 AC and pop, staying atop the latter for four weeks starting January 3, 1970. Luckily for Stevens, he later had a big hit of his own [see 133—"Everything Is Beautiful"].

B.J. Thomas was not the second choice for the song either. Bobby Vinton claimed in his autobiography that he was offered the tune but wanted too much money to do it. Regardless, Thomas was thrilled to do it, having admired David and Bacharach for years. "It was great," he said. "Those guys are some of the greatest composers of all time. It was maybe the highlight of my recording career."

But doing "Raindrops..." was not easy when the tune first was cut to use in the film. "I had just done a series of one-nighters over two weeks in the Midwest and my voice was shot," he said. "I just barely squeaked through the movie version." He laughed when he recalled that one movie executive praised his work in the first screening, guessing that his scratchy vocal was an intentional effort to approximate how Paul Newman would sound singing in the film!

Six weeks later, Thomas was in better vocal shape when he did a stronger version of the song in the studio. At the same session, a Herb Alpertesque horn fadeout was added to end the tune. The whole effort made "Raindrops..." his biggest hit, although Barbara Mason got some action in the middle of 1970 when her cover went to #38 R&B and bubbled under at #112.

"Raindrops..." won the Oscar for Best Song, and Bacharach won one for Best Original Score for his work on *Butch Cassidy*. At the Grammys, "Raindrops..." earned nominations for Song of the Year, Best Contemporary Song, and Best Contemporary Male Vocal Performance, while the *Butch Cassidy* soundtrack won for Best Original Score Written for a Motion Picture or a TV Special. And even the man who rejected the tune had praise for it. As Ray Stevens told this author, "You couldn't have sung it better than B.J."

128 Without Love (There Is Nothing)

TOM JONES

Parrot 40045

January 31, 1970 (1 week)

Writer: Danny Small

Producer: Peter Sullivan

"My songs all have one thing in common," Tom Jones told Digby Diehl in *TV Guide*. "They're all very big songs, very loud songs. Every song I do in the act is like the closer. I've got to rip it to shreds. I've got to get inside each song and tear it apart."

Jones certainly sounded like he did that with his remake of "Without Love (There Is Nothing)." The tune was first a hit for Clyde McPhatter in 1957, who took it to #4 R&B and #19 pop. Later remakes to chart were by Ray Charles in 1963 (#15 R&B and #29 pop), and Oscar Toney, Jr. in 1968 (#47 R&B and #90 pop). Jones got to #1 AC and #40 R&B chart with his version, plus peaked at #5 pop the weeks of January 31 and February 7, 1970. It was his highest-charting pop song since "What's New Pussycat?" reached #3 on the Hot 100 on July 31 and August 7, 1965, and only one song afterward did better—"She's a Lady," which hit #2 pop on March 20, 1971.

The success Jones enjoyed on the charts was no doubt in part due to the exposure he got on his weekly TV series. *This Is Tom Jones*, seen on ATV in England where he taped it, ran on the ABC-TV network from February 7, 1969 through January 15, 1971, and aired in 32 countries in 1970. Though it contained his trademark bumping and grinding to his music, a habit which Jones said developed when he had to conduct a band behind him while singing, the variety show was somewhat more restrained than his concerts, where women were already throwing their keys and underwear to him in unabashed adoration. Still, the very existence of Jones' weekly TV showcase vexed critics who felt he was all posture and had little talent vocally.

Jones conceded that the critics were right to some extent. "I still don't sing technically proper, except something like 'Delilah' with long notes, and pretty controlled," he told Diehl. "It's how far you push your voice, you've got to know your limits." But as he told Mike Hennessey in *Billboard* later in 1970, "I think my singing has become more grown-up, more mature. There is more light and shade in what I do than there used to be."

For whatever reason, Jones' singing alone must have had appeal with AC radio programmers at least, for after "Without Love (There Is Nothing)" he racked up his third consecutive #1 AC hit. For more details, see 134—"Daughter of Darkness."

129 I'll Never Fall in Love Again

DIONNE WARWICK

Scepter 12273

February 7, 1970 (3 weeks)

Writers: Hal David (words), Burt Bacharach (music)

Producers: Burt Bacharach, Hal David

The recording triumvirate of Dionne Warwick, Hal David, and Burt Bacharach, which lasted from 1962 to 1971, brought all three great critical and commercial success with AC, pop, and R&B audiences. "We were known at the time as the triangle marriage that worked," joked Warwick about her association with the music writers and producers. The dynamite combination of Warkwick's exquisite phrasing and the adventurous stylings of David and Bacharach was fully in evidence on her debut solo single with them, "Don't Make Me Over," which hit hit #21 pop and #5 R&B in 1963. A year later, "Anyone Who Had a Heart," her first AC single, peaked at #2.

Warwick had two more #2 AC entries in the 1960s, "Theme From *The Valley of the Dolls*" in 1968 and "This Girl's in Love With You" in 1969, both of which held their position for four weeks. She finally cracked the top with a Bacharach-David composition which was not designed for her to sing.

In 1968 Bacharach and David worked on a musical version of the 1960 Oscar-winning movie *The Apartment* called *Promises, Promises*. Warwick released the title song as a single late in 1968, and it hit #7 AC, #19 pop, and #47 R&B. Another song in the show was "I'll Never Fall in Love Again." Bacharach told Paul Zollo in *Songwriters on Songwriting* that "I'll Never Fall in Love Again" was the quickest song he wrote with David and it came to him when he was hospitalized for pneumonia (as an in-joke, pneumonia was mentioned in the lyrics).

Warwick said the song was written for *Promises, Promises* while the show was already in previews in Boston. To promote the show, jazz great Ella Fitzgerald released "I'll Never Fall in Love Again" as a single. It bombed, so Bacharach and David offered it to their favorite artist.

"I thought they were a little bit left of the line. I mean, how did you cover Ella Fitzgerald?" said Warwick. But she did it, and the song became identified with her in America, making #6 pop the week of February 7, 1970, as well as #1 AC and #17 R&B. There had been earlier efforts on the tune, including Johnny Mathis (#35 AC) and even Bacharach himself (#18 AC, #93 pop), both in 1969, but neither approached Warwick's success. In England, however, Bobbie Gentry took the tune to #1 the week of October 18, 1969.

Warwick saw *Promises, Promises* both in previews and on Broadway. "I thought it was exciting," she said of Bacharach and David's work. But she decided against doing the musical because "At that moment in my life, I knew I was not ready for the exposure in that field." She certainly was confident vocalizing, however, as "I'll Never Fall in Love Again" won her a Grammy for Best Contemporary Pop Female Vocal Performance. One year earlier, "I'll Never Fall in Love Again" also got a Grammy nomination for Song of the Year.

130 Bridge Over Troubled Water
SIMON AND GARFUNKEL

Columbia 45079

February 28, 1970 (6 weeks)

Writer: Paul Simon

Producers: Paul Simon, Art Garfunkel, Roy Halee

In the summer of 1969, Paul Simon strummed his guitar and wrote two verses of what would become one of his most famous compositions, "Bridge Over Troubled Water," while his singing partner Art Garfunkel acted in the film *Catch-22*. "I knew the minute I wrote 'Like a bridge over troubled water I will lay me down' that I had a very clear image," Simon recalled to Joe Smith in *Off the Record*. "The whole verse was set up to hit that melody line. With certain songs you just know it."

Garfunkel asked Simon to write another verse for the tune. Simon complied, but felt it was not as strong as his previous lyrics. Nonetheless, the part which starts "Sail on silver girl" before the chorus remained in the final record. The instruments were recorded when Garfunkel added his soaring tenor in the studio shortly after Christmas of 1969.

When Simon and Garfunkel presented their album to Columbia Records President Clive Davis, they asked him what song he thought should be the first single. "It just has to be 'Bridge Over Troubled Water,'" Davis recalled saying in his memoirs *Clive: Inside the Record Business*, which Davis wrote with James Willwerth. The selection surprised Simon and Garfunkel, who had believed he would choose "Cecilia" as the initial 45. Davis wrote that he told them if "Bridge Over Troubled Water" hit, it could become a classic. And it did.

"Bridge Over Troubled Water" ruled at #1 for six weeks simultaneously on the AC and pop charts. The tune swept the 1970 Grammy Awards too, winning statuettes for Record of the Year, Song of the Year, and Best Contemporary Song, and the LP named after it won Album of the Year.

The next year Aretha Franklin won a Grammy for Best Rhythm and Blues Female Vocal Performance for her version of "Bridge Over Troubled Water" which went to #1 R&B for two weeks plus reached #6 pop and #40 AC. A few months prior to that, Buck Owens released a rendition that hit #9 country and bubbled under at #119. In 1979 Linda Clifford took her cover to #41 pop and #49 R&B, and a decade later the Dramatics' version peaked at #93 R&B.

With the possible exception of Franklin's record, the covers of "Bridge Over Troubled Water" have long been forgotten in favor of the original by Simon and Garfunkel. It is consistently ranked as one of the best pop singles of all time by listeners and critics, and still gets heavy airplay as an "oldie." Due to creative tensions, the duo broke up shortly after its release, but did do a few temporary reunions, one of which resulted in "My Little Town" in 1975 [see 279].

131 Let It Be
THE BEATLES

Apple 2764

April 11, 1970 (4 weeks)

Writers: John Lennon, Paul McCartney

Producer: George Martin

Remarkably, the most successful group on *Billboard*'s Hot 100 and Top LPs charts notched only three entries on the AC chart during the years they recorded together. In fact, those three came as the Beatles were dissolving. The first was "Something," which peaked at #17 in late 1969. The last was "The Long and Winding Road," which climbed to #2 in mid-1970. Between them was "Let It Be," a single released as John Lennon, Paul McCartney, George Harrison, and Ringo Starr were going their separate ways.

Like most tunes with a joint author credit of Lennon and McCartney, "Let It Be" actually was written by just one of them. In this case it was McCartney in honor of his late mother Mary, who is mentioned in the lyrics. McCartney sang lead and played piano, Lennon and Harrison provided harmony vocal and instrumental backup, and Starr was drummer. Joining them at organ was Billy Preston. They began recording the tune on January 25, 1969, in Apple Studios in London, then completed it in nine takes six days later. Overdubbing took place April 30, 1969, and again on January 4, 1970, with the latter resulting in two different mixes of the song, with one used for the single and the other on the *Let It Be* LP.

At first, the Beatles could not agree on whether to release both LP and single. Harrison suggested they let veteran producer Phil Spector work on the tracks. Spector added orchestrations which horrified producer George Martin, according to *The Beatles Recording Sessions* by Mark Lewisohn. "And I know [McCartney] was particularly upset with 'Let It Be' and 'The Long and Winding Road,' with all of the strings and choirs," Martin said. Engineer Peter Bown concurred with that assessment to Lewisohn: "We got the remixes done to the satisfaction of those concerned and the album came out. It had my name on it, the only one that did. . . .The only problem was that it was the worst of the lot."

Americans disagreed, as "Let It Be" the single topped the AC and pop charts on April 11, 1970, staying atop the latter for two weeks, and *Let It Be* the LP led off the album chart for four weeks starting June 13, 1970. In 1971 Joan Baez returned "Let It Be" to the AC chart at #5. In 1987 McCartney was part of the benefit group Ferry Aid who covered the tune to help dependents of the Zeebruggee Ferry disaster on March 6 of that year, where nearly 200 people died. Ferry Aid's "Let It Be" went to #1 for three weeks in 1987 in Britain (the Beatles' original had stopped at #2).

Incidentally, the Beatles did make the AC chart with a few singles released after their breakup (e.g., "Got to Get You Into My Life," which hit #9 in 1976). And all of the "Fab Four" except Lennon made it to the AC top in later years as solo artists.

132 For the Love of Him

BOBBI MARTIN

United Artists 50602

May 9, 1970 (2 weeks)

Writers: Bobbi Martin, Al Mortimer

Producer: Henry Jerome

Barbara Anne Martin, born in Brooklyn, New York, on November 29, 1943 and raised in Baltimore, Maryland, had her AC and pop chart debuts in 1965 with "Don't Forget I Still Love You" (#2 AC, #19 pop). She made the AC chart later that year with "I Can't Stop Thinking of You" (#9 AC, #46 pop), "I Love You So" (#16 AC, #70 pop), "I Don't Want to Live (Without Your Love)" (#21 AC, #115 bubbling under), and "There Are No Rules" (#29 AC). But after "Oh, Lonesome Me" made #64 country in 1966, she was off the charts until "For the Love of Him" in late 1969.

Producing the hit was Henry Jerome, who said, "Originally I discovered Bobbi when I was an A&R man with Decca on the Coral label." Jerome left Decca to do A&R for United Artists in the late 1960s, and "When Bobbi's contract was up at Coral, I signed her over to UA."

To generate enthusiasm for her there, he had her perform at a music industry convention in Nashville. Delays kept her off until 2 a.m., but Jerome noted, "She broke the house up. They gave her a standing ovation." The appearance con-

vinced UA officials to let Jerome record an album with her in the spring of 1969 in Nashville, albeit with what Jerome termed a "big band backup" playing the music.

The album was nearly complete when Michael Lipton, UA's vice president of sales, heard a tune Martin co-wrote called "For the Love of Him." "You've got to put it in," he told Jerome. The producer heeded the advice and got Chet Atkins and other top Nashville session musicians to play on the record. Jerome said that session consisted of "Just the singers, the rhythm, and Bobbi," but he took the tape and added orchestral backing in New York.

Lipton put the single out the week before Thanksgiving 1969, and Jerome said it sold at least 30,000 copies despite getting airplay only on AC stations at first. Then in January 1970, UA's ownership company Transamerica bought Liberty Records. When Liberty's Philadelphia promo man, now absorbed into UA, heard the song, he told Jerome, "I think that's a hit record" and pushed it in his market. It subsequently spread throughout the country, making #1 AC and #13 pop by the spring of 1970.

But Jerome left UA when the company moved to Los Angeles, and without the UA-Jerome combination, Martin had no other hits. "She got married, had a child, the family thing took over, they lived in Dallas," Jerome said. He still talked with her by phone some in 1998. Jerome said he liked working with Martin and thought highly of her hit. "It's every woman's story in the world," he said. He also was flabbergasted in 1998 when British singer Shirley Bassey cut "For the Love of Him" on a CD package. "I wanted the thing and I called the importer, and it's just magnificent," he said.

Left to right:
producer Henry Jerome,
engineer Selby Coffen,
and Bobbi Martin

133 Everything Is Beautiful

RAY STEVENS

Barnaby 2011

May 23, 1970 (3 weeks)

Writer: Ray Stevens

Producer: Ray Stevens

Ray Stevens said, "'[I think] everything is beautiful in its own way' is an old Indian proverb, but I could be wrong," about his #1 pop and AC hit. His first AC entry, it hit #1 pop the week of May 30, 1970, and stayed there for two weeks and also went #39 country.

Stevens needed a theme song for his TV variety hour which served as the summer replacement for *The Andy Williams Show* in 1970. As most of his songs that had hit the Hot 100 since his debut in 1961 were novelties, he needed a straightforward tune. But creating one was not easy.

"I wrote songs in the basement and sort of chained myself down to the piano for three days," he said. After at least 20 efforts, he came across the "everything is beautiful" concept. It took him an hour to complete the tune. Then, after three tries in the studio, he finally recorded a take of the song which pleased him.

For the background chorus, Stevens used children from Oak Hill Elementary from Nashville. "I wanted to put in the kids singing, as one of my daughters was in the second grade and the other was in kindergarten," he said. "We gathered them up and put their voices in a portable recorder."

He won a Grammy for Best Male Contemporary Vocal for the song, but Glen Campbell accepted the award at the ceremony as Stevens was in Australia at the time. The record also got him Grammy nominations for Song of the Year, Best Contemporary Song, and Best Arrangement Accompanying a Vocalist.

There were over 200 covers of "Everything Is Beautiful." One, by Jake Hess, won a Grammy for Best Sacred Performance, Musical. When asked if he thought his song has religious overtones, he said, "I guess you could say in some ways it's inspirational. But it's more an explanation of logic. It's a song that tries to clarify how people look at things."

Born Ray Ragsdale in Clarksdale, Georgia, on January 24, 1939, Stevens hit the AC and pop charts with novelty and "straight" singles in the 1970s. His last entry on both, "I Need Your Help Barry Manilow," went to #11 AC and #49 pop in 1979. He made the country chart with novelties through the 1980s.

In the summers of 1991, 1992, and 1993 Stevens headlined a theater in Branson, Missouri, but sold it due to the pressures of doing two shows a day six days a week at the facility. He concentrated on "family matters" during the mid-1990s and avoided touring. In 1997 he released the LP *Ray Stevens' Christmas Through a Different Window*. He said future recordings will be novelty songs as "I think that's how people perceive me and, let's face it, you've got to go with the flow."

134 Daughter of Darkness

TOM JONES

Parrot 40048

June 13, 1970 (1 week)

Writers: Les Reed, Geoff Stephens

Producer: Peter Sullivan

In 1970 the career of Tom Jones was at its peak. In addition to releasing hit records and having his own TV show, Jones embarked on a tour of America which had him appear before more people and gross more money than any other group in show business history, including the Beatles. To keep himself in check, he brought his wife Linda and their son along with him on tour, but Mrs. Jones did not enjoy watching her husband perform the way other women did. As Tom told John Bardin in *Coronet* at the time, "She doesn't like to be with everyone else in the audience, seeing my hips move around. She knows what's going through other women's minds, and she'd rather not be there."

But money was money, so Jones kept up the pace and scored his third consecutive #1 AC hit with "Daughter of Darkness," which also made #13 pop in the summer of 1970. Believe it or not, singing background on the tune was a young Elton John.

Jones barely missed the AC top again with his next release, "I (Who Have Nothing)," which hit #2 AC for three weeks and #14 pop. The record after that, "Can't Stop Loving You," also did well, making #3 AC and #25 pop by the start of 1971. When Peter Sullivan left after six successful years of records that had started with 1965's "It's Not Unusual," Jones' manager Gordon Mills replaced him. Mills' first outing with Jones went well, as "She's a Lady" became a #2 pop hit and #4 AC entry in the spring of 1971. But around that time Jones' TV show in America was canceled by ABC, and the reduced exposure was probably responsible for a slowdown in entries for Jones. In 1974–75 only AC entries were "Somethin' 'Bout You Baby I Like" at #23 and "Pledging My Love," which stalled at #19.

Sensing they needed to go in another direction, Jones and Sullivan worked on a country tune. "Say You'll Stay Until Tomorrow" went to #1 country the week of February 26, 1977, as well as #3 AC and #15 pop. It seemed to be a comeback hit, yet Jones learned to his regret that doing country songs meant some people thought he only could or should do that genre of music, and he had no crossover success on the Hot 100 after "Say You'll Stay Until Tomorrow" for more than a decade. On the AC chart, he managed three meager follow-ups, ending with "Darlin'" at #54 in 1981.

Jones then shocked nearly everyone with a bombastic version of Prince's funky hit "Kiss" in late 1989. It hit #31 pop but led to no further Hot 100 entries. In the 1990s, Jones went back to what he had been doing throughout much of the 1980s—performing at Las Vegas and a few other clubs. Still pumping and grinding, he was also still looking good.

135 The Wonder of You

ELVIS PRESLEY

RCA 47-9835

June 20, 1970 (1 week)

Writer: Baker Knight

Producers: Elvis Presley, Felton Jarvis

In 1958 Baker Knight wrote "The Wonder of You," which became a #25 pop entry the next year for Ray Peterson. A rerelease of Peterson's record in 1964 hit #70 pop. Five years later, John Davidson did a version which went to #38 AC. It may have been one of those versions or another which Elvis Presley heard and decided to do in his stage show in Las Vegas when he appeared at the International Hotel from January 26 through February 23, 1970.

"I think it was Elvis's idea, because most of the time it *was* his idea," laughed Glen D. Hardin, who did the arrangement for Presley's version and played on the piano for the track. Hardin was not with Presley when the singer made his debut at the International Hotel in the summer of 1969, but he was there six months later. Hardin thought he was joining the band as a pianist, but found that his skills as an arranger were also in demand.

When Presley asked Hardin to do an arrangement for "The Wonder of You," Hardin had very little time to do it, as rehearsals for the show had ended and Presley and company were doing two one-hour shows almost every night. "Back in those days, there was an awful lot of stuff we'd do without rehearsal," he said. Luckily for Hardin, he only had to arrange the instrumental parts of the song and not the vocals. "Sometimes I'd sketch out a vocal part if I had ideas, but generally Elvis did everybody's singing parts," Hardin said. "He was just very, very good at it." Backing Presley on "The Wonder of You" were the Joe Guercio Orchestra, the Sweet Inspirations, the Imperials Quartet, and Millie Kirkham.

Recorded live on February 17, Presley's "The Wonder of You" reached #1 AC plus #9 pop for three weeks starting June 27, 1970, and its B-side, "Mama Liked the Roses," also received airplay in some markets. "The Wonder of You" also went to #37 country in 1970 and stayed at #1 in the United Kingdom for six weeks.

Hardin was with Presley through 1975 and recalled that while the Vegas shows later went down to a schedule of just one a day, the circus-like atmosphere for the singer and his band never died down. "It was pretty frantic," he said. "People were flying in from all over the world." But it was not just Presley fans who wanted their attention. "People would grab you. Everyone would have a song or a movie script or a gold mine for Elvis," he noted.

Presley had another #1 AC hit later in 1970, "You Don't Have to Say You Love Me" [see 141].

136 A Song of Joy

MIGUEL RIOS

A&M 1193

June 27, 1970 (2 weeks)

Writers: Orbe (words), Waldo de Los Rios (musical adaptation), Ludwig van Beethoven

Producer: Hispavox

Born in Granada, Spain, in 1944, Miguel Rios began singing at age 6 and two years later was in his school's choir. During the 1960s he pursued a professional musical career in Spain, but had little luck elsewhere until he recorded a tune based on the final movement of famed classical composer Ludvig van Beethoven's *Ninth Symphony*.

Known as "Himno a la Alegría" in Spanish and given that subtitle on the American release, "A Song of Joy" commemorated the bicentennial of Beethoven's birth. Rios collaborated on the production with conductor Waldo de Los Rios, who also served as composer of the tune. It became a hit in Spain in 1969.

When A&M officials in America received "A Song of Joy" to consider for release in the United States, they turned it down. But two A&M representatives in the company's Toronto office, Liam Mullen and Jerry La Coursière, had faith in its potential and broke it in Canada, where it became a hit. The tune's success then spread to America, where it peaked at #14 pop and #1 AC, and the record eventually sold more than 4 million copies worldwide, also topping the charts in Germany.

Flush with this success, Rios toured Canada, the United States, the United Kingdom (where "A Song of Joy" went to the top 20), and even Australia to promote his next single "Like an Eagle" in 1971. But unlike an eagle, that record did not soar anywhere near the heights of "A Song of Joy," and he went back to performing mostly in Spain.

However, Beethoven's *Ninth Symphony* was not forgotten by Apollo 100, an instrumental group of studio musicians who recorded it as a track on an album of classical compositions using modern rock sounds called *Master Pieces* in 1972. The hit single off that album was "Joy," which despite the similar name was based on Bach and not Beethoven, specifically Bach's "Jesú, Joy of Man's Desiring." "Joy" went to #2 AC for three weeks as well as #6 pop, but "Beethoven 9," the Apollo 100 adaptation of the piece which inspired "A Song of Joy," remained only on the album. It belatedly got released as a single in 1977 on the Eurogram label in America, but flopped.

Miguel Rios remained a popular recording artist nearly 30 years after the release of "A Song of Joy," not just in Spain but also in Latin America, where he toured with some other Spanish acts in the late 1990s. His label Hispavox, which had begun operations in 1955, became part of the massive EMI Records in Spain after the government became less involved in the record industry. And Waldo de Los Rios, who had a #25 AC and #67 pop entry in 1971 with his "Mozart Symphony No. 40 in G Minor," committed suicide on March 28, 1977. He was 42 years old.

137 (They Long to Be) Close to You

THE CARPENTERS

A&M 1183

July 11, 1970 (6 weeks)

Writers: Burt Bacharach, Hal David

Producer: Jack Daugherty

The first time "(They Long to Be) Close to You" appeared on a record was on the B-side of Richard Chamberlain's #12 AC and #42 pop entry of 1963, "Blue Guitar." Dionne Warwick cut the tune again in 1965, but deejays preferred the other side of that single, "Here I Am," as well, and it went to #11 AC and #65 pop. The tune might have been forgotten forever had it not been for Burt Bacharach's regard for the Carpenters.

Karen Carpenter (born March 2, 1950) and her brother Richard (born October 15, 1946) originally recorded as part of the Richard Carpenter Trio; Wes Jacobs rounded out the threesome on bass and tuba while Richard played piano and Karen was on drums. The trio was together from 1965–67 and in 1966 had a recording contract with RCA. Karen and Richard then became part of Spectrum, which lasted a year, before trying to succeed by themselves. In April 1969 A&M Records signed them, and before the end of the year their cover of the Beatles' "Ticket to Ride" debuted on the charts. It peaked at #19 AC and #54 pop.

Burt Bacharach liked the record, and he eventually contacted the Carpenters about doing a medley of his tunes for a benefit on February 26, 1970. A&M's co-owner Herb Alpert suggested the Carpenters try "(They Long to Be) Close to You," but after working up an arrangement Richard decided not to include it in the medley. But prodding from Alpert and others encouraged the Carpenters to record the song on their own. It made #1 AC and pop, topping the latter for four weeks staring July 25, 1970.

"I'm very grateful to Richard Carpenter for making that record the way that they heard it," Bacharach told Paul Zollo in *Songwriters on Songwriting*. "Because the way that I heard it was very different and not very good. I made the first few records of it with the wrong groove, wrong feel. Richard came in and nailed it."

The Carpenters' "Close to You" (Richard was the one who put the "They Long to Be" part in parentheses) earned a Grammy for Best Contemporary Vocal Performance by a Duo, Group or Chorus plus a nomination for Record of the Year. They also won the Grammy for Best New Artist.

Several other artists redid "Close to You" over the next 20 years, including jazz guitarist Gabor Szabo (#40 AC, 1971), Jerry Butler featuring Brenda Lee Eager (#91 pop and #6 R&B, 1972), B.T. Express (#82 pop and #31 R&B, 1976), and Gwen Guthrie (#69 R&B, 1987). In 1992 George LaMond used parts of the song for backing for his single "Baby, I Believe in You," which hit #66 pop. But most people associated "Close to You" with the Carpenters. It became the first of an incredible 15 #1 AC hits for the duo, with the next being "We've Only Just Begun" [see 140].

138 I Just Can't Help Believing

B.J. THOMAS

Scepter 12283

August 22, 1970 (1 week)

Writers: Cynthia Weil (words), Barry Mann (music)

Producer: Chips Moman

B.J. Thomas followed his monster hit "Raindrops Keep Falling on My Head" [see 127] with "Everybody's Out of Town." That single fared moderately well, going to #3 AC and #26 pop in the spring of 1970, although Thomas conceded some might have viewed it as a disappointment commercially since it failed to equal "Raindrops. . . ." "It was a good song, maybe ahead of its time," he said of "Everybody's Out of Town."

There was no disputing the impact of "I Just Can't Help Believing," however. The tune brought him back to the pop top 10, peaking at #9, and became the second of his four #1 AC hits. It pleased Thomas as well, since he described "I Just Can't Help Believing" as "one of my favorites." As he recalled, "I went back to Memphis to record a couple of songs that Barry Mann and Cynthia Weil sent down. One was 'I Just Can't Help Believing' and the other was 'Here You Come Again.'" The latter was a #1 country, #2 AC, and #3 pop hit for Dolly Parton in late 1977, the same year the version by Thomas came out. Though he enjoyed the former tune, Thomas said it took a little time in the studio to lay down the tracks. "It took two days to get it right," he said.

Though he did not make the country chart with the tune, "I Just Can't Help Believing" did make the listings in versions by David Frizzell in 1970 (#36) and David Rogers in 1974 (#59).

In some ways, "I Just Can't Help Believing" is an appropriate phrase to describe Thomas' AC career up to when the song became a hit. Though his vocal sound had been smooth ever since he cracked the Hot 100 in 1966 with a #8 remake of Hank Williams' "I'm So Lonesome I Could Cry," he did not enter the AC chart until "It's Only Love" went to #37 in mid-1969. Somehow, such Thomas favorites as "The Eyes of a New York Woman" (#28 pop in 1968) and "Hooked on a Feeling" (#5 pop in 1969), which continue to get airplay today, failed to make the AC cut.

B.J. Thomas actually came onto the pop charts billed as the lead singer of a band called the Triumphs, of which he had been a member since his high school days. He was born in Hugo, Oklahoma, on August 7, 1942, and raised in Rosenberg, Texas.

In the wake of "I Just Can't Help Believing," Thomas became a frequent visitor to the AC and pop charts over the next two years. His simultaneous 1971 pop/AC entries in chronological order were "Most of All" (#2 AC and #38 pop), "No Love At All" (#4 AC and #16 pop), "Mighty Clouds of Joy" (#8 AC and #34 pop), and "Long Ago Tomorrow" (#13 AC and #61 pop), but his next #1 entry, "Rock and Roll Lullaby," came in 1972 [see 167].

139 Snowbird

ANNE MURRAY

Capitol 2738

August 29, 1970 (6 weeks)

Writer: Gene MacLellan

Producer: Brian Ahern

It was impossible to listen to an AC, pop, or country radio station throughout most of the 1970s and 1980s without hearing an Anne Murray song sometime during the programming day. She amassed an impressive list of hits on all three charts, and nearly all of her eight #1 AC hits either topped or came close to topping the country and pop listings. But it all had to begin someplace, and for Murray that someplace was a little number called "Snowbird."

Born in Springhill, Nova Scotia, Canada, on June 20, 1945, Morna Anne Murray gained notice in Canada for singing on TV programs. She began recording first for the ARC label in 1969, but her initial entry onto the charts in America did not come until the following year, after she met songwriter Gene MacLellan. "I was doing a television show in Halifax, Nova Scotia, and he came down to guest on the show," recalled Murray. Her husband told her to listen to his melodies. "Well, I was just stunned," noted Murray, "because I never heard original material. All the singing I was doing were other people's songs."

MacLellan gave her a tape of his songs, and Murray and her family loved what they heard. So Murray recorded "Snowbird," and she and Capitol record executives agreed it should be released on her first single for the company—as the B-side. "Just Biding My Time" was the tune everyone expected would be a big hit.

"Somebody in Cleveland flipped it. I mean, what are the chances of flipping a single by a new artist?" noted Murray. But Clevelanders loved it and the song generated increasing airplay which led to success in other markets. Still, Murray had her doubts about how the record would do. "I said, 'Oh, well, it won't do anything,' but when it hit the 40s on the chart, I realized I was wrong," Murray noted. "Snowbird" eventually peaked at #8 pop and #10 country as well as #1 AC and went on to become a million seller in the United States alone. In addition, "Snowbird" earned Murray two Grammy nominations, for Female Contemporary Vocal Performance and Best New Artist of 1970.

Even though it's been nearly three decades since it became a hit, Murray has found that "Snowbird" remains a popular tune for her to sing in concert. "People from the audience request that all night long," she said. "It's amazing to me."

Murray recorded another MacLellan song, "Put Your Hand in the Hand," but the Canadian quintet Ocean released it as a single a few months ahead of her in 1971, going to #4 AC and #2 pop, and her version managed only #67 country. She had nothing to worry about, however, for the following year she discovered another writer who would put her on top again—Kenny Loggins [see 188—"Danny's Song"].

140 We've Only Just Begun

THE CARPENTERS

A&M 1217

October 10, 1970 (7 weeks)

Writers: Paul Williams (words), Roger Nichols (music)

Producer: Jack Daugherty

If ever there was a prophetic title for a song, "We've Only Just Begun" was it for the Carpenters. The smash single, the follow-up to "(They Long to Be) Close to You" [see 137], proved the duo would be no one-hit wonder group. It spent the longest number of weeks at #1 on the AC chart of any of their hits, plus had four weeks at #2 pop behind the Jackson Five's "I'll Be There" starting October 31, 1970.

"We've Only Just Begun" was also a fitting description of its songwriting team, Paul Williams and Roger Nichols, who had been working together and on separate projects at A&M Records for two years. Williams was an unemployed actor when he came to A&M ("I always said I showed up at A&M Records in a stolen car," he joked) and wrote songs with Biff Rose before Nichols needed a lyricist. "We've Only Just Begun" was Williams and Nichols' first top 10 pop and #1 AC hit.

"Almost everything we wrote was recorded—album cuts, B-sides—but not single material," Williams recalled of the pre–"We've Only Just Begun" days. Their lucky break came when a former songwriting partner of Nichols', Tony Asher, had an unlucky break and injured himself during a skiing accident. Asher had just been asked to work on a tune for a commercial, but given his predicament he let Williams and Nichols do the job instead.

The song was for Crocker Bank of California, which wanted to attract young couples as clients. The bank's selling slogan was "You've got a long way to go. We'd like to help you to get there. Crocker Bank." Using that theme, Williams said, "We sat down and wrote the first verse of the commercial and finished it as a complete song just in case anyone wanted to record it."

As it turned out, there were two "anyones" for the song. One was the Carpenters, who knew Williams and Nichols' work because their song "I Kept On Loving You" was the B-side of "(They Long to Be) Close to You." The other was Mark Lindsay, lead singer of Paul Revere and the Raiders. Lindsay also pursued a solo singing career in 1969, which led to eight AC entries, the biggest being "And the Grass Won't Pay No Mind" at #5 in 1970. Lindsay recorded "We've Only Just Begun" before the Carpenters did, but their version left his in the dust. Ironically, Lindsay opened for the Carpenters in one of their early tours and co-starred with them in a summer series on NBC-TV in 1971 titled *Make Your Own Kind of Music.*

"We've Only Just Begun" became the first of three compositions by Williams and Nichols performed by the Carpenters to reach #1 AC. The next was "Rainy Days and Mondays" [see 151].

141 You Don't Have to Say You Love Me

ELVIS PRESLEY

RCA 47-9916

November 28, 1970 (1 week)

Writers: Vicki Wickham and Simon Napier-Bell (words–English), V. Pallavicini and P. Donaggio (music)

Producer: Not Known

"You Don't Have to Say You Love Me" was originally an entrant in the 1965 Italian San Remo Song Contest as "Io che non vivo (senzate)." With new English lyrics Dusty Springfield popularized the tune and reached #8 AC and #4 pop in 1966. The next year Arthur Prysock got to #120 bubbling under with his rendition. In 1968 the Four Sonics took their effort to #89 pop and #32 R&B.

Then on June 6, 1970 in Nashville, Elvis Presley recorded his version of "You Don't Have to Say You Love Me" with a large number of backing musicians and singers, including the Imperials and the Nashville Edition vocal groups. James Burton, bandleader for Presley since 1969, said he believed Presley himself had picked the tune to cut as a record and was influenced as to how it should sound by the group he had on stage with him in Las Vegas in 1969 and 1970.

"I remember that Elvis was really digging the big orchestra sound, and he was getting into the pop sound then," Burton said. The bandleader noted Presley particularly loved the horns and string sections he heard in concert. "He really enjoyed. . .the power he got from the orchestra. . . .He went through that time period where the big band thing of the horns made him feel good on stage."

Burton, who was also Presley's lead guitarist, picked many of the musicians who were Presley's backing band from 1969–76, including bassist Joe Osborne, pianist Glen D. Hardin, and drummer Ronnie Tutt.

Presley's "You Don't Have to Say You Love Me" just missed the pop top 10, hitting #11 and sharing the position there with its flip side, "Patch It Up," plus made #56 country. In 1977 the Floaters covered it and made #28 R&B.

Presley did surprisingly well on the AC chart in the early 1970s following "You Don't Have to Say You Love Me," usually better than he did on the Hot 100. He got a pair of #2 singles on the chart in 1971, "I Really Don't Want to Know" (#21 pop) and "I'm Leavin'" (#36 pop), and a total of nine songs made the AC top 10 through the end of 1974. Additionally, some B-sides of pop hits for Elvis charted on the AC roster alone, such as "The Sound of Your Cry," the flip of "It's Only Love," which stopped at #19 in late 1971, and "It's a Matter of Time," the back side of "Burning Love," which went to #9 AC in 1972.

In 1975 Presley rode atop the AC chart one last time, with "My Boy" [see 254].

142 It's Impossible

PERRY COMO

RCA 0387

December 5, 1970 (4 weeks)

Writers: Sid Wayne (words–English),
    Armando Manzanero (music)

Producer: Ernie Altschuler

B y 1970 it was going on 12 years since Perry Como's last top 10 pop hit, 1958's "Kewpie Doll," which hit #6. In fact, its flip side "Dance Only With Me," which reached #12, was the last Como single to crack the pop top 20. The singer remained a familiar face on television and kept constantly releasing new material, so he had not disappeared from public view. It was not impossible for "It's Impossible" to break the trend, but according to Como's longtime manager Mickey Glass, it did take some doing.

"They released 'It's Impossible,' and it did OK, but disc jockeys kept playing it," said Glass. Once the tune topped the AC chart, RCA got ready to release the follow-up "I Think of You." But "It's Impossible" gained more airplay on pop stations following its AC triumph, and "All of a sudden 'It's Impossible' became a really big song," Glass said. The record peaked at #10 on the Hot 100 the week of January 23, 1971, more than four months after its release.

"It's Impossible" was originally sung in Spanish in 1968 (the music was by Armando Manzanero, a singer/songwriter from Mexico). The soul group the New Birth took their rendition of "It's Impossible" to #52 pop and #12 R&B in late 1971. Como did the song along with five others submitted to him by producer Ernie Altschuler, according to Glass.

Como's version earned him a Grammy nomination for Best Male Pop Vocal Performance, which he lost to James Taylor for "You've Got a Friend" [see 153]. It was his first Grammy nomination since he won the first award given for Best Male Vocal Performance in 1958 for "Catch a Falling Star." The tune also gave him his first top 10 hit in the United Kingdom in 11 years when it went to #4 in 1971. (His previous hit there had been "Delaware" at #3 in 1960.)

Such longevity in the music industry is a rather rare phenomenon. Explaining why Como could continue to be so popular over the years, Glass said, "His appeal is his relaxed attitude, and the way he treats people. If someone comes up to him, he'll talk to them for an hour."

The follow-up to "It's Impossible," "I Think of You," went to #5 AC and #53 pop. The returns continued to diminish when the next Como single, "My Days of Loving You," managed to go only to #31 AC while not making the Hot 100 in late 1971. The 45 after that, however, would become Como's third #1 AC hit following "Stop! And Think It Over" [see 88] and "It's Impossible." [See 193—"And I Love You So."]

One Less Bell to Answer
THE 5TH DIMENSION

Bell 940

January 2, 1971 (1 week)

Writers: Hal David (words), Burt Bacharach (music)

Producer: Bones Howe

"One Less Bell to Answer," one of the Fifth Dimension's biggest hits, peaked at #2 pop for two weeks starting December 26, 1970, behind George Harrison's "My Sweet Lord," plus #4 R&B and #1 AC. The inspiration, according to Hal David in Dylan Jones' *Ultra Lounge: The Lexicon of Easy Listening*, came at a dinner party he and Burt Bacharach attended in London, where the hostess said, "When you arrive, don't ring the bell, just come in. It'll make one less bell for me to answer." But Bacharach has a different version. He has said that his then-girlfriend Angie Dickinson remarked, after hearing doorbells at Bacharach's pad in London, "One less bell to answer when I get out of here." Either way, David turned the line into the story of a woman ruminating on her lover's departure from her life.

"We liked the song and we wondered, 'Why isn't Dionne [Warwick, who usually sang Bacharach and David's tunes] doing this?'" Marilyn McCoo said of the Fifth Dimension's first reaction to the tune. (Rosemary Clooney had a rendition of "One Less Bell to Answer" which went to #34 AC in 1968.)

Then while doing *Portrait*, their first LP for Bell Records after leaving Liberty's subsidiary Soul City, McCoo was hired to act and the rest of the group to appear in a TV show, *It Takes a Thief*. "We were in the process of writing the album, and we thought it would be a great way to promote 'Puppet Man,'" McCoo said, referring to a song the group performed on the show. However, as part of the plot three chords of a song were needed to break some glass and explode a bomb in a hotel room, and music from "One Less Bell to Answer" was the best choice for the job. The group had no problem with the song being used that way because, as McCoo said, "At the time, we didn't believe 'One Less Bell to Answer' would be a single."

The first single off *Portrait*, "The Declaration," sputtered to #35 AC and #64 pop. "Puppet Man" followed but reached only #31 AC and #24 pop. When "Save the Country" then made #10 AC and #27 pop, some Bell executives wanted "One Less Bell to Answer" released, but the quintet weren't sure the ballad would have wide appeal. "Then they told us about this deejay in New Orleans who really believed in the song and who had called the record company and said 'You should release this song,'" McCoo remembered. When the record hit #2 on New Orleans' local airplay chart, Bell released it as a single.

Despite her initial skepticism, McCoo was proud to have a hit with "One Less Bell to Answer." "Women have come up to me and told me it's the divorced women's national anthem," she said. She did think that the group should have gotten a Grammy nomination for the tune, but thought maybe the voters had problems deciding whether to classify the record as a soloist or group entry, given her lead vocal on it.

1971

144 Watching Scotty Grow

BOBBY GOLDSBORO

United Artists 50727

January 9, 1971 (6 weeks)

Writer: Mac Davis

Producers: Bob Montgomery, Bobby Goldsboro

Like "Honey" [see 104], "Watching Scotty Grow" was one of the few records sung by Bobby Goldsboro which he did not write. Although many fans asked him about his "son," Scotty wasn't Goldsboro's son, but the son of composer Mac Davis [see 175—"Baby, Don't Get Hooked on Me"]. Remembering the genesis of "Watching Scotty Grow," Goldsboro said that he had run into record producer Jerry Fuller in an L.A. clothing store. Fuller told Goldsboro the songs Davis was giving him were more in Goldsboro's style, so Goldsboro had Davis meet him at his hotel room to play some material for him.

One tune Goldsboro heard during that night with Davis was "Watching Scotty Grow." "I loved it," he said. "I thought it would be perfect for me." Yet an executive with United Artists expressed skepticism. "I just don't think anyone will buy a record from a father to a son," the childless man told Goldsboro. His underlings concurred, so "Watching Scotty Grow" only became a cut on Goldsboro's LP *We Gotta Start Lovin'*.

"They put it out and within two weeks, it was being played like a single," Goldsboro said. Released as a 45, "Watching Scotty Grow" went to #1 AC, #11 pop, and #7 country. He and Davis became close friends thereafter.

Goldsboro's first chart single, 1963's "Molly," hit #17 AC and #70 pop. In 1964 "See the Funny Little Clown" went to #3 AC and #9 pop. Goldsboro was a pop regular for the next nine years but did not become a similar AC favorite until after 1968's "Honey," which also made him a country chart staple. From 1972 to 1975 he hosted a TV variety series that was sold to individual stations, and his singing career began to wind down. During that period, 1973's "Summer (The First Time)" was his last pop entry at #21, and his positions on the AC and country charts were even lower. His last AC record was "Alice Doesn't Live Here Anymore" (#34 in 1981), and his last country single was "Lucy and the Stranger" (#49 in 1982).

Goldsboro, who was born in Marianna, Florida, on January 18, 1941, later moved to Alabama, where he attended Auburn. Dropping out of college after two years, he formed the Webs, a band in which he played lead guitar and which backed up Roy Orbison from 1962 to 1964. In 1962 he signed a contract with Laurie Records as a soloist. Twenty years later Goldsboro moved back to Florida, but through the rest of the '80s he also spent time in Nashville. In the early 1990s, he composed music for Burt Reynolds' CBS-TV comedy series *Evening Shade*.

"The past 10 years I've been doing children's books and videos," Goldsboro said in 1998. He was particularly busy doing music for *Swamp Critters of Lost Lagoon*, a series for the Discovery Channel. "That's the greatest outlet for a writer, because I've written 160 songs over the last three years for the show," he said. However, it's doubtful that any of them will do for him what he got from "Honey" and "Watching Scotty Grow."

145 If You Could Read My Mind

GORDON LIGHTFOOT

Reprise 0974

February 20, 1971 (1 week)

Writer: Gordon Lightfoot

Producers: Lenny Waronker, Joe Wissert

Up through the late 1960s, about the only way a Canadian artist could get a hit in the United States was to relocate to America. In the 1970s, Gordon Lightfoot became an exception to this rule, basing himself north of the U.S. border yet still collecting a fair number of hits in the States.

Lightfoot became an established name in his native Canada almost immediately after he began recording there for Chateau Records in 1962. By the late 1960s Lightfoot had gained some attention in the United States for his songwriting skills (he wrote "Early Mornin' Rain" for Peter, Paul and Mary) and for his performing talent as a vocalist and guitarist, getting a Grammy nomination in 1968 for Best Folk Performance for "Did She Mention My Name." Lightfoot credited a lot of this early attention in America to his manager Albert Grossman, who also handled Peter, Paul and Mary. "I'm sure that Albert had a lot to do with it," he said. "He was a good manager." But he had no singles make the pop or AC charts until "If You Could Read My Mind" made its debut in late 1970.

"If You Could Read My Mind" took shape during a period of several weeks in 1969 when Lightfoot composed several songs. "I was inspired to write a lot of new tunes at the time. I had a new record contract," he noted. He came up with them "over a summer vacation time in an old empty house," and remembered that "If You Could Read My Mind" hit him rather fast. "Sometimes if you can get a chord progression going and a title, it can come pretty quickly," he said.

But any songwriter can tell you that a well-written tune is likely to go nowhere if it doesn't have the proper promotion. "If You Can Read My Mind" was out on the market for eight months before Ron Saul, head of promotions at Warner Records, pushed airplay for it in Seattle. The song became popular there, and subsequently spread across America. Lightfoot admitted that at the time he hadn't been aware of the gap between release and promotion ("We spent actually quite a bit of time finding out exactly what took place," he said), but he was grateful nonetheless for finally getting a hit in the United States.

"If You Could Read My Mind" went to #5 pop for three weeks starting February 20, 1971, in addition to #1 AC. Lightfoot received his second Grammy nomination for "If You Could Read My Mind" for Best Male Pop Vocal Performance. Following that, Lightfoot had a few lean years in America but came back strong in 1974, when he had his second #1 AC hit. For more details, see 221—"Sundown."

146 For All We Know
THE CARPENTERS

A&M 1243

February 27, 1971 (3 weeks)

Writers: Robb Wilson and Arthur James (words),
  Fred Karlin (music)

Producer: Jack Daugherty

"As 'We've Only Just Begun' had peaked, Karen and I were concerned with what song should follow as a single," recounted Richard Carpenter in the liner notes to the Carpenters' 1991 anthology *From the Top*. "We had been touring almost constantly and, as a result, I had little time to be listening to, or writing, new material. "We had arrived in Toronto to open the show for Engelbert Humperdinck and the night before opening our manager, Sherwin Bash, suggested that we relax by seeing a movie. He recommended *Lovers and Other Strangers*. Great suggestion. As we were to discover, 'For All We Know' was written for this film. Karen and I loved it immediately and recorded it upon returning home."

In the movie, the vocalist was the little-known Larry Meredith, whose version did not get released. As for the song's writers, Robb Wilson and Arthur James were pseudonyms for Arthur Griffin and Robb Royer of the group Bread. According to David Gates of that group, the two had to use pseudonyms on the record because "They were under contract, and this was outside the realm of what they could use their names for."

"For All We Know" peaked at #3 pop the week of April 3, 1971, behind the Temptations' "Just My Imagination (Running Away With Me)" at #1 and Janis Joplin's "Me and Bobby McGee" at #2. It also won the Oscar for Best Song, although it was Petula Clark and not the Carpenters who performed it at the Academy Awards ceremony.

Following the success of this song, the Carpenters scored the next year by singing another Oscar-nominated tune, "Bless the Beasts and Children," from the movie of the same name. This time the film's producer and director Stanley Kramer asked the Carpenters to do the song on the soundtrack and they agreed. As a single it reached #26 AC and #67 pop in early 1972 as the B-side to "Superstar" [see 157].

Given these two successes, it may seem odd that the Carpenters did not do more music from films. The reason may be the sour experience they had when performing "Bless the Beasts and Children" at the Academy Awards. "We were badly treated at the 1972 Oscars," Richard told Joyce Haber in *The Los Angeles Times*. He claimed he had to play on a "tacky, whitewashed piano on rollers," and Karen added, "We paid to bring in a piano ourselves, and then they wanted to paint it silver." Richard noted that "There was no one to do makeup. I had to do my own," and Karen concluded, "We just walked out when it was over." They were asked to sing "The Way We Were" [see 208] at the 1974 ceremony, but remembering what had happened before, they turned the offer down.

Thankfully they did not give up doing music on record, and they scored another #1 AC hit shortly after "For All We Know" with "Rainy Days and Mondays" [see 151].

147 (Where Do I Begin) Love Story
ANDY WILLIAMS

Columbia 45317

March 20, 1971 (4 weeks nonconsecutive)

Writers: Frances Lai, Carl Sigman

Producer: Dick Glasser

To say "(Where Do I Begin) Love Story" was a hot property for artists to record in 1971 would be an understatement. On Columbia Records alone, three major artists recorded their versions of the theme from the 1970 tear-jerking film *Love Story*, based on the novel by Erich Segal and starring Ryan O'Neal and Ali McGraw. Columbia, wanting to be fair to Andy Williams, Tony Bennett, and Johnny Mathis, all of whom sang the song, had a novel idea: They released all three records the same day.

The Williams version had several advantages. One was that Williams had a weekly variety series on NBC-TV at the time to promote his version. "I must have done it on the show 12 times," he said. Another, believed Williams, was that he and producer Dick Glasser designed their single expressly to be a pop and AC hit. "Tony's was a little slow, and Mathis's was more of an album cut," Williams opined. Neither competitor made the AC or pop chart with their 45s, although Bennett did bubble under to #114.

"Where Do I Begin" became a big hit for Williams, his first pop top 10 hit since 1963's "Can't Get Used to Losing You" [see 26]. It peaked at #9 pop the week of April 3, 1971. Concerning this return to success, he said, "I was thrilled." He also recorded it in German, Spanish, Italian, and Japanese. Williams noted an odd fact about the Japanese release: "In Japan they sold 600,000 copies in English and 600,000 copies in Japanese."

The 1971 recording that came closest to Williams' success with the song was an instrumental rendition by Henry Mancini, which made #2 AC for two weeks and #13 pop. Others fell shorter, including one by the song's composer Frances Lai, whose single went to #21 AC and #31 pop. Roy Clark had a banjo version that made #74 country, while in 1972 Nino Tempo and April Stevens' vocal try languished at #113.

Williams had no other song do quite as well as "Where Do I Begin," but he kept making the AC and pop charts through 1976. His last entry on both was "Tell It Like It Is" (#17 AC, #72 pop).

In 1992 Williams established the Andy Williams Moon River Theater in Branson, Missouri, where he appears each year from April through December to do his hits including, "Where Do I Begin." "I don't tour anymore at all," he said. "I do make records. . . .Mostly, I just come to Palm Springs and play golf." For a man who was one of the top AC acts of the 1960s and 1970s, he's definitely earned the right to take it easy.

148 When There's No You

ENGELBERT HUMPERDINCK

Parrot 40059

April 3, 1971 (1 week)

Writers: Les Reed, Jackie Rae

Producer: Gordon Mills

Since it took him nearly a decade to break through in the music industry, Engelbert Humperdinck knew exactly who got him his success and often thanked him profusely—his manager Gordon Mills. "Gordon made me do something about my talent. I can't brag for myself, so I needed someone to brag for me," Humperdinck told *Life*. Mills cast him in a more romantic and subdued singing role than his other major client, Tom Jones, a strategy which led to Humperdinck's success starting in 1967.

But it was a delicate balancing act for Mills, as he had to keep both Jones and Humperdinck from thinking he was favoring one over the other, and sometimes it seemed that if one singer got something, the other had to get the same or an equivalent. For example, after Jones got his own TV show on ABC late in 1969, *The Engelbert Humperdinck Show* arrived on ABC on January 21, 1970. Unfortunately, Humperdinck did not click with viewers as well as Jones and went off the network on September 19, 1970, four months before Jones departed.

Nonetheless, Humperdinck can crow about having four

#1 AC hits to Jones' three, with Humperdinck's hits spread out over more than a decade. His first was "Am I That Easy to Forget" [see 101] in early 1968, followed three years later by "When There's No You."

Based on "Vesti La Giubba" from the opera *Pagliacci*, "When There's No You" was co-written by Les Reed, who wrote several hits for both Jones ("It's Not Unusual") and Humperdinck ("The Last Waltz"). Although it was an AC chart-topper, "When There's No You" did only middling business on the Hot 100, stopping at #45. Later in 1971 came "Another Time, Another Place" from Humperdinck, and it became his last top 10 AC and top 60 pop entry for five years, peaking at #5 AC and #43 pop.

Humperdinck was clearly losing popularity after 1971, and after "Love Is All" made #91 pop and #33 AC in 1973, he did not have an entry on the Hot 100 for three years. As with Jones, who suffered a similar decline around the same time, the problem may have stemmed from the departure of his longtime producer Peter Sullivan and replacement Gordon Mills' effort to recreate Sullivan's sound. ("When There's No You" was Mills' first single produced after Sullivan left in 1970.) From 1973 to 1975 Humperdinck did have four singles make the AC chart between "Love Is All" and "After the Lovin'," but the only one to crack the AC top 30 was 1975's "This Is What You Mean to Me" at #14.

But Mills was shrewd enough to work on getting his client another hit, even if it meant he had to stop producing him, which in fact he did. The result, released in 1976, became Humperdinck's biggest hit of the 1970s [see 320—"After the Lovin'"].

149 If

BREAD

Elektra 45720

April 24, 1971 (3 weeks)

Writer: David Gates

Producer: David Gates

Bread rose in 1967 when David Gates, born in Tulsa, Oklahoma, on December 11, 1940, joined forces with Robb Royer to produce the latter's group the Pleasure Faire after years of being behind the scenes in the music world. (Among Gates' writing credits was the 1963 hit "Popsicles and Icicles," which went to #2 AC and #3 pop.) Royer had been writing a few songs with his pal James Griffin, and after the Pleasure Faire dissolved, the trio decided to start recording as their own unit. The group's name was inspired by the lettering on a bread truck; they all thought the word had a sort of universal appeal yet could be taken a number of ways.

"Make It With You" was the AC and pop debut for Bread, and it was a strong one, reaching #4 AC and #1 pop in the summer of 1970. The next release, "It Don't Matter to Me," moved them up two notches to #2 AC while hitting #10 pop around the end of 1970. By this time drummer Mike Botts had joined the trio. Then came "If."

Gates vividly recalled the creation of the tune. "My family had all gone to bed at maybe 10 o'clock at night, and I sat down at my kitchen table with a guitar," he said. He started strumming and the opening chords and words came to him immediately. Within an hour and a half he completed the tune. "I've never, never had a song come that fast to me. They almost never do that," he said. Gates noted, "I kind of wrote it with my wife in mind." He also said that he designed it to be a timeless tune, so the lyrics weren't specifically directed toward her.

"If" went to #4 pop the week of May 15, 1971 as well as becoming the shortest-titled #1 AC record. However, despite "Make It With You" hitting #5 in the U.K. in 1970, Bread's "If" failed to make the U.K. chart. But in 1975 two covers of the song did make the U.K. chart, one a #22 entry by the male vocal duo of Yin and Yan and the other a #1 hit by actor Telly Savalas.

"I was there when it went to #1 in two weeks," Gates said of the Savalas version. "*Kojak* [the TV series starring Savalas] was huge in England, and they tried to get us together to perform." The two never did cross paths, however.

Savalas did the tune by speaking the words rather than singing them. That made the record odd enough, but Gates said he first heard it on a Los Angeles radio station which played Frank Sinatra's vocal version underneath the talking of Savalas. "I said, 'What is that?'" Gates laughed in recalling the occasion.

"If" was the first of a quartet of Bread #1 AC hits. The next was "Baby I'm-A Want You" [see 160].

150 Me and You and a Dog Named Boo

LOBO

Big Tree 112

May 15, 1971 (2 weeks)

Writer: Kent Lavoie

Producer: Phil Gernhard

"That's the one we've been waiting for," producer Phil Gernhard told Roland Kent Lavoie when the latter penned and sang "Me and You and a Dog Named Boo." The tune became the first pop and AC entry for Lavoie under the stage name of Lobo, and he would compile three other #1 AC hits during the 1970s.

Lobo worked with Gernhard, who served as his producer and manager. Gernhard's production credits stretched back at least as far as the 1960 #1 pop and R&B hit "Stay" by Maurice Williams and the Zodiacs, which he co-produced with Johnny McCullough. In the 1970s he became producer and manager of several acts from Florida. One of them was Jim Stafford, who was in vogue from 1973 to 1975 with novelty hits he and Gernhard produced. Four of them made the AC chart in 1973 and 1974, with the highest charting of the quartet being "My Girl Bill" at #9 in 1974.

Stafford had been in a band called the Legends in the 1960s along with Lavoie, but it was not through that band that Lavoie came in contact with Gernhard. After singing in a few other bar bands, Lavoie got married and then played guitar in local clubs in the Tampa–Clearwater Beach area of Florida before meeting Gernhard. The two agreed to work together, and Lavoie cut a few local releases in Atlanta before "Me and You and a Dog Named Boo" convinced Gernhard it had the makings of a national hit. When he cut the record, Lobo not only sang but played rhythm guitar on the session.

For his name on the record, Gernhard decided Lavoie should become Lobo, the Spanish word for wolf. "I chose the billing of Lobo to play it safe," Gernhard told *Billboard* in 1973. "The name symbolizes the image of being a loner, a lone wolf. I figured it could be used for either a group or a soloist, whichever was better in the current market. And frankly, if the record had stiffed, I could start fresh without the stigma of a flop next to my name."

On the pop chart "Me and You and a Dog Named Boo" went to #5 the weeks of May 15 and 22, 1971 while staying at #1 AC. A cover by Stonewall Jackson that same year went to #7 country.

Gernhard and Lobo never got to #1 pop with their records, although Gernhard did reach that peak in 1976 when he and his partner Tony Scotti recorded the Bellamy Brothers doing "Let Your Love Flow." The next of Gernhard and Lobo's #1 AC records was "I'd Love You to Want Me" [see 180].

Rainy Days and Mondays

THE CARPENTERS

A&M 1260

May 29, 1971 (4 weeks)

Writers: Paul Williams (words), Roger Nichols (music)

Producer: Jack Daugherty

"Rainy Days and Mondays" contained what lyricist Paul Williams said is one of his favorite lines from any of his songs, "What I got they used to call the blues." Yet Williams himself admitted he nearly got the blues trying to complete the song.

"It took me forever to find out why rainy days and Mondays always got him down," he said. In fact, Williams noted, "I think that Roger [Nichols, his writing partner] and I finished the third verse in the car when we were headed to Bones Howe to give it to the Fifth Dimension." But Howe, the Fifth Dimension's producer, turned it down. Karen and Richard Carpenter, who had previously cut Williams and Nichols' "We've Only Just Begun" [see 140], heard it in a stack of demos and decided to give it a shot.

Veteran session musician Tommy Morgen played the distinctive harmonica solo used at the start of the song. He said it was the shortest session he ever had for a record—20 minutes. When he arrived, Richard Carpenter told him he was having trouble with Morgen's part. "I know what I want, but I can't write it out," he told Morgen. After they talked about what Carpenter desired, Morgen nailed his solo in one take.

The crux of the song's lyrics came from a source familiar to Williams. "My mother, who passed away in the mid-1970s, was a chronic mumbler," he said. One day Williams asked her, "What's the matter now, Mom?" and she grumbled back, "I'm feeling old." He extended that feeling into a lyrical lament, and thus was "Rainy Days and Mondays" born.

Apart from hitting #1 AC, "Rainy Days and Mondays" stalled at #2 pop for the weeks of July 19 and 26, 1971, behind "It's Too Late" [see 152]. It was the second of five Carpenters singles to stop at #2 pop, the first having been "We've Only Just Begun." In 1975 the Intruders cover of "Rainy Days and Mondays" went to #81 R&B.

Given the acclaim for "We've Only Just Begun" and "Rainy Days and Mondays," it seems surprising that the Carpenters didn't go on to release a number of singles by Williams and Nichols in the future, but the only one was "I Won't Last a Day Without You" [see 220], and that came in 1974, two years after they originally put out the song on their *A Song for You* album. Williams blamed this situation partly on himself, noting that by 1973, he had begun to pursue more solo projects, both writing and performing. But he thought that Richard Carpenter's discovery of a writing partner to do more material also had something to do with it. "Richard had a great collaborator in John Bettis, and I think all of a sudden they had gotten into things they had wanted to record," he said.

"Rainy Days and Mondays" was the Carpenters' fourth consecutive #1 AC single. The next was "Superstar" [see 157].

152 It's Too Late

CAROLE KING

Ode 66015

June 26, 1971 (5 weeks)

Writer: Carole King

Producer: Lou Adler

Though the AC chart listed only "It's Too Late" as Carole King's debut single on that listing, most people were also familiar with the 45's flip side, "I Feel the Earth Move." The impact of both hits, which held the #1 slot on the Hot 100 for five weeks beginning June 19, 1971, made King a household name in the early 1970s, though she had been recording and writing music for over a decade.

Born Carole Klein in Brooklyn, New York, on February 9, 1942, King's first record, "Baby Sittin'," came out in March 1959; it was followed by "Oh, Neil," a response song to Neil Sedaka's "Oh! Carol" written in honor of her. But while the latter went to #9 pop in late 1959 and established a singing career for Sedaka, King's songs flopped. Over the next decade, Carole and her then-husband Gerry Goffin concentrated on writing tunes and doing demos for artists. The numerous hit writing credits for the Goffin-King songwriting team include "Will You Love Me Tomorrow" (as performed by the Shirelles, #1 in the U.S. and #3 in the U.K.), "(You Make Me Feel Like) a Natural Woman," and "Go Away Little Girl" [see 22]. Only two of her sporadic recordings in the 1960s made the Hot 100—"It Might As Well Rain Until September" (#22 in 1962) and "He's a Bad Boy" (#94 in 1963).

In late 1968 King and a few musician friends formed a group called the City, but their LP died. Undaunted, she planned to record on her own again and in 1970 released the album *Carole King: Writer*. It fared better than the City's effort and generated positive reviews, so the next year she followed it with another LP, *Tapestry*.

Tapestry spent 15 weeks at #1 on the LP chart starting June 19, 1971, and stayed on that chart for more than 300 weeks. It generated two hit singles (the other was "So Far Away" backed with "Smackwater Jack," which made #3 AC and #14 pop in late 1971), and earned King four Grammys, including Album of the Year, Record of the Year (for "It's Too Late"), Song of the Year (for "You've Got a Friend" [see 153]), and Best Female Pop Vocal Performance (for the title tune).

In the liner notes to *Carole King: A Natural Woman*, producer Lou Adler said that when he did *Tapestry*, "I had a definite theme in mind, to have that lean, almost demo-type sound, with a basic rhythm section and Carole on the piano, playing lots of her figures. Those are things everyone liked about her demos."

"It's Too Late" bubbled under to #108 in 1972 for Bill Deal and the Rhondells. A year later, the Isley Brothers took their version to #39 R&B. "I Feel the Earth Move" went to #25 pop in 1989 in a rendition by Martika. But most people associate King with both songs, and they were still heavy airplay favorites on oldie stations at the end of the 1990s.

153 You've Got a Friend

JAMES TAYLOR

Warner Brothers 7498

July 31, 1971 (1 week)

Writer: Carole King

Producer: Peter Asher

"Oh, I've seen fire and I've seen rain," notes James Taylor in the first verse to the chorus of his breakthrough 1970 hit "Fire and Rain," and indeed by then the singer-songwriter had packed a lot of living in his lifetime. Born in Boston, Massachusetts, on March 12, 1948, he found himself shuttling between that state and North Carolina as he grew up because his father Isaac was dean of the medical school at the University of North Carolina in Chapel Hill. (His mother was no slouch either, having been a lyric soprano at the New England Conservatory of Music.)

Taylor, who fought depression as a teenager, spent some time in a mental hospital before emerging in New York City with his first professional group, the Flying Machine, in 1967. The group lasted less than a year, and Taylor pursued a solo career. In 1968 he went to London and signed with the Beatles' Apple label, but his singles and LP there generated little interest, possibly because their release coincided with another stay in a mental hospital. No such problems existed in 1969, when he recorded his *Sweet Baby James* LP for Warner with Peter Asher and got his first pop and AC entry from the initial single on the album, "Fire and Rain" (#7 AC, #3 pop).

After "Fire and Rain," a rerelease of the 1969 Apple single "Carolina on My Mind" made #67 pop. The next Taylor single to chart was "Country Road" in 1971, which hit #9 AC and #37 pop. Following it was "You've Got a Friend."

The song which gave Taylor his first #1 AC hit was one written by Carole King and included as a track on her *Tapestry* album before his version appeared. Though King and Taylor became good friends while she worked on *Tapestry*, she has denied that he or anyone else was the source of the lyrics for the tune.

"That song was as close to pure inspiration as I've ever experienced," King told Paul Zollo in *Songwriters on Songwriting*. "The song wrote itself. It was written by something outside of myself. It was written by something outside of myself through me." King concluded that "That song is one of the examples of that process where it was almost completely written by inspiration and very little if any perspiration."

"You've Got a Friend" hit #1 pop the week of July 31, 1971. Besides earning King a Grammy for Song of the Year, "You've Got a Friend" nabbed Taylor a statuette as well for Best Male Pop Vocal Performance plus got another nomination for Record of the Year. In 1971 a cover by Roberta Flack and Donny Hathaway made #8 R&B, #29 pop, and #36 AC and took a Grammy nomination for Best Rhythm & Blues Performance by a Duo or Group, Vocal or Instrumental.

Taylor had three other #1 AC hits. The next was "How Sweet It Is (To Be Loved by You)" [see 270].

154 If Not for You

OLIVIA NEWTON-JOHN

Uni 55281

August 7, 1971 (3 weeks)

Writer: Bob Dylan

Producers: Bruce Welch, John Farrar

Breathy singer Olivia Newton-John scored the first of her nine #1 AC hits in the 1970s with "If Not for You," which also was her AC and pop chart debut in America. She did so with help from her producer John Farrar, who also produced her other AC chart toppers. Like Newton-John, Farrar was a native Australian, and both had moved to Great Britain during their early years of struggling to make it in the music business.

The two of them worked together first in Australia on a television variety series in the 1960s called *The Go Show*, where Newton-John was a featured singer and Farrar was guitarist for the program's backup band the Strangers. "She went to England a couple of years before me," Farrar recalled. "I was asked to join a group in England. Turned out her boyfriend was in the group." That boyfriend was Bruce Welch of the rock group the Shadows, whom Newton-John began dating in 1966. She and Welch never married, but Farrar eventually wed the other former singer of *The Go Show*, Pat Carroll, who also emigrated to England from Australia.

When Peter Gormley became Newton-John's agent, he set up Farrar to be her producer in 1970. (She had done one single earlier, "Till You Say You'll Be Mine" in 1966, but did no recording after that British 45 flopped.) After three singles went nowhere, Newton-John scored a hit in 1971 with "If Not for You."

The tune's writer, Bob Dylan, first cut the song on his 1970 album *New Morning*. But according to Clive Davis in his memoirs *Clive: Inside the Record Business*, although Davis suggested that Dylan put the song out as a single, Dylan resisted. When Newton-John's version came out, it became such a hit so fast that it was too late to release Dylan's version and generate much airplay or sales.

Newton-John was not wild about the song but took the advice of Gormley and recorded it. However, she had not heard Dylan's original, according to Farrar. "It was off a George Harrison album when we first found it," he said (the album was Harrison's 1970 LP *All Things Must Pass*). "I guess it was a pretty hip tune at the time."

Indeed it was. "If Not for You" became John's first entry in the United Kingdom and America, going to #25 pop as well as #1 AC in the latter. Over the next year she had two more AC entries which peaked at #34, "Banks of the Ohio" in 1971, which also made #94 pop, and "What Is Life," another cover of a tune they heard on *All Things Must Pass*, which did not make the Hot 100. It took Newton-John two more years to get back to #1 AC [see 230—"I Honestly Love You"].

155 Beginnings

CHICAGO

Columbia 45417

August 28, 1971 (1 week)

Writer: Robert Lamm

Producer: James William Guercio

Believe it or not, there was a time when Chicago was not being played on the radio. The band had its first #1 AC hit in 1971 and notched up its eighth 26 years later, the longest span between #1 hits for any AC act. The act's original title—The Big Thing—was prophetic, but what is really amazing is how most of the players have stayed with the band for more than 30 years, an incredible achievement in the often volatile, conflict-ridden pop music world.

Formed in Chicago (of course) in 1967, the seven-member band consisted of lead singer and bassist Peter Cetera, trumpeter Lee Loughnane, trombonist James Pankow, woodwind player Walt Parazaider, guitarist Terry Kath, keyboardist Robert Lamm, and drummer Danny Seraphine. All were born and raised in Chicago in the mid to late 1940s except Lamm, who was born in Brooklyn, New York, in 1945. They released their first LP in 1969 not as the Big Thing but under a new name, Chicago Transit Authority, which, due to complaints from city government officials, had been shortened within a year to its final form.

Chicago's debut single, "Questions 67 and 68," only went to #71 on the Hot 100, while the follow-up, "Beginnings," failed to make any chart. It was not until the next year when "Make Me Smile" went to #7 pop that successful 45s for the group began to happen. And after "25 or 6 to 4" went to #4 in the summer of 1970, the group broke onto the AC chart when its follow-up, "Does Anybody Really Know What Time It Is?," went to #5 AC and #7 pop near the end of 1970. A rerelease of "Beginnings" soon followed and put Chicago at #1 AC and #7 pop.

"The first time, we couldn't get arrested playing it," noted Loughnane of "Beginnings." "Thank God FM was starting at the time, because college stations started playing the whole album." Though not sure of the exact reason why "Beginnings" was rereleased, Loughnane thought that "It definitely had potential and they probably checked it out in a few test markets."

"Beginnings" set the pattern of horn-dominated, jazz-influenced rock which Chicago specialized during the early to mid-1970s. It was one of the songs the group rehearsed for six to seven months on the road before including it in the debut LP. "We tried to get it so perfect," Loughnane recalled. "It was not as loose as we normally played. Thank God we knew the songs as well as we did."

The B-side of "Beginnings," "Colour My World," generated some airplay of its own and was listed along with "Beginnings" on the pop chart (the tune previously served as the flip side to "Make Me Smile"). The record's success may have influenced Columbia's next move, which was rerelease "Questions 67 and 68," which went to #34 AC and #24 pop in late 1971. Chicago returned to #1 AC in 1974; see 227—"Call on Me."

156 The Night They Drove Old Dixie Down

JOAN BAEZ

Vanguard 35138

September 4, 1971 (5 weeks)

Writer: Robbie Robertson

Producer: Norbert Putnam, Jack Lathrop

Joan Chandos Baez was arguably the most famous female folk singer of the 1960s and 1970s, but some knew her as much for her political activism as for her songs. Born in Staten Island, New York, on January 9, 1941, she was raised in California and got her first attention nationally with her professional debut at the Newport Folk Festival in July 1959 while attending Boston University. A few years later she helped Bob Dylan launch his career. Her popularity in the 1960s relied largely on live performances and albums. Three of her singles made the Hot 100 during the decade, the biggest being the only one to make the AC chart, 1965's "There but for Fortune" (#50 pop, #16 AC). This pattern changed dramatically in 1971.

"The Night They Drove Old Dixie Down" was an unusual song for civil rights activist Baez, given the focus of its lyrics, which are the words of a Southerner remembering the Civil War. The tune originally appeared on the Band's self-titled 1969 LP and the B-side to "Up on Cripple Creek," the group's #25 pop entry in early 1970. The Band's main connection to Baez was that the group was Bob Dylan's initial backup group. Band guitarist Robbie Robertson wrote the tune for the group, but drummer Levon Helm sang lead on it.

Robertson told Paul Zollo in *Songwriters on Songwriting* that finishing "The Night They Drove Old Dixie Down" was not easy. "This was another one that took me months and months, maybe eight to ten months, to write. . . .Because I only had the music for it. I didn't know what the song was about at all. And if everyone would go, I would sit down at a piano and I would play these chords and go over it. And then one day, the rest of it came to me. But it took a long, long time. And sometimes you have to wait it out. And I'm glad I waited it out."

Done by Baez, "The Night They Drove Old Dixie Down" became a #1 AC and #3 pop smash, reaching the latter the week of October 2, 1971, behind Rod Stewart's "Maggie May" at #1 and Donny Osmond's "Go Away Little Girl" at #2. It also snagged Baez a Grammy nomination for Best Female Pop Vocal Performance. On the country chart, a cover by Don Rich and the Buckaroos made #71 in 1970 and a cover by Alice Creech hit #33 in 1971.

Baez had four more entries make both the AC and pop charts, ending with the highest-charting follow-up on both, 1975's "Diamonds and Rust" (#5 AC, #35 pop). Largely absent from the music scene in the 1980s, she came back in the 1990s with three well-received albums, *Play Me Backwards* (1992), the live *Ring Them Bells* (1995), and *Gone From Danger* (1997). The latter contained the song "Reunion Hill," written by Richard Shindell, which some viewed as a sequel to "The Night They Drove Old Dixie Down."

157 Superstar

THE CARPENTERS

A&M 1289

October 9, 1971 (2 weeks)

Writers: Leon Russell, Bonnie Bramlett

Producer: Jack Daugherty

Bette Midler may not have realized it at the time, but her frequent guest appearances on *The Tonight Show Starring Johnny Carson* in the early 1970s provided other artists with ideas on what songs to record. It happened most dramatically with multiple covers of "Delta Dawn" [see 198], but Midler was also the reason the Carpenters decided to record "Superstar."

In the liner notes to the anthology *From the Top*, Richard Carpenter wrote that "Late one evening during the period in which we were recording our third album, I happened to tune into *The Tonight Show*. Bette Midler, who was then relatively unknown, was guesting and on this particular show sang 'Superstar.' I felt the song was a hit and a natural for Karen. "When the time came to release our version as a single, I was vacillating between 'Superstar' and 'Let Me Be the One,' being concerned that the lyrics to the former were a little unconventional for a Carpenters record—even though we'd changed the lyric 'sleep' to 'be.' Jerry Moss [one of the co-founders of A&M Records], who strongly believed in 'Superstar,' felt I was worrying needlessly and made up my mind for me. Thanks, Jerry."

While "Let Me Be the One" was only a track on the Carpenters' self-titled 1971 LP, "Superstar" became a single and went to #1 AC plus #2 pop for the weeks of October 16 and 23, 1971, behind Rod Stewart's double-sided #1 hit "Maggie May" and "Reason to Believe." It also got Richard Carpenter a Grammy nomination for Best Arrangement Accompanying Vocalists. The B-side of the record, "Bless the Beasts and Children," also got some airplay and went to #26 AC and #67 pop. For more details on that song, see 146—"For All We Know."

Midler did release "Superstar" in 1972 as the B-side to her first pop and AC entry "Do You Want to Dance?" In 1984 Luther Vandross cut the tune as part of a medley with "Until You Come Back to Me (That's What I'm Gonna Do)," and made #5 R&B and #87 pop with it.

The Carpenters' version of "Superstar" came onto the AC chart at the same time the duo finished work on a musical variety series for NBC-TV called *Make Your Own Kind of Music*. It ran from July 20 through September 7, 1971 on Tuesday nights and starred the Carpenters along with Al Hirt and Mark Lindsay. It was the only TV series Karen and Richard did as regulars, but they did host several network specials through the rest of the 1970s as their musical appeal remained steady during much of the decade.

158 Never My Love
THE 5TH DIMENSION

Bell 45134

October 23, 1971 (1 week)

Writers: Dick Addrisi, Don Addrisi

Producer: Bones Howe

Dick Addrisi was awakened one night in 1967 by a call from his brother Don, who said he had a great idea for a song. Don's girlfriend had asked him, "Will there ever come a time when you grow tired of me?" and he had responded, "Never, my love." Their song found its way to the Association, who took it to #2 pop for two weeks starting October 7, 1967, behind the Box Tops' "The Letter." But despite the group's previous success on the AC chart, the tune somehow failed to make the listings at the time. So did a cover by the Sandpebbles, which went to #98 pop in 1968.

The Association's record was still fresh in the minds of the Fifth Dimension when their producer mentioned remaking the song. "Bones talked about doing it and we questioned that, because it was a big hit for the Association and we felt there hadn't been enough years since then," said Marilyn McCoo, lead singer of the group.

But the idea passed the group test (at least three of the five members had to approve doing it), so they recorded it as a track on *The 5th Dimension/Live!!*, an LP supposedly recorded live at Caesar's Palace in Las Vegas. Later, however, McCoo confessed that "Never My Love" was actually recorded in the studio and the applause added at the end.

Released as a single, "Never My Love" was the Fifth Dimension's fourth #1 AC song and also hit #12 pop and #45 R&B. McCoo said it became a bigger hit than the group had anticipated it would be.

Some revivals of "Never My Love" made *Billboard* charts after the Fifth Dimension's effort. Blue Swede had a version which went to #7 pop in 1974. The song's writers, the Addrisi Brothers, took it to #80 pop and #28 AC in 1977. Vern Gosdin's "Never My Love" hit #9 country in 1978 with a harmony vocal by Janie Fricke. And in 1988 Chill Factor, a Chicago trio, hit #62 R&B. Ten years later, BMI announced "Never My Love" had been played on the airwaves over 7 million times, making it the #2 song licensed by BMI most played on radio and TV stations for all time behind only "You've Lost That Lovin' Feelin'."

"Never My Love" was the 14th AC entry for the Fifth Dimension, a streak which began when their Grammy-winning "Up-Up and Away" hit #9 AC in 1967. The group had formed a year earlier originally under the title the Versatiles, with McCoo joined by Billy Davis Jr., Florence LaRue, Lamont McLemore, and Ron Towson. Their first released single was "I'll Be Loving You Forever," but it was their second 45, "Go Where You Wanna Go," which was their first pop entry, peaking at #16 on the Hot 100 in early 1967. "Up-Up and Away" came two singles later.

The Fifth Dimension had one more #1 AC hit after "Never My Love." See 178—"If I Could Reach You."

159 Peace Train
CAT STEVENS

A&M 1291

October 30, 1971 (3 weeks)

Writer: Cat Stevens

Producer: Paul Samwell-Smith

If you were listening to a song on the radio in the early 1970s espousing peace and love sung by a male vocalist, chances were excellent that the singer was Cat Stevens. The bearded tenor wrote most of his own hits, usually emphasizing his own experiences, and he typically came across as sort of a last-gasp hippie until he decided to give up recording toward the end of the decade.

Born Steven Georgiou in London on July 21, 1947, he was the son of a Greek father and a Swedish mother. Stevens grew up in Soho, London, and claimed his early musical influences were Greek music, early rock and roll, and even *West Side Story*. When he was 17 he dropped out of art school to pursue a music career, though he did attend Hammersmith College in 1966.

His first English hit was "I Love My Dog," which went to #28 in the United Kingdom in the fall of 1966. His next U.K. entry was "Matthew and Son," which went to #2 behind the Monkees' "I'm a Believer" in January 1967. The following month, a song he wrote for the Tremeloes, "Here Comes My Baby," hit #4 in Great Britain and gave him his first success in America when their record made #13 pop too.

Stevens had three other entries in England through the end of 1967. Then in 1968 he contracted tuberculosis, and after taking more than a year to recuperate, he returned to the music scene with a more introspective writing style. The change in approach finally paid off, getting Stevens onto the charts in America in 1971. His pop and AC debut was "Wild World," which hit #11 pop and #21 AC. Next came "Moon Shadow," which made #30 pop and #20 AC, followed by "Peace Train."

Describing "Peace Train" to Nik Cohn in *The New York Times* in 1971, Stevens said, "It's sort of an up, full of hope, about how people's heads are getting more together and everyone is climbing on the train. But the message doesn't matter too much, it's more of a mood. "I don't really believe that there's going to be peace in this age; it would take a ridiculous mind to think that, because there are so many different nationalities and attitudes, all struggling against each other. All I meant was to write something happy for a change, so that audiences could groove to it, without thinking anything too heavy."

"Peace Train" chugged its way to #7 pop for three weeks starting November 6, 1971, as well as #1 AC. The next Stevens single also made #1 AC and became his second consecutive top 10 pop hit; see 169—"Morning Has Broken."

Baby I'm-A Want You

BREAD

Elektra 45751

November 20, 1971 (1 week)

Writer: David Gates

Producer: David Gates

"**B**aby I'm-A Want You" was not an effort to mimic or mock an Italian speech pattern, insisted writer-producer David Gates. As he explained, "I had this melody and I wanted the syllables to work. I had to put the 'I'm-A' in there and I thought, 'God, is this going to be accepted?'" Getting over his worry, he went ahead and finished the tune, with the suspect line intact. And, just for good measure, he put "baby, I'm-a need you" in the second line of the first chorus.

Linguists may have winced, but "Baby I'm-A Want You" proved irresistible to listeners and record buyers, who took it to #1 AC and #3 pop. It peaked at the latter position for two weeks starting November 27, 1971. The first week Isaac Hayes' "Theme From Shaft" was #1 and Cher's "Gypsys, Tramps and Thieves" was #2, while "Shaft" moved to #2 the following week as Sly and the Family Stone's "Family Affair" assumed the top spot.

Gates said he didn't think the lyrics really affected the song's popularity anyway. "I think it was more the melody and chord structure that made it work," he said. Along those same lines, he noted that he adjusted the original key for the song from G to A flat on his guitar to make it a little less high. There were no keyboards on the tune because Gates said, when he tried to write the song using the piano, "it was horrible. It just didn't work."

What did work was having Larry Knechtel replace guitarist Robb Royer, who decided to leave the quartet amicably. On "Baby I'm-A Want You," Gates said, "He played bass on that record. Did a great job." Knechtel was a session musician, but he had spent a few years in the early 1960s as a member of Duane Eddy's band the Rebels. He also provided music for the mid-1960s ABC-TV music variety series *Shindig*.

"I had known him for many years," Gates recalled about bringing Knechtel into the group. The musician's familiarity and reputation made him a natural for the recording studio, and his willingness to tour ensured that he would become a regular member of Bread.

After "Baby I'm-A Want You," Bread had two back-to-back #3 AC singles in 1972 with "Everything I Own," which went to #5 pop, and "Diary," which halted at #15 pop. All three singles came from the *Baby I'm-A Want You* album, as did one single which was released ahead of them, the non-AC pop entry "Mother Freedom" in 1971, which reached #37.

Stephanie Winslow's 1980 remake of "Baby I'm-A Want You" went to #35 country.

Left to right:
James Griffin, Larry Knechtel,
David Gates, Mike Botts

161 All I Ever Need Is You

SONNY AND CHER

Kapp 2151

November 27, 1971 (5 weeks)

Writers: Jimmy Holiday, Eddie Reeves

Producer: Snuff Garrett

Sonny Bono, born February 16, 1935, and Cherilyn LaPierre, born May 20, 1946, met as session singers for Phil Spector in the early 1960s. After dating for a while, they married, even though Cher was in her teens. They recorded as Caesar and Cleopatra that same year, 1963, but got nowhere. However, when they cut "I Got You Babe" in 1965, the result was a #1 pop smash, and for several years they were considered a leading "hippie" couple in the music industry.

But the hits had dried up by the end of 1967, and Sonny and Cher made nightclub appearances just to stay solvent. Luckily for them, CBS-TV programming head Fred Silverman saw their shows and signed them to star in a variety show on the network starting August 1, 1971. The response was so positive that the duo was once again in demand as recording artists, and "All I Ever Need Is You" became their first Hot 100 entry in nearly four years as well as their AC debut.

Eddie Reeves came up with most of "All I Ever Need Is You." Jimmy Holiday added a few verses, then Reeves presented it to Kenny Rogers. Rogers rejected the tune, which wound up on a Ray Charles album. Sonny and Cher's producer Snuff Garrett heard the album and cut the track on the duo.

Nearly eight years after "All I Ever Need Is You" made #1 AC and #7 pop the week of December 25, 1971, none other than Kenny Rogers covered it with Dottie West. They hit #1 country the week of April 21, 1979, as well as #38 AC and #102 bubbling under. "It was always ironic in my mind that when I wrote this little love ballad, I did a demo imitating Kenny Rogers, and he turned it down, and it comes around to him and he eventually does record it," Reeves told Tom Roland in *The Billboard Book of Number One Country Hits.*

Sonny and Cher had only two more AC entries, both in 1972—"A Cowboy's Work Is Never Done" (#4 AC, #8 pop) and "When You Say Love" (#2 AC, #32 pop). They announced their divorce in 1974, thus ending their successful TV show, where the gangly Cher and diminutive, mustachioed Sonny traded jokes about each other before doing songs and sketches. Each then failed doing their own variety show, so in 1976 they tried a reunion series on CBS, but it ended a year later.

Cher continued her recording career [see 570—"If I Could Turn Back Time"], while Sonny went into politics. He was mayor of Palm Springs, California, from 1988 to 1992, and in 1994 was elected to the U.S. House of Representatives for the 44th Congressional District, which included Palm Springs and environs, a position he held until his death in January 1998, after a skiing accident. Cher's heartfelt eulogy at his funeral a few days later was heard by many ardent Sonny and Cher fans.

1972

162 An Old Fashioned Love Song
THREE DOG NIGHT

Dunhill 4294

January 1, 1972 (1 week)

Writer: Paul Williams

Producer: Richard Polodor

Vocalist Danny Hutton (born in Buncrana, Ireland, on September 10, 1942) came up with the idea in 1968 of having a pop group featuring three lead singers. Joined by fellow music veterans Cory Wells (born in Buffalo, New York, on February 5, 1942), whom Hutton met when the latter toured with Sonny and Cher, and Chuck Negron (born in the Bronx, New York, on June 8, 1942), whom they met through mutual friends, the trio formed the nucleus of Three Dog Night. Other group members were Michael Allsup (guitarist), Jimmy Greenspoon (keyboardist), Joe Schermie (bassist), and Floyd Sneed (drummer).

The group took their name from an Australian way of describing the relative coldness of a particular night by citing the number of pooches you'd need in your bed to keep warm. A "three dog night," therefore, is very, very cold.

Three Dog Night scored 21 pop hits from 1969–75, beginning with "Try a Little Tenderness," which went to #29. The AC chart proved impervious to the group's charms until "Out in the Country" gave them their debut on it in 1970, going to #11 AC and #15 pop. The next three singles made only the pop chart, including "Joy to the World," the group's second #1 on the Hot 100 following 1970's "Mama Told Me (Not to Come)." Then came "An Old Fashioned Love Song."

"At the time that came out, we were getting good demos," Hutton said. He, Wells, and Negron listened to the demos submitted to them and, based on how they reacted to each song, sorted them into piles as "Good," "Maybe," and "No." "I think when we heard that, the three of us all put it in the 'Good' pile," Hutton said.

Despite its appeal as a demo, "An Old Fashioned Love Song" left a little to be desired as a finished record. "We had to work a long time to come up with the ending," noted Hutton. That ending included sounds from a talkbox, a guitar device that makes the instrument sound like a person's voice. "We had one of those talkboxes, and we had a big, huge garbage can, and we plugged the guitar into the garbage can and we spun it," Hutton said.

With Negron singing the verses and the other men joining in the chorus for "three-part harmony," as the lyrics put it, "An Old Fashioned Love Song" stayed at #4 on the Hot 100 for three weeks beginning December 18, 1971, with the single going to #1 AC on the last week of that run. In 1972 female vocalist Jerri Ross took her rendition to #58 country.

After "An Old Fashioned Love Song," Three Dog Night checked into the AC chart in 1972 with "Never Been to Spain" (#18 AC, #5 pop) and "The Family of Man" (#27 AC, #12 pop). The group returned to the top with the next release, "Black and White" [see 176].

163 Cherish
DAVID CASSIDY

Bell 45150

January 8, 1972 (1 week)

Writer: Terry Kirkman

Producer: Wes Farrell

A leading heartthrob in America during the early 1970s, David Cassidy got much TV and music exposure as part of the made-for-television rock group the Partridge Family. He played Keith Partridge during the show's run on ABC-TV from 1970–74, and his popularity as the fictional group's lead singer turned tunes sung on the TV show into real-life hits.

Cassidy, born in New York City on April 12, 1950 to actor Jack Cassidy and actress Evelyn Ward, concentrated on acting over singing while growing up with his mother, who divorced his father when David was 5. He got a role in a short-lived Broadway show in 1968, *The Fig Leaves Are Falling*, then won several guest shots on TV shows in Hollywood, including *Marcus Welby, M.D.* He got the job on *The Partridge Family* without the producers knowing the woman playing his mother on the show, Shirley Jones, was actually his stepmother, as she had married Jack Cassidy.

Jones and Cassidy were the only actors on *The Partridge Family* who sang both on the show and on records. The first Partridge Family single released, "I Think I Love You," went to #8 AC and #1 pop in 1970, and led to fans demanding more from Cassidy. A spinoff solo career was a natural. "Cherish," Cassidy's first solo single, was a cover of the #1 pop and #38 AC hit by the Association in 1966. Cassidy did the song at the request of his producer, but not willingly. "Wes Farrell would present a bunch of songs to me and, in the beginning, I hated a lot of them," Cassidy told Deidre Rockmaker in *Goldmine* in 1991. "He basically had the control and made the decisions. I could have offered a certain amount of influence but not a lot. I had to sort of, 'Shut up, kid, and sing.'"

"Cherish" made #1 AC plus #9 pop for three weeks starting December 25, 1971. Cassidy had two more entries make both AC and pop in 1972—"Could It Be Forever" (#13 AC, #37 pop) and "How Can I Be Sure" (#3 AC, #25 pop)—but didn't return to either chart for nearly two decades. Partridge Family records had also fallen out of favor by the end of 1972, and when the show ended in 1974, Cassidy spent the rest of the 1970s releasing sporadic solo singles, which had little success in America.

Cassidy spent most of the 1980s doing acting gigs. In 1990 he got a recording contract with the Enigma label after playing some of his demos on a Los Angeles radio station. "Lyin' to Myself" brought Cassidy back to #25 AC and #27 pop, but that was it for recording success and he went back to stage work. In November 1996 he began starring in the "EFX" show at the MGM Grand Hotel in Las Vegas, Nevada, a job he still held in 1998.

164 American Pie—Parts I & II

DON MCLEAN

United Artists 50856

January 15, 1972 (3 weeks)

Writer: Don McLean

Producer: Ed Freeman

The song that encapsulated the story of rock and roll for a generation of Americans had its genesis when Don McLean wrote the lines "A long, long time ago" in reflecting on his feelings about February 3, 1959, "the day the music died," when Buddy Holly, the Big Bopper, and Richie Valens died in a plane crash. He came up with a chorus pretty quickly but didn't complete the song until three months later, when he added allusions to musicians from Bob Dylan ("the jester") to Mick Jagger ("Jack Flash"). The final version summed up his feelings about the progress of popular music from the dawn of rock and roll (which he had lived through, having been born on October 2, 1945, in New Rochelle, New York) to the early 1970s.

When McLean went into the studio with producer Ed Freeman to cut the song, they found that the musicians had no feeling for the rhythm changes they wanted. "And then this one piano player named Paul Griffin, who had worked with Bob Dylan, started running 'American Pie' down, and he played the ass off that song," McLean told Joe Smith in Off the Record. "It just started bouncing all over the place. He really pumped the thing and drove it. And with my guitar in his ear, and him jumping around on piano, it came together."

The tune ran nearly 8½ minutes, but McLean refused to have it edited down to a single, so it took up both sides of a 45. That unusual setup did not stop sales or airplay. "American Pie" topped the AC and pop charts for three weeks simultaneously starting January 15, 1972, and stayed one extra week atop the Hot 100 on February 5, 1972.

"American Pie" became so huge that McLean felt suffocated by the song for a time. He told Edward Kiersh in Where Are You Now, Bo Diddley? that "'American Pie' became my hook that everything revolved around, and, God, was I skewered with it. It was like being an ex-Beatle, people wouldn't question Paul McCartney about anything else. 'American Pie,' 'American Pie.'. . .It was horrible. . . .Every time I'd have another record I'd be asked, 'But is it as big as 'American Pie'? It was a draining, totally annoying experience."

McLean did go on to later success, penning a #1 AC hit for Perry Como [see 193—"And I Love You So"] and getting another #1 AC hit with "Wonderful Baby" [see 262]. But it was "American Pie" which everyone identified with him. His Grammy nominations for Record of the Year, Song of the Year, and Pop Male Vocal Performance of the Year came from "American Pie."

By the mid-1980s McLean had come to terms with his hit, which had inspired Lori Leiberman to write Roberta Flack's 1973 #1 pop and #2 AC hit "Killing Me Softly With His Song." As he told Kiersh, "I got a lot of flak for 'American Pie,' but people have chosen it as their anthem. . . .It's a great song, people cherish it."

165 Hurting Each Other

THE CARPENTERS

A&M 1322

February 5, 1972 (2 weeks)

Writer: Gary Geld, Peter Udell

Producer: Jack Daugherty

The quintet of Ruby and the Romantics is best remembered for the 1963 #1 pop hit "Our Day Will Come," which, despite its smooth sound, did not make the AC chart. The group did make the listings five times later in 1963 and 1964, with their highest AC entry being 1963's "Hey There Lonely Boy" at #5. They kept recording the rest of the decade even though they stopped making the pop chart in 1965. One of their later releases was "Hurting Each Other," which made #113 bubbling under in 1969. By that time the group, which began with lead singer Ruby Nash Curtis being backed by four males, had been transformed into a female trio with Curtis joined by Denise Lewis and Cheryl Thomas.

Ruby and the Romantics' failed version of "Hurting Each Other" might have marked the end of the song's exposure had it not been for Richard Carpenter, who heard the tune because it was a release on A&M, his label. "The Nick DeCaro arrangement combined a bossa nova rhythm in the verses and rhythm ballad feel in the choruses," he recalled in the liner notes to the Carpenters anthology From the Top. "I figured it for a hit. (Wrong.) Recalling the song a couple of years later, I rearranged it and 'Hurting Each Other' became our seventh single release."

The Carpenters' "Hurting Each Other" went to #1 AC plus #2 pop for two weeks starting February 26, 1972, behind "Without You" at #1 [see 166]. It became the Carpenters' sixth consecutive #1 AC after their first single, a remake of the Beatles' "Ticket to Ride," went to #19 in early 1970. But that string ended with the release of the next 45, "It's Going to Take Some Time," a cover of a track from Carole King's 1971 LP Music written by King. "It's Going to Take Some Time" spent some time at #2 AC—four weeks, to be exact—but never could gain enough strength to claim the top spot.

After that came "Goodbye to Love," which perturbed some Carpenters fans and AC programmers, who thought its fuzz guitar solo by Tony Peluso sounded too much like rock music. That kind of reaction may have been why it, too, only went to #2 AC (for one week), although it did better on the pop chart than "It's Going to Take Some Time." The latter made only #12 on the Hot 100 following six consecutive top 10 entries, while "Goodbye to Love" brought them to #7 pop.

But those two failures to make the top proved to be only a brief interruption of the Carpenters' streak, and their next 45 got them back to #1 AC. See 189—"Sing."

166 Without You

NILSSON

RCA 0604

February 19, 1972 (5 weeks)

Writers: Pete Ham, Tom Evans

Producer: Richard Perry

To many music fans, the semioperatic ballad "Without You" is the most memorable record by Nilsson (born Harry Edward Nelson III in Brooklyn, New York, on June 15, 1941). It certainly was the only one guaranteed for release when producer Richard Perry started laying out the *Nilsson Schmilsson* album with the artist in 1971.

"We began the album with one song that we both felt very strongly about, the Badfinger song 'Without You,' but otherwise he had only bits and pieces of songs, none of which he wanted to consider," Perry said in *The Record Producers*, by John Tobler and Stuart Grundy. When Nilsson heard the song on the 1970 Badfinger LP *No Dice*, he took it to Perry and told him it would hit number one.

Badfinger, a quartet led by guitarist Pete Ham and bassist Tom Evans, had previously hit the top 10 pop with three singles from 1970 to 1972—"Come and Get It," "No Matter What," and "Day After Day." Ironically, the latter peaked at #4 the week of February 5, 1972, with "Without You" behind it at #5. "Without You" then reached #1 two weeks later for a four-week stay atop the Hot 100. It also hit #1 in the United Kingdom.

Nilsson's career did not start with "Without You." He wrote music for TV shows and movies, including "Best Friend," the theme from the 1969–72 TV series *The Courtship of Eddie's Father*. Chartwise, his career took off when his first top 10 hit, "Everybody's Talkin'," bubbled under as a single in 1968 to #113, then hit #2 AC and #6 pop a year later after it was heard in the movie *Midnight Cowboy*.

"Everybody's Talkin'" also nabbed Nilsson a Grammy for Best Contemporary Male Vocal Performance. He won that honor again for "Without You," while other nominations went to Perry for Record of the Year and *Nilsson Schmilsson* for Album of the Year. But Nilsson found it hard to match the success of "Without You." He cracked the pop top 20 again only with "Coconut" in 1972, while he hit the AC chart in 1973 with "Remember (Christmas)" at #21 (#53 pop) and "As Time Goes By" at #35 (#86 pop), and then "Daybreak" at #37 in 1974 (#39 pop). He recorded no more LPs after 1976's *That's the Way It Is*.

"Without You" continued to prosper on the charts. The song appeared at #95 R&B in 1975 by Ruby Winters, and at #79 country in 1979 by Susie Allanson and #12 country in 1983 by T. G. Sheppard. On the AC chart it went to #41 in 1973 in a medley by the Pastors with "I Need You" and "Isn't Life Strange," and to #48 in 1991 by Air Supply. In 1994, Mariah Carey's remake reached #3 pop.

Nilsson went into semiretirement in the late 1970s and worked on film projects in the 1980s. He died in his sleep at home on January 15, 1994, after a long period of ill health.

167 Rock and Roll Lullaby

B.J. THOMAS

Scepter 12344

March 25, 1972 (1 week)

Writers: Cynthia Weil (words), Barry Mann (music)

Producers: Steve Tyrell, Al Gorgoni

Although the lyrics to "Rock and Roll Lullaby" use the phrase "rock and roll" several times, the emphasis is not on driving, loud music but on building a soft, nostalgic mood by recreating some of the memorable sounds of pop music during the 1950s and 1960s. "We wanted to make it real authentic," said B.J. Thomas, and to that extent a concerted effort was made by him and his producers to get as many original artists as possible to provide backing vocals or instrumentation.

Thomas, who at the time was not working with his long-time producer Chips Moman, collaborated with Steve Tyrell and Al Gorgoni on what he called "probably the best produced song I've ever done." Gorgoni even got out of the control booth to play on the record. Thomas said that for the guitar part, "Al Gorgoni tried to get the George Harrison sound until Duane Eddy [who contributed his distinctive twangy guitar playing] came in at the end."

Also involved was Barry Mann, who had co-written Thomas's last #1 AC hit [see 138—"I Just Can't Help Believing"] and had also recorded on his own, his releases including the 1961 novelty "Who Put the Bomp (in the Bomp, Bomp, Bomp)," which went to #7 pop. "Barry played piano," Thomas said. Backup vocalists included Dave Sommerville of the Diamonds, a popular doo-wop group of the 1950s ("Little Darlin'," "The Stroll") and the prolific Blossoms, the background singing group for many artists in the 1960s. They and their lead singer Darlene Love were used often by Phil Spector in his pop masterpieces of the early 1960s, and they also provided the actual vocals for two hits by the Crystals, "He's a Rebel" (#1 pop in 1962) and "He's Sure the Boy I Love" (#11 pop in 1963).

Thomas said there was another artist he hoped to have on the record who did not pan out. "We got Brian Wilson on the phone and he agreed to sing with us," he said, referring to the reclusive member of the Beach Boys. But after his verbal commitment, no one could locate him in California in time to do the session, so other singers provided a Beach Boys–style wail in the background instead.

"Rock and Roll Lullaby" went to #15 pop and #1 AC in the spring of 1972. It was popular abroad, too, and Thomas noted that "We sold a million copies in Brazil." But he wasn't to achieve comparable success for another three years. "That's What Friends Are For" (not the #1 AC Dionne Warwick hit of 1985) went only to #38 AC and #74 pop, and its follow-up, "Happier Than the Morning Sun," made just #31 AC and #100 pop. "Songs" in 1973 did even worse, making #41 AC while failing to crack the Hot 100. Thomas' next hit was in 1975 [see 252—"(Hey Won't You Play) Another Somebody Done Somebody Wrong Song"].

168 The First Time Ever I Saw Your Face

ROBERTA FLACK

Atlantic 2864

April 1, 1972 (6 weeks)

Writer: Ewan MacColl

Producer: Joel Dorn

The first time ever you heard Roberta Flack's voice may have been on her debut album *First Take* when it came out in 1969, or maybe in a duet with Donny Hathaway in 1971 (see 172), but it was most likely when "The First Time Ever I Saw Your Face" became a hit in 1972. The tune was actually a cut on *First Take*, which was revived when Clint Eastwood used it as background music for his film *Play Misty for Me*, and became a hit after over a minute of the album track had been edited out to make the song more appealing to radio stations to play at just over four minutes.

"The First Time Ever I Saw Your Face" rode atop the AC chart before staying at #1 pop for six weeks starting April 15, 1972. It also made #4 R&B. Flack actually had gotten her first solo single on the AC and pop charts two months prior to its debut with a cover of Carole King's "Will You Still Love Me Tomorrow" at #15 AC and #76 pop, but it was quickly forgotten in the wake of the other tune.

The single won Grammys for Record of the Year and Song of the Year, but surprisingly Flack lost Best Female Pop Vocal Performance to Helen Reddy even though Flack was nominated for her work on the *Quiet Fire* album and Reddy was competing just with her single "I Am Woman." However, *Quiet Fire* did not contain "The First Time Ever I Saw Your Face," which might have worked against it.

In fact, the history of "The First Time Ever I Saw Your Face" predated that of *First Take*. English folk singer Ewan McColl wrote and first recorded the tune in 1963 for his wife Peggy Seeger, sister of legendary folk singer Pete Seeger. Flack reportedly said her inspiration to record the song was her black cat Sancho Panza.

Born in Asheville, North Carolina, on February 10, 1939, Flack grew up in Arlington, Virginia. She started out as a classical pianist, earning a music scholarship to Howard University when she was 15. After graduation she taught music in a North Carolina high school for a time, but she also played club gigs, and when jazz musician Les McCann heard her at a Capitol Hill club, he urged her to pursue a career as a singer. Atlantic Records signed her in 1969, when she cut *First Take*.

She had decent success after "The First Time Ever I Saw Your Face," returning to #1 AC twice over the next two years, first in a duet with Donny Hathaway [see 172—"Where Is the Love"] and then by herself in 1974 [see 226—"Feel Like Makin' Love"].

169 Morning Has Broken

CAT STEVENS

A&M 1335

May 13, 1972 (1 week)

Writers: Eleanor Farjeon (words), Cat Stevens (music)

Producer: Paul Samwell-Smith

Though he wrote the lyrics and music for most of his hits, Cat Stevens adapted a previous piece of writing to score his second #1 AC hit, "Morning Has Broken." Recounting how the tune came to him to Paul Gambaccini of *Rolling Stone*, Stevens said, "I was in a bookstore and I heard there was a religion section upstairs and something said, yes, go up there, and I went and came to this book of hymns and opened it up and started to read the words. It took about 45 minutes to really understand them. Then it was all getting very heavy, so I left and learned the melody later, because I can't pick up a melody from looking at printed music."

Stevens added some of his own music to the final product, and "Morning Has Broken" became his highest-charting pop entry as well as a #1 AC single, stopping at #6 on the Hot 100 the weeks of June 3 and 10, 1972. One other Stevens single matched the same peak of #6 pop, and that was 1974's "Another Saturday Night," which went to #13 AC.

Between "Morning Has Broken" and "Another Saturday Night," Stevens had three moderately successful singles make both the AC and pop charts—"Sitting" at #17 AC and #16 pop in late 1972, "The Hurt" at #38 AC and #31 pop in 1973, and "Oh Very Young" at #2 AC for one week and #10 pop in the spring of 1974. But after "Another Saturday Night" Stevens failed to crack the top 25 of either chart, and only two other singles made the AC chart after that, both halting at #33 pop. "Two Fine People" in 1975 crept to #39 AC, while "(Remember the Days of the) Old Schoolyard" managed to make #28 AC in 1977.

Two years later, Stevens had his last Hot 100 entry with "Bad Brakes" at #83. The poor showing did not concern him, however, as he had become a devout convert to Islam. He changed his name to Yusuf Islam and forsook virtually everything connected with his music career to work for the Muslim cause in the United Kingdom. Stevens even publicly endorsed a call by Muslim militants in the late 1980s for the death of British author Salman Rushdie, whose book *The Satanic Verses* was condemned as blasphemous by Islamic leaders. In protest, some radio stations refused to play Stevens' old records altogether.

On March 16, 1998, Cat Stevens resurfaced in public in London, still going by Yusuf Islam, to promote two songs he had written for a charity LP benefiting victims of the Bosnian conflict. He himself sang one called "The Little Ones," but said that did not mean he was returning to performing.

170 The Candy Man
SAMMY DAVIS JR.

MGM 14320

May 20, 1972 (2 weeks)

Writers: Anthony Newley, Leslie Bricusse

Producers: Mike Curb, Don Costa

After his success with "I've Got to Be Me" [see 112], based on previous goodwill he had established with Berry Gordy, Davis signed with Motown for a two-album deal. But the first album released in 1971 bombed, as did its only single "I'll Begin Again" from the Broadway musical *The Rothchilds*, which had the distinction of being the only 45 released on the Motown subsidiary label Ecology. As Motown never confirmed when the second LP was forthcoming, Davis bought the unreleased material and sold it to MGM Records President Mike Curb, who signed him.

Curb's real reason for signing Davis was not the Motown recordings but a desire for him to do a track of "The Candy Man" by the Mike Curb Congregation, a sort of in-house young singing act at MGM. "The Candy Man" was the opening song heard in the 1971 movie *Willy Wonka and the Chocolate Factory*, wherein actor Aubrey Woods, playing a candy store owner, sings the praises of Wonka's products to a passel of candy-craving schoolchildren. The soundtrack and the movie went nowhere with the public initially, although the film later became a cult classic. But Curb still had faith in "The Candy Man," so when the Congregation's version generated no interest, he went after Davis.

Davis recalled in his autobiography *Why Me?* that his initial reaction when asked to cut the tune was negative: "It's horrible. It's a timmy-two-shoes, it's white bread, cutems, there's no romance. Blechhh!" But Curb persevered and Davis took only two takes to complete the session, even ad-libbing so that the congregation's backing vocals could come in in the middle of the record. The outcome for Davis was that the album of Motown material tanked while "The Candy Man" hit #1 AC then topped the Hot 100 for three weeks in June of 1972, despite the ridiculous accusation made by some that the song's lyrics promoted drug use.

The popularity of the record flabbergasted Davis, but it gave him renewed respect for the power of record buyers. He told aspiring singers in *Why Me?* to "go out there and play it by ear, but leave a lot of room for the people to discover something you're doing. Because it's the people who lay it on you." No one ever laid it on Davis again in terms of hit records. "The People Tree" used the Mike Curb Congregation too but only hit #16 AC and #92 pop in late 1972. It was the last Hot 100 entry for Davis. His last AC entry was "Baretta's Theme (Keep Your Eye on the Sparrow)," which went to #42 AC and #101 bubbling under in 1976. He made the country chart as late as 1982 with "Smoke, Smoke, Smoke (That Cigarette)," and even returned to Motown to record briefly in 1984.

Sammy Davis Jr. died from throat cancer on May 16, 1990. He was 64 years old.

171 Song Sung Blue
NEIL DIAMOND

Uni 55326

June 3, 1972 (7 weeks)

Writer: Neil Diamond

Producers: Tom Catalano, Neil Diamond

Neil Diamond, whose often introspective songwriting combined with a dynamic performing style inspired intense devotion from his fans, was one of the hottest artists on the AC chart in the 1970s and 1980s. Though his songs often became hits when performed by acts as diverse as the Monkees and UB40, it is his own recordings which easy listening music fans made into the biggest AC hits and which they remember the best.

Born in Brooklyn, New York, on January 24, 1941, Diamond wrote his first song, "Hear Them Bells," as a teenager. He recorded several demos in 1958 and 1959, but "Blue Destiny," "A Million Miles Away," and "A Good Kind of Lonely" did not attract anyone's attention and went nowhere. He finally got a record released on the Duel label in 1960 in a duet with his fellow Lincoln High School senior Jack Packer, but "What Will I Do?" by Neil & Jack, as the label read, stirred no action.

Undaunted, Diamond kept writing in the early to mid-1960s and even got a contract with Columbia Records to do one single, yet neither "At Night" or its B-side, "Clown Town," caused any flurry of activity among record buyers or radio programmers in 1963. He finally debuted on the Hot 100 in 1966 with "Solitary Man," which hit #55. Its follow-up "Cherry, Cherry," brought him to #6 pop and became the first of six consecutive releases to make the top third of the Hot 100 through the end of 1967.

Diamond did not emerge on the AC chart until his 1969 triumph "Sweet Caroline (Good Times Never Seemed So Good)," which made #3 AC and #4 pop. Three years later, he reached the summit there with "Song Sung Blue."

The liner notes to the 1996 Neil Diamond anthology *In My Lifetime* quotes the artist's thoughts to "Song Sung Blue" with the following: "This is one to which I never paid too much attention. A very basic message, unadorned. I didn't even write a bridge to it. I never expected anyone to react to 'Song Sung Blue' the way they did. I just like it, the message and the way a few words said so many things. I recorded the song strictly for that reason. I had no idea it would be a huge hit or that people would want to sing along with it."

"Song Sung Blue" did have a large impact on Diamond's career. Besides its long run at #1 AC, it also made #1 on the pop chart the week of July 1, 1972. It won Diamond Grammy nominations for Record of the Year and Song of the Year. And it became his unofficial theme song for the rest of the 1970s at least (for example, when he came onto the 1977 Academy Awards to give the Best Song Oscar, the orchestra struck up "Song Sung Blue"). Diamond would score seven more #1 AC entries, the next being "Longfellow Serenade" [see 236].

172 Where Is the Love

ROBERTA FLACK AND DONNY HATHAWAY

Atlantic 2879

July 22, 1972 (1 week)

Writers: Ralph MacDonald, William Salter

Producers: Joel Dorn, Arif Mardin

Jerry Wexler of Atlantic Records was frustrated in his attempts to turn Roberta Flack and Donny Hathaway, her former classmate at Howard University in Washington, D.C, into a top singing duo during the early 1970s. First he tried having them cover "You've Got a Friend" from Carole King's *Tapestry* LP, but James Taylor's competing 45 beat them out and they stalled at #36 AC and #29 pop instead. Then he tried them on a remake of the Righteous Brothers' #1 pop hit of 1964, "You've Lost That Lovin' Feeling," and did even worse, missing the AC chart while going only to #71 pop.

But salvation for Wexler was at hand, and ironically it came from two more students at Howard University. Ralph MacDonald and William Salter originally wrote "Where Is the Love" for the Fifth Dimension. MacDonald was quoted in *The Billboard Book of #1 Rhythm and Blues Hits* by Adam White and Fred Bronson as saying, "We wrote it with them in mind. They had a hit called 'Up-Up and Away,' and my partner William Salter and I had an argument. I said 'It's a white group' and he said, 'It's a black group.'. . .We felt we could do something for this group, and we came up with 'Where Is the Love.' And we could never get it to them."

As a result, MacDonald pitched "Where Is the Love" to Atlantic Records, and ended up playing percussion on the track. Flack and Hathaway also contributed to the track's instrumentation by playing keyboards.

Flack and Hathaway's "Where Is the Love" hit #1 R&B the week of August 5, 1972, and peaked at #5 pop the week of August 12, 1972. It had frequent revivals, beginning with Sergio Mendes and Brasil '77 at #36 AC in 1973. In 1977 Ralph McDonald got it to #76 R&B, then in 1989 a version by Robert Brookins featuring Stephanie Mills made #18 R&B. In 1995 Jesse and Trina's cover went to #40 R&B, followed a year later by "Never Leave Me Alone," a #33 pop single by Nate Dogg using part of the Flack and Hathaway original. At the Grammy Awards Flack and Hathaway won for Best Pop Vocal Performance by a Duo, Group or Chorus.

Flack and Hathaway reunited in 1978, when their duet "The Closer I Get to You" went to #3 AC and #2 pop. Less than a year later, on January 13, 1979, Hathaway committed suicide by jumping off the 15th floor of the Essex House hotel in New York City. He was 33 years old. A year later, material he recorded previously with Flack came out as the singles "You Are My Heaven" (#46 AC, #47 pop) and "Back Together Again" (#56 pop).

173 Alone Again (Naturally)

GILBERT O'SULLIVAN

MAM 3619

July 29, 1972 (6 weeks)

Writer: Gilbert O'Sullivan

Producer: Gordon Mills

The top-selling single of 1972 was "Alone Again (Naturally)," which did not strike its composer and singer as anything special. Record buyers throughout America disagreed and sent it to #1 simultaneously on the pop and AC charts for six weeks beginning July 29, 1972. An annoying by-product of the popularity of "Alone Again" was that Gilbert found himself repeatedly having to deny that he was anything like the depressed, introverted character portrayed in the hit song. (Just to set the record straight, O'Sullivan did not weep when his dad died, was not, at the time the song was released, close to marriage and had never been stood up at the altar, and his mother was alive. He later married and had two children.)

"You don't have to experience something to be sincere about it. That's really my philosophy. Most of my songs are fictitious, but it's an understanding of a subject. After all, you can't write about potential suicides or death of people if you don't take the thing seriously and have some sincerity in the way you do it. Otherwise, it will come across as fairly crass," O'Sullivan told Barry Scott in *We Had Joy, We Had Fun*.

The tune garnered three nominations but no wins at the Grammys a few months later, with nods going for Record of the Year, Song of the Year and Best Male Pop Vocal Performance. "Alone Again (Naturally)" also hit the country chart in 1973 in a version by Brush Arbor that hit #72.

The artist was born Raymond O'Sullivan in Waterford, Ireland, on December 1, 1941, and moved to Swindon, England, with his family in 1960 before being rechristened in 1967 when he signed to CBS Records to make his debut as a recording artist. (He previously worked with such forgotten bands as the Doodles, the Prefects, and Rick's Blues.) Some sources say the name change was prompted by his producer and manager Gordon Mills, but O'Sullivan disagreed, noting that he did not meet Mills until 1969. (Mills did later produce all of Gilbert's hit singles.)

It took nearly two years before O'Sullivan and Mills finally began to record new tunes. Their first effort, "Nothing Rhymed," only bubbled under to #114 in the United States in 1971. A year later came "Alone Again," which O'Sullivan told Scott was not the first song under consideration for release.

O'Sullivan remembered, "Decision time came and everybody thought 'Out of the Question' was more commercial than 'Alone Again (Naturally).' At the 11th hour, Gordon said, ' "Alone Again" isn't commercial, but it's a better song, so let's go with it.'"

"Out of the Question" did get released later, but only after "Clair" also hit #1 AC [see 181].

174 The Guitar Man

BREAD

Elektra 45803

September 9, 1972 (1 week)

Writer: David Gates

Producer: David Gates

Since David Gates wrote and produced "The Guitar Man," it is obvious what he played on the record, right? Wrong. "The guitar player on that was Larry Knechtel," Gates said, referring to the rather un-AC, slightly raucous instrumental part of the tune. "I couldn't do it, James [Griffin] couldn't do it, but Larry could." Gates recalled that Knechtel nailed the section in only three takes.

Another false assumption would be that the group cheering at the end was a live audience at the end of a recording session. "The ending on that record was the best of any I've been involved with," Gates said. He liked the changes in sound, which he likened to the theme from the 1965 James Bond film *Goldfinger*, and he liked the cheering, which was edited into the song after being recorded at an unlikely source for a Bread single—a Doors concert." Gates said, "If you listen real close, in the audience some guy says, 'The Doors!'"

Gates also thought his inspiration for the lyrics came from an authentic feeling "for all those guys out there who love to play, they don't care how many people are in the audience." But he found it strange that he has never heard directly from any "guitar man" who enjoyed and appreciated the message of his song.

"The Guitar Man," while making the top of the AC chart, just missed the pop top 10, peaking at #11 in 1972. Knechtel's wailing guitar proved to be no obstacle in getting easy listening play for the song, something that had not happened with a few previous Bread singles such as "Let Your Love Go," which stopped at #28 pop in early 1971. For those Bread singles which did make the AC chart, the group had an impressive record: All 11 of their AC singles made at least the #4 position.

Following "The Guitar Man," Bread had one more #1 AC hit with "Sweet Surrender" [see 182]. But shortly thereafter, Gates thought the sound of Bread went stale. Of Bread's attempt to come up with a new album in 1973, he said, "We had run out of the collective chemistry of the co-writing things. It was just pathetic, I thought, the quality of the songs and the group's attitude." Gates dissolved the group the same year, though there were to be a number of reunions in their future and as of 1998 it was not out of the question that Bread would do a CD. For more information on Bread's later years, see 182.

175 Baby Don't Get Hooked on Me

MAC DAVIS

Columbia 45618

September 16, 1972 (3 weeks)

Writer: Mac Davis

Producer: Rick Hall

Fans of Elvis Presley were caught unaware in 1969 when Ol' Swivel Hips decided to get serious and sang the social protest song "In the Ghetto." The song registered at #3 pop and #8 AC and brought attention to its songwriter, guitarist Mac Davis. The curly-haired Davis, born in Lubbock, Texas, on January 21, 1942, promptly launched his own career as a vocalist after spending much of the 1960s in minor jobs in the music industry.

His early singing efforts in 1970 left a lot to be desired hit-wise. "Whoever Finds This, I Love You" was his AC and pop debut, stopping at #25 AC and #53 pop. He then had two AC entries in 1970 which bubbled under, "I'll Paint You a Song" (#14 AC, #110 bubbling under) and "I Believe in Music" (#25 AC, #117 bubbling under). The latter did get covered by several artists, including Marian Love, whose 1971 take went to #27 AC and #111 bubbling under, and became a hit in 1972 for the group Gallery, who took it to #22 pop and #12 AC. By the time Gallery's version was peaking, Davis finally had his own hit with "Baby Don't Get Hooked on Me."

Davis recounted in *Billboard* how his producer Rick Hall wanted him to write a song with a catchy hook. "So I came up with this phrase and melody line, 'baby don't get hooked on me.' Hall tells me, 'Now that sounds like a number one record. Let's cut it.' Hell, I hadn't even written it yet. So the band made up a skeleton chord progression. I wrote the song that night and we cut it the next day. I thought it was super-egotistical and pretentious, but Columbia released it as a single anyway."

One man's super-egotism and pretentiousness proved to be another's favorite tune as "Baby Don't Get Hooked on Me" went to #1 both AC and pop, topping both charts for three weeks, although its pop run began the week of September 23, 1972.

Riding on the wave of popularity of "Baby Don't Get Hooked on Me," Davis had several AC and pop singles over the next two years, including "Everybody Loves a Love Song" (#13 AC, #63 pop) in 1972, "Dream Me Home" (#32 AC, #73 pop), and "Your Side of the Bed" (#28 AC, #88 pop) in 1973 and "One Hell of a Woman" (#20 AC, #11 pop) in 1974. He also won a spot hosting his own musical variety series on NBC-TV airing off and on from 1974 to 1976. During that period, he returned to the #1 AC spot with "Stop and Smell the Roses" [see 232].

176 Black and White
THREE DOG NIGHT

Dunhill 4317

October 7, 1972 (1 week)

Writers: David Arkin, Earl Robinson

Producer: Richard Polodor

A song Danny Hutton heard during a vacation gave his group Three Dog Night a second #1 AC and third #1 pop hit. The only Three Dog Night hit to top both charts, "Black and White" made the summit of the Hot 100 the week of September 16, 1972, three weeks ahead of doing so on the AC chart. "I used to go to England every Christmas, and I was over in Holland and checked into the big hotel there," Hutton recalled. A song was playing on the radio as he entered the room. Its end chorus caught Hutton's ear, so he called the radio station and asked them what the record was. The single was "Black and White," done by a Jamaican group named Greyhound. Released in 1971, the song hit #6 on the United Kingdom chart but stirred little interest in America. Greyhound had two more records on the U.K. chart in 1972 ("Moon River" and "I Am What I Am") before disappearing from it entirely.

When Greyhound's version failed in America, Three Dog Night cut its own rendition. While noting that "The basic [instrumental] track was incredible," Hutton hated his early singing attempts. "I had a very hard time coming up with a vocal," he said. "I did it with accents, nothing worked." Then after three days of trying, Hutton hit on the right timbre to use. "For some reason, I thought of Gene Pitney, that fast vibrato, and I got it."

After "Black and White" became a hit for Three Dog Night, the group met one of the song's writers backstage after a concert in Los Angeles. Earl Robinson told them he and David Arkin (father of actor Alan Arkin) composed it in 1955 to celebrate the first anniversary of the U.S. Supreme Court's ruling banning segregation from public schools. Hutton admitted that the verses were not the main reason he cut the song. "I just did it because I loved the choruses."

Three Dog Night kept making the AC chart through the release of "Til the World Ends" in 1975 (#11 AC, #32 pop). Shortly thereafter the group disbanded, with an old track, "Everybody Is a Masterpiece," making only #44 AC in 1976.

In 1981 Hutton and co-vocalist Cory Wells re-formed Three Dog Night with a few other original backing musicians, including keyboardist Jimmy Greenspoon and guitarist Michael Allsup. The other lead vocalist, Chuck Negron, did not rejoin the group. He battled a drug dependency for years before becoming a touring solo performer and doing his own LP in 1996. "He's nice and healthy now," said Hutton.

As for Three Dog Night, "We do between 80 and 100 gigs a year," Hutton said. In 1998 they planned to do their first LP of new material since the 1970s, and Hutton sounded optimistic about what they would record. "I don't want to go back in[to the studio] unless you got the hits," he said.

177 Garden Party
RICK NELSON & THE STONE CANYON BAND

Decca 32980

October 14, 1972 (2 weeks)

Writer: Rick Nelson

Producer: Rick Nelson

After being off the charts since the mid-1960s, Rick Nelson returned in 1969 at #27 AC and #33 pop with "She Belongs to Me." The record listed the artist as "Rick Nelson and the Stone Canyon Band." The latter consisted of Tom Brumley and Randy Meisner, who later joined the Eagles, and the group emphasized folk and rockabilly, not the sounds associated with Rick's earlier career. He did not take that into consideration when he reluctantly accepted a date to play an oldies show in Madison Square Garden in New York City in 1971, where his new material was not well received.

"The Garden crowd wanted the old Ricky Nelson," he told Edward Kiersh in *Where Are You Now, Bo Diddley?* "After a while, I realized that, so the hurt went away. I had disappointed them. That booing wasn't a putdown, it was just a tribute to what I had done in the past."

Sticking to his principles, however, Nelson went to Great Britain and recorded "Garden Party," a sparsely produced tune in which he stated unequivocally that he refused to be a musician if he had to live on his old glories. An apparently sympathetic public took the song to #1 AC, #6 pop, and #44 country.

"It was an important song for me, I was able to express my real feelings, and the public accepted it," he told Kiersh. "You'd think that MCA would've been happy, they had themselves a big seller. In fact, though, I created a monster with 'Garden Party.' Just when the record was doing real well I got this call from Mike Maitland, the MCA president. I thought he was calling to congratulate me, but instead he tells me, 'You spent too much money, you need a producer.' I couldn't believe it. Not only did they stop promoting the album, but they also wanted to limit my freedom. . . .It was clearly the beginning of the end of our relationship."

"Palace Guard," the follow-up to "Garden Party," went only to #65 pop in 1973, his last Hot 100 entry. The next year "Windfall," the title tune to Nelson's newest LP, went to #46 AC, and shortly thereafter MCA dropped him from the company. He continued to record for seven more years, but efforts like his LPs *Intakes* (1977) on Epic and *Playing to Win* (1981) on Capitol plus singles like "Dream Lover" (#29 AC in 1979, his last entry on the chart) generated little interest.

With his recording career at a standstill, Nelson did occasional acting jobs and around 200 concerts a year. It was going to one of those dates that he and his band died in a plane crash in DeKalb, Texas, on December 31, 1985. He was not to see his daughter Tracy become a successful actress, or his twin sons Gunnar and Matthew have a hit recording career in the 1990s as Nelson, or his induction into the Rock and Roll Hall of Fame in 1987.

178 If I Could Reach You

THE 5TH DIMENSION

Bell 45261

October 28, 1972 (1 week)

Writer: Landy McNeill

Producer: Bones Howe

Marilyn McCoo said the Fifth Dimension encountered "If I Could Reach You" at the same time they met its composer Landy McNeill. "He was a young writer who Bones was working with. . . .As a matter of fact, he performed ['If I Could Reach You'] for us live." McCoo said she would have preferred to hear the song on a demo because "I've never felt comfortable saying to a writer, 'I don't like it,' to his face."

Thankfully, in this case she didn't have to do that. "I really liked the song first time I heard it. . . .I just really enjoyed singing that song," McCoo said. She may have enjoyed it too much, as she wanted to improvise on parts of it more than Howe wanted her to do. "He really wanted to keep it straight," McCoo said. "I wanted to do some variations to put something on it." In the end, Howe won out, but McCoo noted, "I ended up being able to bend a couple of notes."

"If I Could Reach You" went to #10 pop the week of November 25, 1972, after being #1 AC. It was the last #1 AC

and last top 30 pop song for the group. They had five more singles on the AC chart ending with "No Love in the Room," which went to #11 AC and #105 bubbling under in early 1975. In November of that year, McCoo and her husband Billy Davis Jr. decided to leave the group.

"We just felt like we weren't looking for the same things anymore," McCoo said. She said they felt the Fifth Dimension was doing the same musical approach with decreasing success and "other members were afraid to change it." She and Davis wanted a change, so they left.

While the Fifth Dimension faded away shortly thereafter (their cover of Diana Ross's "Love Hangover" was their last pop entry, hitting #80 on the Hot 100 in 1976), McCoo and Davis Jr. had several entries from 1976–77 as a duo, the biggest being "You Don't Have to Be a Star (To Be in My Show)," which went to #1 pop and #6 AC in 1977. In the 1980s McCoo was quite visible on television, hosting the musical variety series *Solid Gold* from 1981–84 and acting on the NBC-TV soap opera *Days of Our Lives* from 1986–87.

In 1998 McCoo and Davis toured with "It Takes Two," a show consisting of songs that were hits when done by various combinations of two artists. "We are singing the great duets of the '60s, '70s, and '80s," McCoo said. But they did not forget their Fifth Dimension roots. "We did a reunion performance and tour with the group in 1992," McCoo said. Since then, McCoo and Davis have done three or more shows a year with the other original members "under very special conditions," as she put it. The Fifth Dimension have also toured in the 1990s, with original members Florence LaRue and Lamont McLemore plus three others.

179 I Can See Clearly Now

JOHNNY NASH

Epic 10902

November 4, 1972 (4 weeks)

Writer: Johnny Nash

Producer: Johnny Nash

Potential teen idol in the 1950s, reggae-influenced musician of the 1960s and 1970s, virtual recluse by the 1980s and 1990s—Johnny Nash has been many things over the years. One of his career highlights was certainly "I Can See Clearly Now," which was #1 AC and pop simultaneously for four weeks starting November 4, 1972, plus made #38 R&B.

Nash's professional career had started nearly two decades before the rise of "I Can See Clearly Now." Born in Houston, Texas, on August 19, 1940, he was the first African-American to be a regular performer on local television there, on KPRC-TV's *Matinee* show. His success there earned him a regular spot on the daily CBS-TV series *Arthur Godfrey Time* in the late 1950s, by which time he had his first pop hit with "A Very Special Love" at #23 in 1958. He had three more pop entries over the next year: "Almost in Your Arms" (#78, 1958), "The Teen Commandments" with Paul Anka and George Hamilton IV (#29, 1959), and "As Time Goes By" (the song from the 1942 movie *Casablanca*; #43, 1959). By this time, his career as a teen idol seemed unlikely to pan out, so he took a different tack.

In the early 1960s Nash visited Jamaica and found himself inspired by the reggae music played there. He started his own labels JoDa and then JAD and became one of the few artists at the time to write, produce, promote, and distribute his own records. All his work finally paid off in 1968, when "Hold Me Tight" went to #5 pop and was his first AC entry at #20. The B-side of that record, a remake of "Cupid," went to #38 AC and #39 pop in late 1969, then he had no other singles until "I Can See Clearly Now," which he recorded with Bob Marley's Wailers backing him.

Riding on the success of "I Can See Clearly Now," Nash played his first American club date in seven years in 1973 at The Whisky in Los Angeles. But his reign on the charts was to be short-lived. "Stir It Up," written by Marley, did go to #6 AC and #12 pop in the spring of 1973, but "My Merry-Go-Round" in mid-1973 made only #34 AC and #77 pop, and its follow-up, "Ooh What a Feeling," fared worse, going to just #38 AC and #103 bubbling under. Three years later came his last AC single, "(What a) Wonderful World," which made #34 AC and #103 bubbling under.

A few other Nash singles made the British chart in the late 1970s but after that he reportedly retired from performing. Despite Nash's inactivity, "I Can See Clearly Now" remained popular. An instrumental version in 1973 by Lloyd Green made #36 country. A 1978 Ray Charles cover got to #35 R&B. And in 1994 reggae artist Jimmy Cliff redid the tune for the soundtrack for the movie *Cool Runnings* and got to #18 pop and #98 R&B.

180 I'd Love You to Want Me

LOBO

Big Tree 147

December 2, 1972 (1 week)

Writer: Kent Lavoie

Producer: Phil Gernhard

"Me and You and a Dog Named Boo" [see 150] gave Lobo a big splash on the AC and pop charts in 1971, but it was nearly two years before he had another single of similar magnitude. The follow-up to "Me and You and a Dog Named Boo" was a double-sided single, and the split airplay was probably a factor in keeping the record from becoming a hit. "I'm the Only One" was listed as the A-side on the AC chart, with "She Didn't Do Magic" as the flip; on the Hot 100, the positions were reversed. The sides were listed together, and the record went only to #14 AC and #46 pop.

In the fall of 1971 Lobo offered "California Kid and Reemo," but few were interested in trying it, as it got to just #19 AC and #72 pop. In the summer of 1972 "A Simple Man" was only a slight improvement, going to #17 AC and #56 pop. Lobo's next release, however, was "I'd Love You to Want Me," which went to #1 AC after nearly reaching the top on the pop chart, stopping at #2 the weeks of November 18 and 25, 1972, behind "I Can See Clearly Now" [see 179]. It took longer to charm the British, with the tune failing to chart in its initial release in 1972 but going to #1 in the United Kingdom in a reissue in 1974. In the end, "I'd Love You to Want Me" sold over a million copies.

In 1982 Lobo provided a backing vocal for Narvel Felts in the latter's cover of "I'd Love You to Want Me." It went to #58 country on the Lobo label. Felts also recorded two follow-ups for Lobo Records that year, "Sweet Southern Moonlight" and "Roll Over Beethoven."

Lobo was born Roland Kent Lavoie in Tallahassee, Florida, on July 31, 1943. As a teenager he joined the Legends, a rock outfit which included future music stars Gram Parsons, an album rock legend who died in 1973 at age 26, and Jim Stafford. Regarding the latter, Lobo told Barry Scott in *We Had Joy, We Had Fun* that "All I remember was this shy little boy who used to hang around in high school. He was a year behind me. Mr. Quiet, Mr. Practice-His-Guitar. I [hadn't] seen him for five or six years. He was over in St. Petersburg [Florida], and he asked me to come and hear some songs. . . .Man, he came out and started his first show. I couldn't believe he was a comedian. I just absolutely fell on the floor. The guy was great."

Both Lobo and Stafford did well in the 1970s, although Lobo had the bigger hits. He earned his third #1 AC entry two months after "I'd to Want Me" with "Don't Expect Me to Be Your Friend" [see 185].

181 Clair

GILBERT O'SULLIVAN

MAM 3626

December 9, 1972 (3 weeks)

Writer: Gilbert O'Sullivan

Producer: Gordon Mills

"Clair" marked the first time a female's proper name appeared alone in the title of a #1 AC hit. And unlike Gilbert O'Sullivan's previous #1 AC hit "Alone Again (Naturally)" [see 173], the title and song concerned an actual human being—the daughter of his manager and producer, Gordon Mills. O'Sullivan told Barry Scott in *We Had Joy, We Had Fun*, "[Mills] and his wife. . .were almost like parents to me. I used to babysit for them. [Clair] was one of their children. She was the youngest. So, I'd be sort of babysitting every now and then and I kind of got attached to her. As a thank-you to the parents for being so good to me, I wrote the song." The giggling heard at the end of the song came from Clair herself.

Besides its AC showing, "Clair" also nestled into the #2 slot on the Hot 100 the final week of 1972 and the first week of 1973, blocked the first week by Billy Paul's "Me and Mrs. Jones" and the second by "You're So Vain" [see 184]. The song also hit #1 in O'Sullivan's native Great Britain.

O'Sullivan's later singles included "Out of the Question" (#17 pop, #2 AC), "Get Down" (#7 pop, #3 AC), and "Ooh Baby" (#25 pop, #24 AC), all in 1973; "Happiness Is Me and You" (#62 pop, #23 AC) in 1974; and "You Are You" (#17 AC) in 1975. In 1976, growing weary of his working partnership with Mills, he tried to break the contract between them, but spent over a decade litigating to regain the rights to his music and the right to record with other producers. During this period, O'Sullivan was able to get only one album released, the self-produced *Southpaw* in 1980. A single from that LP, "What's in a Kiss?" was a top 20 hit in the United Kingdom but only went to #13 on the AC chart and failed even to bubble under.

In 1989 O'Sullivan released his *In the Key of 'G'* album in England, but could find no American record company willing to distribute it in the United States. The next year he returned to the U.K. singles chart with "So What," but the title kind of summed up the record's performance, as it peaked at #70. The same year, O'Sullivan created a stage production based on his life which ran in England under the title *Every Song Has Its Play*. Since then he has lived on Jersey (one of the Channel Islands), virtually out of sight for most Americans until 1998, when Rhino Records released *The Best of Gilbert O'Sullivan*, a rerelease of a 1991 greatest hits album, which became his first release stateside in nearly two decades.

182 Sweet Surrender

BREAD

Elektra 45818

December 30, 1972 (2 weeks)

Writer: David Gates

Producer: David Gates

"It's about the only song I wrote for Bread while on a Bread tour," noted David Gates in describing the creation of "Sweet Surrender," adding that for some reason whenever the group was on the road, he found it difficult to complete a song. Gates had gotten a riff on his guitar, in his hotel room, that struck him as interesting. He went to fellow guitarist Larry Knechtel's room and said, "Hey, listen to this." Knechtel liked what he heard and Gates went on to complete his composition.

With sly references to such topics as the women's liberation movement of the period (mentioned in the "You keep your rights" line), "Sweet Surrender" definitely was not the typical Bread song of romantic longing. "That's just a happy song," Gates said. "It's not meant to be anything deep or meaningful."

"Sweet Surrender" surrendered to the #15 pop slot in addition to #1 AC. Its follow-up was "Aubrey," which held at #4 AC and #15 pop in early 1973. That same year Gates and the others broke Bread up and pursued their own interests, with Gates establishing a solo career that generated eight entries on the AC chart, the biggest being "Goodbye Girl" from the Neil Simon movie of the same name, which rose to #3 AC and #15 pop in 1978.

But before that triumph, Bread reunited in 1976 at the urging of the record company, who observed that the group's old material still sold well and generated airplay and realized that the quartet owed them two albums under their original contact. Regarding the reunion, Gates said, "I had my doubts, because I didn't think the chemistry had returned." Nonetheless, he appreciated working with Knechtel, James Griffin, and Mike Botts again, and they generated two hits in 1977, "Lost Without Your Love" (#3 AC, #9 pop) and "Hooked on You" (#2 AC, #60 pop).

Nearly 20 years later, in 1996 and 1997, Gates, Knechtel, Griffin, and Botts had a second go-round as Bread, playing venues such as South Africa, New Zealand, and some Asian countries where they remained popular. "It was great," he said, although no new material came out of the reunion tour.

Back on his own, Gates worked both for himself and for others. "I'm just songwriting and doing projects," he said in 1998, noting that in 1994 he had co-produced an album for country singer Billy Dean as well as done his own solo LP. "If something interesting comes along, I'll do it."

Gates added that he still enjoys performing as well, though he does not plan to do any more concerts with Bread at present. "I do maybe 20 concerts a year, orchestra things. . . .If I can go out and do 20 a year, I'm happy."

183 Been to Canaan

CAROLE KING

Ode 66031

January 13, 1973 (1 week)

Writer: Carole King

Producer: Lou Adler

Carole King's success with *Tapestry* [see 151—"It's Too Late"] continued with its follow-up in late 1971, *Music*. Although *Music* did not achieve the massive sales of the earlier album, it did well enough to stay at #1 for three weeks starting January 1, 1972 and generated the hit single "Sweet Seasons," which peaked at #2 AC and #9 pop. The next album after that was *Rhymes and Reasons*, which peaked at #2 in late 1972 and spun off King's second #1 AC song, "Been to Canaan," which also went to #24 pop; the song refers to Canaan, Connecticut, the rural community which served as King's new home during the recording of the album. She wrote most of the LP's songs there, and in fact *Rhymes and Reasons* was the first King album to feature all new songs, half of which were written by King alone.

Producer Lou Adler recalled in the liner notes to *Carole King: A Natural Woman* that for *Rhymes and Reasons* "We added strings, a big difference from the first two albums. And we kept the horns. But there also was more of an R&B feel to the rhythm section, something that Carole, of course, has roots in as far as her writing and piano playing. She played electric piano and organ as well as piano, and we had David T. Walker on guitar and Harvey Mason on drums—we were getting more into session players on this album."

She had also begun to lose some of her fear of performing in public by this time, though she never appeared totally confident with the concept. King was nervous at her debut at the Troubadour in West Hollywood, California, on May 18, 1971, but buoyed by good reviews there, she went on to do several more concerts over the next few years, including an all-star benefit concert for Democratic presidential candidate George McGovern along with Barbra Streisand and James Taylor on April 15, 1972, prior to recording *Rhymes and Reasons*.

King followed *Rhymes and Reasons* with *Fantasy*, which peaked at #6 on the LP chart in the summer of 1973. It contained two moderately successful singles, the first a double-sided entry. On the pop chart, "You Light Up My Life" (not the Debby Boone #1 hit of 1977; see 340) went only to #67, while its flip, "Believe in Humanity," reached #37, but on the AC chart both sides were listed together and peaked at #6, with "You Light Up My Life" listed first. King then surprised her fans with "Corazon," a tune she sang in Spanish, which went to #5 AC and #37 pop.

Her next album, *Wrap Around Joy*, proved to be a bigger success on the charts than *Fantasy*. It included King's third #1 AC hit; see 248—"Nightingale."

1973

184 You're So Vain

CARLY SIMON

Elektra 45824

January 20, 1973 (2 weeks)

Writer: Carly Simon

Producer: Richard Perry

When it comes to "You're So Vain," hardly anybody cares about the fact that its original title was "Bless You Ben," or that it earned Carly Simon a Grammy nomination for Best Female Pop Vocal Performance, or that it was her first #1 on both the AC and pop charts. No, what they really want to know is, who is this narcissist Simon was writing about?

Often-mentioned candidates are then-husband James Taylor, Mick Jagger, and Warren Beatty. Simon has publically ruled out Taylor, but not Beatty and Jagger, and has admitted the portrait is a composite one. Beatty's reputation as a womanizer was well established by 1972, but some think Jagger is a more likely suspect and that Simon had him do background vocals on the song as a subtle way of indicating that the lyrics *were* about him.

Producer Richard Perry gave his perspective on the subject to John Tobler and Stuart Grundy in *The Record Producers.* "It's about a compilation of men that Carly had known, but primarily Warren Beatty," he said. "Mick Jagger got involved because Carly had become friendly with him some months before and felt that it would be good for Mick to sing backgrounds." Perry himself put his own mark on the single by having the song recorded three times, each with a different drummer, before getting the result he wanted.

Ironically, the song about the unidentified louse appeared on Simon's LP titled *No Secrets,* which went to #1 for five weeks starting January 13, 1973, based largely on the strength of "You're So Vain." The single went to #1 pop for three weeks starting January 6, 1973. The tune also became her first and highest-charting single on the British pop chart when it peaked at #3 in early 1973.

Simon was born in New York City on June 25, 1945. Her first *Billboard* chart exposure came in 1964 when she and her sister Lucy hit #73 pop as the Simon Sisters with "Winkin,' Blinkin,' and Nod." When Lucy decided to get married, the two disbanded and Carly embarked on a solo career that did not generate any excitement until she charted AC and pop with her single "That's the Way I've Always Heard It Should Be" in 1971. It hit #6 AC and #10 pop and helped her claim the Grammy for Best New Artist of 1971.

On both charts during the 1970s Simon proved to be a top-selling artist, both solo and on a few duets with her husband, James Taylor (the two divorced in 1983). Her "Haven't Got Time for the Pain" came close to bringing her back to the top in 1974 when it peaked at #2 AC. She finally did return to #1 AC in 1977 with "Nobody Does It Better" [see 337].

185 Don't Expect Me to Be Your Friend

LOBO

Big Tree 158

February 3, 1973 (2 weeks)

Writer: Kent Lavoie

Producer: Phil Gernhard

"Don't Expect Me to Be Your Friend" was the third Lobo single to go to the pop top 10. Coincidentally, it was also the third #1 AC single for him for two weeks before going to #8 pop the weeks of February 17 and 24, 1973. It marked the last time a Lobo single made the pop top 20. It was also the second release from Lobo's album *Of a Simple Man.* The same year Lobo released one other single from the album, "There Ain't No Way," but it went to just #29 AC plus #68 pop. Its B-side, "Love Me for What I Am," which was not on *Of a Simple Man,* also got some airplay before the end of 1973 and made #86 pop.

"Love Me for What I Am" was on Lobo's album *Calumet,* whose first single was "It Sure Took a Long, Long Time." That 45 needed only a brief time to get to #3 AC while stalling at #27 pop in the spring of 1973. In the summer of 1973 came "How Can I Tell Her," another *Calumet* cut which made #4 AC and #22 pop. The last single from the album was titled appropriately "Standing at the End of the Line;" it came in at #25 AC and #37 pop.

Lobo did better, at least on the AC chart, with "Rings" in 1974 (#8 AC, #43 pop) and "Don't Tell Me Goodnight" in early 1975 (#2 AC for one week, #27 pop). But after "Would I Still Have You" reached #44 AC in the summer of 1975, Lobo was off both charts for four years. He and his longtime producer Phil Gernhard went their separate ways as Lobo tried to reestablish himself on a few labels.

The dwindling appeal for Lobo as the mid-1970s approached was just fine with the critics, as Lobo had never been one of their favorite acts. In *The Rolling Stone Record Guide,* Dave Marsh commented, "It is surprising that Lobo of Spanish origin sings in a gentle, Jose Feliciano style of folk pop. All the hits are [on *The Best of Lobo* LP], for anyone who still cares."

But some did care enough to give Lobo a place back in the limelight by 1979, when he got his fourth #1 AC hit as well as his seventh top 30 pop entry. For more details, see 373—"Where Were You When I Was Falling in Love."

186 Dueling Banjos

ERIC WEISSBERG AND STEVE MANDELL

Warner 7659

February 17, 1973 (2 weeks)

Writer: Arthur Smith

Producer: Eric Weissberg

Guitarist Arthur Smith wrote and recorded an instrumental tune in 1955 called "Feuding Banjos," with Smith playing tenor banjo and Don Reno joining him on five-string banjo. It was not a chartbuster, but in 1972 the tune reappeared in the popular movie *Deliverance*, performed on the soundtrack by Eric Weissberg and Steve Mandell, and demand grew for it to be released as a single. When it came out as a 45 by Weissberg and Mandell under the title "Dueling Banjos," Smith received no credit for writing it initially and had to sue to get his share of the profits (he got nearly $200,000). Weissberg and Mandell got similarly cavalier treatment, with some singles listing the artist simply as *Deliverance*.

It was the author of *Deliverance*, James Dickey, who was responsible for the tune being included in the movie. The story goes that after Dickey heard the song on the radio he wrote it into the screenplay, in a scene where Ronny Cox, playing one of the four men heading down the river, strummed the tune as a way to communicate with a mute mountain boy. For the filming, Weissberg and Mandell taught the actors how to fake playing their instruments.

The men performing the tune on record were both veteran session musicians. Back in the early 1960s Weissberg had been a member of the Tarriers, a folk group, and had known Mandell for 15 years when their song became a hit. After its success, Weissberg formed a group called Eric Weissberg and Deliverance which included Mandell, guitarist Charlie Brown, bassist Tony Brown, and drummer Richard Crooks.

"Dueling Banjos" made #2 pop for four weeks starting February 24, 1973, behind Roberta Flack's "Killing Me Softly With His Song," plus made #5 country. It won the Grammy for Best Country Instrumental Performance. The album named after the tune by Weiss and Mandell went to #1 on the LP chart for three weeks starting March 17, 1973.

The popularity of the instrumental inspired several imitations, such as "Dueling Guitars" by Jay and Chet. Arthur Smith got into the act by bringing out his "Battling Banjos Polka" too. But the only one to make any sort of impact, oddly enough, was comedian Martin Mull, with his parody "Dueling Tubas," which went to #92 pop.

Unfortunately for Weissberg and Mandell, the mania for their instrumental never did anything for their careers as artists. "Dueling Banjos" was their only single to make the AC and pop charts. Eric Weissberg and Deliverance came out with their follow-up album *Rural Free Delivery* in the fall of 1973, but it vanished quickly, peaking at #196 on the LP chart during a two-week run. The group last charted in 1975 with a #91 country single "Yakety Yak," a noninstrumental cover of the #1 pop hit for the Coasters in 1958.

187 Last Song
EDWARD BEAR

Capitol 3452

March 3, 1973 (2 weeks)

Writer: Larry Evoy

Producer: Gene Martynec

In the September 6, 1969 issue of *Billboard*, Capitol Records announced it had acquired distribution rights for the Canadian trio Edward Bear. The group, which took its moniker from the original name of Winnie the Pooh in the books written by A.A. Milne, consisted of lead singer Larry Evoy, guitarist Danny Marks, and organist Paul Weldon. When the announcement was made, Edward Bear had been in existence for roughly two years, and had just come off a tour on which it was the unlikely opening act for the hard-rock group Led Zeppelin.

The threesome scored its first chart entry in America in 1970 when "You, Me and Mexico" went to #38 AC and #68 pop. But Capitol's efforts at promoting the band seem half-hearted at best in hindsight. Edward Bear recorded a follow-up to "You, Me and Mexico" called "You Can't Deny It" while the former record was still on the chart, yet the record company did not release it until six months later, destroying any forward momentum for getting onto the American charts the single may have had.

Then, in late 1972, Edward Bear's fortune changed when "Last Song" pushed them to the top of the AC chart. Capitol had so much faith in the single that they released it with a picture sleeve, a rather unusual move considering how relatively unknown the band was at the time. "Last Song" also went to #3 pop the weeks of March 3 and 10, 1973, behind Roberta Flack's "Killing Me Softly With His Song" at #1 and "Dueling Banjos" [see 186] at #2. It also earned the band several Juno Awards, Canada's highest musical honors for native acts.

But "Last Song" became an ironic commentary on the career, as they never had another major hit. The follow-up single, "Close Your Eyes," did moderately well, going to #11 AC and #37 pop. But no other subsequent Edward Bear single ever cracked either chart, although "Walking On Back" did bubble under to #115 in the summer of 1973. Around the time "Close Your Eyes" made the AC and pop listings, Paul Weldon, who also owned a jacket and graphic design business, left the trio, and his eventual replacement was Bob Kendall. (Roger Ellis replaced Danny Marks as guitarist in 1970.)

Given the group's inability to follow up "Last Song" successfully, Capitol stopped releasing Edward Bear singles in America in 1974. Edward Bear continued to record in Canada through 1976, when Evoy left the group to try a solo career. He failed to make either the AC or pop listings with his efforts, and Edward Bear went into musical hibernation on the charts as well as thereafter. In 1990 the original lineup recorded a few new songs for a greatest hits LP released in Canada only.

188 Danny's Song
ANNE MURRAY

Capitol 3481

March 17, 1973 (2 weeks)

Writer: Kenny Loggins

Producer: Brian Ahern

Through constant airplay on rock stations and its frequent inclusion on the group's live and greatest hits albums, "Danny's Song" is thought by some Loggins and Messina fans to have been a big hit single for the group, which in fact it was not. It was, however, an outstanding ballad on the duo's first LP, 1972's *Sittin' In*, and one of those to take notice of it was Anne Murray. "I just lifted it off the Loggins and Messina album, and I found out later he [Kenny Loggins] wrote it for his brother Danny on the occasion of [Danny's] first baby," Murray said. "He didn't have any money, so he wrote them a song." He created his composition in 1970.

The song also served as a gift of sorts for Murray on the charts, as it brought her back to the top on the AC, pop, and country listings for the first time since "Snowbird" [see 139]. "Danny's Song" went to #7 pop and #10 country and got Murray her second Grammy nomination for Best Female Contemporary Vocal Performance (the first was for "Snowbird"). Murray later said of "Danny's Song" that though the tune had touched her right away, it took on a deeper appeal once she had her first child in 1976. "Whenever I was singing that song, it was very meaningful," she said.

While Murray popularized one of their songs, Kenny Loggins and partner Jim Messina hit paydirt with another tune they themselves recorded, "Your Mama Don't Dance," which went to #19 AC and #4 pop. They had four more AC entries through 1975, with the highest chart position going to "Thinking of You" in 1973 (#7 AC and #18 pop). In 1977 Loggins embarked on a successful solo career which—incredibly—did not garner him a #1 AC hit until 20 years later [see 663—"For the First Time"].

To add to the irony, Loggins' cousin Dave Loggins managed to score #1 AC 23 years before Kenny did with "Please Come to Boston" [see 225]. And Dave later sang a duet with Murray in 1984, the #10 AC entry, "Nobody Loves Me Like You Do."

But let's get back to Murray in 1973. The other two singles Murray released after "Danny's Song" did fine on the AC chart but floundered on the other two rosters. "What About Me" went to #2 AC, #20 country, and #64 pop, while "Send a Little Love My Way" made it to #10 AC, #79 country, and #72 pop.

Luckily for Murray, Loggins loved her version of "Danny's Song" and became interested in giving her more material to use in the future. Thanks to a chance encounter, another song written by Loggins gave Murray her next across-the-board smash [see 210—"Love Song"].

189 Sing

THE CARPENTERS

A&M 1413

March 31, 1973 (2 weeks nonconsecutive)

Writer: Joe Raposo

Producers: Richard Carpenter, Karen Carpenter

The answer to the question "What Carpenters hit was done first by Kermit the Frog?" is "Sing." "Sing" was originally a track on the 1970 LP *Sesame Street*, based on the popular children's show on public television which began in 1969 and was still running strong three decades later. The star Muppet (from *marionette* and *puppet*) of the show was Kermit the Frog, who also assumed duties as host of *The Muppet Show*, a weekly TV series popular worldwide from 1976–81.

But while Kermit sounded in good voice singing "Sing," the hit 45 from the album turned out to be the novelty "Rubber Duckie" by the Muppet Ernie, which went to #36 AC and #16 pop. Like Kermit's, Ernie's voice was that of head "Muppeteer" Jim Henson, who died unexpectedly at the age of 53 on May 16, 1990. Ernie and Kermit continued on *Sesame Street* with others providing their voices.

The Carpenters, however, did not hear the song first on either the TV show or its soundtrack LP. Richard Carpenter described how they came across it in the liner notes to the 1991 anthology *From the Top*. "In early 1973, Karen and I were guesting on an ABC television special, 'Robert Young With the Young.' Also guesting were Arte Johnson, Sandy Duncan and a group of the 'young.' One of the songs featuring the cast was 'Sing,' originally written for *Sesame Street*. Karen and I thought the song could be hit (most of our associates thought we were nuts) and selected it as the debut single from the [1973] album *Now and Then*."

With a few notes changed from the original and backing vocals provided by the Jimmy Joyce Children's Choir, "Sing" by the Carpenters went to #1 AC as well as #3 pop the weeks of April 21 and 28, 1973, the first week behind "Tie a Yellow Ribbon Round the Ole Oak Tree" at #1 [see 190] and Vicki Lawrence's "The Night the Lights Went Out in Georgia" at #2, and the second week by "Tie a Yellow Ribbon" at #1 and War's "The Cisco Kid" at #2. The Carpenters' version earned Grammy nominations for Best Pop Vocal Performance by a Duo, Group or Chorus and Best Arrangement Accompanying Vocalists.

A few months after "Sing" came out, Karen Carpenter recorded the song in Spanish as "Canta" following requests from a few radio stations. That rendition did not make the AC or pop charts, but "Sing" remained a special favorite for the Carpenters, as they did it on one of their last TV appearances on an ABC special on April 26, 1980.

After "Sing" ran its course, the Carpenters notched their eighth #1 AC hit [see 196—"Yesterday Once More"].

Left to right: Joyce Wilson, Tony Orlando, Telma Hopkins

190 Tie a Yellow Ribbon Round the Ole Oak Tree

TONY ORLANDO AND DAWN

Bell 45318

April 7, 1973 (2 weeks nonconsecutive)

Writers: Irwin Levine, L. Russell Brown

Producers: Hank Medress, Dave Appell

"I didn't want to cut 'Yellow Ribbon,' because I thought it was a novelty song," admitted Tony Orlando of the song which always will be associated with him and his two backup singers Telma Hopkins and Joyce Wilson, who were known as Dawn. The composition came to his attention via his producer Hank Medress, but its stylized sound worried Orlando. "My heart is rhythm and blues, and I didn't want to go that way," he said.

Orlando said he also wondered how "Tie a Yellow Ribbon . . ." could be part of Dawn's plans at the time. "We were doing an album called *Tuneweaving*, and it was a little bit more eclectic in its appeal," he said. Typical of that LP's songs was "Freedom for the Stallion," which Dawn cut before it became a #63 pop hit for the Hues Corporation later in 1973. In fact, "Tie a Yellow Ribbon. . ." is so different, according to Orlando, that "It's the one song that doesn't fit the record."

Prior to recording it, Orlando pitched the tune to others like Bobby Vinton, but none would cut it. "We kept resisting the song," Orlando said. "Finally, after about three months, I looked at [Medress], and he was so persistent, so I said yes." What really tipped the scales, he said, was when Joyce Wilson's sister Pam Vincent heard the song and told him, "That will be your biggest hit."

Cutting the tune took only one or two takes, Orlando recalled. The first release off *Tuneweaving*, "Tie a Yellow Ribbon. . ." exploded. It hit #1 in America and England, riding the crest of the Hot 100 for four weeks starting April 21, 1973. Tony Orlando and Dawn merited a Grammy nomination for Best Pop Vocal Performance by a Duo, Group or Chorus for it, while "Tie a Yellow Ribbon. . ." earned another nomination for Song of the Year. Eventually more than 1,000 covers of the song appeared, making it one of the most recorded pieces of pop music ever. Yet none of them had a scintilla of the success of Tony Orlando and Dawn's version. (The closest was Johnny Carver, whose effort, titled "Yellow Ribbon," went to #5 country in 1973.) Worldwide, at least 6 million copies of Tony Orlando and Dawn's rendition were sold.

Orlando eventually suggested that it be used as the theme for Tony Orlando and Dawn's self-titled CBS-TV variety series, which debuted on July 3, 1974 as a summer series and returned in December for a two-year run. More to his amazement, he found that "Tying a yellow ribbon for someone who's been kidnapped or held prisoner became popular." Even in the 1990s, Americans were tying yellow ribbons while soldiers went to battle in the Persian Gulf War.

"Tie a Yellow Ribbon. . ." was the first of three #1 AC hits for Tony Orlando and Dawn. Their next was "Say, Has Anybody Seen My Sweet Gypsy Rose" [see 199].

191 You Are the Sunshine of My Life

STEVIE WONDER

Tamla 54232

April 28, 1973 (2 weeks)

Writer: Stevie Wonder

Producer: Stevie Wonder

*L*ittle Stevie Wonder The 12 Year Old Genius read the title of the #1 1963 album by the artist born Steveland Morris in Saginaw, Michigan, on May 13, 1950. Nearly four decades later, Wonder, no longer little or prepubescent, was still regarded as a genius. The blind pianist was one of the most talented artists to pop out of the gusher of soul acts on the Motown label and had compiled a stack of hit platters on the pop and R&B charts before getting his due on the AC side.

Wonder showed enough promise as a musician that Motown president Berry Gordy, Jr., signed him to the company in 1960, where he did backup work until "Fingertips," a wild live single recording of Wonder in concert, went to #1 pop and R&B in 1963. Several 45s followed over the next few years but failed to match "Fingertips" until "Uptight (Everything's Alright)" went to #3 pop and #1 R&B, heralding a decade-long string of top pop and R&B hits.

Wonder's AC bow came in late 1966, when "A Place in the Sun" went to #29 while hitting #9 pop. He then was off the roster for nearly three years, unless one counted the instrumental version of "Alfie" he did in 1968, which was billed as "Eivets Rednow" (his name spelled backward) and made #11. "My Cherie Amour" in 1969 made #3, followed by "Yester-Me, Yester-You, Yesterday" at #10. Other entries thereafter were "Never Had a Dream Come True" at #31 in 1970, "If You Really Love Me" at #10 in 1971, and "Superstition" at #38 in early 1973.

Then came his beautiful ballad "You Are the Sunshine of My Life," a tune Wonder wrote three years before recording it. After the opening electric piano section, Jim Gilstrap and Gloria Barley do brief solos, then Wonder takes over the vocals for most of the rest of the track.

"You Are the Sunshine of My Life" went to #1 pop the week of May 19, 1973, plus #3 R&B. It won a Grammy for Best Male Pop Vocal Performance and was nominated for Record of the Year and Song of the Year. In 1978 Marty Mitchell's cover reached #34 country.

A few months after "You Are the Sunshine of My Life" was released, on August 16, 1973, Wonder survived an accident in which he was knocked unconscious by logs falling from a truck. Although he suffered a permanent loss of his sense of smell as a result, he recuperated otherwise, going on to several more hits, plus Grammy wins, during the 1970s. He did not, however, have another #1 AC hit until 1979 [see 376—"Send One Your Love"].

121

192 Daniel

ELTON JOHN

MCA 40046

May 12, 1973 (2 weeks)

Writers: Bernie Taupin (words), Elton John (music)

Producer: Gus Dudgeon

One of Elton John's most popular, but most misunderstood, hits was "Daniel," the first of 16 #1 AC hits credited to him. Some speculated the lyrics grew from actual events in the life of John's longtime collaborator Bernie Taupin, but Taupin vigorously denied it. Like the protagonist in the tune, Taupin did have an older brother, but his name wasn't Daniel. "Daniel's nobody," he told *Rolling Stone*. "I don't have any set idea on who he is. I just started the song with that corny rhyme, 'plane' and 'Spain.' That first line came first, and the rest of the song grew from it."

Taupin's original song had more verses than the four John sang, and some fans wondered why John deleted them (he claimed the song simply ran too long). Taupin said the missing verses told listeners that Daniel was a war veteran, which would explain the story line better, but fans have speculated there is more to it than that, a fact which irks Taupin. "That

whole 'Daniel' thing, that's just part of the myth," he told Craig Rosen in *Billboard* in 1997. "It's just one of those things that people just pick up on. There are a lot of other songs where there probably was something chopped off. . . .The only reason it became such an issue with 'Daniel' was because some people thought the last verse totally changed what the song was about. I don't remember what the last verse was, so I don't know whether it did or not, but I doubt it. I seriously doubt it."

What was left of "Daniel" was enough to entice the general public to take it to #1 AC and #2 pop, hitting the latter peak the week of June 2, 1973, behind "My Love" [see 194]. John got a Grammy nomination for Best Male Pop Vocal Performance for his work on it. The album on which "Daniel" appeared, *Don't Shoot Me I'm Only the Piano Player*, stayed at #1 on the LP chart for two weeks starting March 3, 1973. It included the previous single to "Daniel," "Crocodile Rock," which went to #1 pop for three weeks but only #11 AC in 1973.

Rolling Stone reported that during his 1973 concerts, Elton John told his audiences about "Daniel," "There are only a few songs that a writer composes that mean a lot to him after years have passed. Even though this hasn't been out for a year yet, I know this will last for me. It is one of my favorites." It remained a concert staple of John's throughout the 1990s. In 1991 Wilson Phillips covered "Daniel" on the tribute album *Two Rooms—Celebrating the Songs of Elton John & Bernie Taupin*, and it made #7 AC as a result of airplay from the LP.

193 And I Love You So

PERRY COMO

RCA 0906

May 26, 1973 (1 week)

Writer: Don McLean

Producer: Chet Atkins

Some RCA executives thought it would be a good change of pace to have Perry Como record with veteran country producer Don McLean in Nashville in the early 1970s. It turned out they were at least right about "And I Love You So," which made #29 pop as well as #1 AC.

"Chet Atkins heard the song," recalled Como's manager Mickey Glass. "It was on Don McLean's album." McLean was a hot artist at the time thanks to "American Pie" [see 164], and many artists had started looking in 1971 at his songs for possible material to cover. In fact, Bobby Goldsboro released a version, "And I Love You So," which went to #8 AC, #83 pop, and #48 country.

But Como confessed his ignorance about the songwriter to *Rolling Stone*. "To be honest, I knew 'American Pie' but I'd never met Don McLean, and I'd never heard his version of the song until Chet Atkins asked me to listen to it. I heard the record for the first time in Nashville, and we cut it during the winter of this year. I was there when Chet taped the music and then I did the singing two days later."

Beyond its pop success, "And I Love You So" also generated Como a Grammy nomination for Best Male Pop Vocal Performance. It was his last Grammy nomination to date.

Following "And I Love You So," Como virtually vanished from the Hot 100 but still made the AC chart frequently through 1976. His biggest hit in this period was a double-sided single in 1974. "I Don't Know What He Told You" reached #8 while the flip, "Weave Me the Sunshine," landed at #5. Como's last entry on the chart was 1983's "As My Love for You," which got to #45.

Como kept recording for RCA until 1987, ending a 43-year run with the company, and continued to perform six years after that before calling it quits in his early eighties. "The last thing he did was a Christmas show in Ireland in 1993," Glass said.

Como has enjoyed being out of the limelight for most of the 1990s. "I talk to him once every week," Glass said. "But he's definitely retired. He doesn't want to do anything. He doesn't want to do any interviews." Glass said he still gets job offers for the octogenarian, which Como always turns down despite the impressive amounts of money involved. Those wanting to hear Como will have to settle for records and the radio until and if he changes his mind.

194 My Love

PAUL McCARTNEY AND WINGS

Apple 1861

June 2, 1973 (3 weeks)

Writer: Paul McCartney

Producer: Paul McCartney

James Paul McCartney, born in Liverpool, England, on June 18, 1942, left the Beatles in 1970, but didn't release a single until 1971, when he cut "Another Day," which went to #4 AC and #5 pop, followed by "Uncle Albert/Admiral Halsey," which made #9 AC and #1 pop. In 1972 "Mary Had a Little Lamb" got to #29 AC and #28 pop, and the next year he finally reached #1 AC with "My Love."

"My Love" was one of many songs he wrote about his wife Linda over the years. Born Linda Louise Eastman in

Linda and Paul McCartney

New York on September 24, 1941, she met McCartney during promotions for the *Sgt. Pepper's Lonely Hearts Club Band* LP in 1967 and wed him on March 12, 1969. He installed her as a keyboardist and singer in his band after he talked her into pressing a few keys on the piano for his *Ram* album before teaching her how to play.

"We really had a few rows as he tried to teach me," she recalled to Hunter Davies in *The Washington Post*. "He really put me through it."

Linda became part of a group backing Paul called Wings. When it started in 1971, Wings consisted of Linda, Denny Laine on guitar, and Denny Seiwell on drums. "The name Wings just came into my head when Linda was having Stella," McCartney told Davies. "She was in Kings College Hospital, where she'd had Mary, and I went round with my camp bed as I'd done before to watch the birth. This time it was a Caesarean and I wasn't allowed in. I sat next door in my green apron praying like mad." "Wings of an angel," chimed in Linda. "That's what he was thinking about."

But Wings underwent a fair amount of turmoil, with guitarist Henry McCullough joining in 1972 only to leave a year later with Seiwell. Rumors were that some musicians felt Linda was unqualified for the band, a suspicion confirmed by Paul when he told Davies that "I could sense a feeling among the others of 'Linda's holding us back.'"

Even Paul admitted that "Perhaps I did have doubts now and again about Linda on keyboard. I did once say to her in a row that I could have had Billy Preston. It just came out. I said I was sorry about an hour later. . . .I don't have to explain her away. She's my wife and I want her to play. But she had to take a lot of stick."

"My Love" went to #1 AC and pop simultaneously for three weeks starting June 2, 1973, followed by one more week at #1 pop. Its success led the album on which it appeared, *Red Rose Speedway*, to ride atop the LP chart the same three weeks "My Love" was #1 AC. It also was the only single released from that album.

Linda McCartney succumbed to breast cancer after three years of fighting the disease on April 17, 1998. She was 56 years old.

195 Boogie Woogie Bugle Boy

BETTE MIDLER

Atlantic 2964

June 23, 1973 (2 weeks)

Writers: Don Raye (words), Hughie Prince (music)

Producer: Barry Manilow

Bette Midler, born in Honolulu, Hawaii, on December 1, 1945, established her career in the early 1970s by offering inimitable song interpretations, with outrageous, often bawdy stage patter between tunes. Nearly 30 years later, that pattern remained intact, only now she performed before thousands of fans per concert rather than dozens of gay men clad in towels at the Continental Baths in New York City, where she got her start. Midler's club popularity won her some guest shots on *The Tonight Show Starring Johnny Carson*, which was taped in New York City in the early 1970s. By the time of her chart debut with "Do You Want to Dance?" in early 1973 at #8 AC and #17 pop, she was a familiar face to many late-night TV viewers.

The single after "Do You Want to Dance?" was to be Midler's take on "Delta Dawn," but a competing version by Helen Reddy led Atlantic Records to push the B-side, "Boogie Woogie Bugle Boy," instead. (For more details on "Delta Dawn," see 198.) "Boogie Woogie Bugle Boy," originally an Oscar nominee for Best Song from the film *Buck Privates* in 1941 when it was a #6 pop hit for the Andrews Sisters, also appeared on Midler's album *The Divine Miss M*.

Barry Manilow, at the time Midler's arranger and a producer of *The Divine Miss M*, told *Rolling Stone* the LP cut of "Boogie Woogie Bugle Boy" produced by Joel Dorn was not considered acceptable to be a single. "It was like piecemeal. . . .It fades in and out and there's four girls sometimes, and there's two girls sometimes," Manilow said. "And he also used this effect of hanging the mike in the middle of the studio so that you get that old-fashioned effect like a cloud over the thing."

But when Atlantic President Ahmet Ertegun heard Midler do "Boogie Woogie Bugle Boy" at a faster pace with more horns on a Burt Bacharach TV special late in London, he had Manilow produce that rendition as a 45. The result was a top 10 AC and pop hit, with the tune peaking at #8 on the latter for two weeks starting July 21, 1973.

One more song from *The Divine Miss M* came out in 1973, "Friends." It went to #40 pop and #9 AC. Some pop radio stations also played the B-side, Midler's remake of the Dixie Cups' #1 pop hit of 1964, "Chapel of Love."

The success of "Do You Want to Dance?" and "Boogie Woogie Bugle Boy" won Midler the Grammy for Best New Artist of 1973. "Boogie Woogie Bugle Boy" also caught her a Grammy nomination for Best Female Pop Vocal Performance, and the LP *The Divine Miss M* got a nomination for Album of the Year. But Midler found that her initial wave of success was hard to ride. She did not have another top 10 AC or pop hit until 1980 [see 385—"The Rose"].

196 Yesterday Once More
THE CARPENTERS

A&M 1446

July 7, 1973 (3 weeks)

Writers: Richard Carpenter, John Bettis

Producers: Richard Carpenter, Karen Carpenter

While on tour in the summer of 1972, the Carpenters decided to add some rock and roll tunes of the 1950s and 1960s to their repertoire, an idea which their concert fans greatly approved of. They decided to take the concept a step farther and include some of what they did on their *Now and Then* album in 1973.

"The 'oldies' were enjoying a resurgence in popularity during the early '70s, much to Karen's and my delight," Richard Carpenter noted in the anthology *From the Top*. "I thought it would be nice to write a song about this and use the piece to 'bookend' the 'oldies' medley we were planning to record. The resulting 'Yesterday Once More' became one of our most popular recordings worldwide."

On the LP the tunes heard between the first go-round of "Yesterday Once More" and its minute-long reprise were, in order, "Fun Fun Fun," "The End of the World," "Da Doo Ron Ron," "Deadman's Curve," "Johnny Angel," "The Night Has a Thousand Eyes," "Our Day Will Come," and "One Fine Day." After doing the vocals, guitarist Tony Peluso served as the ostensible "deejay" between the tunes.

Released as a single by itself, "Yesterday Once More" nearly went to #1 pop as well as AC, stopping at #2 the week of July 28, 1973, behind Jim Croce's "Bad, Bad Leroy Brown." In fact, "Yesterday Once More" was the last of five singles by the Carpenters which came in as the #2 runner-up on the Hot 100, the others being "We've Only Just Begun," "Rainy Days and Mondays," "Superstar," and "Hurting Each Other."

One single that did reach the #1 pop was, appropriately, "Top of the World," which came after "Yesterday Once More." In an odd twist, "Top of the World" went only to #2 AC for two weeks. The tune had been on the Carpenters' 1972 LP *A Song for You*, but Richard admitted he misjudged its potential and did not release it as a 45 at the time. It proved to be quite popular in live shows and got decent airplay for an album track, and when Lynn Anderson took her rendition to #2 country, #34 AC, and #74 pop in 1973, it convinced him the song deserved a shot as a single. The 45 used a revised, remixed version with a new vocal by Karen and not the original on *A Song for You*.

As for "Yesterday Once More," it was a chart entry once more in 1981, ironically in a medley. The Spinners combined the song with "Nothing Remains the Same" and reached #45 AC, #32 R&B, and #52 pop.

197 Touch Me in the Morning
DIANA ROSS

Motown 1239

July 28, 1973 (1 week)

Writers: Michael Masser, Ron Miller

Producers: Michael Masser, Tom Baird

Diana Ross had finished filming *Lady Sings the Blues*, her first movie role and one that would give her an Oscar nomination for Best Actress, when she recorded her first #1 AC hit, "Touch Me in the Morning." As J. Randy Taraborrelli recounted in his book *Call Her Miss Ross*, the decision to do the song came from Motown's president Berry Gordy, who had doubts about how the film and its soundtrack would do. He asked Ron Miller for a tune that would be a smash should the film or its music fail. Miller had the song's title floating in his head as a good one to use for Ross, but he needed more inspiration to do lyrics to match music written by newcomer Michael Masser.

"So I analyzed Diana as a person and realized that she was a contemporary woman who was probably liberal about expressing her sexual values, like most Cosmo women in a '70s society," he told Taraborrelli. "Once, it was the man who might give a woman the brush-off after a one-nighter telling her 'nothing's gonna last forever'; now it could be the other way around. So I started writing. I wanted something more adult than 'Baby Love,' but pop and r&b enough to cover all the markets. It was a cold, calculated, precise job of crafting."

Ross considered the song nothing more than an album track, but Gordy felt otherwise. Ross and Miller argued several times during rehearsal and recording over what key the tune should be sung in, and Miller claimed that he eventually bluffed Ross into thinking he was recording her in A-flat instead of B-flat, which he thought was her natural key. Ross went through 12 takes of the song and Miller edited them almost from one word to another to produce the single which went onto the market.

But before the song was finally released, Gordy heard Miller's production and decided a new, shorter ending was in order for the single. Ross, who had endured losing the Oscar to Liza Minnelli in *Cabaret* and watching her only 45 from *Lady Sings the Blues*, "Good Morning Heartache," stall at #8 AC and #37 pop, was hardly in the mood to record with Miller again. But she did it, and saw "Touch Me in the Morning" go to #1 pop the week of August 18, 1973, plus #5 R&B. It earned Grammy nominations for Best Female Pop Vocal Performance and Best Arrangement Accompanying a Vocalist.

"You're a Special Part of Me," a duet with Marvin Gaye, was the follow-up to "Touch Me in the Morning" and reached #43 AC and #12 pop in late 1973. Ross did better on the AC chart with her next single, "Last Time I Saw Him" [see 211].

Delta Dawn

HELEN REDDY

Capitol 3645

August 4, 1973 (2 weeks)

Writers: Alex Harvey, Larry Collins

Producer: Tom Catalano

Though several other female vocalists took a shot at "Delta Dawn," the one having the biggest AC and pop hit with it was Helen Reddy, who, coincidentally, had once had one of its co-writers open for her. Helen Reddy did not get the song directly from Alex Harvey, but she had worked with him before she sang "Delta Dawn." "He had been my opening act at a club in Denver called Marvelous Marv's," she remembered.

But neither Harvey, who never sang on a national hit, or his collaborator Larry Collins, who sang some now-forgotten rockabilly records with his sister Lorrie in the mid-1950s as the Collins Kids, wrote "Delta Dawn" for Reddy. Harvey did it first on a solo LP for Columbia. A backup vocalist on the session, Tracy Nelson, took a liking to the tune, and a strange chain of events was set in motion.

Nelson sang the song with her group, Mother Earth, at the Bottom Line club in Manhattan. One Mother Earth fan, Bette Midler, became so captivated by "Delta Dawn" that she sang it on a guest shot on *The Tonight Show Starring Johnny Carson.* Billy Sherrill, at the time a producer for up-and-coming 13-year-old country singer Tanya Tucker, saw the show and had Tucker cut the song as a single. Tucker's version went to #6 country and #72 pop in 1972. It was her first entry on both charts.

Amid the crossover success, Midler went into a recording studio to do "Delta Dawn." But another producer, Tom Catalano, had his own idea of making "Delta Dawn" a big pop hit, so he did a session with instruments alone and created a track which he had designed to use with the vocals of Barbra Streisand. Streisand rejected the tune, so Catalano offered it to Reddy's husband and manager Jeff Wald, who urged her to do the song.

"I really didn't think it was for me," Reddy confessed. But she was hot at the time, having scored with "I Am Woman," which hit #1 pop and #2 AC for two weeks in 1972, followed by "Peaceful," which made #12 pop and again #2 AC for two weeks in 1973, and to keep the momentum going she followed Wald's advice and recorded "Delta Dawn."

Meanwhile, Midler's version of "Delta Dawn" came out at the same time, but Atlantic, fearing that their release would be beaten in competition with the one by a somewhat more established artist, promoted the ostensible B-side, "Boogie Woogie Bugle Boy" [see 195]. With no competition, Reddy's record hit #1 pop the week of September 15, 1973, a month after topping the AC chart.

Reddy vaguely recalled the inspiration for "Delta Dawn." "I think there really was some woman," she said. "Every town has its crazy lady." For Reddy, that crazy lady gave her the first of eight #1 AC hits, with the next being "Leave Me Alone (Ruby Red Dress)" [see 206].

199 Say, Has Anybody Seen My Sweet Gypsy Rose

TONY ORLANDO AND DAWN

Bell 45374

August 18, 1973 (3 weeks)

Writers: Irwin Levine, L. Russell Brown

Producers: Hank Medress, Dave Appell

The first record from Tony Orlando and Dawn was actually billed as just Dawn. For "Candida," Tony Orlando lent his voice as a favor to producer Hank Medress. Orlando thought the record would die and that he would continue to work for CBS Records' publishing arm, April-Blackwood Music, where he had worked since 1966.

But then "Candida" went to #8 AC and #3 pop in 1970, and its success changed everything for Orlando. The follow-up "Knock Three Times," did even better, going to #2 AC and #1 pop in 1971, so it convinced Orlando to quit his job and try his hand at musical performance a second time. The group's billing became Dawn featuring Tony Orlando.

In his first go-around as an artist, from 1961 to 1963, Orlando found brief fame as a teenage soloist. Born Michael Anthony Orlando Cassavitis in New York City on April 3, 1944, he never went to high school. Orlando recalled, "The first time I was on the road, I was 16." After his solo vocals stopped selling, Orlando worked behind the scenes in the music business, until "Candida" scored.

Also thrust into the spotlight were two formerly anonymous backup singers who became known as Dawn, Telma Hopkins (born in Louisville, Kentucky, on October 28, 1948) and Joyce Vincent Wilson (born in Detroit, Michigan, on December 14, 1946). Both had been session musicians before deciding to tour and record with Orlando.

Supplying many of the group's hits were songwriters Irwin Levine and L. Russell Brown. They wrote "Knock Three Times" and "Tie a Yellow Ribbon. . ." [see 190]. On the heels of the latter song's success, they proposed a follow-up to Medress. "Irwin Levine, the lyricist of the two, had this love for [Al] Jolson," Orlando said. "He said, 'Hank, I'd like to write some songs that could have been written in the early 1900s.'" They formed the basis of what became the 1973 LP Dawn's New Ragtime Follies. Its first single was "Say, Has Anybody Seen My Sweet Gypsy Rose."

"This was so against the grain at the time, but I took a gamble," he said. But he liked the song and especially the production job by Medress and Appell, so it went out. "Say, Has Anybody Seen My Sweet Gypsy Rose" ended up nearly topping the AC and pop charts, as did its predecessor, peaking at #3 on the Hot 100 the week of September 15, 1973, behind Helen Reddy's "Delta Dawn" at #1 [see 198] and Marvin Gaye's "Let's Get It On" at #2.

The single also was the last 45 billed as Dawn featuring Tony Orlando. Thereafter, it was Tony Orlando and Dawn doing each record, including the group's third #1 AC hit [see 256—"He Don't Love You (Like I Love You)"].

200 Loves Me Like a Rock

PAUL SIMON

Columbia 45907

September 8, 1973 (2 weeks)

Writer: Paul Simon

Producers: Paul Simon, Phil Ramone, Muscle Shoals Sound

The phrase "Simon and Garfunkel" had become so familiar by 1971 that it was a shock to learn the duo was planning to split to pursue individual projects. But over the last few years together Paul Simon, born in Newark, New Jersey, on November 5, 1941, and Art Garfunkel had had quite different ideas on how they wanted to pursue their music careers, and so they decided to go in different directions.

Simon's first solo post-Garfunkel single was "Mother and Child Reunion," which reached #4 both pop and AC in 1972. It was not his first solo single; in 1963 he snuck onto the Hot 100 at #97 with "The Lone Teen Ranger" on a record credited as by "Jerry Landis." He followed "Mother and Child Reunion" with "Me and Julio Down by the Schoolyard" (#22 pop, #6 AC) and "Duncan" (#52 pop, #30 AC) in 1972 and "Kodachrome" (#2 pop and AC) in 1973. Then he finally returned to the top of the AC slate with "Loves Me Like a Rock," a song which Simon's boss Clive Davis of Columbia Records claimed in his memoirs became popular with AM stations after "Kodachrome" hit and forced its release.

Seeking a grittier sound, Simon cut "Loves Me Like a Rock" with the Dixie Hummingbirds gospel group doing backing vocals, even though the lyrics were not necessarily spiritual. When he completed taping the voices and guitar parts, he gave them to drummer Roger Hawkins and asked him to come up with backing music for the tracks.

"He wanted us to put instruments on the tape, so we did," Hawkins told Max Weinberg in The Big Beat. "David [Hood, the bassist] and I overdubbed on the tape. I think it was the second time through that we got it. Now, if you listen to the record, it really drags terribly toward the fade. The tempo goes down drastically." Hawkins stressed to Weinberg he had nothing to do with the change in pace.

Hawkins added that "when Paul sings 'Love me like a rock. . .' there's a hole there to do something, and I thought, 'Well, s—t, maybe the bass drum would sound like a rock.' A lot of times the lyrics of the song just dictate what you should play."

"Loves Me Like a Rock" nearly matched its AC success on the pop chart by reaching #2 on the Hot 100 the week of October 6, 1973, behind Cher's "Half-Breed." On the R&B chart the Dixie Hummingbirds released their own version and went to #72 in 1973. Simon received a Grammy nomination for Best Male Pop Vocal Performance for his work on There Goes Rhymin' Simon, on which "Loves Me Like a Rock" appeared.

The follow-up to "Loves Me Like a Rock" was "American Tune," which hit #8 AC and #35 pop in late 1973. He would top both charts nearly two years later [see 289—"50 Ways to Leave Your Lover"].

201 My Maria

B.W. STEVENSON

RCA 0030

September 22, 1973 (1 week)

Writers: B.W. Stevenson, Daniel Moore

Producer: David N. Kerschenbaum

When Louis "B.W." Stevenson learned that his record company, RCA, wanted him to be a pop artist rather than a bluesy rock and roller, he was not thrilled to say the least. But it was the artist's first chance to make his name nationally, so he acquiesced. He got a little action in 1972 with "Say What I Feel," which gave him his AC debut at #38 while going to #114 bubbling under, then found better success the next year.

Stevenson reached #66 pop and #31 AC with Daniel Moore's "Shambala," but Three Dog Night stunted its growth on both charts by releasing a competing cover at the same time which went to #3 both AC and pop. Nevertheless, RCA thought progress was being made, so they drafted Moore to create a follow-up for Stevenson. Moore had only what was termed in Jan Reid's *The Improbable Rise of Redneck Rock* as "an interesting guitar piece" on hand, but RCA executives thought it had potential. Stevenson drafted lyrics for it, and the result was "My Maria," which became Stevenson's biggest hit.

With veteran session guitarist Larry Carlton playing on the piece, "My Maria" halted at #9 pop the week of September 29, 1973 after having reached #1 AC. It probably was helped by the fact that Three Dog Night did not cover it, as they had the predecessor. The song's most unusual element was Stevenson yodeling the title in the chorus while background singers chanted other lyrics behind him.

Stevenson was born in Dallas, Texas, on October 5, 1949. His nickname B.W. stood for "Buckwheat." As a teenager he worked in bar bands, then went to study voice at North Texas State in Denton before transferring to Cooke County Junior College and then serving in the Air Force.

Stevenson, whose professional singing career started in Austin, Texas, hardly emanated star quality, as he wore a stovepipe hat atop his hairy, chubby face and was given to stage fright. Yet RCA thought he could be a popular act, and "My Maria" appeared to make the company's belief in him a good bet. However, when his follow-up, "The River of Love," only went to #32 AC and #53 pop in early 1974, and later that year "Little Bit of Understanding" reached just #40 AC without making the Hot 100 at all, the label lost interest in promoting him. Stevenson had no more AC entries, and only one more single on the Hot 100, 1977's "Down to the Station," at #82 on Warner.

On April 28, 1988, Stevenson died after heart surgery, at age 38. Eight years later the country duo of Brooks and Dunn, composed of Kix Brooks and Ronnie Dunn, had a #1 country and #79 pop entry with their remake of "My Maria."

202 I'm Coming Home

JOHNNY MATHIS

Columbia 45908

September 29, 1973 (1 week)

Writers: Thom Bell, Linda Creed

Producer: Thom Bell

Chances are that "Chances Are" and other Johnny Mathis hits would have been #1 on an AC chart had there been one in the 1950s. Mathis, born in San Francisco, California, on September 30, 1935, originally came to New York City in 1956 to sing jazz for Columbia Records, but label head Mitch Miller realized he had better potential as a balladeer. His first pop entry was "Wonderful! Wonderful!" in 1957 (the same year "Chances Are" hit #1 for one week on the Most Played by Jockeys chart), and other memorable Mathis hits from the decade included "It's Not for Me to Say," "The Twelfth of Never," and "Misty."

Mathis made his AC debut in 1962 with "Gina," which held at #2 for three weeks while making #6 pop. He became a regular visitor on the chart over the next decade, even though after 1965 most of his AC singles missed the Hot 100. Many of his late 1960s and early 1970s records were covers, but in 1973 Mathis decided to change that approach and asked Columbia President Clive Davis to hook him up with Thom Bell to do new material.

"I told Clive I would love to sing some of Tommy's music and, fortunately, we did the album called *I'm Coming Home*," Mathis told Bil Carpenter in *Goldmine* in 1993. "Linda Creed and Thom Bell wrote all the songs for me and I had long conversations with them and I remember, it was the first time I'd ever done anything like that. And they took all my thoughts, all my little quirks and then, all of a sudden, before we could get the company behind the record, Clive Davis was fired."

In Mathis' view, the dismissal of Davis hurt the promotion Columbia did for the album, which Mathis thought was some of his best work to date. "Tommy understood my voice so well and he wrote in a register that is so pleasing to listen to, as far as I'm concerned, and of course, Linda Creed's words were very much what was in my heart. So I was really happy with the results and over the years, I've performed those songs many times and, in fact, I still do. They're some of my favorite songs."

The LP's title tune, "I'm Coming Home," was prophetic in that it returned him to the Hot 100 after more than a four-year hiatus ("Love Theme From *Romeo and Juliet* [see 117] made #96 in 1969). "I'm Coming Home" peaked at #75 pop and also became Mathis' first R&B entry since "What Will Mary Say" stopped at #92 in 1963.

In 1974, Bell had a bigger hit with his production of "I'm Coming Home" with the Spinners, which went to #18 pop and #3 R&B. However, Mathis would end up having a #1 AC, pop, and R&B record just four years later [see 348—"Too Much, Too Little, Too Late"].

ART GARFUNKEL

Columbia 45926

October 6, 1973 (4 weeks)

Writer: Jimmy Webb

Producers: Art Garfunkel, Roy Halee

Art Garfunkel's versatility was often overlooked by those who regarded him as a lesser light compared to Paul Simon. In fact, Garfunkel had a solo acting career, with leading roles in such films as *Catch-22* and *Carnal Knowledge*, both in 1970. And Garfunkel's solo singing career during the 1970s, while not exactly up to Simon's level, was quite successful, with Garfunkel scoring three #1 AC hits by himself.

Born in Forest Hills, New York, on November 5, 1941, Garfunkel met Simon when they were in sixth grade in Queens, New York. The two eventually sang together, and by their teens were pursuing a professional career as a vocal duo. Calling themselves Tom and Jerry (Garfunkel was Tom), they cracked the pop chart in early 1958 with "Hey, Schoolgirl," which peaked at #49. But Garfunkel left Simon for a time, earning a master's degree in mathematics from Columbia University. They reunited in the 1960s, and once "The Sounds of Silence" hit #1 pop in 1966, they stayed together as a successful team until 1971.

For his debut solo LP *Angel Clare*, Garfunkel sought the assistance of Jimmy Webb, who ended up contributing almost all the tunes on the album. Webb recalled his meeting with Garfunkel about potential songs to Paul Zollo in *Songwriters on Songwriting*. "I went up to San Francisco to see Artie. I came down to the studio and Artie says, 'Hi.' We don't even know each other very well. And I said, 'What do you want me to do?' And he said, 'Well, just do everything.'

"They turned the tape machine on, and I played and sang for two days. I played and sang everything I knew. And he still has those tapes. I mean, when I ran out of songs I started playing Baptist hymns. I started playing 'Come Now, Fount of Every Blessing.' And he said, 'That's great. Have you got some more of those?' And we started doing Baptist hymns. We did Baptist hymns for an afternoon. . . .And in all that material was 'All I Know' tucked in there somewhere."

Webb's composition of "All I Know," which owed much to the hymns he had learned while his father was a preacher, gave Garfunkel (then billed only by his surname), his first solo #1 AC entry and top 10 pop hit. It peaked at #9 on the Hot 100 the week of November 10, 1973.

Three other singles made the AC chart under the "Garfunkel" billing in 1974 following "All I Know"—"I Shall Sing" (#4 AC, #38 pop), "Traveling Boy" (#30 AC, #102 bubbling under), and "Second Avenue" (#6 AC, #34 pop). He returned to #1 AC the next year with "I Only Have Eyes for You" [see 276], and later sang other tunes by Webb when the latter wrote for an orchestral concert called *The Animals' Christmas* in 1983.

204 Paper Roses

MARIE OSMOND

MGM 14609

November 3, 1973 (1 week)

Writers: Janice Torre, Fred Spielman

Producer: Sonny James

Marie Osmond broke onto the country chart with "Paper Roses," which stayed at #1 there for two weeks starting November 10, 1973, and she was still making the chart in 1995, with "What Kind of Man (Walks on a Woman)." Between these singles she did a TV series, had some crossover successes on the AC and pop chart, and. . .well, let's not get ahead of ourselves.

Olive Marie Osmond was born in Ogden, Utah, on October 13, 1959; when she was 14, she joined her five older brothers (who toured as the Osmonds; see 273—"The Proud One") as a performer on stage. Sensing that she had potential, MGM President Mike Curb signed her to his label, as he had done with the Osmonds. "Paper Roses," which Marie sang in Nashville with strings added later, was her first release. A failure when done first by Lola Dee in 1955, the tune went to #5 pop in 1960 when sung by Anita Bryant, and Marie's version reached that same peak on the Hot 100 in 1973. Marie also earned Grammy nominations for Best New Artist and Best

Female Country Vocal Performance for the song.

Recalling doing "Paper Roses" to Barry Scott for *We Had Joy, We Had Fun*, she said, "I remember walking in the studio and thinking, 'Good grief!' I'd seen my brothers do all this stuff, but it's really different when all of a sudden everybody's waiting for you to sing it right."

She got over her fears but had only one other AC entry, a remake of Connie Francis' #4 pop hit of 1958, "Who's Sorry Now," which went to #21 AC and #40 pop in 1975. She also charted in the 1970s with another remake of another top 10 pop Anita Bryant single, "In My Little Corner of the World" (#33 country and #102 bubbling under in 1974); "'A' My Name Is Alice" (#85 country in 1976), and "This Is the Way I Feel" (#39 pop). She gained more attention in the late 1970s co-hosting a variety show with her brother Donny [see 228—"I'm Leaving It (All) Up to You"].

Marie got her own variety show on NBC-TV in 1980, but it went off the air within a year. She married briefly and had a child, then resumed her country career full throttle in 1982, notching three country #1 hits—"Meet Me in Montana" with Dan Seals in 1985, "There's No Stopping Your Heart" in 1986, and "You're Still New to Me" with Paul Davis in 1986. She also co-hosted the ABC-TV series *Ripley's Believe It or Not* with Jack Palance from 1985–86.

After "Like a Hurricane" reached #57 in 1990, Marie was off the country chart for five years until "What Kind of Man (Walks on a Woman)" hit. She also returned to acting in 1995, starring in the ABC-TV sitcom *Maybe This Time*, but it lasted just five months. In 1998 her primary activity was co-hosting a daily TV show with her brother Donny.

205 The Most Beautiful Girl
CHARLIE RICH

Epic 11040

November 10, 1973 (3 weeks)

Writers: Norro Wilson, Billy Sherrill, Rory Bourke

Producer: Billy Sherrill

The most popular country crooner of the mid-1970s was Charlie Rich, a one-time rockabilly artist who had been recording nearly two decades by the time "The Most Beautiful Girl" became a hit. He had been making the country chart on a regular basis since 1968 but did not really break through until "Behind Closed Doors" hit #1 there on April 28 and May 5, 1973, also making #8 AC and #15 pop. The official follow-up was an even bigger triumph for him. (Rich's old record label RCA released "Tomorrow Night" after "Behind Closed Doors," but it got only to #29 country.) "The Most Beautiful Girl" emerged after some give and take between three songwriters, including Rich's producer Billy Sherrill.

Norris "Norro" Wilson made the AC chart as an artist only once, in a 1968 remake of "Only You" [see 242] which made #24. Afterward he concentrated his efforts on songwriting in the country field and scored a #1 hit on that chart in early 1973 with "Soul Song" for Joe Stampley.

While working on a song with Rory Bourke called "Hey, Mister," about a man jilted by his girlfriend, they found themselves stymied when they tried to describe the characteristics of the pretty woman who had run out on their guy. Then as Wilson told Tom Roland in *The Billboard Book of Number One Country Hits*, it hit them that they were trying to do the impossible because "Everybody's got a most beautiful girl or guy. Whoever that person is, is the most beautiful in the world to somebody." With that in mind, they refashioned "Hey, Mister" into "The Most Beautiful Girl."

Wilson pitched the song to producer Billy Sherrill, but Sherrill was not sold on it until he heard another Wilson composition called "Mama McCluskey" and decided to combine a little of that tune with what Bourke and Wilson had written. Sherrill cut "The Most Beautiful Girl" first with Joe Stampley, but his version was not released. Instead, the tune became the follow-up to "Behind Closed Doors" for Charlie Rich as well as his biggest hit.

"The Most Beautiful Girl" was a triple #1 hit on the AC, pop, and country charts. On its last week leading the AC chart it was #1 country for three weeks starting November 24, 1973, then topped the Hot 100 the weeks of December 15 and 22, 1973. Its follow-up, "There Won't Be Anymore," also went to #1 country the weeks of March 9 and 16, 1974, but fell short of that mark on the AC and pop charts, making #15 AC and #18 pop.

Rich topped the AC chart once more, with "A Very Special Love Song" [see 229], the single after "There Won't Be Anymore."

206 Leave Me Alone (Ruby Red Dress)
HELEN REDDY

Capitol 3768

December 1, 1973 (4 weeks)

Writer: Linda Laurie

Producer: Tom Catalano

"Ambrose (Part Five)," sung by Linda Laurie, is not what most people would term a "golden oldie," as it only went to #52 on the Hot 100 in 1959. Yet Helen Reddy did remember the single and its singer quite well. "She had a very strange sort of voice," Reddy said. That fond memory helped Laurie when Reddy decided to record Laurie's composition "Leave Me Alone (Ruby Red Dress)" as her follow-up to "Delta Dawn" [see 198].

Reddy said she had no idea why the phrase "Ruby Red Dress" was in parentheses. She also remembered that at least one radio station had a contest among its listeners to see who could guess how many times she sang "leave me alone" on the track. "I think it was like 43 times," she said. However many times she said it, the repetition didn't keep the song from topping the AC chart and making #3 pop for two weeks starting December 29, 1973. The first week Jim Croce's "Time in a Bottle" [see 207] and Charlie Rich's "The Most Beautiful Girl" [see 205] at #2 impeded her progress to the top, while the second week "Time in a Bottle" remained at the top and Steve Miller's "The Joker" took over the #2 slot.

For her stage shows in the 1990s, Reddy often did a sort of medley based on a "ruby" motif, which opened with her backing musicians playing "Ruby," the theme from the movie *Ruby Gentry*, and then "Ruby Baby," a #2 pop hit for Dion in 1963, before she sang "Leave Me Alone (Ruby Red Dress)." "It's the only way I can bear to do it in concerts nowadays," she said. Reddy has also done the song in a medley along with "Delta Dawn" and "Angie Baby" [see 238] as part of a collection of tunes featuring slightly "out-of-it" (to put it delicately) females.

In addition, "Leave Me Along (Ruby Red Dress)" was the only one of Reddy's eight #1 AC songs to be popularized by her first and then covered by another artist who made a *Billboard* chart. In this case, it was a version by Arleen Harden, who took the tune to #72 country in the summer of 1974.

The song also has the distinction of staying longer at the top of the AC chart than any of her other hit singles. The four-week run of "Leave Me Alone. . ." was double that of its predecessor, "Delta Dawn," as well as that of her next #1 hit, "Keep On Singing" [see 215].

207 Time in a Bottle

JIM CROCE

ABC 11405

December 29, 1973 (2 weeks)

Writer: Jim Croce

Producers: Terry Cashman, Tommy West

The ironies associated with "Time in a Bottle"—from its creation to its eventual success—are myriad. The first is the fact that Jim Croce (pronounced "CROW-chee") wrote the lyrics after his wife Ingrid announced that she was pregnant, in December 1970. "I think, with him recognizing the birth of his own child, there was a sense of his mortality that made him write a song about immortality," Ingrid said in a 1997 documentary about her husband on the VH-1 cable channel series *Behind the Music*. The next irony was that Croce's own time with the son he wrote the song for, was limited due to his heavy touring schedule.

Then, despite the appeal "Time in a Bottle" had for Croce and his friends, it was not issued as a single from his LP *You Don't Mess Around With Jim*. First came the title track, which went to #9 AC and #8 pop and was his debut on both charts. Then came "Operator (That's Not the Way It Feels)," which hit #11 AC and #17 pop. Both 45s came out in 1972, but "Time in the Bottle," written the same week as the other two, stayed only on the album.

The final set of ironies centers around Croce's tragic death. After a concert in Natchitoches, Louisiana, at Northwestern Louisiana University on September 20, 1973, where Croce performed "Time in a Bottle" as an encore, he and five others died when a chartered plane crashed shortly after takeoff. The crash occurred less than two weeks after an ABC-TV movie called "She Lives" featured "Time in a Bottle" in the background. Given the circumstances, demand for release of the tune built, and by the week of December 29, 1973, "Time in a Bottle" was #1 on the pop and AC charts, where it stayed for two weeks. So Croce's biggest hit, dealing with the need for more time, came after time had run out for him. The album, *You Don't Mess Around With Jim*, hit #1 for five weeks after the single had dropped from the top spots.

The classical feel of "Time in a Bottle" was created by heavy use of harpsichord, guitar, and bass and by its waltz pattern. Contrary to what some believe, it was not the first single issued after Croce died. That was "I Got a Name," which went to #4 AC and #10 pop in the fall of 1973. Similarly, it is not true that Croce, born in Philadelphia, Pennsylvania, on January 10, 1943, had been in and out of the music world since his college days, mostly doing coffee houses and bar gigs. In 1968 he and Ingrid did an album for Capitol, but the record sold poorly. Croce, discouraged, survived over the next few years by doing whatever came along—and by selling his guitars—until the release of *You Don't Mess Around With Jim* ensured his success as a full-time musician.

Croce had several chart entries after "Time in a Bottle." The biggest was "I'll Have to Love You in a Song" [see 216].

208 The Way We Were

BARBRA STREISAND

Columbia 45944

January 12, 1974 (2 weeks)

Writers: Marvin Hamlisch, Alan Bergman, Marilyn Bergman

Producer: Marty Paich

Barbra Streisand sang two different versions of "The Way We Were"; one of them was used on two different albums, plus revived as part of three different medleys. In fact, the simple melody has a rather complex history, which began with the 1973 movie of the same name starring Streisand and Robert Redford.

When it was decided that Streisand would sing a title tune for the film, the assignment of creating it fell to old pals of hers. Marvin Hamlisch, her pianist when she did *Funny Girl* on Broadway, wrote the score, while the married couple of Alan and Marilyn Bergman, who had worked on the theme for Streisand's 1972 movie *Up the Sandbox*, became lyricists.

"But there were two 'Way We Weres' because Marilyn and Alan, being very creative and very prolific writers, finished eight weeks before we needed it," Streisand told the audience at a tribute on June 6, 1980 for the Bergmans to benefit the ACLU Foundation of Southern California, and her words were later included as part of the Streisand anthology *Just for the Record*. "And they said, 'Gee, well, we never had the opportunity to write a second lyric to the same song. . . .So they wrote another lyric to it, to another melody, by the way, by Marvin Hamlisch. . . .To distinguish it from 'The Way We Were' #1, we call it 'The Way We Weren't.'" All parties agreed the first worked better for the picture, so it was the one used.

The confusion did not end with the song selection. Album buyers in 1974 could purchase two different Streisand LPs titled *The Way We Were*. One was the soundtrack with the title song. The other was a new collection of Streisand tunes, also with the title song. The former peaked at #20, while the latter made #1 for two weeks starting March 16, 1974.

Voters at the Oscars and Grammys had no confusion over which "The Way We Were" they were hearing (it was the first version), and the song was awarded an Oscar for Best Song and a Grammy for Song of the Year. Surprisingly, the tune failed to get Grammy nominations for Record of the Year or Best Female Pop Vocal Performance for Streisand.

"The Way We Were" reappeared on the AC chart by two different artists, each time as part of a medley. The Lettermen combined it with "Touch Me in the Morning" [see 197] and went to #31 in 1974, while Gladys Knight and the Pips sung it with "Try to Remember" in 1975 and got to #2, as well as #11 pop and #6 R&B. And in 1979 the Manhattans used it in yet another medley, with "Memories," and went to #33 R&B.

Despite the song's convoluted history, it was big enough to give Streisand her first #1 hit on the Hot 100 after a decade of entries there. It rode that position for three weeks starting February 2, 1974. Streisand had another double AC and pop song three years later [see 324—"Love Theme From *A Star Is Born* (Evergreen)"].

1974

209 Love's Theme
THE LOVE UNLIMITED ORCHESTRA

20th Century 2069

January 26, 1974 (2 weeks)

Writer: Barry White

Producer: Barry White

The first part of the name Love Unlimited Orchestra referred to the female R&B trio Love Unlimited—Diane Taylor, Linda James, and Linda's sister Glodean—a group which had been groomed by writer/singer/producer Barry White (later Glodean's husband) and which scored its biggest hit in 1972 (#6 R&B, #14 pop) with "Walkin' in the Rain With the One I Love." The "Orchestra" was the 40-piece orchestra which backed up White on his own records.

When White went to do the last song for Love Unlimited's *Under the Influence of Love* album, "Love's Theme," he met with Russ Regan, head of 20th Century Records, and told him that the track without vocals would do fine as a single. Regan disagreed, but suggested that even if it did happen, the artist should be listed as the Barry White Orchestra since White had written and produced the cut. But White had power and influence at the label, having scored earlier as a solo artist in 1973 with his first hits "I'm Gonna Love You Just a Little More Baby" (#1 R&B, #3 pop, #27 AC) and "I've Got So Much to Give" (#5 R&B, #32 pop, #46 AC), so out went the Love Unlimited Orchestra with "Love's Theme."

Describing the tune to Guy Aoki in *Goldmine* in 1993, White said, "Strings were always used as a background instrument. Barry White took the violins from the background and put 'em up front, where they came at you like some aggressive guitar line. . . .I like to think that strings can play rhythm lines, which I made them play."

The single captivated the public and went on to top both the AC and pop charts, hitting the latter the week of February 9, 1974. On the R&B chart it made #10. The Love Unlimited female trio's vocal rendition did not become a single, but in 1974 Andy Williams recorded a version with lyrics which went to #16 AC.

Four other Love Unlimited Orchestra instrumentals made the pop, R&B, and AC charts: 1974's "Rhapsody in White" (#34 AC, #48 R&B, #63 pop), 1975's "Satin Soul" (#39 AC, #23 R&B, #22 pop), 1976's "My Sweet Summer Suite" (#30 AC, #28 R&B, #48 pop), and 1977's "Theme From King Kong (Pt. 1)" (#27 AC, #15 R&B, #68 pop). Two other singles also made the R&B chart, 1975's "Forever in Love" (#22) and 1976's "Midnight Groove" (#91). The Love Unlimited Orchestra kept releasing singles through 1983, though none charted after 1977.

Barry White never fared as well on the AC chart as Love Unlimited Orchestra, but he was a top R&B and pop performer for a number of years. Born in Galveston, Texas, on September 12, 1944, he grew up in Los Angeles. White performed with several groups from 1961–65, then, after meeting the trio that was to become Love Unlimited, worked mainly as a producer and manager until the late 1960s and early and mid-1970s, when he cut several top-selling singles. White sat out much of the 1980s, but in 1990 he took 37 musicians out on tour for one more fling as conductor of the Love Unlimited Orchestra while he started a new string of R&B solo hits. Both moves delighted his longtime fans, and in late 1994 White released a platinum album, *The Icon Is Love*.

210 Love Song
ANNE MURRAY

Capitol 3776

February 9, 1974 (1 week)

Writers: Dona Lyn George, Kenny Loggins

Producer: Brian Ahern

Though she had a huge success with Kenny Loggins' "Danny's Song" [see 188], Anne Murray did not meet the songwriter in person until months after she recorded the song. As Murray told the story, "I was hosting *The Midnight Special* [a late-night NBC-TV music series in the 1970s], and he was in a recording session somewhere nearby and I hadn't met him. A mutual friend introduced us."

Loggins and Murray then went into what she described as a "washroom" to hear him play two tunes for her, "Love Song" and "Watching the River Run." She loved them both and recorded the tunes for her *Love Song* LP, with the guitar track for "Love Song" performed by Mason Williams [see 107—"Classical Gas"]. Loggins and his partner Jim Messina also recorded "Love Song" for their 1973 album *Full Sail*, but as with "Danny's Song," it was Murray's single which made the charts. (Loggins and Messina did release "Watching the River Run" as their own single. It went to #36 AC and #71 pop in 1974.)

Murray said she considered that encounter lucky because she had always admired Loggins "as a writer and singer" and because their subsequent friendship went far beyond the hit that the meeting engendered.

Her third #1 AC hit, "Love Song," also went to #5 country and #12 pop. But perhaps the sweetest triumph for Murray was that it finally won her her first Grammy, for Best Country Female Vocal Performance. She won over an impressive field of contenders, among them Dolly Parton ["Jolene"], Tanya Tucker ["Would You Lay With Me (In a Field of Stone)"], Dottie West ["Last Time I Saw Him"] and Tammy Wynette ["Woman to Woman"].

"I can remember that Grammy in particular," Murray said. "I was backstage and very, very nervous, and Bette Midler came backstage and said, 'Would you people lighten up?!'" Midler's statement cracked the ice, as did the alcohol the singer offered to anyone who wanted some, er, refreshment during the ceremony. But, Murray noted, she was embarrassed by the fact that her dress strap broke that evening.

Another memorable moment came that same night when Murray met one of her singing idols and was floored by what he said to her. "John Lennon told me 'You Won't See Me' was the best cover version of a Beatles song he'd ever heard," she said. For more details on that hit, see 222.

211 Last Time I Saw Him

DIANA ROSS

Motown 1278

February 16, 1974 (3 weeks)

Writers: Michael Masser, Pam Sawyer

Producer: Michael Masser

Diana Ross notched her only back-to-back solo #1 AC entries when "Last Time I Saw Him" went to the top of the chart following "Touch Me in the Morning" [see 197]. Like the latter, "Last Time I Saw Him" was co-written by Michael Masser, but this tune had a more upbeat edge, even sprinkling in a hint of Dixieland jazz toward the end. Besides its AC peak, it went to #14 pop and #15 R&B in 1974. That same year Dottie West's cover hit #8 country.

"Last Time I Saw Him" and "Touch Me in the Morning" made Ross a force to reckon with on the AC chart, something she could not claim when she was part of the Supremes (originally called the Primettes) from 1960–69. That trio, composed initially of her, Mary Wilson, and Florence Ballard (replaced in 1967 by Cindy Birdsong), charted an impressive 12 #1 pop hits from 1964–69, but despite performances at such adult venues as the Copa and many appearances on *The Ed Sullivan Show*, the group didn't hit the AC chart until its last #1 pop hit, 1969's "Someday We'll Be Together," made #12 in late 1969. The Supremes went on (Jean Terrell became lead singer in the 1970s and Lynda Lawrence replaced Birdsong in 1972) but had only seven other entries make the AC chart from 1970–72, none reaching as high as "Someday We'll Be Together," before they broke up in 1977.

Ross, however, born as Diane Earle on March 26, 1944, kept chugging along as a solo act in the 1970s. Childhood friends from Detroit, Michigan, said she had always struck them as a determined person. Ross helped form the Primettes, which started as a quartet, and got the attention of Motown head Berry Gordy, who stuck with the group even after most of its efforts in the early 1960s flopped. Then "Where Did Our Love Go?" made #1 pop in 1964, and the Supremes were on their way to stardom. Ross, who sang lead, was groomed for special exposure, and by 1967 the group was billed as Diana Ross and the Supremes. Three years later, Ross began her solo career.

The first Ross single released was "Reach Out and Touch (Somebody's Hand)," which made #18 AC and #20 pop. "Ain't No Mountain High Enough," the follow-up, did better, getting to #6 AC and #1 pop in late 1970. She had one more top 10 AC single—1973's "Good Morning Heartache" at #8—before the one-two punch of "Touch Me in the Morning" and "Last Time I Saw Him."

The next single by Ross after "Last Time I Saw Him" was the unimpressive "Sorry Doesn't Always Make It Right," which hit only #17 AC without making the Hot 100. But she rebounded strongly with her next 45, "Theme From Mahogany (Do You Know Where You're Going To)" [see 280].

212 Seasons in the Sun

TERRY JACKS

Bell 45432

March 9, 1974 (1 week)

Writers: Jacques Brel, Rod McKuen

Producer: Terry Jacks

"Seasons in the Sun," written in 1961 by Belgian Jacques Brel, had been translated to English by Rod McKuen a decade before Terry Jacks turned it into a #1 hit in America, Canada, and Great Britain. The Kingston Trio had the first version recorded in English in 1964. Eight years later, the Beach Boys recorded an unreleased rendition. The guitarist at that session was Terry Jacks. Jacks' revival landed at #1 pop for three weeks and was #1 simultaneously on the AC chart for the middle week of that run.

Jacks, born in Winnipeg, Canada, was not an unknown singer when he cut "Seasons in the Sun," but relatively few people knew that he and then-wife Susan Jacks charted as the Poppy Family in the early 1970s. That duo's biggest success was "Which Way You Goin' Billy?" in 1970 (#2 pop, #6 AC). He and Susan divorced in 1973 after six years of marriage, and she went on to a minor career, having only one charted tune, "You're a Part of Me," which hit #18 AC and #90 pop in 1975. In the meantime, Terry created one of the biggest hits of the 1970s after meeting Jacques Brel.

"He told me he wrote the song in Tangiers about a whorehouse," Jacks told Barry Scott in *We Had Joy, We Had Fun*. "He said it was written about an old man who was dying of a broken heart because his best friend had been goofing around with his wife. It was written in march form. The song had a mystique to it. It never left my mind."

Following the Beach Boys' decision not to release the song, and the death of a best friend, Jacks rewrote the lyrics to describe the impact of a young person's death. Adding to the melancholy tone were plaintive guitar strokes from Link Wray. After the song became a hit in Canada, Bell Records released it in the States, where it became an instant success. Incredibly, Jacks never performed the tune outside Canada while it was on the way up.

Jacks' next release was another Brel tune, "If You Go Away." Coincidentally, its peak at #68 pop was the same high point reached in 1967 by Damito Jo with her version of the tune. "If You Go Away" stopped at #29 AC and was his last entry on that chart. Jacks' final Hot 100 song was "Rock 'n' Roll (I Gave You the Best Years of My Life)," which made #97 for one week in late 1975 but was a #15 pop hit that same year for Mac Davis.

Over the next 15 years Jacks recorded only intermittently and confined most of his activities to his native Canada. He told Scott in the early 1990s that he had no plans to return to singing in any studio. Instead, much of his efforts went to fighting water pollution among Canada's major tributaries. His love for the water extended to his boat, where he lived for several months each year. Its name? Why, *Seasons in the Sun*, of course.

213 Sunshine on My Shoulders

JOHN DENVER

RCA 0213

March 16, 1974 (2 weeks)

Writer: John Denver, Dick Kniss, Mike Taylor

Producer: Milt Okun

"Sunshine on My Shoulders" was the first #1 AC hit sung by John Denver, but it was not the first one to be written by him. That distinction belonged to Peter, Paul and Mary's version of "Leaving on a Jet Plane" [see 126]. However, "Sunshine on My Shoulders" did begin a streak of four consecutive #1 AC hits for the singer, and Denver eventually had a total of nine chart-toppers.

In *Take Me Home*, Denver's autobiography, he recalled the inspiration for the record: "I had written the song in a fit of melancholy one wet and dismal late-winter/early-spring day in Minnesota—the kind of day that makes every Minnesotan think about going down to Mexico. On one hand, it was about the virtues of love. On another, more deeply felt level, it reached out for something the whole world could embrace."

The result was the low-key but optimistic "Sunshine on My Shoulders," which began acoustically with Denver and his guitar, then gained more instruments as the tune progressed. Yet the beautiful composition did not attract much attention when it appeared as the B-side to another Denver single in the summer of 1973, "I'd Rather Be a Cowboy," which went to #25 AC and #62 pop. It was not until the record came out in early 1974 that "Sunshine on My Shoulders" moved to the top of the AC and pop charts, making the latter the week of March 30, 1974. It also made #42 country.

In his autobiography, Denver remembered its rise and analyzed why the song had more appeal the second time around. "When it was released initially the song didn't impress the industry as anything special. Its meaning didn't sink in. But while the war in Vietnam was winding down to a disastrous finale, the song suddenly reached out to touch a deep chord of need in the country. Just when there was so much going on in the world that was costing us dearly, and things were seemingly out of control, here was a dove coming back with news of dry land. Or at least a song that soared upward, and took its audience back home."

Denver may have been right, but it should also be noted that the song was prominently featured in a TV movie called *Sunshine*, which aired on CBS on November 9, 1973 (it was the favorite melody of the dying female lead). The song became a theme tune when *Sunshine* became a NBC-TV series from March 6 through June 19, 1975.

When "Sunshine on My Shoulders" emerged as a hit, it propelled the *John Denver's Greatest Hits* LP to #1 on the album chart for three weeks starting March 30, 1974. It was Denver's first LP to do so, and he would have two more follow-ups reach the same peak, each assisted by several tunes which hit #1 AC.

214 A Very Special Love Song

CHARLIE RICH

Epic 11091

March 30, 1974 (2 weeks)

Writers: Billy Sherrill, Norro Wilson

Producer: Billy Sherrill

"A Very Special Love Song" was the fourth consecutive #1 country hit for Charlie Rich as well as his second #1 AC entry after "The Most Beautiful Girl" [see 205]. Actually, "A Very Special Love Song" was the official follow-up to "The Most Beautiful Girl," as the song released between the two singles, "There Won't Be Anymore," came from the vaults of RCA Records, which hoped to capitalize on the newfound success, on Epic, of their former artist. "There Won't Be Anymore" was written by Rich himself, while "A Very Special Love Song" came from the co-writers of "The Most Beautiful Girl," Billy Sherrill and Norro Wilson.

Commenting on the song's introduction and the music between the verses, Wilson told Tom Roland in *The Billboard Book of Number One Country Hits* that "That little melodic thing was inspired by 'The Theme From *The Summer of 42'* [a 1971 film starring Jennifer O'Neill]. I don't think I stole from them all, but that's my favorite theme of all time. There's not

a similarity, and yet, you can understand what I was thinking about and where I was coming from." Anyone wanting to compare "A Very Special Love Song" to "Theme From *The Summer of 42*" can check out two instrumental versions of the latter which made the AC chart, one by Peter Nero in 1971 (#6) and the other by the Biddu Orchestra in 1975 (#10).

As for what inspired the title, Wilson told Roland, "We needed something for Charlie, and he [Billy] said, 'Let's write for him a very special love song.'" It indeed proved to be special in terms of chart performance, reaching #1 AC plus #1 country for three weeks starting April 6, 1974, and #11 pop.

"A Very Special Love Song" won Wilson and Sherrill Grammys for Best Country Song, but surprisingly Rich was not nominated for his work on the tune, even though he had won the previous year for Best Male Country Vocal Performance for his singing on "Behind Closed Doors."

The follow-up to "A Very Special Love Song," "I Don't See You in My Eyes Anymore," was also a #1 country hit; it made #9 AC in the summer of 1974, but faltered on the pop chart, peaking at #47. "I Don't See You. . ." also was actually another RCA release of old material, so its poor performance on the Hot 100 probably did not discourage Rich. A remake of a tune that had been #5 pop hit for the Stardusters in 1949, the song was written by the team of Bennie Benjamin and George David Weiss.

In the fall of 1974, Rich returned to #1 AC with another concoction by Sherrill and Wilson. For details on that, see 229—"I Love My Friend."

215 Keep On Singing

HELEN REDDY

Capitol 3845

April 13, 1974 (2 weeks)

Writers: Danny Janssen, Bobby Hart

Producer: Tom Catalano

"Keep On Singing" was the second of singer Austin Roberts' three singles to make both the AC and pop charts. The first was 1972's "Something's Wrong With Me," which made #16 AC and #12 pop, and the last was 1975's "Rocky," which reached #22 AC and #9 pop. Between them was "Keep On Singing" in early 1973, which stopped at #22 AC and #50 pop. Despite Roberts' so-so showing, Helen Reddy managed to hear the song on her car radio and became enchanted by it. "I had a little Fiat Spider at the time," she recalled. "I said, 'Now that's a great song, but the tempo's too slow.' It was dirgelike."

Reddy thought she would do a more upbeat version of "Keep On Singing" sometime but nothing materialized until her father passed away. The song's lyrics—about how a singer would be a star in the future and make people happy by singing songs—struck her as advice her father might have given her. So, Reddy remembered, "After my father died, I said, 'Hey, let's do that song.'"

She dedicated "Keep On Singing" to her father, but not long after the song was released two more deaths—her mother's and a close friend's—made it difficult for Reddy to feel up to promoting the song. "My parents' funerals were 10 weeks apart to the day," she said. "I don't look back on this time too fondly."

"Keep On Singing" never did make the top 10 of the Hot 100, peaking at #15 there a year after Roberts' rendition, and it was to be the last Reddy single to spend more than one week helming the AC chart.

Singing was indeed an integral part of Reddy's young life. Born in Melbourne, Australia, on October 25, 1941, she was a third-generation performer. Her dad, Max Reddy, was a writer, producer, singer, and actor, while her mom, Stella Lamond, also sang and acted. They encouraged their child to join them onstage as early as age 4, and Helen toured with them while growing up. By the mid-1960s she had her own TV show, where she sang twice a week.

In 1966 Helen won a talent contest with the first prize being a trip to New York City. She expected to conquer Manhattan, but record labels showed no interest. In 1967 she met Jeff Wald, who became her husband and manager. At Wald's urging, the couple moved to Los Angeles the following year and after much work secured a deal with Capitol Records in 1970. They did extensive promotion for Reddy's first Capitol single, a version of "I Don't Know How to Love Him," which surpassed the original done by Yvonne Elliman in *Jesus Christ Superstar* [see 330—"Hello Stranger"], peaking at #12 AC and #13 pop. It was the first of 24 AC entries for Reddy.

216 I'll Have to Say I Love You in a Song

JIM CROCE

ABC 11424

April 27, 1974 (1 week)

Writer: Jim Croce

Producers: Terry Cashman, Tommy West

One day in early 1973 Jim Croce came home to his wife Ingrid in Lyndell, Pennsylvania, hoping to relax after a grueling tour schedule that had him doing about 300 dates a year. Instead of a blissful "welcome home," however, he was met with some hard questions. Ingrid wanted to know why they had so little money despite the touring and the previous year's success with the best-selling LP *You Don't Mess Around With Jim*.

In fact, Croce had sold most of his royalty rights a few years earlier, which limited how much cash he could get for his work, but he did not care to discuss the matter, even when confronted by his wife. ("I would press, and I know that was something you didn't do with Jim," Ingrid said in a 1997 documentary on Croce for VH-1's *Behind the Music* series.) Upset, Jim walked away from Ingrid. "He went downstairs, and he started to play, like he always did when he wrote, and he wrote 'I'll Have to Say I Love You in a Song.' And the next morning, he came up early in the morning and sang it to me," Ingrid recalled.

"I'll Have to Say I Love You in a Song" went onto Jim's 1973 LP *I Got a Name*. The title track of that album was released first and hit #4 AC and #10 pop, then came "Time in a Bottle" from *You Don't Mess Around With Jim* [see 207]. Finally, "I'll Have to Say I Love You in a Song" emerged in early 1974 as a single. In addition to leading the AC chart, it also hit #9 pop and #68 country, the latter being Croce's only country hit.

The song's success was impressive because Croce had died on September 20, 1973, and therefore only the record company and friends and family could promote his tunes. It was not to be the last posthumous release for the artist. Later in 1974 another track from *I Got a Name*, "Workin' at the Car Wash Blues," went to #9 AC and #32 pop. The following year around Christmas came the release of "Chain Gang Medley," which included the old Sam Cooke hit plus "He Don't Love You" and "Searchin'" and went to #22 AC and #63 pop in early 1976. His final chart entry for a single was "Mississippi Lady," which bubbled under to #110 in the spring of 1976.

After Jim's death, Ingrid stayed in San Diego, where she and her late husband had moved in the fall of 1973 shortly before he died. She opened a restaurant in his honor called Croce's, which contained memorabilia of her husband. Their son A.J., now in his twenties, began pursuing a musical career as well and spoke lovingly of the father he never knew on the VH-1 documentary.

217 TSOP (The Sound of Philadelphia)

MFSB FEATURING THE THREE DEGREES

Philadelphia International 3540

May 4, 1974 (2 weeks)

Writers: Kenny Gamble, Leon Huff

Producers: Kenny Gamble, Leon Huff

MFSB, which stood for Mother-Father-Sister-Brother, was the collective name for roughly 34 musicians ranging in age from 26 to 73 who provided the instrumental backing on nearly all of the Philadelphia International releases of the 1970s and other earlier records made by writer/producers Kenny Gamble and Leon Huff. The group existed as early as the first Gamble and Huff hit production, "(We'll Be) United" by the Intruders, in 1966. Two years later, several musicians later to be part of MFSB performed on the instrumental "The Mule" as the James Boys. It reached #82 on the Hot 100.

A later group of Philadelphia International musicians recorded under the name the Family, which did not break the AC or pop chart. They also kept busy backing such top R&B artists as Jerry Butler and the Spinners. By the time MFSB recorded its first album in 1973, the ensemble had as its leaders drummer Earl Young, guitarists Bobby Eli and Norman Harris, bassist Ronnie Baker, percussionist Larry Washington, organist Lenny Pakula, and conductor Don Renaldo.

After the first album emerged, the group got a call from Don Cornelius, producer and host of the popular TV dance series *Soul Train*. Cornelius wanted to update the show's looks and sounds when it began its fourth season nationally in November 1973, so he asked Gamble and Huff to come up with a new theme song. Cornelius liked Gamble's basic melody, but did make a few alterations. "I had the tempo speeded up three or four times as fast as it started out," Cornelius told *Rolling Stone*. "I kept saying, 'It's got to be faster, even faster,' until we got the tempo I wanted."

After recording the tune with MFSB, Gamble, Huff, and group arranger Bobby Martin augmented the track with strings, horns, and vocal backing in the late summer of 1973. The latter came from Gamble and Huff's girl group the Three Degrees, but member Sheila Ferguson told *Rolling Stone* later that their participation was inadvertent. "Kenny Gamble was finishing up with some girls on the TSOP chorus and told us to try the 'Let's get it on' part."

"TSOP" topped the Hot 100 on April 20 and 27, 1974, and the R&B chart on April 20, 1974, before doing the same on the AC chart. While the record was the only MFSB release to make the latter, the group did have a few other minor successes on the other charts with such entries as "Love Is the Message" (also with the Three Degrees; #42 R&B and #85 pop, 1974), "Sexy" (#2 R&B and #42 pop, 1975), and "The Zip" (#72 R&B and #91 pop, 1975). The group continued to chart R&B through 1978's "Use Ta Be My Guy." As for the Three Degrees, they later got their own #1 AC hit [see 239—"When Will I See You Again"].

218 The Entertainer

MARVIN HAMLISCH

MCA 40174

May 18, 1974 (1 week)

Writer: Scott Joplin

Producer: Marvin Hamlisch

Although Scott Joplin's ragtime was out of favor by the time of the Depression, the era in which the 1973 film *The Sting* was set, director George Roy Hill knew that the ragtime sound was exactly what he wanted as theme music. To adapt Joplin's songs he picked Marvin Hamlisch, a rehearsal pianist he had worked with on Broadway a decade earlier.

When the Juilliard-educated Hamlisch, born in New York City on June 2, 1944, went to work on the picture, he knew he wasn't a known Hollywood name. He had helped write "The Way We Were" [see 208], but that movie and song were not yet out. Nonetheless, he tackled the project with confidence.

"I was well aware that there were other musicians who knew the music of Scott Joplin far more intimately than I, men who had popularized Joplin's famous piano rags," Hamlisch wrote in his autobiography *The Way I Was*. "But the truth is, none of them had experience in the movies. I knew how to write for film, marrying music to the length of each scene, and I could also play the piano 'rags'—those Julliard piano lessons were about to pay off.

"George had chosen some pieces from the world of Scott Joplin that he wanted to use. I examined the entire Joplin library and chose my favorites." One of those was "The Entertainer," written in 1902. There was no chance anybody could have a copy on wax of the song by Joplin, since he wrote his tunes only on piano rolls before his death in 1917.

As the soundtrack for *The Sting* gained popularity after its release in early 1974 (it eventually peaked at #1 for five weeks starting May 4, 1974), demand grew for "The Entertainer" to become a 45. The result was an AC chart-topper and a #3 hit on the Hot 100, kept out of the apex there behind the one-two combination of Ray Stevens' "The Streak" and the Jackson Five's "Dancing Machine," respectively, during the weeks of May 18 and 25, 1974.

Hamlisch won an Oscar for Best Score for *The Sting* (he contributed his own ragtime songs to it) and a Grammy for Best Pop Instrumental Performance for "The Entertainer" and for Best New Artist. Despite the latter honor, he charted only one LP after *The Sting* soundtrack. Titled *The Entertainer*, it used his hit along with some other Joplin rags and Hamlisch originals and peaked at #170 in 1974.

"The Entertainer" also proved to be Hamlisch's only entry on the AC and pop charts. Yet he was never away from the music world, appearing in many concerts and often serving as guest conductor for various bands in the following decades. As for the song, vocalist J.R. Bailey adapted "The Entertainer" with lyrics in 1975. His record went to #77 R&B.

219 Help Me

JONI MITCHELL

Asylum 11034

May 25, 1974 (1 week)

Writer: Joni Mitchell

Producers: Joni Mitchell, Henry Lewy

Singer/songwriter Joni Mitchell always considered herself an album artist. This was apparent when her 1996 retrospective LP *Hits* had several tracks which never made the charts. One of them did, however, and that was her biggest 45, "Help Me."

Mitchell co-produced "Help Me" with Henry Lewy, who had previously produced Crosby, Stills and Nash. Lewy had met Mitchell when she was dating David Crosby in the early 1970s. When offered the chance to work with Mitchell instead of CS&N, Lewy jumped at the chance (he recalled telling the men that "You guys are driving me crazy.") Eventually, he and Mitchell worked together on 13 albums.

"Help Me" was recorded during the sessions for Mitchell's *Court and Spark* album. "That was when we were with Tom Scott and his band [backing Mitchell], and she was going out with the drummer," an amused Lewy said. "She played the guitar." Most of the recording on "Help Me" took about one day, with the instrumental track laid first followed by Mitchell's vocal. Lewy thought Mitchell may have doubled her vocal at a later date, but not long after cutting the lead. "The whole album was done very quickly," he said.

Lewy said he knew they had a hit during the playback. "When we did it, I said, 'That's fantastic! You can sing along with it.'" He confirmed that feeling when the record came out. "When I heard it on the radio, the drums were perfect. I said, 'We did a great record.'"

Officials with the Grammys agreed and gave "Help Me" a nomination for Record of the Year. The song went to #1 AC and #7 pop, peaking on the latter the week of June 8, 1974. It spurred *Court and Spark* to reach #2 on the album chart for four weeks in 1974, the best showing of any LP by Mitchell.

Mitchell, born Roberta Joan Anderson in Fort McLeod, Alberta, Canada, on November 7, 1943, created her stage name by using her middle name and her first husband's surname. She came to New York in 1966 and released her first album in 1968. Her AC and pop chart debut was in 1970 with "Big Yellow Taxi" (#33 AC, #67 pop).

She fared decently after "Help Me" with "Free Man in Paris" in 1974 (#2 AC, #22 pop) and a live version of "Big Yellow Taxi" in 1975 (#27 AC, #24 pop), but had her last AC entry in 1976 with "In France They Kiss on Main Street" (#32 AC, #66 pop). She had only minor pop entries afterward. Lewy said record executives wanted her to do more singles-oriented tunes, but she always told them, "I don't care."

Nevertheless, Mitchell's album work remained so strong that she was inducted into the Rock and Roll Hall of Fame in 1997. Lewy believed she deserved the honor, saying, "She was a very good person to work with. I enjoyed every minute of it. . . .Even now she's great."

220 I Won't Last a Day Without You

THE CARPENTERS

A&M 1521

June 1, 1974 (1 week)

Writers: Paul Williams (words), Roger Nichols (music)

Producers: Karen Carpenter, Richard Carpenter,
* Jack Daugherty*

Paul Williams described "I Won't Last a Day Without You," which he co-wrote with Roger Nichols, as "maybe my favorite of our songs." Asked why, he said, "Lyrically, I really like it. All of Roger's music is wonderful. . . .I love the chorus of 'I Won't Last a Day Without You.' I like that it refers very casually to an American icon." (The icon he meant was the song "Over the Rainbow" from the 1939 musical movie *The Wizard of Oz*. The reference comes in the first line of the chorus, which says, "When there's no getting over that rainbow.") Karen and Richard Carpenter cut the tune originally as part of their 1972 LP *A Song for You*, and it was released two years later as a single.

Between its appearance as an album track and the single that became a hit, "I Won't Last a Day Without You" came out as two different singles. Williams himself came out in the spring of 1973 with his effort, which made #40 AC while bubbling under to #106. In the fall of the same year, Maureen McGovern's take reached #14 AC and #89 pop.

In 1975 Al Wilson tried his hand at "I Won't Last a Day Without You" in a medley with "Let Me Be the One," getting to #39 AC, #70 pop and #18 R&B. Vince and Dianne Hatfield got it to #83 country in 1981. But none came close to matching the popularity of the Carpenters' rendition, which went to #11 pop as well as #1 AC.

Williams knew that the lyrics he wrote to this and other hit songs done by the Carpenters, like "We've Only Just Begun" [see 140] and "Rainy Days and Mondays" [see 151], were part of the overall appeal of the Carpenters' records, but he also felt that it was a special ingredient contributed by Karen that made them magical. "The combination of innocence and sensuality in her voice," he said. "There was amazing clarity and real sensuality to her voice. . . .They were so conservative, her soulfulness had to shine past their image."

Nearly two decades after her death, Williams still felt sorrow and confusion over Karen Carpenter's passing. "What a waste. And I was just a hardcore cocaine, drunk addict who did it till the wheels fell off, and she lived this sheltered life and died," he said. The irony was not lost on Williams, who in the early 1990s came to terms with his own demons and dropped the drugs and alcohol. He is now pursuing a writing and performing career in country music while living in southern California.

221 Sundown

GORDON LIGHTFOOT

Reprise 1194

June 8, 1974 (2 weeks)

Writer: Gordon Lightfoot

Producer: Lenny Waronker

It was to be three years—and at least three releases—after the success of "If You Could Read My Mind" [see 145] before Gordon Lightfoot had another hit. The singles that did make the charts were "Talking in Your Sleep" in 1971 (#11 AC, #64 pop), "Beautiful" in 1972 (#30 AC, #58 pop), and "You Are What I Am" (#32 AC, #101 bubbling under). The release of "Sundown" shattered that pattern.

Recalling the inspiration for the tune, Lightfoot said, "I went through the divorce procedure in the early 1970s. . . .I was living a sort of footloose style, and a song like 'Sundown' could be valid, for a song at that time." Prodded to explain more, he added, "There was a lot more freedom during those years. Let's say I was not answerable to anyone." But lest anyone think that philosophy remained with the artist, Lightfoot quickly pointed out that eventually he did settle down and get married.

Besides its AC success, "Sundown" hit #1 pop the week of June 29, 1974 and became Lightfoot's first country entry, peaking at #13. The *Sundown* album was #1 on the LP chart for two weeks starting June 22, 1974. Producing all the songs was Lenny Waronker, who had severed his working relationship with Joe Wissert so the two men could pursue separate projects. Waronker and Wissert had produced Lightfoot's previous hit, "If You Could Read My Mind," and Lightfoot had worked with Wissert as a solo producer, but the rest of Lightfoot's hits came with Waronker as his only producer.

Lightfoot remembered that the popularity of "Sundown" was not a pressing concern for him at the time of its release, 1974. "I was more interested in the 'making a living' aspect at the time," he mused. Yet he did recall when he heard the news about the hit status of "Sundown"—his band was appearing at the Methodist Hall in Belfast, England, while on tour. "Our promoter came onstage to make an announcement we were #1 in America," Lightfoot said. "A great cheer came up."

Lightfoot said the appeal of "Sundown" was simple: "It had a good beat, and the message was a kind of slinky message." He also noted that in America at least, major radio programmers singled it out early as a potential hit to play, leading many stations to put it onto their play lists.

After "Sundown," the next Lightfoot single was from the same album and also went to #1 AC. See 233—"Carefree Highway."

222 You Won't See Me

ANNE MURRAY

Capitol 3867

June 22, 1974 (2 weeks)

Writers: John Lennon, Paul McCartney

Producer: Brian Ahern

Anne Murray is an avid Beatles fan. The one song of theirs which stuck in her mind the most was "You Won't See Me," a composition which, despite the credit, was written solely by Paul McCartney and recorded at the last session for the 1966 *Rubber Soul* LP. Even though the Beatles never released the song as a single, Murray was reluctant to cover it. "First of all, I thought the Beatles were the Second Coming," she said. "So when we did a Beatles song, we had to do something different or better."

It took contributions from two of her band members to convince Murray to give it a shot. "Skip Beckwith, the bass player, came up with this bass line so different from the Beatles that it caught me," she said. And Diane Brooks, one of her backup singers, devised vocals that Murray thought were unique as well, so "You Won't See Me" followed "Love Song" [see 210] as Murray's new release for 1974. It became her fourth #1 AC hit and third top 10 pop entry after "Snowbird" and "Danny's Song," peaking at #8 on the Hot 100. (Incidentally, even though it was a Beatles cover, Murray's "You Won't See Me" did not make the British pop chart and neither did "Love Song" or "Danny's Song." In fact, after "Snowbird" peaked at #23 in the United Kingdom in 1970, Murray charted there only four times through 1980's "Daydream Believer" at #61 [see 382 for more details on that song]. She was much more successful in North America.)

Officials in the country division of Capitol Records objected to the release of "You Won't See Me," saying they doubted the tune would appeal to the country stations that usually played Murray's songs. To placate them, Murray recorded a distaff version of George Jones' #1 country hit of 1962, "She Thinks I Still Care." As the B-side to "You Won't See Me," "He Thinks I Still Care" went to #1 country for two weeks beginning July 6, 1974.

Being the Beatlemaniac that she is, Murray covered two other songs by the Liverpool lads. In 1975 she did "Day Tripper," which the Beatles took to #5 pop in 1966 as the flip side to "We Can Work It Out." Murray's version went to #40 AC and #59 pop but failed to make the country chart. And in 1980 she released as a 45 "I'm Happy Just to Dance With You," a record the Fab Four took to #95 pop in 1964 when it was part of the *A Hard Day's Night* soundtrack. For Murray it went to #13 AC, #64 pop, and even #23 country.

Between "Day Tripper" and "I'm Happy Just to Dance With You," Murray had some up-and-down years. The down period was 1975–77, when her songs hit the lower echelons of the AC, pop, and country charts—if they hit them at all. That changed in 1978 when "You Needed Me" firmly put her back in the spotlight. It was her first #1 pop hit, but surprisingly went to only #3 AC and #4 country. Be that as it may, Murray was back in position to score four more #1 AC hits, starting with the follow-up to "You Needed Me" [see 361—"I Just Fall in Love Again"].

223 Annie's Song

JOHN DENVER

RCA 0295

July 6, 1974 (3 weeks)

Writer: John Denver

Producer: Milt Okun

John Denver wed the former Ann Martell in 1967, well ahead of any major musical success he was to have in life. Seven years later, she provided him with the inspiration for his second double #1 AC and pop hit, which coincidentally stayed atop both charts the longest of any of Denver's #1 songs.

"I wrote 'Annie's Song' riding up a ski lift one day early in 1974," Denver wrote in his autobiography *Take Me Home*. "It was soon after our first serious separation, and we'd just come back together." Denver was on the lift early when there were no other riders, which led his mind to wander and notice the beauty of the sky around him. "Then I became aware of the other people skiing, the colors of their clothes, the birds singing, the sound of the lift, the sibilant sound of the skiers going down the mountain. All of these things filled up my senses, and when I said this to myself, unbidden images came one after the other. The night in the forest, a walk in the rain. The mountains in springtime. All of the pictures merged and then what I was left with was Annie."

The entire song came to him on the 10-minute ride on the lift. After Denver skied down the mountain, he went back to his office and composed the song on his guitar. Despite the fact he wrote and titled it in honor of his wife, her name never appeared in the lyrics.

Before *Annie's Song* was released John and Ann had separated for the first time. Denver blamed the separation on their being apart from each other so frequently and on a lack of communication. Sadly, those problems got worse over time, and Ann asked him for a divorce on June 9, 1982—the couple's 15th wedding anniversary. The two were divorced a year later. Denver married Cassandra Delaney in 1988, but they divorced in 1991.

"Annie's Song" fell out of the #1 AC spot the same week it topped the Hot 100, on July 27, 1974, for two weeks. During that period, John and Ann's son Zak was born. On the country chart the record hit #9. It also hit #1 in Britain, and somewhat surprisingly was Denver's only single of the 1970s to enter the English charts.

As the first single to be released from Denver's *Back Home Again* LP, "Annie's Song" did fantastically well, matching the success of his previous single "Sunshine on My Shoulders" [see 213]. The next single was the title tune from the album, and it too went to #1 AC [see 234]. And the following year, Denver sang "Annie's Other Song" as a track from his LP *An Evening With John Denver*.

224 You and Me Against the World

HELEN REDDY

Capitol 3897

July 27, 1974 (1 week)

Writers: Paul Williams, Kenneth Lee Asher

Producer: Tom Catalano

While much of Helen Reddy's material came picked for her courtesy of her producers, it was not the case with at least one songwriter. "I adore Paul Williams, who wrote the lyrics [for 'You and Me Against the World']," she said. "For a long time, there was a Paul Williams song on each of my albums."

Among some of the Williams compositions which Reddy recorded as album tracks were "What Would They Say?" on 1972's *I Am Woman* and "If We Could Still Be Friends" on 1973's *Long Hard Climb*. Impressed by the way she did his tunes and noting her pulling power as an artist, Williams's publishing company sent over a demo of "You and Me Against the World" for Reddy to consider. "It was haunting," Reddy said. "It was absolutely meant to be a standard. But it was written as a man-to-woman love song." Looking for another angle to do the tune, Reddy came up with the idea of doing it as a song from a parent to a child. "I was a single parent for two years, and that 'You and Me Against the World' really locked onto how I was feeling," she said.

Her producer Tom Catalano suggested that Reddy use her daughter Tracy, the one whom she had raised alone for two years, to speak at the opening and closing of the song, including a touching "I love you, Mommy" at the end. Reddy laughed as she remembered, and could not figure out why some people thought that it was her son who did the dialogue with her rather than Tracy. (Tracy was born in the early 1960s, after Helen's marriage to an older musician, a union that lasted only a few months; her son, born in the 1970s, was the child of Helen and her second husband, Jeff Wald.)

Reddy was less amused when her label Capitol decided to edit the dialogue for the song's release as a single (some AC and pop stations nevertheless played the uncut album track). And though "You and Me Against the World" did fine on the Hot 100, peaking at #9 for two weeks starting the week of September 7, 1974, Reddy recalled that Paul Drew, programming head of the influential RKO chain of radio stations, told her he regretted that he did not add the song to his stations' playlist sooner or it might have gone to #1 pop as well as AC.

In any case, the inspirational lyrics of "You and Me Against the World" had a greater impact than the pop charting would suggest. "To this day, when people come up to tell me which songs touched them, it's always 'I Am Woman' or 'You and Me Against the World,'" she said.

Reddy was to score a greater pop success with her next song, which was described as many things, but inspirational was not one of them. For more details, see 238—"Angie Baby."

225 Please Come to Boston

DAVE LOGGINS

Epic 11115

August 3, 1974 (1 week)

Writer: Dave Loggins

Producer: Jerry Crutchfield

Never as famous as his cousin Kenny Loggins, Dave Loggins nonetheless gained a measure of respect within the music industry for his writing talents, even though only one of his compositions, "Please Come to Boston," became a hit. Born in Mountain City, Tennessee, on November 10, 1947, Dave Loggins briefly attended East Tennessee State University before dropping out to pursue a musical career in New York City. Around the same time Kenny was working in rock groups, but while Kenny found success rather easily in the early 1970s, teaming up with Jim Messina, cousin Dave had to struggle for his moment in the pop spotlight.

Dave released his debut album on Vanguard in 1972, *Personal Belongings*. It sold poorly, but a Three Dog Night cover of one song on that album, "Pieces of April," became a hit at #6 AC and #19 pop in 1972. Loggins released his version in 1979, and it went to #22 AC.

In 1974 Loggins switched from Vanguard to Epic and finally got the breakthrough he sought. "Please Come to Boston" peaked at #5 pop the weeks of August 10 and 17, 1974, after topping the AC chart, and also earned him a Grammy nomination for Best Male Pop Vocal Performance. It was not, however, a harbinger of long-term success.

Loggins recorded on Epic for seven more years, but apart from the aforementioned "Pieces of April" in 1979, he had no other singles to hit the charts except when the follow-up to "Please Come Home to Boston," "Someday," went to #57 pop in late 1974. Similarly, only the album containing "Please Come to Boston," 1974's *Apprentice (In a Musical Workshop)*, was able to crack *Billboard*'s Top 200 LP chart.

Without a permanent label, Loggins wrote country songs in the early 1980s. He also made the country chart providing vocals for duets with Anne Murray ("Nobody Loves Me Like You Do" at #1 country and #10 AC in 1984) and Gus Hardin ("Just As Long As I Have You" at #72 in 1985). The Murray duet was to be his last entry on the chart, and those two entries were not strong enough to suggest Loggins had drawing power as a country act, and he remained unsigned.

For the rest of the 1980s, Loggins gave up recording to concentrate on being a country composer. Among his credits were "Forty Hour Week (for a Livin')" with Lisa Silver and Don Schlitz, which made #1 country in 1985 for Alabama, and "Love Will Find Its Way to You" with J.D. Martin, which made #1 country in 1988 for Reba McEntire. At this writing he was still writing songs in Nashville, but apparently had no plans for a recording or performing comeback.

226 Feel Like Makin' Love

ROBERTA FLACK

Atlantic 3025

August 10, 1974 (2 weeks)

Writer: Eugene McDaniels

Producer: Rubina Flake

The writer of "Feel Like Makin' Love," Eugene McDaniels, was familiar with hit records, having scored a few of them himself as an artist in the 1960s. As Gene McDaniels, he had several pop and R&B hits during the early 1960s, including "A Hundred Pounds of Clay" and "Tower of Strength," but only one of them crossed over to the AC chart, "It's a Lonely Town (Lonely Without You)" at #20 AC in 1963. Nine years later he returned to the chart under the name of Universal Jones, singing "River," which made only #37 AC.

McDaniels concentrated more on songwriting during the 1970s, and one of his tunes that made an album was "Compared to What," which appeared on Roberta Flack's 1970 LP *First Take*. He made another sale to the artist in 1974 with a tune inspired by his assistant, Morgan Ames.

Gene had run into him as Ames was packing to leave a woodsy lodge at Lake Arrowhead, California. As McDaniels told Adam White and Fred Bronson in *The Billboard Book of #1 Rhythm and Blues Hits*, when he asked Ames why he was leaving, the response was, "Gotta get back to town. I feel like makin' love." The phrase made such an impression on McDaniels that he finished the tune within a half hour.

The main obstacle "Feel Like Makin' Love" faced was that Joel Dorn, who was supposed to be producing the album, left after a disagreement with Flack, who had to take over the production tasks (the listed producer, "Rubina Flake," was Flack). That delayed the release of the material somewhat, but it did not matter. "Feel Like Makin' Love" was another of the relatively rare triple chart #1 hits. It went to #1 R&B for five weeks starting August 3, 1974, before hitting the top of the AC and pop charts the following week of August 10, 1974 (it stayed only one week leading the Hot 100). Three months later jazz-fusion keyboardist Bob James performed an instrumental version of the tune which made #88 pop.

"Feel Like Makin' Love" earned Grammy nominations for Record of the Year, Song of the Year, and Best Female Pop Vocal Performance, the third consecutive year a Roberta Flack single scored nominations in all three categories following "The First Time Ever I Saw Your Face" [see 168] and "Killing Me Softly With His Song." But unlike the first two efforts, not one award came out of them. ("Killing Me Softly With His Song," which reached #2 AC and #1 pop in 1973, swept all three categories.)

Between "Killing Me Softly With His Song" and "Feel Like Makin' Love," Flack had one single released in 1973, "Jesse," which made #3 AC and #30 pop. Her singles over the next four years did not perform nearly as well, but she got back to #1 AC in 1978 [see 351—"If Ever I See You Again"].

227 Call on Me

CHICAGO

Columbia 46062

August 24, 1974 (1 week)

Writer: Lee Loughnane

Producer: James William Guercio

Lee Loughnane had a definite inspiration for writing "Call on Me." "It was my first wife," he said. "We were separated at the time. But. . .I felt we could still be friends and she could call on me." (He no longer feels that way.)

Loughnane also remembered that there had been rumors that Chicago bandmate and lead singer Peter Cetera claimed to have co-written the song. As Loughnane explained, the band had liked "Call on Me" but felt it needed some changes, so Peter did alter a couple of lyrics. But, said Loughnane, he "didn't do enough to rewrite it. . . .I wrote the frigging song!"

Loughnane also addressed another myth some Chicago detractors have circulated—that the group was a slavish imitation of Blood, Sweat and Tears right down to using that band's producer, James William Guercio.

"He asked for *us*," Loughnane said, and noted that Guercio had stayed with the band through 11 albums, longer than he stayed with Blood, Sweat and Tears. "Call on Me" required Loughnane to work with him a bit more than usual on a record, but the trumpeter enjoyed collaborating with Guercio. "He was a bit of a Hitler, but he got great sounds," Loughnane said.

All members of Chicago wrote for the band, so when asked if there was much competition for Loughnane to get "Call on Me" on the *Chicago VII* album, he responded, "You got that right! There was competition and a bit of a hierarchy. Robert [Lamm] did most of the writing early, but then Peter and Danny [Seraphine] started writing a good amount by the time 'Call on Me' occurred." Each writer lobbied to get his tune on an album, and Loughnane admitted he was "tenuous and afraid they wouldn't like it" when he presented "Call on Me" for their consideration. Luckily, it made the cut.

"Call on Me" hit #6 pop for two weeks on August 10 and 17, 1974, before it topped the AC chart. It was the fourth song to make the AC chart in the wake of Chicago's first #1 AC hit "Beginnings" [see 155]. The other three were 1972's "Saturday in the Park" (#8 AC, #3 pop), 1973's "Just You 'n' Me" (#7 AC, #4 pop), and 1974's "(I've Been) Searchin' So Long" (#8 AC, #9 pop).

Later in 1974, the group scored its first *consecutive* #1 AC hit with the follow-up to "Call on Me," "Wishing You Were Here" [see 240].

228 I'm Leaving It (All) Up to You

DONNY AND MARIE OSMOND

MGM 14735

August 31, 1974 (1 week)

Writers: Don Harris, Dewey Terry, Jr.

Producer: Mike Curb

Donny Osmond began his music career with his brothers and started a concurrent solo career in 1971, but he did not become an AC chart-topper until he teamed with his sister Marie to do remakes of old songs. "I'm Leaving It (All) Up to You" hit #1 pop and AC when done in 1963 by Dale and Grace [see 34]. It was revived on the country charts in 1970 by Johnny and Jonie Mosby, who took it to #18, and in 1978 by Freddy Fender, who took it to #26. But only Donny and Marie's version made the AC, pop, and country charts, hitting #4 pop the week of September 14, 1974, plus #17 country.

The song's crossover success astounded Donny. "What surprised me about 'Leaving It (All) Up to You' was it gave me a country award [on the American Music Awards for Best Country Duo or Group], and I'm the farthest thing from country," he said. "When I look at that videotape, the look on my face was 'You've got to be kidding!'" Of course, anyone who watched their variety show *Donny and Marie* on ABC-TV from January 16, 1976 through May 6, 1979, knows that Marie boasted "I'm a little bit country," while Donny proclaimed, "I'm a little bit rock and roll."

Donny admitted he was unfamiliar with earlier versions of the song. In fact, he did not know why he and Marie added "All" in the middle of the title verse or, for that matter, that it was not in the original version of the song.

He did know how he and Marie became an act. "Our career basically started at Caesar's Palace, I'm thinking 1974," he said. During their performance in Las Vegas together, which was part of the Osmonds act at the time, the two sang "Where Is the Love" [see 172]. MGM President Mike Curb heard about the teaming and had Donny and Marie become a recording act. "I'm Leaving It (All) Up to You" was the first single they released and also their most successful entry on the charts.

While some people's idea of torture would be having to work constantly with their brother or sister, Donny said that although there were times when they got on each other's nerves, mostly it went smoothly. "You learn how to get along with each other, you learn how to treat each other," he said. "In retrospect, I have to say that there was a mutual respect for each other, particularly in concert."

The two garnered another #1 AC hit [see 244—"Morning Side of the Mountain"], and Donny also topped the chart again with his brothers, the Osmonds [see 273—"The Proud One"]. The highest AC entry he had as a soloist was "Sacred Emotion," which made #4 in 1989, although "Go Away Little Girl" did hit #1 pop in 1971 (it went to #14 AC).

229 I Love My Friend

CHARLIE RICH

Epic 20006

September 7, 1974 (1 week)

Writers: Billy Sherrill, Norro Wilson

Producer: Billy Sherrill

Charlie Rich's first listings on the AC chart, in 1970, weren't exactly blockbusters. "July 12, 1939" went to #39 on the listing for a total of two weeks, and later that year he returned with "Nice 'N' Easy," a tune he had done back in 1964 when it bubbled under to #131, but it got only to #34.

Three years passed before Rich returned with his biggest hit to that point, "Behind Closed Doors." It made #8 AC and set off a string of seven consecutive top 20 AC singles for the singer/pianist. The last of those seven was "I Love My Friend," which also became Rich's third #1 AC hit.

Talking about the song to Tom Roland, for *The Billboard Book of Number One Country Hits*, co-writer Norro Wilson noted that "We wondered when we said 'I love my friend' if we were offering some strange message. If it sounded that way, it wasn't meant to. We thought it was very delicate, and if anybody listens to it closely, I think it has a lot of stuff to say. It was kind of a left-field thing."

After its AC peak, "I Love My Friend" hit #1 country the week of October 5, 1974, becoming Rich's sixth consecutive country chart-topper. It also made #24 pop.

To score some of the heat from Rich's success at the time, RCA released an old track of his as a single after "I Love My Friend." "She Called Me Baby," a tune written by Harlan Howard which Rich recorded about a decade earlier for RCA, went to #1 country for his seventh consecutive time, though it fared poorly on the other two charts, making only #41 AC and #47 pop. Rich's "real" follow-up came out in early 1975, but "My Elusive Dreams" reached only the top five on the country chart while going to #16 AC and #49 pop.

That Rich had not yet lost all momentum, however, was proved when his next record, "Every Time You Touch Me (I Get High)," went back to #1 AC [see 266]. But Rich's crossover appeal was waning, as the latter record's follow-up, "All Over Me," went only to #33 AC while missing the Hot 100. His next try, "Since I Fell for You" in 1976, did better, going to #11 AC and #71 pop, but it was his last Hot 100 entry. However, "The Silver Fox," as Rich was called by some, did continue to make the AC and country charts through the rest of the 1970s, with his last AC entry being "Life Goes On" at #13 in 1979.

I Honestly Love You

OLIVIA NEWTON-JOHN

MCA 40280

September 14, 1974 (3 weeks)

Writers: Peter Allen, Jeff Barry

Producer: John Farrar

"That was a song that came in the mail, a demo sent to us for Olivia's consideration," Olivia Newton-John's producer John Farrar said of "I Honestly Love You." "We heard it and we did it."

Writers Jeff Barry and Peter Allen originally intended for Allen to do the song himself, but took a chance on Newton-John cutting it, no doubt because the latter was a hot artist at the time, having scored hits in 1973 with "Let Me Be There" (#3 AC, #6 pop) and in 1974 with "If You Love Me (Let Me Know)" (#2 AC for two weeks, #5 pop). The result was Newton-John's second #1 AC hit after "If Not for You" [see 154]. Allen had to wait until 1976 to get his first AC entry, "The More I See You" at #38, and until 1981 to make his pop debut with "Fly Away" at #55 (not the John Denver tune of the same name in which Newton-John provided vocals).

What Farrar remembered best about "I Honestly Love You," besides Newton-John's vocal, was that the recording was cut in a cramped studio in London where space was so tight that it wasn't easy for all the musicians to cut their parts. "We crammed the string section in there somehow," he said.

After a three-week run atop the AC chart, "I Honestly Love You" hit #1 pop the weeks of October 5 and 12, 1974, plus made #6 country. The single won Grammys for Record of the Year and Best Female Pop Vocal Performance, as well as nominations for Song of the Year. Incidentally, despite all the success and attention to the record, Farrar said he never met the tune's writers Barry and Allen (Allen died of AIDS on June 18, 1992).

MCA rereleased "I Honestly Love You" by Newton-John in 1977, and it got to #49 AC and #48 pop. Farrar said he did not recall the reason why the song came out again (the reason for cutting the B-side, "Don't Cry for Me Argentina," was clear). In 1978 the soul group the Staples did a rendition which went to #68 R&B. Two decades later, Newton-John remade "I Honestly Love You" with David Foster as her producer and got to #18 AC on July 18, 1998. About that remake, Farrar said, "It sounded great."

With the rerelease and rerecording, plus the stays atop the AC and pop chart which were the longest for any Newton-John until 1980, "I Honestly Love You" was a particularly noteworthy hit in chart terms for the singer, and remained a concert fan's favorite. "I think that meant a lot to her, that song," Farrar concluded.

231 Tin Man

AMERICA

Warner 7839

October 5, 1974 (1 week)

Writer: Lee Bunnell

Producer: George Martin

Yes, it's true; the group America did include a member born in England. That would be Dewey Bunnell, born in 1952 nine months before fellow band member Gerry Buckley, but later than the other original member Dan Peek, who was born in Panama City, Florida, in 1950. To complicate the genealogy even more, Buckley's mother actually was British even though he was born in Texas, and Bunnell later became an American citizen.

The three, who met in the late 1960s at London's Central High School, which was designed to teach children of American expatriates working in London, shared a love of playing guitars and singing. Originally they were part of a quintet called the Daze, but after two members of that unit left, the remaining three stuck together and called themselves America.

The trio of guitar men scored in their homeland with "A Horse With No Name," a dead ringer vocally for Neil Young. It went to #1 for three weeks on the Hot 100 in 1972 as well as #3 AC. Two other America singles made the top 10 of both charts in 1972, "I Need You" (#7 AC, #9 pop) and "Ventura Highway" (#3 AC, #8 pop).

"Ventura Highway" came off America's second LP. But their third album, 1973's *Hat Trick*, proved a relative disappointment saleswise, although one of the singles from it, "Muskrat Love," became a #1 AC hit for the Captain and Tennille [see 318]. In the face of *Hat Trick*'s lack of success, America brought out the big guns, hiring as producer George Martin, the man who did the deed for the Beatles.

"That whole project was special in a lot of ways," Bunnell said of America's fourth album, 1974's *Holiday*. "We went back to England. It was great working with George. It's like we knew each other. We were familiar with the Beatles, of course, and we had that British sense of humor. We really enjoyed it."

Bunnell wrote the tune which became the initial single released from the album, "Tin Man." Bunnell confirmed that the inspiration for the song was the film *The Wizard of Oz* (which would be obvious, based on the song's title and words to those familiar with the movie); he had these comments about the movie and the tune: "My favorite movie, I guess. I always loved it as a kid. Very obscure lyrics. Great grammar—'Oz never did give nothing to the Tin Man.' It's sort of a poetic license."

"Tin Man" clanked its way to the top of the AC chart while it stalled at #4 pop for three weeks starting November 9, 1974. "That was a thrill," Bunnell said of the song's popularity. "It was good to be back in the spotlight too." The follow-up to "Tin Man" also hit #1 AC [see 247—"Lonely People"].

232 Stop and Smell the Roses

MAC DAVIS

Columbia 10018

October 12, 1974 (1 week)

Writers: Mac Davis, Doc Severinsen

Producer: Gary Klein

The musical activites of Carl H. "Doc" Severinsen, the flashy bandleader on *The Tonight Show Starring Johnny Carson* from 1967–92, went beyond that late-night talk show. He played with some big bands of the 1940s and 1950s, including the Tommy Dorsey Orchestra from 1949–50, and from 1966–77 made the AC chart three times with minor instrumental records. But his biggest AC impact was with a song he inspired Mac Davis to write, "Stop and Smell the Roses."

Severinsen actually met Mac's mother before he met Mac—at an airport, where she told him about her rising songwriting son. "He was a frequent guest on *The Tonight Show* in the early 1970s. . . .Mac and I, we always spoke and got to be friends," Severinsen said.

Then Severinsen approached him after one show with a song idea he had. He had been describing symptoms of an ailment that was bothering him to a female doctor in Florida when she told Severinsen, "I tell you what you need to do. You need to stop and smell the roses."

"I thought I had something there, but I wasn't a songwriter," noted Severinsen. So he told Davis he had what he thought was a sure hit song idea. "I hear that all the time," an unimpressed Davis said. But the phrase must have grown on him, for a month later a music publisher told Severinsen that the song was coming out and that Severinsen was listed as co-writer.

"Mac had gone on vacation in Hawaii and wrote a song about it," Severinsen explained. He was astonished that Davis had given him partial credit for the tune. "He could've gone ahead and written the song and not done that," noted the grateful bandleader.

"Stop and Smell the Roses" went to #1 AC, #40 country, and #9 pop for two weeks starting October 26, 1974, the only other top 10 pop hit for Davis as a singer after "Baby Don't Get Hooked on Me" [see 175]. Severinsen enjoyed the record and its hit status but added, "Della Reese was a frequent guest on *The Tonight Show*, and I'll be damned if she didn't come on one night to do the song and sang a gospel version. And that's the way it needs to be done."

By the time "Stop and Smell the Roses" came out, Davis had his own musical variety series on NBC which lasted through 1976. Afterward, his chart activity died down. His last AC record was 1978's "Music in My Life" at #22. "I haven't seen Mac in a while," Severinsen said in 1998, and indeed he did very little of note after a run of country entries through 1986. His last major release was a 1996 CD titled *Will Write Songs for Food* on Sony Music, following two years of starring as the lead character in *The Will Rogers Follies* musical on Broadway and on tour across America.

233 Carefree Highway
GORDON LIGHTFOOT

Reprise 1309

October 19, 1974 (1 week)

Writer: Gordon Lightfoot

Producer: Lenny Waronker

The title may sound like a fanciful invention on Gordon Lightfoot's part, but there really was a Carefree Highway running through Arizona. "I was driving through Flagstaff to Phoenix late one night, and the big sign 'Carefree Highway' appeared," Lightfoot said. Thinking it a good title for a song, Lightfoot took the corner of the contract for the car he had rented for his drive and wrote down the two words. By the time he arrived in Phoenix, Lightfoot had finished the song. As he was on tour, he did not fine-tune "Carefree Highway" until the run of concert dates ended two weeks later. It then took him a day to get "Carefree Highway" into the composition he recorded.

Officials at Lightfoot's label Reprise decided the song would be a worthy follow-up to his smash "Sundown" [see 221], but Lightfoot said the record did not come out as well as he had hoped. "Lenny [Waronker, his producer] and I, when we looked back a few years later, we decided we would've liked to have done that again." Lightfoot said he felt he could give a better performance for the song on record and added, "There's a few like that." He added that the song reflects a restlessness that he no longer feels now that he has settled down and married. "Things have changed a lot," he said. "If we look at the responsibilities we have acquired and family responsibility, the party at the moment doesn't matter."

"Carefree Highway" became Lightfoot's first back-to-back #1 AC hit as well as top 10 pop hit following "Sundown," reaching #10 on the Hot 100 the weeks of November 9 and 16, 1974. It also was his second country entry after "Sunshine," peaking at #81 there ("Sundown" went to #13 country).

Lightfoot had been on a lot of highways by the time the song hit. Born in Orillia, Ontario, Canada, on November 17, 1938, he went to Los Angeles in 1958 to study piano at Westlake College, then spent some time in England before returning to Canada. In 1960 he took up the guitar and two years later made his first record. In the mid-1960s he and Jim Whalen played as a duo called the Two Tones, but by the end of the decade he had made a name for himself as one of Canada's most successful singer/songwriters and by the middle of the 1970s he had achieved a similar reputation in the United States.

There would be one more #1 AC hit for Lightfoot after "Carefree Highway." See 260—"Rainy Day People."

234 Back Home Again

JOHN DENVER

RCA 10065

October 26, 1974 (2 weeks)

Writer: John Denver

Producer: Milton Okun

"Back Home Again," the title track from John Denver's LP, took him only 15 days in the studio to complete. It became his first #1 country hit the week of November 30, 1974, plus #5 pop the weeks of November 9 and 16, 1974.

Denver was not accepted by all quarters of the country music world. While "Back Home Again" won the Country Music Association's award for Song of the Year in 1975 and the group also named Denver the country music entertainer of the year, Charlie Rich burned the card announcing his win at one awards show. Nevertheless, he stayed a frequent visitor on that chart into the 1980s, including two other trips to #1 in 1975 with "Thank God I'm a Country Boy" and "I'm Sorry" [see 274].

Denver never felt the need to categorize himself as a pop, middle-of-the-road, or country artist. As he told one interviewer, "People still call me a folk singer because I play an acoustic guitar, but I'm a contemporary singer/songwriter." The only generalization about his songs he would agree to was that they were optimistic. As he told *The New York Post* in 1973, "I want my music to take people away from songs like 'Sister Morphine.' I want people to feel the goodness in their own lives. It's funny, but I have the capacity to make people happy. . . .I really am an oddity."

Several critics agreed, although not to Denver's advantage. For example, Loraine Alterman of *The New York Times* condemned "Back Home Again" as being lightweight and banal and added, "What bothers me most about Denver's music is that it's so boring. . . .Even though [he] does possess a good voice, it's not expressive enough to make him sound anything more than pleasant."

Of course, for every critic who disdained Denver there were hundreds of thousands of other fans in America who clamored for every bit of his music. His concerts attracted people ranging in age from children to septugenerians who enjoyed not only his singing and guitar playing but also jokes and even juggling, a talent he had developed just in case he needed to fall back on something while his music career stagnated. Obviously, he did not have to throw too many balls up in the air to entertain people.

"Back Home Again" was the third consecutive #1 AC hit and top 20 pop entry for Denver. He extended his streak to four on both counts with his next release, "Sweet Surrender" [see 246]. Coincidentally, that single came from his first live recording, although it appeared first on his *Back Home Again* album.

235 My Melody of Love

BOBBY VINTON

ABC 12022

November 9, 1974 (1 week)

Writers: Henry Mayer, Bobby Vinton

Producer: Bob Morgan

"My Melody of Love" earned Bobby Vinton the nickname "The Polish Prince" due to its theme of ethnic pride and refrain of "Moja droga, ja cie kocham," which translated as "My dearest, I love you." In his autobiography, *The Polish Prince*, Vinton said he saw the song as a declaration of pride for any minority, a claim confirmed by the use of other foreign phrases as "Besame mucho" and "C'est si bon" in the lyrics, plus Vinton's statement that when he performed the tune, "The audience responds with a warmth of feeling I've never had for any other song or story."

Vinton adapted "My Melody of Love" from a German tune by Henry Mayer while doing some shows in Las Vegas. The tune had previously been translated into English by Brian Blackburn and recorded as "Don't Stay Away Too Long" by the British duo of [Lennie] Peters and [Dianne] Lee; that version went to #3 in the United Kingdom in 1974 but flopped in America. Seven companies rejected Vinton's demo until Jay Lasker of ABC Records accepted it, telling Vinton, "We'll sell two million copies of this." A stunned Vinton responded, "Two million! I'll take a million, I'll take 90th on the charts—I'll take anything."

While Lasker corralled his promotion staff to get behind the record, Vinton plugged the song in cities in the North and Midwest with large Polish populations such as Detroit and Cleveland. The record broke first in Buffalo and went on to peak at #3 pop for two weeks in November 1974, first behind "Whatever Gets You Through the Night" by John Lennon at #1 and "Do It ('Til You're Satisfied)" by B.T. Express at #2, then "I Can Help" by Billy Swan at #1 and "Do It" at #2 the second week.

The accolades accorded to "My Melody of Love" were numerous. "I ran out of wall space in my office for all the plaques and citations, all the keys to the city, all the statues and paintings that have come from admirers of 'My Melody of Love,'" wrote Vinton. Mayor Richard Daley of Chicago proclaimed January 18, 1975, as "Bobby Vinton Day" and joined him in singing "My Melody of Love" to an enthusiastic crowd. And Vinton's promotion of the song on many talk shows, including *The Merv Griffin Show*, where he debuted "My Melody of Love," led to him getting his own variety series, *The Bobby Vinton Show*. The series, which was sold individually to TV stations, ran from 1975–78.

On the music front, Vinton never equaled the performance of "My Melody of Love." The best he could do was the follow-up, "Beer Barrel Polka," which also had a Polish theme and which made #5 AC and #33 pop in 1975. His last AC entry was "Let Me Love You Goodbye" at #45 in 1981. He then had several records make the lower rungs of the country chart through 1989. In the 1990s he recorded occasionally as well as appeared in concert in Branson, Missouri, often.

236 Longfellow Serenade

NEIL DIAMOND

Columbia 10043

November 16, 1974 (1 week)

Writer: Neil Diamond

Producer: Tom Catalano

Though it marked the 22nd time Neil Diamond appeared on the chart, "Longfellow Serenade" was only his second #1 AC hit, the first being 1972's "Song Sung Blue" [see 171]. He arrived in the runner-up position four times. "Cracklin' Rose" peaked at #2 for one week in the fall of 1970 while making it to the top of the Hot 100 the week of October 10, 1970. Next was "I Am. . .I Said," which held at #2 for two weeks in 1971 while stopping at #4 pop. "Stones," in late 1973, just missed making #1 for three weeks in 1971 while going to #14 pop, and the following year "Walk on Water" had two weeks at #2 AC and one at #17 pop.

All of those hits were on the Uni label, which Diamond joined in 1968 when his original label, Bang Records, wavered on releasing "Shilo," claiming the song was not as upbeat as previous Diamond hits like "You Got to Me" and "I Thank the Lord for the Night Time," both top 20 pop hits in 1967. By the time Bang did issue "Shilo" in 1968, Diamond was on Uni, and by the following year he had become a staple on the AC chart.

Bang would not be denied, however, and during the early 1970s the label reissued singles or tracks from old Diamond albums to use as 45s while he was putting out new material on Uni. Diamond fared pretty well considering he was competing with himself, as Bang released "Shilo" (#8 AC and #24 pop in 1970) and "Solitary Man" (his first hit in 1966, which he surpassed in 1970 by going to #6 AC and #21 pop). Bang's 1966 B-side to "Solitary Man," "Do It," also made both charts in late 1970 (#25 AC and #36 pop), as did a song Diamond wrote which became a #1 pop hit for the Monkees in 1966, "I'm a Believer" (#31 AC and #51 pop in 1971).

In 1973 Diamond switched labels again, this time to Columbia, and after doing the soundtrack for the movie *Jonathan Livingston Seagull*, he released his first hit single for the label a year later. In the liner notes for his anthology *In My Lifetime*, Diamond described "Longfellow Serenade" with the statement, "Occasionally I like using a particular lyrical style which, in this case, lent itself naturally to telling the story of a guy who woos his woman with poetry." The title referred to poet Henry Wadsworth Longfellow.

"Longfellow Serenade" stalled at #5 on the Hot 100 the weeks of November 23 and 30, 1974. Surprisingly, he did not have another pop top 10 hit until he teamed with Barbra Streisand to sing "You Don't Bring Me Flowers" in 1978. The duet hit #1 for two weeks starting December 2, 1978, but somehow made only #3 AC. Diamond had better luck when three songs released between "Longfellow Serenade" and "You Don't Bring Me Flowers" did top the AC chart, the first being "I've Been This Way Before" [see 251].

237 Laughter in the Rain

NEIL SEDAKA

Rocket 40313

November 23, 1974 (2 weeks)

Writers: Phil Cody (words), Neil Sedaka (music)

Producers: Neil Sedaka, Robert Appere

When Neil Sedaka made his celebrated "comeback" to the American pop music world in the mid-1970s, he chose "Laughter in the Rain" to make his return. "I felt there was a magic about it," he said of the record. "It had my optimism. I like to look up and laugh under duress."

Sedaka and Phil Cody wrote "Laughter in the Rain" together, in upstate New York. Sedaka composed the bulk of the melody. "I wrote it backwards, with the chorus first— 'Ooh, I hear laughter in the rain,'" he recalled. He said the lyrics had no particular inspiration other than describing romantic images like "holding hands with the one I love." The musicians used on the session were James Taylor's backing band, including guitarist Danny Kortchmar. "The lyric was wonderful. The record was perfect," Sedaka said.

"Laughter in the Rain" came out first in England, where Sedaka retreated in the early 1970s after his recording career in America stalled, despite many pop successes as a solo artist

in the late 1950s and early 1960s (e.g., "Oh Carol" and "Calendar Girl"). It went to #15 in the summer of 1974. But the song really impressed Elton John, who signed him to his Rocket label, a subsidiary of MCA Records in America. "He agreed with me it would be the first single off *Sedaka's Back* [his 1974 LP in the United States]," Sedaka said.

Sedaka remained worried about his record's appeal, and his fears seemed to be confirmed when a competing version came out a couple of weeks before his record was due to be released. "I was riding in the car and I heard somebody sing 'Laughter in the Rain,'" Sedaka said. "It was Lea Roberts. She was magnificent." He told Elton John about Roberts' cover, and as a result John and his manager "killed it," in Sedaka's words, by promoting Sedaka's original heavily on interviews and other promotional activities. Roberts ended up going only to #69 R&B and #109 bubbling under before virtually vanishing from the charts.

After making #1 AC, Sedaka's "Laughter in the Rain" took more than two months before it topped the Hot 100 the week of February 1, 1975. "It was the thrill of a lifetime," he said of the song's success. "A dream come true. I had always wanted to come back. . . .A lot of people said I would never come back."

Sedaka celebrated his return with a concert at the Troubadour club in Los Angeles in early 1975. Among those seeing him were Elton John, Andy Williams, Neil Diamond, James Taylor, and a duo who would cover one of Sedaka's tunes with great success in 1975. Their names were the Captain and Tennille [see 263—"Love Will Keep Us Together"].

238 Angie Baby
HELEN REDDY

Capitol 3972

December 7, 1974 (1 week)

Writer: Alan O'Day

Producer: Joe Wissert

"I think it has every necessary element to be a hit song," said Helen Reddy about "Angie Baby." She claimed this was the one record she never had to push radio stations into playing. And though the Rolling Stones had had a #1 pop hit called "Angie" a year earlier, there was no possibility that listeners would confuse the two songs. Anyone familiar with the Reddy song knows that Mick Jagger would find her "Angie Baby" quite a bit harder to deal with than Angela Bowie, whom he sang about in "Angie."

"It's a very well-crafted song," Reddy said. "I always thought it was a very psychological song." Its obscure lyrics have left the tune open to interpretation, and Reddy has refused to comment on what the story line really is, partly because she has enjoyed hearing different people's views. She said the disparate interpretations have amused and puzzled her and usually gave her more insight into the person from whom she heard the explanation than into the song itself. When pressed for one of the descriptions of "Angie Baby" she has heard, Reddy said, "There was one guy who obviously had a lot of hostility to my gender, because he said, 'Then at the end, he kills her!'" she said with a laugh.

Although Reddy remained mum on the tune, writer Alan O'Day finally spilled the beans, talking to Barry Scott for *We Had Joy, We Had Fun*. "Angie had great power," O'Day said. "It turned out she wasn't crazy, she was just very, very smart and used the magic powers at her command to physically shrink this guy and put him into the radio. He was her pawn. It's kind of the ultimate women's lib song. It's the only song that actually goes further into women's lib than 'I Am Woman.'"

O'Day had actually written "Angie Baby" for Cher. When either Cher or someone on her staff rejected the submission, Jeff Wald picked it up for his wife and client Helen Reddy. She used Joe Wissert rather than Tom Catalano to produce the song, but preferred not to say why the change was made, only commenting that "I used a wide variety of producers over my career."

"Angie Baby" became Reddy's third #1 pop hit, peaking atop the Hot 100 the week of December 28, 1974, and her fifth consecutive #1 AC hit, an unprecedented streak at the time. The string began with "Delta Dawn" [see 198]. Before that single, Reddy had five songs make the AC chart. They were "I Don't Know How to Love Him" (#12) and "Crazy Love" (#8) in 1971, "No Sad Song" (#32) and "I Am Woman" (#2 for two weeks) in 1972, and "Peaceful" (#2 for two weeks) in 1973. Her follow-up to "Angie Baby" would also hit #1 AC [see 253—"Emotion"].

239 When Will I See You Again
THE THREE DEGREES

Philadelphia International 3550

December 14, 1974 (1 week)

Writers: Kenny Gamble, Leon Huff

Producers: Kenny Gamble, Leon Huff

Cooing "oooo, ahhh" before the main lyrics, the Three Degrees took "When Will I See You Again" to the AC chart apex as well as #2 pop, where it stopped behind "Kung Fu Fighting" in December 1974, and #4 R&B. It was their biggest hit after doing vocals on "TSOP (The Sound of Philadelphia)" [see 217]. But they never matched the impact of either hit before or afterward, a result the group blames on the paradox of their popularity in other countries, like England and Japan, being so great that they never had time to exploit their potential in the United States when the tunes were peaking.

The Three Degrees were, as their name suggests, a trio. The original members of the all-female group were Fayette Pinkney, Shirley Porter, and Linda Turner. They first hit the pop chart in 1965 at #80 with "Gee Baby (I'm Sorry)," but by 1967 Porter and Turner had left the group and been replaced by Sheila Ferguson and Valerie Holiday. They got back on the charts in 1970 when their remake of a 1958 #15 pop hit for the Chantels, "Maybe," went to #29 pop and #4 R&B.

In 1973 the Three Degrees joined the Philadelphia International label. They also began touring more outside America, and during the summer of 1973 they performed "When Will I See You Again" at the Tokyo Music Festival. The song became a big hit in Japan, and was subsequently released in other countries. But the timing of its U.S. release proved to be problematic because the Three Degrees were so busy working concert dates overseas. As Holiday told Marc Taylor for *A Touch of Classic Soul: Soul Singers of the Early 1970s*, "The demand for us became so big that we were constantly working. Before we would finish one tour, another one had already been booked. We were constantly out of the States so we couldn't fully capitalize on the song being a hit here."

The group's lack of visibility in America while their hit was rising to the top was probably the reason none of their singles cracked the Hot 100 again. They did make the R&B chart occasionally through 1979, with two entries there also making the AC chart, 1975's "Take Good Care of Yourself" (#24 AC) and 1979's "Woman in Love" (#50 AC).

In the 1980s and 1990s the Three Degrees toured the world constantly, with "When Will I See You Again" naturally a highlight at each performance. Only Holiday remained in the lineup, as Pinkney and Ferguson had left to start families. Helen Scott had replaced Pinkney in 1976. After Ferguson departed in 1984, several replacements came and went; in 1989 Cynthia Garrison assumed the post.

240 Wishing You Were Here
CHICAGO

Columbia 10049

December 21, 1974 (1 week)

Writer: Peter Cetera

Producer: James William Guercio

While recording at his studio at his Caribou Ranch in Colorado, producer James William Guercio managed to get some special guests to do background vocals for Chicago's song "Wishing You Were Here." "I think Jimmy Guercio was wooing the Beach Boys at the time," trumpeter Lee Loughnane recalled. "Peter [Cetera, Chicago's lead singer] had idolized the Beach Boys for years." His idols became backup to Cetera's tenor as he sang his composition "Wishing You Were Here."

"Wishing You Were Here" broke Chicago's streak of four consecutive top 10 hits on the pop chart, but only barely—it peaked at #11 on the Hot 100 in late 1974. However, it did become Chicago's third #1 AC hit after "Beginnings" [see 155] and "Call on Me" [see 227]. The song's success prompted Chicago and the Beach Boys to team up for some tour dates the following year, and, amazingly, in 1989 and 1996.

Of course, Chicago went out plenty of times on its own, touring every summer of every year from 1967 to 1998. Nowadays, the schedule is not as grueling as the 200 or so dates the group averaged in the 1970s, but as Loughnane said when describing their current tours, "It's more fun now, because it really isn't supposed to be happening for a group for this long. I've never had to get a job anywhere else."

The 45 released after "Wishing You Were Here" didn't fare quite as well as its predecessor. "Harry Truman" managed to go to only #23 AC and #13 pop in 1975. A bigger hit was "Old Days," which rocketed to #3 AC and #5 pop in the summer of 1975. But its follow-up, "Brand New Love Affair (Part I and II)," was a lackluster performer, hitting only #27 AC and #61 pop in the fall of 1975. An improvement on that was *its* follow-up, 1976's "Another Rainy Day in New York City," which made #2 AC for a week and #32 pop.

Like "Call on Me," "Wishing You Were Here" came from the *Chicago VII* LP, which hit #1 on the album chart the week of April 27, 1974. The two albums preceding it, *Chicago V* and *Chicago VI*, also topped that chart, the former for nine weeks beginning August 19, 1972 and the latter for five weeks starting July 28, 1973. About the only chart honor the members of Chicago had yet to take was a #1 pop single. They would get that in 1976 with their fourth chart-topper; see 314—"If You Leave Me Now."

241 Mandy

BARRY MANILOW

Bell 45613

December 28, 1974 (2 weeks)

Writers: Scott English, Richard Kerr

Producers: Barry Manilow, Ron Dante

The song which launched Barry Manilow's career was one he had not written, even though he was a composer; had been forced into recording by his record label's president; and had been a flop for its co-writer a few years earlier in America. It had even had its title changed and its origins misrepresented. Although the genesis of "Mandy" may be more dramatic than the ballad itself, to Barry Manilow fans, all that matters is that it put him into the big time.

"Mandy" began as "Brandy" when Scott English and Richard Kerr created it on an out-of-tune piano one rainy Tuesday in London in 1971. English recorded it by himself, and it went to #12 in the United Kingdom that year. But in America it went only to #91 on the Hot 100, for two weeks in March 1972, and the single and English were forgotten quickly stateside.

But two important facts should be noted. One, "Brandy" was not English's only U.S. pop entry, as he made the Hot 100 in 1964 at #77 with "High on a Hill." And, despite some reports to the contrary, "Brandy" was not about a dog. English explained in the liner notes to Manilow's *The Complete Collection and Then Some. . .* that a reporter called him at 7 a.m. asking who Brandy was. "I would have said anything to get rid of him, so I spat out the first thing that come to mind. 'It was about a dog like Lassie and I had her sent away. Now you go away!' I said and hung up on him. I guess I'll have to live with that story."

In 1974 Clive Davis became president of Bell Records and dismissed most of the roster except for Manilow. Davis liked the artist's first albeit unsuccessful album and stage show and felt he needed a hit single. He sent him "Brandy." Manilow eventually was hooked by the song, even though he did not consider himself an interpreter and so didn't like using other writers' tunes. To learn the song, he played it slowly, but at the recording session he did it more like English's up-tempo version. Davis hated it.

Manilow recalled what happened next in *The Complete Collection and Then Some. . .* "So I played 'Brandy' as a ballad and Clive closed his eyes and smiled and murmured, 'That's better. That's it.'. . .And we recorded the ballad version of 'Mandy' right then and there and my life was never the same."

"Brandy" became "Mandy" to avoid confusion with "Brandy (You're a Fine Girl)," a #1 pop and #7 AC hit in 1972 for the Looking Glass. On his first take Manilow mistakenly said "Brandy," but two takes later came the one which was the hit. "Mandy" topped the Hot 100 the week of January 18, 1975, after doing so on the AC chart, and later won a Grammy nomination for Record of the Year. Manilow's life really never *was* the same after "Mandy."

242 Only You
RINGO STARR

Apple 1876

January 11, 1975 (1 week)

Writers: Buck Ram, Ande Rand

Producer: Richard Perry

1975

After the Beatles dissolved, the solo career of Ringo Starr, born Richard Starkey in Liverpool, England on July 7, 1940, was spectacular in the early to mid-1970s. He garnered two #1 pop hits, "Photograph" in 1973, which hit #3 AC, and "You're Sixteen" in 1974, which made #2 AC. Two other songs also made the AC chart (1971's "It Don't Come Easy" at #24 AC and #4 pop, and 1974's "Oh My My" at #24 AC and #5 pop) before he finally topped the listing with "Only You."

"Only You" had made the AC chart once previously, in a version by Norro Wilson; it reached #24 there as well as #68 country. But starting in 1955, it was an evergreen on the pop chart, first hitting for the Platters (whose manager, Buck Ram, had co-written the tune) at #5 as well as #1 R&B for seven weeks, then for the Hilltoppers, whose cover went to #8 pop. In 1959 Franck Pourcel's French Fiddles offered an instrumental version which reached #9 pop, and another instrumental cover by Mr. Acker Bilk [see 13—"Stranger on the Shore"] made #77 in 1963. Six years later Bobby Hatfield, one of the Righteous Brothers, sang it again and it went to #95 pop.

The next major revival of the song grew out of fellow ex-Beatle John Lennon's involvement in Starr's 1974 LP *Goodnight Vienna*. "He [Lennon] had written the title song well in advance of the sessions and had done a demo of it, so we had this wonderful piece of material with which to kick the album off, and in addition to that, he came up with the idea of redoing the oldie 'Only You,' which was the first single from that album and a top five record in this country," producer Richard Perry reported in John Tobler and Stuart Grundy's *The Record Producers*. (Actually, the song hit #6 pop.) "He not only played guitar on that session, and piano on the title track, but he also helped Ringo through all the vocals, just standing there and helping to infuse him with the spirit and singing backgrounds with him."

The follow-up to "Only You," "No No Song," hit #3 pop but was the last solo hit for Starr. No singles released after the *Goodnight Vienna* LP cracked the pop top 25, and he had only one other AC entry, 1976's "A Dose of Rock and Roll," which went to #44 AC and #26 pop. He recorded sporadically after the late 1970s, with albums released in 1981, 1983, 1991, and 1998. Since 1994, Starr has spent much of his time touring with his All-Starr Band composed of former members of other rock groups, with all doing each other's hits.

As for the future of "Only You," it bubbled under to #122 in 1964 when done by Wayne Newton and hit the country charts in 1978 for Freddie Hart (#34), in 1982 for Reba McEntire (#13), and in 1986 for the Statler Brothers (#36).

243 Please Mr. Postman

THE CARPENTERS

A&M 1646

January 18, 1975 (1 week)

Writers: Brian Holland, Robert Bateman, William Garrett, Georgia Dobbins

Producers: Richard Carpenter, Karen Carpenter

The first song on a Motown label to reach #1 on the Hot 100 was "Please Mr. Postman" by the Marvelettes, originally a quintet. It topped the pop chart the week of December 11, 1961, in addition to staying seven weeks atop the R&B chart starting November 13, 1961. Group member Georgia Dobbins got the early version of the tune from William Garrett before making her contributions along with two other writers. Gladys Horton sang lead on the track.

Nearly 13 years later, the Carpenters revived "Please Mr. Postman." As Richard explained in the liner notes to the Carpenters' anthology *From the Top*, "Karen and I had always liked it and I had considered recording it for some time. Listening to the basic 'track' of this song can be a fairly boring experience, as it is only four chords repeating themselves. Our engineer, Ray Gerhardt, upon first hearing the 'track,' hated it and thought we had taken leave of our senses. Of course as more was added to it, the recording took shape and Ray ultimately just disliked it. We loved it and thought it could be a hit. Released in the fall of 1974, 'Postman' was a smash worldwide. A simple but magical song."

"Please Mr. Postman" became the only Carpenters single after "(They Long to Be) Close to You" to make #1 pop as well as AC. It topped the Hot 100 on January 25, 1975, a week after leading the AC roster, and was their third single to be #1 pop along with "Close to You" and "Top of the World." The 45 became the 10th Carpenters tune to top the AC chart, making them the first act ever to reach that number. The single was also the first remake of a Motown tune to go to #1 AC.

Two other revivals of "Please Mr. Postman" hit the charts in later years. In 1981 the Originals sang it in a medley with "Waitin' on a Letter" and got to #74 R&B. Two years later an outfit called Gentle Persuasion reached #82 pop with its rendition.

In 1982 the Carpenters remade one more song popularized by the Marvelettes. "Beachwood 4-5789" made #17 pop in 1962 in its original version. As done by the Carpenters, it reached #16 AC and #74 pop.

But before "Beachwood 4-5789" came out, the Carpenters released several other singles which led the AC chart. The follow-up to "Please Mr. Postman" was the first of these to do so [see 258—"Only Yesterday"].

244 Morning Side of the Mountain

DONNY AND MARIE OSMOND

MGM 14765

January 25, 1975 (1 week)

Writers: Dick Manning, Larry Stook

Producer: Mike Curb

"Morning Side of the Mountain" was Donny and Marie Osmonds' follow-up to their first #1 AC hit, "I'm Leaving It (All) Up to You" [see 228], and like that record it was a new version of an old tune. Tommy Edwards made the pop chart with two renditions of the song, first in 1951, when it peaked at #24, and then in 1959, when it stopped at #27. Donny and Marie surpassed both his tries when "Morning Side of the Mountain" peaked at #8 pop in 1974. Also like their previous single, it was producer Mike Curb who had thought of redoing an older song with Donny and Marie. "He was the one coming up with all those songs," Donny said. "I was so young at the time, I didn't know I had veto power to not do them."

Donny and Marie continued to make the pop and AC charts through 1978's "On the Shelf" (#25 AC, #38 pop), although none of the singles equaled the first two's success. The duo fared better on television hosting their own variety show, which came about after ABC-TV's new president Fred Silverman saw them co-host *The Mike Douglas Show* for a week in 1975 and let them do their own series a year later.

After the cancellation of *Donny and Marie* in the spring of 1979, the brother and sister act split up for almost 20 years. Donny pursued a stage career during the 1980s, then returned to the charts in 1989 after a 13-year absence with "Soldier of Love," which hit #20 AC and #2 pop. But the revival petered out within two years, and he went back to the stage and personal appearances. Marie's career in the 1980s and early 1990s is detailed in the entry on her solo #1 AC hit "Paper Roses" [see 204].

But as the old saying goes, what goes around comes around. In 1997 Donny and Marie announced they would do a daily variety TV show sold to individual stations for launching in the fall of 1998. "It's been kicked around since we did the original show," Donny said, adding that originally he was going to host his own talk show until others suggested he have Marie serve as co-host. Also in 1997, Donny announced that a compilation video of highlights of the old *Donny and Marie* series were available for purchase via the QVC cable shopping channel.

Donny said he is looking forward to working professionally with his sister again, but do not expect many reprises of their old hits. "I don't think we're going to dwell on it," he said.

245 Best of My Love

THE EAGLES

Asylum 45218

February 1, 1975 (1 week)

Writers: Glenn Frey, Don Henley, J.D. Souther

Producer: Glyn Johns

"Best of My Love" topped the AC chart for a week before making #1 on the Hot 100. The group logged four other pop chart-toppers through 1979 ("One of These Nights," "New Kid in Town" (also #2 AC for three weeks in 1977), "Hotel California," and "Heartache Tonight"), but could only hit #1 on the AC chart once more—with a reunion record in 1995 [see 648—"Love Will Keep Us Alive"]. Strangely, despite its representative Eagles sound of country-influenced rock and pop music, "Best of My Love" failed to crack the country chart.

Glenn Frey (born in Detroit, Michigan, on November 6, 1948) and drummer Don Henley (born in Gilmer, Texas, on July 22, 1947) formed the Eagles in 1971 after serving as backup musicians for Linda Ronstadt on tour. They added Bernier Leadon as lead guitarist and Randy Meisner as bassist. Although Frey and Henley acted as principal song-writers for the group, a composition by Frey and Jackson Browne, "Take It Easy," gave the Eagles their first AC and pop entry, peaking at #12 on both in 1972.

Another writing pal of Frey's was J.D. Souther, who might have joined the Eagles were it not for his desire to be a solo performer. When Frey and Henley began writing songs for the 1974 album *On the Border*, "Best of My Love" took shape, but they had difficulty completing it, as Souther told Stephen Bishop in *Songs in the Rough*. "I knew he [Frey] had the little guitar riff that's in the beginning, this little C-tuning thing he has. And we were talking on the phone and he said, 'We got this thing and it needs a bridge.'" Souther gave them one, and the result, with Henley on lead vocal, was the group's first #1 hit.

By the time "Best of My Love" was released in late 1974, guitarist Don Felder had become the fifth Eagle. Leadon left at the end of 1975, and Joe Walsh replaced him. Then Meisner departed in 1979, with Timothy B. Shmit taking his place. In 1982 the band split up. Members pursued successful solo careers, with Henley returning to #1 AC with a duet with Patty Smyth in 1992 [see 622—"Sometimes Love Just Ain't Enough"].

"Best of My Love" resurfaced in 1993 on a tribute album by country musicians titled *Common Thread: The Songs of the Eagles*. The following year, despite over a decade of saying they would not do so, Frey, Henley, Felder, Walsh, and Shmit reunited for the Hell Freezes Over tour, for which they recorded new material plus sang old hits, including "Best of My Love." They also had another #1 AC hit in 1995. See 648—"Love Will Keep Us Alive."

246 Sweet Surrender

JOHN DENVER

RCA 10148

February 8, 1975 (1 week)

Writer: John Denver

Producer: Milt Okun

"Sweet Surrender" was the second #1 AC title to be used on two different chart-topping hits (the first was "I'll Never Fall in Love Again"), having previously been used by Bread [see 182]. Originally done on his *Back Home Again* LP in 1974, Denver's "Sweet Surrender" was deemed the tune to have the most potential as a lead single from the 1974 live double album *An Evening With John Denver*, recorded during his summer concerts at the Universal City Amphitheater in Los Angeles, California.

"Sweet Surrender" topped the AC charts as it went to #7 country and #13 pop. It was another success for the former Henry John Deutschendorf Jr., who was born in Roswell, New Mexico, on New Year's Eve 1943. (He told Olga Curtis of *The Denver Post* that his stage surname became Denver when a record producer decided "Deutschendorf wouldn't fit on a record label.") Denver's father was a lieutenant colonel in the Air Force and the family moved frequently. "I had kind of a lonely childhood," he admitted to Starkey Flythe Jr. in *The Saturday Evening Post*. "We never stayed any place long enough to make friends."

Things changed for the lonely child in the seventh grade, when his grandmother gave him a guitar. He became proficient on the instrument and played in local bands when he was a teenager. He went to Texas Tech University in Lubbock, Texas, with the intention of studying architecture, but in the middle of his junior year, against the advice of his parents and friends, he dropped out and went to Los Angeles to pursue fame and fortune as a musician. In the early 1960s he did a couple of singles as a soloist for Capitol Records, but none of them were released.

A hint of success came Denver's way in 1965 when he won the job of new lead singer for the Chad Mitchell Trio after Mitchell decided to leave the group. But folk music was on its way out, and after the trio disbanded in early 1969, Denver became a solo singer again. Luckily for him, in late 1969 his composition "Leaving on a Jet Plane" became a hit for Peter, Paul and Mary [see 126], and the association with that single brought him more bookings and opportunities in the 1970s.

Denver followed "Sweet Surrender" with another cut on *An Evening With John Denver* which had appeared first on *Back Home Again*. "Thank God I'm a Country Boy" was a raucous raveup that went to #1 pop and country but proved a mite too untamed for the taste of some AC programmers and listeners, as it got to only #5 there. No worry, though; Denver managed to top all three charts with his next single, "I'm Sorry" [see 274].

247 Lonely People

AMERICA

Warner 8048

February 15, 1975 (1 week)

Writers: Catherine Peek, Dan Peek

Producer: George Martin

All three members of America sang. No problem. They all played guitar too. Not a problem either, given their fondness for acoustic music. But all three also wrote and wanted their own material included in each album. Was that a difficulty? Not at all, remembered America member Dewey Bunnell: "It's funny, we all worked on our own songs, independently of each other, and then brought them to the project." From there, all members would agree on what tunes to do, and each album contained a roughly equal mix of tunes from each of them. "We all had the same feeling of what was good and balanced the albums. We didn't want resentment."

Bunnell felt that Dan Peek favored songs with a country and rock feeling, while Gerry Buckley specialized in ballads. He believe their approach worked well commercially as well as personally because "Each one of us wrote songs that were hits."

In Peek's case, the biggest hit song was "Lonely People," the first single after "Tin Man" [see 231]. He actually was listed as co-writer of the composition with his wife, Catherine.

"Cathy wrote the lyrics, I think, but I don't know what inspired it," Bunnell said. "It had a little bit of 'Eleanor Rigby' to it." Whatever led to its creation, the end result was success, although the song's pop chart performance (#5 on the Hot 100 the week of March 8, 1975) didn't match its #1 AC status.

Following "Lonely People" came the release of America's fifth LP, 1975's Hearts, and its lead single "Sister Golden Hair," which went to #1 pop but only #5 AC. Two other singles came after that 45 finished its run. "Daisy Jane" did a respectable showing of #4 AC and #20 pop, while "Woman Tonight," which came out at the end of 1975, was not a Christmas season hot seller or radio favorite and went only to #41 AC and #44 pop.

History, America's 1975 greatest hits album, did better. In addition to the group's current successes at the time, the LP included "Lonely People," "Sister Golden Hair," and "Daisy Jane." It was the last of five top 10 albums for the group, peaking at #3.

In 1976 America returned to #1 AC with "Today's the Day." It would be the last hit for the group, as well as one of the last singles to feature all the original members. For more details, see 303.

248 Nightingale

CAROLE KING

Ode 66106

February 22, 1975 (1 week)

Writers: Carole King, David Palmer

Producer: Lou Adler

The album Wrap Around Joy turned out to be a family affair of sorts for Carole King. For one thing, she gave birth to her first son, Levi, on April 23, 1974, shortly after the album was recorded. But another element was the inclusion of her daughters on one song that was to become King's third #1 AC hit.

In the liner notes to Carole King: A Natural Woman, producer Lou Adler said, "Louise and Sherry sang background on 'Nightingale.' They were about 14 and 12 then, and Carole wanted very much to involve her daughters. She was in the studio, taught them all the parts, and sang it with them." Louise Goffin, King's daughter by Gerry Goffin, became a solo artist in 1979 and garnered her own AC entry in 1988 with a single, "Bridge of Sighs," which went to #41.

As for "Nightingale," it was King's last single to crack the pop top 10, peaking at #9 the week of March 1, 1975. It was the second single from Wrap Around Joy, which hit #1 on the album chart for the week of November 9, 1974 and was described by Adler as "a good, solid album." David Palmer collaborated with King in writing all the songs for the LP.

The first single from Wrap Around Joy was "Jazzman," which hit #4 AC and #2 pop in late 1974 and earned King a Grammy nomination for Best Female Pop Vocal Performance. She received another Grammy nomination that same year for Best Recording for Children, for her work on Really Rosie, a soundtrack to a CBS-TV animated special which hit #20 on the album chart in 1975 and was the follow-up to Wrap Around Joy.

But in spite of the chart successes and the honors, all was not well for King personally. In 1975, she and her second husband, Charles Larkey, were divorced. King moved to a ranch in Idaho, hoping her life would settle down, but the relocation did not solve several problems she faced at the time. As Adler later recalled, "She was going through some real turbulence in her life, and there was some turbulence between us, too. . . .It was just a very unsettled time for her, for me, and for us together."

Yet King kept writing, and she presented Adler with 12 new tunes to record in the fall of 1976. One of these, "Only Love Is Real," became King's second consecutive #1 AC hit and fourth #1 AC smash overall [see 292]. Unfortunately, it also marked the beginning of the end of the streak of hits for King.

249 Poetry Man

PHOEBE SNOW

Shelter 40353

March 1, 1975 (1 week)

Writer: Phoebe Snow

Producer: Dino Airali

When she was four years old, Phoebe Laub, born in New York City on July 17, 1952 and raised in New Jersey, saw some boxcars in the trainyards near her home. One of them had the name "Phoebe Snow" on it "in letters five or six feet high," she recalled. "And I said, 'I'll use that.'" Thus, she became Phoebe Snow, despite some ribbing from other children.

As a grownup, Snow performed nightly in Greenwich Village in the early 1970s until "One guy came in one night and offered me a contract," she said. She considered she was discovered rather quickly, yet she recorded her self-titled debut LP in 1974 which contained her first and biggest single, "Poetry Man."

Snow reluctantly admitted who inspired her to write "Poetry Man." "I was very, very smitten with a married man who was older than me," she said. She emphasized that the crush happened when she was young and she never pursued a married man afterward. However, she also remembered that when her mother heard the song, the first words out of her mouth were, "OK, who are you sleeping with?" Snow said the song's production was more jazz-oriented than she preferred. "Honestly, it wouldn't have been my first choice," she said, adding that at the time she viewed herself as an acoustic guitarist who happened to sing.

"Poetry Man" peaked at #5 on the Hot 100 the week of April 12, 1975, as well as #1 AC. Its success helped Snow get a Grammy nomination for Best New Artist. She recalled the Grammys as "Totally mind-blowing..., a huge head trip" and said she really lost her composure when she saw Aretha Franklin performing live at the ceremony.

Following "Poetry Man," Snow had little success on the pop chart except with "Gone at Last," a duet with Paul Simon in 1975 (#23 pop, #9 AC). She did better on the AC chart, including two entries in 1989, "If I Can Just Get Through the Night" (#13) and "Something Real" (#29).

Snow has also done well on the album chart, but denied that she considers albums her natural format. "I think to try to pre-conceive whether something is a single or an album cut—I am so tired of people prognosticating that. . . .I think it's silly to second-guess what will work," she said.

Regular TV viewers have probably heard Snow's voice many times—on voiceover singing in commercials. "I think my very first one was in 1979 for AT&T," she said. Snow said she does just two or three jingles each year because with her distinctive alto voice, "They can't bury me in the mix."

In 1998 Snow released an album called *I Can't Complain*, a statement which she said summed up her feelings about her career. "It's a little bit folky, but some rock and blues. It sounds like a contemporary alternative record," she said. Those hoping to hear more of her in the "Poetry Man" mode will probably be disappointed. "I never intended to be a jazz artist," she said. "That takes a heavy amount of background."

250 Have You Never Been Mellow

OLIVIA NEWTON-JOHN

MCA 40349

March 8, 1975 (1 week)

Writer: John Farrar

Producer: John Farrar

John Farrar said "Have You Never Been Mellow" was the result of "Just desperately trying to come up with a song I hoped Olivia liked." He got an idea for a song from her musicians on the road. "I remember being on a tour with her in America; all the guys in the band were using 'mellow' as their favorite word," he said.

From that memory grew "Have You Never Been Mellow," a plea from a woman to her lover to slow down and enjoy their romance which became the second #1 AC hit for Newton-John to top the pop chart too after "I Honestly Love You" [see 230]. "Have You Never Been Mellow" topped both charts the week of March 8, 1975, plus went to #3 country, and earned Newton-John a Grammy nomination for Best Female Pop Vocal Performance.

Two consecutive #1 hits were something Newton-John might have dreamed about growing up in Australia, although she was born in Cambridge, England, on September 26, 1948. She grew up in an academic family: her grandfather Max Born was a Nobel Prize–winning physicist and her father Bryn was a professor of German. In 1953, when "Livvy" was 5, Bryn accepted a job offer to be dean of Ormond College in Melbourne, Australia. She showed an early interest in music, playing songs on the piano when she was quite young. When Newton-John was 11, her parents were divorced; she moved with her music-loving mother to an apartment, and her musical pursuits became even more important to her. By age 14 Newton-John was part of an all-female singing jazz quartet called the Sol Four. Two years later she did a TV variety series, *The Go Show*, where she met John Farrar, a guitarist in the show's backup band, the Strangers, and another female singer, Pat Carroll, later to be Mrs. John Farrar.

In 1954, at age 17, with her mother's encouragement, Newton-John moved to London and cut her first single there a year later. It bombed. After that she played dreary clubs—and longed for Australia—until Carroll came over too. Carroll and Newton-John became roommates for a time and also appeared as a duo, but when Carroll went back to Australia, Newton-John was forced to fend for herself. In 1971 she finally took off as a singer, with "If Not for You" [see 154].

The success of "I Honestly Love You" and "Have You Never Been Mellow" made Newton-John the most popular female singer in America in the mid-1970s. She got her third consecutive #1 AC hit later in 1975 with "Please Mr. Please" [see 267].

251 I've Been This Way Before

NEIL DIAMOND

Columbia 10084

March 15, 1975 (1 week)

Writer: Neil Diamond

Producer: Tom Catalano

"I've Been This Way Before," which made #34 pop as well as #1 AC, came out as a single to follow up the success Neil Diamond had with "Longfellow Serenade" [see 236]. As Diamond related in the liner notes to his anthology *In My Lifetime*, the tune had actually been done as part of Diamond's first movie work, writing songs for the soundtrack of *Jonathan Livingston Seagull*, the film adaptation of Richard Bach's best-selling novel of the same name. "I didn't finish in time," he said. "That's one of my disappointments about the project. It should have been in the movie. . . ."

The liner notes also quote Diamond as saying that he had a difficult time doing the score. At first, he said, ""I didn't have the vaguest idea of how to write songs from a seagull's point of view. So I turned it down. Then I thought a little more and decided to try it. I figured nobody else had much more insight into writing for a seagull, so why not?

"I threw myself into that project as completely as I ever had before. It was a spiritual story and I had to understand the spiritual nature of its lead character before I could write a note. After about six months of studying various spiritual approaches to life, I was able to make my first breakthrough, which became the first song written—'Be.' When it finally came to me, I remember feeling very elated. After that, the rest of the songs came relatively easily."

"Be" was the first single from the soundtrack, and it went to #11 AC and #34 pop toward the end of 1973. Another movie tune, "Skybird," went to #24 AC and #75 pop in the spring of 1974. The mediocre chart performances of both were indicative of the response Diamond received for his score. While the soundtrack hit #2 on the album chart and won Diamond a Grammy for Best Original Score Written for a Motion Picture or Television Special, he failed to get even an Academy Award nomination for the score or songs. And many film critics voiced disapproval with Diamond's work, such as the comment in *Leonard Maltin's Movie and Video Guide* that it was "overbearing."

Although Diamond was to score five other #1 AC entries over the next seven years, only one of them was, like "I've Been This Way Before," written for a movie. That was "America," from the soundtrack for the 1980 remake of *The Jazz Singer*, a film in which Diamond acted as well [see 405]. But that's getting ahead of the story. The next chart-topper was "If You Know What I Mean" [see 305].

252 (Hey Won't You Play) Another Somebody Done Somebody Wrong Song

B.J. THOMAS

ABC 12054

March 22, 1975 (1 week)

Writers: Chips Moman, Larry Butler

Producer: Chips Moman

The longest title of a #1 AC song, "(Hey Won't You Play) Another Somebody Done Somebody Wrong Song" came from the writing duo of B.J. Thomas' occasional producer Chips Moman and Chet Butler. "We cut an album and needed one more song," Thomas said. A musician at the session remembered Moman and Butler's song and suggested it, but Moman was reluctant to cut it. "He was embarrassed. He didn't think it was finished," Thomas recalled. When Thomas heard the song, he fell for it immediately. "It was one of those very few songs that sounded like a hit," he said. And despite being in what he called the "tail end" of his drug addiction, Thomas did the vocals for the record along with the 12 album tracks in one day.

"(Hey Won't You Play) Another Somebody Done Somebody Wrong Song" gave Thomas his fourth #1 AC hit and brought him back to #1 pop when it peaked atop the Hot 100 the week of April 26, 1975. It also became his first country chart entry, topping that chart as well the week of May 17, 1975. "It was just a great song," Thomas said. Voters at the Grammys concurred, naming the tune as Best Country Song. Surprisingly, Thomas was not even nominated for his singing on the record.

After 1975, Thomas' musical career took new directions. He began performing gospel as well as secular music, though his refusal to stop doing the latter made some hardline Christians question his devotion to religion. His pop music success shrank quickly, with only his 1977 remake of the Beach Boys' "Don't Worry Baby" breaking the top 40 on the Hot 100 (it went to #17 pop and #2 AC for two weeks). After 1978 only one more record made the pop chart—1983's "Whatever Happened to Old Fashioned Love," which made #93 pop and #13 AC.

"Whatever Happened to Old Fashioned Love" also became his second #1 country hit, and Thomas scored several entries on that chart from 1975–86, including another #1 country hit in 1983, "New Looks From an Old Lover." During this period, other singles he released made only the AC chart, from 1979's "God Bless the Children" (#38) to 1982's "But Love Me" (#27). By the late 1980s Thomas had pretty much vanished from the charts, although the theme to the ABC-TV sitcom *Growing Pains* he sang with Dusty Springfield, "As Long As We Got Each Other," made #7 AC in 1989. The record was credited to artist "Steve Dorff and Friends" (Dorff produced the 45).

In the late 1990s Thomas continued to tour and record popular and contemporary Christian music. "I kind of do it all in the same deal," he said. "I really like a song if it has a spiritual element. I believe we're all eternal spirits, so I'll do the best that I can while I'm here."

253 Emotion
HELEN REDDY

Capitol 4021

March 29, 1975 (1 week)

Writers: Patti Dahlstrom (words–English),
Veronique Marie Sanson (music)

Producer: Joe Wissert

Follow an eerie song like "Angie Baby" with a French tune? Unthinkable to most artists, yet Helen Reddy did it in 1975 with "Emotion." And she offered no apologies for doing so. "I like a wide variety of music," she said. "My taste is very eclectic." She noted that she had no albums with themes on them, and most of them used several different composers. This technique upset some music critics who did not like her versatile selections, she believed.

But Reddy and her producers had confidence in the mix-and-match approach because it worked for her. When it came to doing her albums, she said, "We would collect songs. There would be a big cardboard box of demos, and we would pick out what we'd like." One tune making the cut was "Emotion," which was first done with the lyrics in French.

"It was originally a French tune called 'Amoreuse,'" Reddy said. "And there were two sets of lyrics in English." Reddy believed there was a singer in the United Kingdom who recorded the other English words to the melody but did not recall who that was or who wrote those lyrics.

Unlike some of her other hits, Reddy has a certain fondness for "Emotion." "I would love to do it in the original French," she said. "That would be fun." But in terms of the pop chart, "Emotion" was somewhat of a disappointment, peaking at #22 in the spring of 1975. It was the first Helen Reddy single not to make the top 20 on the Hot 100 since "No Sad Song" hit #62 in early 1972.

Reddy wasted no tears over this development. In fact, she did not have much time to do anything except work during this period, as she was in demand for tours, TV shows (she hosted *The Midnight Special* late Friday night NBC series from 1975–76 and frequently showed up on it through its run from 1973–81), and even movies. (She played a nun in *Airport 1975*.)

She conceded that it had probably been difficult to do all those tasks plus record and promote her tunes without cracking under the pressure. "It's all a blur," she said. "I remember being a guest on Johnny Carson [host of *The Tonight Show*], and he asked me, 'What's the one thing you don't have that you want?' and I stunned him by saying, 'Eight hours of sleep.'"

The next single after "Emotion" was "Bluebird," a tune written by Leon Russell. The 45 ended her six consecutive #1 AC singles record, flying only to #5 AC and #35 pop in the summer of 1975. She rebounded to #1 AC with her following release, "Ain't No Way to Treat a Lady" [see 275].

254 My Boy
ELVIS PRESLEY

RCA PB-10191

April 5, 1975 (1 week)

Writers: Phillip Coulter and Bill Martin (words–English),
Jean Bourtayre and Claude Francois (music)

Producer: Not Listed

In 1971 actor Richard Harris sang "My Boy" as one of the entrants at the third Radio Luxembourg Grand Prix music contest. Much to the anger of the audience in Luxembourg, who liked the tune, the song failed to finish among the top three selected at the event. In the wake of the controversy, Harris cut a version of the song and reached #13 AC and #41 pop. Three years later Elvis Presley recorded a cover of "My Boy," and four years later the song was released.

Presley's bandleader James Burton felt the singer did the tune because of its lyrics. "He loved the story. That really struck him," Burton said. Presley did not have a son, but he did have a daughter, Lisa Marie, the child of Elvis and Priscilla Beaulieu Presley, his wife from 1967 to 1973. "He loved that little girl," Burton said.

Recorded in Memphis, Tennessee, on December 13, 1973, "My Boy" came out first on Presley's 1974 LP *Good Times*. Promotional copies of the single for radio stations had it backed with "Loving Arms" from that album, but by the time the 45 came out commercially, RCA had replaced "Loving Arms" with "Thinking of You," a tune on Presley's latest album *Promised Land*.

"My Boy" by Presley hit #1 AC, #20 pop, and #14 country. He had four more singles hit the AC and pop charts over the next two years—"T-R-O-U-B-L-E" (#42 AC, #35 pop), "Hurt" (#7 AC, #28 pop), "Moody Blue" (#2 AC for two weeks, #31 AC), and "Way Down" (#14 AC, #18 pop)—before his untimely death on August 16, 1977 from heart failure attributed to years of abuse of prescription drugs.

A posthumous release of "My Way" hit #6 AC and #22 pop in late 1977. Two other remixed versions of Presley's music charted a few years later, "Guitar Man" in 1981 (#16 AC, #28 pop) and "The Elvis Medley" in 1982 (#31 AC, #71 pop). But the demand for Presley records and related merchandise has never really died, particularly in Memphis, where his house Graceland is a huge tourist attraction, a sort of mecca for Elvis fans.

In 1998 those fans had a special treat when a multimedia concert showing old Presley footage along with a live band and singers appeared at various locations around America. "It's just like Elvis being there," noted Burton, who played guitar in the event, as he had more than 25 years earlier. He admitted he still missed the King of Rock and Roll.

For the final word on Presley, the following words of Burton seem appropriate: "He loved everything and loved doing live shows. He was just a downhome Southern gentleman, a wonderful guy and a great entertainer."

255 The Last Farewell

ROGER WHITTAKER

RCA 50030

April 12, 1975 (1 week)

Writers: Roger Whittaker, Ron A. Webster

Producer: Dennis Preston

A four-year-old song done by a little-known artist hardly seems the makings of an international hit, but "The Last Farewell" was exactly that. It went to #1 in 11 countries, #2 in the United Kingdom, and #19 on America's Hot 100 in addition to #1 AC. The record sold more than 11 million copies worldwide.

The voice behind "The Last Farewell" was Roger Whittaker, born in Nairobi, Kenya, on March 22, 1936. Though he graduated from the University of Bangor in Wales in 1962 with a bachelor of science degree, he found that singing was taking more of his time and interest than a career in medicine. When some recording he did for the university prompted Fontana Records to offer him a contract, he decided to become a vocalist.

His first single was "The Charge of the Light Brigade." He debuted on the British pop chart in 1969 with "Durham Town (The Leavin')," which hit #12. Four more entries followed over the next two years, during which time "The Last Farewell" came into existence.

As Whittaker said, "I had a radio series in 1971 in Eng- land, and one of the ideas I had was to invite listeners to send their poems or lyrics to me and I would make songs out of them. We got a million replies, and I did one each week for 26 weeks." A man named Zack Lawrence did arrangements for each song, which included backing by a full orchestra. One selected was "The Last Farewell," a poem by Ron Webster, who was a silversmith from Birmingham, England.

"The Last Farewell" appeared on Whittaker's 1971 LP *A Special Kind of Man* but generated no excitement initially. "I didn't think it was going to be a hit," Whittaker said. But then the wife of a program director for the Atlanta, Georgia, radio station WSB heard "The Last Farewell" in 1975 when she went to Canada and requested that her husband play it on air. "I don't remember the name of the guy, but they played it once and kept on playing it and there it was," Whittaker said. Its success eventually spread throughout the world.

Whittaker credited the song's appeal to the opening, a Wagnerian-like piece played on a French horn. He said he could not remember the name of the musician but did know they used Lawrence's initial horn arrangement.

Though it was his only Hot 100 entry, "The Last Farewell" was the fourth of 10 AC singles for Whittaker, starting with "New World in the Morning" (#12, 1970) through "You Are My Miracle" (#35, 1979). He also hit #91 country in 1983 with "I Love You Because" [see 28].

Whittaker has no hits in America in the 1990s, but has remained a popular touring artist in the country and around the world. "I do about 180 concerts a year," he said. He also does occasional recording in England and Germany, and spends a lot of time with his family in the rural west of England.

256 He Don't Love You (Like I Love You)

TONY ORLANDO AND DAWN

Elektra 45240

April 19, 1975 (1 week)

Writers: Jerry Butler, Clarence Carter, Curtis Mayfield

Producers: Hank Medress, Dave Appell

When Tony Orlando and Dawn switched in 1975 to Elektra Records, they found an executive willing to let them change their style. "David Geffen was the person who really leaned on us to go more on the R&B side," Orlando said. But it was the opinion of an actress and her then-husband that decided them on what single to do first.

"I went to the Golden Globe Awards and I'm in the hallway singing with Peter Wolf," said Orlando, referring to the lead singer of the J. Geils Band. "At that time, he was married to Faye Dunaway. They were oldies freaks, and we started singing in the lobby." When Orlando sang "He Will Break Your Heart," a #7 pop and #1 R&B hit for co-writer Jerry Butler in 1960, Wolf and Dunaway recommended he remake the tune.

"He Will Break Your Heart" had hit the charts often after 1960 (#91 pop for the Righteous Brothers in 1966, #120 bubbling under for Freddie Scott in 1967, and #68 country and #104 bubbling under for Johnny Williams in 1972), but Orlando took their advice. "I always loved Jerry Butler, and I always loved Curtis Mayfield," he said.

But, he noted, "What used to bug me about that song is I never heard 'He will break your heart' in the lyrics." He did remember the opening phrase, "He don't love you, like I love you," and thought most listeners did too, so he got permission from Mayfield to change the title. As "He Don't Love You (Like I Love You)," it peaked at #1 on the Hot 100 two weeks after topping the AC chart and stayed there for three weeks.

The group charted for two more years, but after "Sing" peaked at #7 AC and #58 pop, Orlando announced his retirement from show business at a concert in Cohasset, Massachusetts, on July 22, 1977. The next year he returned to performing as a solo act, but his 45s "Don't Let Go" (#48 AC, 1978) and "Sweets for My Sweet" (#20 AC and #54 pop, 1979) generated little enthusiasm, so he concentrated on personal appearances and some acting work.

In 1993 Orlando substituted for an ill Roy Clark at the latter's theater in Branson, Missouri. He so enjoyed the experience that he established the Tony Orlando Yellow Ribbon Music Theater there, where he appears from April through December yearly, doing two shows a day six days a week. He and Wayne Newton have since opened a bigger theater in Branson, where Orlando performs regularly.

Orlando has fond memories of working with Telma Hopkins and Joyce Wilson. "Those two girls were super talented girls," he said. They had no plans to do a reunion as of mid-1998. Asked if they all still talk with each other, Orlando said, "Not as much as we should. But if those girls are ever in trouble, I'd be there. And I'm sure they'd be there for me." As for Tony's feeling about how his career has gone, he said, "I've got no complaints. It's been great."

257 It's a Miracle

BARRY MANILOW

Arista 0108

April 26, 1975 (1 week)

Writers: Barry Manilow, Marty Panzer

Producers: Barry Manilow, Ron Dante

Barry Manilow wrote "It's a Miracle," perhaps his most upbeat hit with the possible exception of "Copacabana," in 1973, just after finishing a tour with Bette Midler as her pianist for three weeks of sold-out concerts across America. He had returned to his New York City apartment in the middle of the night still high from excitement, and the next morning found it impossible to resume his former low-key lifestyle. Instead, as he recalled in his autobiography, *Sweet Life*, "I went to the piano the next day and wrote, 'You wouldn't believe where I've been,' the opening lines to 'It's a Miracle.' Little did I know that that tour would be the shortest and easiest tour I would ever do."

In the liner notes to Manilow's anthology *The Complete Collection and Then Some. . .*, co-writer Marty Panzer recalled that the singer called him to tell Panzer he stole the idea of the song's title from him. Manilow said, "Well, every time I call you and tell you about some incredible thing that's happened, you say the same thing. Every time. So I'd like to use it as the title." A confused Panzer asked Manilow, "You wrote a song called 'Holy S—t!'?"

Midler did not record "It's a Miracle," but Manilow did on his second album. Released as the follow-up to "Mandy" [see 241], "It's a Miracle" went to #12 pop as well as topping the AC chart. Manilow did not like the idea of singing other people's compositions at the time, and was grateful that his first solo hit was one he had written himself.

It may have been a miracle to Manilow that he had a successful singing career at all. Born Barry Alan Pincus in Brooklyn, New York, on June 17, 1946, Manilow studied music after high school first at the New York College of Music and then Juilliard. He wrote a score for an off-Broadway musical called *The Drunkard* and served as music director for *Callback!*, a TV series on the CBS affiliate in New York City, before he began an active performing career in the late 1960s singing with Jeanne Lucas for several years.

His big break was an odd one—being the in-house pianist at the Continental Baths, an all-male establishment. There he met Bette Midler, where he eventually became her musical director and arranger as well as a pianist. That provided the launching pad from which he tried his own solo vocal records.

258 Only Yesterday
THE CARPENTERS

A&M 1677

May 3, 1975 (1 week)

Writers: John Bettis (lyrics), Richard Carpenter (words)

Producer: Richard Carpenter

The Carpenters' 11th #1 AC entry was "Only Yesterday," which also became their 12th top 10 pop single by reaching #4 on the Hot 100 the weeks of May 24 and 31, 1975. In the liner notes to the Carpenters anthology *From the Top*, Richard Carpenter wrote that it "became a hit in a number of countries" (but not quite as big as its forerunner "Please Mr. Postman" [see 243]).

"Please Mr. Postman" and "Only Yesterday" both came from the Carpenters' 1974 LP *Horizon*. By the time that album came out, several patterns involving the Carpenters were set. As in the case of "Only Yesterday," if Richard wrote a tune, his collaborator would be John Bettis. Frequently used players on their records were guitarist Tony Peluso and bassist Joe Osborn. The latter had produced and engineered the early, now-rare records of the Richard Carpenter Trio in 1965–66 with Karen and Richard joined by bassist Wes Jacobs.

The main change from the early 1970s for the Carpenters themselves, apart from Richard doing more writing, producing, and arranging, was that Karen no longer played drums in concert, owing to the need for her to be in front of the band when performing in public. (For the most part on the early Carpenters records, busy session player Hal Blaine was the drummer so she could concentrate on singing.)

But by 1975 there were signs of trouble. During a performance in Las Vegas Karen collapsed. It was the first indication that she was suffering from anorexia nervosa, an eating disorder that was pretty much unknown at the time. The Las Vegas concerts also created problems for the Carpenters; their opening act, Neil Sedaka, proved to be more popular among audiences than themselves, which Richard resented. For more details on this, see 272—"Solitaire," the last song from *Horizon* to be released as a single.

In addition, Karen and Richard were both suffering from studio fatigue. "Around the time of *Horizon* we started to get tired. It took a long time to do that album and I was wearing out," Richard told *Billboard*'s Paul Grein in 1981. This flagging stamina was not obvious in later recordings, all of which sounded top-notch, but the Carpenters did start to do less well on both the AC and pop charts through the rest of the 1970s, with only three more #1 AC hits coming after "Only Yesterday" in that decade—"Solitaire," "There's a Kind of Hush (All Over the World)" [see 293], and "I Need to Be in Love" [see 304]. After that, it took them another five years to top the AC chart again [see 408—"Touch Me When We're Dancing"].

259 The Immigrant
NEIL SEDAKA

Rocket 40370

May 10, 1975 (1 week)

Writers: Phil Cody (words), Neil Sedaka (music)

Producers: Neil Sedaka, Robert Appere

Neil Sedaka has mentioned often that "The Immigrant" was his tribute to John Lennon, who had fought immigration officials in the United States over his right to stay in the country. (Rumors had it that the Nixon administration considered Lennon unfit to live in America given his history of drug use.) But Sedaka drew on his personal experience for the tune as well. "I also have immigrant grandparents," he said. "They came from Istanbul, Turkey, in the 1900s."

Sedaka, born in Brooklyn, New York, on March 13, 1939, had known Lennon several years before writing "The Immigrant." "We were at Los Angeles at a party, and then in New York when he moved there with Yoko [Ono]," he said. Lennon appreciated the record and called to thank him for it. "I still have a copy of him talking about 'The Immigrant,'" said Sedaka of Lennon, who was murdered in 1980.

"The Immigrant" became Sedaka's second #1 AC hit after "Laughter in the Rain" [see 237]. But Sedaka saw his record stop at #22 pop in the spring of 1975 while a cover of another song from his *Sedaka's Back* LP, "Love Will Keep Us Together," became a bigger hit when done by the Captain and Tennille as a single [see 263]. He appreciated their work but regretted he did not release the latter song, rather than "The Immigrant," after "Laughter in the Rain," although he thought both were fine tunes. Nonetheless, he liked "The Immigrant" enough to continue doing it in concert through the late 1990s.

All of Sedaka's mid-1970s tunes were co-produced by Robert Appere, whom Sedaka described as "Very talented. Very nervous. He was very hyper but very nice to me." For an artist used to cutting four songs in a three-hour session during the 1950s and 1960s, Sedaka found himself thrown somewhat at the beginning by Appere's contemporary approach. "We went on for weeks, changing the drum sounds and later on overdubbing the strings. . . .It was a long procedure."

But Sedaka grew to appreciate the changes, which allowed him to double-track his voice on "The Immigrant," among other luxuries, for a deeper, broader final result. "Robert Appere took great pains with the sounds, and it was not as gimmicky or piercing as the old days," Sedaka said.

The "old days" were the 1950s, when "The Diary" went to #14 pop in 1959 and became the first of 20 pop entries through 1966. After that Sedaka became primarily a writer of tunes for others until returning to the American charts in 1974 with "Laughter in the Rain." "Laughter in the Rain" and "The Immigrant" were his first two AC entries. After "That's When the Music Takes Me" hit #7 AC and "Bad Blood" made #25 AC, Sedaka returned to top the charts with a remake of his oldie "Breaking Up Is Hard to Do" [see 286].

260 Rainy Day People
GORDON LIGHTFOOT

Reprise 1328

May 17, 1975 (1 week)

Writer: Gordon Lightfoot

Producer: Lenny Waronker

Gordon Lightfoot used his personal experience of being rootless and fun-loving as the basis for "Rainy Day People." "That was written, I believe, in the early 1970s," he said. "It had to do with the lifestyle and the insecurity of relationships. I could feel what was happening in the song, because I had nothing permanent in it." But Lightfoot emphasized that the lyrics for "Rainy Day People" did not apply to any specific person to the point where he or she would recognize themselves in the storyline. "There was nothing in there that was going to offend," he said. "I knew that people would hear the songs, and I tried to be careful about what I put in there."

"Rainy Day People" became Lightfoot's third consecutive #1 AC single, but stopped at #26 pop and #47 country. It was his last #1 AC entry. In 1976 "The Wreck of the Edmund Fitzgerald" went to #9 AC and #2 pop for two weeks, but it was the last major success for Lightfoot. He came close to the top of the AC roster when "The Circle Is Small (I Can See It in Your Eyes)" reached #3 AC and #33 pop in 1978, but after that his records rarely made the charts. He went on to have only three more 45s on the AC chart, "Dream Street Rose" in 1980 (#25 AC), "Baby Step Back" in 1982 (#17 AC and also #50 pop, his last Hot 100 entry), and "Anything for Love" in 1986 (#13 AC).

By the 1990s Lightfoot and his band settled down to a routine of about 40 touring dates a year in North America as well as some occasional recording. He released his most recent album, titled *A Painter Passing Through*, on Painter Records in 1998 and admitted, "It makes it an especially exciting year when we have an album out." He added that his urge to write songs remains, but he has a more leisurely approach to doing records, saying that when it comes to when he will be finishing another one, "It possibly could be another three or four years." When not on the road, Lightfoot lives in Toronto, Canada, and is active as an environmentalist.

Asked what he looked forward to doing in the future, Gordon joked a little, saying, "What I want to do is head into the 21st century. I'm very happy that I've been able to survive and stay in commission."

261 99 Miles From L.A.
ALBERT HAMMOND

Mums 6037

May 24, 1975 (1 week)

Writers: Hal David (words), Albert Hammond (music)

Producers: Hal David, Albert Hammond

Albert Hammond is better known for his 1972 #5 pop and #2 AC hit "It Never Rains in Southern California" than "99 Miles From L.A.," which despite going to #1 AC halted at #91 on the Hot 100, the worst performance by a #1 AC single on the pop chart since John Gary's "Cold" failed even to bubble under in late 1967. Hammond went on to be a successful songwriter in the 1980s, which is how he got started in the business in the 1960s prior to becoming a vocalist.

Born in London, England, on May 18, 1942, Hammond grew up in Gibraltar, Spain. From age 16 to 18 he and his brother toured as the Diamond Boys, then he went to England and joined a group called Los Cuico Ricardos. In 1966 he started collaborating on songs with Mike Hazelwood, and they hit in England and America with "Little Arrows" (a #38 AC and #16 pop entry for Leapy Lee in 1968) and "Gimme Dat Ding" (a #20 AC and #9 pop single for the Pipkins in 1970) from a British children's musical called *Oliver and the Overlord* which they scored.

Hammond and Hazelwood also sang in the group the Magic Lanterns in 1971, with Hammond doing vocals on "One Night Stand," which made #74 pop in America. Then he took a year off and ended up getting his own recording contract on Mums Records in 1972.

His first solo single was "Down by the River," which made only little waves, going to #38 AC and #91 pop. Two months later "It Never Rains in Southern California" nearly reached the top, but Hammond learned that following up a hit can be a difficult task. He tried with eight more pop entries through 1975, three of which made the AC chart—"Half a Million Miles From Home" at #26 AC and #87 pop in late 1973, "I'm a Train" at #15 AC and #31 pop in 1974, and finally "99 Miles from L.A." The latter was his last 45 on the AC and pop charts.

With the relative failure of "99 Miles From L.A.," Hammond switched to Epic Records from 1976–77 and then Columbia in 1981–82, but all his output was met with disinterest. He fared better as a writer, getting #1 AC hits with "Nothing's Gonna Stop Us Now" [see 514] and "One Moment in Time" [see 550], among numerous hit credits.

It was a mixed blessing for him to write hit songs but not be the singer. "I'm jealous when they do it and they have a hit," he admitted to Barry Scott in *We Had Joy, We Had Fun.* "I'm very happy for them, but I'm jealous. I'm an artist too. I love to sing and perform and go on the road." If Hammond did any of the latter in the late 1990s, it would have been hard to find him—there was no listing for Hammond in *Billboard's 1998 International Talent and Touring Directory,* and at press time he had yet to put out another album.

262 Wonderful Baby

DON MCLEAN

United Artists 614

May 31, 1975 (1 week)

Writer: Don McLean

Producer: Joel Doran

"I had done an enormous amount of work from 1968 to 1970. I was playing nightclubs all the time and opening other acts. I was always on tour with some big act and my name was around a lot and I was putting a lot of effort into it, and then 'American Pie' came out and I just went into outer space. It's that simple." That's what Don McLean told Kristin Baggelaar and Donald Milton in *Folk Music: More Than a Song* about his professional career before "American Pie" became such a megahit [see 164]. Prior to that record, McLean debuted on the AC chart with "Castles in the Air," which dented the chart at its last place of #40 for the week of February 27, 1971. That tune became the B-side to the follow-up to "American Pie," "Vincent," which hit #12 pop and #2 AC in 1972. That song was a tribute to Vincent Van Gogh, and a tribute to another artist was to give McLean his second #1 AC hit.

In the wake of "American Pie," McLean decided not to work for a year, telling Baggelaar and Milton that he "got reacquainted with friends that I had lost contact with for years. . .and in 1975 I started doing some good hard work again." Part of that labor came from promoting his album *Homeless Brother*, released in late 1974. A single from that LP was "Wonderful Baby," and McLean dedicated it to silver screen dancing icon Fred Astaire. It peaked at the summit of the AC chart but managed only to get to #93 on the Hot 100.

McLean has speculated that the media's obsession with "American Pie" and his refusal both to interpret the song's sometimes obscure lyrics or defend its implicit dismissal of rock and roll in favor of folk music made him persona non grata among music critics to the point where his later work in the 1970s, like "Wonderful Baby," was ignored. He claimed the lowest point was after a 1973 concert in Sarasota Springs, Florida, where he muttered he would not perform "American Pie" anymore. A reporter overheard his statement and ran it as fact, and McLean said the publicity helped lower his concert and album business considerably in the United States.

Indeed, McLean did not make the AC or pop charts again for six years after "Wonderful Baby." He mainly worked overseas until 1981, when his biggest post-"American Pie" hit, a remake of Roy Orbison's "Crying," made #2 AC and #5 pop. His last pop and AC entry was a 1981 remake of "Castles in the Air," which ascended to #7 AC and #36 pop. McLean then returned to tour and record in America fairly steadily if not spectacularly through the late 1990s. Before that, in the late 1980s, he had managed to get a few entries onto the country chart.

263 Love Will Keep Us Together

THE CAPTAIN AND TENNILLE

A&M 1672

June 7, 1975 (1 week)

Writers: Howard Greenfield (words), Neil Sedaka (music)

Producer: Daryl Dragon

The biggest-selling single of 1975, "Love Will Keep Us Together," got the Captain and Tennille off to a rousing start. It was the first of five consecutive #1 AC and top five entries for the married duo, discounting "Por Amor Viviremos," a #49 pop single which was "Love Will Keep Us Together" sung in Spanish and released after the English version's success. And love really has kept the Captain and Tennille together, as the two are still married and still performing the tune more than 25 years later.

Neil Sedaka wrote "Love Will Keep Us Together" as one of two final tunes he did with longtime partner Howard Greenfield in 1971; the other was the appropriately titled "Our Last Song Together." Sedaka said the song was based on the singing styles of the Beach Boys, Al Green, and the Supremes. He included it on his 1974 "comeback" LP in America, *Sedaka's Back*, but he did not release the track as a single.

The acclaim accorded Sedaka's album got the attention of Kip Cohen, head of A&R (artists and repertoire) at

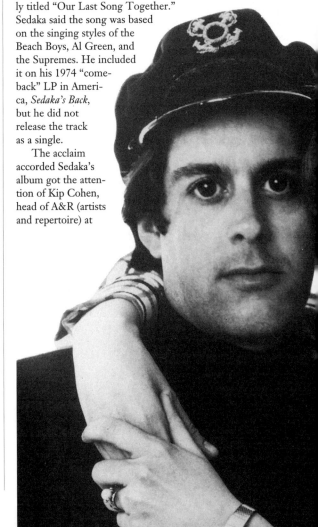

A&M Records. He felt one of the songs would be right for the Captain and Tennille's debut album. The Captain and Tennille listened to Sedaka's LP and agreed to do "Love Will Keep Us Together." The Captain, whose real name is Daryl Dragon, had worked out an arrangement on piano with his wife Toni Tennille within two weeks.

Other then the new arrangement, "Love Will Keep Us Together" stayed the same as Sedaka's album cut, although as a tribute to him near the end, Tennille threw in "Sedaka is back." The two disagreed as to who thought of including it. "When we were fooling around in rehearsal, one of us did it," said Tennille. But Dragon said the idea came from one of the A&M secretaries who provided rhythm clapping at the end of the session and applauded after "Sedaka is back" was sung.

On one thing everyone had to agree: "Love Will Keep Us Together" was a #1 AC and pop hit, staying at #1 on the Hot 100 for four weeks starting June 21, 1975. Tennille credited appearances on *American Bandstand* and *The Dinah Shore Show* with popularizing the record.

"Love Will Keep Us Together" also earned Grammy nominations for Record of the Year, Song of the Year, and Best Pop Vocal Performance by a Duo, Group or Chorus, winning for the first one. "We thought, 'That's it, we don't have a chance' when it wasn't Song of the Year," Tennille recalled of the event. But their names popped out when Stevie Wonder and Joan Baez presented Record of the Year.

Tennille kept Wonder's envelope announcing their win in Braille. As for Baez, Tennille said, "She looked at us like we came out from under a rock." Sedaka loved the Captain and Tennille's cover of his song. "It was a perfect pop record," he said. In 1976 Wilson Pickett's version of "Love Will Keep Us Together" went to #69 R&B.

264 Wildfire

MICHAEL MURPHEY

Epic 50084

June 14, 1975 (1 week)

Writers: Michael Murphey, Larry Cansler

Producer: Bob Johnston

Dallas, Texas, native Michael Martin Murphey co-wrote "Wildfire" in 1968 shortly after the dissolution of the Lewis & Clarke Expedition, a duo in which he went by the name of Travis Lewis and partner Owen Castleman called himself Boomer Clarke. The act hit the Hot 100 in 1967 at #64 with "I Feel Good (I Feel Bad)." Eight years later, both men were on the chart simultaneously but separately; Owen, now Boomer Castleman, made it with "Judy Mae," which stopped at #33, and Murphey with "Wildfire." It was Castleman's last chart appearance, but for Murphey it was one of several stops in his growing solo career.

Murphey planned to put "Wildfire" on his debut album for A&M Records, but the company rejected it, so he charted first with "Geronimo's Cadillac," which reached #37 pop in 1972. Co-author and fellow Texas schoolmate and recording artist Larry Cansler also had no luck in getting Warner Brothers executives to OK his version for release. But both retained faith in the song, which got a good response when Murphey played it on tour.

Yet Murphey considered the song worthy only of being an album track. "I thought it was too obscure, too fantasy, too wrapped up in the west for a single that would appeal to everybody," he told *Rolling Stone* (the song told of a girl's love for a pony named Wildfire). Murphey changed his mind after a new element was added in the studio.

"The piano player [Jac Murphy] played me a piece by Scriabin, very modern and not real flowery like most classical pieces," he said. "I really fell in love with it, so I said, 'Can you put this in the key of E?' He did, and we tacked it onto the beginning of 'Wildfire.' That made the song connect for me." That part was left off the single, but many AC and pop stations played the album version with the piano solo during and after the song's run on the charts.

"Wildfire" peaked at #3 pop the weeks of June 21 and 28, 1975, behind "Love Will Keep Us Together" [see 263] at #1 and "When Will I Be Loved" by Linda Ronstadt at #2. Murphey followed it with "Carolina in the Pines" (#4 AC and #21 pop in 1975).

Seven years later, he made #1 country with "What's Forever For," which also went to #4 AC and #19 pop. Thereafter he worked as a country artist and changed his billing to include his middle name. By the 1990s Murphey had made Taos, New Mexico, his home base between tours and record sessions.

Murphey recorded a new version of "Wildfire" on his 1997 LP *The Horse Legends*. He told Deborah Evans Price in *Billboard* that "'Wildfire' is the thing that broke my career wide open and, on some level, still keeps it fresh. Because that song appeals to kids, and always has, it's kept my career fresh. I've always got a new generation coming along."

265 Midnight Blue
MELISSA MANCHESTER

Arista 0116

June 21, 1975 (2 weeks)

Writers: Carole Bayer Sager, Melissa Manchester

Producer: Vini Poncia

By staying atop the #1 spot on the AC chart for two weeks, "Midnight Blue" became the first single in 1975 to spend more than one week leading the listing. That string—24 consecutive different AC chart toppers—remains a record nearly 25 years later. But that is not "Midnight Blue's" only distinction. It gave Melissa Manchester her first and so far only #1 AC hit. It also became her first top 10 pop hit, peaking at #6 the week of August 9, 1975. But all its achievements left Manchester with a mixed feeling, despite the fact she co-wrote the tune.

"The idea of a single is preposterous in that it is not going to represent your whole point of view," Manchester told Penelope Ross for *Rolling Stone*. "But sure, I'm looking for a hit single. I was thrilled about 'Midnight Blue.' If that's the only song I'm remembered for, it won't be so fine. I have other things on my mind. To play a concert and have people genuinely acknowledge something on the second side and the fourth cut, that's just a treat."

Manchester was born in the Bronx, New York, on February 15, 1951. Her father was David Manchester, who had been playing bassoon with the Metropolitan Opera Orchestra in New York City for 20 years by the time "Midnight Blue" became a hit. She attended the High School of the Performing Arts in Manhattan, and at the same time managed the impressive task of being a writer with the Chapell Music publishing firm (age 16 to 18). After high school, Manchester attended the New York University School of the Arts to study songwriting. Her teacher there was Paul Simon.

After leaving the university, Manchester became one of the Harlettes, Bette Midler's backup singing group of women. Her early career bore similarities to that of Midler's arranger at the time, Barry Manilow. Both signed with Arista Records after being on Bell as unsuccessful vocalists. Manchester's first two albums, both on Bell, 1973's *Home to Myself* and 1974's *Bright Eyes*, generated no AC or pop entries, but 1975's *Melissa*, on Arista, did with "Midnight Blue."

The follow-up to "Midnight Blue," "Just Too Many People," hit #2 AC and #30 pop. She was a frequent visitor on both charts through the early 1980s, even managing to eclipse the pop peak of "Midnight Blue" with 1982's "You Should Hear How She Talks About You," which went to #5 on the Hot 100 and #10 AC. She continued to record and tour the rest of the 1980s and 1990s but none of her releases has had much success on the charts.

266 Every Time You Touch Me (I Get High)
CHARLIE RICH

Epic 50103

July 5, 1975 (1 week)

Writers: Charlie Rich, Billy Sherrill

Producer: Billy Sherrill

He had the majority of his success in the country field, but Charlie Rich worked in various musical genres before making his name in Nashville in the 1970s. Born in Colt, Arkansas, on December 14, 1932, Rich grew up on a small cotton plantation farm. He learned gospel music from his Southern Missionary Baptist parents, blues from the field hands, and country from the Saturday night radio broadcasts from the Grand Ole Opry in Nashville. Yet when Rich started doing music professionally, it was playing in a jazz band in a small combo while stationed in the Air Force at Enid, Oklahoma, during the Korean War.

After being discharged in 1955, Rich went into farming, but found time to play some nighttime gigs in Memphis, Tennessee. His talents were noticed, and he signed with Sun Records, Presley's original label. Rich struck success with his third release, the rockabilly-tinged "Lonely Weekends," which made #22 pop in 1960. But he had no other hits with Sun, so he strayed to RCA and then Mercury, getting to #21 pop in 1965 on the latter's Smash imprint with "Mohair Sam." He then went to Hi Records, but in 1968 Rich made a decision which changed the direction of his career.

"After leaving Hi, Sy Rosenberg, my manager, went over and talked to Epic Records," Rich told *Billboard* in 1975. "He came back and mentioned that Billy Sherrill, who had engineered some of my records at Sun, was now a producer at Epic. Sy said that the company wasn't offering any cash advance for signing, but I felt that because I'd be working with Billy, it was the best thing to do. And it was."

"Every Time You Touch Me (I Get High)" was among more than 10 top 10 country hits Rich had during the 1970s. It hit #3 country and #19 pop in addition to #1 AC. It was the last of his four #1 AC hits, all of which Sherrill co-wrote, and earned a Grammy nomination for Rich and Sherrill for Best Country Song. Rich was nominated the same year for Best Inspirational Performance for his LP *Silver Linings*. He would have one last Grammy nomination for his 1978 #1 country duet with Janie Fricke, "On My Knees," for Best Country Vocal Performance by a Duo or Group.

Rich's follow-up to "On My Knees," "I'll Wake You Up When I Get Home," hit #3 country in 1979 and was his last top 10 entry on that chart. His final entry on the country chart was "You Made It Beautiful" at #47 in the summer of 1981. He continued performing at various venues until his death from a blood clot on July 25, 1995. He was 62 years old.

267 Please Mr. Please

OLIVIA NEWTON-JOHN

MCA 40418

July 12, 1975 (3 weeks)

Writers: Bruce Welch, John Rostill

Producer: John Farrar

The writers of "Please Mr. Please," Bruce Welch and John Rostill, were both members of Cliff Richard's backing group, The Shadows. Hugely popular in England during the late 1950s and all of the 1960s, Richard somehow never transferred much of his success to America during those years, even in the wake of the British invasion of 1964, when his highest-charting tune from that period, "It's All in the Game," became a #10 AC and #25 pop entry. For some reason, he had his first million seller in the United States a year after "Please Mr. Please," getting to #30 AC and #6 pop with "Devil Woman." He made the AC chart nine times after that through 1984, including a duet with Olivia Newton-John, "Suddenly," from the 1980 film Xanadu [see 388—"Magic"].

According to producer John Farrar, Welch and Rostill wrote "Please Mr. Please," for Newton-John. "They intended it to be a country song," Farrar noted. That explained why the lyrics made references to beer and jukeboxes, with the singer imploring her listener not to play the B-17 selection on the latter, as it was the song she shared with the lover who had left her, another staple of country music.

"Please Mr. Please" did not top the country charts, however, but it did become a top 10 single there, as it did on the pop chart, peaking at #3 the week of August 9, 1975, behind "Jive Talkin'" by the Bee Gees at #1 and "I'm Not in Love" by 10cc at #2. It was the most blatant pandering to the country audience since Newton-John had first broken into that market with "Let Me Be There" in 1973 (a top 10 country, AC, and pop hit, getting to #3 AC), and further incensed the country traditionalists who resented Newton-John being counted as one of their own, not least because she recorded in England and not Nashville.

Newton-John acknowledged that she was an unusual breed of country star in 1974 when she accepted her Grammy for Best Female Country Vocal Performance over the likes of Marie Osmond, Dottie West, and Tammy Wynette, saying, "It's probably the first time an English person won an award over Nashville people." But Farrar said she did not realize until later just how much some other acts disliked her. (The same year she got her Grammy some members of the Country Music Association formed the Association of Country Entertainers after Olivia was named the CMA's Female Vocalist of the Year.)

"I heard there was a lot of resentment down there to her," Farrar recalled. "But we were in England and sort of isolated from it at the time." Indeed, Farrar was more concerned about getting hits, and he had another one on the AC chart with the single after "Please Mr. Please," "Something Better to Do" [see 277].

268 Rhinestone Cowboy

GLEN CAMPBELL

Capitol 4095

August 2, 1975 (1 week)

Writer: Larry Weiss

Producers: Dennis Lambert, Brian Potter

The biggest record of Glen Campbell's career was "Rhinestone Cowboy," his first #1 pop hit as well as a chart topper on AC and country too. He liked the lyrics just as much as the music ("there'll be a load of compromising" hit home with him as a musician), and it remained one of his favorite songs even though during the time it became a hit his wife Billie announced she wanted to separate.

Larry Weiss wrote "Rhinestone Cowboy" and recorded it on an album in 1974; the song was also released as a single. Reviewing the 45 in its March 16, 1974 edition, Billboard commented that Weiss sounded like Neil Diamond. (Campbell's judgment was that Weiss was "kind of" similar to Diamond.) The Weiss take on "Rhinestone Cowboy" managed to go only to #24 AC.

However, Campbell happened to hear the tune on the radio in Los Angeles and liked it, so he bought a cassette and listened to the record in Australia during a 1974 tour of one-night shows across the continent. The airlines were on strike, so he had plenty of time to learn the tune while traveling along winding roads between tour stops. ("We were over there like three weeks," Campbell recalled. "Man, that was a tough row to hoe.") Coincidentally, when Campbell returned to America, Al Coury, vice president of promotions and A&R (artists and repertoires) at Capitol Records, presented him with a song he thought would be right for Campbell to record. The song was "Rhinestone Cowboy." With that extra bit of encouragement, Campbell recorded the tune, but not quite the way Weiss had done it. "I did it faster, because I wanted it to be a little more up-tempo," he said. He did vocal tracks for the melody first, then electronically overdubbed his voice to supply the harmony for the record.

Campbell's "Rhinestone Cowboy" galloped to the top spot of the AC, country, and pop charts in that order. It made #1 country three weeks after doing so on the AC chart starting August 23, 1975, and held there for three weeks. Then on September 6, 1975, "Rhinestone Cowboy" led the Hot 100 for two weeks. At the Grammy Awards, "Rhinestone Cowboy" notched nominations for Record of the Year, Song of the Year, and Best Male Pop Vocal Performance.

During the period when the song was most popular, Campbell and Weiss became friends. Unfortunately, Campbell was not able to stop Weiss from trying to make a film out of the tune, a goal which resulted in a critical and commercial disaster called Rhinestone in 1984 starring Sylvester Stallone and Dolly Parton. Commenting on the movie, which he saw on television first rather than in a theater, Campbell said, "That was a total farce. If I'd been Larry, I'd sue them."

But Campbell had no such complaints about the song. "I'd like to find another one like that," he said.

269 At Seventeen

JANIS IAN

Columbia 10228

August 9, 1975 (2 weeks)

Writer: Janis Ian

Producer: Brook Arthur

Janis Ian, born Janis Eddy Fink in Farmingdale, New Jersey, on April 7, 1951, had one of the oddest chart careers on the Hot 100, scoring only three entries there during a period of 14 years, with two of them being a top 20 hit. Her debut was "Society's Child (Baby I've Been Thinking)," a song about miscegenation she wrote in 1965 that hit #14 pop in 1967. Her swan song came in 1981 when "Under the Covers" went to #71. Between those records came her best-known tune, "At Seventeen."

"People know my name from '[At] Seventeen,' that song's special, you only get one of those once in a while," she told Edward Kiersch in Where Are You Now, Bo Diddley? "Anyone could have written it, though. . . .It's a song about growing up, the transitions we all go through. . .[T]he song makes that journey so personal. . . .It could really silence audiences, and that's magic, wonderful magic."

Beside hitting #1 AC, "At Seventeen" peaked at #3 pop on September 13 and 20, 1975, behind "Rhinestone Cowboy" [see 268] at #1 and "Fallin' in Love" [see 271] at #2 the first week, and then David Bowie's "Fame" at #1 and "Rhinestone Cowboy" at #2 the second. The tune also claimed a Grammy nomination for Song of the Year and won Ian a Grammy for Best Female Pop Vocal Performance.

"At Seventeen" was not Ian's first AC entry. While "The Man You Are in Me" bubbled under at #104 in 1974, it gave her an AC debut of #33. For the rest of the decade she was a fairly consistent presence on the AC listings, although "At Seventeen" was the only one to make the Hot 100 as well. After "The Man You Are in Me" came "When the Party's Over" in early 1975 (#20), then "At Seventeen," followed by "In the Winter" (#21) in late 1975, and three consecutive entries in 1976, "Boy I Really Tied One On" (#43), "I Would Like to Dance" (#28), and "Roses" (#37). She ended her AC streak with two more 45s, 1978's "That Grand Illusion" (#43) and 1980's "The Other Side of the Sun" (#47).

Afterward, Ian recorded fairly steadily on a variety of labels through the late 1990s, but none of her singles or albums clicked like the acoustic guitar sound and lyrics of "At Seventeen" or the LP which included the song, Between the Lines, which went to #1 the week of September 20, 1975. In 1993 Ian acknowledged she was a lesbian in the gay rights magazine The Advocate, 17 years after she had been "outed" in the New York weekly The Village Voice. She was still contributing a regular humorous column to the The Advocate through 1997, while she continued to write, record, and tour.

270 How Sweet It Is (To Be Loved by You)

JAMES TAYLOR

Warner 8109

August 23, 1975 (1 week)

Writers: Brian Holland, Lamont Dozier, Eddie Holland

Producers: Lenny Waronker, Russ Titelman

"How Sweet It Is (To Be Loved by You)" was the biggest pop hit Marvin Gaye had in the 1960s until his seven-week run at #1 on the Hot 100 with "I Heard It Through the Grapevine" in late 1968. His "How Sweet It Is" went to #6 pop and #4 R&B in early 1965. A year later, another group on the Motown label, Junior Walker and the All Stars, took their spin on it to #18 pop and #3 R&B. Nine years later, the song made the Hot 100 once more, this time at the top spot.

"James wanted to do a Marvin Gaye song, so we threw some ideas around in the studio," producer Russ Titelman told Rolling Stone. "Finally, it came down to 'Stubborn Kind of Fellow' [Gaye's first pop and R&B entry, peaking at #46 pop and # R&B in 1962] or 'How Sweet It Is.' Kortch [guitarist Danny Kortchmar] started playing a Curtis Mayfield thing for 'How Sweet' that fit right in, and that decided it." Taylor's then-wife Carly Simon added backing vocals to the track after James sang his part, while the sizzling sax solo in the middle of the tune came courtesy of David Sanborn.

The same Rolling Stone article noted that co-writer Brian Holland approved of the new version. So did the general public, as Taylor's "How Sweet It Is" peaked at #5 pop for two weeks starting August 30, 1975, in addition to its AC victory. Taylor failed to make the R&B chart with his effort, but five years later Tyrone Davis's got to #36 on that chart.

The record certainly was sweet for Taylor in terms of chart success. He had not had a solo top 10 pop hit since "You've Got a Friend" [see 153], although he did make #5 pop and #10 AC in 1974 in a duet with Carly Simon in their remake of another oldie, "Mockingbird." Other releases between 1971–74 fared less well. "Long Ago and Far Away," the follow-up to "You've Got a Friend," made only #31 pop and #4 AC. In early 1973 his "Don't Let Me Be Lonely Tonight" stopped at #14 pop as well as #3 AC. And after "Mockingbird," Taylor's next single, "Walking Man," missed the Hot 100 completely while going to #26 AC in late 1974.

In late 1975 Taylor missed the top again when "Mexico" got only to #49 pop and #5 AC. However, his next single brought him back to the #1 AC [see 310—"Shower the People"].

"How Sweet It Is" was the second cover of a Motown tune to make #1 AC after the Carpenters' "Please Mr. Postman" [see 243]. Later remakes with this same distinction were the Captain and Tennille's "Shop Around" [see 300], Rod Stewart with Ronald Isley doing "This Old Heart of Mine" [see 580], and Paul Young's "What Becomes of the Brokenhearted" [see 612].

271 Fallin' in Love

HAMILTON, JOE FRANK AND REYNOLDS

Playboy 6024

August 30, 1975 (1 week)

Writers: Dan Hamilton, Ann Hamilton

Producer: Jim Price

"Fallin' in Love" was a piece of advice the song's co-writers Dan and Ann Hamilton took to heart, as they were husband and wife when the song reached #1 both on the AC and pop charts, hitting the latter first for the week of August 23, 1973. "Fallin' in Love" was a surprise crossover to the R&B chart as well, getting to #24 there. In 1976 a cover by the soul group New Birth got to #51 R&B.

The Hamiltons never wrote another hit as big as "Fallin' in Love," nor did the group who popularized it come near its success. Hamilton, Joe Frank and Reynolds were three men who were part of the T-Bones, an instrumental act which had a #3 pop hit in 1966 with "No Matter What Shape (Your Stomach's In)." Their full names were Dan Hamilton, Joe Frank Carollo, and Tommy Reynolds, and all got to use their voices when they debuted at #4 on both the AC and pop charts in 1971 with "Don't Pull Your Love," later a #1 AC hit as part of a medley for Glen Campbell [see 297].

"Don't Pull Your Love" proved to be a tough tune to follow. In 1971 they released "Annabella" (#21 AC and #46 pop) and "Daisy Mae" (#41 pop), but were off both charts for more than three years even though they released material on the Dunhill label. During this period Reynolds left the group to become a minister in Texas in 1972. Alan Dennison replaced him, but Dunhill kept the billing as Hamilton, Joe Frank and Reynolds both so listeners wouldn't be confused and in the hope that the familiar names would stir memories of the 1971 hit.

In 1974 the relatively new Playboy music label, an outgrowth of the men's magazine of the same name, signed Hamilton, Joe Frank and Reynolds and saw the investment pay off with "Fallin' in Love." But the group was only a little bit more successful following up that hit than they had been with the immediate follow-ups to "Don't Pull Your Love." "Winners and Losers" made #3 AC and #21 pop in early 1976, followed by "Everyday Without You" at #7 AC and #62 pop in the spring of 1976. On the next 45, "Light Up the World With Sunshine," the band's title was now Hamilton, Joe Frank and Dennison, but that did not reverse their chart pattern, as they made only #21 AC and #67 pop. The next tune, "Don't Fight the Hands (That Need You)," was their last AC and pop entry at #50 AC and #72 pop in the fall of 1976.

Hamilton, Joe Frank and Dennison had their last album released in 1977. Not long afterward, Playboy Records became defunct, but the trio did not. The group toured some as an oldies act under its original, more familiar title in the 1980s and 1990s. Dan Hamilton died on December 23, 1994, in North Hollywood, California, at age 48 (he was born in Wenatchee, Washington, on June 1, 1946).

272 Solitaire

THE CARPENTERS

A&M 1721

September 6, 1975 (1 week)

Writers: Phil Cody (words), Neil Sedaka (music)

Producer: Richard Carpenter

Howard Greenfield had been Neil Sedaka's musical collaborator for most of the singer's career during the 1950s and 1960s. Feeling that their work together was growing stale, they parted professionally in an amicable way, and in the 1970s Sedaka started working with lyricist Phil Cody. "We were both writers for Screen Gems," Sedaka said. "His lyrics were very poetic and painted beautiful pictures."

One of their earliest compositions was "Solitaire." "I wrote it in upstate New York," Sedaka recalled. "I had a home in the Catskill Mountains. Phil and I would write there. The melody came first, as it did in those days. I was inspired by my classical training." But though he employed his studies of Chopin as a guide to setting up the tune, he was also influenced by the music of Roberta Flack. "I was inspired by a couple of things on the radio by her, and I wanted to do something in her style," he said. "Also, Harry Nilsson was very popular at the time and his style was very harmonic, and I used that too." The mood of the end product affected Sedaka the first time he listened to it, noting that "I could not make it through the song. I cried."

"Solitaire" made its initial appearance on a Sedaka album released only in Great Britain. The first to chart with it as a single was Andy Williams, who took it to #23 AC in 1973 and to #4 in the United Kingdom in 1974. "He made us change the lyric," Sedaka said, adding that Williams thought the line "A little hope goes up in smoke" could be interpreted as a drug reference. "I didn't like it as much as mine."

Then in 1975 Karen and Richard Carpenter released their version of the tune after hearing Sedaka do it in concert. "I was their opening act for six weeks," he said. Their "Solitaire" went to #17 pop as well as #1 AC. Sedaka enjoyed their rendition better than the Williams single. "I was thrilled with the record. I thought the record was a little slow, but it was beautiful," he said.

Unfortunately for Sedaka, while he was touring with the Carpenters, reception to his show became too strong for Richard Carpenter's comfort, and Carpenter fired him. The rift between them remained more than 20 years later, according to Sedaka. "Unfortunately, she passed on, and he's never spoken to me since." Sedaka didn't break with "Solitaire," however. "I still sing it at all my shows," he noted. "It's a showstopper."

273 The Proud One

THE OSMONDS

MGM 14791

September 13, 1975 (1 week)

Writers: Bob Gaudio, Bob Crewe

Producer: Mike Curb

Despite having been in the music business for a decade, as well as regulars on *The Andy Williams Show* on NBC-TV from 1962–67, in the 1970s the Osmonds constantly found themselves being compared to the Jackson Five due to their breakthrough soundalike hit, 1971's "One Bad Apple." It was their first pop and AC hit, making #1 pop and #37 AC; it even sounded enough like Michael Jackson and his brothers to make #6 R&B, the group's only appearance on the soul chart. But the Osmonds managed to do better on the AC chart, scoring a #1 hit there later and a total of seven entries versus only one for the Jackson Five (1970's "I'll Be There").

The Osmonds were a quintet consisting of five brothers born and living in Odgen, Utah. In descending age they were Alan (born June 22, 1949), Wayne (born August 28, 1951), Merrill (born April 30, 1953), Jay (born March 2, 1955), and Donny (born December 9, 1957). Donny became the group's heartthrob and concurrently with the group's success began a solo career and a duo with his sister Marie [see 228—"I'm Leaving It (All) Up to You"].

Though mostly a favorite on the Hot 100, a few Osmond singles did make it onto the AC chart, including "Let Me In" in 1973 (#4 AC, #36 pop) and "Love Me for a Reason" in 1974 (#2 AC, #10 pop). Finally in 1975, the group reached the summit with a song Frankie Valli took to #68 pop in 1966, "The Proud One." Though several fans have told Donny it is one of their favorite Osmond records, it is not one of his. "I didn't really think much about the song," Donny said. "I remember recording it and doing the harmonies." Donny also said he has never listened to Valli's version of the song.

"The Proud One" hit #22 pop in addition to its AC success. Its follow-up, "I'm Gonna Still Need You," went only to #38 AC, and "I Can't Live a Dream," released in 1976, became the last AC and pop entry for the group, going to #38 AC and #46 pop.

When Donny headlined an ABC–TV variety series with Marie from 1976–79, his brothers joined him on the show. In 1980 the Osmonds broke up but reunited two years later as a quartet without Donny called the Osmond Brothers. They scored 11 moderate country entries from 1982–86. In 1992 they opened their own music theater in Branson, Missouri, and had several other family members join them onstage occasionally, including Alan's five sons, known as the Osmond Boys.

A footnote: Donny said he planned to have the Osmond Brothers as guests on his and Marie's talk show in its first season (1998–99). As he put it, "It's going to be really weird interviewing my brothers."

274 I'm Sorry

JOHN DENVER

RCA 10353

September 20, 1975 (2 weeks)

Writer: John Denver

Producer: Milt Okun

"I'm Sorry" was the first and only John Denver single to reach #1 on the AC, pop, and country charts. It went to #1 AC first; on its second week atop that chart it also peaked at #1 on the Hot 100, and a few weeks later, the week of November 8, "I'm Sorry" was #1 country.

On the flip side of "I'm Sorry" was "Calypso," Denver's tribute to environmental oceanographer and deep sea diver Jacques Cousteau and his vessel the *Calypso*, and Denver's share of the proceeds from the single went to the Cousteau Society.

"Calypso" hit #2 pop for four weeks after "I'm Sorry" hit #1 pop; it was listed as the lead side of the single starting the week of October 11, 1975 and held the runner-up position on the Hot 100 behind Neil Sedaka's "Bad Blood" for the first three weeks and Elton John's "Island Girl" the last. (It was never listed on the AC chart.)

Regarding the genesis of that song, Denver told Marcia Seligson in *Playboy* that "I was walking the deck of the *Calypso* the day I met Captain Jacques Cousteau, and suddenly the chorus of 'Calypso' came to me. . . .Then for months I struggled to write the verses that had to be totally different from the chorus, because I wanted them to sound classical, while the chorus is a sea chantey." It took him several months, but then one day driving his jeep, the lyrics and melody came to Denver, and he finished his song.

In addition to his activities on behalf of the Cousteau Society (he also became a board member), Denver involved himself in several other environmental and social lobbying groups. Among them were the Friends of the Earth, the World Wildlife Fund, Environmental Action, and the Wilderness Society. He worked extensively on projects to combat hunger, and yet somehow found time through all of these activities to enjoy his hobbies of photography, skiing, and flying.

With one side of his latest single topping three charts and the other coming close to topping the Hot 100 as well, Denver was at his peak of popularity. (His previous single, "Thank God I'm a Country Boy," also netted him his first Grammy nomination, in the Best Male Country Vocal Performance category.) Although Denver never again hit #1 on the pop or country charts, he did get four more chart-toppers on the AC listing, with the next one being "Fly Away" [see 284].

275 Ain't No Way to Treat a Lady

HELEN REDDY

Capitol 4128

October 4, 1975 (1 week)

Writer: Harriet Schock

Producer: Joe Wissert

"It's a song about respect," said Helen Reddy of her seventh #1 AC hit, "Ain't No Way to Treat a Lady." Written by Harriet Schock ("A friend to this day," Reddy noted), it went to #8 pop for two weeks starting the week of October 11, 1975. The single was her last to crack the pop top 10.

Reddy earned her second and last Grammy nomination for Best Female Pop Vocal Performance for her work on "Ain't No Way to Treat a Lady." But the artist who appalled Christian conservatives with her acceptance speech for her first Grammy in the same category in 1972 for "I Am Woman" (she had said, "I want to thank everyone concerned at Capitol Records, my husband and manager Jeff Wald, because he makes my success possible, and God, because She makes everything possible") was unmoved by the honor. She was frank about her reasons. "By that time, I didn't care, because I came to realize that the Grammys were a bunch of crap," she said. "I have not been a member of NARAS [the National Academy of Recording Arts and Sciences, which oversees the Grammys] for a long time." (For the record, Reddy lost to Janis Ian for "At Seventeen" [see 269].)

In fact, Reddy said she never had the obsession with Grammys or music sales that some artists have. "I'm more concerned with how many lives I touched," she said.

After "Ain't No Way to Treat a Lady," Reddy nearly scored another #1 AC triumph with her follow-up, "Somewhere in the Night," which halted at #2 AC for one week while making #19 pop by early 1976. The tune, written by Will Jennings and Richard Kerr, beat out a competing version released at the same time by Batdorf and Rodney, who took it to #24 AC and #69 pop in late 1975. Batdorf and Rodney, whose full names were John Batdorf and Mark Rodney, had only one other entry on the charts, the predecessor to "Somewhere in the Night," titled "You Are a Song" (#22 AC and #87 pop in the fall of 1975). In early 1975 Barry Manilow took his rendition of "Somewhere in the Night" to #4 AC and #9 pop.

Reddy came back to #1 AC in 1976 with her next single, "I Can't Hear You No More" [see 315]. The title was ironic, since after that 45 left the chart, she faced declining airplay and sales for the rest of the decade. The woman who had been one of the most dominant female vocalists for the first half of the 1970s (during that period only Olivia Newton-John had more AC chart-toppers) ended the decade with almost no chart activity at all.

276 I Only Have Eyes for You

ART GARFUNKEL

Columbia 10190

October 11, 1975 (1 week)

Writers: Al Dubin (words), Harry Warren (music)

Producer: Richard Perry

"I Only Have Eyes for You" was written in the 1930s and first heard in the 1934 film *Dames*, starring Joan Blondell. The act to have a big hit with it at the time was Ben Selvin, whose version got to #2 on the hit parade that year. Forty-one years later, Art Garfunkel revived "I Only Have Eyes for You," but he did so unintentionally.

In a 1975 interview on a British Broadcasting Corporation radio program called *My Top 12* and transcribed on an unofficial fan Web site for Garfunkel on the Internet, the singer recalled how he did "I Only Have Eyes for You." "Well, we recorded—I say we, Richard Perry and I—recorded 'I Only Have Eyes for You' in the most unusual way. We were going to the studio that night and our plans for something else that we had intended to record fell through that night. So we had the musicians booked and no material. This is a situation I have never been in before. I have always been mindful of all the many young talents, the people who don't have the resources to get into the studio, how precious it is to have studio time. Here am I going off and not even knowing what I'm going to record.

"So Richard said, 'Let's do "I Only Have Eyes for You," it's a favorite of mine and I've been wanting to do it for many years. I have an idea of the kind of record I'd like to make.' And very fearfully—I say fearfully because I have never proceeded in this kind of casual way—I said, 'Well, alright, let's try and see what we can do tonight.'"

It took them only four hours to get the basic track ready. Garfunkel considered it to be the most spontaneous recording he had done up to that point in his career.

"I Only Have Eyes for You" hit #1 in the United Kingdom in 1975 as well as #1 AC in America, but on the U.S. pop chart it did not get quite as high, reaching #18. It was Garfunkel's second solo #1 AC hit after "All I Know" [see 203].

Other versions of "I Only Have Eyes for You" to chart after the 1930s were by the Flamingos in 1959 (#3 R&B, #11 pop), Cliff Richard in 1964 (#109 bubbling under), the Lettermen in 1966 (#4 AC, #72 pop), Jerry Butler in 1972 (#20 R&B, #85 pop), Mel Carter in 1974 (#39 AC, #104 bubbling under), the Chicago-based soul group Heaven and Earth in 1979 (#63 R&B), and the New York-based quartet the Funky Poets in 1994 (#81 R&B).

277 Something Better to Do
OLIVIA NEWTON-JOHN

MCA 40459

October 18, 1975 (3 weeks)

Writer: John Farrar

Producer: John Farrar

"**I** do not know where that came from," writer/producer John Farrar admitted about the notion for "Something Better to Do." "Sort of a stage, 1940s song. . . .One of those stupid songs, I guess."

Farrar may not have much respect in hindsight for his "Something Better to Do," but that easygoing, shuffling tune became his and Olivia Newton-John's fifth #1 AC hit as well as their sixth top 20 pop tune, peaking at #13. However, since their previous five singles all made at least #6 pop, "Something Better to Do" arguably could be considered a mild disappointment.

Apart from some woodwind instrumental sections, "Something Better to Do" emphasized Newton-John's singing voice. "It was very open that way," Farrar said. "She had this lovely, pure quality that was great to hear at the time," he said. Yet Farrar admitted the spotlight on Newton-John's vocal may not have been so pronounced if he had been planning to release it on its own. "I don't think I expected it to be a single," he said. "I expected it to be a silly song."

Silly or not, "Something Better to Do" was the leadoff single to Newton-John's new album released in the fall of 1975, *Clearly Love*. Coming off two albums which peaked at #1, *If You Love Me, Let Me Know* (the week of October 12, 1974) and *Have You Never Been Mellow* (the week of March 15, 1975), the #12 peak of *Clearly Love* was something of a letdown, even though the album did become a million seller. As Farrar recalled, "That was the last album I think we did in England, and it wasn't received that well. I remember at the time being grateful just that they found something off that album."

Actually, they, being MCA Records, released one more single of material from *Clearly Love*, "Let It Shine" backed with "He Ain't Heavy. . .He's My Brother" [see 285]. It became Newton-John's only double-sided AC entry, although in 1979 she scored on the Hot 100 with "Totally Hot," which went to #52 for a few weeks, followed by "Dancin' 'Round and 'Round," which reached #82. In contrast, "Let It Shine" and "He Ain't Heavy. . .He's My Brother" were listed as one entry.

278 The Way I Want to Touch You
THE CAPTAIN AND TENNILLE

A&M 1725

November 8, 1975 (2 weeks)

Writer: Toni Tennille

Producer: Morgan Cavett

Contrary to popular belief, the Captain and Tennille were not married when they did "Love Will Keep Us Together" [see 263], but they were in wedded bliss by the time "The Way I Want to Touch You" hit #1 AC. Ironically, that song was written by Toni Tennille as a way to express her growing romantic interest in Daryl Dragon, nicknamed "the Captain."

Tennille, born in Montgomery, Alabama, on May 8, 1943, met Dragon, born in Los Angeles on August 27, 1942, when he auditioned for her in 1971 in San Francisco as keyboardist for a rock musical she co-wrote called *Mother Earth*. Dragon, the son of symphony conductor Carmen Dragon, got the job, but when the musical's run ended in Los Angeles, he had to go back to touring with the Beach Boys, whom he had joined on tour beginning in 1967. (He got the nickname of "the Captain" from Mike Love of the Beach Boys from the cap he wore onstage.) Tennille joined him as a "Beach Girl" singing backup for the group and began to look at Dragon in a different light.

"I started having romantic feelings about him in 1972, 1973," she said. She channeled her emotions into composing "The Way I Want to Touch You." "I actually wrote that one when Daryl and I were at an airport hotel in Passaic, New Jersey," she said. "Very romantic."

When Dragon first saw the song, he missed its implications. "I don't think I really got the message," he admitted. Tennille agreed and joked, "No, he didn't. He's a little dense." Dragon said what he *did* notice about the song were its bass notes and chords, which reminded him of something Brian Wilson would write for the Beach Boys. He came up with an arrangement and the two cut the song as a demo along with four other songs, including "Disney Girls," which became the original B-side to "The Way I Want to Touch You." Leaving the Beach Boys behind, the Captain and Tennille pressed 500 copies of the record on their Butterscotch Castle label for $250. It generated some airplay and sales, leading to its release on the Joyce label and then A&M in 1974, with the latter signing the duo to do an album.

After "Love Will Keep Us Together" hit, A&M decided to rerelease "The Way I Want to Touch You." This time it hit #1 AC and #4 pop, peaking on the latter the week of November 29, 1975. Tennille was thrilled that the tune had finally broken through nationally. "It's always nice to have the one that you wrote be a hit," she said.

279 My Little Town
SIMON AND GARFUNKEL

Columbia 10230

November 22, 1975 (2 weeks)

Writer: Paul Simon

Producers: Paul Simon, Art Garfunkel, Phil Ramone

Art Garfunkel and Paul Simon's big breakthrough on the Hot 100 was their #1 hit of early 1966, "The Sounds of Silence," but the record did not cross over to the AC side, a surprising development given the song's mellow quality. Following several other major pop hits ("Homeward Bound," "I Am a Rock"), Simon and Garfunkel did not crack the AC chart until 1968 with "Scarborough Fair," which reached #5 AC and #11 pop. The record came from the soundtrack of the movie *The Graduate*, as did the follow-up, "Mrs. Robinson," which went to #4 AC and #1 pop. The next year they took "The Boxer" to #3 AC and #7 pop.

After the success in 1970 of "Bridge Over Troubled Water" [see 130], the duo continued to hit the AC chart, first with "Cecelia" (#31 AC, #4 pop) and then "El Condor Pasa" (#6 AC, #18 pop) in 1970. They charted again in 1972 with "For Emily, Wherever I May Find Her" (#27 AC, #53 pop), but by that time the two men were on separate career paths. Three years later Simon brought them back together to do a song that casual listeners may think involves warm reminiscences of Simon's youth, but in fact does not.

"That song isn't about me," Simon told Timothy White in *Rock Lives*. "It isn't autobiographical in any sense. The song is about someone who hates the town he grew up in. Somebody happy to get out. I don't know where the idea came from.

"It originally was a song I was writing for Artie [Garfunkel]. I was gonna write a song for his new album, and I told him it would be a nasty song, because he was singing too many sweet songs. It seemed like a good concept for him. As I was teaching it to him, we would be, aaah, harmonizing. So he said, 'Hey, why don't you do this song with me on the record?' So I said, 'Yeah, sure, why not.'"

"My Little Town" reached #9 on the Hot 100 the week of December 13, 1975. The resulting production ended up on 1975 solo LPs of both Paul Simon (*Still Crazy After All These Years*) and Art Garfunkel (*Break Away*), and solo follow-ups from both artists also hit #1 AC in 1976. For Garfunkel's 45, see 288—"Break Away," and for Simon's single, see 289—"50 Ways to Leave Your Lover."

The duo reunited one more time in the studio in 1977. The result was another #1 AC hit for them in 1978 along with James Taylor [see 344—"What a Wonderful World"].

280 Theme From *Mahogany* (Do You Know Where You're Going To)
DIANA ROSS

Motown 1377

December 6, 1975 (1 week)

Writers: Michael Masser, Gerry Goffin

Producer: Michael Masser

In 1975 Diana Ross followed her Oscar-nominated performance in *Lady Sings the Blues* with *Mahogany*, a box office hit which nonetheless produced a lot of unhappy memories for participants. Critics hated the soap opera storyline and gave mixed reviews to the acting, original director Tony Richardson left after Motown head Berry Gordy decided he could do a better job as director, Gordy and Ross fought vehemently during filming and left with a serious rift in their personal and professional relationships to each other. . .you name it. Even the movie's theme song, despite its wide popularity and critical praise, was controversial.

As J. Randy Taraborrelli wrote in his book *Call Her Miss Ross*, "Prior to [the single's] release, Gordy and Michael Masser, who also composed the soundtrack to the film, argued over the music mix; Gordy wanted one version released and Masser another. As a last resort, Masser snuck into the recording studio and erased the version Gordy liked. At first Berry was furious, but then he began to laugh. 'That little blond s**t-head,' he said with a grin. 'Okay. Release his version.'"

That disagreement was a minor snag considering what happened next. After topping the AC chart in late December and doing the same on the Hot 100 the week of January 24, 1976, as well as making #14 R&B, the Academy of Motion Picture Arts and Sciences announced that the song was "qualitatively ineligible" to be considered for nomination for Best Song from a movie. Protests by music executives eventually got the decision reversed, but the song lost to "I'm Easy" [see 306].

As for Ross's movie career, the film she did after *Mahogany*, the 1978 adaptation of the hit Broadway musical *The Wiz*, was a huge financial flop, and her performance as Dorothy was panned by most critics. To date, Ross has not appeared in another film.

But "Theme From *Mahogany*" did give her a second tune to top both the AC and pop charts after "Touch Me in the Morning" [see 197] and her third #1 AC hit. She continued to make both listings regularly through the rest of the 1970s, although her highest-charting AC single in that period, 1976's "I Thought It Took a Little Time (But Today I Fell in Love)," made #4 AC while only getting to #47 pop.

Incidentally, for a time after the record's release, "Do you know where you're going to?" was a frequently heard gag question used by those who worked for "The Boss" (Ross's nickname in the business) and even by Ross herself. Ross may not have known it then, but one place she was going to—albeit six years later—was back on top of the AC and pop chart with the biggest hit of her career [see 409—"Endless Love"].

281 I Write the Songs
BARRY MANILOW

Arista 0157

December 13, 1975 (2 weeks)

Writer: Bruce Johnston

Producers: Ron Dante, Barry Manilow

Probably no other song created so much dissension between Barry Manilow and Clive Davis, the president of Manilow's label Arista Records, as "I Write the Songs." After the success of "Mandy" [see 241] Manilow had vowed that he would sing only tunes he had written, but Davis had different ideas, and he sent Bruce Johnston's composition "I Write the Songs" to Manilow.

"I began writing the words to 'I Write the Songs' while driving on the San Diego Freeway and then I rushed home to see if I could add some verses and a bridge," Bruce Johnston is quoted in the liner notes to Manilow's anthology *The Complete Collection and Then Some.* "I put it all together and found that I'd written a song about where I think music comes from."

While working on his second album at his apartment in August of 1975, Manilow received several versions of "I Write the Songs" from Davis via a messenger. "Attached was a note saying what huge potential the song had for me," recalled Manilow in his autobiography, *Sweet Life.* "Three artists had already recorded the song, with no success. I listened as its writer Bruce Johnston sang it, then as David Cassidy sang it and finally the Captain and Tennille's version.

"It was an intriguing song. The melody was simple but the lyric was ambitious. It gave credit to 'music' for having written every song. 'I am music, and I write the songs,' the lyric went. I liked that. . . .The problem with the song was that if you didn't listen carefully to the lyric, you would think that the singer was singing about himself. It could be misinterpreted as a monumental ego trip."

A month later, Manilow met with Davis and argued, "Clive, I can't do this song!". . .They'll think I'm bragging!" To which Davis shot back, "Barry, it's a major hit record for you. Nobody will think you're bragging. And even if they do, you *do* write songs that make the young girls cry."

Not wanting to jeopardize his career over the matter, Manilow recorded the song. "Ron [Dante] and I used every commercial trick we could think of on it. I changed keys three times, the orchestra was huge, we used tons of background vocals, and I hit the highest note I've ever sung at the end. To this day, when I listen to that song, I swell with pride at our work on the record."

"I Write the Songs" became Manilow's second #1 AC and pop hit after "Mandy." It rode atop the Hot 100 the week of January 17, 1976. It received Grammy nominations for Record of the Year and Song of the Year and won for the latter category.

And, in light of its success, Manilow dropped his "no covers" policy. In fact, of his 13 #1 AC hits, Manilow wrote only three.

282 Country Boy (You Got Your Feet in L.A.)
GLEN CAMPBELL

Capitol 4155

December 27, 1975 (1 week)

Writers: Dennis Lambert, Brian Potter

Producers: Dennis Lambert, Brian Potter

Glen Campbell's production team of Dennis Lambert and Brian Potter specifically wrote "Country Boy (You Got Your Feet in L.A.)" for him to record. He loved the biographical tune ("I still do that on stage," he said), and so did AC listeners, who made it his first consecutive #1 AC entry following the success of "Rhinestone Cowboy" [see 268]. It progressed almost as well on the country and pop listings, halting at #3 country and #11 pop in the summer of 1975. Campbell also received a Grammy nomination for Best Male Country Vocal Performance for his work on the tune.

Campbell really was a country boy with his feet in Los Angeles. He grew up in Arkansas, the youngest of seven sons, and proved to be so proficient on the guitar that he could be heard on local radio at age 6. He did some touring with various bands before arriving in Hollywood by 1960 and becoming a member of the Champs instrumental group of "Tequila" fame. He remained based in Los Angeles the next two decades, during which time he went from being a background guitar player to a familiar personality in several media, including a few movies (he acted alongside John Wayne in *True Grit* in 1969).

Prior to "Rhinestone Cowboy" and "Country Boy (You Got Your Feet in L.A.)," Campbell's popularity did decline somewhat. He still made the charts, but his singles were not matching the success rate of the previous three years when he topped the AC and country listings several times. The best he could manage on the Hot 100 was #45 in 1973 with "I Knew Jesus (Before He Was a Star)," which also made #26 AC and #48 country. His AC high was #13 in 1974 with "Houston (I'm Comin' to See You)," which went to #20 country and #68 pop. He did his biggest chart number on the country slate in 1973 with "Bonaparte's Retreat," which also made #42 AC. However, the latter single didn't make the Hot 100, the first single of Campbell's since 1967 that had failed to do so. But in 1995 "Rhinestone Cowboy" and "Country Boy (You Got Your Feet in L.A.)" were proof that Campbell was back in hit form.

Campbell said of Lambert and Potter, the producers of "Rhinestone Cowboy" and "Country Boy (You Got Your Feet in L.A.)": "They were great. But they made a mistake. They made a track to a song before I heard it first." The ultimate result of their decision to plan a record for Campbell without prior approval was that Campbell and the duo parted company. But before that happened, Capitol released one more single produced by them which made #1 AC [see 297—"Don't Pull Your Love/Then You Can Tell Me Goodbye"].

1976

283 Times of Your Life

PAUL ANKA

United Artists 737

January 3, 1976 (1 week)

Writers: William M. Lane, Roger S. Nichols

Producer: Bob Skaff

Anyone watching TV or listening to the radio in 1975 likely heard "Times of Your Life" as part of a Kodak commercial on the former and a single on the latter. It was the first time a song popularized by an advertising campaign led to a #1 AC hit.

Recalling the song's history, Paul Anka said, "The commercial came first. I met with Kodak and went through a bunch of songs with them. . . .We talked about the philosophy of the campaign. We knew it was the 'times of your life' campaign which was the philosophy, so we went from there."

Kodak may have planned for "Times of Your Life" just to be a pleasant way to sell film, but Anka had bigger plans for the tune. "I thought. . .we had a chance to hit with it as a single," he said. His instincts proved right, as "Times of Your Life" became an AC and pop hit, reaching #7 on the Hot 100 the week of February 7, 1976. The tune became a standard part of his act as well. "It's a big, big portion of my show, especially in places like Singapore, Hong Kong. In Asia it was a huge, huge success," he noted. During his act, the song plays while film of him and his family comes on screen. In effect, it's Anka recalling the times of his life for his fans.

Anka was born in Ottawa, Canada, on July 30, 1941. He began recording in 1956 and hit the following year with "Diana," which went to #1 pop. He had several more pop hits through 1963, then disappeared from the chart for six years. Luckily, unlike some of his contemporary "teen idols," Anka had cultivated a stage act appealing to adults which kept him busy during the lean years. He began playing Las Vegas in 1958 and was still there 40 years later.

Anka's first AC was "Goodnight My Love" (#2 in 1969). He had a few more entries through "Do I Love You" (#14 in 1971). He was then quiet on the chart until 1974, when "(You're) Having My Baby" went to #5 AC and #1 pop. With Odia Coates, his singing partner from "(You're) Having My Baby," Anka notched up three more hits before "Times of Your Life"—"One Man Woman/One Woman Man" (#5 AC, #7 pop) in 1974 and "I Don't Like to Sleep Alone" (#8 AC and pop), and "(I Believe) There's Nothing Stronger Than Our Love" (#3 AC, #15 pop) in 1975.

His last pop entry was "Hold Me 'Til the Mornin' Comes," which hit #40 pop and #2 AC in 1983. He hit the AC chart last with "Second Chance," which made #14 AC in 1984. He continued recording in the 1990s, with many releases geared to the Spanish-language market. He released his 123rd LP in 1998 and is still a popular nightclub performer.

284 Fly Away

JOHN DENVER

RCA 10517

January 10, 1976 (2 weeks nonconsecutive)

Writer: John Denver

Producer: Milt Okun

When John Denver created "Fly Away," he asked Olivia Newton-John to add a backing vocal to enhance its sound. Given that her sound was just as familiar in pop and country circles as Denver's was, listeners could easily identify the woman singing the title phrase in response to Denver, and her contribution no doubt helped "Fly Away" to become a smash. Besides hitting #1 AC, "Fly Away" soared to #13 pop and #12 country.

Naturally, the high profiles of the two artists fueled rumors of a possible romance. Asked by Marcia Seligson of *Playboy* about the speculation that he and Newton-John were having an affair, Denver said, "I heard that once and didn't hear anything more about it. Not a bad notion." (He was joking, of course.)

By the time "Fly Away" came out, *Newsweek* announced that "John Denver, at 32, is the most popular singer in America." But his appeal was not limited to records. His friendly face and pleasant demeanor were perfect for television, and in the early 1970s he not only played on the traditional music variety series and specials but also served as guest host on a few of them, including *The Midnight Special* and *The Tonight Show Starring Johnny Carson*. He also got dramatic roles in such series as *McCloud* and *Owen Marshall, Counselor at Law*, and his music was featured on documentaries and other shows. In 1974 he even wrote and sang the theme song for ABC-TV's short-lived dramatic series *The New Land*.

ABC executives, wanting to capitalize on Denver's popularity, offered him the chance to host his own weekly variety series. As Denver preferred touring, he turned down the offer but did do four music specials for them, one of which, "An Evening With John Denver," won the Emmy in 1975 for Best Musical Variety Special. And there were more TV appearances to come in the late 1970s.

Shortly after "Fly Away" came out in late 1975, Denver released the Yuletide single "Christmas for Cowboys," which made only #58 pop and never appeared on the AC chart. It appeared on his *Rocky Mountain Christmas* LP of the time, which could also be purchased with the *Windsong* LP, which contained "Fly Away," in an album package called the *John Denver Gift Pak*. An earlier Christmas tune, 1973's "Please, Daddy," had made #69 pop but got no AC action. Denver's most successful Noel-themed project which nonetheless failed to make the AC chart was his 1979 album with the Muppets, the certified platinum *A Christmas Together*. The Muppets and Denver reteamed a few years later for a similar LP, *Rocky Mountain Holiday*.

Flying away from the 1975–76 Christmas season, Denver continued to do well, getting his next #1 AC hit with "Looking for Space" [see 294].

285 Let It Shine/He Ain't Heavy... He's My Brother

OLIVIA NEWTON-JOHN

MCA 40495

January 17, 1976 (2 weeks)

Writers: Linda Hargrove (1st); Bobby Russell, Bobby Scott (2nd)

Producer: John Farrar

The girl who sang backgrounds on "Fly Away" followed it onto the #1 AC slot with her own double-sided hit. Producer John Farrar recalled that it had not been originally intended for both sides of Olivia Newton-John's last single of 1975 (the recent composition, "Let It Shine," backed with a remake of an older hit, "He Ain't Heavy. . .He's My Brother") to get airplay on both sides, but they did nonetheless, on both the pop and AC charts. "That was a surprise," Farrar said.

"Let It Shine" was by Linda Hargrove, a Nashville songwriter. "That was something that came in the mail, unsolicited," Farrar said. He and Newton-John liked it enough to give it a try on her *Clearly Love* album.

But getting airplay at the same time was "He Ain't Heavy. . .He's My Brother," a tune inspired by the slogan used for Father Flanagan's Boys Town orphanage in Nebraska. The first to have success with the song in America were the Hollies, who took it to #7 pop in early 1970. At the end of that year Neil Diamond released his own version, getting to #20 pop plus #4 AC.

"I think Olivia wanted to do that," Farrar said. "We both liked it, thought it was a great song." They were not alone, as Bill Medley also redid the tune in 1988 and got to #49 AC with it.

The one-two punch of "Let It Shine" and "He Ain't Heavy. . .He's My Brother" resulted in Newton-John's fifth consecutive #1 AC hit and sixth overall #1 AC 45, but on the pop chart it was a different story, as the single struggled to #30. It was her worst chart performance there since "Banks of the Ohio" made #94 in 1971. On the country chart "Let It Shine" hit #5, but the other side did not. However, "He Ain't Heavy. . .He's My Brother" did make the country chart two years later in a cover by June Neyman which made #93. And interestingly, Newton-John's greatest hits album in 1977 contained "Let It Shine" but not "He Ain't Heavy. . . ."

The relative pop failure of the double-sided single didn't have much effect on Newton-John's overall career, which remained in high gear throughout 1976 and included headlining her first TV variety special on ABC. And of course she had a hammerlock on the AC chart. Her next single, "Come On Over" [see 295], gave Newton-John her sixth consecutive #1 AC hit, tying her with fellow Australian Helen Reddy, and she beat Reddy before the year was out with an unprecedented seventh #1 AC hit in a row, "Don't Stop Believin'" [see 315].

286 Breaking Up Is Hard to Do

NEIL SEDAKA

Rocket 40500

February 7, 1976 (1 week)

Writers: Howard Greenfield (words), Neil Sedaka (music)

Producers: Neil Sedaka, Robert Appere

The idea of doing Neil Sedaka's upbeat #1 pop and #12 R&B hit of 1962, "Breaking Up Is Hard to Do," as a ballad grew out of a request from Lenny Welch, the artist best known for his 1963 hit "Since I Fell for You" (#3 AC, #4 pop), that Sedaka write a song for him. Sedaka, finding that "Breaking Up. . ." worked well at a slower tempo, gave the more deliberate rendition to Welch, and it reached #8 AC, #27 R&B, and #34 pop in 1970.

Then Sedaka put the song into his act as an encore, and, he remembered, "The audience reaction was very exciting." In 1975, during his American comeback, he decided to record the song himself. At the time he was the opening act for the Carpenters, and, noted Sedaka, "Richard Carpenter heard it and very graciously said he would arrange the string section."

Sedaka's ballad redo of "Breaking Up Is Hard to Do" went to #8 pop the week of February 21, 1976, in addition to #1 AC. It was the first time a singer had two different versions of the same song make the pop top 10. It also had the unique distinction of getting Grammy nominations for Best Rock and Roll Recording of 1962 and Song of the Year of 1976. (The only Grammy award Sedaka actually got was for Record of the Year for "Love Will Keep Us Together.") Sedaka's perspective on the two versions was "As a rock and roll song it was fine and lovely and sweet, but it showed more maturity to do it as a ballad."

Other versions of "Breaking Up Is Hard to Do" to make the charts were from the Happenings (#67 pop in 1968), the Partridge Family (#28 pop and #30 AC in 1972), Heaven Bound with Tony Scotti (#101 bubbling under in 1972), and Jimmy Bee (#91 R&B in 1976).

After "Breaking Up Is Hard to Do" Sedaka lost some of his comeback momentum. He had no further #1 AC or top 10 pop hits and found himself off both charts for three years. In 1980 a duet with his daughter Dara, "Should've Never Let You Go," did get to #3 AC and #19 pop, but he had no other Hot 100 entries after that and had only three other AC singles over the next four years, with the last being "Rhythm of the Rain" at #37 in 1984.

But Sedaka had an established name in the pop music field and continued to maintain a busy presence touring, though recording infrequently, in the 1980s and 1990s. "I'm still working six to seven months a year. I do concerts, casinos," he said. In addition to his U.S. tours, he tours most often in Great Britain, Australia, and Italy, when not at home in New York City. As for what Sedaka hopes to accomplish as the year 2000 approaches, he said, "I live it day to day. I'm still glad people come out to see me."

287 Paloma Blanca

THE GEORGE BAKER SELECTION

Warner 8115

February 14, 1976 (1 week)

Writer: Johannes Bowens

Producer: Hans Bouwens

George Baker was the stage name of Dutch singer and songwriter Hans Bouwens, born on December 8, 1944. He served as the vocalist, guitarist, pianist, flautist, organist, and mandolin player for his sextet, the George Baker Selection, so-named in 1969 after being called Soul Invention for two years before that. The group scored its first hit in America in 1970 with "Little Green Bag," which went to #21 pop. The follow-up, "Dear Ann," made #93 pop in mid-1970, and in the fall of 1970 came "I Wanna Love You," which bubbled under to #103.

But when the group's American distributor, Colossus Records, went bankrupt in 1971, other U.S. labels had little interest in trying the group's releases in the United States. By 1974, however, the George Baker Selection had deemphasized its rock influences in favor of a more middle-of-the-road approach. This paid off handsomely the next year when

"Paloma Blanca" (Spanish for "white dove") made the U.S. charts in late 1975, peaking at #1 AC, #26 pop, and even #33 country. It was #1 in Holland, Austria, Belgium, Germany, New Zealand, South Africa, and Sweden, and also sold well in Great Britain, France, and Italy.

Jeanne Bot, who operates the official Internet Web site for the George Baker Selection along with her husband Cor Bot in Holland, recalled the creation of that tune: "George Baker always said he wrote 'Paloma Blanca' in ten minutes. He was playing on his recorder and so he found the melody of 'Paloma Blanca.' I think it became a hit across the world because the melody is so lovely; when you hear it you can't just sit down, and when you're not in the mood, this song will cheer you up."

There have been at least 125 covers of "Paloma Blanca," but the one known best in most parts of the world is undoubtedly the George Baker Selection version. Although the group had no other chart entries in America after the hit fell off the listings, they were still active in the late 1990s, mainly in their native Holland, and by that time claimed to have sold more than 20 million records worldwide. The member who has lasted the longest in Selection, besides Bouwens, is drummer Jan Hop.

"At this moment George Baker still gives his shows, he writes songs for other artists and he's working in his own studio," said Bot. "So, you see, he is very busy, and we are very happy that we can go to his shows and see him singing. He's a great artist."

288 Break Away
ART GARFUNKEL

Columbia 10273

February 21, 1976 (1 week)

Writers: Benny Gallagher, Graham Lyle

Producer: Richard Perry

In their book *The Record Producers* John Tobler and Stuart Grundy quote Richard Perry as having a very favorable opinion of his work with Art Garfunkel on the latter's *Break Away* album. "In many ways, that album is my favorite of all the albums that I've made, my personal favorite. . ., the only one that I consistently like to take with me when I travel. It has such a wonderful consistency of mood—we set out to do a 'make out' album, a real old-fashioned 'make out' album for teenagers, although it certainly isn't teenage music, but something that would have a consistency of mood.

"I don't think I've ever really done an album quite like that, with no intentional uptempo numbers, and in fact, I usually like to combine a great deal of variety in my albums, but this was one where the variety had to be limited from the standpoint that it really couldn't get too raucous, or even approach it, and I discovered that those are the kind of albums that I enjoy listening to the most. On some classical albums that they have, I edit out the robust sections. . .but listening back to Artie's album, it still holds up wonderfully for me."

The first release from *Break Away* was not the title tune, but a remake of "I Only Have Eyes for You" [see 276], followed by his reunion duet with Paul Simon, "My Little Town" [see 279]. "Break Away" came next, complete with beautiful background vocals supplied by David Crosby and Graham Nash. While it topped the AC chart, it was a relative disappointment on the pop listing, getting only to #39.

A year later, Garfunkel came out with another single, "Crying in My Sleep," which did poorly, getting to just #25 AC without cracking the Hot 100. He rebounded in 1978 with a song he cut with Simon and James Taylor [see 344—"(What a) Wonderful World"], but singing alone he generated little interest on the pop charts thereafter. In 1979 his "In a Little While (I'll Be on My Way)" got only to #12 AC without registering on the pop side, while his remake of "Since I Don't Have You" made #5 AC but just #53 pop.

Garfunkel had his last Hot 100 entry in 1981 with "A Heart in New York" at #66, which also made #10 AC. After that his only major AC entry, in 1988, was yet another remake of an old tune, "So Much in Love," at #11.

289 50 Ways to Leave Your Lover
PAUL SIMON

Columbia 10270

February 28, 1976 (2 weeks)

Writer: Paul Simon

Producers: Paul Simon, Phil Ramone

Art Garfunkel's old partner Paul Simon followed him at #1 AC with a song much more funky than "Break Away." Opening with a military drumroll, "50 Ways to Leave Your Lover" perfectly reflected the volatile up-and-down nature of male-female relations in the 1970s, albeit in a lighthearted manner.

Simon discussed the tune with Timothy White in *Rock Lives.* "I woke up one morning in my apartment on Central Park, and the opening words just popped into my mind: 'The problem is all inside your head, she said to me. . .' That was the first thing I thought of. So I just started building on that line. It was the last song I wrote for the album, and I wrote it with a Rhythm Ace, one of those electronic drum machines, so maybe that's how it got that sing-sing 'Make a new plan Stan, don't need to be coy Roy' quality. It's basically a nonsense song."

One writer's nonsense was the general public's charm as "50 Ways to Leave Your Lover" topped the AC and pop music charts, doing so on the latter for three weeks starting February 7, 1976. Two covers of the song made the country chart, one by Bob Yarborough in 1976 which went to #85, and another by Sonny Curtis in 1980 which reached #70.

"50 Ways to Leave Your Lover" won Simon a Grammy nomination for Record of the Year of 1976, the year after Simon won Grammys for Album of the Year and Best Male Pop Vocal Performance from the LP which contained the single, *Still Crazy After All These Years.* The reason for the single's later nomination was that it was released after the eligibility period for the 1975 awards. *Still Crazy After All These Years* also went to #1 on the album chart the week of December 6, 1975.

Despite its evident commercial appeal, "50 Ways to Leave Your Lover" was not the first or even the second single off *Still Crazy After All These Years.* The first 45 released was "Gone at Last" with Phoebe Snow [see 249—"Poetry Man"] and the Jessy Dixon Singers, which went to #9 AC and #23 pop in 1975, followed by "My Little Town," [see 279], which went on both Simon's LP and Garfunkel's *Break Away* album. After "50 Ways to Leave Your Lover," the fourth single released from the LP was its title tune, which went to #5 AC and #40 pop in 1976.

In 1977 Simon had another hit with "Slip Slidin' Away" (#4 AC and #5 pop), and returned to #1 AC in 1978 with "(What a) Wonderful World" [see 344]. Surprisingly, he had only one more single on either the top 10 or the pop or AC chart; that was in 1980, when "Late in the Evening" hit #7 AC and #6 pop.

290 Lonely Night (Angel Face)
THE CAPTAIN AND TENNILLE

A&M 1782

March 13, 1976 (1 week)

Writer: Neil Sedaka

Producers: Daryl Dragon, Toni Tennille

The Captain and Tennille went back to Neil Sedaka as the source for their #1 AC hit, "Lonely Night (Angel Face)." The song had first been done by Sedaka on his 1975 album *The Hungry Years*, but like the other Sedaka song done by the Captain and Tennille, "Love Will Keep Us Together" [see 263], it was not released as a single. However, when the Captain and Tennille did "Lonely Night," they had finally met Sedaka in person, through the co-writer of "Love Will Keep Us Together," Howard Greenfield.

"Howie, when he heard 'Love Will Keep Us Together' and saw it go up the charts, called up A&M and said, 'Who are these people? I want to meet them,'" Toni Tennille recalled. She and husband Daryl Dragon ("the Captain") arranged to get together with Greenfield, who had remained in contact with Sedaka even though they no longer wrote songs together. "I think Neil was at Howard Greenfield's house when we heard it," she said of "Lonely Night." "We just liked the tune, thought it was cute." The Captain and Tennille's version added jungle sounds in the background, which Tennille said makes it rather wild when they involve the audience in the song in concert.

Besides hitting #1 AC, "Lonely Night" peaked at #3 pop for three weeks on the Hot 100 starting March 27, 1976, the first week behind the Four Seasons' "December 1963 (Oh, What a Night)" at #1 and Gary Wright's "Dream Weaver" at #2, and the last two behind Johnnie Taylor's "Disco Lady" at #1 and "Dream Weaver" at #2. Tennille said she didn't believe that Sedaka minded too much having another of his songs covered as a hit by the duo. "Neil had had so many hits over the years done by other artists. But I think in a way he was envious. We certainly gave him credit when we did the songs." (Sedaka told me he likes the Captain and Tennille. "They're lovely people," he said.)

The Captain and Tennille did another Sedaka song as a single, "You Never Done It Like That," which made #14 AC and #10 pop in 1978. It was their first top 10 pop song since 1976's "Muskrat Love" [see 318], and while they had several pop and AC entries in the months between those songs, most made top 10 AC while failing to crack the pop top 60. The exception was "Can't Stop Dancin'," which made #12 AC and #13 pop in 1977. The duo has said the variety series they did on ABC-TV from September 20, 1976 through March 14, 1977, which they hated, was partly to blame for their diminished record sales during that time. (Incidentally, that show's theme was "Love Will Keep Us Together.")

But that's getting ahead of the story, for after "Lonely Night," the Captain and Tennille returned to #1 AC with "Shop Around" [see 300].

291 Venus
FRANKIE AVALON

De-Lite 1578

March 20, 1976 (1 week)

Writer: Ed Marshall

Producer: Billy Terrell

In the 1950s Frankie Avalon, born Francis Avallone in Philadelphia on September 18, 1939, had several top 10 hits, the biggest being "Venus," which hit #1 pop for five weeks starting March 9, 1959, plus made #10 R&B. In the 1960s he concentrated on film work as his music career died down, although one of his last hits, "You Are Mine" in 1962, made the AC chart at #7 as well as #26 pop. He was most visible professionally as an actor in beach party movies with Annette Funicello. But in the 1970s Avalon found himself yesterday's news, and his early efforts to revive his musical career were initially met with indifference.

"Prior to [Paul] Anka's comeback the two of us tried to make a joint deal with some companies with him producing and writing and me singing," Avalon told Dennis Hunt of the *Los Angeles Times*. "But they all turned us down." Then Anka scored with "You're Having My Baby" in 1974, and Avalon considered other options, including a contract to work six days a week for seven months in Hawaii, which he nearly took. But he decided to hold out for another chance to go into the recording studio.

"Fourteen different labels passed on me, and then Billy Terrell of DeLite Records came up with the idea of remaking 'Venus' disco style," he told Bob Gilbert and Gary Theroux in *The Top Ten*. "I wasn't too thrilled about it. I really didn't want to touch that song. It was such a big record, and such a good record. How do you top a song like that?"

Nonetheless, the new "Venus" did well enough to reach #1 AC, #46 pop, and #97 R&B. It was his only other AC appearance apart from "You Are Mine" and his first entry on any singles chart since 1962. Avalon's final verdict on the tune, quoted in *The Top Ten*, was "It was all right, but I still prefer the original."

Despite his mixed feelings about the 45's success, it did lead to Avalon getting a contract to do an album for DeLite. "It's aimed at the 28- to 40-year-old, middle-of-the-road [MOR] set because 'Venus' is mostly played on MOR stations and that's the audience that I appeal to now," he told Hunt in 1976.

But the LP did not become a hit, and after doing a summer variety series on CBS that year titled *Easy Does It*, Avalon started touring the oldies circuit again, which he was still doing at the end of the 1990s, often appearing with fellow teen idols Fabian and Bobby Rydell. Interestingly, Rydell also made the AC chart in 1976 with a disco redo of one of his old hits, "Sway," but it only went to #27 while failing to make the pop chart.

Johnny Mathis also did a version of "Venus" in 1968. It bubbled under to #111.

292 Only Love Is Real

CAROLE KING

Ode 66119

March 27, 1976 (1 week)

Writer: Carole King

Producer: Lou Adler

"Sounds a bit like 'It's Too Late,'" wrote an anonymous *Billboard* reviewer in describing Carole King's newest single in 1976, "Only Love Is Real." Indeed "Only Love Is Real," like the earlier release, did reach the top of the AC chart, but its peak of #28 pop was considered a disappointment at the time. Producer Lou Adler later took some of the blame for the relative failure of both the single and the album from which it came, *Thoroughbred*.

"I didn't think *Thoroughbred* had a definite direction," Adler said in the liner notes to *Carole King: A Natural Woman*. "To tell you the truth, as a producer, I just didn't have a real fix on all the songs. We were also using a lot of people who weren't with her before, and even though they were good players, the sessions didn't seem as comfortable as they had in the past." Adler added, "We didn't come out of *Thoroughbred* with a strong single. Truth is, by that time, Carole and I had probably lost whatever chemistry that had made us a good match for so many years."

After "Only Love Is Real" came out, the next single from *Thoroughbred* emerged. "High out of Time" was the worst-performing King single since the 1960s, her first song since "It's Too Late" not to crack the pop top 40 or the AC top 10. It went to #40 AC and #76 pop in the middle of 1976.

Working apart from Adler, King's recording career began to fizzle in the late 1970s. "Hard Rock Cafe" did well enough to go to #8 AC and #30 pop in 1977, but 1977's "Simple Things" and "Morning Sun" missed the Hot 100 completely while going to only #37 and #43, respectively, on the AC chart. She bounced back in 1980 with a slower-paced remake of a tune she co-wrote for the Chiffons in the 1960s, "One Fine Day," which went to #11 AC and #12 pop, but it was a brief reversal of fortune for her. She had one more pop entry, 1982's "One to One," which hit #45 on the Hot 100 while going to #20 AC, and got a few more songs onto the AC chart into the 1990s.

But King had nothing to worry about in terms of respect from her peers. In 1990 she was voted into the Rock and Roll Hall of Fame, and in 1995 singers as varied as Rod Stewart to Celine Dion recorded tunes from her biggest album on the LP *Tapestry Revisited—A Tribute to Carole King*. She was still popping up for public appearances in the 1990s, but King surely knows that she really doesn't need to do anything else professionally to ensure her place in the musical canon as one of the biggest and best singer/song-writers of the 20th century.

293 There's a Kind of Hush (All Over the World)

THE CARPENTERS

A&M 1800

April 3, 1976 (2 weeks)

Writers: Les Reed, Geoff Stephens

Producer: Richard Carpenter

Herman's Hermits never had an AC single, but anyone listening to pop music during the mid-1960s could hardly miss them. The quintet from Manchester, England, led by singer Peter "Herman" Noone along with bassist Karl Green, guitarists Keith Hopwood and Derek Leckenby, and drummer Barry Whitwam, was even more popular in America than in their native country, scoring two #1 pop hits in 1965 ("Mrs. Brown You've Got a Lovely Daughter" and "I'm Henry VIII, I Am") and 14 top 20 pop hits, from 1964's "I'm Into Something Good" to 1967's "Don't Go Out in the Rain (You're Going to Melt)." The next to last of those top 20 hits was "There's a Kind of Hush," which made #4 pop in the spring of 1967.

Like all Herman's Hermits hits, "There's a Kind of Hush" came from writers outside the group, in this case Les

Reed and Geoff Stephens, who co-wrote several other tunes together, including "Daughter of Darkness" for Tom Jones [see 134].

The Carpenters' "There's a Kind of Hush (All Over the World)" was a fairly faithful cover of the Hermits version, though they did add the second line of the chorus in parentheses to distinguish it from the original. It made #12 pop as well as #1 AC and would be the last top 20 pop hit for the duo until "Touch Me When We're Dancing" in 1981 [see 408]. Despite its relatively high chart showing, Richard Carpenter must not have thought too highly of the remake, for it did not make *From the Top*, the 1991 four-CD authorized Carpenters anthology, while other, less successful tunes did.

By the time Brian Collins' cover of "There's a Kind of Hush" went to #47 country (the last time it charted), Herman's Hermits were history. Peter Noone did make the AC chart as a soloist, first in 1974 with "Meet Me on the Corner Down at Joe's Cafe" at #22 and then 15 years later with a remake of his old group's first hit, "I'm Into Something Good," from the movie *The Naked Gun*, which went to #19.

As for the Carpenters, they had their sixth consecutive and 14th overall #1 AC hit with their next release after "There's a Kind of Hush," "I Need to Be in Love" [see 304]. Somewhat surprisingly, that single would be only the third #1 AC hit with a writing credit for Richard Carpenter, in spite of much praise for his work in the studio. However, he did produce the majority of the Carpenters singles after 1972.

294 Looking for Space

JOHN DENVER

RCA 10586

April 17, 1976 (1 week)

Writer: John Denver

Producer: Milt Okun

"It's about looking for the definition of who you are, by finding out where you are, not only physically, but mentally and emotionally," John Denver told Craig Rosen in *The Billboard Book of Number One Albums* about "Looking for Space." The tune, which also went to #29 pop and #30 country, would have been the third consecutive #1 AC single for Denver, but for a Christmas single after "Fly Away," which did not chart [see 284].

The album on which "Looking for Space" appeared, *Windsong*, went to #1 on the LP chart the weeks of October 18 and 25, 1975. The LP's title became the name of a fledgling label Denver established to expose new talent, but its main success story was the Starland Vocal Band, whose "Afternoon Delight" hit #5 AC and #1 pop in 1976 and won them the Grammy for Best New Artist (much to Grammy voters' dismay, they had few chart entries after that).

Despite the fact that "Looking for Space" was Denver's seventh #1 AC hit, close observers might remember that he had spent three years of on-and-off acceptance on the charts before hitting his stride in 1974. He debuted on the AC and pop charts in 1971 with "Take Me Home, Country Roads" (backed by Bill Danoff and Taffy Nivert, later of the Starland Vocal Band) at #3 AC and #2 pop. Efforts to follow it over the next year were mixed at best, with 1971's "Friends With You" at #4 AC and #47 pop, followed by "Everyday" at #21 AC and #81 pop and "Goodbye Again" at #23 AC and #88 pop in 1972.

He did not have a real hit again until late 1972, when "Rocky Mountain High" came out and reached #3 AC and #9 pop, but that was followed by another mediocre year, in which "I'd Rather Be a Cowboy" made #25 AC and #62 pop, while "Farewell Andromeda (Welcome to My Morning)" got to #20 AC and #89 pop. Then came "Sunshine on My Shoulders" [see 213], and Denver's hot streak began.

The follow-up to "Looking for Space," "It Makes Me Giggle," broke Denver's run of #1 AC hits, stopping at #9 AC (it also made #60 pop). As the song was the leadoff on Denver's 1976 album *Spirit*, its poor chart performance was a disappointment. The next single from the LP, "Like a Sad Song," got him back to #1 AC [see 316]. But by then, Denver's high standing in the music business had begun to fall, and he was never again to chart consecutive #1 AC hits.

295 Come On Over
OLIVIA NEWTON-JOHN

MCA 40525

April 24, 1976 (1 week)

Writers: Barry Gibb, Robin Gibb

Producer: John Farrar

In January of 1976 John Denver's "Fly Away" [see 284] was bumped from the top of the AC chart by Olivia Newton-John's combination of "Let It Shine" backed with "He Ain't Heavy. . .He's My Brother," and three months later she did it again, knocking off his "Looking for Space" with "Come On Over," from the Bee Gees' 1975 album, *Main Course*. This time out, Newton-John's single reached a higher peak on the pop chart by stopping at #23, which was also a seven-point improvement over her last single.

Although Newton-John had never worked directly with the Bee Gees (the *brothers Gibb*) on a single, they admired each other's work. There were also some similarities between the two. Both Newton-John and the Gibb brothers had been born in Great Britain yet had grown up in Australia, and the harmonies of both found favor with American record buyers many times during the 1970s. In addition, Newton-John recorded "I Can't Help It" with the Bee Gees' youngest brother Andy in 1980 and got to #8 AC and #12 pop.

"I think that was on the [Bee Gees'] *Main Course* album, which we used to love to play on the tour bus," said John Farrar. Indeed, "Come On Over" was on *Main Course* but did not get released as a single; "Jive Talkin'," "Nights on Broadway" and "Fanny (Be Tender With My Love)" came out instead, letting Newton-John release her own version.

Newton-John told Gerry Wood in *Billboard* that her singing on "Come On Over" was a conscious effort to stretch beyond the breathy vocal style which had characterized much of her earlier work. "I really love that song—and I'm getting confidence in doing songs like that. In each album I try to add something different. But I'd also like to keep what I established myself with. Because I don't use all my voice, people think that I have much less voice than I actually use. On the next album I show more voice than ever before."

"Come On Over" went to #5 country in addition to its AC and pop standings. It also became the title tune of an album which Farrar would rather forget, from a period he would rather forget. Asked what he thought the problem was he and Newton-John's crew were facing at the time, he said, "I think the material. It was like we had this huge peak and went into a valley for awhile." He also felt it was due to overexposure of Newton-John's singles on the AC, country, and pop airwaves.

But AC programmers did not seem to share Farrar's negative feelings, as Newton-John got yet another #1 hit on the chart before the end of 1976 [see 313—"Don't Stop Believin'"].

296 Tryin' to Get the Feeling Again
BARRY MANILOW

Arista 0172

May 1, 1976 (1 week)

Writer: David Pomeranz

Producers: Ron Dante, Barry Manilow

"Tryin' to Get the Feelin' Again" was the title song of Barry Manilow's third LP, but the first single released from that album was "I Write the Songs" [see 281]. Recalling "Tryin' to Get the Feelin' Again" in Manilow's anthology *The Complete Collection and Then Some. . .*, composer David Pomeranz noted that he wrote the tune in "moody San Francisco" in 1974.

Said Pomeranz: "I liked the main melody from the start—it just felt right. I worked like the devil on the lyric. I wrote it at home, while driving, at the piano, on the roof, in bathrooms, at parties—I think I was even still working on it after Barry had already put it in his show! It was so emotional for me that, for a while, I didn't think I could play or sing it without crying. It's good when that sort of thing happens—makes it all worthwhile."

Pomeranz recorded it on his debut LP in 1976, but found it overshadowed by Manilow's cover. "This is another one of those rare cuts that was done all together, live, and in a few takes," Manilow wrote in his anthology. "It seems to have an urgency and a 'liveness' that many of the other records don't have." (Actually, it was not all that "live": it was edited, and lost in the released single was a bridge mentioning "meditation and poem.")

As a single, "Tryin' to Get the Feelin' Again" went to #10 the weeks of May 22 and 29, 1976. On the AC chart, it became the second of five consecutive #1 hits for Manilow. That streak could have been eight if "Could It Be Magic" had not faltered at #4 AC between "It's a Miracle" and "I Write the Songs" in 1975 (it finished at #6 pop).

Manilow had actually written and recorded "It Could Be Magic" in 1971 under the pseudonym Featherbed. He composed it on the piano in his Manhattan apartment. "I had been playing Chopin's Prelude in C Minor and took a break," Manilow recounted. "After a glass of wine and dinner, I went back to the piano and wrote 'Could It Be Magic.' When I played back the cassette tape and listened to it, I realized that I had stolen the chord changes for the chorus from Chopin's prelude! Thank goodness the melody and verses were my own."

Manilow sent the song to his collaborator Adrienne Anderson, who worked on the lyric, and then contacted Tony Orlando, who produced it in an up-tempo bubblegum style which Manilow disliked. Nonetheless, he sang on the record. In the mid-1970s, Manilow remade it in more of a classical flavor, and that version became a hit. It was the last single released before the *Tryin' to Get the Feelin' Again* LP came out.

297 Don't Pull Your Love/ Then You Can Tell Me Goodbye

GLEN CAMPBELL

Capitol 4245

May 8, 1976 (1 week)

Writers: Dennis Lambert, Brian Potter (1st);
*   John D. Loudermilk (2nd)*

Producers: Dennis Lambert, Brian Potter

"Don't Pull Your Love/Then You Can Tell Me Goodbye" was the second (and to date the last) medley to top the AC chart, coming seven years after "Aquarius/Let the Sunshine In" [see 115]. Its medley form was sort of a subliminal accident. Glen Campbell had started to do "Don't Pull Your Love" in front of his producers Dennis Lambert and Brian Potter, who had written the tune years earlier. "I was singing it to them on guitar," Campbell recalled. "I wanted to sing it slow, and when I went to the chorus, I sang, 'Kiss me each morning. . . .' I didn't even know that was another song." Campbell unwittingly had segued into the start of "Then You Can Tell Me Goodbye," and Lambert and Potter enjoyed what he did so much that they all decided to record the two tunes together.

Hamilton, Joe Frank and Reynolds originally scored a hit with "Don't Pull Your Love" in 1971, going to #4 both on the AC and pop charts. They later hit #1 on both charts with "Fallin' in Love" [see 271]. Campbell said he believed the trio did appear on his TV show in the early 1970s to sing "Don't Pull Your Love." Sam and Dave also cut the tune in 1971 and went to #36 R&B and #102 bubbling under.

As for "Then You Can Tell Me Goodbye," the nine-member vocal group the Casinos first popularized the tune in 1967, when it reached #6 on the Hot 100. (Campbell said the Casinos definitely did not do his TV show.) The next year Eddy Arnold released a version which made #1 for two weeks on the country chart as well as #6 AC and #84 pop. In 1979 Toby Beau took "Then You Can Tell Me Goodbye" to #7 AC and #57 pop.

The "Don't Pull Your Love/Then You Can Tell Me Goodbye" medley went to #4 country and #27 pop in addition to topping the AC chart. But Campbell said the song might have become an even bigger hit had it been promoted properly. The decision by his then-manager to release the medley as a single without first informing Capitol's promotional department of his intentions made it difficult for Capitol to mount an effective publicity campaign.

"Don't Pull Your Love/Then You Can Tell Me Goodbye" was Campbell's sixth #1 AC hit as well as third consecutive AC chart topper. That string ended with the release of his next tune, "See You on Sunday," which made only #15 AC and #18 country and failed to make the Hot 100. Campbell came back strongly with his next single, which topped the AC, pop, and country charts [see 325—"Southern Nights"].

298 Welcome Back
JOHN SEBASTIAN

Reprise 1349

May 15, 1976 (2 weeks)

Writer: John Sebastian

Producers: Steve Barri, John Sebastian

Designed to exploit the name of the TV series on which it was the theme, the title "Welcome Back" was an apt way to describe how fans of John Sebastian felt about his return to the tops of the charts. As lead singer of the Lovin' Spoonful in the 1960s, he had racked up seven top 10 pop entries, from "Do You Believe in Magic" in 1965 through "Nashville Cats" in 1967 (no Lovin' Spoonful song ever crossed over to the AC chart). But after Sebastian, born in New York City on March 17, 1944, went solo, he experienced a seven-year hitless drought.

Then Alan Sachs, the producer of a new ABC-TV series in 1975 called *Welcome Back, Kotter* starring Gabe Kaplan and a young John Travolta, told his agent he wanted a theme that sounded like the Lovin' Spoonful. Dave Bendet, Sachs' agent, just happened to represent Sebastian as well, and after meeting Sachs and reviewing a description of the show, Sebastian agreed to do a theme.

After rejecting his own inaugural attempt, Sebastian came up with a second effort that pleased everyone enough to become the show's opening and closing song. But there were no plans to make it a single, and it was recorded initially with just one verse. Sebastian was considered past his prime commercially, and his label, Warner Brothers, was thinking of dropping him from its roster until "Welcome Back" became a top request among disc-buying TV viewers.

"What happened was record stores began to call their distributors and say, 'We're getting 10 requests a day for this television theme song—where's the record?'" Sebastian told John DeAngelis in an interview in the July 1997 issue of *Discoveries* magazine. "And they went, 'There is no record.' So they rushed me into the studio." Sebastian cut the tune and several more for an LP called *Welcome Back,* but he felt that rushing into album production ultimately hurt the chances of anything but the single becoming a hit. Indeed, no follow-ups to "Welcome Back" made the AC chart, although one single, "Hideaway," did reach #95 pop later in 1976. As for "Welcome Back" itself, it topped the Hot 100 on the week of May 8, 1976, two weeks before doing the same on the AC chart.

Although the popularity of "Welcome Back" did get Sebastian more work creating music for television and movie projects, it was not until 15 years later, in 1993, that he released another new LP, *Tar Beach.* Four years later, Sebastian, heading a group called the J-Band, came out with another album, *I Want My Roots.* Between these two releases, the Nickelodeon cable channel repeated episodes of *Welcome Back, Kotter,* which ended its TV run in 1979, to modest success.

299 Silly Love Songs
WINGS

Capitol 4256

May 29, 1976 (1 week)

Writer: Paul McCartney

Producer: Paul McCartney

Following the success of "My Love" [see 194], Paul McCartney decided to continue with his group concept and released his singles throughout the 1970s under the Wings title rather than his name. The ones making the AC chart after "My Love" were "Live and Let Die," the theme to the James Bond movie of the same name, which peaked at #8 AC and #2 pop in 1973; "Band on the Run" (#22 AC and #1 pop in 1974); "Sally G" (#7 AC and #17 pop in 1975); and "Listen to What the Man Said" (#8 AC and #1 pop in 1975).

Then, in 1976, came "Silly Love Songs." McCartney recalled the circumstances surrounding the creation of the tune to Tom Mulhern in the July 1990 issue of *Guitar Player* magazine.

"I had been accused around that time of singing too much about love. I said, 'Hey, wait a minute! It's the best thing!' Love definitely beats hate, and it's definitely kind of cool, at least in my book. But it can be perceived as sort of sloppy. "So I wrote this song and asked, 'What's wrong with silly love songs?' I wrote it on holiday in Hawaii. I just had piano and chords, and then I wanted to have a melody on bass. We really pushed the bass and drums right out front. But it drove the song along quite nicely. Pushed it hard. We wanted to make something you could dance to, so you *had* to."

The combination of its tempo changes and overlapping choruses resulted in a final playing time of over five minutes, making it theoretically too long for most radio station programmers at the time. But it was a record by McCartney, who still reigned as one of the hottest artists in 1976, so they gave the song airplay and listeners eagerly bought it up. "Silly Love Songs" peaked at the top of the Hot 100 a week before it did so on the AC chart, and stayed there for five weeks. *Billboard* ranked it as the number one song of the year for 1976.

In addition, the album from which it came, *Wings at the Speed of Sound*, hit #1 the week of April 24, 1976 and stayed there for seven weeks. It contained a follow-up single which also went to #1 AC [see 308—"Let 'Em In"]. Later that year McCartney released a live album from his group's summer tour titled *Wings Over America*, and "Silly Love Songs" was the only cut from *Wings at the Speed of Sound* to be included. Like its predecessor, *Wings Over America* peaked at #1 too, during the week of January 22, 1977.

300 Shop Around
THE CAPTAIN AND TENNILLE

A&M 1817

June 5, 1976 (1 week)

Writer: William Robinson, Berry Gordy

Producers: Daryl Dragon, Toni Tennille

Smokey Robinson originally wrote "Shop Around," which took him 10 minutes to finish, for fellow Motown artist Barrett Strong in 1960, as Strong had recorded one of the label's earliest hits with "Money (That's What I Want)," which went to #23 pop and #2 R&B for six weeks. However, when Motown President Berry Gordy heard "Shop Around," he rearranged the words and music and suggested that Robinson's wife Claudette Rogers sing lead on the song with Robinson's group the Miracles.

A few days after releasing Rogers' vocal version, Gordy awakened her, Robinson, and the rest of the Miracles in the wee hours of the morning and had them come into the Motown studios in Detroit to redo the tune with a faster beat. The new rendition, with Smokey as lead singer, proved to be a hit, giving Motown its first pop top 10 at #2 and its first #1 R&B record in 1961, and even inspired an answer record, Debbie Dean's "Don't Let Him Shop Around," which made #92 pop in 1961.

Fifteen years later, "Shop Around" finally made the AC chart, but in a remake by the Captain and Tennille (Daryl Dragon and his wife, Toni Tennille). Asked who or what inspired them to redo the tune, Tennille said, "Actually, it was Daryl, kind of. He used to play this piece on the piano, very classical actually."

Dragon said he did not really recognize what he was playing when he did the song one day. "I never even listened to the lyrics," he said. But Tennille did, and an idea hit her on how to approach the tune. "I said, 'Why don't we do it from a girl's perspective?'" she recalled.

With that concept in mind, the Captain and Tennille cut "Shop Around" and saw it go to #4 pop as well as #1 AC, peaking on the Hot 100 the week of July 10, 1976. The uptempo song became a favorite in concert for the duo, according to Tennille. "The audience in our show still loves that song and to sing along with it."

Tennille recalled that initially Detroit radio stations refused to give the song airplay "because it was Smokey's tune. But he said, 'Please play it, because it's a hit.'" Tennille, who described Robinson as a "fabulous, fabulous talent," said she and Dragon later met him and he thanked them for their record.

"Shop Around" was the fourth of five #1 AC songs for the Captain and Tennille. The last chart-topper was "Muskrat Love" [see 318].

301 Save Your Kisses for Me

THE BROTHERHOOD OF MAN

Pye 71066

June 12, 1976 (1 week)

Writers: Tony Hiller, Martin Lee, Lee Sheridan

Producer: Michael J. Powell

The Brotherhood of Man was originally a studio group featuring such singers as Tony Burrows and Johnny Goddison. They had two entries in America in 1970, "United We Stand" (#15 AC, #13 pop) and "Where Are You Going to My Love" (#11 AC , #61 pop). But after "Reach Out Your Hand" went to #77 pop in 1971, the group disappeared from the American charts for five years, although members continued to record in England.

In 1973 the Brotherhood of Man became the quartet of Martin Lee, Lee Sheridan, Nicky Stevens, and Sandra Stevens. The members were session singers and songwriters. Their moment of glory took three years before it occurred.

"We wanted to enter the Eurovision Song Contest," Sheridan recalled, referring to the annual event wherein each member country in the European Broadcasting Union submits one entry to a panel that then picks that year's best composition winner. "We needed a song to do for it, so we wrote 'Save Your Kisses' ourselves." Sheridan claimed that he, Martin Lee, and Tony Hiller wrote roughly equal amounts of the music and lyric. As the songwriters, the Brotherhood of Man were able to nominate who they wanted to sing their tune at the judging, and so naturally they picked themselves.

"Save Your Kisses for Me" dealt with a dad going to work and leaving his 3-year-old girl home for the day. Recalling performing the song at Eurovision, Sheridan said, "We were very nervous. We were on first, which was a good thing, to get it out of the way." The song had good lyrics and music, plus wide popularity across the Continent at the time (it had already reached #1 on the United Kingdom chart), and "Save Your Kisses for Me" won the Eurovision Song Contest by the largest margin ever.

In America, the song proved to be a mild hit, peaking at #27 pop as well as #1 AC. Its potential on the Hot 100 may have been limited due to a competing cover by Bobby Vinton at the same time which went to #75 on that chart. There was even a version by Margo Smith which made #10 country. In any event, "Save Your Kisses for Me" became the last charted entry in America for the Brotherhood of Man.

In their homeland the Brotherhood of Man managed two #1 follow-ups, "Angelo" in 1977 and "Figaro" in 1978. They were labeled by some as ABBA imitators, which did not bother Sheridan. "That was bound to happen, because we were both two boys and two girls. And that was a tribute, because we knew they were a great group."

The last entry for the Brotherhood of Man in Great Britain was "Lightning Flash," which went to #67 in 1982. "The band is still going today. It's the same lineup for 25 years," noted Sheridan in 1998. The group does most of its shows in England, averaging about 80 concerts a year.

302 Never Gonna Fall in Love Again

ERIC CARMEN

Arista 0184

June 19, 1976 (1 week)

Writer: Eric Carmen

Producer: Jimmy Ienner

"There have always been two camps of Eric Carmen fans," noted Carmen in the liner notes to his 1997 retrospective LP *The Definitive Collection*. "There's one camp that loves everything that happened with the Raspberries and hates everything I've done since then. And there's another camp that really likes all the solo stuff and can't ever imagine why I did rock 'n' roll. So I've always straddled that fence—not necessarily wisely—but I just thought that you should be able to do both things. . . .I found it very limiting to be stuck with either one or the other, which I'm afraid is an easier thing for record companies and radio to deal with."

Eric Carmen, born in Cleveland, Ohio, on August 11, 1949, was originally trained in classical piano, at the Cleveland Institute of Music. Later he learned to play drums (badly, according to him), guitar, and bass. After a brief stint in the late sixties with a popular Cleveland group called Cyrus Erie, Carmen became lead singer of the Raspberries, a rock band that scored several entries on the Hot 100 between 1970 and 1974, the biggest being 1972's "Go All the Way" at #5, but none crossed over to the AC chart. In contrast, his solo career found him making both charts with ease, though usually peaking higher on the AC than pop chart.

Such was the case with "Never Gonna Fall in Love Again," which topped the AC chart while getting to #11 on the pop chart. It was the follow-up to his first solo hit, "All by Myself" [for more details on that song, see 662]. Carmen wrote both songs around the same time for his 1975 debut LP, *Carmen*, and both were derived from Rachmaninoff.

"I think for 'Never Gonna Fall in Love Again,' the theme for the chorus was from Rachmaninoff's Second Symphony, whereas the theme for the verse of 'All by Myself' was from Rachmaninoff's second Piano Concerto No. 3," Carmen wrote in *The Definitive Collection*. "You know, I think I used up most of his good stuff, but I'm always looking. When I was reading a biography of Rachmaninoff, I found that. . . he had actually gotten [both melodies] from other sources. One he heard from an Italian organ grinder playing, and the other a friend gave him. I thought, geez, what a nice friend."

Though from the same source as "All by Myself," "Never Gonna Fall in Love Again" sounded more optimistic than the first hit despite its title and some depressing lyrics due to a flowing woodwinds section and a strong vocal performance by Carmen. Its follow-up, "Sunrise," was even more upbeat and reminiscent of Carmen's days with the Raspberries. The final song off his debut LP, it went to #33 AC and #34 pop.

Carmen later returned to #1 AC with a song he co-wrote for the movie *Footloose* [see 457—"Almost Paradise"] and then as a soloist again with "Make Me Lose Control" [see 543].

303 Today's the Day

AMERICA

Warner 8212

June 26, 1976 (2 weeks)

Writer: Dan Peek

Producer: George Martin

"Today's the Day" marked two transitions for America. It signaled the loss of one founding member, and it also marked a change in label affiliation. The latter occurred rather effortlessly, but the former was more problematic.

"That was our last major song from the whole Warner Brothers era," said Dewey Bunnell about the single. The group would have one more single release, "Amber Cascades," which went to #17 AC and #75 pop, before emerging on Capitol Records. "Today's the Day" did better than "Amber Cascades" by hitting #1 AC and #23 pop in mid-1976, but it did not chart as high as earlier efforts, like "Tin Man" [see 231]. Bunnell attributed this showing to the fact that "We were getting to be a little old news by then, I think."

The writer of "Today's the Day" was Dan Peek, and he decided to leave the group around the time the single came out. Bunnell said he and Gerry Buckley, the other member of America, were not shocked by Peek's move. Peek had become a born-again Christian and felt he needed to work apart from the other two as he espoused his religious beliefs.

"He really went his separate way," Bunnell said. "I haven't seen him for a few years now." He still remains in contact with Peek via Christmas cards, but they have not met in person for some time.

Bunnell said Buckley decided against finding someone to fill Peek's position. "He was irreplaceable," Bunnell said. "We had gone to school together, made our band together. It wouldn't have been the same." As a consequence of this decision, he said, "We didn't do Dan's songs in concert for years and years." But by the 1990s, due to requests from their fans, they had started to include some Peek tunes in the lineup.

The new America struggled for six years, getting only one pop entry, "California Dreamin'" in 1979, which hit #56, and two AC singles, "All My Life" at #48 in 1979 and "All Around" at #45 in 1980. (Peek got on the charts in 1979 with "All Things Are Possible," which made #6 AC and #78 pop.) In 1982 Bunnell and Buckley had a brief comeback spearheaded by "You Can Do Magic," which went to #5 AC and #8 pop, followed by 1983's "Right Before Your Eyes" (#16 AC, #45 pop) and "The Border" (#4 AC, #33 pop), the latter being the last pop charting for the group. America's swan song on the AC listings was "(Can't Fall Asleep to a) Lullaby," which went to #26 in early 1985.

Bunnell announced in early 1998 that as far as America's current activities were concerned, "We're always working. We're a touring band and doing a 100-plus date tour this year." When at home in the studio in Los Angeles, the group also worked on a new album, *Human Nature*, released by Oxygen Records in New York that year.

304 I Need to Be in Love

THE CARPENTERS

A&M 1828

July 10, 1976 (1 week)

Writers: John Bettis and Albert Hammond (words and music), Richard Carpenter (music)

Producer: Richard Carpenter

In the liner notes to the Carpenters anthology *From the Top*, Richard Carpenter described "I Need to Be in Love" as "Karen's favorite of all the songs we recorded and one we all felt would chart higher than it ultimately did." Though it made #1 AC, "I Need to Be in Love" only got to #25 pop, the first Carpenters single to fall short of the pop top 20 since 1970. It was a trend which continued the rest of the late 1970s.

For some reason the follow-up to "I Need to Be in Love" was "Goofus," a remake of a 1932 tune. It went only to #4 AC, making it the first Carpenters single not to make #1 or #2 since 1970, and just #56 pop. Coming off that debacle, the Carpenters' first 45 of 1977 was "All You Get From Love Is a Love Song," which did better pop-wise at #35 while reaching #4 AC.

"Calling Occupants of Interplanetary Craft," subtitled "The Recognized Anthem of World Contact Day," came next and got to #18 AC and #32 pop. A cover of a #62 pop entry, "Calling Occupants," recorded in the spring of 1977 by a Beatles imitation group named Klaatu, it was one of the oddest Carpenters records ever, with "spacey" sounds and large background vocals. By the way, Richard Carpenter admitted the subtitle was a joke—there really was no such thing as "World Contact Day."

In 1978 the Carpenters' stock on the Hot 100 fell further when "Sweet, Sweet Smile" went only to #44 and "I Believe You" got to just #68. In fact, "I Believe You," which came out around Christmas time, probably got less airplay on top 40 radio stations at the time than the Carpenters' perennial Christmas favorite, "Merry Christmas Darling," first released in 1970. The tunes did do fine on the AC roster, with "Sweet, Sweet Smile" at #7 and "I Believe You" at #9, but the decrease in pop action encouraged the Carpenters to try a different tack.

In 1979 producer Phil Ramone cut a solo album with Karen Carpenter, but after it was finished in 1980, she requested that the completed project not be released. (Richard did not record or tour that year "for personal reasons," as he put it.) The material remained in the A&M vaults until 1989, when it was released as the LP *Karen Carpenter*. One single from the album, "If I Had You," reached #18 AC while missing the Hot 100.

After the solo effort, Karen and Richard teamed up again for a new album. Their first release gave them their 15th #1 AC hit [see 408—"Touch Me When We're Dancing"].

305 If You Know What I Mean

NEIL DIAMOND

Columbia 10366

July 17, 1976 (2 weeks nonconsecutive)

Writer: Neil Diamond

Producer: Robbie Robertson

"If You Know What I Mean" arrived on the heels of the relative failure of its predecessor, "The Last Picasso." Though that single went to #7 AC in the summer of 1975, it did not make the Hot 100 at all, the first Neil Diamond 45 not to since the 1960s. "The Last Picasso" was the third single off Diamond's *Serenade* LP after two #1 AC hits, "Longfellow Serenade" [see 236] and "I've Been This Way Before" [see 251], and the fact that it came out nearly a year after the album was released did not help its chances.

On the other hand, "If You Know What I Mean" was the first single off the *Beautiful Noise* album released in 1976. The producer of the LP was Robbie Robertson, guitarist and singer with the rock group the Band, who had previously hit #1 AC when he wrote "The Night They Drove Old Dixie Down" for Joan Baez [see 156]. His friendship with Diamond extended to having the artist make a guest appearance in the 1976 documentary about the Band's final concert titled *The Last Waltz*.

That a middle-of-the-road artist like Diamond would appear at a rock concert, much less have a member of the Band produce him, surprised some observers, but it was no big deal to him. As Diamond told David Wild in *Rolling Stone* in 1988, "I never tried to fit in because that meant conforming what I could write or what I could do to a certain set of rules. . . .The last group I joined was the Boy Scouts, and they threw me out for nonpayment of dues. So I suppose you could say that I've always gone my own way."

Diamond wrote in the liner notes to his anthology *In My Lifetime* that "If You Know What I Mean" "was one of my stronger songs, one of the strongest I'd written in a long time. It reflected some of the intensity of the times and the whole songwriting world I had been living in. It is a song about the loss of innocent dreams."

Besides topping the AC chart, "If You Know What I Mean" just missed being a top 10 pop hit for Diamond, peaking at #11 on the Hot 100. Two other singles came from the *Beautiful Noise* album. The first follow-up, "Don't Think. . .Feel," reached #4 AC and #43 pop. The second, the title song of the LP, reached #8 AC but, like "The Last Picasso," failed to dent the pop chart.

In December 1977, a year after the "Beautiful Noise" single debuted on the AC chart, Diamond claimed another #1 AC hit with "Desiree" [see 343]. It was his fifth of eight songs to top that chart.

306 I'm Easy

KEITH CARRADINE

ABC 12117

July 24, 1976 (1 week)

Writer: Keith Carradine

Producer: Richard Baskin

Thanks to his composition "I'm Easy," Keith Carradine is the only member of his famous acting family—including father John and brothers David and Robert—to have an Oscar. "I'm Easy," which appeared in the Robert Altman's 1975 movie *Nashville*, won Keith a statuette for Best Song, the only Oscar earned by the movie despite multiple nominations. Unfortunately for Keith, "I'm Easy" failed to lead to a successful singing career.

Born in San Mateo, California, on August 8, 1949, Keith Carradine decided to follow in his father's footsteps and studied drama at Colorado State University in the late 1960s. He made his motion picture debut in *McCabe and Mrs. Miller* in 1971 (also directed by Altman).

For *Nashville*, Altman wanted the cast to write and sing their own country songs. His novel approach got largely negative reactions from music critics and the general public when the actors' records came out, with no one too interested in hearing, for example, the vocalizing efforts of Ronee Blakely or Henry Gibson (Gibson's "200 Motels" was the B-side to "I'm Easy").

But Carradine had come to the project having already written "I'm Easy," when he did the Los Angeles production of the stage musical *Hair* in 1969. The song fit perfectly with his character Tom Frank, an egocentric, narcissistic singer. After the song's critical and commercial success—it made #17 pop as well as #1 AC—Carradine sang a few dates in clubs across America, trying to be taken seriously as a vocalist himself.

"My time is important, because I'm trying to balance two things, film and music," he told Donna Landry in *The Washington Post*. "I have to be careful about what I do. Especially with film—I can't commit myself to something unless I can totally commit myself to it."

Carradine did not have to worry about the balancing act for long, as his 1977 follow-up LP to "I'm Easy" flopped, virtually ending his recording career. He did not do another album until 1988, when the unsuccessful *Land Where Dreams Are Made* came out on Open Sky. He had more success two years later, when the original cast album of the Broadway musical *The Will Rogers Follies* came out, featuring Carradine, as Rogers, singing, acting, and doing roping tricks. But during most of the 1980s and 1990s the bulk of his work consisted of acting—in numerous TV productions and the occasional movie (e.g., 1984's *Choose Me*.)

You'll Never Find Another Love Like Mine

LOU RAWLS

Philadelphia International 3592

July 31, 1976 (1 week)

Writers: Kenny Gamble, Leon Huff

Producers: Kenny Gamble, Leon Huff

L ou Rawls, born on December 1, 1935, made his first LP for Capitol in 1961, but it was 15 long years before he scored a truly big hit, "You'll Never Find Another Love Like Mine." Lou, who had been part of the Pilgrim Travelers gospel group in the late 1950s, switched over to secular music in the early 1960s. He first gained notice as a prominent response voice to Sam Cooke on Cooke's double-sided 1962 hit "Bring It On Home to Me" and "Having a Party," then, in 1965, broke onto the pop and AC chart on his own with "Three O'Clock in the Morning" (#27 AC, #83 pop).

Rawls spent the rest of the 1960s hitting the pop and R&B charts fairly regularly, with his biggest single on them being "Love Is a Hurtin' Thing" in 1966 (#1 R&B, #13 pop). He returned to the AC chart in 1969 with "Your Good Thing (Is About to End)" (#35 AC). Two years later he moved from Capitol to MGM and scored with "A Natural Man," which made the top 20 on the AC, pop, and R&B charts. But Rawls thought that most of his MGM material was "bubblegum music," and he faltered for five years until he moved to Philadelphia International, the hottest source of R&B hits at the time, where he got to record a tune written by the company's founders, Kenny Gamble and Leon Huff. Philadelphia did no damage to their reputation when they released Rawls doing "You'll Never Find Another Love Like Mine." Concerning the tune, Rawls told Tom Vickers in *Rolling Stone* that "When I heard it, I knew it was a winner because of the words. Those words will never miss. For your average man or woman, that is their theme song: 'All right, sucker, you gonna mess around, and you're gonna miss me.'"

Rawls' interpretation of "You'll Never Find Another Love Like Mine" went to #1 R&B for two weeks starting July 24, 1976, plus #2 pop for two weeks starting September 4, 1976 behind the Bee Gees' "You Should Be Dancing" at #1 the first week and KC and the Sunshine Band's "(Shake, Shake, Shake) Shake Your Booty" the second week. A year later, jazz saxophonist Stanley Turrentine's instrumental version of the tune made #68 R&B.

For the rest of the 1970s Rawls stayed with Philadelphia

International. His best-charting follow-up was "Lady Love," which went to #5 AC and #24 pop in 1978. He last charted AC and pop with "Wind Beneath My Wings" in 1983 (#10 AC, #65 pop), though Bette Midler's version was a bigger hit, at #2 AC and #1 pop. In the 1980s and 1990s, Rawls continued to record and tour, and was also an active fundraiser for several charities, such as the United Negro College Fund and Easter Seals.

308 Let 'Em In

WINGS

Capitol 4293

August 7, 1976 (1 week)

Writers: Paul McCartney, Linda McCartney

Producer: Paul McCartney

Paul McCartney scored his only consecutive #1 AC hits when "Let 'Em In" followed up "Silly Love Songs" [see 299]. Besides getting to #1 AC, "Let 'Em In" held at #3 pop for four weeks starting August 14, 1976. The first three weeks it stood behind "Don't Go Breaking My Heart" at #1 [see 312] and "You Should Be Dancing" by the Bee Gees at #2. In its final week at #3 (September 4, 1976), "Let 'Em In" followed "You Should Be Dancing" at #1 and "You'll Never Find Another Love Like Mine" at #2 [see 307]. "Let 'Em In" also earned McCartney a Grammy nomination for Best Arrangement Accompanying Vocalists.

Despite such novel touches as a whistle playing a marching tune in the background and references to "Phil and Don" (the Everly Brothers, who were a major influence on Paul McCartney), many critics found "Let 'Em In" to be unsubstantial, a complaint made often about McCartney's work during the 1970s. The adverse critical reaction did not escape his attention.

"Yeah, I know a lot of critics haven't liked our music," McCartney told Lynn Van Martre in *The Chicago Tribune*. "Lightweight music, that's what they've called it. . . .I don't get overly angry at what the critics have said about our records. Well, sometimes it does bother me a little. But there's nothing I can do about it anyway, at least until the next album. There's nothing to do now but enjoy the tour."

By "the tour" McCartney's meant his first solo tour along with Wings, which he did in 1976 while he was enjoying much commercial and critical success. Five years later he disbanded Wings even though they continued to generate hit singles through the rest of the 1970s, the highest-charting on the AC roster being "With a Little Luck" at #5 in 1978. In the 1980s he returned to the AC pole position twice in duets: with Stevie Wonder on "Ebony and Ivory" [see 422] and with Michael Jackson with "The Girl Is Mine" [see 432], both in 1982. His name was often on the chart for the rest of the decade, and his best effort was "No More Lonely Nights" at #2 AC for four weeks in 1984.

During the 1990s McCartney was still showing up on the AC chart, but several of his tunes failed to make the Hot 100, such as "Put It There" in 1990 (#11) and "Off the Ground" (#27) in 1993. In 1997 he released his *Flaming Pie* LP, his first in four years. Although the album generated some of the best reviews in McCartney's career, none of its songs became hits.

In 1977 a Billy Paul cover of "Let 'Em In" that included speeches by slain civil rights leaders the Rev. Martin Luther King Jr. and Malcolm X reached #91 R&B.

309 I'd Really Love to See You Tonight

ENGLAND DAN AND JOHN FORD COLEY

Big Tree 16069

August 21, 1976 (1 week)

Writer: Parker McGee

Producer: Kyle Lehning

Two male duos dominated the easy listening field in the 1970s. One was England Dan and John Ford Coley. The other was Seals and Croft. The fact that "England" Dan Seals was the brother of Jim Seals of Seals and Croft didn't seem to confuse fans. As Coley said, "The only thing that made us the same was, we were both a duo." The main difference between the two groups on the AC chart was that England Dan and John Ford Coley reached the top four times, whereas Seals and Croft did not ("We May Never Pass This Way Again," "Get Closer," and "You're the Love" stalled at #2).

Coley, born October 13, 1948, met England Dan, born February 8, 1948, when they were growing up in Austin, Texas. In the mid-1960s both were in high school and both joined a group which eventually came to be known as Southwest F.O.B. (Freight on Board). The band scored a #56 pop hit in 1968 with "Smell of Incense," but had no further successes. In 1970 Dan and Coley left the group to become a duo and go in their own musical direction.

"Dan and I had been singing and working on different songs. . . .It was just kind of a natural flow, and we began having fun doing songs acoustically," Coley said. Their rather odd name had two sources. Jimmy Seals came up with the first part, said Coley, explaining that Dan liked to try to imitate Britons but, because of his Texas accent, made a poor job of it and Jimmy thought "England Dan" would be catchy. As for Coley himself, he formed his new professional name by getting rid of the middle name on his birth certificate, Edward, and substituting "Ford."

Their first single was "New Jersey" on A&M, which bubbled under to #103 in 1971. For five years, nothing else by the duo made the charts, but they stayed busy. "We did a tremendous amount of touring," Coley said. He said they were a popular opening act because "We had two acoustic guitars. Therefore, there was no stage turnover." But they did want a hit, and their producer Kyle Lehning thought he had found them one with "I'd Really Love to See You Tonight."

Coley said that when he and Dan first got the song, they thought it was more suited for a female. Nonetheless, their demo of the tune earned them a contract offer from executives at Big Tree Records. The execs proved to be right when "I'd Really Love to See You Tonight" went to #1 AC and #2 pop, behind Wild Cherry's "Play That Funky Music" on the latter for two weeks starting September 25, 1976.

Coley said he was surprised by the song's success and its Grammy nomination for Best Pop Vocal Performance by a Duo, Group or Chorus. It was the duo's biggest hit ever. In 1978 a remake by Jacky Ward and Reba McEntire went to #20 country.

310 Shower the People

JAMES TAYLOR

Warner 8222

August 28, 1976 (1 week)

Writer: James Taylor

Producers: Lenny Waronker, Russ Titelman

In the early 1970s Lenny Waronker teamed with Russ Titelman to form a working duo of record producers. Describing their process of doing business in the studio, Waronker said, "It was just working together, bouncing off each other, seeing if someone had an idea." One of the acts they got to handle by the middle of the decade was one of the biggest signed to Warner Records—James Taylor.

Taylor came to Waronker and Titelman with some ideas of doing covers [see 270—"How Sweet It Is (To Be Loved by You)"] along with some of his own compositions, including "Shower the People." The two men were impressed with what Taylor had done so far with the latter. "He had done a demo of it that was nearly complete," Waronker said. "Certainly the vocals, a lot of them, were used on the final record." However, the instrumentation left something to be desired, and in the age before synthesizers, they had to make do with a "voice organ" played by Randy Newman to back Taylor up.

To contribute to the background choral sound, Taylor himself recorded the parts and brought them back to the studio. "He went out and had people sing, I think, maybe two octaves or three octaves, a note just for a few minutes," Waronker said. Taylor did that part during the course of one weekend and used mainly women, including his then-wife Carly Simon. Waronker remembered that the vocals weren't exactly what they were looking for, but "added to the overall vibe." With the vocals and instrumentals down pat, Waronker said the rest of the session with Taylor came together quickly. When it came out, "Shower the People" stormed its way to #1 AC and #22 pop.

Only one more single from Taylor came on Warner, 1976's "Woman's Gotta Have It," a remake of Bobby Womack's 1972 #60 pop hit which went only to #20 AC. The next year Taylor switched to Columbia Records and scored another #1 AC hit [see 337—"Handy Man"]. He remained a frequent visitor on the AC chart through 1981, even getting airplay on "Summer's Here," the B-side of the main entry "Hard Times," which reached #23 AC and #72 pop.

After taking a break for a few years, Taylor came back with three big favorites on the AC chart—a remake of the Buddy Holly composition "Everyday" in 1985 (#3 AC, #61 pop) and "Only One" (#6 AC) and "That's Why I'm Here" (#8 AC) in 1986. He kept making the chart often into the 1990s, although, like the last-named singles, most of his entries did not make the Hot 100. In the early 1990s, like several other venerable acts of the time, many of his AC entries were album cuts, such as 1991's "Copperline" (#13). Taylor's most recent album was 1997's *Hourglass*, but he remained a strong concert draw in 1998.

311 Summer

WAR

United Artists 834

September 4, 1976 (1 week)

Writers: Sylvester Allen, Harold Ray Brown, Morris Dickerson, Gerald Goldstein, Lonnie Jordan, Charles Miller, Lee Oskar, Howard Scott

Producer: Gerald Goldstein

The name "WAR" is in capital letters for "Impact, like when you think of the letter 'S' on Superman," said Lonnie Jordan, the one remaining original group member. A keyboardist, Jordan joined drummer Harold Brown, bassist Morris "B.B." Dickerson, saxophonist Charles Miller, and guitarist Howard Scott to form the Creators, a band whose first release was "Burn, Baby, Burn" in 1965. Then Dickerson left the band and Scott was inducted into the Army, prompting the group to break up. Scott's return in 1968 led the other Creators sans Dickerson to form a band called the Night Shift, which included bassist Peter Rosen and percussionist Papa Dee Allen.

Rosen invited producer/writer Jerry Goldstein to check out the band. Rosen brought along Eric Burdon and out-of-work harmonica player Lee Oskar. Both ultimately joined the band, with Burdon becoming the group's lead singer. When Rosen died of a drug overdose, Dickerson returned to the group, now called WAR. Jordan said the new name had come about after Goldstein saw the group one night in their street clothes and said, "Thank God I know you guys! You guys look like you came from a battlefield!" But, as Jordan noted, "We were warring against poverty, injustice, things like that, not military warring."

Eric Burdon and WAR went to #3 pop in 1970 with "Spill the Wine." In 1971, without Burdon, WAR scored six hits that made both the pop and R&B top 10 charts. The last one was "Summer," which like all WAR hits was credited to all members, although Jordan said he was the principal contributor.

"I was in the Sound City Studios in the [San Fernando] Valley when we recorded that song," Jordan recalled. "I was playing an old piano and this melody I was playing on that piano was captured on tape by the engineer there." Goldstein came up with the idea of the song being about summer and recalling his childhood days, which were a little different from Jordan's. "He was relating to Brooklyn and I was relating to Compton [California]," laughed Jordan. Nevertheless, both men's memories became part of the lyrics of "Summer."

"Summer," which hit #7 pop and #4 R&B, was one of only three AC entries WAR had. They first hit with "All Day Music" at #12 in 1971 and last made it with "Groovin'" at #30 in 1985. Their other hits were too funky for AC programmers to handle.

Though they had no top 30 pop hit after "Summer," WAR remained popular on the soul and LP charts with sporadic releases in the 1980s and 1990s coupled with intensive touring. In 1997 the group released *The Latin Collection* LP, and an album of new material titled *Grooves and Messages* appeared in 1998.

312 Don't Go Breaking My Heart
ELTON JOHN AND KIKI DEE

Rocket 40585

September 11, 1976 (1 week)

Writers: Ann Orson, Carte Blanche (pseudonyms for Elton John and Bernie Taupin)

Producer: Gus Dudgeon

Elton John had sung background for several other artists during the 1970s, most notably on Neil Sedaka's "Bad Blood," which went to #1 pop and #25 AC in 1975, but he never recorded a bona fide duet with another vocalist until "Don't Go Breaking My Heart." The idea to do the song came from John himself.

As he told Cliff Jahr in *Rolling Stone* in 1976, "I was messing around in the studio one day on the electric piano and came up with the title line. I made a hasty phone call to Barbados and said, 'Write a duet,' and Taupin nearly died 'cause he'd never done one. It's very hard anyway."

To sing the other part, John drafted Kiki Dee, born Pauline Matthews in Yorkshire, England, on March 6, 1947, who was best known in America for "I Got the Music in Me," a #12 pop hit in 1976, though she also made the AC chart with "Love Makes the World Go Round" at #16 in 1971 and "Once a Fool" at #25 in early 1976. John, an enthusiastic believer in her talent, signed her to his Rocket record label.

"When Elton invited me to sing 'Don't Go Breaking My Heart,' he'd already completed his vocal and had sung my part in falsetto voice, and so consequently we were never in the studio at the same time," Dee recalled in *Billboard* in 1997. John recorded his part of the tune at Eastern Sound Studios in Toronto, Canada, in March 1976, then Kiki Dee taped her vocals in London.

The completed "Don't Go Breaking My Heart" went to #1 pop for four weeks starting August 7, 1976, before topping the AC chart. John and Dee earned Grammy nominations for Best Pop Vocal Performance by a Duo, Group or Chorus. In 1994 John redid the tune in a peppy dance version with drag queen RuPaul in place of Dee and reached #92 pop.

John and Dee reunited several times in later years, though none of their efforts were anywhere near as popular as "Don't Go Breaking My Heart." Among them were "Loving You Is Sweeter Than Ever" in 1981, "True Love" in 1983, and a cameo mention and appearance in the video of Dee in John's "Wrap Her Up," which went to #20 pop in 1985. Dee sang background on his "Can You Feel the Love Tonight" in 1994 [see 643], but has never had another AC entry to follow "Don't Go Breaking My Heart."

John, however, did get plenty of other AC singles, including the #1 follow-up to "Don't Go Breaking My Heart," "Sorry Seems to Be the Hardest Word" [see 321].

313 Don't Stop Believin'
OLIVIA NEWTON-JOHN

MCA 40600

September 18, 1976 (1 week)

Writer: John Farrar

Producer: John Farrar

"Don't Stop Believin'" was the title tune for the first U.S. album produced by John Farrar for Olivia Newton-John. Production was originally supposed to be done in southern California, but that was not to be.

"When I first came to America, we went into record in Los Angeles, and I had the wrong players," Farrar said. "Larry Carlton [a top Los Angeles session guitarist] said, 'You need to have the right players.'" Farrar took his advice and pulled Newton-John to Nashville, where musicians were familiar with her country-flavored pop sound. There is where they cut "Don't Stop Believin'," a tune whose inspiration Farrar said he no longer recalls.

Whatever the source, "Don't Stop Believin'" went to #33 pop as well as #1 AC, making it Newton-John's seventh consecutive Farrar-produced #1 AC hit. But the streak could not last and in fact ended with the next 45, "Every Face Tells a Story," which also came from the *Don't Stop Believin'* LP but got only to #6 AC. That song's #55 pop peak was also the worst pop performance by a Newton-John single in five years.

She came back to #1 AC after "Every Face Tells a Story" with "Sam" [see 326]. But after that, Newton-John's performances on the AC chart became just as shaky as on the Hot 100, with 1977's "Making a Good Thing Better" going to only #20 AC as well as #87 pop. What saved her from a possible permanent downturn on the charts was her starring role in 1977's movie adaptation of the Broadway hit *Grease*. The film actually gave her bigger hits on the Hot 100 than the AC chart, for while "Hopelessly Devoted to You," "You're the One That I Want," and "Summer Nights" were all top five pop singles, they got only to #7, #23, and #21 AC, respectively. But the movie did open up new doors for Newton-John, and she played the lead in two other films, *Xanadu* (1980) and *Two of a Kind* (1983), the latter a disastrous reunion with her *Grease* costar John Travolta.

Newton-John also branched out musically in the late 1970s, venturing into rock- and dance-flavored material. As a result, the one-time AC queen saw such efforts as "Totally Hot" (1979), "Heart Attack" (1982), "Tied Up" (1983), and "Twist of Fate" (1983) shut out from the AC listings. But Newton-John never became totally hard-edged, as evidenced by the 30 AC entries she *did* chart from 1978 to 1983, with the later singles including her last #1 AC hit to date, "Magic" [see 388].

314 If You Leave Me Now

CHICAGO

Columbia 10390

September 25, 1976 (1 week)

Writer: Peter Cetera

Producer: James William Guercio

In the opinion of trumpeter Lee Loughnane, "If You Leave Me Now" was a milestone for Chicago in that it changed the way radio stations perceived the group. "If You Leave Me Now" offered a distinct change of pace from the usual brass-heavy instrumentation with its muted horns and emphasis on Peter Cetera's lead vocals. As a result, Loughnane said, "The next hits after that were ballads. Everybody decided we were a ballad band with tenor vocals."

That change in direction did not disturb him, he said, although he also noted that the appearance of the tune surprised him and a few other Chicago horn players. "We had actually finished that album [Chicago X] and the horn players had already gone home when Peter presented it to Jimmy Guercio," he said. "The first time we heard it, it was on the radio."

"If You Leave Me Now" gave Chicago its first #1 pop hit, riding atop the Hot 100 for the weeks of October 23 and 30, 1976, and became Chicago's fourth #1 AC hit. It earned the band its first Grammy for Best Pop Vocal Performance by a Duo, Group or Chorus, as well as nominations for Record of the Year and Album of the Year for Chicago X.

Chicago soon found that a massive hit like "If You Leave Me Now" was not easy to follow. Only one record released in the next two years cracked the top 10 on either the pop or AC chart—"Baby, What a Big Surprise," which made #8 AC and #4 pop in the fall of 1977. Doing less well were "You Are on My Mind" (#17 AC and #49 pop in 1977), "Little One" (#40 AC and #44 pop in 1978), and "Take Me Back to Chicago" (#39 AC and #63 pop).

On January 23, 1978, guitarist Terry Kath died as the result of a self-inflicted gunshot wound; the death was accidental. Loughnane recalled that when he and the other musicians heard the news, their initial reaction was that the band was over. But, said Loughnane, "It didn't take us that long to realize there were six of us alive, and we were successful, and he'd want us to go on without him." Donnie Dacus replaced Kath for only a year, and there was no regular guitarist until DeWayne Bailey came on board at the end of the 1980s.

In the wake of the tragedy, Chicago rebounded in the fall of 1978 with "Alive Again," which went to #39 AC and #14 pop. They hit the same pop peak with the follow-up in early 1979, "No Tell Lover," which made #5 AC. But the hits soon leveled off again, and 1980's disappointing "Thunder and Lightning," which reached #46 AC and #56 pop, was the last Chicago record on either chart for nearly two years. Luckily, the group came back and notched another double pop-AC hit; see 425—"Hard to Say I'm Sorry."

315 I Can't Hear You No More

HELEN REDDY

Capitol 4312

October 2, 1976 (1 week)

Writers: Gerry Goffin (words), Carole King (music)

Producer: Joe Wissert

Carole King's first solo LP, 1970's Writer: Carole King, included a song King co-wrote with her ex-husband Gerry Goffin called "I Can't Hear You No More." Six years later, Helen Reddy revived the tune, but not because she wanted to cover it. "That was the record company really putting its foot on my shoulder and saying, 'You have to have a disco hit,'" Reddy said, sighing at the memory.

While "I Can't Hear You No More" led the pack of the AC rankings, it went only to #29 on the pop chart. Part of that relatively poor showing for Reddy could be attributed to the fact that the B-side, "Music in My Life," also got some airplay on pop radio outlets (it failed to do so on AC radio stations) and split the following for the record. When asked about "Music in My Life," Reddy paused and then let out, "Another true piece of tripe! Those were songs I was pressured to sing. I would rather not have a hit than do them."

She definitely did not have a hit with her follow-up to "I Can't Hear You No More," called "Gladiola." It got to only #10 AC in late 1976, her lowest showing on that chart in nearly five years, and failed to even make the Hot 100. "You're My World," which came in mid-1977 and made #18 on the Hot 100 and #5 AC, seemed to mark a reversal of Reddy's pop slide, but the turnabout was short-lived. "The Happy Girls," released in the fall of 1977, reached an unimpressive #14 AC and #57 pop.

Through the rest of the decade, Reddy released a few more 45s, with several either missing the Hot 100 or making the lower rungs of the chart. Her last entry on both the AC and pop charts was, ironically, "I Can't Say Goodbye to You," which hit #42 AC and #88 pop in mid-1981 on MCA Records (she had left Capitol in 1979). Since then, and into the late 1990s, Reddy has released albums only sporadically, which doesn't bother her at all.

"Of all the media I've been in, that's the one I've had the least experience in," she said. She has continued to pursue her acting career, working on Broadway, on London's West End, and on tour in England playing the female lead in the musical Blood Brothers. She continues to do occasional concerts for her fans.

Asked what she wanted to do as the millennium approached, Reddy said, "I'm just looking to live my life. I'm very happy now." Both her daughter and son are grown and she has become a grandparent. Her home base is Los Angeles, where she has a house, but she also has apartments in New York City, London, and Rio de Janeiro.

316 Like a Sad Song

JOHN DENVER

RCA 10774

October 9, 1976 (1 week)

Writer: John Denver

Producer: Milt Okun

The title of John Denver's tune "Like a Sad Song" was ironic in that it summed up how his releases had been going heading into the late 1970s. Though it made #1 AC, the song got only to #36 pop and #34 country. After that, the performances of his 45s on all charts were mostly unimpressive.

Part of this downturn for Denver may have been due to overexposure. On TV, he could be seen frequently headlining his own specials plus hosting the Grammys a few times starting in 1978. He made his motion picture acting debut in the popular comedy *Oh, God!*, with George Burns as the title character, in 1977. Add to that the endless tours, including one concert series with Frank Sinatra, who later covered "Like a Sad Song," plus his extensive charitable and personal causes, and the result, as Denver agreed in a 1977 interview with Marcia Seligman for *Playboy*, was Denver burnout for many consumers. In the interview, Denver noted that he had been at home for only four weeks in 1976. "Everything started to suffer," he said.

Denver's AC chart performances yo-yoed between excellent and awful as a result, though not quite as bad as on the Hot 100, where he struggled just to make the top 40 after 1977. His first two releases after "Like a Sad Song" both peaked at #13 AC in 1977—"Baby, You Look Good to Me Tonight" (also #65 pop) and "My Sweet Lady" (also #32 pop), the latter of which he had originally recorded back in 1971. In late 1977 he hit strongly with "How Can I Leave You Again," which held at #2 AC for four weeks while getting to #44 pop, and his next three also did decently AC-wise. "It Amazes Me" went to #9 AC and #59 pop in 1978, followed by two at #10 AC, "I Want to Live" (also #55 pop) in 1978 and "What's on Your Mind" (also #107 bubbling under) in 1979.

But from 1979 to 1982 Denver's releases were almost as weak on the AC chart as they were on the pop chart. "Garden Song" in 1979 got only to #31 AC without making the pop chart, and 1980's "Autograph" (#20 AC, #52 pop) and "Dancing With the Mountains" (#43 AC, #97) appeared on few record buyer's wish lists. "Some Days Are Diamonds (Some Days Are Stone)" did return him to the pop top 40 (at #36) in 1981, but its #12 AC showing was a far cry from what he had been doing just a few years earlier. And "Perhaps Love," a duet with opera great Plácido Domingo which got Denver one of his rare appearances on the British chart, failed to stir up much interest stateside, going only to #22 AC and #59 pop in 1982.

Denver did have one more #1 AC hit left in him, and it came as the follow-up to "Perhaps Love" [see 421—"Shanghai Breezes"].

317 Fernando

ABBA

Atlantic 3346

October 16, 1976 (2 weeks)

Writers: Benny Andersson, Stig Andersson, Bjorn Ulvaeus

Producers: Benny Andersson, Bjorn Ulvaeus

ABBA was Sweden's biggest export of the mid- to late 1970s, a group of two fresh-faced, then-married couples whose ability to come up with catchy melodies and sing phonetically in many different languages assured their place in pop music history. Their two #1 AC chart hits only hint at how popular ABBA was—and is—worldwide.

The quartet's title comes from the initial letter of the first name of each member—Agnetha, Bjorn, Benny, and Anni-Frid ("Frida"). All were born in Sweden except Frida Lyngstad, who was born in Narvik, Norway, on November 15, 1945. The first to team up were guitarist Bjorn Ulvaeus, born in Gothenburg on April 25, 1945, and keyboardist Benny Andersson, born in Vallinby on December 16, 1946. Bjorn was part of the Hootenanny Singers and Benny a member of the Hep Stars, both popular Swedish acts, when they met while touring on the road. They recorded together in 1966 but remained in their respective groups through the end of the 1960s, by which time the men had found two female soloists who became interested in them personally as well as professionally. For Benny it was Frida, and for Bjorn it was Agnetha Faltskog, born in Jonkoping on April 5, 1950.

A last-minute booking in Gothenburg in November 1970 led the women to work onstage with the men as a group named Festfolk, translated as "party people" or "engaged couples," according to John Tobler in *ABBA Gold: The Complete Story*. Slowly the act jelled; their first American release was "People Need Love" on Playboy Records in 1972, which listed them as "Bjorn & Benny." In 1973, now named ABBA, they released "Ring, Ring," which they hoped would get the nod as the Swedish entry for that year's Eurovision contest. (For details on Eurovision, see 103—"Love Is Blue.") "Ring, Ring" failed, but ABBA tried again in 1974, and their tune "Waterloo" not only won the right to represent Sweden but also took first prize at Eurovision and went on to #6 on the Hot 100 in America. ABBA's hit streak had begun.

"Fernando" originally appeared in Swedish on Frida's 1975 solo LP, *Frida Ensam;* later, English vocals were overdubbed and the song was released as an ABBA tune. Benny and Bjorn tried doing it first at a recording session on August 5, 1975 in various musical genres—tango, country, and western, even polka. Finally, on September 3, 1975, they recorded the final version of the song with an emphasis on woodwinds which made it sound somewhat classical and Scandanavian.

In addition to being #1 AC for two weeks, "Fernando" peaked at #13 on the Hot 100, the group's best showing there since "Waterloo." (In England it was the second of nine #1 hits ABBA had on that chart.) The follow-up, "Dancing Queen," was the group's only #1 on the Hot 100. They had another #1 on the AC chart with "The Winner Takes It All" [see 397].

318 Muskrat Love
THE CAPTAIN AND TENNILLE

A&M 1870

October 30, 1976 (4 weeks nonconsecutive)

Writer: Willis Alan Ramsey

Producers: Daryl Dragon, Toni Tennille

The memory of helping bring "Muskrat Love" to prominence seemed both to tickle and embarrass Dewey Bunnell at the same time. Bunnell was one of three members of America, whose version of "Muskrat Love" became a minor chart entry in 1973, hitting #11 AC and #67 pop. But the first act to do the song was its composer Willis Alan Ramsey, who had originally called his song "Muskrat Candlelight."

"We heard his album on Shelter [Records]," Bunnell recalled. "At that point in our careers, we were young and totally devouring music around us." "Muskrat Love" became one of the few outside tunes the group ate up in an effort to get a hit. "It's a silly song in retrospect, I suppose, but we liked it," he said.

Though its showing on the Hot 100 made it one of the lesser entries for America, the group did like it enough to include in America's greatest hits LP of 1975 and on their live stage album in 1977. Nevertheless, Bunnell said the group does not perform it on stage anymore, as it has become more identified with the Captain and Tennille. But, he noted, "I guess it proves we could at least spot a hit."

Toni Tennille of the Captain and Tennille remembered thinking, when she heard America's record, that it wasn't doing well because you couldn't understand the words. Resolving to find out what was being sung, she told her husband Daryl Dragon ("The Captain") they needed to find a lyric sheet for a song called "Muskrat Love." Upon hearing the request, Daryl said, "I thought Toni had lost her mind." But they found one despite the song's relative obscurity, and Tennille was excited when she read the words. "I said, 'Daryl! This is about two muskrats! This is a hoot!'" Somehow she convinced him to record the tune with her.

Their "Muskrat Love" became a hit, making #1 AC plus #4 pop for five consecutive weeks starting November 20, 1976. Tennille recalled it was requested often in concert. At one point, she said, "I had to put a twice-a-night limit on singing 'Muskrat Love.'"

The Captain and Tennille made the pop and AC chart for three years after "Muskrat Love," with the highest-charting effort thereafter being their second-to-last single to reach the charts, "Do That to Me One More Time," which made #1 pop and #4 AC in 1980. They continued to tour as a duo in the 1980s and 1990s, but both made time for solo projects, such as Tennille's short-lived 1980 TV talk show, Tenille's big band stints, and Dragon's work with his boogie band. In 1998 Tennille assumed the lead role in the American touring company of the Broadway musical *Victor/Victoria*. (In 1997 she had auditioned for the part on Broadway which Julie Andrews had originated, but lost out to Racquel Welch.)

319 This One's for You
BARRY MANILOW

Arista 0206

November 13, 1976 (1 week)

Writers: Barry Manilow, Marty Panzer

Producers: Ron Dante, Barry Manilow

"This One's for You" was the title tune for Barry Manilow's fourth solo album. Following in the steps of "Tryin' to Get the Feeling Again" [see 296], the title tune of his previous LP, "This One's for You" was released as a single, only in this case it was the lead 45 from the album.

Recalling the tune in the liner notes to his anthology *The Complete Collection and Then Some . . .,* Manilow noted, "I remember the exact moment when Marty [Panzer, the co-writer] read me this lyric. I was hooked from the very first line, 'This one'll never sell.' It wouldn't have mattered if the rest of the lyric had been about a lamb chop, I loved it. When he read me the rest, I couldn't wait to get to the piano because I could hear the melody in my head."

Manilow did the demo for "This One's for You" as a spare piano version, and some of the lyrics in that version were later deleted from the final cut. As for its chart performance, despite its topping the AC roster, "This One's for You" stopped at #29 pop in the fall of 1976. The song was the first Manilow 45 to fail to reach the pop top 10 after five consecutive singles had made it.

Another Manilow-connected single which was out at the same time but which did not make the pop top 10 was "Street Singin'" by Lady Flash, the name for the trio of females who sang backup for Manilow (Monica Burruss, Delta Byrd, and lead singer Lorraine Mazzola, who had been a member of the girl group Reparta and the Delrons from 1966–73.). The single, which went to #27 pop without making the AC chart, was arranged, produced, and written by Manilow and became the only charted record for the three women.

Shortly after "Street Singin'" and "This One's for You" peaked, Manilow was interviewed by Dennis Hunt of *The Los Angeles Times*. Concerning his position in the music scene, Manilow told Hunt: "Some say I'm too middle-of-the-road, some say I'm too bubblegum, some say I'm trying to replace Perry Como, some say this, some say that. I'd be a fool to worry about the negative stuff because I'm not going to change what I do. I like it and so do a lot of other people."

Manilow was right about the last statement. After "This One's for You" came "Weekend in New England," which became his sixth #1 AC hit and fourth top 10 pop hit. For more details, see 323.

320 After the Lovin'

ENGELBERT HUMPERDINCK

Epic 50270

December 4, 1976 (2 weeks)

Writer: Richie Adams, Alan Bernstein

Producers: Joel Diamond, Charlie Calello

Charlie Calello was an arranger/producer based in New York City when he teamed with Joel Diamond, a producer and music publisher who was trying to get "After the Lovin'" recorded by Tom Jones. Jones rejected the tune, but he was sharing managers with Engelbert Humperdinck at the time, and Humperdinck decided to record it.

When Calello got involved in the project, he learned that at least two earlier versions of the song had already been produced. As arranger, he made a conscious decision not to listen to them, so, as he put it, he could get his own ideas on how to "conceptualize the song."

"What I had in my mind when. . .I saw the lyric was, the song actually sounded to me like there was a stripper, like he was seducing a lady," Calello said. He decided to make "After the Lovin'" his version of a contemporary redo of David Rose's old hit "The Stripper" [see 15], though the Calello song was slower in tempo than the earlier tune and his horns were not as brassy.

Before Humperdinck recorded his vocal to the instrumental tracks, his management and associates heard what Calello and Diamond had done. "It was obvious to everyone that 'After the Lovin'' was a hit," Calello said. Everyone, that is, except Humperdinck's record company London. Calello remembered thinking at the time that London was using their supposed dislike of the record as an excuse to dump Humperdinck from their artist roster. London did relinquish control of "After the Lovin'" and Humperdinck, but CBS Records executive Steve Popovich bought both the singer and the record, as well as two other artists handled by Humperdinck's management, Tom Jones and Gilbert O'Sullivan.

Signed to CBS's subsidiary label Epic, Humperdinck's "After the Lovin'" was the most successful acquisition made in the deal with London in America. It went to #8 pop the week of January 22, 1977, as well as #1 AC and #40 country, his first entry on the latter chart. The single was Humperdinck's first top 10 pop hit since 1967's "Release Me (And Let Me Love Again)," and his first #1 AC hit since "When There's No You" in 1971 [see 148]. It was Humperdinck's third #1 AC single.

The success of "After the Lovin'" gave Humperdinck more momentum on the AC chart over the next two years, although only one song in that period, "Goodbye My Friend," also made the pop chart (#37 AC, #97 pop). He was back on both charts by the start of 1979 with "This Moment in Time" [see 359].

321 Sorry Seems to Be the Hardest Word

ELTON JOHN

MCA/Rocket 40645

December 18, 1976 (1 week)

Writers: Bernie Taupin (words), Elton John (lyrics)

Producer: Gus Dudgeon

Born Reginald Kenneth Dwight in Pinner, Middlesex, England, on March 25, 1947, pianist Elton John got his stage name by combining the first names of two members of his first group, Bluesology, Elton Dean and Long John Baldry. Bluesology, which John formed in 1966, had not generated much enthusiasm anywhere, but when John met lyricist Bernie Taupin in 1969, the two men formed a partnership that would create a bounty of solo hits for John in the early to mid-1970s.

John's first pop entry was "Border Song" at #92 in 1970, followed near the end of the year by "Your Song," which gave him an AC debut of #9 as well as a pop peak of #8. Thereafter John was a regular on both charts, although his more frenetic or soul-like records ("Saturday Night's Alright for Fighting," "Bennie and the Jets," "The Bitch Is Back" and "Lucy in the Sky With Diamonds") did not get AC airplay. "Daniel" [see 192] and "Don't Go Breaking My Heart" [see 312] made #1 AC, and early John tunes that were AC hits included "Honky Cat" at #6 in 1973 and "Goodbye Yellow Brick Road" at #7 in early 1974. In 1976 he made a single that was available only to radio stations, "Love Song," which made #18 AC on airplay alone.

But 1976 heralded a slight downturn in John's popularity. The singer, who had just scored the first two albums to debut at #1 on *Billboard*'s LP chart in 1975 (*Captain Fantastic and the Brown Dirt Cowboy* followed by *Rock of the Westies*) saw his 1976 album *Blue Moves* go only to #3, a relative disappointment given his track record. John was philosophical about what happened.

"I think people had enough of me by the time of *Blue Moves*," John told Ed Harrison in *Billboard* in 1978. "I put out an awful lot of product." Some people, though John was not one of them, thought his admission of his bisexuality in *Rolling Stone* that year was also a turnoff.

John took full blame for the way the project turned out. "I can't blame MCA for not selling *Blue Moves*, because the record was in the stores and radio stations had it. People didn't want to buy it. It's as simple as that. I didn't help it any. I didn't do any promo because I was too tired. I didn't even do a promo film for 'Sorry Seems to Be the Hardest Word.'"

"Sorry Seems to Be the Hardest Word" did make #6 pop for two weeks starting December 25, 1976, which definitely made the song a hit, if not the album from which it came. John then decided to drop Taupin as his writing partner for the rest of the 1970s. With new collaborators and a little luck, he got back to #1 AC in 1979 [see 370—"Mama Can't Buy You Love"].

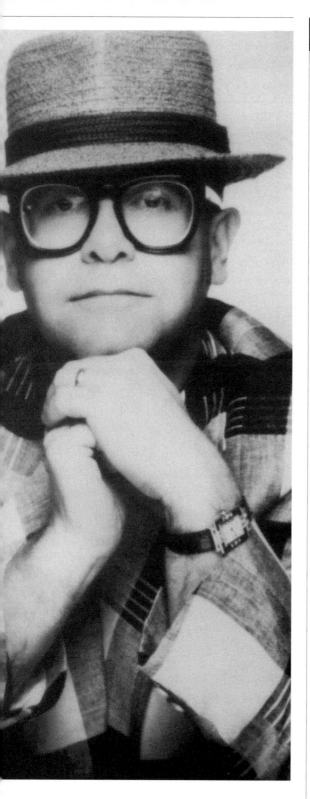

322 Torn Between Two Lovers

MARY MACGREGOR

Ariola America 7638

December 25, 1976 (2 weeks)

Writers: Phil Jarrell, Peter Yarrow

Producers: Peter Yarrow, Bary Beckett

"Mary MacGregor was a background singer for me," said Peter Yarrow in recalling the woman who sang "Torn Between Two Lovers." MacGregor joined Yarrow during the 1970s period during which he and the other members of Peter, Paul and Mary embarked on separate projects [see 27—"Puff the Magic Dragon"]. But the tune was originally intended for a male vocalist.

Yarrow said the major change he made when he decided to cut the tune with a distaff slant was the opening line, which had originally read, "I'm not the kind of guy who can lead a double life." Some of Yarrow's listeners were not pleased with the results of his alterations, which had a woman seeing two men rather than vice versa. "I realized when it was considered for Mary MacGregor that for a woman to be presented sympathetically as to having two lovers, that was upsetting to men," Yarrow said.

Some of those not bothered by the woman with two lovers issue but familiar with Yarrow's previous folk-oriented work *were* put off by the lush orchestration and unabashed middle-of-the-road melody. Yarrow said he enjoyed recording the song at the famed Muscle Shoals Studio in Alabama with "the best rhythm section in America," yet acknowledged how upsetting the record had been to some of his fans. "I think if you were to play it with just a guitar and bass, it wouldn't sound too poppy," he said. "[But] it does sound poppy. . . .There were some people shocked by it."

"Torn Between Two Lovers" became a #1 AC hit over a month before it climbed to #1 pop for the weeks of February 5 and 12, 1977. Rather unexpectedly, "Torn Between Two Lovers" also went to #3 country. In 1979 the song served as a title for a TV movie featuring Lee Remick as an adulterous socialite.

Born in St. Paul, Minnesota, on May 6, 1948, Mary MacGregor found it difficult to match the success of "Torn Between Two Lovers," which was her debut on the AC and pop charts. Six of her songs, the first two of which were also written by Yarrow, made the AC chart in the wake of "Torn. . ." In chronological order, they were "This Girl (Has Turned Into a Woman)" (#27 AC, #46 pop) and "For a While" (#38 AC, #90 pop) in 1977, "I've Never Been to Me" (#29 AC) and "The Wedding Song (There Is Love)" (#23 AC, #81 pop) in 1978, "Good Friend" (#11 AC, #39 pop) in 1979, and "Dancin' Like Lovers" (#31 AC, #72 pop) in 1980.

323 Weekend in New England

BARRY MANILOW

Arista 0212

January 8, 1977 (1 week)

Writer: Randy Edelman

Producers: Ron Dante, Barry Manilow

"I was stunned that this became a hit," said Barry Manilow in the liner notes to his anthology *The Complete Collection and Then Some. . .* about "Weekend in New England." "The song is a beauty and I tried to create a record that had the passion and power that I believed was inherent in the song. . . .'Weekend in New England' was a ballad that started out very tiny and ended very tiny. It sounded very legitimate, not rock- or dance-oriented. It was written in 3/4 time—a waltz. And besides, the title never appeared in the song!"

Discussing his composition in the same anthology, Randy Edelman said, "The music for 'Weekend' was written on an old Steinway upright in New Jersey in the house where I grew up. I wrote the lyrics on a plane and included the song on a solo album I was recording." Roughly a year after Edelman cut his version, Arista President Clive Davis told him if he made a few changes and put a new arrangement on the song, he would submit it to Manilow for consideration.

Manilow's take on "Weekend in New England" climbed to #10 pop for two weeks starting February 26, 1977, in addition to making #1 AC. Manilow played piano on the track in addition to singing the tune. Composer Edelman made the AC listings twice as a solo act himself, with "Everybody Wants to Find a Bluebird" in 1975 (#18 AC, #92 pop) and "Concrete and Clay" in 1976 (#11 AC, #108 bubbling under).

"Weekend in New England" was Manilow's sixth #1 AC and seventh consecutive top 30 pop hit, and by this time his fan base was so strong that plenty of female listeners would no doubt have been happy to take him for a weekend in New England or anywhere else for that matter. But Manilow insisted that his career always came first in his life, a fact that probably disappointed some of his detractors as well as his admirers.

"I'm consumed with my work," he told Chip Brion in *Us.* "I'm dedicated to it, I live for it. I don't have star friends, I don't go to crazy parties just to be seen. I don't rip hotel rooms apart while I'm on tour. Sure, I'll throw a tantrum once in a while. But nobody pays attention to me anyway! . . . If I'm boring, then I'm boring. I don't care. If the press and the critics want to dump on me, let 'em. It's going to get worse, as far as that's concerned, so I'm totally prepared for it."

But as far as the AC chart was concerned, Manilow was doing just fine. He got his fifth consecutive #1 on the listings a few months later with "Looks Like We Made It" [see 332].

1977

324 Love Theme From *A Star Is Born* (Evergreen)

BARBRA STREISAND

Columbia 10450

January 15, 1977 (6 weeks)

Writers: Barbra Streisand, Paul Williams

Producers: Barbra Streisand, Phil Ramone

W ho could have predicted that the theme song to Barbra Streisand's movie *A Star Is Born* would be written by Streisand herself? Certainly not Streisand. But Streisand's character was supposed to be a contemporary singer/songwriter, and she felt she needed to practice playing guitar in order to be believable in the role. So Streisand enlisted lyricist Lori Barth to be her instructor for the film.

One of their rehearsals proved pivotal. Streisand had asked Barth to play some of her own music; then, becoming extremely upset at the thought that she did not have Barth's songwriting talent, she ran out crying and hid in a bathroom. In a *Playboy* interview, Streisand recalled that her boyfriend Jon Peters, who was also producing the film, consoled her. "It was really this lovely moment, he was comforting me and saying, 'You can do it. You can do anything you set your mind to. Try to write a song!'" Emboldened, Streisand later did just that, using guitar chords she was learning from Barth.

The tune was strong enough to be chosen as the film's theme. As with other songs in *A Star Is Born*, the lyricist was to be Paul Williams. "I held off writing lyrics to 'Evergreen' to the last second," he said. "I knew it was a great song she had written." Initially, Williams' and Streisand's collaborative relationship was rocky. "I think I was intimidated by her, and my reaction to intimidation is a little glibness," he said. The barbs he aimed at Streisand did not make getting the song done a quick task, but when it was finished, nobody was complaining about how long it had taken. Looking back, Williams said he enjoyed working with her, saying "She was terrific." He also said, "She was really demanding. She was a perfectionist."

Though the film met with mixed reviews, there were only raves for "Evergreen," which won the Oscar for Best Song and the Grammy for Song of the Year (actually a tie for the latter with "You Light Up My Life"—see 340). "The partying almost killed me, but it was great," Williams joked about the wins. On a more serious note, he said, "For someone in the Midwest who came to Hollywood to break into the business, it was spectacular."

In addition, "Evergreen" became Streisand's second double-#1 AC and pop single, staying atop the latter chart for three weeks starting March 5, 1977. The soundtrack was at #1 on the LP chart at the same time, peaking there for six weeks starting February 12, 1977. Also worth noting is that Streisand recorded "Evergreen" in Spanish, Italian, and French. The song showed up again in 1982, as the B-side to Streisand's "Memory," from the Broadway musical *Cats*, and the record made #9 AC and #52 pop.

325 Southern Nights

GLEN CAMPBELL

Capitol 4376

February 26, 1977 (4 weeks nonconsecutive)

Writer: Allen Toussaint

Producer: Gary Klein

"S outhern Nights" was the second Glen Campbell single to top the AC, pop, and country charts, the first being "Rhinestone Cowboy" [see 268]. Although many listeners probably assumed the song was Campbell's, and was about his own happy childhood, the writer was actually Allen Toussaint, a leading writer and producer of New Orleans soul music during the 1960s.

Toussaint told *Goldmine* in 1997 how his childhood life inspired the song. "When I did it, I did it as a communication vehicle to share a mode of how I felt; a culmination of a lot of life—me as a little boy, coming up and visiting the people in the country. Sitting out on the porch when it's getting dark at night and all the old folk telling those stories behind me. And you feel so secure, because everything that's important in the whole world is right here—there's Aunt Jenille over here, and Uncle Ed, and over there, Uncle Moey.

"Those evenings would get very quiet because there wasn't as much electronics to buzz the area. No television . . .of course. The houses didn't have any electricity so the way people communicated and what they did in the evenings was so different. . . .I wanted to bring all those feelings to the moment."

Toussaint's recording of "Southern Nights" generated no national action, and it was only by chance that Campbell heard the song. "Jimmy Webb played that for me, and I thought it was a joke," he said. What did not seem right about the record to him was the placement of some of the lyrics, which struck Campbell as being random, and the fact that "It was hard to understand."

But what he did make out of the words and the melody touched him, so Campbell decided to cut the tune with a few changes. "I put in the 'old man' part at the end," he said in describing alterations to the lyrics. Because the original opening ("done on a saxophone playing through a Leslie speaker") left him cold, he also played a guitar shuffle to kick off the tune.

"Southern Nights" topped the AC chart first before doing the same on the country listings for two weeks starting March 19, 1977. It reached the pinnacle of the Hot 100 on April 30, 1977, but only for a week.

Campbell contacted Toussaint after cutting the song. "I called him when it was #1 across the board. I apologized to him and said I understood if he was upset with me changing his song. He said, 'No, man, you gave it such a lift.'" Toussaint reinforced that opinion in the *Goldmine* article, telling interviewer Emily Gaul that "I like Glen's [version] because he made it into a real song."

326 Sam

OLIVIA NEWTON-JOHN

MCA 40670

March 12, 1977 (2 weeks)

Writers: Don Black, John Farrar, Hank Marvin

Producer: John Farrar

Even people who already thought Olivia Newton-John was somewhat old-fashioned as a singer might have been taken by surprise when her first release of 1977 was a waltz. "It just worked out that way," producer John Farrar said of the 3/4 time for "Sam," a rare hit he wrote not by himself but with two collaborators, Don Black and Hank Marvin.

Farrar said that he had done a lot of the song long before it was finished. First, he and friend Hank Marvin came up with the music. Later Black, whose work as a lyricist included the #1 pop hits "To Sir With Love" in 1967 and "Ben" in 1972, worked with Farrar in creating words for his composition. "I think Hank had a couple of verses, and I did the chorus on it," Farrar said.

Unlike some of his other songs which became singles, Farrar said "Sam" struck him as a hit as soon as he heard it in the studio. "I remember when we recorded in Nashville, it went down great," he said.

"Sam," a name which Farrar said did not refer to an actual person, made #20 pop as well as #1 AC in 1977. It was Newton-John's seventh top 20 pop entry and first to make that part of the Hot 100 since "Something Better to Do" [see 277]. Despite the fact that some of her other singles hit higher peaks, Newton-John enjoyed "Sam" enough to include it in her anthology *Back to Basics—The Essential Collection 1971–1992.*

Farrar continued to work with Newton-John constantly for eight years after "Sam," through the 1985 single and LP title tune "Soul Kiss," which reached #20 both on the AC and pop charts. He and Newton-John teamed up again in 1989 to do her album for children, *Warm and Tender.* In the 1990s Farrar was based in Los Angeles, and he did some work with Tim Rice on a few musical projects.

As for Newton-John, she had become less involved in the music industry by the mid-1980s. She started a chain of clothing stores she called Koala Blue, and took time off to be with her husband and daughter. Her songs did not fare as well on either the AC and pop charts as previous efforts (e.g., a 1988 single, "The Rumour," written by Elton John, went to just #33 AC and #62 pop in 1988), and she began to record infrequently. Her anthology in 1992 included four new tunes, but she had little time to promote them as she was being treated for breast cancer. (One cut, "I Need Love," made #96 pop, and another, "Deeper Than a River," got to #20 AC.) The cancer treatments were successful, but the 1990s brought other traumas, including divorce and the bankruptcy of her company. In 1998 Newton-John finally released an album of all-new material, her first in a decade.

327 Don't Give Up on Us

DAVID SOUL

Private Stock 45129

April 9, 1977 (1 week)

Writer: Tony Macauley

Producer: Tony Macauley

In the hopes of finding a breakout hit, Private Stock label head Larry Uttal sent David Soul a song written by Howard Greenfield and Neil Sedaka called "One More Mountain to Climb" for Soul to add to his debut LP for the company. Then Uttal changed his mind and told Soul to drop "One More Mountain to Climb" in favor of another tune called "Don't Give Up on Us." Soul complied again, and the result was a #1 AC and pop hit, topping the latter the week of April 16, 1977. The 45 also hit #1 in the United Kingdom for four weeks starting January 15, 1977.

The song's popularity worried Soul somewhat, because it was not the exact direction he wanted to take as a singer. "I don't want to sell a few million copies and then disappear," Soul told Dennis Hunt of the *Los Angeles Times* in 1977. "Uttal is singles-oriented and he's geared to capitalizing on me while I'm hot. But I want him to put some of the money I'm making for his company back into developing me so I can become an album-selling artist and have longevity." Neither happened; both Soul's music career and Private Stock were virtually dormant by 1980.

Soul's other main job in 1977 was starring on the ABC-TV crime drama *Starsky and Hutch,* and he had misgivings about that too. He found himself under contract to do the series after the network bought it when it was a TV movie in 1975, and he hated the show, complaining that it was "formula TV." But the exposure did not hurt sales for "Don't Give Up on Us."

Born David Solberg in Chicago, Illinois, on August 28, 1943, he made his musical and TV mark in the mid-1960s playing "The Covered Man," a singer wearing a ski mask on *The Merv Griffin Show.* He even released a song with that title in 1966 on MGM, but had shed the image by the time he landed a starring role on the ABC-TV program *Here Come the Brides* from 1968-70. During the last year on the show he released a single on Paramount Records, but it bombed, and he had no other recording deals until Private Stock in 1976.

Soul did not stretch his recording success much past "Don't Give Up on Us." Two other Private Stock 45s made both the pop and AC charts in 1977 before he disappeared on both—"Going In With My Eyes Open" (#14 AC, #54 pop) and "Silver Lady" (#23 AC, #52 pop).

In 1995, after having acted in three more series after *Starsky and Hutch* ended in 1979 (the last being *Unsub* on NBC in 1989) and almost 20 TV movies, Soul left Hollywood for London. He told *Entertainment Weekly* in 1997 that "I had to get out of L.A. It was like being at a bad party." That same year, his first album in 15 years, *Leave a Light On,* was released in Europe.

328 Right Time of the Night

JENNIFER WARNES

Arista 0223

April 16, 1977 (1 week)

Writer: Peter McCann

Producer: Jim Ed Norman

"Right Time of the Night" arguably came at the right time in the career of Jennifer Warnes (pronounced "warns"). Born in Seattle, Washington, on March 3, 1947, she grew up in Anaheim, California, and before graduating high school sang at local venues and state fairs. She was so confident in her future as a pop vocalist that she turned down a scholarship to study opera in college. At age 19 she made her first album on London Records, billing herself as Jennifer.

Pat Paulsen, another Orange County native, caught her act and finagled an audition for her on *The Smothers Brothers Show*, the CBS-TV variety program on which he appeared. She became a regular on the show from 1967–69 as "Jennifer Warren," and made two more albums on Warner Brothers, still as just Jennifer, before going on a tour of Europe after the TV series ended. Unfortunately, when she got back from the tour, she learned that Warner Brothers had dropped her. Warnes spent much of the 1970s struggling and trying to regroup.

Then Warnes got her chance for an album on Arista Records, but prospects for her self-titled LP looked bleak when label president Clive Davis told her and her producer Jim Price he heard no songs he could promote as hit singles on it. Davis made two late additions to the album. "Clive picked 'I'm Dreaming' and 'Right Time of the Night,' and he brought in Jim Ed Norman, who arranges strings for the Eagles, to give those songs very explicit tracks," Warnes told Ariel Swartley in *Rolling Stone*. Under Norman's production, "Right Time of the Night" became Warnes' first AC and pop entry, reaching #1 AC and #6 pop the weeks of May 7 and 14, 1977. "I'm Dreaming" became the follow-up, and it made #9 AC and #50 pop.

The composer of "Right Time of the Night," Peter McCann, made the AC and pop charts himself at the same time with "Do You Wanna Make Love" (which peaked at #22 AC and #5 pop) while Warnes was climbing up the chart with his other composition. McCann had auditioned for Davis, but the executive liked "Right Time of the Night" better than "Do You Wanna Make Love" and did not care for McCann as a singer. McCann signed with 20th Century Records instead.

Over the next five years, Warnes stayed with Arista, charting fairly regularly on the AC and pop charts. However, the only song that came close to the popularity of "Right Time of the Night" was "I Know a Heartache When I See One" (#14 AC, #19 pop). Her biggest successes in the 1980s were duets, with Joe Cocker on "Up Where We Belong" in late 1982 (#3 AC, #1 pop) and with Bill Medley on "(I've Had) the Time of My Life" [see 528]. In the 1990s, she has continued to record and tour frequently.

329 When I Need You

LEO SAYER

Warner Brothers 8332

April 23, 1977 (1 week)

Writers: Albert Hammond, Carole Bayer Sager

Producer: Richard Perry

Briton Leo Sayer charted initially in his homeland in late 1973 with "The Show Must Go On," which peaked at #2 in the United Kingdom. But a cover by Three Dog Night in America became the hit version when it went to #4 pop in 1974, and Sayer did not make an impact in the United States until his second album, 1974's *Just a Boy*, prompted the release of "Long Tall Glasses (I Can Dance)," which peaked at #9 pop. Unhappily for Sayer, his co-writer and co-producer David Courtney left for a solo career, and his next album, 1975's *Another Year*, got nowhere in the United States. Sayer's manager, Adam Faith, then took things into his own hands and set up his client to work with producer Richard Perry, who had scored many previous hits with other artists including Nilsson [see 166—"Without You"] and Carly Simon [see 184—"You're So Vain"].

Sayer submitted material early for his fourth album, which eventually would become the *Endless Flight* LP, but Perry nixed all of it. Instead, he looked for material submitted by other writers. Perry described the history of "When I Need You" to John Tobler and Stuart Grundy in *The Record Producers*: "It was another huge hit and I think represented a different side of Leo, his best and truest side—there are very few people who can convey an intimate song like that quite the way he can. It was written by another dear and old friend, Carole Bayer Sager, along with Albert Hammond, and as soon as they brought me the song, I knew it was a hit, and I felt it would be excellent for Leo."

Sayer heard a demo of the song done by Hammond. "I just heard this song and flipped," he told Barry Scott in *We Had Joy, We Had Fun*. "I thought it was great. I was going through this situation where my wife, my ex-wife now, was back at home in England and I was in America in the studio missing her. Everything that I wanted to try and put into a song was already in this song. So I couldn't turn it down."

"When I Need You" topped the AC chart three weeks before doing so on the Hot 100. The record also crossed over to the R&B chart, hitting #94, and earned Sayer a Grammy nomination for Best Male Pop Vocal Performance. In 1978 Lois Johnson covered the song and made #63 country.

On the heels of his success with "When I Need You," Sayer told Ben Fong-Torres of *Rolling Stone*, "I'm happily married to a great girl who's my friend as well as my lover. . . .I've got a great band with me now, I've got Richard Perry, who can actually make my voice sound like God if need be. I've got everything I need. I'm living a good life." Despite that, Sayer did not hit #1 AC or return to the pop top 10 until three years later, with "More Than I Can Say" [see 395].

330 Hello Stranger

YVONNE ELLIMAN

RSO 871

April 30, 1977 (4 weeks)

Writer: Barbara Lewis

Producer: Freddie Perren

The first single from Yvonne Elliman, born in Honolulu, Hawaii, on December 29, 1951, was 1971's "I Don't Know How to Love Him," which she sang in the rock opera *Jesus Christ Superstar*. Her singing in a club attracted the attention of Andrew Lloyd Webber and Tim Rice, the writer/producers of *Jesus Christ Superstar*. Said Elliman: "They came up to me afterward and they said, 'You are our Mary Magdalene.'" At the time Elliman thought Mary Magdalene was the mother of Jesus, so when she heard "I Don't Know How to Love Him," the romantic song puzzled her. Once that misconception was cleared up, she played Magdalene, on stage, on the album, and later in the 1973 movie.

"I Don't Know How to Love Him" hit #15 AC and #28 pop, but it was bested by a cover from Helen Reddy which peaked at #12 AC and #13 pop in 1971. Elliman did another *Jesus Christ Superstar* tune, "Everything's Alright," which climbed to #25 AC and #92 pop in 1971. She did not make either chart after that until "Love Me" reached #5 AC and #14 pop in late 1976.

After "Love Me" came "Hello Stranger," a tune Barbara Lewis first took to #3 pop and #1 R&B in 1963. A duo called Fire and Rain took their version to #24 AC and #100 pop in 1973. "I really liked the Barbara Lewis version. It's always been a favorite of mine," Elliman said. She said her producer Freddie Perren intentionally copied the sounds of the Lewis record, and she imitated the singer's phrasings as well. According to Elliman, Lewis liked the near-remake of her cut ("She called me up on the phone and thanked me for doing it and I thanked her"). So did the record buyers, as the song hit #15 pop and #57 R&B in addition to #1 AC. "Hello Stranger" returned to the R&B chart at #20 in 1985 (Carrie Lucas, featuring the Whispers) and at #40 in 1990 (She, featuring Kim Waters).

Meanwhile, Elliman's career took off in 1978 with "If I Can't Have You," a #1 pop and #9 AC from the movie *Saturday Night Fever*. The next year "Moment by Moment," the theme song to another, less successful John Travolta film, went to #32 AC and #59 pop. Later that year her "Love Pains" went to #33 AC and #34 pop. "After that, I met my husband, and then we had a baby," she said. "There was no thought of continuing my career."

Speaking backstage after singing "If I Can't Have You" at a *Saturday Night Fever* reunion in New York City on January 31, 1998, she noted it was her first public singing appearance in 17 years. "This felt real good tonight," she commented, indicating that while she has been a happy housewife in southern California, she may go back into the studio again. As she put it, "Even my children are saying, 'Mom, why don't you sing?'"

331 Margaritaville

JIMMY BUFFETT

ABC 12254

May 28, 1977 (1 week)

Writer: Jimmy Buffett

Producer: Robert Putnam

More than 20 years after it became a hit, "Margaritaville" was a cottage industry for its singer Jimmy Buffett. Besides being a song, "Margaritaville" was the name of a merchandise store and cafe in Buffett's home base of Key West, Florida, in 1984 and in New Orleans in 1992, plus the name for a record label distributed by MCA in the 1990s. Buffett even wrote a movie script based on the song, but as of this writing it has not been filmed.

As for "Margaritaville" the song, the initial idea came to Buffett in Key West. He was watching tourists hit the town on a Memorial Day weekend, and they looked out of place. But it was not until 1973, when he was sitting at a bar in Austin, Texas, at the end of a tour, that the song came together.

"I was working on it, and I didn't have a title for it—I was sitting in a bar and had a wonderful frozen margarita, one of the best ones I ever had," Buffett said in a 1989 interview with the *Solid Gold Summer Hits* radio program. "That's where I said, 'Margaritaville'—that's the title I need for this tune. I had 'wasting away' and I had a fill-in word there. . .I was looking for the hook. After the little bar experience, I plugged it in."

One stanza Buffett wrote did not make the final record, but he later performed it often in concerts. "Margaritaville," listed on Buffett's lyric sheet as "Wastin' Away Again in Margaritaville," ended up at #1 AC, #13 country, and #8 pop the week of May 28, 1977.

Buffett did much more than just "Margaritaville," of course. He was born in Pascagoula, Mississippi, on December 25, 1946, but his family moved to Mobile, Alabama, when he was two years old. Buffett earned a double major in history and journalism from the University of Southern Mississippi in Hattiesburg, Mississippi. For a short time after graduating, he was a staff reporter at *Billboard*, contributing the Nashville news to the Music Capitals of the World column. But his burning desire was to be a singer, and in 1970 he left *Billboard* to release his first album, *Down to Earth*, on the Barnaby label.

He made Key West his home in 1971, and debuted on the AC chart in 1973 with "Grapefruit—Juicy Fruit" at #23. 1974's "Come Monday" broke him on the Hot 100 at #30 plus #3 AC, his biggest chart song until "Margaritaville." But no other 45s matched "Margaritaville," and his last pop entry was 1981's "It's My Job" at #57. Buffett made the AC chart only sporadically thereafter, including "Another Saturday Night" at #29 in 1993, yet his albums remained steady sellers into the 1990s, and he remains a top concert draw among his devoted fans, who are known as "Parrot Heads." As for "Margaritaville," by the late 1990s it had managed over 3 million plays over radio and TV airwaves.

332 Looks Like We Made It

BARRY MANILOW

Arista 0244

June 4, 1977 (3 weeks)

Writers: Richard Kerr, Will Jennings

Producers: Ron Dante, Barry Manilow

A few years before writing "Looks Like We Made It," Richard Kerr and Will Jennings collaborated on the song "Somewhere in the Night," which was done both by Helen Reddy and by the duo Batdoft and Rodney before Barry Manilow covered the tune in 1978. But it was Manilow alone who could take credit for popularizing 1977's "Looks Like We Made It."

"We wrote this one in Richard's flat in London where he banged away at a huge upright piano he called Old Joanna," Jennings related in Manilow's anthology *The Complete Collection and Then Some*. . . ."He gave me another of those beautiful, over-the-top-don't-spare-the-melodrama melodies, with at least two melodic hooks in the verse and two more in the chorus. All this accomplished with much good wine and Indian food in between writing sessions and much hilarity.

"Richard and I have often remarked on the people, millions of them in the world, who misunderstood the lyric of 'Looks Like We Made It.' It is a rather sad and ironic lyric about making it apart and not together, and of course everyone thinks it is a full on, positive statement. I don't know. Perhaps it is. . .in a way." Kerr recalled that it was a beautiful sunny day when they wrote the song, and they closed the curtains and dimmed the lights to avoid the temptation of going outside.

After hitting #1 AC the week of June 4, "Looks Like We Made It" got to the top of the Hot 100 the week of July 23. It would be Manilow's last #1 pop hit following "Mandy" [see 241] and "I Write the Songs" [see 281]. The song was on Manilow's current live album release, and its success no doubt helped the LP reach #1 the week of July 16. Manilow later performed the song in concert as part of a medley with "Send in the Clowns" from the Broadway musical *A Little Night Music*.

Manilow's streak of five consecutive #1 AC hits ended after "Looks Like We Made It." "Daybreak," a tune Manilow co-wrote with Adrienne Anderson, could not get past #7 AC and #23 pop when released as the follow-up. Manilow also made #33 AC near the end of 1977 with "It's Just Another New Year's Eve," but that was a live recording released as a promotional single to radio stations and was not available commercially, which is why it did not make the Hot 100.

After those two records, Manilow returned to the head of the AC listings with "Can't Smile Without You" [see 345]. He did have six more #1 AC entries after "Looks Like We Made It," but never more than two consecutively.

333 It's Sad to Belong

ENGLAND DAN AND JOHN FORD COLEY

Big Tree 16088

June 25, 1977 (5 weeks)

Writer: Randy Goodrum

Producer: Kyle Lehning

A fter the unexpected success of "I'd Really Love to See You Tonight" [see 309], England Dan and John Ford Coley found it a bit difficult to adjust to their newfound popularity. Coley said that when he learned while touring in Toronto that "I'd Really Love to See You Tonight" had become a gold record (over 1 million sold), "I went, 'Wow! I got a gold record. Now what do I do?' "

Fortunately, Parker McGee, the writer of "I'd Really Love to See You Tonight," had another song ready for them to record, called "Nights Are Forever Without You." England Dan and John Ford Coley thought this tune, unlike McGee's earlier submission, was appropriate for them to sing and they recorded it enthusiastically. It went to #6 AC and #10 pop in the fall of 1976.

Other songwriters took note of the sales and radio activity for the duo and decided to submit their own work to see if they could get a piece of the action. One was Randy Goodrum, whom Coley described as "a real nice guy." Goodrum offered "It's Sad to Belong" to the duo's production heads and they passed it to the singers, who agreed to do the tune. Goodrum went on to write several other #1 AC hits after this, from "Bluer Than Blue" [see 350] to "I'll Be Over You" [see 504].

Coley said part of the appeal of "It's Sad to Belong" was probably its story line, about a married person falling in love with someone outside the marriage. "It sounded like there were so many people in that situation," he said. But Coley also gave credit to Big Tree executives, who, he said, "were very aggressive in their manner of marketing. They would go out and meet radio stations and thank them personally for playing our records."

"It's Sad to Belong" made #21 pop in addition to its five-week #1 AC run in the summer of 1977. For its follow-up, Foley himself became the writer, penning "Gone Too Far," which did not quite live up to its title when it stopped at #8 AC and #23 pop in the fall of 1977. "We were trying to write as many things as we could ourselves," Coley recalled, adding that while he and England Dan liked much of the material they received from other artists, they worried that relying too much on outside sources would result in a "continuity loss" in quality. Nonetheless, "Gone Too Far" was the only single written by either member of the duo to be considered a hit.

The follow-up to "Gone Too Far" brought them back to #1 AC. See 346—"We'll Never Have to Say Goodbye Again."

334 My Heart Belongs to Me

BARBRA STREISAND

Columbia 10555

July 30, 1977 (4 weeks)

Writer: Alan Gordon

Producers: Gary Klein, Charlie Calello

An unpublicized fact about the production of the movie *A Star Is Born* was the doubts Barbra Streisand had about the way the songs sounded. "She recorded the music for *A Star Is Born* and didn't like it," recalled Charlie Calello. So her manager Charles Koppelman contacted his cousin, producer Gary Klein, about trying his hand on the tunes. Klein brought along Calello, who had worked with Klein previously as arranger on the Klein-produced hit "Southern Nights" [see 325].

They completed work on four songs for Streisand, but none of their mixes saw the light of day. "By the time we finished the records, the movie was such a success that she left them alone," Calello said. But she did like them enough to use for her next studio album. One of the tunes chosen for that album was "My Heart Belongs to Me." Calello produced "My Heart Belongs to Me" first as a single, sung by its writer Alan Gordon, but Gordon's release was quite different from the lushly orchestrated Streisand rendition—"more leveled," said Calello—and it promptly disappeared into obscurity.

Calello rehearsed the song with Streisand by playing it to her on piano while she sang it. During that first session, they worked out the song's introduction and break, which were different from Gordon's record. Calello went back to his hotel room after the rehearsal, but Streisand was bubbling with ideas on what to do with the song and contacted him there. "She would call me every 10 minutes. 'Charlie! I can sing it higher!'" laughed Calello. "Seriously," he added. "She was really a motivating factor in making that record better."

For the instrumental track, Calello and Klein used the top session players in Los Angeles at the time, including drummer Jeff Porcaro, later of Toto, and guitarist Larry Carlton. "I think David Foster played piano," Calello said. "We cut the track at 7 o'clock at night to 4 in the morning." The next day, with 40 to 50 musicians in an orchestra present, they recorded Streisand's vocal twice. After hearing the final product, Streisand told Calello, "That's beautiful, Charlie!" He said Streisand, at least for this recording, was nowhere near the perfectionist terror her reputation suggested.

"My Heart Belongs to Me" was the second consecutive #1 AC hit and top 10 pop entry for Streisand following "Love Theme From *A Star is Born* (Evergreen)" [see 324]. It stopped at #4 pop the weeks of July 30 and August 6, 1977. Its follow-up did not emerge until a year later, but it also hit #1 AC; see 352—"Songbird."

335 Sunflower

GLEN CAMPBELL

Capitol 4445

August 27, 1977 (1 week)

Writer: Neil Diamond

Producer: Gary Klein

Neil Diamond wrote "Sunflower" but did not release it on an album or as a single. That honor went to Glen Campbell, whose production staff worked on the backing tracks first. "The guys actually did it out in San Francisco and knew that he [Diamond] wasn't doing it," Campbell said. It did moderately well as a single, hitting #1 AC, #39 pop, and #4 country in the summer of 1977, and Campbell liked it enough to continue doing it in concert in the 1990s, sometimes introducing it on stage with the help of his daughter.

"Sunflower" was the last #1 AC for Campbell, and his singles started to do poorly on the AC and pop charts after 1977. The effort that came closest to a hit was 1978's entry "Can You Fool," which made #7 AC, #16 country, and #38 pop. Two singles in 1979 made the AC chart without hitting the Hot 100, "I'm Gonna Love You" (#38) and "My Prayer" (#42), and he had only three more AC entries through his last, 1983's "I Love How You Love Me," which got only to #35 AC (his last pop entry was 1981's "I Love My Truck," which went to #94).

Campbell blamed his declining sales on his label, Capitol; he said they didn't have the right type of people in the promotional department for his records. He left Capitol in 1981, but the replacement companies promoted him only to country and not AC or pop listeners.

On Atlantic America from 1982–86, Campbell remained a staple on the country charts, with his highest-charting effort during his time there being "A Lady Like You" at #4 in 1985. MCA had him for most of the rest of the 1980s and he continued as a chart regular there too, with his best outing being 1988's "Still Within the Sound of My Voice," which went to #5.

Campbell returned to Capitol in the 1990s, but mostly made only the lower rungs of the country ladder, with cuts from his albums which were not released as singles. This change in fortune seemed not to perturb Campbell too much, as by then he had declared himself a born-again Christian and was in demand for singing before Christian audiences as well as secular ones. "I love to play," he said." I do half Christian and half secular dates." In 1998 he vowed not to go out on the road so much anymore, but also noted that he did more touring in 1997 than in the early 1970s. Campbell lives with his family in Phoenix, Arizona, which he has considered his hometown since moving there on September 18, 1981. He still plans to record in the future and said he is looking for songs about love and life in general.

336 Handy Man

JAMES TAYLOR

Columbia 10557

September 3, 1977 (1 week)

Writers: Otis Blackwell, Jimmy Jones

Producer: Peter Asher

"Handy Man" was an upbeat ditty complete with whistling when originally done by Jimmy Jones in 1960. His version went to #2 pop and #3 R&B. Then in 1977 James Taylor transformed the song into a languid ballad that topped the AC chart and also made #4 on the Hot 100 for two weeks beginning September 10, 1977. It proved to be Taylor's last top 10 pop hit to date.

Otis Blackwell is credited with writing much of "Handy Man," but Jones is quoted in *The Top Ten* by Bob Gilbert and Gary Theroux as having added a substantial element to the song. "One night I was in bed worried, because I had to pay my rent the next day, and I didn't have any money," he said.

"Now, I had been thinking about 'Handy Man,' but couldn't get that song to hang together right. Then about one or two o'clock in the morning, the punch hit—the 'come-a, come-a' rhythm idea. My wife was pregnant at the time, but I woke her up in the middle of the night and said, 'Hey, how do you like this? Come-a, come-a, come-a?' And she said, 'Aw, all right, whatever,' 'cause to her it didn't sound like anything at all. But I knew that it did."

While Jones sang "come-a, come-a" in a peppy manner, as did Del Shannon in a remake which went to #22 pop in 1964, Taylor took the same lines and stretched them out to give them and the rest of the lyrics almost a mournful quality. The radical revision impressed Grammy voters to the extent that they awarded him with a statuette for Best Male Pop Vocal Performance and nominated the LP from which it came, *JT*, for Album of the Year. By the time that happened, Jimmy Jones had faded into obscurity, having had only one more hit, "Good Timin'," which reached #3 pop and #8 R&B in 1960.

The B-side to Taylor's "Handy Man," "Bartender's Blues," generated enough response on country radio stations to go to #88 country in the summer of 1977. Another rendition of "Handy Man" also cropped up on the country chart five years later when Joel Hughes took it to #75.

The same week "Handy Man" peaked on the pop chart, James' younger sister Kate Taylor entered the AC chart with her remake of a soul tune, Betty Everett's 1964 hit "It's in His Kiss (The Shoop Shoop Song)." Kate went to #13 AC and #49 pop with her rendition, which was produced and arranged by James. Taylor had no more solo #1 AC hits but did return to the peak position when he sang with Art Garfunkel and Paul Simon in 1978 [see 344—"(What a) Wonderful World"].

337 Nobody Does It Better

CARLY SIMON

Elektra 45413

September 10, 1977 (7 weeks)

Writers: Carole Bayer Sager (words), Marvin Hamlisch (music)

Producer: Richard Perry

"Nobody Does It Better" reteamed Carly Simon with producer Richard Perry, with whom she had not worked since her 1975 LP *Playing Possum*. Their reunion proved fruitful as "Nobody Does It Better" rocketed her back to solo hit status, a position she had not been in since "You're So Vain" in 1972 [see 184]. Not only did the song have a long run atop the AC chart but it also stayed three weeks at #2 pop in late October 1977 behind the powerhouse "You Light Up My Life" [see 340].

Though Perry no longer produced Simon after 1975, he thought of her when two songwriter chums of his showed him their early work on music for the James Bond film *The Spy Who Loved Me*, slated for 1977 release. Perry elaborated on the circumstances in *The Record Producers* by John Tobler and Stuart Grundy. "When I heard the song 'Nobody Does It Better,' which was long before it was to be included in the film, and Marvin Hamlisch and Carole Bayer Sager, two very close friends of mine who wrote it, saw how enthusiastic I was about it, they submitted it to the producer, Cubby Broccoli," said Perry. "He immediately loved it." He also said that as soon as he knew that it was going to be the theme for *The Spy Who Loved Me*, he felt that Carly would be the perfect person to sing it. "When Carly heard it, she liked the song very much, and we got together shortly afterwards and made the record."

The result was a hit and an Oscar-nominated Best Song, losing to "You Light Up My Life." The tune also earned Grammy nominations for Song of the Year and Best Female Pop Vocal Performance.

After "Nobody Does It Better," Simon had one other top 10 pop hit, "You Belong to Me," which went to #4 AC in 1978. That same year a duet with her husband James Taylor, "Devoted to You," went to #2 AC and #36 pop (they divorced in 1983). In the 1980s she made occasional appearances on the AC and pop charts with several of the singles being songs from motion pictures. The most important of these to her despite its rather meager chart showing of #11 AC and #49 pop in 1989 was probably one she wrote, "Let the River Run" from *Working Girl*, which won the Oscar for Best Song and the Grammy for Best Song Written Specifically for a Motion Picture or Television. During the 1990s Simon made only the AC chart, generally with album tracks. In May 1998 she announced she was battling breast cancer.

"Nobody Does It Better" was the first James Bond theme to make #1 AC. The second came six years later [see 442—"All Time High"].

338 Just Remember I Love You

FIREFALL

Atlantic 3420

October 29, 1977 (2 weeks)

Writer: Rick Roberts

Producer: Jim Mason

Guitarist Jock Bartley met vocalist Rick Roberts when the latter replaced Gram Parsons in the Flying Burrito Brothers band in 1970. "He and I found out that we both lived in Boulder [Colorado]," Bartley said. Roberts subsequently launched a solo career, and later approached Bartley about working together.

Returning to Boulder, they found bassist Mark Andes, formerly with the Spirit and Jo Jo Gunne bands. Then Roberts recruited guitarist and songwriter Larry Burnett from Washington, D.C. "Basically, we started Firefall and played with a local drummer until that didn't work, and Rick brought in Michael Clarke instead," Bartley said. The quintet's name came from Roberts, who remembered that in the 1950s Firefall was the name of a tourist attraction in Yosemite National Park involving a burning bonfire that was hurled off a cliff.

Firefall recorded their first self-titled LP for Atlantic in 1975, with David Muse added at keyboards. Released in 1976, the song which became their big hit was "You Are the Woman," which hit #6 AC and #9 pop. This tune, like most Firefall hits, was written by Roberts. "Rick wrote from a left-brain, not necessarily formula-type of way, but with an eye to commercial success," Bartley said.

For their second LP, they accepted Atlantic's suggestion to go back and write a few more songs after submitting their first efforts. They also changed "Just Remember I Love You." "We thought, 'We should recut this over again.' It was a little slow and didn't have the pizzazz we wanted," Bartley said. He and Andes added a few guitar licks and "more oomph." Bartley believed that without the changes, the song might not have become the hit it was, going to #11 pop and being played more than 2 million times on radio stations.

The song's background vocals were by Timothy B. Schmit, a member of the Eagles from 1977–80. Roberts and Clark knew him from previous recording work and producer Jim Mason asked him to be on the record. "Timothy is all over that, particularly the end," Bartley said. "Great singer."

By 1981, all the founding members of Firefall had left the group except Bartley, possibly due to the way Atlantic viewed the band. "They wanted us to be a light rock band, and we thought, 'We're a rock band that does some ballads,'" Bartley said. As the sole owner of the band's name, Bartley continued to cut records and tour with new musicians.

Firefall last charted with "Always" in 1983 (#24 AC, #59 pop). The Boulder-based group still tours and records occasionally. Bartley noted that a lot of couples still request "Just Remember I Love You," saying they played it when they fell in love or got married. "I'm really happy that the songs we have to play now have stood the test of time," Bartley noted. "The main thing Firefall always had was really good songs."

339 We're All Alone

RITA COOLIDGE

A&M 2551

November 12, 1977 (1 week)

Writer: William "Boz" Scaggs

Producer: David Anderle

Born in Nashville, Tennessee, on May 1, 1944, Rita Coolidge led a group called R.C. and the Moonpies while attending Florida State University. After graduating with an art degree, she went to Memphis to do session work. Her voice attracted the attention of several artists. Joe Cocker and the folk duo of Bonnie & Delaney had her tour with their acts as well as sing, and her work on stage won raves.

Coolidge first skirted the Hot 100 as a soloist the week of May 10, 1969, with "Turn Around and Love You," which hit #96 on Pepper Records, but she did not "officially" start her solo career until A&M Records signed her in 1971. A year later, her first A&M single to chart was "Fever," backed with "My Crew." "Fever" stalled at #76 pop while "My Crew" got airplay on a few stations, including some AC ones in 1973, where it hit #38 and became the first of her 17 AC entries. During the early to mid-1970s Coolidge also had a few hit duets with her husband Kris Kristofferson (they were married from 1973 to 1980)

It was not until 1977 that she had her first solo hits, including "We're All Alone." "The record company president Jerry Moss had called me into his office one day to talk about songs," Coolidge said. He showed her Boz Scaggs' Silk Degrees LP, a #2 album for five weeks in 1976 which spun off four singles onto the Hot 100, "It's Over" (#38), "Lowdown" (#3 pop and his first AC entry at #11), "What Can I Say" (#42 pop, #35 AC), and "Lido Shuffle" (#11 pop in 1977). Surprisingly, "We're All Alone," an album cut and the B-side to the last two singles, was not promoted by Scaggs' label Columbia. Moss thought it could be big and told Coolidge to cut it.

"We're All Alone" had been covered earlier by Frankie Valli in 1976, who went to #27 AC and #78 pop with it, and Tanya Tucker's older sister La Costa, who took the song to #75 country in the spring of 1977. But Coolidge, who did not hear Valli's or La Costa's versions, was coming off a hit with "(Your Love Has Lifted Me) Higher and Higher" (#5 AC and #2 pop in the summer of 1977), and that momentum brought attention to the follow-up, "We're All Alone." "After 'Higher and Higher,' and I imagine it still happens in the music business, it was the idea of going on something hot [uptempo] with a ballad," she said of the timing.

Coolidge's "We're All Alone" went top 10 AC and pop, reaching #7 on the latter for four weeks beginning November 26, 1977. It even made #82 country. And, as Coolidge later learned, "At some point, maybe three years after it was a hit, it was the theme song of a soap opera in Brazil."

Coolidge went on to have several more hit singles, including another at #1 AC [see 442—"All Time High"].

340 You Light Up My Life
DEBBY BOONE

Warner/Curb 8455

November 19, 1977 (1 week)

Writer: Joe Brooks

Producer: Joe Brooks

In the 1977 film *You Light Up My Life*, the heroine, played by Didi Conn, cuts the title tune in a recording studio with one take and, at the end of the film, sees the tune go up a pop chart similar to the Hot 100 to hit #1. In this case, life imitated art, as Debby Boone's cover stayed at #1 pop an impressive 10 weeks starting October 15, 1977 and also got to #1 AC and #4 country for a week. But Boone's version was not the one heard in the film.

Debby Boone was born in Hackensack, New Jersey, on September 22, 1956. Her father, Pat Boone, never hit #1 AC but might have had the chart been in existence in the 1950s, as most of his hits were in that decade. Debby was part of the Boone Sisters, a gospel-oriented quartet featuring her three siblings, from 1969 until her decision to go solo in 1977.

The success of "You Light Up My Life" was due to an odd set of circumstances. According to Pat, Joe Brooks, who wrote and directed the film as well as the title song, wanted to release the soundtrack rendition done by Kacey Cisyk as a single. But she refused to sign the contract, so he cut it with Debby instead. Cisyk finally did get her version out, but only after Boone hit #1. To make matters worse, the single listed the artist as "Original Cast" rather than by her name. It went only to #80 pop in four weeks. (Cisyk did get to #33 AC in 1978 with her recording of the title tune of the movie *The One and Only*, but had no further success. She died in 1998.)

Apart from a minor note or phrasing change, the vocal and backing track on the two versions are so similar that it hard to tell who is singing, Boone or Cisyk. Boone told Dennis Hunt of *The Los Angeles Times* that "Even some of my friends thought I was singing the song in the movie."

"You Light Up My Life" won a host of awards, including the Oscar for Best Song and the Grammy for Song of the Year. "You Light Up My Life" also got Grammy nominations for Record of the Year and Best Female Pop Vocal Performance, and Boone won the Grammy for Best New Artist.

Nothing Boone did later came close to having the success of "You Light Up My Life." She did have eight more AC entries through 1981's "Perfect Fool" at #37, but most did not even bubble under, although 1980's "Are You on the Road to Lovin' Me Again" hit #1 country. She has since alternated between being a stay-at-home mother and starring in various stage productions.

341 How Deep Is Your Love
THE BEE GEES

RSO 882

November 26, 1977 (6 weeks)

Writers: Barry Gibb, Robin Gibb, Maurice Gibb

Producers: Barry Gibb, Robin Gibb, Maurice Gibb, Karl Richardson, Albhy Galuten

Atlantic producer Arif Mardin raved one day to arranger Karl Richardson about the next group they would record in Miami following their work with the Average White Band. "They sing like angels," boasted Mardin. He was referring to the Bee Gees.

The brothers Gibb—Barry (born September 1, 1947) and twins Maurice and Robin (born December 22, 1949)—were born in Manchester, England, but lived in Australia from 1958–67 before returning to England and becoming a top worldwide singing trio. Their falsetto harmonies found favor in America first on the Hot 100, when "New York Mining Disaster 1941" went to #14 in 1967. Their AC chart debut was 1971's "Lonely Days," which hit #28.

Mardin produced the group's "Jive Talkin'," which made #9 AC and #1 pop, in 1975, and was planning a follow-up when the Bee Gees' manager Robert Stigwood switched his RSO label from Atlantic Records to PolyGram. Atlantic subsequently refused to let Mardin work with the trio. Richardson decided to stick with the Bee Gees, and they said, "We'll just do it ourselves." But after 10 days of working with them as producer, Richardson decided that he needed help with their next album, so he called in his friend Albhy Galuten from England. Together, the five of them had another #1 pop hit in 1976 with "You Should Be Dancing" (#25 AC). Then Stigwood had them do music for a film, which was eventually titled *Saturday Night Fever*. One of the songs for the film was the mellow "How Deep Is Your Love."

Richardson said that contrary to some reports, "How Deep Is Your Love" was written for the movie and intended to be sung by the Bee Gees. "We made the record in France," he said. "I remember Barry came down around noontime to [pianist] Blue Weaver. He said, 'Blue, have I got a record for you!'" The Bee Gees, Richardson, and Galuten made the demo of "How Deep Is Your Love" in France, but not the final version. "At the time, I remember, we only had a month in France to [mix the album]," Richardson said. But the group had booked studio time in Miami afterward, so they did the final vocal and instrumental tracks in Florida instead.

Releasing the ballad "How Deep Is Your Love" as the first single off a disco-oriented album puzzled some, but Richardson thought it was appropriate. "It was right around Christmas time. . . .I think the thing was kind of magical," he said. "How Deep Is Your Love" ended up going to #1 AC and pop, staying atop the latter chart three weeks starting December 24, 1977.

"How Deep Is Your Love" was released as a single before the movie came out in every country in which it was to be shown. The song's success helped *Saturday Night Fever* become one of the biggest-selling soundtracks ever (more than 20 million copies sold) and earned the Bee Gees a Grammy for Best Pop Performance by a Duo, Group or Chorus with Vocal.

In 1995 the male vocal quartet Portrait revived "How Deep Is Your Love," taking it to #51 R&B and #93 pop.

1978

342 Just the Way You Are

BILLY JOEL

Columbia 10646

January 7, 1978 (4 weeks)

Writer: Billy Joel

Producer: Phil Ramone

William Martin Joel, born on Long Island, New York, on May 9, 1949, was anything but an overnight sensation when "Just the Way You Are" hit. He formed his first band in 1964, but the Echoes, which later became the Lost Souls, never went much beyond the bar band circuit. In the late 1960s he and some other gents from his hometown toured as the Hassles, and then he and the Hassles' drummer Jon Small formed a hard-rock duo named Attila, but Attila's noisy instrumentals were virtually unlistenable and sold few copies.

Embarking on a solo career in the early 1970s, the pianist got a contract with Columbia Records and made his AC and pop chart debut in 1974 with his autobiographical "Piano Man" at #4 AC and #25 pop. But after his 1974 follow-ups, "Travelin' Prayer" (#31 AC, #77 pop) and "The Entertainer" (#30 AC, #34 pop), he was off the charts for nearly three years until he clicked with the ballad "Just the Way You Are." "I was in the middle of a meeting with someone, and 'Just the Way You Are' popped out of my head," he told Joe Smith in *Off the Record.* "I said, 'I gotta go home right now and write this song.' I just stopped the meeting. That's how all my songs get written. It's another dimension."

But, as he told Timothy White in *Rock Lives,* getting his band to do the song was not as easy as creating it. "First of all, we weren't even serious about the song. Everybody was down on it and thought it was too goofy and sappy. Liberty [DeVitto, the group's drummer] didn't even want to play on it. 'I'm not Tito Puente!' he said. 'I won't play that oily cocktail lounge cha-cha/samba crap!'

"I couldn't explain the tune to anyone. The track never really made much sense until I added the wordless vocal that winds its way through the track, giving it some glue and some texture."

It had more than texture, for "Just the Way You Are" got Joel to #1 AC and #3 pop for the weeks of February 18 and 25, 1978, behind the Bee Gees' "Stayin' Alive" at #1 and Andy Gibb's "(Love Is) Thicker Than Water" at #2. It was his best showing on both charts. Additionally, Joel won a Grammy for Song of the Year for the tune. Barry White covered "Just the Way You Are" in 1979 and got to #45 R&B and #102 bubbling under.

Devotees of "Just the Way You Are" were disappointed when in 1982 Joel divorced his wife Elizabeth, for whom he had written the tune. However, he kept her brother on his payroll to handle his finances, a move he later bitterly regretted. But that, as they say, is another story.

343 Desiree

NEIL DIAMOND

Columbia 10657

February 4, 1978 (1 week)

Writer: Neil Diamond

Producer: Bob Gaudio

"To me it's a song with a great groove," Neil Diamond wrote about "Desiree" in his liner notes to his anthology *In My Lifetime*. "That's about it. I wrote it in my beach house so there's definitely some ocean vibes going on in that one." The fictional woman described in "Desiree" (pronounced "DEZ-ur-ray") became a real #16 pop hit for Neil Diamond in 1978 and also led the pack for a week on the AC chart. He recorded it in 1977 for his *I'm Glad You're Here With Me Tonight* LP. Another track on the album would receive more attention for him, even though it was not released as a single.

"You Don't Bring Me Flowers" was written originally by Diamond along with the husband and wife songwriting team of Alan and Marilyn Bergman as, of all things, the theme song to *All That Glitters*, a 1977 TV sitcom in which men and women switched traditional roles (the men were sex objects and wore revealing outfits, for example). The show died a quick death and did not use the composition, which was intended to be a torch song as done by a man. Diamond did a straightforward version for *I'm Glad You're Here With Me Tonight*.

As luck would have it, Diamond's colleague Barbra Streisand heard it and recorded the tune for her *Songbird* LP [see 352] in the same key. A deejay in Louisville, Kentucky, Gary Guthrie, cut both versions together into a "duet," and its popularity led Diamond and Streisand to redo the song for real on another session. The new "You Don't Bring Me Flowers" hit #1 pop for two weeks starting December 2, 1978, but made only #3 AC.

Nonetheless, the new duet became the title track for Diamond's new LP in 1978, which generated a few more hits for him. "Forever in Blue Jeans" went to #2 AC for two weeks in 1979 along with reaching #20 pop, followed by "Say Maybe," which reached #3 AC despite a rather unimpressive peak of #55 pop.

Diamond's next LP, *September Morn*, had a title song which reached #2 AC for one week in 1980 as well as #17 pop. Another single from the album, "The Good Lord Loves You," became the first Diamond single since 1974's "Skybird" not to make the AC top 10 after 11 consecutive singles before it had done so. "The Good Lord Loves You" was one of Diamond's worst-performing singles on both the AC and pop charts, peaking at #23 AC and #67 pop.

Luckily for Diamond, his next LP was the soundtrack for his remake of the movie *The Jazz Singer*, and it earned him his sixth #1 AC hit [see 405—"America"].

344 (What A) Wonderful World

ART GARFUNKEL WITH JAMES TAYLOR AND PAUL SIMON

Columbia 10676

February 11, 1978 (5 weeks)

Writers: Barbara Campbell, Lou Adler, Herb Alpert

Producer: Art Garfunkel

The British music industry celebrated 25 years of charting records (1952 to 1977) in the United Kingdom in a television show in October 1977. One of the special's segments was the acceptance ceremony for the Britannia Award to Paul Simon and Art Garfunkel. The duo's "Bridge Over Troubled Water" single and LP from 1970 [see 130] won the Brittannia as the best in their respective categories.

As part of the event, Simon and Garfunkel sang a few tunes for the show and, according to Garfunkel in *Rolling Stone*, "we got the feeling of singing together again. Then we thought of James as an interesting third element." "James" was James Taylor, whose 1976 LP *In the Pocket* used Garfunkel as a contributing vocalist. Simon and Garfunkel first considered redoing the oldie "Bring It On Home to Me" before settling on "(What A) Wonderful World." Both songs had been hits for the late soul artist Sam Cooke. "We all have this thing for Sam Cooke," Garfunkel explained. In the case of "(What A) Wonderful World," Cooke took the song to #12 pop and #2 R&B in 1960. Later remakes came from Herman's Hermits, who got it to #4 pop in 1965, and Johnny Nash, who went to #34 AC, #66 R&B, and #103 bubbling under in 1976.

Of the trio's version, Garfunkel commented, "The tempo and feel are James'. We had two rehearsals to get the vocals right—we traded off the parts—then we took it into the studio." Garfunkel had the only album of the three to contain the song, 1978's *Watermark*. "(What A) Wonderful World" with three-part harmonies made #17 pop in 1978.

In 1981, Simon and Garfunkel reunited for a concert in New York City's Central Park in 1981, but other than that remained apart professionally. Simon remained a fairly popular and critically admired musician over the next decade. His *Graceland* album was a huge critical success and moderate commercial one in 1986, scoring a hit single with "You Can Call Me Al" (#15 AC, #23 pop). Less successful was his 1989 follow-up, *Rhythm of the Saints*. In the 1990s he spent much of his time working on a Broadway musical called *The Capeman*, which opened on January 29, 1998 but closed two months later after tepid reviews and ticket sales. Nevertheless, he remained well respected within the music industry.

Garfunkel took more varied avenues, usually away from the music world, over the next two decades. Garfunkel admitted to Beth Johnson in *Entertainment Weekly* in 1998 that "I was quite reclusive in the '80s." He hardly recorded at all for 15 years, dabbling instead in everything from writing a book of poetry (1989's *Still Water*) to literally walking across the United States. Then he released two albums, 1996's *Across America* and 1997's *Songs From a Parent to a Child*, and announced plans to do another solo album and even write his autobiography.

345 Can't Smile Without You

BARRY MANILOW

Arista 0305

March 18, 1978 (2 weeks nonconsecutive)

Writers: Geoff Morrow, Chris Arnold, David Martin

Producer: Ron Dante, Barry Manilow

"In 1975, my wife Debbie was working at a greeting card store," recounted David Martin about "Can't Smile Without You," the song he co-wrote with Geoff Morrow and Chris Arnold, in the Barry Manilow anthology *The Complete Collection and Then Some*. . . . "One evening she gave me a card. The card was completely plain except for a small blue badge on the front. On the badge was a mouth drooping at the corners and a tear rolling down the cheek. Across the top of the card were simply the words 'Can't Smile Without You.'

"I was immediately drawn to the slogan and during the drive home from Hampstead to Harrow [England], a journey of about 30 minutes, the song was written. As a token of my love for Debbie, I recorded the song myself in 1975 and although it got a lot of airplay in the U.K., it missed becoming a hit." In 1976 Engelbert Humperdinck included the song as a track on his album *After The Lovin'*, as did the Carpenters on their LP *A Kind of Hush*, but the tune gained little attention in either version.

Then Clive Davis, president of Arista, heard the tune and presented it to Manilow for consideration. Manilow was less than enthusiastic, as he recalled in his anthology's liner notes. "It went against every sophisticated musician bone in my body. It was so simple. It was so sweet. It was so, so. . .commercial! I resisted recording it for the longest time. But Clive wouldn't give up. He kept insisting that I give it a try. Finally, I gave in. I decided that I would treat it with a big smile; like a vaudeville piece, with lots of key changes, a whistle in the intro and a real take-home ending. I had even made plans to include a tap dance solo!" That latter part was edited out of the final record, but the whistling and bright finish remained.

In his autobiography *Sweet Life*, Manilow claimed that the song's power was so great, it inspired a woman with severe depression to leave her house. He also enjoyed doing the song in concert, as it "had become the favorite part of my show. During the song, I would pick someone at random out of the audience to sing with."

"Can't Smile Without You" also made #3 pop for three weeks, starting April 22. Holding it back from the top there was the Bee Gees' "Night Fever" at #1 and Yvonne Elliman's "If I Can't Have You" at #2. Manilow's next AC chart-topper came in May—"Even Now" [see 349].

346 We'll Never Have to Say Goodbye Again

ENGLAND DAN AND JOHN FORD COLEY

Big Tree 16110

March 25, 1978 (6 weeks)

Writer: Jeffrey Comanor

Producer: Kyle Lehning

A duo named Deardorff and Joseph (Danny and Marcus) cut "We'll Never Have to Say Goodbye Again" first, but with a slightly different title, "Never Have to Say Goodbye Again," and it became their one and only chart entry, bubbling under at #109 in the spring of 1977. For John Ford Coley, the song brought back bittersweet memories. On the positive side, he enjoyed reminiscing about its writer Jeffrey Comanor, who had his only hit with this record. "He's a chiropractor down in Georgia," Coley said. "He's also written some very interesting books." Coley also found "We'll Never Have to Say Goodbye Again" an enjoyable record to sing, but the circumstances surrounding his and England Dan's work on it made it somewhat painful to recall. "That song was at a very stressful point in our career," Coley said.

England Dan and John Ford Coley decided to cut the song, but then their ex-manager Marcia Day encouraged her new client Maureen McGovern to do the song as well. When the duo's management heard about the cover, a licensing battle ensued over who had the rights to do the song, followed by a similar battle for control between the record companies representing each act. (Eventually Dan and Coley were allowed to release their version as a single.)

The conflict upset England Dan and John Ford Coley, who did not participate in the power struggle. "Poor Maureen McGovern," Coley said. "We were just saying, 'Maureen, we don't know anything about this.'" The result may not have been optimal for McGovern, but "We'll Never Have to Say Goodbye Again" did allow the two men to return to #1 AC and top 10 pop for the third time on each chart. On the Hot 100, the single peaked at #9 for two weeks starting April 15, 1978. Like most of their tunes, noted Coley, in this one "Dan actually did the majority of the leads, and I did the majority of the harmonies."

England Dan and John Ford Coley released three more singles after "We'll Never Have to Say Goodbye Again" in 1978, but none fared particularly well. "You Can't Dance" stopped at #22 AC and #49 pop in the summer of 1978, and the next two singles failed to make the pop chart. "If the World Ran Out of Love Tonight" ran out of gas at #41 AC in the fall of 1978, and "Westward Wind," a composition written by Coley, blew only to #31 AC near the end of 1978.

Happily for the duo, they had one more hit ready to go in 1979 [see 364—"Love Is the Answer"].

347 Feels So Good

CHUCK MANGIONE

A&M 2001

May 13, 1978 (1 week)

Writer: Chuck Mangione

Producer: Chuck Mangione

For Chuck Mangione, "Feels So Good" was a happy by-product of doing his album of the same name. "I didn't go into the studio to make a single," he recalled. He was doing only six instrumental numbers, none of which had titles at first. According to Mangione, most of the A&M executives saw no potential for any of them outside the LP, asking him, "Where are the singles on this album?" Then one exec, Barry Korkin, came up with the idea of paring "Feels So Good" down from nine minutes to three and a half for radio play (Mangione called the editing "major surgery"). The 45 kept intact the two principle attributes of "Feels So Good," a punchy guitar solo by Grant Geissman and the laid-back sounds Mangione blew on his favorite instrument, the fluegelhorn. It also included James Bradley Jr. on drums and Charles Meeks on bass.

"[The fluegelhorn] is a very odd instrument," Mangione noted. "It kind of looks like a trumpet in the sixth month of pregnancy. It's in the same key, but a darker, more mellow instrument." He took up the instrument during his studies at the Eastman School of Music in the early 1960s when he saw Miles Davis perform in person. To Mangione, "It was like finding the right baseball glove."

Prior to "Feels So Good," Mangione had only minor AC and pop chart success. His single "Hill Where the Lord Hides" went to #32 AC and #76 pop in 1971; then "Chase the Clouds Away" went to #96 pop in 1975, "Bellavia (Belle Veeya)" to #49 AC in 1976, and "Land of Make Believe" to #86 pop in 1977. But "Feels So Good" became a hit on both charts, topping the AC list and peaking at #4 pop the week of June 10, 1978. It also became his first entry on the R&B chart, where it reached #68.

Mangione believes that part of the tune's appeal was that it sounded so different from the disco beat prevalent over the airwaves in 1978. "Radio at the time was saturated with *Saturday Night Fever*," he said. The popularity of the single extended to the *Feels So Good* LP, which became Mangione's biggest triumph on the album chart when it reached #2 for two weeks in 1978 behind—what else?—*Saturday Night Fever*.

At the Grammys, "Feels So Good" got a Record of the Year nomination, but Mangione won only for his *Children of Sanchez* album for Best Pop Instrumental Performance. Written for a movie soundtrack, the title tune was the follow-up to "Feels So Good" and fared much worse, reaching only #44 AC and #104 bubbling under.

But Mangione was not finished yet. He had another hit on both charts two years later with "Give It All You Got" [see 381].

348 Too Much, Too Little, Too Late

JOHNNY MATHIS AND DENIECE WILLIAMS

Columbia 10693

May 20, 1978 (1 week)

Writers: Nat Kipner, John Vallins

Producer: Jack Gold

When Johnny Mathis came back to the Hot 100 after more than four years with "I'm Coming Home" [see 202], it appeared he might be ready to have more hits there. But after "Life Is a Song Worth Singing" went to #54 pop and #8 AC in early 1974, he was off the chart again for another four-year stretch. When he reentered the Hot 100 in 1978, it was with the biggest hit of his career.

"Too Much, Too Little, Too Late" was a Mathis–Deniece Williams duet. At the time, Williams, born in Gary, Indiana on June 3, 1951, was best known for her 1977 solo single "Free" (#2 R&B, #25 pop, #38 AC), but she was not the Mathis team's first choice.

"We called Minnie Riperton first," Mathis told Bil Carpenter in *Goldmine* in 1993. "Then, we called a couple of other people and they just weren't around, they weren't available. We had the song and I was in the studio and I had to get it done. So we called Deniece Williams and she said, 'Great, sure.' And that's how that happened."

Mathis decided to go with Williams because he knew she could harmonize with him while he sang the melody. The combination clicked beautifully as "Too Much, Too Little, Too Late" went to #1 not only AC but also pop and R&B. The record first led the R&B listings for four weeks starting April 15, 1978, topped the AC chart two weeks after that, and finally hit #1 pop on June 3.

"The minute we did that single, we went in and did an album, which was great fun and that's another thing I like a lot because Deniece wrote several of the songs on the album and they were just there for me and that was thrilling," Mathis said. Included on the LP was the follow-up to "Too Much, Too Little, Too Late," a remake of the Marvin Gaye–Tammi Terrell 1968 #1 R&B hit "You're All I Need to Get By," which went to #10 R&B, #16 AC, and #47 pop. In 1984, Mathis and Williams reunited to do the Major Harris #1 R&B hit of 1975, "Love Won't Let Me Wait," and got to #14 AC, #32 R&B, and #106 bubbling under.

Mathis had other AC entries without Williams in the late 1970s and early 1980s, but they became infrequent around that time and most missed the Hot 100. The one exception was "Friends in Love," a duet with Dionne Warwick, which made #5 AC, #22 R&B, and #38 pop in 1982. Nevertheless, he continued recording for Columbia into the 1990s and toured often as well. But in spite of his continuous activity and considerable career success on the AC charts, Mathis will probably be best remembered for his 1950s pop classics.

349 Even Now

BARRY MANILOW

Arista 0330

May 27, 1978 (3 weeks)

Writer: Marty Panzer (words), Barry Manilow (music)

Producer: Ron Dante, Barry Manilow

Manilow described "Even Now" in his autobiography *Sweet Life* as "one of my personal favorites, which never fails to move me. It reminded me of the great times I had collaborating with Marty [Panzer]. Marty and I had written 'Even Now' in Florida on Golden Beach." After two tries, the melody for the tune was finished.

Panzer explained the motivation for his lyrics in the liner notes to Manilow's anthology *The Complete Collection and Then Some...* "I wanted to write a song that said, 'I miss you, because you're worth missing.' Most songs said, 'I'm lonely—and I miss you.' 'I'm unhappy—and I miss you.' 'My life is not as good—and so, I miss you.' I wanted to say, 'I miss you—because you're wonderful. Whether I'm happy, or sad, has nothing to do with it. I miss you because you are an extraordinary person, whose value exists independent of my state of mind, or the condition of my life.' I wanted to say, 'I miss you, because you're worth missing. Even now.'"

"Even Now" was the title song of a Manilow LP which merited a Grammy nomination for Album of the Year. Manilow also won a Grammy that same year for Best Male Pop Vocal Performance for his work on another track on the album, "Copacabana." As a single, "Copacabana" went to #6 AC and #8 pop and surprised Manilow and Arista executives when radio stations requested it be released as a single. Everyone had regarded the song, which later served as the basis for a television movie starring Manilow, as a novelty track and did not consider it a likely candidate for a 45. Manilow claimed it took him less than 15 minutes to come up with the music for the lyrics written by Bruce Sussman and Jack Feldman for "Copacabana."

"Ready to Take a Chance Again" followed "Copacabana," and it reached #5 AC and #11 pop. Norman Gimbel and Charlie Fox wrote the tune expressly for Manilow to sing for the movie *Foul Play*, and Manilow agreed to do it. In return, "Copacabana" appeared in the film as well. "Ready to Take a Chance Again" also earned an Oscar nomination for Best Song.

Next up was "Somewhere in the Night," Manilow's final song to chart in 1978, which went to #4 AC and #9 pop. Nearly a year later, Manilow got back on the charts with "Ships," which songwriter Ian Hunter wrote in honor of his father. That made #4 AC and #9 pop too. Then came "When I Wanted You," which returned Manilow to #1 AC [see 380].

350 Bluer Than Blue

MICHAEL JOHNSON

EMI America 8001

June 17, 1978 (3 weeks)

Writer: Randy Goodrum

Producer: Brent Maher, Steve Gibsons

Born in Alamosa, Colorado, on August 8, 1944, Michael Johnson grew up in Denver and by age 13 was playing gigs on guitar with his 20-year-old brother Paul. After attending Colorado State College, he toured America in the 1960s, studied guitar at the Conservatory of Liceo in Barcelona, Spain, and joined the Chad Mitchell Trio in 1967–68 when John Denver was a member.

His first LP was the unsuccessful *There Is a Breeze* on Atlantic Records in 1972. Vocalist Gene Cotton worked with Johnson on the album, and when Johnson went to play on a later session by Cotton, Johnson contacted its producer, Brent Maher, and asked him to produce some songs with Johnson as singer on spec. Maher said he would. Johnson in the meantime released two LPs in the Midwest on his Sanskrit label in 1975 and 1977.

The two went through demos to see what material Johnson could record. "He played me 'Bluer Than Blue,' and I was amazed no one had recorded it," Johnson said. They did the song basically like the demo, although Johnson noted that "We changed one of the verses into, I guess you would call it a coda." Then Johnson hoped someone would pick up the record, which was done without a contract.

"I spent my life's savings on that song," Johnson recalled. "We shopped it to, oh, six or seven labels before EMI America wanted it." What really made Johnson confident in how strongly the company believed in the tune was that EMI rush-released "Bluer Than Blue" while he was in final negotiations for a contract.

"Bluer Than Blue" went to #12 pop as well as the top of the AC chart. Later in 1978 Beverly Heckel's rendition went to #56 country. Johnson did an "acoustic, scaled-down version" on his 1997 Intersound LP *Then and Now*.

A few follow-ups to "Bluer Than Blue" hit the AC and pop charts: "Almost Like Being in Love" went to #4 AC and #32 pop in 1978 and "This Night Won't Last Forever" went to #5 AC and #19 pop in 1979. But after 1981's "You're Not Easy to Forget," which went only to #32 AC, Johnson stopped cracking both charts. "It was during the techno pop days, and only Phil Collins and a few other balladeers made it," he said.

Regrouping with Maher and his backing musicians, Johnson entered the country charts in 1985 and scored two #1 hits in 1987, "Give Me Wings" and "The Moon Is Still Over Her Shoulder," among many other entries. Regarding the switch in music styles, Johnson said, "It was easy as anything, because it was the same producer and same band."

Johnson lives in Nashville now. He tours, records for the Intersound label, and is not above doing some backup work for other musicians at local clubs. "I'm no longer trying to be part of the big music horse race, just enjoying the music in my life," he said.

351 If Ever I See You Again

ROBERTA FLACK

Atlantic 3483

July 8, 1978 (3 weeks)

Writer: Joe Brooks

Producer: Joe Brooks

Given the massive popularity of "You Light Up My Life" [see 340], composer Joe Brooks decided to write another movie featuring a title song, only this time he would be the star. But *If Ever I See You Again* was panned by most critics, who accused Brooks of letting his egomania run rampant when he cooked up his story about a songwriter rejuvenated by the love of a pretty new woman, played by Shelley Hack, and though the title song did reach the top AC spot, it went only to #24 pop and #37 R&B.

While "If Ever I See You Again" failed to recapture the commercial and critical heights of his previous hit (garnering no Grammy or Oscar nominations), it did bring Roberta Flack her biggest solo hit since "Feel Like Makin' Love" in 1974. She actually had spent the bulk of 1975–77 working on her *Blue Lights in the Basement* album, which was released in 1978, and the few stray single releases which appeared in that period, 1975's "Feelin' That Glow" (#38 AC, #76 pop) and 1977's "25th of Last December" (#28 AC), attracted little notice.

The death of her former singing partner Donny Hathaway in 1979 inspired the release of a few more tunes by the duo after "If Ever I See You Again," and Flack did not have another solo entry on the AC chart until 1982, when "Making Love" from the movie of the same name went to #7 AC and #13 pop. Two other Flack solo 45s came out after it in 1982, the most she had ever done in one calendar year, with "I'm the One" making #10 AC and #42 pop and "In the Name of Love" getting to just #24 AC.

In 1983 Flack made Peabo Bryson her new recording partner and from 1983–1984 they scored three entries on the AC chart, the biggest being "Tonight, I Celebrate My Love" at #4 in 1983. After that, the next recording to meet with some success was her 1988 single "Oasis," but it made only #13 AC. She did much better in 1991, when her duet with Maxi Priest, "Set the Night to Music," made #2 AC and #6 pop.

Flack spent much of the 1990s concentrating on benefits and personal appearances, making several guest appearances on *The Rosie O'Donnell Show* in 1997 alone. She was then, and still is, a much admired and respected artist. When not on the road, Flack lives in New York City.

352 Songbird

BARBRA STREISAND

Columbia 10756

July 29, 1978 (2 weeks)

Writers: Dave Wolfert, Stephen Nelson

Producer: Gary Klein

Bad timing may be the reason that "Songbird," a #1 AC hit and a title tune for a Streisand album, is not one of her better-remembered songs. The trouble began in the production phase. Gary Klein had produced Streisand's last hit, "My Heart Belongs to Me" [see 334], with the assistance of Charlie Calello, but Calello was left out of the next record despite his work on the predecessor to "Songbird." Calello blamed it on Streisand's manager, Charles Koppelman, who was related to Klein. "After ['My Heart Belongs to Me'], Koppelman got his cousin Gary in there, and business was business," Calello said. "If they could save money, they would."

When it came out, "Songbird" did fine as an AC follow-up but lagged somewhat in the pop listings, reaching only #25 there. Part of the problem may have been that a few weeks after it was on the market, Columbia also released Streisand singing the title song of a new movie. "Love Theme From *Eyes of Laura Mars* (Prisoner)" went to only #48 AC but peaked at #21 pop around the same time "Songbird" reached its maximum, and the competition between the two for sales and airplay possibly hurt their potential on the Hot 100.

Streisand has endured plenty of ups and downs in her entertainment career, which has encompassed much more than just singing. Born in Brooklyn, New York, on April 24, 1942, she struggled as a nightclub performer until cracking up critics and audiences with her witty portrayal of Miss Marmelstein in her 1962 Broadway debut *I Can Get It for You Wholesale*. A recording contract with Columbia followed, but Streisand did not crack the AC or pop charts until 1964, when she sang "People" from her Broadway hit *Funny Girl* [see 42].

In the 1960s Streisand became an AC chart favorite, and although she did not get another #1 AC until nearly 10 years after "People," she did have three memorable #2 AC entries—"He Touched Me" in 1965, from the short-lived Broadway musical *Drat! The Cat* (#53 pop); "Stout-Hearted Men," from the old Broadway musical *The New Moon* in 1967 (#92 pop); and "Stoney End," her first foray into contemporary, rock-flavored music in 1970 (#6 pop). She did better in the mid-1970s, as "Songbird" became her third consecutive #1 AC hit after "Love Theme From *A Star is Born* (Evergreen)" and "My Heart Belongs to Me."

After "Songbird," Streisand went without a #1 AC hit for two years. Her closest effort was "The Main Event/Fight," a disco number from her film *The Main Event* which hit #2 AC and #3 pop in 1979. It took a collaboration with the Bee Gees to bring her to the top again [see 392—"Woman in Love"].

353 My Angel Baby

TOBY BEAU

RCA 11250

August 12, 1978 (1 week)

Writers: Danny McKenna, Balde Silva

Producer: Sean Delaney

Strange as it may sound, it was a one-time producer of Kiss, Sean Delaney, who spotted what started out as a quintet called Toby Beau and went to work with the band on "My Angel Baby" and the rest of the debut LP in England. All the band members were classmates born and raised in the Rio Grande Valley of Texas, where they formed their group in 1975. The name came from a shrimp boat one of them saw in the Gulf of Mexico.

As for the membership and their duties, Balde Silva did guitars and harmonica, Danny McKenna handled the guitar, Ron Rose played the guitar, banjo, and mandolin, Rob Young strummed on drums, and Steve "Zip" Zipper was on bass. The hours spent on rehearsal and recording paid off when McKenna and Silva's "My Angel Baby," featuring a harmonica solo in the middle and Silva in fine falsetto form hitting the last note, got to #1 AC and #13 pop in the summer of 1978.

"My Angel Baby" did not have an immediate follow-up, although there was one promotional single issued to radio stations called "Three You Missed, One You Didn't." In 1979 Toby Beau charted again with "Then You Can Tell Me Goodbye," which had previously hit #1 AC in a medley by Glen Campbell [see 297]. At #7 AC and #57 pop, it was their last entry on the AC chart. About a year later, Toby Beau made the Hot 100 for the last time, when "If I Were You" peaked at #70.

Toby Beau released only three albums after their first one in 1978. McKenna departed after the first album, and Silva was the only original member left by the time of the group's third album in 1980. He called it quits a year later after the LPs kept failing to make *Billboard*'s Top 200 album chart.

Silva and the rest of the band disappeared into obscurity in the 1980s. But everything old is new again, so the saying goes, and that even applies to a one-hit wonder like Toby Beau.

By the late 1990s Silva had revived the Toby Beau name for a duo in which he served as singer/songwriter/guitarist while Rennetta Dennett joined him as singer/keyboardist. The new-look Toby Beau was surprisingly successful, and during the summer of 1998 they were often seen doing cruise ship gigs off the Gulf of Mexico when they were not living at home in southeastern Texas.

354 Three Times a Lady

THE COMMODORES

Motown 1443

August 19, 1978 (1 week)

Writer: Lionel Richie

Producers: James Anthony Carmichael, the Commodores

The Commodores could have been the Commodes had the group's trumpeter William King put his finger just slightly higher when he picked their name at random from a dictionary. Formed as a combination of members of the Mighty Mystics and the Jays, two bands based in Tuskegee, Alabama, the Commodores originally consisted of King, vocalist and saxophonist Lionel Richie, guitarist Thomas McClary, and keyboardist Milan Williams in the late 1960s. When the group got the chance to open for the Jackson Five in 1971, bassist Ronald LaPread and drummer Walter "Clyde" Orange were part of the mix as well.

It was not until 1974 that a Commodores single made the charts. "Machine Gun," an instrumental, went to #7 R&B and #22 pop. They had several other vocal hits before cracking the AC chart in 1977 with "Easy," which made #14 AC, #4 pop, and #1 R&B. The next year "Three Times a Lady" gave the Commodores their first #1 AC entry.

"The only thing I can tell you about 'Three Times a Lady' is out of all the songs we did, as soon as the first note of the song was sung in the studio, we knew it was a hit going in," said Orange. "We said, 'Yeah!'" "Three Times a Lady" was three times a #1 hit, topping the AC, pop, and R&B chart. It led the Hot 100 and the R&B listings simultaneously the weeks of August 12 and 19, 1978. The tune also made the country chart in covers by Nate Harvell in 1978 (#23) and Conway Twitty in 1984 (#7). At the Grammys "Three Times a Lady" was nominated for Song of the Year plus earned the Commodores a nomination for Best Pop Vocal Performance by a Duo, Group or Chorus.

The next three years after "Three Times a Lady," the Commodores hit the AC, pop, and R&B chart frequently. But in 1982 Lionel Richie's solo work began to gain prominence [see 430—"Truly"] and he left the group. After that, the Commodores found their chart fortunes fading fast. J. D. Nicholas replaced Richie, but only one song in the post-Richie era could be considered a hit—"Nightshift," a tribute to Marvin Gaye which made #2 AC, #3 pop, and #1 R&B for four weeks in 1985. A switch from Motown to Polydor in 1986 did not change the momentum, and by 1988 the group was off the charts.

Nonetheless, a decade later the Commodores' name still had enough pull to keep them on a busy touring schedule across America. Those in the 1998 lineup who had been with the group longest were King, Orange, and Nicholas.

355 Fool (If You Think It's Over)

CHRIS REA

United Artists 1198

September 9, 1978 (3 weeks)

Writer: Chris Rea

Producer: Gus Dudgeon

"Fool (If You Think It's Over)" was part of Chris Rea's album Whatever Happened to Benny Santini? The LP title and the tune of the same name in the album refer to the time in 1975 when Rea signed with his first record company and they wanted to call him Benny Santini "just because me dad's an Irish-Italian with an ice-cream business!" he wailed to Mark Williams in Rolling Stone. Thankfully, that name did not stick, and Rea made it on his own with his birth name.

Born in Middlesborough, Cleveland, in the United Kingdom on March 4, 1951, Rea (pronounced "REE-ah") went into the music business in the late 1960s, first playing in a band called Cattermole, Rea and Taylor, then in a conglomeration called the Beautiful Losers. After the Benny Santini ordeal, he got a new solo record deal through Brian Reza, an employee at Magnet Music in London who had heard his demos.

"Brian sent out me demos to various producers, and Gus Dudgeon shared a strong interest," Rea told Williams. From their collaboration came "Fool (If You Think It's Over)," Rea's first chart entry in America and the United Kingdom. In his homeland the single went only to #30, but in the United States it made #12 pop as well as #1 AC, and Rea got a Grammy nomination for Best New Artist.

Many critics hearing the tune claimed Dudgeon made Rea sound very similar to his previous high-profile client, Elton John, a charge Dudgeon quickly dismissed. "People do that with every artist I produce," he told Williams. "They even said that about the first Joan Armatrading. If he sounds like anyone, I'd say it was a little bit of Joe Walsh."

But despite the record's success, Rea left Dudgeon shortly thereafter, saying that "Dudgeon and I both agree now that I'm not the sort of artist he should produce." At the same time, the title track of Whatever Happened to Benny Santini? became the follow-up to "Fool (If You Think It's Over)" and hit #71 pop in America. Thereafter Rea's popularity in the United States went into a decline, and he had virtually no chart entries there for a decade, although he amassed a string of singles that made the U.K. listing starting in the mid-1980s. He had a brief return to the American airwaves in 1989 when his "On the Beach," a song he originally recorded in 1986 and later remade, became his second AC single at #9 and "Working on It" made #73 pop.

In the 1990s, Rea, although virtually ignored in America, continued to be a chart favorite in Europe. At last report he was living in Cookham, England.

356 Right Down the Line

GERRY RAFFERTY

United Artists 1233

September 30, 1978 (4 weeks nonconsecutive)

Writer: Gerry Rafferty

Producer: Hugh Murphey, Gerry Rafferty

Guitarist and singer Gerry Rafferty, born in Paisley, Scotland, on April 16, 1947, began his professional recording career in 1964 when he joined the Mavericks, a band from Paisley. He left the group and joined the London band the Humblebums a few years later but remained in contact with Mavericks keyboardist Joe Egan, who had stayed in Scotland to study languages. After the Mavericks disintegrated, Rafferty cut a failed solo album, *Can I Have My Money Back?*, then he and Egan later reunited to form Stealers Wheel, where the duo sang vocals accompanied by Rod Coombes on drums, Luther Grosvenor on guitar, DeLisle Harper on bass, and Paul Pilnick on guitar.

With the famous duo of Jerry Leiber and Mike Stoller producing them, Stealers Wheel had three singles make both the AC and pop charts—"Stuck in the Middle With You" (#13 AC, #6 pop) and "Everyone's Agreed That Everything Will Turn Out Fine" (#23 AC, #49 pop) in 1973 and "Star" (#6 AC, #29 pop) in 1974.

Stealers Wheel broke down not long thereafter, but because of legal complications involving the group, Rafferty was blocked from recording solo for much of the 1970s. The support he got from his wife during this period led Rafferty to dedicate "Right Down the Line" to her. "She had stood by me through some really heavy times," Rafferty told Craig Rosen in *The Billboard Book of Number One Albums*. "It was just my way of saying thanks."

"Right Down the Line" was the second single from the album *City to City*, which managed to dethrone the wildly popular *Saturday Night Fever* soundtrack to hit #1 on the LP chart the week of July 8, 1978. The first was "Baker Street," which made #2 pop and #4 AC in the summer of 1978. "Right Down the Line" made #12 pop as well as #1 AC in the fall of 1978. One other 45, "Home and Dry," came off *City to City*, and it went to #26 AC and #28 pop.

Rafferty found it hard to match the success of *City to City*. In 1979 he had two fairly successful singles, "Days Gone Down (Still Got the Light in Your Eyes)" at #17 both AC and pop and "Get It Right the Next Time" at #15 AC and #21 pop. Rafferty, apparently unable to heed the advice of the latter title, never again appeared on the AC or pop charts.

357 Love Is in the Air

JOHN PAUL YOUNG

Scotti Brothers 402

October 7, 1978 (2 weeks)

Writers: Harry Vanda, George Young

Producers: Harry Vanda, George Young

He is often identified as Australian, but John Paul Young was actually born in Glasgow, Scotland, in 1953, though his family later moved to the land down under. Young worked five years full-time as a sheet-metal worker before he started playing piano professionally. He first did weekend gigs, joining a band called Elm Tree, and also appeared in an Australian stage production of *Jesus Christ Superstar*.

But Young really did not hit his stride until he began collaborating with writer/producers Harry Vanda and George Young. The two guitarists had been part of Australia's biggest rock group of the 1960s, the Easybeats (their "Friday on My Mind" hit #16 pop in 1967), but went out on their own in the 1970s, calling themselves Flash and the Pan. Their only American chart entry under the latter name was in 1979 with "Hey, St. Peter," which made #76 pop. They also produced the heavy-metal rock band AC/DC, whose members Angus and Malcolm Young were George's younger brothers.

For Young, Vanda and Young wrote "Yesterday's Hero," which became a #1 smash in Australia. It was Young's first release in the United States, and it did moderately well there, cresting at #42 pop. But nothing else from the artist charted until "Love Is in the Air." The song was the title tune for an album of Young's material in America which was the first release by the Scotti Brothers label, named after founders Ben and Tony Scotti. Vanda and Young wrote all but two songs on the LP. "Love Is in the Air" was by far the most successful single from it, making #1 AC plus #7 pop the weeks of October 14 and 21, 1978. It was an international hit, as it also went to #5 in Great Britain.

After "Love Is in the Air" finished its run in America, "Lost in Your Love" came out and went to an unimpressive #28 AC and #55 pop in early 1979. Thereafter Young made neither the pop or AC chart in America as interest in him dropped off rapidly. By 1983 Young's album *One Foot in Front* was available in America only as a German import. It sold few copies.

In 1993 a rerecorded version of Young doing "Love Is in the Air" produced by David Hirschfelder along with the old Vanda and Young duo appeared in the Australian movie *Strictly Ballroom*. The remake did become a single but failed to generate any activity in America, although it did go to #49 in the United Kingdom in late 1992. Later in the 1990s the song did get airplay in the United States as background music in phone commercials.

358 Time Passages

AL STEWART

Arista 0362

November 11, 1978 (10 weeks)

Writers: Al Stewart (words), Peter White (music)

Producer: Alan Parsons

Living up to its name, "Time Passages" stayed at #1 on the AC chart for 10 weeks through January 13, 1979, the longest run of any song at the top since "Love Is Blue" stayed there 11 weeks in 1968. No other record reached 10 or more weeks at #1 afterward until Billy Joel's "The River of Dreams" in 1993 [see 638].

The man behind "Time Passages" was Al Stewart, born in Glasgow, Scotland, on September 5, 1945. When asked why a Scotsman would give up his native land to live in California's Bay Area, Stewart replied, "Have you been to Scotland? No? Then you've answered your question!" All kidding aside, Stewart noted that he left Scotland after he was three years old when his family moved to Bournemouth, England. He thinks that change of location attracted him to California because Bournemouth is "coincidentally the only town in England that has palm trees."

Stewart started recording commercially in 1966 with an unsuccessful single. He stayed in the business for a decade until his big breakthrough in early 1977 with the single "Year of the Cat," which hit #8 both pop and AC. Surprisingly, it was his only 45 to make the U.K. chart, peaking at #31 there. In America, he followed up the song with "On the Border" (#23 AC, #42 pop) before scoring his highest-charting tune the next year, the title track of his 1978 LP. "*Time Passages* was my eighth album," Stewart said.

Although "Time Passages" mentions specific days and events in its lyric, Stewart said that there was nothing particular which inspired him to compose them, only that they came to him spontaneously. "It's one of those sort of nebulous things. 'Time Passages'—it's a phrase that stuck in my mind. I have very little idea about what it's about."

His memories of his producer Alan Parsons are more distinct. "He was and still is an avid fan of magic. He's the only producer I know of who likes pulling playing cards out of your ears." As producer and music leader of the Alan Parsons Project, he scored his own AC and pop hits in the early to mid-1980s, the biggest being "Eye in the Sky," which hit #3 on both charts in 1982.

"Time Passages" peaked at #7 pop the weeks of December 9 and 16, 1978. Its follow-up, "Song on the Radio," made #10 AC and #29 pop in 1979. But after "Midnight Rocks" went to #13 AC and #24 pop in 1980, no more Stewart singles made the charts. Nevertheless, he did record seven LPs after "Time Passages" and continued touring through the late 1990s. Said Stewart: "I put the odd album out now and then. Basically, when someone pays me, I do it. I keep thinking I need to get a proper job someday, but I've survived 35 years without gainful employment, so why do it?"

359 This Moment in Time
ENGELBERT HUMPERDINCK

1
9
7
9

Epic/MAM 50632

January 20, 1979 (2 weeks)

Writers: Alan Bernstein, Ritchie Adams

Producer: Joel Diamond

Less than three years after his third #1 AC, "After the Lovin'" [see 320], Engelbert Humperdinck surprised prognosticators by notching his fourth AC chart topper with "This Moment in Time." It scored less effectively on the other charts, however, making only #58 pop and #93 country. "This Moment in Time" also became the title tune for the last album by Humperdinck to make the *Billboard* LP chart. It peaked at #164 in the summer of 1979.

By this moment in time in Humperdinck's career, he had gotten used to living and recording in Los Angeles, which he had done for much of the 1970s. In June 1979, as the *This Moment in Time* album was peaking, *The Sunday Telegraph* of London asked him whether he would return to England following the announcement that the government was cutting the highest tax rate for its citizens from 83 to 60 percent. Humperdinck told reporter Richard Holliday that "Although I am extremely pleased with the new tax situation in England, I don't think it will influence my decision to return." It did not; 20 years later, he is still in America.

Humperdinck might have also noted that he was doing better on the American charts than in the United Kingdom at the time. His last entry on the British charts was all the way back to 1973's minor single, "Love Is All." But in America he continued to chart the rest of the 1970s, even after "This Moment in Time." In 1979 his version of "Can't Help Falling in Love" went to #44 AC, followed that same year by "A Much, Much Greater Love" at #39 AC.

He returned to the Hot 100 in 1980 with "Love's Only Love" at #83 pop plus #28 AC, then hit the AC listing again in 1981 with "Don't You Love Me Anymore?" at #41. In 1983 " 'Til You and Your Lover Are Lovers Again" became his last entry on the AC, pop, and country charts, peaking at #17 AC, #39 country, and #77 pop.

After 1983 Humperdinck's career lost its luster, with his recordings getting little note critically or commercially. That is not to say his popularity vanished, however. On October 23, 1989, Humperdinck got his own star on the Hollywood Walk of Fame, and in the 1990s he remained a popular draw in Las Vegas. But as he headed toward the turn of the century—and his mid-sixties—it appeared doubtful he would score another hit. Then again, the former Arnold Dorsey has in the past confounded those who counted him out before his time, so who knows what will happen? If nothing else, he at least can be happy that he still leads rival Tom Jones in total #1 AC hits, with his four to Jones' three.

360 Lotta Love

NICOLETTE LARSON

Warner 8664

February 3, 1979 (1 week)

Writer: Neil Young

Producer: Ted Templeman

Born in Helena, Montana, on July 17, 1952, Nicolette Larson grew up in Kansas City, Missouri, and came to California when she was 21. Her big break in show business was singing on a Commander Cody LP which led to her touring with Cody when he opened for Joan Baez. She then became a top session vocalist singing behind the likes of the Doobie Brothers, Arlo Guthrie, Van Halen, Linda Ronstadt, and others.

One day while at Ronstadt's house, Neil Young dropped by and asked Ronstadt if she knew any strong backup singers he could use. She introduced him to her friend, and Larson went on to sing on Young's album *Comes a Time*. Her work on it impressed Warner Brothers executives enough to sign Larson as a solo performer. Ironically, *Comes a Time* came out in September 1978, about the same time Larson's debut LP was released, and both contained versions of a song Young composed and let Larson record—"Lotta Love."

"I got that song off a tape I found lying on the floor of Neil's car," Larson was quoted as saying in a 1997 Associated Press article. "I popped it in the tape player and commented on what a great song it was. Neil said, 'You want it? It's yours.'" She learned the tune on an acoustic guitar. Released as her first single, Larson's "Lotta Love" peaked at #8 pop on February 17, 1979, in addition to its AC success.

Unfortunately, Larson's professional and personal relationship with Young dissolved soon after "Lotta Love" became a hit. She told *People* in 1979 that she and Young dated until "he just disappeared. I haven't seen him since." Luckily, she fared better with her pal Ronstadt, who hooked Larson up with producer Ted Templeman and even sang backup on Larson's album. Templeman sang on it too, having had musical experience as part of Harpers Bizarre [see 99—"Chattanooga Choo Choo"].

Larson found that following up "Lotta Love" was not easy. Two other singles from her debut LP charted lower in 1979, "Rhumba Girl" (#38 AC, #47 pop) and "Give a Little" (#19 AC, #104 bubbling under). She came back slightly with "Let Me Go, Love," a duet with Michael McDonald which made #9 AC and #35 pop in 1980, but then had only one more single on both charts—1982's "I Only Want to Be With You," which hit #15 AC and #53 pop.

Sensing a need to change, Larson switched to country music in 1985 and scored six hits within a two-year period, the biggest being "That's How You Know When Love's Right," which climbed to #9 in 1986. But despite being named best new vocalist by the Academy of Country Music in 1985, she found her success there limited as well. Nonetheless, she continued to record and tour until her death on December 16, 1997, from complications due to cerebral edema. She was 45 years old.

361 I Just Fall in Love Again

ANNE MURRAY

Capitol 4675

February 10, 1979 (4 weeks)

Writers: Steve Dorff, Gloria Sklerov, Harry Lloyd, Larry Herbstritt

Producer: Jim Ed Norman

Anne Murray, in explaining its appeal to her, said "'I Just Fall in Love Again' is just a wonderful song," although she couldn't quite understand its appeal to one music genre —country. "It didn't seem the least bit country to me, especially with the classical piano part." Despite Murray's opinion, "I Just Fall in Love Again" stayed at #1 country for three weeks starting March 24, 1979, two weeks after its final stay at #1 on the AC chart. On the pop chart the single peaked at #12.

Murray was not the first person to cut "I Just Fall in Love Again." The Carpenters put the tune on the duo's 1977 LP *Passages*, and Dusty Springfield also took a shot at it before Murray recorded vocals for it. "I knew Dusty had done it, and I thought, 'What the hell?' It hadn't been in rotation anywhere," said Murray.

Though she thought the tune had its own appeal, Murray acknowledged that the fact that it came after "You Needed Me" probably helped get both airplay and sales. "I was kind of on a roll after 'You Needed Me,'" she said. Like "You Needed Me," which made only #3 AC despite hitting #1 pop in 1978, "I Just Fall in Love Again" was produced by Jim Ed Norman. He came onto the scene after Murray severed her working relationship with Brian Ahern, who oversaw a number of her hits, including "Snowbird" and "You Won't See Me."

"It was time," Murray said in describing the amicable breakup. "Brian and I had done a lot of albums together." After they split in the mid-1970s she did two LPs with other producers which fared poorly. When she went looking for a new producer, Norman fit what she wanted. "Jim Ed seemed to be very solid in his head about what I should do. I was very impressed with his resolve. It's kind of nice to work with someone who takes charge in the studio."

With Norman at the helm, "I Just Fall in Love Again" was the first of four consecutive #1 AC hits for Murray. The first two following it, "Shadows in the Moonlight" [see 367] and "Broken Hearted Me" [see 374], also went to #1 country, a feat no other act has been able to equal. More curious is the fact that "I Just Fall in Love Again," "Broken Hearted Me," and "Daydream Believer" (the fourth consecutive #1 AC hit; see 382) all peaked at #12 on the pop chart. And despite their critical and commercial acclaim, this quartet, all released in 1979–80, got no Grammy nominations. But the often-nominated Murray did not go completely without nominations during this period. She was up in 1979 for Best Recording for Children for her *Anne Murray Sings for the Sesame Street Generation* album.

362 Crazy Love
POCO

ABC 12439

March 10, 1979 (7 week)s

Writer: Russell Young

Producer: Richard Sanford Orshoff

The one constant in the ever-changing country-rock group Poco was guitarist Rusty Young, born in Long Beach, California, on February 23, 1946 and raised in Colorado. In 1968 he joined lead guitarist Jim Messina, rhythm guitarist Richie Furay, drummer George Grantham, and bassist Randy Meisner (replaced by Timothy B. Schmidt in 1969) to form Poco. Their albums through 1977 sold much better than their singles. Their Hot 100 debut was 1970's "You Better Think Twice" at #72, with four more entries the next seven years. Two of them hit the AC chart, 1975's "Keep On Tryin'" (#23 AC, #50 pop) and 1977's "Indian Summer" (#39 AC, #50 pop).

By then Poco had gone through some personnel changes. Messina left in 1971 to team with Kenny Loggins. Paul Cotton replaced him. Then in 1973 Furay departed, as did Grantham and Schmidt in 1977. Young and Cotton found replacements in Charlie Harrison, Kim Bullard, and Steve Chapman, but realized ABC Record executives might have doubts about the act given the defections. Young said those concerns eased when "We went in and played 'Crazy Love' and 'Heart of the Night' for the record company."

Regarding the creation of "Crazy Love," Young said, "I was living in Los Angeles and I was working in a house paneling a wall. Almost the whole chorus, 'It happens all the time' and so on, came to me at once. It only took half an hour to write." At first he was worried that some people would confuse "Crazy Love" with the Van Morrison song of the same name, but that ended when "I just remembered Richie always said that stuff didn't matter." Richie was right. "Crazy Love" became Poco's biggest hit, going to #17 pop and winning the *Billboard* award for Adult Contemporary Song of the Year. "I'm so glad I got to experience that," Young said about having a hit.

But then MCA Records bought out ABC and fired many executives who backed Poco. Though "Heart of the Night," the follow-up to "Crazy Love," went to #5 AC and #20 pop in 1979, it would be the last hit Poco had on MCA. "It turned into something unpleasant for us," Young said of the office politics at MCA. By 1984 he and the rest of Poco had disbanded.

In 1989 the first incarnation of Poco, including Meisner, reunited. "I saw Richie at some point and he called me and asked if I would be interested in getting the original band together," he said. Though they had a #2 AC and #18 pop hit with "Call It Love," Young had expected the reunion to do better commercially. He was, nonetheless, glad it occurred.

In the late 1990s Young was touring occasionally under the Poco name. However, his main occupation was writing songs for country artists like Bryan White in Nashville.

363 I Never Said I Love You
ORSA LIA

Infinity 50004

April 28, 1979 (1 week)

Writers: Hal David, Archie Jordan

Producers: Hal David, Archie Jordan

Hal David wrote his first songs in the 1940s, but did not get his biggest commercial and critical hosannas until he met Burt Bacharach in the late 1950s. The two began working together regularly in the early 1960s and created a host of hits for various artists, especially their favorite, Dionne Warwick. But by the time David and Bacharach's score for the 1973 movie *Lost Horizon* came out, the two had split up. David had trouble finding a new partner, and he had few hits to show for his efforts during the rest of the 1970s.

The decade wasn't a total loss. In 1973 he and Henry Mancini wrote "Send a Little Love My Way" for the film *Oklahoma Crude*, which Anne Murray sang and took to #10 AC and #72 pop. And in 1975 he helped Albert Hammond write "99 Miles from L.A." [see 261]. But he had no luck with Marty Robbins' cut of his "A Man and a Train," which he wrote with Frank DeVol for the movie *Emperor of the North* (1973), or trying to get a musical called *Brainchild*, composed by Michel Legrand, off the ground in 1974. (The show was canned after two weeks of pre-Broadway tryouts in Philadelphia).

Still looking for a sure-fire collaboration, David spotted Archie Jordan. They wrote "It Was Almost Like a Song," a #19 AC hit for Ronnie Milsap in 1977 that got a Grammy nomination as Best Country Song. Energized by this triumph, the two men stuck together as writer/producers and worked on an artist they thought had promise named Orsa Lia. Lia, born in Virginia, had sung jingles for commercials on television for a few years before getting a shot at a regular recording gig with David and Jordan.

The trio's first single together was "I Never Said I Love You," a song which was a *Billboard* Recommended Pick in its review of pop music. But "I Never Said I Love You" never really took off on the Hot 100, peaking at #84 in April 1979 before getting to #1 AC.

Shortly after "I Never Said I Loved You" hit #1 AC, Lia was pictured in *Billboard* recording duets with her Infinity label mate Dobie Gray (best remembered for his 1973 million seller "Drift Away" at #12 AC and #5 pop) under David and Jordan's production. But that project resulted in no pop or AC chart entries, and in 1980 David left Jordan and Lia to become president of ASCAP (the American Society of Composers, Authors and Publishers) and work for protections for songwriters.

David once told Marilyn Goldstein in *Newsday* that "The important thing is what one does, not one's name. The songs live, the writer doesn't. You just hope your songs outlast you." That certainly looks like it will happen with his tunes with Bacharach, but not for the rarely revived "I Never Said I Love You."

364 Love Is the Answer

ENGLAND DAN AND JOHN FORD COLEY

Big Tree 16131

May 5, 1979 (2 weeks)

Writer: Todd Rundgren

Producer: Kyle Lehning

"Of all the songs we released as singles, that was my favorite," John Ford Coley said of "Love Is the Answer," written by rock singer Todd Rundgren. "The song first of all had a classical base, and the middle had a gospel section which I loved."

"Love Is the Answer" was the answer for England Dan and John Ford Coley after a slight slump in 1978 during whch three of their singles flopped. Beside its #1 AC status the record made #10 pop for two weeks starting May 26, 1979. Sadly, during this time of chart success, the two failed to stay together. Explaining their split, Coley blamed it on interference from others who created dissension between him and England Dan to satisfy their own needs. "The whole story is you kind of lose sight of stuff," he said. "You have people coming in saying, 'You should do this, you should do that,' and it pulls you away from one another."

Both men eventually figured they could not reconcile and perform together. "When we decided that would be it, we decided it when 'Love Is the Answer' was a hit, so we said, 'Let's go out on top,'" Coley said. He added, "That was a real hard breakup. When Dan and I split, it was really a cold turkey situation." In fact, the collaboration between the two had lasted longer than either of their first marriages.

Without the duo to promote them, the few remaining singles from England Dan and John Ford Coley after "Love Is the Answer" generated little response. "What Can I Do With This Broken Heart" hit #12 AC and #50 pop in 1979, and the belated releases of "In It for Love" in 1980 and "Part of Me Part of You" in 1981 made #45 AC and #75 pop, and #42 AC, respectively.

England Dan became known as England Dan Seals in 1980, but his single "Late at Night" made only #28 AC and #57 pop. Then going as Dan Seals, he developed a very successful solo career in country music beginning in 1983, scoring 11 hits in that field from 1985-90. One of them, "Bop," made #10 AC and #42 pop in 1986. As for Coley, he did music for TV shows and movies, and got a number of acting jobs, appearing in such films as *Scenes From the Goldmine* (1987) and *Dream a Little Dream* (1989) and such TV shows as *America's Most Wanted.*

Speaking in 1998 of the possibility of a reunion with England Dan, Coley discounted it. "There's still a lot of things that need to be cleared up," he said. He was on speaking terms with Seals but noted "We haven't seen each other for 12 years." Coley concluded, "I've got so many things I want to do, the last thing I want to do is dig up bones."

365 Just When I Needed You Most

RANDY VANWARMER

Bearsville 0334

May 19, 1979 (2 weeks nonconsecutive)

Writer: Randy Vanwarmer

Producer: Dell Newman

Following his father's death when he was 15, Randall Van Wormer (the pronounciation, "warmer," motivated the change in spelling), born in Indian Hills, Colorado, on March 30, 1955, went to England with his mother. When he was about 16, he flew back to the States to finish high school. According to Vanwarmer, he met a girl there and fell in love, but she left him when he was 18 and that heartbreak was the inspiration for "Just When I Needed You Most."

During the 1970s Vanwarmer signed with Bearsville Records in London to cut some records. Albert Goldman, head of Bearsville's American parent company Warner Brothers, let Vanwarmer's producer Dell Newman record Vanwarmer's initial batch of tunes in Nashville in 1976. Unfortunately, the label refused to release the records cut there.

Upset, Vanwarmer moved to Goldman's hometown of Woodstock, New York, in 1978 to try to do another record and impress the label head. Warner Brothers finally decided to release one of his tunes, but needed a B-side. "I picked 'Just When I Needed You Most,'" Vanwarmer said. The company made that song the A-side once they heard the finished product.

Vanwarmer believed the attention-getter in the song was an instrumental passage in which he replaced a synthesizer with a unique sound from a unique musician. "John Sebastian played autoharp," Vanwarmer revealed. "He was very happy to do it." Sebastian [see 298—"Welcome Back"], lived in Woodstock at the time, played around with the song after a mutual friend of his and Vanwarmer's, guitarist Paul Butterfield, gave him a copy of it.

"Just When I Needed You Most" made #1 AC and #4 pop for two weeks starting June 16, 1979, and #71 country. But it was his only AC entry and top 40 pop hit. Regarding the lack of a big followup, Vanwarmer said, "I think. . .that I was kind of into new wave music, and that record was where I was at at age 18." And, although his label encouraged him to release other material, to show that he was more than a balladeer, he noted, "Really, the stuff that was different wasn't very good."

In 1985 Vanwarmer moved to Nashville following two other pop entries, "Whatever You Decide" (#77 in 1980) and "Suzi" (#55 in 1981). Though he had country entries in 1988 with "I Will Hold You" (#53) and "Where the Rocky Mountains Touch the

Morning Sun" (#72), he became primarily a songwriter for other artists. He had several country hits credited to him such as 1992's #1 "I'm in a Hurry (And Don't Know Why)" for Alabama.

"I'm very happy with the way things happened," he said. "My goal was to become a songwriter rather than an artist." He plans to stay busy in Nashville into the 21st century because "It's the one place in the country, and maybe the world, where you tell somebody, 'I'm a songwriter,' and nobody says, 'So what's your day job?'"

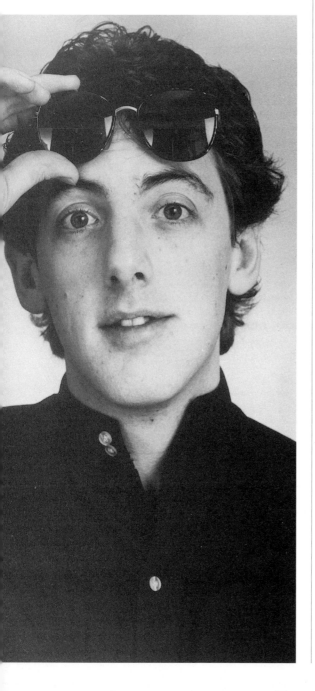

366 She Believes in Me

KENNY ROGERS

United Artists 1273

May 26, 1979 (2 weeks)

Writer: Steve Gibb

Producer: Larry Butler

Although Kenneth Donald Rogers, born in Houston, Texas, on August 21, 1938, was America's favorite country-pop balladeer from the late 1970s to the mid-1980s, he did not get there overnight. He emerged from high school with a band called the Scholars, then joined the Bobby Doyle Trio as a bass player. Neither group was a hit. By the time he joined the Kirby Stone Four and later the New Christy Minstrels, in the late 1960s, both groups were past their heyday.

However, in 1967 Rogers and three other members of the New Christy Minstrels—Thelma Camacho, Mike Settle, and Terry Williams—formed a group called the First Edition along with Mickey Jones. A year later their psychedelic relic hit "Just Dropped In (To See What Condition My Condition Was In)" was the group's first pop entry, peaking at #5. In 1969 "But You Know I Love You" was their second pop entry at #19 and first AC single at #18.

When the group's "Ruby, Don't Take Your Love to Town" went to #6 both AC and pop in the summer of 1969, it was under the billing of Kenny Rogers and the First Edition. He held lead singer status with the group as it amassed several more entries and even taped its own TV musical variety series, *Rollin' on the River*, from 1971–73. When the show ended, the group split up, having last hit the AC chart in 1971 with "Fools" (#4 AC, #51 pop), and the Hot 100 with "School Teacher," which hit #91 in 1972.

Several hitless years followed for Rogers as a soloist until "Lucille" became a multichart hit, making the top 10 of the AC, pop, and country listings in 1977. A few other Rogers songs received decent airplay and sales afterward, but none went top 10 AC, pop, and country again until 1979's "She Believes in Me."

Rogers said he looks for lyrics first when doing a song, and the words to "She Believes in Me" attracted him because it had what he thought were the best ingredients for a ballad. "I look for ballads that say what every man wants to say and what every woman wants to hear," he said.

Like Three Dog Night—and no doubt some other artists—Rogers and his producer Larry Butler had a system of reviewing submitted songs, putting them into boxes marked "yes," "maybe," and "no," and giving the "maybes" one more listen by the two to see if they felt like doing the song. "I think 'She Believes in Me' was 'yes' all the way," Rogers said.

"She Believes in Me" went to #1 for two weeks on the country chart starting June 9, 1979, and to #5 pop for two weeks beginning July 7, 1979. Another Rogers, the unrelated D. J. Rogers, covered the song and went to #66 R&B in 1980. Kenny would have even bigger success on all the charts with his next release, "Lady" [see 393].

367 Shadows in the Moonlight

ANNE MURRAY

Capitol 4716

June 16, 1979 (3 weeks)

Writers: Rory Bourke, Charlie Black

Producer: Jim Ed Norman

Rory Bourke already had one co-writing credit, joined by Norro Wilson and Billy Sherrill, for a #1 AC and country hit with "The Most Beautiful Girl" in 1973 [see 205]. He notched a second double success with a different partner with "Shadows in the Moonlight," which also became the sixth #1 AC hit for Anne Murray.

Bourke's collaborator for this song was Charlie Black. "I had a couple of ideas laying around, little bits and pieces of tunes and ideas," Black told Tom Roland in *The Billboard Book of Number One Country Hits*. "I had a few lines and a few things that went together in the chorus of 'Shadows.'" Bourke continued the story "He showed up at my house and played me part of the chorus of 'Shadows in the Moonlight' and said, 'What do you think?' I said, 'I think we better write this right away.'"

But while Bourke and Black were happy with their final creation, Anne Murray admitted she was not bowled over when she first heard it. "It didn't get me immediately, but it did get Jim Ed Norman, who said, 'You've got to do this song,'" Murray remembered. As Norman was her producer, Murray took his word for it.

For listeners who heard the final version of "Shadows in the Moonlight," some of the highlights were a guitar solo by Bob Mann and a saxophone segment near the end of the record by Don Thompson. Combined with Murray's strong vocals, the result for her was a #25 pop hit (the lowest pop peak of any of her #1 AC hits) and a #1 county entry in addition to her AC success. The tune topped the country chart for the week of July 21, 1979, three weeks after it had peaked on the AC listings. "I was lucky in that a lot of these [songs] were crossovers," Murray noted. "It was more universally accepted then."

Prior to "Shadows in the Moonlight," Bourke and Black worked together with Kerry Chater to write "I Know a Heartache When I See One" in 1979. That song also was a multiple chart entry, hitting #10 country, #14 AC, and #19 pop for Jennifer Warnes [see 328—"Right Time of the Night"].

"Shadows in the Moonlight" was the follow-up to "I Just Fall in Love Again" and taken from Murray's 1979 LP *New Kind of Feeling*, which peaked at #23. The follow-up to "Shadows in the Moonlight" was "Broken Hearted Me," the leadoff single from the late 1979 album *I'll Always Love You*, which peaked at #24 and contained Murray's final #1 AC single, "Daydream Believer" [see 382]. None of Murray's LPs produced more than two #1 AC hits, except of course her greatest hits albums.

368 Lead Me On

MAXINE NIGHTINGALE

Windsong 11530

July 7, 1979 (7 weeks nonconsecutive)

Writers: Allee Willis (words), David Lasley (music)

Producer: Denny Diante

Allee Willis and David Lasley had been songwriting partners for some time before they created "Lead Me On." "We first wrote in 1974, a song for Bonnie Raitt called 'Got You on My Mind,'" Lasley said. They also wrote for Rosy, a trio Lasley was in with two women, before they split up when Willis moved to California.

When Lasley sang backup vocals for James Taylor in the fall of 1977, he came to Los Angeles and started working again with Willis. The duo wrote tunes for the Almo Irving music publishing company. One of the many songs Lasley and Willis created on the Almo Irving lot was "Lead Me On." "We got the chorus and the verse and went screaming into our publisher and asked, 'Do you think this is a hit?' and they said, 'Yes we do,' and we finished it in 30 minutes," Lasley said. He recalled that he and Willis alternated playing piano when one of them got stuck on a chord to play. In terms of the lyrics, he noted, "It was a song somewhat about what both of us were going through then in our relationships."

With Lasley's voice on the demo, Shelly Weiss of Almo Irving promoted the song and found an interested listener in Denny Diante, who produced Maxine Nightingale. Nightingale, born in Wembly, England, on November 2, 1952, had two entries on the pop and AC charts in 1976, "Right Back Where We Started From" (#5 AC, #2 pop) and "Gotta Be the One" (#22 AC, #53 pop), but there had been no chart activity since then. Recalling his initial reaction to learning that Nightingale was doing the tune, Lasley admitted, "Nobody went 'Yeah!' like if it had been Aretha [Franklin]."

Willis sang background on Nightingale's record, which came out first in the United Kingdom and did not generate much activity. But Diante was unfazed. "He was the one who really believed in it and remastered it and sped it up," Lasley said in describing the version released in the United States. Although the song's seven-week stay at the top of the AC chart was nonconsecutive, Lasley thinks the consistent airplay was what led to the song's eventual strong showing on the pop chart (#5 the week of September 22, 1979) and respectable position on R&B (#37).

Lasley and Willis grew to appreciate Nightingale. "She's very sweet, and she reminded me a lot of Kiki Dee," he said. They wrote "Take Your Heart" for her 1980 album following up the song, but it flopped. "Lead Me On" proved to be Nightingale's AC swan song and next-to-last pop entry before "(Bringing Out) the Girl in Me" went to #73 in late 1979. After her "Turn to Me" reached #17 R&B in 1983, she virtually disappeared from the music scene.

But Lasley has not forgotten his love for "Lead Me On." "I have a soft spot in my heart for that one," he said.

369 Morning Dance
SPYRO GYRA

Infinity 50011

July 28, 1979 (1 week)

Writer: Jay Beckenstein

Producers: Jay Beckenstein, Richard Calandra

Co-founder, co-producer, co-manager, writer—Jay Beckenstein, born on June 14, 1951, basically was Spyro Gyra despite its name and somewhat fluid membership. Beckenstein started the group in late 1975 with his high school pal Jeremy Wall, and they played together at bars in Buffalo, New York, with Beckenstein on sax and Wall on keyboards. Their first LP came out in 1977, and Beckenstein selected the group name Spyro Gyra simply because he liked the way it sounded. They had their first charted single in 1978 with "Shaker Song" (#16 AC, #90 pop).

Recalling composing "Morning Dance," Beckenstein said, "I just wrote it at the piano for the most part. The name came after the tune, so I wasn't looking at matching the song to the title." However, Beckenstein did think he wrote the piece in the morning.

When "Morning Dance" came out in 1979, joining Beckenstein and Wall on the record were Rubens Bassini on percussion, Jim Kunzdorfer on bass, and Ken Reinhardt on drums. "The band was in transition right when we were making our record," Beckenstein noted. "I frankly was experimenting with a few different bands at the time." And, despite the fact that none of the other musicians lasted long with the group, Beckenstein credited one of them with making "Morning Dance" a hit. "The thing that made 'Morning Dance' successful, it was two reasons. It had a nice melody, and it was Rubens, who laid a great percussion part on it."

"Morning Dance" reached #24 pop and #60 R&B as well as #1 AC. But its popularity as a representative example of "jazz fusion" led some critics who didn't like the genre to dismiss Spyro Gyra and its tunes. Looking back, Beckenstein commented, "The term 'jazz fusion' at the time to me, was very broad. It meant. . .jazz combined with other things, and I never thought it was a negative." He had listened to other musicians such as Miles Davis who combined soul and rock in their compositions and enjoyed doing it in his work as well.

Spyro Gyra had three other AC entries after "Morning Dance": "Catching the Sun" (#15 AC, #68 pop) and "Percolator" (#48 AC, #105 bubbling under) in 1980 and "Cafe Amore" (#14 AC, #77 pop) in 1981. All were instrumentals. Beckenstein continued to work with various musicians as leader of Spyro Gyra in the 1980s and 1990s.

In the spring of 1998 Spyro Gyra released its 21st album. "We tour 80 to 100 dates a year, always have, and have got a rock solid following," Beckenstein said. "We think of ourselves as the Grateful Dead of jazz." For the future, he hopes to continue to write music that appeals to people yet shows he is not stagnant in his approach. "It's important to grow and change," he said.

370 Mama Can't Buy You Love
ELTON JOHN

MCA 41042

August 25, 1979 (1 week)

Writers: Leroy Bell, Casey James

Producer: Thom Bell

After "Sorry Seems to Be the Hardest Word" [see 321] ran its course in 1976, Elton John had a second single released from the same album, *Blue Moves*, but "Bite Your Lip (Get Up and Dance!)" went only to #28 pop in early 1977 without making the AC chart, the worst performance by an Elton John 45 on the Hot 100 since "Tiny Dancer" went to #41 in 1972. Feeling he needed something new to rejuvenate what looked to be musical stagnation, in 1977 John went to Philadelphia and recorded some tracks with Leroy Bell and Casey James, a songwriting duo associated with that city's burgeoning soul sound.

"The sessions were fantastic and Elton was a real pro," Bell told *Billboard*. "Then one day someone called me and said they weren't being released. I just said 'Next page' and didn't worry about it. When MCA finally released it, the record sold more than one million copies. Maybe their timing was right."

What happened was that after three songs, John decided to abandon the project and focus his efforts elsewhere. After his second greatest hits album came out in the fall of 1977, John released "Ego," a single which did even worse than "Bite Your Lip" by stopping at #34 pop in 1978. Next came "Part-Time Love," which was a slight improvement over the previous 45, going to #22 pop and #40 AC in late 1978.

"Part-Time Love" was the first single from John's 1978 LP *A Single Man*. The second was "Song for Guy," an instrumental which despite getting to #37 AC was a complete washout on the pop ledger, only bubbling under to #110 in the spring of 1979. Figuring they had nothing else to lose and wanting to keep John's name in front of the public before his next album came out, MCA released "Mama Can't Buy You Love" along with "Are You Ready for Love" and "Three-Way Love Affair" on a record titled *The Thom Bell Sessions*, plus released it as a 45 as well in the summer of 1979.

By itself as a single, "Mama Can't Buy You Love" peaked at #1 AC plus #9 pop the weeks of August 25 and September 1, 1979. It also hit #36 R&B and even earned him a Grammy nomination for Best Male Rhythm and Blues Vocal Performance. It was the first #1 AC hit by John which he did not write.

Despite the success of "Mama Can't Buy You Love," the other two songs from *The Thom Bell Sessions* did not become singles. Instead, MCA released the title song of John's LP *Victim of Love* in the fall of 1979. The single went only to #31 pop, while the album was John's first not to sell a million copies since *11-17-70* in 1971. But he rebounded in 1980 with "Little Jeannie" [see 386].

371 Different Worlds

MAUREEN MCGOVERN

Warner/Curb 8835

September 8, 1979 (2 weeks)

Writers: Norman Gimbel (words), Charles Fox (lyrics)

Producer: Michael Lloyd

Here's a quiz. How many motion picture theme songs in the 1970s were sung by Maureen McGovern? The answer: Lots. Her first hit, "The Morning After," went to #6 AC and #1 pop in 1973 after winning the Academy Award for Best Song for the movie *The Poseidon Adventure*. She followed it with "Nice to Be Around" from *Cinderella Liberty* in 1973 (#28 AC, #101 bubbling under), "We May Never Love Like This Again" from *The Towering Inferno* in 1975 (#20 AC, #83 pop), and "Can You Read My Mind" from *Superman* in 1979 (#5 AC, #52 pop). Yet it was a TV theme song which gave McGovern, born in Youngstown, Ohio, on July 27, 1949, her #1 AC hit.

"I had recorded 'We Could Have It All' with [Charlie Fox and Norman Gimbel] for the movie *The Last Married Couple in America*," recalled McGovern. "We had a great, great working relationship. They asked me if I would do their theme 'Different Worlds,' and I did."

McGovern said she liked "Different Worlds" because "It was just a fun pop song." It was the opening song for the ABC-TV sitcom *Angie* starring Donna Pescow as a waitress who wed a rich doctor played by Robert Hays. Debuting on February 8, 1979, it did well through the autumn of that year, but too many time slot changes hurt its ratings, and *Angie* ended its run on October 2, 1980.

The initial success of *Angie* led "Different Worlds" to hit #1 AC and #18 pop. Gimbel and Fox achieved a similar crossover hit in 1976 with the self-titled theme from *Happy Days*, which peaked at #7 AC and #5 pop. "Happy Days," sung by Pratt and McClain, had something else in common with "Different Worlds": it was the title theme song for a Paramount Pictures sitcom airing on ABC.

Despite her success with "Different Worlds," McGovern did no more TV themes and very few movie tunes afterward. "I actually walked away from recording by the end of the 1970s," she said. "There was more to me than a three minute and ten second record." Oddly, "Different Worlds" helped McGovern show that to others.

When Linda Ronstadt left *The Pirates of Penzance* musical on Broadway in the early 1980s, McGovern got the job to replace her. "Someone had heard 'Different Worlds' and said 'She can hit those high notes,'" laughed McGovern. After 14 months with the show she left to pursue other musical alternatives.

Her plans in the late 1990s included promoting the 1997 LP *The Music Never Ends—The Lyrics of Alan and Marilyn Bergman*, working on a project of children's songs, possibly making albums of country and Gershwin music, and taking her one-woman 90-minute show on the road. Talk about your different worlds!

372 Rise

HERB ALPERT

A&M 2151

September 22, 1979 (1 week)

Writers: Andy Armer, Randy Badazz

Producers: Herb Alpert, Randy Badazz

"Rise" was the fifth #1 AC entry for Herb Alpert, but it came 11 years after his last one, "This Guy's in Love With You" [see 106]. He dropped the Tijuana Brass name for his 1979 hit, but not his distinctive vibrant trumpet sound. Ironically, it was while Alpert was trying to redo some of his Tijuana Brass hits that he decided to do "Rise."

A nephew of Alpert's, Randy Badazz, suggested the trumpeter remake his hits in a disco vein. But early into the project Alpert hated what he heard and called off the project. Badazz then offered Alpert a concoction he wrote with his friend Andy Armer called "Rise," and Alpert found that if he did the song at a slower groove than the disco beat of the time, it sounded fine.

"I know disco's not the rage anymore, but I also know that lots of people still dance," Alpert told *Rolling Stone* about "Rise." "I wanted to plug into that—not to make another routine disco record, but to take some of those elements and come up with something I'd have fun playing." That element did appeal to some, but the fact that "Rise" played in the background for some scenes on ABC-TV's then-popular daily soap opera *General Hospital* did not hurt either.

"Rise" rose to #1 on both the AC and pop charts, staying atop the latter for two weeks starting October 20, 1979. It also became Alpert's first top 10 R&B entry when it floated to #4 (he previously made his R&B debut with "Skokiaan," an instrumental duet with Hugh Masekela which went to #87 in 1978). The record also won him a Grammy for Best Pop Instrumental Performance.

Alpert returned several times to the AC and pop charts through the mid-1980s. The one single that had the closest sales impact to "Rise" failed to hit the AC chart, however. "Diamonds," featuring a vocal by Janet Jackson, went to #1 R&B for two weeks and #5 pop in 1987. But Alpert was not able to build up any lasting momentum on the Hot 100 or AC charts, and "Making Love in the Rain," which went to #21 and #35 later in 1987, proved to be his swan song on both. Alpert did make the R&B chart a few more times, however, including "North on South St.," which made #40 in 1991.

In 1997 "Rise" rose again to #1 pop when used as a backing track for "Hypnotize" by the late rapper the Notorious B.I.G. By then Alpert and Jerry Moss had sold A&M Records, which they created in 1962 for $500 million, to PolyGram Records (it was sold in 1989), and Alpert did his last A&M album in 1992. In 1994 he and Moss formed Almo Sounds, a label distributed by Geffen Records, where Alpert put out his all-instrumental LP *Second Wind* in 1996. Two years later he was still active in several Almo Sounds projects, and was also planning to do more recording.

373 Where Were You When I Was Falling in Love

LOBO

MCA/Curb 41065

September 29, 1979 (2 weeks)

Writers: John Samuel Lorber, Jeff Silbar, Steve Jobe

Producer: Bob Montgomery

After enjoying a fair amount of popularity during the early 1970s, Lobo experienced a downturn. After leaving the Big Tree label in 1975, where he had earned all of his hits, and doing unproductive singles for Warner Brothers from 1976–78, he managed to come back in 1979 on MCA with a tune not written with him in mind.

"Where Were You When I Was Falling in Love" was a composition done in Nashville in 1979 by a trio of men. "We were staff songwriters at a company called House of Gold Music, and worked with Bob Montgomery," said co-writer Jeff Silbar. In fact, Sam Lorber was Silbar's next-door neighbor. Recalling the idea for the song and who contributed what parts to it, Silbar said, "I would say it was three songwriters getting together to make somebody a hit. It was a great title."

Lorber, Silbar, and Jobe did not participate in the production of Lobo's take on their tune, but according to Silbar they enjoyed the final record because it sounded pretty much the way they had done the song themselves. "We made a demo very close to the original version, except for the background vocals, which was the producer's idea," he said. The trio were also pleased that they had given Lobo a hit after several years of drought.

"Where Were You When I Was Falling in Love" went to #23 pop in addition to its two-week stay atop the AC chart. Unfortunately for Lobo, he could get only one more record on both listings after that, "Holdin' On for Dear Love," which peaked at #13 AC and #75 pop in early 1980. The next year he moved into country music and made that chart with three singles on his own Lobo label from 1981–82: "I Don't Want to Want You," "Come Looking for Me," and "Living My Life Without You." (Long before, in 1974, Lobo had established his own music publishing company, Boo Publishing.) He had no other entries there until two in 1985 on the Evergreen label, "Am I Going Crazy (Or Just Out of My Mind)" and "Paint the Town Blue." The latter tune, a duet with Robin Lee, was Lobo's last charting anywhere. Lobo assumed a low profile for the rest of the 1980s and 1990s and apparently no longer tours or records.

374 Broken Hearted Me

ANNE MURRAY

Capitol 4773

October 13, 1979 (5 weeks)

Writer: Randy Goodrum

Producer: Jim Ed Norman

In the wake of his success with "You Needed Me," writer Randy Goodrum felt a need to get another hit with Anne Murray. "I certainly didn't put any pressure on him, but he just kept sending me songs," she said. After several submissions, "Broken Hearted Me" was the one which appealed to the vocalist. It became her seventh #1 AC hit and fourth #1 country hit, peaking on the latter chart the week of December 1, 1979, three weeks after falling off the top of the AC chart. On the pop chart it peaked at #12.

Murray meant it in a complimentary way when she said that Goodrum had a "feminine side" to him when it came to writing songs for her. "'Broken Hearted Me' is so heartfelt," she said. Murray also noted that although "Broken Hearted Me" was more downbeat than "You Needed Me," which was an ode of thanks from one lover to another, it still touched a mass audience.

However, recording "Broken Hearted Me" was anything but easy for Murray. "I had chronic sinusitis, and of course you can't do anything about it," she said. "I couldn't get the breath that I needed." Murray was also pregnant, and the recording session, she remembered, was quite a chore. Yet Murray summoned up enough strength to sound like her regular self, and most listeners would notice nothing amiss in "Broken Hearted Me."

"Broken Hearted Me" was the third #1 AC hit for Randy Goodrum in three years. In 1977 he made it with "It's Sad to Belong" with England Dan and John Ford Coley [see 333], and in 1978 the one which did the trick for him was "Bluer Than Blue" by Michael Johnson [see 350].

Murray always has been quick to thank songwriters like Goodrum for bringing their work to her. "I feel so lucky to have been associated with these songs," she said while recounting her #1 AC hits. "I believe a lot in being in the right place at the right time." But Murray also noted that it was not all luck that helped her earn her hits. "A good song is a good song," she said. She insisted that she never looked at a song as a country or pop or AC hit, but cared only about how it appealed to her.

That strategy must have worked, for Murray continued to make all three charts into the 1980s, beginning with her first #1 AC record of that decade, "Daydream Believer" [see 382]. As for Goodrum, he penned several more hit tunes for other artists in the 1980s, including co-writing "Who's Holding Donna Now" for DeBarge [see 478].

375 You're Only Lonely

J. D. SOUTHER

Columbia 11079

November 17, 1979 (5 weeks)

Writer: J. D. Souther

Producer: J. D. Souther

When you are the one-time roommate of Glenn Frey and Jackson Brown, it makes it easier to get to write songs and play music with them, as John David "J.D." Souther (pronounced "SOW-ther" and having nothing to do with where he was born, which was Detroit, Michigan) found out in the 1970s. In the late 1960s, a few years after some local success with his high school band in Amarillo, Texas, John David and the Cinders, Souther came to Los Angeles and roomed with the two other musical hopefuls.

With Frey, Souther formed a group called Longbranch Pennywhistle in 1970, which went nowhere. Next came his debut solo album, 1972's *John David Souther*, which also flopped. Then in 1974 the Souther, Hillman, Furay Band debuted and hit #27 pop with "Fallin' in Love" (not the Hamilton, Joe Frank and Reynolds hit). Unfortunately, nothing else by Souther and his bandmates Chris Hillman and Richie Furay charted, so he spent the next few years primarily cranking tunes out for others, including "Best of My Love" for the Eagles [see 245].

Souther did release another solo LP in 1976, to relatively little notice, then set about recording his third one in an unusual manner. Rather than play the same tune constantly to get the track down at a session, Souther told Judson Klinger in *Rolling Stone* that "We played those songs like sets, every afternoon, for weeks and weeks. And I loved the way it was sounding."

One tune included in the sets was "You're Only Lonely," which became his first solo hit, going to #1 AC, #7 on the Hot 100 the weeks of December 15 and 22, 1979, plus #60 country by the start of 1980. Regarding the song's success, Souther told Klinger, "It doesn't change the shape of your nose or give you the football letter you didn't get in high school, but it does sort of hand you back your ticket, stamped 'Validated, you were right. You can do this.'"

The momentum Souther created with "You're Only Lonely" evaporated when the follow-up, "White Rhythm and Blues," went only to #46 AC and #105 bubbling under in the spring of 1980. The following year he teamed with James Taylor to do "Her Town Too," a #5 AC and #11 pop entry, his last single on both charts. In 1982 his duet with Linda Ronstadt, "Sometimes You Just Can't Win," went to #27 country as the flip side of Ronstadt's #29 pop hit "Get Closer." Souther continued in the music business afterward, but his profile during the 1980s and 1990s was rather low.

376 Send One Your Love

STEVIE WONDER

Tamla 54303

December 22, 1979 (4 weeks)

Writer: Stevie Wonder

Producer: Stevie Wonder

Five years before receiving critical and commercial favor with "I Just Called to Say I Love You" from the movie *The Lady in Red*, Stevie Wonder scored a hit with "Send One Your Love," written first as a melody for a little-seen documentary.

Based on the book of the same name by Christopher Bird and Peter Tompkins, *The Secret Life of Plants* was the first film produced by Michael Braun, who co-wrote the screenplay with Tompkins and the movie's director Walon Green. As its name implied, the motion picture dealt with the life cycles of various flora and fauna using time-lapse photography and miniature cameras.

To have a blind man score such a visual piece struck a few critics as a ridiculous notion, but not Braun. "The reason I wanted Stevie to score in the first place is that it's about unseen things—the insides of seeds and plants—and he has about as much right to write about that as a composer who can see," he told Paul Grein in *Billboard*. But Braun did acknowledge that scoring the film with Wonder had not been easy. "When I first approached Stevie, I told him if he could write the songs we would edit the footage to his music," he told Grein. "But he said he wanted to do it the regular way—sitting down at an editing machine and composing. Obviously he couldn't do that, so I described each scene to him practically frame-by-frame, and he went from there."

Wonder constructed songs as the score for the film, then wrote lyrics for them which he sang on the soundtrack LP titled *Journey Through the Secret Life of Plants*. While the film did unimpressive business, the album became a hit, and included two versions of "Send One Your Love." The vocal rendition, featuring a harmonica solo, became a single and stayed at #4 pop for four weeks starting December 22, 1979. It also made #5 R&B. The LP's other "Send One Your Love" was what *Billboard* reviewer Cary Darling termed "A near cocktail lounge instrumental version."

With its #1 AC peak, "Send One Your Love" was Wonder's biggest hit on the chart since "You Are the Sunshine of My Life" in 1973 [see 191]. Two singles made #1 pop in 1977, but on the AC chart "I Wish" made only #23 and "Sir Duke" stopped at #3. Also that year, "Isn't She Lovely," a track from the album on which the previous two songs appeared, *Songs in the Key of Life*, made #23 and was the first album cut to make the AC chart without being on a single.

One other single from *Journey Through the Secret Life of Plants* came out after "Send One Your Love." "Outside My Window" reached #43 AC and #52 pop. But Wonder rebounded quickly and notched another #1 AC hit two years later [see 422—"Ebony and Ivory"].

377 Deja Vu

DIONNE WARWICK

Arista 0459

January 19, 1980 (1 week)

Writers: Adrienne Anderson (words), Isaac Hayes (music)

Producer: Barry Manilow

Some artists have off years in recording. Dionne Warwick seemed to have an off decade—most of the 1970s. Her headaches started when her longtime writer/producer team of Burt Bacharach and Hal David ended their professional working relationship around 1972, depriving Warwick of her main source of songs. Then from 1972–78 she managed only four AC entries, of which only two made the Hot 100. Admittedly, one of these was her first #1 pop hit, 1974's "Then Came You" with the Spinners, which peaked at #3 AC.

But otherwise Warwick, who had taken to adding an "e" to the end of her surname, had no big hits until 1979's "I'll Never Love This Way Again," which made #5 on both the pop and AC charts. Following it up was "Deja Vu," a song which was instrumental in getting together Warwick with Barry Manilow, the producer of that tune and "I'll Never Love This Way Again."

"It was a culmination of things that occurred," Warwick remembered. "Isaac Hayes and I toured together. He wrote the melody basically for me on tour." But Hayes had trouble coming up with lyrics for the song, so Warwick found a writer—Adrienne Anderson, who just happened to be friends with Barry Manilow.

Manilow recorded for Arista Records, the same label which signed Warwick. When he learned she was recording new material for the label, he offered to produce her. "It was something Barry pushed to do," Warwick said. "He convinced me he had the ability to do what I wanted him to do."

Their collaboration on "Deja Vu" certainly paid off, going not only to #1 AC but also #15 pop and #25 R&B. The follow-up to "Deja Vu," "After You," went only to #10 AC, #33 R&B, and #65 pop in the spring of 1980. But that relative disappointment mattered little, since Warwick clearly was back on top. In fact, her next-released 45, which came out in the fall of 1980, returned her to #1 AC [see 391—"No Night So Long"]. By that time Manilow no longer was producing her, but the two did sing a duet in 1985, a remake of the Bee Gees' 1972 pop hit "Run to Me," which made #12 AC.

By the way, it is not surprising to report that Warwick, who served as spokesperson for infomercials of the Psychic Friends Network in the early 1990s, believes in the concept of *déjà vu* (a French saying meaning "the illusion of having previously experienced something actually being encountered for the first time"), although she did laugh at first when asked about it. "I think déjà vu just happens to everyone," she said. "I bet people feel they've been through something several times."

235

378 Yes, I'm Ready

TERI DESARIO WITH KC

Casablanca 2227

January 26, 1980 (2 weeks)

Writer: Barbara Mason

Producer: Harry Wayne Casey

Barbara Mason's debut chart single "Yes, I'm Ready" was her biggest hit at #5 pop and #2 R&B in 1965. Mason rerecorded the song in 1973, when it bubbled under to #125, and again in 1980, but by then buyers favored a rendition by another musician and his protégé.

Harry Wayne Casey, born in Miami, Florida, on January 31, 1951, does not remember why he chose to remake "Yes, I'm Ready" other than it was one of his favorite songs of the 1960s, when he met his future singing partner. "I went to elementary and high school with Teri DeSario," he said. "We were in talent shows together. I always admired her voice, and after high school, I always kept in touch with her, what she was doing."

What Casey was doing in the 1970s was producing hits, particularly as lead singer of KC and the Sunshine Band. There he scored five #1 pop hits, including "Please Don't Go," which peaked at #27 AC in 1979, and a #2 pop and #1 R&B hit, "Keep It Comin' Love," which reached #36 AC in 1977. It was while reviewing new records in release one day in 1978 that he caught up with DeSario.

"I got to Casablanca and I saw a song by Teri DeSario called 'Ain't Nothing Gonna Keep Me From You.' I thought it was a great record," he said. He encouraged a Miami radio station to play it, and the record went to #43 pop. DeSario learned what had happened, contacted KC and thanked him, and told him that her career was not going as well as she had hoped. KC took over managing her and convinced Neil Bogart, president of Casablanca Records, to let him produce her second album.

DeSario had not considered doing remakes, but on a flight to Los Angeles with KC, he convinced her that an updated "Yes, I'm Ready" would be a hit. "I don't know if it was going to be a duet originally. I think it was Neil's idea," KC said. As the first single off DeSario's album, it topped the AC chart a month before it reached #2 pop for two weeks in March 1980 behind Queen's "Crazy Little Thing Called Love." It also hit #20 R&B.

The duo's follow-up was a remake of Martha and the Vandellas' 1964 hit "Dancing in the Streets," which hit #66 pop but missed the AC chart. DeSario then toured with KC and the Sunshine Band as an opening act or "special guest." She and KC last charted with "Don't Run (Come Back to Me)," which held at #12 AC and #103 bubbling under in 1983.

After three albums together, DeSario "decided she didn't want to do touring anymore," according to KC, and settled in Los Angeles to do everything from vocal coaching to gospel music. As for KC, he went on tour again in 1990 after a five-year layoff and performed "Yes, I'm Ready" in concert assisted by his backup singers Maria DeCrescenzo and Beverly Foster.

379 Longer
DAN FOGELBERG

Full Moon 50824

February 9, 1980 (1 week)

Writer: Dan Fogelberg

Producers: Dan Fogelberg, Norman Putnam, Morty Lewis

One of the most popular AC acts of the 1980s, Dan Fogelberg often confounded radio programmers by following ballads with releases of hard rock tunes like "The Power of Gold" and "Missing You." In fact, Fogelberg's recording career has been much more adventurous and wide-ranging than listening only to his four #1 AC hits would lead one to think.

Born Daniel Grayling Fogelberg in Peoria, Illinois, on August 13, 1951, the singer/songwriter grew up with parents who loved music. His father was an ex-bandleader who taught music in schools and private practice, and his mother studied opera singing in college. Fogelberg took piano lessons from his father before reaching his teens but preferred plucking guitar instead. He began to write songs as an adolescent, but nothing of note happened until he attended the University of Illinois in Champaign-Urbana and performed at a club called the Red Herring. His singing there attracted the attention of music agent Irving Azoff, who convinced Fogelberg to leave college and join him in Los Angeles to pursue a recording career.

Azoff got Fogelberg signed to Columbia in 1971. His debut LP, *Home Free*, came out the following year but contained no hit singles and did poorly. His next album release, 1974's *Souvenirs*, did generate a hit 45—"Part of the Plan," which gave him his AC and pop debuts at #22 AC and #31 pop in 1975. Three years later, he had a bigger pop hit with "The Power of Gold"; that tune went to #24 on the Hot 100, but its rocking sound kept it off the AC chart. Then in 1979 came the release of "Longer," the first song since "Part of the Plan" that Fogelberg was sure would be a hit.

In the liner notes to his 1997 retrospective album *Portrait: The Music of Dan Fogelberg*, the artist described "Longer" as "The song I jokingly referred to as 'the song that put me on the elevators.' I wrote it while on a vacation in Maui in 1979 while lounging in a hammock one night and looking up at the stars. It just seems this song was drifting around the universe, saw me, and decided I'd give it a good home." Fogelberg played acoustic guitar while Jerry Hey provided a solo on the fluegelhorn.

"Longer" nearly topped the pop chart as well as AC, staying at #2 the weeks of March 15 and 22, 1980, first behind "Crazy Little Thing Called Love" by Queen and then Pink Floyd's "Another Brick in the Wall." "Longer" even made it to the country chart, where it peaked at #85.

The follow-up to "Longer" was "Heart Hotels," which made #3 AC and #21 pop. Toward the end of 1980, Fogelberg released another album, which gave him four hit singles, including another #1 AC hit [see 416—"Leader of the Band"].

380 When I Wanted You
BARRY MANILOW

Arista 0481

February 16, 1980 (1 week)

Writer: Gino Cunico

Producers: Barry Manilow, Ron Dante

In 1976 an aspiring singer/songwriter from Los Angeles named Gino Cunico released his debut album on Arista Records. While it had virtually no impact in the marketplace, it certainly caught the attention of Barry Manilow, who covered two tunes heard on the record. One of them, "When I Wanted You," was written by Cunico himself.

Cunico's rendition of "When I Wanted You" came out in the fall of 1976 after his first single, "Daydreamer," made only #43 AC in mid-1976 (and was his only single to make any chart). Reviewing "When I Wanted You," a *Billboard* reviewer's comments were telling, if not prescient: "The producer of Arista's hottest female act, Melissa Manchester [referring to Vini Poncia; see 265—"Midnight Blue"], gives this the feel of a smash ballad by the label's hottest male act, Barry Manilow." Apparently Manilow fans wanted the real thing and not an imitation, for while Cunico's single bombed, Manilow's take on it three years later went to #1 AC and #20 pop.

To add insult to injury, Manilow got another hit out of a Cuncio flop. Cunico's follow-up to "When I Wanted You," in December 1976, was "Can't Smile Without You." Despite the tune's being rerecorded to insert the call letters for major radio stations in 25 markets, including New York, Chicago, and Philadelphia, it went nowhere—but did become a #1 AC hit for Manilow a few years later [see 345].

"When I Wanted You" was Manilow's first hit in the 1980s, becoming his 16th top 10 AC and top 30 pop single. But his notorious reliance on ballads for success was beginning to have a negative effect, even on the AC chart, where in 1979 Ray Stevens managed to reach #11 with his bitingly humorous parody "I Need Your Help Barry Manilow."

Manilow, however, argued that people who saw him only as a romantic love singer were getting the wrong impression of him. "The words I sing best to a melody are words about love," he explained to Robert Windeler in *People*. "Listening only to my singles, you'd think that's all I sing about. On albums I do take it a step or two further. I'm possibly breaking through into slightly new ground with more intelligent lyrics than 'Baby, oh, baby' and more sophisticated rhythm and arrangements that go beyond a guitar and a drum. Arranging is my strongest suit."

Despite his protestations, Manilow remained identified with slow, heavily produced ballads into the 1980s, and it was in that very mold that he scored his 11th #1 AC hit in 1981 [see 413—"The Old Songs"].

381 Give It All You Got
CHUCK MANGIONE

A&M 2211

February 23, 1980 (3 weeks nonconsecutive)

Writer: Chuck Mangione

Producer: Chuck Mangione

Chuck Mangione got his second #1 AC hit after "Feels So Good" [see 347] by way of a TV network president. As Mangione explained, "In 1976 during the Summer Olympics, I noticed they played a lot of my music. I heard 'Chase the Clouds Away' and other songs of mine." ABC Sports staff member Doug Wilson had gotten his network to play the tunes because he was a Mangione fan. When Mangione played Lincoln Center in New York City in the late 1970s, Wilson brought his boss, ABC Sports President Roone Arledge. Arledge asked Mangione if he would like to do the official theme of the 1980 Winter Olympics, to be played during ABC's coverage. "Of course I said yes, and that's where 'Give It All You Got' came from," Mangione said.

Arledge gave Mangione no suggestions on what sort of instrumental to write. Mangione said he did have an inspiration: "My vision was to think about the athletes and their efforts to do their best now. They're giving it all they've got. And we almost got to be like the athletes because we also got to perform the song at the ceremonies for a world-wide audience."

ABC used a slower version of "Give It All You Got" as background music for instant replays. It appeared on Mangione's 1980 LP *Fun and Games* as "Give It All You Got, But Slowly" along with the original. "Give It All You Got" went to #18 pop, #32 R&B, and #1 AC, and got a Grammy nomination for Best Instrumental Composition. *Fun and Games* was nominated for Best Jazz Fusion Performance.

Born Charles Frank Mangione in Rochester, New York (about a four-hour drive from Lake Placid, the site of the 1980 winter Olympics), he and older brother Gaspare ("Gap") liked jazz as children, so their father let them meet touring musicians like Dizzy Gillespie. "My dad would invite them over to our house for spaghetti and some wine. I thought every kid had Dizzy at his house for one week," he said.

Mangione studied at the Eastman School of Music from 1958–63, earning a B.A. During this time he and Gap recorded as the Jazz Brothers in 1960, and he did a solo LP, *Recuerdo*, in 1962. After teaching music and playing as a sideman, a break came in 1970, during a stint conducting the Rochester Philharmonic on some of his songs: he won a contract with Mercury to do his LP *Friends and Love*. By 1972 he had formed the Chuck Mangione Quartet, serving as musical director as well as fluegelhornist.

He last charted AC in 1980 at #49 with the title track from *Fun and Games*. In the 1990s he toured and did matinees which stipulated that no one over 18 could attend without being accompanied by a child. He wants children to enjoy jazz music the way he did as a kid, for as he noted, "You've got to get them while they're young."

382 Daydream Believer
ANNE MURRAY

Capitol 4813

March 1, 1980 (1 week)

Writer: John Stewart

Producer: Jim Ed Norman

If Anne Murray could score a hit covering a tune by the "Fab Four"—the Beatles' "You Won't See Me" [see 222]—then why couldn't she do the same with one by the so-called "Prefab Four," TV's the Monkees, whose act was based on the Beatles? She could, and she did.

"In 1968 I was in Halifax, Nova Scotia, and did a show called *Let's Go*. It was a teenybopper show, and I sang the week's hits," Murray remembered. One of them was "Daydream Believer" by the Monkees, which peaked at #1 pop for four weeks starting December 2, 1967. About a decade later, Murray recalled that she said, 'We've got to do that one too'" and had her band cover it.

The original version, sung by Davy Jones (the short English one), did not cross over to the AC chart. The Monkees did make the listings twice, however, first during their 1960s heyday with "Good Clean Fun," which made #29 AC and #82 pop in 1969, and then in 1986, when Jones, Mickey Dolenz, and Peter Tork reunited to do "That Was Then, This Is Now," which went to #24 AC and #20 pop. (The other Monkee, Mike Nesmith, did not rejoin the group to tour until the group's 20th anniversary, 11 years later.) Ironically, the Monkees' follow-up to "That Was Then, This Is Now" was a remixed version of "Daydream Believer," which reached #79 on its second go-round on the Hot 100 in 1986 but failed again to make the AC chart.

It was a different story for Murray's "Daydream Believer," as it not only topped the AC chart but made #12 pop and, surprisingly, #3 country, even though Murray changed the song very little except for a few notes and some lyrics to make them more appropriate for a woman to sing. In fact, Murray had the bulk of her 1980s hits on the country chart, where she scored six #1 entries after "Daydream Believer," ranging from "Could I Have This Dance" in 1980 to "Now and Forever (You and Me)" in 1986. She still appeared often on the AC and pop charts, but her records peaked at lower positions there.

In the 1990s Murray had more success as a touring act than on the charts, having virtually disappeared from the pop and AC listings while notching up a few country entries. Based in Toronto, she remained active in the record business, however, with more than 30 albums to her credit. Her most recent was 1997's *An Intimate Evening With Anne Murray—Live!*

"I had never done a live album," marveled Murray. But when she taped a TV special in Halifax, which included her doing duets with fellow recording artists and fans Bryan Adams and Celine Dion, the decision was made to release the tracks as a live production. Many of her old #1 AC hits were on the album as well, including the one that started it all for her, "Snowbird" [see 139].

383 Lost in Love

AIR SUPPLY

Arista 0479

March 22, 1980 (6 weeks nonconsecutive)

Writers: Graham Russell

Producers: Robie Porter, Rick Chertoff, Charles Fisher

Air Supply was a vocal duo consisting of two Mutt 'n' Jeff types, the 6-foot-5, sandy-haired Graham Russell and the 5-foot-7, curly-haired Russell Hitchcock. The two banded together after meeting in 1976 during an Australian production of the stage musical *Jesus Christ Superstar*, and became one of the most popular AC acts of the early 1980s.

Hitchcock, born in Melbourne, Australia, on June 15, 1949, and Russell, born in Nottingham, England, on June 1, 1950, before emigrating to Australia at age 17, picked the name "Air Supply" because they were both Geminis, an "air" sign on the astrological chart. The two shared a love of music, but both hailed from working-class families, and each had done his fair share of odd jobs and singing in pubs Down Under before they found each other doing *Jesus Christ Superstar*. In the production Russell played the apostle Peter, and Hitchcock alternated between the role of Jesus and that of his betrayer, Judas.

While still in the musical, they created their own demos of songs written by Russell, but once they had their first hit, they left the show to tour and promote their music. But within a few years their popularity in Australia had faded, and in the late 1970s, Russell went to England in an attempt to pitch their songs and crack the European market. While there, he read that "Lost in Love," which Air Supply's Australian label Big Time Records had sold to Arista for distribution in America, was going up the charts in the United States.

"I begged, borrowed and stole enough money to get us to Los Angeles," Russell recalled Davin Seay of *People*. "I called Clive Davis and all he wanted to know was why I wasn't back in Australia recording an album."

Meanwhile, "Lost in Love" went to #1 AC plus #3 pop for four weeks starting May 3, 1980. Ahead of it were Blondie's "Call Me" at #1 and Christopher Cross's "Ride Like the Wind" at #2 the first three weeks, with Lipps, Inc.'s "Funkytown" replacing "Ride Like the Wind" at #2 the final week. Later in 1980 a cover by Dickey Lee with Kathy Burdick came out and reached #30 country.

While Russell's efforts to sell Air Supply in England never amounted to much (the duo had only three entries there from 1980–93, and "Lost in Love" was not one of them), they became a top act in America. "Lost in Love" was their first AC entry and #1 AC hit, followed by "Here I Am (Just When I Thought I Was Over You)" in 1981 [see 412].

384 Three Times in Love

TOMMY JAMES

Millenium 11785

March 29, 1980 (1 week)

Writers: Tommy James, Rick Serota

Producer: Tommy James

Tommy James and the Shondells were one of the most successful rock groups on the Hot 100 in the 1960s, scoring #1 hits with "Hanky Panky" (1966) and "Crimson and Clover" (1968). They did not cross over to the AC chart until 1969, when "Crystal Blue Persuasion" made #27 while going to #2 pop for three weeks. The following year James, born Thomas Jackson in Dayton, Ohio, on April 29, 1947, broke up with the 1966–70 Shondells (he had originally cut "Hanky Panky" in 1963 with a different Shondells incarnation, but that's another story). As a soloist, his "Draggin' the Line" in 1971 hit #6 AC and #4 pop, but shortly after "Love Song" in 1972 (#40 AC, #67 pop), James was off both charts through the end of the decade.

James' difficulties in the 1970s started when his record label Roulette became K-Tel, a company primarily interested in promoting its discount compilation LPs rather than his material. He signed with Fantasy Records but found them more involved in the movie business (they had an interest in 1975's *One Flew Over the Cuckoo's Nest*) than his two albums for them, 1976's *In Touch* and 1977's *Midnight Rider*. In late 1978 he left Fantasy.

During these years James toured constantly and added new material to his act, refusing to be an "oldies" attraction, and he felt audiences responded to his new songs just as strongly as they had to his 1960s hits. He told Jeff Tamarkin in *Goldmine* in 1980 that it was in early 1979 that he decided to make a serious effort to score another hit. "I brought the guitar player to live in my house, my drummer came in later, and I said, 'We're going to write.' I swear it was like a straight shot, it was like a bullet. It couldn't have happened any faster. Ronnie Serota (my guitar player) and I sat down and the first song we wrote was 'Three Times in Love.' Suddenly it was all coming back to me."

Within three weeks James, Serota, and other members of the band did demos of "Three Times in Love" and got a contract with Millenium Records, a division of RCA. "By November 1979, we had cut three sides—'Three Times in Love,' 'Long Way Down,' and 'You Got Me.' 'Three Times in Love' was the obvious hit," James said. "It came out so fast and so good. I knew it was the right song. We released 'Three Times in Love' and it immediately took off."

"Three Times in Love" became James' first #1 AC hit as well as his first pop entry since 1973, peaking at #19 in the spring of 1980. Unfortunately, it was his last AC entry, and he managed only one more on the Hot 100, 1981's "You're So Easy to Love," which made #58. In the 1990s he became primarily an oldies touring act, though a few new records of him in concert were released.

385 The Rose
BETTE MIDLER

Atlantic 3656

May 10, 1980 (5 weeks)

Writer: Amanda McBroom

Producer: Paul A. Rothchild

Contrary to some reports, *The Rose* was not technically Bette Midler's film debut. She appeared in a bit part in the 1966 movie *Hawaii* when it was filmed in the state where she grew up. But *The Rose* was the picture which put the entertainment world on notice that the bawdy broad of records, nightclubs, and TV shows could more than hold her own on the big screen.

Based on the life of Janis Joplin, but with enough changes made to prevent her family from filing a lawsuit charging infringement, *The Rose* told of a hard-driving female rock artist who rose to the top but was burnt out in the process. The business pressure side of the story was one Midler could relate to, having seen her career get a huge shot of popularity in 1973 with "Boogie Woogie Bugle Boy" [see 195] and a Grammy win for Best New Artist, only to endure commercial disappointment during the rest of the 1970s with indifferently received singles. Her five unexceptional releases from 1974–78 were remakes of "In the Mood" in 1974 (#18 AC, #51 pop), and "Strangers in the Night" (#45 AC) and "Old Cape Cod" (#36 AC) in 1976, followed by "You're Moving Out Today" (#11 AC, #42 pop) in 1977 and "Storybook Children (Day-break)" (#37 AC, #57 pop) in 1978.

Two songs from *The Rose* soundtrack became singles in their own right. The first was Midler's remake of "When a Man Loves a Woman," which got only to #35 pop without making the Hot 100. The second was "The Rose," which out-of-work actress Amanda McBroom wrote two years before the film went into development. The song became a hit without a chorus, an element deemed almost always necessary for a tune to be a hit.

"The emotion seems to be what makes the record work," McBroom said in *The Top Ten* by Bob Gilbert and Gary Theroux. "It's real and poignant because Bette just sounds so whipped." "The Rose" peaked at #3 pop in addition to getting #1 pop. On the Hot 100 it was held out of the top spot the week of June 28, 1980, by Paul McCartney's "Coming Up (Live at Glasgow)" at #1 and Lipps Inc.'s "Funkytown" at #2.

At the Oscars Midler got a nomination for Best Actress, but somehow "The Rose" failed to get a mention in the Best Song category. In contrast, the Grammys gave Midler a statuette for Best Female Pop Vocal Performance and nominations for Record of the Year and Song of the Year.

Midler went on to several other movie roles in the 1980s, but it was another decade before she reached #1 AC again [see 591—"From a Distance"].

386 Little Jeannie

ELTON JOHN

MCA 41236

June 14, 1980 (2 weeks)

Writers: Gary Osborne (words), Elton John (music)

Producers: Clive Franks, Elton John

John's erratic chart numbers in the late 1970s, and the fact that by then he had dropped much of the flamboyant, flashy wardrobe that had prompted one critic to dub him "the Liberace of rock," led some observers to wonder whether John had the goods to deliver hits in the 1980s. He proved that he did with "Little Jeannie," his first single of the decade.

"Little Jeannie" was John's biggest pop hit since "Don't Go Breaking My Heart" hit #1 in 1976. Beside being #1 AC, "Little Jeannie" went to #3 for four weeks starting July 19, 1980, behind Billy Joel's "It's Still Rock and Roll to Me" at #1 the first two weeks and Paul McCartney's "Coming Up (Live at Glasgow)" and "Magic" [see 388] at #2 the first and second weeks respectively. For the last two weeks that "Little Jeannie" held at #3, "Magic" was at #1 and Joel's "It's Still Rock and Roll to Me" at #2.

At the time, there was a hiatus in the working relationship between John and lyricist Bernie Taupin, so John employed Gary Osborne to do the job for this tune. It was the first single off John's 1980 album *21 at 33*, the 33-year-old John's 21st album.

Despite its popularity in 1980, those attending John's concerts in the 1990s rarely heard the tune performed. John explained to Timothy White in *Billboard* in 1997 that "A song like 'Little Jeannie' was a nice little song, but it just doesn't work live, whereas a song like 'Healing Hands' is even more vibrant on stage than it is on record."

Another thing "Little Jeannie" did not do was return John back to consistent hit-making form. Its follow-up "(Sartorial Eloquence) Don't Ya Wanna Play This Game No More?" got just to #45 AC and #39 pop in the fall of 1980. In 1981 John switched from MCA to Geffen, but his album *The Fox* failed to sell a million copies and spun off two disappointing singles, "Nobody Wins" at #23 AC and #21 pop, and "Chloe" at #16 AC and #34 pop. However, "Nobody Wins" does have the distinction of being the first Elton John single to be produced by Chris Thomas, who would be the artist's favorite producer during the 1980s and 1990s.

In 1982 John got back to the top 20 pop listing when his tribute to his late pal John Lennon, "Empty Garden (Hey Hey Johnny)," went to #18 AC and #13 pop. The two men also worked together before Lennon's tragic slaying in 1980, with John singing backup on Lennon's #1 pop hit of 1974 "Whatever Gets You Through the Night" and Lennon returning the favor by singing "I Saw Her Standing There" in concert with John, a performance taped and released as the B-side of John's #1 pop hit of 1975 "Philadelphia Freedom." The 45 after "Empty Garden (Hey Hey Johnny)" brought John back to #1 AC [see 426—"Blue Eyes"].

387 Let Me Love You Tonight

PURE PRAIRIE LEAGUE

Casablanca 2266

June 28, 1980 (3 weeks)

Writers: Jeff Wilson, Dan Greer, Steve Woodard

Producer: John Ryan

Formed in Cincinnati in 1971, Pure Prairie League first stirred national action with "Amie" in 1975 (#20 AC, #27 pop). By that time high school student Vince Gill had opened for the group at a concert in Oklahoma. Little did he know that in 1979 he would become the band's lead singer.

Gill, born in Norman, Oklahoma, on April 12, 1957, came with a friend to a Pure Prairie League audition after the departure of George Ed Powell and Larry Gorshom, guitarists and vocalists for the group since 1976 (Craig Fuller was lead vocalist/guitarist from 1971–75). Besides singing and guitar playing, Gill also wrote songs, and the group used his talent extensively. "I think I wrote maybe half of each album," he said.

But he did not write "Let Me Love You Tonight." That came from Jeff Wilson, who had joined the group as another guitarist after Gill was already on board. Other band members were keyboardist Michael Connor, drummer Billy Hinds, and bassist Mike Reilly. "We did that record out in Van Nuys, California," Gill recalled. "All in all, a pretty fun project. It was a neat time for the band because it was a new label for them."

The Pure Prairie League had switched from RCA to Casablanca by 1980, and, according to Gill, Casablanca wanted to be known for more than their disco hits with acts like Donna Summer. "They wanted to prove they could have a pop hit and did it with us. I don't want to know how, and I don't want to know why," Gill said with a laugh in remembering the circumstances.

With David Sanborn's sax providing flavor, "Let Me Love You Tonight" peaked at #10 pop the weeks of July 12 and 19, 1980, while riding atop the AC listings. It was the band's second AC entry and third pop one. ("Two Lane Highway" hit #97 the week of June 28, 1975 after "Amie.") After "Let Me Love You Tonight," two more singles made the pop chart in 1980, then came the last AC and second-to-last pop entry, 1981's "Still Right Here in My Heart" (#4 AC, #28 pop). The follow-up, "You're Mine Tonight," was the last pop 45, stopping at #68.

In 1982 Gill left the band. "My wife was pregnant, and I did want to pursue a solo career," he said. The parting was amicable, as he had told the band at his initial audition that he did not want to be part of it forever. Apparently, the rest of the group felt the same way, as the band broke up shortly thereafter.

Gill's first solo country entry was 1984's "Victim of Life's Circumstances" at #40. By the 1990s, he had grown more popular, with #1 country hits like "I Still Believe in You" and "The Heart Won't Lie." Gill occasionally sang "Let Me Love You Tonight" in concert, but he said that many fans were confused when he did it, having no idea that he "had a life" before 1990.

388 Magic

OLIVIA NEWTON-JOHN

MCA 41247

July 19, 1980 (5 weeks)

Writer: John Farrar

Producer: John Farrar

When Olivia Newton-John agreed to star in the movie *Xanadu*, her producer and writer John Farrar found he had to do much more for the film than he did with her previous motion picture *Grease* (he wrote and produced "You're the One That I Want" for the film but let others handle other songs and productions for it as well). When it came to scoring the film and doing the musical numbers, Farrar said, "I had to write the script pretty much."

The eerie "Magic" played in the movie during a sequence where Newton-John's character, a muse (another character looked up the word's definition in a dictionary—it was that kind of a movie), had a roller skating fantasy. "She was trying to encourage this guy to do this dream," Farrar recalled. Like the rest of the film, which also included Gene Kelly dancing with Newton-John, the scene was hard to swallow, but the music stood in its own.

Farrar said "Magic," with its extensive sound effects, took a bit of time to get into final shape. "We worked hard on that one," he said. "Quite a while to record, and about three days mixing it." But the results paid off handsomely as "Magic" went to #1 both AC and pop, staying at the top pop spot for four weeks starting August 2, 1980. "I thought it was a good song, but I didn't know it would be a single," admitted Farrar.

"Magic" was not the first single released from *Xanadu*. That distinction went to "I'm Alive" by the Electric Light Orchestra, who got to #48 AC and #16 pop. After "Magic" reached its AC peak, the title song sung by Newton-John with the Electric Light Orchestra came out and made #2 AC for two weeks plus #8 pop. Simultaneously, the Electric Light Orchestra charted with another film tune, "All Over the World," at #46 AC and #13 pop. Then came "Suddenly," a duet with Cliff Newton that Farrar thought would do better than "Magic." It ended up going to #4 AC and #20 pop. On the *Xanadu* soundtrack, Newton-John's songs were on the first side and the Electric Light Orchestra's took up the second side.

After *Xanadu* made a profit despite critical brickbats, Newton-John made one more film in the 1980s, *Two of a Kind* in 1983. She did not return to the screen again until she did a small role in the 1996 drama *It's My Party*. That film's director was Randall Keiser, who had directed Newton-John in *Grease*. With the successful 20th-anniversary rerelease of that film in 1998 there was talk that Newton-John would start acting again, but so far she has not.

389 Why Not Me

FRED KNOBLOCK

Scotti Brothers 518

August 23, 1980 (2 weeks)

Writers: J. Fred Knobloch, Carson Whitsett

Producers: James Stroud, D. Barrett

J. Fred Knobloch, born in Jackson, Mississippi on April 28, 1953, was playing professionally by age 13. By the time he was 20 he was performing solo at clubs and working as a session guitarist at Malaco Studios in Jackson. It was while backing such soul greats as Eddie Floyd and Dorothy Moore that he became friends with drummer James Stroud and pianist Carson Whitsett.

Knobloch remembered the night when the words to "Why Not Me" hit him. "It was rainy like hell, and I wrote the lyrics down," he said. He went over to Whitsett's house, and the latter played the piano to come up with the music. "It didn't take very long to do, probably a couple of hours," Knobloch said. "He came up with what I thought was beautiful music."

Knobloch mulled over what to do with the song. Finally, encouraged by Whitsett, Knobloch went to Los Angeles in the summer of 1979 to cut the tune with Stroud as his producer. Nigel Olsson, formerly a drummer for Elton John from 1971–76, played on the session.

Roughly six months later, Knobloch got an agreement with the Scotti Brothers label to distribute "Why Not Me." "I guess they thought I was good looking and talented enough to sign me," joked Knobloch. "Why Not Me" went to #1 AC, #18 pop, and #30 country in the summer of 1980. The company listed his last name as "Knoblock" on the record. "I guess they thought it'd be easier to spell," he said.

The follow-up to "Why Not Me," "Let Me Love You," went only to #53 country and was lost quickly as Scotti Brothers promoted the next single, "Killin' Time," a duet with actress Susan Anton which made #5 AC, #28 pop, and #10 country. The idea was that Knobloch would help Anton break through on radio and she would help him get into television, but neither really happened. Still, Knobloch enjoyed recording and touring with Anton. "She's a sweetheart, great working with her," he said.

Knobloch did not enjoy having record executives make more decisions for his career. In 1981 his last AC entry was "Memphis," which went to #28 AC, #10 country, and #102 bubbling under. "That was when the suits started to take over and control compositions," said Knobloch. He left Los Angeles for Nashville in January 1983, and concentrated on writing and producing songs rather than recording for a few years.

In 1986 he returned as an artist on the country chart as part of Schuyler, Knobloch and Overstreet, also known as S-K-O (Thom Schuyler and Paul Overstreet were the S and the O). They hit #1 country in 1987 with "Baby's Got a New Baby." Later that year Craig Bickhardt replaced Overstreet, making it S-K-B, but in 1989 they made a mutual decision to disband.

In the 1990s Knobloch concentrated on writing and producing songs, once again in Nashville. Performing-wise, "I play the odd gig," as he put it. He is married with two children and said in 1998 that he was quite content with his life.

Don't Ask Me Why

BILLY JOEL

Columbia 11331

September 9, 1980 (2 weeks)

Writer: Billy Joel

Producer: Phil Ramone

Billy Joel created his first homage to the early 1960s school of rock music with his perky, Phil Spector–like ditty "Don't Ask Me Why," his first #1 AC hit since "Just the Way You Are" in 1978. It made #19 pop as well as #1 AC.

"Don't Ask Me Why" was Joel's third single off his LP *Glass Houses*, which had hit #1 on the album chart for six weeks starting June 14, 1980 and got a Grammy nomination as Album of the Year, with Joel winning the Best Male Rock Vocal Performance for his work on the LP. The 45s from that album preceding "Don't Ask Me Why" on the charts were "You May Be Right" (#48 AC, #7 pop) and "It's Still Rock and Roll to Me" (#45 AC, #1 pop for two weeks) in 1980. Later, another 45 from the album, "Sometimes a Fantasy," made the Hot 100, but only at #36.

Joel had not been absent from the AC or pop charts between "Just the Way You Are" and *Glass Houses*, however—far from it, in fact—although some of his singles missed the AC chart because they were too, shall we say,

"untamed." In chronological order, his 45s in 1978 and 1979 were "Movin' Out (Anthony's Song)" (#40 AC, #17 pop), "Only the Good Die Young" (#24 pop), "She's Always a Woman" (#2 AC for two weeks, #17 pop), and "My Life" (#2 for five weeks, #3 pop) in 1978, and "Big Shot" (#14 pop) and "Honesty" (#9 AC, #24 pop) in 1979.

In 1981 two songs which Joel had cut earlier in his career became hits. "Say Goodbye to Hollywood," which he wrote in 1976, made #35 AC and #17 pop, while "She's Got a Way" went to #4 AC and #23 pop. Then in 1982 he released his *The Nylon Curtain* album, with songs dealing with social issues and concerns rather than romantic themes. His singles charting from that LP were "Pressure" (#20 pop), "Allentown" (#19 AC, #17 pop), and "Goodnight Saigon" (#56 pop).

Touring and promotion for the album were held up to a degree when Joel was injured in a motorcycle accident on Long Island, New York in 1982, and for a time it was feared that he would not be able to play the piano again. To the contrary, he created a batch of optimistic yet nostalgic songs which would give him his greatest success on the Hot 100. For more details, see 444—"Tell Her About It."

No Night So Long
DIONNE WARWICK

Arista 0527

September 20, 1980 (3 weeks)

Writers: Will Jennings (words), Richard Kerr (music)

Producer: Steve Buckingham

Dionne Warwick took nearly 10 years to score her first two #1 AC hits, but then needed only eight months between her second and third one. "No Night So Long," which followed "Deja Vu" [see 377], made Warwick the first artist to score two #1 AC entries in the 1980s. She would do well the rest of the decade, garnering three other #1 AC records.

Warwick described the composers of "No Night So Long," Will Jennings and Richard Kerr, as "Brilliant songwriters and very sensitive persons who I've grown to admire as people." They also wrote Barry Manilow's hit "Looks Like We Made It" [see 332].

To produce the tune, Warwick did not use Barry Manilow, who produced her comeback hits a few months earlier, but enlisted Steve Buckingham instead. "I'd met him in Nashville, and he, like Barry, had a desire to work with me," she said. Buckingham also produced her 1981 LP *Hot! Live and Otherwise.*

"No Night So Long" did not do quite as well on the pop and R&B chart as it did on the AC listings. It peaked at #23 pop and #19 R&B. After four follow-ups on the AC chart—"Easy Love" in 1980 (#12), "Some Changes Are for Good" in 1981 (#23), and "Friends in Love" with Johnny Mathis (#5) and "For You" (#14) in 1982—Warwick hit #1 AC again with "Heartbreaker" [see 431].

While doing these songs, Warwick increased her work schedule by hosting *Solid Gold*, a weekly musical variety series sold to local TV stations. She served as hostess from 1980–81 and again from 1985–86. Though it would seem to be an ideal venue for her to perform her own material, Warwick said that was not the case. "It didn't feature my songs primarily," she said. "When I was on the charts, then I sang my song." Other times, she typically sang other artists' hits or did duets with the artist on his or her hit. She also remembered that, surprisingly, doing the show on top of her recording and concert work "really wasn't difficult. . . .On *Solid Gold*, we taped two shows a day."

Warwick had been used to working since she started singing in her church choir at the age of six. Born Marie Dionne Warwick in East Orange, New Jersey, on December 12, 1940, she worked primarily in the gospel field, including singing with her sister Dee Dee Warwick, who had a minor solo career, and her aunt Cissy Houston, who later gave birth to Whitney Houston.

By the late 1950s, she had become a prominent backup vocalist in studio sessions. But it was not until 1962—when she met Burt Bacharach and Hal David and made a name for herself as a solo singer with "Don't Make Me Over"—that Warwick's substantial singing career really took off.

392 Woman in Love

BARBRA STREISAND

Columbia 11364

October 11, 1980 (5 weeks)

Writers: Barry Gibb, Robin Gibb

Producers: Barry Gibb, Karl Richardson, Albhy Galuten

Maurice Gibb said in the 1997 videotape *Keppel Road: The Life and Times of the Bee Gees* that his brothers got involved in writing and producing the *Guilty* album for Barbra Streisand as the result of a question from reporters. "They asked us, 'Who would you love to produce?' We said, 'Barbra Streisand.' Then a week later Charles Koppelman [who would become executive producer of *Guilty*] called us. 'I read in the paper you'd love to do Barbra.'" Streisand was interested in the Bee Gees too, so Koppelman put her together with them.

It was primarily Barry Gibb, the oldest Gibb, who wrote and produced the bulk of *Guilty*, according to co-producer Karl Richardson. And despite what some of the current publicity said, Richardson insisted that Maurice and Robin *did not* sing on the album. "Barry did all the backgrounds," he said. "They may say Bee Gees, but it was just him for male vocals." A few female session singers in Los Angeles also provided backup, he said.

Richardson said the Bee Gees were so hot at the time thanks to *Saturday Night Fever* [see 341—"How Deep Is Your Love"] that they had to turn down many artists who wanted them as producers. "I think Barry loved Barbra's voice," he said of the client they decided to accept. It didn't take the eldest Gibb long to compose tunes for her, and Richardson remembered that it was only a couple of months before they were in the studio cutting them.

One of those tunes, and the first to be released as a single, was "Woman in Love." Richardson said Streisand liked the liberationist slant of the lyrics. "She thought it was cool that she was singing some of these things," he said. So did her fans, who took the song to #1 AC and pop, riding atop the latter for three weeks starting October 25, 1980. It earned Grammy nominations for Record of the Year, Song of the Year, and Best Female Pop Vocal Performance. The LP on which it appeared, *Guilty*, also got a Grammy nod for Album of the Year and was #1 on the LP chart for three weeks starting October 25, 1980.

Regarding working with Streisand, Richardson said, "She was gorgeous. I think what happened is we were working with her when she was trying to put together the movie *Yentl*, so she relied on us to make a lot of the decisions. . . .I think she respected the decisions we all were making." Barry sent mixes of each day's work on songs to Streisand's house for input during part of the recording, Richardson noted, and this allowed her to critique at home.

Richardson found Streisand to be on time and ready to work at every session and not at all as demanding as her reputation suggested. "She was a dreamboat. I never had a problem with her," he concluded.

Another tune from *Guilty* later made #1 AC; see 400—"What Kind of Fool."

393 Lady

KENNY ROGERS

Liberty 1380

November 15, 1980 (4 weeks)

Writer: Lionel Richie

Producer: Lionel Richie

Though Kenny Rogers and Larry Butler had created such hits together as "She Believes in Me" [see 366], at the start of the 1980s Rogers decided it was time to end their working relationship. Rogers feared the duo could be getting stale, and he was also intrigued by the possibility of exploring a new avenue, thinking perhaps he could use Lionel Richie, the Commodores' lead singer, who had helped produce the group's hits.

"I had heard 'Three Times a Lady' [see 354] and 'Still,' and I always thought they were country songs with an R&B track," Rogers said, referring to previous Commodores records. Citing Ray Charles as another example of what he meant, Rogers said he wanted to do R&B songs with a country vocal bent. "It's the simplicity of [R&B] that gives it its international appeal," he said of the genre.

After putting some feelers out to Richie's colleagues, the singer agreed to see Rogers. At their first meeting, in Las Vegas, after they talked about working together and what each wanted, Richie presented him with a song. Said Rogers, "He only had 'Lady' with the one word and the melody." But though Rogers usually wanted to hear lyrics first, the melody and Richie's humming the rest of the tune won him over. "Lady" became a single and a track on Rogers' *Greatest Hits* LP, and the results were astounding.

"Lady" became one of the rare singles to make the AC, pop, country, and R&B charts. It hit the top of the first three (it was Rogers' first #1 pop hit and his R&B debut), and stayed atop the Hot 100 for six weeks starting November 15, 1980. "Lady" helmed the country list the week of November 22, 1980 and got to #42 R&B.

Furthermore, with the success of "Lady," Rogers' *Greatest Hits* album hit #1 for two weeks starting December 13, 1980. And at the Grammys, "Lady" merited nominations for Record of the Year, Song of the Year, and Best Male Pop Vocal Performance. All the acclaim from so many different sources pleased Rogers. "That was validation for the concept, I thought," he said. "That song, it's just a universal song of love and commitment."

Rogers worked with Richie for his next album, which included several #1 AC hits starting with "I Don't Need You" [see 407]. And Richie, whose stature within the industry grew as a result of their joint successes, eventually left the Commodores to launch a successful solo career [see 430—"Truly"]. "Lady" certainly was no tramp for either of them.

394 Never Be the Same
CHRISTOPHER CROSS

Warner 49580

December 13, 1980 (2 weeks)

Writer: Christopher Cross

Producer: Michael Omartian

"Never Be the Same" was the third single off Christopher Cross's huge self-titled debut album. It spun off three other 45s—"Ride Like the Wind" (#24 AC, #2 pop) and "Sailing" (#10 AC, #1 pop) in 1980 and "Say You'll Be Mine" (#15 AC, #20 pop) in 1981—and earned him four Grammys, for Best New Artist and Album, and for Record and Song of the Year (the latter two for "Sailing"). It was an impressive beginning.

Christopher Geppert, born in San Antonio, Texas, on May 3, 1951, began playing drums in a band called the Psychos in seventh grade. "We played church socials and junior high makeout parties," Cross told Lynn Van Matre of *The Chicago Tribune*. "Nobody else wanted to sing, so I did." He switched to guitar in high school, finding it easier to write songs that way. In 1970 he cut a privately pressed regional single using the surname "Cross" for the first time.

Cross and his band spent much of the 1970s playing covers of other groups' tunes at clubs. "Then we'd use that money to rent studio time to make demo tapes of our own material to send to Warner Brothers," he told Van Matre. "They were the only record company we were really interested in." In 1978, a Warner representative who saw their show Halloween night in Austin, Texas, gave them the go-ahead to work out a recording agreement with the company for an album to be produced in 1979.

When his LP came out in 1980 he opened for Fleetwood Mac and also the Eagles. Don Henley of the latter group sang on the Cross album, as did Michael McDonald of the Doobie Brothers, J. D. Souther, and Nicolette Larsen. Cross told Richard Harrington of *The Washington Post* that McDonald was the first to come into the studio after his friend, producer Michael Omartian, played him what Cross had done. "That started the ball rolling. . . .But they wouldn't have sung for a new artist if they didn't like it. You couldn't pay them, they're already rich," he said.

Cross told Paul Grein in *The Los Angeles Times* he thought the success of his album due to the appeal to women. "Take 'Never Be the Same': That's a very structured little package of music: It doesn't take many listens to get all the pieces right—it's A, B, C," Cross said. "And there are no hidden meanings in the lyric: It's about a broken heart, and that housewife has had her heart broken quite a few times, just like I have. My audience seems to be 70 percent women, and they're all crying and thinking about their sophomore boyfriends who kissed them off."

Despite that somewhat condescending characterization of his audience, Cross did get plenty of men and women to listen to his next #1 AC hit [see 410—"Arthur's Theme (Best That You Can Do)"].

395 More Than I Can Say
LEO SAYER

Warner 49565

December 27, 1980 (3 weeks)

Writers: Sonny Curtis, Jerry Allison

Producer: Alan Tarney

Bobby Vee came to prominence after he replaced Buddy Holly on a bill in Fargo, North Dakota, following the plane crash of February 3, 1959, that killed Holly, Ritchie Valens, and the Big Bopper. Two years later he took "More Than I Can Say," a song written by two members of Holly's backup band the Crickets, Sonny Curtis and Jerry Allison, to #61 pop. But fate had bigger plans in store for the tune, as it was revived nearly two decades later as a hit when Leo Sayer attempted to complete his album *Living in a Fantasy*.

"It was just a throwaway attempt at an oldie," Leo Sayer told Steve Pond in *Rolling Stone*. "We had the album almost finished, but we needed one more tune because I hadn't written enough songs. Alan [Tarney, his producer] and I were watching television in the studio one morning when we saw a commercial for Bobby Vee's greatest hits. 'More Than I Can Say' was one of those. Alan looked at me and said, 'You'd be great singing that!' We went into a record store that afternoon, bought the record and had the song recorded that night. Now it's my fastest hit ever."

Sayer's version of "More Than I Can Say" peaked at #2 on the Hot 100 for five weeks beginning December 6, 1980 in addition to topping the AC chart. Keeping it from #1 pop were "Lady" by Kenny Rogers [see 393] for the first three weeks and then the late John Lennon's "(Just Like) Starting Over" for the last two.

The song marked Sayer's first pop top 10 entry after "Long Tall Dances (I Can Dance)" in 1975 and "You Make Me Feel Like Dancing" (his AC debut at #19) and "When I Need You" [see 329] in 1977. On the AC chart, the artist, born Gerard Hugh Sayer in Shoreham-by-the-Sea, Sussex, England, on May 21, 1948, also scored with "How Much Love" in 1977 (#27 AC, #17 pop) and "Raining in My Heart" in 1978 (#9 AC, #47 pop).

The latter single came from Sayer's self-titled 1978 LP, the last album he did with producer Richard Perry. A 1979 album with his original songwriting partner David Courtney called *Here* failed to chart, so he hooked up with Tarney for *Living in a Fantasy* and told Pond it was a refreshing experience. "Alan had a new approach that felt really good," he said. "It was the simplest album I've ever recorded—no traumas, no troubles with musicians. Alan played everything but the drums, he was an ideal band all in one guy."

But Alan was not an ideal hitmaker for Sayer. After "Living in a Fantasy," the follow-up to "More Than I Can Say," hit #12 AC and #23 pop in early 1981, Sayer was unable to return to either chart. His label, Warner, dropped him in America, and for most of the 1980s and 1990s Sayer found no others willing to sign him stateside. However, he did continue to perform and record in Europe.

396 I Love a Rainy Night

EDDIE RABBITT

Elektra 47066

January 17, 1981 (3 weeks)

Writers: Eddie Rabbitt, Even Stevens, David Malloy

Producer: David Malloy

His first record came out in 1964, but Edward Thomas Rabbitt was nothing more than a struggling songwriter in Nashville for the rest of the 1960s. His first taste of fame came after he wrote "Kentucky Rain," which became a #3 AC and #16 pop hit for Elvis Presley in 1970. The royalties from that hit kept him going financially until he finally got another solo recording contract in 1974 with Elektra. That same year he had his first of many country chart entries with "You Get to Me," which went to #34.

The bearded Rabbitt, born in Brooklyn, New York, on November 27, 1944, debuted on the AC chart in 1976 with "Rocky Mountain Music" at #48. It was a #1 hit on the country chart, as were the next six singles to cross over to the AC chart before Rabbitt had his biggest hit, "I Love a Rainy Night."

"I Love a Rainy Night" came to light after producer David Malloy told Even Stevens and Eddie Rabbitt about the growing fascination in the United Kingdom for rockabilly, a hybrid of country and rock that had all but disappeared by the late 1950s. Something about the description prompted Rabbitt to seek out a melody using the phrase "I Love a Rainy Night" which he had stored in an old Army foot locker.

The writers combined the melody and words with a rhythmic pattern Malloy had going from snapping fingers to clapping hands, but it wasn't until percussionist Farrell Morris stepped in that they got what they wanted. "In about three hours' time he laid down two tracks of snaps and two tracks of claps and that was it," Malloy told Tom Roland in *The Billboard Book of Number One Country Hits.*

With its catchy beat in place, "I Love a Rainy Night" became a #1 hit on the AC, pop, and country charts. It was atop the country chart the week of January 17, 1981, then went to #1 pop for two weeks starting February 28, 1981, after a three-week AC run. Rabbitt nearly returned to the AC top again with two singles that hit #2 on the chart, "You and I," a duet with Crystal Gayle in 1982, and "You Can't Run From Love" in 1983.

The AC appeal of Rabbitt soon faded after the latter hit, and he last made the chart in 1985 with "A World Without Love" at #35, his 17th AC entry. He continued to have considerable popularity on the country chart through 1990, when he had his last #1 country hit with "On Second Thought." In all, he had 17 #1 country hits. Rabbitt died on May 7, 1998 after fighting lung cancer for a year.

1981

The Winner Takes It All

ABBA

Atlantic 3776

February 7, 1981 (2 weeks)

Writers: Benny Andersson, Bjorn Ulvaeus

Producers: Benny Andersson, Bjorn Ulvaeus

"I think that the simplest and [yet] still sophisticated song is 'The Winner Takes It All,'" Benny Andersson told Fred Bronson in the liner notes to the 1994 anthology *ABBA: Thank You for the Music*. "It's two short themes, not a verse and a chorus. It's just a tune and a little bridge. It goes around and around and still it's not boring. A good performance by Agnetha as well." Benny and Agnetha Faltskog, who sang lead, thought it was the best song ABBA ever did.

Originally titled "The Story of My Life," "The Winner Takes It All" was recorded on June 6, 1980 after an earlier effort failed. Bjorn Ulvaeus is quoted in *ABBAmania Volume 1: The Singles* by Pete Bingham, Bernadette Dolan, and Michael Clough as saying "I have never written any lyrics as quickly as I did for this track. I don't think it took me longer than an hour, it sounded just right."

"The Winner Takes It All" was the last American top 10 pop hit for ABBA when it peaked at #8 in 1981. It was their second #1 AC hit after "Fernando" [see 317]. By the time it peaked in America Benny and Frida Lyngstad had announced their divorce. (They had been living together for eleven years, but for only two of those years were they married.) Since Benny and Frida's breakup came hard on the heels of Bjorn and Agnetha's divorce (in 1979, after eight years of marriage), it didn't surprise anyone when ABBA split up in 1982.

For whatever reason—perhaps listeners sensed the inevitable—ABBA releases after "The Winner Takes It All" did poorly in the United States. Charting in 1981 were "Super Trooper" (#14 AC, #45 pop), "On and On and On" (#90 pop), and "When All Is Said and Done" (#10 AC, #27 pop). "The Visitors" in 1982 was their last Hot 100 entry, peaking at #63. The final AC chart single, "One of Us," climbed to #33 in 1983, two years after it had been recorded and a year after the group dissolved.

Frida and Agnetha then released solo LPs until the end of the 1980s, when they both retired. In America Frida hit #13 pop in 1983 with "I Know There's Something Going On," while Agnetha also charted pop that same year with "Can't Shake Loose" at #29 and in 1988 with "I Wasn't the One (Who Said Goodbye)," a duet with Peter Cetera which made #93. Benny and Bjorn did songwriting only, scoring with "One Night in Bangkok," a #3 pop hit for Murray Head in 1985.

In the 1990s, with ABBA personnel concentrating their activities in Sweden, groups like Bjorn Again, Voulez Vous, and ABBAcadabra, which specialized in remakes of ABBA's songs, flourished in Europe (less so in America), as did re-releases of their music everywhere. Despite the renewed visibility of the quartet's music, there has been no announcement of a future reunion.

398 Smoky Mountain Rain

RONNIE MILSAP

RCA 12084

February 21, 1981 (1 week)

Writers: Kye Fleming, Dennis Morgan

Producers: Ronnie Milsap, Tom Collins

Ronnie Milsap has had enormous success in his 25 years as a country artist, with 35 #1 songs on that chart; it may surprise some to learn that music was not his first career choice. Milsap, who was born in Robbinsville, North Carolina, on January 16, 1946, has been blind since birth and attended the North Carolina's State School for the Blind in Raleigh during his childhood. Though Milsap's musical talents were evident from an early age—he could play classical piano and guitar before he was 13—he planned to be a lawyer.

In 1965, however, Scepter Records signed Milsap as a musician for pop and R&B sessions at the label's New York City offices and his legal aspirations were forgotten. He moved to Memphis in 1968, where he played in numerous sessions and concerts, but left in 1972 after Charlie Pride and Conway Twitty convinced him he could be a country artist in Nashville. RCA Records agreed and signed Milsap in April 1973.

Milsap's country chart debut, "I Hate You" backed with "(All Together Now) Let's Fall Apart," reached #10 in June 1973. A year later "Pure Love" was his first #1 country hit. But Milsap retained a fondness for pop and R&B music, and after four years, he began doing material that would let him cross over to other charts. His first crossover success was 1977's "It Was Almost Like a Song," another #1 country hit which went to #7 AC and #16 pop. Over the next few years he had a few other crossovers while still hitting #1 country, and such was the case with "Smoky Mountain Rain."

"Smoky Mountain Rain" came from songwriters Kye Fleming and Dennis Morgan. "They worked for a publishing company that is run by a good friend of mine named Tom Collins," Milsap said. Collins, Milsap's co-producer, thought two of Fleming and Morgan's songs could be combined into one composition for Milsap. The title came from Milsap himself.

"We were sitting around the office and I made the comment, 'Even though I went to school in Raleigh, I grew up in the Smoky Mountains. I wish I had a song about it.' Then Dennis said, 'Let's work on it,'" Milsap recalled.

Milsap played piano for the track under Collins' guidance. "He reminded me I played on 'Kentucky Rain' with Elvis, and Elvis wanted 'piano thunder.' Tom said, 'You ought to do the same,'" Milsap said. He also played the introduction on his piano, which "has kind of a signature lick on the front of the song."

Included as the only new song on his greatest hits LP, "Smoky Mountain Rain" went to #24 pop while topping the AC and country charts. The song became part of Milsap's standard repertoire in concert as well. "It's popular everywhere we go," he said. "It's especially popular in the Smokies, of course." He returned to #1 AC two years later with "Any Day Now" [see 423].

399 9 to 5

DOLLY PARTON

RCA 12133

February 28, 1981 (2 weeks)

Writer: Dolly Parton

Producer: Gregg Perry

Dolly Parton, born in Sevier County, Tennessee, on January 19, 1946, is one of the queens of country music, yet her recording career choices invariably have raised a few eyebrows in that conservative field. Some were stunned when she split from Porter Wagoner in 1974 after seven years of doing duets with him while keeping a successful solo act. On the heels of that decision, she cracked the AC and pop charts for the first time in 1974 with "Jolene," her second of 24 #1 hits on the country chart. "Jolene" went to #44 AC and #60 pop.

There were a few more crossover hits following "Jolene," but then Parton went after the pop market in earnest, and in 1977 "Here You Come Again" hit #1 country as well as #2 AC and #3 pop. But Parton had some other surprises in store for her fans. Her comic performance in the 1980 film *9 to 5* impressed critics and the general public so much that the theme song, which she had written on the set, was nearly overlooked.

"I remember writing the song on the back of my script and using my fingernails to create a rhythm as I sang it," Parton wrote in her autobiography *Dolly: My Life and Other Unfinished Business*. "I would get inspirations for different parts of the song at different times. Any time I started working on it, the women on the set would just naturally gather around to listen. My hairdresser would start clacking her brushes together in time to the rhythm I had set up. The script supervisor would chime in, slapping her clapboard in time.

"Before long, I had created a whole section of backup singers made up of all the working women around me. Because of what the song had to say, I thought that was especially appropriate. It was also a heap of fun. That helped inspire me in writing the lyrics and made the song as special as it is."

"9 to 5" landed at #1 on the country chart first, the week of January 24, 1981, then made #1 pop for two weeks starting January 21, 1981, before doing the same on the AC chart. The tune won an Oscar nomination for Best Song and a Grammy for Best Country and Western Song. The only glitch was a plagiarism suit filed against Parton by a couple who said they had written some of the words, but the courts didn't agree and Parton eventually won.

When *9 to 5* became a TV series in 1982, Parton's sister Rachel Dennison assumed the Parton role. Phoebe Snow initially sang the theme song, but by the time the sitcom finished its run on ABC in 1983, Parton's version of "9 to 5" was the theme, as it was on the revival in syndication from 1986–88. Parton herself went on to score another #1 AC, pop, and country hit in 1982 [see "Islands in the Stream" at 446].

400 What Kind of Fool

BARBRA STREISAND AND BARRY GIBB

Columbia 11430

March 14, 1981 (4 weeks)

Writers: Barry Gibb, Albhy Galuten

Producers: Barry Gibb, Albhy Galuten, Karl Richardson

After the triumph of "Woman in Love" [see 392], the second single off Barbra Streisand's *Guilty* album was the title tune, a duet with co-producer Barry Gibb which had been intended only to be a solo recording for her. "Charles Koppelman [executive producer of *Guilty*] always heard it as a duet," explained co-producer Karl Richardson. To help Gibb in singing, the producers had to change the key for him and add a few musicians. "Guilty" went to #5 AC and #3 pop in late 1980.

Another duet followed as a single, although this one, "What Kind of Fool," had always been intended as a Gibb–Streisand number. Regarding Barry's vocal contribution, Richardson said, "He did the demo first. Barbra sang to the demo, then he came back and replaced a couple of things after he had heard what she was doing."

"What Kind of Fool" went to #1 AC while becoming the third consecutive top 10 pop hit for Streisand, peaking at #10 there for three weeks starting March 21, 1981. One more single from *Guilty* followed, but "Promises," a solo Streisand effort, was a relative disappointment, getting only to #8 AC and #48 pop.

By this time Gibb, Richardson, and Galuten had worked together as co-producers for five years, and Richardson said the trio functioned fine together because they each had a unique perspective to contribute. "Barry's the creative force," he said. "Albhy was the musical guru. . .more of an arranger/producer. My forte has always been as an arranger."

Streisand and the Bee Gees' coalition went their separate paths after *Guilty*, with the Bee Gees' crew producing Dionne Warwick [see 431—"Heartbreaker"] and Kenny Rogers [see 446—"Islands in the Stream"]. "At that point, we parted ways," noted Richardson, as Albhy Galuten moved to Los Angeles while he and the Bee Gees stayed in Miami. The brothers Gibb would have a #1 AC hit in 1989 [see 569—"One"]. Richardson did musical production work while based in Miami. "I still see Barry every six months or so. We trade Christmas cards," said Richardson.

As for Streisand, she continued to be one of the most-played artists on AC stations throughout the 1980s, with most of her single releases making the top 10 on the chart, although she had only one more #1 AC hit in that decade [see 448—"The Way He Makes Me Feel"]. She had less success in the 1990s as her releases became more infrequent. In the late 1990s a duet she did with Celine Dion, "Tell Him," stalled at #5 AC for three weeks starting November 8, 1997. Nonetheless, in late 1998 she could still, on the basis of her overall chart performance since the 1960s, be labeled the most successful female ever on the AC listings.

401 Angel of the Morning

JUICE NEWTON

Capitol 4976

April 11, 1981 (3 weeks)

Writer: Chip Taylor

Producer: Richard Landis

There were seven singles on the country chart by Juice Newton before she had what her bandleader and road manager Otha Young called her "breakthrough record," namely "Angel of the Morning." The vocalist, born Judy Kay Newton in New Jersey on February 18, 1952, and raised in Virginia Beach, Virginia, had her first entry in 1976 as lead singer of the trio Silver Spur with "Love Is a Word."

But Silver Spur, which formed in 1974 in Los Angeles, failed to get any other country entries thereafter and broke up in 1978. Young had been a member of the group but did not want to pursue a solo career in front of the microphones and decided to work for Newton instead. "It crossed my mind occasionally, but I never considered myself a lead singer," he said. As for the group's other member, Young said, "Tom Keely felt he needed to move on. He felt his roots were back in the [San Francisco] Bay area."

Newton then entered the country chart as a solo act several times in 1979 and 1980, but no 45s did exceptionally well. The highest-charting one was 1979's "Let's Keep It That Way," which held at #37. That situation changed when a remake of a song previously a hit 13 years earlier established Young as a top artist in the early 1980s.

"Angel of the Morning" went to #7 pop and #37 AC in 1968 when sung by Merrilee Rush. The next year a rendition by Bettye Swann bubbled under to #109, followed in 1970 by a version from Connie Eaton which went to #34 country. Eight years later another cover by Melba Montgomery went to #22 country.

Young said it was neither his nor Newton's idea to redo the tune, but that it had come from Richard Landis, who had gotten it from Steve Myers in the promotions department at Capitol. Myers felt the song could be a hit again for Newton, and she and Landis agreed. So did Young, who said that "Juice has always and still excels at doing old standards."

Beside hitting #1 AC, "Angel of the Morning" went to #4 pop for four weeks beginning May 2, 1981. The record was Newton's debut on the AC chart, and also made #22 country. (She had been on the Hot 100 once before, at #86 in 1978 with "It's a Heartache.") Newton notched her first Grammy nomination for Best Female Pop Vocal Performance for her singing on the record.

Recalling the popularity of the record, Young said, "It was great. We actually were on the road on a broken-down motor home when we heard it was on the charts." But Young added it did not go to the heads of the artist and her entourage. "We didn't go out and start buying stuff, let's put it that way."

402 Morning Train (Nine to Five)
SHEENA EASTON

EMI-America 8071

May 2, 1981 (2 weeks)

Writer: Florrie Palmer

Producer: Christopher Neil

The 1980 British Broadcasting Corporation 1980 documentary "The Big Time" certainly lived up to its name in terms of starting unknown singer Sheena Easton on the road to eventual worldwide prominence. The special showed the struggling Easton going from $40-a-night gigs with a band called Something Else to a professional makeover and finally a deal with Deke Arlon as her manager. The only thing she did not have when the show aired was a hit.

But after "The Big Time" aired, Easton's second single, "Nine to Five," went to #3 on the United Kingdom chart, and her first, "Modern Girl," which initially made only #56 in early 1980, went to #6. These successes convinced EMI-America to try the singer in America. The first release was to be "Nine to Five," but since Dolly Parton already had a single out by that name [see 399], it was retitled "Morning Train (Nine to Five)." The record became a simultaneous #1 AC and pop hit the weeks of May 2 and 9, 1981.

"Morning Train (Nine to Five)" was the first of a plethora of AC and pop hits for Easton during the 1980s. Born Sheena Shirley Orr in Belshill, near Glasgow, Scotland, on April 27, 1959, she became Sheena Easton due to an eight-month marriage to actor/singer Sandi Easton from whom she separated in 1979 and was divorced in 1981.

She had better luck on the music charts, getting four top 10 AC entries and six top 10 pop hits during the 1980s alone. Her biggest AC single after "Morning Train" was "We've Got Tonight," a duet with Kenny Rogers which held at #2 for five weeks in 1983. Her other top 10 AC hits were "For Your Eyes Only," the theme song of the James Bond film of the same name, at #6 in 1981; "You Could Have Been With Me," at #6 in 1982; and "Almost Over You" at #4 in 1984.

But after 1989's "The Arms of Orion" with Prince went to #21 AC and #36 pop, Easton, now a citizen of the United States, couldn't get another hit. In 1996 MCA dropped her after her 10th studio album, *My Cherie*, failed to make the *Billboard* Top 200 LP chart. Later that year she played Rizzo in the Broadway revival of *Grease* for 10 weeks, but she still hoped that her future would include another recording contract.

"I'm totally admitting there's not a large market for my kind of pop music in the States," Easton told Chuck Taylor in *Billboard*. "When I turn on the radio, I realize the kind of songs I relate to aren't getting played a lot. I think there's a season, so to speak, and that it comes back around."

403 Sukiyaki
A TASTE OF HONEY

Capitol 4953

May 16, 1981 (2 weeks)

Writers: Rokusuke Ei, Hachidai Nakamura

Producer: George Duke

When A Taste of Honey won the Grammy for Best New Artist after the #1 pop and R&B hit "Boogie Oogie Oogie" in 1978, cynics began denouncing the award when the group was unable to score again the following years despite numerous efforts. In the midst of dealing with their detractors in 1980, the group went from a quartet to a duo of lead singers, a change that led to A Taste of Honey finally coming up with a second hit.

Formed in Los Angeles in 1972 and named after the Herb Alpert hit of the same name [see 62], A Taste of Honey went through some personnel changes before arriving at the lineup of vocalists Janice Marie Johnson and Hazel Payne, who also played guitar and bass respectively, plus drummer Donald Johnson and keyboardist Perry Kimble. "Boogie Oogie Oogie" was their first chart entry. On the heels of that hit, only one song hit both the pop and R&B charts—1979's "Do It Good," which hit #79 pop and #13 R&B. Feeling the need for change, A Taste of Honey dropped Johnson and Kimble before beginning work on their 1980 LP *Twice and Sweet*.

It was Janice Marie Johnson who thought about redoing "Sukiyaki" by Kyu Sakamoto [see 29]. She received permission to do an English translation of the tune, but interpreters found that it could come out three different ways— as a man on his way to an execution, as a man trying to stay confident despite life's ups and downs, or as a love gone bad. "Me being the hopeless romantic I am, I decided to write about a love gone bad," she told Adam White and Fred Bronson in *The Billboard Book of #1 Rhythm and Blues Hits*. After working on the lyrics for two weeks, Johnson feared her song would be too simplistic, but her producer George Duke told her to go by her instinct, so she kept them.

"Sukiyaki" was the third single released from their LP after unimpressive response to "Rescue Me" (#16 R&B) and "I'm Talkin' 'Bout You" (#64 R&B) in 1980. Besides its AC triumph, where it became the group's first entry on that chart, "Sukiyaki" also went to #1 R&B the week of May 9, 1981, and to #3 pop for three weeks starting June 13, 1981, behind "Bette Davis Eyes" by Kim Carnes and "Stars on 45 Medley" by Stars on 45.

The popularity generated by "Sukiyaki" did not remain with A Taste of Honey long. "I'll Try Something New" in 1982 hit #9 R&B, #29 AC, and #41 pop but was the group's last AC and pop entry. One more single, "We've Got the Groove," made #75 R&B before Johnson and Payne parted ways, with Johnson charting only one single as a solo act, 1984's "Love Me Tonite" (#67 R&B). But before they broke up, the girls did have time to sing "Sukiyaki" on tour in Japan with Sakamoto prior to his death in 1985.

404 How 'Bout Us
CHAMPAIGN

Columbia 11433

May 30, 1981 (2 weeks)

Writer: Dana Walden

Producer: Leo Graham

Champaign took its name from the Illinois city which served as home base for the sextet. Its biggest hit, "How 'Bout Us," went to #12 pop and #4 R&B in addition to #1 AC.

Recalling the band's start, percussionist Rocky Maffit said, "Four of the original members of the band had a recording studio. They were recording demos for songs they had written." The four were keyboardist Michael Day, bassist Michael Reed, guitarist Leon Reeder, and keyboardist Dana Walden. Maffit was at the drama department at the University of Illinois when he met Day, who was producing a record for another person in the department, and Day convinced the others to let Maffit audition. Reed had left and singers Pauli Carman and Rena Jones had joined by the time Champaign began work on "How 'Bout Us" in 1980.

Walden wrote "How 'Bout Us" a few years earlier before letting the group try it, Maffit recalled. "It was a song done in a number of different styles. I think there was a country and western version." Finally, they came up with a demo which sounded very similar to the final record, with Carman, Jones, and Reeder singing harmony.

"We sent out tapes to all the major labels, and I think most of the labels that heard 'How 'Bout Us' wanted us," Maffit said. "I think a few wanted to buy the song outright, but Dana held out that they had to take us with it, which I thank him for doing." They signed with Infinity, but switched to Columbia when Infinity went bankrupt.

"How 'Bout Us" hit in America and most of Europe, so Champaign toured overseas. "Two days after I got married, my wife and I were flying to Amsterdam," Maffit said. But the group was not happy that Leo Graham, the producer assigned to them, picked the rest of the tunes on the first album. Apparently neither was the general public, for the follow-up 45, "Can You Find the Time," missed the charts in 1981. Two years later Champaign had another hit with the appropriately titled "Try Again," which made #6 AC, #23 pop, and #2 R&B, but no other successes followed, and by 1985 the band had broken up.

Rena Jones married Michael Day and the two became worldwide touring Christian musicians. Dana Walden went to California to write scores for movies and TV shows. Pauli Carman performed in Asia, while Leon Reeder worked with computers in Chicago. Maffit remained in Champaign (Illinois), but often lectured on percussion in cities around the world. He noted that the group seemed to be popular most everywhere but Champaign, and had never even been given a key to the city in appreciation for their hit records.

Grayson Hugh and Betty Wright's remake of "How 'Bout Us" went to #15 AC, #67 pop, and #30 R&B in 1990.

405 America
NEIL DIAMOND

Capitol 4994

June 13, 1981 (3 weeks)

Writer: Neil Diamond

Producer: Bob Gaudio

Neil Diamond's motion picture acting debut—and swan song—was a role in the 1980 remake of *The Jazz Singer*. Al Jolson starred as the cantor's son in the first version—also the first Hollywood "talkie," where spoken dialogue was part of the dramatic action—in 1927, and Danny Thomas played the lead in a second version, in 1953. Thirty years later Diamond played the lead in film version number three, and while the public and critics alike noted that his acting abilities onscreen left much to be desired, the music had more impact.

For *The Jazz Singer*, Diamond wrote and sang songs for the film as well as acted along with Sir Laurence Olivier, who played his father. His score included three songs which were also released as singles—"Love on the Rocks," "Hello Again," and "America."

"Love on the Rocks" came out first. Diamond's writing partner Gilbert Becaud loved scotch on the rocks, so that was the title used for the demo of the song until new lyrics transformed it into a serious ballad. It went to #3 AC and #2 pop for three weeks in early 1981. Then came "Hello Again," which went into the film after officials with Columbia Records picked "September Morn" to use as the title song for Diamond's LP on that label before *The Jazz Singer* soundtrack came out on Capitol. "Hello Again" went to #3 AC while arriving at #6 pop.

"America" was the final single released from the movie. Diamond wrote in the liner notes to his anthology *In My Lifetime* that "America" was "One from the heart for my grandparents who made the journey and passed on the folklore of it to their grandchildren. I am just passing it on to my kids and theirs." Beside its AC success, "America" made #8 pop for three consecutive weeks beginning the week of June 13, 1981.

While none of the individual tunes from *The Jazz Singer* won Oscar or Grammy nominations, Diamond did get a Grammy nomination for Best Album of Original Score Written for a Motion Picture or a Television Special. He lost to John Williams for the movie *Raiders of the Lost Ark*.

Given that and the picture's poor box office receipts, some might have viewed *The Jazz Singer* as something of a disaster, but Diamond had his own unique way of looking at it in terms of his career. "From 'Cherry Cherry' to 'The African Trilogy' to *Jonathan Livingston Seagull* to 'America,' I've had a very strange kind of weird path, but at least it's been my path," he told David Wild in *Rolling Stone* in 1988.

Ironically, Diamond had another single after "America" that was inspired by a movie. For more details, see 429—"Heartlight."

406 All Those Years Ago

GEORGE HARRISON

Dark Horse 49725

July 4, 1981 (1 week)

Writer: George Harrison

Producers: George Harrison, Ray Cooper

Beatles fans called him "the shy one" in the early years, but George Harrison had proved himself to be much more than that by the time the group dissolved in 1970. Overshadowed by the John Lennon–Paul McCartney writing machine, the guitarist nonetheless wrote some of the most beautiful compositions in the Beatles' output, among them "Something" and "Here Comes the Sun." He continued having success as a soloist in 1970s, though like all the ex-Beatles he found it a bit rockier to have hits outside of the band.

Harrison was born in Liverpool, England, on February 25, 1943. He became a member of the Quarrymen, the forerunner of what was to be the Beatles, in 1958 with his acoustic guitar rendition of the Bill Justis instrumental hit "Raunchy." In 1968 he became the first Beatle to do a complete album apart from the group, but *Wonderwall Music* spun off no singles. Instead, his first independent 45 was 1970's "My Sweet Lord," which gave him debuts on the pop and AC charts at #1 and #10 respectively.

During the 1970s five other singles of Harrison's made the AC chart: 1971's "What Is Life" (#31 AC, #10 pop), 1973's "Give Me Love (Give Me Peace on Earth)" (#4 AC, #1 pop), 1977's "Crackerbox Palace" (#20 AC, #19 pop), and 1979's "Blow Away" in 1979 (#2 AC for one week, #16 pop) and "Love Comes to Everyone" (#38 AC only). He finally reached the AC summit with a tribute to his slain musical comrade Lennon titled "All Those Years Ago."

"All Those Years Ago" was meant originally for fourth Beatle Ringo Starr to record on his 1981 LP *Stop and Smell the Roses*, on which Harrison and McCartney played. "I was writing that expressly for Ringo, but I never had words, and I never actually played it for him—although I got him to play on my final track," Harrison told Timothy White in *Goldmine* in 1992. "I don't remember exactly why he didn't record it himself. I think he'd done his *Roses* album by the time I'd finished writing it."

With Starr on drums and McCartney doing backup vocals, "All Those Years Ago" was the first single to use all the surviving Beatles after Lennon's death, and that, coupled with its touching lyrics about how Lennon was "the one who made it all clear," made it nearly unstoppable on the charts. It nearly reached #1 pop as well as AC, held out of the top of the Hot 100 for three weeks starting July 4, 1981, behind Kim Carnes' "Bette Davis Eyes."

Six years after "All Those Years Ago," Harrison did score a #1 hit on both the pop and AC charts. For more details, see 529—"Got My Mind Set On You."

407 I Don't Need You

KENNY ROGERS

Liberty 1415

July 11, 1981 (6 weeks)

Writer: Rick Christian

Producer: Lionel Richie

"Lady" [see 393] was supposed to be a one-song test of compatibility between Kenny Rogers and Lionel Richie. "I really just wanted him to write a song for me," Rogers said. Then Richie decided to produce "Lady" too, and the song seemed to take on as life of its own after that. In the wake of its huge success, and the fact that the two men hit it off so well, Rogers named Richie as the producer of his next LP *Share Your Love With Me*. "I just loved the way he thought," Rogers recalled of Richie. "He had the innate ability to say the simplest things and put them to beautiful music and everybody can relate to them."

However, it soon became apparent for both that Richie would not be able to write all the songs for the album, so he and Rogers agreed to accept a few outside tunes, but only ones on which they both agreed. "I Don't Need You" fell into that category.

"It's still to this day one of my favorite songs," Rogers said of "I Don't Need You." He loved its lyrics particularly. However, he noted, "I don't think I've ever met Rick Christian, the guy who wrote it."

"I Don't Need You" was the first single from *Share Your Love With Me*. Apart from being #1 AC, it also went to top the country chart and #3 pop on August 15 and 22, 1981. On the pop chart it stayed behind "Endless Love" at #1 [see 409; ironically, a song sung in part by Lionel Richie] and "Theme from 'Greatest American Hero' (Believe It or Not)" by Joey Scarbury at #2. "I Don't Need You" was not the only single with Rogers' voice to appear shortly after "Lady" was released. "What Are We Doin' in Love," a duet between Rogers and his frequent singing partner Dottie West, went to #1 country the week of June 13, 1981 as well as #7 AC and #14 pop.

By the time of "I Don't Need You," Rogers had become fairly entrenched on the AC, pop, and country charts. He was especially potent on the country ledger, scoring 17 consecutive top 10 entries from 1977's "Lucille," his first country #1, to "I Don't Need You." Of those 17, 12 went to #1. His AC streak had "I Don't Need You" as his eighth consecutive top 10 song there since "She Believes in Me" [see 366], with two singles nearly topping the chart in that time, 1979's "You Decorated My Life" (#2 for one week) and 1980's "Don't Fall in Love With a Dreamer" with Kim Carnes (#2 for four weeks).

On the pop chart, "I Don't Need You" was his ninth consecutive top 20 entry since 1979's "The Gambler" hit #16. He extended his records on all three charts with his next single, "Share Your Love With Me" [see 411].

408 Touch Me When We're Dancing

THE CARPENTERS

A&M 2344

August 22, 1981 (2 weeks)

Writers: Terry Skinner, J. L. Wallace, Ken Ball

Producer: Richard Carpenter

"Touch Me When We're Dancing" brought the Carpenters back to prominence after a lean period during the late 1970s. It was their first #1 AC hit since "I Need to Be in Love" [see 304] and first top 20 pop single (#16) since "There's a Kind of Hush (All Over the World)" [see 293]. Its mellow pace and sound made it sound like a natural creation for the Carpenters, although they were not the first to do the record.

The song's writers, Terry Skinner, J. L. Wallace, and Ken Ball, first cut the tune under the group name of Bama (they were session musicians in Muscle Shoals, Alabama) and it reached #42 AC and #86 pop in 1979 on the Free Flight label. Ironically, the country group Alabama covered the tune after the Carpenters, going to #1 country with it the week of November 29, 1986.

The Carpenters had three more singles make the AC and pop charts over the next year, "(Want You) Back in My Life Again" (#14 AC, #72 pop), "Those Good Old Dreams" (#21 AC, #63 pop), and "Beechwood 4-5789" (#16 AC, #74 pop). While the latter was on the charts, Karen Carpenter recorded her last vocals in April 1982.

On February 4, 1983, Karen died of cardiac arrest after collapsing in her parents' home in Downey, California. Some, including Richard, believed the strain on her heart came from more than seven years of fighting the eating disorder anorexia nervosa while trying to continue to record and tour. (At one point she weighed only 80 pounds.)

Richard found it difficult getting over his sister's death but managed to pull himself together and finish their album *Voices of the Heart* for release in the fall of 1983. Two singles from the LP made the AC chart, "Make Believe It's Your First Time" (#7) in 1983 and "Your Baby Doesn't Love You Anymore" (#12) in 1984. Richard spent the rest of the 1980s working mainly on several compilation albums of Carpenters material, plus his own solo LP titled *Time*. One single from it, "Something in Your Eyes," with Dusty Springfield, went to #12 AC in 1987.

On his own in the 1990s, Richard toured, did some shows, and remixed some old Carpenters tunes for various projects, including several documentaries about the group or his sister. It seems inevitable that Richard's career will always be linked with his sister's, but that is not necessarily a negative for him. The Carpenters' legacy going into the 21st century—15 #1 AC hits, more than any other duo or group, plus legions of devoted fans—would be hard for him or anyone else to match.

409 Endless Love

DIANA ROSS AND LIONEL RICHIE

Motown 1519

September 5, 1981 (3 weeks)

Writer: Lionel Richie

Producer: Lionel Richie

As 1981 dawned, Diana Ross had severed her 20-year tie with Motown and jumped to RCA, and Lionel Richie, lead singer for the label's top act, the Commodores, was coming into prominence with his solo work as a writer. Then a series of odd circumstances led to Ross and Richie teaming up to give Motown its biggest hit ever up to that time.

When director Franco Zeffirelli asked Richie to compose a title tune for his film *Endless Love*, starring Brooke Shields, Richie submitted an instrumental rejected by other Commodores as not worthy of appearing on an LP by the group. An impressed Zefferelli encouraged Richie to write lyrics to the melody—and to consider doing it as a duet with Diana Ross.

Ross explained her and Motown's involvement to J. Randy Taraborrelli in *Call Her Miss Ross*: "At first it wasn't a Motown single. I didn't come into the picture until later. Lionel's agreement was with PolyGram (Records and Pictures). When I got into the picture, Lionel and I agreed that it was only fair that Motown get the single. [Actually, Motown president Berry Gordy insisted on it.] I was really pleased with it because it was one of the most beautiful songs I've ever recorded."

Due to their heavy schedules, the two had to record the song in the early morning hours in Reno, Nevada, between concert dates. The tune went to #1 AC, pop, and R&B, staying at #1 on the Hot 100 for nine weeks starting August 15, 1981, and on the R&B for seven weeks starting August 22, 1981. Given this popularity, it was surprising that another Ross-Richie duet on the Endless Love soundtrack, "Dreaming of You," was not released as a follow-up single.

Nobody cared much for the film, but the record did earn an Oscar nomination for Best Song (at the ceremonies Bette Midler cracked that it was "from the endless movie Endless Love") and Grammy nominations for Song of the Year, Record of the Year, and Best Pop Performance by a Duo or Group with Vocal.

Richie scored several more #1 AC hits starting with "Truly" in 1982 [see 430]. But Ross never got there again despite frequent recording and touring through the mid-1990s, by which time she had gone back to Motown. It hardly hurt her, however, as she seemed to find her own "endless love" when she wed Norwegian multimillionaire Arne Naess in 1986.

"Endless Love" nearly reached #1 pop again when a version by Luther Vandross and Mariah Carey stopped at #2 the week of October 1, 1994 (it also made #7 R&B). Ironically, ahead of it was "I'll Make Love to You" by Boys II Men, who stayed at #1 for 14 weeks with that song, putting it ahead of the first "Endless Love" as the Motown single with the most weeks at #1 pop.

410 Arthur's Theme (Best That You Can Do)

CHRISTOPHER CROSS

Warner 49787

September 26, 1981 (4 weeks)

*Writers: Burt Bacharach, Christopher Cross,
    Carole Bayer Sager, Peter Allen*

Producer: Michael Omartian

After he won four Grammys for his debut album [see 394—"Never Be the Same"], Christopher Cross was contacted by Burt Bacharach to work on songs. The result of their collaboration, helped by contributions from Bacharach's wife Carole Bayer Sager and performer Peter Allen, was "Arthur's Theme (Best That You Can Do)," the upbeat title song from the amusing Dudley Moore comedy *Arthur*, a sleeper hit in 1982.

"Arthur's Theme" proved that those who thought Cross would be unable to match his initial success were dead wrong, as the song got the Oscar for Best Song plus Grammy nominations for Record of the Year, Song of the Year, and Best Male Pop Vocal Performance. But Cross admitted to Paul Grein of *The Los Angeles Times* that writing "Arthur's Theme," his first experience with a songwriting collaboration, was a somewhat disorienting experience for him.

"Songwriting is a very personal experience," he told Grein. "It's like making love with someone for the first time. You have your technique and they have theirs and you've got to feel each other out." Nonetheless, doing the song was not that complicated, as it took him only one night to hash it out with his co-writers.

The popularity of "Arthur's Theme" brought Cross recognition as a leading figure in adult contemporary music, a status that he relished. "I'm an adult," he said. "I love that kind of music. If there's a Led Zeppelin song on the radio and an Anne Murray tune, I'll pick the Anne Murray tune. Why get heavy for the sake of being heavy? What's the point in writing a bunch of stuff nobody can understand?"

"Arthur's Theme" boded well for Cross as he prepared to release his sophomore album in 1983, but he acknowledged that "I realize that sometimes—I don't think in my case, but sometimes—success is short-lived." Asked by Grein how he thought he would do with his next album, Cross said, "If it stops right now and my second album comes out and goes down the tubes and I'm forgotten, I can still be on my deathbed and say, 'I put out an album and it went double platinum and had a #1 single and I won all these Grammys. Now what did *you* do?'"

He did not die, but Cross's next album, titled *Another Page* in honor of the new girlfriend in his life, did not do nearly as well as his first. Its first two singles, "All Right" (#3 AC, #12 pop) and "No Time for Talk" (#10 AC, #33 pop), performed decently, though not as spectacularly as was expected. The third, however, did get him back to #1 AC [see 450—"Think of Laura"].

411 Share Your Love With Me

KENNY ROGERS

Liberty 1430

October 24, 1981 (2 weeks)

Writers: Al Braggs, Deadric Malone

Producer: Lionel Richie

The first person to popularize "Share Your Love With Me" was Bobby "Blue" Bland, who reached #42 pop with his rendition in 1964. He would probably have gone even higher on the R&B chart, but *Billboard* did not publish a chart that year. Aretha Franklin had no such obstacle in 1969 when her "Share Your Love With Me" went to #1 R&B for five weeks starting August 23, 1969, as well as making #13 pop. But it was the earlier version which led to Kenny Rogers recording the song.

"This was a song I had loved when I was a kid. Bobby 'Blue' Bland sang this when I was young," said Rogers, who actually was in his twenties when Bland's take became a hit. Nevertheless, "Share Your Love With Me" stuck with him, and he and members of his group, the First Edition, sang it along with Gladys Knight and the Pips during the latter group's visit to his band's TV series *Rollin' on the River* in the early 1970s.

But he did not get around to recording the theme until nearly a decade later when Lionel Richie was producing him. Despite Franklin's considerable success with her cover, Rogers and Richie felt they had a shot at a hit. "It was just one of those songs whose statement I loved," Rogers said. An interesting bit of trivia from Rogers is that he corrected the lyrics, which, as sung by Bland, implied that he was in love with a man, and when Franklin did her version, she unthinkingly changed the gender, which made it sound as if she were in love with a woman.

When Rogers' full album with Richie came out, its title was *Share Your Love With Me*. But rather than use the title tune as the first single, the two decided to go with "I Don't Need You" [see 407] instead. But after a few radio stations started playing the tune as a follow to "I Don't Need You," they decided to release "Share Your Love With Me" as the second 45 from the album.

"Share Your Love With Me" shared time in the upper reaches of the AC, pop, and country charts, going to #5 country and #14 pop (the first time any version of that tune had cracked the latter two) in addition to helming the AC chart. In 1983 the song returned to the R&B chart when Lanier and Co. took it to #57.

Rogers' "Share Your Love With Me" became the fourth of eight #1 AC hits for the artist. His next to top the chart was "Through the Years" [see 418].

412 Here I Am (Just When I Thought I Was Over You)

AIR SUPPLY

Arista 0626

November 7, 1981 (3 weeks)

Writer: Norman Sallitt

Producer: Harry Maslin

After their breakthrough hit "Lost in Love" [see 383], Air Supply went on a tear over the next year and a half, scoring four consecutive top 5 AC and pop singles through "Here I Am (Just When I Thought I Was Over You)." In chronological order, the records were "All Out of Love" in 1980 (#5 AC, #2 pop for four weeks) and "Every Woman in the World" (#2 AC for two weeks, #5 pop) and "The One That You Love" (#2 AC for five weeks, #1 pop) in 1981.

Then came "Here I Am (Just When I Thought I Was Over You)," which made #5 pop the weeks of November 21 and 28, 1981 as well as #1 AC. It was only the second single by Air Supply not written by Graham Russell, who sang leads along with his partner Russell Hitchcock in the group. The first 45 with that distinction was "Every Woman in the World," composed by Dominic Bugatti and Frank Musker. Russell claimed that most of his songs for the group were inspired by his girlfriend in Australia.

The hit streak for Air Supply was quite a surprise to industry observers, many of whom regarded them as schmaltzy Barry Manilow imitators (the fact that they recorded on Manilow's label Arista was further ammunition). However, Hitchcock and Russell themselves were not particularly surprised, even though in the late 1970s they had so little well-paying work in their native Australia that Russell had to sell some of his instruments and personal possessions.

Russell thought it was due to timing. "When we had our first hit in 1980, it was because we were filling a vacuum," he told Howard Reich of *The Chicago Tribune*. "It was the heyday of hard rock, and there weren't that many ballads coming out in the United States, so fans jumped on our sound. I think they missed tunes like 'Yesterday' and those kind of sweeter songs the Beatles used to do."

As their popularity solidified in America, Hitchcock and Russell decided to continue living and recording in Australia and at the same time to tour in concert and appear on TV frequently in the United States. Their strategy worked fine, at least for a while. The follow-up to "Here I Am (Just When I Thought I Was Over You)," "Sweet Dreams," made #4 AC and #5 pop, and the record after that, "Even the Nights Are Better" [see 424], gave Air Supply its third and final #1 AC hit in 1982.

413 The Old Songs

BARRY MANILOW

Arista 0633

November 28, 1981 (3 weeks)

Writers: David Pomeranz, Buddy Kaye

Producer: Barry Manilow

"The Old Songs" was in a certain sense an old song, as its co-writer David Pomeranz cut it before Manilow did it. The Pomeranz release went nowhere, but Manilow's name had more drawing power, and when his version emerged in 1981, it went to #1 AC and #15 pop. While Manilow's version was atop the AC listings, a cover by Frederick Knight reached #74 on the R&B chart.

The single marked a comeback of sorts for Manilow. The follow-up to his previous #1 AC entry, "When I Wanted You," in 1980 [see 380] had been "I Don't Want to Walk Without You," which despite going to #2 AC for two weeks stalled at #36 pop, his worst showing there to date. He rebounded with his next effort, "I Made It Through the Rain," at #10 pop and #4 AC in late 1980, but then he went even lower when the following 45, "Lonely Together" (the first single he produced by himself), made only #45 pop and #7 AC in the spring of 1981.

But doing a tune called "The Old Songs" inevitably drew potshots from critics, who said Manilow's ballads all sounded like his old songs. It was a comment he thought had some validity, albeit with a few caveats.

As he told Tony Kornheiser in *The Washington Post* in 1980, "When I'm making them [singles], they don't sound the same, but when I hear them back-to-back they begin to. Maybe it's because I'm the same singer with the same voice. I really like the records I make. They're great records. I hear 'em on the radio and I say, 'Awwright, that sounds good. That sounds like someone put a lot of work into it.'

"The only thing I might change is the order in which they're released. . . .The singles come out because they tell me the album will fail if I don't release it. So the choice is failure or success—I don't want to fail. I want my albums to succeed because there's great stuff on them. If the single takes off, it catapults the album and the good stuff gets out there."

After "The Old Songs" had taken off, Manilow followed it with another #1 AC single, "Somewhere Down the Road" [see 417]. It marked the last time he had consecutive #1 AC hits. "The Old Songs" also had the distinction of being Manilow's last top 20 pop entry until 1983's "Read 'Em and Weep" [see 449].

414 Yesterday's Songs

NEIL DIAMOND

Columbia 02604

December 19, 1981 (6 weeks)

Writer: Neil Diamond

Producers: Neil Diamond, Dennis St. John

Neil Diamond brought out his middle-age anxieties via his tune "Yesterday's Songs." As he explained in his liner notes to his anthology *In My Lifetime*, the tune was "Written in the early eighties when I guess I doubted that any of my early songs would be remembered. . . before UB40 turned 'Red, Red Wine' into a reggae hit and [the 1994 film] *Pulp Fiction* spotlighted 'Girl, You'll Be a Woman Soon.'"

Both "Red, Red Wine" and "Girl, You'll Be a Woman Soon" were from the late 1960s period when Diamond somehow failed to make the AC chart. "Red, Red Wine" went to #62 pop for him in 1968, and even had a cover by Vic Dana make the Hot 100 at #72 plus #30 AC in 1970. But it really did not become popular until UB40's rendition, which hit #34 pop first in 1984 and then #1 pop for a week in October 1988. On the second go-

round the UB40 single made #13 AC. The "Girl, You'll Be a Woman Soon" reference involved a remake done by the rock group Urge Overkill which appeared in *Pulp Fiction* and hit #59 pop by early 1995.

In fact, despite Diamond's fear of becoming yesterday's singer/songwriter, by 1982 a number of covers of his 1960s songs had appeared: Deep Purple did "Kentucky Woman" in 1968, which peaked at #38 pop; Junior Walker and the All Stars' covered "Holly Holy," which made #75 pop in 1971; Bert Kaempfert and then Bobby Womack both did takes on "Sweet Caroline," Kaempfert's going to #24 AC in 1970 and Womack's to #51 pop in 1972; and T. G. Sheppard redid "Solitary Man," which hit #29 AC and #100 pop in 1972.

As for "Yesterday's Songs," the record made #11 pop in early 1982 in addition to its AC peak. The single was the first taken from Diamond's *On the Way to the Sky* album, and its six-week run at #1 AC was the best performance of any Diamond single except for the seven-week span of "Song Sung Blue" [see 171]. The follow-up to "Yesterday's Songs" was the title tune from the LP, which went to #4 AC and #27 pop in the spring of 1982. A third single from *On the Way to the Sky*, "Be Mine Tonight," maxed out at #2 AC for three weeks but only hit #35 pop at the same time in the summer of 1982.

The next single after "Be Mine Tonight" was "Heartlight" [see 429]. It became Diamond's eighth and to date final #1 AC hit.

415 The Sweetest Thing (I've Ever Known)

JUICE NEWTON

Capitol 5046

January 30, 1982 (1 week)

Writer: Otha Young

Producer: Richard Landis

With the crossover success of "Angel of the Morning" [see 401], Juice Newton became a familiar presence on the AC and pop as well as country charts. Its follow-up, "Queen of Hearts," became Newton's highest-charting single on the Hot 100, stopping at #2 for two weeks in the summer of 1981 (it also went to #2 for three weeks on the AC chart). The record earned Newton her second Grammy nomination for Best Female Country Vocal Performance.

For Newton's next 45, she released a tune she had originally done in 1975 as part of the trio Silver Spur, where she sang lead joined by Tom Keely and her future bandleader/road manager Otha Young. "I actually wrote ["The Sweetest Thing (I've Ever Known)"] in the early 1970s. Juice sang that on her first album," Young said. Nothing particularly inspired him to create the tune. "I didn't have an idea except I wanted to write a classic country song." The Newton–Silver Spur release failed, but the song did have enough appeal that an artist named Dottsy (her full name was Dottsy Brodt) covered it in 1976 and it went to #86 country.

But Newton, Young, and others connected to the country singer believed in 1981 her newfound appeal left the possibility open to do the song again. "We felt it hadn't gotten a proper shot on the first album, so we decided to recut it," he said. "It's kind of an unusual thing to do." The version released had the same lyrics but a slightly different arrangement.

"The Sweetest Thing (I've Ever Known)" went to #1 country the week of January 30, 1982. The single was Newton's first of four #1 hits on the country chart. On the pop chart, the record held at #7 on the Hot 100 for two weeks starting February 13, 1982, and became her third consecutive top 10 pop hit. For the AC chart, "The Sweetest Thing" became Newton's second #1 there.

For the follow-up to "The Sweetest Thing," Newton offered "Love's Been a Little Bit Hard on Me." It made #4 AC, #7 pop, and #30 country in the summer of 1982. It was her lowest showing on the latter chart since "Angel of the Morning." Next came Newton's final #1 AC hit, "Break It to Me Gently" [see 428], which broke her string of four consecutive top 10 pop hits.

Incidentally, Newton was an accomplished songwriter in her own right, although she composed none of her three #1 AC hits. Her "Sweet Sweet Smile" was a #7 AC and #44 pop record for the Carpenters in 1978, for example. Newton also did well as an equestrian at some events in the 1980s, but this hobby as well as songwriting generally took a backseat to her performing endeavors.

DAN FOGELBERG

Full Moon 02647

February 6, 1982 (2 weeks)

Writer: Dan Fogelberg

Producer: Dan Fogelberg, Marty Lewis

The leader of the band in Dan Fogelberg's eyes was his father Lawrence, who conducted big bands in the 1940s before settling down in Illinois to teach music. When Fogelberg wanted to quit the University of Illinois to try his luck in the L.A. music scene, his dad agreed to let him do so on the condition that he return to college if his career choice hadn't worked out within a year. Young Fogelberg's career did take off, and "Leader of the Band" was a song expressing appreciation from son to father, right up to the line "Thank you for the freedom when it came my time to go."

In the liner notes to *Portrait: The Music of Dan Fogelberg*, he recalled that "Leader of the Band" was "A one-day wonder that I would never have dreamed could have been a hit. My manager, Irving Azoff, heard the track and had it released. Great instincts. One of my most emotional memories was playing it for my father for the first time. He truly gave me more than I could ever repay."

"Leader of the Band" was the third sin-gle released from Fogelberg's 1980 album *The Innocent Age*. The first was "Same Old Lang Syne," a song about a real-life encounter with a former sweetheart of Fogelberg's which took him more than a year to write and incorporated the New Year's Eve perennial tune "Auld Lang Syne." The record went to #8 AC and #9 pop in early 1981. Next up was "Hard to Say," written by Fogelberg at a resort while recuperating from surgery, which clung to #2 AC for three weeks and #7 pop. "Leader of the Band" gave Fogelberg his third consecutive top 10 hit when it went to #9 on the Hot 100 the weeks of March 6 and 13, 1982.

After "Leader of the Band," one more hit came out of *The Innocent Age*. "Run for the Roses," written for ABC Sports' coverage of the 1980 Kentucky Derby, went to #3 AC and #18 pop. Like the other songs on *The Innocent Age* and Fogelberg's previous album, which included "Longer" [see 379], it had been recorded at various studios whenever the urge to write and record hit the artist. There were six studios used in all—Northstar in Boulder, Colorado; Rudy Records, Wally Heider Studio, and Sunset Sound in Los Angeles; the Record Plant in Sausalito, California; and the Caribou Ranch at Nederland, Colorado.

"Leader of the Band" reappeared on Fogelberg's next LP, 1982's *Greatest Hits*, along with two new compositions. The first of the two released was "Missing You," which despite its hard-driving sound managed to go to #6 AC as well as #23 pop in late 1982. The other one became Fogelberg's third #1 AC hit when released as a single [see 436—"Make Love Stay"].

417 Somewhere Down the Road
BARRY MANILOW

Arista 0658

February 20, 1982 (2 weeks)

Writers: Cynthia Weil (words), Tom Snow (music)

Producer: Barry Manilow

Cynthia Weil was well established as a lyricist working with her husband Barry Mann by the time she met Tom Snow, another successful songwriter with credits that included 1979's "Deeper Than the Night" for Olivia Newton-John. "I approached her at a BMI Awards dinner first," he said. Then he went through her publisher, making an official offer to be Weil's writing partner. One of their earliest successes was "Somewhere Down the Road."

"Somewhere Down the Road" was not written for any particular artist, according to Snow. It followed his typical pattern of writing with Weil. "All my collaborations with Cynthia, I wrote the melody first," he said. "She kept the melody for a time and wrote a beautiful lyric for it."

Once the president of Arista Records heard the demo, the tune's future was assured. "Clive Davis loved the song and put it on hold for a year for Barry Manilow," Snow said. Manilow changed the lyrics somewhat, although Snow declined to say exactly how he altered it, but kept the music fairly intact. "That was a really quite intimate sound," he said of Manilow's record.

Besides making #1 AC, "Somewhere Down the Road" went to #21 pop. It was the first Manilow single to make #1 AC without cracking the top pop 20 since "This One's for You" in 1976 [see 319], but that slightly disappointing showing did not bother co-writer Snow. "I was pleased with the results on the charts," he said. Possibly some record buyers and listeners may have confused the tune with the similarly titled "Somewhere in the Night," which Manilow took to #4 AC and #9 pop in 1979.

Manilow kept a constant presence on the AC and pop charts for two years before returning to top the former once again with "Read 'Em and Weep" in 1984 [see 449]. The singles released in chronological order during this period were "Let's Hang On" (#6 AC and #32 pop in 1982), "Oh Julie" (#24 AC and #32 pop in 1982), "Memory" from the musical *Cats* (#8 AC and #39 pop in 1982), and "Some Kind of Friend" (#4 AC and #26 pop in 1983).

As indicated by the Hot 100 positions listed for the latter songs, Manilow was starting to lose his appeal among pop music deejays and listeners in the wake of "Somewhere Down the Road," and in fact of all Manilow's later songs, only "Read 'Em and Weep" would make a better showing on the pop chart. After "Read 'Em and Weep," had only two minor Hot 100 entries, 1986's "I'm Your Man" at #86 and 1988's "Hey Mambo" at #90. His support at AC stations did not decline as dramatically, but by the mid-1980s, Manilow's hitmaking single days were over.

418 Through the Years
KENNY ROGERS

Liberty 1444

March 6, 1982 (2 weeks)

Writers: Steve Dorff, M. Panzer

Producer: Lionel Richie

After scoring two #1 AC hits back to back with "I Don't Need You" [see 407] and "Share Your Love With Me" [see 411], Kenny Rogers faltered when the third single spun off from his LP *Share Your Love With Me*, "Blaze of Glory," got shot down at #9 country, #25 AC, and #66 pop. It was his worst performance on all three charts since the 1970s. He quickly rebounded at the start of 1982 with the fourth song from the album, "Through the Years."

Rogers recalled reading that the song was one of the top five requested songs at weddings and anniversary celebrations. He gave much of the credit to its songwriter Steve Dorff, who remained active into the 1990s writing a lot of music for television programs, including the theme to the situation comedy *Growing Pains*.

"Through the Years" returned Rogers to familiar territory—the top or close to it of the AC, pop, and country charts. Its best pop showing was at #13, while the record claimed a #5 spot on the country listings.

But Rogers' consistently strong showings on the AC, pop, and even R&B charts brought charges from some critics in public and some envious musicians in private that he was not "true" country. Although Rogers saw it differently, feeling that he was a singer who appreciated and celebrated musical diversity in his work, he acknowledged that he was "kind of a moving target." He said, "I'll move off into jazz for awhile, and then country and then rock and roll and then R&B. . . .When I hear a song, I call on a different influence. I don't get stagnant in one influence."

Rogers said that even the way he sings his hits can be affected by the crowd which comes to see him. "Even today, if I play before a country audience, I feel so pop. And if I play before a pop audience, I feel so country. I just do them the best I can."

After "Through the Years," Rogers stopped working with Lionel Richie as his producer. Richie began doing his own solo LP, which would give him superstar status. Fans who admired both artists thought it was a shame that the two could not find a duet to do together. Rogers did say they looked for one, and he also tried to get Richie to sing with him on a later record [see 463—"What About Me?"]. At least, as Rogers noted, "He and Michael Jackson did a lot of background vocals for my record."

The next #1 AC for Rogers came a few months after "Through the Years" [see 427—"Love Will Turn You Around"].

419 Key Largo
BERTIE HIGGINS

Kat Family 02524

March 20, 1982 (2 weeks)

Writers: Sonny Limbo, Bertie Higgins

Producers: Sonny Limbo, Scott Macellan

The title came from the 1948 film starring Humphrey Bogart and wife Lauren Bacall, but Bertie Higgins insisted that as far as his hit song went, "It's not about the movie *Key Largo*. It's about old movies in general and how it affected a couple." (In fact, according to Higgins, the "couple" it described was him and his wife, Beverly Seaberg. They were separated when he wrote the song, but, said Higgins, "She heard it on the radio and came back to me," Sadly, by early 1998, Bertie and Beverly had separated again.)

Higgins co-wrote "Key Largo" with Sonny Limbo ("He gave me the line 'Here's looking at you, kid,'" Higgins said), and the song hit #1 AC, held at #8 pop for two weeks starting April 17, 1982, and even made #50 country. It was his first entry on each chart, but hardly his entrance into the music industry.

Elbert Higgins was born in Tarpon Springs, Florida, on December 8, 1944. His great-great-grandfather was German poet Johann Wolfgang van Goethe, who wrote the classic novel *Faust*. From 1964–1966 Higgins was drummer for the Roemans, a group of musicians who backed pop singer Tommy Roe. "The Roemans released four or five singles on their own," he recalled. But none were hits, and after serving his time in the Army as a draftee, he returned home at age 23, got married, had two kids, and played guitar at clubs a couple of nights each week.

When he was 29, Higgins quit his day job and pursued club work full time. For five years he did mostly original material in local clubs. "I decided at age 34 to move back to Atlanta where the Roemans were based originally," he said. But he was both poor and divorced by the time he persuaded Joel Katz, head of the Kat Family label, to let him record. "I had to beg him to do it," Higgins said. "Turned me down three times."

But Higgins found that having a hit record caught him off guard. "I said, 'What am I going to do now?' It was pretty frightening." However, he thought bad management was mainly to blame for his poor showing after "Key Largo": only one more Hot 100 entry ("Just Another Day in Paradise," which hit #46 pop and #10 AC in mid-1982), one other AC single after that ("When You Fall in Love" at #34 in late 1983), and a few tunes which made the country chart through 1989.

By 1998 Higgins had finished his sixth album and was planning to tour Asia. While he still tours in America, he believes his records are hard to program because they do not fit any current radio format. "I've been pretty hard to pigeonhole," he said. "Maybe that worked against me." Though based in Tarpon Springs in 1998, he said he may move to Las Vegas in the future.

420 Chariots of Fire—Titles
VANGELIS

Polydor 2189

April 3, 1982 (5 weeks)

Writer: Vangelis

Producer: Vangelis

Composer, arranger, producer, performer—you name the job and Vangelis probably did it while he was working on the theme for the movie *Chariots of Fire*. Born Evangelos Papathanassiou in Velos, Greece (about 200 miles north of Athens), on March 29, 1943, Vangelis composed his first tune at age 4. He wrote and recorded music as part of the Greek band Formynx before moving to Paris as a 25-year-old. There, he teamed with Demis Roussos and the two recorded as Aphrodite's Child for a few years before he began to pursue a solo career. He relocated to London in 1974.

Prior to *Chariots of Fire*, Vangelis had written music for a few European movies, such as the 1973 French film *Amore*. But none of them earned him the popular or critical acclaim he won after producer David Puttnam selected him to do music for *Chariots of Fire*.

Vangelis did not write his score on paper, preferring to watch the movie on his video screen and then add the musical elements electronically, with considerable use of a synthesizer. It took him about a month to score *Chariots of Fire*. He told William Tuohy of the *Los Angeles Times* that "I very much enjoyed doing *Chariots of Fire*, and found it very exciting to be able to bring something more to the film. It was a period film but I tried to develop music that would sound right—but not just seem like conventional music of the time."

Vangelis's music was the pulsating instrumental heard over the opening credits as runners competing for the Olympics ran near crashing waves. Polydor first released the single under the prosaic title of "Titles," but as the movie caught on with critics and scored several Academy Award nominations in early 1982, the renamed "Chariots of Fire" 45 stormed up the charts. By the time *Chariots of Fire* won several Oscars including Best Picture and Best Original Score for Vangelis at the Academy Awards ceremony on March 29, 1982, "Chariots of Fire" was the #1 AC hit of that week.

The record also hit #1 pop the week of May 8, 1982, and the soundtrack was #1 on the album charts for four weeks starting April 17, 1982. "Chariots of Fire" also received a Grammy nomination for Record of the Year.

"Chariots of Fire" was the only solo AC and pop entry for Vangelis. Later in 1982 he returned to both charts as part of Jon & Vangelis, a duo composed of him and Yes lead singer Jon Anderson, with "I'll Find My Way Home" (#41 AC, #51 pop). (Anderson also sang on Vangelis's first single release in America, "So Long Ago, So Clear" in 1976.) Over the next two decades, Vangelis concentrated on writing movie themes for movies, and his credits include *Blade Runner* (1982), *The Bounty* (1984), and *1492: The Conquest of Paradise* (1992).

421 Shanghai Breezes

JOHN DENVER

RCA 13071

May 8, 1982 (1 week)

Writer: John Denver

Producers: John Denver, Barry Wyckoff

More than six years passed after John Denver's "Looking for Space" topped the AC listing [see 294] before he returned to #1 on that chart with "Shanghai Breezes." "Shanghai Breezes" was also Denver's highest-charting tune on the Hot 100 since "Looking for Space" (#31 and #29, respectively).

"Shanghai Breezes" did not make the country chart, but several follow-ups did, including Denver's last AC entry, "Dreamland Express," which made #34 AC and #9 country in 1985. His AC entries between "Shanghai Breezes" and "Dreamland Express" were few—"Seasons of the Heart" (#23 AC, #78 pop) in 1982, "Wild Montana Skies" with Emmylou Harris (#26 AC) in 1983, "Love Again" with Sylvie Vartan (#30 AC, #85 pop; his last pop entry) in 1984, and "Don't Close Your Eyes, Tonight" (#37) in 1985.

For the rest of the 1980s, Denver made a few infrequent appearances on the country chart. "And So It Goes," his 1989 duet with the Nitty Gritty Dirt Band at #14, was his swan song there.

The 1990s were fairly tough for Denver. He divorced Cassandra Delaney in 1991. He pleaded guilty to a DWI arrest on August 21, 1993, and was fined and sentenced to probation. Exactly one year later, on August 21, 1994, he faced another drunk driving charge; this time it went to trial and ended in a hung jury. Recording deals were rare for him, although he did get a live two-record set called *The Wildlife Concert*, which had been taped February 23 and 24, 1995 in New York City, released by Legacy Records in 1995.

In early 1997 Denver told a reporter, "The last five or six years have been the hardest part of my life." But he kept writing songs in hopes of another album deal and stayed busy making appearances for charity events, with a camp for deaf children in Aspen, Colorado being a favorite beneficiary. One of his last public appearances was at a cystic fibrosis fundraiser at a Baltimore Orioles baseball game on September 20, 1997. He sang his old favorite "Thank God I'm a Country Boy," which regularly played during the Orioles' seventh-inning stretch in games.

On October 12, 1997, Denver drove to an airport in Monterey, California, near his second home near Carmel, California (he split his time between there and Denver, Colorado). Planning to fly over Clint Eastwood's new golf course in the area, he got into a single-engine home-built plane and took off. Denver never returned, as his plane crashed off the California coast. Denver was 53 years old.

422 Ebony and Ivory

PAUL MCCARTNEY WITH STEVIE WONDER

Columbia 02860

May 15, 1982 (5 weeks)

Writer: Paul McCartney

Producer: George Martin

Stevie Wonder displayed publicly his affection for Beatle Paul McCartney when he took his cover of the Beatles' "We Can Work It Out" to #13 pop in 1971. Likewise, Paul McCartney and his wife Linda announced their fondness for Wonder when they pressed "We love you" in Braille into the upper left-hand corner of the back of the 1973 Wings LP *Red Rose Speedway*. But it was not until almost a decade later that Wonder and McCartney, two of the biggest artists of the 20th century, got together to do a song.

The tune, appropriately, was a McCartney composition that noted how black and white keys on pianos "live together in perfect harmony" and asked why human beings can't do the same. It marked the first time either artist had been part of a duet on a single. (Wonder did sing on "Pops, We Love You," a tribute to Motown founder Berry Gordy's late father, with Marvin Gaye, Smokey Robinson, and Diana Ross in 1979. It went to #59 pop.)

"The thing about that song, working with Stevie Wonder—Stevie is such a consummate musician—working with someone that good really keeps you on your toes," McCartney told Tom Mulhern in *Guitar Player* magazine in July 1990. "He did the drumming on that, but we started off with a rhythm box, one of the first Linn drum machines. . . . After we put a track down with that, Stevie did the drums, and then we did the vocals. So I figured I had to put down a good bass part. I sat around and tried to work out something that would sympathize with the record; I was quite pleased with it."

Evidently McCartney was not the only person contented with the end product, for "Ebony and Ivory" topped the AC and pop charts simultaneously starting the week of May 15, 1982, with the tune spending two extra weeks at #1 on the Hot 100 after that. It did come up short on the R&B chart, stalling at #8 there.

The popularity of "Ebony and Ivory" propelled McCartney's *Tug of War* album to #1 for three weeks starting May 29, 1982. The other singles from *Tug of War* were "Take It Away" (#6 AC, #10 pop) and the title tune (#31 AC, #53 pop), both in 1982. Since the song was a Columbia record, Motown artist Stevie Wonder has yet to include it on any of his albums.

"Ebony and Ivory" racked up Grammy nominations for Record of the Year, Song of the Year, and Best Pop Performance by a Duo or Group With Vocal, plus McCartney's *Tug of War* LP was a finalist for Album of the Year.

Though McCartney and Wonder did not team up again on record after "Ebony and Ivory," McCartney did another duet with a high-profile artist which hit #1 AC. For more details, see 432—"The Girl Is Mine."

423 Any Day Now

RONNIE MILSAP

RCA 13216

June 19, 1982 (5 weeks)

Writers: Bob Hilliard (words), Burt Bacharach (music)

Producers: Ronnie Milsap, Tom Collins

During his time recording at Scepter Records in the mid-1960s, Ronnie Milsap recalled, "I got to meet a lot of R&B singers and thought that was what I'd want to be." One of those artists was Chuck Jackson, whose biggest hit was "Any Day Now," which reached #23 pop and #2 R&B in 1962. Milsap decided Jackson's hit would work well for him too, even though several others had some success in covering the song before Milsap, including Percy Sledge, who went to #86 pop and #35 R&B in 1969 with his rendition, and Don Gibson, who took it to #26 country in 1979.

But Milsap's effort surpassed theirs, perhaps due to a change in the introduction where he played the piano in the key of F. It hit #1 on the country chart in the middle of its five-week run atop the AC chart. In fact, Milsap remembered being handed an award from *Billboard* for having the biggest AC hit of 1982 with "Any Day Now." He also recalled with a laugh that "Ever since that record came out, I keep getting messages from Chuck saying, 'Where is my money? Send me my money!'"

On the pop chart, "Any Day Now" went to #14, making it Milsap's second-highest-charting hit on the Hot 100, beaten only by 1981's "(There's) No Gettin' Over Me," which made #2 AC for four weeks. "It was one of those songs that helped to bridge what I was trying to do in country and appeal to all the charts," Milsap said. "You can't do that today. It almost feels like a lockout." He credited his manager Dan Cleary for pushing his songs to AC and pop radio stations as well as country ones.

"Any Day Now" was one of 10 consecutive singles to hit #1 for Milsap on the country chart from 1980–83, as was his earlier #1 AC hit, "Smoky Mountain Rain" [see 398]. A year after that streak ended, Milsap stopped hitting the Hot 100, and even his AC entries dwindled to one per year, with his 1987 duet with Kenny Rogers, "Make No Mistake, She's Mine," being his last AC entry until 1991's "Since I Don't Have You." He continued to make the country chart into the 1990s, but the songs didn't rise as high as previous efforts, and he and RCA parted company in 1993 after 20 years of work together.

In 1998, Milsap was based in Nashville, where he likes to live, and was signed with Warner Brothers. "I'm going to continue making records," he said, adding that he also tours roughly two to three months each year. While not thrilled with the musical segregation that has made it increasingly difficult to come up with crossover hits, he can handle doing the country market because in terms of the types of songs played, "The country format is so much wider today than it used to be."

424 Even the Nights Are Better

AIR SUPPLY

Arista 0692

July 24, 1982 (4 weeks)

Writers: Terry Skinner, J. L. Wallace, Ken Ball

Producer: Harry Maslin

Songwriters Terry Skinner, J. L. Wallace, and Ken Ball formed the group Bama in 1979, but their work didn't get much recognition until two of their tunes hit #1 AC within a year's period. The first was "Touch Me When We're Dancing" by the Carpenters [see 408], and the second was "Even the Nights Are Better," the third #1 AC hit for Air Supply in three years.

"Even the Nights Are Better" peaked initially on the AC chart over a month before doing the same on the Hot 100. It made #5 pop the weeks of September 4 and 11, 1982. It was the group's last top 10 pop hit except for 1983's "Making Love Out of Nothing At All," which went to #2 both AC and pop.

Between "Even the Nights Are Better" and "Making Love Out of Nothing At All," Air Supply came out with two 45s that coincidentally both peaked at #38 pop, "Young Love" in 1982, which made #13 AC, and "Two Less Lonely People in the World," which did better by going to #4 AC in 1983. There were no more Air Supply singles until 1985, when "Just As I Am" made #3 AC and #19 pop. But by this time, many radio programmers and record buyers had begun to choke on Air Supply's light ballad style, and "Just As I Am" became the last top 10 AC and top 20 pop entry by the group.

Later in 1985 Air Supply released "The Power of Love (You Are My Lady)," a #13 AC and #68 pop single which was a #1 AC and pop hit nine years later for Celine Dion [see 640]. The following year "Lonely Is the Night" failed to reverse Air Supply's declining fortunes by getting only to #12 AC and #76 pop. It was the last Air Supply 45 to go onto the Hot 100.

Taking stock of their shrinking popularity, Russell Hitchcock and Graham Russell ended their partnership in 1988 to pursue solo careers. Niether fared well, though Hitchcock did return to the AC chart. His first solo 45, a remake of "What Becomes of the Brokenhearted?" hit #39, followed three years later by "Caught in Your Web (Swear to Your Heart)," an album cut from the soundtrack of the movie *Arachnophobia* which got to #9. As neither song made the Hot 100, Hitchcock decided later in 1991 to rejoin Russell and inflate Air Supply again.

The first Air Supply LP of the 1990s, *The Earth Is. . .*, had a #48 AC entry with a cut from the album, a redo of Nilsson's "Without You" [see 166]. Another album cut, "Goodbye," from the 1993 album *The Vanishing Race*, made the AC chart for one week at #48 in 1993. Obviously, the resurrected Air Supply was not bowling over their old AC fans in the 1990s, but at the end of the decade, Russell and Hitchcock's concert act, at least, was still playing at venues across America.

425 Hard to Say I'm Sorry

CHICAGO

Full Moon/Warner Brothers 29979

August 21, 1982 (3 weeks)

Writers: Peter Cetera, David Foster

Producer: David Foster

In the early 1980s Chicago suffered a few setbacks that made some question whether the group would survive. As the band's singles received less airplay, their albums began to do poorly too, with *Chicago XIV*, released in 1980, becoming their first LP not to be certified gold (it peaked at #71). *Chicago—Greatest Hits, Volume II* fared even worse in 1981, going only to #171 for five weeks. And by then Columbia had dropped the act, feeling the group's time had come and gone.

Undaunted, Chicago signed with Full Moon and planned its 16th album with veteran producer David Foster at the helm. The first song released from it in the summer of 1982 was "Hard to Say I'm Sorry," which Foster co-wrote with lead singer Peter Cetera. It was heard in the critical and commercial movie bomb *Summer Lovers* about a three-way love affair between a man and two women he adores equally. "The movie was in the process of being created when we presented the record to them," said trumpeter Lee Loughnane in recalling how the song became part of the film.

The failure of *Summer Lovers* did not keep "Hard to Say I'm Sorry" from hitting #1 on the AC and pop charts, although not simultaneously (the record topped the Hot 100 for two weeks after the AC run starting the week of September 11, 1982). Though not nominated for an Oscar for Best Song, "Hard to Say I'm Sorry" did net Chicago a Grammy nomination for Best Pop Performance by a Duo or Group With Vocal.

For longtime fans who might have thought "Hard to Say I'm Sorry" was too bland, Foster provided a raveup ending with keyboards and horns on the album version that reminded them of the free-form jams Chicago did to wind up their songs back in the 1970s on their long LP renditions of tunes like "Beginnings." "I think Foster came out with that, and most radio stations didn't play it. They played it till it faded out on the changeover," Loughnane said. "It sort of took us back to the FM, extended album days. We still play it like that in concert."

In 1997 "Hard to Say I'm Sorry" reappeared on the pop and AC charts when Peter Cetera sang a few lines along with the R&B vocal group Az Yet. The credits were Az Yet featuring Peter Cetera, with Foster and Babyface as co-producers. The single peaked at #8 pop in May and #14 AC in August. Asked his opinion of the remake, Loughnane said, "It's OK. I think it helped our careers and gave us appeal to younger kids."

Chicago notched two AC-pop hits after "Hard to Say I'm Sorry." "Love Me Tomorrow" went to #8 AC and #22 pop in the fall of 1982, then two years later "Hard Habit to Break" brought them to #3 on both the AC and pop chart. Their next single took them to #1 AC for a sixth time; see—"You're the Inspiration."

426 Blue Eyes
ELTON JOHN

Geffen 29954

September 11, 1982 (2 weeks)

Writers: Gary Osborne (words), Elton John (music)

Producer: Chris Thomas

"**B**lue Eyes" was the last single released before Elton John permanently reunited with his old lyricist Bernie Taupin for the rest of the 1980s and 1990s. Supplying words for this tune was Gary Osborne, who also did the chore for John's previous #1 AC record [see 386—"Little Jeannie"].

On the pop chart "Blue Eyes" did well enough to reach #12 and net John a Grammy nomination for Best Male Pop Vocal Performance. John, however, failed to pick up a statuette for the 13th time (the 12th was the same night; he had earlier missed a win in the Video of the Year category). He would miss again in 1984, failing to get Best Male Rock Vocal Performance, before finally claiming a Grammy in 1986, as part of Dionne and Friends, for Best Pop Performance By a Duo or Group With Vocal [see 485—"That's What Friends Are For"].

John hit #12 pop again with the follow-up to "Blue Eyes," "I'm Still Standing," which went to #28 AC as well in 1983. Then he went back to raucous rock and roll with "Kiss the Bride," which got no AC airplay but made #25 pop in 1983, and ended the year with another ballad, "I Guess That's Why They Call It the Blues," which made #2 AC for three weeks as well as #4 pop.

"Sad Songs (Say So Much)" came out in 1984 and nearly cracked #1 AC, staying at #2 for six weeks, while also reaching #5 pop. His other two singles of 1984, "Who Wears These Shoes?" and "In Neon," made #11 AC while getting to #16 pop and #38 pop respectively. "Wrap Her Up" was his only entry in 1985, but it did get to #20 pop without making the AC chart.

In 1986 "Nikita" landed at #3 AC and #7 pop, followed by "Heartaches All Over the World" at #55 pop. His name was in parentheses when he duetted with Jennifer Rush on "Flames of Paradise" in 1987, which made #32 AC and #36 pop. He ended 1987 by releasing a live recording with the Melbourne Symphony Orchestra done on December 14, 1986 in Syndey, Australia, of "Candle in the Wind," a track he recorded on his 1973 LP *Goodbye Yellow Brick Road*. It went to #2 AC for two weeks and #6 pop and later became a hit again under tragic circumstances (the death of Princess Diana) in 1997 [see 670—"Something About the Way You Look Tonight"]. Another recording with the symphony, "Take Me to the Pilot," failed to make the Hot 100 but did get to #37 AC in the spring of 1988.

John then got his highest-charting pop solo hit since the 1970s with his next release, which also was his eighth #1 AC entry [see 545—"I Don't Wanna Go On With You Like That"].

427 Love Will Turn You Around
KENNY ROGERS

Liberty 1471

September 25, 1982 (2 weeks)

Writer: Kenny Rogers, David Malloy, Thom Schuyler, Even Stevens

Producers: Kenny Rogers, David Malloy

By 1982 Kenny Rogers had sold millions of records and was a familiar television personality, having appeared on that medium in music specials and even made for TV movies (*The Gambler* and several sequels). So why not have Rogers as the lead in a film? Rogers' first starring effort was *Six Pack*, and while not a blockbuster, it did provide him with a few enjoyable memories, one of which was doing "Love Will Turn You Around."

"We were just looking for a song in there," Rogers said about the story behind "Love Will Turn You Around." He met with songwriters David Malloy, Thom Schuyler, and Even Stevens, showed them the movie and "I just told them what I wanted to say." Specifically, that was "I'm a race car driver, and here's what's got me going, the love for this girl, played by Erin Gray."

From that information, the trio created "Love Will Turn You Around," though they gave Rogers writing credit for putting his piece into the final work (Rogers said in Nashville the policy is known as the "word for a third" of credit). The record became a double #1 hit, topping both the AC and country charts, doing so on the latter chart the week of September 4, 1982. The single was his first #1 country hit since "I Don't Need You" a year earlier [see 407]. "Love Will Turn You Around" also made #13 on the Hot 100 and garnered Rogers a Grammy nomination for Best Male Country Vocal Performance.

But Rogers found that making movies for release in theaters is not as easy as recording songs. "When you do a feature film, it can take. . .months to do it," he said. In fact, Rogers made more per hour doing concerts between shooting scenes than he did from his cut of the movie proceeds. Also, the schedules for non-TV films are often delayed, sometimes for months, which can easily interfere with tour dates set up on the basis of the original schedule. In contrast, TV movies have shorter schedules—usually two months. Said Rogers about the TV movies he did: "We produced them ourselves, so I could work some days and be off others to tour when we needed."

Rogers also believed that *Six Pack* could have done better if he had used bigger names to support him rather than be its only star. "We assumed that at the time I would be strong enough to draw in feature films," he said. "And that's a different world than television."

Nonetheless, *Six Pack* did make its money back, and did not adversely affect his career. He came close to the top of the AC chart in 1983 with "We've Got Tonight" with Sheena Easton (#2 for five weeks) and "All My Life" (#2 for two weeks) before scoring an AC, pop, and country #1 hit with "Islands in the Stream" [see 446].

428 Break It to Me Gently

JUICE NEWTON

Capitol 5148

October 9, 1982 (2 weeks)

Writers: Diane Lampert, Joe Seneca

Producer: Richard Landis

Brenda Lee scored her ninth top 10 pop hit in early 1962 with "Break It to Me Gently," which peaked at #4 on the Hot 100. Twenty years later, Juice Newton did the tune and brought it back to hit status.

"That was one where Juice and I had a habit of going out to get Patsy Cline records," said her road manager and bandleader Otha Young, referring to a period when they were buying oldies. "We went out and got a Brenda Lee record, and as soon as that came on, we gave a look to each other and did it with the band."

"Break It to Me Gently" stalled at #2 country for two weeks in the fall of 1982 in addition to being #1 AC. On the pop chart it stopped at #11 and was the last Newton single to make the pop top 20. The song did get Newton her first Grammy Award for Best Female Country Vocal Performance, but Young bemoaned the fact that Newton and her entourage got stuck in traffic and didn't make it to the ceremony in time to receive the award in person.

Newton's run of entries on the AC and pop charts came to a halt within two years of "Break It to Me Gently." Her last AC entry was 1984's "A Little Love," which went to #7 AC. The follow-up to that song, "Can't Wait All Night," was her final single on the Hot 100, peaking at #66 in 1984.

Over the next seven years, Newton continued to make the country chart, hitting #1 with "You Make Me Want to Make You Mine" in 1985 and "Hurt" and "Both to Each Other" in 1986. The latter was a duet with Eddie Rabbitt which was a cover of the #1 AC hit "Friends and Lovers" [see 501]. Her last entry was "When Love Comes Around the Bend," which came around to #40 before dropping off the chart in 1989.

During most of the 1990s Newton did occasional live performances, but concentrated much of her time on raising her children in southern California. In 1998 she released her first LP in 11 years, *The Trouble With Angels*, which included remakes of "Angel in the Morning," "The Sweetest Thing (I've Ever Known)," and "Love's Been a Little Bit Hard on Me," and began to tour more extensively. "We want to expand Juice's popularity," Young said as he described what he hoped will be increased activity for the band into the 21st century.

429 Heartlight

NEIL DIAMOND

Columbia 03219

October 23, 1982 (4 weeks)

Writers: Neil Diamond, Burt Bacharach, Carole Bayer Sager

Producers: Neil Diamond, Burt Bacharach, Carole Bayer Sager

Count Neil Diamond among the millions of movie lovers who enjoyed *E.T. The Extra-Terrestrial*, the 1982 fantasy blockbuster from Steven Spielberg. "Carole Bayer Sager, Burt Bacharach and I went to see *E.T.*," recalled Diamond in his anthology *In His Lifetime*. "After the movie, we went to their apartment and came up with a simple musical statement that we all felt very sincerely."

"Heartlight" peaked at #5 pop for four consecutive weeks starting the week of November 13, 1982. It was the last #1 AC hit for Diamond and also his last single to penetrate the pop top 30. Nobody realized it at the time, but Diamond's popularity on the charts had already started to wane.

The first three follow-ups to "Heartlight" did fine on the AC chart if not too impressively on the Hot 100. "I'm Alive" in 1983 hit #4 AC and #35 pop; "Front Page Story" did not make first-page news by going to #65 pop as well as #5 AC in mid-1983; and "Turn Around" did not live up to its title on the pop chart, getting only to #62 on that list, though it did make #4 AC. The performance of the follow-up to "Turn Around" in late 1984, "Sleep With Me Tonight," was even worse: it went only to #24 AC and was the first of Diamond's 1980 songs not to make the Hot 100. Next up, the yuletide "You Make It Feel Like Christmas" made only #28 AC in early 1985.

Diamond's last entry on the Hot 100, the synthesizer-heavy title song to his *Headed for the Future* LP, was released in mid-1986, amid some bad publicity revealing that Columbia Records executives had rejected the album as first submitted. The version that was distributed went to #10 AC but only #53 pop. Throughout the rest of the 1980s Diamond released singles which almost always made the top 20 of the AC chart despite no pop action. The biggest of these were in 1989, when "This Time" and "The Best Years of Our Lives" made #9 and #7, respectively. Diamond kept charting AC into the 1990s, but by this time Columbia had stopped releasing 45s by the artist and AC stations were playing album cuts instead.

Diamond took these career changes in stride. Though he was no longer the dominant male solo singer on the charts he had been from the late 1960s through early 1980s, he continued to be a top-drawing concert attraction and, through the end of the decade, was still regularly releasing albums with new material. And Diamond plans to continue doing so as long as possible. As he put it in *In My Lifetime*, "There's something inside of me that is released when I'm able to write music. And I think I'll need that release for as long as I live."

430 Truly

LIONEL RICHIE

Motown 1644

November 20, 1982 (4 weeks)

Writer: Lionel Richie

Producers: Lionel Richie, James Anthony Carmichael

Music ran in the genes of Lionel Brockman Richie, Jr., born in Tuskegee, Alabama, on June 20, 1949. As a child he learned the piano from imitating his grandmother's playing, which consisted primarily of classical pieces. Richie grew up in Tuskegee, then went to high school in Joliet, Illinois. After high school, he started at the Tuskegee Institute with the intention of being a minister, but after a semester he learned that was not where his interests lay.

While attending Tuskegee Institute, he was invited to join an R&B group being formed locally in 1970, the Commodores. "When I went to Tuskegee Institute, I took my saxophone along to learn how to play it," Richie told Lynn Van Matre of *The Chicago Tribune*. "That's right, I hadn't a clue how to play when I first joined the Commodores there. Thomas McClary, the guitar player, asked if I wanted to play with this group at a school talent show, and I said sure. It wasn't until two years later that I told the rest of the Commodores that I was winging it in the beginning."

After graduating from Tuskegee with a major in economics and a minor in accounting, Richie stayed with the Commodores. They were known as one of the top funk bands of the 1970s, but Richie typically wrote the group's ballads to add some contrast in the mix. His writing and singing lead on songs like "Easy" in 1977 (#14 AC, #4 pop) and "Still" in 1979 (#6 AC, #1 pop) got him noticed by others in the band.

"As time went on, I started writing songs and singing them, and eventually I was singing more and more," he told Van Matre. "Then it was lead singer Lionel Richie. It just evolved. Then one day Kenny Rogers called and wanted me to produce a song for him." The result was 1980s "Lady" [see 393]. Following "Lady" and 1981's hit duet with Diana Ross, "Endless Love" [see 409], there was pressure on Richie to start a solo recording career and he left the Commodores in 1982. The title of his last hit with them, a #5 AC and #4 pop entry in 1981, might have been spoken by numerous Commodores fans when they heard the news— "Oh No."

Richie's first single from his self-titled debut album was "Truly," which made #1 pop for two weeks starting November 27, 1982, plus #2 R&B for nine weeks. The tune won him a Grammy for Best Male Pop Vocal Performance. It also was the first of an incredible 11 #1 AC hits, with the next being his follow-up to "Truly," called "You Are" [see 435].

431 Heartbreaker

DIONNE WARWICK

Arista 1015

December 18, 1982 (1 week)

Writers: Barry Gibb, Maurice Gibb, Robin Gibb

Producers: Barry Gibb, Karl Richardson, Albhy Galuten

When Arista President Clive Davis decided to attend a Florida wedding in 1981, he had no idea that the trip would the provide his label with another #1 AC hit for Dionne Warwick. "That was another brainstorm of Clive Davis," Warwick recalled. "He ran into Barry Gibb at a restaurant, he and his wife Linda. And Barry said he wanted to work with me." Davis pitched the idea to Warwick, who agreed to try it. So now she could count a Bee Gee as well as Barry Manilow as one of her producers. "That's the joy of recording and being in this world of entertainers," she said. "You meet some incredible people."

Barry and his brothers Maurice and Robin gave Warwick their song "Heartbreaker" to record. "Actually, it didn't attract me," Warwick confessed. But she trusted their judgment, or as she put it, "If the writer and the producer of the project definitely know what it's about, it's up to me to help them," so she recorded it, with Barry Gibb's prominent vocal providing harmony in the background. Her decision certainly turned out to be a wise one in terms of commercial appeal.

"Heartbreaker" became Warwick's first top 10 pop hit since "I'll Never Love This Way Again" in 1979. The song peaked at #10 on the Hot 100 the week of January 15, 1982 and also made #14 R&B. Regarding the success of a song she hadn't liked, Warwick said, "I cried all the way to the bank." She remembered she had had similar misgivings about a 1968 Burt Bacharach and Hal David song, "Do You Know the Way to San Jose"?, because the "Whoa whoa, whoa whoa, whoa whoa, whoa whoa whoa, whoa" lyrics at the beginning and end of the tune bothered her. She was wrong about that one too; it peaked at #4 AC, #10 pop, and #23 R&B.

Two other singles from her work with Gibb made the AC chart. "Take the Short Way Home" went to #5 AC in 1983 as well as #41 pop and #43 R&B, while its follow-up, "All the Love in the World," reached #16 AC plus bubbled under to #101.

Warwick then joined with Luther Vandross to do "How Many Times Can We Say Goodbye," a #4 AC, #27 pop, and #7 R&B duet in 1983. Two years later, she returned to the AC listings with the title song from the short-lived ABC-TV series *Finders of Lost Love*, a duet with Glenn Jones which went to #12 AC and signaled her renewed working relationship with Burt Bacharach. That connection paid off even better later in 1985 with "That's What Friends Are For" [see 485].

432 The Girl Is Mine

MICHAEL JACKSON AND PAUL McCARTNEY

Epic 03288

December 25, 1982 (4 weeks)

Writer: Michael Jackson

Producer: Quincy Jones

Born in Gary, Indiana, on August 29, 1958, Michael Jackson rose to prominence in 1970 when he and his four brothers, then known as the Jackson 5, hit #1 pop with "I Want You Back." After more hits, Jackson started a concurrent solo career in 1971 with "Got to Be There," which went to #4 pop and became his first AC chart entry at #14. Other pop, AC, and R&B hits followed over the next decade.

Then he asked Paul McCartney to join him in doing "The Girl Is Mine," "which I knew would be right for his voice and mine working together," Jackson wrote in his autobiography *Moonwalk*. The two disagreed on when and how they met in the 1970s, but it is known that McCartney wrote "Girlfriend" for Jackson, which McCartney recorded for his 1978 LP *London Town*, while Jackson did his version on his 1979 LP *Off the Wall*.

"Then we wrote 'Say Say Say' and 'The Man' together and then he wrote 'The Girl Is Mine'," McCartney recalled in *Rock Lives* by Timothy White. The first two tunes appeared on McCartney's 1983 LP *Pipes of Peace*. "The Girl Is Mine" went onto Jackson's 1982 LP *Thriller* and became the first single from that album, going to #1 R&B for three weeks starting January 15, 1983 and #2 pop for three weeks starting January 8, 1983, behind Hall and Oates' "Maneater" the first week and Men at Work's "Down Under" the last two, in addition to its AC peak. It also prompted one individual to sue Jackson unsuccessfully for plagiarism. Jackson wrote in *Moonwalk*, "When I was sued by someone I had never heard of for 'The Girl Is Mine,' I was quite willing to stand on my reputation. I stated that many of my ideas come in dreams, which some people thought was a convenient cop-out, but it's true."

The six follow-ups to "The Girl Is Mine" placed in the top pop 10, the first time seven singles from one LP ever did so. Four made the AC chart—"Billie Jean" (#9), "Human Nature" (#2), "P.Y.T. (Pretty Young Thing)" (#37), all in 1983, and "Thriller" (#24) in 1984. *Thriller* held at #1 for 37 weeks starting February 27, 1983, and at the end of 1997 still held the record as the biggest-selling LP of all time, with more than 25 million copies sold. *Thriller* also netted Jackson eight Grammys, including Album of the Year and Best Male Pop Vocal Performance.

Jackson returned to #1 AC in 1987 [see 524—"I Just Can't Stop Loving You"], but before that relations between him and McCartney had cooled, when Jackson bought the rights to the Beatles music catalog. McCartney told White he had wanted the rights but obstacles prevented him from getting them, then added, "Anyway, Michael's got it, and all's fair in love, war and business, I suppose. But it is a little galling now to find that I own less of 'Yesterday' than Michael Jackson!"

433 Baby, Come to Me
PATTI AUSTIN WITH JAMES INGRAM

Qwest 50036

January 22, 1983 (3 weeks)

Writer: Rod Temperton

Producer: Quincy Jones

Patti Austin, born in New York, New York, on August 10, 1948, said she knew producer Quincy Jones "just about all my life." Jones was her godfather, having known her father Gordon Austin, a jazz trombonist. Later Jones produced her biggest hit, "Baby, Come to Me."

Austin started singing professionally at age 4 and cutting singles in 1969 with her debut "The Singing Tree," which made #46 R&B. But though she continued to record and do commercial jingles, Austin had no chart activity until 1977's "Say You Love Me" became her second R&B entry at #63. She made seven more R&B singles through 1981.

Jones produced some of Austin's singles in the 1970s on A&M before setting up his Qwest label under Warner Records. He also liked James Ingram, who sang lead on "Just Once" (#7 AC, 1981) and "One Hundred Ways" (#5 AC, 1982) on 45s billed as "Quincy Jones featuring James Ingram." Regarding Ingram's participation on "Baby, Come to Me," Austin said, "I think Quincy was trying to keep James going until he got signed to Qwest."

Austin said that while recording the tune with Jones, "I think he asked James to do some kind of masculine roar in the song. Hence we had James going 'Hey!' in the middle of the song." Ingram's improvised shout cracked him and Austin up, but Jones said, "That's it!" and put it in the record.

"Baby, Come to Me" stopped at #37 R&B and #73 pop when first released in early 1982. Luckily, the ABC-TV daily serial *General Hospital* began using the song as background music. But Austin said that alone did not spur sales. "There was a radio station in Florida that started playing the record when they [recapped] the day's events on the soap operas whenever it came time to do *General Hospital*," she said. That exposure led the song to sell 20,000 copies one weekend. After much reluctance plus pressure from Austin and others, Warner rereleased the tune in the fall of 1982.

"Baby, Come to Me" topped the Hot 100 the weeks of February 19 and 26, 1983, and also made #9 R&B. "It felt great in a way and it felt horrible in a way, because it was a duet," Austin said of the hit. When she toured with Ingram, some people assumed they were a team. (They had another single in 1983, "How Do You Keep the Music Playing," which made #5 AC and #45 pop.) "It was tough getting my individual identity back," she said. But she did, and even managed to perform "Baby, Come to Me" solo in a novel way. "A long time I did the song doing me and him, imitating James' voice," she said. In 1984 a Stephanie Winslow version of "Baby, Come to Me" went to #42 country.

Austin and Ingram continued to hit the AC and R&B charts separately into the 1990s. By the end of the decade Austin was living in northern California and touring in a one-woman show.

434 Shame on the Moon

BOB SEGER

Capitol 5187

February 12, 1983 (2 weeks)

Writer: Rodney Crowell

Producer: Jimmy Iovine

Gritty rock shouter Bob Seger was the most unlikely artist to reach the AC chart peak since WAR [see 311 —"Summer"], but he did it nonetheless with one of his few hits not written by him. Struggling country singer Rodney Crowell composed the tune and recorded it, with little fanfare, before Seger covered it.

"Don Henley turned me on to Crowell, who he was listening to a lot, in 1980, but I didn't buy one of his records til '82," Seger told Fred Bronson in *Billboard's Hottest Hot 100 Hits*. "When I heard 'Shame on the Moon,' I just stopped and thought, 'Wow, this is a great song!' I played it for everyone in the band, and they said, 'Sure, let's do it.' . . . It's more like a western song—a cowboy song—than it is a country and western song. And the track is flawless, the best and tightest track on the album. We cut it in like two hours, and everybody decided it was the miracle track."

At first, Seger's producer Jimmy Iovine did not share the band's enthusiasm for the song. He finally warmed to it when Seger and his pal Don Henley did the background vocals. Officials with Capitol Records were quicker to respond to the song, making it the first single released from Seger's otherwise all-rock LP *The Distance* in late 1982.

"Shame on the Moon" nearly matched its AC peak on the pop chart. The record stayed at #2 for four weeks starting February 26, 1983. Keeping it from the top the first week was "Baby, Come to Me" [see 433], and then, for the last three weeks, Michael Jackson's "Billie Jean." "Shame on the Moon" also became Seger's first country hit, peaking at #15 on that chart in 1983. His singing on *The Distance* LP, which went to #5, earned him a Grammy nomination for Best Male Rock Vocal Performance.

Seger, born in Dearborn, Michigan, on May 6, 1945, had been a favorite on the Detroit music scene since the 1960s. He first recorded in 1966 and charted initially in 1967 with "Heavy Music (Part 1)," which went to #103 bubbling under. The next year he cracked the Hot 100 with the frenetic organ-powered hit "Ramblin' Gamblin' Man" at #17, but was nearly a decade before he cracked the pop top 40 again with "Night Moves," which peaked at #4 in 1977.

The following year Seger made his AC chart debut with "Still the Same," which made #27 AC and #4 pop. He appeared only occasionally on the listings, as most of his singles were too raucous for the format, including "Shakedown," his first #1 pop hit in 1987. The closest he came to #1 AC after "Shame on the Moon" was "The Real Love," which hit #4 in 1991 as well as #24 pop. He remained quite active recording and touring through the late 1990s.

435 You Are

LIONEL RICHIE

Motown 1657

February 26, 1983 (6 weeks)

Writers: Brenda Richie, Lionel Richie

Producers: Lionel Richie, James Anthony Carmichael

Frustration during a recording session for easygoing Lionel Richie? That scenario sounded unlikely, yet that is what happened when the singer worked on "You Are" for his first solo album. He was not upset with the song itself, which he co-wrote with his wife Brenda, or the instrumental tracks he co-produced with James Anthony Carmichael, who had been his producer when he was with the Commodores. No, Richie was disgusted with the background vocalists who were to join him in the chorus.

One observer of the session for "You Are" was Richard Marx [see 568—"Right Here Waiting"]. The struggling musician came to Hollywood at Richie's urging, and when he and his dad got to the studio, they witnessed Richie and others' frustration as the backup singers failed to give him what he wanted on the song. "The more we sat down and watched the session, the more unhappy they were," Marx recalled.

After having worked on the vocals unsuccessfully for four days, an unusual event took place as Marx was recruited to try doing backup. "There was this long, long pause, and Lionel went out and said, 'Go out there and sing a third above the melody,'" Marx said. Richie liked what he heard and they ending by getting the whole thing done in one day. Marx ended up singing backgrounds on three other songs on Richie's debut LP.

"You Are" went to #4 pop for two weeks starting March 26, 1983, plus #2 R&B for three weeks in addition to its six-week run at #1 AC, the longest for any Richie tune except for 1984's "Hello" [see 453], which also stayed at #1 for six weeks.

While "You Are" was at #1 AC, Richie accepted his first Grammy for his singing on his previous #1 AC hit, "Truly" [see 430]. He had come very close to not attending the ceremony. His ambivalence was understandable, given that he had been nominated almost every year since 1977 without winning in various singing, writing, and producing categories, and had failed to win seven times during the previous year's ceremony alone. But his manager and wife Brenda talked him into going. "I'm glad they did," he said. "If I had missed accepting my Grammy in person, I'd be kicking myself the rest of my life."

Richie would win several more Grammys over the next year to compensate for his earlier disappointments. He also kept his hot streak going by getting another single to #1 AC [see 439—"My Love"].

436 Make Love Stay

DAN FOGELBERG

Full Moon 03525

April 9, 1983 (1 week)

Writer: Dan Fogelberg

Producers: Dan Fogelberg, Marty Lewis

By the 1980s it had become commonplace to introduce a new single or two by including it on an artist's "best of" package to interest buyers and convince them they were getting more than old material. Such was the case with "Make Love Stay," the second 45 off Dan Fogelberg's *Greatest Hits* LP of 1982. The first was "Missing You," which Fogelberg described in his liner notes to *Portrait: The Music of Dan Fogelberg* as "A somewhat disco-y production of a song I wrote while driving from Santa Fe to the ranch in Colorado." That single managed to go to #6 AC as well as #23 pop in late 1982. Its success paved the way for the release of "Make Love Stay."

While it didn't quite become a "great hit" for Fogelberg on its own, "Make Love Stay" did make #29 on the Hot 100 as well as top the AC chart. Beyond the usual acoustic guitar and vocals from Fogelberg, "Make Love Stay" was distinguished by some nice work on the drums and congas by Fogelberg's longtime studio musician Russ Kunkel, who also played on many sessions for James Taylor. Fogelberg commented in *Portrait* that "Make Love Stay" was "A sinuous piece written around a chapter of Tom Robbins' 'Still Life With Woodpecker.' Recorded (with my band) on a day off in L.A. [at Sunset Sound Studios] while on tour in 1982. [The song was] a musical question that, unfortunately, eludes me still."

Another elusive question might have been why "Make Love Stay" was the third Fogelberg single to carry "Hearts and Crafts" as its B-side. The same song appeared on the flip of "Same Old Lang Syne" in 1980, then returned on the back of "Missing You," the predecessor to "Make Love Stay." It probably was reused because it was a favorite of Fogelberg's, who included it on *Portrait* as well.

After "Make Love Stay" was gone from the charts, Fogelberg returned in 1984 with "The Language of Love," which reached #14 AC and #13 pop. He described that composition as "A sardonic look at communication (or the lack of it) in relationships. Angry, cynical, yet frighteningly true." It was also the last Fogelberg single to crack the pop top 40.

"The Language of Love" did have one thing in common with "Make Love Stay"—it featured a flip side song that would reappear, in this case, "Windows and Walls," the title tune of Fogelberg's new album. "Windows and Walls" became the B-side to the follow-up to "The Language of Love," "Believe in Me," a song that was to become the fourth #1 AC hit for Fogelberg [see 456].

437 It Might Be You

STEPHEN BISHOP

Warner 29791

April 16, 1983 (2 weeks)

Writers: Alan and Marilyn Bergman (words),
Dave Grusin (music)

Producer: Dave Grusin

One of the most frequently Oscar-nominated, and Oscar-winning, lyricists are the husband-and-wife duo Alan and Marilyn Bergman. Their first success was "The Windmills of Your Mind," which won the 1968 Academy Award for Best Song when it appeared in *The Thomas Crown Affair*. Several nominations plus one more Best Song win later (for "The Way We Were" from the film of the same name; see 208), the duo found themselves in contention once again in 1982 with "It Might Be You," a tune they wrote when they were assigned to work on the film *Tootsie*.

Tootsie, a farce starring Dustin Hoffman, who dresses like a woman to land acting roles, turned into one of 1982's biggest box office hits. The Bergmans contributed lyrics to "It Might Be You" with the music of Dave Grusin, who also did the score for the movie.

The production team designated "It Might Be You" for two sequences, according to Alan Bergman. In the first one, Hoffman's cross-dressing character, Dorothy, visits the home of the father of Jessica Lange's character and reveals how strongly "she" is attracted to Lange. "He's never made a commitment to a woman, but masquerading as a woman he's learning to become a better man," Bergman noted. "The tentative commitment of 'Something's telling me it might be you' is a big step in the right direction," added Marilyn Bergman.

Then at the end of the movie, "Dorothy" both reveals her identity and makes a definite commitment to be with Lange's character. When the tune plays there, Alan said, "At the end of the song it's 'It *must* be you.' So there is closure."

The decision to use Stephen Bishop as the vocalist for "It Might Be You" was a calculated one designed to reflect the androgynous theme of the movie. "We needed somebody who had that voice that you really couldn't really tell was a man or a woman," Alan said. "Stephen has a wonderfully ambiguous voice." Bishop, himself a songwriter, first made the AC chart in 1976 with "Save It for a Rainy Day," which peaked at #6 and had four more singles make the listing before "It Might Be You" gave him his first #1 AC hit.

"It Might Be You" also made #25 pop and looked to be a good bet to win Best Song, given the popularity of it and *Tootsie*. Unfortunately for the Bergmans, they had written lyrics for two other tunes in contention for Best Song that year— "How Do You Keep the Music Playing" from *Best Friends* and "If We Were in Love from *Yes, Giorgio*. All lost to "Up Where We Belong" from *An Officer and a Gentleman*, a tune which reached #3 AC and #1 pop when sung by Joe Cocker and Jennifer Warnes. The Bergmans had to deal with another multiple-nomination loss the next year [see 448—"The Way He Makes Me Feel"].

I Won't Hold You Back
TOTO

Columbia 03597

April 30, 1983 (3 weeks)

Writer: Steve Lukather

Producer: Toto

"It's a ridiculous name. I've always hated it," said guitarist Steve Lukather of his band's title, Toto. The group wanted a name that would be easy to say in any language, and they hit upon using a variation on original lead singer Bobby Kimball's birth surname of Toteaux. Lukather thought the spelling provided a double meaning, with the second being a reference to Dorothy's dog Toto, in *The Wizard of Oz*.

Regardless of what they called themselves, Lukather and the other members of Toto had known each other since their days as teenagers working with a touring group called Rural Still Life. "We were good friends since 1972," he said. The "we" at the time referred to bassist David Hungate, keyboardists David Paich and Steve Porcaro, and Steve's drummer brother Jeff Porcaro. All grew up in the San Fernando Valley in California, and after their Rural Still Life days they became session musicians in Los Angeles. Lukather said Toto formed after Boz Scaggs' 1976 tour, on which Lukather, Paich, and Steve Porcaro all played. Kimball, who was not on the tour, came into the fold as lead vocalist, while Hungate

rejoined them as bassist.

The group recorded its self-titled first LP in 1977 and debuted on the Hot 100 the next year with "Hold the Line," which went to #5. Two singles later Toto cracked the AC chart in 1979 with "Georgy Porgy" (#49 AC, #48 pop). In 1982 the group reached its pinnacle of success with five singles released from their *Toto IV* album, four of them making the AC chart. The biggest pop hit was "Africa," which made #1 on the Hot 100 the week of February 5, 1983, while getting to #5 AC. But on the AC chart, Lukather's song "I Won't Hold You Back" took the top honors.

"I remember writing that song in 1980, 1981," he said. "They were mixing something at Cherokee Studios and I was playing on the piano." The Porcaro brothers heard his melody and recommended he make a song out of it, but it took him some time. He wrote the chorus first, then the verse lyrics, and the bridge last. For the final recording, Lukather said, "Timothy Schmidt [formerly of the Eagles] came in and sang background vocals for me. When I heard it, I had tears in my eye."

"I Won't Hold You Back" peaked at #10 pop the week of May 7, 1983. By that time, each member of Toto had won at least four Grammys that year, including the one they all got for Album of the Year for *Toto IV*. "We were laughing," Lukather recalled of the ceremony. "We were, 'You must be joking!' It was a beautiful night. . . .I didn't even vote for myself [for Album of the Year]. I voted for Donald Fagen [with *The Nightfly* LP]."

Lukather added, "The critics hated us and were appalled that we won." The public did not seem to mind, as Toto returned to #1 AC three years later [see 504—"I'll Be Over You"].

Left to right:
Michael Porcano,
David Paich,
Joseph Williams,
Steve Lukather,
Jeff Porcano

439 My Love
LIONEL RICHIE

Motown 1677

May 21, 1983 (4 weeks)

Writer: Lionel Richie

Producers: Lionel Richie, James Anthony Carmichael

"My Love" is a perhaps overused title for several different songs since the 1960s. The first version charted before the AC listing began in 1960 with Nat "King" Cole joined by Stan Kenton and reached #47. Paul McCartney's 1973 version, a tribute to his wife, made #1 AC and pop [see 194], and earlier Petula Clark had a #1 pop and #4 AC hit in 1965 with a bouncy rendition using the words in the chorus. Julio Iglesias and Stevie Wonder took a version to #14 AC and #80 pop in 1988, and six years later the country group Little Texas got to #1 country and #83 pop with their "My Love."

But the most successful "My Love" on the AC chart was cut by Lionel Richie. The song had a country feel to it, enhanced no doubt by the fact that Kenny Rogers sang harmony on it. Richie's version was #5 pop the week of June 11, 1983, plus #6 R&B. It was the third and last single from his self-titled debut album, and like the previous two 45s it made #1 AC, which no doubt helped the LP sell more than 4 million copies in America alone.

But the release of three ballads back to back led some critics to claim Richie had lost his funky grooves and become bland. He noted the comments and planned for his next album, *Can't Slow Down*, to have more variety to it. "But I never want to go too fast and leave any of my fans behind," he told *Jet* magazine. "The whole point is to take people with me." Richie believed he had attracted different fans than the ones who followed him with the Commodores, and he did not plan to unleash a round of loud tunes that might turn them off, just to please the critics.

A few months after "My Love" peaked, Bill King of *The Atlanta Journal-Constitution* asked Richie what he would do if he came out with an album without a hit single on it. Richie responded, "I've thought about that many times. I think I would probably laugh. I didn't take this seriously to start. I was an economics major and accounting minor in school. What I'm doing here, I have no foundation for. . . . It would probably bring me to reality."

He didn't need to worry about that happening for a few years, however, as his second album got him four #1 AC hits, beginning with "All Night Long (All Night)" [see 447].

440 Never Gonna Let You Go
SERGIO MENDES

A&M 2540

June 18, 1983 (4 weeks)

Writers: Cynthia Weil (words), Barry Mann (music)

Producer: Sergio Mendes

The once-hot U.S. career of Sergio Mendes, who was big in the late 1960s, when he scored hits like "The Fool on the Hill" [see 108], went stone cold in the 1970s after he left the A&M label. Mendes drifted into unsuccessful singles, all of which missed the Hot 100 and only three of which hit the AC chart before 1983, including "Love Music" at #24 in 1973 and "The Real Thing" at #50 in 1977. What kept him financially solvent during the 1970s was performing in foreign countries for roughly half of each year.

Still, Mendes itched for another recording contract in America, and after putting together a three-song demo tape he secured a deal with his old label A&M as co-founder Herb Alpert signed him back as an artist. He spent a year and a half working on his first album of the 1980s, and it paid off by getting a hit with "Never Gonna Let You Go."

Barry Mann and Cynthia Weil wrote "Never Gonna Let You Go" in 1981. "I spent three weeks on that melody," Mann told Fred Bronson in *Billboard's Hottest Hot 100 Hits*. "I was going to write something for Maurice White. He asked me to come up with something for Earth, Wind and Fire." That soul group passed on the song, but Dionne Warwick recorded it in 1982 for an album.

Mendes's keyboardist Robbie Buchanan brought "Never Gonna Let You Go" to his attention as a potential song. "All the other songs on the album were up and festive," Mendes told Dennis Hunt of *The Los Angeles Times*. "I needed a ballad on the album, just to change the pace a bit. 'Never Gonna Let You Go' seemed like a good one." When Sergio Mendes cut his version, it featured Joe Pizzulo and Leza Miller on vocals.

"Never Gonna Let You Go" went to #4 pop for four weeks starting July 9, 1983, as well as #1 AC and #28 R&B. It was Mendes's biggest AC and pop hit since "The Fool on the Hill." Mendes followed it with "Rainbow's End," with Dan Sembello as lead vocalist, and that went to #6 AC and #52 pop.

But after 1984's "Alibis" went to #5 AC and #29 pop, Mendes had no other big hits. He did not make the Hot 100 again, and had only four other singles on the AC chart through 1987. When Mendes did "Never Gonna Let You Go," he dropped his decades-old practice of adding "Brasil," followed by the two last digits of a year, to the group's billing, but reverted to it toward the end of his AC run.

Even without any hits, Mendes remained active recording and touring through the 1980s while living in southern California. In the 1990s, as in the 1970s, a considerable amount of his work was outside of the United States, particularly in Spanish-speaking countries.

441 All This Love
DEBARGE

Gordy 1660

July 16, 1983 (3 weeks)

Writer: Eldra DeBarge

Producers: Eldra DeBarge, Iris Gordy

Although there were 10 children in the DeBarge family of Grand Rapids, Michigan, the group signed with Motown in 1980 as a quartet consisting of Eldra "El" DeBarge (born June 4, 1961), the group's lead singer and vocalist; his older brothers Mark, a trumpeter and saxophonist, and Randy, a bassist; and the oldest sibling, their sister Bunny (born March 15, 1955), also a lead singer. Their musical inspiration came from their mother, who was a gospel singer.

Their first album, *DeBarge*, attracted little attention in 1981, but 1982's *All This Love* LP did much better. It contained the group's first single to make the R&B chart, "Stop! Don't Tease Me"; first to make the Hot 100, 1983's "I Like It" at #31 pop; and the first to dent the AC chart, "All This Love."

As with much of DeBarge's early material, El DeBarge wrote and produced "All This Love." Co-producing the track with him was Iris Gordy, the niece of Motown president Berry Gordy, which was no doubt a factor in the label's decision to promote the single.

Also present on the track was another DeBarge brother, keyboardist James, who, like Mark and Randy, was older than El. His introduction into the group met with some resistance from Motown, according to El in an interview with Dennis Hunt of *The Los Angeles Times*. "The company didn't want to add a new face just when we were starting to get recognized," he said.

DeBarge's version of "All This Love" went to #5 R&B and #17 pop while spending three weeks atop the AC chart. In 1994 Patti LaBelle revived the tune and made #42 R&B.

Three months after "All This Love" peaked, DeBarge came out with a new album, *In a Special Way*, with its first single being "Time Will Reveal" at #12 AC and #18 pop. Its follow-up, "Love Me in a Special Way," came out in 1984 and went to #21 AC and #45 pop. That same year, James married Janet Jackson of the Jackson family, another Motown group, and one with which DeBarge was often compared. They had been seeing each other two years prior to the wedding, but the marriage was a disaster; it was annulled after just six months. Jackson turned her frustration over the way she felt she had been treated into material for many of the songs in her hit 1986 album *Control*.

As for the rest of DeBarge, they concentrated on their music and generated their biggest hit ever in 1985 with "Rhythm of the Night" [see 473].

442 All Time High
RITA COOLIDGE

A&M 2551

August 6, 1983 (4 weeks)

Writers: John Barry, Tim Rice

Producer: John Barry

Following in the steps of artists ranging from Shirley Bassey to Paul McCartney, Rita Coolidge became the designated vocalist for the 13th James Bond film, *Octopussy*. An "insider" with the film's producer, Albert R. "Cubby" Broccoli, played an instrumental part in getting her to sing "All Time High."

"Cubby Broccoli had a daughter at that time at home, and she worked with him on the films, and she had the idea I should do the film," Coolidge said. To prod her father to have Coolidge do the theme, she played the vocalist's records at dinner to interest him. Eventually one night he asked, "Who is that? That's the person I want to do it," and Coolidge learned through A&M executives she would be doing the theme for *Octopussy*.

Coolidge flew to London to record with John Barry and an orchestra, but found that "All Time High" was not quite ready. "Tim [Rice, Barry's collaborator] was still doing lyrics when I got there," she said. "It was a little close, down to the wire." She believed Rice had other ongoing projects which affected how much time he had to do the words for the song and therefore the tune suffered somewhat, as he did them at the last minute. "It was just like even after we did the record, the song felt a little incomplete," she said. "But people loved it."

Indeed they did. "All Time High" did well on the AC and pop charts, hitting #36 on the latter. It also got a huge amount of exposure by being on *Octopussy*, one of the top moneymaking films of 1983. But despite its popularity and praise, the record did not get an Oscar nomination for Best Song. "I was a little surprised it didn't get nominated, but I didn't expect anything at the outset," Coolidge said.

Because Coolidge still felt "All Time High" was not a finished work, she often, in concerts in the 1980s and 1990s, had her backing musicians open with the song as an overture; that way she didn't have to sing it herself.

"All Time High" was the last Hot 100 entry for Coolidge and nearly the same on the AC chart, with just "Only You" (#37 AC in 1983) and "Something Said Love" (#15 AC in 1984) coming after it. Between "We're All Alone" [see 339] and "All Time High," she had three songs make the pop top 40 and the AC top 10—"The Way You Do The Things You Do" (#9 AC, #20 pop) and "You" (#3 AC, #25 pop) in 1978 and "I'd Rather Leave While I'm in Love" (#3 AC, #38 pop) in 1980.

Coolidge remained active in the 1980s and 1990s, recording, touring, and publicizing the needs of American Indians. (She is a Cherokee.) Her most recent LP, *Thinkin' About You*, came out on the Innerworks label in 1998. As for the future, she said, "I'll just still be singing."

443 How Am I Supposed to Live Without You

LAURA BRANIGAN

Atlantic 89805

September 3, 1983 (3 weeks)

Writers: Michael Bolton, Doug James

Producer: Jack White

The belting vocals of Laura Branigan were often heard in the early 1980s, but by the middle of the decade her popularity had declined. She racked up five consecutive top 20 pop and top 30 AC songs from 1982–84 before falling out of favor, with her biggest on the AC chart being "How Am I Supposed to Live Without You."

Born in Brewster, New York, on July 3, 1957, Branigan worked as a session vocalist for cult singer/songwriter Leonard Cohen before trying for her own career in the early 1980s. Her Hot 100 debut, "All Night With Me," got to #69 in the spring of 1982, but its follow-up, "Gloria," was an international smash, a remake of a 1979 tune cut by its writer Umberto Tozzi in Italy that made #2 pop and #28 AC in early 1983. Her next single, "Solitaire," kept up the pace, hitting #7 pop and #16 AC, and then came "How Am I Supposed to Live Without You."

"How Am I Supposed to Live Without You" was originally supposed to be cut by Air Supply. However, when co-writer Michael Bolton refused to let Arista president Clive Davis alter part of the chorus, Davis released the song and Branigan recorded it as written. The ballad went to #1 AC and #12 pop and would become an even bigger hit more than six years later when redone by Bolton himself [see 575].

Branigan had two more top 20 pop songs after "How Am I Supposed to Live Without You" in 1984, "Self Control" at #4 pop and #5 AC and "The Lucky One" at #20 pop and #13 AC. In 1986 she recorded another tune written by Bolton, "I Found Someone," but it stalled at #25 AC and #90 pop. She would have only one more tune make both the AC and pop charts, 1987's "Power of Love" at #19 AC and #26 pop. Ironically, another strong-lunged singer, Celine Dion, would have much more success with the tune six years later [see 640].

After her self-titled 1990 album went only to #133 on the LP chart and produced no hits ("Moonlight on Water" made only #59 pop while "Never in a Million Years" just went to #22 AC), Branigan released material only sporadically during the rest of the 1990s, and with little success. Her remake of Donna Summer's #44 AC and #2 pop hit of 1979 "Dim All the Lights" on her 1995 *Best of Branigan* LP generated some interest on the dance chart but nothing on the others, and 1997's *Over My Heart* LP sank quickly after its release as well.

444 Tell Her About It

BILLY JOEL

Columbia 04012

September 24, 1983 (2 weeks)

Writer: Billy Joel

Producer: Phil Ramone

On his *The Nylon Curtain* album of 1982 Billy Joel created songs which touched on such themes as job layoffs and the effects of the Vietnam War. He later described *The Nylon Curtain* to Stephen Holden of *The New York Times* as "an elaborate studio album that took a year to make and whose songs were difficult to play live." For his next LP, he did a complete turnaround and focused on the pleasures and occasional pains of his life when he was growing up in Long Island. They were also a lot easier to play in concert.

In a release to *The Atlanta Journal-Constitution*, Joel stated that "I'd just gotten off the road from the Nylon Curtain tour when I started working on *An Innocent Man*. Suddenly, there were a lot of women around. I felt like I'd just come out of a cocoon. I was in love with fifteen of them at once." (He ended up going with model Christie Brinkley.)

Continuing, Joel noted, "Usually I agonize over every note. But this time the songs came pouring out of me as if they had a life of their own. I wrote 10 songs in seven weeks—something I've never done before."

As Joel wrote the new tunes, he realized they represented a readymade theme for the new album. "All the songs are based on the old records I loved as a kid. It's a guy enjoying the courtship rituals—making out, dating, love, slow dancing—and the insecurities that go with it—the gamut of passions that come with romance."

Regarding "Tell Her About It," Joel said, "I was picturing the Supremes or Martha and the Vandellas. Those girl groups always sang, 'Listen girl. . .you gotta do this.' I turned it around. . . .The whole point of the song is that you should communicate to somebody when you're in love with them, despite the insecurity it brings." For the song's video, Joel kept the nostalgic atmosphere of the tune going by pretending he was a guest singer on *The Ed Sullivan Show*. That was a reasonable notion, given that his inspiration for "Tell Her About It," the Supremes, appeared often on that show in the 1960s (Sullivan at least once forgot their names and introduced them as "The girls").

As the leadoff single to *An Innocent Man*, "Tell Her About It" performed excellently, going to #1 AC and pop simultaneously the week of September 24, 1983, followed by an additional week atop the Hot 100. The hits just kept coming on the AC chart after that, as of the six singles released from *An Innocent Man*, four made #1 AC, including "Tell Her About It."

445 True
SPANDAU BALLET

Chrysalis 42720

October 8, 1983 (1 week)

Writer: Gary Kemp

Producers: Tony Swain, Steve Jolley, Spandau Ballet

"True" was the 10th consecutive entry in the United Kingdom for Spandau Ballet, a quintet formed in London in 1979 that was far more popular in their native country than in America. Vocalist Tony Hadley was the front man for the group, which included Gary Kemp as its guitarist and keyboardist, his brother Martin Kemp as bassist, John Keeble as drummer, and Steve Norman as saxophonist and percussionist. Gary Kemp also served as the group's primary songwriter.

A band known for its sartorial splendor, especially in its videos, Spandau Ballet was composed of men from working-class families. They did share a love of fashion and soul-based rhythms that came through in their club performances in England, and their appearances led them to a recording contract within a year of their creation.

Their first song to make the British chart was "To Cut a Long Story Short," which hit #5 in 1980. Spandau Ballet then had six other tunes make the top 20 of the U.K. chart before "True," the highest-charting being "Chant No. 1 (I Don't Need This Pressure On)" at #3 in 1981, but none of them made an impression on American buyers.

That trend changed with the romantic "True," recorded by Spandau Ballet at the Compass Point Studios in the Bahamas. The single hit #1 for four weeks in Great Britain starting the week of April 30, 1983, before crossing the ocean and peaking at #1 AC plus #4 pop for four weeks starting October 8, 1983. Spandau Ballet even made the R&B chart with the tune, peaking at #76.

"True" would be Spandau Ballet's only #1 hit. Its follow-up, "Gold," hit #2 in the U.K. while making #17 AC and #29 pop in 1984. "Communication," a #12 British entry before "True," came after "Gold" in America and made #59 in the spring of 1984. "Only When You Leave" was the group's last AC and pop single, hitting #35 AC and #34 pop in mid-1984.

Spandau Ballet's following may have died in the United States by the mid-1980s, but the group remained an English favorite through the rest of the decade. The last recorded new product by Spandau Ballet came out in 1989, when "Be Free With Your Love" reached #42 on the British chart. The following year the Kemps received excellent critical notices for their performances as true-life twin murderers in The Krays. But the only member of Spandau Ballet to establish a significant solo musical career was Tony Hadley, who had a few entries on the U.K. chart starting in 1992 with "Lost in Your Love" at #42.

"True" had a brief revival when the rap duo PM Dawn sampled "True" for their record "Set Adrift on Memory Bliss." The tune hit #1 on the Hot 100 the week of November 30, 1991.

446 Islands in the Stream
KENNY ROGERS WITH DOLLY PARTON

RCA 13615

October 15, 1983 (4 weeks)

Writers: Barry Gibb, Robin Gibb, Maurice Gibb

Producers: Barry Gibb, Karl Richardson, Albhy Galuten

Having lost Lionel Richie [see 418], Kenny Rogers turned to the Bee Gees. He was not a total stranger to the group, having been at Maurice Gibb's wedding to Lulu in 1969, but this was their first time working together professionally. Barry, Maurice, and Robin Gibb agreed to do an album with him if only they could write and produce the songs, a condition which Rogers agreed to.

One of the tunes Rogers tried to record was "Islands in the Stream," a title inspired by the Hemingway novel of the same name, but "I just couldn't get into it." Then the Bee Gees told him that "Originally this was written as an R&B duet." Duets not being a foreign concept to Rogers, he considered doing it with a female. When Dolly Parton's name came up, the idea was greeted with enthusiasm by everyone involved, but no one knew how to get her to do the record.

Luckily, Rogers' manager had the connection. "Ken Kragen knew her manager, Sandy Gallin, and he asked her to do it," Rogers said. Parton accepted, and so the Bee Gees produced them in the studio. The sheer magnitude of the talent involved at the session impressed even Rogers, who recalled that "It was electric, more so than anything I knew before."

Music fans across America heartily agreed, as "Islands in the Stream" hit the peak of the AC, pop, and country charts. After two weeks at #1 AC, it topped the pop and country charts October 22 and 29, 1983, while staying at the AC pole position at the same time. Rogers and Parton also won a Grammy nomination for Best Pop Performance by a Duo or Group With Vocal.

The next year Rogers and Parton teamed up again to do a Christmas TV special, The Greatest Gift of All, and the title tune made #40 AC, #53 country, and #81 pop in early 1985. Later that year the Rogers-Parton duet "Real Love" went to #1 country the week of August 24, 1985, plus #13 AC and #91 pop. But when he and Parton did "Love Is Strange" in 1990, all it managed was #21 country. Concerning their waning appeal then, Rogers said, "I think we got too dangerously identified with each other." Rogers saw Parton less as he pursued other projects in the 1990s, but he said, "I still consider her a good friend."

The other two singles Rogers did with the Bee Gees fared respectably. "This Woman" hit #2 AC for three weeks in 1984 as well as #23 pop, but only its B-side, "Buried Treasure," made the country chart at #3. After that one, "Eyes That See in the Dark" reached #4 AC, #30 country, and #79 pop. Then came Rogers' eighth #1 AC hit [see 463—"What About Me?"].

447 All Night Long (All Night)
LIONEL RICHIE

Motown 1698

November 12, 1983 (4 weeks)

Writer: Lionel Richie

Producers: Lionel Richie, James Anthony Carmichael

For his sophomore LP, *Can't Slow Down*, Lionel Richie came out a tad funkier than he had on his debut release. "This album has a little bit for everybody," Richie told Bill King of *The Atlanta Journal-Constitution*. "You've got some people that like Lionel Richie sweet. You've got some people who like Lionel Richie sentimental, like Hallmark Cards. . . .I don't want to lose those people. They're the ones that discovered me. You don't walk away from them trying to be hip. But I do like to catch them off guard. Be unusual, but still make the records approachable."

Of the "off guard" selections on his album, Richie told King, "Besides 'All Night Long,' I went and got Steve Lukather, the lead guitar player from Toto, to come in and nail me one of the all-time great rock solos I've ever heard on 'Running With the Night.' Instead of Lionel Richie the balladeer, that will be Lionel Richie the rocker."

Both up-tempo songs did surprisingly well on both the AC and pop charts. "Running With the Night" made #6 AC and #7 pop in early 1984, although some AC stations did edit out Lukather's guitar solo. But "Running With the Night" was not the leadoff single for *Can't Slow Down*; "All Night Long (All Night)" was.

The song had a Caribbean flavor which Richie enhanced with the Jamaican chant "Tom be lid de say di moi ya, yeah, jambo, jumbo." He admitted in *USA Today* that "I was worried about getting the right words and about pronouncing them right. My wife's gynecologist is Jamaican, so for a week I was after him. Finally he said, 'Look, Lionel, I'm right in the middle of an appointment, can we talk later?'"

"All Night Long (All Night)" was a triple #1 on *Billboard*'s charts. It made #1 R&B for seven weeks starting October 22, 1983, then moved over to the AC and pop charts where it began a simultaneous #1 AC and pop run of four weeks from November 12, 1983. "All Night Long (All Night)" also got Grammy nominations for Record and Song of the Year and Best Male Pop Vocal Performance. Richie later performed the tune to a worldwide audience at the closing ceremonies of the 1984 Summer Olympics in Los Angeles, California.

And in the "silly but interesting trivia" category, *Billboard* Chartbeat writer Paul Grein noted in his November 12, 1983 column reader Steve Nadel's observation that Richie's #1 AC solo hits formed the complete sentence "You are truly my love all night long." (Author's note: To get that sequence you have to reverse the titles of the first and second hits.)

448 The Way He Makes Me Feel
BARBRA STREISAND

Columbia 04177

December 10, 1983 (2 weeks)

Writers: Alan and Marilyn Bergman (words),
Michel Legrand (music)

Producers: Phil Ramone, Dave Grusin

When Barbra Streisand finally got the chance to do her long-awaited movie adaptation of Isaac Bashevis Singer's story *Yentl*, she discussed the project with her good friends, lyricists Alan Bergman and his wife Marilyn. "We long had the idea of musicalizing the story," said Alan Bergman. "It's the inner life of the character that leant itself to a musical interior monologue."

Michel Legrand and the Bergmans created the score of the film, which Streisand starred in, directed, and co-wrote. *Yentl* is the story of a woman in late-nineteenth-century Poland who must masquerade as a man in order to attend a yeshiva, a talmudic academy for males only. "We discussed places where songs would occur in the script," said Bergman. After Legrand created the melodies, the Bergmans wrote the lyrics for songs in the movie, all of which were sung by Streisand.

Two tunes in *Yentl* earned Oscar nominations for Best Song, "Papa, Can You Hear Me?" and "The Way He Makes Me Feel." Regarding the inspiration for the latter, Alan explained it related to one of the central dilemmas for Streisand's character in *Yentl*. "She is being sexually awakened by a young man [played by Mandy Patinkin] but obviously cannot tell him how she feels," he said.

For the single release of "The Way He Makes Me Feel," Streisand did not use the movie soundtrack version. She redid her vocal and used a different, more modern arrangement. "I liked it a lot," Bergman said of the single. "The picture was in its period, so there were no drums on the score, no pianos. . . .In order to bring more attention to the song, there was an attempt to contemporize the orchestrations."

The revised "The Way He Makes Me Feel" reached #40 pop in addition to #1 AC in late 1983. "Papa, Can You Hear Me?," the follow-up to "The Way He Makes Me Feel," only made #26 AC without cracking the Hot 100. Both tunes lost the Oscar to "Flashdance. . .What a Feeling" from *Flashdance*. The Bergmans, who had been competing against themselves for Best Song in prior years [see 437—"It Might Be You"], took the situation in stride. "The most important thing for us is the nominations and the attention to the songs that they afford," said Mr. Bergman.

The Bergmans could take consolation in that they and Legrand won Best Score Adaptation for *Yentl*. But Streisand found herself locked out of any Oscar nominations in the Best Actress, Director, or Writing categories despite considerable box office success and critical acclaim for her work. Streisand and the Bergmans went onto further movie and musical successes through the 1990s, although nothing since "The Way He Makes Me Feel" has attained the #1 AC spot.

449 Read 'Em and Weep

BARRY MANILOW

Arista 9101

December 24, 1983 (6 weeks)

Writer: Jim Steinman

Producer: Jim Steinman

In late 1982 Barry Manilow was doing relatively well on the AC chart, but he had been through several years of declining popularity (his last top 10 pop hit was in late 1980 with "I Made It Through the Rain," which finished #10 pop plus #4 AC). The song chosen for him to break his streak was "Read 'Em and Weep," a tune first popularized by Meat Loaf on his 1981 LP *Dead Ringer*. Writer Jim Steinman also produced Meat Loaf's rendition.

Manilow recalled the scenario in his autobiography *Sweet Life*. "I had finished recording Jim Steinman's 'Read 'Em and Weep,' and everyone at Arista was very excited about it. When I listened to it, I felt proud of my interpretation, but once again, there was an emptiness about singing a song I hadn't written. I felt especially distant from this record because, due to the craziness of the tour [in Great Britain in 1983], I hadn't even been able to produce or arrange the song."

Then Manilow read "some especially negative press clippings about my music," and while he did not note whether reading them made him weep, he did say that "my empty feelings about 'Read 'Em and Weep' made me reevaluate my entire public image." He decided that from then on he would do the music he wanted to do and not what was dictated to him, even if it cost him some of his following.

"Read 'Em and Weep" became Manilow's biggest hit on the AC chart, spending #1 six weeks there, and while it did not reach the pop top 10, its peak of #18 on the Hot 100 made it his best showing on that chart since "The Old Songs" hit #15 in 1981 [see 413]. Manilow even grew to like the song as done in concert. "It was a very well-written, dramatic song, and as a performer, I was really able to sink my teeth into it," he wrote. "But it was emotionally draining for me each night, because I was feeling so ambiguous about its success."

There wasn't any ambiguity about the fact that no Manilow single after "Read 'Em and Weep" made the Hot 100. Following the AC-only appearances in 1984 of "You're Looking Hot Tonight" (#25) and "When October Goes" (#6), Manilow released a jazz album he recorded with other top musicians including Mel Torme called *Paradise Cafe*. The switch did not turn off his AC fans, as the title tune hit #24 in 1985.

Manilow kept making the AC charts with his singles on a fairly regular basis through 1990. In the 1990s he scaled back his recording activities in favor of concert performances, where he remained a very popular artist with a devoted fan base, primarily though not exclusively female.

1984

450 Think of Laura
CHRISTOPHER CROSS

Warner 29658

February 4, 1984 (4 weeks)

Writer: Christopher Cross

Producer: Michael Omartian

Christopher Cross meant to release his second album earlier than at the start of 1983, but two things got in the way, one professional and one personal. The first was that the unexpected popularity of "Arthur's Theme (Best That You Can Do)" [see 410] tied him up touring and promoting that record in 1981–82. "'Arthur' was great for my international market," he told Dennis Hunt of *The Los Angeles Times*. "I wasn't big overseas before that. After 'Arthur,' my first album came out in a lot of countries for the first time."

The second was that while he was promoting "Arthur's Theme," Cross' seven-year marriage collapsed. He and his wife separated in 1981, and the divorce became final a year later in July 1982. "It was time consuming and emotionally consuming," he told Hunt. "I wanted to handle things the right way. I was concerned about my son [seven-year-old Justin] and how he was going to handle it. When that kind of stuff is on your mind, you're not in great shape to write."

But he did finally create new songs, thanks to a new love in his life, and one of them, the mournful "Think of Laura," got a jolt in popularity by being featured on ABC-TV's daily soap opera *General Hospital* as the character of Luke Spencer, played by Anthony Geary, pined for his missing wife Laura. It was the second tune that the soap had helped get to #1 AC, the first being "Baby, Come to Me" [see 433].

"Think of Laura" went to #9 pop the weeks of February 4 and 11, 1984, while riding atop the AC chart. Its success did not translate to its follow-up, "A Chance for Heaven." Although that tune was designated as the swimming theme from the Official Music of the Summer Olympics in Los Angeles in 1984, it went only to #16 AC and #76 pop. More than a year passed before his next entry, "Charm the Snake," became his last Hot 100 entry, at #68 pop. Cross had two more AC entries after that, "Loving Strangers" from the film *Nothing in Common* at #27 in 1986 and "I Will (Take You Forever)" with Frances Ruffelle at #41 in 1988.

By the end of the 1980s Cross had moved away from Los Angeles, dropping out from recording as well for a few years. His next album was 1992's *Rendezvous*, but few made an appointment to buy it. He did not give up, however, and in June 1998 he came out with his seventh LP, a double-CD set titled *Walking in Avalon* that attracted little attention.

In the late 1990s, given his long absence from the charts, it appeared unlikely that Cross would get another chart-topper in what was left in his career, but that did not appear to bother him. As he said in a statement on his official Web site on the Internet, "Once I stopped worrying about my next #1 hit and focused on fulfilling my promise as an artist within myself, I think it's all come together for me."

451 An Innocent Man
BILLY JOEL

Columbia 04259

March 3, 1984 (1 week)

Writer: Billy Joel

Producer: Phil Ramone

Billy Joel told Melinda Newman in *Billboard* in 1997, "'An Innocent Man' was written to evoke the same kind of feelings that I got when I heard Ben E. King and the Drifters [do] those Leiber and Stoller songs with a little bit of Latin lilt in [them], with that bass, boom, like 'Under the Boardwalk' or 'Stand By Me.' Also, there's a high note in that recording—that was done in 1983—and I had a suspicion that was going to be the last time I was going to be able to hit those notes, so why not go out in a blaze of glory? That was the end of Billy's high note."

Joel told Stephen Holden of *The New York Times* that the *An Innocent Man* album "was a romantic tribute to my rhythm and blues roots and the discovery of love when you're a teenager." He also made clear that if anyone thought he had a few leftover tunes from this or any other LP, he or she was wrong. "When I'm doing an album, I only complete 10 or 11 songs," he told Holden. "If I don't like something I've started, rather than continuing to work on it, I toss it into the trash can. There's no backlog of Billy Joel material. You'll never hear my basement tapes, because there are none." (Joel did do a live album in 1981 titled *Songs in the Attic*, but the title referred to mostly obscure material he cut and released on earlier LPs and not any tracks that were in company vaults.)

Referring to his writing process, Joel said, "While I get ideas for songs all the time, I've found that the pressure to record has been the major motivation factor for me to finish anything. Once I get an idea, I write it down in a notebook. Six months later, when it has marinated, I'll look at it and probably think of something better. . . .Then when I finally go into the studio, 80 percent of the actual recording process consists of cutting things out, changing, revising and editing.

"I write the tunes first and then the lyrics, which are dictated by the mood of the music. Though the two have to fit together, for me the language is really secondary. It's the strangest thing. . . .It may take me a year to figure out why I wrote some of the songs I did, why I said some of the things I said, and what I really meant."

A lot of music buyers apparently wanted to put their minds to the meaning of Joel's songs in 1984, as a remixed version of his first solo album, 1971's *Cold Spring Harbor*, got onto the album chart for a few weeks along with *An Innocent Man*. It peaked at #158, while *An Innocent Man* got to #4 on the LP chart and ended up selling more than seven million copies. "An Innocent Man" the single made #10 pop the week of February 25, 1984 before getting to #1 AC.

452 Got a Hold On Me
CHRISTINE MCVIE

Warner 29372

March 10, 1984 (4 weeks)

Writers: Christine McVie, Todd Sharp

Producer: Russ Titelman

Keyboardist Christine McVie, best known as the other female vocalist in Fleetwood Mac along with Stevie Nicks, has done solo albums twice. The first one came in 1969, when she was part of a sexually mixed aggregation called Chicken Shack, following some work playing for the Spencer Davis Group. At that time she was going by her maiden name of Christine Perfect (she was born in Birmingham, England, on July 12, 1943).

"I had married John McVie [in 1968]," she recalled to Robert Palmer of *The New York Times*. "And I had quit playing with Chicken Shack. I was quite happy being a housewife. But I had sung a soul ballad on my last album with Chicken Shack, and a British music paper gave me an award for it—top female vocalist of the year."

Her manager at the time convinced her to cut an album and do a few concerts, to wring out as much success from that award as possible, but the LP flopped. Then personnel changes in her husband's band, Fleetwood Mac, led her to take over the keyboard position in the group in 1970, and her stab at a solo career was forgotten until Sire Records reissued the LP in 1976 as *The Legendary Christine Perfect Album* to capitalize on McVie's newfound celebrity as a member of Fleetwood Mac. At the same time, her relationship with John McVie deteriorated and their marriage broke up, though the divorce was not enough to make her leave what was one of the hottest bands in the world at the time. [For more details on the history of Fleetwood Mac, see 526—"Little Lies."] But when Nicks and Lindsay Buckingham took time off to do solo LPs in the early 1980s, McVie figured she would do one too.

Most of the tunes on her self-titled album were as mellow as her vocals on such Fleetwood Mac favorites as "You Make Loving Fun" and "Hold Me." "Maybe it isn't the most adventurous album in the world, but I wanted to be honest and please my own ears with it," she told Christopher Connelly of *Rolling Stone*. "I tend to like the traditional sound: three-part harmony, guitar and piano. I mean, a well-played guitar is a joy forever."

The debut single from the album, "Got a Hold on Me," got ahold of the #1 AC post while stopping at #10 pop the week of March 24, 1984. One other 45 came from the LP, "Love Will Show Us How," which made #32 AC and #30 pop. After their releases McVie concentrated on her work with Fleetwood Mac, and even though she left the group for a few years in the 1990s, she has yet to put out another solo album.

453 Hello
LIONEL RICHIE

Motown 1722

April 7, 1984 (6 weeks)

Writer: Lionel Richie

Producers: Lionel Richie, James Anthony Carmichael

With "Hello," Lionel Richie greeted the British charts with the longest-running #1 song by a Motown artist since 1978, when Richie's own "Three Times a Lady," when he was with the Commodores, also notched five weeks. Oddly, during the week of May 5, 1984, "Hello" was #1 in the United Kingdom and "Against All Odds (Take a Look at Me Now)" by Phil Collins was #2, while on the pop chart in America the positions of those two records were reversed. The same week, "Hello" began a three-week run atop the R&B chart as well. The following week, May 12, the song went to #1 on the Hot 100 for two weeks. That made "Hello" the first record since "Karma Chameleon" by Culture Club to be #1 pop in both America and England and the first record to be #1 AC, pop, and R&B simultaneously since Richie's "All Night Long (All Night)" [see 447].

But "Hello" was not the immediate follow-up to "All Night Long (All Night)." Another up-tempo number from *Can't Slow Down*, "Running With the Night," came out in late 1983 and peaked at #6 AC as well as #7 pop. A hit but not a megahit, the record broke Richie's string of five consecutive #1 AC songs. "Hello" put him back on top and started a second wave of four back-to-back AC chart-toppers.

Richie had originally written "Hello" for his 1982 solo debut album, but his wife Brenda Richie argued that it should be included it on *Can't Slow Down*, which is where it ended up. Besides singing on the tune, Richie did vocal arrangements and played piano.

In July 1984, shortly after "Hello" reached its peak, a songwriter named Marjorie Hoffman White claimed that Richie had "completely incorporated" the melody of a tune she copyrighted in 1978 called "I'm Not Ready to Go" for "Hello." However, despite the backing of a musicologist who concurred with her charge, White did not get a songwriting credit for "Hello" and Richie remained the sole writer for the tune.

"Hello" was Richie's last #1 on the pop and R&B charts until "Say You, Say Me" in 1985 [see 484]. On the AC chart, however, he led the listing with his next release, "Stuck on You" [see 459], later in 1984. Before the end of 1984, Richie had also made it onto the AC chart as a writer and producer, with "Missing You," a tribute to Marvin Gaye sung by Diana Ross that went to #4 AC and #10 pop.

454 The Longest Time
BILLY JOEL

Columbia 04400

May 19, 1984 (2 weeks)

Writer: Billy Joel

Producer: Phil Ramone

Billy Joel doo-wopped his way through a rare a capella AC and pop hit in "The Longest Time," the fourth single from his *An Innocent Man* LP and the third one to reach #1 AC. It fell short of that mark on the pop chart, but the #14 showing was quite respectable.

In an article for *The Atlanta Journal-Constitution* in 1984, Joel noted about "The Longest Time" that "All the background voices are me—the bass part, the high parts, the harmonies. . . .I didn't want to at first. I said, 'Well, the problem with doing your own background is you sound too much like yourself—you don't get enough personality.' . . .so I sang one voice as if I were black, another as if I were an Italian from Newark. The bad part wasn't staying in key, it was staying in key as an Italian from Newark."

"The Longest Time" did remind several listeners of doo-wop records of the 1950s and early 1960s, but some politically correct critics condemned Joel for not including any black actors when he did the video for the song except for a cleaning man who comes upon Joel and his friends singing at the end of the song. The stereotyped role of the black actor may have been the issue, because there had been no controversy when Joel's other neo-doo-wop tune on *An Innocent Man*, "Uptown Girl," came out as a single and video prior to "The Longest Time," although it featured no blacks either. (For the record, what it did have was future wife Christie Brinkley attempting to dance with Joel and several other actors playing auto mechanics cum chorus line boys.)

"Uptown Girl," which came out between "Tell Her About It" and "An Innocent Man," went to #2 AC for four weeks and #3 pop in late 1983. The paean to the Four Seasons falsetto sound earned him a Grammy nomination for Best Male Pop Vocal Performance. His only other Grammy nomination in connection with *An Innocent Man* was for Album of the Year.

Phil Ramone, who spent nearly a decade producing Joel's albums, including *An Innocent Man*, had high praise for him and his song selection when he talked with Lynn Van Matre of *The Chicago Tribune* in 1985. "Here's a guy who is very eclectic, who is afraid to say the same thing twice, which makes a great common bond for both of us. Looking back, it's been an amazing time. I would say that I'm a good editor of the songs he brings in. The fact that he bounces songs off of me is delicious. Once he gets into the studio, he really gets into it. He's here on time every day and he feels guilty if he leaves too early."

After "The Longest Time," Joel had one more #1 AC hit from *An Innocent Man* [see 460—"Leave a Tender Moment Alone"].

455 Time After Time
CYNDI LAUPER

Portrait 04432

June 2, 1984 (3 weeks)

Writers: Cyndi Lauper, Rob Hyman

Producer: Rick Chertoff

In conversation Cyndi Lauper sounded like Betty Boop crossed with Bugs Bunny, but when she sang, the diminutive orange-haired vocalist was serious and pure, able to sing both rockers and ballads with ease. Her success with the moody "Time After Time" after her initial breakthrough with the novelty "Girls Just Wanna Have Fun" (#2 pop, 1984) showed she had enough talent to be more than a one-hit wonder.

Born in Queens, New York, on June 20, 1953, Lauper began singing professionally in clubs in the early 1970s, but by the middle of the decade she had grown tired of performing others' hits in small venues. That approach changed in 1977 when she partnered with keyboardist/saxophonist John Turi to form Blue Angel, a band which finally got a record contract in 1980. Its self-titled album received solid critical notices, but a lack of sales and dissension among band members led to Blue Angel dissolving two years later. The next year (1983), Lauper signed her own solo record deal.

"I decided to just go ahead and do it, though I hadn't written many songs," she was quoted in Irwin Stambler's *Encyclopedia of Pop, Rock and Soul* as saying. "I had broken my partnership with John Turi—and I didn't like the idea of just singing other people's songs. But for my debut album, producer Rick Chertoff and I selected songs that allowed me to keep my integrity and that meant something to me. And I wrote some too."

"Time After Time" was one of those she wrote. The second single from Lauper's *She's So Unusual* album, it went to #1 AC first, then #1 AC and pop simultaneously for two weeks starting June 9, 1984. It also went to #78 R&B. At the Grammys "Time After Time" got a nomination for Song of the Year and *She's So Unusual* for Album of the Year. But the only statuette Lauper claimed that night was for Best New Artist.

Three other top 30 pop singles came off *She's So Unusual*, but only one of them made the AC chart—"All Through the Night," which hit #4 in late 1984. With her wide range of funk- and rock-related songs, she scored much more often on the Hot 100 than the AC chart the rest of the 1980s, with her only 45s to make the latter being "True Colors" at #5 in 1986, "What's Going On" at #29 in 1987, and "I Drove All Night" at #43 in 1989.

That last song was virtually her last entry on the pop chart until 1995, when "Hey Now (Girls Just Want to Have Fun)," a remake of her first hit for the movie *To Wong Foo*, hit #87. Lauper in fact recorded infrequently during the 1990s, but could still be seen occasionally on the movie screen (e.g., *Life With Mikey*) and on television (a guest spot on *Mad About You*). What she will do next is anybody's guess.

456 Believe in Me

DAN FOGELBERG

Full Moon 04447

June 23, 1984 (1 week)

Writer: Dan Fogelberg

Producers: Dan Fogelberg, Marty Lewis

"Believe in Me" was nearly a one-man operation by Dan Fogelberg, as he did not only guitar and vocals for it but bass as well. The only other musician in the studio when it was recorded on May 25, 1983, was Mike Hanna on acoustic guitar. In his liner notes to *Portrait: The Music of Dan Fogelberg*, the singer/songwriter cryptically wrote that "Believe in Me" was "One of my best love songs. Written at my old house in Nederland, Colorado, while building the ranch. Obviously, all was not well."

The latter statement could have described many things, although it appears to be a comment on his married life, which began after he moved into the ranch he built in Colorado and ended in divorce after a few years. During his newlywed period, he wrote the song "Lonely in Love," which he later admitted was an odd theme to sing for someone in his position.

After "Believe in Me" peaked at #48 pop, Fogelberg hit the Hot 100 only twice more, with "Go Down Easy" (#85 in 1985) and "She Don't Look Back" (#84 in 1987). He was more successful on the AC chart, with "Believe in Me" being followed by "Sweet Magnolia and the Traveling Salesman" in 1984 (#36), then "Go Down Easy" in 1985 (#6), and "Lonely in Love" (#2) and "Seeing You Again" (#15), both in 1987. His biggest recent AC success was a medley of the old Cascades hit "Rhythm of the Rain" [see 24] with the Beatles' "Rain," which went to #3 in 1990.

The decline in Fogelberg's popularity may have been because he released songs only sporadically in the late 1980s and 1990s (generally two to three years between records), or because his subject matter had less appeal to listeners. He wrote songs about the environment, many of them critical of what was done during the Reagan and Bush administrations, and others dealing with metaphysical and spiritual concerns regarding the Earth. Fogelberg knew such material might have serious problems commercially, but was committed to writing music about the concerns that interested him as an artist and human being.

In the late 1990s, between working on his albums and touring, Fogelberg based himself at his home in Colorado and continued to refuse to compromise his artistic vision. "You've got to just follow your heart and do your best work," he told Paul Zollo about his philosophy of life in an article in *Portrait*. "For better or worse, I have followed my heart. There is no doubt in my mind or heart that everything I've done is exactly what I've intended to do."

457 Almost Paradise . . . Love Theme From *Footloose*

MIKE RENO AND ANN WILSON

Columbia 04418

June 30, 1984 (1 week)

Writers: Eric Carmen, Dean Pitchford

Producer: Keith Olson

"Almost Paradise" was the only one of five singles released from the soundtrack to the movie *Footloose* to top the AC chart. Deniece Williams' "Let's Hear It for the Boy" went to #3 AC, while Bonnie Tyler's "Holding Out for a Hero," Shalamar's "Dancing in the Sheets," and the title track sung by Kenny Loggins all missed the AC chart while hitting the pop top 40. (Williams' and Loggins' records hit #1 pop, and the album itself made #1 for 10 weeks starting April 21, 1984.)

The first vocalist the producers contacted for the song was Ann Wilson, lead singer of the group Heart. "They had this song and wanted to put together this duet," she said. "They asked me who I wanted to sing with. And I said Lou Gramm, Paul Rodgers, I gave them this whole list of names. And then they came back and said, 'You're singing with Mike Reno.' And I said, 'Oh, OK!'"

Reno, lead singer for the group Loverboy, had *not* been on Wilson's list. She had nothing against him. It was just that his band's hard-driving sound did not seem right for the song. She remembered that nothing about the demo seemd to point to Reno. "The demo was real amazing, Eric Carmen singing with a piano. It was really gospelly," she said.

Wilson said she had no objection to trying him. But just before the day they planned to record the song in Chicago, the one time when neither group was touring, she fell in her hotel room, breaking her wrist. Although she was in a lot of pain, the session went ahead as planned. And Wilson, worried that drugs given to ease her pain could affect her singing, did the song with no painkillers whatsoever.

Though Dean Pitchford co-wrote the script and all the songs for *Footloose*, he was not directly involved in producing the song in terms of the vocals, Wilson recalled. "By the time we got to the studio, the track was already laid down," she said. Keith Olson supervised Wilson and Reno's efforts on the song.

"Almost Paradise" peaked at #7 pop the weeks of July 14 and 21, 1984. When told it would possibly be released as a single from the album, Wilson said she had an "I'll believe it when I see it" attitude. However, she was less amazed by its success as a 45 than she was by another development. "I was most surprised by how it became a prom and wedding song," she said.

Though she said of "Almost Paradise" that "I've always loved it. I thought it was a great song" and "It was very good for [Heart]," she and Reno did not record another song together again and saw each other only occasionally afterward. Heart never did the song in concert, but that was not the case with Wilson's next #1 single [see 491—"These Dreams"].

458 If Ever You're in My Arms Again

PEABO BRYSON

Elektra 69728

July 7, 1984 (4 weeks)

Writers: Cynthia Weil, Michael Masser, Tom Snow

Producer: Michael Masser

Robert Peabo Bryson, born in Greenville, South Carolina, on April 13, 1951, and raised in Mauldin, South Carolina, first became familiar to AC listeners primarily as a duet partner before he notched his own solo success with "If Ever You're in My Arms Again." Though he recorded initially on Bang in 1970, he did not get a permanent record deal until 1977 with Capitol. His "Reach for the Sky" gave Bryson his debut on the R&B chart in 1977, but he remained largely unfamiliar outside the soul market until he switched to Elektra in 1983.

"Capitol saw me as a 'ghetto' artist," Bryson complained to Dennis Hunt of *The Los Angeles Times*. "They thought I could sell only to blacks; they wouldn't see my pop potential. It all boiled down to money. They were making money on me in the black market. It was a low-overhead situation for them. To push me as a pop artist in the expensive pop market would have cost a lot of money. And they didn't want to spend the money."

Bryson's first AC entry was "Lovers After All," a duet with Melissa Manchester that made #25 in 1981 as well as #54 pop and # R&B. Three consecutive duets he did with Roberta Flack then made the AC chart—"Tonight, I Celebrate My Love" (#4 in 1983), "You're Looking Like Love to Me" (#5 in 1984), and "I Just Came Here to Dance" (#15 in 1984). But none of them had the impact of his first solo hit, "If Ever You're in My Arms Again."

"I co-wrote that one with Michael Masser, and he and I made a feeble attempt to do a lyric," Tom Snow recalled. Once their attempts proved nonproductive, they gave the melody to Snow's erstwhile writing partner Cynthia Weil. "She liked the music and got a lyric for it."

Snow said he and Masser embarked on writing together because "We were having hits at the same time." They did not plan to do it specifically for Peabo Bryson, but Snow remembered thinking that Masser, an active producer as well as songwriter, probably had it in mind to produce the song himself. Masser did produce the Bryson version, with Snow playing keyboards on the session. Despite the success of this collaboration, it was the only hit record he and Masser wrote together.

"If Ever You're in My Arms Again" was a hit on three different formats, making #1 AC, #6 R&B, and #10 pop (the pop position was held for three weeks beginning August 18). Bryson returned to the top of the AC chart in 1993, in a duet with Regina Belle [see 628].

459 Stuck on You

LIONEL RICHIE

Motown 1746

August 4, 1984 (5 weeks)

Writer: Lionel Richie

Producers: Lionel Richie, James Anthony Carmichael

With the ascension of "Stuck on You," Lionel Richie had the distinction of being the first artist to have at least one single from the same album on the AC chart every week for a year. The string began when "All Night Long (All Night)" entered the listing the week of September 24, 1983 and ended when "Stuck on You" departed from the #1 in September 1984.

"Stuck on You" held at #3 pop for two weeks starting August 25, 1984. The first week it stood behind Ray Parker Jr.'s "Ghostbusters" at #1 and Tina Turner's "What's Love Got to Do With It" at #2, and the second week "What's Love Got to Do With It" was at #1 while John Waite's "Missing You" took over the #2 spot. It also went to #8 R&B and #24 country. "Stuck on You" was the first Richie single to make the country chart, but two years later another of his tunes got there: "Deep River Woman" with Alabama hit #10 [see 511—"Ballerina Girl"].

But at the same time that Richie was broadening his appeal, some fans complained that he was selling out the audience base that had brought him success. The Promoters Association, a group of prominent black concert promoters, announced a boycott of Richie's 1984 tour in the May 12, 1984 issue of *Billboard*, claiming he was ignoring them in favor of Caucasian promoters. The group's founder, Jesse Boseman, claimed that "Richie's situation is gross. Blacks helped make Richie when he was with the Commodores. He had a black manager and a black base. Now he has a booking agent, Howard Rose, who has stopped adequate black participation."

Richie's manager at the time, Ken Kragen, responded to the charges with the following statements: "Those promoters—black and white—who helped Richie when he first went out last fall have dates on this tour. I don't know what they [the protesting promoters] did for the Commodores, but this is a separate career." While acknowledging that black attendance at Richie's last tour was only two to five percent of the audience, Kragen said that plans were afoot to do much advertising for Richie's concerts on black-owned radio stations, and for Richie to make contributions to the black community with some of the money that would come from Richie's reported $8.5 million contract with Pepsi.

The controversy never quite resolved itself, although Richie's black audiences did not get appreciably bigger over the years and remained overwhelmingly white. As for "Stuck on You," it found new life in 1998 when it appeared as background music for a TV commercial for a starch product.

285

460 Leave a Tender Moment Alone

BILLY JOEL

Columbia 04514

September 8, 1984 (2 weeks)

Writer: Billy Joel

Producer: Phil Ramone

David Sheff, a music critic for *Playboy*, probably wasn't aware of it, but something he said gave Billy Joel the idea for his sixth #1 AC hit, "Leave a Tender Moment Alone." "I had the melody. . .and I needed a lyric," Joel recalled in a 1984 article in the *Atlanta Journal-Constitution*. "I have a notebook that I put all my lyrics in, and I had a phrase on the top of a page with a line under it. [Sheff] once pointed out that when I play piano I always throw in a lot of kitsch after anything tender, so I'd written 'Leave a Tender Moment Alone' in my book. I figured it would be a good title for a song. Then I leafed back 10 pages and I found lyrics I'd written. It was magic."

"Leave a Tender Moment Alone" was Joel's fourth and final #1 AC single from his *An Innocent Man* LP. It went to #27 pop as well as #1 AC, and its relative success encouraged Columbia to release a sixth single from the album, something rarely done at the time for any artist and never done with Joel before. That 45 was "Keeping the Faith," which went to #3 AC and #18 pop in early 1985.

Regarding "Keeping the Faith," he said, "This song wraps up the whole mood of the album. To some people, the music might sound like I'm a nostalgia freak or something, and I'm not. I had to explain to myself why I'd done it too. What I'm trying to say is that this is where I came from. The song says I'm not living in the past, I'm celebrating today. I'd never have had the first if I'd never have hung out with the wild boys and heard the old music. I'm just carrying on a rock and roll tradition, keeping the faith."

After "Keeping the Faith" finished its chart run, Columbia issued Billy Joel's *Greatest Hits Volume I and Volume II* in the summer of 1985 with a few new tunes that came out as singles. "You're Only Human (Second Wind)" was a return to serious concerns for Joel as it addressed the idea of suicide prevention (years earlier, Joel had considered himself suicidal). It went to #2 AC for three weeks plus #9 pop, his first top 10 pop hit since "An Innocent Man" in 1984 [see 451]. The other single was "The Night Is Still Young," which made #13 AC and #34 pop in the fall of 1985.

In 1986 Joel released *The Bridge*, an album that contained a song which would become his seventh #1 AC single and 19th top 20 pop entry [see 509—"This Is the Time"].

461 Drive

THE CARS

Elektra 69706

September 22, 1984 (3 weeks)

Writer: Ric Ocasek

Producers: Robert John "Mutt" Lange, the Cars

The Cars sped into the playlists of album rock and top 40 stations for six years before veering onto the AC chart with "Drive." The quintet, formed in Boston in 1976, consisted of Ric Ocasek as lead singer and guitarist, Benjamin Orr as bassist and occasional lead singer, Elliot Easton as guitarist, Greg Hawkes as keyboardist, and David Robinson as drummer. (In the early 1970s, Ocasek, Orr, and Hawkes had worked together as a trio.) Robinson gave the group its name, and by 1978 rock and pop fans became familiar with it via decent airplay for two singles, "Just What I Needed" (#27 pop, their debut on the Hot 100) and "My Best Friend's Girl" (#35 pop). The highest-charting pop tune for the Cars during the early years was "Shake It Up," which went to #4 in 1982.

Ocasek wrote "Drive," as he had the group's previous singles. "I write lyrics pretty fast," Ocasek said to Irwin Stambler for *The Encyclopedia of Pop, Rock and Soul*. "I usually write five songs at a sitting in a three-day period. I might write five songs and then not do any more for a few weeks until I feel in the mood again, then do five more. If there's an album project coming up, I pick the ones I like."

Sung by Orr and promoted by an intriguing music video directed by actor Timothy Hutton, "Drive" not only coasted into the #1 AC spot but was a #3 pop hit for three weeks. Its pop run started September 29, 1984. The first two weeks it was behind Prince's "Let's Go Crazy" at #1 and John Waite's "Missing You" and Stevie Wonder's "I Just Called to Say I Love You" [see 462] at #2 the first and second weeks respectively. For the third week "I Just Called to Say I Love You" was #1 and "Let's Go Crazy" was #2.

Five more Cars singles hit the AC chart through 1988's "Coming Up You," which hit #12. That same year, the Cars broke down because members wanted to pursue individual projects. Ocasek and Orr both had solo singles make the AC chart in 1986 (Ocasek's "Emotion in Motion" went to #8 and Orr's "Stay the Night" made #2), but those were the only solo successes by any members of the Cars.

While promoting a new album in an interview on *Showbiz Today* on the Cable News Network (CNN) which aired September 16, 1997, Ocasek doubted there ever would be a reunion of the Cars. He said most groups come together again either to recapture their past glory or to make a profit, and with that in mind, "I'm willing to leave alone what I had, and I don't need the money."

462 I Just Called to Say I Love You
STEVIE WONDER

Motown 1745

October 13, 1984 (3 weeks)

Writer: Stevie Wonder

Producer: Stevie Wonder

The inspiration for "I Just Called to Say I Love You" came to Stevie Wonder either in July 1976 or 1977 (he has given both years in interviews). The melody came first. Oddly, he thought of it first as something he might do with ex-Beatles John Lennon and Paul McCartney. As he told Lisa Anderson in *The Chicago Tribune*, "It was summertime, I was feeling good, and I imagined the voices of myself and John and Paul singing it together."

Then in 1984, his friend Dionne Warwick urged him to contribute to the soundtrack to *The Woman in Red*, an American adaptation of a French farce with Gene Wilder as the star. He reworked the 1976 melody and added lyrics to create "I Just Called to Say I Love You." Wonder claimed he wrote the lyrics with no particular person in mind.

The result was one of the most popular ballads by Wonder since "You Are the Sunshine of My Life" [see 191]. As he told Anderson, "'I Just Called' is like 'Sunshine of My Life' as far as the feeling, how it has been accepted and how people are responding to it."

"I Just Called to Say I Love You" was an across-the-board smash, being #1 AC, pop, and R&B simultaneously for three weeks starting October 13, 1984. It also earned him an Academy Award for Best Song, although some wanted him to return the Oscar when they learned he had written part of it years earlier and not specifically for a movie. But as the tune had not been released commercially prior to appearing in *The Woman in Red*, the issue died quickly.

The record was the best solo performance Wonder had on the AC chart since "Send One Your Love" hit #1 in 1980 [see 376]. He hit the same position in 1982 with his duet with Paul McCartney, "Ebony and Ivory" [see 422], but otherwise he struggled on the chart in the early 1980s, with only two other singles making the AC top 20, "I Ain't Gonna Stand for It" at #20 in 1981 and "That Girl" at #10 in 1982.

One other Wonder song from *The Woman in Red* soundtrack became a single in late 1984. "Love Light in Flight" wound up going to #10 AC and #17 pop in early 1985. After that 45 faded, Wonder finally released his album *In Square Circle*, which had been delayed by the success of "I Just Called to Say I Love You." That LP's first single, "Part-Time Lover," became a #1 AC hit [see 482].

463 What About Me?

KENNY ROGERS WITH KIM CARNES AND JAMES INGRAM

RCA 13899

November 3, 1984 (2 weeks)

Writers: Kenny Rogers, David Foster, Richard Marx

Producers: Kenny Rogers, David Foster

"What About Me?" went through two proposed sets of singers before it finally emerged as a song that would hit all four charts. Rogers wrote "What About Me?" with producer David Foster and Richard Marx, later a singer himself [see 568—"Right Here Waiting"], as a grand ballad. "It was like a three-way love song," Rogers said. "Everybody involved said, 'Hey, what about me?' I think it's a beautiful record."

The trio aimed to make the final song big not only in terms of production value but also in terms of the marquee value of the two singers who were to sing with Rogers. "It was originally going to be me, Lionel Richie, and Barbra Streisand," Rogers said. But Rogers claimed when Richie read a *Billboard* report about how "hip" he had become as a solo artist, he decided against doing the song. Informed of the news, Streisand dropped out as well.

The initial replacements for Richie and Streisand were Jeffrey Osborne and Olivia Newton-John. Newton-John backed out first. "She got a call from Barry Gibb and he had a duet with her coming out soon, and he didn't want the competition," Rogers said. And then Osborne had an album coming out that conflicted with the planned release of "What About Me?" so he left the project too

Undaunted, the group went to the well one more time and came up with Kim Carnes and James Ingram. "Kim Carnes was in the New Christy Minstrels with me in the 1960s," Rogers said. This trio was the one which finally made it to the recording studio, and they ended up hitting the AC, pop, country, and R&B charts with their single. The song came closest to its AC success on the Hot 100, where it hit #15, while going to #57 R&B and #70 country.

"What About Me?" was Rogers' second and last R&B entry, the first being "Lady" [see 393]. A year later Rogers charted for the last time on the Hot 100, when "Morning Desire" went to #72. He kept making the AC and country charts into the early 1990s, but his singles on both did not fare nearly as well as they had in previous years. Upset with the lack of radio airplay given to his 1992 LP for Giant Records, he waited four years before releasing a Christmas album called *The Gift*, which he said sold well despite the fact that it too got little airtime.

Rogers is looking into the future with his label Dreamcatcher, which he established in 1998. "I'll be able to sign new artists, do other things as well," he said. "It'll be for my new product and new artists." It remains to be seen if he or any of the others on Dreamcatcher will be able to compile the type of hits on AC, pop, and country which Rogers had during his heyday.

464 Penny Lover

LIONEL RICHIE

Motown 1762

November 17, 1984 (4 weeks)

Writers: Lionel Richie, Brenda Harvey Richie

Producers: Lionel Richie, James Anthony Carmichael

An anonymous *Billboard* singles reviewer described Lionel Richie's "Penny Lover" as "Another of his unfailingly effective universal-appeal ballads." It also was Richie's eighth #1 AC hit overall and fourth #1 AC hit from his album *Can't Slow Down*. On the other charts, "Penny Lover" held at #8 pop for the weeks of December 1 and 8, 1984, plus made #8 R&B.

"Penny Lover" was Richie's first solo #1 to credit a co-writer, in this case his wife Brenda Richie. As with the previous hits James Anthony Carmichael was co-producer. (Carmichael tried doing his own LP in 1995, but *Instant Funk*, on which he served as singer, bandleader, and percussionist, was a flop.)

Shortly after "Penny Lover" arrived on the AC chart, Paul Grein, in a *Billboard* review of a Richie concert in Costa Mesa, California, wrote: "Richie should be less concerned that too many ballads will slow down the show. [His] emphasis on ballads may have been a problems before 'All Night Long' and 'Running With the Night,' but it is no longer." While Grein liked Richie's take on "Penny Lover" and other slower-paced tunes, he was dismayed by his cursory takes on his ballads with the Commodores such as "Easy." And as for "All Night Long," Grein found it living up to its name in performance in concert, with "seemingly endless drum solos" and a bunch of breakdancers inappropriately dressed up in New Wave outfits for the Caribbean-flavored song.

But while his live shows may have had their drawbacks, there was no denying that "Penny Lover" and the album on which it appeared, *Can't Slow Down*, were immensely popular with both the public and critics. Besides the success on the charts, *Can't Slow Down* won the Grammy for Album of the Year, and Richie and co-producer Carmichael tied with David Foster as Producers of the Year, Non-Classical. Richie also got nominations for Song of the Year and Best Male Pop Vocal Performance, both for the third single released from the album, "Hello" [see 453].

In 1985 Richie did not release an album but did maintain a high profile with two #1 AC hits, "We Are the World" by USA for Africa, which he co-wrote [see 472], and "Say You, Say Me," the theme song for the movie *White Nights* [see 484]. Those two songs brought the number of #1 AC hits written or co-written by Richie to 12, placing him just ahead of Burt Bacharach, who scored his 11th AC #1 hit with the song which replaced "Say You, Say Me," "That's What Friends Are For." But although it took Bacharach 24 years to write 11 #1 AC hits, Richie wrote his 12 within seven years.

465 Sea of Love

THE HONEYDRIPPERS

Es Paranza 99701

December 15, 1984 (1 week)

Writers: George Khoury, Phil Battiste

Producers: Nugetre, the Fabulous Brill Brothers

Atlantic Records chairman Ahmet Ertegun built his company on rhythm and blues records in the 1940s and 1950s, so when Led Zeppelin lead singer Robert Plant expressed an interest in doing an album to cover some of the soul tunes from the era, Ertegun was intrigued. Plant and Ertegun became co-producers on the project (the "official" credits, "Nugetre" and "The Fabulous Brill Brothers" is a fiction), and enlisted guitarists Jeff Beck and Jimmy Page, bassist Nile Rodgers, and pianist Paul Shaffer to make up a group they dubbed the Honeydrippers.

"It was just a session. I was called as a studio musician," said Shaffer, bandleader for *The Late Show Starring David Letterman*, about his involvement with the Honeydrippers. Dave Matthews (not the guitarist with his own band but a New York arranger for James Brown) drafted Shaffer to do the gig, which took place over one Saturday and Sunday weekend.

Shaffer assumed that either Plant or Ertegun, or both, picked "Sea of Love" to remake. The song was originally a #2 pop and #1 R&B hit for Phil Phillips in 1959. Phillips, whose real name was John Baptiste, first wrote the tune as an attempt to impress a woman while he was bellhopping at the Chateau Charles in Lake Charles, Louisiana, then continued, with the help of his producer George Khoury, to fine-tune it.

Surprisingly, Shaffer played on all the takes of the Honeydrippers album except the "Sea of Love" cover. "'Sea of Love' was recut in England," he said. But he did play the tune with the group when they appeared on NBC-TV's *Saturday Night Live* and in the Meadowlands in New Jersey.

Released as the first cut off the Honeydrippers LP, "Sea of Love" went to #3 pop the week of January 5, 1985, as well as #1 AC. One other single followed it, "Rockin' at Midnight," a remake of "Good Rockin' Tonight" which made #38 AC and #25 pop.

The easy-listening sound of "Sea of Love" astonished some Led Zeppelin fans accustomed to Plant singing harder-edged ditties like "Whole Lotta Love." But in spite of the Honeydrippers' popularity, which included a million-selling album, there was no follow-up to the project, a decision Shaffer attributed to Plant. "He's the kind of guy who likes to do new things and move on. He didn't want to repeat the success of what he thought was a novelty."

Other remakes of "Sea of Love" were by the Kit Kats in 1967 (#130 bubbling under) and Del Shannon in 1982 (#36 AC, #33 pop). In the late 1980s, Phil Phillips also produced a version of his song with five of his children—the group was billed as the Fire Ants—but it generated little activity.

466 Do What You Do

JERMAINE JACKSON

Arista 9279

December 22, 1984 (3 weeks)

Writers: Ralph Dino, Larry DiTomaso

Producers: Jermaine Jackson, Dick Rudolph

Jermaine Jackson found himself the odd man out of the Jackson family musical dynasty in 1976 when the rest of his brothers left Motown and signed with the Epic label. He remained because he was married to Hazel Gordy, daughter of Motown head Berry Gordy, Jr., and did not want to displease his powerful father-in-law. The decision might have hurt for a time, however, for while Michael, Jackie, Tito, Marlon, and Randy Jackson prospered during the late 1970s on their new label, Jermaine was hitless until the 1980s.

Born in Gary, Indiana, on December 11, 1954, the fourth child of Joe and Katharine Jackson, Jermaine Jackson got his first taste of being a soloist while part of the Jackson Five. The bassist's first single, "That's How Love Goes," went to an unimpressive #46 pop in 1972, but its follow-up, a remake of "Daddy's Home," made #9 pop in 1973. He had only two other songs make the pop chart in the 1970s, "You're in Good Hands" at #79 in 1973 and "Let's Be Young Tonight" at #55 in 1976.

In 1979 Stevie Wonder wrote and produced two top 40 hits for Jackson which charted in 1980, "Let's Get Serious" at #9 pop and #1 R&B and "You're Supposed to Keep Your Love for Me" at #34 pop. Only one more hit emerged through 1983, 1982's "Let Me Tickle Your Fancy" at #18, before Jackson rejoined his brothers for an album and tour titled *Victory* in 1984. That same year Jackson left Motown for Arista, and in 1987 he severed one of the last ties with his old company when he divorced Hazel Gordy.

But back to the Arista deal. Label head Clive Davis, wanting to give a big push to his newly signed artist, served as executive producer of the *Jermaine Jackson* LP. Its first single was "Dynamite," which blew away nearly everything Jackson had done in the 1980s by reaching #15 pop. Its follow-up, the laid-back, sultry "Do What You Do," fared even better, going to #1 AC in his debut on the chart, plus #13 pop and #14 R&B. A special treat on the single was its B-side, Jermaine's duet with his brother Michael called "Tell Me I'm Not Dreaming," which had earned a lot of airplay when the album first appeared, in 1984, but could not be released as a 45 at the time due to contractual difficulties.

Jermaine became less germane to the music world after "Do What You Do," getting just five singles on the pop chart afterward through the rest of the 1980s. Only one of them, 1986's "I Think It's Love," made the AC chart, peaking at #5. In 1991, signed to LaFace Records, Jermaine generated some headlines with "Word to the Badd!" The record, viewed as an attack on his brother Michael's success, brought Jermaine more controversy than sales, as it peaked at #78 pop. His musical activities the rest of the 1990s were very low-key.

1985

467 All I Need

JACK WAGNER

Qwest 29238

January 12, 1985 (2 weeks)

Writers: Glen Ballard, Clifton Magness, David Robert Pack

Producers: Glen Ballard, Clifton Magness

The first soap opera actor to hit #1 on a *Billboard* chart was Rick Springfield, whose "Jessie's Girl" topped the Hot 100 for two weeks starting August 1, 1981. But Springfield, who starred as Dr. Noah Drake on ABC-TV's daily serial *General Hospital,* scored only three entries on the AC chart, none of which peaked higher than #16. It was another *General Hospital* actor, Jack Wagner, who became the first to lead the AC listings, with his ballad "All I Need."

Wagner was born in Washington, Missouri, on October 3, 1959. He began playing guitar at age 14 but considered a golfing career until he got a scholarship to study acting at the University of Arizona. After graduating from the U of A in 1982, he moved to Los Angeles and started working in Hollywood. Wagner, initially billed as Jack P. Wagner, landed a role on the cable soap opera *A New Day in Eden,* and joined the cast of *General Hospital* in 1983.

Expanding his horizons in 1984, Wagner nailed a recording deal with Quincy Jones' Qwest Records. Recalling "All I Need," he said that "It was the first single I had cut for my album." Asked if the single's success caught him off guard, he said, "Totally. It actually died its first time out, and then it caught on at Y-100 in Miami and then spread across the country to be a hit."

"All I Need," which Wagner introduced on *General Hospital* on July 4, 1984, as his character Frisco Jones, peaked at #2 pop behind Madonna's "Like a Virgin" the same two weeks it was #1 AC. But efforts to reproduce its popularity were largely unsuccessful. The follow-up, "Lady of My Heart," stumbled at #34 AC and #76 pop. Later in 1985, "Too Young" proved too weak when it only got to #15 AC and #52 pop. In early 1986 he teamed with Valerie Carter to do "Love Can Take Us All the Way," but the record made only #15 AC, his last entry on the chart. He got back on the Hot 100 in 1987 with "Weatherman Says," but it stalled at #67 and proved to be his final single there. That same year, Jones ended his recording work with Qwest and left *General Hospital.*

In the 1990s Wagner was married to Kristina Malandro, who had played his love interest Felicia Cummings on *General Hospital* (she stayed with the show and changed her billing to Kristina Wagner). After a stint on *Santa Barbara* in 1991, which ran on NBC-TV opposite *General Hospital,* Wagner joined the nighttime Fox-TV soap opera *Melrose Place,* playing devious Dr. Peter Burns in 1994, a role he still held four years later. Asked in 1998 if he had any plans to return to the recording studio, Wagner answered simply, "No."

468 You're the Inspiration
CHICAGO

Full Moon 29126

January 26, 1985 (2 weeks)

Writers: Peter Cetera, David Foster

Producer: David Foster

"You're the Inspiration" marked the second time for Chicago that an AC chart-topper for the group was written by lead singer Peter Cetera and Chicago producer David Foster. The first was "Hard to Say I'm Sorry" [see 425], which also made #1 pop. "You're the Inspiration" did not equal that achievement on the Hot 100, stalling at #3 the weeks of January 19 and 26, 1985, behind Madonna's "Like a Virgin" at #1 and "All I Need" [see 467] the first week and "Like a Virgin" at #1 and Foreigner's "I Want to Know What Love Is" at #2 the second.

Around the time "You're the Inspiration" became a hit, it became apparent that relations between the band and Cetera were strained. "It was obvious he was more and more unwilling to go on the road, and I think that was the crux of the matter," Chicago trumpeter Lee Loughnane said. "He wanted to do a solo LP." Cetera's departure a few months later was not acrimonious, although Loughnane has wondered what might have happened if the split hadn't taken place. "If we had stayed together and all of us kept from killing each other, we would have been playing arenas and selling even more of our hits," he said.

Chicago held auditions to replace Cetera and the winner was, well, let Loughnane tell it. "Jason [Scheff] had presented a song to Warner Brothers because he had heard Cetera had left the band and offered to get it to Peter Cetera," Loughnane said. Instead, Scheff took Cetera's position as singer and bassist, and Loughnane was impressed with him. "He played rings around Peter, and he's improved 500 percent as a vocalist and is a more consistent singer than Peter."

After Scheff joined, the hits kept coming. Among them were "Will You Still Love Me?" in early 1987 (#2 AC for three weeks and #3 pop), "If She Would Have Been Faithful" in the summer of 1987 (#9 AC and #17 pop), and "I Don't Wanna Live Without Your Love" in 1988 (#5 AC and #3 pop). The follow-up to the latter became the seventh Chicago #1 AC entry; see 553—"Look Away."

By the way, Cetera remade "You're the Inspiration" along with the Chicago hits "Baby What a Big Surprise" and "If You Leave Me Now" [see 314] in 1997 on the River North anthology of his solo career titled *You're the Inspiration, A Collection.* Discussing this move with Chuck Taylor in *Billboard,* he said, "The only thing I'm nostalgic about is the Beatles, not my old stuff, not Chicago's old stuff. That's one reason I'm happy about doing updated versions of things I wrote 15 or 20 years ago. I think the new versions are better." A single of "You're the Inspiration" with Az Yet doing background vocals on it as a replay of their cover of "Hard to Say I'm Sorry" went to #77 pop the weeks of October 25 and November 1, 1997.

469 Careless Whisper
WHAM! FEATURING GEORGE MICHAEL

Columbia 04691

February 9, 1985 (5 weeks)

Writers: George Michael, Andrew Ridgely

Producer: George Michael

Americans took longer than Britons to succumb to the charms of Wham!, a duo formed in England in the early 1980s with lead singer and songwriter George Michael, born Georgios Kyriacos Panayiotou in Bushey, England on June 25, 1963, and guitarist Andrew Ridgely, born in Bushey on January 26, 1963. After several years of recording, the two men broke onto the Hot 100 in 1983 with "Bad Boys," at #60.

Finally in 1984, "Wake Me Up Before You Go-Go" gave them the breakthrough in America they craved, hitting #4 AC and #1 pop. Its follow-up, "Careless Whisper," also hit #1 pop, for three weeks starting February 16, 1985, plus #1 AC and #8 R&B. Since Ridgely played no part in the recording, singles initially billed George Michael as the artist until it was decided to use the group name so that people would associate it with the previous hit.

While "Careless Whisper" peaked on the AC chart, Michael assessed the song frankly to John Pareles of *The New York Times.* Noting he composed it when he was 17, he said, "I wasn't secure enough to write something that would expose my feelings, so it's very clichéd in a lot of its terms."

In fact, Michael felt he had matured noticeably as a composer by 1985, telling Pareles that "I think I've gotten rid of every songwriting influence I've ever had. Most of them I've aped to some degree, and I'm not ashamed of that; I've been learning to write well-structured commercial songs. With the next album, we'll be trying to experiment with our own sound."

There would be only one more Wham! album, as it became quite evident to everyone that Michael was doing almost all the work on the music. A telling comment at the time came from Michael's and Ridgely's manager, Simon Napier-Bell, who informed David Thomas of *The Times* of London that "George decided very young that he wanted to be a pop star and so he sat down and decided how to do it. If you like, Wham! is George Michael's solo career."

Michael started his official solo career a year after "Careless Whisper." His first 45 without the Wham! designation was "A Different Corner," which hit #6 AC and #7 pop before the release of the last two Wham! singles in 1986, "The Edge of Heaven" (#22 AC, #10 pop) and "Where Did Your Heart Go?" (#33 AC, #50 pop). Also in 1986 he and Ridgely gave their farewell performance as Wham! in London's Wembley Stadium.

In the late 1980s Ridgely dabbled in race car driving, and it was clear by 1990 that his own effort to have a solo music career had flopped. By the end of the 1990s he was concentrating on conservation and environmental concerns. Michael, however, managed several hits, including another #1 AC in 1988 [see 540—"One More Try"].

470 Too Late for Goodbyes

JULIAN LENNON

Atlantic 89589

March 16, 1985 (2 weeks)

Writer: Julian Lennon

Producer: Phil Ramone

When Julian Lennon was born in Liverpool, England, on April 8, 1963, his father John Lennon held him up and announced, "Who's going to be a famous little rocker like his dad?" Julian must have absorbed what his father said, for by the time he was in his early twenties, the first child to be born to any of the Beatles had completed his first album.

Before that occurred, Julian had to sort through an array of emotions regarding his father. John Lennon had married Yoko Ono when Julian was five, which did not bother him too much because he lived nearby in Kensington, England, with his mother, Cynthia Powell Lennon, and his grandmother. But John left for New York City when Julian was eight, and Julian felt abandoned. Then came John's murder when Julian was 17, and the massive publicity surrounding it made Julian's life even more difficult. But Julian did indeed want a career as a "rocker," as his dad put it, so he quietly made cassettes of his music at home, putting out a demo tape when he was 20.

After more than a dozen record companies rejected him, he was signed by Charisma. Julian's debut album was recorded at Valotte, a French country chateau, and *Valotte* became the title of his first album. The title tune, which was also the first single released from the LP, went to #4 AC and #9 pop. Next up was "Too Late for Goodbyes."

Some speculated that "Too Late for Goodbyes" and a few other songs on *Valotte* were about the loss of his father and that he was consciously trying to mimic John Lennon's sound. Producer Phil Ramone told Lynn Van Matre of *The Chicago Tribune* that "He's not consciously doing his dad or impressions of his dad. But there are some very interesting lyrics there."

"Too Late for Goodbyes" went to #5 pop the week of March 23, 1985, while finishing up its run at #1 AC. Its follow-up, "Say You're Wrong," went to #21 pop and #6 AC and was his last entry on the latter chart. One more *Valotte* single, "Jesse," went to #54 pop in 1985.

Despite his strong debut, the junior Lennon never had another hit as big as *Valotte* and its singles. He had only two other Hot 100 entries, "Stick Around" at #32 in 1986 and "Now You're in Heaven" at #93 in 1989. Nevertheless, he continued to record and tour through the late 1990s. In 1998 fans could chose between Julian's new album and the first one of his half-brother, John and Yoko's son, Sean Lennon. However, neither LP became a big seller.

471 One More Night

PHIL COLLINS

Atlantic 89588

March 30, 1985 (3 weeks)

Writer: Phil Collins

Producers: Phil Collins, Hugh Padgham

Diminutive, bald Phil Collins was hardly the image of a romantic music star, but he was just that to many of his female fans in the 1980s, who adored his sensitive ballads, like "One More Night." It was quite a triumph for a man who spent roughly two decades in the entertainment industry before getting worldwide acclaim.

Born in London, England, on January 30, 1951, Collins became a professional actor when he was still a lad. He had some decent parts, including the role of the Artful Dodger in the London stage production of *Oliver!*, but he became disenchanted with the acting business when his part was excised from a children's film and switched to a musical career instead.

Collins joined the band Flaming Youth in 1969, then became drummer with the struggling British rock band Genesis in 1970. In 1975, when Peter Gabriel left the group, he moved up to being their lead singer as well as drummer [for more details, see 503—"Throwing It All Away"]. He also took part in a jazz-fusion quintet called Brand X, a group which had no AC or pop singles but did get three chart entries on *Billboard*'s album listing from 1976–79.

In 1981 Collins, while still part of Genesis, released his first solo album, which spun off two #19 pop singles, "I Missed Again" and "In the Air Tonight." He made his AC debut more than a year later with his remake of the Supremes' #1 hit of 1966, "You Can't Hurry Love," which went to #9 AC and #10 pop. He had two more AC entries before the release of "One More Night"—the Oscar-nominated "Against All Odds (Take a Look at Me Now)," which made #2 AC for six weeks and #1 pop for three weeks in 1984, and "Easy Lover," a duet with Philip Bailey which reached #15 AC and #2 pop in 1985.

"One More Night" hit #1 AC and pop for two weeks simultaneously starting March 30, 1985, followed by one week atop the AC chart alone. It also went to #80 R&B. The tune came from *No Jacket Required*, which made #1 for seven weeks starting March 30, 1985 on the album chart. Other hit singles from the album were "Sussudio" (#30 AC, #1 pop), "Don't Lose My Number" (#25 AC, #4 pop), and "Take Me Home" (#2 AC, #7 pop). The latter had backing vocals from Sting and Peter Gabriel—yes, the same Peter Gabriel Collins had replaced in Genesis nearly a decade earlier.

"I don't know why this album did as well as it has done," Collins told Gary Graff of the Knight-Ridder Newspapers Syndicate. "I wrote the songs the same way I wrote the other songs—maybe there's just something in there that hit a few nerves."

Collins hit a few more nerves with his next #1 AC hit [see 483—"Separate Lives"].

472 We Are the World

USA FOR AFRICA

Columbia 04839

April 20, 1985 (2 weeks)

Writers: Michael Jackson, Lionel Richie

Producer: Quincy Jones

"We Are the World" was not the first record whose profits provided relief for famine-stricken victims in Africa in the mid-1980s. "Do They Know It's Christmas?," sung by a host of British artists known collectively as Band Aid, hit #1 in the United Kingdom and #13 pop in America in 1984. But "We Are the World," due to the sheer weight of the musical talent involved, sparked more interest and was a broader-based hit in America, reaching #1 AC, pop, and R&B and #76 country.

The project came together a few days before Christmas 1984 when Harry Belafonte, disturbed by reports of the lack of food in Africa caused by a drought, called Ken Kragen, whose client Kenny Rogers had picked up the fight against world hunger led by Harry Chapin, who was killed in an automobile accident in 1981. Belafonte suggested an all-star concert to raise money, but Kragen told him they could do better with a single. Lionel Richie agreed to write the tune, and Quincy Jones signed on as producer. Richie tried to get Stevie Wonder as a co-writer, but when he was unavailable, Jones hooked him up with one of his artists, Michael Jackson. It was decided to make the song an anthem, but nothing emerged until January 15, 1985, when Jackson, using two melodic ideas from Richie, presented a demo with music played on drums, piano, and strings, plus words to the chorus. Six days later, Richie and Jackson completed the lyrics in two and a half hours. Studio musicians recorded the final instrumental track on January 22 in six takes.

The final recording session came on January 28, 1985, in A&M Studios in Hollywood, after the American Music Awards. At 9 p.m., artists began to filter into the session. Around 10:30 p.m., Band Aid organizer Bob Geldof gave a sobering talk to participants about the suffering in Africa, then Jones and Kragen told them how profits from the single would be spent, including 10 percent for the hungry and homeless in America. The chorus was finished by 2 a.m., and the solos, ending with Bruce Springsteen's, were done by 6:45 a.m.

The list of artists who participated, now known as United Support of Artists (USA) for Africa, were chosen to fit in with the "world" theme. They were, in alphabetical order, Dan Aykroyd, Harry Belafonte, Lindsey Buckingham, Kim Carnes, Ray Charles, Bob Dylan, Sheila E., Bob Geldof, Daryl Hall and John Oates, James Ingram, the Jacksons, La Toya Jackson, Michael Jackson, Al Jarreau, Waylon Jennings, Billy Joel, Cyndi Lauper, Huey Lewis and the News, Kenny Loggins, Bette Midler, Willie Nelson, Jeffrey Osborne, Steve Perry, the Pointer Sisters, Lionel Richie, Smokey Robinson, Kenny Rogers, Diana Ross, Paul Simon, Bruce Springsteen, Tina Turner, Dionne Warwick, and Stevie Wonder.

The production won Best Record, Song, and Pop Performance by a Duo or Group with Vocal honors at the Grammy Awards, but neither the awards nor the $60 million plus raised by the project mattered to Belafonte, Geldof, and Kragen as much as the hope that the project had changed some people's attitudes, making them more compassionate and generous.

473 Rhythm of the Night

DEBARGE

Gordy 1770

May 4, 1985 (1 week)

Writer: Diane Warren

Producer: Richard Perry

"Rhythm of the Night" was the first #1 AC hit for Diane Warren, who would compile more than 10 similar hits over the next decade by herself or in collaboration with other partners. For this assignment the prolific songwriter was asked to write a song for the karate film *The Last Dragon* and not specifically for DeBarge.

Warren recalled what inspired the song's lyrics and peppy beat: "I had just gotten my first drum machine, so actually being able to keep a good rhythm might have inspired it," she said.

"Rhythm of the Night" was a triple #1 chart-topper. It hit #3 pop the weeks of April 27 and May 4, 1985, behind "We Are the World" [see 472] at #1 and Madonna's "Crazy for You" at #2. It also made #1 R&B the week of April 27, 1985, followed by #1 AC a week later.

DeBarge contributed only "Rhythm of the Night" to *The Last Dragon* soundtrack, with the rest of the tunes coming from other Motown artists ranging from Stevie Wonder to the film's star, Vanity. None of them came within striking distance of the popularity of "Rhythm of the Night," which became DeBarge's second #1 AC hit after "All This Love" [see 441]. It also served as the title of DeBarge's 1985 LP, which would end up having three other singles released from it, including the group's third #1 AC hit, "Who's Holding Donna Now" [see 478].

While "Rhythm of the Night" reached its peak, rumors flew that the eldest DeBarge brother, Bobby, wanted to join his sister Bunny and brothers El, James, Mark, and Randy in the group. At the time, El told Dennis Hunt of *The Los Angeles Times* that "We won't let [Bobby] in. The group is big enough now. Besides, he probably couldn't make full use of his talent in this group. We'd probably clash too. It's better for him to go solo."

El was wrong. By 1986 Bobby, along with another DeBarge brother, Tommy, had joined the group. Bobby and Tommy had no solo hits but had been members of the band Switch, where Bobby played keyboardist and Tommy was its bassist. The sextet had a few pop and R&B hits in the late 1970s on the Gordy label prior to DeBarge being signed to it, with the highest-charting pop tune being "There'll Never Be" at #36 on the Hot 100 in 1978. But the public turned off Switch in the 1980s, leaving the two men to join their siblings' group. Bobby died of AIDS-related complications on August 16, 1995. He was just 36 years old.

474 Smooth Operator

SADE

Portrait 04807

May 11, 1985 (2 weeks)

Writers: Helen Folosade Adu, St. John

Producer: Robin Millar

The parents of Helen Folosade Adu dubbed her Sade (pronounced "shar-DAY"), using part of her middle name, when Nigerians refused to call her by her English name after she was born in Ibadan, a village near Lagos, the capitol of Nigeria, on January 16, 1959. In 1963 Sade's family returned to England, living first in Essex and then Holland-on-Sea. At age 17 Sade went to London's St. Martin's School of Art, where she studied fashion and design for three years.

After Sade's graduation in 1980, a friend, Lee Barrett, got her to audition to sing backup for a group called Pride. She got the job, but had to take modeling assignments and design menswear while Pride struggled in the early 1980s. Then Barrett encouraged Sade and some other members of Pride, including saxophonist/guitarist Stuart Matthewman, to develop their own sets to do during breaks at Pride's shows. Sade and crew began to upstage Pride, and when Sade attracted widespread attention for her vocalizing at a 1983 concert at the Institute of Contemporary Arts in England, Barrett felt the smaller group had the talent to go out on their own.

In October 1983 Barrett signed Sade, Matthewman, bassist Paul Denman, keyboardist Andrew Hale, and drummer Paul Cooke to a recording contract (by 1985 Cooke had been replaced by Dave Early). With the four men backing her, Sade's first hit in the United Kingdom came soon thereafter as "Your Love Is King" reached #6 in the spring of 1984. In the summer of 1984 "When Am I Gonna Make a Living" was released, going to #36, followed in the fall by "Smooth Operator," which made #19.

Sade's first release in America was "Hang On to Your Love." While that 45 went nowhere, "Smooth Operator" broke her out big time. It went to #5 pop for two weeks starting May 18, 1985, as well as #1 AC and #5 R&B. Her English debut, "Your Love Is King," came out next; it did OK on the AC chart at #8 but came up short on the Hot 100 at #54. Her next single, "The Sweetest Taboo" [see 488], which came out the end of 1985, hit big on both charts, and Sade won the Grammy for Best New Artist of 1985.

Sade and her group had not really expected such rapid transatlantic success. "What has happened is really not believable," she told Walter Leavy in *Ebony*. "We thought after our third or fourth album we would begin to expand the audience that we already had in England. We just didn't think people would pick up on what we were doing so quickly."

475 Suddenly

BILLY OCEAN

Jive 9323

May 25, 1985 (2 weeks)

Writer: Billy Ocean

Producers: Keith Diamond, Billy Ocean

The man born Leslie Sebastian Charles in Trinidad on January 21, 1950, became one of the top AC and pop performers in America in the mid-1980s, almost a decade after observers had predicted such success. Billy Ocean scored a modest disco pop hit in 1976 with "Love Really Hurts Without You" at #22 on the Hot 100, which also went to #2 in the United Kingdom. But in the United States he could not get another entry on that chart until 1984, when "Caribbean Queen (No More Love on the Run)" established his chart dominance by going to #1 pop and #7 AC.

Billy Ocean got the idea for his stage name while appearing in London clubs at the age of 19 under various guises (his family moved to London when he was seven and did not want him not to pursue music). The surname "Ocean" came from the 1961 "Rat Pack" film starring Frank Sinatra and Dean Martin, *Oceans 11*, which in turned inspired a Trinidad soccer team to name itself after the movie. But his recording career progressed slowly during the 1970s, and in fact when "Love Really Hurts Without You" became a hit, he was an installer of windshield wipers at a Ford plant in England.

He dropped his installation work, and while he had no more success in America during the 1970s, he did have three top 20 hits in the United Kingdom within a year after "Love Really Hurts Without You"—"L.O.D. (Love on Delivery)," "Stop Me (If You've Heard It All Before)," and "Red Light Spells Danger." He did have R&B success in the United States in 1981 with "Nights (Feel Like Getting Down)," but didn't really attract many American listeners until "Caribbean Queen."

Another Trinidad-born man, Keith Diamond, produced Ocean on "Caribbean Queen" and did the same honors for the other singles released from the album on which the tune appeared, 1984's *Suddenly*. The first follow-up was "Loverboy," which went to #2 pop in early 1984. Then the album's title tune "Suddenly" came out as a 45 and hit #4 pop for two weeks starting June 8, 1985, plus #5 R&B in addition to #1 AC. It was Ocean's third top five pop hit and second top 10 AC entry. There was one more cut off the *Suddenly* album which became a single, "Mystery Lady," and it went to #5 AC and #24 pop.

Ocean scored his next #1 AC hit a year later, with "There'll Be Sad Songs (To Make You Cry)" [see 496].

Axel F
HAROLD FALTERMEYER

MCA 52536

June 8, 1985 (2 weeks)

Writer: Harold Faltermeyer

Producer: Harold Faltermeyer

"Axel F" was the first #1 AC instrumental since "Chariots of Fire—Titles" hit the top more than three years earlier [see 420]. Like that earlier hit, "Axel F" was the theme song of a movie, in this case *Beverly Hills Cop* starring Eddie Murphy as cop Axel Foley. But "Axel F" was a funkier groove than "Chariots of Fire" and relied even more extensively on synthesizers and sound effects, a result no doubt of composer Harold Faltermeyer's training under Georgio Moroder during the late 1970s.

Born in Munich, Germany, on October 5, 1952, Faltermeyer came to prominence while in his mid-twenties working for Moroder as the arranger and keyboardist of kinetic, disco-influenced soundtracks, such as the ones to the movies *Midnight Express* (1978) and *American Gigolo* (1980). Although he branched out on his own in the early 1980s to write and produce music, he did not attract much notice until the success of "Axel F."

"Axel F" was just one of several instrumentals Faltermeyer contributed to the soundtrack to *Beverly Hills Cop*, including "Shoot Out" and "The Discovery," but it was the only one released as an A-side. In fact, the week after "Axel F" finished its reign on the AC chart, the soundtrack made #1 on the album chart for two weeks. Other hits from the soundtrack in 1985 were "The Heat Is On" (#36 AC, #2 pop) by Glenn Frey, "Neutron Dance" (#23 AC, #6 pop) by the Pointer Sisters, and "New Attitude" (#17 pop) and "Stir It Up" (#41 pop) by Patti LaBelle.

"Axel F" went to #1 AC but stopped at #3 pop for three weeks starting June 1, 1985. The first two weeks "Everything She Wants" (Wham!) and "Everybody Wants to Rule the World" (Tears for Fears) held the top two spots. In the third week "Everybody Wants to Rule the World" began its second week at #1 while Bryan Adams' "Heaven" got to #2. The tune also peaked at #13 R&B and earned Faltermeyer a Grammy nomination for Best Instrumental Composition.

While "Axel F" has been his only single to grace the AC and pop charts, Harold Faltermeyer has hardly been inactive since 1985. He did the theme for the movie *Fletch* starring Chevy Chase later in 1985 which got to #74 on the British chart ("Axel F" went all the way to #2 there earlier that year). In 1986 he won a Grammy for Best Pop Instrumental Performance by an Orchestra, Group or Soloist when he collaborated with Steve Stevens to do the "Top Gun Anthem" from the movie of the same name (he got a Grammy nomination for Best Instrumental Composition for the same tune). He continued to concentrate on creating soundtracks more than a decade after that, with his most recent work including the film *Frankie* (1995) and the CD-ROM *Jack Orlando* (1997).

The Search Is Over
SURVIVOR

Scotti Brothers 04871

June 22, 1985 (4 weeks)

Writers: Frank Sullivan, Jim Peterik

Producer: Ron Nevison

The roots of Survivor go back more than 25 years. "I had known Mark [Droubay, Survivor's original drummer] since 1973," said Frankie Sullivan, Survivor's guitarist. Sullivan was in a band called Mariah from 1973–75, and Droubay opened for the group. Then through a mutual acquaintance he met keyboardist Jim Peterik, former lead singer of the group Ides of March, whose "Vehicle" hit #2 pop in 1970. With the addition of Stephan Ellis on bass and Dave Bickler as lead singer, Survivor was in place by late 1978.

The group's first entry was 1980's "Somewhere in America," which made #70 pop. But what really made the band a household name was "Eye of the Tiger," the theme from the movie *Rocky III*, which went to #1 pop for six weeks and became their first AC entry in 1982, peaking at #27. Two years later, Bickler left, and Jimi Jamison became the new vocalist for Survivor.

Survivor had several pop entries in 1983 and 1984 after "Eye of the Tiger" but did not return to the AC chart until 1985, with "The Search Is Over," which Sullivan wrote with Peterik. "He and I had a good songwriting career," Sullivan said. "Both of us were really heads-on in co-writing music and the lyrics." Sullivan also said that the two really had no formula for creating songs, but "were always picky about lyrics because we believed that was what sold the song."

He said he had a difference of opinion with Peterik over the wording of the second verse, a battle which he won despite Peterik's displeasure with the passage. When "The Search Is Over" became a #1 AC hit, joked Sullivan, "I said, 'Jim, it's really a shame those second verse lyrics messed up the song.'" As for the song's overall meaning, Sullivan said, "When we started out, it was more a friendship song, but then we turned it into a love song."

"The Search Is Over," the third single released from Survivor's *Vital Signs* LP, peaked at #4 pop the week of July 13, 1985. Sullivan liked both the song and the success. "We loved ballads, and when you're a songwriter you love to write ballads. I think 'The Search Is Over' was our best commercial ballad."

Survivor continued to make the AC and pop charts until its swan song on both in 1989, "Across the Miles" (#16 AC, #74 pop). After a four-year hiatus, the original lineup returned and went back to performing as Survivor except for Peterik, who went to a re-formed Ides of March. In 1998 they were working on a new album, slated for release the following year.

478 Who's Holding Donna Now

DEBARGE

Gordy 1793

July 20, 1985 (3 weeks)

Writers: David Foster, Jay Graydon, Randy Goodrum

Producer: Jay Graydon

DeBarge scored its only consecutive #1 AC hits when "Who's Holding Donna Now" followed "Rhythm of the Night" [see 473] as the second single off the *Rhythm of the Night* LP. In addition to its run atop the AC chart, "Who's Holding Donna Now" stopped at #6 pop the week of August 10, 1985, and also went to #2 R&B for four weeks.

By this time tenor El DeBarge had earned special notice among fans for his good looks and lead singing of DeBarge's tunes, and much of the group's fan mail was addressed to him. When asked in 1985 whether he was leaving the group, El candidly told Dennis Hunt of *The Los Angeles Times* that "With all the questions everybody is making me think about a solo career [but] I'm not really ready. . . ."

What the answer would be was pretty obvious when the third 45 from the *Rhythm. . .* album, "You Wear It Well," billed the group as "El DeBarge with DeBarge." As any student of music history can tell you, once a member of a group gets special mention before the band itself, that person almost always begins a solo career, and El did so after "You Wear It Well" went to #46 pop and the last 45 from the group's album, "The Heart Is Not So Smart," made #17 AC and #75 pop in early 1986.

Thereafter DeBarge did not make the charts, although the group continued with brothers Bobby and Tommy after El left. (Bunny, the only female DeBarge in the band, recorded a solo album in 1987, *In Love*, that did not sell well.)

El had a good year in 1986; three top 20 AC singles were released: "Who's Johnny" from the film *Short Circuit* (#18 AC, #3 pop), "Love Always" (#8 AC, #43 pop), and "Someone" (#20 AC, #70 pop). That same year yet another DeBarge, Chico, made his pop debut with "Talk to Me, " which went #21 on the Hot 100, but his career slid in the 1990s as he spent much of the decade in jail on charges of conspiracy to sell drugs.

Though El faced no such problems, he too seemed to fade away for much of the decade. He sang on part of the all-star single "The Secret Garden (Sweet Seduction Suite)" in 1990 with Quincy Jones, Al B. Sure!, James Ingram, and Barry White (it got to #26 AC and #31 pop), but his other 1990s activities didn't generate much interest. His 1994 LP *Heart, Mind & Soul* got only to #137 on the album chart during a quick seven-week run. However, he remained the most visible of the DeBarge musical group members in 1998, doing several concerts that year.

479 Everytime You Go Away

PAUL YOUNG

Columbia 04867

August 10, 1985 (2 weeks)

Writer: Daryl Hall

Producer: Laurie Latham

Pop-soul stylist Paul Young spent several years of struggling before finding success, but when it did come, it was on both sides of the Atlantic. Born in Bedfordshire, England, on January 17, 1956, he grew up taking lessons in piano and bass while working at a Vauxhall auto factory. In the mid-1970s Young sang and played harmonica with Streetband, a group which cut two albums but fell apart a year after their first single, "Toast," came out in 1978 (it did get to #18 on the U.K. chart).

After that event Mick Pearl, the bassist with Streetband, joined Young to form an octet called Q-Tips, where Young had more leeway to indulge in his love of soul music. "We never had any hits," he recalled to Tom Popson in *The Chicago Tribune*. "There was a demand for that music on the dance floor, though. We used to play college circuits, and we'd always pack a place. We had a great name for being an entertaining band, and we lived off that for three years without earning any money from record sales." (Q-Tips recorded one live and one studio album, neither of which generated much enthusiasm.)

After that ensemble's failure, Young embarked on a solo career. His third single, "Wherever I Lay My Hat (That's My Home)," became his first British chart entry, getting to #1 there for three weeks starting July 23, 1983. He had four consecutive top 10 entries after that, ending with "Everytime You Go Away" at #4 in the spring of 1985. The song was a cover of a track from Daryl Hall and John Oates' 1980 album *Voices*.

"My album [*The Secrets of Association*] needed a commercial track," he told Dennis Hunt of *The Los Angeles Times*. "Everything on it is so different. It's like a musical maze. I thought people might find it hard to listen to, even my hard-core fans. You need a gateway into the album, something to make it accessible. A publisher sent me 'Everytime You Go Away' and I eventually used that as the commercial song."

Young admitted he resisted the idea at first. "It was too obvious, too commercial, too rock 'n' soul. Now I'm glad I changed my mind about it."

"Everytime You Go Away" went to #1 pop the week of July 27, 1982, before going to #1 AC. It earned Grammy nominations for Song of the Year and Best Male Pop Vocal Performance, and did far better than his previous three singles released in America, only one of which, 1984's "Come Back and Stay," made the AC chart (it hit #40 AC and #22 pop). The others were "Wherever I Leave My Hat" at #70 pop in 1983 and "Love of the Common People" at #45 in 1984.

It took Young more than five years to get his next #1 AC hit. See 588—"Oh Girl."

480 Cherish

KOOL AND THE GANG

De-Lite 880869

August 24, 1985 (6 weeks)

Writers: Ronald Bell, James Taylor, Kool and the Gang

Producers: Jim Bonneford, Ronald Bell, Kool and the Gang

Kool and the Gang officially began in 1969, and during its first decade the band specialized in funk grooves exemplified by their biggest pop hits, "Jungle Boogie" (#4 pop, #2 R&B) and "Hollywood Swinging" (#6 pop, #1 R&B), both in 1974. But toward the end of the 1970s the hits dried up. Then the band became even more popular in 1979 with new lead singer James "J.T." Taylor (no relation to sweet baby James).

Taylor's distinctive voice provided the group that year with hits ranging from party tunes like "Ladies' Night" (#8 pop, #1 R&B) to mellower material like "Too Hot" (#5 pop, #3 R&B). "Too Hot" also became the first of the group's eight singles on the AC chart, peaking at #11. Other AC entries were "Celebration" (#34 AC, #1 R&B and pop) in 1981, "Joanna" (#2 AC and pop, #1 R&B) in 1984, and "Fresh" (#5 AC, #9 pop, #1 R&B) in 1985. Then came "Cherish," which hit #1 R&B on September 14, 1985, the fourth week it was atop the AC chart, and made #2 pop for three weeks starting September 21, 1985 ("Money for Nothing" by Dire Straits kept it from the top there).

Though "Cherish" was credited to all six members of Kool and the Gang plus producer James Bonneford, keyboardist Curtis Williams said Taylor and Ronald Bell wrote most of the tune, with Taylor doing the lyrics and Bell the music. "It was a song inspired while we were recording the initial [music] tracks in Nassau," Williams said. The band members stayed with their families in beachfront condos which gave them lovely views throughout the day and night, and the experience was such a pleasure that Taylor wrote "Cherish" both as a reflection of the love everyone felt at the time, and as how the band should appreciate the opportunities they had received from their continuing success.

However, "Cherish" was a ballad unlike any the group had done before. Williams credited his fellow keyboardist Bell, brother of group founder and bassist Robert "Kool" Bell, with setting the mood with his melodic introduction that made it easy to record the tune. "Once Ronald was in with the main motif, everything else kind of fell into place," he said. "It was a smooth transition from the funk to that."

The group, which at the time also included drummer George Brown and guitarist Charles Smith, thought the song was something special, but Williams said they were not sure it was necessarily going to be a hit. "You never really know, but people who heard the initial mix of it thought it was beautiful," he said.

After "Special Way" hit #6 AC and #72 pop in 1987, Taylor left the group for a solo career, but neither he nor the band fared well, with Kool and the Gang falling off the AC and pop charts entirely. In 1995 Taylor rejoined the band, which has been touring worldwide since that time.

481 Saving All My Love for You

WHITNEY HOUSTON

Arista 9381

October 5, 1985 (3 weeks)

Writers: Gerry Goffin (words), Michael Masser (music)

Producer: Michael Masser

Not long after making her AC debut in 1984 singing with Teddy Pendergrass in "Hold Me" (#6 AC, #46 pop), Whitney Houston started to work on her first solo album. The initial single from the LP was "You Give Good Love" in 1985, which went to #4 AC, #3 pop, and #1 R&B. For the follow-up, Arista President Clive Davis considered releasing "All at Once," but a performance by Houston of "Saving All My Love for You" at the Roxy in Los Angeles convinced Davis to put that song out instead, and it proved to be an even bigger hit than "You Give Good Love."

"'Saving All My Love' could have been written in the thirties," song co-writer Gerry Goffin told Paul Zollo on *Songwriters on Songwriting*. "I've got to give a lot of credit to Michael Masser. When he used to play me his melodies, I used to laugh because they sounded like traditional ballads. And I said, 'I don't think a traditional ballad is going to make it in today's market.' But I'd write to them anyway 'cause I liked his music. And I'm glad he proved me wrong."

Houston was not the first artist to cut "Saving All My Love for You." In 1978 Marilyn McCoo and Billy Davis Jr. did the tune as a track for their album *Marilyn & Billy*. Masser removed and replaced some parts of the McCoo and Davis version when he produced it for Houston.

"Saving All My Love for You" topped the AC, pop, and R&B charts, though not at the same time. It peaked on the R&B chart first the week of September 7, 1985; a month later it spent three weeks leading the AC chart, and the following week (October 26, 1985) got to #1 on the Hot 100. The record won Houston a Grammy for Best Female Pop Vocal Performance (she was nominated for Best Female Rhythm and Blues Vocal Performance for "You Give Good Love").

In addition, "Saving All My Love for You" became the second of four hit singles released from the *Whitney Houston* album, which peaked at #1 on the LP chart for 14 weeks starting March 8, 1986. And it was the first in a string of five consecutive #1 AC and pop hits, the next being "How Will I Know" [see 489]. Masser was not the sole producer of the album, however. Others who worked on *Whitney Houston* were Jermaine Jackson, Kashif, and Narada Michael Walden.

482 Part-Time Lover
STEVIE WONDER

Tamla 1808

October 26, 1985 (3 weeks)

Writer: Stevie Wonder

Producer: Stevie Wonder

Mix two Supremes hits from the mid-1960s, "My World Is Empty Without You" and "You Can't Hurry Love," and you have the melody for "Part-Time Lover." Or so said the song's writer and singer Stevie Wonder, who got his fifth #1 AC, ninth #1 pop, and 17th #1 R&B hit with the tune. It was his second record to top all three charts; the first, "I Just Called to Say I Love You" [see 462], had come just a year earlier.

"Part-Time Lover" was the first single released from Wonder's album *In Square Circle*. While he might have borrowed the music from earlier Motown hits, the lyrics were his original creation, although he left open exactly who or what, if anyone or anything, might have inspired them.

"Sure, a lot of the songs I write are from my own direct experiences," Stevie Wonder told David Nathan in *Pulse* magazine. "I remember when I was breaking up with a girl and I was like, seeing this *other* girl. I came home and some guy called up and disguised his voice, tried to sound like one of her girlfriends to see if she was around." Asked if that experience inspired "Part-Time Lover," Wonder said, "Well, let's say that after I wrote that, I thought about how many people might get into trouble behind that song!"

Wonder, who sang and played synthesizers and drums on the record, wasn't the only notable name attached to the song's production. Luther Vandross contributed some to the lead vocal, while singing backup were Philip Bailey, lead singer of Earth, Wind and Fire, and Wonder's ex-wife Syreeta Wright. Wright had reached #2 on the AC chart in 1980 in a duet with Billy Preston titled "With You I'm Born Again."

"Part-Time Lover" was a full-time success for Wonder on the charts. Besides #1 AC, it topped the Hot 100 the week of November 2, 1985, and stayed at #1 R&B for six weeks starting October 19, 1985. It also went to #1 on the dance/disco club play and dance/disco 12-inch singles sales charts (listings which evolved out of a dance chart *Billboard* started in September 1974), making it the first song ever to top five different *Billboard* charts.

In addition to its record-setting chart success, "Part-Time Lover" also contributed to Wonder's ever-growing tally of awards. The tune got him a Grammy nomination for Best Male Pop Vocal Performance, and he won the Grammy for Best Male R&B Vocal Performance for the entire *In Square Circle* album. The follow-up to "Part-Time Lover" also made #1 AC [see 486—"Go Home"].

483 Separate Lives
PHIL COLLINS AND MARILYN MARTIN

Atlantic 89498

November 16, 1985 (3 weeks)

Writer: Stephen Bishop

Producers: Arif Mardin, Phil Collins, Hugh Padgham

Phil Collins found himself close but not a winner for the second year in a row as "Separate Lives" followed 1984's "Against All Odds (Take a Look at Me Now)" as a nonwinning Oscar nominee for Best Song. As with "Against All Odds," Collins did not perform the tune at the ceremony, leaving that honor to its composer, Stephen Bishop, who had sung another Oscar-nominated tune, 1983's "It Might Be You" [see 437].

Bishop created "Separate Lives" in 1982 when director Taylor Hackford told him about his latest project, *White Nights*, a drama about a Russian dancer (played by Mikhail Baryshnikov) who defects from the Soviet Union. Intrigued, Bishop wrote "Separate Lives" using his experience with his ex-girlfriend, actress Karen Allen, as one of the basic elements for the lyrics, which he said dealt more with anger than love. He ended up giving the song to Phil Collins to record, but Atlantic Records president Doug Morris felt it should be a duet and suggested that Collins sing with an unknown named Marilyn Martin. For the last few years Martin, a native of Louisville, Kentucky, had been singing background vocals on albums and on tour for artists ranging from Joe Walsh to Stevie Nicks.

Collins agreed to work with Martin. "We overdubbed vocals by Marilyn Martin with great results," co-producer Arif Mardin told Fred Bronson in *Billboard's Hottest Hot 100 Hits*. Mardin, who had worked with Collins on "Against All Odds," joined him again to do "Separate Lives." Their second joint venture went to #1 AC first for two weeks before being #1 pop simultaneously the week of November 30, 1985. It was Collins' fourth #1 pop hit as a soloist or part of a duo and second #1 AC hit under the same category, following "One More Night" [see 471].

The popularity of "Separate Lives" did not, however, lead to a successful solo career for Martin. By herself she only charted one record on the Hot 100, 1986's "Night Moves" at #28, followed by one AC entry that same year, "Move Closer" at #34. In contrast, Collins would have many more #1 AC hits after "Separate Lives," the first being "Groovy Kind of Love" [see 549].

Replacing "Separate Lives" at #1 AC was "Say You, Say Me," also from *White Nights*. It was the first time that two songs from the same movie hit #1 AC back to back, and the second time, following "Endless Love" and "Arthur's Theme (Best That You Can Do)" in 1981, that two Oscar-nominated tunes were consecutive #1 AC hits. In both cases, the second record which hit #1 was the one to claim the Oscar for Best Song.

Say You, Say Me

LIONEL RICHIE

Motown 1819

December 7, 1985 (5 weeks)

Writer: Lionel Richie

Producers: Lionel Richie, James Anthony Carmichael

Taylor Hackford, the director of *White Nights*, had originally asked Richie to write the title tune for the film, but after a few weeks of trying—unsuccessfully—to write a song with that title, Richie came up with "Say You, Say Me." The director loved it. He was not the only one, as the record ended up winning the Oscar for Best Song, the first time a black writer had won since Isaac Hayes claimed the statuette for his tune "Theme From *Shaft*" in 1971.

Richie told Robert E. Johnson of *Jet* magazine that when he won the Oscar for the tune, "I went over to hug my wife, and that was a good response. But I had to check first of all to make sure that the name Lionel Richie was called. That was Lionel Richie's name, wasn't it? Then I went over to hug my mother, and she said, 'Go on up there —they might change their minds.'"

Back in Richie's home state of Alabama, his father called him after the win. "His voice cracked as he said, 'Son, I've got to tell you—you have no idea how proud I am,'" Richie told Johnson. Richie also talked to his grandmother Adelaide Foster, who had inspired him to become a pianist, for about an hour after the Academy Award ceremonies.

"Say You, Say Me" became a virtual cottage industry of awards for Richie. Among other honors, it won a Golden Globe, an American Music Award, and the People's Choice Award for Favorite Song From a Motion Picture. Richie had wanted to release the new album he was working on, tentatively titled *Say You, Say Me*, at the same time as the single, but interruptions in his work schedule, including concerns about his family, forced him to delay the album until August 1986.

The failure to get "Say You, Say Me" on an album while the single was out (due to Richie's contract with Motown, Atlantic Records could not put the song on the soundtrack LP) was about the only disappointment connected to the tune, which topped the AC, pop, and R&B charts. After leading the pop chart first, it went to #1 on the Hot 100 for four weeks starting December 21, 1985. Ending its AC and pop run, it finally hit #1 R&B for two weeks starting January 11, 1986.

"Say You, Say Me" did get on Richie's 1986 album, but by then the title was *Dancing on the Ceiling*. That album's first #1 AC single was "Love Will Conquer All" [see 506].

1986

485 That's What Friends Are For

DIONNE AND FRIENDS

Arista 9422

January 11, 1986 (2 weeks)

Writers: Burt Bacharach, Carole Bayer Sager

Producers: Burt Bacharach, Carole Bayer Sager

During the 1960s Dionne Warwick and Burt Bacharach had reached almost every level of acclaim for her work except for getting a #1 pop single. The two did reach that peak working with others, but it was not until "That's What Friends Are For" that Warwick and the composer, working together, could claim credit at the top spot.

Ironically, the song had not been designed for Warwick. "What happened is I had just gotten back together with Burt after a long sabbatical. He and Carole [Bayer Sager, his partner] had written about five or six songs I looked at in the studio one night," said Warwick. Later that night, she was watching a movie which had a tune that caught her fancy. "I heard this wonderful melody, and I sat up in my bed, and I knew it was Burt. It was Rod Stewart singing it in *Night Shift*." Sure enough, Stewart was the first to record "That's What Friends Are For," but his version on *Night Shift*, a 1982 comedy starring Michael Keaton, generated little attention and did not get released as a single.

Warwick admitted she was not *sure* that Bacharach had written the song since she did not see his name on the credits at the time. When he confirmed that he had done it, she decided she wanted to record it.

In keeping with the "friends" theme of the tune, the decision was made to have a few other artists join Warwick. "They know about my friendships and how vital they are to me," she said. She got on the phone and tracked down Gladys Knight, Stevie Wonder, and Elton John because "Those particular folks were in Los Angeles at the time." Warwick remembered that John had to squeeze the recording session in between shopping for his manager's birthday that night and attending the party.

With each artist taking one of the choruses, "That's What Friends Are For" took on a special life of its own, and again in keeping with the friends theme, Warwick and the others agreed to give any profits from the song to help the American Foundation for AIDS Research. "We filmed the video after the session, when we decided the song should be given to benefit the fight against AIDS," she noted. The song raised more than $1 million.

"That's What Friends Are For" was a triple #1 hit, topping the pop chart for four weeks starting January 18, 1986, and giving Warwick her first R&B #1 for three weeks starting January 25, 1986. She, Knight, Wonder, and John also won Grammys for Best Pop Vocal Group Performance, and "That's What Friends Are For" won the Song of the Year Grammy as well as a nomination for Record of the Year.

486 Go Home

STEVIE WONDER

Tamla 1817

January 25, 1986 (1 week)

Writer: Stevie Wonder

Producer: Stevie Wonder

Stevie Wonder replaced himself at #1 AC when "Go Home" took over the top spot from "That's What Friends Are For," the first time an artist had accomplished that particular feat. "Go Home" also hit #10 pop the week of February 1, 1986, as well as #2 R&B for two weeks.

A *Billboard* singles reviewer described "Go Home" as "Conflicted emotions set to a deep-cut, pumping groove; if the breezy 'Part-Time Lover' [the single preceding 'Go Home'; see 482] was a monster crowd-pleaser, its darker follow-up is altogether more subtle and affecting." An earlier review in the same publication of *In Square Circle*, the album containing "Go Home," called the tune "superb" but considered the numbers "I Love You Too Much" and "Spiritual Walkers" as even better bets for being hits as singles (neither were).

The fact that *In Square Circle* even got out to the public felt like a triumph to some Motown staff members, as it was virtually Wonder's first album of all-new music in the 1980s (*Hotter Than July* came out in 1985). Wonder told *USA Today* in 1985 that "It just took me a long time to get the songs I wanted. I usually come up with the music first and then come up with an idea about the song. I sing a lyric out loud and change it right away if it sounds like too many other words. I practice piano every day and sing other people's songs when I do."

At least two years before the album was released, Wonder played parts of it to Motown president Jay Lasker, who was impressed by what he heard. But he and Motown founder Berry Gordy were not thrilled at the amount of time Wonder, ever the perfectionist, was taking to do *In Square Circle*. As Gordy told *Rolling Stone*, "Five years is much too long to spend on making an album. We disagree tremendously on that. He could have had two or three albums out in that time." (In fact, Wonder did do the soundtrack to *The Woman in Red* in 1984, but Motown had only reluctantly agreed to let him do that and delay *In Square Circle* to 1985.)

Wonder had a hat trick of #1 AC hits when the follow-up to "Go Home," "Overjoyed," reached the top a few months later [see 493]. It was the first time in his career he had three consecutive #1 AC hits from the same album, so maybe Wonder was right in taking in his time with *In Square Circle*.

487 My Hometown
BRUCE SPRINGSTEEN

Columbia 05728

February 1, 1986 (1 week)

Writer: Bruce Springsteen

Producers: Bruce Springsteen, Jon Landau, Steve Van Zandt, Chuck Plotkin

By the time "My Hometown" hit #1 AC, Bruce Springsteen was the hottest name in rock and roll. His tour in the summer of 1985 was a sellout in huge venues across America, and his album *Born in the U.S.A.* was a multimillion-selling smash which stayed #1 on the LP chart for seven nonconsecutive weeks in 1984 and 1985 starting July 7, 1984. The album had seven top 10 pop hits, with the last released being "My Hometown."

The tune was one of the first songs Springsteen recorded for *Born in the U.S.A.* Some critics had a field day with the contradiction between the way some listeners construed the lyrics—as a celebration of the singer's birthplace—and what they were really about—a man brooding about the loss of employment and the doubtful future his children faced. Like many of the songs on the album, Springsteen wrote them to critique what had happened to America under Ronald Reagan's presidency, but some, including Reagan himself, thought he was offering patriotic odes to the times.

"My Hometown" peaked at #6 pop for two weeks starting January 25, 1986. The previous month the tune's B-side, a 1975 live, revved-up performance of "Santa Claus Is Coming to Town," had gotten a little airplay on some stations. It also appeared on the massive five-record set *Bruce Springsteen & the E-Street Band Live/1975–85*, which hit #1 on the album chart for seven weeks starting November 29, 1986 and confirmed that there was no rock and roll star bigger than Springsteen in the mid-1980s.

That had not always been the case, of course. Springsteen's hometown was Freehold, New Jersey, where he was born on September 23, 1949. He ventured into playing clubs in New Jersey and Greenwich Village in New York before he was 20, but gained little notice until he formed his E-Street Band in 1973 with saxophonist Clarence Carter as an original member. He made his debut on the Hot 100 with "Born to Run" at #23, but did not get a top 10 pop hit until 1980's "Hungry Heart."

Anyone not familiar with Springsteen prior to 1984 became well acquainted with him that year as he started reeling off the hits from *Born in the U.S.A.*, beginning with "Dancing in the Dark" at #2 pop for four weeks, the highest performance on that chart for any of his singles. His fourth 45 from the LP, "I'm on Fire," a subdued, brooding tune, gave him his AC debut at #6 in 1985.

Springsteen had a handful of later singles make the AC chart in the 1980s and 1990s (e.g., "Human Touch" at #8 in 1992), but the days when he could sell out just about any arena were over (he stopped working with the E-Street Band in 1989). Yet Springsteen remains one of the most respected rock and roll artists among critics and fans alike, and in March 1999 was one of the inductees in the Rock and Roll Hall of Fame.

488 The Sweetest Taboo
SADE

Portrait 05713

February 8, 1986 (1 week)

Writers: Helen Folosade Adu, Martin Ditcham

Producer: Robin Millar

Like her first #1 AC hit, "Smooth Operator" [see 474], "The Sweetest Taboo" also peaked at #5 pop, in this case the week of March 1, 1986, plus #3 R&B. Sade's LP on which "The Sweetest Taboo" appeared, *Promise*, hit #1 on the album chart the first two weeks after "The Sweetest Taboo" peaked at #1 AC.

Detractors grumbled that chart positions were not the only similarity between "The Sweetest Taboo" and "Smooth Operator." To them Sade's silky-smooth vocals were bland and lacked passion, making all of her songs, with their jazz-pop cocktail lounge instrumental backing, sound the same. The vocalist scoffed at that notion in an interview with Mick Brown of *The Sunday Times* in London.

"I think the reason my singing technique has come under such close scrutiny is because we've sold a lot of records," Sade said. "People start getting suspicious and treating you as if you should be as good as Aretha Franklin, which is a little unfair. I'm not trying to be her, or anybody else. I consider myself much more to be a storyteller and a tunemaker than a great vocal stylist. I think I'm good for somebody who's only been singing three years, and I'm improving all the time."

She elaborated on her singing style to Charles Shaar Murray of *Rolling Stone*. "I'm not over the top; I'm not wacky. I'm fairly understated, and that reflects in the way I sing. I don't necessarily think that you have to scream and shout to move somebody. Sometimes. . .to me I'm really putting something in and really saying something. "But when it comes out the other end and people hear it, they think it sounds very understated. Maybe at the right time, with the right song, I will belt and I will go over the top, but I don't think that to overstate is the best way of putting something across."

To date, "belting" has not been a feature of any Sade single. She remained a fairly constant AC artist through 1988, with such singles as "Never As Good As the First Time" (#6 AC, #20 pop) and "Is It a Crime" (#32 AC) in 1986 and "Paradise" (#3 AC, #16 pop) and "Nothing Can Come Between Us" (#21 AC) in 1988. After a four-year absence from the charts she came back in 1992 with "No Ordinary Love" (#14 AC, #28 pop) and then "Kiss of Life" (#20 AC, #78 pop) in 1993. Since then, Sade has kept a low profile in America, although she remains available for bookings.

489 How Will I Know
WHITNEY HOUSTON

Arista 9434

February 15, 1986 (1 week)

Writers: George Merrill, Shannon Rubicam, Narada Michael Walden

Producer: Narada Michael Walden

"How Will I Know" was the first foray into writing for other artists for the duo of George Merrill and Shannon Rubicam, who had previously made the music charts under the group name of Boy Meets Girl [see 555—"Waiting for a Star to Fall"]. A&M executives wanted them to write a song for Janet Jackson, who was working on her heavily anticipated album *Control*, so they cranked out "How Will I Know." Unfortunately for them, Jackson's management felt the tune was not in the spirit of what they wanted on the LP and declined to use it.

"We kind of ignored it for a while," said Rubicam. But others at Merrill and Rubicam's publishing company remembered the song, and when Arista President Clive Davis heard their demo of the song, he declared it would be perfect for Whitney Houston's debut album. He sent it to Houston's producer Narada Michael Walden.

Walden thought a few changes were necessary to make the song a hit. Rubicam recalled that Walden wrote some new bars of music, and needed some words for them. "We wrote some additional lyrics, and we got it to Whitney, which was a stroke of good luck." The initial version of the song came to them quickly, Rubicam added. "We might have taken an hour to write it. We never do that anymore!" Merrill said that the demo took them only one afternoon to complete as well.

Merrill and Rubicam had no idea that "How Will I Know" would be released as a single. "We were happy to have it on the album," Merrill said. They thought the song appealed to Walden because "It had a lot of spunk," said Merrill. "Lively and a lot of spunk," added Rubicam.

Apparently those qualities appealed to A&M honchos as well, for "How Will I Know" became the third release off Whitney's debut LP. It hit #1 on the AC, pop, and R&B charts, topping the Hot 100 for two weeks starting February 15, 1986, and the R&B chart for the week of March 8, 1986.

The timing of the release for "How Will I Know" after Houston's previous "You Give Good Love" and "Saving All My Love for You" [see 481] helped its success and aided in cementing her fame, according to Merrill. "I have to say, I felt it was time for an up-tempo to get across-the-board appeal for her," he said. As for what the songwriters got out of the record, Rubicam said she remembered vividly the first time she heard the tune on radio from a car going by and realized that she had written a hit.

The combination of Merrill, Rubicam, Walden, and Houston worked together on a record one more time after "How Will I Know." The result proved to be just as popular as the first song [see 520—"I Wanna Dance With Somebody (Who Loves Me)"].

490 Sara
STARSHIP

Grunt 14253

February 22, 1986 (3 weeks)

Writers: Ina Wolf, Peter Wolf

Producers: Dennis Lambert, Peter Wolf, Jeremy Smith

Starship descended from Jefferson Starship, which in turn grew out of the 1960s rock band Jefferson Airplane. That lineage meant little to the only Starship member who also was part of Jefferson Airplane, Grace Slick. "This band has absolutely nothing to do with the past," she told Steve Pond of *Rolling Stone*. "I'm the only one who's been around for that long, and I could care less."

Slick joined Jefferson Airplane in 1966, a year after singer Marty Balin and guitarist/singer Paul Kantner formed the group with singer Signe Anderson, bassist Bob Harvey (replaced shortly thereafter by Jack Casady), guitarist Jorma Kaukonen, and drummer Alexander "Spence" Spencer. Slick replaced Anderson while Spencer Dryden took over the other Spencer's spot as drummer in 1966. In 1967 the band had two great psychedelic hits, "Somebody to Love" (#5 pop) and "White Rabbit" (#8 pop), but had little success from then through the early 1970s.

In 1974, the group became Jefferson Starship, with Slick, Kantner, drummer John Barbata, guitarist Craig Chaquico, violinist Papa John Creach, and bassists David Freiberg and Pete Sears. "Miracles" in 1975 became the group's first AC appearance (#17) and biggest pop hit (#3).

Jefferson Starship had a few more shared AC and pop successes through 1978, the biggest AC hit being "With Your Love" at #6 AC and #12 pop in 1976. They continued to make the Hot 100 in the early 1980s, albeit sporadically, and the cast changes continued. Mickey Thomas replaced Balin in 1979, and in 1982 Donny Baldwin was the group's sixth drummer. In 1984 Kantner left the group and sued for ownership of its name, with an out-of-court settlement letting the rest of the band continue as Starship. Creach, Freiberg, and Sears had dropped out by the time of Starship's 1985 album, leaving only Slick, Thomas, Baldwin, and Chaquico.

Going against the Jefferson tradition, members of Starship accepted songs from writers outside the group in an effort to expand the fan base. This worked well as "We Built This City" went to #37 AC and #1 pop in late 1985, followed by the ballad "Sara" getting to #1 AC and pop, topping the latter chart the week of March 15, 1986.

But longtime Jefferson Airplane fans loathed the change. As Thomas told Pond, "What I hate more than anything is this idea that we're selling out. . . . Jefferson Airplane, in the eyes of the public now, really stood for something, for these high ideals, and was spokesman for a generation and all that kind of stuff. And now Starship is just kind of making well-crafted, commercial pop songs. But I just don't think the comparison is fair." Fair or not, the new Starship did claim several hits. The next one on the AC chart came in 1987 [see 514—"Nothing's Gonna Stop Us Now"].

491 These Dreams
HEART

Capitol 5541

March 15, 1986 (3 weeks)

Writers: Bernie Taupin, Martin Page

Producer: Ron Nevison

Heart formed in Seattle in 1974 when guitarist/keyboardist Nancy Wilson joined the band of her sister Ann Wilson, who had been vocalist since 1970 of what was first known as the Army and then, from 1972–74, as White Heart. Generally a quintet, Heart had many personnel changes over the years. Guitarist Howard Leese, who joined the group in 1980, was, besides the Wilsons, the longest-lived member.

Heart's first Hot 100 entry, "Crazy on You" (#35 pop in 1976), set the pattern of its predominately thumping rock sound. From 1977–81 Heart slowed down to make the AC chart three times prior to "These Dreams," the first time with "Dreamboat Annie" in 1977 (#17 AC, #42 pop). But after 1981 the group's airplay and sales slumped, so the Wilsons agreed to their record label's demand to use outside material rather than write most of their own songs, as they had in the past.

Discussing this change, Ann Wilson said, "It was easy in the beginning, when they gave us great songs like 'These Dreams.'" But she objected to letting Nancy and not her sing lead. "It was not without a struggle," she said. "I really wanted to sing the song, but it was decided she should do it because the lyrics were very wispy and dreamy."

But Nancy had a cold when "These Dreams" was to be recorded. "She said, 'I don't feel like singing. My throat is pretty scratchy,'" Ann recalled. The protest failed. When "These Dreams" became Heart's first #1 both AC and pop, topping the latter the week of March 22, 1986, Nancy found to her dismay that producers and fans wanted her to recreate that gravelly sound on future songs.

"These Dreams" was the third of four top 10 pop songs released from Heart's self-titled LP which also made #1 on the album chart the week of December 21, 1985. It was the first of those singles to make the AC chart, after "What About Love?" and "Never," and its follow-up, "Nothin' At All," made #40 AC and #10 pop. "These Dreams" also carried a special dedication on the album to longtime Heart fan Sharon Hess. "At the time we were making the *Heart* album, she had terminal leukemia," noted Ann. "She came out and hung in the studio a couple of days." Shortly thereafter, Hess died at age 21.

Heart made the AC and pop charts occasionally into the early 1990s. Then in 1991, an impromptu concert with pals Sue Ennis and Frank Cox led to a new venture: the Wilsons formed an acoustic quartet called the Lovemongers. The new group's first LP, *Whirlygig*, came out in 1998. While the Lovemongers were touring that spring, Ann announced she would tour during the summer as Heart featuring Ann Wilson, so Nancy could take time off to have a baby.

Ann felt confident she could keep both bands going. "We still want to do Heart," she said. "The Lovemongers can be anything we want it to be, too."

492 Secret Lovers
ATLANTIC STARR

A&M 2788

April 5, 1986 (1 week)

Writers: David Lewis, Wayne Lewis

Producers: David Lewis, Wayne Lewis

Formed in White Plains, New York, in 1976, Atlantic Starr was originally a nine-piece unit led by brothers David, Wayne, and Jonathan Lewis. Joining them in the lineup was lead singer Sharon Bryant (born in Westchester County, New York, on August 14, 1956), plus Clifford Archer, Porter Carroll, Joseph Phillips, Damon Rentie, and William Sudderth. They moved to the Los Angeles area in 1978 and got their first R&B entry that year with "Stand Up" at #16. Atlantic Starr compiled four more singles on the chart through 1981, with the highest being "When Love Calls Me" at #5 in 1981, but could not cross over to the AC chart or Hot 100.

They did get on the latter listing in 1982 when "Circles," a #2 R&B 45, also got to #38 pop. But it did not lead to a long-term affair with the Hot 100, as plenty of their singles failed to hit the chart or got only low positions on it. In fact, just their two top 10 R&B singles from 1983–85 got on the Hot 100, "Touch a Four Leaf Clover" at #4 R&B and #87 pop in 1983 and "Freak-A-Ristic" at #6 R&B and #90 pop in 1985.

By the time "Freak-A-Ristic" came out, Atlantic Starr had whittled itself down to just the Lewises, Phillips, and new female lead singer Barbara Weathers (Rentie had left the group in 1980 and been replaced by Koran Daniels, who left along with Archer, Carroll and Sudderth a few years later). Sharon Bryant tried a solo career but came away with little to show for it other than two moderately performing singles in 1989, "Let Go" at #2 R&B and #34 pop and "Foolish Heart" at #7 R&B and #90 pop. She also sang with her old Atlantic Starr comrade Porter Carroll on the 1990 single "The Real Thing" for saxophonist Marion Meadows, which reached #44 R&B. The realigned Atlantic Starr finally got the crossover hit they had been wanting with the Lewises' laid-back ballad "Secret Lovers," released in late 1985.

"Secret Lovers" went to #3 pop for the weeks of March 22 and 29, 1986, behind "These Dreams" [see 491] at #1 and "Sara" [see 490] at #2 the first week and Falco's "Rock Me Amadeus" at #1 and "These Dreams" at #2 the second. It also was #4 R&B. The tune was the fourth single from their *As the Band Turns* LP. Following it was "If Your Heart Isn't in It," which made #4 R&B, #11 AC, and #57 pop.

Atlantic Starr faltered with the 45 after that, "Armed and Dangerous," as it made only #86 pop in the fall of 1986, but they came back in full force a year later with another multi-chart hit [see 518—"Always"].

493 Overjoyed
STEVIE WONDER

Tamla 1832

April 12, 1986 (2 weeks)

Writer: Stevie Wonder

Producer: Stevie Wonder

After the somewhat funky groove of "Go Home" [see 486], Stevie Wonder returned to familiar AC territory with the keyboard-heavy ballad "Overjoyed." Like his previous odes of affection, he claimed it was written for no one in particular. "When I write my love songs, I think of the people in my life—my children, my mother, brothers and sisters, all the loves of my life," he told Donna E. Haupt in *Life* magazine.

"Overjoyed" was a moderate hit for Wonder, going to #1 AC, #8 R&B, and #24 pop. It was the third single from his *In Square Circle* album. One more 45 followed it, "Land of La La," but it was a washout, not making the AC chart and getting only to #86 pop.

In 1987 Wonder had another single emerge which failed to get onto the AC roster. "Skeletons" climbed to #19 pop and #1 R&B. Another #1 R&B hit came in 1988 with "You Will Know," but the record performed less spectacularly for him on the other charts, getting to #16 AC and #77 pop. He then had two duets come out in the summer of 1988, both of which stopped at #80 pop; "My Love" with Julio Iglesias managed to cross over to #14 AC, but "Get It," with Michael Jackson, did not live up to its title, missing the AC listing entirely.

The 1990s have been the toughest decade for Wonder in terms of hits since he got into the music business. His "Keep Our Love Alive" made #44 AC in 1990 without making the Hot 100, something a Stevie Wonder single had never done before. He did the soundtrack for the movie *Jungle Fever* in 1991, but the music did not have the same appeal that his work for *The Woman in Red* had seven years earlier [see 462—"I Just Called to Say I Love You"]. Only one single, "Gotta Have You," made the Hot 100, but it topped out at a measly #92 and missed the AC chart totally.

Wonder waited four more years before releasing another album, and although *Conversation Piece* got to #16 on the album chart in 1995, few people talked about the LP or its singles, none of which were hits, as they had with previous Wonder records. But despite the dearth of recent hits, Wonder is highly respected within the music industry, and in 1996 he received the Grammy's Lifetime Achievement Award.

Though he had no album out in 1998, he could be heard singing on two soundtracks of films, "True to Your Heart" in *Mulan* and "Masta Blasta '98" with Wyclef Jean on *How Stella Got Her Groove Back*. Whatever he does next matters little; his place in history is secure, and he will be remembered as one of the leading creative musical forces of the 20th century.

494 Greatest Love of All
WHITNEY HOUSTON

Arista 9466

April 26, 1986 (5 weeks)

Writers: Michael Masser, Linda Creed

Producer: Michael Masser

"Greatest Love of All" went to #22 AC, #24 pop, and #2 R&B when done originally by George Benson in 1977 for *The Greatest*, the autobiographical film about Muhammed Ali starring the boxing champ as himself. It became a favorite tune for Whitney Houston to perform while an aspiring singer, and she sang it when Arista head Clive Davis spotted her in action at the club Sweetwater's in Manhattan when she was 19.

Houston, born in Newark, New Jersey, on August 9, 1963 and raised in East Orange, New Jersey, has spent most of her lifetime involved with music at some level. Her mother is Cissy Houston, the leader of the Sweet Inspirations backup group which has sung behind many major artists including Aretha Franklin, and Dionne Warwick is a cousin. She has fond memories of hearing and being with these ladies as their careers prospered during the late 1960s and early 1970s.

"I was only 6 or 7 at the time and didn't realize history was being made—I just loved the way 'Aunt Ree' [her nickname for Franklin] sang and how she made people feel," Houston told Stephen Holden in *The New York Times*. "Dionne was a legend when I was growing up and has always been like a second mother. But my mom was my biggest influence."

Despite all the talent around her, she told Holden it took her a little time to learn she had musical talent for a career. "Although I started singing in the church choir when I was 7, it wasn't until I was 12 or 13 that I realized I was a singer and that this gift God gave me was something I could spread around," she said. She backed up Lou Rawls and Chaka Khan, among other artists, in her early teens, then at 15 went to sing in clubs with her mother. At first she did one solo per show, then several and then finally had her own act.

Davis spent $270,000 to produce Houston's first album, quite above the normal amount laid out for a new artist, but he was convinced she was something special. He had her do "Greatest Love of All" under the supervision of Michael Masser, the song's co-writer, but its potential as a single was overlooked initially. Originally it was the B-side of her first solo single, "You Give Good Love," in 1985, then became her fourth and final single from her LP *Whitney Houston*. Her version went to #1 pop for three weeks starting May 17, 1986, and #3 R&B as well as #1 AC.

Houston told Lynn Norment in *Ebony* her opinion of the importance of "Greatest Love of All": "Our young people need to hear that song and realize that it's all about loving yourself. If you can love yourself through all your rights and wrongs and faults, then that's the greatest love of all. That's the message."

495 Live to Tell
MADONNA

Sire 28717

May 31, 1986 (3 weeks)

Writers: Madonna, Patrick Leonard

Producer: Patrick Leonard

Branded a one-hit wonder in 1983 when the peppy "Holiday" went to #16 pop in her Hot 100 debut, Madonna proved her many critics wrong by succeeding in the recording industry beyond even her own wildest dreams. There were a number of reasons for her success, and certainly one of them was the expansion of Madonna's range, from dance ditties to introspective ballads such as "Live to Tell," which she recorded for *At Close Range*, a film starring actor Sean Penn, her then-husband.

Madonna made her AC debut in 1984 with the follow-up to "Holiday," called "Borderline," which made #23 AC and #10 AC. She had six more singles make the chart before "Live to Tell," with wildly varying results, in sharp contrast to her showing on the Hot 100 from 1983–93, when 27 consecutive Madonna singles made the pop top 20. For example, "Angel" made #5 AC, the same peak it had on the pop chart, but "Material Girl," a song so associated with her it became her nickname, made only #38 AC for two weeks while going to #2 pop.

"Live to Tell" began as a melody Patrick Leonard wrote for a film called *Fire With Fire*. Madonna, who hired Leonard to be musical director of her 1985 tour, agreed to write the lyrics for him. But after Paramount Pictures rejected the tune for *Fire With Fire*, Madonna thought it would work fine for *At Close Range* and wrote lyrics accordingly. Though it was designed for a man to sing, Madonna ended up cutting the tune, needing only one take to do it.

In concert Madonna's performance of "Live to Tell" was a showstopper. With a large picture of herself projected in the background, she stood front and center by herself, singing the song. Toward the end, the picture darkened, and Madonna dropped to her knees, then got herself back up and stood tall, usually to tremendous applause.

Upon witnessing the scene, *Rolling Stone* reporter Mikal Gilmore asked her if the scenario was her commentary on ill-fated icon Marilyn Monroe, a person Madonna often found herself measured against. "Actually, I think 'Live to Tell' is about something very different," she responded. "It's about being strong, and questioning whether you can be that strong, but ultimately surviving." She later clarified to Gilmore that "Marilyn Monroe was a victim, and I'm not. That's why there's really no comparison."

With "Live to Tell" hitting #1 AC and pop, the latter the week of June 7, 1986, Madonna certainly was not a sufferer. She would go on to have several more #1 AC hits, the first being "La Isla Bonita" in 1987 [see 517].

496 There'll Be Sad Songs (To Make You Cry)

BILLY OCEAN

Jive 9432

June 21, 1986 (1 week)

Writers: Wayne Brathwaite, Barry J. Eastmond, Billy Ocean

Producer: Barry J. Eastmond, Wayne Brathwaite

Billy Ocean's previous #1 AC hit, "Suddenly" [see 475], was the "particular song" which inspired co-writer Barry J. Eastmond to add words to a melody he had floating in his head for a time. Eastmond said in *The Billboard Book of Number One Hits* by Fred Bronson that "The lyrics came out of a story my wife told me about a friend of hers. She had just broken up with the fellow she had been going out with for years. There was a particular song that always made her think of her boyfriend.

"She was at a party given by her new boyfriend and the song came on and reminded her of the old boyfriend. She broke down. . .we thought that was an interesting story so we wrote the song around it."

"There'll Be Sad Songs (To Make You Cry)" topped the AC chart before doing the same on the R&B and pop listings. It was #1 R&B the weeks of June 28 and July 5, 1986 and #1 pop the week of July 5, 1986.

Ocean had some ups and downs between "Suddenly" and "There'll Be Sad Songs (To Make You Cry)." "Mystery Lady" came out in the summer of 1985 and went to #5 AC but only #24 pop, a relative disappointment given that Ocean's previous two singles ("Suddenly" and "Caribbean Queen") had made the top 10 both AC and pop. Later in 1985 Ocean's remake of the Beatles' #2 AC and #1 pop hit of 1970, "The Long and Winding Road," was a washout, going only to #24 AC without making the Hot 100.

Then Ocean, Eastmond, and Wayne Brathwaite co-wrote almost all of the songs for Ocean's *Love Zone* album in 1986, which came out after "There'll Be Sad Songs (To Make You Cry)" was released. Eastmond, who joined Brathwaite as the album's producer, had played keyboards and synthesizers on Oceans's previous LP *Suddenly*. That tune, however, was not the three men's first collaboration out as a single. That distinction went to "When the Going Gets Tough, the Tough Get Going" from the soundtrack of the movie *The Jewel of the Nile*, which made #2 AC and pop in early 1986.

After "There'll Be Sad Songs" had run its course, the next single was the title tune from *Love Zone*, which made #5 AC and #10 pop. The third release of the LP was "Love Is Forever," which went to #1 AC at the end of 1986 and gave Ocean his fourth consecutive top 5 AC and top 20 pop single [see 508].

497 No One Is to Blame

HOWARD JONES

Elektra 69549

June 28, 1986 (1 week)

Writer: Howard Jones

Producers: Phil Collins, Hugh Padgham

Virtually every British record label turned him down in the early 1980s, but Howard Jones was not a man who took no for an answer in his quest for show business success. He finally secured a deal when his stage show displayed his one-man-band versatility: Jones played drum machines, fancy keyboards, synthesizers, and other gadgets while he sang, and a mime acted out scenarios during songs. But Jones's early reliance on machines (he also experimented with sequencers, filters, and other specialized equipment) led detractors to claim he was interested more in sounds than substantial lyrics, a charge which he disputed.

"The words take priority," he told Parke Puterbaugh in *Rolling Stone*. "I can say that categorically, because I just feel embarrassed if the words aren't saying something—at least posing a question or provoking some kind of reaction."

Born to Welsh parents in Southampton, England, on February 23, 1955, Jones had a herky-jerky childhood, having to live in some 18 different locales including, at one point, Canada. His higher education ended at age 21 when he got fed up with studying classical piano in the Royal Northern School of Music in Manchester, England, and went out on his own. His activities during the late 1970s in Manchester included playing in various bands and teaching piano, and he had his own late-night slot on a local radio station doing piano instrumental versions of popular hits of the time under the name of John Howard.

He then spent three years in a plastic-wrap factory, first as a shop worker and then as a buyer in the front office, and those years made him realize that if he was serious about having a career in music, he needed to take action as soon as possible. "If there's one experience in my life I couldn't do without, it was that," he told Puterbaugh.

After landing a record deal, Jones's first 45 on the United Kingdom chart was "New Song" in 1983, which went to #3. Its follow-up, "What Is Love," became his highest-charting tune, peaking at #2. He had four more top 10 hits in Britain through "Look Mama," which stalled at #10 in mid-1985.

In 1986 "No One Is to Blame" made #16 on the British chart. Although it was on his *Dream Into Action* LP, Jones had "No One Is to Blame" rerecorded for single release under the production of Phil Collins, a fan of Jones' music. Collins also played drums and sang backup on the cut.

"No One Is to Blame" stopped at #4 the week of July 5, 1986 after peaking at #1 AC. Jones would have another #1 AC after that [see 566—"Everlasting Love"].

498 Your Wildest Dreams

THE MOODY BLUES

Threshold 883906

July 5, 1986 (2 weeks)

Writer: Justin Hayward

Producer: Tony Visconti

The Moody Blues have the odd distinction of being the only act to score just one top 10 pop hit per decade in the 1960s, 1970s, and 1980s. Their American chart debut was "Go Now!" which made #10 in 1965. Several 45s later, a rerelease of their flop 1968 single "Nights in White Satin" surged to #2 pop for two weeks in 1972, and also gave the group its first AC entry at #37. Nearly 14 more years passed until they cracked the top 10 of the Hot 100 again, when "Your Wildest Dreams" went to #9 pop and #1 AC.

"I believe a lot of young people were introduced to the Moody Blues by 'Your Wildest Dreams,' which coincided with a kind of fascination about the Sixties," opined lead vocalist and guitarist Justin Hayward in the liner notes to the Moody Blues' 1994 retrospective LP *Time Traveller*. "There's always been a certain amount of looking backwards within our music; about searching and seeking some kind of enlightenment. A lot of that can be understood by knowing what's happened before you. . . ."

The Moody Blues' own past consisted of five musicians getting together in Birmingham, England, in 1964. They were drummer Graeme Edge (born March 30, 1942), guitarist and singer Denny Laine (born Brian Hines on October 29, 1944), keyboardist and singer Mike Pinder (born December 19, 1942), flautist and singer Ray Thomas (born December 29, 1942), and bassist Clint Warwick (born June 25, 1940). Laine and Warwick left a year after "Go Now!" hit and were replaced by Hayward (born October 14, 1946) and bassist and singer John Lodge (born July 20, 1943). The lineup stayed intact until 1978, when Patrick Moraz, the former keyboardist for the rock group Yes, assumed Pinder's duties through early 1992.

For the most part the hits of the Moody Blues did not cross over from pop to the AC chart. Between "Nights in White Satin" and "Your Wildest Dreams," only two of the group's singles managed that feat: "Driftwood," which made #38 AC and #59 pop in 1978, and "The Voice," which stopped at #16 AC and #15 pop in 1981. In fact, after "Your Wildest Dreams," the group had few other hit singles. The follow-up, "The Other Side of Life," hit #18 AC and #58 pop in 1986, then "I Know You're Out There Somewhere" became the last Moody Blues single to make the Hot 100 when it went to #30 pop and #9 AC in 1988. Its follow-up, "No More Lies," went only to #15 AC. The group would not score again on the AC chart until "Say It With Love" reached #31 in 1991.

At the end of the decade, although their hitmaking days appeared to be over, the Moody Blues continued to record and tour, signed to PolyGram Records.

499 Glory of Love

PETER CETERA

Full Moon 28662

July 19, 1986 (5 weeks)

Writers: Peter Cetera, David Foster, Diane Nini

Producer: Michael Omartian

The popularity of "Glory of Love" did not surprise singer Peter Cetera. "I really was expecting a number one single," he told Lynn Van Matre in *The Chicago Tribune*. "Why? Because I just really felt that this song, which meant so much to me, would mean a lot to a lot of other people, too.

"You know, there's an old saying about how if you give yourself 100 percent [to a project], that's all you can ask. And I really gave *more* than 100 percent of myself on that song—and on the whole solo album. It was the first time in my life that I worked on an album and wanted to listen to it more than one time when it was done."

Cetera had worked on plenty of albums in his life, having been the lead singer for Chicago for nearly 20 years before going full-time into his solo career. Born in Chicago on September 13, 1944, he actually did his first solo album in 1981 while still putting his tenor voice at the front of Chicago records, but that LP generated little sales activity or airplay. In the mid-1980s, after wanting to leave the group for several years, he finally did so. He told Van Matre that Chicago's "jazz-rock music never was me. I was always the rock and roller, trying to get out."

One of the first projects he took on as a soloist was "Glory of Love," written for the movie *The Karate Kid II*. What appealed to Cetera about the tune was its lyrics. His wife, Diane Nini, had helped write a few verses. It was to be her only writing credit on a hit record, although she had provided background noises for "Mononucleosis," an odd track on 1974's *Chicago VII* album.

"I think that every man sees himself that way, and I think that every lady sees that song as being about looking for the man who is going to die for her honor," he told Van Matre. "I think the secret dream of everybody in the world, man or woman, is to be the fairy tale prince or princess."

"Glory of Love" hit #1 both AC and pop, topping the latter chart for two weeks starting August 2, 1986. It also received an Oscar nomination for Best Song. Cetera contributed to the song's writing along with David Foster, who had been Chicago's producer during the early 1980s. It was his first solo entry on the AC and pop charts, and was the only hit from *The Karate Kid II* soundtrack.

Cetera followed "Glory of Love" with another #1 AC and pop hit, "The Next Time I Fall," a duet with Amy Grant [see 505]. He also sang on another Oscar-nominated Best Song in 1989, "After All," with Cher [see 563].

500 Words Get in the Way

MIAMI SOUND MACHINE

Epic 06120

August 23, 1986 (2 weeks)

Writer: Gloria Estefan

Producer: Emilio Estefan

In October of 1975, a woman named Gloria Fajardo auditioned with her cousin Merci to sing with a weekend band called Miami Sound Machine. Emilio Estefan, the head of the band, hired them not only because he liked their voices but because they would be the only women to sing lead in a Latin band in Miami, Florida. The novelty worked, and what began as a part-time venture eventually grew into the biggest act coming out of Miami during the mid-1980s.

Gloria was a baby when her father, Jose Manuel Fajardo, a former bodyguard to President Fulgencio Batista, fled to Miami after Fidel Castro's takeover of Cuba in 1959. In 1961, Fajardo took part in the ill-fated C.I.A.-backed Bay of Pigs invasion of Cuba, and spent 18 months in a Cuban prison before President John F. Kennedy negotiated his release.

Later, Fajardo volunteered for service in the Vietnam War. During that conflict, he was exposed to Agent Orange, and returned home a very sick man. His daughter Gloria tried to cope with her grief through singing by herself and playing guitar.

A year after Gloria joined Miami Sound Machine, she and Emilio began a relationship, and they were married on September 1, 1978. A year earlier the group had released its first album, *Renacer*, locally, but Emilio had bigger plans and by 1981 had given up his day job to work at Miami Sound Machine full time. From 1981–83 Miami Sound Machine released four albums in Spanish on CBS Records' Hispanic division Discos CBS International, garnering #1 hits in Panama, Peru, and and Venzuela. During this period a few members quit, including Merci,

"Words Get in the Way" went to #5 pop the week of September 20, 1986.

Clockwise
from top left:
Kiki Garcia,
Marcos Avila,
Gloria Estefan,
Emilio Estefan

501 Friends and Lovers
GLORIA LORING AND CARL ANDERSON

USA Carrere 06122

September 6, 1986 (2 weeks)

Writers: Paul Gordon, Jay Gruska

Producer: Yves Dessca

Born in New York City on December 10, 1946, Gloria Loring was a busy TV singer in the 1960s and 1970s. "I did about 400 variety shows," she said, including 32 appearances on *The Merv Griffin Show* in one year. Her first acting job was as vocalist Liz Curtis on NBC-TV's daily soap opera *Days of Our Lives*.

Loring had recorded as early as 1968 on MGM, but when she got to *Days* she told an associate producer she feared she never would have a hit. "I said the only way I could do it is if I found a wonderful song and it was tied onto a story line on the show," she recalled.

The associate producer knew that another actor on the soap had sung "Friends and Lovers," but the tune had attracted little attention. The producer played the demo for Loring. "It got to the end of the first chorus and I said, 'That's a hit song if I ever heard one,'" she said.

"Friends and Lovers" became the show's theme song for Kimberly Brady, played by Patsy Pease, and Shane Donovan, played by Charles Shaughnessy. As Loring's character sang "Friends and Lovers" every other week, it generated much fan mail and requests for copies.

But Loring heard the song as a duet, and she wanted it to be released as a single that way. She tried Al Jarreau, but he was on tour at the time. Then Loring's boyfriend took her to see Carl Anderson, born in Lynchburg, Virginia, on February 27, 1945 and best known for playing Judas in the Broadway and movie productions of *Jesus Christ Superstar*. Loring remembered that she had said, after leaving the show, "Oh, he's got a fabulous voice."

She and Anderson recorded "Friends and Lovers" but, she noted, "Every major music company turned it down." Finally Carrere Records, a label distributed in America by CBS, planned to release it. Legal delays held up the release for a year, and Loring, worried that the song would never come out, took to calling it "Friends and Lawyers."

When "Friends and Lovers" finally saw the light of day, it was still being played on the soap and getting much fan mail, and the song went to #2 pop for two weeks starting September 27, 1986, behind "Stuck With You" [see 502]. It also made #54 R&B. Loring said the song's appeal was "The simple musical melody, very listenable, just lovely, combined with a lyric that's just classic. 'I'll be your friend, and I'll be your lover'—you can't top that." Despite her feelings that the song deserved to be a hit, however, she was amazed at the route it had taken to get there. "That was an absolute miracle for that to have happened," she said. "I just consider the whole process a gift from God."

Loring released a few LPs afterward, but had no other AC entries after "Friends and Lovers." She sang the song with Anderson on a few TV shows and concerts, but mostly they pursued separate careers. Anderson did have some minor R&B hits, and Loring continued to tour, record, and act through the '90s.

502 Stuck With You
HUEY LEWIS AND THE NEWS

Chrysalis 43019

September 20, 1986 (3 weeks)

Writers: Chris Hayes, Huey Lewis

Producers: Huey Lewis and the News

Huey Lewis was born Hugh Cregg III in New York City on July 5, 1950, and raised in Mill Valley, California. He began playing harmonica after high school and eventually joined the country-rock band Clover in 1972. They had success in Great Britain but none in America despite much touring, and had broken up by 1979. During that time in England he changed his professional name to Huey Lewis.

Later in 1979, Lewis sent out demo tapes under the

name Huey Lewis and American Express. The latter was really a group of friends with whom Lewis sang at a hangout in Corte Madera, California. The tapes eventually led to them signing with Chrysalis Records. The group planned to release its first LP for Chrysalis when, according to Lewis, "Their legal department was afraid we were going to be sued by American Express." To head off potential legal problems, the band became Huey Lewis and the News.

The self-titled *Huey Lewis and the News* LP in 1980 flopped, but in 1982 Lewis and his group hit with their second album, *Picture This*, and its single, "Do You Believe in Love," which went to #7 pop. The next LP, 1984's *Sports*, hit #1 and contained five top 20 pop singles, including the first AC entry, "If This Is It," which made #5.

The hits kept coming through mid-1985, when "The Power of Love" from the movie *Back to the Future* gave Huey Lewis and the News its first #1 pop hit and #6 AC charting. Pressured by Chrysalis executives to get out a new album fast, Lewis cranked out the lead single for the projected album, "Stuck With You," along with News lead guitarist Chris

Hayes. (Other members of the News were Mario Cipollina on bass, Johnny Colla on sax, Bill Gibson on drums, and Sean Hopper on keyboards.)

"Chris wrote the music and I wrote the words," Lewis recalled. "The melody was hummed out by both of us. It was very quick." He said the lyrics, which despite the title indicated the singer was "happy to be stuck with you," were inspired by his wife. "My wife and I had been married 10 years at the time," he said.

"Stuck With You" was #1 AC and pop simultaneously for three weeks starting September 20, 1986. The album from which it came, *Fore!*, also hit #1. Lewis kept hitting the AC chart into the 1990s, with two songs, "Doing It All For My Baby" in 1987 and "Perfect World" in 1988, making #2.

Though Huey Lewis and the News releases have not been as popular in the 1990s as their music was in the previous decade, the group has continued to record and tour frequently. In 1998 the group began working on a new album for Elektra, with all-new material, their first such LP in four years.

Huey Lewis and the News
(Lewis is fourth from the left)

503 Throwing It All Away
GENESIS

Atlantic 89372

October 11, 1986 (2 weeks)

Writers: Anthony Banks, Phil Collins, Mike Rutherford

Producers: Genesis, Hugh Padgham

Genesis had its genesis in England in 1966, when the group was formed and made its first recording for British Decca in 1968. Peter Gabriel sang lead vocals, with Tony Banks on keyboards, Anthony Phillips on guitar, Mike Rutherford on guitar and bass, and Chris Stewart on drums. The drumming position underwent a great amount of changeover initially, with Stewart replaced by John Silver in 1968 and then John Mayhew in 1969. Mayhew left the next year along with Phillips, and their respective replacements were Phil Collins and Steve Hackett.

In December 1972 the group made their American concert debut, and a year later their fourth English album, *Selling England by the Pound*, became their first U.S. release. But they remained a cult album group even in the United Kingdom, where they did not get their first chart entry on the singles listing until 1974, with "I Know What I Like (In Your Wardrobe)," which made #21.

In August 1975 Gabriel left the group, and Collins, who also recorded with a band called Brand X for a time, remained on drums while assuming Gabriel's role as lead singer. Hackett left in 1977, the same time Genesis made a concerted effort to attain success on the pop charts in order to survive as a band. "Your Own Special Way" got them their Hot 100 debut that year when it went to #62, but Genesis really broke through in 1978 when "Follow You Follow Me" made #21 AC, their first entry on the chart, and #23 pop. However, the group had a spotty track record through the mid-1980s, with only two top 20 pop hits in this period making the AC chart as well—1980's "Misunderstanding" (#32 AC, #14 pop) and 1984's "That's All!" (#7 AC, #6 pop).

The ascension of Collins' solo career in 1985 [see 471— "One More Night"] drew attention to Genesis' 1986 releases, and finally he, Banks, and Rutherford got the due they deserved, though some old fans still missed Gabriel.

Collins admitted that his approach did occasionally make him seem like the odd man out. "The basic difference between me and Pete and Tony and Mike is that lyrically they're a bit emotionally screwed up," Collins told Rob Hoerburger in *Rolling Stone*. "They went to boarding schools all their lives, only saw their families on holidays, while I went to a regular school, went home every day. They would never put 'I love you' in a lyric, whereas I think nothing of it."

Judging by the title and lyrics of "Throwing It All Away," the group's first #1 AC hit, it seems safe to say that Collins didn't have much to do with the writing. That song also went to #4 pop the weeks of October 11 and 18, 1986. Genesis would score again in 1987 with "In Too Deep" [see 519].

504 I'll Be Over You
TOTO

Columbia 06280

October 25, 1986 (2 weeks)

Writers: Steve Lukather, Randy Goodrum

Producers: Toto

After the success of the *Toto IV* album [see 438—"I Won't Hold You Back"], Toto went through three lead singers in as many years. Original vocalist Bobby Kimball was followed by Fergie Fredericksen, but his work on "Stranger in Town" in 1984 (#30 pop) and "Holyanna" in 1985 (#71 pop) did not thrill the group or their audience. In 1986 Joe Williams, son of conductor John Williams, became the lead.

Regarding those years, Toto guitarist Steve Lukather said, "It was terrible. Lead singers, they always think it's about them. . . .It's hard to fit someone into something pre-existed." He said none of the singers left because they wanted to go, and even admitted that Williams was not his choice as new vocalist. The issue really did not matter to him, however, because he sang lead on Toto's 1986 hit "I'll Be Over You."

"That song was written in about 15 minutes," he said. "Randy [Goodrum] and I used to live behind my mother down in the [San Fernando] Valley." Through mutual friends the two met and wrote at least two songs together before creating "I'll Be Over You."

"I came up with the opening, the riff. It just fell into place, and Randy wrote the lyrics, and it just came together," Lukather said. He planned to give the song to an unnamed artist, but then at a meeting with Toto members, "I just played it for the guys, and they flipped."

As with his "I Won't Hold You Back," Lukather's "I'll Be Over You" hit #1 AC and did well on the pop chart too, cresting at #11. "It was ironic that I sang both of those songs," he said. Lukather recalled that while he brought a hard edge to Toto's music, "I've been the one writing the ballads for the band."

But Toto's hitmaking days wilted after "I'll Be Over You." Its follow-up, "Without Your Love," went to #7 AC and #38 pop in 1987. The following year "Pamela" made #9 AC and #22 pop, but was the group's last Hot 100 entry. "Anna," released later in 1988, was their AC swan song, reaching #47.

On August 5, 1992, Toto drummer Jeff Porcaro died at age 38. "He was like my big brother I never had," Lukather said. "I talked with him the day he died." Lukather bitterly denounced reports which called Porcaro's death drug-related. "Did we do drugs? Yeah, tons of them. Were we doing them at the time of his death? No. The guy had a bad heart. That's how he died."

The rest of Toto continued to record. Of their 1995 LP *Tambu*, Lukather cracked, "It sold a million copies worldwide and five copies here." In 1998 the band released the *Toto 20* album of unreleased material, and worked on a new LP for 1999. The 1998 lineup was Lukather, David Paich, Mike Porcaro (Jeff's brother, who replaced David Hungate as bassist in 1983), and Simon Phillips on drums. Jeff's other brother, Steve Porcaro, left in 1988.

505 The Next Time I Fall

PETER CETERA WITH AMY GRANT

Full Moon 28597

November 8, 1986 (2 weeks)

Writers: Bobby Caldwell, Paul Gordon

Producer: Michael Omartian

Amy Grant was mainly known as a contemporary Christian recording artist when she branched out and scored a big success dueting with Peter Cetera in "The Next Time I Fall." She got her part courtesy of Cetera's producer, Michael Omartian. "He knew me because of the work we had done in contemporary Christian music," she said. "He was always one to keep the doors open for me."

When "The Next Time I Fall" came to Cetera's attention, plans were to do it with a female singer. "Michael said, 'I would love for you to sing it with Amy Grant.' Peter said, 'Who?'" Grant recalled. Omartian told Cetera to trust him on this one and give the singer he did not know a shot at it.

Remembering the recording session, Grant said, "I fly in. Pete was there in the studio and was very nice. What I didn't know was that they were keeping the door open for another vocalist." But Grant's vocal, which she felt blended well with Cetera's, erased any doubts they had about using her on the final record.

Grant had been a fan of Cetera's since his days with Chicago in the 1970s. "'Saturday in the Park' was one of the first cool tunes I learned on the piano," she said. "I was a fan since grade school." And she admitted that when they first started recording, "I was still bright-eyed and in awe of somebody I knew only from radio and records. We had great laughs during the session."

For his part, Cetera praised Grant's work on the record. "I thought she was a great choice because she was looking to make a pop crossover, and I like what she stands for," he told Lynn Van Matre of *The Chicago Tribune*. "She was real excited about the idea too. I think I was a good choice for her, since I have a good reputation as a hardworking singer."

Regarding her own approach in the studio, Grant said she is hardworking too, but noted, "I'm not anywhere near a perfectionist, and I would prefer emotion over perfection any day of the week."

People with the Grammy Awards must have felt they got both emotion and perfection with Cetera and Grant's performances, as they awarded them a Grammy nomination for Best Pop Performance by a Duo or Group. On the charts, "The Next Time I Fall" went to #1 pop the week of December 6, 1986, three weeks after it fell from the top of the AC listing, giving Grant her first #1 AC and pop hit and Cetera his second as a soloist [see 499—"Glory of Love"].

Even with all the success, there were no plans for Grant and Cetera to record together again, although Grant noted that "Our paths have crossed since then." Cetera has done a few duets since then with other women, however. "When he does that, every time, I feel that twinge that an old girlfriend feels— 'You're singing with who?!'" Grant joked.

506 Love Will Conquer All

LIONEL RICHIE

Motown 1866

November 22, 1986 (2 weeks)

Writers: Lionel Richie, Cynthia Weil, Greg Phillinganes

Producers: Lionel Richie, James Anthony Carmichael

When Lionel Richie's 1986 LP *Dancing on the Ceiling* came out in 1986, many wondered whether the album would keep Richie's string of hits going. Happily, the answer was yes, but that did not mean he was using exactly the same old approach to achieving that hit status.

As his manager Ken Kragen told Linda Moleski in *Billboard*, "What Lionel went for with this album was to make sure that it covered a broad spectrum of tastes. He tries to push it a little farther each time without abandoning what the base of his audience is."

The first single off the album was the up-tempo title tune, but "Dancing on the Ceiling" made only #3 AC, ending four consecutive #1 AC hits for him, as well as #2 pop for two weeks. The next single from the LP, "Love Will Conquer All," with its more laid-back groove, did get to #1 AC, plus went to #9 pop for two weeks starting November 29, 1986, as well as #2 R&B. As for the *Dancing on the Ceiling* album, it went to #1 for two weeks starting September 27, 1986.

Joining Richie in writing "Love Will Conquer All" was veteran songwriter Cynthia Weil ("I Just Can't Help Believing," "If Ever You're in My Arms Again," and many more), and session musician Greg Phillinganes. It was one of the few times Richie co-wrote one of his hits.

Regarding his composing process, Richie told *Ebony* that he wrote "from a sincere base." He said, "I am the songs I write. It's not that I'm calculating or that I sit down to write a particular way. It just comes. God's the writer here."

At about the same time in his life, Richie told Jack Matthews of *The Los Angeles Times* that he planned to make his movie acting debut soon. "Now that I feel comfortable as a solo artist, I'm ready to take on the challenge," he said. "I think, to be successful, you have to keep going to the edge, doing things people don't expect from you. I've done that with my music. Lionel Richie going to the movies is certainly Lionel Richie going to the edge." (As it turned out, personal problems in the late 1980s and early 1990s caused Richie to delay his film debut until 1996, when he landed a role in *The Preacher's Wife*, starring Denzel Washington and Whitney Houston.)

Richie promoted "Love Will Conquer All" with a 40-city concert tour which started in Phoenix, Arizona, on September 29, 1986, as well as a special on the HBO cable channel.

The next release after "Love Will Conquer All" also hit #1 AC [see 511—"Ballerina Girl"].

507 The Way It Is
BRUCE HORNSBY AND THE RANGE

RCA 5023

December 6, 1986 (2 weeks)

Writer: Bruce Hornsby

Producers: Bruce Hornsby, Elliot Scheiner

Bruce Hornsby moved to Los Angeles with his wife in 1979 with the intention of breaking into the industry, but it was not until seven years later that he finally had his own solo success marked by the #1 AC and pop hit "The Way It Is." He was born in Williamsburg, Virginia, on November 23, 1954, and his years of growing up in Virginia, encountering people's prejudices and racist views, served as the basis for the song's lyrics, which came to him before the music did.

"I wrote it in the fall of 1985 in my garage in Van Nuys," Hornsby recounted to Paul Zollo in *Songwriters on Songwriting*. "Little tract home on Heartland Street, every house looks the same. . . .I had this song I was working on called 'The Way It Is.' I put it down on cassette and felt really good about this song. I really liked it. I never had any notion that it would be a hit or anything.

"I had never played any of these work tapes for anybody. But I brought the tape into the house for my wife to hear, and said, 'Hey, Kathy—listen to this.' I played her this tape, and she listened to it, and all she said afterwards was, 'That's pretty funny.' Pretty funny? What a reaction. It was just something perfunctory for her to say to have something to say. And that lack of enthusiasm and saying that inexplicable statement sent me into months of self-doubt about the song."

It took at least three months before Hornsby pulled the tape out again and recorded it for a demo. The recording was the umpteenth demo he had sent to record companies, but "The Way It Is" sparked the interest of RCA executives, who decided to sign him. For a man whose biggest show business credit previously had been playing piano for Sheena Easton on tour in 1983, the signing alone was cause for rejoicing.

The first single release for Hornsby and his backing group the Range was not "The Way It Is" but "Every Little Kiss," which stalled at #37 AC and #72 pop in the fall of 1986. "The Way It Is" was its follow-up, and despite those who predicted the song would never be anything more than a B-side, it performed much better than "Every Little Kiss," hitting #1 pop on December 13, the second week it was at #1 AC. At the 1986 Grammys Hornsby was named Best New Artist.

The next single release by Bruce Hornsby and the Range also went to #1 AC. See 513—"Mandolin Rain."

508 Love Is Forever
BILLY OCEAN

Jive 9540

December 20, 1986 (3 weeks)

Writers: Billy Ocean, Wayne Brathwaite, Barry J. Eastmond

Producers: Wayne Brathwaite, Barry J. Eastmond

Given how much success resulted from their *Suddenly* album, music observers were surprised when the Jive label replaced Billy Ocean's producer Keith Diamond with Wayne Brathwaite and Barry J. Eastmond, the latter a keyboardist on *Suddenly*, for Ocean's next album, *Love Zone*. Ocean told Dennis Hunt in *The Los Angeles Times* that it was a decision beyond his control.

"It was politics," Ocean said. "I don't get involved in politics anymore. I learned my lesson at CBS. I was paranoid after that experience. I wasn't going to fall into that political trap again." Regarding his relationship with Diamond, Ocean told Hunt, "I haven't talked to him. . . .There was nothing personal in what happened. It was just business. It wasn't my decision. I might work with him again. Who knows?"

To date Ocean has not reunited with Diamond. It should be noted, however, that the change did not affect his hit status, as *Love Zone* generated three hit 45s—the title tune, "There'll Be Sad Songs (To Make You Cry)" [see 496]," and "Love Is Forever." The latter tune made #1 AC, #10 R&B, and #16 pop in late 1986, and, like all but one cut on the *Love Zone* album, was written by Ocean, Brathwaite, and Eastmond and recorded in London.

Less than two years later Ocean was back on the charts with yet another producer, Robert John "Mutt" Lange, who co-wrote with Ocean the hit "Get Outta My Dreams, Get Into My Car," which reached #5 AC and #1 pop in the spring of 1988. (Ocean may not have worked with Brathwaite and Eastmond again because he reportedly like working late at night while the producers favored early-morning hours.) Its follow-up, "The Colour of Love," did even better on the AC chart, coming in at #2 while stalling at #17 pop. Interestingly, "The Colour of Love" made Ocean's *Greatest Hits* LP in 1989 while "Love Is Forever" did not, even though the latter had higher peaks on the AC and pop charts.

By then the tide of musical popularity had crested and was receding for Ocean. In 1989 his "Licence to Chill" made only #32 pop. He did not chart again until 1993, when "Everything's So Different Without You" went to just #43 AC with two weeks on the chart while missing the Hot 100. That same year Ocean had his first single on the British listing in five years and it too was a disappointment; "Pressure" stalled at #55.

By about 1995 Ocean had disappeared from the U.S. music scene. At last report he was still living in London.

509 This Is the Time

BILLY JOEL

Columbia 06526

January 10, 1987 (3 weeks)

Writer: Billy Joel

Producer: Phil Ramone

The idea for "This Is the Time" came to Billy Joel when he thought about his wedding to supermodel Christie Brinkley. However, the couple mentioned in "This Is the Time" exchanged their vows on a beach during wintertime, whereas Joel and Brinkley had their ceremony on a yacht moored in New York Harbor in early spring, 1985.

Ruminating over the song with Melinda Newman in *Billboard* in 1997, Joel said, "One of the most difficult things to maintain is a relationship, and that's really what this song is about: 'Let's remember this good time, because we're going to remember this when times get tough.' It didn't mean I thought we should stay in that moment, because I said, 'It will not last forever.'"

Cynics may note that Joel and Brinkley's marriage did not stay "in that moment," as the two divorced in 1994. But there was little sign of discord while "This Is the Time" was becoming Joel's seventh #1 AC hit and 20th top 20 pop hit, reaching #18 on the Hot 100 in early 1987. The B-side of the single, though it got little airplay, rates a mention because it was a duet between Joel and another famous native New Yorker, Cyndi Lauper, called "Code of Silence."

"This Is the Time" was the third single on Joel's *The Bridge* album, although the first 45, "Modern Woman," actually came out before the LP, on the soundtrack to the movie *Ruthless People*. "Modern Woman" went to #7 AC and #10 pop, followed by "A Matter of Trust," which stopped at #17 AC and #10 pop. The final single, "Baby Grand" in 1987, featured Joel with his idol Ray Charles, whom he met at the USA for Africa session [see 472—"We Are the World"]. It made #3 AC and #75 pop.

It was natural that the styles and sounds on *The Bridge* should be divergent, given Joel's overall approach to the LP. As he told Stephen Holden in *The New York Times*, "The only premise for *The Bridge* when I started was that it not be a concept album."

Joel released a live album of him performing in Russia in the fall of 1987 called *Kohu,ept* (on which he did "A Matter of Trust" and "Baby Grand" but, interestingly, not "This Is the Time"), then came out two years later with a new studio album, *Storm Front*, which led off with his hit "We Didn't Start the Fire" at #5 AC and #1 pop in 1989. However, it would be nearly four years before he had his next #1 AC hit [see 638—"The River of Dreams"].

1987

510 At This Moment
BILLY VERA AND THE BEATERS

Rhino 74403

January 31, 1987 (1 week)

Writer: Billy Vera

Producer: Jeff Baxter

B illy Vera, born William McCord, Jr., in Riverside, California, on May 28, 1944, first scored on the pop chart as a singer with two duets with Judy Clay in 1968, "Storybook Children" (#54) and "Country Girl—City Man" (#36). Later that year his solo hit "With Pen in Hand" went to #43 pop and became his first AC entry at #25. Thirteen years later he returned to the Hot 100 with "At This Moment."

"At This Moment" came from Vera's own experience. "I met this girl that I started to date, and when I met her, she was breaking up with another guy," he said. "A couple of days later I wrote the first two-thirds of this song, and I couldn't finish it. Then about nine months later, when we broke up, I finished it."

Vera played it with eight other musicians known as the Beaters one night in January 1981 at the Los Angeles club the Roxy. The live performance was recorded and hit #79 pop in September 1981. At one of Vera's club performances in the mid-1980s, "At This Moment" caught the fancy of Michael Weithorn, a supervising producer for the NBC-TV comedy series *Family Ties*. He thought the song would be perfect to use in a scene between the show's young couple, played by later real-life husband and wife Michael J. Fox and Tracy Pollan.

Vera and his group rerecorded roughly 30 seconds of the song for the show. When it aired, viewers deluged Vera and NBC with fan mail and calls. Sensing the song had hit potential now, Vera called record companies, but none wanted to recut "At This Moment." Desperate, he called Richard Foos of Rhino Records, whose label specialized in reissuing old material, and made a deal to rerelease the original "At This Moment." But the episode featuring the song had already been rerun once by that time and was unlikely to be shown again anytime soon, so it looked as if the record would die.

In September 1986, the season opener of *Family Ties* featured the song again as the couple broke up. Vera hadn't known about the new airing, and the reaction took him by surprise. "I came home from going out on a date and there were about 25 calls and people going nuts," he said.

"At This Moment" made #1 AC plus #1 pop for two weeks starting January 24, 1987, #42 country, and #70 R&B. A number of record company execs called him to do new songs. Signed to Capitol, he only had one other AC entry, 1988's "Between Like and Love," which went to #9. Undaunted, Vera did fine in the 1990s, doing some acting and voiceover work for commercials, liner notes for several blues compilations, and a few gigs with the Beaters, usually in the southern California area.

Vera had one favorite piece of fan mail regarding "At This Moment." "I got a note from Elvis Costello at the time it came out. I can't remember his exact words, but it was something like, 'Man, when a record like yours becomes #1, it gives me hope that you don't have to make bulls__t to make #1.' Coming from him, it made me feel real good."

511 Ballerina Girl
LIONEL RICHIE

Motown 1873

February 7, 1987 (4 weeks)

Writer: Lionel Richie

Producer: Lionel Richie, James Anthony Carmichael

L ionel Richie managed a double-sided hit with the fourth single from his *Dancing on the Ceiling* album. The A-side, "Ballerina Girl," hit #7 pop the week of February 21, 1987, and also went to #5 R&B in addition to #1 AC. But Richie also got a decent amount of airplay with his duet with Alabama, "Deep River Woman," which made #28 AC and #71 pop. However, though no one could have known it at the time, "Ballerina Girl" was the last Richie tune to crack the pop top 10.

The follow-up to "Ballerina Girl," "Se La" (pronounced "say lah"), which went to #5 AC and #20 pop, was the final single released from *Dancing on the Ceiling*. The chart performance of singles from that album—five top 20 pop and three #1 AC—was almost as good as that of its predecessor, *Can't Slow Down*, which got five top 10 pop and four #1 AC hits.

Dancing on the Ceiling was to have a follow-up sometime before the end of the 1980s. But circumstance conspired to prevent that from happening. As Richie told an Associated Press reporter in 1996, "I was just going to take off a year and sort of chill out for a moment and go back. And during that year, my father became very ill, and I was not going back into the studio or go on the road until he finished his thing."

Richie's father died in 1990. Then Richie and his wife Brenda went through an acrimonious divorce, ending what had appeared to be a picture-perfect marriage, plus his best friend contracted the AIDS virus. "Well, needless to say, it caught me so far off guard, and I was not ready for those one-two-three punches," he said. An anxious Motown asked him to complete a new album, but all he felt like doing was a few new tunes for a 1992 greatest hits compilation called *Back to Front*. Two of those tunes became 45s, "Do It to Me" (#3 AC, #21 pop and #1 R&B) and the less successful "My Destiny" (#7 AC).

Not pleased with his relationship with Motown, Richie left the label for Mercury but did not release an album there for another four years. When *Louder Than Words* came out in 1996, it was a major disappointment, spinning off no hit singles and stopping at #28 on the album chart while failing to sell a million copies. He tried again in 1998 with an album called *Time*, which included a remake of the hit he wrote for Kenny Rogers, "Lady" [see 393], the song which arguably set Richie in motion to become a solo singer in the first place.

You Got It All

THE JETS

MCA 52968

March 7, 1987 (2 weeks)

Writer: Rupert Holmes

Producers: Don Powell, David Rivkin

Don Powell, a former manager of Stevie Wonder, so enjoyed a family act he caught one night in Minneapolis that he offered to manage and produce the group, which consisted of eight brothers and sisters. He was not similarly enchanted with the names they were using—Quasar or the Wolfgramm Phenomenon (their family name was Wolfgramm)—and suggested they look for a catchier handle. Inspired by Elton John's hit "Bennie and the Jets" and one of the gangs from the musical *West Side Story*, they became the Jets.

The Wolfgramms had emigrated to Minneapolis from Tonga in the South Pacific. The children began performing professionally in 1981. When Powell signed them to MCA Records in 1985, they ranged in age from 19 to 11. Leroy, the eldest, was keyboardist and guitarist. In descending age, the rest were Haini, the bassist; Rudy, the drummer; Eddie, the percussionist; Eugene, a singer; Kathi, a keyboardist; and Elizabeth and Moana, both vocalists.

Their first release was "Curiousity," which peaked at #8 R&B in 1985. Its follow-up, "Crush on You," did even better, going to #4 R&B and #3 pop in 1986. Next up was "Private Number," which went to #28 R&B and #47 pop. They followed it with their fourth single from their self-titled debut LP, a ballad called "You Got It All."

"We heard the song 'You Got It All' and knew it was a hit," Rudy said. "The vocals, just hearing Rupert Holmes sing it [on the demo tape], did it for us." Holmes, who wrote the tune, is best remembered for his 1979 hit "Escape (The Piña Colada Song)," which peaked at #8 AC. The Jets got to hear his song because Powell's and Holmes' attorneys were good friends, according to Rudy.

"You Got It All" was the Jets' AC debut. It nearly duplicated its AC peak on the R&B chart, where it reached #2, and the Hot 100, where it held at #3 the week of March 7, 1987, behind Bon Jovi's "Livin' on a Prayer" at #1 and "Jacob's Ladder" by Huey Lewis and the News at #2.

The Jets did little production-wise for the song, leaving that to Powell and a man named David Rivkin. "That record, we were basically young and just contributed our vocals and played our instruments," Rudy said. However, he did think his sister Elizabeth's assured vocal contributed much to its success. "Liz was basically the talented one singing," he said. "At 12 years old, she sounded very mature."

Taking off from "You Got It All," the next three Jets singles all missed the AC chart but fared well pop and R&B. "Cross My Heart" hit #7 pop and #11 R&B in 1987, followed by "I Do You" (#20 pop, #19 R&B) in late 1987 and then "Rocket 2 U" (#6 pop, #5 R&B) in early 1988. The single after "Rocket 2 U" landed the Jets back at #1 AC [see 542—"Make It Real"].

513 Mandolin Rain
BRUCE HORNSBY AND THE RANGE

RCA 5087

March 21, 1987 (3 weeks)

Writer: Bruce Hornsby

Producers: Bruce Hornsby, Elliot Scheiner

"Rural Southern highbrow" was how Bruce Hornsby described the music on his group's first LP to Bill Barol of *Newsweek*. The album relied heavily on folk music influences, including mandolin and violin, although those instruments were not typically the ones played by the Range, which Hornsby formed in 1984.

Making up the Range, a name Hornsby picked for its rural connotations, were guitarists David Mansfield and George Marinelli, drummer John Molo, and bassist Joe Puerta. The lineup stayed intact until 1990, when Peter Harris replaced Mansfield. Hornsby sang and played keyboards with the group, something he had been doing since, at age 17, he realized that despite his height (6 foot 4) he had no future as a basketball player. Before forming the band, he studied music at the University of Miami in Florida. Hornsby had a wide range of musical influences, including country crooner George Jones and jazz pianist Keith Jarrett.

After Bruce Hornsby and the Range broke through with "The Way It Is" [see 507], the next single they did was "Mandolin Rain," a 45 that went to #4 pop the week of March 21, 1987 plus #38 country and #1 AC. The group then had a third hit from their debut LP, a remixed version of their first single, "Every Little Kiss," which went to #3 AC and #14 pop, a big jump from its #37 AC and #72 pop peak in 1986.

Adding to Hornsby's reputation was the showing of "Jacob's Ladder," a tune he had written that Huey Lewis and the News took to #1 pop the week of March 14, 1987. Not unexpectedly, Bruce Hornsby and the Range became the opening act on tour for Huey Lewis and the News in 1987.

Popular as a lead singer and as a songwriter, Hornsby faced the question of what approach he would take to keep his momentum going in both those fields. "I'm not really concerned with trying to find what the people will like, because that's the wrong way to go about it," Hornsby told Laura Van Tuyl in *The Christian Science Monitor*. "That's what we did to get this far. . . .So it'd be a little stupid for me, now that we've got commercial success, to turn around and think, 'OK, now I gotta write a hit.' We're not going to do that."

Nonetheless, Bruce Hornsby and the Range ended up getting their third #1 AC hit in 1988 with "The Valley Road" [see 541]. Apparently his "rural Southern highbrow" music was just what AC programmers and listeners wanted to hear at the time.

514 Nothing's Gonna Stop Us Now
STARSHIP

Grunt 5109

April 11, 1987 (2 weeks)

Writers: Diane Warren, Albert Hammond

Producer: Narada Michael Walden

On the heels of their newfound popularity with such tunes as "Sara" [see 490], Starship recorded "Nothing's Gonna Stop Us Now" for the comedy *Mannequin*, starring Andrew McCarthy. Their producer Narada Michael Walden recorded most of the instrumental tracks for "Nothing's Gonna Stop Us Now" while the band was on tour in 1986, then did their vocals when they finished doing the concerts.

"Nothing's Gonna Stop Us Now" received an Oscar nomination for Best Song, the first for prolific songwriter Diane Warren. Asked how she felt about it, she said, "It was pretty cool, but it would've been even cooler to win!" The victor in that contest was "(I've Had) The Time of My Life" [see 528]. Warren and co-writer Hammond were only nominees at the Grammys too, as "Nothing's Gonna Stop Us Now" lost out in the Best Song Written Specifically for a Motion Picture or Television Show category to "Somewhere Out There" from the film *An American Tail*.

On the charts, "Nothing's Gonna Stop Us Now" made #1 pop the week of April 4, 1987, and stayed there the following week while hitting #1 AC, then spent a second week at #1 AC while dropping from the pole position on the Hot 100. It also made #1 in the United Kingdom, the first chart-topper ever there for the group in any of its incarnations, including Jefferson Airplane and Jefferson Starship, but that was to be their last entry on that chart.

In the summer of 1987 Starship had its last top 10 pop hit, ironically with a tune called "It's Not Over ('Til It's Over)," at #9. The single did not make the AC chart, nor did "Beat Patrol" at #46 pop later in 1987. In 1988 "Set the Night to Music" reached #9 AC without cracking the Hot 100, but by that time vocalist Grace Slick had left the band. The following year she and other members of the 1966 lineup of Jefferson Airplane—Marty Balin, Jack Casady, Paul Kantner, and Jorma Kaukonen—worked together again as the original group.

Starship kept going, now composed of bassist Brett Bloomfield and keyboardist Mark Morgan along with singer Mickey Thomas, guitarist Craig Chaquico, and drummer Donny Baldwin, but the hits were rare now. They cut "Wild Again" for the Tom Cruise movie *Cocktail* but got only to #73 pop in 1989. "It's Not Enough" did get to #30 AC and #12 pop in 1989 but was the last Starship record to make the AC chart. In later 1989, after "I Didn't Mean to Stay All Night" got to #79 pop, Starship broke up.

However, in 1998 a rejuvenated Starship (Starship Featuring Mickey Thomas) could be seen on tour in venues across America. Not part of the group was Slick, who declined to any more concerts, feeling rock and roll should not be sung by middle-aged people.

515 The Finer Things
STEVE WINWOOD

Island 28498

April 25, 1987 (3 weeks)

Writers: Steve Winwood, Will Jennings

Producers: Russ Titelman, Steve Winwood

Bluesy white soul artist Steve Winwood was born in Great Barr, a suburb of Birmingham, England, on May 12, 1948. Growing up, he was influenced by soul music, particularly that of Ray Charles, and learned how to play the piano and guitar. He came to prominence while still a teenager as part of the Spencer Davis Group, a quartet which included Winwood's brother Muff at bass and scored two pop hits in 1967 with "Gimme Some Lovin'" at #7 and "I'm a Man" at #10, both of which had Winwood singing lead. But that same year Winwood grew tired of the group and became a member of another quartet called Traffic.

Traffic, which originally included drummer Jim Capaldi, guitarist Dave Mason, and flautist Chris Wood, performed less well on the pop chart than did the Spencer Davis Group during its seven-year run. Ironically, its highest-charting single was a remake of "Gimme Some Lovin'," which hit #68 on the Hot 100 in 1971. During a low period for Traffic, Winwood also became part of the supergroup Blind Faith, along with Eric Clapton, drummer Ginger Baker, and Rick Grech. Blind Faith's only album got to #1 on the LP chart the weeks of September 20 and 27, 1969.

After Traffic crashed in 1974, Winwood embarked on a solo career but attracted little attention until 1981, when his single "While You See a Chance," went to #17 AC and #7 pop. He had three other 45s make the Hot 100 through 1982, but would have to wait four more years before getting his second AC entry with "Higher Love," which made #7 AC and #1 pop in 1986.

"Higher Love" also won Grammys for Record of the Year and Best Male Pop Vocal Performance, plus a nomination for Song of the Year. Its two follow-ups, "Freedom Overspill," which went only to #20 pop, and then "The Finer Things," both came off the same LP containing "Higher Love," *Back in the High Life.*

Winwood created "The Finer Things" along with Will Jennings. Regarding his use of a collbarator, Winwood told Stephen Bishop in *Songs in the Rough* that "I like co-writing. I do write lyrics and have written lyrics, but delegation is the art of leadership! No, it's not really that. But I feel my lyrics are more intuitive, whereas the music I probably understand more thoroughly. The music has to be intuitive, too, but I feel I understand the science and intellectual content of music more than I do literature, perhaps. And Will, who as I say is a professor and a scholar, understands the English language, and several others, too."

"The Finer Things" reached #8 pop for three weeks starting April 18, 1987 while getting to #1 AC. The next Winwood single after it was his album's title tune; see 522—"Back in the High Life Again."

516 Just to See Her
SMOKEY ROBINSON

Motown 1877

May 16, 1987 (1 week)

Writers: J. George, L. Pardin

Producers: Peter Bunetta, Rick Chudacoff

"Just to See Her" was a bittersweet hit for Smokey Robinson in many respects. It was the first #1 AC hit for Robinson, whose ethereal voice had virtually defined easy-listening soul since he began recording for Motown in 1960 as lead singer of the Miracles (the group, formed in high school as the Matadors in 1955, recorded two years prior to Motown). It also was his first top 10 pop hit since "Being With You" in 1981. And, when the song peaked at #8 pop the week of July 4, 1987, the English group ABC entered the Hot 100 with a tribute song titled "When Smokey Sings," which peaked at #5 11 weeks later.

But amid these triumphs came word that Berry Gordy was looking to sell Motown Records, which he founded in 1959 and built into one of the world's biggest black-owned businesses. In June 1988, MCA bought Motown. For Robinson, who had worked for the company from the start as an artist, writer, producer, and executive, it hurt that Motown was no longer its own entity in a field dominated by media conglomerates. Cushioning the blow was the fact that MCA retained him as a solo artist. He was also getting his personal life in order, dealing with drug addiction, the consequences of marital indiscretions, and other problems detailed in his autobiography, *Smokey: Inside My Life* with David Ritz.

Robinson, born in Detroit, Michigan, on February 19, 1940, did hit #1 AC in 1976 as a writer [see 300—"Shop Around"]. By then he was three years into his solo career after splitting with the Miracles. It was not until 1980 that he cracked the AC chart and pop top 10 with "Cruisin'," a surprisingly late time for a man who had six top 10 pop entries with the Miracles between 1960 and 1970. From 1981–86 he had seven AC entries, although after "Being With You" in 1981, none hit the pop chart.

"Just to See Her" emerged from Robinson's LP *One Heartbeat,* on which Berry Gordy served as executive producer. "It was a little like the old days, with him critiquing and pushing me to my limits," Robinson wrote of working with his old boss. "Berry will never change. Even during my most recent tour, he didn't leave my Las Vegas show before redoing the light show and sound mix."

Robinson got his first Grammy for "Just to See Her" for Best Male Rhythm and Blues Performance. The song also went to #2 R&B. But after the follow-up, "One Heartbeat," peaked at #2 AC and #10 pop in 1987, Robinson had no more big hits, although "Everything You Touch" in 1990 was #2 AC for three weeks. Robinson's musical legacy, however, is assured, as he was inducted into the Rock and Roll Hall of Fame in 1987.

517 La Isla Bonita

MADONNA

Sire 28425

May 23, 1987 (1 week)

Writers: Madonna, Patrick Leonard

Producers: Madonna, Patrick Leonard

Though the area described was a flight of fancy (there is no San Pedro Island) Madonna told Stephen Holden of *The New York Times* that she considered "La Isla Bonita" her tribute to "the beauty and mystery of Latin American people."

Originally designed by Patrick Leonard to be sung by Michael Jackson, with whom Leonard worked on the 1984 Victory tour with the Jacksons, "La Isla Bonita" made #4 pop for three weeks starting May 2, 1987. It was the fifth and final single from Madonna's *True Blue* album, which had peaked at #1 on the LP chart for five weeks starting August 16, 1986. The LP came out after its first single, "Live to Tell," had peaked [see 495]. The other 45s seemed to generate their own publicity.

"Papa Don't Preach," the second single from *True Blue*, is the tale of an unwed teenager who announces she is going to give birth to her child and raise it. The tune aroused the ire of critics on the left of the political spectrum, who thought she was making a veiled attack on abortion rights, and on the right, who thought she was condoning illegitimacy. Madonna insisted neither was the case. In any event, all the attention over the song's message, plus heavy airplay to a touching video dramatizing the tune featuring Danny Aiello as the father of Madonna's character, got it to #16 AC and #1 pop in 1986.

Next up was "True Blue," a throwback to the "girl group" sound of the 1960s that went to #5 AC and #3 pop. Then came "Open Your Heart," a more rock-oriented tune that upset some not because of its sound but because of the explicit imagery in the video. Madonna was seen wearing a black corset with a whip in her hand posing sexually for clients looking at her via private booths at an adults-only performance. It was not the first time Madonna had shocked viewers. When she did "Like a Virgin" on an awards ceremony on MTV in the mid-1980s, she writhed on the ground in a wedding gown in a sequence that left hostess Bette Midler momentarily at a loss for words. Midler later got back at Madonna in her 1985 comedy LP *Mud Will Be Flung Tonight* by paraphrasing the song's chorus and saying, "Madonna, like a virgin, touched for the very first time . . .the very first time today!" In any event, "Open Your Heart" got to #12 AC and #1 pop in 1987.

After "La Isla Bonita," Madonna was off the charts until 1989 save for a couple of singles from her movie *Who's That Girl?* Her next #1 AC hit was "Cherish" [see 571]

518 Always
ATLANTIC STARR

Warner 28455

May 30, 1987 (2 weeks)

Writers: Jonathan Lewis, David Lewis, Wayne Lewis

Producers: David Lewis, Wayne Lewis

"Always" was the second #1 AC hit for Atlantic Starr following "Secret Lovers" [see 492]. The three Lewis brothers, who led the group, came up with the melody in a somewhat unusual way.

"Wayne would play keyboards and drums and I would play keyboards and Jonathan would play keyboards," David Lewis told Adam White and Fred Bronson in *The Billboard Book of Number One R&B Hits*. "Just different parts, because that's all we had at the time, a drum machine and a keyboard. That's how we put it together on a four-track. And then Wayne took it home and did the lyrics." Regarding the lyrics, Wayne said, "At the end of the phrases, I kept coming up with 'Always,' so I said, 'Why not just call it 'Always'?"

Written as a duet, "Always" featured David Lewis and Barbara Weathers singing lead. Lewis cut his part in Los Angeles, while Weathers taped hers in New York. The single became a #1 hit on the charts, first #1 on the R&B chart on May 16 and 23, 1987, followed by #1 AC and then #1 pop the week of June 13, 1987.

However, the follow-up to "Always," "One Lover at a Time," did not fare as well, getting only to #10 R&B and #58 pop in 1987. Two other singles over the next year got only on the R&B chart—"All in the Name of Love" and "Thankful."

Weathers left Atlantic Starr in 1988 after four years with the band for an unexceptional solo career (she got only three entries on the R&B chart in 1990 and 1991, with the highest being 1990's "The Master Key" at #13). Her replacement was Porscha Martin, whom David and Wayne picked after reviewing more than 100 candidates. The first single on which she sang lead, "My First Love" in 1989, went to #1 R&B

But nothing ever seemed stable with the women in the group. Martin was gone by the time "Love Crazy" went to #7 AC and #75 pop in 1991, replaced by Rachel Oliver. (Joseph Phillips also left the band.) Oliver sang with them on their biggest hit since "Always," 1992's "Masterpiece," which went to #3 both R&B and pop. "Masterpiece" was written by Kenny Nolan, who had top 10 AC hits in 1977 singing "I Like Dreamin'" at #4 and "Love's Grown Deep" at #3. But by 1994, Oliver too was gone, and Aisha Tanner was the new female lead. The group continued to be active into the late 1990s, but they rarely scored a hit outside the R&B market.

519 In Too Deep
GENESIS

Atlantic 89316

June 13, 1987 (3 weeks)

Writers: Phil Collins, Mike Rutherford, Anthony Banks

Producers: Genesis, Hugh Padgham

The 1986 *Invisible Touch* album gave Genesis something few groups ever achieve: five singles which hit top 5 pop and four which made top 10 AC. The string started with the title tune, which went to #3 AC and #1 pop in the summer of 1986, followed by "Throwing It All Away" [see 503], which got to #1 AC and #4 pop.

Next up was "Land of Confusion," a rather blaring track whose sound kept it off the AC chart but got it to #4 pop in early 1987. The sinewy "Tonight, Tonight, Tonight" returned them to the AC roster at #8 while going to #3 pop. Then came the last release from *Invisible Touch*, "In Too Deep." According to Phil Collins, drummer and lead vocalist of the trio, all these successes were the result of a concentrated focus on music for the album.

"It was completed in three months of hard, intense work," Collins told Stephen Holden in *The New York Times*. "Instead of writing material ahead of time, what we've always done is go into the studio and improvise. We each have our own drum machine, and often what evolves is based on drum-machine patterns that set up a mood out of which comes a song.

"During this process, I sing along with the rhythms. Everything gets put on cassette. Then we plow through and find the bits that work and develop them. The lyrics are written much later by different individuals. The words for 'Invisible Touch,' 'Tonight, Tonight, Tonight,' and 'In Too Deep' were mine, while Mike Rutherford wrote 'Land of Confusion' and 'Throwing It All Away.'" (It should be noted that for all of the tracks each member of Genesis received writing credit, including guitarist Rutherford and keyboardist Tony Banks.)

"In Too Deep" went to #3 pop the week of June 27, 1987, behind "I Wanna Dance With Somebody (Who Loves Me)" [see 520] at #1 and "Head to Toe" by Lisa Lisa and the Cult Jam at #2, as well as #1 AC. The album from which it came, *Invisible Touch*, also peaked at #3 but sold more than six million copies in America alone.

There was no follow-up LP to *Invisible Touch* until 1991's *We Can't Dance*. In 1989 Collins released another successful solo album [see 574—"Another Day in Paradise"], while Rutherford scored around the same time with his own group Mike + the Mechanics [see 560—"The Living Years"]. When the men finally did regroup, they notched their third #1 AC hit [see 617—"Hold On My Heart"].

520 I Wanna Dance With Somebody (Who Loves Me)

WHITNEY HOUSTON

Arista 9598

July 4, 1987 (3 weeks)

Writers: George Merrill, Shannon Rubicam

Producer: Narada Michael Walden

Arista President Clive Davis was only one of many who asked songwriters George Merrill and Shannon Rubicam to give Whitney Houston another tune to record for her second LP. (They had created one of the biggest hits from her debut album, "How Will I Know" [see 489].) They obliged and whipped up "Waiting for a Star to Fall," but that composition was rejected. (Ironically, Merrill and Rubicam later made their own hit recording of the song in 1988 under their group name Boy Meets Girl [see 555].)

Having to do a second song for submission could have been an ego-deflating experience for the songwriters, since "How Will I Know" had won easy approval for recording by Houston. Yet Merrill said they had no doubt that "I Wanna Dance With Somebody" was a Houston record. "We were confident in what we had done," he said.

But whereas Houston's producer Narada Michael Walden had made the two rewrite some lines in "How Will I Know," he made no changes in the words used in the demo for "I Wanna Dance With Somebody." The sound, however, was a different matter altogether.

"I think when he first heard it, I don't think he was sure what direction to take it in," noted Merrill. "Our demo with Shannon singing was almost rock, and he did almost calypso." Rubicam agreed, saying that "They pretty much changed direction on it."

Nevertheless, Merrill added, "I think he did a fantastic job. It's so bright. . . .It's probably what Whitney wanted to do." It proved to be what radio listeners and consumers wanted to hear and buy as well. The first single released from the *Whitney* LP, "I Wanna Dance With Somebody," rode atop the Hot 100 for two weeks starting June 27, 1987, and nearly did the same on the R&B chart, stopping at #2 there for two weeks. Houston snagged a Grammy for Best Female Pop Vocal Performance for her work on the song.

Surprisingly, "I Wanna Dance With Somebody" marked the last collaboration between the songwriters and Houston. Merrill and Rubicam said it was because Houston switched to Babyface to produce her next LP, *I'm Your Baby Tonight*, and he and Houston were interested in pursuing a different musical direction, one more attuned to ballads.

"We submitted things over time, and we stay in touch with Clive," Rubicam said in explaining the current status of their relationship. She added, "If we ever get to write for her in the future, we'll get a jump on it immediately."

The follow-up to "I Wanna Dance With Somebody" was another #1 AC triumph for Houston. See 525—"Didn't We Almost Have It All."

521 Moonlighting

AL JARREAU

MCA 53124

July 25, 1987 (1 week)

Writers: Al Jarreau (words), Lee Holdridge (music)

Producer: Nile Rodgers

Jazz-influenced vocalist Al Jarreau, born in Milwaukee, Wisconsin, on March 12, 1940, earned an M.A. in psychology from the University of Iowa before going into music as a career. He first charted on the R&B ledger in 1976 with "Rainbow in Your Eyes," a tune off his debut album which went to #92. Jarreau had five more entries there from 1977–80 until he broke through on the other charts in 1981 with "We're in This Love Together," which made #6 AC, #6 R&B, and #15 pop.

In the 1980s Jarreau became a constant presence on the AC, R&B, and pop charts, and for a period from 1982–83 went by only his surname, during which time he reached #2 AC with "Mornin'" in 1983. He finally reached the top spot four years later with "Moonlighting."

According to Jarreau, he got involved with "Moonlighting" through a phone call by Lee Holdridge, a composer and arranger and writer for TV and film. "[Holdridge] was called in to do some music for a pilot," Jarreau said. "We all know what that means. It's a tossup, baby."

But Jarreau was attracted by Holdridge's pitch. Holdridge wanted him to do lyrics and sing the theme, and said, "We haven't met at all, but I like your music, and the producers are big fans of your songs." Holdridge also told him about the show's concept and stars (he had to fumble through his papers to find the male lead—"He was looking for Bruce Willis's name. Who knew?" laughed Jarreau), and played the melody to Jarreau. Enticed, the singer went to work on the theme of the project.

"I put together a lyric that I thought would fit the characters," Jarreau said. But he admitted he had no idea that the series, which would become *Moonlighting* and air on ABC-TV from 1985–89, would become such a big hit. "You can never predict those things," he said, adding that "People in Oslo, Norway, and Jakarta, India, come up to me and talk about 'Moonlighting'!" (Jarreau now regrets that despite the recognition he got for *Moonlighting*, he never even got to meet Willis or Cybill Shepherd, the show's stars. "I think there was a big missed opportunity there," he said. "I was always interested in doing a little acting myself, and just a walk-on would have been nice.")

Expanded into a full-length song, "Moonlighting" was an across-the-board chartmaker. Beside #1 AC, it went to #23 pop and #32 R&B. Thereafter the hits slowed for Jarreau, and in 1994 he left Warner, the company to which he had been signed since the 1970s ("Moonlighting" was released on MCA) for PolyGram. After a tour of Europe in mid-1998, he planned to record an album tentatively titled *Tomorrow Today* on his new label by the spring of 1999 and do a tour to support it.

522 Back in the High Life Again

STEVE WINWOOD

Island 28472

August 1, 1987 (3 weeks)

Writers: Steve Winwood, Will Jennings

Producers: Russ Titelman, Steve Winwood

"The song 'Back in the High Life Again' originally had an island-like feeling on it, very up and Caribbean-like," producer Russ Titelman recalled in a 1996 *Billboard* article about his career. "When Steve first played it for me on piano, that's the sense I got from it. I brought Jimmy Bralower in for some drum programming, and when he and Steve got together they slowed it down. It turned into a more plaintive, churchy, heartbreaking song; plus Stevie plays mandolin on it."

Titelman first met Winwood while doing George Harrison's self-titled 1979 LP. His work with Winwood on the album *Back in the High Life* took eight months, but it was worth it in terms of popular appeal. It peaked at #3 on the LP chart and earned Titelman and Winwood Grammy nominations for Album of the Year and Producers of the Year, Non-Classical.

"Back in the High Life Again," featuring James Taylor as a backup vocalist, was the fourth single from the album and second to hit #1 AC [see 515—"The Finer Things"]. It peaked at #13 pop. There would be no more songs released from the album.

Around the time the single peaked, Winwood stunned observers and officials at Island Records by announcing he was ending his 20-year connection the label. He signed with Virgin for a reported $13 million. To get a few more bucks from their now-former artist while he was hot, Island decided to release some old Winwood material as new singles. A remix of "Valerie," a 1982 single which hit #70 pop and did not chart AC then, fared much better its second time out by going to #2 AC for three weeks and #9 pop in 1987. Island followed it with another remix, this time the title cut to his 1982 flop LP *Talking Back to the Night*, and it went to #7 AC and #57 pop.

In his native England, only "Valerie" charted, hitting #19. It stayed on the U.K. chart for 8 weeks, and that, plus the earlier 4-week run there (in 1982, to #51), added up to a total of 12 weeks, the longest stay of any solo single of his to date on that chart. Somewhat surprisingly, Winwood has yet to break into the top 10 chart in Britain, with his highest placement being "Higher Love" at #13 in 1986. In fact, "Back in the High Life Again" went only to #53 for a two-week run there.

Given his increased popularity in America, it surprised few observers when Winwood announced he had married a woman from Tennessee and was going to relocate to that state while continuing to record. He used the successful formula of *Back in the High Life* as a pattern for his next LP, *Roll With It*. That album's title tune became Winwood's next #1 AC hit [see 544].

523 Love Power

DIONNE WARWICK AND JEFFREY OSBORNE

Arista 9567

August 22, 1987 (1 week)

Writers: Carole Bayer Sager (words), Burt Bacharach (music)

Producers: Carole Bayer Sager, Burt Bacharach

Besides having hit singing careers, the Spinners, Johnny Mathis, Luther Vandross, Barry Manilow, Willie Nelson, Kashif, Howard Hewett, and Jeffrey Osborne have another common element—they all have at one time or another done a duet with Dionne Warwick. It's something she is proud of. "I became known as the duet queen of the industry," she said. "How can you not love it when people want to sing with you?"

In the case of getting Jeffrey Osborne, it was Warwick and her writing/producing team of Carole Bayer Sager and Burt Bacharach who drafted the singer for "Love Power." As Warwick explained, "Carole and Burt wanted to do a duet. We looked for the right person, and Jeffrey was it." She added that they wrote "Love Power" with her in mind.

Osborne, born in Providence, Rhode Island, on March 9, 1948, was lead singer of the soul group L.T.D. when it hit the pop and R&B charts from 1976–80. He then left for a solo career and had seven entries on the AC chart from 1982–87 prior to "Love Power." The biggest single on the listing from this period was "You Should Be Mine (The Woo Woo Song)," which made #2 for two weeks in the summer of 1986.

"Love Power," which also went to #12 pop and #5 R&B, was a rebound chartwise for Warwick after the follow-up to "That's What Friends Are For" [see 485], "Whisper in the Dark," stumbled at #7 AC, #49 R&B, and #72 pop in 1986. She did duets with Kashif in 1987 ("Reservations for Two," which went to #7 AC, #62 pop, and #20 R&B) and Howard Hewett in 1988 ("Another Chance to Love," which hit #24 AC and #42 R&B) before she and Osborne reteamed in 1989. However, their duet "Take Good Care of You and Me" made only #25 AC and #46 R&B.

In the 1990s Warwick remained largely absent from the recording scene, though she still performed on stage. Then in 1998 she put out her first album in years, *Dionne Sings Dionne*, on the RiverNorth label (ending nearly 20 years with Arista Records). The LP included some remakes of her old tunes, plus new material and gospel songs. (Warwick got her musical start in the gospel genre, but did not sing it much on record.) Warwick also planned to tour in support of the new release.

In addition, Warwick planned to work on something she said she has wanted to do for many years, a work detailing the history of African-Americans. She will pursue this project while living in Brazil, her home base as of the mid-1990s onward.

524 I Just Can't Stop Loving You

MICHAEL JACKSON

Epic 07253

August 29, 1987 (3 weeks)

Writer: Michael Jackson

Producer: Quincy Jones

In the wake of *Thriller* [see 432—"The Girl Is Mine"], Michael Jackson toured with his brothers in 1984 to promote their LP *Victory* and then did a follow-up solo LP. (Incredibly, despite fame on the pop and R&B charts, the Jackson 5 made the AC chart only once with "I'll Be There" at #24 in 1970.) It was nearly three years before Jackson released *Bad*.

Jackson wrote in his autobiography *Moonwalk* that *Thriller* loomed large while doing *Bad*. "In the end, it was worth it because we were satisfied with what we had achieved, but it was difficult too. There was a lot of tension because we felt we were competing with ourselves."

Critics of *Bad* agreed. To them, the LP followed the formula of *Thriller*, with "Dirty Diana" the rock song with a crunching guitar solo à la "Beat It" in *Thriller* and "I Just Can't Stop Loving You" the slow-tempo duet in the mode of "The Girl Is Mine." "I Just Can't Stop Loving You" might have had even more similarities to that hit with Paul McCartney if Jackson had sung with superstars Barbra Streisand or Whitney Houston, but he settled on virtual unknown Siedah Garrett to sing a few verses and the chorus, albeit without credit. (Garrett also co-wrote and sang backup on "Man in the Mirror" on *Bad*.)

"Several people have asked me if I had anybody in mind when I wrote '[I] Just Can't Stop Loving You,'" Jackson wrote. "And I say that I didn't, really. I was thinking of somebody while I was singing it, but not while I was writing it."

"I Just Can't Stop Loving You" peaked at #1 AC, pop, and R&B, doing it on the latter two the week of September 19, 1987 only. It was the lead single from *Bad*, which spawned seven top 20 pop singles and was the #1 LP for six weeks starting September 26, 1987. Of its other 45s, the closest to come near #1 AC was "Man in the Mirror," a #2 AC and #1 pop hit in 1988. At the Grammys *Bad* was nominated for Album of the Year and Jackson for Best Male Pop Vocal Performance for his work on *Bad*.

In the 1990s Jackson had several releases hit #1 pop and R&B but fall short of that spot on the AC chart. The biggest of these was "You Are Not Alone," the first song ever to *enter* the Hot 100 at #1 (the week of September 2, 1995). But Jackson's bizarre personal life, including a payoff to a plaintiff on charges of child molestation, a brief marriage to Elvis Presley's daughter Lisa Marie, and a claim to have fathered a boy with one of his employees, left some fans cold. In 1997 he missed the pop top 40 with a new single for the first time since 1979, when "Blood on the Dance Floor" got only to #42 pop. Only time will tell if this was the beginning of the end to the reign of the "King of Pop."

525 Didn't We Almost Have It All

WHITNEY HOUSTON

Arista 9616

September 19, 1987 (3 weeks)

Writers: Michael Masser, Will Jennings

Producer: Michael Masser

Another Whitney Houston ballad meant another #1 AC hit for the vocalist in 1987. "Didn't We Almost Have It All" became the fifth consecutive AC chart-topper for Houston. But by this time some listeners felt that her formula was wearing thin, and Houston's new tune faced some unexpected competition from, of all things, a takeoff on the song by the American Comedy Network.

The ACN was a group of ex-deejays whose spoof on the forced collapse of the Bell Telephone Company, "Breaking Up Is Hard on You (a/k/a Don't Take Ma Bell Away From Me)," made #47 AC and #70 pop in 1984. President and general manager Andy Goodman and vice president and creative director Bob James wrote and produced "Don't My Songs All Sound the Same," using the melody of Houston's hit with biting lyrics about her tendency to emote in big, ultimately boring ballads.

"Our feeling is it's legitimate parody. . . .We really say things. If something seems a little too puffed up—just not human enough—we bring it back down to earth. We're sort of like the court jesters," James told Paul Grein in *The Los Angeles Times*. To sing a vocal resembling Houston's, ACN enlisted Bertilla Baker, at the time a singer in Broadway productions.

Liz Kiley, music director of KOST-FM Los Angeles, told Grein she heard few complaints about the novelty tune. "We get a lot of listener requests for it," she said. "They'll call in and ask for that and another Whitney Houston song, so I don't think the audience takes it as a negative either."

Regardless of the parody, "Didn't We Almost Have It All" was #1 AC and pop simultaneously the weeks of September 26 and October 3, 1987. It also went to #2 R&B. The album on which it appeared, *Whitney*, went to #1 for 11 weeks starting June 27, 1987, and fell from the top just a week before "Didn't We Almost Have It All" hit #1 AC. The tune also earned a Grammy nomination for Song of the Year, with Houston getting nominations for pop and R&B vocals for other tunes on *Whitney*.

The follow-up to "Didn't We Almost Have It All" was the upbeat "So Emotional" (it was not in response to the satire, as it was released prior to that tune), which got to #1 pop and #5 R&B but only #8 AC. That was just an aberration for Houston, of course. She returned to the top of the AC listing with the next 45 after "So Emotional," "Where Do Broken Hearts Go" [see 536].

526 Little Lies
FLEETWOOD MAC

Warner 28291

October 10, 1987 (4 weeks)

Writers: Christine McVie, Eddy Quintela

Producers: Lindsey Buckingham, Richard Dashut

Little lies have not been as much of a problem for Fleetwood Mac as huge egos and quick tempers have. The group, which some refer to as rock's longest-running soap opera, has undergone several transformations since its start, but most people in America associate it with the quintet which had a string of hits in the 1970s—founding members Mick Fleetwood and John McVie, McVie's one-time wife Christine, Lindsey Buckingham, and Buckingham's one-time girlfriend Stevie Nicks.

John McVie and Fleetwood were drummer and bassist respectively with John Mayall's Bluesbreakers in England along with guitarist Peter Green when the three left in 1967 and teamed with guitarist Jeremy Spencer to form Fleetwood Mac. The group had a #1 hit in the United Kingdom, the instrumental "Albatross," before getting their Hot 100 debut at #55 in 1970 with another instrumental, "Oh Well—Pt. I." That same year Green and Spencer left and McVie joined on keyboards, followed by Bob Welch as guitarist from 1971–74.

The ensemble moved to California in 1975. Joining them the following year were guitarists Lindsey Buckingham and vocalist Stevie Nicks (replacing Welch), and from the start of 1976 through 1980 the revamped Fleetwood Mac charted 10 consecutive top 20 pop hits and 9 top 50 AC entries (1980's "Over My Head" made #20 pop and #32 AC). With their growing popularity came some acrimonious interviews, and some of their lyrics detailed the deteriorating relationships among the principles, most notably Buckingham's bitter words about Nicks on "Go Your Own Way" (#10 pop, #45 AC) followed by her mellower but still cutting words about him on "Dreams" (#1 pop, #11 AC).

"Dreams" was the highest-charting AC entry for Fleetwood Mac until 1982's "Hold Me" went to #7. The group fared better on the charts during the 1980s than in the 1970s even though all pursued solo projects between group work at the time. (For information about Christine McVie's career, see 452—"Got a Hold on Me.") They finally got to the top in 1987 with "Little Lies."

McVie wrote "Little Lies" with her husband Eddy Quintela, whom she wed in 1986. "The idea of the lyric is 'If I had the chance, I'd do it differently next time. But since I can't, just carry on lying to me and I'll believe—even though I know you're lying,'" McVie told Timothy White in *Rock Lives*. White also mentioned, but did not confirm, the rumor that the lyrics were based on her 1978–1980 relationship with the late Dennis Wilson of the Beach Boys.

"Little Lies" went to #4 pop the weeks of November 7 and 14, 1987, as well as #1 AC. Its follow-up went to #1 AC too; see 530—"Everywhere."

527 Breakout
SWING OUT SISTER

Mercury 888016

November 7, 1987 (2 weeks)

Writers: Swing Out Sister

Producer: Paul Staveley O'Duffy

"I couldn't imagine three other people who are as different as we are actually working together," Swing Out Sister's drummer Martin Jackson told Amy Duncan in *The Christian Science Monitor*. "I think you'd have a hard job finding anything we have in common."

Happily, Jackson and his cohorts, vocalist Corinne Drewery and keyboardist Andy McConnell, related to each other musically. The trio from Great Britain were first the duo of Jackson and McConnell, and were known for their use of electronic samples of various sounds along with music from their instruments. Drewery was a fashion designer with her own business when she decided to take a shot at a singing career. Though initially hesitant to work with the two due to their "electro" reputation, she nevertheless found some common ground with Jackson and McConnell and recorded a demo tape with them. A friend came up with the group's name of Swing Out Sister.

"We took tapes around for quite awhile, to general apathy, really," Jackson told Duncan. "PolyGram finally signed us for two singles—the first one came out, 'Blue Mood,' and sort of swan-dived, straight down without a trace. I think it sold a staggering 800 copies in total."

But the second 45, "Breakout," broke out to #4 on the United Kingdom chart in late 1986 and encouraged Mercury in the United States to release the record in America. It went to #1 AC plus #6 pop for the weeks of November 14 and 21, 1987. It earned them a Grammy nomination for Best Pop Performance by a Duo or Group With Vocal.

The trio acknowledged that "Breakout" was an odd mélange of musical genres. "When people ask any one of us to describe our music, we really couldn't say, because it's a kind of fusion of our separate influences and tastes," Drewery told Duncan. She favored a straight-ahead pop approach to her vocals, while Connell favored jazzy arrangements on piano (he counted Miles Davis and Weather Report as his inspirations) and Jackson did rock-oriented drumming.

Somehow it all came together, and Swing Out Sister became a popular act on both sides of the Atlantic through the rest of the 1980s. They did better on the AC chart than the Hot 100 during this time, with the single after "Breakout," "Twilight World," going to #7 AC and only #31 pop in early 1988, followed by the AC-only "Surrender" at #37 in 1988. In 1989 "Waiting Game" hit #6 AC and #89 pop, but its follow-up, "You On My Mind," made only #23 AC.

That same year Jackson left Swing Out Sister. Drewery and McConnell carried on and even managed to return #1 AC in 1992 [see 624—"Am I The Same Girl"].

528 (I've Had) The Time of My Life
BILL MEDLEY AND JENNIFER WARNES

RCA 5224

November 21, 1987 (4 weeks)

Writers: Frank Previte, John DeNicola, Donald Markowitz

Producer: Michael Lloyd

Formerly best known as part of the Righteous Brothers [see 589—"Unchained Melody"], Bill Medley established a solo singing career in the 1980s with several pop and AC entries starting with 1981's "Don't Know Much" [see 573]. Ironically, he had his biggest success in the decade with a duet sent to him by Jimmy Ienner, the executive producer of the soundtrack of the 1987 movie *Dirty Dancing*.

Not familiar with Ienner or the project, he asked for more details about the song and the movie. Upon learning its title, Medley recalled that he exclaimed, "My God! It sounds like a porno movie! I can't do that while my folks are alive!" Ienner explained the title referred to a style of dancing and not sex, which calmed Medley somewhat.

Although Medley never learned much about the concept and stars of the film (Patrick Swayze and Jennifer Grey), he did listen to "(I've Had) The Time of My Life." He liked the tune but noted that on the demo, "Whoever was singing on it was singing way up," and Medley, a baritone, had to adjust the song to his range. But there was a problem. "They wanted me to go to New York, and that was right when my wife was expecting our child," Medley said. Medley turned down the offer, preferring to help with the delivery of their baby.

But Ienner proved persistent. Then he told Medley, "Jennifer Warnes [see 328—"Right Time of the Night"] wants to do it with you." Medley replied, "OK, if I can do it in California." (Medley believed the tune was always planned as a duet, but Warnes was the first potential partner presented to him.)

Medley admitted he and Warnes doubted the potential of the project as a whole. "We didn't have a clue that the movie and the song were going to take off," he said. But they did, and "(I've Had) The Time of My Life" hit #1 pop as well as AC the week of November 28, 1987.

Given the success of "(I've Had) The Time of My Life," which also won the Oscar for Best Song, it was surprising that Medley and Warnes did not do a follow-up even though it was the only tune they sang in the movie. Medley, who would have only one more AC entry after this record (1988's "He Ain't Heavy, He's My Brother" at #49), noted that "Off and on over the years, Jennifer and I have discussed doing stuff together." Though nothing was definite, Medley said they may do an album together sometime in the future.

The week before "(I've Had) The Time of My Life" peaked at #1 AC, the *Dirty Dancing* soundtrack began the first of 18 weeks at #1 on the album chart. That streak was due not only to the popularity of this song but to a follow-up hit from the soundtrack, "She's Like the Wind" [see 534].

529 Got My Mind Set On You
GEORGE HARRISON

Dark Horse 28178

December 19, 1987 (4 weeks)

Writer: Rudy Clark

Producers: Jeff Lynne, George Harrison

"I never listen to the radio to keep up with current trends," proclaimed George Harrison to Iain Blair in *The Chicago Tribune*. Appropriately, he returned to the AC chart after a long layoff (following the #1 AC success of 1981's "All Those Years Ago" [see 406]) with "Got My Mind Set On You." The tune was first recorded by James Ray in 1962 but went nowhere until Harrison redid it a quarter century later. A week after it dropped out of the #1 AC spot, on January 16, 1988, the single also made #1 pop.

Harrison had not been idle during the six years between hits, but had not enjoyed much success. In 1982 he released an album called *Gone Troppo* which faltered horribly, going only to #108 on the LP listings for a seven-week run and generating just one 45 which made the Hot 100, "Wake Up My Love" at #53. Following that album's failure, rumors flew that Harrison had become a recluse, a claim he denied. "The truth is, during the long layoff, I was always writing and putting down demos at my home studio," he told Blair. "But apart from needing that break, it was also a matter of finding the right producer. I wanted to collaborate with someone, but it had to be someone I could work with and who wouldn't disrespect my past."

That someone turned out to be Jeff Lynne, a longtime Beatles admirer whom Harrison met through their mutual friend, guitarist Dave Edmunds. Lynne and Harrison put together the latter's *Cloud Nine* album and, with "Got My Mind Set On You" as its debut single, watched it soar to a #8 peak on the LP roster, the highest position for any of his albums since *Extra Texture (Read All About It)* hit the same number in 1975.

The follow-up to "Got My Mind Set On You" from *Cloud Nine* was "When We Was Fab," an affectionate look at Harrison's old Beatles days, which climbed to #10 AC and #23 pop in 1988. The third 45 from the album, "This Is Love," stumbled at #20 AC without making the Hot 100.

After *Cloud Nine* had run its course, Harrison once again became relatively invisible. He had two LPs released which generated meager activity in sales or airplay, 1989's *Best of Dark Horse 1976–1989* and 1992's *Live in Japan*. He also participated in the two albums collecting Beatles material from the vaults which hit #1 on the LP chart, *Anthology 1* (1995) and *Anthology 2* (1996), but otherwise he has been strangely silent.

530 Everywhere
FLEETWOOD MAC

Warner 28143

January 16, 1988 (3 weeks)

Writer: Christine McVie

Producers: Lindsey Buckingham, Richard Dashut

By the time "Everywhere" peaked at #1 AC and #14 pop in early 1988, the man who co-produced the tune, Lindsey Buckingham, was no longer part of Fleetwood Mac. He left the quintet in mid-1987 after more than 12 years with the group.

"His heart wasn't into it," Fleetwood Mac co-founder Mick Fleetwood told David Silverman of the *Chicago Tribune*. "But we thought he would stick it out. There are easier ways to start a tour than to have your guitarist walk out."

Buckingham was so talented it took two guitarists to replace him—Billy Burnette, of the Burnette music dynasty (Dorsey was his father, Johnny his nephew, and Ricky his cousin) and a member of the Zoo (Fleetwood's band on the side) and Rick Vito. It really was a poor time for Buckingham to leave, though, for "Everywhere" was one of five singles released from Fleetwood Mac's *Tango in the Night* LP to make both the AC and pop chart. The others were, in chronological order, "Big Love" (#23 AC, #5 pop), "Seven Wonders" (#13 AC, #19 pop), and "Little Lies" [see 526] in 1987 and "Family Man" (#23 AC, #90 pop) in 1988. "Everywhere" came after "Little Lies" and became the second #1 AC hit for the band as well as their only consecutive #1 AC hit.

As a solo act Buckingham, born in Palo Alto, California, on October 3, 1947, had most of his success in the early 1980s when he did his own material between tours and recordings for Fleetwood Mac. His "Trouble," released in the fall of 1981, got to #14 AC and #9 pop in early 1982, followed the next two years by Hot 100–only singles, 1983's "Holiday Road" from the movie *National Lampoon's Vacation* (#82) and 1984's "Go Insane" (#23).

In 1992 he charted twice on the AC ledger with "Countdown" (#32) and then "Soul Drifter" (#38), but neither made even a dent on the pop side.

The other members of Fleetwood Mac during its late 1970s to late 1980s heyday—Mick Fleetwood, Christine McVie, John McVie, and Stevie Nicks—also recorded their own solo projects, but of them only the women made the AC chart. McVie had a #1 AC hit in 1984 [see 452—"Got a Hold on Me"], while Nicks had six solo entries from 1981–89, the highest charting being 1981's "Leather and Lace" with Don Henley at #10 AC and #6 pop.

The Buckingham-less Fleetwood Mac forged ahead and toured in 1988. The new sextet even managed to get another #1 AC hit in 1989 [see 557—"As Long As You Follow"].

1988

531 Could've Been

TIFFANY

MCA 53231

February 6, 1988 (1 week)

Writer: Lois Blaisch

Producer: George Tobin

"Could've Been" could've been a hit for its writer had not circumstances surrounding it worked out the way they did. As Lois Blaisch recalled, she came up with the tune when "I was dating a fellow. It was a true-to-life experience. . . .Basically, I got my hopes up and got swept up by a tall, dark and handsome guy. The relationship was over by the time the roses he sent me were drooping."

She wrote the song, she said, "because I was so heartbroken." She performed it as part of a duo which toured nightclubs in California. At a show at the Hungry Hunter in Thousand Oaks, California, a man who worked for producer George Tobin heard her doing the tune and asked if she would get a tape of it to his boss. "He [Tobin] had me play it three times in a row," Blaisch said. Impressed, he had her cut a demo of it in a studio.

Originally Blaisch believed she would get to record "Could've Been." "It was to be an artist deal for me, but it didn't happen," she noted. Instead, the record went to Tiffany, a teenage hopeful. Born Tiffany Darwisch in Norwalk, California, on October 2, 1971, Tiffany would have a #1 pop and #38 AC hit in late 1987 with a remake of Tommy James and the Shondells' "I Think We're Alone Now" before "Could've Been" emerged as its follow-up.

Tiffany took "Could've Been" to #1 AC and pop simultaneously the week of February 6, 1988, followed by an extra week leading the Hot 100. For the two weeks before the single reached #1, Tiffany's self-titled LP with "Could've Been" led the album chart. Blaisch described her reaction to its success as "Kind of a half-dream for me," since she did not sing on the record. Regarding Tiffany's vocal, Blaisch said, "I thought she was a really good singer but didn't put enough resignation in it." However, she did take consolation in the fact that Tiffany copied the phrasing in her vocal for the tune.

Three more entries made the AC chart under Tiffany's name, with the last being "Hold an Old Friend's Hand," an AC-only single at #37 in mid-1989. By that time Tiffany's fan base, composed primarily of other adolescent girls, had transferred to other artists, including New Kids on the Block. (NKOTB opened for Tiffany on tour in early 1989, but within a few months they had become so much more popular that Tiffany became the opening act instead.) In the 1990s she retired from show business to get married and raise a family. But Blaisch remained more musically active, earning three Grammy nominations and writing music for such TV series as *Touched by an Angel* and *Promised Land* while continuing to perform and do recording work.

532 Can't Stay Away From You

GLORIA ESTEFAN AND THE MIAMI SOUND MACHINE

Epic 07641

February 13, 1988 (1 week)

Writer: Gloria Estefan

Producers: Emilio and the Jerks

Who exactly were "Emilio and the Jerks"? Well, Emilio was Gloria Estefan's husband, born March 4, 1953, who fled his native Cuba with his father in 1966 when he was 13. After two years in Madrid, Spain, Emilio got a student visa to study in Miami. In the early 1970s he got a job in Bacardi's Miami marketing division, but also played the accordion in his spare time at restaurants for tips.

In 1973 a co-worker of Emilio's asked him to perform at a private party. To help out, he got two other musicians to join him, bassist Juan Marcos Avila and drummer Enrique "Kiki" Garcia. The combination worked, and through perseverance Emilio developed a band with drums, congas, horns, keyboards, and a few other instruments. Initially called the Miami Latin Boys, the group became Miami Sound Machine with the introduction of Gloria Fajardo in 1975, who three years later became Emilio's wife.

The "Jerks" were producer-drummer Joe Galdo and his partners Lawrence Dermer and Rafael Vigil. From the mid-1980s through 1988, they arranged and performed, in the studio, the bulk of the Miami Sound Machine's material. Although they did not play in concert with Miami Sound Machine, their rhythm and synthesizer programs were parts of the group's on-stage presence. The only band members the Jerks dealt with directly were Emilio and Gloria. "[Gloria] was naturally musical, and a real hard worker," Galdo told Daisann McLane in *Rolling Stone*. "No prima donna groove. If there was something wrong with a track at four in the morning, she'd say, 'Okay, let's work on it.'"

Emilio met the Jerks when both were working on a commercial jingle. The Jerks' tracks for an aerobics project called *Salsa-cize* intrigued Emilio, and he signed them to work for his band. But when Emilio tried to put the Jerks under a five-year exclusive contract with the group, they balked, feeling they were not getting enough credit or royalties for their work in the studio. Shortly after the success of "Can't Stay Away From You," the Jerks and Emilio parted company.

Other changes were in the wind. In 1987, a year after Miami Sound Machine's top 10 pop and AC successes with several tunes, including "Words Get in the Way" [see 500], the group was renamed Gloria Estefan and Miami Sound Machine to draw more attention to its lead singer. Two singles came out that year under the new name, "Rhythm Is Gonna Get You" (#31 AC, #5 pop) and "Betcha Say That" (#19 AC, #36 pop), before the release of "Can't Stay Away From You."

"Can't Stay Away From You" peaked at #6 pop the week of March 5, 1988, three weeks after it topped the AC chart. Replacing it at #1 on the AC chart was a tune by another band from Miami, Exposé.

533 Seasons Change
EXPOSÉ

Arista 9640

February 10, 1988 (1 week)

Writer: Lewis A. Martinee

Producer: Lewis A. Martinee

In the 1960s "girl groups" ranging from the Supremes to the Chiffons flourished on the pop music scene, but by the early 1980s the concept seemed dated. That did not deter Miami-based producer Lewis A. Martinee, who decided to give the world a new female singing and dancing trio called Exposé.

"I really formed it in late 1982," he said. "Then in 1983 I released my own record, and then in 1984 Arista signed it." The next year Exposé scored a #19 hit on *Billboard*'s Disco/Dance chart with "Point of No Return." But there were problems with the three vocalists at the time—Sandee Casanas, Ale Lorenzo, and Laurie Miller. "One of the girls didn't like to travel, things happened," Martinee said. "It was just better to use a new lineup."

Through various connections he found Gioia (pronounced "JOY-uh") Bruno, Ann Curless, and Jeanette Jurado. Bruno recalled that "I had been singing in New York, really rock. I came down here [to Miami] to check the scene." When asked to be part of Exposé, "I was sort of hesitant, because it was not my sort of music." But she joined anyway.

In 1987 Exposé broke onto the Hot 100 with "Come Go With Me" at #5. A remake of "Point of No Return" also hit #5 pop, followed by "Let Me Be the One," which charted #7 pop. Toward the end of 1987 Arista released "Seasons Change," which also peaked simultaneously at #1 pop and AC (the first entry on the latter) the week of February 10, 1988.

"The inspiration for that was, I think, I was about to turn 30," Martinee said. "It's really a song about years gone by and how seasons change." Bruno said she thought the big success of the group's first three Hot 100 records encouraged Arista President Clive Davis to release the ballad. "We were in Japan when it came out and went to #1," she remembered. "It felt great. It was exciting."

However, Bruno felt that she didn't have much input into group decisions, and grew tired of her somewhat limited role (on most songs, including "Seasons Change," Jurado sang lead while Bruno did "a lot of the demo work, the ad-libbing stuff in the background," as she put it). She did like recording and touring with Curless and Jurado, noting that "We had a great time, got to do a lot of things together. We were like sisters." But when she became ill in 1991, Bruno left the group.

In 1996 Bruno became lead singer of the Miami-based hard-rock group Wet. They recorded their first LP the following year, but by 1998 she had left the band to work on her own projects. Before those events, Exposé managed one more #1 AC hit [see 636—"I'll Never Get Over You (Getting Over Me)"].

534 She's Like the Wind
PATRICK SWAYZE FEATURING WENDY FRASER

RCA 5363

February 27, 1988 (2 weeks)

Writers: Patrick Swayze, Stacy Widelitz

Producer: Michael Lloyd

The movie *Dirty Dancing* allowed Patrick Swayze not only to show off the footwork which had led him into a show business career but also display his singing voice. The funny thing is that the song which allowed him this forum, "She's Like the Wind," had been written for a different Swayze movie.

Swayze, born in Houston, Texas, on August 18, 1952, composed the tune with the help of Stacy Widelitz. (Widelitz was none too pleased when several pressings of "She's Like the Wind" spelled his name "Stacey," furthering the misconception held by some that Stacy Widelitz was a female.) Widelitz recalled of working with Swayze that "He and I actually had become friends in the early 1980s. We wrote the song for a different movie. The movie was *Grandview, U.S.A.* [1984]."

Widelitz was not the originator of the song. "Patrick always had an idea for the germ of the song," Widelitz said. "And then he asked me, 'Do you want to help finish up the song?'" Widelitz said he did and noted, "We reworked it

entirely." Among the changes were adding the hook and two more sections to the tune.

When they did the demo for the song, Wendy Fraser, Widelitz's girlfriend at the time, sang backgrounds prominently. "She was a great singer," said Widelitz. The producer of the final version, Michael Lloyd, used her in his record too.

After "She's Like the Wind" failed to make *Grandview, U.S.A.*, Swayze pitched the song to be included in *Dirty Dancing*. Its acceptance pleased him and Widelitz, but they had no inkling it would make any impact outside the film. "No one expected it to be a big album, even when we were working on it," Widelitz said. "We were all very, very shocked."

The soundtrack became a hit and spawned several hit singles, including "(I've Had) The Time of My Life" [see 528], followed by "She's Like the Wind." It peaked at #1 AC plus made #3 pop for three weeks. The first week, George Michael's "Father Figure" at #1 and the Pet Shop Boys and Dusty Springfield's "What Have I Done to Deserve This" at #2 held it from the top, while the last two weeks "Father Figure" and "Never Gonna Give You Up" [see 535] stopped it.

According to Widelitz, the record was popular because "It really fit with his character. The lyric is about a guy who thinks he's not good enough for a girl he wants." And the fact that it was the romantic lead of the film singing a ballad in a love story did not hurt either, he added.

Swayze sang on the soundtracks of *Next of Kin* and *Road House*, both 1989 movies, but the albums and singles from the films flopped. He and Widelitz continued to work together on various projects through the 1990s, but Swayze concentrated more on straight acting roles, appearing in films ranging from *Ghost* (1990) to *Black Dog* (1998).

535 Never Gonna Give You Up
RICK ASTLEY

RCA 5347

March 12, 1988 (3 weeks)

Writers: Mike Stock, Matt Aitken, Pete Waterman

Producers: Mike Stock, Matt Aitken, Pete Waterman

The booming voice of Rick Astley seemed to take the world by storm from 1987–88 as "Never Gonna Give You Up" became a big hit in many nations. But unlike most of the other singers produced by the English dance production trio of Mike Stock, Matt Aitken, and Pete Waterman, Astley managed to have more than just a few hits under their guidance. He also later wrote and produced his own material with considerable success.

Born Richard Paul Astley in Newton-le-Willows in Lancashire, England, on February 6, 1966, he sang in his church choir while growing up. At age 6 he started taking piano lessons. While still quite young, he learned to play drums, and later learned the guitar as well. While in school he and some fellow students formed a band, called Give Way.

In his late teens Astley became the drummer for a band called FBI; at the same time he worked for his father's garden shop company, building sheds and driving delivery trucks. At one FBI wedding gig Astley replaced the band's lead singer, who couldn't be there. The response was enthusiastic, and Astley eventually became FBI's lead singer and songwriter.

In 1985 FBI won a band contest and got to play at a club where producer Pete Waterman saw him singing. The producer, impressed, signed the artist and prepped him for stardom. He had Astley sing without credit on an unsuccessful 45 by O'chi Brown called "Learning to Live" in 1986, then used him in a few other projects, including the all-star benefit record "Let It Be" by Ferry Aid in April 1987 [see 131], before "Never Gonna Give You Up" came out as a single.

Recorded in October 1986, mixed January 1, 1987, and released six months later, "Never Gonna Give You Up" was Astley's first chart entry in Great Britain and went to #1 for five weeks starting August 29, 1987. It became the #1 song of the year there, and also topped the chart of nearly every other European country before going to #1 AC and pop simultaneously for two weeks starting March 12, 1988, plus another week at #1 AC alone.

Observers were surprised that the vocals behind the tune were so strong, given that they were sung by a relatively untrained voice. Astley credited it to the music he heard as a youth. "I'm influenced by a lot of black American artists," Astley told Stephen Holden in *The New York Times*. "Luther Vandross is one of my favorites, and I like James Ingram and Jeffrey Osborne."

He was heard a great deal more after "Never Gonna Give You Up," with his next #1 AC hit coming later in 1988 [see 548—"It Would Take a Strong Strong Man"].

536 Where Do Broken Hearts Go

WHITNEY HOUSTON

Arista 9674

April 2, 1988 (3 weeks)

Writers: Frank Wildhorn, Chuck Jackson

Producer: Narada Michael Walden

When Frank Wildhorn learned in 1987 that Chuck Jackson, an executive at Solar Records, had produced Wildhorn's composition "One More Night" with an artist named Donna Washington, he decided to meet him. He found that Jackson also had such 1970s hits as "This Will Be" and "I've Got Love on My Mind" for Natalie Cole on his list of credits, and the two men began a collaboration. Not long after they started working together, they created their first joint tune, which would be their biggest hit together.

"He called me from work and said, 'I have a great title—Where Do Broken Hearts Go," Wildhorn said. By the time Jackson got home, Wildhorn had virtually finished the song, but Jackson did come over to polish it. Then while making a demo of it with a vocal, piano, and drum machine, Wildhorn designed the tune to appeal to Whitney Houston, whose first album he had heard and loved.

"I tailored the melody to at least something I thought she would enjoy," Wildhorn said. The demo went to Houston's mentor, Arista President Clive Davis, who listened to it and liked it except for one thing. "We need a bridge," Davis told him.

Wildhorn wrote two or three bridges but faced an unusual obstacle: He didn't have the money to record a demo tape. So he taped himself singing the suggested additions. The final verdict from Davis' office, according to Wildhorn, was "We love bridge number two. And don't you ever sing your songs again!"

There was a period between the song's acceptance and its appearance on the album which made Wildhorn wonder when—if ever—it might appear, but when the *Whitney* album came out in 1987, "Where Do Broken Hearts Go" was on it. As that album's fourth single it peaked at #1 pop for two weeks starting April 23, 1988, plus made #2 R&B. It was her seventh consecutive #1 pop hit, but only her sixth #1 AC entry, as the previous release, "So Emotional," had gotten only to #8 AC.

The *Whitney* album had one more 45 released from it. However, "Love Will Save the Day" was a relative disappointment in comparison to the prior hits, reaching #10 AC and #9 pop. Houston rebounded with her next entry in late 1988, "One Moment in Time" [see 550].

Wildhorn later went on to do music for such Broadway productions as *Jekyll and Hyde* (1997) and *The Scarlet Pimpernel* (1998). "The Whitney thing was kind of the end of my pop career," he said. But, he also noted, "All of my Broadway stuff was made possible by, among other things, 'Where Do Broken Hearts Go.'"

537 Anything for You

GLORIA ESTEFAN AND THE MIAMI SOUND MACHINE

Epic 07759

April 23, 1988 (3 weeks)

Writer: Gloria Estefan

Producer: Emilio Estefan

Gloria Estefan and the Miami Sound Machine's 1987 tour was to end in the spring of 1988, but with the success of "Anything for You," six more months were added to it. "We went from playing 5,000-seat halls to playing 30,000 in like two weeks," recalled Estefan's younger sister and on-tour assistant Becky Fajardo to Daisann McLane in *Rolling Stone*.

"Anything for You" was a landmark of sorts for Estefan and crew, as it became their first #1 pop song as well as third #1 AC song. It topped the Hot 100 the week of May 14, 1988. "Anything for You" also earned Estefan and the Miami Sound Machine their first Grammy nomination for Best Pop Vocal Performance by a Duo or Group with Vocal for the song's Spanish and English version. On one side of the single, "Anything for You" was sung in English; on the other side, it was sung in Spanish.

In the United Kingdom, "Anything for You" peaked at #10, becoming the Miami Sound Machine's second top 10 hit there, after the single "Dr. Beat," which made #6 in 1984. But between "Dr. Beat" and "Anything for You," the group had only one other entry in Great Britain, with "Bad Boy" making #16 in 1986.

Like its predecessor "Can't Stay Away From You" [see 532], "Anything for You" was a slow, somewhat downbeat ballad which appeared on the Miami Sound Machine album *Let It Loose*. Originally recorded with just Estefan's vocals backed with a piano, the group later recut it with an arrangement which included more instrumental tracks. It was the last song done for the album.

In the wake of the success with "Anything for You," some observers deemed the Miami Sound Machine a great "crossover" success from Latin music, a designation which bothered Gloria. "Crossover is a weird word to use," she told Judy Hevrdejs in *The Chicago Tribune*. "To me, music has always been an emotional thing. I don't think you have to intellectualize, categorize or understand what it is. If it reaches you and teaches you, then that's what music is for.

"In a way, it's frustrating. We're strongly Hispanic and we live in Miami. It's all part of us, so it's hard when people try to pigeonhole you." She told Hevrdejs that during the group's Spanish-only recording days in the early 1980s, they did not do salsa but "pop-oriented songs with Spanish lyrics." But at the same time, she continued to sing in Spanish even on her English-oriented albums because "I didn't want them [her Latin fans] to think I ever forgot about them or would ignore these fans."

After "Anything for You" ran its course, the Miami Sound Machine's next single hit #1 AC as well [see 546—"1-2-3"].

538 I Don't Want to Live Without You

FOREIGNER

Atlantic 89101

May 14, 1988 (1 week)

Writer: Mick Jones

Producers: Frank Filipetti, Mick Jones

Foreigner came together in 1976 and quickly became a favorite of album-oriented rock stations for the rest of the decade with hard-driving hits like "Feels Like the First Time" (their first Hot 100 entry, peaking at #4 in 1977) and "Dirty White Boy" (#12 pop in 1979). In the 1980s they softened their sound somewhat and ended up getting a #1 AC hit with "I Don't Want to Live Without You."

The original Foreigner was made of six longtime musicians. Mick Jones (born in London, England, on December 27, 1944) had been a session guitarist in the 1970s for everyone from Jerry Lee Lewis to George Harrison when he decided to form a band. He brought in first guitarist/keyboardist Ian MacDonald (born in London on June 25, 1946), whom he met at a recording project, and keyboardist Al Greenwood (born in New York City), who had been in a group called Storm. Later joining them were vocalist Lou Gramm (born in Rochester, New York, on May 2, 1950), bassist Ed Gagliardi, and drummer Dennis Elliott. They stayed together until Rick Wills replaced Gagliardi in 1979; then Greenwood and McDonald left in 1980.

In 1981 "Waiting for a Girl Like You" gave the group its AC debut at #5 while going to #2 pop for an unprecedented 10 weeks. It was the band's sixth top 10 hit without making #1 pop, a situation which changed when Foreigner's single "I Want to Know What Love Is" topped the Hot 100 in 1985 while getting to #3 AC. It was the second AC entry for the group, with two more following before the release of "I Don't Want to Live Without You": "That Was Yesterday" in 1985 (#24 AC, #12 pop) and "Say You Will" in 1988 (#41 AC, #6 pop).

Jones and Gramm had composed all of the previous singles which made the charts, and Jones wrote "I Don't Want to Live Without You," which made #5 pop the week of May 28, 1988, two weeks after leading the AC listing. Unfortunately, after that tune left the charts, Foreigner's popularity began to dwindle. Gramm, who as a soloist had a #5 pop hit in 1987 with "Midnight Blue," scored by himself again in 1990, when his "Just Between You and Me" made #4 AC and #6 pop. Gramm left the band in 1991 to create a group called Shadow King, and Willis left in 1992.

But Gramm's band attracted little attention, so he returned to Foreigner in 1992. His rejoining did not end Foreigner's slide in the 1990s, and none of the albums and singles they released generated much in the way of sales or airplay. However, the group continued to be a hot touring property through the end of the decade.

539 Shattered Dreams

JOHNNY HATES JAZZ

Virgin 99383

May 21, 1988 (1 week)

Writer: Clark Datchler

Producers: Calvin Hayes, Mike Nocito

Johnny Hates Jazz was a transatlantic trio consisting of Britons Clark Datchler and drummer/keyboardist Calvin Hayes (the son of famous producer Mickie Most) with American Mike Nocito. Datchler handled lead vocals. Before they met, Datchler had been a songwriter with Warner Brothers Music in Los Angeles before he returned to England to try a solo singing career that produced a few unsuccessful singles. Hayes played in various bands as a teenager, then became a producer/A&R staff member at RAK Records in London. Nocito engineered recordings for several British groups including the Cure, Duran Duran, Pink Floyd, and the Thompson Twins. The three met at a London recording studio in 1986 when Datchler was recording by himself.

"Shattered Dreams" went to #5 in the United Kingdom in mid-1987. The group had several other entries there over the next year, although none of them reached as high as the first. Among them were "I Don't Want to Be a Hero" (#11) and "Turn Back the Clock" (#12) in 1987, then "Heart of Gold" (#19) and "Don't Say It's Love" (#48) in 1988. The latter was their last British chart entry.

The American charts were in a year-behind time warp with the group as "Shattered Dreams" went to #1 AC plus #2 on the Hot 100 for the weeks of May 21 and 28, 1988, while "One More Try" [see 540] held #1. Its follow-up, "I Don't Want to Be a Hero," apparently didn't want to be a hit either, stopping at #15 AC and #31 pop. That was the last single by Johnny Hates Jazz to make the Hot 100, although one more 45 after it, the previous British hit "Turn Back the Clock," made #5 AC. The material on their debut album in the United States included contributions from Kim Wilde and the Art of Noise's Anne Dudley, who was also a writer and producer.

Toward the end of 1988 Datchler left the group and Phil Thornalley, a member of the British technorock group the Cure, became the lead singer, but to no avail. British audiences no longer cared about the trio, and given the disappointing sales and airplay for "I Don't Want to Be a Hero" and "Turn Back the Clock," Virgin did not feel inclined to promote the group in America either. So with one #1 AC and #2 pop single, Johnny Hates Jazz vanished from the AC and pop listings within a year after some pundits had predicted they would be the next big group from Great Britain. Shattered dreams, indeed.

540 One More Try

GEORGE MICHAEL

Columbia 07773

May 28, 1988 (3 weeks)

Writer: George Michael

Producer: George Michael

When George Michael left Wham! officially behind in 1986 [see 469—"Careless Whisper"], he found himself going gangbusters in his new solo career. The first example of this was "I Knew You Were Waiting (For Me)," a duet with Aretha Franklin which went to #1 pop and #2 AC in the spring of 1987. Then came his 1987 LP *Faith*, which generated six singles, four of which crossed over to the AC chart. The LP itself went to #1 on the album chart for 12 weeks starting January 16, 1988.

The first 45 from *Faith* was "I Want Your Sex," a track too funky in sound and controversial in lyrics for most AC stations to play. Nonetheless, it did get to #2 pop. Then came the album's title tune, "Faith," which made #5 AC and #1 pop in late 1987, becoming the first of four consecutive #1 pop hits from the album. Next came "Father Figure," which reached #3 AC and #1 pop before the release of "One More Try."

Like all the previous singles from *Faith*, "One More Try" was written, produced, and sung by Michael. But, as its chart performance showed, it was a much more soulful ballad than his earlier efforts. The tune hit #1 R&B the week of June 18, 1988 as well as #1 pop and AC simultaneously for three weeks starting May 28, 1988.

A few months after "One More Try" peaked, Michael described to Liz Nickson of *Life* magazine his songwriting method. "I do it all in my head," he said. "I have almost a photographic memory for my own ideas. I don't have to put them down, because if they're good, they do stay. I have songs in my head that are three years old, and I have the complete arrangements, the string arrangements, everything. My publisher goes white when I tell him that. He says, 'You only have to bump your head and you lose millions of dollars.'"

Fortunately, he managed to keep his thoughts in his head while *Faith* kept spinning off hit singles. His next 45 from *Faith*, "Monkey," went to #1 pop but proved to be too raucous for AC stations to program. But the last single from the album, "Kissing a Fool," went to #1 AC [see 552]. All these successes were capped off by Michael winning the Grammy for Album of the Year with *Faith*, but strangely none of the tunes got a nomination for Record of the Year or Song of the Year. Michael got only one other nomination that year, for Best Male Pop Vocal Performance for "Father Figure."

541 The Valley Road
BRUCE HORNSBY AND THE RANGE

RCA 7645

June 18, 1988 (1 week)

Writers: Bruce Hornsby, John Hornsby

Producers: Bruce Hornsby, Neil Dorfsman

As with most of his songs, Bruce Hornsby said "The Valley Road" came to him from personal experience, in this case from the mismatched relationships he observed while growing up in southern Virginia. "Every year, some rich girl would get involved with some country guy, and they would act irresponsibly and have to deal with the ramifications," he told Lynn Van Matre in *The Chicago Tribune*. From such doomed affairs sprung forth "The Valley Road."

Hornsby emphasized to Van Matre that despite his group's tendency to deal with social issues in their music, they did not intend to be preachy or polemical. "I think the best we can do as musicians is to help create awareness or heighten awareness of problems, and we try, in our own hopefully subtle fashion, to do just that," he said. "Our approach. . .is more of a humble one. We're not politicians, that's not our trade, but there are some issues that we feel are important, so we write about them. . . .We also like to tell a story, like in 'The Valley Road,' or paint a picture."

"The Valley Road," which Hornsby co-wrote with his brother John, went to #5 pop the week of July 2, 1988, as well as #1 AC. It was the group's last top 10 pop and #1 AC single. "Look Out Any Window" went to #7 AC and #35 pop in the fall of 1988, then Hornsby and crew were off the charts until 1990, when "Across the River," a number featuring Jerry Garcia of the Grateful Dead on guitar, reached #8 AC and #18 pop. (Hornsby took over keyboards for the Grateful Dead temporarily when that band's Brent Mydland died of a drug overdose in 1990 at age 37.) The fall of that year "Lost Soul," with an early vocal by Shawn Colvin [see 668—"Sunny Came Home"], made only #18 AC and #84 pop.

In 1991 Hornsby and the Range came out with "Set Me in Motion," a tune from the movie *Backdraft*, and got stopped at #25 AC while failing to make the Hot 100. In the wake of that disappointment Hornsby dropped the Range and decided to record solo, but his sendoff single, "Harbor Lights," went only to #13 AC and got nowhere on the pop chart. In late 1998, he had yet to score a solo hit.

That lack of chart action probably did not faze Hornsby, who got his recording contract during the mid-1980s thinking he was not making commercial songs anyway. As he told Van Matre in 1988, "I care about the music, and the rest of it doesn't mean that much to me."

542 Make It Real
THE JETS

MCA 53311

June 25, 1988 (3 weeks)

Writers: Linda Mallah, Rick Kelly, Don Powell

Producers: Michael Verdick, Rick Kelly, Don Powell

Jets manager and co-producer Don Powell extended his credits with the group when he co-wrote "Make It Real" with Rick Kelly and Linda Mallah. This song put the Jets at #1 AC for a second time [see 512—"You Got It All"].

"Make It Real" was recorded hastily. As drummer Rudy Wolfgramm recalled, "We had the second album, the *Magic* album, done. We were on tour and everything was done, but they had an idea, so we did 'Make It Real' on the road."

The group had to go to a studio in Texas in which they had never worked to record "Make It Real." It took them an hour to finish the song. When they heard it, Rudy said, "It blew us all away." An impressive feat, given that it had taken the group six months to record the other nine songs on *Magic*. As with "You Got It All," Rudy credited the vocals of his young sister Elizabeth as the record's highlight. "Liz was on fire, man. She hit it," he said.

Also like "You Got It All," "Make It Real" was the fourth single released from the album following more up-tempo numbers. As Rudy explained, "'Make It Real' just had a life of its own. A deejay in Miami started playing it and it overtook 'Rocket 2 U.'" As "Rocket 2 U" slipped down the Hot 100 from its #6 peak, "Make It Real" came onto the chart and went to #4 pop for two weeks starting June 25, 1988, plus #1 AC and #24 R&B.

The *Magic* LP featured one less Jet than the group's debut album, as Eugene Wolfgramm stopped recording with his seven brothers and sisters. "He was really looking for a solo career," noted Rudy. As Gene Hunt, he teamed with Joe Pasquale to form Boys Club. They charted AC with "I Remember Holding You" at #8 in 1988 and "The Loneliest Heart" at #39 in 1989. Eugene remained solo in the 1990s, and the group did not replace him.

The remaining Jets found it hard to follow "Make It Real." When "The Same Love" reached #15 AC and #87 pop in 1989, it was their last entry on both charts. "Special Kind of Love" in 1990 was their last R&B single, peaking at #83. But the group kept going into the 1990s, with the line-up toward the end of the decade being Rudy, Leroy, Haini, Moana and three new members, one a cousin of the Jets and the others two friends of the family. Rudy, who became the group's leader and manager, said his brother and two sisters who retired from the group did so after their weddings. "Everybody's married but me and Moana," he said.

Though their 1998 LP *Love Will Lead the Way* combined pop and Christian music, Rudy said the group continues to play the old material and look for new mainstream hits. And when it comes to favorites in concert, he noted, "Every time we play 'Make It Real,' the place just goes nuts."

543 Make Me Lose Control

ERIC CARMEN

Arista 9686

July 16, 1988 (3 weeks)

Writers: Eric Carmen, Dean Pitchford

Producer: Jimmy Ienner

After his successful debut LP which included the 1976 #1 AC single "Never Gonna Fall in Love Again" [see 302], Eric Carmen had some hits over the next decade, but it was an up-and-down affair. He had one AC and pop hit per year for the first three years after "Never Gonna Fall in Love Again," namely "She Did It" (#26 AC, #23 pop) in 1977, "Change of Heart" (#6 AC, #19 pop) in 1978, and "Baby, I Need Your Lovin'" (#30 AC, #62 pop) in 1979. At the same time, two of his compositions proved to be bigger pop hits for Shaun Cassidy—"That's Rock and Roll," #3 in 1977, and "Hey, Deanie," #4 in 1978.

He had no hits of his own in the 1980s until 1985's "I Wanna Hear It From Your Lips" peaked at #10 AC and #35 pop, followed by "I'm Through With Love" at #16 AC and #87 pop. He had scored a bigger triumph a year earlier when he co-wrote "Almost Paradise" with Dean Pitchford for Mike Reno and Ann Wilson [see 457]. Then in late 1987 he finally returned to the top 10 of both charts with "Hungry Eyes" from the soundtrack of the movie *Dirty Dancing*, which peaked at #2 AC and #4 pop. On the heels of that success, he reteamed with Pitchford to write "Make Me Lose Control."

Carmen described "Make Me Lose Control" in the liner notes to his 1997 retrospective LP *The Definitive Collection* as "An odd record because it was all by itself. The song wasn't part of an album, but it was an interesting experience to jump back into the studio with Jimmy Ienner after 10 years. [Ienner had produced Carmen's debut LP.] 'Make Me Lose Control' started out as 'Long Live Rock & Roll,' and I've heard from some of my friends that on the Internet all the Raspberries fans now have somehow gotten copies of 'Long Live Rock & Roll'. . .and they're discussing it amongst themselves."

In its final version, "Make Me Lose Control" distinguished itself from other songs out at the time by the chorus, which was repeated near the end sung a capello. It went to #3 on the Hot 100 the week of August 13, 1988, behind Steve Winwood's "Roll With It" at #1 [see 544] and Breathe's "Hands to Heaven" at #2. Longtime fans of Carmen got a treat with the B-side of the record—Carmen's version of "That's Rock and Roll."

The follow-up to "Make Me Lose Control" was "Reason to Try," the theme NBC-TV used for the 1988 Summer Olympics. Despite the exposure, the single managed to go only to #87 on the Hot 100. After that appearance, Carmen had no success as a recording artist on the pop or AC charts for the next decade, but he remain active in touring and recording work.

544 Roll With It

STEVE WINWOOD

Virgin 99326

August 6, 1988 (2 weeks)

Writers: Steve Winwood, Will Jennings

Producers: Steve Winwood, Tom Lord Alge

When Steve Winwood left Island Records after 20 years to sign with Virgin, he went to Dublin, Ireland, and Toronto, Canada, to record his first album with his new label. The title track became its first release. coming out as a single a few weeks before the LP debuted.

"Roll With It" featured Winwood doing his best vocal imitation of Ray Charles, whom he said was his biggest musical influence. The pumping horn section consisted of the Memphis Horns' Wayne Jackson on trumpet and Andrew Love on saxophone. The record reminded people of some soul shouters from the 1960s. According to Winwood, that was intentional.

"With *Roll With It* [the album] I certainly did get back to the sort of early records that were an influence on Spencer Davis," he told Chris Welch in *Roll With It*, referring to his old band. "I really did want to identify with the old group on that last album. It was a musical statement about the Spencer Davis Group and I think it succeeded with songs like 'Dancing Shoes' and 'Roll With It.'"

Incredibly, the funky tune caught favor with AC radio and hit #1 there a week after the record started the first of four weeks at #1 on the Hot 100. On the week of August 20, 1988, when it fell out of #1 AC and spent its last week at #1 pop, Winwood's album *Roll With It* hit #1 on the LP chart. During this period the tune also peaked at #30 on the R&B chart, where Winwood last appeared 21 years earlier as part of the Spencer Davis Group when "I'm a Man" hit #48.

At the Grammys, nominations went to "Roll With It" for Record of the Year and the LP for Album of the Year, and Winwood also nailed a nomination for Best Male Pop Vocal Performance. However, he got more controversy than acclaim for the single after "Roll With It." "Don't You Know What the Night Can Do?" did not bother critics with its sounds or words, but with the circumstances surrounding the release. It came out at the same time the makers of Michelob beer used it as background music for its commercials, leading some to grouse that Winwood had sold out and cared more about getting money than creating songs.

Winwood denied the charges. He said he had let the Anheuser-Busch company use "Don't You Know. . ." because he understood that the commercial would air only after the song been out as a single, but to his surprise the advertisement came on while the 45 hit the airwaves. Either despite the situation or because of it, "Don't You Know What the Night Can Do?" made #2 AC for three weeks and #6 pop.

There was no brouhaha over the next single from Winwood, just more success. "Holding On" became his fourth #1 AC hit in 1989 [see 558].

545 | I Don't Wanna Go On With You Like That

ELTON JOHN

MCA 53345

August 20, 1988 (1 week)

Writers: Elton John, Bernie Taupin

Producer: Chris Thomas

"I Don't Wanna Go On With You Like That" holds the distinction of being the Elton John single which had the most number of promotional versions released for radio stations. There was one just with Elton John and a backing guitar, one seven-and-a-half minute remix by dance music producer Shep Pettibone, who worked often with Madonna, and even one tagged with the improbable title "The Pub Dub." Given such a push for the song by MCA, it was hardly surprising that "I Don't Wanna Go On With You Like That" was a huge hit in America, becoming John's eighth #1 AC hit. The song also made #2 pop the week of August 27, 1988, behind "Monkey" by George Michael.

But in his native United Kingdom, "I Don't Want to Go On With You Like That" went only to a disappointing #30. John had in fact been somewhat frustrated on the English chart, as despite a plethora of releases only one of his songs—"Don't Go Breaking My Heart"—made #1 there, and that was a duet with Kiki Dee. On his own, John notched 16 other top 10 entries in Great Britain, with the closest to #1 being 1972's "Rocket Man" at #2 and 1985's "Nikita" at #3. He finally did reach the peak in the United Kingdom by himself in 1990 [see 572—"Healing Hands"].

Producing "I Don't Want to Go On With You Like That" was Chris Thomas, who had produced many of John's records in the early 1980s, from 1981's "Nobody Wins" to 1984's "In Neon," but hadn't worked with him for three years. Thomas's work in music studios went all the way back to the 1960s, when he assisted George Martin on producing the Beatles, and in the 1970s Thomas went on to produce several other artists including Procol Harum, the Pretenders, and the Sex Pistols.

Following up "I Don't Wanna Go On With You Like That," John released one more single from his *Reg Strikes Back* album. "A Word in Spanish" made #4 AC and #19 pop in late 1988. In the spring of 1989 he had another top five AC and top 20 pop entry with a duet with Aretha Franklin called "Through the Storm" (#3 AC, #16 pop), which was the title tune for Franklin's 1989 album but did not make any of John's LPs.

546 | 1-2-3

GLORIA ESTEFAN AND THE MIAMI SOUND MACHINE

Epic 07921

August 27, 1988 (1 week)

Writers: Gloria Estefan, Enrique Garcia

Producers: Emilio and the Jerks

"1-2-3" landed at the last-named spot on the Hot 100, peaking behind "Roll With It" [see 544] at #1 and George Michael's "Monkey" at #2 the week of August 20, 1988. It also made #54 R&B, the group's third single on that chart after "Conga" made #60 and "Bad Boy" hit #74, both in 1986. "1-2-3" also went to #9 in the United Kingdom in 1988 and had enough appeal to rechart at #72 the last week of that year in Great Britain as well.

Ironically, by the time "1-2-3" reached its top position in America, co-writer Enrique "Kiki" Garcia, drummer for the Miami Sound Machine since 1975, left the group. He complained to Daisann McLane in *Rolling Stone* that the group was dead in his mind. "There is no Miami Sound Machine," he said. "There is Gloria and Emilio telling a bunch of hired musicians what to do."

Estefan and her husband prospered well without Garcia, who had co-written earlier up-tempo triumphs like "Conga" and "Rhythm's Gonna Get You." Under the billing of just Gloria Estefan, the singer-producer combo had hits in 1989 with "Don't Wanna Lose You" (a #2 AC entry for five weeks and #1 pop single) and "Get On Your Feet" (a #5 AC and #11 pop record), and would have several other #1 AC hits in later years.

Emilio offered no apologies about the group being dropped in favor of his wife. In fact, he thought it was the proper thing to do. "She's been the lead singer for years but no one knows her name," he told Jefferson Graham in *USA Today*. "They always called her 'that girl from the Miami Sound Machine.' In the Grammys, she could only be nominated in the group category, not as a singer. This was the record company's idea, and I like it."

Before Gloria became a solo act officially, and around the time "1-2-3" was popular, she and the band had rejected an offer to appear on the popular NBC crime drama *Miami Vice*, set in the group's hometown. The reason was because the story line called for the band to be playing a party thrown by drug dealers. Estefan told Russ DeVault of *The Atlanta Constitution* in 1988 that "They even wanted us to play ourselves. But we said, 'No—people have enough trouble distinguishing fact from fiction. We never did that in real life, so why on TV?'"

Gloria did get plenty of television exposure which she approved later, however, including being a host of the American Music Awards on January 22, 1990. By then, she had another #1 AC hit [see 577—"Here We Are"].

547 One Good Woman

PETER CETERA

Full Moon 27824

September 3, 1988 (4 weeks)

Writers: Peter Cetera, Patrick Leonard

Producer: Peter Cetera, Patrick Leonard

Peter Cetera was fairly quiet in 1987 after his one-two punch of successive #1 AC and pop hits "Glory of Love" [see 499] and "The Next Time I Fall" with Amy Grant [see 505]. His "Big Mistake" lived up to its title by going only to #61 pop while failing to make the AC chart in early 1987, while his other 45, "Only Love Knows Why," reached #24 AC without cracking the pop chart.

That same year Cetera planned to collaborate with writer/producer Patrick Leonard, but the latter's commitments to Madonna's *Who's That Girl* tour interfered. With free time on his hands, he produced a solo album for Agnetha Faltskog, formerly of ABBA, called *I Stand Alone*, and wrote the title track and sang a duet with her. Their "I Wasn't the One (Who Said Goodbye)" went to #19 AC and #93 pop in the spring of 1988. (Cetera obviously appreciated Faltskog's work in ABBA, as he covered that group's #15 pop hit "SOS" two decades later.)

By the time "I Wasn't the One" peaked, Leonard had finished his obligations with Madonna and he and Cetera were co-writing and co-producing Cetera's album *One More Story*. "*One More Story* came out in the summer of 1988 and led off with the single 'One Good Woman,'" wrote Michelle Finch in the fall 1996 edition of the Peter Cetera Fan Club newsletter titled *One More Story*. "Though it was originally intended to be a song for the movie *Big*, Peter took it back when the movie people wanted to change too much of it. Good move on Peter's part; the song sounds great as it stands, and many fans obviously agreed because the song hit the top 10 all over the world.

"As an added bonus, in the video fans caught a glimpse of a young Claire Cetera, Peter's daughter—the object of Peter's 'fatherhood' songs 'Daddy's Girl' and 'One More Story,' and later on 'Apple of Your Daddy's Eye.'"

"One Good Woman" went up to #4 pop the week of October 1, 1988, after finishing a four-week run atop the AC chart. Its follow-up, "Best of Times," was not as fortunate, getting only to #22 AC and #59 pop.

In 1989 Cetera made a move into movie music. He contributed "No Explanation" to the soundtrack of *Pretty Woman*, which came out in 1990. But he gained more fame and praise the same year from a duet with Cher, which appeared in the film *Chances Are* and became his fourth #1 AC hit [see 563—"After All"].

548 It Would Take a Strong Strong Man

RICK ASTLEY

RCA 8663

October 1, 1988 (1 week)

Writers: Mike Stock, Matt Aitken, Pete Waterman

Producers: Mike Stock, Matt Aitken, Pete Waterman

Rick Astley astounded the detractors who considered him to be a one-hit wonder ("Never Gonna Give You Up" [see 535]) racking up six more consecutive top 10 entries in the United Kingdom through 1989. The first two, "Whenever You Need Somebody" and "When I Fall in Love/My Arms Keep Missing You," came out in Great Britain in 1987 and not in America, and they hit #3 and #2 respectively. After them in 1988 came "Together Forever," and that made #2 in England while going to #2 AC and #1 pop later in America.

Following "Together Forever" in the United States was "It Would Take a Strong Strong Man," which went to #10 pop the week of September 17, 1988 before peaking atop the AC chart two weeks later. Like its predecessors, "It Would Take a Strong Strong Man" was an up-tempo number suitable for dancing, a style of music Astley appreciated.

"I like dance music," Astley told Stephen Holden of *The New York Times*. "I'm happy doing what I'm doing and want to get more deeply into it."

But his massive success, which also resulted in a Grammy nomination for Best New Artist, inevitably brought questions about what if anything Astley was trying to say with his music. Asked by *People* what he thought the message of his LP was, Astley said, "Blah-dee-blah. It's me first album, and I'm not particularly trying to put any messages across. I'm not Peter Gabriel. We can't all be."

Still, the criticism that he was just a puppet to the writer/producer team of Mike Stock, Matt Aitken, and Pete Waterman rankled him. (It was true that the trio often received more credit for their songs which were hits in England and/or America than the artists who did the songs, such as Hazell Dean, Samantha Fox, and Bananarama.) To rectify the situation, Astley decided in 1988 to write and produce his own material. His first self-produced single was another peppy concoction, "She Wants to Dance With Me," which made #5 AC and #6 pop in America in early 1989.

Later in 1989 Astley had two more AC and pop entries, "Giving Up on Love" at #11 AC and #38 pop and a remake of the Temptations' 1966 #13 pop hit "Ain't Too Proud to Beg" at #16 AC and #89 pop. He let a year go by before releasing his next album, *Free*, in 1991; that album contained the single "Cry for Help" [see 598], which became his third—but to date last—#1 AC hit.

549 Groovy Kind of Love
PHIL COLLINS

Atlantic 89017

October 8, 1988 (3 weeks)

Writers: Toni Wine, Carole Bayer Sager

Producers: Phil Collins, Anne Dudley

When the soundtrack album *Playing for Keeps* came out in early 1988, demand among AC stations for a Phil Collins tune to play was so great that his cut "We Said Hello Goodbye" went to #34 on the chart, even though it had been on his 1985 album *No Jacket Required*. So when Collins released a new single later in 1988, which also came from a soundtrack, no one was surprised that it was an even bigger success, even though that one would come from a soundtrack as well.

"Groovy Kind of Love" was written by Toni Wine and Carole Bayer Sager in 20 minutes in the mid-1960s and originally was a #2 pop hit for the Mindbenders in 1966, the group's second biggest hit in America behind the #1 pop smash of 1965 "Game of Love." "Game of Love" was released with Wayne Fontana and the Mindbenders listed as the artists, and when lead singer Fontana left for a solo career in October 1965, "Groovy Kind of Love" was the only hit he or the group had after "Game of Love." It came to the Mindbenders' attention via Don Kirshner, who employed Wine and Sager as staff writers in his company and pushed the tune to the Mindbenders knowing they needed songs at the time.

In an interview in the People Online Internet Web site on May 19, 1998, Sager recalled that "Groovy Kind of Love" was her first effort at a hit song and gave her the wrong impression of how quickly her songwriting career would develop. "I was pretty young and thought it was going to be pretty easy, and then I found out I had to wait eight more years until I had 'Midnight Blue' by Melissa Manchester," she recalled.

In Collins' remake of "Groovy Kind of Love," he took the upbeat tune into a more mournful mood even while keeping intact the lyric "groovy," the 1960s slang phrase meaning something was good in the beholder's judgment. Regarding the redo, Sager said, "Phil Collins, when he recorded 'Groovy Kind of Love,' took it into his world, which was totally cool." Or "totally groovy," as one might have said in the 1960s.

Actually, Collins got the idea for a new version of "Groovy Kind of Love" while working on a production of the song for another vocalist, Stephen Bishop [see 437]. Collins, who was slated to play the title role in the movie *Buster*, told Bishop that he thought "Groovy. . ." would work well for him in the soundtrack for the film and Bishop agreed to let Collins do the song.

Collins earned a Grammy nomination for Best Male Pop Vocal Performance for his work on the tune. Besides going to #1 AC, "Groovy Kind of Love" also topped the pop chart the weeks of October 22 and 29, 1988.

Another tune sung by Collins on the *Buster* soundtrack hit #1 AC a few months later; see 556—"Two Hearts."

550 One Moment in Time
WHITNEY HOUSTON

Arista 9743

October 29, 1988 (2 weeks)

Writers: John Bettis, Albert Hammond

Producer: Narada Michael Walden

When his label Arista got rights to release the official album of the 1988 Summer Olympics, Clive Davis commissioned his top artist Whitney Houston to be one of several acts to do songs for the LP. The result was "One Moment in Time," the second single, and the highest-charting 45, released from the album. (The first single from the album, the Four Tops' "Indestructible," made #20 AC and #35 pop, while the third one, Eric Carmen's "Reason to Try," got only to #87 pop without cracking the AC chart.)

"One Moment in Time" went to #1 AC, #5 pop, and #22 R&B. Houston received a Grammy nomination for Best Female Pop Vocal Performance for her singing on it, and NBC-TV used it in their coverage of that year's game.

After "One Moment in Time," members of Houston's camp took seriously the criticism that she was doing too many ballads at the expense of her R&B following, and over the next few years, she did a few more upbeat tunes. Her duet with childhood pal Aretha Franklin, "It Isn't, It Wasn't, It Ain't Never Gonna Be" proved too much of a soul shouter for the taste of AC programmers in 1989, and apparently for a few pop radio station managers as well, because it got only to #41 on the Hot 100. Then in 1990 she released the slinky "I'm Your Baby Tonight" as the leadoff single to her album of the same name and got to #7 AC and #1 pop.

Three other singles came from the *I'm Your Baby Tonight* LP, all peaking in 1991: "All the Man That I Need" [see 595]; "Miracle," which went to #4 AC and #9 pop; and "My Name Is Not Susan" at #44 AC and #20 pop. Also, Houston wowed the audience at Super Bowl XXV on January 17, 1991 with a powerhouse rendition of "The Star Spangled Banner"; a recording of her performance went to #48 AC and #20 pop a few weeks later, and the single ending up selling over a million copies.

By the time 1992 rolled around, Houston had tried virtually every possible source to get a hit, from old tunes to new songs, using both famous and unknown talent, and promoting the tunes everywhere from television to sports events. About the only area she had not mined was songs for and in movies. That policy would change with her ninth #1 AC single, which would become her biggest AC and pop hit ever [see 627—"I Will Always Love You"].

551 How Can I Fall?

BREATHE

A&M 1224

November 12, 1988 (2 weeks)

Writers: David Glasper, Marcus Lillington

Producer: Bob Sargeant

The name of the group Breathe came about by default. As lead singer David Glasper explained in the British magazine *Smash Hits*, "It was the name for a song that we had at the time. . . .What happened was we needed a name for the band so that we could do gigs in the local area and we panicked, so we thought, 'Right, let's just call it "Breathe" for the moment and then we can change it later.' But we never did."

Breathe began as a trio of Glasper (born January 4, 1965 or 1966, depending on the source), guitarist/keyboardist and programmer Marcus Lillington (born February 28, 1967), and drummer Ian "Spike" Spice (born September 28, 1966). They all hailed from Yately in Surrey, England, and started playing together as adolescents. Reportedly Lillington asked Glasper to come to a rehearsal with Spice after seeing him act in a stage musical called *Boyfriends*.

In 1984 the trio became a quartet with the addition of Michael "Mick" Delahunty as bassist. They recorded four singles, the first being "Don't Tell Me Lies" in 1985, before "Hands to Heaven" broke them onto both the British and American charts. In the United Kingdom "Hands to Heaven" made #4, while in the United States it peaked at #2 both AC and pop, with AC stations playing it two months before top 40 ones did.

The next record released in America was "How Can I Fall?" (in England, it was "Jonah," which reached #60, followed by "How Can I Fall?" at #48). Besides going to #1 AC, "How Can I Fall?" went to #3 pop the weeks of December 3 and 10, 1988, held out of the top by "Baby, I Love Your Way/Freebird Medley" by Will to Power and "Look Away" [see 553], which stood at #1 and #2 respectively the first week and switched positions the second week. By the time "How Can I Fall?" finished its chart run, Delahunty no longer was part of the group, and Breathe began to run out of air on the charts.

A new release of "Don't Tell Me Lies" in 1989 did well, going to #5 AC and #10 pop, but then "All This I Should Have Known" in mid-1989 only made the AC chart at #34. Breathe rebounded in the fall of 1990 with "Say a Prayer" at #3 AC and #21 pop, but it was almost a last gasp for them. After billing themselves as "Breathe featuring David Glasper," their next single, "Does She Love That Man?," was their last to chart in America, going to #17 AC and #34 pop in early 1991.

552 Kissing a Fool

GEORGE MICHAEL

Columbia 08050

November 26, 1988 (1 week)

Writer: George Michael

Producer: George Michael

George Michael could do virtually no wrong in 1988. He scored two #1 AC hits, the first being "One More Try" [see 540], followed by "Kissing a Fool," which reached #5 pop the week of November 28, 1988, and also went to #33 R&B. Both came from his #1 album *Faith*, which had four other hit singles from it.

He kept his hot streak going into 1989 with "Heaven Help Me," a duet with the otherwise hitless Deon Estus that made #3 AC and #5 pop. He released another album in 1990 and scored with "Praying for Time" at #4 AC and #1 pop (his ninth #1 on that chart either by himself or as part of Wham!) and "Freedom," a tune different from his 1985 Wham! song of the same name that reached #27 AC and #8 pop in late 1990 and earned him a Grammy nomination for Best Male Pop Vocal Performance.

In 1991 he had only middling success with his double-sided single "Waiting for That Day" (#22 AC and #27 pop) backed with "Mother's Pride" (#41 AC and #46 pop). He came back strongly at the end of the year, and went into 1992 with "Don't Let the Sun Go Down on Me," a duet with Elton John which became his tenth pop and fourth AC #1 hit [see 611]. After that, his 1992 single "Too Funky" proved to be just that for the AC chart, but it did go to #8 pop.

Michael remade two Queen hits in a tribute to Freddie Mercury which hit the charts in 1993. "Somebody to Love" went to #42 AC and #30 pop, but "Killer/Papa Was a Rollin' Stone" made only #69 pop. He then had a bitter contract dispute with Sony Records and asked that his association with the label be terminated. It was, and in 1995 he began recording for DreamWorks, the new label led by David Geffen and Steven Spielberg. But even though his album *Older*, released in 1996, made #6 on the LP chart, it was considered a disappointment commercially and critically and left his musical future in doubt.

His private life was another matter altogether. On April 7, 1998, a policeman charged Michael with doing an unspecified lewd act by himself in the men's room of a park in Beverly Hills, California. Three days later he apologized for the incident to his fans in an interview with Jim Moret on *Showbiz Today* on the Cable News Network (CNN), saying he felt stupid for acting in a reckless manner. He also acknowledged having same-sex lovers for the last 10 years but added, "I do want people to know that the songs that I wrote when I was with women were really about women. And the songs that I've written since have been fairly obviously about men."

553 Look Away

CHICAGO

Reprise 27766

December 3, 1988 (1 week)

Writer: Diane Warren

Producer: Ron Nevison

The first #1 hit for Chicago not written by a group member was "Look Away." As trumpeter Lee Loughnane remembered, "HK Management [which handled Chicago] put the feelers out and asked Diane [Warren] to put out some songs." Warren, who also co-wrote Chicago's previous single, "I Don't Want to Live Without Your Love," wrote many AC hits before and after this song, ranging from "Nothing's Gonna Stop Us Now" for Starship in 1987 [see 514] to "How Do I Live" for LeAnn Rimes in 1997 [see 669]. With a lead vocal by keyboardist Bill Champlin, "Look Away" topped the Hot 100 a week after it left #1 AC, staying there the weeks of December 10 and 17, 1988.

Although it became the group's seventh #1 AC hit and third #1 pop hit, Loughnane felt it did not help the band as much as it should have because the emphasis was so much on the vocals and there were very few horns used. "To this day, many people don't realize that was a Chicago song. We play it in concert and some go, 'Why are they singing that?'" he said.

Part of the tendency to "look away" from the horns had been in evidence with the group's pre–Ron Nevison producer, David Foster, who produced Chicago from 1982–87. Discussing his technique, Loughnane said, "He has a formula for recording which he still uses today. It doesn't usually incorporate the band as much as we wanted." But, he noted, "We hired him to be the producer and go out and be the best producer he could, and his method got us hits, so we didn't really complain."

The downplaying of brass did have some benefits for Loughnane. "It got me playing more guitars and keyboards and singing," he said. But he also admitted that he thought Chicago records of the late 1980s did not use enough trumpets and trombones.

As to the decision to seek outside songwriters, Loughnane said that although the band would have preferred to keep writing and recording as a group activity, they also wanted "to get the best possible song for each album." He thought that at this period, Chicago got the best of both worlds because group members could do their own material and pick and choose the cream of the crop submitted to them as well.

In the aftermath of the success of "Look Away" came the singles "You're Not Alone" (#9 AC and #10 pop) and "We Can Last Forever" (#12 AC and #55 pop) in 1989 and "What Kind of Man Would I Be?" (#2 AC for four weeks and #5 pop) in late 1989 and early 1990. By that time original member Danny Seraphine had left the group, but otherwise Chicago stayed intact as it entered the 1990s. Still, it was not until the end of that decade that the band scored another #1 AC hit; see 666—"Here in My Heart."

554 Giving You the Best That I Got

ANITA BAKER

Elektra 69371

December 10, 1988 (1 week)

Writers: Anita Baker, Skip Scarborough, Randy Holland

Producer: Michael J. Powell

The soaring jazz-influenced vocals of Anita Baker on "Sweet Love" in 1986 must have convinced some music lovers they had discovered a bright new vocalist, but Anita Baker, born in Toledo, Ohio, on January 26, 1958, actually was the lead singer of a group named Chapter 8 from 1976–83, a unit which could muster only three chart entries from 1979–80, and those were on the R&B listing. Baker's first solo single was a double-sided R&B entry in 1983, "No More Tears" (#49) backed with "You Will Be Mine" (#87), and she had only R&B singles until "Sweet Love" brought her to #2 R&B, #3 AC, and #8 pop in 1986.

Three more singles through 1987 went to the top 10 on the AC and R&B charts while making the top 50 pop listing—"Caught Up in the Rapture," "Same Ole Love (365 Days a Year)," and "No One in the World." She then went back to work on her next album and used some members of Chapter 8 with whom she retained ties: Michael J. Powell, the former group leader, was producer; Vernon Fails was on keyboards; and Valerie Pinkston did background vocals for "Giving You the Best That I Got."

Baker received "Giving You the Best That I Got" from writer Skip Scarborough after he attempted to have a few other artists record it, including Howard Hewett. She requested lyric changes, including her scatted introduction for the tune, and a slight increase in tempo, before she cut the song.

"Giving You the Best That I Got" hit #1 R&B the weeks of November 12 and 19, 1988, before going to #1 AC three weeks later. The week of December 17, the record reached its pop peak of #3 behind "Look Away" [see 553] at #1 and "Every Rose Has Its Thorn" by Poison at #2. It won Grammy nominations for Record of the Year and Song of the Year, while Baker claimed a statuette for Best Female Rhythm and Blues Vocal Performance.

The *Giving You the Best That I Got* album went to #1 for four weeks starting December 24, 1988, although Baker admitted to David Silverman in *The Chicago Tribune* that its release was held up by her belief that the tracks needed to be redone. "There were plenty of times in the studio when I wanted to put the tape machine through the wall and just start over," she said. Her manager was so frustrated by her actions that he sent a set of completed tapes to be mastered one afternoon while she was out of the studio. Baker went to the mastering company and, she noted, "They were even more surprised when I asked them to trash the masters. We did a second, and then a third mix of the songs before we got what we wanted."

Though she has not had as big a hit since "Giving You the Best That I Got," Baker remained a popular recording and touring act into the late 1990s.

555 Waiting for a Star to Fall

BOY MEETS GIRL

RCA 8691

December 17, 1988 (1 week)

Writers: George Merrill, Shannon Rubicam

Producer: Arif Mardin

George Merrill, the male half of Boy Meets Girl, met Shannon Rubicam at the wedding, in Seattle, of Susan Boeing, a member of the Boeing family, of aircraft fame. Merrill, born in Renton, Washington, on January 10, 1956, and Rubicam, born in Seattle, Washington, on October 11, 1951, sang in the choir loft at the event and struck up a friendship that led them to become partners professionally and later socially.

But before that happened, they had landed a contract with A&M Records and scored a #39 pop single in 1985 with "Oh Girl" billed as Boy Meets Girl. Then they wrote hits for Whitney Houston [see 489—"How Will I Know"]. Finally, in the summer of 1988, they wrote their own biggest hit and also got married. "Waiting for a Star to Fall" was originally intended for Whitney Houston. Explaining the inspiration for the song, Rubicam said, "It actually was fairly literal. We were sitting at the Greek Theater [in Los Angeles] when Whitney was in concert, and I saw a star fall."

Houston's representatives nixed the song. Merrill and Rubicam were not sure why. "We didn't get a specific word," Rubicam said. "Although the song had the right elements, it wasn't right for Whitney at the time," suggested Merrill. "They may have thought it was too pop," added Rubicam.

Their demo eventually came to Robert Palmer, who planned to cut it. Then their producer Arif Mardin heard the demo and "gently goaded him into not doing that," according to Merrill. "Waiting for a Star to Fall" became a Boy Meets Girl record, with Mardin underlining the song's hooks with layers of instruments. "He took it up several notches with key changes and that sort of stuff," Rubicam said. The result gave Boy Meets Girl its AC debut at #1 and a pop hit that peaked at #5 the weeks of December 17 and 24, 1988.

Having sung a hit thrilled the couple in a way their songs for Houston could not. "That was actually our dream," said Rubicam. "To us, everything felt right and complete." But their popularity did not last long. The follow-up, "Bring Down the Moon," went to #28 AC and #49 pop in early 1989. Then the duo vanished completely from both charts.

While claiming that the follow-up 45 had a lack of promotion, Merrill and Rubicam said their own work on the next Boy Meets Girl album in 1992 was poor, and they and RCA executives agreed not to release it. "None of us was quite happy with it," Merrill noted. "We probably overproduced and overwrote it."

Merrill and Rubicam kept afloat as songwriters in the 1990s. But they planned a performing comeback. "We think we're definitely ready to do another Boy Meets Girl album," Rubicam said. At the end of 1998, they were planning to record the LP first, then look for a label to release it.

556 Two Hearts

PHIL COLLINS

Atlantic 88980

December 24, 1988 (5 weeks)

Writers: Phil Collins, Lamont Dozier

Producers: Phil Collins, Lamont Dozier

Phil Collins made his dramatic movie acting debut starring as the lead in *Buster*, a comedy-adventure about the real-life story of Buster Edwards, who masterminded what was termed the "Great Train Robbery of 1963" in England. He got the job on the strength of playing a villain on a guest spot of the NBC-TV crime show *Miami Vice*. The movie was to have its premiere before the royal family, but protesters complained that the movie glorified Edwards and convinced them not to attend the event.

As for Collins' work on the film, he planned only to act in it, not write for it. But when he was talked into doing music as well, he enlisted the help of Lamont Dozier, whom he had admired as a songwriter, particularly his compositions with brothers Brian and Eddie Holland for the Motown label in the 1960s. (He covered their "You Can't Hurry Love," a #1 pop smash for the Supremes, and got to #9 AC and #10 pop with his version in 1983.) The two of them came up with the bouncy "Two Hearts," which had some melodic similarities to "You Can't Hurry Love."

"Two Hearts" went to #1 AC and pop, going atop the latter for the weeks of January 21 and 28, 1989. It also grabbed an Oscar nomination for Best Song. But Collins had mixed feelings about its success, feeling that the stylized sound and the fact that it followed another "poppy" song from the film, "Groovy Kind of Love" [see 549], might foster listeners' false perception of him as a frivolous artist.

"Although I wouldn't change anything if I could do it over again, what happened was that in ['Buster'] the songs were done for a project, not as Phil Collins' solo material," he told David Silverman in *The Chicago Tribune*. "I made that distinction and maybe I gave people too much of the benefit of the doubt to do it themselves. But that music was for something specific; when they became hits there was really no control. I went into the film saying I didn't want to do anything with the music, which was understood by the producer and the director. But I eventually wrote the lyrics because I was Buster and thought I would be able to write them as the character, but with the intention of having someone else sing it."

Not happy with his image as a fluffy pop singer, Collins did an about-face and examined a societal dilemma for the subject matter of his next single, which definitely was not from a movie. The result was "Another Day in Paradise" [see 574].

557 As Long As You Follow

FLEETWOOD MAC

Warner 27644

January 28, 1989 (1 week)

Writers: Christine McVie, Eddie Quintela

Producers: Greg Ladanyi, Fleetwood Mac

"As Long As You Follow" topped the AC chart but proved to be one of Fleetwood Mac's lowest-charting tunes on the pop ledger, going only to #43 in early 1989. It was the only new track on the band's *Greatest Hits* album, but even though Christine McVie and Eddy Quintela wrote it, it certainly was no "Little Lies" [see 526].

In 1990 "Save Me" was the first single off the *Behind the Mask* album, the first Fleetwood Mac LP to feature guitarists/vocalists Billy Burnette and Rick Vito as a replacement for Lindsey Buckingham. Though it reached #6 AC, "Save Me" had a pop peak of #33 and was considered a disappointment. A definite flop was its follow-up, "Skies the Limit," which got to #10 AC but failed to make the Hot 100. Then defections started hitting the band.

In September 1990 Christine McVie and Stevie Nicks announced that they intended to leave at the end of that year's tour. Mick Fleetwood and John McVie tried to continue with the remaining members, but a year later Vito left also. In 1992 Fleetwood and John McVie unveiled their individual efforts, but Fleetwood's *Zoo* and McVie's *Gotta Band* did not elicit much enthusiasm in any quarters. The release of the Fleetwood Mac 45 "Paper Doll" near the end of 1992 met with virtually no notice, going only to #32 AC and #108 bubbling under.

However, that same year presidential aspirant Bill Clinton used Fleetwood Mac's "Don't Stop" as the theme song for his drive to be chief executive of America. When he won, the Fleetwood Mac lineup of the late 1970s reunited at Clinton's inaugural ball to play the tune. Yet the reunion was just a one-shot deal, and in 1994 Fleetwood and John McVie tried an old/new combination: McVie with vocalist Bekka Bramlett and Dave Mason and Billy Burnette. The resulting LP, 1995's *Time*, was so unsuccessful that Fleetwood disbanded his group.

A few more twists lay ahead, however. Buckingham invited Fleetwood to play on material designed for the former's solo album, then John McVie came to play bass, followed eventually by Christine McVie and Stevie Nicks. The result was the 1997 LP *The Dance*, which the group promoted extensively on tour and TV appearances.

"Lindsey was very much the focus of how it all got back together," Fleetwood told Amy Hanson in *Goldmine* in 1997. "I've gotten real close to Lindsey over the last year, to a place we've never been before."

That's where Fleetwood Mac stood in late 1998. As for where it will go in the future, probably none of the band members know the answer.

1989

558 Holding On
STEVE WINWOOD

Virgin 99261

February 4, 1989 (2 weeks)

Writers: Steve Winwood, Will Jennings

Producers: Steve Winwood, Tom Lord Alge

"Holding On" was the third single released from Steve Winwood's *Roll With It* album after the title tune and "Don't You Know What the Night Can Do?" It was also the second #1 AC hit from the album after "Roll With It" [see 544], and nearly became the album's third top 10 pop hit as well, stopping short at #11 on the Hot 100. Like Winwood's three previous #1 AC songs, "Holding On" was co-written by him with Will Jennings, a former English teacher who started writing songs in 1971 and began creating tunes with Winwood 10 years later for the latter's *Arc of a Diver* LP.

After "Holding On" ended its reign, one more 45 came from the *Roll With It* album. "Hearts on Fire" did not really catch fire, going only to #22 AC and #53 pop in 1989. A year later, Winwood came out with his *Refugees of the Heart* LP, and its debut single, "One and Only Man," went to #9 AC and #18 pop. The next and final 45 from the album was 1991's "I Will Be Here," but it flopped, making only #40 AC while missing the Hot 100 entirely. This decreasing success rate was a signal that Winwood would not be nearly so popular in the 1990s as he had been in the previous decade, even though by now he was living in Nashville rather than his native England.

In the early 1990s Winwood did a few dates with Jim Capaldi, his old cohort from their group Traffic, and in 1994 he and Capaldi recorded a new Traffic album called *Far From Home*. The LP generated no hits and fared only modestly on the album chart, peaking at #33, but Winwood and Capaldi enjoyed their reunion in concerts nonetheless. In June of that year the group opened for no less than the Grateful Dead.

In 1997 Winwood released *Junction 7*, his first solo album after *Refugees of the Heart*. The seven-year layoff between releases might have hurt, as the album did not become a best-seller (it stopped at #123 on the LP chart) and produced no hits on the AC or pop chart, even though he did several TV shows and toured extensively to promote it.

Regarding the disappointing performance of *Junction 7*, Winwood told Dean Goodman of the Reuters news service that "I like my music to reach as many people as possible. But over 35 years or whatever, it's impossible to keep on the crest of the wave. Over a period of time, you have to learn how to surf." One has a feeling that given Winwood's talents, he will be able to surf comfortably into the 21st century.

559 When I'm With You
SHERIFF

Capitol 44302

February 18, 1989 (1 week)

Writer: Arnold Lanni

Producer: Stacy Heydon

Five musicians in Canada corralled themselves in Toronto in the summer of 1979 to form Sheriff: lead singer Freddy Curci, guitarist Steve DeMarchi, drummer Rob Elliott, bassist Wolf Hassell, and keyboardist Arnold Lanni. They had only one entry on the Hot 100 to show for four years of work, and that was "When I'm With You," which originally went to #61 in the summer of 1983. Given their lack of success, the group dissolved that same year.

Afterward, Curci and DeMarchi "committed to each other musically" in 1985 and fronted a group called Alias. According to Curci, in 1988 the president of Capitol called them and said, "Do you know you're going to have a hit?" They did not, and thought it was an Alias record at first. Then they learned that the potential hit was "When I'm With You." A Las Vegas radio DJ who felt that current releases were not up to snuff had started playing the tune as if it was a new release. "It was like the most requested song there, and Capitol jumped on it and made us very happy," Curci said.

However, the pleasant feelings shared by the former group members did not extend to Capitol's idea of reforming Sheriff. Curci and DeMarchi were committed to Alias, and Lanni and Hassel were to become a duo called Frozen Ghost, which had put out a #69 pop tune in 1987, "Should I See." Thus, Sheriff was destined to be a one-hit wonder.

On its second go-round, "When I'm With You" made #1 pop the week of February 4, 1989, followed by #1 AC two weeks later. Although Lanni is listed as the song's sole writer, Curci said in 1998, "We just won a 10-year lawsuit that said we all did it." Curci said he was thrilled by the hit even though the group no longer existed. "I'll take a hit whenever it happens," he said.

Actually, Curci did have a few more hits when Alias started charting in 1990. "More Than Words Can Say" made #2 both pop and AC, followed by "Waiting for Love" in 1991, which went to #13 pop and #17 AC. Curci thought news surrounding the circumstances of Sheriff's hits helped in getting attention to the Alias releases. "Any publicity is good publicity," he noted.

Alias scored no more hits and remained low-key for most of the rest of the 1990s. But in 1998, Curci and DeMarchi started work on a new Alias record. "We put Alias back together and I'm going to do a solo tour," said Curci. Curci also hoped to get out his second solo record (his first was not released in America). He is currently based in Los Angeles.

560 The Living Years
MIKE + THE MECHANICS

Atlantic 88964

February 25, 1989 (4 weeks)

Writers: Mike Rutherford, B. A. Robertson

Producers: Christopher Neil, Mike Rutherford

When the first Mike + the Mechanics album came out in 1985, group founder Mike Rutherford was on tour with his main group Genesis and so was at first unable to promote it. It seemed logical that this Rutherford project would sink just as quickly as his two prior solo albums, *Smallcreep's Day* (1979) and *Acting Very Strange* (1982). Luckily, interest in the new band picked up in 1986, and three top 40 pop singles came from the debut album, all of which stopped at #7 AC—"Silent Running (On Dangerous Ground)," "All I Need Is a Miracle," and "Taken In."

These successes thrilled Rutherford, who told Iain Blair of *The Chicago Tribune* that "I formed the group because I wanted to do something away from Genesis, but not just on my own. I wanted to work with some different people, without the pressure of being in a supergroup, and just see where it took me." Joining him were singers Paul Carrack and Paul Young (not the British soul singer), drummer Peter Van Hooke, and keyboardist Adrian Lee.

Two years later, Mike + the Mechanics released "The Living Years," which at nearly 5 1/2 minutes in length seemed unlikely to get airplay. When writing the song Rutherford had worried more about subject matter than length. "It's about missed opportunities, and it's based on my own real-life experiences and those of the co-writer, B. A. Robertson," Rutherford told Blair. "To put the song in some sort of perspective, I felt that my life had been pretty easy until the last year." (At the end of 1986 Rutherford's father died while he was on tour, followed a few weeks later by his father-in-law's death.) "When B.A. also lost his father around the same time, we decided to try and write a song about it."

There was more than a 40-year age difference between Rutherford and his father when the latter died at age 80. "Looking back, I just feel that our relationship was too formal, too reserved in a way. It's sad—I was never able to tell my father that I loved him, and now it's too late to express all those feelings. And those are the things I should have said during 'the living years,' which is where the title comes from," he said. However, Rutherford added, "It's a very delicate area, and we were both worried that the song might turn into some schmaltzy number. But as we were recording it, I found I was becoming quiet and then, once I heard Paul Carrack singing it, I knew it'd work."

"The Living Years" was #1 AC and pop, riding atop the latter the week of March 25, 1989. But the follow-up, "Nobody Knows," made only #41 AC, and two years later another 45, "Everybody Gets a Second Chance," was another AC-only entry at #24, all of which led Mike + the Mechanics to close shop while Rutherford once again concentrated on Genesis.

561 You Got It
ROY ORBISON

Virgin 99245

March 25, 1989 (2 weeks)

Writers: Jeff Lynne, Roy Orbison, Tom Petty

Producer: Jeff Lynne

Roy Orbison's life story sounds as highly dramatic as one of his many pop hits. Born in Vernon, Texas, on April 23, 1936, the guitarist made his pop debut in 1956 as the lead singer of the Teen Kings with "Ooby Dooby" at #59. His next entries came in 1960, first "Up Town" at #72 and then "Only the Lonely," which went to #2 and was the first of ten top 10 pop hits for him.

Orbison made the pop chart often during the early 1960s, with three records going on the AC chart too in 1963—"In Dreams" (#3 AC, #7 pop), "Falling" (#7 AC, #22 pop), and "Pretty Paper" (#10 AC, #15 pop). Then when "Oh, Pretty Woman" stayed at #1 pop for three weeks in 1964, he left Monument Records for MGM Records in hopes of film offers. But his only MGM movie was *The Fastest Guitar Alive* in 1968, and his MGM 45s from 1965–67 failed to crack the pop top 20. After 1968 Orbison was off the charts for 13 years.

Meanwhile, his wife Claudette died in a motorcycle accident in 1966 and two of his sons died at a fire in his home in 1968. He later remarried, but professionally he found the 1970s difficult, especially in America. After trying a few tunes on MGM in the early 1970s, he did not record much the rest of the decade, except for albums in 1977 and 1979.

In 1980 Orbison's duet with Emmylou Harris, "That Lovin' You Feelin' Again," went to #10 AC and #55 pop. But one single does not a comeback make, so Orbison and his wife developed a strategy for him to get one in 1985.

"Barbara and I felt we had to put everything in order in my career," he told Steve Pond in 1988 in *Rolling Stone*. "We never had the right management, the right agency, the right record company all at once. And then a couple of things happened. [The film] *Blue Velvet* came out with 'In Dreams' in it. Then there was the Rock and Roll Hall of Fame [which inducted him in 1987], and then Virgin got in touch. So there has been a concerted effort for the career to make sense for the last three years."

With his Virgin deal Orbison got help writing "You Got It" from Jeff Lynne and Tom Petty, members of the supergroup the Traveling Wilburys to which Orbison belonged in 1988. But on December 6, 1988, before the song was released, Orbison died of a heart attack. He was only 52 years old.

"You Got It" peaked at #9 pop the week of April 15, 1989 after reaching #1 AC, plus hit #7 country. It earned Orbison a posthumous Grammy nomination for Best Male Pop Vocal Performance. He had a few other AC entries thereafter, including "Crying," a duet he did with k.d. lang in 1987 which went to #40 in 1993.

In 1995 Bonnie Raitt remade "You Got It" for the movie soundtrack for *Boys on the Side*. It went to #33 pop.

562 Eternal Flame

THE BANGLES

Columbia 68533

April 8, 1989 (2 weeks)

Writers: Susanna Hoffs, Billy Steinberg, Tom Kelly

Producer: Davitt Sigerson

Formed in Los Angeles, California, in 1981 as the Bangs, the Bangles broke nationally in 1986 when "Manic Monday" went to #2 pop and #10 AC. The four women were guitarist Susanna Hoffs (born in Los Angeles on January 17, 1959), drummer Debbi Peterson (born August 22, 1961), her sister and lead guitarist Vicki Peterson (born January 11, 1958), and bassist Michael Steele (born June 2, 1954).

After "Manic Monday" came "If She Knew What She Wants" in 1986 (#24 AC, #29 pop) and "Walking Down Your Street" in 1987 (#33 AC, #11 pop). Two years later, "Eternal Flame" became the group's fourth and last AC entry.

Hoffs recalled the song's inspiration. "It was kind of a silly story," she said. "The Bangles were on tour. We were on our day off, and we decided to go to Graceland." Graceland is the late Elvis Presley's estate in Memphis, Tennessee. One attraction is an eternal flame at Presley's grave. But Hoffs said, "The day we were there, the flame was not lit." The irony of that stuck in her mind, and she told the story to her songwriting pal Billy Steinberg.

"When I said the words 'eternal flame,' he stopped and something sparked in him," she noted. Steinberg told her that as a child he used to see an eternal flame at his synagogue. Intrigued by the notion, Hoffs said, "The two of us started writing some ideas, with the 'eternal flame' being a title lyric."

As was their custom, Hoffs and Steinberg took their proposed lyrics to Tom Kelly, who wrote the melody with them as all three crafted the final lyrics and notes to their satisfaction. Hoffs then had to convince the other Bangles to record "Eternal Flame." It wasn't easy, as each Bangle had her own songs she wanted on the group's album. "There were a whole lot of ideas floating around," Hoffs said.

But producer Davitt Sigerson "had the idea of doing a sparse, kind of music box sound, like the demo," and encouraged the group to do the song even though it was not their typical "bass and drums grounded kind of arrangement," according to Hoffs. During recording, she sang lead with just keyboard backing, which intimidated her at first but then pleased her. "It was really nice to have all this space to sing into," she said. The other Bangles added their harmonies afterward.

"Eternal Flame" went to #1 pop the week of April 1, 1989 before being #1 AC. Six months later, the Bangles broke up. "It was a point where everybody kind of needed some space," Hoffs said. She would love to work together with the other Bangles anytime, noting "There was a great chemistry there."

Hoffs pursued a solo singing career which included the 1991 single "My Side of the Bed" (#27 AC, #30 pop). As for the future, she said, "I'm still writing songs, looking forward to making more albums and continuing to be a working musician, hopefully."

563 After All

CHER AND PETER CETERA

Geffen 27529

April 22, 1989 (4 weeks)

Writers: Dean Pitchford (words), Tom Snow (music)

Producer: Peter Asher

Tom Snow worked primarily with Cynthia Weil as a writing partner during the 1980s with such hits as "Somewhere Down the Road" [see 417] and "If Ever You're in My Arms Again" [see 458], but he did have time to collaborate with others; one was Dean Pitchford. As Snow explained, "Dean and I had. . .written 'Let's Hear It for the Boy' for Deniece Williams and 'You Should Hear How She Talks About You' for Melissa Manchester." The former was a #3 AC and #1 pop hit in 1984 from the movie *Footloose* which won an Oscar nomination for Best Song. Pitchford and Snow received the same honor again five years later when they created "After All" for the film *Chances Are*, starring Cybill Shepherd.

"We were appointed by Michael Bell and the late Emile Ardilino," Snow said, referring to the film's respective producer and director. "They needed a song for the wedding scene at the end of the movie." With that information as a guide, Snow and Pitchford crafted "After All."

What the gentlemen did not know at the time was who was going to do the song, but, said Snow, they "thought it was meant to be a duet because of the nature of the wedding scene." The two who ended up singing "After All" were Cher and Peter Cetera. The release of the song as a single marked the first time Cher did a duet on a 45 with someone other than Sonny Bono.

"After All" went to #6 pop the week of May 13, 1989 plus #1 AC. Nearly a year later at the Academy Awards ceremony, Pitchford and Snow got the opportunity to be in the audience of the show and see James Ingram and Melissa Manchester sing "After All" as one of the Best Song nominees. "They did a really good job," Snow said. But Snow and Pitchford did not get a chance to get onstage themselves, as the winner that year was "Under the Sea," from the movie *The Little Mermaid*.

Both Cher and Cetera returned to the #1 AC spot with their own solo hits following "After All," which was her second AC chart-topper and his fourth. Cher did it first with "If I Could Turn Back Time" [see 570], while it was over three years before Cetera returned to the top, with "Restless Heart" [see 621].

.38 SPECIAL

A&M 1273

May 20, 1989 (2 weeks)

Writers: Max Carl, Jeff Carlisi, Cal Curtis

Producer: Rodney Mills

The writers took a second try at "Second Chance," and that may have helped the tune become the highest-charting hit for the rock band .38 Special. Ironically, the band member who suggested revising the tune, guitarist Danny Chauncey, didn't think the second effort was much better than the first.

Chauncey had joined the group in 1987 shortly after Max Carl joined as the other guitarist. They came aboard after founding .38 Special members Steve Brookins and Don Barnes had left. The other members, including lead singer Donnie Van Zandt, bassist Larry Junstrom, and guitarist Jeff Carlisi, had been with the band since it started in 1975 in Jacksonville, Florida.

"I believe I heard what was to become the song before we had rehearsals at Jeff's house in Atlanta," recalled Chauncey about "Second Chance." When he heard it then, "The chorus sang, 'I never wanted anyone else but you.' I thought it was lame." Carl had written the chorus, but Carlisi thought Chauncey's opinion was valid, so he went to Los Angeles and rewrote the song with the chorus featuring the opening line "This heart needs a second chance."

The rest of the band liked the new lyrics except for Chauncey. "I thought it was awful when it was rewritten. . . . To me, there was just no edge to the melody," he admitted. But being new to the band and not wanting to make waves, he kept quiet about it.

Helping him endure taping the song was his producer. "Rodney Mills is just one of those great producers," Chauncey said. "He knows when to lay off and when to come forward. I think he was aware I was not too fond of the song." To involve Chauncey in it more, he had the guitarist play lead for much longer than had been planned prior to recording. "I was really answering Max's vocal with the guitar," he said.

Although .38 Special had been cutting albums since 1977, "Second Chance" became the group's only AC entry when it peaked atop the chart after stopping at #6 pop on May 6, 1989. The group did have success in other genres, making the Hot 100 with 15 singles from 1980–91 starting with "Rockin' Into the Night" in 1980 (#43 pop).

After 1991, Max Carl left the band and Barnes returned in his place. Carlisi later dropped out and was not replaced. Chauncey, Barnes, Van Zandt, and Junstrom did not release another album until *Resolution* in 1997, as their manager Mark Spector advised them to tour until they came up with songs he thought would do well in the contemporary music market.

Heading into the 21st century, Barnes said the group's goals were "I think just to continue to improve our songwriting. We're all fans of popular music, and its changing affects our music. . . .You'll still be hearing from us for a long time."

Left to right:
Don Barnes,
Danny Chauncey,
Donnie Van Zant,
Larry Junstrom

565 Miss You Like Crazy
NATALIE COLE

EMI 50185

June 3, 1989 (1 week)

Writers: Michael Masser, Gerry Goffin, Preston Glass

Producer: Michael Masser

Natalie Cole seemed to spend the early part of her career avoiding comparisons with two other people: the first was her father Nat "King" Cole, the balladeer who raised her along with five other children in Los Angeles, California; the second was Aretha Franklin.

Natalie was born on February 6, 1950. She sang with her father on stage and recorded a Christmas tune with him when she was six, and they appeared together sporadically until her mid-teens, when she found out she was not as interested in Nat's smooth pop style of music as in another genre. "He was not a rock and roll singer, but he turned me on to it," Cole told Dale Adamson of *The Houston Chronicle* in 1978. "It was like he said, 'Here, you do it. I can't.' . . ."

Natalie Cole had a nervous breakdown after her father's death in 1965, and when she recovered she went on to get an undergraduate degree in sociology. But after graduating in 1972, she found that she wanted to sing professionally again. She got a manager in 1973, then a contract with Capitol, her father's label, in 1975. That same year her effervescent debut single "This Will Be" went to #1 R&B, #6 pop, and #45 AC. Unfortunately, her powerful vocals reminded many critics of Aretha Franklin, a comparison that was reinforced when Cole won the Grammy for Best Female R&B Vocal Performance for "This Will Be," a category Franklin, the Queen of Soul, had won for eight years.

Cole remained a steady performer on the pop, R&B, and AC charts through 1980, with her highest AC single being "Someone That I Used to Love" at #3 in 1980. Her career took a downturn due to a severe drug problem in the early 1980s, and she really did not come back until "I Live for Your Love" went to #2 AC, #13 pop, and #4 R&B in early 1988. A year later she finally topped the AC chart with "Miss You Like Crazy."

The tune began as one of at least 20 songs composer Preston Glass sent to Michael Masser several years earlier. Masser made his contributions to the melody and then Gerry Goffin added words before the completed song went to Cole for consideration to record.

"Miss You Like Crazy" went to #1 AC and R&B the week of June 3, 1989, then reached #7 pop the weeks of July 8 and 15, 1989. It solidified Cole's comeback, which continued strong through the 1990s, by which time Cole also began an acting career to complement her extensive recording and touring schedule.

566 Everlasting Love
HOWARD JONES

Elektra 69308

June 10, 1989 (2 weeks)

Writer: Howard Jones

Producer: Chris Hughes, Ross Cullum, Ian Stanley

The title "Everlasting Love" charted twice on the AC listing, first in 1974 with a #15 hit by Carl Carlton which later went to #31 AC in 1981 when done as a duet by Rex Smith and Rachel Sweet, and then in 1978 when Andy Gibb took his version to #8, but it did not top the chart until the third go-round, with Howard Jones. "Everlasting Love" was the second #1 AC hit for Jones following "No One Is to Blame" [see 497], but in spite of his two hits on the chart Jones actually did much better on the Hot 100, scoring more than double the number of entries he had on the AC chart. He had in fact made his American chart debut in 1984 with "New Song" at #27 pop, followed by "What Is Love?" at #33 pop.

In 1985 he finally crossed over to the AC chart with "Things Can Only Get Better," which made #38 AC as well as #5 pop, and its follow-up, "Life in One Day," at #16 AC and #19 pop. But his next release, "Like to Get to Know You Well," was a pop-only affair, getting to #49 on the Hot 100.

After "No One Is to Blame" hit top 5 AC and pop, Jones did not make the AC chart for nearly three years until "Everlasting Love," even though two 45s made the Hot 100 during the period, 1986's "You Know I Love You. . .Don't You?" at #17 and 1987's "All I Want" at #76.

The follow-up to "Everlasting Love" (which surprisingly did not fare well in his homeland, peaking at #62 on the U.K. chart in 1989) was "The Prisoner," which made #30 pop without cracking the AC chart in 1989. Three years later, Jones had his last AC and pop entry with "Lift Me Up" at #10 AC and #32 pop.

"Everlasting" definitely was not the term to use to describe Jones' career in the 1990s. His albums during the decade (1992's *In the Running*, 1993's *Best of Howard Jones*, and 1996's *Live Acoustic America*) all failed to make *Billboard*'s Top 200 LP chart. Jones seemed to be having a hard time updating his sound to what contemporary listeners wanted in the 1990s, as did a lot of other English "new wave" acts from the 1980s at the time (e.g., Duran Duran and Culture Club, to name just two of a myriad of artists). But he kept making music and touring. Jones had a few dates in America in 1998, and his fan club remained active, hoping that he would be able to make a comeback.

567 If You Don't Know Me By Now

SIMPLY RED

Elektra 69297

June 24, 1989 (6 weeks)

Writers: Kenny Gamble, Leon Huff

Producer: Stewart Levine

Curly redhead Mick Hucknall, the lead singer of Simply Red, was one of a wave of British singers in the 1980s who stormed the United States with vocals influenced by American soul music. His throbbing emoting on "Holding Back the Years" broke his group onto the U.S. charts at #4 AC and #1 pop in 1986. The song was then rereleased in Great Britain, where it went to #2 (on its first try there, in late 1985, it stopped at #51).

Simply Red had debuted in England with the single "Money's Too Tight (To Mention)," which hit #13 in 1985. Elektra released that tune in America the same year but got little reaction; however, it did go to #28 pop in 1986 as the follow-up to "Holding Back the Years" and paved the way for future entries by Simply Red.

The initial composition of Simply Red, based in Manchester, England, was Hucknall, born June 8, 1960, bassist Tony Bowers, drummer Chris Joyce, keyboardists Tim Kellett and Fritz McIntyre, and guitarist Sylvan Richardson. Although the group had to wait three years to have another hit as big as "Holding Back the Years," they were hardly inactive, getting to #27 pop with "The Right Thing" in 1987, #28 AC with "Maybe Someday" in 1987, and "It's Only Love" at #19 AC and #57 pop in 1989.

"If You Don't Know Me By Now" put Simply Red back in the winner's circle by going to #1 both pop and AC the week of July 15, 1989, plus #38 R&B. The tune had been a frequent visitor to the soul chart ever since Harold Melvin and the Blue Notes, the original vocalists of the tune, took it to #1 R&B on November 18 and 25, 1972. It charted again there at #82 in 1975 by Lyn Collins, #49 in 1982 by Jean Carn, and #79 in 1986 by Patti LaBelle. Also in 1989, Joe Stampley's version went to #59 country.

Despite the multiple covers, "If You Don't Know Me By Now" had always been considered a Harold Melvin and the Blue Notes tune thanks to the powerful lead singing of Teddy Pendergrass. Hucknall admitted following in his footsteps was a challenge. "For a singer to sing other people's songs, it is like singing another vision of the world," Hucknall said in a press release shown on Elektra's Web site on the Internet. "The challenge for me is always, 'How am I going to make that sound like Simply Red? How am I going to interpret it my way?' It's something I hope I will always do."

Simply Red had a few more singles make the AC and pop charts in 1991–92. In 1995 the group released its fifth LP, *Life*, then followed it with an album of covers of old songs called *Blue*. Neither did much business, but at the end of the 1990s, Simply Red's act was still a staple at smaller venues.

568 Right Here Waiting

RICHARD MARX

EMI 50219

August 5, 1989 (6 weeks)

Writer: Richard Marx

Producers: Richard Marx, David Cole

Richard Marx has explained in interviews that he wrote "Right Here Waiting" for his wife Cynthia Rhodes when they were apart for a period of three months, separated "only geographically, not emotionally," as he put it. But what is less publicized is that he nearly gave the song to Barbra Streisand.

Streisand contacted Marx two weeks before he wrote "Right Here Waiting" seeking material for her latest LP. After he gave her the tune, she left a message on his phone. "She said, 'Richard, call me back. The music is beautiful, but we have to change the lyrics, because I'm not right here waiting for anybody,'" Marx recalled with a chuckle.

Friends of Marx's encouraged him to believe that the song was fine as is, so he included it on his *Repeat Offender* LP. As the second single off the album, it hit #1 AC and pop, leading the latter for three weeks starting August 12, 1989, and also propelled *Repeat Offender* to #1 on the album chart the week of September 2, 1989. Marx also got a Grammy nomination for Best Male Pop Vocal Performance for the tune.

Recalling the circumstances which led to the song, Marx said his wife was in South Africa making a film and he was on his first tour. He made plans to visit her during a two-week break in his tour, but the South African government denied his visa, fearing that he would protest that country's apartheid policy ("Which actually I would have," Marx said). Marx's reaction was to throw himself into his work.

One day when his pal and fellow musician Bruce Gaitsch took a phone call, the words and music to "Right Here Waiting" came to Marx. "It's the only time in my life where I wrote a song so easily," he said. But, said Marx, he had no plans to release it commercially until many of the people who had heard the demo "encouraged me to do it on the album."

Marx was still uncertain whether to use such a personal song, which would also add another ballad to *Repeat Offender*, but he decided to go ahead. "'Right Here Waiting' recorded as quickly as I wrote it," he said. Confessing that he never thought the song would be a hit, he recognized its potential only when the label chose to release it as a single.

"Right Here Waiting" followed the hard-rocking leadoff single from *Repeat Offender*, "Satisfied," which hit #1 on the Hot 100 the week of June 24, 1989 without making the AC chart. Marx did have reservations about the decision of his record company to follow "Right Here Waiting" with another "soft" single, "Angelia," which went to #2 AC for two weeks and #4 pop in 1989. He thought listeners would forget he also did rock songs, and said it made EMI look at him as "the ballad cash cow." "Balladeer" was not exactly a title the rock and roller enjoyed being labeled with, even though it did give him several successes, including "Keep Coming Back" [see 609].

569 One

THE BEE GEES

Warner 22899

September 16, 1989 (2 weeks)

Writers: Barry Gibb, Maurice Gibb, Robin Gibb

Producers: Barry Gibb, Maurice Gibb, Robin Gibb, B. Tench

After the release of the *Saturday Night Fever* soundtrack in 1977, in which the Bee Gees had a prominent role, the group found themselves "typecast" as disco kings, even though the first song from the LP was the ballad "How Deep Is Your Love" [see 341]. They had #1 pop hits through 1979 with "Stayin' Alive" (#28 AC), "Night Fever" (#19 AC), "Too Much Heaven" (#4 AC), "Tragedy" (#19 AC), and "Love You Inside Out" (#15 AC), but in the 1980s many people wrote them off as high-pitched tenors whose talents were limited to singing dance tunes. Their 1981 releases "He's a Liar" and "Living Eyes" made only #30 pop and #45 pop, respectively. The two singles from the *Saturday Night Fever* sequel, 1983's *Staying Alive*, didn't do much better: "The Woman in You" went to #31 AC and #24 pop and "Someone Belonging to Someone" made #22 AC and #49 pop.

Sensing the mood was against them at the time, the brothers Gibb went into producing and writing for other artists in the early to mid-1980s, including Barbra Streisand [see 392—"Woman in Love"], Dionne Warwick [see 431—

"Heartbreaker"], and Kenny Rogers [see 446—"Islands in the Stream"].

In 1987 the Bee Gees put out "So You Win Again," which was a top 10 hit in many countries but a disappointment in America, where it got only to #50 AC and #75 pop. Asked about the song's failure to get much airplay on U.S. radio stations, Barry Gibb told Adam White in *Rolling Stone* that "They just couldn't see past [*Saturday Night*] *Fever*. There were people who were afraid to go on a Bee Gees record."

Undeterred, the trio tried again two years later with "One." Robin Gibb told White he thought the timing for the group's latest material was right. "Radio has changed a lot since *ESP* [their album containing 'So You Win Again'] was out," he said. "If you look at this week's *Billboard* charts, you see Donna Summer, the Doobie Brothers, Donny Osmond, Elton John, Paul McCartney. Two or three years ago, some of those same artists wouldn't have been played on American radio. . . .A good record should be judged on its merits and should be heard. Hopefully, that will swing in our favor."

It certainly did in the case of "One," which reached #1 on the AC chart, although peaking a little bit short of that on the Hot 100 at #7 pop the week of September 30, 1989. Nevertheless, it was the group's first top 10 pop hit in a decade, certainly a happy accomplishment for the band.

The Bee Gees continued to put out new product through the late 1990s as well as tour frequently, although none of their singles has had anything close to the success of "One." If nothing else, they have at least come to terms with their disco heritage: in 1998, they performed at a concert saluting the 20th anniversary of *Saturday Night Fever*.

If I Could Turn Back Time

CHER

Geffen 22886

September 30, 1989 (1 week)

Writer: Diane Warren

Producers: Diane Warren, Guy Roche

Cher's solo singing career actually started in 1964 as she recorded under the names Cherilyn and Bonnie Jo Mason. No records under these pseudonyms charted, but when she and her then-husband Sonny Bono cracked the Hot 100 in 1965, a solo singing career for her began concurrently as "All I Really Want to Do" went to #15 pop that year. Despite a few top 10 pop successes over the next two years ("Bang Bang" and "You Better Sit Down Kids"), she did not cross over to the AC chart until 1971, when her #1 pop hit "Gypsies, Tramps & Thieves" made #6 AC.

The next year, "The Way of Love" and "Living in a House Divided" both made #2 AC, but though Cher had seven singles make the top 10 on that chart through 1974, she couldn't manage to get to the top. After her breakup with Bono in 1974 she was hitless until 1979, when her disco hit "Take Me Home" reached #19 AC and #8 pop. But shortly thereafter Cher curtailed her music activities for much of the early and mid-1980s to concentrate on her acting career, which paid off handsomely when she won the Oscar for Best Actress for her work on *Moonstruck* in 1987. That same year, Cher went back to the studio and got her first AC and pop entry in more than eight years with "I Found Someone," which reached #33 AC and #10 pop. Two years later, writer Diane Warren presented Cher with her biggest hit chartwise since the 1970s—"If I Could Turn Back Time."

Guy Roche, co-producer and arranger of the record, recalled that taping Cher's vocal was about the easiest part of the project. "It was great," he said. "She really got excited about it. She thought it would be a big hit."

However, doing the instrumental tracks for "If I Could Turn Back Time" was nowhere near as painless. "We had to do so much more music for her vocal that it became a nightmare in mixing. . . .More synthesizers, more guitars. I think there were even two drum sessions." It took over two months for Roche and Warren to get the record together, but all their efforts paid off. "If I Could Turn Back Time" went to #1 AC and #3 pop, hitting the latter peak the weeks of September 23 and 30, 1989, behind Milli Vanilli's "Girl I'm Gonna Miss You" at #1 and Warrant's "Heaven" at #2.

Cher had a few other pop and AC hits through the 1990s. In 1998 Simon & Schuster published her memoirs, titled *The First Time*, and the same year Cher released a dance record, "Believe," which hit #1 in the U.K. and several other European countries before starting to climb up the Hot 100 at the end of the year.

571 Cherish

MADONNA

Sire 22883

October 7, 1989 (2 weeks)

Writers: Madonna, Patrick Leonard

Producers: Madonna, Patrick Leonard

"Cherish" is the first title to appear atop the AC chart in three different versions. David Cassidy was there first with his remake of the Association's hit in 1972 [see 163], followed by Kool and the Gang's mellow take in 1985 [see 480]. When Madonna did her "Cherish," it was with an eye toward the old "girl group" sound of the 1960s.

Madonna and her collaborator Patrick Leonard wrote "Cherish" in the same week as "Like a Prayer." They both became part of the *Like a Prayer* album, which peaked at #1 on the LP chart for six weeks starting April 22, 1989 based on the success of the title song, which was the first single released from it.

"Like a Prayer" raised a furor not necessarily for its music, but for the *Like a Prayer* video, which featured an array of religious imagery, including crosses (some burning), stigmata, children from a church choir; explicitly sexual poses, and intimate scenes featuring Madonna and a black man. Naturally, conservatives complained and Madonna scored a hit, getting to #3 AC and #1 pop.

"Express Yourself" followed "Like a Prayer," and despite another provocative video showing Madonna amid shirtless working men in an industrial factory, it attracted little criticism and got to #12 AC and #2 pop. Then came "Cherish." With a striking video of hunky "mermen" (male mermaids) swimming in the waves, including Madonna's then-current boy toy Tony Ward, while Madonna frolicked on the shore, "Cherish" went all the way to #2 on the Hot 100 the weeks of October 7 and 14, 1989, behind "Miss You Much" by Janet Jackson.

"Cherish" came out the same week Madonna turned 31. Born Madonna Louise Ciccone in Bay City, Michigan, on August 16, 1958, she was interested in the arts as a young child, but was devastated, at age 6, when her mother died. She moved to New York during the late 1970s, where she became a member of the Alvin Ailey Dance Troupe. In the early 1980s she was briefly a member of the Breakfast Club, a group that later made #36 AC in 1987 with "Kiss and Tell." Stephen Bray, also a Breakfast Club member, produced her *True Blue* album. But her ambition was to make it as a solo singer, and after "Holiday" cracked the Hot 100 in late 1983, she was set to become a superstar.

After "Cherish," the final two singles from *Like a Prayer* were "Oh Father" (#20 pop) and "Keep It Together" (#32 AC, #8 pop). She did not have her next #1 AC hit until 1994 [see 642—"I'll Remember"].

572 Healing Hands

ELTON JOHN

MCA 53692

October 21, 1989 (1 week)

Writers: Bernie Taupin (words), Elton John (music)

Producer: Chris Thomas

"Healing Hands" appeared on Elton John's 1989 album *Sleeping With the Past*, an appropriately named venture as he and Bernie Taupin wrote songs they felt reflected their musical roots. "You know, when we started writing together back in '69, our inspiration came from the same records and artists—Ray Charles, Jackie Wilson, Otis Redding, Sam and Dave, etc.," John mused to Iain Blair of *The Chicago Tribune*. "So we decided this time to take the spirit and vigor of those '60s classics and try and make an '80s record that captured all of that—a white soul record for the '80s."

John's collaborator Taupin and producer Chris Thomas remained on hand once again for this effort, but this time the album was recorded in Denmark. When Blair asked why, John said, "Because I think our best albums have always been the ones where I've just gone off and lived at the studio and concentrated on nothing but the music, and hopefully it paid off this time, too." In Denmark, John was able to focus solely on his album.

His fans might have debated whether it paid off musically, but in terms of sales John was right on target, as *Sleeping With the Past* became another million seller for him. He told Blair the process he and Taupin went through to decide which songs would be used on the album was fairly rigorous. "We ended up writing nearly 20 songs together, but only kept 10," he said. Of the 10, "Healing Hands" became the first one released as a single and made #13 pop as well as #1 AC.

The next 45, "Sacrifice," almost matched the U.S. success of "Healing Hands" by getting to #3 AC and #18 pop, but it far surpassed that song's performance in the U.K. "Healing Hands" had gone to an unimpressive #45, and at first "Sacrifice" did only a little better, making #55 at the end of 1989. But a few months later Steve Wright, a deejay at Britain's Radio One station, put "Sacrifice" in rotation. Listener reaction was strongly positive, prompting John's label to rerelease the song, backing it with "Healing Hands." The new single gave John his first solo #1 hit in the United Kingdom for five weeks starting June 23, 1990.

There was one more hit in America off *Sleeping With the Past*. "Club at the End of the Street" went to #2 AC for four weeks while making #28 pop in 1990. Later that year it was time for another greatest hits collection by John, which included yet another #1 AC hit [see 592—"You Gotta Love Someone"].

573 Don't Know Much

LINDA RONSTADT FEATURING AARON NEVILLE

Elektra 69261

October 28, 1989 (5 weeks)

Writers: Barry Mann, Cynthia Weil, Tom Snow

Producer: Peter Asher

In 1967 "Tell It Like It Is" provided Aaron Neville, born in New Orleans on January 24, 1941, a #2 pop and #1 R&B hit, but the recording success that some expected would follow didn't materialize until more than 20 years later. After "Tell It Like It Is" Neville embarked upon a rather low-key musical career, working often in the 1970s and 1980s with his siblings Art, Charles, and Cyril as part of the Neville Brothers.

What brought Aaron Neville back to prominence was the release of "Don't Know Much," a duet with Linda Ronstadt. The two had been friends for at least four years before they were able to set aside time to record together. "We hooked up at the World's Fair in 1984 when she was there with Nelson Riddle and I was there with the Neville Brothers," Neville recalled. They found that their voices blended well, plus "She said she was a fan of mine, and I was a fan of hers," so they decided to work together, but it wasn't until 1988 that their schedules permitted the collaboration.

One of the first tunes the two tried was "Don't Know Much." "Steve Tyrell, he brought us that song," Neville said. "As soon as we heard it, we loved it."

Barry Mann, a co-writer of "Don't Know Much," was the first to record the song, releasing it on an album of his for Casablanca in 1980. A year later, "Don't Know Much" made its AC and pop chart debut in a version by Bill Medley, who landed it at #29 AC and #88 pop. In 1983 Bette Midler took a stab at the song under the title "All I Need to Know," but it did only slightly better than Medley's effort, halting at #39 AC and #77 pop.

As done by Ronstadt and Neville, "Don't Know Much" went to #2 pop the week of December 23, 1990, behind "Another Day in Paradise" [see 574], in addition to #1 AC. Ronstadt and Neville won a Grammy for their work, in the Best Vocal Performance by a Pop Group or Duo category, while "Don't Know Much" was nominated for Song of the Year. Recalling all the acclaim for the duo, Neville said, "It was great. We got to be good friends."

Both Neville and Ronstadt were at the ceremony to accept their award, as they performed the song on the show. Incredibly, they were to get another #1 AC hit the next year and win the same category as well with it [see 578—"All My Life"].

574 Another Day in Paradise

PHIL COLLINS

Atlantic 88774

December 2, 1989 (5 weeks)

Writer: Phil Collins

Producers: Phil Collins, Hugh Padgham

The lyrics to "Another Day in Paradise" made the song one of Phil Collins' more controversial offerings. Some people considered his "think twice" commentary on the large number of homeless people he saw on the street to be a heartfelt response to the situation. But others saw Collins as a johnny-come-lately, who, after a career typified by tunes dealing with love and other, less weighty concerns was writing about social problems only because that approach was in vogue at the time.

Collins rejected the criticism. "When I started work on the new album, I wasn't thinking I'll write something serious," he told David Silverman of *The Chicago Tribune*. "I don't have those preconceptions. But I do know that, unfortunately, I'm tarred with a certain brush now. Now as soon as you hear a drum machine and it's a Phil Collins record, people say, '"In the Air Tonight," he's done that.'

"But I also didn't sit down with a sheet of paper and say I want to touch on serious issues. I don't write like that. I write and whatever comes out, comes out. It's just that this time I've been more direct. As I've gotten a little older, I've gotten more direct. Why hide the anger?"

"Another Day in Paradise" came to him during an 18-month period of working on tunes for his new album (initially, the working title was "Homeless"). In interviews, he noted that he had witnessed people needing money in both London and Washington, D.C., among other locales, and that, as he described in the song, he had been indifferent to their plight while working on his LP.

With backup vocals by David Crosby, "Another Day in Paradise" went to #1 AC and pop, getting atop the latter for four weeks starting December 23, 1989. It won the Grammy for Record of the Year and earned nominations for Song of the Year and Best Male Pop Vocal Performance. It came from the album *. . .But Seriously*, which went to #1 for three weeks starting January 6, 1990, and got a Grammy nomination for Album of the Year.

The follow-up to "Another Day in Paradise" was "I Wish It Would Rain Down," a louder and less lyrically charged single than its predecessor, which made #3 both AC and pop and featured Eric Clapton on guitar. After that came the more romantic "Do You Remember?" [see 582], which became Collins's sixth #1 AC hit either as a soloist or as part of a duet.

575 How Am I Supposed to Live Without You

MICHAEL BOLTON

Columbia 73017

January 6, 1990 (2 weeks)

Writers: Michael Bolton, Doug James

Producer: Michael Omartian

"How Am I Supposed to Live Without You" was the first #1 hit written by Michael Bolton when it charted first in a version by Laura Branigan in 1983 [see 443]. Six years later, he decided to record his own rendition of the song he had co-written, and got to #1 AC, plus #1 pop for three weeks starting January 20, 1990. It was Bolton's first #1 on either the pop or AC chart, but he would fare well on both through much of the 1990s.

Bolton composed "How Am I Supposed to Live Without You" with Doug James in 1983. Both men had sold several tunes to other acts individually in the early 1980s, but nothing major became of them. An executive with CBS Songs, a publishing firm, introduced James and Bolton and suggested they try writing together.

James said in *The Billboard Book of Number One Hits* by Fred Bronson that "'How Am I Supposed to Live Without You' was the first song I wrote with Michael, and the first song I wrote for CBS. We got the best part of it done in one session. It took, if my memory is correct, three sessions. We had the age-old problem—the second verse was tough as nails to write. It was very difficult."

At that time Bolton was concentrating on songwriting, so the tune went out for consideration by other acts. Air Supply was to do it first, but they wanted to change the lyrics, which eventually led to Laura Branigan doing it. "When we first heard Laura's, we thought it was good, but it was not quite what we had envisioned," James said. "I love to hear her version—she's got a wonderful voice, and did a good job on it."

But the general public seemed to like Bolton's version better, as Branigan's effort stalled at #12 pop. The same could be said about the National Academy of Recording Arts and Sciences, whose membership awarded Bolton the Grammy for Best Male Pop Vocal Performance for his singing on this tune (Branigan did not get a nomination for her vocal on it).

The success of his version of "How Am I Supposed to Live Without You" marked a turning point for Bolton, who was to hit the top of the AC chart many more times, after spending much of the 1980s getting recognition more as a songwriter than a vocalist. (Another tune he co-wrote, "I Found Someone," got to #25 AC and #90 pop for Laura Branigan in 1986 and #33 AC and #10 pop for Cher in 1988.) He admitted to Daniel Rosenthal in *The Chicago Tribune* that "I love it when other artists have hits with my songs, but I think if it continued happening while my own solo career was floundering, it would be a different story."

Bolton had his next hit later in 1990 with "When I'm Back on My Feet Again" [see 583].

576 Downtown Train
ROD STEWART

Warner 22685

January 20, 1990 (1 week)

Writer: Tom Waits

Producer: Trevor Horn

The sultry "Tonight's the Night (Gonna Be Alright)" (1976) got banned by several radio stations due to its lyrics, but incredibly this #1 pop smash for eight weeks was the first of Rod Stewart's records to cross over onto the AC chart, stopping at #42. It was virtually the first time in any context he made the AC listing despite having nearly a decade of high-profile recording activity under his belt, including singing lead for the Jeff Beck Group from 1967–69, singing lead for the Faces from 1969–75, and making the Hot 100 consistently with solo entries from 1971–76.

Roderick Stewart, born in London on January 10, 1945, worked as a folk singer in Europe in the early 1960s. By the middle of the decade he was involved in the recording industry, but his U.S. breakthrough didn't come until 1971, with the double-sided #1 pop hit "Maggie May/Reason to Believe." Though nothing charted quite that well until "Tonight's the Night," he did maintain a constant presence on the pop chart through solo singles like "You Wear It Well" (#17 in 1972) and with Faces in 45s like "Stay With Me" (also #17 in 1972). After "Tonight's the Night" hit, Stewart got a few singles on the AC chart through the 1980s, although his activity on it came nowhere near to matching his success on the Hot 100, probably because his gravelly voice and vibrant instrumental backing seemed too powerful for the format.

Among the three other AC singles he had in the 1970s, the highest charting was 1978's "You're in My Heart (The Final Acclaim)," which made #17. His early to mid-1980s outings were sparse, with only 1980's "I Don't Want to Talk About It" (#44) and 1984's "Some Guys Have All the Luck" (#32) making the roster until 1986's "Love Touch," from the movie *Legal Eagles*, gave him his first top 10 AC single at #5. Two other 45s released in 1988, "Forever Young" and "My Heart Can't Tell You No," hit #3 AC. Then came "Downtown Train."

Recorded in September 1989, "Downtown Train" went to #3 pop for three weeks starting January 27, 1990. The first two weeks "How Am I Supposed to Live Without You" [see 575] was #1, with "Pump Up the Jam" by Technotronic featuring Felly and then "Opposites Attract" by Paula Abdul with the Wild Pair at #2. The last week "Opposites Attract" was #1 and "Two to Make It Right" by Seduction was #2.

"Full credit must be lavished upon my good friend and high-flying executive, Mr. Rob Dickins of WEA London, for drawing my attention to this beautiful Tom Waits song," wrote Stewart in the liner notes to his anthology *Storyteller.* "Downtown Train" did more then get to #1; it earned Stewart a Grammy nomination for Best Male Pop Vocal Performance. Stewart got to #1 AC again later in 1990 [see 580—"This Old Heart of Mine"].

577 Here We Are
GLORIA ESTEFAN

Epic 73084

January 27, 1990 (5 weeks)

Writer: Gloria Estefan

Producers: Emilio Estefan, Jorge Casas, Clay Ostwald

"Here We Are" has the distinction of being the longest-running #1 AC single for Gloria Estefan, surpassing her previous high mark, the three-week run atop the chart with "Anything for You" in 1988. "Here We Are" also went to #6 pop the week of March 3, 1990. On the British chart it made #23.

The single also marked the first time two names appeared at #1 AC under the producer heading. They were Jorge Casas and Clay Ostwald, who also co-wrote Gloria's 1989 hit "Get On Your Feet" with John De Faria. Casas, Ostwald, and De Faria all joined the Estefan troupe in December 1986 after meeting Gloria and Emilio while doing a concert in Miami with their group the Company. The Company was made up of the three men plus several other artists who would work with the Estefans in the future, including singer Jon Secada, whose #2 AC hit of 1992, "Just Another Day," featured Gloria as a background vocalist.

Besides being a producer and arranger, Casas also was a bassist. He produced several other artists apart from Estefan including Secada, Matt Bianco, and David Coverdale and Jimmy Page. He also contributed as a bassist or co-producer or both in such diverse projects as Frank Sinatra's *Duets II* album in 1994 and the 1996 soundtrack to the movie version of the Broadway musical *Evita*. In 1994 he served as co-producer and co-arranger of the halftime show during the Super Bowl, and also played bass for the event. In 1998 he could be glimpsed in the movie *There's Something About Mary* in the band in the closing credits (he was the second from the left).

Ostwald was a keyboardist who also served as Gloria's assistant musical director during the 1990s. His production résumé away from the Estefans included work with Julio Iglesias, Buster Poindexter, and Laura Branigan. He came to Miami in 1979 to study at the University of Miami and graduated with a music degree in studio music and jazz in 1983. Two years before that, he began playing locally in Miami with the pre-Estefan Company.

After rearranging "Anything for You" and "1-2-3" for the Estefans and seeing them become big hits, Casas and Ostwald were drafted as co-producers of the *Cuts Both Ways* album. Because of the success of the album and of singles from it, including "Here We Are," the two continued to work with the Estefans well into the 1990s.

The next single after "Here We Are," "Oye Mi Canto (Hear My Voice)," broke Estefan's string of six consecutive top five AC entries by finishing at #31. On the pop chart it fared even less well, going to #48. But Estefan rebounded with her following release, which became her sixth #1 AC hit [see 584—"Cuts Both Ways"].

578 All My Life

LINDA RONSTADT FEATURING AARON NEVILLE

Elektra 64987

March 3, 1990 (3 weeks)

Writer: Karla Bonoff

Producer: Peter Asher

Aaron Neville claimed that working with Linda Ronstadt on duets like "All My Life" and "Don't Know Much" [see 573] was a pleasant experience, even though he was in the intimidating position of singing not only for her but also her longtime producer Peter Asher. The duets certainly were nice for Ronstadt, as they gave her the only #1 AC hits she had after having made the chart fairly consistently for almost two decades.

Ronstadt, born in Tucson, Arizona, on July 17, 1946, debuted on a *Billboard* chart in 1967 with "Different Drum," a #13 pop hit, as one of the folk-rock trio, the Stone Poneys (the other two were guitarist Bobby Kimmel and keyboardist Ken Edwards). Her AC chart debut was "Long Long Time," which made #20 in 1970. Her best effort prior to "Don't Know Much" and "All My Life" was "Ooh Baby Baby," a remake of the Miracles' 1965 #13 pop and #4 R&B hit, which got to #2 for two weeks in early 1979.

Neville said a friend of Ronstadt's brought "All My Life" to her attention. "Linda loved the song and thought it would be great as a duet," he said. Neville agreed when he heard it, and the two recorded it.

But Neville said that as with the previous single, he and Ronstadt did numerous vocal takes on the song before settling on a final mix. "We both did it till we were satisfied," he said. "We wanted it to be perfect."

The similarity of "All My Life" to "Don't Know Much" did not end there. Though "All My Life" made only #11 pop, a lower ranking than "Don't Know Much," it did, like its predecessor, top the AC chart. Ronstadt and Neville also won their second Grammy in as many years for Best Vocal Performance by a Pop Group or Duo.

Neville, convinced they would never get two Grammys in a row, didn't even attend the ceremony. He found out about the win in a grocery store parking lot in New Orleans, after a friend who had been shopping in the store came back to the car and told Neville that he had heard about the win from a fellow shopper.

After "All My Life" came the release of one more Ronstadt-Neville duet, "When Something Is Wrong With My Baby," which went to #5 AC and #78 pop in mid-1990. The two later worked together on other musical projects [see 605—"Everybody Plays the Fool"], and hope to do more in the future. "We're still talking about trying to get the record companies to let us do something," he said in 1998.

579 Love Will Lead You Back

TAYLOR DAYNE

Arista 9938

March 24, 1990 (4 weeks)

Writer: Diane Warren

Producer: Ric Wake

Why did Lesley Wundermann, born in Baldwin, New York, on March 7, 1963, decide to change her professional name to Taylor Dayne? She said it was in order to get the most out of previous recording contracts which prevented her from working under her birth name without severe financial consequences. Her new first name became Taylor because, she said, "We wanted a name that wasn't necessarily identified with one gender," while the Dayne surname was picked from a book of names for babies.

As Taylor Dayne, she moved into the big time musically with the release in late 1987 of "Tell It to My Heart," which went to #7 pop, as did its follow-up, "Prove Your Love." Both were bouncy dance hits, but Dayne followed them in 1988 with the softer "I'll Always Love You" and did even better. The song went to #3 pop, marked her debut on the AC chart, at #2, and hit #21 R&B.

All the hits were produced by Ric Wake, who discovered Dayne and guided her career ascension. "When we began together, he just loved what was coming out of my voice," she said. She added that while she and Wake usually trust each other's instincts when it comes to the music business, "We've had our head buttings."

Dayne said she did not have to argue with Wake when it came to recording "Love Will Lead You Back." She was hooked once she heard the demo. "It was just a magical song. You could hear it. There were no ifs, ands, or buts," she said.

Originally intended for Whitney Houston, "Love Will Lead You Back" led Dayne to the top of the AC and pop charts for the first time on each. She reached the zenith of the Hot 100 in the middle of her AC run, for the week of April 7, 1990. Recalling that time, Dayne said, "It's a great feeling. I think we were on *Arsenio* [*The Arsenio Hall Show*] that night and he announced we were #1."

Dayne followed "Love Will Lead You Back" with another composition from its writer Diane Warren, "I'll Be Your Shelter." That record went to #15 AC and #4 pop. There were a few more singles to make both the AC and pop charts during the early 1990s, including her 1993 remake of Barry White's "Can't Get Enough of Your Love," which made #15 AC and #20 pop.

Still touring and recording in 1998, Dayne continued to mix dance tunes and ballads in her repertoire. As to whether she finds herself somewhat pigeonholed as a dance singer despite the success of "Love Will Lead You Back" and other tunes, she said, "It's so hard to say. I think the public just likes things that are fun and good and hit them. As for ballads, a ballad is a ballad. If it hits people's hearts, and you know it, it just soars."

580 This Old Heart of Mine
ROD STEWART (WITH RONALD ISLEY)

Warner 19983

April 21, 1990 (5 weeks)

Writers: Brian Holland, Lamont Dozier, Eddie Holland

Producers: Bernard Edwards, Trevor Horn

In 1989 Rod Stewart won the Grammys' Living Legends Award, but he proved he was not ready for retirement by any means, as he scored his second consecutive #1 AC hit with "This Old Heart of Mine." The tune was actually a remake of a remake, as Stewart had covered the tune originally in 1976, going to #83 pop.

The first artists to popularize "This Old Heart of Mine" were the Isley Brothers, who went to #6 R&B and #12 pop in 1966. Songwriters Brian and Eddie Holland and Lamont Dozier also produced that tune, as they had the album track version for the Supremes' 1966 LP, *The Supremes A Go Go*. (The Supremes were the act for which they normally wrote.) Three years later, fellow Motown artist Tammi Terrell got to #67 pop and #31 R&B with the song.

Stewart's "This Old Heart of Mine" went to #10 pop the week of May 26, 1990, after finishing its run atop the Hot 100. The idea of teaming Stewart with the song's original singer, Ronald Isley, for the remake did not come from Stewart. In the liner notes to his anthology *Storyteller*, Stewart extended a "Special thanks to Michael Ostin, head of Warner Bros. A&R in Los Angeles, whose idea it was to bring us both together."

That tune was not the only cover Stewart did in 1990. He cut a new rendition of his #44 AC and #46 pop entry of 1980, "I Don't Want to Talk About It," for *Storyteller*, and the song got so much AC airplay as an album track this time around, it went to #2 on the chart. It also kept Stewart's hot streak on the AC chart going, being his sixth consecutive top five AC entry for Stewart. The streak continued in 1991 as Stewart charted with top AC singles "Rhythm of My Heart" (#2 AC, #5 pop), "The Motown Song" (another nod to the company which created "This Old Heart of Mine," this time featuring the Temptations; it went to #3 AC and #10 pop), and "Broken Arrow" (#3 AC, #20 pop).

In 1992 "Your Song" fell shy of the AC top five, but just barely, peaking at #6 AC and #48 pop. The tune appeared on the 1991 tribute album to Elton John and Bernie Taupin called *Two Rooms*, and Stewart donated all the money he received from it, including royalties, to AIDS charities across the world.

Later in 1992, Stewart released another album, *Vagabond Heart*, and one track from the album, released in a live version a year later, became a hit. [See 634—"Have I Told You Lately."]

581 Hold On
WILSON PHILLIPS

SBK 07322

May 26, 1990 (1 week)

Writers: Chynna Phillips, Glen Ballard, Carnie Wilson

Producer: Glen Ballard

"Wilson Phillips" was not a single person, but the trio of Carnie Wilson, born April 29, 1968, her sister Wendy Wilson, born October 16, 1969, and their friend Chynna (pronounced "CHIGH-nuh") Phillips, born February 12, 1968. They were the children of future members of the Rock and Roll Hall of Fame: Carnie and Wendy's dad was Brian Wilson of the Beach Boys and Chynna was the daughter of Michelle Phillips of the Mamas and the Papas. When they decided to become a group, they considered such monikers as Entropy and the Girls, Ladies First, Pretzels With Mustard, Sound Thought, and Zen Girls before settling on their surnames.

Their first hit emerged when their producer Glen Ballard gave the group some instrumental tracks to consider for their album. When Chynna heard what would become "Hold On" in her car, she sang along with the track and, with a few additional lyrics from Carnie, it emerged as Wilson Phillips' first single.

However, as Ballard told Christopher Connelly of *Rolling Stone*, they "were concerned that it wouldn't be commercial enough" and so to promote "Hold On," the trio spent a grueling three-month tour going to radio stations and conventions, sometimes doing four different towns a day. The effort paid off in getting airplay and concert dates for them, as Carnie told Alice Ansfield of *Radiance* magazine. "Before we knew it, we were in Japan and our record company called and told us that 'Hold On,' our first single, had gone to number one. I'll never forget that moment. It was 4 a.m. when I got that call. I screamed and then cried. Then I screamed and cried some more! Wendy had been sleeping next door, and she heard me and didn't know what was going on! It was the best feeling in the whole world."

"Hold On" hit #1 AC two weeks before topping the Hot 100 the week of June 9, 1990. It earned Grammy nominations for Song of the Year and Best Pop Performance by a Duo or Group with Vocal. In addition, Wilson Phillips got nominations for Best New Artist and Album of the Year.

Carnie told Chuck Eddy of the *Philadelphia Inquirer* she was not surprised by the popularity of "Hold On," but gave much of the credit to the words of the song. "You know what, it's a very realistic thing," she said. "The idea that we always dig our own grave or make our own mess." But the overall message of "Hold On" wasn't pessimism; the lyrics also say we can survive our mistakes if we can "hold on for one more day." Carnie told Ansfield that "We got letters from people who had been suicidal who, after hearing 'Hold On,' chose to live. It was very moving for all of us."

"Hold On" was the first of three consecutive #1 AC hits for Wilson Phillips. The next was "Release Me" [see 587].

582 Do You Remember?

PHIL COLLINS

Atlantic 87955

June 2, 1990 (5 weeks)

Writer: Phil Collins

Producers: Phil Collins, Hugh Padgham

Stephen Bishop was generous to Phil Collins in more ways than one. After letting Collins cover a song which might have become a hit for himself [see 549—"Groovy Kind of Love"], Bishop agreed to sing backup on "Do You Remember?" It was a good move, at least for Collins, since the song became Collins' first #1 AC hit of the 1990s.

"Do You Remember?," the third single released from Collins' . . .*But Seriously* album, went to #4 pop the week of June 30, 1990. In the United Kingdom, the song did not make the chart until it was released as a single toward the end of 1990 in a live version which appeared in Collins' album *Serious Hits. . .Live!* That album was recorded on his concert tour in 1990.

Two other singles from . . .*But Seriously* charted in America after "Do You Remember?" The first was "Something Happened On the Way to Heaven," which had the demo ver-

sion of "Do You Remember?" as its B-side. It made #4 pop and #2 AC for two weeks. Then "Hang In Long Enough" lived up to its title to get to #38 AC and #23 pop in early 1991. That same year, Atlantic issued a promotional CD single called "Who Said I Would" which made #73 pop.

But in the 1990s Collins faced decreasing success on the charts, especially in comparison to his Hot 100 heyday in the 1980s. The man who in the years from 1984–89 had seen almost all his singles make the pop top five was now failing to make even the top 20. "Hero," a duet with David Crosby, got to only #44 pop in 1993, while its follow-up, "Both Sides of the Story," stalled at #25. "Everyday," in 1994, did not do much better, stopping at #24, while "Dance Into the Light" stumbled at #45 in late 1996.

However, Collins did do somewhat better on the AC chart, particularly with "Hero," which reached #3 there. And in late 1998, he was holding the #2 slot behind "I'm Your Angel" [see 677] with his remake of "True Colors," a #5 AC and #1 pop hit for Cyndi Lauper in 1986. In 1997 he was a top U.S. concert draw, selling out several large arenas, but given the lukewarm response to his most recent work, Collins may be performing in smaller venues in the future, at least in the United States. Although his acting career continued through the decade—including *Hook* in 1991; the voices of Muk and Luk in *Balto* in 1995; and a U.K. TV film, *In My Life* (about his own life), in 1998, there is no indication that he plans to make film work a priority in the 21st century.

583 When I'm Back On My Feet Again

MICHAEL BOLTON

Columbia 73342

July 7, 1990 (3 weeks)

Writer: Diane Warren

Producer: Michael Bolton

Though Warren had known Bolton for about a year before he did "When I'm Back on My Feet Again," she did not write the song specifically for him. "I just wrote the song, or I should say the song wrote itself. . . .I was thinking about my dad who had recently passed away, and it just came pouring out." Her late father also was the inspiration behind a later #1 AC hit, "Because You Loved Me" [see 657].

In a chat on America Online on March 15, 1998, Bolton talked about "When I'm Back on My Feet Again." "Well, it's about recovery, but recovery of every type. It's amazing how that song keeps coming back to me in the form of stories. . .people like Oral Hershiser and other athletes and people in all walks of life. They have expressed how important that particular song was to them while they were going through extremely difficult times. It never ceases to amaze me how important music can be to people."

Bolton was familiar with Hershiser, a major league pitcher, no doubt because he himself was a big baseball fan. In fact, Bolton formed a softball group with his entourage which challenged other bands, celebrities, radio station employees, and even league teams in competitions throughout the 1990s. The Bolton Bombers typically played games the day before, the day of, or the day after one of his concerts to raise money for charity, with Bolton playing infield. By 1997 he had his own instructional video about the game, *Michael Bolton's Winning Softball: Hit Harder, Play Smarter*, with Bomber coach Dave Carroll featured as well.

"When I'm Back On My Feet Again" went to #7 pop the week of August 4, 1990, after finishing its run at the helm of the AC chart. It became his second #1 AC hit after "How Am I Supposed to Live Without You" [see 575]. Prior to that single, Bolton had four entries on the AC chart as a singer. The first was "That's What Love Is All About," which made #3 in 1987, followed by "(Sittin' On) The Dock of the Bay" at #19 and "Walk Away" at #14 in 1988, and "Soul Provider" at #3 in 1989. All the songs except "Walk Away" were top 20 pop hits as well ("Walk Away" did not make the Hot 100).

Though it came a few months after "How Am I Supposed to Live Without You," "When I'm Back on My Feet Again" was not a consecutive #1 AC hit for Bolton, as "How Can We Be Lovers," which came out between those singles, missed the top spot by two, making #3 both AC and pop. However, in 1991 Bolton did kick off a streak of four consecutive #1 AC hits [see 600—"Love Is a Wonderful Thing"].

584 Cuts Both Ways

GLORIA ESTEFAN

Epic 73395

July 28, 1990 (1 week)

Writer: Gloria Estefan

Producers: Emilio Estefan, Jorge Casas, Clay Ostwald

Cuts Both Ways, Gloria Estefan's 1989 album, produced four AC and pop entries prior to the release of the title tune as a single. Among them was the previous #1 AC entry, "Here We Are" [see 577]. Next came "Cuts Both Ways," which made #44 pop in the United States and #49 in the U.K.

But although the title tune may not have been a high-charting pop tune on either side of the Atlantic, "Cuts Both Ways" cut many ways musically, making *Billboard*'s dance and Latin charts as well as the AC and pop ones and showcasing the versatility that give Estefan's records such wide appeal. Indeed, Estefan's broad-based popularity led some producers of theatrical or motion picture projects to contact her about acting in them. For a long time Estefan turned them down, saying she was more comfortable with the touring lifestyle and the music industry in general, although she did contribute to a few soundtracks, such as that for the 1994 Sylvester Stallone adventure flick *The Specialist*, which featured her remake of "Turn the Beat Around." Finally, in late 1998, it was announced that Estefan would make her motion picture acting debut in *50 Violins*, starring Meryl Streep and scheduled for release in 1999.

Nearly all the songs on the *Cuts Both Ways* album were written or co-written by Estefan. It took over two years to compile the songs that eventually made the cut for the LP.

"I've written most of my songs in the last year when I've been alone in hotel rooms or in the tour bus," Estefan told Russ DeVault in his "Night Beat" column for *The Atlanta Constitution* in 1989. "I'm the type of person who can't stand being in one place for very long, and I really enjoy being on the road. Besides," she joked, "being away from my family gives me something to write about."

Apart from the road, Estefan insisted she was pretty much a traditional wife and mother, concentrating on raising her son Nayib, who was born in 1980. She was active in the antidrug efforts of the late 1980s, and in March 1990 she met President George Bush to discuss her work in that area. Estefan was also active in community affairs in Miami. Yet just when it seemed that Estefan had it all—success in work, marriage and family, and community life—and before "Cuts Both Ways" reached the top of the AC chart, she was in a horrible accident that could have ended her career [for more details, see 596—"Coming Out of the Dark"].

585 Vision of Love

MARIAH CAREY

Columbia 73348

August 4, 1990 (3 weeks)

Writers: Mariah Carey, Ben Margulies

Producers: Rhett Lawrence, Narada Michael Walden

The Columbia label expected a lot out of Mariah Carey when they signed her in 1989. Before her debut LP came out, the label made a deal for the unknown vocalist to sing the national anthem before the first of the National Basketball Association (NBA) finals in 1989. And her first video was found unacceptable, so they trashed it and started over again at a reported cost of $450,000. But if such behavior was unusual, it hit the mother lode for the label, as Mariah Carey became its top female act during the early and mid-1990s on the AC, pop, and R&B charts.

Carey had done some background vocals for CBS soul artist Brenda K. Starr before going to a party with Starr in December 1988, where she dropped off a demo tape for CBS Records President Tommy Mottola. After leaving the party, Mottola popped the demo in his limo tape deck. Once he heard Carey's seven-octave voice, he had the driver return to the party so he could speak to her. His verdict to Chris Smith of *New York* magazine: " Mariah is one of the greatest singers ever."

When Carey cut her first album in 1989, CBS, wanting to make sure she was not lost among new musical artists, not only promoted her album but also decided to fine-tune her image. ("We don't look at her as a dance-pop artist," said Columbia President Don Ienner to Rob Tannenbaum in *Rolling Stone*. "We look at her as a franchise.") To that end, Columbia brought in producer Narada Michael Walden, who previously produced Whitney Houston, to oversee Carey's debut. Carey told Tannenbaum she would have preferred that her partner, Ben Margulies, handle the chore instead. "I wasn't open to working with a superstar producer," she said.

Tannenbaum also discovered that Carey did not like the layers of instrumentation backing her on "Vision of Love." At a session at which he saw her and two backup singers rehearsing the song with spare accompaniment, he asked why this method of singing hadn't made the record. Carey stopped work only long enough to answer, "It wasn't my choice to do so much production."

Nonetheless, radio programmers and the general public loved what they heard, and "Vision of Love" became a triple chart-topper, going to #1 R&B for two weeks starting August 11, 1990 and #1 pop for four weeks starting August 4, 1990 in addition to #1 AC.

Carefully choosing her words, this is how she summed up her experience in cutting her first records to Tannenbaum: "I wasn't used to working that way. I think it worked out okay in the end." It was "okay in the end" for her second single too [see 590—"Love Takes Time"].

586 Come Back to Me

JANET JACKSON

A&M 1475

August 25, 1990 (3 weeks)

Writers: Janet Jackson, Terry Lewis, James Harris III

Producers: Jimmy Jam, Terry Lewis

The youngest of nine children in the Jackson musical clan, Janet Jackson, born in Gary, Indiana, on May 16, 1966, made her professional debut at age seven singing with the Jackson 5 onstage in Las Vegas. Initially, however, she concentrated on acting rather than follow in their footsteps, getting regular roles on the situation comedies *Good Times* (1977–79) and *Diff'rent Strokes* (1981–82) before going into music. Her debut single in 1983, "Young Love," went only to #64 pop, hardly an indication of things to come.

After a role on the TV drama *Fame* from 1984–85, Jackson came out in 1986 with her *Control* album. Her biting "What Have You Done for Me Lately" became her AC debut at #38 while getting to #4 pop, and was the first of six singles from Control to make top 20 pop. Of that group, two others made the AC chart, 1986's "When I Think of You" at #10 and 1987's "Let's Wait Awhile" at #2.

When it came time to do the follow-up to *Control*, Jackson again enlisted the help of the writers and producers who had worked on the first album, Terry Lewis and James "Jimmy Jam" Harris III. The LP became *Rhythm Nation 1814*, where "1814" was a reference to the year "The Star Spangled Banner" was written.

"We went into *Rhythm Nation* not having any concept at all, just an idea of what we didn't want to do: We didn't want to do *Control II* and we didn't want any record company involvement," Harris told Greg Kot of *The Chicago Tribune*. After four months of work, the trio developed a theme: lyrics about the world around Jackson. The final version included sound bites of news stories between cuts, to give the album a socially relevant feel.

"Come Back to Me" was the fifth single released from *Rhythm Nation 1814*. It peaked at #2 R&B plus #2 pop the weeks of August 18 and 25, 1990, held out of the top of the Hot 100 behind "Vision of Love" [see 585]. The tune became one of seven top five pop singles released from *Rhythm Nation 1814*, which topped the album chart for four weeks starting October 28, 1989. Only three of those seven singles made the AC chart. Besides "Come Back to Me," there was "Escapade," which made #16 AC and #1 pop for three weeks in early 1990 prior to "Come Back to Me," and "Love Will Never Do (Without You)," which made #33 AC and #1 pop for one week in early 1991.

Jackson continued to make the AC chart occasionally through the end of the 1990s, although she was more popular on the R&B and pop charts. Her most recent LP was *The Velvet Rope* in 1997.

587 Release Me

WILSON PHILLIPS

SBK 07327

September 15, 1990 (1 week)

Writers: Wilson Phillips

Producer: Glen Ballard

"I've been singing ever since I remember," Carnie Wilson of Wilson Phillips told Alice Ansfield of *Radiance* magazine in 1996. "I was hearing *Pet Sounds* [the Beach Boys album on which her father Brian Wilson performed] in my mother's womb!. . .At home, Daddy would play music or music would be on."

Her younger sister Wendy got similar exposure, and before either was five they were performing in their home. "We used to sing by the fireplace mantle, using broomsticks as microphones!" Carnie said. "We'd sing Fleetwood Mac, the Carpenters. We were always performing for whoever came to the house."

Despite their dad Brian Wilson's problems with drugs and alcohol, the girls were able to pursue their interest in music during high school and both aimed for a professional career after graduation. Carnie said Brian taught her how to hear and arrange harmony, skills which were invaluable for her.

In 1986 Owen Elliot, daughter of the late Cass Elliot of the Mamas and the Papas, asked Carnie, Wendy, and other children of 1960s rock stars like Donovan and Jerry Garcia to record a song to benefit charities. None were interested except the Wilson girls and their friend Chynna Phillips. "I said, 'Hey, let's just do it,'" Carnie recounted. "So the four of us started to sing Heart and Stevie Nicks [songs]. Wendy and I taught Chynna how to sing harmony, and we all decided to form a group. But Owen was clearly a solo artist. She's now pursuing her own career."

The girls first tried to work with veteran producer Richard Perry, a friend of Chynna's mother (Michelle Phillips of the Mamas and Papas). When they disagreed on his approach to their music, Perry set them up with producer Glen Ballard. "We worked with Glen for two years until, OK, we had enough songs to get a record deal," Carnie said.

The trio attracted attention from many labels, but they signed with SBK Records when company founder Charles Koppelman promised them they would be a top priority there. In 1989 they worked on their first album and included "Release Me," which was under consideration to be the initial single until "Hold On" [see 581] got the nod instead. "Release Me" was the second straight #1 AC and pop hit for Wilson Phillips, staying atop both charts the week of September 15, 1990, followed by an additional week leading the Hot 100. It was a feat neither Brian Wilson nor Michelle Phillips had ever accomplished in their groups.

In 1990, Brian told Steve Daugherty and Maria Eftimiades of *People* magazine, "I'm so damn proud of Wendy and Carnie. I've been following their record's chart position like I used to do with my own songs when I was their age. I haven't called to congratulate them, probably because I know I was awkward as a parent and I'm a little nervous. But God, they make me proud."

Brian finally reconciled with his daughters in 1993. By then, they had scored their third double #1 AC and pop hit [see 597— "You're in Love"].

588 Oh Girl
PAUL YOUNG

Columbia 73377

September 22, 1990 (3 weeks)

Writer: Eugene Record

Producer: Pete Wingfield

Because he did not write his own material, vocalist Paul Young often did covers of other artists' tunes, such as his first #1 AC hit, "Everytime You Go Away" [see 579], and its follow-up, "I'm Gonna Tear Your Playhouse Down," a remake of Ann Peebles' 1973 single which bubbled under to #111. His effort on the latter went to #13 pop without crossing over to the AC chart. When he did not do "oldie" material, however, he mostly struck out, as was the case for him in 1986 when his "Everything Must Change" made #36 pop and "Some People" got only to #65 on the Hot 100. During the same period he had a similar lack of success on the British pop chart, and by the end of the 1980s Young looked to be washed up.

However, he came back strong in 1990 with a remake of "Oh Girl." Eighteen years earlier, the Chi-Lites' original version, written by the quartet's lead singer Eugene Record, had made it to #1 both pop (the week of May 27, 1972) and R&B (the weeks of May 27 and June 3). In Britain the Chi-Lites' record performed even better: in 1972 it got to #3, and in 1975, backed with a reissue of their 1971 hit "Have You Seen Her," went to #5. Back in America, in 1982 Con Hunley reached #12 country with his take on the tune, and in 1988 Glenn Jones took his rendition to #38 R&B.

Regarding his philosophy on what old tunes to do, Young told Merle Ginsberg of Rolling Stone that "I'd never cover a song I think there's a definitive version of." He explained to Ginsberg that he considered "definitive versions" such records as Percy Sledge's "When a Man Loves a Woman" [which Michael Bolton remade in 1991; see 607] and anything by Otis Redding. Apparently he didn't think that any of the existing takes on "Oh Girl" was definitive.

Young's version went to #8 pop the week of October 6, 1990 after topping the AC chart. It was his first AC entry in five years since "Everytime You Go Away." But there was no successful follow-up to the record for a while, although Young did make the AC chart in 1991, when a cut from an album by an Italian singer named Zucchero, a duet called "Senza Una Donna (Without a Woman)," received enough AC airplay to get it to #23.

The next year Young got back to #1 AC on his own for a third time. For more details, see 612— "What Becomes of the Brokenhearted."

589 Unchained Melody
THE RIGHTEOUS BROTHERS

Verve Forecast 871882

October 13, 1990 (2 weeks)

Writers: Hy Zaret (words), Alex North (music)

Producer: Phil Spector

The Righteous Brothers, composed of baritone Bill Medley and tenor Bobby Hatfield, prospered in the mid-1960s but made the AC chart only once then, with an instrumental called "Rat Race" that got to #37. Medley went solo in 1968 after six years of working with Hatfield, then rejoined him in 1974. They had two AC and pop hits that year, "Rock and Roll Heaven" (#38 AC, #3 pop) and "Dream On" (#6 AC, #32 pop). Their best AC showing came 16 years later.

"Unchained Melody" first peaked at #4 pop in 1965 for the Righteous Brothers as the B-side of "Hung on You." "It was not intended for 'Unchained Melody' to be a hit," Medley said. He also said that at the time he and Hatfield each did one solo song on their LPs, one of which was "Unchained Melody." Hatfield sang "Unchained Melody," and Medley claimed that although Phil Spector took credit for producing that song, "I produced it."

In 1990 Medley and Hatfield's "Unchained Melody" was featured during a pottery-making scene in the popular movie Ghost, which got the song a lot of attention. Medley had unpleasant memories of a similar situation, when the appearance of the duo's "You've Lost That Lovin' Feeling" in the 1986 film Top Gun had also attracted attention, but the record company that owned the rights to the song refused to rerelease it. Not wanting that to happen again, Medley produced a remake of "Unchained Melody" with Hatfield singing.

"I went to Mike Curb [head of Curb Records] and said, 'Mike, this is a slam dunk,'" Medley said. Curb agreed and pressed a half-million copies. So while radio stations played the old version, record stores sold the new version. This split the song's pop performance; the original went to #13 in 1990 while the Curb redo made #19. On the airplay-only AC chart there was no such divided action and the old "Unchained Melody" made #1.

The remake aided the duo's visibility and bank accounts ("We weren't making any royalties off our old product," Medley said), but Medley later regretted the move. "Redoing your old stuff is not a bright thing to do. There's no way to recapture the magic," he said.

No other tunes by the duo made the pop or AC charts in the 1990s, but they remained popular performers, particularly in Las Vegas, where they appeared often when not living in southern California. "I spent about 90 percent of my time being a Righteous Brother," Medley said in 1998. "Starting next year, I'm going to start doing more Bill Medley stuff."

"Unchained Melody" has been unchained on the charts. Nine different renditions have made the pop chart. The highest charting was by Les Baxter, whose take hit #1 in 1955, the same year it had an Oscar nomination for Best Song from the film Unchained. In the United Kingdom "Unchained Melody" was the first song to hit #1 there in three different versions—Jimmy Young in 1955, the Righteous Brothers in 1990, and Robson Green and Jerome Flynn in 1995. The AC chart had only one other cover besides the Righteous Brothers, a non–Hot 100 take by George Benson which reached #27 in 1979. Most recently, LeAnn Rimes took the song to #3 country in 1997.

590 Love Takes Time

MARIAH CAREY

Columbia 73455

October 27, 1990 (1 week)

Writers: Mariah Carey, Ben Margulies

Producer: Walter Afanasieff

Mariah Carey wrote "Love Takes Time" with the idea of putting it on her second album. But when CBS Records President Tommy Mottola heard the song, he insisted on adding it to her debut LP, despite the fact that some copies were already in record stores. The song became Carey's second single after "Vision of Love" [see 585].

After its week atop the AC chart, "Love Takes Time" went to #1 R&B the week of November 10, 1990 plus #1 pop the same week for a three-week run. The #1 AC/pop/R&B performance of "Love Takes Time" matched the success of "Vision of Love," a formidable and unprecedented achievement by a new artist.

Carey's work on these songs and others did not go unnoticed at the Grammy Awards, where her label had submitted her as a candidate for Record, Song, and Album of the Year plus Best New Artist, the first person to be considered in all those categories since Christopher Cross in 1980. She won for Best New Artist and the one other category in which she was nominated as well, Best Female Pop Vocal Performance.

A native of Long Island, New York, Mariah Carey was born on March 27, 1970. "I think my mother chose Mariah because it would be a good stage name," Carey told Chris Smith of *New York* magazine. However, in other interviews Carey revealed that her first name came from the tune "They Call the Wind Mariah" from the stage and screen musical *Paint Your Wagon*. Her mother was a singer too, having spent two years as a vocalist with the New York City Opera.

Some accused Carey of being "a white girl trying to sing black." In an interview with Lynn Norment of *Ebony* she answered all those unenlightened critics once and for all: "My father is black and Venezuelan, my mother is Irish. That makes me a combination of all those things. I am a human being, a person. What I am not is a white girl trying to sing black."

When Carey was four, her mother gave her vocal lessons, and Carey listened to and appreciated a wide range of artists, from Billie Holliday and Sarah Vaughn to Gladys Knight, Stevie Wonder, and Al Green. She also studied lyrics and arrangements, and by the time she was a teenager Carey was able to write her own songs. At age 18, she was working as a waitress in New York while shopping her demo tapes to various companies, but the transition from unsigned artist to an affiliation with a major record company—Columbia Records—was accomplished in a remarkably brief time [see 585].

Her next #1 AC hit came in 1991 with "I Don't Wanna Cry" [see 601].

591 From a Distance

BETTE MIDLER

Atlantic 87820

November 3, 1990 (6 weeks)

Writer: Julie Gold

Producer: Arif Mardin

Following her triumph in 1980 with "The Rose" [see 385], Bette Midler had a recording slump for much of the 1980s, with only two AC entries until 1989. "My Mother's Eyes," from the soundtrack of her 1980 concert film *Divine Madness*, made #8 AC and #39 pop in early 1981, and "All I Need to Know" hit #39 AC and #77 pop in 1983 [for more details on that tune, see 573]. Only two other singles made the pop chart during the same period, 1983's "Favorite Waste of Time," which made #78, and 1984's remake of the Rolling Stones' "Beast of Burden," which halted at #71.

By the mid-1980s Midler was concentrating on acting in movies, scoring in such farces as *Down and Out in Beverly Hills* and *Ruthless People*. In 1989 her dramatic film *Beaches* included her rendition of "Wind Beneath My Wings," which went to #2 AC for two weeks and #1 on the pop chart, her first on the latter. Her next single was "From a Distance."

"From a Distance," first recorded roughly five years earlier by Nanci Griffith, was the first hit written by Julie Gold, who had previously worked as a secretary for the pay cable channel Home Box Office (HBO) in New York City. Gold wrote "From a Distance" at a time when several events were shaking up her emotional life, among them her thirtieth birthday and her brother's impending marriage. Most disturbing was a stint on jury duty: despite Gold's sympathy for the defendant, who had killed a man only after being harassed by him for years, she had ultimately voted to convict.

Gold did her first draft at work before completing the tune on piano. Recalling the story behind the tune to Stephen Bishop in *Songs in the Rough*, she noted that "when you're trapped at your desk or in your life, not seeing what or who you know you're put on Earth to be, the line 'God is watching us' just sort of comes to you. As it did me."

Another line about "even though we are at war" led some to adopt "From a Distance" as an anthem for American soldiers fighting in the Persian Gulf in Operation Desert Storm at the time. The circumstances did not hurt the popularity of "From a Distance," which nearly led both the AC and pop charts, falling one shy on the latter the week of December 15, 1990, when it stayed at #2 behind "Because I Love You (The Postman Song)" [see 593]. Gold's tune won her a Grammy for Song of the Year, while Midler notched another Best Female Pop Vocal Performance nomination for her work on the single.

Midler did not have a song with the impact of "From a Distance" after it hit, but she hardly needed one. With her brash quips and unique delivery, and a legion of devoted fans, she was sure to remain a popular movie, TV, and stage personality heading into the 21st century.

592 You Gotta Love Someone

ELTON JOHN

MCA 53953

December 15, 1990 (5 weeks)

Writers: Bernie Taupin (words), Elton John (lyrics)

Producer: Don Was

"You Gotta Love Someone" gave Elton John his 10th #1 AC hit along with the sixth one he had co-written with Bernie Taupin. It was a striking success for the singer on the AC chart in comparison with its showing on the Hot 100, where it stopped at #43 in early 1991, proving to be John's worst showing there since "Heartache All Over the World" in 1986 made #55 pop. "You Gotta Love Someone" also was one of the few new tunes on John's 1990 retrospective anthology box set *To Be Continued*, which contained almost all of his old hits.

The success of "You Gotta Love Someone" came 20 years after John first made the AC chart with "Your Song" in 1970. It too was co-written with Taupin, who was born on May 22, 1950, and grew up in Lincolnshire, England, as the son of a farmer.

When he aligned with John in 1969, the two began writing in an unusual fashion, doing their work separately via mail or, by the 1990s, faxing each other's contribution to a song. "I don't think we ever collaborated on a song in the same room," John told Taupin on the *Storytellers* show on VH-1 in 1997, and Taupin agreed with him.

Taupin did work with others apart from John on various tunes, but few netted him the amount of attention his collaborations with John did. He did score two #1 pop hits in collaborations with others with "We Built This City" for Starship in 1985 and "These Dreams" for Heart in 1986 [see 491]. Another rare exception was "How You Gonna See Now," a #22 AC and #12 pop entry in 1978 for Alice Cooper which Cooper and Taupin wrote along with Dick Wagner.

In 1996 Taupin, who followed his father's footsteps and became a farmer himself, albeit living in California, tried his hand at performing and recording. His band, called Farm Dogs, toured and made a few records over the next few years, but neither of those activities generated anywhere close to the acclaim he got in his work with John on songs like "You Gotta Love Someone."

For producing "You Gotta Love Someone," John enlisted the services of Don Was, but the relationship did not last long. After George Michael produced John's next #1 AC hit [see 611—"Don't Let the Sun Go Down on Me"], John went back to using Chris Thomas as his regular producer.

1991

593 Because I Love You (The Postman Song)

STEVIE B

LMR 2724

January 19, 1991 (2 weeks)

Writer: Warren Allen Brooks

Producer: Stevie B

Despite the subtitle, songwriter Warren Allen Brooks did not get the idea for "Because I Love You (The Postman Song)" from a letter deliverer. "'Because I Love You' to me is a spiritual song. It was God talking to me, telling me that he loved me. . . .It was like I had written him a letter. . .and he was telling me that he got my letter, that he cared, and that whenever I needed him, he'd be there," Brooks said in *The Billboard Book of Number One Hits* by Fred Bronson.

"I turned it into a pop song where the audience thinks it's about a male/female relationship, but it's really about me and God having a personal relationship," he added. "I did the music first, then the lyrics."

Performing "Because I Love You" was Brooks' friend Stevie B, who had heard the tune at least five years earlier when he and Brooks were a duo called Friday Friday and predicted it would be a smash. He was right in that respect. "Because I Love You (The Postman Song)" went to #1 pop for four weeks starting December 8, 1990, before getting to #1 AC.

Born Steven Bernard Hill in Miami, Florida, he formed a band in high school called LUV, which stood for Love, Unity, and Virtue, before attending college and then trying a recording career. His debut solo release on his Midtown label, 1980's "Sending Out for Love," is now a collector's item, and during the years following that release he saved enough money to get his own recording studio and make more demos. One of his tunes, "Party Your Body," became a hit in Miami thanks to local airplay and then received national distribution on the independent LMR label, which signed Stevie B to a contract. "Party Your Body" went to #69 R&B in late 1987.

In 1988 Stevie B finally cracked the pop chart with "Dreamin' of Love" at #80. Six more 45s followed, all of which missed the AC chart and fell short of the pop top 10, until "Because I Love You" became Stevie B's biggest hit.

"Because I Love You" was also the first and only #1 AC and pop hit for LMR. Hill had another AC entry after "Because I Love You," the follow-up 45, "I'll Be by Your Side," which reached #16 AC and #12 pop in the spring of 1991. Contract disputes with LMR prevented him from recording for a time, and when he returned to recording later in the 1990s, his releases generated much less airplay and sales in America. However, he remained popular enough outside the country to tour overseas in 1998.

594 The First Time

SURFACE

Columbia 73502

February 2, 1991 (2 weeks)

Writers: Bernard Jackson, Brian Simpson

Producers: Surface

"The First Time" existed originally as sheet music that a writer named Brian Simpson finished in 1986. When his friend Bernard Jackson, a member of the R&B trio called Surface, reviewed the material, he immediately asked that Simpson put the tune on tape so he could listen to it. "Around 4:00 in the morning, I took the tape in the bedroom and started writing. It was a special song. It reminded me of Chicago, and I heard a little Earth, Wind and Fire in it. I heard drama," Jackson said in *The Billboard Book of Number One Hits* by Fred Bronson.

Jackson took what he had done to other members of the band and they recorded the resulting composition, "The First Time," at Simpson's garage in Van Nuys, California, which officially became a studio when a truck of recording equipment pulled up to his house. Jackson sang lead vocals. Their label Columbia felt the result was strong enough to be the first 45 from Surface's LP *3 Deep*.

"The First Time" was not the first #1 R&B hit for Surface, as "Closer Than Friends," "Shower Me With Your Love," and "You Are My Everything" had all hit in 1989. But once "The First Time" got to #1 there on January 19, 1991, it rode atop the Hot 100 for two weeks starting January 26, 1991 and then peaked on the AC chart.

Besides singer/songwriter Jackson, Surface included bassist/saxophonist Dave "Pic" Conley, a one-time horn player for the 1970s jazz-rock ensemble Mandrill, and guitarist/keyboardist David Townsend, whose father Ed Townsend had a #13 pop solo hit in 1958 with "For Your Love." Townsend and Conley had met in a band called Port Authority before deciding to become songwriters. They met Jackson because Townsend and Jackson shared the same godfather, who in 1984 suggested they check each other out. The three men worked as staff songwriters in New Jersey before going to Los Angeles to pursue their own career as Surface, a name Conley had used earlier in a duo to which he belonged.

In 1987 the first Surface LP came up, and "Happy" proved to be a crossover hit, going to #24 AC and #20 pop as well as #2 R&B. The trio had one more AC entry, "Shower Me With Your Love" at #3 in 1989, before "The First Time."

Subsequently, Surface sank below the hit line on the AC and pop charts, as the group was last seen on those listings with the follow-up to "The First Time," "Never Gonna Let You Down," which went to #17 on each. However, the group did stay together and have continued to tour into the late 1990s.

595 All the Man That I Need

WHITNEY HOUSTON

Arista 2156

February 16, 1991 (4 weeks)

Writers: Dean Pitchford, Michael Gore

Producer: Narada Michael Walden

Dean Pitchford and Michael Gore first worked together creating tunes for the 1980 film *Fame*. After that, one of their first projects was composing "Red Light" for singer Linda Clifford. She liked the tune so much she asked the duo to write an LP's worth of songs for her. One of them was "All the Man That I Need."

"We wrote it on a Sunday afternoon," Pitchford said. "I came up with the title and Michael said, 'Oh, it's a really good title. Leave it with me.' And I said, 'No, let's finish it now.'" Pitchford remembered they did at least the chorus that afternoon if not the whole song.

But, according to Pitchford, there was a great deal of confusion over how to promote Clifford's album, and "All the Man That I Need" died. Then in 1982, the female soul trio Sister Sledge covered it along with male vocalist David Simmons, and it hit #45 R&B. "They kind of pushed and pulled it into another kind of song," Pitchford said.

In 1986, Pitchford had dinner with Arista President Clive Davis. When he got out of their cab after supper, Pitchford told Davis, "I've never done this, but I think I have a song for Whitney's new album." Despite Davis' positive reaction ("Your lovely song is great"), it was nearly four years after that before Houston's version of "All the Man That I Need" emerged in public. The first problem was that Davis heard it around the time Houston's second LP was to come out and it was too late to make that album. Pitchford held the song for Houston for more than two years. Then Pitchford faxed some new words to the song to Houston's producer, Narada Michael Walden, a year before the record's release.

"I had always wanted to revise the lyrics," Pitchford said. "And I thought if Whitney does it, this will be the definitive version." But he did not hear back from anyone about the changes, which he described as "a little tweak to the second verse" and a few other differences, until Davis called him in Toronto, Canada, to play him Walden's mix of the tune and he heard Houston singing the new lyrics.

Another holdup was Houston's singing. "Clive kept on sending her back to the studio and didn't think the vocal was up to what he wanted," Pitchford said. When Pitchford finally met Houston after the record came out, she told him she could not get what Davis wanted until she realized that she could sing the tune in honor of God. "Suddenly, it transformed the song for her," he said, and with the religious angle in mind, Houston nailed the tune.

"All the Man That I Need" hit #1 pop for two weeks starting February 23, 1991, plus #1 R&B on March 2 and 9, 1991, in addition to #1 AC. Pitchford's final verdict on Houston's take was "I thought it was just thrilling."

596 Coming Out of the Dark

GLORIA ESTEFAN

Epic 73666

March 16, 1991 (2 weeks)

Writers: Gloria Estefan, Emilio Estefan, Jon Secada

Producers: Emilio Estefan, Jorge Casas, Clay Osterwald

On March 20, 1990, near Tobyhanna, Pennsylvania, a speeding truck hit Gloria Estefan's tour bus from behind, knocking the sleeping vocalist from her bunk and breaking her back. The accident could have been worse for her, as Estafan narrowly escaped permanent paralysis, and the injuries of husband Emilio and son Nayib were less serious than they might have been. Ten days after an operation in a New York hospital in which a bone graft from her hip and steel rods were used to repair the injuries to her spine, Estafan was flown back to her home in Miami.

The first few weeks after the incident Estefan could not even dress herself, but after three months of hydrotherapy she regained her ability to walk. "It wasn't until a month ago that I started feeling pretty much the way I did before the accident," she told Stephen Holden in *The New York Times* in January 1991. "Now, I can do almost everything I did before, but I have to do things in different ways that are healthier for my back."

Being bedridden for so long could have been frustrating for others, but Estefan used her recuperation time judiciously. "It was the first time in 15 years when I've had nothing else to think of except writing," she told Holden. The first tune she created was "Coming Out of the Dark."

"I didn't start to write until about three months after the accident," she said. "The song was closely related to the whole experience. It was also the first song I tried to sing. My doctor had told me that injury might affect my singing, but thank God it didn't."

For the chorus of "Coming Out of the Dark," Estefan enlisted the help of fellow Miami vocalist Betty Wright, who had made the AC chart in 1990 with a duet with Grayson Hugh on "How 'Bout Us" [see 404]. Wright organized a backing chorus for the title tune, which could be heard prominently on the final version.

After hitting #1 AC, "Coming Out of the Dark" went to #1 pop the weeks of March 30 and April 6, 1991. It also made #60 R&B. Estefan followed "Coming Out of the Dark" with "Seal Our Fate," which stumbled to a disappointing #44 AC and #53 pop. "Can't Forget You" came out quickly after "Seal Our Fate" and got all the way to #2 AC, but it too came up short on the Hot 100, stalling at #43. She did better with another #2 AC single after that, "Live for Loving You," at #22 pop.

For the rest of the 1990s Estefan was a familiar name on the AC and pop charts, while maintaining a strong base overseas with her Spanish-language—as well as English-language—hits. For her 1998 album *Gloria!* she concentrated on dance music rather than ballads.

597 You're in Love
WILSON PHILLIPS

SBK 07343

March 30, 1991 (4 weeks)

Writers: Wilson Phillips, Glen Ballard

Producer: Glen Ballard

After Wilson Phillips scored two #1 AC and pop hits with "Hold On" and "Release Me" (making Wilson Phillips the first artist with more than #1 AC hit to have each of the AC chart-toppers reach #1 pop too), the group stumbled a bit when their next release, "Impulsive," went to #2 AC and #4 pop at the end of 1990. They rebounded with their next song, "You're in Love," for which their producer Glen Ballard wrote the chorus and Carnie and Wendy Wilson and Chynna Phillips wrote the verses. It was the AC chart-topper for three weeks before going to #1 pop as well the week of April 20, 1991. "You're in Love" also earned a Grammy nomination for Best Pop Performance by a Duo or Group with Vocal.

Speaking to Alice Ansfield of *Radiance* magazine, Carnie summarized why the group thought those three songs got to the top: "People were hungry for a new sound. I think the harmonies were pleasing, we had a nice blend. The lyrics were uplifting, honest and inspiring. They described young love and relationships and life. People related to it."

A year later the trio released its second LP, *Shadows and Light*. The women were intimidated by their previous LP's huge sales, and all were in therapy while doing *Shadows and Light*. "How do you follow up a 10-million seller?" Carnie told Ansfield. "We were scared s__tless." *Shadows and Light* sold over three million copies and while the singles were not as spectacularly successful as the ones from their debut, they did fairly well. "You Won't See Me Cry" hit #4 AC and #20 pop, followed by "Give It Up" at #12 AC and #30 pop and "Flesh & Blood" at #17 AC and #119 bubbling under at the end of 1992.

Then Phillips stunned Carnie and Wendy by saying she was becoming a solo artist. "That was real hard for Wendy and me," said Carnie. "It was too soon. I was very upset for about six months. I felt I was letting people and fans down. I loved our group so much, I didn't want it to stop there."

After Wendy and Carnie recorded a 1993 Christmas LP called *Hey Santa*, SBK dropped them but kept Phillips. Phillips' solo career flopped, although she made news in 1995 when she wed actor Billy Baldwin. Meanwhile, when promoting *Hey Santa* on the nationally syndicated radio program *The Howard Stern Show*, Carnie riposted cracks from the controversial "shock jock" host so well that a producer signed her to do a national TV talk show, *Carnie*. But work on the show frustrated Carnie, not only because the ratings were disappointing but because she had no artistic control over guests or topics. *Carnie* lasted only one season, 1995–1996.

In 1997 Carnie and Wendy rechristened themselves as the Wilsons and released an album of that name on the Mercury label. Their dad Brian Wilson co-produced two songs and sang on four of them on the LP. But the LP and three singles from it bombed, and at the end of the decade it was up in the air whether another Wilsons album would ever be made.

598 Cry for Help
RICK ASTLEY

RCA 2774

April 27, 1991 (1 week)

Writers: Rick Astley, Rob Fisher

Producers: Rick Astley, Gary Stevenson

For his third #1 AC hit, Rick Astley enlisted the help of collaborators to write and produce "Cry for Help," a much slower-paced entry that his two previous chart-toppers. Co-writer Rob Fisher was part of the Climie Fisher duo (the "Climie" was singer Simon Climie) of England who had a #12 AC and #23 pop hit in 1988 in the United States with "Love Changes (Everything)." (They had many other hits in their native country.) Backing Astley on the tune was noted gospel singer Andraé Crouch and his choir, who, although they had no previous AC or pop entries, were familiar to secular music fans from their appearances and wins on the Grammy Awards.

"Cry for Help" reached #7 pop the weeks of May 4 and 11, 1991, after topping the AC chart. The single was his last #1 AC hit and fifth and final entry in the pop top 10. Its follow-up, "Move Right Out," did poorly in comparison, getting to #29 AC and #81 pop.

After a year's layoff, Astley returned in 1993 with his *Body & Soul* album, which bombed in America, spending only a week at #185 in October on the LP chart while producing no big hit. For most of the rest of the decade, Astley engaged in fewer music-related activities, concentrating more on his wife and family.

But in the June 1, 1998 edition of the *Manchester Evening News*, producer Pete Waterman announced he had re-signed Astley to his label. Waterman, along with Mike Stock and Matt Aitken, had been one Astley's original writers and producers, and had also helped groom the singer for stardom. "I just bumped into Rick in the street the other day and he said, 'Have a listen to this,'" Waterman told the paper. "He played me some of his new stuff and it's great. We're getting it back together again. As a singer, he is looking stronger than ever."

Whether this reunion of Waterman and Astley will work in America going into the 21st century is a big question mark, given there were not many hits produced by Waterman in the United States in the late 1990s. But Astley has surprised his critics in the past, lasting a lot longer and being more successful than they had predicted, and a few of his fan clubs are still around, so perhaps a comeback is in the cards for the soulful, deep-voiced singer.

599 Baby Baby

AMY GRANT

A&M 1549

May 4, 1991 (3 weeks)

Writers: Amy Grant (words), Keith Thomas (music)

Producer: Keith Thomas

Christian singer Amy Grant solidified her pop appeal in 1991 with "Baby Baby," a tune Keith Thomas gave to her. "I met Keith because he wrote songs with my husband Gary Chapman before I married him," she said. She clarified that this was when she was a 19-year-old junior in college in the fall of 1980. "I did a benefit in Nashville. My manager Mike Blanton helped me put a band together. Keith was the piano player."

When Thomas played her the melody to "Baby Baby," she knew it was a smash. "An absolute moron could've sung the ABC's to it and had a hit," Grant asserted. But she created lyrics with more depth than that. "My daughter Millie was six weeks old at the time, and she inspired them," Grant said.

The song did not upset Grant's Christian fans but, she said, "The video caused a big stir." Originally she proposed to A&M an idea involving many babies in one room, but the label rejected it. Instead, they proposed that she sing the tune to a man portraying her lover. "I said, 'OK, let's try it.' I had never done a video with anyone else in my scenes," she said, noting that for "The Next Time I Fall" [see 505], she had never appeared in any shots with Peter Cetera.

"What I felt was unbelievable relief to be working with somebody else," she noted. "I don't even like making videos." However, she did not use her husband in the video "because there would be kind of an awkwardness for both of us," she said. Grant had to interview prospective actors to find her love interest for the video. "Jamie Stein walked in and he was so disarming and real goofy," she said. "We just had real chemistry between us. . . .It was never weird for a minute." She noted that even when they had to act amorous in strange ways (in one scene she jumped on his back), once the director yelled "Cut!" they quickly dissolved into laughter.

But Grant's more fundamentalist fans did not find the video amusing, and some felt she had sold out her religion. To that charge, Grant said, "I think people are uncomfortable with change. It's just unsettling. The reaction over the years has been so much more positive."

At any rate, she got more immediate praise from secular listeners, as "Baby Baby" reaped Grammy nominations for Record of the Year, Song of the Year, and Best Female Pop Vocal Performance. Regarding those achievements, Grant said, "I knew it was true when people say it's an honor just to be nominated. I never believed for a minute that I would win, and I didn't, but it was just amazing to be up there. I think my whole family went up to New York that year."

"Baby Baby" also became Grant's first #1 solo AC and pop hit, initially topping the Hot 100 on April 27 and May 4, 1991. She got her next #1 AC hit a few months later [see 608—"That's What Love Is For"].

600 Love Is a Wonderful Thing

MICHAEL BOLTON

Columbia 73719

May 25, 1991 (4 weeks nonconsecutive)

Writers: Michael Bolton, Andy Goldmark

Producers: Walter Afanasieff, Michael Bolton

Born in New Haven, Connecticut, on February 26, 1953, Michael Bolotin was the youngest of three children. His father was George Bolotin, a New Haven Democratic ward chairman, and his grandfather and grandmother had been Russian immigrants. Michael started studying the sax when he was 7, and when his parents separated three years later, he concentrated even more on music. By the time he was 11, he was able to play the guitar, and by age 14 he was singing in a local bar band called the Nomads, a group which even managed to get two singles released on Epic Records a year after he joined.

In the 1970s, still going by Bolotin, he got record deals as both a solo act and as part of a hard-rock unit called Blackjack. Blackjack, a quartet formed in New York City, consisted of Bolotin, guitarist Bruce Kulick, bassist Jimmy Haslip, and drummer Sany Gennaro. Their self-titled album of 1979 got to #127 on the LP chart, thanks largely to the leadoff single, "Love Me Tonight," which went to #62 pop and was their only 45 to chart. The group dissolved shortly thereafter, and Bolotin, living in an apartment in New Haven with his wife and three kids, had to scramble to provide for them all on his meager wages.

"It's not hard for me to access this view of that apartment," Bolton told Steve Doughterty in *People*. "I'm sitting at the kitchen table, wondering how I'm going to pay my rent and feed my children. I used to just stare. I would go in and out of the most depressing thoughts, trying to imagine some way out of the situation. That was the darkest period, when I didn't see any light at the end of the tunnel." But in 1983, now calling himself Michael Bolton, he finally found success when his co-creation with Doug James, "How Am I Supposed to Live Without You" hit #1 AC [see 575]. More hits followed, and eventually he returned to singing on his own in the studio.

He still wrote while singing, and he and Andy Goldmark collaborated on the title tune to his *Soul Provider* album as well as the cut "Love Is a Wonderful Thing." The latter song got to #4 pop the week of June 15, 1991 after having peaked earlier on the AC chart.

But "Love Is a Wonderful Thing" turned out to be not so wonderful when, in 1994, a judge ruled that Bolton and Goldmark had copied "significant" elements of a 1966 Isley Brothers tune with the same name and ordered them to pay monetary damages to the Isleys. Perhaps as a result of the controversy, "Love Is a Wonderful Thing" was conspicuously absent the year after the ruling when Bolton's album *Greatest Hits 1985–1995* came out.

601 I Don't Wanna Cry

MARIAH CAREY

Columbia 73743

June 8, 1991 (1 week)

Writers: Mariah Carey, Narada Michael Walden

Producer: Narada Michael Walden

When Mariah Carey cut her self-titled debut album, she co-wrote all 11 cuts, 6 of them with Ben Margulies. Regarding his work with her, Margulies told Stephen Holden in *The New York Times* that "She had the ability just to hear things in the air and to start developing songs out of them. Often I would sit down and start playing something, and from the feel of a chord, she would start singing melody lines and coming up with a concept."

"I Don't Wanna Cry" was not a collaboration with Margulies, but it had much in common with their previous singles, "Vision of Love" [see 585] and "Love Takes Time" [see 590], including anguished vocals about failed relationships, disappointments in life, and the like. "A lot of those songs were written when I was kind of struggling, before I had a record deal," she told Hillel Italie in *The Chicago Tribune*. "It was a harrowing emotional time in my life. . . . They weren't necessarily all about relationships, but they were about things happening in my life."

Her personal relationships soon became public knowledge when it became known that she was dating her boss, Tommy Mottola, chairman of Sony Music Entertainment, the parent company of Columbia Records. The two wed on June 5, 1993, in a lavish ceremony attended by more than 300 people, including many top music artists and executives. But it was not a storybook marriage. Carey preferred to roller-skate and hang out with friends her age at night, while the middle-aged executive favored staying at home in their mansion. On May 30, 1997, the two of them separated. The following year Carey briefly dated professional baseball player Derek Jeter, and when they broke it off, they cited intense media scrutiny as a cause.

The fourth single from the *Mariah Carey* LP, "I Don't Wanna Cry," went to #1 pop for two weeks starting May 25, 1991, plus #2 R&B. It was a return to form for her on the charts, as her previous single, "Someday," had made it only to #5 AC ("Vision of Love" and "Love Takes Time" had both been #1 AC) and was also the first Carey song not to reach #1 R&B. However, the four tunes did all hit #1 pop, the first time that had ever happened for the first four singles by an artist, and it made her the only woman besides Whitney Houston and Janet Jackson to get four #1 pop hits from one album.

Carey's hit train did not stop after "I Don't Wanna Cry." Her next #1 AC hit was "Can't Let Go" in 1992 [see 610].

602 Rush, Rush

PAULA ABDUL

Virgin 98828

June 29, 1991 (5 weeks)

Writer: Peter Lord

Producers: V. Jeffrey Smith, Peter Lord

An only slightly oversimplified version of Paula Abdul's career reads like an American teenage girl's dream: become a hit cheerleader, break into show business, and eventually make it big as a solo star, with admiring fans and handsome boyfriends galore.

Born June 19, 1962, Abdul grew up in the San Fernando Valley region of California. In the early 1980s she became a member of the cheerleading squad for the professional Los Angeles Lakers basketball team, and later lead choreographer for the group. That led to doing choreography for various artists' music videos, including Janet Jackson, and a regular stint on *The Tracey Ullman Show* on the Fox TV network in the late 1980s. Once she tried her own hand at recording, success was not long in coming. She had two 45s on the pop chart in 1988, "Knocked Out" at #41 and "(It's Just) The Way That You Love Me" at #88, before "Straight Up" in 1989 went to #1 pop and gave her an AC debut of #39. She had three more #1 pop hits—"Forever Your Girl" (#11 AC) and "Cold Hearted" in 1989 and "Opposites Attract" (#45 AC) in 1990—before she did "Rush Rush," which became her only #1 AC hit and was the fifth of six consecutive #1 pop hits from 1989–91.

"I remember when 'Opposites Attract' was a hit, I received a cassette of 'Rush Rush' and I carried it everywhere I went," she told Craig Rosen of *The Billboard Book of Number One Albums*. "I couldn't wait to record it." She wanted the ballad to be the first release from her *Spellbound* album because, as she told Rosen, "It showed versatility and a different side of me and won me some new fans." It also made #1 AC and pop, running on the latter for five weeks starting June 15, 1991, and #20 R&B. *Spellbound* also went to #1 on the album chart for two weeks starting June 8, 1991.

There were four more singles from *Spellbound* after "Rush Rush"—"The Promise of a New Day" at #26 AC and #1 pop and "Blowing Kisses in the Wind" at #5 AC and #6 pop, both in 1991, and "Vibeology" at #16 AC and "Will You Marry Me?" at #17 AC and #19 pop in 1992. Appropriately, the latter song debuted a few weeks before Abdul wed actor Emilio Estevez, the son of actor Martin Sheen, on April 29, 1992.

Unfortunately for Abdul, both the marriage and her recording career went sour in the mid-1990s. While her 1995 LP *Head Over Heels* did get to #18 on the album chart, it produced no major hits, and for a few years she did no recording or touring. In 1998, she announced plans for a new album, but in early 1999, nothing had been released.

603 (Everything I Do) I Do It for You

BRYAN ADAMS

A&M 1567

August 3, 1991 (8 weeks)

Writers: Bryan Adams, Robert John "Mutt" Lange,
Michael Kamen

Producer: Robert John "Mutt" Lange

Canadian rocker Bryan Adams was a pretty regular presence on the Hot 100 during the 1980s but had only one #1 pop hit during the period, 1985's "Heaven." He doubled his tally with "(Everything I Do) I Do It for You," which he co-wrote for the movie *Robin Hood: Prince of Thieves* starring Kevin Costner, when the tune become a simultaneous #1 AC and pop entry for most of its run, going to #1 pop for seven weeks starting July 27, 1991.

While its long runs atop the AC and pop listings were impressive, "Everything I Do" was an even bigger hit in the United Kingdom, where it stayed at #1 for an unprecedented 16 weeks—an excellent performance for a tune that had been buried during the end-of-film credits, reportedly because the movie's producers felt it was too modern for the rest of the soundtrack.

"(Everything I Do) I Do It for You" cleaned up critically as well as commercially, getting an Oscar nomination for Best Song. It also claimed the Grammy for Best Song Written Specifically for a Motion Picture or for Television, as well as notched Grammy nominations for Record of the Year, Song of the Year, and Best Male Pop Vocal Performance.

In a Web site on the Internet called "Bryan Adams Heaven" run by a woman who identified herself only as Connie, Adams was quoted as saying that he and his collaborator/producer Robert John "Mutt" Lange got involved with the project at the request of Michael Kamen, who wrote the film's score. "He was incredibly precious about who else was going to be involved in the writing process, to the point he actually nixed Mutt and me out of the music credits even though we wrote half the melody, we created middle eights, a structure and bridges. . . .When the song turned out to be a rock ballad, he lost his mind, and we compromised by not taking musical credit," reported Adams. He also was not thrilled with the idea that he do the song as a duet with Kate Bush and reportedly told Kamen, "You worry about the film score—I'll worry about the song."

Although Adams did get another #1 AC hit later (see 652—"Have You Ever Really Loved a Woman?") nothing before or since "Everything I Do" matched that song's overwhelming popularity. In fact, after one concert in 1991, Robert Sandall of the *Sunday Times* of London asked Adams if it was getting to be a chore for him to do the tune. Adams responded with a smile and said, "Ask me again in 20 years."

604 Time, Love and Tenderness

MICHAEL BOLTON

Columbia 73889

September 28, 1991 (2 weeks)

Writer: Diane Warren

Producers: Walter Afanasieff, Michael Bolton

Even though her tune "When I'm Back on My Feet Again" gave Bolton a huge hit [see 583], songwriter Diane Warren said she did not feel that she created "Time, Love and Tenderness" with that success in mind. "I just wrote the song and thought it would be perfect for Michael," she said in a 1998 fax to this author. "I had played him part of it when I was writing it and he had loved it, so when we got together a couple of months later, I played it for him complete, and it was the final song he cut for his album as well as the title of the album."

Regarding the inspiration for the tune, Warren said, "I loved the title and what the song had to say. I thought it had a very positive, healing quality."

Ahh, but what did Bolton think about when doing a love song like "Time, Love and Tenderness"? Asked this question on a chat on American Online on March 15, 1998, Bolton responded, "It really varies, of course, depending what is going on in my life. And I think the most important thing is that whenever I sing, I draw upon my personal experience, so what my audience feels is something I have or am presently feeling. That is what makes it REAL, that's the strongest way to communicate whatever I'm singing about."

Bolton could probably have used some more time, love, and tenderness while his song was peaking. After a two-year separation, he and his wife Maureen were divorced in 1991, and they had some serious disagreements about how to divvy up assets accumulated during those two years. He later became such an eligible bachelor that gossip had him romantically paired with every female celebrity he came in contact with, possibly excepting talk show host Oprah Winfrey, a devoted fan who had him on her show several times. Among the famous names he did acknowledge seeing were actress Nicolette Sheridan, who had previously dated actor Harry Hamlin, and actress Ashley Judd, whose older sister Wynonna Judd, a country superstar, made occasional forays onto the AC chart during the 1990s beginning with "She Is His Only Need" at #25 in 1992.

"Time, Love and Tenderness" got to #7 pop for three weeks starting September 14, 1991. On its last peak week on the Hot 100 it topped the AC chart for two weeks. It was Bolton's fourth #1 AC hit and second consecutive one, with his next coming with the follow-up to it later in 1991 [see 607—"When a Man Loves a Woman"].

605 Everybody Plays the Fool
AARON NEVILLE

A&M 1563

October 12, 1991 (1 week)

Writers: J.R. Bailey, Rudy Clark, Kenneth Williams

Producer: Linda Ronstadt,

More than two decades before his son Cuba Gooding Jr. won the Oscar for Best Supporting Actor for his role in *Jerry Maguire*, Cuba Gooding had his greatest success as lead singer of the soul trio the Main Ingredient. The group's biggest hit was "Everybody Plays the Fool," which made #3 pop, #25 AC, and #2 R&B in 1972. Nearly 20 years later, "Everybody Plays the Fool" became a hit again, this time as the first solo #1 AC hit for Aaron Neville.

The idea for remaking the song can be traced to Ronstadt's drummer, Russ Kunkel, who joined Neville and Ronstadt in concert during the early 1990s. "Russ. . .came up with that," Neville said. "He did it in a reggae style and he shared it with us when we were on tour."

Neville added that during the 1970s he and his brothers, who recorded as the Neville Brothers, covered "Everybody Plays the Fool" in their act, so it was not a foreign tune to him. And regarding the reaction of the man who first sang it, Neville said, "I met Cuba Gooding. I was a big fan of his. He told me he liked it."

Neville's "Everybody Plays the Fool," which appeared on his LP *Warm Your Heart*, went to #8 pop the week of October 19, 1991 in addition to its AC success. Two other songs from that album made the AC chart only: "Somewhere, Somebody," which entered the listing in late 1991 and peaked at #6, and "Close Your Eyes" with Linda Ronstadt, which went to #38 in 1992. Ronstadt also co-produced the album.

A few more singles came afterward, but none approached the popularity of "Everybody Plays the Fool." The best Neville could muster was "Don't Take Away My Heaven," which did reach #4 AC but only #56 pop. Nonetheless, he kept busy recording for A&M Records and touring through most of the 1990s. And, although the three #1 AC hits that Neville made early in the decade are certainly enough to ensure that he will be remembered, he said he wants to do more.

In 1998 Neville, who lives in New Orleans when not on tour, was planning projects for another Neville Brothers album, and also looking forward to recording some spirituals and a capella jazz music. The same year a tune by his son, bassist Ivan Neville, "Not Just Another Girl," hit #26 pop. "I'm looking forward to being around for a long time," he said.

606 Too Many Walls
CATHY DENNIS

Polydor 867134

October 19, 1991 (2 weeks)

Writers: Cathy Dennis, Anne Dudley

Producers: Cathy Dennis, Phil Bodger

The kinetic dance hit "C'mon and Get My Love" was most Americans' first introduction to British vocalist Cathy Dennis. She sang lead on the tune, which made #10 pop in 1990, and even got billing as part of the studio group, D Mob ("D Mob Introducing Cathy Dennis"). The group was history after the follow-up, "That's the Way of the World," only went to #59 pop, but Dennis was to have several solo hits in the early 1990s which crossed over to the AC chart

Born circa 1968 in Norwich, England, the young Cathy Dennis appreciated the music of such artists as Stevie Wonder, Joni Mitchell, and Laura Nyro. She made her AC debut in 1991 with "Touch Me (All Night Long)," which got to #32 plus #2 pop for two weeks. It was the second single released from her 1990 *Move to This* album, which incorporated the work of several producers, including Dancin' Danny D, the mastermind behind D Mob. The LP's first single, "Just Another Dream," had made #9 pop in early 1991, but the third, "Too Many Walls," became her highest-charting AC entry and also reached #8 pop the week of September 21, 1991.

Describing "Too Many Walls" to Elysa Gardner of *Rolling Stone*, Dennis said, "I think it's the best song on the album, especially in terms of lyrics. The other songs are fun, but they can be quite vacant." She wrote the lyrics to a melody provided by Anne Dudley, keyboardist for the English techno-pop trio the Art of Noise before the group broke up in 1990.

Dennis claimed that the words grew out of a personal incident involving her and her lover, but would not specify what split them apart, telling Gardner only that it involved religion. "The song's about when you want to be together with someone, but other people's opinions and prejudices get in the way," she said.

Discussing the differences between mellow tunes like "Too Many Walls" and her previous upbeat singles, Dennis said, "With dance music, it's easy to get a groove happening, but it's more difficult to really make a song—to not end up with just hooks. With 'Too Many Walls,' the music itself was very natural, very instinctive, but the lyrics took more concentration."

After "Too Many Walls," Dennis faded rather quickly from public view in America. She had one more 45 from *Move to This*, "Everybody Move," which made #90 pop, then got "You Lied to Me" to #32 pop in 1992, "Irresistible" to #6 AC and #61 pop in early 1993, and "Moments of Love" to #8 AC in 1993. Since then, she has been little heard from in the United States, but has continued to record and tour in the U.K.

607 When a Man Loves a Woman

MICHAEL BOLTON

Columbia 74020

November 2, 1991 (4 weeks)

Writers: Cameron Lewis, Arthur Wright

Producers: Walter Afanasieff, Michael Bolton

Bassist Cameron Lewis and organist Arthur Wright wrote "When a Man Loves a Woman" for their lead singer Percy Sledge in the mid-1960s, and despite numerous covers, the great soul lament will always be associated first with Sledge. His original version topped the R&B chart first for four weeks starting May 7, 1966, and then the pop chart for two weeks starting May 28, 1966.

That same year Esther Phillips changed genders in the lyrics, and her "When a Woman Loves a Man" made #26 R&B and #73 pop. Two other reverse-gender renditions appeared later, at #35 pop in 1980 by Bette Midler and at #45 AC in 1987 by Carrie McDowell. Covers on the country chart were by John Wesley Ryles in 1976 (#72), Jack Grayson and Blackjack in 1982 (#18), and Narvel Felts in 1987 (#60).

Given the song's familiarity, one might have expected Michael Bolton to try a totally different approach when he recorded it for his *Time, Love and Tenderness* LP, but he kept the vocals mostly in line with what Sledge had done. He claimed he was using the same philosophy he employed when he redid "Georgia on My Mind" on his previous album, *Soul Provider*.

"The main thing when I'm doing a song like 'Georgia [on My Mind]' or the others is that I'll never get modern with one of those songs," Bolton told Joe Brown of *The Washington Post*. "I don't want to lose the essence or feel of those songs. I don't want to do a technique thing, you know: 'Here's a great song, and now we'll take it to the future.' I love these songs for what they are, so I want to remain as true to that spirit as possible. And I want to express what I can so people will say, 'I really like this version,' not 'Oh, that blows away the original version.'"

Bolton got reactions at both extremes to his "When a Man Loves a Woman" remake at the Grammy Awards ceremony a few months after it had gone to #1 AC and pop, hitting the latter the week of November 23, 1991. He received the statuette for Best Male Pop Vocal Performance for his work on the tune, but it was upsetting to some that he didn't acknowledge Percy Sledge, whose version had gotten him nominated for Best Male R&B Vocal Performance 25 years earlier but who hadn't won.

Bolton presented the Song of the Year award to songwriter Irving Gordon for creating "Unforgettable," which Natalie Cole revived in a duet with her late father via computer-age wizardry, and Gordon said in his acceptance speech, "It's nice to have a song come out that doesn't scream, yell and have a nervous breakdown while it talks about tenderness. It's nice to have a song accepted where you don't have a hernia when you sing it." Gordon later denied he was referring to Bolton.

The brouhahas eventually faded, but Bolton's career did not. He got another #1 AC hit in 1992 [see 613—"Missing You Now"].

608 That's What Love Is For

AMY GRANT

A&M 1566

November 30, 1991 (2 weeks)

Writers: Amy Grant, Michael Omartian, M. Mueller

Producer: Michael Omartian

"When I first started writing songs when I was a kid, I wrote about everything, mostly relationships, because that was what was most intriguing to me at that time," said Amy Grant, born in Augusta, Georgia, on November 25, 1960. But she got her first serious offer as a recording artist from Myrrh Records, a gospel label, in the late 1970s. "They asked if I could do a Christian record. It was wonderful," said Grant, a born-again Christian.

Grant's contemporary Christian music about faith and religion paid off as early as 1979, when her album *My Father's Eyes* got her a Grammy nomination, her first, for Best Gospel Performance, Contemporary or Inspirational. She claimed the statuette in that category in 1982 for her *Age to Age* LP and became arguably the most popular performer of contemporary Christian music during the early 1980s. "Sometime around 1984, 1985, I became a lot more interested in broadening the subject matter I was writing about," Grant said. "I was not trying to seek a broader audience. I was not dissatisfied with the gospel world."

But she did want to write about more secular concerns like love, so Grant found herself being promoted by A&M's pop division in 1985 with her single "Find a Way." It was her AC and pop debut at #7 AC and #29 pop. Her next two 45s in 1985 were not impressive— "Wise Up" made #34 AC and #66 pop and "Everywhere I Go" got only to #28 AC—but a 1986 duet with Peter Cetera was a huge hit and made her name familiar to secular audiences [see 505—"The Next Time I Fall"]. From 1986-89, three singles did modestly well on the AC chart, but Grant did not have another big AC and pop hit until 1991's "Baby Baby" [see 599]. "Every Heartbeat," which made #2 both pop and AC, was next, and then came "That's What Love Is For."

"I did a rewrite on that," Grant recalled. "It was a finished song, and I don't do rewrites to get a piece of the music publishing, but it went a little angle I didn't want it to go. I can't even remember now what it was. I know Michael insisted I put my name on it."

"That's What Love Is For" peaked at #7 pop the week of November 23, 1991. Grant said the decision to release the song as a single came from A&M and not from her. "I might have an opinion about what song I want released, but they make the final call," she said.

Grant scored several other pop and AC hits after "That's What Love Is For" during the 1990s. In 1998 she did a 22-city Christmas tour, and a new album was set for release in 1999.

609 Keep Coming Back
RICHARD MARX

Capitol 44753

December 21, 1991 (4 weeks)

Writer: Richard Marx

Producer: Richard Marx

Born in Chicago, Illinois, on September 16, 1963, Marx started singing at age five, doing advertising jingles written by his father. The performing bug stayed with him throughout his childhood in Chicago. Though Marx liked his home town, he realized that its music production scene was limited, and he took off for Los Angeles as soon as he graduated from high school.

According to Marx, he had sent material to Lionel Richie, and though he had headed west "really without the intention of singing background vocals for Lionel," that was how he got his first big break, doing so initially for the song "You Are" [see 435]. But he wanted his own singing career, and after a few other ventures, such as co-writing Kenny Rogers' hit "What About Me" [see 463], Marx broke onto the AC and pop charts with "Should've Known Better," which hit #20 AC and #3 pop in 1987. "Keep Coming Back" was his second #1 AC hit after "Right Here Waiting" [see 568].

The lyrics to "Keep Coming Back" deal with a man's love for a woman who doesn't reciprocate his feelings. Asked if this obsessive love story caused his wife to wonder what inspired it, Marx said that was not a concern. "She's always been aware I wrote songs about past relationships, relationships I never had, friends' relationships," he said.

Marx focused more on getting the right sound for the record. "I wanted to write an old-fashioned R&B song," he said. To set the proper mood, he got veteran musicians such as guitarist Greg Phillinganes to lay the music tracks, and Marx said they did a speedy job. "Literally, I turned the tape on and let them play it," he said. Adding to the soulful flavor was a background vocal from Luther Vandross, whom Marx first met at an American Music Awards ceremony. Saying that he had always been a fan, Marx said of Vandross, "Luther's probably the only guy I would consider as a friend" among fellow vocalists.

Marx produced "Keep Coming Back" and the rest of his album by himself after co-producing his first two albums with David Cole. "Initially, David and I, the stuff we were going to do, I was going to produce and he was going to mix and engineer," Marx said. Co-producing worked better, particularly with Cole offering suggestions to Marx on his vocals, but Marx felt he could do fine on his own for his third LP. "To me, that's my favorite part of working—producing," Marx added.

"Keep Coming Back" was not planned to be a single, but Marx went along with releasing it as a 45 after his manager Allen Kovac and others enjoyed it. It peaked at #12 pop and #71 R&B as well as #1 AC and made Marx feel his venture into R&B was a success. "It convinced me that, yeah, I was able to do that kind of music," he said.

610 Can't Let Go

MARIAH CAREY

Columbia 74088

January 18, 1992 (3 weeks)

Writers: Walter Afanasieff, Mariah Carey

Producer: Walter Afanasieff, Mariah Carey

The first release off Mariah Carey's 1991 sophomore album *Emotions* was the title tune, which went to #1 pop and R&B but failed to make the top on the AC chart as well, stopping at #3, in what was to be a typical pattern for a Carey release. In fact, Carey has had nearly twice as many #1 pop hits as #1 AC. Among the songs which fell short of the mark on the AC chart while making #1 on the Hot 100 were "Someday" (1991), "Dreamlover" (1993), "Hero" (1993), "Fantasy" (1995), and "Always Be My Baby (1996).

The follow-up to "Emotions" got to #1 on the AC chart only. "Can't Let Go" made #2 on the Hot 100 the week of January 25, 1992, behind Color Me Badd's "All 4 Love," plus #2 R&B. In addition, Carey got a Grammy nomination for Best Female Pop Vocal Performance for her work on the entire album *Emotions*, but lost to Bonnie Raitt's "Something to Talk About."

Carey wrote "Can't Let Go" with Walter Afanasieff, a writer/producer previously associated with Michael Bolton. It was one of several tunes they wrote for *Emotions* which made the final grade among Columbia executives. To create the song, Afanasieff played chord progression on the piano and Carey improvised melodies and lyrics for the tune; then they polished it to final form. However, Afanasieff was not the only producer who worked with Carey on *Emotions*; David Cole and Robert Clivilles, who scored several pop and dance hits as the writers and producers for C & C Music Factory in the early 1990s, helped write and produce the title song.

There was one more single from *Emotions* after "Can't Let Go." "Make It Happen" was the first single by Carey after six previous 45s not to go to #1 on the AC, pop, or R&B charts. Its #13 AC peak was the first time a Carey song had not made the AC top five, and its #5 pop showing was also a new low. Of course, most other artists would be ecstatic to have a tune get to those levels, especially if it was their "worst"-performing single.

Carey once told Lynn Norment of *Ebony* that "I don't let stuff like this go to my head, because success isn't a scale for talent. I don't want to be a 'big star,' but I want to be respected as an artist." She already had that respect from most observers of the music business and was to gain even more as she got her fifth #1 AC hit a few months later with "I'll Be There" [see 619].

611 Don't Let the Sun Go Down On Me

GEORGE MICHAEL WITH ELTON JOHN

Columbia 74086

February 8, 1992 (2 weeks)

Writers: Elton John, Bernie Taupin

Producer: George Michael

One of the strongest mutual admiration friendships in show business had to be between George Michael and Elton John. Michael often cited John's work as an inspiration for his music, while John once said that Michael was "the greatest songwriter of his generation." The two men first teamed up on record for "Wrap Her Up," a #20 pop hit in 1985 credited to John with Michael on lead. Michael also did backgrounds on "Nikita," a #3 AC and #7 pop in 1986. That same year John played piano on "The Edge of Heaven," which made #22 AC and #10 pop.

Five years later, in March 1991, the two did what was to be their biggest hit together when John joined Michael in concert at London's Wembley Stadium, where they taped a live version of John's #3 AC and #2 pop hit of 1974, "Don't Let the Sun Go Down on Me." (In 1974 the song netted John a Grammy nomination for Best Male Pop Vocal Performance and was itself nominated for Song of the Year.)

John said he always had a soft spot for the song. "Sometimes something sticks out, like 'Don't Let the Sun Go Down On Me.' I remember writing that and 'Someone Saved My Life Tonight' and thinking they were special. . . . There are lots of songs that I've written that I think are as good as 'Don't Let the Sun Go Down On Me,' but haven't come out as well on record," he told Timothy White in *Billboard* in 1997.

Co-writer Bernie Taupin told Craig Rosen in *Billboard* that he offered a piece of advice for John on how to do the tune. "I remember when I wrote that; I gave it to him and said, 'Think Phil Spector when you do this.'" (Actually, John reportedly considered it more Beach Boys–influenced.)

When John did the tune with Michael, he came onstage as a surprise guest singing the third verse. The two sang the title lyric together. It was not the first time the men had shared the stage together; John and Michael performed "Candle in the Wind" when John popped up at George's first American concert as a solo performer on April 5, 1988.

The remake of "Don't Let the Sun Go Down On Me" hit #1 pop the week of February 1, 1992, and a week later led the AC listings. Michael and John received Grammy nominations for Best Pop Vocal Performance by a Duo or Group. Proceeds from the single went to charities for AIDS and nine other causes.

612 What Becomes of the Brokenhearted

PAUL YOUNG

MCA 54331

February 22, 1992 (2 weeks)

Writers: James Dean, Paul Riser, William Witherspoon

Producer: Arthur Baker

After an appearance in a tribute to South Africa's President Nelson Mandela in 1988, Paul Young took a self-imposed rest of three years to be with his family; during that time he worked on music only occasionally, and releases were rare [see 588—"Oh Girl"]. He came back in America with a remake of a Motown hit which had charted several times previously, "What Becomes of the Brokenhearted."

The song had been a favorite in Great Britain, going to the top 10 in the United Kingdom for Jimmy Ruffin in 1966, when it reached #10 (the same year it went to #7 pop and #6 R&B in the United States), and again in a reissue in 1974, when it made #4. In 1980 Dave Stewart brought it back to #13 in Britain with a vocal by Colin Blunstone. Another version by Russell Hitchcock, formerly of Air Supply, made #39 AC in 1988.

When Young did the song, it was part of the soundtrack to the movie *Fried Green Tomatoes* starring Kathy Bates and Jessica Tandy. It wound up being a #1 AC and #22 pop entry in 1992, and the last new song most people in the United States heard by him for the rest of the 1990s. In 1993, Young left his record company and management in England, and the new label could not get him a contract to release material in America. He toured Europe, particularly the United Kingdom and France, in 1994 and 1995, and even did a brief reunion of a few shows with his old band the Q-Tips.

In 1996 Young had such a low profile in America that a reporter with *People* magazine included him in a "Where Are They Now?"–type feature, even though Young had been off the charts only a scant four years and was working on a new album. Still, Young admitted he was not killing himself to be at the top of the musical heap, especially with three children to raise with his wife, former model Stacey Smith. "As long as we've got enough for the family, and I'm doing what I love, I've got nothing to be cutthroat about," he said. For her part, Smith said, "He's not very good about painting the garden fence, but he will vacuum up the biscuits the kids leave in the carpet."

In 1997, after two years of work, Young released *Paul Young*, but the album flopped in America. Young has, however, remained active in music in the United Kingdom, and his performances have included a few shows in the London area with a band called Los Pacaminos.

613 Missing You Now
MICHAEL BOLTON FEATURING KENNY G

Columbia 74184

March 7, 1992 (3 weeks)

Writer: Walter Afanasieff

Producers: Walter Afanasieff, Michael Bolton

The friendship between Michael Bolton and saxophonist Kenny G was in place well before the two collaborated on "Missing You Now." For one thing, Kenny G played with Bolton on the single version of Bolton's remake of "Georgia on My Mind," which went to #6 AC and #36 pop in 1990 (however, on the 1989 album *Soul Provider*, which contained the redo, Michael Brecker provided the background music). Bolton got a Grammy nomination for Best Male Pop Vocal Performance for that record, and when he sang "When a Man Loves a Woman" at the following year's Grammys, a record for which he won in the category he lost the previous year, Kenny G backed him on that as well.

"Missing You Now" was the third single released from Bolton's *Time, Love and Tenderness* LP, which went to #1 on the album chart the week of May 25, 1991. Written by his co-producer Walter Afanasieff, the single peaked at #12 pop while topping the AC chart. (Coincidentally, Afanasieff and Kenny G co-wrote the latter's 1990 song "Going Home," a #5 AC and #56 pop record which earned them a Grammy nomination as Best Instrumental Composition.) The last 45 from the album, "Steel Bars," a song he co-wrote with none other than Bob Dylan, received a fair amount of airplay as an album track on pop and AC stations and ended up peaking at #7 AC.

After "Missing You Now," Kenny G scored his own solo hit [see 629—"Forever in Love"], and had another #1 AC duet, this time accompanying Peabo Bryson [see 635—"By the Time This Night Is Over"]. He had done duets with other artists prior to the one with Bolton. Among his collaborators have been Natalie Cole, Aretha Franklin, Aaron Neville, and even Frank Sinatra (on "All the Way" and "One for My Baby" on the *Duets* album). His "We've Saved the Best for Last" with Smokey Robinson went to #4 AC and #47 pop.

"On duets, I take a back seat to the singer, because the words and the voice are primarily the song," Kenny G told Joe Brown of *The Washington Post*. "I don't mind—I like playing around the vocal as opposed to trying to compete with it. I just play the way I play no matter who the singer is."

Kenny G has also played sax on record, although not featured as part of a duet, for Dionne Warwick ("Love Power"), Whitney Houston ("All the Man That I Need"), and Johnny Gill ("My, My, My"), and on various albums for singers Freddie Jackson, Kashif, and Lenny Williams, among many others.

614 Save the Best for Last
VANESSA WILLIAMS

Wing 865 136-4

March 28, 1992 (3 weeks)

Writers: Wendy Waldman, Jon Lind, Phil Galdston

Producer: Keith Thomas

The birthplace of "Save the Best for Last" was an apartment in Los Angeles which a friend of Phil Galdston let him use to work on his latest project. "Jon Lind and I were writing another song which we had been working on for quite some time," recounted Galdston. In frustration, Galdston started messing around with the piano. "I just began to play that opening theme, and Jon said, 'Hey, what's that?' and pretty soon we had the music."

The melody came to them quickly, Galdston remembered. "We took a break, worked on the music for a while, and it took 27 minutes. Jon asked, 'What do you think we ought to call it?' and I pulled out the title 'Save the Best for Last' from my notebook with song titles."

But both men needed to work on the other tune before going on with "Save the Best for Last," and Galdston had to return to his home base of New York City. "How can we work on this one?" Lind asked. Recalling another songwriting buddy with whom he had been working for five years, Galdston said, "Why don't I show it to Wendy Waldman?" He had to meet Waldman in Nashville in March 1989, so he brought the song to her.

"As soon as I played it for her, she loved it," Galdston said. The only thing which bothered her were the lyrics, which used the title "Save the Best for Last" to refer to a person bitter over a relationship's dissolution. "She looked at me and said, 'No, no, it's way too positive for that.'" She suggested new opening lines, and they finished the lyrics in three days. "I remember in the middle we called Jon and told him what we had, and he was real enthusiastic," Galdston said.

Galdston had doubts about the ballad's commercial potential, but his worries diminished somewhat when his son Jesse, who was five at the time, said, "This is a great song." Vanessa Williams put a contractual hold on the tune after hearing the demo which Waldman sang, and it finally came out as a single in early 1992.

"Save the Best for Last" was a triple #1 smash, topping the pop charts for five weeks starting March 21, 1992, and leading the R&B and AC charts simultaneously for three weeks starting March 28, 1992. Williams earned a Grammy nomination for Best Female Pop Vocal Performance for her work on the tune, which itself won nominations for Record of the Year and Song of the Year. "It was a thrill on so many levels," Galdston said of the song's commercial and critical praise. What he really liked was that Williams and her producer consulted the writers to make sure the proper points were emphasized, and that "the song and the writers were treated with the utmost respect."

In 1993, Williams had another #1 AC; see 631—"Love Is."

615 Tears in Heaven

ERIC CLAPTON

Reprise 19038

April 18, 1992 (3 weeks)

Writers: Eric Clapton, Will Jennings

Producer: Russ Titelman

"Clapton is God" proclaimed blues fans in graffiti on London city walls in 1965, but for a long time you wouldn't have found evidence of that status by looking at the AC chart. Born Eric Patrick Clapp in Ripley, England, on March 30, 1945, he gained prominence as the lead guitarist for the Yardbirds rock group starting in 1963. After he left the Yardbirds in 1965, he joined several groups during the late 1960s and early 1970s (Cream, Blind Faith, Derek and the Dominoes) before going solo in 1973. His "I Shot the Sheriff" hit #1 pop in 1974, but he did not crack the AC chart until 1978 with "Lay Down Sally" at #25. He had three more entries through 1983's "I've Got a Rock N' Roll Heart" at #6, then returned to the chart nine years later in a song inspired by one of the worst tragedies in his life.

On March 20, 1991, Clapton's 4-year-old son Conor accidentally fell to his death from a window in the 53rd-floor New York City apartment of Clapton's ex-wife, Conor's mother, Lori Del Santo. Del Santo didn't realize what had happened until she called Conor for lunch, then noticed that a window had been left open by a cleaner who normally did not work at the building. Hysterical, she called Clapton, who arrived there within a half hour.

"I was in a state of shock," Clapton told Bill Frost of the London Times. "I was shown the open window. All I remember was there was nothing there. You might feel a breeze, but other than that it did not look any different from how it would normally look. It could not have been anyone's fault. I do not know if the man who opened the window was even aware there was a child in the apartment. He was not to blame."

Clapton poured his sorrow over his loss of Conor into a song called "Tears in Heaven" he did for the movie Rush. Recalling the tune in Billboard in 1996, producer Russ Titelman credited Celtic harp player Gayle Levant's work as crucial to making the song a hit. "Just listen to Gayle's ethereal harp on 'Tears of Heaven.' It really helps make that record what it is. But it was very difficult for Eric to record the vocal on that song since it concerned the loss of his son. It was hard for all of us when it came to that moment."

The mournful "Tears in Heaven" stayed at #2 pop for four weeks starting March 28, 1992, behind "Save the Best for Last" [see 614], as well as #1 pop. It won Record of the Year and Song of the Year at the Grammys, as did Clapton's LP containing the song, Unplugged, for Album of the Year, and Clapton for Best Male Pop Vocal Performance. Also, Unplugged went to #1 on the album chart for three weeks starting March 13, 1993.

Clapton had another #1 AC hit from a movie four years later [see 658—"Change the World"].

616 Hazard

RICHARD MARX

Capitol 44796

May 9, 1992 (1 week)

Writer: Richard Marx

Producer: Richard Marx

"Hazard" may be better known by some listeners as "The River," since that phrase is the one most frequently repeated in the lyrics, but Marx, thinking of the title tune of Bruce Springsteen's 1980 LP, resisted the temptation to give the song that name. Instead, after deciding his lyrics dictated setting the events in Nebraska, he called up officials there to get a list of all two-syllable towns which he might use. Ultimately he went with "Hazard," a place which really exists, with a population of 54.

The location is about the only clear aspect of the lyrics, which deal with a murder mystery. "The first chorus of 'I swear I left her by the river' came to me and I thought, 'Where did that come from?'" Marx recalled. Being a mystery buff himself, he crafted a story which asks the listener to figure out whether the protagonist has killed his missing girlfriend Mary, whom he has been used to meeting at the river in town.

"To this day I get people asking me who killed Mary," Marx said. "A lot of radio stations would run contests asking what happened. I would think to myself, 'There is no answer to this question.'"

Some fans even went so far as to pore over the video for "Hazard" hoping to find clues. (Marx said there weren't any.) Marx insisted he really does not know or care about the outcome of the song's mystery the way others apparently do. He does emphatically deny that the song was inspired by "Ode to Billie Joe." "It wasn't that," he said. "I love a good mystery and enjoy great mystery novels. The story came along because the music dictated it."

"Hazard"—"Or as I called it, 'Has-Weird,'" joked Marx—went to #9 pop the week of April 25, 1992. Modestly, Marx did not credit its success to his writing but deferred to the acoustic guitar playing done by his buddy Bruce Gaitsch. "The guitar work on that was incredible," he said.

He also thanked his wife for encouraging him to do "Hazard" in the first place, as he didn't feel it was a sure hit. "I owe Cynthia for getting it on the record," he said. "I played it for Cynthia, and she flipped. She totally flipped. She said to me, 'If you don't record this song, you're a moron.'"

Marx continues to be somewhat amazed at the lasting appeal of "Hazard," which he still hears on the radio occasionally. "I couldn't believe that the song was recorded by me," he said. "I couldn't believe that it was released as a single."

617 Hold On My Heart
GENESIS

Atlantic 87481

May 16, 1992 (5 weeks)

Writers: Phil Collins, Mike Rutherford, Tony Banks

Producers: Genesis, Nick Davis

The name of the 17th album from Genesis, in 1991, was *We Can't Dance*. "Calling the album *We Can't Dance* is our way of staking a claim," Phil Collins told David Wild of *Rolling Stone*. "We're drawing a line in the sand and saying, 'We're over here. We can't dance. If you're fed up with what you're hearing in the current climate, then move over a little this way and check this out.' We're offering an alternative. Also, it's a title that makes people smile when they hear it."

For the LP, the trio dropped its longtime co-producer Hugh Padgham in favor of Nick Davis. "We all felt it was time for a change," Tony Banks told Wild. Mike Rutherford added, "Because of the way we work, by the time we actually start recording the album, the songs are pretty much worked out. We're open to comments, but really in many ways the songs are self-producing."

One of those "self-produced" songs was the laid-back "Hold On My Heart," the third single from the LP. The first was "No Son of Mine," which came out in late 1991 and made #8 AC and #12 pop, followed by "I Can't Dance" at #26 AC and #7 pop. The next one was "Hold On My Heart," which got to #12 pop as well as #1 AC. After that was "Jesus He Knows Me" at #27 AC and #23 pop, and finally "Never a Time," which landed at #4 AC and #21 pop in early 1993.

With five singles making the top 30 of both the AC and pop charts, it was clear that Genesis was still as popular in America as they had been in the 1980s even though it had been five years since they did their last studio album. But they did have some concerns, the most nagging being the rumor that with Collins' solo career going full speed ahead and Rutherford having success with Mike + the Mechanics, Genesis was going to break up. When Wild asked about the rumor, Banks responded ambiguously, saying that "as far as we're concerned, the band is an ongoing concern, and those sorts of doubts are the kind of thing that has happened throughout the band's history, really."

However, Collins made it official in April 1996 that he was leaving the band for good, forcing Banks and Rutherford to look for a replacement. In 1997 Rutherford and Banks unveiled the new lead singer of Genesis, 28-year-old Ray Wilson, as they promoted their new LP *Calling All Stations*, their first studio album since *We Can't Dance*. Rutherford told *Billboard* at the time that "Singles now are so high profile, they overshadow albums. . . .I just hope this one's taken more as an album." Unfortunately, Neither the LP nor the leadoff single, "Congo," sold very well.

618 If You Asked Me To
CELINE DION

Epic 74277

June 20, 1992 (3 weeks)

Writer: Diane Warren

Producer: Guy Roche

"If You Asked Me To" was written for the last James Bond film to star Timothy Dalton, *Licence to Kill*, with soul powerhouse Patti LaBelle the intended vocalist. "I knew Patti would most likely be the artist to do it, so in the second verse when it says 'Can't go back to being on my own,' I thought that was kind of cool," said writer Diane Warren. (Warren was referring to LaBelle's #1 pop and #2 AC duet with Michael McDonald in 1986, "On My Own.")

LaBelle's version performed curiously poorly on the Hot 100, stopping at #79 pop in 1989, but did much better on the R&B and AC charts (#10 and #11, respectively). It was her first solo entry on the AC listing, although she had previously made the chart with two duets: with Michael McDonald ("On My Own" at #2 for two weeks in 1986) and with Bill Champlin ("The Last Unbroken Heart" at #15 in 1987).

Despite its pop showing, "If You Asked Me To" did become somewhat of a favored tune at weddings. It also attracted the attention of Polly Anthony, an executive at Epic Records who later became president of 550 Records, who thought a promising vocalist at Epic could have a hit with the song even though LaBelle had released her rendition just three years earlier. According to Warren, "Polly Anthony had always loved the song and thought it would be great for Celine [Dion] to record it."

Dion's rendition of "If You Asked Me To" got to #4 pop the week of July 11, 1992, after finishing a three-week run atop the AC chart. It was the first of Dion's many #1 AC hits, but it was not her first single to chart. That was "Where Does My Heart Beat Now," which made an impressive AC and pop debut for her in 1990 when it got to #2 AC and #4 pop.

Her follow-up to "Where Does My Heart Beat Now," 1991's "(If There Was) Any Other Way," performed less spectacularly, going to at #8 AC and #35 pop in 1991, and her next 45, "The Last to Know," did even worse—#22 AC without making the Hot 100. But her duet with Peabo Bryson on the Oscar-winning Best Song "Beauty and the Beast" from the Disney animated musical film of the same name reversed the downward trend by reaching #3 AC and #9 pop in early 1992. "If You Asked Me To" came out after that release.

Dion would sing two other #1 AC hit ballads written by Warren afterward, "Nothing Broken but My Heart" [the follow-up to "If You Asked Me To"; see 623] and "Because You Loved Me" [see 657].

619 I'll Be There

MARIAH CAREY

Columbia 74330

July 11, 1992 (2 weeks)

Writers: Berry Gordy Jr., Hal Davis, Willie Hutch, Bob West

Producers: Walter Afanasieff, Mariah Carey

It's hard for anyone to steal the scene from Mariah Carey when she is doing her vocal gymnastics, but backup singer Trey Lorenz did so when he sang the bridge to "I'll Be There" in a wild falsetto during Carey's appearance on MTV's *Unplugged* music show in March 1992. The live performance met with such enthusiasm at the taping and among home viewers that Carey's remake of the old Jackson 5 hit became a single and another double #1 AC and pop hit for her.

"I met Trey in February 1990, when I was working on my first album," Carey told Timothy White in *Billboard*. "I was recording a song called 'There's Got to Be a Way,' and one of the backup singers was friends with Trey and had brought him down to the studio for the session. I heard someone singing all the high, top notes for me, and I'm like, 'Who is that?' I turned around and it was Trey."

Lorenz sang backup on Carey's *Emotions* album, and also did some dates with Carey in Europe. "But we were also involved in the preparation for *Unplugged*, and people kept saying to do an oldie," Carey recalled. "Two nights before the actual show I decided on 'I'll Be There' and said, 'Trey, why don't you sing the male part?' We had no plans to release the show on record when we originally did it, so the decision to put the song out as a single was a total fluke."

When Lorenz heard that "I'll Be There" would become a record, he had no recollection of his performance and worried about its result. "I was like, 'Whoa! Let me hear it again!'" he told White. "I mean, great goodness, I think we were singing really good that day, but I wasn't so sure about me. I was really relieved when I listened."

While the Jackson 5 original went to #1 both pop and R&B plus #24 AC in 1970, Carey's remake was #1 both AC and pop, peaking on the latter the weeks of June 20 and 27, plus #11 R&B.

With "I'll Be There" a hit, Carey went to work on co-producing Lorenz's solo debut album. The first song that Lorenz, born in Florence, South Carolina, on January 19, 1969, can recall hearing was the Jackson 5 tune "I Want You Back." Lorenz won talent contests and sang in bands while he was growing up, and although he attended Fairleigh Dickinson University in New York and got an advertising degree, music remained his first love. The first single from Lorenz's solo album, "Someone to Hold," which he co-wrote with Carey and Walter Afanasieff, did admirably well, going to #18 AC and #19 pop.

Unfortunately for Lorenz, no other single of his made the AC or pop charts in the 1990s. That was not the case with Carey, of course, who returned to #1 AC in 1995 [see 656—"One Sweet Day"].

620 The One

ELTON JOHN

MCA 54423

July 25, 1992 (6 weeks)

Writers: Bernie Taupin (words), Elton John (music)

Producer: Chris Thomas

A bright, confident tune, "The One" reflected the state of its singer, Elton John, who had been through some troubled personal times prior to 1992. In an article in *Rolling Stone* by Philip Norman, John recounted what he had done since his semiretirement from public life in 1990. After reviewing some known negatives (his divorce after an ill-fated marriage to recording engineer Renate Blauel and his auctioning off his possessions in his mansion in Old Windsor, England, to name just two), John disclosed his private demons to Norman.

"I was cocaine addicted. I was an alcoholic. I had a sexual addiction. I was bulimic for six years," he said. "It was all through being paranoid about my weight but not able to stop eating. So in the end I'd gorge myself, then deliberately make myself sick."

Also, John's ego was so inflated that he would leave a hotel if he objected to something as trivial as the color of a bedspread. He would lock himself in his bedroom for weeks and go through fits of rage. Even his mother, normally a supportive person, had abandoned John, leaving England for Minorca with John's stepfather.

What turned him around was when he fell in love with a man in Atlanta, Georgia. "For the first time, I knew someone I wanted to be totally monogamous with," he said. "Before, I only took hostages." John's companion convinced him they should both treat their chemical dependencies, and John conquered his cocaine and alcohol addictions at the Parkside Lutheran Hospital near Chicago. He joined Alcoholics Anonymous, reconciled with his mother, and went on a diet of no snacks.

Throughout it all, John never lost contact with his longtime writing partner Bernie Taupin, and they crafted their new LP *The One* with his new outlook on life in mind. "This album is the best one I've done since *Captain Fantastic [and the Brown Dirt Cowboy*, in 1975]," John told French radio before starting his European tour. "All the songs seem to have an edge to them. I wanted these songs to be serious. Very morbid. And I didn't want them to be very poppy."

The album's title tune was hardly "morbid." In fact, "joyous" seemed to be a better description for it. As the leadoff single for the album, "The One" went to #1 AC and #9 pop, peaking there the week of September 19, 1992. John got a Grammy nomination for Best Male Pop Vocal Performance.

Two more singles were culled from *The One*, including another #1 AC hit [see 630—"Simple Life"].

621 Restless Heart
PETER CETERA

Warner 18897

September 5, 1992 (2 weeks)

Writers: Peter Cetera, Andy Hill

Producers: Peter Cetera, Andy Hill

In 1992, after a three-year absence from the entertainment world (with the exception of his acting debut in the 1991 TV movie based on Sidney Sheldon's novel *Memories of Midnight*), Peter Cetera released his third solo album, *World Falling Down*. Many of the songs he composed obviously dealt with his recent divorce, and the recording of the LP was complicated, with Cetera recording it at nine different studios. But he felt the effort was worth it.

"This was actually the first time I could write about the other side of love," he told *Billboard*. "I'd try to write a happy love song and I just couldn't do it. Then I got mad and so everything was about hating the world. So I settled on the truth." One song expressing his depressed emotions about his personal life was "Restless Heart." The leadoff single from *World Falling Down*, it made #35 pop as well as #1 AC and was his second #1 AC hit he co-wrote following "One Good Woman" in 1987 [see 567].

In a chat with fans on America Online in 1996, one person asked him how he wrote songs. Cetera responded, "Once again, there is no process for it. I enjoy working with other people in the beginning on chord structure. It comes in different shapes and ways. If I'm involved, writing it has just to happen right out of the air. I can't plan it."

To a question about how labels promoted him, Cetera responded, "I think everybody at one time or another has problems with marketing strategies. You just deal with them as best you can. Patience has not been my number one asset. You just have to hang in there and whatever happens, happens." What happened to Cetera is that he went from Full Moon in the 1980s to Warner in 1992 and then River North in 1995, following the release of two other singles from *World Falling Down*, "Feels Like Heaven," a duet with Chaka Khan which made #5 AC and #71 pop in early 1993, and "Even a Fool Can See," which reached #2 AC and #68 pop in the summer of 1993.

When he switched to River North in 1995, Cetera went on his first tour in a decade, with eight other musicians, including two guitarists and one bassist (he played guitar and bass on a few songs in concert). The set included some songs from Chicago, but he asked promoters not to mention his former group in publicity for the show. "Restless Heart" did make the cut as one of the songs performed.

Cetera's most recent album was his 1998 greatest hits compilation on River North, *You're the Inspiration*.

622 Sometimes Love Just Ain't Enough
PATTY SMYTH WITH DON HENLEY

MCA 54403

September 19, 1992 (4 weeks)

Writers: Patty Smyth, Glen Burtnik

Producer: Roy Bittan

Born in New York City on July 26, 1957, Patty Smyth came to prominence in the 1980s as lead singer of the rock quintet Scandal. Their "heavy" sound won them no airplay on AC stations, but they did reasonably well on the pop chart, making their Hot 100 debut in 1982 with "Goodbye to You" (#65), followed by "Love's Got a Line on You" (#59) in 1983.

In 1984 the band, renamed Scandal featuring Patty Smyth, got its biggest hit when "The Warrior" went to #7 pop. Two follow-ups stalled at #41 pop—"Hands Tied" in 1984 and "Beat of a Heart" in 1985. After taking time off to give birth to a child, Smyth went solo in 1987. Although her singles that year, "Never Enough" (#61 pop) and "Downtown Train" (#95 pop), did not bode well for long-term success, Smyth kept active in the recording world (one effort was singing backup to Dion for his #16 AC and #75 pop entry "And the Night Stood Still" in 1989).

Then came her self-titled album in 1992, on which she wrote seven songs, including the leadoff single, a duet with former Eagle Don Henley, "Sometimes Love Just Ain't Enough" featuring guitarist Glen Burtnik. Besides being #1 AC for four weeks the song made #2 pop for six weeks starting the week of September 26, 1992, behind Boys II Men's "End of the Road" at #1. Smyth and Henley also got a Grammy nomination for Best Pop Vocal Performance by a Duo or Group. Speaking about the song to Larry Flick in *Billboard*, Smyth said, "It's gratifying to watch people have a positive reaction to songs that, in a way, speak about moments of your life. People can sense when you're putting out for them—they dig honesty. But it can be tough to expose so much of yourself to the world."

Smyth's follow-up to "Sometimes Love Just Ain't Enough," "No Mistakes," made #4 AC and #33 pop in early 1993. In 1994 she co-wrote the Oscar-nominated Best Song "Look What Love Has Done" from the movie *Junior*, starring Arnold Schwartzenegger and Danny DeVito, and sang it at the Academy Awards ceremony. She then retreated from the spotlight again for most of the 1990s, except for publicity surrounding her marriage to former U.S. Tennis Association star John McEnroe following his divorce from Tatum O'Neal.

In 1998 Smyth returned to action with a song on the *Armageddon* soundtrack, "Wish You Were Here," and a greatest hits set with new material released in September. "People should get used to the fact that I always go away for a while," she told Jim Bessman in *Billboard*. "I haven't been sitting around since the last album [in 1992], but for some reason I didn't feel like I had anything to say. Then the urge came, and I was inspired to write songs."

Nothing Broken but My Heart

CELINE DION

Epic 74336

October 17, 1992 (1 week)

Writer: Diane Warren

Producer: Walter Afanasieff

The Celine Dion story begins in Charlemagne, Quebec, Canada, where she was born the youngest of 14 brothers and sisters on March 30, 1968. All were involved in the music industry while Dion was growing up, but only Dion really achieved success. Dion told Mike Joyce of *The Washington Post* that "I guess I'm the lucky one. My parents used to tour with other members of my family before I was born."

Dion made her first public appearance singing at the age of 5. Her musical influences as a child came from the records her brothers and sisters played, which included the Beatles, Aretha Franklin, and Stevie Wonder. She eventually developed as an impressive five-octave soprano.

When she was 12, a demo tape with her singing "It Was Only a Dream" found its way to producer Rene Angelil. "She made me cry," he told Edna Gunderson in *USA Today*. "I had

an instinct about her. When I heard Celine singing in front of me, it was so moving. She had so much feeling inside. I couldn't believe a young girl could sing like that." Within a year of meeting Dion, Angelil dropped all his other clients and mortgaged his house to pay for her debut LP. It paid off handsomely, as she chalked up four platinum albums in Canada in her late teens and early twenties. But Celine only spoke and sang in French, and to have a bigger impact worldwide, she would have to learn English.

"When I first started to record in English, it was really scary. I couldn't speak the language and express myself," she told Joyce. "But now I'm much more confident and willing to express my opinion, and that's very important to me. Because I have this dream, and it's a very, very big dream. I want to have an international career, not a hit. I want to record music that I really like. If I wanted to make a hit maybe I'd make a rap record tomorrow, but that's not me. If I record a song and it sells millions of copies, then that's great for all of us, but if it doesn't sell, if it doesn't capture the heart of the people, well, I'm still very young and I'll come back and work harder and record again. I want to be doing this for the rest of my life."

"Nothing Broken but My Heart" was not one of her bigger pop performers, getting only to #29 on the Hot 100, but it was her first consecutive #1 AC hit, after "If You Asked Me To" [see 618].

624 Am I the Same Girl

SWING OUT SISTER

Fontana 864170

October 24, 1992 (1 week)

Writers: Eugene Record, Sonny Sanders

Producer: Paul Staveley O'Duffy

With the departure of drummer Martin Jackson in 1989, the duo of singer Corinne Drewery and keyboardist Andy Connell, who now comprised Swing Out Sister, spent three years off the charts in America. They returned with a golden oldie, 1969's "Am I The Same Girl," which co-writer Eugene Record, one-time lead singer of the Chi-Lites, let his wife cut. Her version went to #33 R&B and #79 pop, but Britons Drewery and Connell were probably more familiar with the version done by Dusty Springfield, which hit #43 on the United Kingdom chart that same year.

To further confuse matters, Acklin's vocal version appeared after an instrumental-only rendition of the tune titled "Soulful Strut" went to #2 AC and #3 pop in early 1969 as done by Young-Holt Unlimited. The latter band belonged to the Brunswick label, as did Acklin, so their track was used as the backing instrumental for her record.

"Am I the Same Girl" by Swing Out Sister went to #1 AC and # pop. Though it was the first single the group did as a cover, Drewery told Dylan Jones in *Ultra Lounge: The Lexicon of Easy Listening* that she favored listening to older tunes such as those by Burt Bacharach over most contemporary records. "I find it difficult to form opinions about a lot of modern music because my head's buried in the past," she said. "A lot of my favorite records seem to have been picked up in the discount rack at Woolworth's. I'll be quite happy if our records end up in the Woollies bargain bin in 10 years' time."

As Woolworth's is now out of business, Swing Out Sister's records won't end up there, but toward the end of the 1990s it was true that their tunes were more likely to be found in the cutout sections of record stores than in the new material areas. "Am I the Same Girl" became the last pop entry for the duo in America, although "Notgonnachange" did make #22 AC in early 1993. In 1994 Swing Out Sister's album *Living Return* appealed to few buyers in England or America, but their following in Japan remained strong enough that they were able to cut another LP in 1997, *Shapes and Patterns*, distributed on the Mercury label in the United States.

Mercury vice president of marketing Marty Maidenberg admitted to Paul Sexton in *Billboard* that promoting *Shapes and Patterns* in America would not be an easy job. "When you have a band like Swing Out Sister, you'd have a a tough time pinpointing their sound. It's pop, it's urban, it's adult, it's jazz. Europe and Japan don't adhere to those rules as much as America does. It crosses over so many different lines, and that's where Swing Out's strength is."

Drewery and Jackson did a few club dates in America to promote the LP, but it bombed. Nonetheless, they announced plans to do another album set for release in 1999.

625 I Will Be Here for You

MICHAEL W. SMITH

Reunion 19139

October 31, 1992 (2 weeks)

Writers: Michael W. Smith, Diane Warren

Producers: Michael W. Smith, Mark Heimermann

"When I sit down to play, I feel like I'm doing what God called me to do," Michael W. Smith wrote in his official Web site on the Internet. "It's an expression of my gratitude. I could never take credit for it. I sit down and play these things and I don't even know what my fingers do. They go here, they go there. I close my eyes and all of a sudden, I'm playing this thing. It's a bit overwhelming how it works."

As a boy, Smith, a native of Kenova, West Virginia, who was born in 1957, wanted to become a baseball player but by the time he was 16 found himself drawn to music instead. His route into a solo music career was through Nashville, in 1978, and by 1982 he was playing keyboards for contemporary Christian artist Amy Grant [see 608—"That's What Love Is For"]. Smith helped contribute to her pop and AC crossover in the mid-1980s by writing two of her tunes, "Find a Way" and "Stay for Awhile."

As an artist, Smith cracked the AC and pop charts in 1991 with "Place in This World" at #5 AC and #6 pop, followed by "For You" the same year at #20 AC and #60 pop. At the same time he recorded more explicitly religious tunes and drew a strong fan base among the contemporary Christian world. Next up in 1992 was "I Will Be Here for You." According to Diane Warren, there were no concerns about how spiritual or secular the lyrics might be. "We just wanted to write a great song," she said. Co-producing the track was Mark Heimermann, who also played keyboards in Smith's band.

"I Will Be Here for You" went to #27 pop as well as #1 AC. In 1993 Smith released "Somebody Love Me," which got to #10 AC and #71 pop. He then remained fairly quiet the rest of the decade (by 1998 he was a father of five, and spent a lot of time with his family), but did set up his own label called Rocketown Records, which began operations in 1996. Chris Rice was the first artist signed by the company. He also wrote an inspirational guidebook called *Friends Are Friends Forever and Other Encouragements From God's Word* in 1997.

In 1998 Smith released an album called *Live the Life* on Jive/Reunion Records. It debuted at #23 on the LP chart, leading some to believe that Smith might again be reaching the secular music world, as he had in the early 1990s, although no singles charted immediately.

626 To Love Somebody

MICHAEL BOLTON

Columbia 74733

November 14, 1992 (5 weeks)

Writers: Barry Gibb, Maurice Gibb, Robin Gibb

Producers: David Foster, Michael Bolton

The Bee Gees originally wrote "To Love Somebody" for consideration by Otis Redding, but the soul great died three months after they composed the tune, so they did the song themselves. Maurice Gibb recalled the composition's creation in the 1997 video *Keppel Road: The Life and Times of the Bee Gees*. "We'd say, 'Let's write Elvis Presley's new record. Let's write the Beatles' new record. What would they write?' And then we'd sing it, it'd be ours. So, 'Let's write a great soul song for Otis Redding.' 'To Love Somebody' was born. And that became our song, even though we wrote it for Otis Redding."

Done by the Bee Gees, "To Love Somebody" became the group's second pop entry in America, peaking at #17 in 1967 while failing to make the AC chart. The song soon generated covers which made the charts. In 1968 the Sweet Inspirations took their version to #74 pop and #30 R&B. The following year James Carr's effort made #44 R&B, while in the United Kingdom a remake by Nina Simone reached #5 there. The country charts saw renditions hit by Narvel Felts in 1977 (at #22) and Hank Williams Jr. in 1979 (at #49).

Between those two singles, Jackie DeShannon gave the song its AC debut when her effort halted at #44 in 1978. In 1990 "To Love Somebody" made the United Kingdom top 10 again when Jimmy Sommerville's try hit #8. When Bolton released his version two years later, he hit #11 pop as well as #1 AC and #16 on the British chart.

"To Love Somebody" was the only single released from Bolton's LP *Timeless (The Classics)*, which hit #1 on the album chart the second week "To Love Somebody" went to #11 pop as well as #1 AC. Two other cuts from the all-remake album, "Reach Out I'll Be There" and "White Christmas," also received a fair amount of airplay on AC and pop stations, with "Reach Out I'll Be There" getting to #8 on the AC chart in early 1993.

The idea of doing an album of remakes came to Bolton following his work on a few other old songs, the most obvious being his version of "When a Man Loves a Woman" [see 607]. Oddly enough in fact, Bolton, who got his start in the music business writing, had not written his last three #1 AC hits. But Bolton fans who worried he had lost his touch for writing his own material were proved wrong a year later when "Said I Loved You. . .But I Lied" became his eighth #1 AC hit [see 639].

627 I Will Always Love You

WHITNEY HOUSTON

Arista 12490

December 19, 1992 (5 weeks)

Writer: Dolly Parton

Producer: David Foster

When the 1992 Academy Award nominations came out, it shocked some that "I Will Always Love You," sung by Whitney Houston in *The Bodyguard*, was not selected for Best Song. After all, the record had set a new mark of success by staying an unprecedented 14 weeks at #1 on the Hot 100 starting November 28, 1992, not to mention an impressive 11 weeks at #1 R&B starting December 5, 1992, in addition to its time atop the AC chart.

But "I Will Always Love You" was ineligible for nomination, having been released commercially before the movie began production—not only once, but twice. Dolly Parton took her original version of "I Will Always Love You" to #1 country the week of June 8, 1974, and four years later a cover by Jimmie Peters went to #84 country. Then Parton revived the tune in a new rendition she performed in the movie *The Best Little Whorehouse in Texas*, in which she played a madam. That record went to #1 country as well the week of October 16, 1982.

Around the same time, Parton managed to cross over with her second 45 and get to #53 pop and #17 AC with it in the fall of 1982. But it would be safe to say that despite all the exposure, most of the noncountry record–buying public was not familiar with the song until Houston's version came out a decade later.

When Houston's rendition became a big hit, gossip columnists, went into overdrive, claiming that Parton was bitter about Houston's success with a song Parton had written for herself. They apparently didn't know about the composer's royalties Parton would rake in. Parton herself laughed off the charges in her autobiography *Dolly: My Life and Other Unfinished Business*, writing "One of the biggest thrills of my entire life happened just recently when Whitney Houston's version of 'I Will Always Love You' became the most played song of the year. I was so proud when I went to New York to pick up my award. You couldn't have hit me in the butt with a red apple I had it so high in the air, but humble at the same time."

Besides that award, and while ineligible for an Oscar, "I Will Always Love You" got Grammys for Record of the Year and Best Female Pop Vocal Performance.

As for what inspired the composition, Parton wrote, "Most people think the song 'I Will Always Love You' was written about me breaking up with some lover, but in fact I wrote it about Porter [Wagoner] and the special, although painfully heart-wrenching, time we spent together." She said that she and Wagoner were musical partners only during their time together from 1967–74 and not lovers, as some have speculated.

628 A Whole New World (Aladdin's Theme)

PEABO BRYSON AND REGINA BELLE

Columbia 74751

January 23, 1993 (6 weeks)

Writers: Alan Menken (music), Tim Rice (lyrics)

Producer: Walter Afanasieff

What would Disney Films have done had they not scooped up off-Broadway composer Alan Menken in the late 1980s to do music for their animated movies? Certainly they would have done without such hits as *The Little Mermaid* (1989), *Beauty and the Beast* (1991), and *Aladdin* (1992), although *Aladdin* had been in development for some time by Menken's original partner, lyricist Howard Ashman.

"Initially. . . , Howard Ashman was playing with the idea of having a live action show at Disney of *Aladdin*," Menken said. "Then that became an assignment to be a musical which we did on the heels of *The Little Mermaid*."

Menken and Ashman created a few songs for *Aladdin* before Ashman died of AIDS-related complications. Then Menken forged ahead on the project with Tim Rice, whom Disney executives recommended to him. He liked working with Rice. "Tim had worked in theater and was pretty witty on his own and had a lot of invention," Menken noted.

While some of Ashman's work was kept, other plans for the movie vanished, such as Aladdin having brothers and a mother. Those changes left the cartoon without a "big ballad moment," as Menken termed it, until he and Rice saw where else they could install it. "There was talk about having a montage with Aladdin flying with Jasmine [his girlfriend] on the carpet over the city. . . .That became the big ballad moment. It was perfectly suited to Tim's style," Menken said.

Menken originally titled the song for the montage "The World at My Feet," but Rice redid the lyrics to make it a duet called "A Whole New World." "We knew pretty instantly that it would be a hit," Menken said. But Columbia Records had rights to the single version of the tune and therefore could decide who would record it.

Michael Bolton and Celine Dion won initial consideration for the job, but Columbia favored Regina Belle and paired her with Peabo Bryson, who had recorded the 45 rendition of "Beauty and the Beast" with Dion a year earlier, making it a #3 AC and #9 pop hit. Belle and Bryson sang together in 1988's "Without You," from the film *Leonard, Part 6*, a box-office flop starring Bill Cosby, but that made only #8 AC and #89 pop. In contrast, their "A Whole New World" went to #1 AC and pop, topping the latter the week of March 6, 1993, plus #21 R&B.

"A Whole New World" won Grammys for Song of the Year and Best Pop Vocal Performance by a Duo or Group, plus a nomination for Record of the Year. Menken also got his third Oscar for Best Song for the tune.

After the wins, "A Whole New World" became the theme songs heard at Disney's parks worldwide. Asked how he felt about being so identified with the organization, Menken said, "I love it. I love the Disney company and my association with them. I put a lot of my eggs in Disney. . . ."

629 Forever in Love

KENNY G

Arista 12482

March 6, 1993 (2 weeks)

Writer: Kenny G

Producer: Kenny G

First things first: The "G" stands for Gorelick, but friends nicknamed him "Kenny G" rather than use his full surname, so that became his professional name as well. With that out of the way, it should be noted that this soprano saxophonist has been the most successful instrumentalist on the AC and pop charts from the late 1980s through the late 1990s, with his biggest solo hit on the AC chart to date being "Forever in Love."

Born in Seattle, Washington, on July 6, 1956, Kenny G was inspired to play music after seeing a saxophonist on *The Ed Sullivan Show* on television when he was 10. He did not attend any music schools, preferring to play in school bands and practicing along with records at home, but proved to be so musically precocious that when he was 17 he became part of the Love Unlimited Orchestra [see 209—"Love's Theme"]. He went to the University of Washington, where he played for the college band, graduating magna cum laude and Phi Beta Kappa with an accounting degree.

At age 22 he joined Jeff Lorber's band and toured America, and impressed Arista's president Clive Davis so much that he got to release his own self-titled album in 1982. In 1984 he released an album titled *G Force*, the same name as his group at the time. The group was billed as Kenny G and G Force for the 1985 follow-up LP, *Gravity*, but 1986's *Duotones* was done by just plain Kenny G. That LP contained "Songbird," his AC and pop debut, and it was a big hit, getting to #3 AC and #4 pop. He started charting fairly regularly on both listings over the next decade.

For his LP *Breathless*, released in late 1992 with 14 songs, Kenny G recorded the tunes in his home studio. One of the instrumentals, "Forever in Love," became the album's biggest hit, going to #1 AC, #18 pop, and #73 R&B. He said the process of recording it was easy because "When I play the saxophone, I feel like I'm singing, I feel like I'm talking."

Kenny G was quoted on Arista's official Web site on the Internet as saying that the inspiration for his songs "comes from many different places and at very unexpected times. That's the beauty of creativity. I feel that really experiencing the moments of our lives is the only way to really live."

Remaining a popular recording and touring artist through the late 1990s, Kenny G has resisted offers to do more than just play the sax. "I have no aspirations to do more than what I'm doing," he told Brown. "In other words, I don't want to be a singer, I don't want to be an actor. I don't want to be a comedian, and I don't want to be an athlete. I am a good golfer, though. I have about a 10 handicap."

630 Simple Life

ELTON JOHN

MCA 54581

March 20, 1993 (3 weeks)

Writers: Bernie Taupin (lyrics), Elton John (music)

Producer: Chris Thomas

Elton John was enjoying the simple life in 1993, having set up residence at an apartment complex in Atlanta, Georgia, in addition to his home in England. His steady boyfriend, a native of Atlanta, remained largely in the background. John told talk show host Oprah Winfrey in 1998 that he liked living in Atlanta both because of the people and because it had a 24-hour airport which allowed him to return home the morning after a concert anywhere in America.

He was also doing great AC-wise: after peaking at #2 on the AC chart, his 1992 single "The Last Song," his tenth consecutive top five AC entry, was still there (it went to #23 pop). The song spoke about the love between a man and his father, something John felt was not there in his own relationship with his dad, who forbid him to do many activities he enjoyed while his mother applauded John's work in music (his mother and father divorced when he was 10, much to John's relief). Profits from "The Last Song" single and video went to six AIDS organizations in America, a cause dear to John, who would later start his own AIDS charity. He was very close to several people who had the disease, including Ryan White, a child from Indiana who had contracted AIDS via blood transfusion and had drawn the nation's attention to the discrimination suffered by people with AIDS.

"The Last Song" also served as the closing tune for the 1993 HBO miniseries about the history of the AIDS crisis, *And the Band Played On*, based on the best-selling book of the same name by Randy Shilts.

Next up after "The Last Song," and the last single from *The One* LP (the first had been the title tune), was "Simple Life," which made #30 pop in addition to #1 AC." Before Christmas of 1993, John came out with his next album, *Duets*, which featured him singing along with 15 of his favorite artists, including George Michael, Don Henley, k.d. lang, Little Richard, and many others. Two singles came out of it, but both were among his lowest-charting pop efforts—"True Love" with Kiki Dee, a remake of the Oscar-nominated Cole Porter tune sung by Bing Crosby and Grace Kelly in 1956's *High Society*, and "Don't Go Breaking My Heart," John's remake of his own duet, this time with drag queen RuPaul in place of Kiki Dee [see 312].

Then in 1994 John had his biggest hit in two years with, of all things, a tune from a children's musical [see 643—"Can You Feel the Love Tonight"].

631 Love Is

VANESSA WILLIAMS AND BRIAN MCKNIGHT

Giant 18630

April 10, 1993 (3 weeks)

Writers: Tonio K., John Keller

Producers: Gerry Brown, Vanessa Williams, Brian McKnight

The first black woman to be named Miss America—and the first one to be dethroned from the post by pageant officials—was Vanessa Williams, born in Tarrytown, New York, on March 18, 1963. Williams had to give up her 1983 crown after *Penthouse* magazine published nude photos of her, taken before the contest, she had not believed would surface in public.

Williams tried unsuccessfully for a few years to shake off the notoriety of the incident and pursue an entertainment career, but few people helped her. Things changed when her husband Ramon Hervey introduced her to Ed Eckstine, a friend who was starting the Wing label on PolyGram Records. After hearing her sing, Eckstine decided to take a chance on Williams and do an album.

"We didn't want to be disposably dancey or 'Here She Is, Miss America'—the exploitation of all that," Eckstine told *Vibe* magazine in 1994. Williams said in the same article they had trouble finding tunes to use on the LP. "For the first record we had virtually no songs given to us. So we had to beg, borrow and steal to get any kind of material." Luckily for them, *The Right Stuff* spun off a few hits, including her AC debut "Dreamin'" in 1989 (it got to #2), and put her firmly in the musical establishment. After the big success of "Save the Best for Last" in 1992 [see 614], she got another #1 AC with "Love Is," a duet with the then-little-known singer Brian McKnight, born in Buffalo, New York, on June 5, 1969.

Before "Love Is" became a single, it appeared on the Fox-TV show *Beverly Hills 90210* playing in background music for a few scenes and during the end credits. It also appeared on the first *Beverly Hills 90210* soundtrack, but the album differed from the single in what backing instruments were used.

"Love Is" went to #3 pop the week of May 15, 1993, behind "That's the Way Love Goes" by Janet Jackson at #1 and "Freak Me" by Slik at #2. It also made #55 R&B in addition to #1 AC. Williams and McKnight earned Grammy nominations for Best Pop Performance by a Duo or Group With Vocal for the record.

After "Love Is," Williams was virtually everywhere the rest of the 1990s, not only on records (her "Colors of the Wind" from the *Pocahontas* soundtrack in 1995 was a big seller and the Oscar winner for Best Song) but also Broadway (a nine-month run as the lead in the musical *Kiss of the Spider Woman* starting June 1994, replacing Chita Rivera), television (various specials and movies, including the 1995 remade-for-television *Bye Bye Birdie*), and movies (extensive credits, including *Hoodlum* and *Soul Food* in 1997 and *Dance With Me* in 1998). For the latter, she had to bill herself as Vanessa L. Williams because another actress named Vanessa Williams had registered earlier with the Screen Actors Guild and requested that she go by a different name.

632 I Have Nothing

WHITNEY HOUSTON

Arista 12527

May 1, 1993 (2 weeks)

Writers: Linda Thompson (lyrics), David Foster (music)

Producer: David Foster

"I got a call saying that there is a script that Kevin Costner has, called *The Bodyguard*, that he wanted me to do," Whitney Houston said to Anthony DeCurtis of *Rolling Stone* when asked about her involvement in the movie. "He wanted me to co-star with him. I went, 'Yeah, sure.' Then I called my agent, and she said, 'Yeah, it's true.' So I read the script. I liked the story, but in the beginning Rachel was very rough, very hard—a little bitch."

Houston said that as shooting progressed she worried less about her character and more about how people would respond to her dramatic acting debut. "I wanted to do some acting, but I mean, I never thought I'd be co-starring with Kevin Costner!" she said. "I thought, 'I'll just get this little part somewhere, and I'll work my way up.' And all of a sudden I get this script, and I said: 'I don't know. This is kind of. . .big.' So I was scared. It took me two years to decide to do it."

It turned out Houston had nothing to worry about. *The Bodyguard* was a box-office hit and did even better in record stores. One of the tunes Houston's character sang, "I Have Nothing," was the third of four Whitney Houston singles from the soundtrack. The first two were "I Will Always Love You" [see 627] and "I'm Every Woman," which reached #26 AC and #4 pop in early 1993.

"I Have Nothing" became the soundtrack's second #1 AC hit, plus third top 10 pop entry, peaking at #4 for five weeks starting April 3, 1993, and third R&B top five single, stopping at #4. With all these hits, it was not surprising that *The Bodyguard* LP containing them held at #1 on the album chart for 20 weeks starting December 12, 1992. "I Have Nothing" also received an Oscar nomination for Best Song.

The fourth single by Houston from the soundtrack was "Run to You," which galloped to #9 AC and #31 pop in mid-1993 and, like "I Have Nothing," had an Oscar nomination for Best Song. Houston sang two other tracks on *The Bodyguard* LP, "Jesus Loves Me" and "Queen of the Night," and the latter got some airplay despite not being available as a commercial single.

Houston went on to star in another films in the 1990s, including *Waiting to Exhale* (1995) and *The Preacher's Wife* (1996), in additional to maintaining a very active and successful recording and touring career. However, as of 1998 "I Have Nothing" was her last #1 AC hit.

633 Tell Me What You Dream

RESTLESS HEART FEATURING WARREN HILL

RCA 62468

May 15, 1993 (2 weeks)

Writers: Josh Leo, Vince Malamed, Timothy B. Schmidt

Producer: Josh Leo

The country quintet of Restless Heart flirted with the AC and pop charts first in 1987 when "I'll Still Be Loving You" got them their debut listings at #3 AC and #33 pop. They had made their country debut two years earlier with "Let the Heartaches Ride" at #23 and went on to score six consecutive #1 country hits from 1986–88, with "I'll Still Be Loving You" and "Why Does It Have to Be (Wrong or Right)" (#11 AC, 1987) from that string crossing over to the AC chart.

Yet Restless Heart, formed in 1983 and composed of lead singer Larry Stewart, drummer John Dittrich, bassist Paul Gregg, keyboardist Dave Innis, and guitarist Greg Jennings, managed only two minor AC crossovers afterward until 1992's "When She Cries," which made #11 pop and #2 AC for seven weeks. It came after Stewart had left the band. In early 1993 Innis left, shortly before the group had its first AC chart-topper, "Tell Me What You Dream."

Though Restless Heart's producer had co-written the song, Dittrich said it was not Leo's idea for them to do it. "Actually there was an A&R person at RCA pop in New York. He came up with this song, and he had no idea that 10 years prior, Josh Leo, Vince Malamed, and Timothy B. Schmidt had written the song for Tim's first solo album after the Eagles broke up." Dittrich said Leo took the idea of redoing the tune in good humor. "Josh said, 'Gee, we thought it was a hit when we wrote it.'"

Restless Heart found themselves with a special guest on the recording. "Warren Hill got involved on the project because the song, as Tim recorded it, had a big saxophone part. RCA had signed Warren with a big deal, so to give him exposure, he got the song and the billing." With Hill's solo in place, "Tell Me What You Dream" went to #43 pop and #1 AC. Curiously, it did not crack the country chart.

But Dittrich, Gregg, and Jennings found that using studio musicians in place of their former bandmates did not satisfy them creatively or commercially and by 1996 they had broken up. Then a fan who was ill made a request. "It was her wish that Restless Heart re-form," Dittrich said. He and the others did a tape for her, and, when they noted that "The vocals were still there, the talent was still there," they made plans to get together again, except for Innis.

In 1998, with all their schedules cleared, the rejuvenated Restless Heart did 10 shows before signing a new record deal. Dittrich had high hopes for the group on the second go-round because, as he noted, everyone this time was "A little older and a little wiser."

634 Have I Told You Lately

ROD STEWART

Warner 18511

May 29, 1993 (5 weeks)

Writer: Van Morrison

Producer: Patrick Leonard

Toward the end of 1992, AC and pop radio stations started playing "Have I Told You Lately," a track from Rod Stewart's album *Vagabond Heart*. But that LP had been out over a year, and its three previously released singles, "Rhythm of My Heart," "The Motown Song," and "Broken Arrow" (all in 1991), had met with decreasing success on the pop chart. That, plus the fact that another Stewart album was due in 1993, kept Warner Records from releasing that version of "Have I Told You Lately," but it went to #33 AC anyway, remaining on the chart well into the spring of 1992.

Mindful of the song's popularity among radio programmers, Stewart redid it for his 1993 LP *Unplugged. . .And Seated*, a recording of his live performance on MTV's series *Unplugged*, with Ronnie Wood, an old mate from the 1970s group Faces, joining him as a special guest on guitar. "Have I Told You Lately" was included in the show, where it was well received, and became the leadoff single for the album.

"Have I Told You Lately" stayed at #5 pop for three weeks starting June 19, 1993, by which time it was #1 on the AC chart. Stewart received a Grammy nomination for Best Male Pop Vocal Performance for the tune.

The song was a cover of a composition Van Morrison created for his 1989 album *Avalon Sunset*. Despite Stewart's getting wider notice for his version of the tune, Morrison enjoyed it enough to do it again in a December 1993 concert released a year later as his LP *A Night in San Francisco*. And in 1995 Morrison revived the tune and recorded it with the Irish folk band the Chieftains. Their version of "Have I Told You Lately" won a Grammy for Best Pop Vocal Collaboration.

Stewart kept going strong in 1993 with another remake released from *Unplugged*, "Reason to Believe," a tune he took to #62 pop in 1971, and a song he cut with Bryan Adams and Sting for the movie *The Three Musketeers* called "All for One," which wound up peaking at #1 pop in 1994. Another track from *Unplugged*, "Having a Party," also came out in 1994, but the real news for Stewart that year was his induction into the Rock and Roll Hall of Fame.

For the rest of the 1990s Stewart continued to record occasionally, although most of his releases failed to get the same level of chart activity that his early 1990s efforts had. An exception was the single "Ooh La La," which was #3 AC for six weeks starting August 15, 1998. Then again Stewart doesn't need any more hits to solidify his stature as one of the leading rock artists of his period.

635 By the Time This Night Is Over

KENNY G AND PEABO BRYSON

Arista 12565

July 3, 1993 (2 weeks)

Writers: Michael Bolton, Diane Warren, Andy Goldmark

Producers: Walter Afanasieff, David Foster

Peabo Bryson had an up-and-down career after his #1 AC hit in 1984, "If Ever You're in My Arms Again" [see 458]. He remained an R&B chart favorite over the next decade, but he wanted to have more crossover successes in the AC and pop fields. Unfortunately for him, his performances on those charts were spotty at best.

Bryson stumbled first when his follow-up to "If Ever You're in My Arms Again," called "Slow Dancin'," got only to #82 pop in 1984. The next 45, 1985's "Take No Prisoners (In the Game of Love)," did just slightly better, at #78 pop and #37 AC. The next year "Love Always Finds a Way" found a way to make #26 AC without cracking the Hot 100.

After a two-year absence, Bryson returned to the AC chart plus the Hot 100 in 1988 with a duet with Regina Belle called "Without You," and a few years later the two collaborated again, creating a bigger AC and pop single [for more details on those songs, see 628—"A Whole New World (Aladdin's Theme)"]. Three more years passed after "Without You" before he crossed over again with "Can You Stop the Rain," a #1 R&B tune that nevertheless made just #11 AC and #52 pop in 1991. For the rest of the early 1990s, it took duets for him to make the AC and pop charts, with the last being "By the Time This Night Is Over."

"By the Time This Night Is Over" first appeared as a track on Kenny G's 1992 album *Breathless*, which also included another duet between Kenny G and vocalist Aaron Neville. One of the co-writers of "By the Time This Night Is Over," Diane Warren, said the big sax solo in the tune was intentional because "it was written for Kenny." Though another co-writer, Michael Bolton, had sung with Kenny G on a previous hit [see 613—"Missing You Now"], it was decided that Bryson would sing on the track instead.

Besides reaching #1 AC, "By the Time This Night Is Over" went to #25 pop and #37 R&B. Interestingly, it was the third #1 AC hit for both men, each of whom had a solo #1 AC hit plus two #1 AC 45s done as part of a duet. And oddly, neither of them released another single which scored as highly on either the pop or AC chart for the rest of the 1990s, although both remained quite busy recording and touring.

As for the fortunes of Bolton, Warren, and co-producers David Foster and Walter Afanasieff, read on. They appeared quite frequently in various combinations atop the AC listings through 1998.

636 I'll Never Get Over You (Getting Over Me)

EXPOSÉ

Arista 12518

July 17, 1993 (1 week)

Writer: Diane Warren

Producer: Guy Roche

Exposé's success with "Seasons Change" in 1988 [see 533] encouraged the group's producer Lewis Martinee to use more ballads on their next few albums. Exposé was originally conceived and promoted as a dance act, but by the early 1990s, the group was putting out LPs that were about half ballads and half up-tempo numbers. Martinee said he had no problem with this change in emphasis since "I've always done ballads."

Despite the new approach, most of Exposé's hits remained too frenetic for the girl trio to make the AC chart too often. Their first release after "Seasons Change," 1989's "What You Don't Know," made #8 pop only, and its follow-up, "When I Look at Him," crossed over to AC and made #3 there as well as #10 pop. "Tell Me Why" hit only the Hot 100, peaking at #9 in early 1990, then came another AC-pop double smash, "Your Baby Never Looked Good in Blue" (#9 AC, #17 pop). In 1992 Exposé returned to pop-only status with "I Wish the Phone Would Ring," which hit #28 on the Hot 100 that fall.

Next up was "I'll Never Get Over You (Getting Over Me)," written by Diane Warren. "Clive Davis [president of Arista] found that song," Martinee recalled. Martinee arranged the tune rather than produce it and managed to give Exposé its last #1 AC hit and pop top 10 entry, with the song peaking on the Hot 100 at #8 the weeks of July 17 and 24, 1993.

By that time, Kelly Moneymaker had replaced Gioia Bruno in the group, joining Ann Curless and Jeanette Jurado. But nothing could take the place of Lewis Martinee when the producer found he had lost his enthusiasm for handling the group he had started a decade earlier. "I basically left the group in 1993," he said. Within a year after his departure, Exposé had stopped making the charts, with their last Hot 100 entry, "In Walked Love," peaking at #84 before vanishing in May 1994. (Exposé had stopped appearing on the R&B chart after "Seasons Change" peaked at #27 in early 1988.)

The members of the group began to pursue their own careers, although they remained under contract to work for the group. Bruno said the last she had heard, Curless was working in New York while Jurado was in Las Vegas. Martinee said that while he and Bruno "always had a good relationship," he does not hear from the other members of Exposé.

Martinee's latest discovery in 1998 was Kristen, the 15-year-old granddaughter of white soul shouter Wayne Cochran, whom Martinee described as "the next Mariah Carey." His album with her was slated to come out in 1999. Those waiting to see if he will come up with "the next Exposé" will have to wait until this venture plays itself out.

637 I Don't Wanna Fight

TINA TURNER

Virgin 12652

July 24, 1993 (7 weeks)

Writers: Lulu, Steve Duberry, Billy Lawrie

Producers: Chris Lord-Alge, Roger Davies

The former Annie Mae Bullock, born in Brownsville, Tennessee, on November 26, 1938, staged one of the greatest comebacks in rock and roll history when in 1984 her "What's Love Got to Do With It" single got to #8 AC and #1 pop, eight years after she had left her abusive husband Ike Turner with nothing more than 36 cents and a credit card in her possession. Turner would go on to have many other pop and AC hits during the 1980s and rather unexpectedly had a big AC triumph in 1993 with "I Don't Wanna Fight."

Tina found her way in the music world when she married guitarist Ike Turner in 1958. With Tina, Ike set up the Ike and Tina Turner Revue, a rollicking stage show featuring his wife as lead vocalist supported by several other harmonizing women. They had their first pop entry in 1960 with "It's Gonna Work Out Fine" and hit the Hot 100 through 1975 with 20 singles, with the highest charting being their 1971 take on the Creedence Clearwater Revival hit "Proud Mary," at #4.

When she left Ike after one beating too many in 1976, Tina struggled for a while, doing game shows like *Hollywood Squares* while trying to get her own record career in order. It took perseverance, but once "What's Love Got to Do With It" hit, she was back on top again with five top 10 pop hits through 1986 alone. The AC chart was more resistant, giving Turner only six entries after "What's Love Got to Do With It" through 1990 until "I Don't Wanna Fight" came out.

"I Don't Wanna Fight" appeared in the movie *What's Love Got to Do With It?*, which was based on her autobiography *I, Tina*, written in 1986 with Kurt Loder. Actress Angela Bassett portrayed Tina in the film, while Laurence Fishburne was Ike Turner. Tina told Greg Kot in *The Chicago Tribune* she would not see the movie because "I'm a critical person; I'm critical of myself. How would I be able to sit there and watch someone portraying me? And I know there's no way they can get me absolutely right, because it's like twenty years in two hours."

On the Hot 100 "I Don't Wanna Fight" peaked at #9 the week of August 14, 1993. It also went to #51 R&B. Turner got a Grammy nomination for Best Female Pop Vocal Performance for the tune. "Why Must We Wait Until Tonight?," the follow-up single from the soundtrack, which was co-written and co-produced by Bryan Adams, fared miserably, getting to #97 pop.

Since "I Don't Wanna Fight" Turner has not had a major hit single, but then again she does not need one. Her concerts in the late 1990s continued to be top sellers, and she had already become a living icon, both as a survivor of abuse and a standout star in the history of rock and roll.

638 The River of Dreams

BILLY JOEL

Columbia 77086

September 11, 1993 (12 weeks)

Writer: Billy Joel

Producer: Dan Kortchmar

"The River of Dreams" washed Billy Joel back to hit status after a rather dry stretch in the early 1990s. He started off fine with "I Go to Extremes" in early 1990, reaching #4 AC and #6 pop, but then floundered the same year when "The Downeaster 'Alexa'" hit just #18 AC and #57. "And So It Goes" got him back to #5 AC but only #37 pop toward the fall of 1990.

Then in 1992 "Shameless," his composition which Garth Brooks made into a #1 country hit in 1991, bombed out at #40 AC while failing to make the Hot 100, his first single to do so since the 1970s. His 1992 take on Elvis Presley's #1 pop hit of 1957, "All Shook Up," did only slightly better, going to #15 AC and #92 pop as a cut from the soundtrack of the film *Honeymoon in Vegas*. But just as his poor chart performance was beginning to seem like a nightmare to Joel, a positive vision got him back on track.

As he told Melinda Newman about "The River of Dreams" in *Billboard*, "It's really a play on the phrase 'stream of consciousness.' The words just came to me. There are Biblical phrases in there, evocations of baptism and resurrection, and a great deal of symbolism in the river and the seas; I'm always using water as a metaphor. I'm still finding out why I wrote that song. That's a difficult one to be able to explain. . . . I feel what it is, but I don't necessarily know what it is."

He elaborated on the VH-1 TV series *Storytellers* in 1997 that a dream really did inspire the song. After waking up one night, he asked his then-wife Christie Brinkley, "Did I walk in my sleep last night?" He paraphrased that question to form the second line of the song's chorus, while the rhythm for the tune came to him while he was showering. He added that the song's three-chord progression was based on a lullaby.

"The River of Dreams," which also made #3 pop the week of October 16, 1993, behind Mariah Carey's "Dreamlover" at #1 and SWV's (Sisters With Voices') "Right Here/Human Nature/Downtown" at #2, served as the title song for Joel's 1993 album, which reached #1 on the LP chart for three weeks starting August 28, 1993. The tune also got Grammy nominations for Record of the Year and Song of the Year, and Joel had a nomination for Best Male Pop Vocal Performance.

Four years after *The River of Dreams* LP emerged, Joel released his *Greatest Hits, Volume 3* album and shocked his fans by announcing first in *Billboard* that he would not be writing any more pop songs, feeling he had done all he could with the genre, and was considering doing music for the theater. Although none of this had come to fruition by the end of 1998, Joel continued to tour some and play his old hits in a number of concerts into 1999.

639 Said I Loved You. . .But I Lied

MICHAEL BOLTON

Columbia 77260

December 4, 1993 (12 weeks)

Writers: Michael Bolton, Robert John "Mutt" Lange

Producers: Michael Bolton, Robert John "Mutt" Lange

When "Said I Loved You. . .But I Lied" hit #1 AC, Michael Bolton had his eighth chart-topper within four years, a feat matched only by John Denver, Barry Manilow, and Lionel Richie. The song also went to #6 pop for two weeks starting January 22, 1994. Bolton received a Grammy nomination for Best Male Pop Vocal Performance for the record.

But despite the success and the nomination, criticism of Bolton increased just as much as, if not more than, his popularity. He discussed the situation with Michael Angeli in *Esquire* in 1993. "I read a review that said Michael Bolton is so mainstream he should have a white stripe running down his back. And I thought, I could be a lot more mainstream. He meant it as an insult, but I don't consider it as such. On the contrary, I haven't hurt anybody. And I've gotten more affirmation and confirmation out of my effort than I could ever bargain for.

"I'm just glad I can sing and do what I love to do for a living while 99 percent of the people I know in the world can't. On top of it, I make people feel good. I think I can deal with that. . . .Does the criticism hurt? Sometimes. At first, it was devastating to me. If you have talent, there's a good chance that you're sensitive; it's like a microphone that picks up everything, and it can give you problems. But to be honest, I'd rather have it that way, because I think you just live a more edifying life."

After the success of "Said I Loved You. . .But I Lied," it was not until 1997 that Bolton released albums full of new material (he was hardly inactive, having toured several times in the mid-1990s, and made many TV and charitable event appearances). One of them was a collection of classical arias. The same year Hyperion published a children's book written by Bolton, *The Secret of the Lost Kingdom*.

But it was his new LP of pop music which attracted the most attention. *All That Matters* featured his version of "Go the Distance" from the 1997 Disney movie *Hercules* [see 667]. He co-produced and co-arranged every cut. Speaking of cuts, Bolton's fans noticed that year that he had cropped his trademark long locks. "I just decided it was time," he said of the change to Melinda Newman in *Billboard*.

640 The Power of Love

CELINE DION

550 Music 77230

February 26, 1994 (4 weeks)

*Writers: Candy de Rouge, Gunther Mende, Jennifer Rush,
    Mary Susan Applegate*

Producer: David Foster

"The Power of Love" had international power from the start. It initially became a #1 hit in the United Kingdom in 1985 for one of its co-writers, Jennifer Rush, who was an American but who recorded the song in Germany under the production of two other co-writers, Candy de Rouge and Gunther Mende. In the United States, Rush's version was not the first to chart. Instead, a cover by Air Supply in 1985, subtitled "You Are My Lady," went to #13 AC and #68 pop, followed in 1986 by Rush's cut which made only #57 pop. (She hit the AC chart in 1987 with "Flames of Paradise" with Elton John at #32 AC and #36 pop.) In 1987 another remake, from Laura Branigan, made #19 AC and #26 pop.

Then seven years later Celine Dion took "The Power of Love" to #1 both AC and pop, hitting the latter for four weeks starting February 12, 1994. It was the singer's first #1 pop hit as well as first #1 AC hit since "Nothing Broken but My Heart" in 1992 [see 623]. She had hardly been inactive in the interim, however, having charted in 1993 with "Love Can Move Mountains" (#8 AC, #36 pop), "Water From the Moon" (#11 AC), and a duet with Clive Griffin on the oldie "When I Fall in Love" from the movie *Sleepless in Seattle* (#6 AC, #23 pop).

Dion was involved in her own power-of-love scenario the same year when on December 17 she wed her longtime manager Rene Angelil at a lavish wedding at Notre Dame Basilica in Montreal at an estimated cost of $500,000. The facts that Angelil was 26 years older than Dion and had discovered her when she was 12 fueled speculation that he had always wanted her more personally than professionally. Both denied the rumors, and Dion asserted that there had been no romantic involvement until she had dated a few other men.

"I had a crush on a hockey player, but it never worked and I cried a lot," she told Edna Gunderson of *USA Today*. "I had a real boyfriend when I was 17. It lasted three or four months. Then came Rene. Life sometimes goes really fast." They started dating when she was 20 and he had been a widower for three years.

"The Power of Love" was the first single off Dion's *The Colour of My Love* album. None of the other three singles from the LP—"Misled," "Think Twice," and "Only One Road"—came near its impact on the charts. But Dion had nothing to cry about, for in 1996 she would release the biggest AC hit ever [see 657—"Because You Loved Me"].

1994

641 Now and Forever

RICHARD MARX

Capitol 58005

March 26, 1994 11 weeks

Writer: Richard Marx

Producer: Richard Marx

When Richard Marx married Cynthia Rhodes, an actress and onetime lead singer of the group Animotion, on January 8, 1989 after four years of dating, he wanted to keep his career and private life separate and so planned not to write songs about their relationship. But after the huge success of "Right Here Waiting" [see 568], he relaxed his attitude and became willing to explore his feelings for her via his records. But nothing after "Right Here Waiting" really took this approach until "Now and Forever."

"I was working on the fourth album and realized I had not written a song addressing our relationship since we had gotten married and had three kids," he said. "I think this is one of those songs which was unique in that the verses are so specific to our relationship." Nonetheless, he noted it had wide appeal because "There's a lot of people who can relate to parts or all of it."

To make "Now and Forever" even more special, Marx went for an acoustic sound and had his father do an arrangement suitable for a string quartet. "I had done so many piano ballads, I wanted to do a guitar ballad," explained Marx.

Marx said the whole process of putting the track down went quickly. "I think it was all of three days recording and mixing," he said. The single was a big hit, not only with its eleven-week run at #1 AC but also its pop peak of #7 for three weeks starting March 19, 1994.

Marx's marriage to Rhodes is so successful that many people ask him what he considers to be the secrets to a happy marriage. "I can only tell you that, first of all, we started out as best friends before we fell in love. . . .There's a lot of laughing. She's really funny. She thinks I am funny," he said. Adding that they never take each other for granted ("I can barely walk through a room without grabbing her") and maintain their companionship ("There's nobody I'd rather hang out with than Cynthia. You'd think she'd be sick of me"), he concluded, "I guess the real answer is that I found the right girl." Another ingredient may be that after the first baby, Rhodes decided to quit her career and become a housewife, quite a change from when they first met. Then, as Marx put it, "I was a cliché, a struggling songwriter in L.A., and she was a movie star."

At the end of the decade, Marx was planning to cut down on touring and spend more time himself with the kids at their Chicago residence. "I still have a presence on radio, but it's tough on white boys right now, white boys singing pop music," he said in early 1998. He wants to do more music for the movies (he sang on a track for the 1997 animated feature *Anastasia*) and producing other people as well as keep recording his songs. Summing up, he said, "I've got to keep doing the best I can do."

642 I'll Remember

MADONNA

Maverick/Sire 18247

June 11, 1994 (4 weeks)

Writers: Madonna, Patrick Leonard

Producers: Madonna, Patrick Leonard, R. Page

Madonna spent the years 1992 and 1993 generating as much controversy as media success, although one could argue that the former often led to the latter. Her $50 oversized book *Sex*, labeled obscene by detractors for its photos of naked people in various poses, some with sadomasochistic overtones, became a best-seller. The provocative stage antics on her "Girlie Tour" drew numerous protests, but didn't keep the tour from being a hit. She got criticism when she complained how boring the town was in Indiana where she was filming *A League of Their Own*, but the movie was a box-office success. And throughout this period she maintained a presence as a top name in the music industry, as confirmed by the reception of "I'll Remember."

Madonna just missed having "I'll Remember" become another #1 pop hit as well as her fourth #1 AC entry, as the tune notched four weeks at #2 pop behind "I Swear" by All-4-One starting the week of May 28, 1994. It was the theme for the movie *Without Honors*, starring Joe Pesci, which already was out of most theaters by the time "I'll Remember" finished its run at the top of the AC listing.

In general, Madonna's singing in films was more successful critically and commercially than her acting. Her first stab with both came in 1985: she sang "Crazy for You" from *Vision Quest*, which got to #2 AC and #1 pop, and also starred in the comedy *Desperately Seeking Susan*, whose "Into the Groove" did not get released as a single until after it received considerable airplay.

Her "Live to Tell" was a hit for her then-husband Sean Penn's movie *At Close Range* in 1986, but when they acted together in *Shanghai Surprise* a year later her performance brought catcalls rather than praise. The same could be said for Madonna's acting in *Who's That Girl?*, but her recording of the title theme and "Causing a Commotion" for the movie became big hits, with "Who's That Girl" going to #5 AC and #1 pop and "Causing a Commotion" to #37 AC and #2 pop. She finally got praise for both acting and singing, in *Dick Tracy*; she had two hits "inspired by" the movie, including her two-million selling single "Vogue" at #23 AC and #1 pop. But her best work on film (until *Evita*—see 649) was probably her 1991 documentary about her own touring and personal life in 1990, *Truth or Dare.*

By the way, the end of 1994 was pretty much business as usual for Madonna. Among other things, Norman Mailer, in an interview/article in *Esquire*, called her a "great artist" and the artist herself showed up at a New York City nightclub wearing pajamas, to promote her album *Bedtime Stories.*

643 Can You Feel the Love Tonight

ELTON JOHN

Hollywood 64543

July 9, 1994 (8 weeks)

Writers: Tim Rice (words), Elton John (music)

Producer: Chris Thomas

The first time Elton John contributed to a soundtrack for a movie was in 1970: he did "Friends," the title tune of the movie, which made #17 AC and #34 pop. He was the Pinball Wizard in the 1975 film *Tommy*, but his version of "Pinball Wizard" did not get released as a single. But almost 20 years later, in 1994, John's melodies for one of Disney's most ambitious animated motion pictures, *The Lion King*, achieved huge success.

John got involved in the project courtesy of collaborator Tim Rice. Rice, who worked on other major musical events, such as *Jesus Christ Superstar*, could pick anyone he wanted to write the score for *The Lion King*, and he approached John with the proposal in 1991, having previously worked with the artist a decade earlier.

John agreed to sing the songs as well as write melodies for them. He found the former an easier task than the latter. "I sat there with a line of lyrics that began, 'When I was a young warthog. . .' and I thought, 'Has it come to this?'" he told Richard Corliss in *Time*. But he got the job done and managed to get a few accomplished musical friends to join him in recording the tunes. In the case of "Can You Feel the Love Tonight," it was Rick Astley and Kiki Dee singing backing vocals for the record.

Besides making #1 AC, "Can You Feel the Love Tonight" went to #4 pop the week of August 6, 1994. The soundtrack went to #1 on the album chart for 10 weeks starting June 16, 1994. The other song from the soundtrack released as a single, "Circle of Life," peaked at #2 AC and #18 pop.

"Can You Feel the Love Tonight" won a bucketful of awards for Rice and John, most notably an Oscar for Best Song. Incredibly, Elton John won his first Grammy for singing solo for this song after more than a quarter century as a recording artist. He won for Best Male Pop Vocal Performance, making it his second Grammy (the first was in 1986—Best Pop Vocal Group Performance for "That's What Friends Are For" [see 485]). "Can You Feel the Love Tonight" also received a Grammy nomination for Song of the Year.

Once the tune became popular, youngsters in airports started coming up to John to tell him they loved his songs for the movie. "That's exactly what I wrote it for," he told Corliss. "I wanted to write melodies that kids would like."

John and Rice wrote three additional tunes for the stage adaptation of *The Lion King*, which opened on Broadway in November 1997. The musical was a smash hit, winning six Tonys, including Best New Musical, and as of January 1999 was still going strong. Not surprisingly, "Can You Feel the Love Tonight" remained as part of the score.

644 Wild Night

JOHN MELLENCAMP/ ME'SHELL NDEGEOCELLO

Mercury 858738

September 3, 1994 (8 weeks)

Writer: Van Morrison

Producers: John Mellencamp, Michael Wanchic

The "rebel rock" image of John Mellencamp, born in Seymour, Indiana, on October 7, 1951, wasn't hurt when he bristled at being called "Johnny Cougar" by his manager Tony DeFries. The aspiring singer reluctantly billed himself as "John Cougar" when he made his Hot 100 debut in 1979 with "I Need a Lover" at #28. But by 1983, after a #1 pop hit ("Jack and Diane") and #2 pop single ("Hurts So Good"), he felt he had earned the right to go by his real name, so as a compromise he became John Cougar Mellencamp and compiled six consecutive top 20 pop singles from 1983–86.

Some thought Mellencamp was too much of a rocker to make #1 AC during his early years, but when he finally did it, it was with "Lonely Ol' Night" at #37 in 1985, hardly a mellow tune. He had only four others cross over during the 1980s, with the highest-charting AC entry being "Cherry Bomb" at #12 in 1988. After nearly a three-year absence, he returned to the chart in 1992 with "Again Tonight" at #46 under the name of John Mellencamp, which he had used on all his releases since 1991. But it still seemed unlikely that he would ever have a big hit on the AC chart.

Enter "Wild Night," a cover of Van Morrison's #28 pop entry of 1971 sung as a duet with a shuffling beat by Mellencamp and Me'Shell Ndegeocello (pronounced "nuh-DAY-gay-OH-CHEL-lo"). Born in Berlin, Germany, on August 29, 1969, Ndegeocello grew up in Washington, D.C. Her dad and brother were musicians. She studied jazz at the Duke Ellington School of the Arts and Howard University before going to New York in 1990, where she played for a group called the Black Rock Coalition before going solo. Madonna heard Ndegeocello as a soloist, and, thinking she had potential as a singer and bass player, signed Ndegeocello to her Maverick label.

Ndegeocello recounted the making of "Wild Night" to Evelyn McDonnell in *Rolling Stone*: "[Mellencamp] called and wanted me to sing. He didn't know I played bass. Pretty much what you hear on 'Wild Night' is the second take. For the first hour I thought my name was 'goddamn it, Me'Shell,' but he was cool." "Wild Night," which Martha Reeves had taken to #74 R&B in 1974, peaked at #3 pop the weeks of September 3 and 10, 1994, behind "I'll Make Love to You" [see 646] at #1 and "Stay (I Missed You)" by Lisa Loeb and Nine Stories at #2. The duo got a Grammy nomination for Best Pop Vocal Collaboration.

Ndegeocello had no hits after "Wild Night," but then again she did not really pursue them. As for Mellencamp, in 1998 came the release of *The Best That I Could Do 1978–1988*, 14 songs from that period. It was to be his last Mercury LP, as he announced after 22 years with the label that he was looking for a new company.

645 All I Wanna Do
SHERYL CROW

A&M 0702

October 29, 1994 (8 weeks)

Writers: David Baerwald, Bill Bottrell, Wynn Cooper,
Sheryl Crow, Kevin Gilbert

Producer: Bill Bottrell

Born in Kennett, Missouri, on February 11, 1962, Sheryl Crow graduated from the University of Missouri in 1984 with a degree in piano and voice, then moved to Los Angeles in 1986 to pursue a singing career. For a few years she found only backup work, including touring 18 months with Michael Jackson on his 1987–88 world tour, but in December 1989 she was signed to Warner/Chappell music as a songwriter and vocalist.

In 1992 she worked on what was to be her debut album on A&M with Hugh Padgham as her producer, but Crow decided that the LP should not be released. The rhythm guitarist did not give up, however, and that same year she teamed with producer Bill Bottrell and a motley crew of his friends who worked on creating songs every Tuesday night through the wee hours of the morning. "As soon as she started coming by, the songs got a lot better thanks to her singing," Bottrell told *People* magazine. One of the songs the group collaborated on was "All I Wanna Do," which became Crow's breakthough hit.

"All I Wanna Do" spent six weeks at #2 pop starting the week of October 8, 1994, held out by "I'll Make Love to You" [see 646], and the LP on which it appeared, *Tuesday Night Music Club*, went to #3 on the LP chart. Crow won Record of the Year and Best Female Pop Vocal Performance Grammys for her work on the single, which also earned a nomination for Song of the Year. Additionally, Crow claimed a statuette for Best New Artist.

Crow found that a few of her own musicians resented all the critical and commercial acclaim that came to her personally. "There were guys in the group who were feeling bitter about the record doing so well," she told Melinda Newman in *Billboard* in 1996. "There's only two of them that struck out at me, [but] I wasn't prepared for it. Bill [Bottrell] said, 'If you only sold 10,000 copies, they'd love you.' . . .I'm still not over it." She also told Newman that "A lot of what I recorded on the last record was while I was drinking or stone-cold drunk."

The more sober Crow shook off the negative vibes, which could have been the result of the fact that all the musicians had other commitments lined up when Crow went to tour in support of her LP. "When you put a band together, it's a crapshoot, and people don't wanna be involved until they know," Crow told Elysa Gardner in *Rolling Stone*. "Now I've got people crawling up my legs, you know? But, hey, I've already got my band from middle America, and we're happy."

Crow continued recording and touring extensively after "All I Wanna Do," although nothing released since then has had as big an impact on the AC chart.

646 I'll Make Love to You

BOYZ II MEN

Motown 2257

December 24, 1994 (3 weeks nonconsecutive)

Writer: Babyface

Producer: Babyface

In 1988 four hopeful men from different parts of the city met at Philadelphia's High School for the Creative and Performance Arts and found they had a lot in common: they shared a love of soul harmony sounds and all were from single-parent households headed by women. They were Michael "Bass" McCary from Logan on the north side, Wanya "Squirt" Morris from the Richard Allen projects, the unrelated Nathan "Alexandervanderpool" Morris (born in Philadelphia on June 18, 1972) from east Philadelphia, and Shawn "Slim" Stockman (born in Philadelphia on September 26, 1973) from southwest Philadelphia. They called themselves Unique Attraction and specialized in a sweet doo-wop/gospel harmony.

During a concert in 1991, the quartet met Michael Bivins, formerly a member of the New Edition quintet, which had been a popular soul act in the 1980s. They impressed him with their version of New Edition's "Can't Stand the Rain," and Bivins, now an artist manager at Motown, signed them to a five-record deal with his label. In his honor, Unique Attraction became Boyz II Men, using the New Edition song "Boys to Men" as inspiration for the group's new name.

Bivins also contributed the rap to Boyz II Men's first single in 1991, "Motownphilly," named in tribute to the two cities whose soul sounds they enjoyed. That went to #3 pop. But it and six other singles released through 1993 paled in comparison with the success they had with their inaugural single of 1994. "I'll Make Love to You" was a multichart #1 hit. Besides its AC success, it was #1 R&B for nine weeks starting August 20, 1994, and even more impressively #1 pop for 14 weeks starting August 27, 1994—four months before it topped the AC chart! The single tied "I Will Always Love You" [see 627] for the longest run atop the Hot 100 with 14 weeks, a number again reached in 1996 by "Macarena" by Los Del Rio (bayside boys mix). The production also earned a Grammy nomination for Record of the Year.

Ironically, the song which knocked "I'll Make Love to You" off its #1 pop perch was Boyz II Men's own single "On Bended Knee," which had a six-week nonconsecutive run on the chart starting December 3, 1994. This meant that during the week of January 14, 1995, Boyz II Men were #1 pop with "On Bended Knee" and #1 AC with "I'll Make Love to You," the first time an artist was #1 on both charts for the same week with a different song. The final irony was that the single which passed the 14-week longest #1 pop mark was a Mariah Carey–Boyz II Men entry a year later [see 656—"One Sweet Day"].

1995

647 I'm the Only One

MELISSA ETHERIDGE

Island 854068

January 7, 1995 (2 weeks nonconsecutive)

Writer: Melissa Etheridge

Producers: Melissa Etheridge, Hugh Padgham

It was a sign of the times when the AC chart yielded its #1 ranking to hard-rocking Melissa Etheridge with "I'm the Only One" in 1995. The woman who considered Bruce Springsteen her inspiration kept her trademark shouted vocals and intense guitar chord playing intact on a song just as tough as any in her repertoire. It was also worthy of notice that she made the top spot after acknowledging that she was a lesbian at the inauguration of President Bill Clinton in January 1993, making her the first woman to head the AC listings after publicly announcing her homosexuality.

Etheridge was born in Leavenworth, Kansas, on May 29, 1961. She left Leavenworth to study guitar at Boston's Berklee College of Music but did not graduate. Instead, she headed west to southern California in 1982 to play various bars. She was discovered by Chris Blackwell, founder of Island Records. Island signed Etheridge, and she cut her first self-titled LP for the company in 1987.

Her first single to make the Hot 100 was "Similar Features" in 1989, which peaked at #94. It and its flip side, "Bring Me Some Water," did much better with album-rock stations, which played the tunes frequently. The first single by Etheridge to make the AC chart was "Dance Without Sleeping," which hit #24 in 1992. The following year "I'm the Only One" was the leadoff single from her LP *Yes I Am*, but as with the previous 45s it generated the bulk of its airplay on rock stations first. Its follow-up, 1994's "Come to My Window," finally got her a name as a successful pop song vocalist when it stopped at #23 on the Hot 100, leading Island to rerelease "I'm the Only One."

Etheridge discussed "I'm the Only One" in a "How I Wrote That Hit Song" column for *Musician* in 1995. "I believe I started it in Austria, going to Vienna. Of course it then takes weeks after to polish it up, but the bulk of it came 'boom'—the melody, and the idea of the chorus," she wrote. She added that "I was excited to perform it live. I felt like in concert it would really grab people. And it has."

"I'm the Only One" became Etheridge's first top 10 pop hit as well as #1 AC entry, peaking at #8 the week of January 21, 1995. It won a Grammy nomination for Best Rock Song, but competed against another song by Etheridge, "Come to My Window," which won her the Best Female Rock Vocal Performance Grammy. She has since had several other hit records (for example, 1996's "I Want to Come Over"), and has also become widely known for her political activism (for example, appearing naked in an ad for People for the Ethical Treatment of Animals with her partner Julie Cypher).

648 Love Will Keep Us Alive

THE EAGLES

Geffen Album Cut

January 28, 1995 (3 weeks)

Writers: Pete Vale, Jim Capaldi, Paul Carrack

Producers: The Eagles, Elliot Scheiner, Ron Jacobs

When the Eagles split apart in 1980, the acrimony between group members, as well as each member's stated desire to pursue a solo career, made observers think the group would never get back together, and in interviews from 1980–1993, they all made it clear they had no reunion ambitions.

Then in 1993 an album featuring country singers covering the Eagles' hits, called *Common Threads*, became a surprise multimillion seller. One of the artists on the LP, Travis Tritt, was asked to do a video for his version of "Take It Easy." "I said the only way I'd do a video is if we got the Eagles back together again," Tritt told Peter Castro in *People*. "Everybody chuckled because nobody thought it could happen. When [Giant, the label which issued *Common Threads*] approached them and they agreed, I was scared to death because I was expecting a fistfight."

But Don Felder, Glenn Frey, Don Henley, Timothy B. Schmidt, and Joe Walsh found that they could and did all want to work together again. The result was a decision to perform in concerts as part of the aptly named Hell Freezes Over tour. It started May 27, 1994 in Irvine, California, and covered 26 other cities, grossing more than $175 million before it ended. The average cost of a top ticket was an unprecedentedly high $100, but Frey defended the price to David Wild in *Rolling Stone* by bringing up what he paid for season tickets to the Los Angeles Lakers basketball team.

"One floor seat for one game to watch the under-.500 Lakers play cost $500," he said. "The Eagles get together once every 14 years, so I think $115, parking including, is not too much to ask. It's all relative. We're competitive with the [Rolling] Stones and Pink Floyd, and we're cheaper than Streisand. . . .And clearly the response has been tremendous. As far as I know, the only people who brought the issue up are press people who are getting their tickets for free."

With the new tour came the idea of doing a few new tunes. While the rowdy "Get Over It" went to #31 AC, the mellow "Love Will Keep Us Alive" started getting airplay before Christmas of 1994 and had enough impact to get to #1 AC within a few weeks. Strangely, Geffen did not release the song as a single, or another track which got a fair amount of airplay too, "Learn to Be Still."

A few weeks prior to the peak of "Love Will Keep Us Alive," *Hell Freezes Over*, the LP containing that song, hit #1 on the album chart for two weeks starting November 26, 1994. But by the end of 1998 that success had not led to a full-scale reunion of the band, and there is no evidence that such a follow-up will happen.

649 Take a Bow

MADONNA

Maverick 18000

February 18, 1995 (9 weeks)

Writers: Babyface, Madonna

Producers: Babyface, Madonna

He recorded some on his own, including his 1990 AC debut "Whip Appeal" at #36, but Kenneth "Babyface" Edmonds found greater success in the 1990s as a producer of such talent as Boyz II Men. His reputation continued to shine when he gave Madonna her longest-lasting single atop both the AC and pop charts with "Take a Bow." Babyface provided a backing vocal to the song, which he also co-wrote and co-produced. Besides getting to #1 pop for seven weeks starting February 25, 1995, "Take a Bow" went to #40 R&B.

Commenting on the song to Barbara Ellen in *New Musical Express*, Madonna said, "Lyrically, ["Take a Bow"] only reflects one side of my personality. I have that side which is . . .willing to, literally, do anything for love. But there's another side too, which is 'Don't f___ with me, I don't need anybody. I can do what I want.'"

"Take a Bow" was—and is—only the second Madonna single to be #1 both pop and AC after "Live to Tell" [see 495]. She had 11 songs which topped the Hot 100 through 1998, and among the nine which did not top the AC chart, one missed the chart entirely ("Justify My Love" in 1991), and two others cracked only the top 30 (1984's "Like a Virgin" at #29 and 1990's "Vogue"). Some other pop top 20 hit singles by Madonna during the 1980s and 1990s missed the AC chart entirely, such as "Oh Father" in 1989, "Hanky Panky" in 1990, and "Rescue Me" in 1991.

After "Take a Bow," much of Madonna's attention over the next year focused on getting the title role in *Evita*, the film version of the 1970s stage musical which had been in development for more than a decade and whose producer and director had considered less controversial stars, such as Barbra Streisand and Meryl Streep, for the lead. Madonna won the Golden Globe Award for Best Actress in a Musical or Comedy for the film when it came out in 1996, but to many people's surprise, she did not get an Oscar nomination.

Perhaps the slight didn't bother her too much, as in 1997 she gave birth to her first child, a daughter she named Lourdes (to probably no one's surprise but his own, Madonna stopped dating the child's father, aspiring actor Carlos Leon, not long after the birth). Then in 1998 she made a move into the "electronica" dance sound and met with a good share of critical approval for her album *Ray of Light*. Its first two singles, "Frozen" and "Ray of Light," became top 10 pop hits, but the latter proved to be too frenetic for AC airplay.

As Madonna approached her 40th birthday in August 1998, VH-1 aired a special reviewing her impact on popular culture during the 1980s and 1990s. Time will tell if they will be doing a similar tribute to her in the 21st century.

650 In the House of Stone and Light

MARTIN PAGE

Mercury 858940

April 22, 1995 (4 weeks)

Writer: Martin Page

Producer: Martin Page

Few people had really heard Martin Page before "In the House of Stone and Light," but they probably knew his music, as he had written several hits for various acts in the 1980s before beginning a solo singing career. Born in Southampton, England, on September 23, 1959, Page considered a professional career as a soccer player before deciding to stick with music. He played bass in soul and reggae clubs in the Southampton area, then became part of a duo called Q-Feel. Then, even though Q-Feel never charted in the United Kingdom, Page decided to try his luck in the United States.

Page's music initially met with relative indifference; Q-Feel only bubbled under to #110 in 1983 with its single "Dancing in Heaven (Orbital Be-Bop)." (However, that single did somehow get to #75 pop in a revival in 1989.) Real success for him came when he pursued songwriting in the mid-1980s, getting hits with "We Built This City" for Starship (#37 AC and #1 pop in 1985), "These Dreams" for Heart in 1986 [see 491], and "King of Wishful Thinking" (#7 AC and #8 pop in 1990) and "Faithful" (#3 AC and #14 pop in 1993) for Go West. He often wrote with Elton John's famous lyricist Bernie Taupin, and after several projects with Taupin, Page decided to record an album featuring himself as lead singer.

"It was time for me to write my own book, make my own statement," Page was quoted as saying on Mercury's official Martin Page Web site. "There had been a lot of preparation up to this point, and I was ready to explore my music as an artist."

He recorded his first album, titled *In the House of Stone and Light*, mostly in his garage at home, with contributions from various musicians he knew including Phil Collins and Robbie Robertson. The title tune became its first single, and "In the House of Stone and Light" made #14 pop while topping the AC chart. The follow-up, "Keeper of the Flame," proved less successful, going only to #83 pop.

"Making this album has been a great adventure of self-discovery," Page noted on the Mercury Web site. "I've chased away some demons and shed my skin, while, in the process, I can tell you I've also had a lot of fun and some great moments doing it."

But the album did not do very well despite the success of "In the House of Stone and Light," peaking at only #161 on the LP chart in 1995. Page may have had "some great moments doing it," but as of mid-1998 he had yet to release a follow-up album to his initial effort.

651 Believe
ELTON JOHN

Rocket 856014

May 20, 1995 (2 weeks)

Writers: Bernie Taupin (words), Elton John (music)

Producers: Elton John, Greg Penny

The huge success of *The Lion King* soundtrack might have been a tough act to follow for other artists, but Elton John kept going with the flow and readied another album of new material with writing partner Bernie Taupin. When he went to work on his 1995 LP *Made in England*, John found that tunes for the project did not come to him automatically. He told Timothy White in *Billboard* that at first he wrote "two or three songs, and then I wrote 'Believe' and felt we'd discard everything and start from there." He used Greg Penny as his co-producer for the album rather than his old favorite Chris Thomas.

"Believe" got to #13 pop as well as #1 AC, making it his 15th hit atop the latter chart and tying him with the Carpenters for most #1 AC hits ever plus giving him an impressive 39th single to make the pop top 20. John got yet another Grammy nomination for Best Male Pop Vocal Performance for his singing on this tune.

John's obvious disappointment with the chart performance of "Believe" in England, where it failed to make the top 10, was captured on tape on a documentary done by his boyfriend which aired on cable television in 1998. The appropriately named *Tantrums and Tiaras* offered intimate glimpses of John at work and at play. There were several examples of his famous temper, including a flare-up during the taping of a video and his stalking out of a tennis match when someone took his picture against his wishes. But John also could be seen in mellower moods: with his mother, who admitted she worried she was going to lose him to drugs, and in his Atlanta apartment, where he unveiled his massive closet full of glasses, shirts, pants, and shoes, among other pieces of his wardrobe, that allowed him to wear a different outfit every day of the year with no repeats.

Two other singles released from *Made in England*, the title tune and "Blessed," fared less well than "Believe." When "Blessed" came out toward the end of 1995, John was occupied with personal projects, including his work for AIDS benefits. He also continued to look for the right diet to help him lose weight and the right wig for his rapidly receding hairline, two physical problems he had been contending with since arriving on the music scene in the 1970s.

John would come back again to #1 AC, but it was on the heels of a tragedy this time. For more details, see 670—"Something About the Way You Look Tonight."

652 Have You Ever Really Loved a Woman?
BRYAN ADAMS

A&M 1028

June 3, 1995 (5 weeks)

Writers: Bryan Adams, Robert John "Mutt" Lange, Michael Kamen

Producers: Robert John "Mutt" Lange, Bryan Adams

Bryan Adams' 1991 hit "(Everything I Do) I Do It for You" [see 603] was the biggest hit on the AC chart that year, but surprisingly it was only the third AC entry for Adams despite nearly a decade during which he was a frequent presence on the Hot 100. It came after 1983's "Straight From the Heart" (#29 AC, #10 pop) and 1985's "Heaven" (#12 AC and #1 pop).

Adams, born in Kingston, Ontario, Canada, on November 5, 1959, wrote his first song at age 15, then spent much of the mid- to late 1970s working to achieve success in the music world. Among other accomplishments, he was lead singer of Sweeney Todd, a Canadian rock outfit. Sweeney Todd went to #90 pop in August 1976 with "Roxy Roller" sung by Nick Gilder, then quickly replaced him with Adams and rereleased "Roxy Roller" with the latter's voice and got to #99 pop in September 1976. Adams also had a disco hit in the late 1970s, "Let Me Take You Dancing." He finally made his pop debut in 1982 with "Lonely Nights" at #84 and then scored 13 top 40 pop hits through 1987 before his triumph with "(Everything I Do)."

After "(Everything I Do)," Adams found himself with a more receptive audience on AC radio. He made the chart over the next year with "Can't Stop This Thing We Started" in 1991 (#40 AC, #2 pop), and "Thought I'd Died and Gone to Heaven" (#36 AC, #13 pop) and "Do I Have to Say the Words?" (#5 AC, #11 pop) in 1992. However, he did not return to the top of the chart until "Have You Ever Really Loved a Woman?" in 1995.

"Have You Ever Really Loved a Woman?" was from the movie *Don Juan DeMarco*, starring Johnny Depp, Marlon Brando, and Faye Dunaway. On a Web site on the Internet called "Bryan Adams Heaven," run by a woman named Connie, Adams was quoted as saying that "the charm of that song is its simplicity—it is really sparse and basically what it is, a flamenco guitar and a voice." He did the tune with the help of the crew from "(Everything I Do)" again, co-writers Robert John "Mutt" Lange and Michael Kamen, even though he had had disagreements with Kamen on their first collaboration.

Adams got a Grammy nomination for Best Male Pop Vocal Performance for the tune, which also received an Oscar nomination for Best Song and was #1 pop and AC simultaneously for five weeks starting June 3, 1995. To date, no more of Adams' movie tunes have made either chart, although Adams has remained active on both. His busy worldwide tour schedule seems likely to continue into the 21st century.

653 I'll Be There for You

THE REMBRANDTS

EastWest Album Cut

July 8, 1995 (7 weeks)

Writers: David Crane, Marta Kauffman, Allee Willis, Phil Solem, Danny Wilde (words); Michael Skloff (music)

Producer: Gavin MacKillop

"Theme songs for TV shows are dead" decreed several network executives in the fall of 1994. They believed that in the multiple-channel world of the 1990s, the idea that viewers would be attracted by a theme tune introducing a show was passé. So what happened? The biggest new show of the 1994–95 season, NBC-TV's sitcom *Friends,* created the most requested TV theme song among radio stations in at least a decade.

"I'll Be There for You" was a peppy concoction that ran during the opening credits of the show. Singing the tune were the Rembrandts, a male singing duo composed of Danny Wilde and Phil Solem. The two men previously had been in a Los Angeles band called Great Buildings before getting onto the charts in 1991 with "Just the Way It Is, Baby" (#12 AC, #14 pop).

Kevin Bright, the executive producer of *Friends,* recruited Wilde and Solem to sing and play "I'll Be There for You" as well as make changes. The two were glad to have the oppor-

tunity to make their own contributions for, as Wilde told John Maynard in *The Washington Post* about the first version of the tune, "It had kind of a sterile sound to it. But we saw the potential and felt we could 'Rembrandt' it up. We definitely put our stamp on it."

At first, "I'll Be There for You" was just a 42-second track played on the TV show's opening and closing. But as listeners deluged radio stations with requests to air the tune and Wilde and Solem's label pressed them to respond, the Rembrandts relented and added "I'll Be There for You" to their current album, called simply *LP*. "It was sort of a corporate choice to put it on the album," Solem told Maynard. "Once we saw the potential of what kind of a spearhead that would give us, we went along with it."

After "I'll Be There for You" had been at #1 on the Hot 100 Airplay chart for eight weeks starting May 20, 1995, EastWest finally released the tune as a single and saw it debut impressively at #18 on the pop chart the week of September 30, 1995 (a song cannot chart on the Hot 100 unless a commercially available single of the tune exists). But its airplay was on the decline already, so it peaked at #17 in October with the help of some action for its B-side, "This House Is Not a Home."

More than three years after it became a hit, "I'll Be There for You" still got occasional airplay on radio while remaining as the theme for the still-popular *Friends.* The Rembrandts have yet to come up with anything nearly as popular, but not for lack of trying. As Solem told Maynard, "If we were to just hang our hat on ['I'll Be There for You'], we'd be toast."

654 Kiss From a Rose

SEAL

ZTT/Sire 17896

August 26, 1995 (12 weeks)

Writer: Seal

Producer: Trevor Horn

Like "I Will Always Love You" [see 627], "Kiss From a Rose" was a #1 AC and pop song in a movie which received no Oscar nomination for Best Song because it did not appear there first. The tune, heard in the hit sequel *Batman Forever* starring Val Kilmer, originally appeared on Seal's self-titled LP, his second album, in 1994, and actually charted that year as a single in the United Kingdom at #20.

Written in 3/4 time, "Kiss From a Rose" was "sort of a medieval folk song" from Seal, according to his producer Trevor Horn. Horn told Ben Cromer in *Billboard* in 1998 that "Seal had a real good demo of 'Kiss From a Rose,' but the bit in the middle he had at the end. I got Betsy Cook to play a string synth on it. She played two or three passes on it, and I grabbed it in the computer and spent three days editing it." Horn said when it came to cutting "Kiss From a Rose" and other tunes on Seal's album, he employed a seven-piece band to use at Peter Gabriel's studio Real World because he felt that on the demos, "the songs really hadn't been performed."

Besides its AC success, "Kiss From a Rose" hit #1 on the Hot 100 the week of August 26, 1995. It also reached #52 on the R&B chart. "Kiss From a Rose" also snagged Grammys for Record of the Year and Song of the Year, and Seal won Best Male Pop Vocal Performance for his work on it. It was a triumph for the singer after having lost in the same later category a year earlier for his singing on "Prayer for the Dying."

Seal was born Sealhenry Samuel in Paddington, England, on February 19, 1963. It took some time, but he finally made his big splash in the music world when his "Crazy" went to #2 in the United Kingdom in 1990. A year later, "Crazy" hit #7 on the pop chart in America. But Seal found it difficult to maintain that success in America, and in 1992, only "Killer" made the Hot 100, and only at the bottom rung, while he compiled five top 40 entries in Great Britain during the same period.

Unfortunately, the popularity of "Kiss From a Rose" was a not a signal that Seal was to have an immediate follow-up success. As of early 1999, his best effort after "Kiss From a Rose" was "Fly Like an Eagle," a remake of Steve Miller's #2 pop and #38 AC hit of 1977. The cover went top 10 both pop and AC in February 1997, and like "Kiss From a Rose," it was included on a movie soundtrack, in this case *Space Jam*, starring basketball great Michael Jordan.

655 As I Lay Me Down

SOPHIE B. HAWKINS

Columbia 77801

November 18, 1995 (6 weeks)

Writer: Sophie B. Hawkins

Producer: Stephen Lipson

Self-described "omnisexual" Sophie B. Hawkins has led what might be termed an adventurous life and career. Hawkins (the "B" stood for Ballantine) was born in New York City sometime in the mid-1960s to mid-1970s. As she put it to Ray Rogers in *Out* magazine, "My age is one thing I'm not out about."

Hawkins moved out of her parents' house at 14 with her boyfriend at the time, a man in his forties, and started taking part in the music scene of the Big Apple in the 1980s. During that decade she became a percussionist with the backing band for Bryan Ferry, the former lead singer and keyboardist of Roxy Music in the 1970s, whose other group members were guitarist Phil Manzanera and horn player Andy Mackay. Roxy Music had one AC entry in 1979, the #38 AC and #44 pop single "Dance Away," while Ferry charted as a solo artist in 1985 with "Don't Stop the Dance" at #26 AC.

In the 1990s Hawkins began her solo singing career and scored a big hit with "Damn I Wish I Was Your Lover," which made #5 pop but, due to its loud sound, not the AC chart. The fact that the person to whom Hawkins sang the song sounded like both a man and a woman led to rampant rumors about her personal life. While saying to Rogers that she had been in love with both males and females, she refused to categorize herself as straight, gay, or bisexual, preferring the term "omnisexual" instead. "I liken 'omnisexual' to different aspects of the personality. . . .I have my spirituality, my intellectuality, my sexuality, my emotionality, among others," she told Ray.

For her second album, *Weaker*, Hawkins included her song "As I Lay Me Down," which became the second 45 after its first single bombed. It first hit the charts back in June of 1995 and looked to be an unsuccessful effort for a time. But Columbia got its promotion staff behind the tune to hype play on radio stations, and Hawkins made a similar effort by doing many TV appearances, including *Live With Regis and Kathie Lee*. One wonders how the born-again Christian co-host of that show, Kathie Lee Gifford, felt about working with a self-proclaimed "omnisexual."

"As I Lay Me Down" got to #6 pop for three weeks starting October 28, 1995, before hitting #1 AC. It also spent an unprecedented 67 weeks on the AC chart, a record at the time when it ended the week of August 30, 1996. But Hawkins did not have long to celebrate that distinction, as the record had been broken within 18 months by "Change the World" [see 658].

656 One Sweet Day

MARIAH CAREY AND BOYZ II MEN

Columbia 78074

December 30, 1995 13 weeks

Writers: Mariah Carey, Michael McCary, Nathan Morris,
Wanya Morris, Shawn Stockman, Walter Afanasieff

Producers: Walter Afanasieff, Mariah Carey

When the 1990s' hottest female singer and top vocal group combined to make "One Sweet Day," the result was gangbusters on the charts. While it did peak at #2 R&B for 9 weeks, "One Sweet Day" spent a new record 13 weeks leading the AC chart. It also stayed on the pop chart at #1 for 16 weeks starting December 2, 1995, the longest ever for a tune on the Hot 100. That run ended the week of March 23, 1996, when "Because You Loved Me" took over as the top pop single. Ironically, "Because You Loved Me" did the same thing to "One Sweet Day" on the AC chart but it ended up having the longest run at #1 AC, staying 6 weeks more than "One Sweet Day" for a total of 19 weeks. And to top everything off, the tune received a Grammy nomination for Song of the Year.

One Sweet Day" appeared only on Carey's album *Daydream*, which hit #1 for four weeks starting October 21, 1995. But Boyz II Men probably benefited more from the hit, as it confirmed the group's growing acceptance in the AC world to the same level they had already achieved in the pop and R&B fields.

The quartet of Michael McCary, Nathan Morris, Wanya Morris, and Shawn Stockman did not make their AC debut until more than a year after they did so on the pop and R&B charts. The song that put them through was "End of the Road," from the Eddie Murphy film *Boomerang*, which despite going to #1 R&B and pop, helming the latter an impressive 13 weeks, got only to #35 AC in the fall of 1992. Before that, from 1991–92, they had scored four entries on both the pop and R&B; in chronological order, they were "Motownphilly," "It's So Hard to Say Goodbye to Yesterday," "Uhh Ahh," and "Please Don't Go." The failure of the smooth, sweet "It's So Hard to Say Goodbye to Yesterday" is a particular mystery, as it fared so well on the other charts, making #1 R&B and #2 pop.

After "End of the Road" and then "In the Still of the Nite (I'll Remember)," a #11 AC tune from the 1993 ABC-TV miniseries *The Jacksons: An American Dream*, on which Boyz II Men appeared, the vocal group did considerably better AC-wise, getting to #1 in 1995 with "I'll Make Love to You" [see 646]. They remained popular on the AC, pop, and R&B charts with fairly regular releases after that into the late 1990s. By that time, Nathan Morris and Shawn Stockman had both recorded solo efforts which were heard in tunes on two different movie soundtracks. Stockman struck first by doing "Visions of a Sunset" in the 1995 film *Mr. Holland's Opus*, featuring an Oscar-nominated performance by Richard Dreyfuss, while Morris sang "Wishes" in the 1996 movie *Kazaam*, featuring professional basketball player and actor (well, at least he *said* he was an actor) Shaquille O'Neal.

1996

657 Because You Loved Me

CELINE DION

550 Music 78237

March 30, 1996 (19 weeks)

Writer: Diane Warren

Producer: David Foster

"My dad truly believed in me when nobody else did," Diane Warren recalled in a personal communication to me in 1998. "He always encouraged me when I was down and was basically my biggest fan and supporter. This song was a way I could really put into words how grateful I was to have had somebody like that in my life."

Warren's tribute to her father became the longest-running #1 AC hit ever, staying atop the chart for much of the spring and summer of 1996 for an incredible 19 weeks. The tune, which appeared in the Michelle Pfeiffer–Robert Redford movie *Up Close and Personal*, also peaked at #1 pop for six weeks beginning March 23, 1996. In the film it served as the love song between Pfeiffer and Redford's romantically involved characters. The motion picture did not rate the commercial and critical success of "Because You Loved Me," partly because although the film was supposed to be based on the life story of NBC-TV reporter Jessica Savidge, the final cut bore little resemblance to the real story of that troubled newscaster's life (she died in a car crash in 1984 before she was 40).

"Because You Loved Me" did nicely in various awards categories, getting an Oscar nomination for Best Song, a Grammy for Best Song Written for a Motion Picture or Television, and Grammy nominations for Record of the Year and Song of the Year as well. Celine Dion also received a nomination for Best Female Pop Vocal Performance on the tune.

Asked by Mike Joyce of *The Washington Post* if she knew "Because You Loved Me" would become such a tremendous success, Dion laughed and said, "I wished I was that smart. I never know. I listen to a lot of songs each year, especially when we're preparing an album. I don't write my songs, so I'm very fortunate that writers send me such great songs. But to me, a hit is a song that I love, that boosts me, and that I can sing with all my heart."

Joyce asked her if by that description she meant she favored ballads, which she told him she did. "My favorite kind of thing to sing is that kind of song," she said. "I like uptempo songs and blues, and great grooves, but for me, it's easier to put my emotions into big ballads like 'Power of Love,' 'The Colour of Love,' and 'Because You Loved Me.' I know I'm always singing about love, but maybe that's because I'm very much in love."

Dion would return to the top of the AC chart later in 1996 with another big ballad, "It's All Coming Back to Me Now" [see 659].

658 Change the World

ERIC CLAPTON

Reprise 17621

August 10, 1996 (13 weeks)

Writers: Tommy Sims, George Kennedy, Wayne Kirkpatrick

Producer: Babyface

When "Change the World" came out after several years in the making, it set a record of 80 weeks on the AC chart. It may not have exactly changed the world, but its year-and-a-half stay on the AC chart, with three of those months being at #1, was something no other 45 had (or has) accomplished.

"It started off as a musical idea Tommy Sims had. It had been hanging out there for a while," recalled co-writer Wayne Kirkpatrick of the tune. Sims developed the title and a basic melody before he put the result down in rough form on tape and let Kirkpatrick hear the song. "Tommy was leaning toward some type of social protest song," Kirkpatrick remembered. "I suggested making it into a love song." With that approach in mind, Kirkpatrick wrote new lyrics for "Change the World." He added that "It wasn't being written for anyone specifically."

When Kirkpatrick finished his part, the song then went to George Kennedy, who contributed his own ideas before submitting the song to get a record deal. Then they finally got an artist to record the song, namely country singer Wynonna, formerly the younger member of the mother-daughter act the Judds, but Wynonna's track was held from release for two years.

A few months after the writers got word that Wynonna's company would include the song in her next album, they were told that Eric Clapton was going to do it for the movie *Phenomenon*. Kirkpatrick said that when they heard the news, "There was a little bit of 'Yeah, I'll believe that when I see it' from us." By this time, it had been nearly five years since Sims started working on it, and Wynonna's version had yet to appear. But Clapton's version did come out and made a huge impact, going to #5 pop the week of August 17, 1996, as well as #1 AC. It also won Grammys for Record of the Year and Song of the Year, and Clapton won a Grammy for Best Male Pop Vocal Performance.

"I'll you the truth, the first time I heard it, I said, 'Well, this sounds great, but I wonder if it'll make it on the radio,'" Kirkpatrick said of the record. The extensive airplay it got was far beyond what Kirkpatrick expected. "I was amazed. . . .I would be looking at *Billboard* and comment, 'Gee whiz, it's still in the top 10!'" he said with a laugh.

Kirkpatrick attributed a great deal of its appeal to the combination of rock star Clapton and R&B producer Babyface doing a song by three writers from the country capital of Nashville. "That covered such a broad category," he said. He also thought the timing of the release was right. "Nothing else like that had been out for awhile." But he said ultimately that he really was not sure what the big selling point of "Change the World" was. "I wish I knew, because I'd do it again!" he laughed.

659 It's All Coming Back to Me Now
CELINE DION

550 Music 78435

November 19, 1996 (5 weeks)

Writer: Jim Steinman

Producer: Jim Steinman

"It's All Coming Back to Me Now" was originally done by its writer Jim Steinman with his group Pandora's Box and published in 1989. The tune held at #2 on the Hot 100 for five weeks starting October 26, 1996, held from the top the first three weeks by "Macarena" by Los Del Rio and "No Diggity" by BLACKstreet (Featuring Dr. Dre) the last two.

The B-side of "It's All Coming Back to Me Now" was also noteworthy. "The Power of the Dream," co-written by David Foster, his wife Linda Thompson Foster, and Kenneth "Babyface" Edmonds, was commissioned to be sung at the opening ceremony of the 1996 Summer Olympics in Atlanta, Georgia, by Dion and telecast to a worldwide audience live. "Three billion people watching you is pretty frightening. This moment is coming very fast now, and I have goose bumps thinking about it," she admitted to Kim Cunningham of *People* on the eve of her performance. Of course, Dion pulled it off without a hitch.

An unpleasant situation resulted when Sony Music nominated "It's All Coming Back to Me Now" for Best Record and Best Female Pop Vocal Performance at the Grammys but not for Best Song. Since Best Song is the category that covers the writer(s) of a tune, it meant that Steinman lost out on a potential nomination, which his manager David Sonenberg said infuriated the writer. When reporter Steve Hochman asked representatives of Sony's Epic Records, of which 550 Music was a subsidiary, to explain why "It's All Coming Back to Me Now" had no Best Song nomination, they refused to comment. But Sonenberg, talking to Hochman in an article in *The Los Angeles Times*, said he learned Sony kept it off the list of 511 Best Song entries for fear it could cancel out the other hit Dion sang in 1996, "Because You Loved Me."

Speaking on behalf of Steinman, Sonenberg told Hochman, "It's wrong to put this in the hands of a record company and let politics take over." But Mike Greene, president of the National Academy of Recording Arts and Sciences (NARAS), which hands out the Grammys, defended the long-held practice of record companies nominating songs and artists for Grammys. "We still believe the creative people at the labels are integral to the entering process for Grammy Awards," he said. "They all know the product." Sonenberg also said that based on past experience he had believed that Sony would nominate "It's All Coming Back to Me Now" and did not learn until after the deadline had passed that Sony had not.

At any rate, Dion emerged unscathed, and was to return to #1 AC just five months later [see 662—"All by Myself"].

660 When You Love a Woman
JOURNEY

Columbia 78428

December 4, 1996 (4 weeks)

Writers: Steve Perry, Jonathan Cain, Neil Schon

Producer: Kevin Shirley

Guitarist Neil Schon and bassist Rick Vallory were among the five men who originally comprised Journey when the group started in 1973. Lead singer George Tickner departed in 1975, leaving the group without a permanent lead singer until Steve Perry joined in 1978. That same year the band debuted on the Hot 100 at #57 with "Wheel in the Sky."

The next year Steve Smith became Journey's drummer, replacing Aynsley Dunbar, who had been with the group since 1974. Then in 1981 Jonathan Cain took over Gregg Rolie's role on keyboards, and the group began a string of top 20 pop hits which crossed over to the AC chart through 1983, the first being "Who's Crying Now" (#14 AC, #4 pop). By 1986, Journey was down to a trio of Cain, Perry, and Schon, but when "Why Can't This Night Go On Forever" peaked at #24 AC and #60 pop in 1987, Journey dissolved shortly thereafter. Perry continued a solo career he had started in the early 1980s (his "Foolish Heart" made #2 AC in 1984), while Cain and Schon became part of the group Bad English, whose biggest hit was "When I See You Smile" at #11 AC and #1 pop in 1990.

Almost a decade after the breakup, Cain, Perry, Schon, Smith, and Vallory reunited to re-form Journey. The first single released was "When You Love a Woman," which some complained sounded just like the group's old material. Perry told Melinda Newman in *Billboard* that was exactly what the band wanted to do.

"Nothing sounds more pretentious than someone being something they're not," he said. "One of the things we've always known is that there are certain musical directions that fit what [our] chemistry is about. We're going to sink or swim being what we are and not by trying to reinvent ourselves and not by trying to be the flavor of the month." Perry also implicitly noted that his career in the industry had been checkered by mentioning that "The music business can be a choke chain, and you have to be aware of that, especially when you still have a few marks around your neck from it."

Prior to 1996, Journey's biggest AC hits were "Open Arms" in 1982 and "I'll Be Alright Without You" in 1987, both stopping at #7. "When You Love a Woman" reached #1 AC as well as #12 pop. The band received a Grammy nomination for Best Pop Vocal Performance by a Duo or Group.

The reborn Journey did not last long before defections occurred. By 1998 Perry and Smith had left Journey again, with their respective replacements being Steve Augeri and Dean Castranova.

661 Un-Break My Heart

TONI BRAXTON

LaFace 24200

January 4, 1997 (14 weeks)

Writer: Diane Warren

Producer: David Foster

Born in Severn, Maryland, on October 7, 1968, Toni Braxton first cracked a *Billboard* chart in 1990 as part of the Braxtons, a vocal quintet featuring her and her sisters Tamar, Towanda, Traci, and Trina. Their "Good Life" went to #79 R&B, but there were bigger things in store for Toni.

When Toni left the group in 1992 (making it a quartet, which then became a trio when Traci defected in 1995), she became a top R&B act, starting with "Give U My Heart," a single billed as Babyface (featuring Toni Braxton), with the tune's producer listed first. The 45 made #2 R&B and #29 pop and kicked off a string of top 10 R&B hits for Braxton. It took a little longer for the pop and AC listeners to fall under her spell, but they had by the mid-1990s, when she had such hits as "Breathe Again" and "You Mean the World to Me."

In the summer of 1996 Braxton finally got her first #1 R&B hit as well as #1 pop triumph with her double-sided entry "You're Makin' Me High/Let It Flow." A few months later Braxton came out with an even bigger hit, "Un-Break My Heart."

"The title really inspired and compelled me to write it," said songwriter Diane Warren. "I thought it was unique and yet it was so simple that I was surprised someone hadn't thought of it before." As to how Braxton got involved, Warren remembered, "I played the song in rough form to Clive Davis and he loved it and gave it to Toni."

"Un-Break My Heart," with a backing vocal by Shanice Wilson, made #1 pop for 11 weeks starting December 7, 1996 before starting an even longer run of 14 weeks on the AC chart. Its run atop the chart was the second-longest in AC history, behind only the 19-week run of "Because You Loved Me," also written by Warren [see 657].

The massive popularity of the song did not really surprise Warren. "I really believed it would be a huge worldwide hit the second I heard Toni sing the song in the studio. I felt it would really be a song a lot of people would relate to," she said.

Despite its enduring popularity, "Un-Break My Heart" did not provide Braxton with financial solvency. In January 1998, to the shock of the music industry, Braxton announced she was filing for bankruptcy protection. Some speculated that she made that move in order to have her record contracts voided. Whatever the truth of the matter, she has continued to work and perform, and in September 1998 began an extended run in *Beauty and the Beast*, playing Belle, the female lead.

662 All By Myself

CELINE DION

550 Music 78529

April 12, 1997 (3 weeks)

Writers: Eric Carmen, Sergei Rachmaninoff

Producer: David Foster

Eric Carmen wrote the rather mournful "All By Myself" after he broke up with a woman he had been with for three years. The melody was an adaptation of Rachmaninoff's *Second Piano Concerto* (Carmen had studied classical music). His version went to #6 AC and #2 pop in 1976.

"It's unbelievable, the life of this song," Carmen mused in the liner notes to his 1997 retrospective LP *The Definitive Collection.* "Last year was pretty amazing, between the Jewel version that was in [the movie] *Clueless,* my version that was in [the movie] *To Die For,* Sheryl Crow doing it on a B-side, and the Babes in Toyland's version, which I thought was possibly the funniest record I ever heard in my life. . . .To me as a songwriter, the ongoing success of this song is the kind of triumph I dreamed of growing up.

"The idea was to write standards—songs that lived beyond your years. This is a song that has been recorded or sung by everyone from Frank Sinatra to Paul Anka to Hank Williams Jr. Stanley Turrentine did a jazz version, and now Celine Dion's having another big pop record with it. Amazing."

The version by Dion differed from the original mainly in that it dropped the false ending Carmen used before reprising the chorus one last time. Her "All By Myself" peaked at #4 pop the weeks of April 5 and 12, 1997 while going to #1 AC. Dion also did the tune in Spanish to appeal to her Latin followers.

Three weeks before "All By Myself" reached its peak, reporter Mary McNamara of *The Los Angeles Times,* in a profile of the singer, specifically mentioned the tune. Describing Dion's voice as "Pure and powerful, without any hitches or quavers or distinguishing scars," McNamara went on to write, "When you listen to Dion sing a sad song, even her no-holds-barred version of 'All By Myself,' you get the feeling she has never had one of those nights—you know, when you sit on the couch chain-smoking, trying to decide between getting drunk, dying your hair black or killing yourself. No one can feel really, *really* bad and sing quite that perfectly, quite that loud, at the same time."

McNamara sounded a touch too cynical to be a true Dion fan, of which there were millions across the world by 1997. She had sold over 20 million records within the last four years alone and ranked that year as the number one selling artist worldwide, as she had the previous two years. To top it off, she would end 1997 singing the theme from the most successful motion picture of the decade and possibly of all time [see 671—"My Heart Will Go On"].

663 For the First Time

KENNY LOGGINS

Columbia Album Cut

May 3, 1997 (2 weeks)

Writers: James Newton Howard, Allen Dennis Rich, Jud Friedman

Producer: Peter Asher

Kenny Loggins had two big album releases in 1997. One was *Yesterday, Today, Tomorrow: The Greatest Hits of Kenny Loggins,* a CD summarizing his 25 years as a music producer, including his first five years as part of the duo Loggins and [Jim] Messina, who created the #4 pop hit "Your Mama Don't Dance" in 1972. Another was a book and CD of new material called *The Unimaginable Life: Lessons Learned on the Path of Love.* While Loggins was doing *The Unimaginable Life,* Columbia Records chairman/president Don Ienner told him he ought to consider recording "For the First Time" from the romantic George Clooney–Michelle Pfeiffer film *One Fine Day.*

"I had been shying away from movies since the old days," Loggins told Chuck Taylor in *Billboard,* recalling the times in the 1980s when his voice graced such hits as the title song for *Footloose* and "Danger Zone" from *Top Gun.* "Image-wise, I thought it was better to stay away and focus on my own stuff."

Yet the lyrics, about not really knowing your partner until you've been together a few years, hit home with Loggins, who felt it captured his feelings about his early relationship with his wife Julia. Loggins said when he recorded the song, "I decided to stay out of the production of it and just be the singer, so I left the madness up to Peter Asher. In the end, I only took a couple days off from my project."

The tune ended up nominated as Best Song at the Oscars, where Loggins performed it on March 30, 1997. It was after that appearance that the song, available only as part of the *One Fine Day* soundtrack and not as a single, started to get big-time airplay on AC stations to the point where it topped the chart a few weeks later.

"For the First Time" was Loggins' first #1 AC hit, a perhaps surprising honor considering the circumstances surrounding its making. "My family and I joke that I managed to get a #1 song in my spare time," he said. One of those family members already had a #1 AC hit himself. Kenny's cousin Dave Loggins had scored with "Please Come to Boston" nearly 23 years earlier [see 225].

Loggins was born in Everett, Washington, on January 7, 1947, and raised in Alhambra, California. Prior to joining Jim Messina he spent time in the bands Gator Creek and Second Helping. Despite his soundtrack reputation, he has scored a few hits away from films, including "Whenever I Call You Friend" with Stevie Nicks in 1978 (#5 pop, #9 AC) and "This Is It" in 1979 (#11 pop, #17 AC).

664 You Were Meant for Me

JEWEL

Atlantic 87021

May 17, 1997 (1 week)

Writers: Jewel, Steve Poltz

Producers: Ben Keith, Peter Collins

"You Were Meant for Me" had the longest consecutive-week run on *Billboard*'s Hot 100 when it finished 65 weeks on the chart on February 21, 1998. Part of that run occurred because its B-side, "Foolish Games," became its follow-up on the chart. On the AC chart, "Foolish Games" got its own listing and peaked at #4 the weeks of October 11 and 18, 1997. But the really amazing part about "You Were Meant for Me" is that it became a hit two years after its first release and after three different mixes were tried.

Born Juel Kilcher in Homer, Alaska, on July 23, 1974, Jewel joined Atlantic Records in the mid-1990s as a vocalist. The label had hoped she would be a breakout success, but that did not happen. Her first single, "Who Will Save Your Soul," stirred little action initially when released in 1995. Then "You Were Meant for Me" got the nod, but executives worried that the version which appeared on her LP *Pieces of You* would not make the grade, so they had it remixed and added guitars. The new "You Were Meant for Me" was meant for no one in terms of appeal. It bombed too.

In the fall of 1995 Jewel toured intensively while Atlantic repromoted "Who Will Save Your Soul" to album rock stations. Its popularity there prompted a rerelease of the single, which peaked at #11 pop in August 1996. Another try with "You Were Meant for Me" seemed in order, but Jewel insisted she redo the track, as she hated the LP and remixed single versions.

As Jewel told Chuck Taylor in *Billboard*, "When I got my album in my hands for the first time, I sat down crying because I hated the way I sang the song so much. The choruses really bothered me. To hear that it was going to be the single, it was like, no, that's my worst nightmare come true. I was appalled."

Her producer Peter Collins liked her new vocal for the single. He told Taylor, "She felt so much more powerfully in control of her voice. She had obviously grown. . .in the two years since [the song] was first recorded." Others agreed, as "You Were Meant for Me" became her first AC entry and also peaked at #2 pop for two weeks, the first the week of April 19, 1997, behind "Can't Nobody Hold Me Down" by Puff Daddy featuring Mase, and the second the week of May 10, 1997, behind "Hypnotize" by the Notorious B.I.G.

Perhaps the person most surprised by "You Were Meant for Me" was Jewel herself. "It's funny, I didn't really see 'You Were Meant for Me' as a single," she said. "It's such a simple song. I thought radio songs had to be 16-track epics. The thing I've really learned about my audience is that any-thing can be a single as long as it touches people."

665 Butterfly Kisses

BOB CARLISLE

Diadem 42456

May 24, 1997 (7 weeks)

Writers: Bob Carlisle, Randy Thomas

Producer: Bob Carlisle

When contemporary Christian singer Bob Carlisle contemplated his daughter Brooke's 16th birthday, the event stirred him considerably. "I was alone in my office one night, and I came to the realization that I don't have this child under my roof for too much longer," he told Deborah Evans Price in *Billboard*. "I pulled out some photos of me walking her on a horse and different things that are depicted in the song, and I just came unglued. The song poured out of me. It was just a gift for her."

Carlisle's wife thought otherwise and convinced him to play it for the head of his label Diadem. All agreed to put it on Carlisle's LP *Shades of Grace*, which came out in the summer of 1996. Christian radio stations played it frequently, and on April 27, 1997, Carlisle and his co-writer Randy Thomas won Dove Awards from the Gospel Music Association for Song of the Year and Inspirational Song of the Year. Following these triumphs, officials at Diadem's parent company Zomba decided to push it to AC stations, where it debuted at #21 on May 10, hit #3 the next week, and then #1 for seven weeks.

But while Carlisle was touring Denmark, MCA Records had its new country act, the Raybon Brothers, consisting of Marty Raybon from the group Shenandoah and his brother Tim, record it May 12 for a quick release. Back in America, Carlisle remixed his original for a more country version, but it was too late. The Raybon Brothers had a bigger pop and country hit with "Butterfly Kisses," peaking at #22 pop and #37 country. Besides being #1 AC, all Carlisle did elsewhere was #45 country. Another cover, this one by Jeff Carson, also charted, at #66 country.

There were no hard feelings between Carlisle and the Raybons about the cover battle. "It's been no secret over the years that Marty Raybon is probably one of my favorite singers in country music. I'm honored that he would even think of doing the song," Carlisle told Price in the *Billboard* piece, which also quoted Raybon as saying, "Carlisle is a magnificent talent. He sings the stew out of it."

Carlisle was virtually unknown before "Butterfly Kisses." Raised in Orange County, California, he spent 20 years in the music business doing everything from singing backup at sessions for artists ranging from Barry Manilow to Poison to spending nine years with the Christian rock group Allies. He seemed to milk "Butterfly Kisses" for all it was worth in 1997, even letting it be the basis of an illustrated children's book in time for Christmas that year.

Still, Carlisle told *Time*, "As wonderful as this is, my life does not revolve around having a hit record. If it all went away, I'd sniffle for a couple of days, but that's all." We'll see what he writes when his son Evan turns 16, around 2003.

666 Here in My Heart

CHICAGO

Reprise Album Cut

July 12, 1997 (1 week)

Writers: Glen Ballard, James Newton Howard

Producer: James Newton Howard

B ill Champlin, who began to sing lead on some Chicago songs in the late 1980s [see 553—"Look Away"], originally sang "Here in My Heart" with no intention of having it be part of the group's repertoire. "It was written as a possible movie song and presented with Bill's voice before it was to go on a Chicago album," said Chicago trumpeter Lee Loughnane. Once the decision was made to have it on the LP, additional lyrics had to be done by producer/writer James Newton Howard and writer Glen Ballard, as only one verse had been composed.

AC programmers liked "Here in My Heart" as an album cut, and it became the group's first hit to make the chart in that format. Ironically, the week it led the chart, former Chicago lead singer Peter Cetera was at #21 AC and #17 pop singing with Az Yet on the latter's remake of "Hard to Say I'm Sorry" [see 425]. (The tune later peaked at #8 pop.) "Here in My Heart" was Chicago's first AC chart appearance since 1991's "You Come to My Senses," which made #11 AC but became one of the few Chicago 45s to fail to make the Hot 100. "Chasing the Wind," the other Chicago song of 1991 released earlier that year, did go to #39 pop as well as #13 AC. In the interim, the group put out a 1995 LP of big band tunes which generated minimal interest.

"Here in My Heart" was also the eighth #1 AC hit for Chicago overall, their first going all the way back to 1971's "Beginnings" [see 155]. In 1998 the group released its second greatest hits LP with two new songs on it, plus was planning to do a long-overdue Christmas album, with Bruce Fairbairn as producer.

The fact that Chicago would be doing multiple best-of albums and had lasted more than three decades boggled Loughnane's mind. "You couldn't possibly have believed something like this would happen when we started out," he said. "We've been very fortunate and worked very hard to stay here. Some things go right, but you still have to work at it." Asked how Chicago has by and large managed to keep the same personnel it had when it started over 30 years ago, Loughnane said, "I think there's a mutual respect for us as individuals. We know that we're trying our best for perfection. I think it shows whenever we're onstage and doing our music, to our fans and to ourselves." As the millennium approached, Loughnane said he and the other members are ready and looking forward to continuing to record and tour as Chicago.

667 Go the Distance

MICHAEL BOLTON

Columbia 78554

July 19, 1997 (3 weeks)

Writers: Alan Menken (music), David Zippel (words)

Producers: Michael Bolton, Walter Afanasieff

B ack in the early 1980s, aspiring songwriter David Zippel moved to New York City and worked together with another hopeful composer named Alan Menken in off-Broadway productions. He had no inkling that 15 years later both men would team again for *Hercules*, a big-budget animated film for the Walt Disney studios.

While Menken was a familiar name to Disney [see 628—"A Whole New World (Aladdin's Theme)"], the company had hired Zippel as a fresh recruit, specifically to work with Menken on *Hercules*. "I think they liked my work on Broadway," Zippel said in explaining how he got the assignment, noting that he had won much praise for his contributions to the musical, *City of Angels*. He also had experience doing tunes for animated films, as he had worked on a musical version of *The Swan Princess* released by another studio in the early 1990s.

Zippel found *Hercules* to be an enjoyable yet laborious project. "Animated films have a rather long incubation period," he noted. "This took about three and a half years between its inception and when it came out."

The decision to use "Go the Distance" as the initial single from *Hercules* caught Zippel off guard because, he explained, "It came rather late in the film. We had written a song for another part of the film and thought it would be the breakout hit." While declining to name the other song, Zippel noted that he and Menken had to change their approach to "Go the Distance." The final lyrics and arrangement emerged as they tried to come up with a song that had a universal theme yet gave Hercules a big moment in the film which also related specifically to his role.

As with all songs from Disney feature-length cartoons of the 1990s, the company decided to have a major musical act sing the tune for a promotional single. The company asked Michael Bolton to do "Go the Distance," and Bolton responded favorably. Zippel and Menken met with him and his co-producer Walter Afanasieff to talk about the tune, but Zippel said other than that he and Menken had nothing to do with the final record. However, he did like what Bolton and Afanasieff created, saying that "I thought it sounded great."

The tune, which Bolton also sang on the *Hercules* soundtrack, went the distance on the AC chart in its ninth week. Its pop peak was a somewhat disappointing #24. However, it did an Oscar nomination for Best Song, the first one for Zippel. Bolton sang it at the Oscar ceremony as well, but it lost to "My Heart Will Go On" [see 671].

After *Hercules*, Zippel continued to work with Disney, with his next project for the studio being the 1998 summer release *Mulan*. "It's a great relationship," he said about working for the company.

668 Sunny Came Home

SHAWN COLVIN

Columbia 78528

August 9, 1997 (4 weeks)

Writers: Shawn Colvin, John Leventhal

Producer: John Leventhal

"Sunny Came Home" was the second release off Colvin's *A Few Small Repairs* LP after "Get Out of This House" became another in a string of her singles to fail to make the Hot 100. Before "Sunny Came Home," singles by the vocalist, whose first album, *Steady On*, came out in 1989, had only made the AC chart. Her first AC entry was in fact the title tune from *Steady On*, and it made #30 in 1990.

That pattern changed with "Sunny Came Home." Colvin told Chuck Taylor in *Billboard* that "It was a hard song to write. I was putting every possible idea into every nook and cranny, and it was still awkward and very frustrating. I thought the song was a dud."

Originally Colvin named her protagonist Sally. In time the woman became Sunny, and ultimately, according to the song's lyrics, she was a lady so upset with her life that she set fire to her house. Such a drastic action shocked some listeners, but not the main writer. "It was fun to write about a character and have her do something far more extreme than I would," Colvin said. "It's not clear to her why she did it, and it's not clear to me either."

"Sunny Came Home" gained popularity first on radio airplay by top 40 stations and then AC stations. However, Columbia Records opted not to release it as a commercial single until 17 weeks after *Billboard* began recording top 40 airplay for the song. When it finally came out as a 45, "Sunny Came Home" debuted at #8 on the Hot 100 the week of July 19, 1997. It ended up peaking at #7 pop while going to #1 AC, but some observers thought the 17-week delay in getting the record out to the buying public prevented it from reaching #1 pop, since its top 40 appeal was waning by then.

Discussing the situation, Tom Corson, senior vice president of marketing for Columbia, told *Billboard* that "Obviously, we didn't need the single to make the song a success at radio. Largely, Shawn's audience is adult, so we wanted to drive album sales first. But when we were hearing back from radio that it was also appealing to a younger audience, we wanted to solidify that group, because they buy singles."

Colvin probably cared less about where the song charted and more that it led her to a busy schedule of tour dates and TV shows the rest of 1997. Born Shanna Colvin in Vermillion, South Dakota, on January 10, 1958, she provided backing vocals for Suzanne Vega before landing her own recording contract. Despite her initial lack of success, she fared well enough with folk-rock fans to convince Columbia to keep her on its roster even though she didn't get a gold LP until *A Few Small Repairs*, which was no doubt because "Sunny Came Home" was on that album.

669 How Do I Live

LEANN RIMES

Curb 73022

September 6, 1997 (11 weeks)

Writer: Diane Warren

Producers: Chuck Howard, Wilbur Rimes

LeAnn Rimes caused quite a stir in country circles in 1996 when she recorded "Blue," a tune planned for Patsy Cline to record before the latter's death in 1963. Deemed too old-fashioned by some modern country stations, the tune nevertheless became a country hit and even crossed over to #26 on the Hot 100. What really astonished people besides Rimes' vocal, which sounded eerily like Cline, was that the singer cut the tune when she was only 13 years old.

Born in Jackson, Mississippi, on August 28, 1982, Rimes grew up in Garland, Texas, while developing a love of music encouraged by her parents. "Blue" introduced her to much of the music-listening public, but strangely it did not make the AC chart. Instead, Rimes had her first AC entry with "How Do I Live," written for the movie Con Air. It was her first major release after winning the Grammy for Best New Artist of 1996.

Rimes was the first to record "How Do I Live," but the film company apparently did not like her version (reportedly they thought she did not sound mature enough) and asked fellow country music thrush Trisha Yearwood to do it. It was Yearwood's version which made the movie and its soundtrack.

Undeterred, Curb Records went ahead and released Rimes' effort to compete against Yearwood's, with Rimes' father Wilbur serving as co-producer. The cover battle was a competition that Rimes at least did not enjoy. "I don't think there's anything positive that ever comes out of being pitted against another artist, which is unfortunately what ended up happening in the press," Yearwood told Deborah Evans Price in Billboard about the controversy. "I hate that it happened, and I really felt uncomfortable about the face-off thing they did at radio where people would play both versions and people would vote. . . .I have nothing but a huge amount of respect for LeAnn and her singing, and I think it's unfortunate the whole thing had to happen."

The "face-off," as Yearwood put it, was interesting in terms of the charts. On the country listings Rimes' rendition stalled at #52 while Yearwood peaked at #2 the week of August 30, 1987. But AC and pop-wise, Rimes was the clear winner, peaking at #2 pop for three weeks starting December 13, 1997, as well as #1 AC. In fact, Rimes' showing on the Hot 100 was the highest ever for a country singer to reach on that chart since Billboard started using its Sound-Scan method of tallying record sales in 1991.

At the Oscar ceremony, it was Yearwood alone who sang the song. It ended up losing to "My Heart Will Go On" [see 671]. Rimes went ahead to compile a few other country hits and tour in 1998, and seemed buoyant in interviews despite the announcement that her parents were planning to get a divorce.

670 Something About the Way You Look Tonight

ELTON JOHN

Rocket 568108

November 22, 1997 (10 weeks)

Writers: Elton John (music), Bernie Taupin (lyrics)

Producer: Chris Thomas

"It is a simple, straight-ahead love song, which I think we do very well," Bernie Taupin said on a 1997 episode of the VH-1 series Storytellers in describing "Something About the Way You Look Tonight." Initially, the song was planned to be the first release from Elton John's 1997 LP The Big Picture. Then John's "Candle in the Wind 1997," a revised version of his 1973 ode to Marilyn Monroe with new lyrics by Bernie Taupin to honor the late Princess Diana of Wales, became its companion tune. John performed "Candle in the Wind" at the princess's funeral on September 6, 1997 and later that day recorded it with Sir George Martin. It was not an easy act for him to do it in public or at a studio that day, as he was quite distraught over the loss of the Princess, who had been seen comforting him at the funeral of their mutual friend, designer Gianni Versace, just a few months earlier.

The combination of the two songs made it the biggest-selling single ever. "Candle in the Wind 1997" and "Something About the Way You Look Tonight" debuted at #1 the week of October 11, 1997 and remained at the top for 14 consecutive weeks through January 10, 1998. That was not a record stay atop the Hot 100, but the 11-million plus U.S. sales figure was a first. (Worldwide, the number of singles sold was more than double that, and all money received went to charities which the late Princess supported.)

However, on the AC chart Billboard treated "Candle in the Wind 1997" and "Something About the Way You Look Tonight" as separate entries. The former tune got only to #5 on September 27, 1997, its second week on the chart, and dropped out of the listings before the end of the year, while "Something About the Way You Look Tonight" still reigned at the top.

"Candle in the Wind" had hit the AC chart previously at #2 for two weeks in 1987 in a "live" version with the Melbourne Symphony Orchestra. It originally appeared in a studio version as a track on John's #1 LP of 1973, Goodbye Yellow Brick Road.

With the appearance of "Something About the Way You Look Tonight," John scored his 16th #1 AC hit, putting him ahead of the Carpenters, whose 15 hits had held the top spot since 1981. He also took the lead in the most number of weeks at #1 AC, getting a total of 49. (That record did not last long; see 674—"To Love You More.") It also marked 28 consecutive years of John having at least one top 40 pop hit per year, breaking the 27-year mark set by Elvis Presley, and put John just behind Presley in terms of total top 40 pop singles. Given his fair lead in these records, it will be up to John to see how far and what sort of new precedents he will set in the future.

1998

671 My Heart Will Go On

CELINE DION

550 Music 78825

January 31, 1998 (10 weeks)

Writers: Will Jennings (words), James Horner (music)

Producers: James Horner, Walter Afanasieff

"Titanic"—the word described not just the ship which crashed into an iceberg and killed more than 1,000 souls in 1912, but also the impact of the movie named after the ship. *Titanic*, released in late 1997, cost more than $200 million to make, largely due to elaborate special effects (which also delayed its premiere, which had been slated for mid-1997), but came out to widespread critical praise and commercial success.

Just as the movie generated big audiences, it also attracted attention for its romantic score, written by James Horner. Ironically, the film's director James Cameron had originally requested that Horner write no pop songs as part of the score.

"Feeling *Titanic* still needed something to sum up [the heroine] Rose's feelings at film's end, Horner secretly commissioned lyricist Will Jennings to compose words for the movie's love theme, sang the song for his friend Celine Dion, invited Dion to record it, and then presented the tape to Cameron," wrote David Browne in *Entertainment Weekly*. Cameron switched his position after hearing the tune, recorded by Dion in May 1997, and included it in the film.

"I loved the song, I loved the movie, and I went into the studio and recorded a song," Dion told Chuck Taylor in *Billboard*. "I gave it as much as any other song recorded in my life, and now, here we are breaking records. It's not something that you think you will ever do. I am very amazed, but at the same time, people are touched by love, by love stories, and by emotion. To me, this is the most important thing."

For those who love to quote statistics on record-breaking performances, "My Heart Will Go On" has been a veritable trivia feast. Its 10-week run at #1 AC gave Dion a total of 45 weeks atop the listings, the most of any female vocalist and behind only Elton John and Lionel Richie in the overall totals. Also, the second week "My Heart Will Go On" was #1 AC, it got a record number of airplays for a single week—9,415—as well as a record number of radio listeners—105 million.

On the pop chart it was the eighth single to debut at #1 on the Hot 100 the first week it was released as a commercially available single on February 28, 1998. It stayed at that position for an additional week. And on the album chart the *Titanic* soundtrack featuring the song in a slightly different version stayed at #1 for 16 weeks starting January 24, 1998, the longest run for any soundtrack since *Dirty Dancing* held at #1 for 18 weeks in 1987. Last but not least, "My Heart Will Go On" won the Oscar for Best Song (as well as a Golden Globe, a Golden Satellite, and an MTV Movie Award), and the movie itself won for Best Picture, among the host of awards it reaped.

672 Truly Madly Deeply
SAVAGE GARDEN

Columbia 78723

April 11, 1998 (11 weeks)

Writers: Darren Hayes (words), Daniel Jones (music)

Producer: Charles Fisher

The fast-paced lyrics of Savage Garden's American break-through single "I Want You" captivated many listeners in the summer of 1997, including daytime talk show hostess Rosie O'Donnell, who loved to sing along with it on her show even though the only words she seemed to know were "cherry cherry cola." She invited the group on her show as the record went on to peak at #4 on the Hot 100.

But Savage Garden, an Australian duo composed of lead singer Darren Hayes and his partner Daniel Jones, learned like many other groups in the past that one pop hit in America does not guarantee further success, and their follow-up, "To the Moon and Back," stopped at #37 pop despite being a huge hit Down Under. Luckily, the two were able to rebound with an even bigger hit than "I Want You." "Truly Madly Deeply" was their return to the top, although it almost did not make it on to their self-titled album.

"I remember sitting in a cafe, writing it," Hayes told Chuck Taylor in *Billboard*. "It was an honest love song and how I was feeling at the time. I had just recently gotten married, and my wife and I were apart for seven months as Daniel and I wrote songs. I rewrote the chorus, and it maintained the feeling that came from a basic, core place. There's not a lot of pretension about the song."

Hayes added that "We had originally called it 'Magic Kisses,' with the same verses and [instrumental] hook, only it was 50 beats per minute faster." But he and Jones then decided to do an acoustic version they thought would serve as a bonus track. However, their producer Charles Fisher had bigger ambitions for the song and installed a few other elements, including background vocals, to increase its potential as a hit single, which it indeed became.

"Truly Madly Deeply" first hit #1 in Australia before making a splash in America. It had a two-week run at #1 pop starting January 17, 1998, before belatedly becoming an AC favorite a few months later. Its 11 weeks atop the AC roster was the longest for any group's initial appearance on the chart since Paul Mauriat's 11 weeks with "Love Is Blue" in 1968.

Discussing the impact of success on their lives, Hayes told Taylor, "A year ago when we were writing, Daniel and I were living on instant noodles. It was not so luxurious. It was a process filled with ambiguity and insecurity, whether the album would ever be released or successful. Then, suddenly, we're expected to know how to make a video, how to take a photograph, how to act in public. . . . We are still learning the act of image in real time. I guess that's growth, that's progression."

Savage Garden toured America the summer of 1998 in the wake of the popularity of "Truly Madly Deeply." Afterward, the duo planned to record a follow-up album in the hope of continuing their worldwide success.

673 You're Still the One
SHANIA TWAIN

Mercury 568452

June 27, 1998 (8 weeks nonconsecutive)

Writers: Shania Twain, Robert John "Mutt" Lange

Producer: Robert John "Mutt" Lange

The name Shania (pronounced "shu-NIGH-uh") is an expression from the Ojibway Indian tribe meaning "I'm on my way." Shania certainly was on her way in 1998, making a huge crossover from country to the AC and pop charts with one of the year's biggest hits, "You're Still the One."

Born Eileen Twain in Windsor, Ontario, Canada, on August 28, 1965, the future country star grew up in Timmons, Ontario, located roughly 500 miles north of Toronto. She was the second of five children in an impoverished household, but she did not let the family's lack of money get her down. As a child she enjoyed listening to rock and country music on the radio, and she started singing in clubs while in her teens.

When Twain was 21, her mother and stepfather were killed in an automobile accident. Twain assumed guardianship of her three younger siblings and went to work as a performer at Deerhurst Resort in Ontario. In 1990, free of familial duties, she adopted the name Shania in honor of her stepfather, an Ojibway, and went to Nashville to audition as a country singer. Three years later her first record was released.

Twain's first country single was "What Made You Say That" in 1993; that song, like its follow-up, "Dance With the One That Brought You," stalled at #55. But two years later, on July 22, 1995, she reached #1 country for the first time with "Any Man of Mine," which stayed there for two weeks. Over the next two years she had four other #1 country entries, including "(If You're Not in It for Love) I'm Outta Here!" and "You Win My Love" and "No One Needs to Know" in 1996, followed by "Love Gets Me Every Time," which stayed at #1 for five weeks starting November 8, 1997.

The following year, Shania hit the chart again with "You're Still the One." It hit #1 country only for the week of May 2, 1998, but it stayed #1 on the country sales chart an amazing 22 consecutive weeks starting March 21, 1998. On the Hot 100 the tune peaked at #2 for eight weeks behind "The Boy Is Mine" by Brandy and Monica starting June 20, 1998. In the fall of 1998, the ABC television network used "You're Still the One" as the theme song in its promotions for the Wednesday night sitcom *Dharma and Greg*.

In January 1999 "You're Still the One" brought more triumph to Twain when it received four Grammy nominations, for Record of the Year, Song of the Year, Best Female Country Vocal Performance, and Best Country Song. The LP on which it appeared, *Come On Over*, received nominations for Album of the Year and Best Country Album. That same album produced Shania's second big crossover hit of 1998, "From This Moment On" [see 676].

674 To Love You More
CELINE DION

550 Music Album Cut

August 8, 1998 (8 weeks nonconsecutive)

Writers: David Foster, Junior Miles

Producer: David Foster

"To Love You More" appeared on Celine Dion's 1997 release *Let's Talk About Love*, an album which Dion decided to record only after she realized how impressive the talent assembled for the project was. The contributors included former Beatles producer Sir George Martin, who produced Dion on a tune by Carole King called "The Reason," and the Bee Gees, who wrote, produced, and sang background on another song, called "Immortality."

The people involved in the album were in turn impressed with Dion. "Working with her is an absolute joy," said Martin in *VH1 to One*, a 1998 documentary on the album. Similar praise came from King and the Bee Gees, but Dion did not let it go to her head, saying in the documentary that "I don't consider myself as a star. I consider myself the baby of [my] family."

While the documentary made little reference to "To Love You More," the song was a major track pushed to radio in 1998 to promote *Let's Talk About Love*. The song worked wonders for the LP, which sold over 24 million copies. *Let's Talk About Love* would probably have made #1 on the LP chart also, but keeping it from the top was the soundtrack to *Titanic*—which of course featured Dion's hit "My Heart Will Go On" [see 671]. But that second-place finish did not mean it was second-place to Dion. "It is, I think, to me the album of my life," she said.

Although Dion had been quoted as saying that she would prefer staying at home with her husband in their Palm Beach mansion to working, her successes in 1997 and 1998 pulled her out on the road for a year-long worldwide tour while "To Love You More" was #1 AC. As she explained to Edna Gunderson of *USA Today* in August of 1998, the eve of her first show on the schedule (in Boston): "'My Heart Will Go On' touched the hearts of a lot of people. I can't just say, 'Sorry, that's it.'"

She also promised that she would do more recording, albeit under her conditions. As she said in her *VH1 to One* interview, "I want to do a better album each time, and if I cannot do that, I will not record." Whether or not Dion has lived up to that vow only her fans can decide, but she did release another LP in 1998, which spawned another #1 AC hit for her [see 677—"I'm Your Angel"].

675 I'll Never Break Your Heart
THE BACKSTREET BOYS

Jive Album Cut

October 17, 1998 (7 weeks)

Writers: Eugene Wilde, Albert Manno

Producer: Timmy Allen

The all-male singing quintet Backstreet Boys, which came together in Orlando, Florida, found they had to score hits in Europe before becoming a top-selling act in their native country. The group consisted of Nicholas Gene Carter (born in Jamestown, New York, on January 28, 1980); Howard Dwaine "Howie D." Dorough (born in Orlando, Florida, on September 22, 1973); Brian Thomas Littrell (born in Lexington, Kentucky, on February 29, 1975); a cousin of Littrell's, Kevin Scott Richardson (born in Lexington on October 3, 1972); and Alexander James "A.J." McLean (born in West Palm Beach, Florida, on January 9, 1978). Littrell and Richardson sang in various church choirs while growing up in Lexington, but in the early 1990s Richardson decided to go to Orlando to pursue a career as a singer/songwriter.

Carter, Dorough, and McLean, who had met frequently at various auditions for stage, TV, and music work in Orlando, found they shared an interest in smooth, harmonized a capella music. When Richardson arrived on the scene, he heard about the trio through the local entertainment grapevine and the four joined forces. Richardson then convinced the others that his cousin Littrell would be a worthy addition to the group (Littrell was, like Carter, a tenor, Richardson a bass, McLean a baritone, and Dorough a falsetto). The vocal quintet took its name from the Backstreet Market, a flea market with a large parking lot where many teenagers liked to hang out.

Their first self-titled album came out in America in 1996, but sales were poor, and the first 45 from that album, "We've Got It Goin' On," made only #69 pop. Undeterred, the Boys went to Europe and made their debut on the U.K. chart that year with another song from *Backstreet Boys*, "We've Got It Goin' On" at #54. Its follow-up (also from the album), "I'll Never Break Your Heart," hit #42. Then a year later, both songs were rereleased and did much better, with "We've Got It Goin' On" making #3 and "I'll Never Break Your Heart" #8. With these overseas successes and others behind them, in 1977 the Backstreet Boys launched a second push in America.

Their first AC entry was "Quit Playing Games (With My Heart)," which went to #2 in the fall of 1997. In May 1998 "As Long As You Love Me" made #3 AC. The next try, the mellow "I'll Never Break Your Heart," on which A.J. was lead singer of each verse, became the group's first #1 AC hit.

By the end of 1998, the Backstreet Boys had spawned numerous copycat groups of adolescent males, such as 'N Sync and 98 Degrees, all of whom had their own devoted followings. The act which hadn't been able to cut it in America just three years earlier was now the hottest, most imitated ensemble in the pop music world.

676 From This Moment On

SHANIA TWAIN

Mercury (Nashville) 566450

December 5, 1998 (1 week)

Writers: Shania Twain, Robert John "Mutt" Lange

Producer: Robert John "Mutt" Lange

"From This Moment On" was one of 16 songs Shania Twain included in her 1997 album *Come On Over*. The unusually large number of tunes (most one-disc releases have 12 to 14 songs at most) was requested by Twain, who explained her reasoning in a press release included on Mercury Nashville's Internet web page. "There was so much that I wanted to achieve. I couldn't have done it in any less than 16 songs—very one of them makes this album feel complete to me. Maybe it's because of the time I was given, I just felt like I couldn't leave any one of them out."

Though she did not discuss the creation of any of the songs on the album specifically, Twain did note that "I love to write stories. Songwriting is my favorite part of what I do. I like to give each song its own personality and attitude and to sing each one in its own style." Given that sentiment, she must have felt unfulfilled when her self-titled debut LP in 1993 came out with only one song that had been written by Twain.

But Twain had an admirer in record producer Robert John "Mutt" Lange, who liked her album so much that he arranged to meet her and liked her so much that the two were married in December 1993. Lange produced Twain's second album, 1995's *The Woman in Me*, which became a major country hit and paved the way for *Come On Over*.

Lange and Twain did all the background vocals on *Come On Over*. For "From This Moment On," Bryan White duetted with Twain, but got only a "guest vocal" credit. However, he did do the song on stage with his co-headliner LeAnn Rimes while they toured in 1998. White, born in Lawton, Oklahoma, on February 17, 1974, and raised in Oklahoma City, had a few country #1 hits of his own, starting with 1995's "Someone Else's Star."

"From This Moment On" first arrived on the country chart as an album track the week of November 15, 1997, being played ahead of "You're Still the One." It peaked at #6 there the week of July 25, 1998. Because "You're Still the One" was still the one being played on AC and pop charts at that time, "From This Moment On" did not get onto those charts until "You're Still the One" had ended its run, in the fall. "From This Moment On" peaked at #4 pop after topping the AC chart the weeks of December 19 and 26, 1998.

Twain began 1999 taping her first starring TV special in Miami with guests Elton John and the Backstreet Boys in January. The show was slated to air two months later on March 3, followed by more recording and touring.

677 I'm Your Angel

R. KELLY AND CELINE DION

Jive 42557

December 12, 1998 (12 weeks)

Writer: R. Kelly

Producer: R. Kelly

With sultry, sensual R&B hits like 1993's "Sex Me (Parts I & II)" and 1994's "Bump N' Grind" (a #1 R&B pop triumph), R. Kelly, who was born Robert Kelly in Chicago, Illinois, on January 8, 1969, hardly came across as the type to crack the AC chart anytime in his career. But the singer/songwriter, who released his first album, *Born Into the '90s*, in 1991, proved he had more than just sex on his mind when his inspirational tune from the Michael Jordan movie *Space Jam*, "I Believe I Can Fly," peaked at #3 AC the week of May 3, 1997. The song's commercial success (it also reached #2 pop for four weeks and #1 R&B) and Grammy nominations for Record of the Year and Song of the Year led to an even bigger AC and pop hit the following year when he teamed with superstar Celine Dion to sing his "I'm Your Angel."

In an America Online chat in 1998 recorded at the Internet Web site www.peeps.com, Kelly talked about the creation of "I'm Your Angel." "I wrote that song for. . .my mom Joann, and baby girl Joann. When I got through it felt like it should be a duet. Celine popped to mind, and she agreed right away. . . .I went to Canada, and came back to the studio to finish it up."

"I'm Your Angel" became a track on both R. Kelly's double-set album *R.* and Dion's first Christmas album, *These Are Special Times*. To promote it on her album, Dion acted on the November 15, 1998 episode of the popular CBS Sunday night drama *Touched by an Angel*, which left time at the end of the program for the North American television premiere of the "I'm Your Angel" video. Anybody who missed that airing had to wait only a week and a half, until November 25, when Dion sang the song byself on the CBS Christmas special, *Celine Dion: These Are Special Times*. After that, the cable music channel VH-1 repeated the show several times before Christmas.

Given all that TV exposure, it was not surprising that "I'm Your Angel" caught on with the listening public quickly, and not just on the AC chart. On the Hot 100, "I'm Your Angel" hit #1 on its sixth week on the chart, on December 5, 1998, and stayed there for six weeks. It also went to #6 R&B for two weeks.

And finally, although "I'm Your Angel" was R. Kelly's first #1 AC hit, it was the ninth #1 AC hit for Celine Dion within seven years, putting Dion ahead of her idol Barbra Streisand, who had eight, and only one hit behind Whitney Houston and Olivia Newton-John, who had each scored with ten chart-toppers.

The Most Weeks at Number One

19	"Because You Loved Me," Celine Dion (1996)	
14	"Un-Break My Heart," Toni Braxton (1997)	
13	"One Sweet Day," Mariah Carey and Boys II Men (1995–96)	
13	"Change the World," Eric Clapton (1996)	
12	"The River of Dreams," Billy Joel (1993)	
12	"Said I Loved You. . .But I Lied," Michael Bolton (1993–94)	
12	"Kiss From a Rose," Seal (1995)	
12	"I'm Your Angel," R. Kelly and Celine Dion (1998–99)	
11	"Love Is Blue," Paul Mauriat (1968)	
11	"Now and Forever," Richard Marx (1994)	
11	"How Do I Live," LeAnn Rimes (1997)	
11	"Truly Madly Deeply," Savage Garden (1998)	
10	"Big Bad John," Jimmy Dean (1961)	
10	"King of the Road," Roger Miller (1965)	
10	"This Guy's in Love With You," Herb Alpert (1968)	
10	"Time Passages," Al Stewart (1978)	
10	"Something About the Way You Look Tonight," Elton John (1997)	
10	"My Heart Will Go On," Celine Dion (1998)	
9	"Hello, Dolly!," Louis Armstrong (1964)	
9	"Somethin' Stupid," Nancy Sinatra and Frank Sinatra (1967)	
9	"Take a Bow," Madonna (1995)	

65	Celine Dion	28	Billy Joel	24	Kenny Rogers
49	Elton John	28	Barry Manilow	23	Mariah Carey
47	Lionel Richie	28	Barbra Streisand	22	Richard Marx
45	Celine Dion	26	Frank Sinatra	22	Stevie Wonder
38	Michael Bolton	25	Neil Diamond	21	Elvis Presley
38	The Carpenters	24	Anne Murray	21	Glen Campbell
31	Whitney Houston	24	Olivia Newton-John	20	Herb Alpert

The Most Number One Hits by Artist (Ties Listed in Alphabetical Order)

16	Elton John	9	John Denver	8	Anne Murray
15	The Carpenters	9	Celine Dion	8	Helen Reddy
13	Barry Manilow	8	Glen Campbell	8	Kenny Rogers
11	Lionel Richie	8	Chicago	8	Barbra Streisand
10	Whitney Houston	8	John Denver	8	Stevie Wonder
10	Olivia Newton-John	8	Neil Diamond	7	Gloria Estefan
9	Michael Bolton	8	Billy Joel		

Number One AC Hits Which Were Also Number One Pop Hits

1961

Wooden Heart	*Joe Dowell*
Michael	*The Highwaymen*
Big Bad John	*Jimmy Dean*

1962

Don't Break the Heart That Loves You	*Connie Francis*
Stranger on the Shore	*Mr. Acker Bilk*
I Can't Stop Loving You	*Ray Charles*
The Stripper	*David Rose*
Roses Are Red (My Love)	*Bobby Vinton*
Go Away Little Girl	*Steve Lawrence*

1963

Walk Right In	*The Rooftop Singers*
Sukiyaki	*Kyu Sakamoto*
Blue Velvet	*Bobby Vinton*
I'm Leaving It Up to You	*Dale and Grace*
Dominique	*The Singing Nun*

1964

There! I've Said It Again	*Bobby Vinton*
Hello, Dolly!	*Louis Armstrong*
Everybody Loves Somebody	*Dean Martin*
Ringo	*Lorne Greene*

1966

The Ballad of the Green Berets	*SSgt. Barry Sadler*
Strangers in the Night	*Frank Sinatra*
Winchester Cathedral	*The New Vaudeville Band*

1967

Somethin' Stupid	*Nancy Sinatra and Frank Sinatra*

1968

Love Is Blue	*Paul Mauriat*
Honey	*Bobby Goldsboro*
This Guy's in Love With You	*Herb Alpert*

1969

Aquarius/Let the Sunshine In	*The 5th Dimension*
Love Theme From *Romeo and Juliet*	*Henry Mancini*
In the Year 2525 (Exordium & Terminus)	*Zager and Evans*
Wedding Bell Blues	*The 5th Dimension*
Leaving on a Jet Plane	*Peter, Paul and Mary*
Raindrops Keep Fallin' on My Head	*B. J. Thomas*

1970

Bridge Over Troubled Water	*Simon and Garfunkel*
Let It Be	*The Beatles*
Everything Is Beautiful	*Ray Stevens*
(They Long to Be) Close to You	*The Carpenters*

1971

It's Too Late	*Carole King*
You've Got a Friend	*James Taylor*

1972

American Pie—Parts I and II	*Don McLean*
Without You	*Nilsson*
The First Time Ever I Saw Your Face	*Roberta Flack*
The Candy Man	*Sammy Davis Jr.*
Song Sung Blue	*Neil Diamond*
Alone Again (Naturally)	*Gilbert O'Sullivan*
Baby Don't Get Hooked on Me	*Mac Davis*
Black and White	*Three Dog Night*
I Can See Clearly Now	*Johnny Nash*

1973

You're So Vain	*Carly Simon*
Tie a Yellow Ribbon Round the Ole Oak Tree	*Tony Orlando and Dawn*
You Are the Sunshine of My Life	*Stevie Wonder*
My Love	*Paul McCartney and Wings*
Touch Me in the Morning	*Diana Ross*
Delta Dawn	*Helen Reddy*
The Most Beautiful Girl	*Charlie Rich*
Time in a Bottle	*Jim Croce*

1974

The Way We Were	*Barbra Streisand*
Love's Theme	*Love Unlimited Orchestra*
Seasons in the Sun	*Terry Jacks*
Sunshine on My Shoulders	*John Denver*
TSOP (The Sound of Philadelphia)	*MFSB featuring the Three degrees*
Sundown	*Gordon Lightfoot*
Annie's Song	*John Denver*
Feel Like Makin' Love	*Roberta Flack*
I Honestly Love You	*Olivia Newton-John*
Laughter in the Rain	*Neil Sedaka*
Angie Baby	*Helen Reddy*
Mandy	*Barry Manilow*

1975

Please Mr. Postman	*The Carpenters*
Best of My Love	*The Eagles*
Have You Never Been Mellow	*Olivia Newton-John*
(Hey Won't You Play) Another Somebody Done Somebody Wrong Song	*B. J. Thomas*
He Don't Love You (Like I Love You)	*Tony Orlando and Dawn*
Love Will Keep Us Together	*The Captain and Tennille*
Rhinestone Cowboy	*Glen Campbell*
Fallin' in Love	*Hamilton, Joe Frank and Reynolds*
I'm Sorry	*John Denver*
Theme From *Mahogany* (Do You Know Where You're Going To)	*Diana Ross*
I Write the Songs	*Barry Manilow*

1976

50 Ways to Leave Your Lover	*Paul Simon*
Welcome Back	*John Sebastian*
Silly Love Songs	*Wings*
Don't Go Breaking My Heart	*Elton John and Kiki Dee*
If You Leave Me Now	*Chicago*
Torn Between Two Lovers	*Mary MacGregor*

1977

Love Theme From *A Star Is Born* (Evergreen)	*Barbra Streisand*
Southern Nights	*Glen Campbell*
Don't Give Up on Us	*David Soul*
When I Need You	*Leo Sayer*
Looks Like We Made It	*Barry Manilow*
You Light Up My Life	*Debby Boone*
How Deep Is Your Love	*The Bee Gees*

1978

Too Much, Too Little, Too Late	*Johnny Mathis and Deniece Williams*
Three Times a Lady	*The Commodores*

1979

Rise	*Herb Alpert*

1980

Magic	*Olivia Newton-John*
Woman in Love	*Barbra Streisand*
Lady	*Kenny Rogers*

1981

I Love a Rainy Night	*Eddie Rabbitt*
9 to 5	*Dolly Parton*
Morning Train (Nine to Five)	*Sheena Easton*
Endless Love	*Diana Ross and Lionel Richie*
Arthur's Theme (Best That You Can Do)	*Christopher Cross*

1982

Chariots of Fire—Titles	*Vangelis*
Ebony and Ivory	*Paul McCartney with Stevie Wonder*
Hard to Say I'm Sorry	*Chicago*
Truly	*Lionel Richie*

1983

Baby, Come to Me	*Patti Austin with James Ingram*
Tell Her About It	*Billy Joel*
Islands in the Stream	*Kenny Rogers with Dolly Parton*
All Night Long (All Night)	*Lionel Richie*

1984

Hello	*Lionel Richie*
Time After Time	*Cyndi Lauper*
I Just Called to Say I Love You	*Stevie Wonder*

1985

Careless Whisper	*Wham! featuring George Michael*
One More Night	*Phil Collins*
We Are the World	*USA for Africa*
Everytime You Go Away	*Paul Young*
Saving All My Love for You	*Whitney Houston*
Part-Time Lover	*Stevie Wonder*
Separate Lives	*Phil Collins and Marilyn Martin*
Say You, Say Me	*Lionel Richie*

1986

That's What Friends Are For	*Dionne and Friends*
How Will I Know	*Whitney Houston*
Sara	*Starship*
These Dreams	*Heart*
Greatest Love of All	*Whitney Houston*
Live to Tell	*Madonna*
There'll Be Sad Songs (to Make You Cry)	*Billy Ocean*
Glory of Love	*Peter Cetera*
Stuck With You	*Huey Lewis*
The Next Time I Fall	*Peter Cetera with Amy Grant*
The Way It Is	*Bruce Hornsby and the Range*

1987

At This Moment	*Billy Vera and the Beaters*
Nothing's Gonna Stop Us Now	*Starship*
Always	*Atlantic Starr*
I Wanna Dance With Somebody (Who Loves Me)	*Whitney Houston*
I Just Can't Stop Loving You	*Michael Jackson*
Didn't We Almost Have It All	*Whitney Houston*
(I've Had) The Time of My Life	*Bill Medley and Jennifer Warnes*
Got My Mind Set on You	*George Harrison*

1988

Could've Been	*Tiffany*
Seasons Change	*Exposé*
Never Gonna Give You Up	*Rick Astley*
Where Do Broken Hearts Go	*Whitney Houston*
Anything for You	*Gloria Estefan*
One More Try	*George Michael*
Roll With It	*Steve Winwood*
Groovy Kind of Love	*Phil Collins*
Look Away	*Chicago*
Two Hearts	*Phil Collins*

1989

When I'm With You	*Sheriff*
The Living Years	*Mike + the Mechanics*
Eternal Flame	*The Bangles*
If You Don't Know Me by Now	*Simply Red*
Right Here Waiting	*Richard Marx*
Another Day in Paradise	*Phil Collins*

1990

How Am I Supposed to Live Without You	*Michael Bolton*
Love Will Lead You Back	*Taylor Dayne*
Hold On	*Wilson Phillips*
Vision of Love	*Mariah Carey*
Release Me	*Wilson Phillips*
Love Takes Time	*Mariah Carey*

1991

Because I Love You (The Postman Song)	*Stevie B*
The First Time	*Surface*
All the Man That I Need	*Whitney Houston*
Coming Out of the Dark	*Gloria Estefan*
You're in Love	*Wilson Phillips*
Baby Baby	*Amy Grant*
I Don't Wanna Cry	*Mariah Carey*
Rush, Rush	*Paula Abdul*
(Everything I Do) I Do It for You	*Bryan Adams*
When a Man Loves a Woman	*Michael Bolton*

1992

Don't Let the Sun Go Down on Me	*George Michael and Elton John*
Save the Best for Last	*Vanessa Williams*
I'll Be There	*Mariah Carey*
I Will Always Love You	*Whitney Houston*

1993

A Whole New World (Aladdin's Theme)	*Peabo Bryson and Regina Belle*

1994

The Power of Love	*Celine Dion*
I'll Make Love to You	*Boyz II Men*

1995

Take a Bow	*Madonna*
Have You Ever Really Loved a Woman?	*Bryan Adams*
Kiss From a Rose	*Seal*
One Sweet Day	*Mariah Carey and Boyz II Men*

1996

Because You Loved Me	*Celine Dion*

1997

Un-Break My Heart	*Toni Braxton*
Something About the Way You Look Tonight	*Elton John*

1998

My Heart Will Go On	*Celine Dion*
Truly Madly Deeply	*Savage Garden*
I'm Your Angel	*R. Kelly and Celine Dion*

Index of Artists

AC Index of Songs

426

Bibliography

BOOKS

Baggelaar, Kristin, and David Milton. *Folk Music: More Than a Song*. New York: Crowell, 1976.

Bingham, Pete, Bernadette Dolan, and Michael Clough. *ABBAmania Volume 1: The Singles*. Wales: Vinyl Addicts, 1997.

Bishop, Steven. *Songs in the Rough*. New York: St. Martin's, 1996.

Bowen, Jimmy, and Jim Jerome. *Rough Mix*. New York: Simon & Schuster, 1997.

Breskin, David. *We Are the World*. New York: Perigee, 1985.

Bronson, Fred. *The Billboard Book of Number One Hits*, 4th ed. New York: Billboard, 1997.

———. *Billboard's Hottest Hot 100 Hits*. New York: Billboard, 1991.

Carr, Roy, and Mick Farren. *Elvis Presley: The Complete Illustrated Record*. New York: Harmony, 1982.

Charles, Ray, with David Ritz. *Brother Ray*. New York: Warner, 1978.

Considine, Shaun. *Barbra Streisand: The Woman, the Myth, the Music*.

Davis, Clive, with James Willwerth. *Clive: Inside the Music Business*. New York: Morrow, 1975.

Davis, Sammy, Jr., *Why Me? The Sammy Davis Jr. Story*. New York: Warner, 1990.

Davis, Skeeter. *Bus Fare to Kentucky: The Autobiography of Skeeter Davis*. New York: Birch Lane Press, 1993.

Denver, John, with Arthur Tobier. *Take Me Home*. New York: Harmony, 1994.

Dexter, Dave, Jr., *Playback*. New York: Billboard, 1976.

Duxbury, Janell R. *Rockin' the Classics and Classicizin' the Rock*. Westport, CT: Greenwood, 1985.

Eng, Steve. *Jimmy Buffett: The Man From Margaritaville Revealed*. New York: St. Martin's, 1996.

Friedwald, Will. *Sinatra! The Song Is You*. New York: Scribner's, 1995.

Gambaccini, Paul, Tim Rice, and Jonathan Rice. *The Guinness Book of Number One Hits*, 3rd ed. Enfield, Middlesex, Great Britain: Guinness, 1994.

Gilbert, Bob, and Gary Theroux. *The Top Ten*. New York: Fireside, 1982.

Hamlisch, Marvin, with Gerald C. Gardner. *The Way I Was*. New York: MacMillan, 1992.

Horstman, Dorothy. *Sing Your Heart Out, Country Boy*. New York: Dutton, 1975.

Jackson, Michael. *Moonwalk*. New York: Doubleday, 1988.

Jacobs, Dick, and Harriet Jacobs. *Who Wrote That Song?* 2nd ed. Cincinnati, OH: Writer's Digest, 1994.

Jancik, Wayne. *The Billboard Book of One-Hit Wonders*, 2nd ed. New York: Billboard, 1998.

Kiersh, Edward. *Where Are You Now, Bo Diddley?* Garden City, NY: Doubleday, 1986.

Laine, Frankie, and Joseph F. Laredo. *That Lucky Old Son*. Ventura, CA: Pathfinder, 1993.

Lamparski, Richard. *Whatever Became Of. . . ? Ninth Series*. New York: Crown, 1985.

Lanza, Joseph. *Elevator Music*. New York: St. Martin's, 1994.

Lee, Peggy. *Miss Peggy Lee: An Autobiography*. New York: Donald I. Prine, 1989.

Lewisohn, Mark. *The Beatles Recording Sessions*. New York: Harmony, 1988.

McAleer, Dave. *Encyclopedia of Hits—The 1960s*. London: Blandford, 1996.

Manilow, Barry. *Sweet Life: Adventures on the Way to Paradise*. New York: McGraw-Hill, 1987.

Murrells, Joseph. *The Book of Golden Discs*, 2nd ed. London: Barrie and Jenkins, 1978.

Parton, Dolly. *Dolly: My Life and Other Unfinished Business*. New York: HarperCollins, 1994.

Reid, Jan. *The Improbable Rise of Redneck Rock*. Austin, TX: Heidelberg, 1974.

Roland, Tom. *The Billboard Book of Number One Country Hits*. New York: Billboard, 1991.

Rosen, Craig. *The Billboard Book of Number One Albums*. New York: Billboard, 1996.

Scott, Barry. *We Had Joy, We Had Fun*. Boston: Faber and Faber, 1994.

Sinatra, Nancy. *Frank Sinatra: An American Legend*. Santa Monica, CA: General Publishing Group, 1995.

Smith, Joe. *Off the Record: An Oral History of Popular Music*. New York: Warner, 1988.

Stambler, Irwin. *The Encyclopedia of Pop, Rock and Soul*, rev. ed. New York: St. Martin's, 1989.

Taraborrelli, J. Randy. *Call Her Miss Ross*. Secaucus, NJ: Birch Lane, 1989.

Taylor, Marc. *A Touch of Classic Soul: Soul Singers of the Early 1970s*. Jamaica, NY: Aloiv, 1996.

Tobler, John. *ABBA Gold: The Complete Story*. New York: St. Martin's, 1993.

———, and Stuart Grundy. *The Record Producers*. New York: St. Martin's, 1982.

Vinton, Bobby. *The Polish Prince*. New York: M. Evans, 1978.

Warner, Jay. *Billboard's American Rock 'N' Roll in Review*. New York: Simon & Shuster, 1997.

Weinberg, Max, with Robert Santelli. *The Big Beat*. New York: Billboard, 1991.

Welch, Chris, with Stevie Winwood. *Roll With It*. New York: Perigee, 1990.

Whitburn, Joel. *Bubbling Under the Hot 100 1959–1985*. Menomonee Falls, WI: Record Research, Inc., 1986.

———. *Pop Memories 1890–1954*. Menomonee Falls, WI: Record Research, Inc., 1986.

———. *Top Adult Contemporary 1961–1993*. Menomonee Falls, WI: Record Research, Inc., 1993.

———. *Top Country Singles 1944–1993*. Menomonee Falls, WI: Record Research, Inc., 1994.

———. *Top Pop Albums 1955–1996*. Menomonee Falls, WI: Record Research, Inc., 1996.

———. *Top Pop Singles 1955–1996*. Menomonee Falls, WI: Record Research, Inc., 1997.

———. *Top R&B Singles 1942–1995*. Menomonee Falls, WI: Record Research, Inc., 1996.

White, Adam, and Fred Bronson. *The Billboard Book of #1 Rhythm and Blues Hits*. New York: Billboard, 1993.

White, Timothy. *Rock Lives*. New York: Henry Holt, 1992.

PERIODICALS

Billboard. Various issues, 1961–1998.
Goldmine. Various issues, 1980–1998.
Rolling Stone. Various issues, 1973–1996.